Easy Learning
French
Dictionary

BEGINNER'S
FRENCH
DICTIONARY

HarperResource
An Imprint of HarperCollins*Publishers*

Easy Learning

French
Dictionary

HarperCollins*Publishers*

Second edition 2001

© **HarperCollins Publishers 1996, 1998, 2001**

HarperCollins Publishers
Westerhill Road, Bishopbriggs, Glasgow G64 2QT, Great Britain

The HarperCollins website address is
www.**fire**and**water**.com

Collins® and Bank of English® are registered trademarks
of HarperCollins Publishers Limited

ISBN 0-00-472403-8

HarperCollins Publishers, Inc
10 East 53rd Street, New York, NY 10022

ISBN 0-06-273751-1

CIP information available on request

The HarperCollins USA website address is
www.harpercollins.com

project management
Ray Carrick, Michela Clari

general editor
Horst Kopleck

editorial coordination
Vivian Marr, Nicola Cooke
second edition
Sharon J. Hunter, Caitlin McMahon

editors

Christine Penman	Daphne Day
Chantal Testa	Harry Campbell
Cécile Aubinière-Robb	Gavin Killip
Hélène Bernaërt	Elspeth Anderson
Caroline Lehni	Joane Siksous
Sabine Citron	

computing staff
Ann Rautenbach

our thanks to the following for their help in researching the project
Maree Airlie, Teresa Alvarez, Phyllis Gautier, Janet Gough, Sharon Hunter,
Mary James, Cordelia Lilly, Carol MacLeod, Jill McNair, Janet Chalmers

illustrations
Richard Anderson

maps
HarperCollins Cartographic

series editor
Lorna Sinclair Knight

Corpus Acknowledgements

We would like to acknowledge the assistance of the many hundreds of individuals and
companies who have kindly given permission for copyright material to be used in The
Bank of English. The written sources include many national and regional newspapers in
Britain and overseas; magazine and periodical publishers; and book publishers in Britain,
the United States and Australia. Extensive spoken data has been provided by radio and
television broadcasting companies; research workers at many universities and other
institutions; and numerous individual contributors. We are grateful to them all.

CONTENTS

INTRODUCTION

Collins Easy Learning French Dictionary is an innovative dictionary designed specifically for anyone starting to learn French. We are grateful to all those teachers who have contributed to its development by advising us on how to tailor it to the needs of their students. We also gratefully acknowledge the help of the examining boards, whom we have consulted throughout this project, and whose word lists and exam papers we carefully studied when compiling this dictionary.

Note on trademarks
Entered words which we have reason to believe constitute trademarks have been designated as such. However, neither the presence nor the absence of such designation should be regarded as affecting the legal status of any trademark.

DICTIONARY SKILLS

Using a dictionary is a skill you can improve with practice and by following some basic guidelines. This section gives you a detailed explanation of how to use the dictionary to ensure you get the most out of it.

The answers to the questions in this section are on page 16.

▶ MAKE SURE YOU LOOK IN THE RIGHT SIDE OF THE DICTIONARY

The French–English side comes first: you look there to find the meaning of a French word. The second part is English–French. That's what you need for translating into French. (To remind yourself which side is which, you could remember the phrase *French first*.) At the top of every page, you will see either **French ~ English** or **English ~ French**, so you can see immediately if you've got the side you want. The middle pages of the book have a blue border so that you can see where one side finishes and the other starts.

> 1   Which side of the dictionary would you need to look up to translate "le vélo"?

▶ FINDING THE WORD YOU WANT

When you are looking for a word, for example **nouveau**, look at the first letter – **n** – and find the **N** section in the French–English side. Look at page 186. At the top of the page, you'll find the words **né → nez**. These are the first and last words on that page. So **nouveau** is not going to be on page 186 because its second letter, **o**, comes after **e**, the second letter of **nez**. You have to go past all the words starting with **ne** and all the words starting with **ni** until you get to words starting with **no**. Scan down these until you find the word you want. Remember that even if a letter has an accent on it, it makes no difference to the alphabetical order.

> 2   Which comes first – "nager" or "nécessaire"?
> 3   Does "nouveau" come before or after "Noël"?
> 4   Does "chou–fleur" come before or after "chocolat"?

▶ MAKE SURE YOU LOOK AT THE RIGHT ENTRY

An entry is made up of a **word**, its <u>translations</u> and, often, example phrases to show you how to use the translations. If there is more than one entry for the same word, then there is a warning box to tell you so. Look at the following example entries:

flat ADJECTIVE
> see also **flat** NOUN

1 <u>plat</u> ◊ *a flat roof* un toit plat ◊ *flat shoes* des chaussures plates
2 <u>crevé</u> (*tyre*) ◊ *I've got a flat tyre.* J'ai un pneu crevé.

flat NOUN
> see also **flat** ADJECTIVE

l' <u>appartement</u> MASC ◊ *She lives in a flat.* Elle habite un appartement.

---

5 **Which of the two entries above will help you translate the phrase "My car has a flat tyre"?**
Look for the two clues which are there to help you:

◇ an example similar to what you want to say
◇ the word ADJECTIVE

Always pay attention to information boxes – they tell you if there is more than one entry for the same word, give you guidance on grammatical points, and tell you about differences between French and British life.

▶ CHOOSING THE RIGHT TRANSLATION

The main translation of a word is shown on a new line and is underlined to make it stand out from the rest of the entry. If there is more than one main translation for a word, each one is numbered. If an entry continues over the page, there is a signpost to indicate this ☞.

Often you will see phrases in *italics*, preceded by a white diamond ◊ . These show how the translation they follow can be used. They also help you choose the translation you want because they give you examples of the context in which it can be used.

bouillant ADJECTIVE
1 <u>boiling</u> ◊ *Faites cuire les pâtes à l'eau bouillante.* Cook the pasta in boiling water.
2 <u>piping hot</u> ◊ *La soupe est servie bouillante.* The soup should be served piping hot.

to **overlook** VERB
1 <u>donner sur</u> (*have view of*) ◊ *The hotel overlooked the beach.* L'hôtel donnait sur la plage.
2 <u>négliger</u> (*forget about*) ◊ *He had overlooked one important problem.* Il avait négligé un problème important.

6 Use the dictionary to translate *"That's a very hard question"*.

Words often have more than one meaning and more than one translation: if you don't **get** to the station on time, you don't arrive on time, but if you say "I don't **get** it", you mean you don't understand. When you are translating from English, be careful to choose the French word that has the particular meaning you want. The dictionary offers you a lot of help with this. Look at the following entry:

> **pool** NOUN
> 1. la flaque (*puddle*)
> 2. l' étang MASC (*pond*)
> 3. la piscine (*for swimming*)
> 4. le billard américain (*game*)

A **pool** can be a puddle, a pond or a swimming pool; **pool** can also be a game. Underlining highlights all the main translations, the numbers tell you that there is more than one possible translation and the words in brackets in *italics* after the translations help you choose the translation you want.

7 How would you translate *"I like playing pool"*?

Never take the first translation you see without looking at the others. Always look to see if there is more than one translation underlined.

Phrases in **bold type** preceded by a black diamond ✦ are phrases which are particularly common or important. Sometimes the phrases have a completely different translation from the main translation; sometimes the translation is the same. For example:

le **dommage** NOUN
   damage ◊ *La tempête a causé d'importants dommages.* The storm caused a lot of damage.
   ✦**C'est dommage.** It's a shame. ◊ *C'est dommage que tu ne puisses pas venir.* It's a shame you can't come.

to **go out** VERB
   1. sortir (*person*) ◊ *Are you going out tonight?* Tu sors ce soir?
   ✦**to go out with somebody** sortir avec quelqu'un ◊ *Are you going out with him?* Est-ce que tu sors avec lui?
   2. s'éteindre (*light, fire, candle*) ◊ *Suddenly the lights went out.* Soudain, les lumières se sont éteintes.

When you look up a word, make sure you look beyond the main translations to see if the entry includes any **bold phrases**.

8 In a job advert you read that applicants *"doivent tous passer une visite médicale"*. What must they all do?

Look up *"visite"* and find the answer as quickly as possible by skimming down the *bold phrases*.

▶ MAKING USE OF PHRASES IN THE DICTIONARY

Sometimes when you look up a word you will find not only the word, but the exact phrase you want. For example, you might want to say "*What's the date today?*". Look up **date** and you will find:

> **date** NOUN
> 1 la <u>date</u> ◊ *my date of birth* ma date de naissance
> ♦**What's the date today?** Quel jour sommes-nous?

Sometimes you have to adapt what you find in the dictionary. If you want to say "*I play darts*" and look up **dart** you will find:

> **dart** NOUN
> la <u>fléchette</u> ◊ *to play darts* jouer aux fléchettes

You have to substitute *je joue* for the infinitive form *jouer*. You will often have to adapt the infinitive in this way, adding the correct ending for **je**, **tu**, **il** etc and choosing the present, future or past form. For help with this, look at the verb tables. **Jouer** is a verb ending in –*er* so it follows the same pattern as **aimer**, which is set out on page 316.

> *9 How would you say "We played football"?*

Phrases containing nouns and adjectives also need to be adapted. You may need to make the noun plural, or the adjective feminine or plural. Remember that some nouns and adjectives have irregular feminine or plural forms and that this is shown in the entry.

> *10 How would you say "The jewels are beautiful"?*

▶ DON'T OVERUSE THE DICTIONARY

It takes time to look up words so try to avoid using the dictionary unnecessarily, especially in exams. Think carefully about what you want to say and see if you can put it another way, using words you already know. To rephrase things you can:

◇ Use a word with a similar meaning. This is particularly easy with adjectives, as there are a lot of words which mean *good*, *bad*, *big* etc and you're sure to know at least one.

◇ Use negatives: if the cake you made was a total disaster, you could just say it wasn't very good.

◇ Use particular examples instead of general terms. If you are asked to describe the sports facilities in your area, and time is short, don't look up *facilities* - say something like "In our town there is a swimming pool and a football ground."

11 You want to ask "*Have you got any pets?*". How could you avoid using the word "*pet*" if you don't know it?

12 How could you say "*The palace of Versailles is huge*" without looking up the word "*huge*"?

You can also often guess the meaning of a French word by using others to give you a clue. If you see the sentence "*j'écoute de la musique rap*", you may not know the meaning of the word **écoute**, but you do know it's a verb because it's preceded by **j'**. Therefore it must be something you can do to music: **listen**. So the translation is: *I listen to rap music.*

13 In a description of a holiday centre you see a picture of bikes and read "*On peut louer des vélos: 20F la journée*". You may not know the meaning of "*louer*", but you can see that you have to pay 20 francs, which gives you a clue to what it could mean. What can you do — ride bikes, borrow bikes or hire bikes?

PARTS OF SPEECH

There are two entries for **flat** because this word can be a noun or an adjective. It helps to choose correctly between entries if you know how to recognize these different types of words.

▶ NOUNS AND PRONOUNS

Nouns often appear with words like *a, the, this, that, my, your* and *his*. They can be singular (abbreviated to SING in the dictionary):

his **dog**   *her* **cat**   *a* **street**

or plural (abbreviated to PL in the dictionary):

the **facts**   *those* **people**   *his* **shoes**   *our* **holidays**

They can be the subject of a verb:

Vegetables *are good* for you

or the object of a verb:

I play ***tennis***

Words like *I, me, you, he, she, him, her* and *they* are pronouns. They can be used instead of nouns. You can refer to a person as *he* or *she* or to a thing as *it*.

> *I bought my mother a box of chocolates.*
>
> **14 Which three words are nouns in this sentence?**
> **15 Which of the nouns is plural?**
> **16 Which word is a pronoun?**

French nouns are either masculine or feminine (abbreviated to MASC and FEM). Masculine nouns are shown by **le**:

le bateau   *le* chien   *le* jardin

11

Feminine nouns are shown by **la**:

        la porte   *la* robe   *la* souris

If a noun starts with a vowel or a vowel sound, then **le** or **la** becomes **l'**:

      *l'*ami   *l'*eau   *l'*orage   *l'*histoire

The plural forms of **le**, **la** and **l'** is **les**. As in English, the plural of most French nouns is made by adding **s**:

      les chiens   *les* portes   *les* tables

If the singular form already ends in **s**, or if it ends in **x**, then you don't have to add anything:

      *l'*ananas   *les* ananas
      la voix   *les* voix

Sometimes, however, the plural form is irregular and this is shown in the entry:

    cheval NOUN (PL les **chevaux**)   **horse** NOUN
      <u>horse</u>   le <u>cheval</u>
                                 (les chevaux PL)

Je me brosse les dents tous les soirs.

17 Two words in this sentence are nouns. Which ones?
18 Are they singular or plural?
19 What is the plural form of "*le choix*"?
20 Look in the dictionary to find the plural form of "*le travail*".

▶ ADJECTIVES

Flat can be an adjective as well as a noun. Adjectives describe nouns: your tyre can be **flat**, you can have a pair of **flat** shoes.

21 "*Dark*" is an adjective in one of these sentences and a noun in the other. Which is which?

I'm not afraid of the dark.
She's got dark hair.

French adjectives can be masculine or feminine, singular or plural, depending on the noun they describe:

un **petit** garçon (MASC SING)
une **petit<u>e</u>** fille (FEM SING = masculine singular + e)
trois **petit<u>s</u>** garçons (MASC PL = masculine singular + s)
trois **petit<u>es</u>** filles (FEM PL = masculine singular + es)

Only the masculine singular form of regular adjectives is shown in the dictionary.

So if you want to find out what sort of shoes **des chaussures plates** are, look under **plat**

If the feminine or the plural form of an adjective does *not* follow the above rules, then the irregular form is shown in the dictionary:

frais ADJECTIVE (FEM SING **fraîche**)
> *see also* **frais** NOUN
1 fresh

fresh ADJECTIVE
frais MASC
fraîche FEM

bon ADJECTIVE, ADVERB (FEM SING **bonne**)
> *see also* **bon** NOUN
1 good

good ADJECTIVE
1 bon MASC
bonne FEM

If the masculine form ends in **s** or **x**, then you don't need to add **s** to make the masculine plural. And if the masculine form ends in **e**, you don't add anything to form the feminine form. But remember – if the adjective ends in **é**, then it behaves like any regular adjective.

MASC SING	FEM SING	MASC PL	FEM PL
gris	grise	gris	grises
anxieux	anxieuse	anxieux	anxieuses
agréable	agréable	agréables	agréables
passé	passée	passés	passées

Some adjectives remain the same whether they're masculine, feminine or plural. This is also shown in the dictionary:

arrière ADJECTIVE (MASC, FEM, PL)
> *see also* **arrière** NOUN
back

back ADJECTIVE, ADVERB
> *see also* **back** NOUN, VERB
arrière MASC, FEM, PL

22 What is the feminine singular form of "*vert*"?
23 What is the masculine plural form of "*aimable*"?
24 What forms can "*heureux*" be?
25 What is the masculine plural form of "*gras*"? And the feminine singular (look in the dictionary for this one)?

She's going to record the programme for me.
His time in the race was a new world record.

Record in the first sentence is a verb. In the second, it is a noun.

One way to recognize a verb is that it frequently comes with a pronoun such as **I**, **you** or **she**, or with somebody's name. Verbs can relate to the present, the past or the future. They have a number of different forms to show this: **I'm going** (present), **he will go** (future), and **Nicola went by herself** (past). Often verbs appear with **to**: **they promised to go**. This basic form of the verb is called the infinitive.

In this dictionary, verbs are preceded by "to", so you can identify them at a glance. No matter which of the four previous examples you want to translate, you should look up to **go**, not **going** or **went**. If you want to translate **I thought**, look up to **think**.

> **26 What would you look up to translate the verbs in these phrases?**
>
> | | | |
> |---|---|---|
> | *I went* | *she's crying* | *he was lying* |
> | *I did it* | *he's out* | *they've gone* |

Verbs have different endings, depending on whether you are talking about **je**, **tu**, **nous**, **ils** etc: **j'aime**, **tu aimes**, **nous aimons**, **ils aiment** etc. They also have different forms for the present, future, past etc. **Nous mangeons** (we eat = present), **nous avons mangé** (we ate = past). **manger** is the infinitive and is the form that appears in the dictionary.

Sometimes the verb changes completely between the infinitive form and the **je**, **tu**, **ils** etc form. For example, *I go* is **je vais**, but *to go* is **aller**, and **nous faisons** (*we do*) comes from **faire** (*to do*). **J'ai fait** (*I have done* or *I did*) also comes from **faire**.

On pages 316-329 of the dictionary, you will find tables of the most important forms of 14 French verbs. And on pages 330-332, you will find a list of the main forms of other French irregular verbs.

▶ ADVERBS

An adverb is a word that describes a verb or an adjective:

> Write **soon**.   Check your work **carefully**.
> They arrived **late**.   The film was **very** good.

In the sentence "*The swimming pool is open daily*", **daily** is an adverb describing the adjective **open**. In the phrase "*my daily routine*", **daily** is an adjective describing the noun **routine**. We use the same word in English but to get the right French translation, it is important to know if it's being used as an adjective or an adverb. When you look up **daily** you find:

> **daily** ADJECTIVE, ADVERB
> [1] quotidien MASC
> quotidienne FEM
> ◊ *It's part of my daily routine.* Ça fait
> partie de mes occupations
> quotidiennes.
> [2] tous les jours ◊ *The pool is open
> daily from 9 a.m. to 6 p.m.* La piscine
> est ouverte tous les jours de neuf
> heures à dix-huit heures.

The examples show you **daily** being used as an adjective and as an adverb and will help you choose the right French translation.

Take the sentence "The menu changes daily".

27 Does "daily" go with the noun "menu" or the verb "changes"?
28 Is it an adverb or an adjective?
29 How would you translate "daily" in this sentence?

▶ PREPOSITIONS

Prepositions are words like **for**, **with** and **across**, which are followed by nouns or pronouns:

*I've got a present **for** David.*   *Come **with** me.*   *He ran **across** the road.*

The party's over.
The shop's just over the road.

30 In one of these sentences "over" is an adjective describing a noun, in the other it is a preposition followed by a noun. Which is which?

▶ ANSWERS

1 the French side
2 **nager**
3 **nouveau** comes after **Noël**
4 **chou–fleur** comes after **chocolat**
5 the first entry (the ADJECTIVE entry)
6 **C'est une question très difficile.**
7 **J'aime jouer au billard américain.**
8 they must all have a **medical examination**
9 **Nous avons joué au football.**
10 **Les bijoux sont beaux.**
11 you could ask "Have you got a cat or a dog?"
12 you could say "Very big."
13 you can **hire** bikes
14 **mother**, **box** and **chocolates** are nouns
15 **chocolates** is plural
16 **I** is a pronoun
17 **dents** and **soirs** are nouns
18 they are both plural
19 **les choix**
20 **les travaux**
21 **dark** in the first sentence is a noun and in the second, it's an adjective
22 **verte**
23 **aimables**
24 masculine singular or plural
25 the masculine plural form is **gras** and the feminine singular form is **grasse**
26 to **go**, to **cry**, to **lie**, to **do**, to **be**, to **go**
27 **daily** goes with the verb **changes**
28 it is an adverb
29 **tous les jours**
30 in the first sentence, **over** is an adjective and in the second, it's a preposition

a VERB *see* **avoir**

> *a* should not be confused with the preposition *à*.

♦ **Il a beaucoup d'amis.** He has a lot of friends.

♦ **Il a mangé des frites.** He had some chips.

♦ **Il a neigé pendant la nuit.** It snowed during the night.

♦ **il y a (1)** there is ◊ *Il y a un bon film à la télé.* There's a good film on TV.

♦ **il y a (2)** there are ◊ *Il y a beaucoup de monde.* There are lots of people.

à PREPOSITION

> *à* should not be confused with the verb form *a*. See also **au (=à+le)** and **aux (=à+les)**.

1️⃣ at ◊ *être à la maison* to be at home ◊ *à trois heures* at 3 o'clock

2️⃣ in ◊ *être à Paris* to be in Paris ◊ *habiter au Portugal* to live in Portugal ◊ *habiter à la campagne* to live in the country ◊ *au printemps* in the spring ◊ *au mois de juin* in June

3️⃣ to ◊ *aller à Paris* to go to Paris ◊ *aller au Portugal* to go to Portugal ◊ *aller à la campagne* to go to the country ◊ *donner quelque chose à quelqu'un* to give something to somebody ◊ *Cette veste appartient à Marie.* This jacket belongs to Marie. ◊ *Je n'ai rien à faire.* I've got nothing to do.

♦ **Ce livre est à Paul.** This book is Paul's.

♦ **Cette voiture est à nous.** This car is ours.

4️⃣ by ◊ *à bicyclette* by bicycle ◊ *être payé à l'heure* to be paid by the hour

♦ **à pied** on foot

♦ **C'est à côté de chez moi.** It's near my house.

♦ **C'est à dix kilomètres d'ici.** It's 10 kilometres from here.

♦ **C'est à dix minutes d'ici.** It's 10 minutes from here.

♦ **cent kilomètres à l'heure** 100 kilometres an hour

♦ **À bientôt!** See you soon! ◊ *À demain!* See you tomorrow! ◊ *À samedi!* See you on Saturday! ◊ *À tout à l'heure!* See you later!

abandonner VERB

1️⃣ to abandon ◊ *Avant les vacances, beaucoup de chiens sont abandonnés par leurs maîtres.* Before the holidays, a lot of dogs are abandoned by their owners.

2️⃣ to give up ◊ *J'ai décidé d'abandonner la natation.* I've decided to give up swimming.

l'**abeille** FEM NOUN
bee

abîmer VERB
to damage

♦ **s'abîmer** to get damaged

l'**abonnement** MASC NOUN
1️⃣ season ticket
2️⃣ subscription (*to* magazine)

s'**abonner** VERB

♦ **s'abonner à une revue** to take out a subscription to a magazine

l'**abord** MASC NOUN

♦ **d'abord** first ◊ *Je vais rentrer chez moi d'abord.* I'll go home first.

aboyer VERB
to bark

l'**abri** MASC NOUN
shelter

♦ **être à l'abri** to be under cover

♦ **se mettre à l'abri** to shelter

l'**abricot** MASC NOUN
apricot

s'**abriter** VERB
to shelter

l'**absence** FEM NOUN
absence

♦ **Il est passé pendant ton absence.** He came while you were away.

absent ADJECTIVE
absent

absolument ADVERB
absolutely

l'**accélérateur** MASC NOUN
accelerator

accélérer VERB
to accelerate

l'**accent** MASC NOUN
accent ◊ *Il a l'accent de Marseille.* He has a Marseilles accent.

♦ **un accent aigu** an acute accent

♦ **un accent grave** a grave accent

♦ **un accent circonflexe** a circumflex

accentuer VERB
to stress

accepter VERB
to accept

♦ **accepter de faire quelque chose** to agree to do something

l' **accès** MASC NOUN
access ◊ *avoir accès à quelque chose*
to have access to something
♦ **"Accès aux quais"** "To the trains"

l' **accessoire** MASC NOUN
1 accessory ◊ *les accessoires de mode* fashion accessories
2 prop

l' **accident** MASC NOUN
accident ◊ *un accident de la route* a road accident ◊ *Caroline a eu un accident de ski.* Caroline had a skiing accident.
♦ **par accident** by chance

accompagner VERB
to accompany

accomplir VERB
to carry out ◊ *Il n'a pas réussi à accomplir cette tâche.* He didn't manage to carry out this task.

l' **accord** MASC NOUN
agreement
♦ **être d'accord** to agree ◊ *Tu es d'accord avec moi?* Do you agree with me?
♦ **se mettre d'accord** to come to an agreement
♦ **D'accord!** OK!

l' **accordéon** MASC NOUN
accordion ◊ *Ray joue de l'accordéon.* Ray plays the accordion.

l' **accoudoir** MASC NOUN
armrest

l' **accrochage** MASC NOUN
collision

accrocher VERB
♦ **accrocher quelque chose à (1)** to hang something on ◊ *Il a accroché sa veste au portemanteau.* He hung his jacket on the coat rack.
♦ **accrocher quelque chose à (2)** to hitch something up to ◊ *Ils ont accroché la remorque à leur voiture.* They hitched the trailer up to their car.
♦ **s'accrocher à quelque chose** to catch on something ◊ *Sa jupe s'est accrochée aux ronces.* Her skirt got caught on the brambles.

s' **accroupir** VERB
to squat down

l' **accueil** MASC NOUN
welcome ◊ *Il nous a remerciés de notre accueil.* He thanked us for our welcome.
♦ **Elle s'occupe de l'accueil des visiteurs.** She's in charge of looking after visitors.

accueillant ADJECTIVE

welcoming ◊ *Ses parents ont été très accueillants.* Her parents were very welcoming.

accueillir VERB
to welcome

accumuler VERB
to accumulate
♦ **s'accumuler** to pile up

l' **accusation** FEM NOUN
accusation

l' **accusé** MASC NOUN
accused ◊ *L'accusé a déclaré que ...* The accused stated that ...
♦ **un accusé de réception** an acknowledgement of receipt

l' **accusée** FEM NOUN
accused

accuser VERB
to accuse ◊ *accuser quelqu'un de quelque chose* to accuse somebody of something

l' **achat** MASC NOUN
purchase
♦ **faire des achats** to do some shopping

acheter VERB
to buy ◊ *J'ai acheté des gâteaux à la pâtisserie.* I bought some cakes at the cake shop.
♦ **acheter quelque chose à quelqu'un (1)** to buy something for somebody ◊ *Qu'est-ce que tu lui as acheté pour son anniversaire?* What did you buy him for his birthday?
♦ **acheter quelque chose à quelqu'un (2)** to buy something from somebody ◊ *J'ai acheté des œufs au fermier.* I bought some eggs from the farmer.

acide ADJECTIVE
see also **acide** NOUN
acid ◊ *Ce pamplemousse est trop acide.* This grapefruit is too acid.

l' **acide** MASC NOUN
see also **acide** ADJECTIVE
acid

l' **acier** MASC NOUN
steel

l' **acné** FEM NOUN
acne ◊ *Il a de l'acné.* He has acne.

acquérir VERB
to acquire

acquis VERB see **acquérir**

acquitter VERB
to acquit ◊ *L'accusé a été acquitté.* The accused was acquitted.

l' **acte** MASC NOUN
act
♦ **un acte de naissance** a birth certificate

l'**acteur** MASC NOUN
actor ◇ *Il est acteur.* He's an actor.
◇ *un acteur de cinéma* a film actor

actif ADJECTIVE (FEM SING **active**)
active
◆ **la population active** the working
population

l'**action** FEM NOUN
action
◆ **une bonne action** a good deed

s'**activer** VERB
1 to bustle about ◇ *Elle s'activait à
préparer le repas.* She bustled about
preparing the meal.
2 to move oneself ◇ *Allez! Active-
toi!* Come on! Get moving!

l'**activité** FEM NOUN
activity

l'**actrice** FEM NOUN
actress ◇ *Elle est actrice.* She's an
actress. ◇ *une actrice de cinéma* a
film actress

l'**actualité** FEM NOUN
current events
◆ **un problème d'actualité** a topical
issue
◆ **les actualités** the news

actuel ADJECTIVE (FEM SING **actuelle**)
present ◇ *le système actuel* the
present system
◆ **à l'heure actuelle** at the present time
*Be careful! **actuel** does not mean
actual.*

actuellement ADVERB
at present
*Be careful! **actuellement** does not
mean **actually**.*

l'**acuponcture** FEM NOUN
acupuncture

l'**adaptateur** MASC NOUN
adaptor

l'**addition** FEM NOUN
1 addition ◇ *Il a fait une erreur dans
son addition.* He made a mistake in
his addition.
2 bill ◇ *L'addition, s'il vous plaît!*
Can we have the bill, please?

additionner VERB
to add up

adhésif ADJECTIVE (FEM SING **adhésive**)
◆ **le ruban adhésif** sticky tape

adieu EXCLAMATION
farewell!

l'**adjectif** MASC NOUN
adjective

admettre VERB
1 to admit ◇ *Il refuse d'admettre
qu'il s'est trompé.* He won't admit
that he made a mistake.

2 to allow ◇ *Les chiens ne sont pas
admis dans le restaurant.* Dogs are
not allowed in the restaurant.

l'**administration** FEM NOUN
administration
◆ **l'Administration** the Civil Service

admirable ADJECTIVE
wonderful

l'**admirateur** MASC NOUN
admirer

l'**admiratrice** FEM NOUN
admirer

admirer VERB
to admire

admis VERB *see* **admettre**

l'**adolescence** FEM NOUN
adolescence

l'**adolescent** MASC NOUN
teenager

l'**adolescente** FEM NOUN
teenager

adopter VERB
to adopt

adorable ADJECTIVE
lovely

adorer VERB
to love ◇ *Elle adore le chocolat.* She
loves chocolate. ◇ *J'adore jouer au
tennis.* I love playing tennis.

l'**adresse** FEM NOUN
address
◆ **mon adresse électronique** my email
address

adresser VERB
◆ **adresser la parole à quelqu'un** to
speak to someone
◆ **s'adresser à quelqu'un (1)** to speak to
somebody ◇ *C'est à toi que je
m'adresse.* It's you I'm speaking to.
◆ **s'adresser à quelqu'un (2)** to go and
see somebody ◇ *Adressez-vous au
patron.* Go and see the boss.
◇ *Adressez-vous aux renseignements.*
Ask at the enquiry desk.
◆ **s'adresser à quelqu'un (3)** to be
aimed at somebody ◇ *Ce film
s'adresse surtout aux enfants.* This
film is aimed mainly at children.

l'**adulte** MASC/FEM NOUN
adult

l'**adverbe** MASC NOUN
adverb

l'**adversaire** MASC/FEM NOUN
opponent

aérien ADJECTIVE (FEM SING **aérienne**)
◆ **une compagnie aérienne** an airline

l'**aérobic** MASC NOUN

☞

aerobics ◊ *Teresa fait de l'aérobic.*
Teresa does aerobics.

l'**aérogare** FEM NOUN
terminal

l'**aéroglisseur** MASC NOUN
hovercraft

l'**aéroport** MASC NOUN
airport

l'**affaire** FEM NOUN
see also **les affaires**
1 case ◊ *une affaire de drogue* a
drugs case
2 business ◊ *Son affaire marche
bien.* His business is doing well.
◆ **une bonne affaire** a real bargain
◆ **Ça fera l'affaire.** This will do nicely.
◆ **avoir affaire à quelqu'un** to deal with
somebody

les **affaires** FEM NOUN
see also **l'affaire**
1 things ◊ *Va chercher tes affaires!*
Go and get your things!
2 business ◊ *Les affaires marchent
bien en ce moment.* Business is good
at the moment. ◊ *Mêle-toi de tes
affaires.* (*informal*) Mind your own
business.
◆ **un homme d'affaires** a businessman
◆ **le ministre des Affaires étrangères** the
Foreign Secretary

l'**affection** FEM NOUN
affection

affectueux ADJECTIVE (FEM SING **affectueuse**)
affectionate

l'**affiche** FEM NOUN
poster

afficher VERB
to put up ◊ *Ils ont affiché les
résultats dehors.* They've put the
results up outside.
◆ **"Défense d'afficher"** "Stick no bills"

affilée
◆ **d'affilée** ADVERB
at a stretch ◊ *Il a travaillé douze
heures d'affilée.* He worked 12 hours
at a stretch.

affirmer VERB
to claim ◊ *David a affirmé que c'était
la vérité.* David claimed it was the
truth.
◆ **s'affirmer** to assert yourself ◊ *Il est
trop timide, il faut qu'il s'affirme.*
He's too shy, he should assert
himself.

l'**affluence** FEM NOUN
◆ **les heures d'affluence** the rush hour

s'**affoler** VERB
to panic ◊ *Ne t'affole pas!* Don't
panic!

affranchir VERB
to stamp

affreux ADJECTIVE (FEM SING **affreuse**)
awful

affronter VERB
to face ◊ *L'Allemagne affronte l'Italie
en finale.* Germany will face Italy in
the final.

afin de CONJUNCTION
◆ **afin de faire quelque chose** so as to
do something ◊ *Je me suis levé très
tôt afin d'être prêt à temps.* I got up
very early so as to be ready on time.

afin que CONJUNCTION
so that
*afin que is followed by a verb in the
subjunctive.*
◊ *Il m'a téléphoné afin que je sois
prêt à temps.* He phoned me so that
I'd be ready on
time.

africain ADJECTIVE, NOUN (FEM SING **africaine**)
African
◆ **un Africain** an African (*man*)
◆ **une Africaine** an African (*woman*)

l'**Afrique** FEM NOUN
Africa
◆ **en Afrique (1)** in Africa
◆ **en Afrique (2)** to Africa
◆ **l'Afrique du Sud** South Africa

agacer VERB
to get on somebody's nerves ◊ *Tu
m'agaces avec tes questions!* You're
getting on my nerves with all your
questions!

l'**âge** MASC NOUN
age
◆ **Quel âge as-tu?** How old are you?

âgé ADJECTIVE
old ◊ *Son père est âgé.* His father's
old. ◊ *Il est âgé de dix ans.* He's 10
years old.
◆ **les personnes âgées** the elderly

l'**agence** FEM NOUN
1 agency ◊ *l'agence pour l'emploi*
the employment agency
◆ **une agence de voyages** a travel
agency
2 office ◊ *Nous avons plusieurs
agences à Londres.* We have several
offices in London.
◆ **une agence immobilière** an estate
agent's

l'**agenda** MASC NOUN
diary ◊ *Je l'ai noté dans mon
agenda.* I have made a note of it in
my diary.
*Be careful! The French word **agenda**
does not mean **agenda**.*

A

s' **agenouiller** VERB
　to kneel down

l' **agent** MASC NOUN
　◆ **un agent de police** a policeman
　◆ **un agent d'entretien** a cleaner

l' **agglomération** FEM NOUN
　town
　◆ **l'agglomération parisienne** Greater
　Paris

aggraver VERB
　to make worse
　◆ **s'aggraver** to worsen

agir VERB
　to act ◊ *Il a agi par vengeance.* He
　acted out of vengeance.
　◆ **Il s'agit de ...** It's about ... ◊ *Il s'agit*
　du club de sport. It's about the sports
　club. ◊ *De quoi s'agit-il?* What is it
　about?
　◆ **Il s'agit de faire attention.** We must
　be careful.

agité ADJECTIVE
　1 restless ◊ *Les élèves sont agités.*
　The pupils are restless.
　2 rough ◊ *La mer est agitée.* The
　sea is rough.
　◆ **un sommeil agité** broken sleep

agiter VERB
　to shake ◊ *Agitez la bouteille.* Shake
　the bottle.

l' **agneau** MASC NOUN (PL les **agneaux**)
　lamb

l' **agrafe** FEM NOUN
　staple (*for papers*)

l' **agrafeuse** FEM NOUN
　stapler

agrandir VERB
　1 to enlarge ◊ *J'ai fait agrandir mes*
　photos. I've had my photos enlarged.
　2 to extend ◊ *Ils ont agrandi leur*
　jardin. They've extended their garden.
　◆ **s'agrandir** to expand ◊ *Leur magasin*
　s'est agrandi. Their shop has
　expanded.

agréable ADJECTIVE
　nice

agréer VERB
　◆ **Veuillez agréer, Monsieur,**
　l'expression de mes sentiments les
　meilleurs. Jean Ormal. Yours
　sincerely, Jean Ormal.

agressif ADJECTIVE (FEM SING **agressive**)
　aggressive

l' **agressivité** FEM NOUN
　aggression
　◆ **faire preuve d'agressivité envers de**
　quelqu'un to be aggressive to
　somebody
　◆ **l'agressivité au volant** road rage

agricole ADJECTIVE
　agricultural ◊ *le matériel agricole*
　agricultural machinery
　◆ **une exploitation agricole** a farm

l' **agriculteur** MASC NOUN
　farmer
　◆ **Il est agriculteur.** He's a farmer.

l' **agriculture** FEM NOUN
　farming

ai VERB *see* **avoir**
　◆ **J'ai deux chats.** I have two cats.
　◆ **J'ai bien dormi.** I slept well.

l' **aide** FEM NOUN
　1 help ◊ *J'ai besoin de ton aide.* I
　need your help. ◊ *appeler quelqu'un*
　à l'aide to call to somebody for help
　◆ **À l'aide!** Help!
　2 aid ◊ *une aide financière* financial
　aid
　◆ **à l'aide de** using ◊ *J'ai réussi à ouvrir*
　la boîte à l'aide d'un couteau. I
　managed to open the tin using a
　knife.

aider VERB
　to help

l' **aide-soignant** MASC NOUN (PL les **aides-**
　soignants)
　auxiliary nurse ◊ *Il est aide-soignant.*
　He's an auxiliary nurse.

l' **aide-soignante** FEM NOUN (PL les **aides-**
　soignantes)
　auxiliary nurse ◊ *Françoise est aide-*
　soignante. Françoise is an auxiliary
　nurse.

aie VERB *see* **avoir**

aïe EXCLAMATION
　Ouch!

aigre ADJECTIVE
　sour

aigu ADJECTIVE (FEM SING **aiguë**)
　sharp (*pain*) ◊ *Il a ressenti une*
　douleur aiguë dans le bas du dos. He
　felt a sharp pain in the small of his
　back.
　◆ **e accent aigu** e acute

l' **aiguille** FEM NOUN
　needle ◊ *une aiguille à tricoter* a
　knitting needle
　◆ **les aiguilles d'une montre** the hands
　of a watch

l' **ail** MASC NOUN
　garlic

l' **aile** FEM NOUN
　wing

aille VERB *see* **aller**

ailleurs ADVERB
　somewhere else
　◆ **partout ailleurs** everywhere else

♦ **nulle part ailleurs** nowhere else
♦ **d'ailleurs** besides

aimable ADJECTIVE
kind

l' **aimant** MASC NOUN
magnet

aimer VERB
1 to love ◊ *Elle aime ses enfants.* She loves her children.
2 to like ◊ *Tu aimes le chocolat?* Do you like chocolate? ◊ *J'aime bien ce garçon.* I like this boy. ◊ *J'aime bien jouer au tennis.* I like playing tennis. ◊ *J'aimerais aller en Grèce.* I'd like to go to Greece.
♦ **J'aimerais mieux ne pas y aller.** I'd rather not go.

aîné ADJECTIVE
see also **aîné** NOUN
elder ◊ *mon frère aîné* my big brother

l' **aîné** MASC NOUN
see also **aîné** ADJECTIVE
oldest child ◊ *Il est l'aîné.* He's the oldest child.

l' **aînée** FEM NOUN
oldest child ◊ *Elle est l'aînée.* She's the oldest child.

ainsi ADVERB
in this way ◊ *Il faut faire ainsi.* This is the way to do it.
♦ **C'est ainsi qu'il a réussi.** That's how he succeeded.
♦ **ainsi que** as well as
♦ **et ainsi de suite** and so on

l' **air** MASC NOUN
1 air ◊ *l'air chaud* warm air
♦ **prendre l'air** to get some fresh air
2 tune ◊ *Elle a joué un air au piano.* She played a tune on the piano.
♦ **Elle a l'air fatiguée.** She looks tired.
♦ **Il a l'air d'un clown.** He looks like a clown.

l' **aire de jeux** FEM NOUN
playground

l' **aire de repos** FEM NOUN
rest area (*on motorway*)

l' **aise** FEM NOUN
♦ **être à l'aise** to be at ease ◊ *Elle est à l'aise avec tout le monde.* She's at ease with everybody.
♦ **être mal à l'aise** to be ill at ease
♦ **se mettre à l'aise** to make oneself comfortable

ait VERB see **avoir**

ajouter VERB
to add

l' **alarme** FEM NOUN

alarm ◊ *donner l'alarme* to raise the alarm

l' **Albanie** FEM NOUN
Albania

l' **album** MASC NOUN
album

l' **alcool** MASC NOUN
alcohol ◊ *Je ne bois pas d'alcool.* I don't drink alcohol.
♦ **les alcools forts** spirits

alcoolisé ADJECTIVE
alcoholic
♦ **une boisson non alcoolisée** a soft drink

les **alentours** MASC NOUN
♦ **dans les alentours** in the area
♦ **aux alentours de Paris** in the Paris area
♦ **aux alentours de cinq heures** around 5 o'clock

l' **algèbre** FEM NOUN
algebra

Alger NOUN
Algiers

l' **Algérie** FEM NOUN
Algeria

algérien ADJECTIVE, NOUN (FEM SING **algérienne**)
Algerian
♦ **un Algérien** an Algerian (*man*)
♦ **une Algérienne** an Algerian (*woman*)

l' **algue** FEM NOUN
seaweed

l' **aliment** MASC NOUN
food

l' **alimentation** FEM NOUN
1 groceries ◊ *le rayon alimentation du supermarché* the grocery department in the supermarket
2 diet ◊ *Elle a une alimentation saine.* She has a healthy diet.

l' **allée** FEM NOUN
1 path ◊ *les allées du parc* the paths in the park
2 drive (*in street names*)
♦ **les allées et venues** comings and goings

allégé ADJECTIVE
low-fat ◊ *un yaourt allégé* a low-fat yoghurt

l' **Allemagne** FEM NOUN
Germany
♦ **en Allemagne (1)** in Germany
♦ **en Allemagne (2)** to Germany

allemand ADJECTIVE, NOUN
German ◊ *Elle parle allemand.* She speaks German.
♦ **un Allemand** a German (*man*)

A

- ◆ **une Allemande** a German (*woman*)
- ◆ **les Allemands** the Germans

aller VERB

see also **aller** NOUN

Present tense:	
je vais	nous allons
tu vas	vous allez
il/elle va	ils/elles vont
Past participle:	
allé	

to go ◇ *Je suis allé à Londres.* I went to London. ◇ *Je dois y aller.* I've got to go. ◇ *Elle ira le voir.* She'll go and see him. ◇ *Je vais me fâcher.* I'm going to get angry.
- ◆ **s'en aller** to go away ◇ *Je m'en vais demain.* I'm going tomorrow.
- ◆ **aller bien à quelqu'un** to suit somebody ◇ *Cette robe te va bien.* This dress suits you.
- ◆ **Allez! Dépêche-toi!** Come on! Hurry up!
- ◆ **Comment allez-vous? – Je vais bien.** How are you? – I'm fine.
- ◆ **Comment ça va? – Ça va bien.** How are you? – I'm fine.
- ◆ **aller mieux** to be better

l' **aller** MASC NOUN

see also **aller** VERB

[1] outward journey ◇ *L'aller nous a pris trois heures.* The journey there took us three hours.
[2] single (*ticket*) ◇ *Je voudrais un aller pour Angers.* I'd like a single to Angers.
- ◆ **un aller simple** a single
- ◆ **un aller retour (1)** a return ticket ◇ *Je voudrais un aller retour pour Londres.* I'd like a return to London.
- ◆ **un aller retour (2)** a round trip ◇ *Il a fait l'aller retour en dix heures.* He did the round trip in ten hours.

allergique ADJECTIVE
- ◆ **allergique à** allergic to ◇ *Je suis allergique aux poils de chat.* I'm allergic to cat fur.

allô EXCLAMATION

Hello! ◇ *Allô! Je voudrais parler à Monsieur Simon.* Hello! I'd like to speak to Mr Simon.

l' **allocation** FEM NOUN
allowance
- ◆ **les allocations chômage** unemployment benefit

s' **allonger** VERB
to lie down ◇ *Il s'est allongé sur son lit.* He lay down on his bed.

allumer VERB

[1] to put on (*light*) ◇ *Tu peux allumer la lumière?* Can you put the light on?
[2] to switch on ◇ *Allume la radio.* Switch on the radio.
[3] to light ◇ *Elle a allumé une cigarette.* She lit a cigarette.
- ◆ **s'allumer** (*light*) to come on ◇ *La lumière s'est allumée.* The light came on.

l' **allumette** FEM NOUN
match ◇ *une boîte d'allumettes* a box of matches

l' **allure** FEM NOUN
[1] speed ◇ *à toute allure* at top speed
[2] look ◇ *avoir une drôle d'allure* to look odd

l' **allusion** FEM NOUN
reference

alors ADVERB
[1] then ◇ *Tu as fini? Alors je m'en vais.* Have you finished? I'm going then.
[2] so ◇ *Alors je lui ai dit de partir.* So I told him to leave.
- ◆ **Et alors?** So what?
[3] at that time ◇ *Il habitait alors à Paris.* He was living in Paris at that time.
- ◆ **alors que (1)** as ◇ *Il est arrivé alors que je partais.* He arrived just as I was leaving.
- ◆ **alors que (2)** while ◇ *Alors que je travaillais dur, lui se reposait.* While I was working hard, he was resting.

les **Alpes** FEM NOUN
Alps ◇ *dans les Alpes* in the Alps

l' **alphabet** MASC NOUN
alphabet

alphabétique ADJECTIVE
alphabetical ◇ *par ordre alphabétique* in alphabetical order

l' **alpinisme** MASC NOUN
mountaineering

l' **alpiniste** MASC/FEM NOUN
mountaineer

l' **Alsace** FEM NOUN
Alsace

l' **amande** FEM NOUN
almond
- ◆ **la pâte d'amandes** marzipan

l' **amant** MASC NOUN
lover

amateur ADJECTIVE (FEM SING **amateur**)

see also **amateur** NOUN

amateur ◇ *Elle est pianiste amateur.* She's an amateur pianist.

l' **amateur** MASC NOUN

see also **amateur** ADJECTIVE

amateur

☞

◆ **en amateur** as a hobby ◊ *Il fait de la photo en amateur.* He takes photos as a hobby.

◆ **C'est un amateur de musique.** He's a music lover.

l' **ambassade** FEM NOUN
embassy

l' **ambassadeur** MASC NOUN
ambassador

l' **ambiance** FEM NOUN
atmosphere ◊ *Je n'aime pas l'ambiance ici.* I don't like the atmosphere here. ◊ *Il y a de l'ambiance dans ce café.* This café has a lively atmosphere.

◆ **la musique d'ambiance** background music

ambitieux ADJECTIVE (FEM SING **ambitieuse**)
ambitious

l' **ambition** FEM NOUN
ambition ◊ *Il a l'ambition de devenir Premier ministre.* His ambition is to be Prime Minister.

◆ **Il a beaucoup d'ambition.** He's very ambitious.

l' **ambulance** FEM NOUN
ambulance

l' **âme** FEM NOUN
soul

l' **amélioration** FEM NOUN
improvement

améliorer VERB
to improve

◆ **s'améliorer** to improve ◊ *Le temps s'améliore.* The weather's improving.

l' **amende** FEM NOUN
fine ◊ *une amende de cinq cents francs* a 500 franc fine

amener VERB
to bring ◊ *Qu'est-ce qui t'amène?* What brings you here? ◊ *Est-ce que je peux amener un ami?* Can I bring a friend?

amer ADJECTIVE (FEM SING **amère**)
bitter

américain ADJECTIVE, NOUN (FEM SING **américaine**)
American

◆ **un Américain** an American (*man*)

◆ **une Américaine** an American (*woman*)

l' **Amérique** FEM NOUN
America

◆ **en Amérique (1)** in America

◆ **en Amérique (2)** to America

◆ **l'Amérique du Nord** North America

◆ **l'Amérique du Sud** South America

l' **ami** MASC NOUN
friend

◆ **C'est son petit ami.** He's her boyfriend.

amical ADJECTIVE (MASC PL **amicaux**)
friendly

amicalement ADVERB
in a friendly way

◆ **amicalement, Pierre** best wishes, Pierre

l' **amie** FEM NOUN
friend

◆ **C'est sa petite amie.** She's his girlfriend.

l' **amitié** FEM NOUN
friendship

◆ **Fais mes amitiés à Paul.** Give my regards to Paul.

◆ **Amitiés, Christèle.** (*in letter*) Best wishes, Christèle.

l' **amour** MASC NOUN
love

◆ **faire l'amour** to make love

amoureux ADJECTIVE (FEM SING **amoureuse**)
in love ◊ *être amoureux de quelqu'un* to be in love with somebody

l' **amour-propre** MASC NOUN
self-esteem

l' **amphithéâtre** MASC NOUN
lecture theatre

amplement ADVERB

◆ **Nous avons amplement le temps.** We have plenty of time.

l' **ampoule** FEM NOUN
1. light bulb
2. blister ◊ *J'ai une ampoule au pied.* I've got a blister on my foot.

amusant ADJECTIVE
amusing

les **amuse-gueule** MASC NOUN
party nibbles

amuser VERB
to amuse

◆ **s'amuser (1)** to play ◊ *Les enfants s'amusent dehors.* The children are playing outside.

◆ **s'amuser (2)** to enjoy oneself ◊ *On s'est bien amusés à cette soirée.* We really enjoyed ourselves at that party.

l' **an** MASC NOUN
year

◆ **le premier de l'an** New Year's Day

◆ **le nouvel an** New Year

l' **analyse** FEM NOUN
1. analysis
2. test (*medical*) ◊ *une analyse d'urine* a urine test

l' **ananas** MASC NOUN

pineapple

l' **ancêtre** MASC/FEM NOUN
  ancestor

l' **anchois** MASC NOUN
  anchovy

ancien ADJECTIVE (FEM SING **ancienne**)
  [1] former ◊ *C'est une ancienne élève.*
  She's a former pupil.
  [2] old ◊ *notre ancienne voiture* our
  old car
  [3] antique ◊ *un fauteuil ancien* an
  antique chair

l' **ancre** FEM NOUN
  anchor

Andorre FEM NOUN
  Andorra

l' **âne** MASC NOUN
  donkey

l' **ange** MASC NOUN
  angel
  ♦ **être aux anges** to be over the moon

l' **angine** FEM NOUN
  throat infection

anglais ADJECTIVE, NOUN (FEM SING **anglaise**)
  English ◊ *Est-ce que vous parlez
  anglais?* Do you speak English?
  ♦ **un Anglais** an Englishman
  ♦ **une Anglaise** an Englishwoman
  ♦ **les Anglais** the English

l' **angle** MASC NOUN
  [1] angle ◊ *un angle droit* a right
  angle
  [2] corner ◊ *à l'angle de la rue* at the
  corner of the street

l' **Angleterre** FEM NOUN
  England
  ♦ **en Angleterre (1)** in England
  ◊ *J'habite en Angleterre.* I live in
  England.
  ♦ **en Angleterre (2)** to England ◊ *Je suis
  allée en Angleterre le mois dernier.* I
  went to England last month.

anglo- PREFIX
  anglo-
  ♦ **les îles Anglo-Normandes** the Channel
  Islands

anglophone ADJECTIVE
  English-speaking

angoissé ADJECTIVE
  stressed ◊ *Il était angoissé à l'idée
  de prendre l'avion.* He was stressed
  about the idea of taking the plane.

l' **animal** MASC NOUN (PL les **animaux**)
  animal

l' **animateur** MASC NOUN
  [1] host ◊ *Il est animateur à la télé.*
  He's a TV host.

[2] youth leader ◊ *Pierre est
animateur au centre sportif.* Pierre is
a youth leader at the sports centre.

l' **animatrice** FEM NOUN
  [1] host ◊ *Elle est animatrice à la télé.*
  She's a TV host.
  [2] youth leader ◊ *Cécile est
  animatrice au centre sportif.* Cécile is
  a youth leader at the sports centre.

animé ADJECTIVE
  lively ◊ *Cette rue est très animée.*
  This is a very lively street.
  ♦ **un dessin animé** a cartoon

l' **anis** MASC NOUN
  aniseed

l' **anneau** MASC NOUN (PL les **anneaux**)
  ring

l' **année** FEM NOUN
  year ◊ *l'année dernière* last year
  ◊ *l'année prochaine* next year

l' **anniversaire** MASC NOUN
  [1] birthday ◊ *C'est l'anniversaire de
  Janet.* It's Janet's birthday.
  [2] anniversary ◊ *un anniversaire de
  mariage* a wedding anniversary

l' **annonce** FEM NOUN
  advert ◊ *J'ai lu votre annonce dans
  le journal.* I saw your advert in the
  newspaper. ◊ *passer une annonce* to
  place an ad
  ♦ **les petites annonces** the small ads

annoncer VERB
  to announce ◊ *Ils ont annoncé leurs
  fiançailles.* They've announced their
  engagement.

l' **annuaire** MASC NOUN
  phone book

annuel ADJECTIVE (FEM SING **annuelle**)
  annual

annuler VERB
  to cancel

anonyme ADJECTIVE
  anonymous

l' **anorak** MASC NOUN
  anorak

l' **ANPE** FEM NOUN (= *Agence nationale
pour l'emploi*)
  job centre ◊ *Je suis allé à l'ANPE.* I
  went to the job centre.

l' **Antarctique** MASC NOUN
  Antarctic

l' **antenne** FEM NOUN
  [1] aerial
  ♦ **antenne parabolique** satellite dish
  ♦ **être à l'antenne** to be on the air
  [2] antenna

l' **antibiotique** MASC NOUN
  antibiotic

l' **antidépresseur** MASC NOUN
antidepressant ◇ *Elle est sous antidépresseurs depuis un mois.* She's been on antidepressants for a month.

l' **antigel** MASC NOUN
antifreeze

les **Antilles** FEM NOUN
West Indies
♦ **aux Antilles (1)** in the West Indies
♦ **aux Antilles (2)** to the West Indies

antipathique ADJECTIVE
unpleasant ◇ *Je le trouve plutôt antipathique.* I find him rather unpleasant.

antipelliculaire ADJECTIVE
anti-dandruff

l' **antiquaire** MASC/FEM NOUN
antique dealer ◇ *Elle est antiquaire.* She's an antique dealer.

l' **antiquité** FEM NOUN
antique ◇ *un magasin d'antiquités* an antique shop
♦ **pendant l'antiquité** in classical times

antiseptique ADJECTIVE
see also **antiseptique** NOUN
antiseptic

l' **antiseptique** MASC NOUN
see also **antiseptique** ADJECTIVE
antiseptic

l' **antivol** MASC NOUN
1 lock (*on bike*)
2 steering lock (*on car*)

anxieux ADJECTIVE (FEM SING **anxieuse**)
anxious ◇ *Il est anxieux de nature.* He's a born worrier.

août MASC NOUN
August
♦ **en août** in August

apercevoir VERB
to see ◇ *J'aperçois la côte.* I can see the shore.
♦ **s'apercevoir de quelque chose** to notice something
♦ **s'apercevoir que ...** to notice that ...

l' **apéritif** MASC NOUN
aperitif ◇ *Venez donc prendre l'apéritif ce soir!* Come round for drinks this evening!

apparaître VERB
to appear

l' **appareil** MASC NOUN
device
♦ **un appareil dentaire** a brace (*for teeth*)
♦ **les appareils ménagers** domestic appliances
♦ **un appareil photo** a camera

♦ **Qui est à l'appareil?** Who's speaking? (*on phone*)

apparemment ADVERB
apparently

l' **apparence** FEM NOUN
appearance

l' **apparition** FEM NOUN
appearance ◇ *Il n'a fait qu'une brève apparition.* He only appeared briefly.

l' **appartement** MASC NOUN
flat

appartenir VERB
♦ **appartenir à quelqu'un** to belong to somebody

apparu VERB *see* **apparaître**

l' **appel** MASC NOUN
1 cry ◇ *un appel au secours* a cry for help
2 phone call
♦ **faire appel à quelqu'un** to appeal to somebody
♦ **faire l'appel** to call the register (*in school*)
♦ **faire un appel de phares** to flash one's headlights

appeler VERB
to call ◇ *Elle a appelé le médecin.* She called the doctor. ◇ *J'ai appelé Richard à Londres.* I called Richard in London.
♦ **s'appeler** to be called ◇ *Comment ça s'appelle?* What is it called? ◇ *Elle s'appelle Muriel.* Her name's Muriel. ◇ *Comment tu t'appelles?* What's your name?

l' **appendicite** FEM NOUN
appendicitis

appétissant ADJECTIVE
appetizing

l' **appétit** MASC NOUN
appetite
♦ **Bon appétit!** Enjoy your meal!

applaudir VERB
to clap (*applaud*)

les **applaudissements** MASC NOUN
applause SING

appliquer VERB
1 to apply
2 to enforce ◇ *appliquer la loi* to enforce the law
♦ **s'appliquer** to apply oneself

apporter VERB
to bring

apprécier VERB
to appreciate

appréhender VERB
to dread ◇ *J'appréhende cette réunion.* I'm dreading this meeting.

apprendre VERB
[1] to learn ◊ *apprendre quelque chose par cœur* to learn something by heart
♦ **apprendre à faire quelque chose** to learn to do something ◊ *J'apprends à faire la cuisine.* I'm learning to cook.
[2] to hear ◊ *J'ai appris son départ.* I heard that she had left.
♦ **apprendre quelque chose à quelqu'un (1)** to teach somebody something ◊ *Ma mère m'a appris l'anglais.* My mother taught me English. ◊ *Elle lui a appris à conduire.* She taught him to drive.
♦ **apprendre quelque chose à quelqu'un (2)** to tell somebody something ◊ *Jean m'a appris la nouvelle.* Jean told me the news.

l'**apprentissage** MASC NOUN
learning ◊ *On dit que l'apprentissage de l'arabe est très difficile.* Learning Arabic is said to be very difficult.

appris VERB *see* **apprendre**

l'**approbation** FEM NOUN
approval ◊ *donner son approbation* to give one's approval

approcher VERB
♦ **approcher de** to approach ◊ *Nous approchons de Paris.* We are approaching Paris.
♦ **s'approcher de** to come closer to ◊ *Ne t'approche pas, j'ai la grippe!* Don't get too close to me, I've got flu!

approprié ADJECTIVE
suitable ◊ *une tenue appropriée* suitable clothes

approuver VERB
to approve of ◊ *Je n'approuve pas ses méthodes.* I don't approve of his methods.

approximatif ADJECTIVE (FEM SING **approximative**)
[1] approximate ◊ *un prix approximatif* an approximate price
[2] rough ◊ *un calcul approximatif* a rough calculation

l'**appui** MASC NOUN
support ◊ *J'ai besoin de votre appui.* I need your support.

appuyer VERB
[1] to press ◊ *appuyer sur un bouton* to press a button
[2] to lean ◊ *Elle a appuyé son vélo contre la porte.* She leaned her bike against the door.
♦ **s'appuyer** to lean ◊ *Elle s'est appuyée contre le mur.* She leaned against the wall. ◊ *Il s'est appuyé sur la table.* He leaned on the table.

après PREPOSITION, ADVERB
[1] after ◊ *après le déjeuner* after lunch ◊ *après son départ* after he had left ◊ *après qu'il est parti* after he had left ◊ *Nous viendrons après avoir fait la vaisselle.* We'll come after we've done the dishes.
[2] afterwards ◊ *aussitôt après* immediately afterwards
♦ **après coup** afterwards ◊ *J'y ai repensé après coup.* I thought about it again afterwards.
♦ **d'après** according to ◊ *D'après lui, c'est une erreur.* According to him, that's a mistake.
♦ **après tout** after all

après-demain ADVERB
the day after tomorrow

l'**après-midi** MASC OR FEM NOUN
afternoon

l'**après-rasage** MASC NOUN
aftershave

l'**aquarium** MASC NOUN
aquarium

arabe ADJECTIVE, NOUN
[1] Arab ◊ *les pays arabes* the Arab countries
[2] Arabic ◊ *la littérature arabe* Arabic literature ◊ *Il parle arabe.* He speaks Arabic.
♦ **un Arabe** an Arab (*man*)
♦ **une Arabe** an Arab (*woman*)

l'**Arabie Saoudite** FEM NOUN
Saudi Arabia

l'**araignée** FEM NOUN
spider

l'**arbitre** MASC NOUN
[1] referee
[2] umpire

l'**arbre** MASC NOUN
tree
♦ **un arbre généalogique** a family tree

l'**arbuste** MASC NOUN
shrub

l'**arc** MASC NOUN
bow ◊ *son arc et ses flèches* his bow and arrows

l'**arc-en-ciel** MASC NOUN (PL les **arcs-en-ciel**)
rainbow

l'**archéologie** FEM NOUN
archaeology

l'**archéologue** MASC/FEM NOUN
archaeologist ◊ *Elle est archéologue.* She's an archaeologist.

l'**archipel** MASC NOUN
archipelago

l'**architecte** MASC NOUN

architect ◊ *Il est architecte.* He's an architect.

l' **architecture** FEM NOUN
architecture

l' **Arctique** MASC NOUN
Arctic

l' **ardoise** FEM NOUN
slate

l' **arène** FEM NOUN
bullring
♦ **des arènes romaines** a Roman amphitheatre
♦ **l'arène politique** the political arena

l' **arête** FEM NOUN
fish bone

l' **argent** MASC NOUN
1 silver ◊ *une bague en argent* a silver ring
2 money ◊ *Je n'ai plus d'argent.* I haven't got any more money.
♦ **l'argent de poche** pocket money
♦ **l'argent liquide** cash

argentin ADJECTIVE, NOUN (FEM SING **argentine**)
Argentinian
♦ **un Argentin** an Argentinian (*man*)
♦ **une Argentine** an Argentinian (*woman*)

l' **Argentine** FEM NOUN
Argentina

l' **argile** FEM NOUN
clay

l' **argot** MASC NOUN
slang

l' **arme** FEM NOUN
weapon
♦ **une arme à feu** a firearm

l' **armée** FEM NOUN
army
♦ **l'armée de l'air** the Air Force

l' **armistice** MASC NOUN
armistice

l' **armoire** FEM NOUN
wardrobe

l' **armure** FEM NOUN
armour ◊ *un chevalier en armure* a knight in armour

arnaquer VERB (*informal*)
to con

aromatisé ADJECTIVE
flavoured

l' **arôme** MASC NOUN
1 aroma
2 flavouring (*added to food*)

arpenter VERB
to pace up and down ◊ *Il arpentait le couloir.* He was pacing up and down the corridor.

arrache-pied

♦ **d'arrache-pied** ADVERB
furiously ◊ *travailler d'arrache-pied* to work furiously

arracher VERB
1 to take out ◊ *Le dentiste m'a arraché une dent.* The dentist took one of my teeth out.
2 to tear out ◊ *Arrachez la page.* Tear the page out.
3 to pull up ◊ *Elle a arraché les mauvaises herbes.* She pulled up the weeds.
♦ **arracher quelque chose à quelqu'un** to snatch something from somebody

arranger VERB
1 to arrange ◊ *arranger des fleurs dans un vase* to arrange flowers in a vase
2 to suit ◊ *Ça m'arrange de partir plus tôt.* It suits me to leave earlier.
♦ **s'arranger** to come to an agreement ◊ *Arrangez-vous avec le patron.* You'll have to come to an agreement with the boss.
♦ **Je vais m'arranger pour venir.** I'll organize things so that I can come.
♦ **Ça va s'arranger.** Things will work themselves out.

l' **arrestation** FEM NOUN
arrest ◊ *en état d'arrestation* under arrest

l' **arrêt** MASC NOUN
stop ◊ *un arrêt de bus* a bus stop
♦ **sans arrêt (1)** non-stop ◊ *Elle travaille sans arrêt.* She works non-stop.
♦ **sans arrêt (2)** continually ◊ *Ils se disputent sans arrêt.* They quarrel continually.

arrêter VERB
1 to stop
♦ **Arrête!** Stop it!
♦ **arrêter de faire quelque chose** to stop doing something
2 to switch off ◊ *Il a arrêté le moteur.* He switched the engine off.
3 to arrest ◊ *Mon voisin a été arrêté.* My neighbour's been arrested.
♦ **s'arrêter** to stop ◊ *Elle s'est arrêtée devant une vitrine.* She stopped in front of a shop window.
♦ **s'arrêter de faire quelque chose** to stop doing something ◊ *s'arrêter de fumer* to stop smoking

les **arrhes** FEM NOUN
deposit SING ◊ *verser des arrhes* to pay a deposit

l' **arrière** MASC NOUN
see also **arrière** ADJECTIVE

back ◊ *l'arrière de la maison* the back
of the house

♦ **à l'arrière** at the back

♦ **en arrière** behind ◊ *Ils sont restés en
arrière.* They stayed behind.

arrière ADJECTIVE (MASC, FEM, PL)

see also **arrière** NOUN

back ◊ *le siège arrière* the back seat
◊ *les roues arrière* the rear wheels

l' **arrière-grand-mère** FEM NOUN (PL les
arrière-grands-mères)
great-grandmother

l' **arrière-grand-père** MASC NOUN (PL les
arrière-grands-pères)
great-grandfather

l' **arrivée** FEM NOUN
arrival

arriver VERB

[1] to arrive ◊ *J'arrive à l'école à huit
heures.* I arrive at school at 8 o'clock.

[2] to happen ◊ *Qu'est-ce qui est
arrivée à Ann?* What happened to
Ann?

♦ **arriver à faire quelque chose** to
manage to do something ◊ *J'espère
que je vais y arriver.* I hope I'll
manage it.

♦ **Il m'arrive de dormir jusqu'à midi.** I
sometimes sleep till midday.

arrogant ADJECTIVE
arrogant

l' **arrondissement** MASC NOUN
district

> *ⓘ Paris, Lyons and Marseilles are
> divided into numbered districts
> called **arrondissements**.*

arroser VERB
to water ◊ *Daphne arrose ses
tomates.* Daphne is watering her
tomatoes.

♦ **Ils ont arrosé leur victoire.** They had
a drink to celebrate their victory.

l' **arrosoir** MASC NOUN
watering can

l' **art** MASC NOUN
art

l' **artère** FEM NOUN

[1] artery

[2] thoroughfare ◊ *les grandes artères
de Paris* the main roads of Paris

l' **artichaut** MASC NOUN
artichoke

l' **article** MASC NOUN

[1] article ◊ *un article de journal* a
newspaper article

[2] item ◊ *les articles en promotion*
items on special offer

l' **articulation** FEM NOUN
joint ◊ *l'articulation du genou* the
knee joint

articuler VERB
to pronounce clearly

artificiel ADJECTIVE (FEM SING **artificielle**)
artificial

l' **artisan** MASC NOUN
self-employed craftsman

l' **artiste** MASC/FEM NOUN

[1] artist

[2] performer

artistique ADJECTIVE
artistic

as VERB *see* **avoir**

see also **as** NOUN

♦ **Tu as de beaux cheveux.** You've got
nice hair.

l' **as** MASC NOUN

see also **as** VERB

ace ◊ *l'as de trèfle* the ace of clubs

l' **ascenseur** MASC NOUN
lift

l' **Ascension** FEM NOUN
Ascension

asiatique ADJECTIVE
Asiatic ◊ *la cuisine asiatique* Oriental
cooking ◊ *le Sud-Est asiatique* South
East Asia

l' **Asie** FEM NOUN
Asia

♦ **en Asie (1)** in Asia

♦ **en Asie (2)** to Asia

l' **aspect** MASC NOUN
appearance

l' **asperge** FEM NOUN
asparagus

l' **aspirateur** MASC NOUN
vacuum cleaner

♦ **passer l'aspirateur** to vacuum

l' **aspirine** FEM NOUN
aspirin

assaisonner VERB
to season

l' **assassin** MASC NOUN
murderer

assassiner VERB
to murder

assembler VERB
to assemble

♦ **s'assembler** to gather ◊ *Une foule
énorme s'était assemblée.* A huge
crowd had gathered.

s' **asseoir** VERB
to sit down ◊ *Asseyez-vous!*
Sit down! ◊ *Assieds-toi!* Sit
down!

assez ADVERB

1 enough ◇ *Nous n'avons pas assez de temps.* We don't have enough time. ◇ *Est-ce qu'il y a assez de pain?* Is there enough bread?

♦ **J'en ai assez!** I've had enough!

2 quite ◇ *Il faisait assez beau.* The weather was quite nice.

l' **assiette** FEM NOUN

plate ◇ *une assiette creuse* a soup plate ◇ *une assiette à dessert* a dessert plate

♦ **une assiette anglaise** assorted cold meats

assis VERB *see* **asseoir**

assis ADJECTIVE

sitting ◇ *Il est assis par terre.* He's sitting on the floor.

l' **assistance** FEM NOUN

1 audience ◇ *Y a-t-il un médecin dans l'assistance?* Is there a doctor in the audience?

2 aid ◇ *l'assistance humanitaire* humanitarian aid

3 assistance ◇ *avec l'assistance de quelqu'un* with the assistance of somebody

l' **assistant** MASC NOUN

assistant ◇ *Il était assistant d'anglais à Tourcoing.* He was an English assistant in Tourcoing.

♦ **un assistant social** a social worker

l' **assistante** FEM NOUN

assistant ◇ *Elle est assistante de français à Oxford.* She's a French assistant in Oxford.

♦ **une assistante sociale** a social worker

assister VERB

♦ **assister à un accident** to witness an accident

♦ **assister à un cours** to attend a class

♦ **assister à un concert** to be at a concert

l' **association** FEM NOUN

association

l' **associé** MASC NOUN

partner (*in business*)

l' **associée** FEM NOUN

partner (*in business*)

s' **associer** VERB

to go into partnership

assommer VERB

to knock out ◇ *Il l'a assommé avec une bouteille.* He knocked him out with a bottle.

l' **Assomption** FEM NOUN

Assumption

assorti ADJECTIVE

1 matching ◇ *des couleurs assorties* matching colours

2 assorted ◇ *des chocolats assortis* assorted chocolates

♦ **être assorti à quelque chose** to match something ◇ *Son sac est assorti à ses chaussures.* Her bag matches her shoes.

l' **assortiment** MASC NOUN

assortment

l' **assurance** FEM NOUN

1 insurance ◇ *une assurance maladie* medical insurance

2 confidence ◇ *parler avec assurance* to speak with confidence

assurer VERB

1 to insure ◇ *La maison est assurée.* The house is insured. ◇ *être assuré contre quelque chose* to be insured against something

2 to assure ◇ *Je t'assure que c'est vrai!* I assure you it's true!

♦ **s'assurer de quelque chose** to make sure of something ◇ *Il s'est assuré que la porte était fermée.* He made sure the door was shut.

l' **asthme** MASC NOUN

asthma ◇ *une crise d'asthme* an asthma attack

l' **astronaute** MASC/FEM NOUN

astronaut

l' **astronomie** FEM NOUN

astronomy

astucieux ADJECTIVE (FEM SING **astucieuse**)

clever

l' **atelier** MASC NOUN

1 workshop

2 studio (*artist's*)

Athènes NOUN

Athens

l' **athlète** MASC/FEM NOUN

athlete

l' **athlétisme** MASC NOUN

athletics ◇ *un championnat d'athlétisme* an athletics championship

l' **Atlantique** MASC NOUN

Atlantic

l' **atlas** MASC NOUN

atlas

l' **atmosphère** FEM NOUN

atmosphere

atomique ADJECTIVE

atomic ◇ *la bombe atomique* the atomic bomb

l' **atout** MASC NOUN

[1] <u>asset</u> ◊ *L'atout principal de ce joueur, c'est sa vitesse.* This player's main asset is his speed.
[2] <u>trump card</u> ◊ *J'avais quatre atouts dans mon jeu.* I had four trump cards in my hand.

atroce ADJECTIVE
<u>terrible</u>

attachant ADJECTIVE
<u>lovable</u> ◊ *un enfant attachant* a lovable child

attacher VERB
<u>to tie up</u> ◊ *Elle a attaché ses cheveux avec un élastique.* She tied her hair up with an elastic band.
♦ **s'attacher à quelqu'un** to become attached to somebody
♦ **une poêle qui n'attache pas** a non-stick frying pan

attaquer VERB
<u>to attack</u>

atteindre VERB
<u>to reach</u>

attendant
♦ **en attendant** ADVERB
<u>in the meantime</u>

attendre VERB
<u>to wait</u> ◊ *attendre quelqu'un* to wait for someone ◊ *J'attends d'avoir un appartement à moi.* I'm waiting until I've got a flat of my own. ◊ *Attends qu'il ne pleuve plus.* Wait until it's stopped raining.
♦ **attendre un enfant** to be expecting a baby
♦ **s'attendre à** to expect ◊ *Je m'attends à ce qu'il soit en retard.* I expect he'll be late.
Be careful! **attendre** *does not mean* *to attend.*

l' **attentat** MASC NOUN
♦ **un attentat à la bombe** a terrorist bombing

l' **attente** FEM NOUN
<u>wait</u> ◊ *deux heures d'attente* two hours' wait
♦ **la salle d'attente** the waiting room

attentif ADJECTIVE (FEM SING **attentive**)
<u>attentive</u>

l' **attention** FEM NOUN
<u>attention</u> ◊ *à l'attention de* for the attention of
♦ **faire attention** to be careful
♦ **Attention!** Watch out! ◊ *Attention, tu vas te faire écraser!* Watch out, you'll get run over!

attentionné ADJECTIVE
<u>thoughtful</u>

atterrir VERB

<u>to land</u>

l' **atterrissage** MASC NOUN
<u>landing</u> (*of plane*)

attirant ADJECTIVE
<u>attractive</u>

attirer VERB
<u>to attract</u> ◊ *attirer l'attention de quelqu'un* to attract somebody's attention
♦ **s'attirer des ennuis** to get into trouble ◊ *Si tu continues, tu vas t'attirer des ennuis.* If you keep on like that, you'll get yourself into trouble.

l' **attitude** FEM NOUN
<u>attitude</u>

l' **attraction** FEM NOUN
♦ **un parc d'attractions** an amusement park

attraper VERB
<u>to catch</u>

attrayant ADJECTIVE
<u>attractive</u>

attrister VERB
<u>to sadden</u>

au PREPOSITION *see* **à**
au is the contracted form of à + le.
♦ **au printemps** in the spring

l' **aube** FEM NOUN
<u>dawn</u> ◊ *à l'aube* at dawn

l' **auberge de jeunesse** FEM NOUN
<u>youth hostel</u>

l' **aubergine** FEM NOUN
<u>aubergine</u>

aucun ADJECTIVE, PRONOUN
[1] <u>no</u> ◊ *Il n'a aucun ami.* He's got no friends. ◊ *Aucun enfant ne pourrait le faire.* No child could do that.
[2] <u>none</u> ◊ *Aucun d'entre eux n'est venu.* None of them came. ◊ *Aucune de mes amies n'aime le football.* None of my female friends like football. ◊ *Tu aimes ses films? – Je n'en ai vu aucun.* Do you like his films? – I haven't seen any of them.
♦ **sans aucun doute** without any doubt

au-delà ADVERB
♦ **au-delà de** beyond ◊ *Votre ticket n'est pas valable au-delà de cette limite.* Your ticket is not valid beyond this point.

au-dessous ADVERB
[1] <u>downstairs</u> ◊ *Ils habitent au-dessous.* They live downstairs.
[2] <u>underneath</u>
♦ **au-dessous de** under ◊ *au-dessous du pont* under the bridge ◊ *dix degrés au-dessous de zéro* ten degrees below zero

au-dessus ADVERB
1. upstairs ◊ *J'habite au-dessus.* I live upstairs.
2. above
• **au-dessus de** above ◊ *au-dessus de la table* above the table

audiovisuel ADJECTIVE (FEM SING **audiovisuelle**)
audiovisual

l' **auditeur** MASC NOUN
listener (*to radio*)

l' **auditrice** FEM NOUN
listener (*to radio*)

l' **augmentation** FEM NOUN
rise

augmenter VERB
to increase

aujourd'hui ADVERB
today

auparavant ADVERB
first ◊ *Vous pouvez utiliser l'ordinateur mais auparavant vous devez taper le mot de passe.* You can use the computer but first you have to key in the password.

auquel PRONOUN (MASC PL **auxquels**, FEM PL **auxquelles**)
auquel is the contracted form of à + lequel.
◊ *l'homme auquel j'ai parlé* the man I spoke to

aura, aurai, auras, aurez, aurons, auront VERB see **avoir**

l' **aurore** FEM NOUN
daybreak

ausculter VERB
• **Le médecin l'a ausculté.** The doctor listened to his chest.

aussi ADVERB
1. too ◊ *Dors bien. – Toi aussi.* Sleep well. – You too. ◊ *Lui aussi parle espagnol.* He too speaks Spanish.
2. also ◊ *J'aimerais aussi que tu achètes le journal.* I'd also like you to get the paper. ◊ *Je parle anglais et aussi allemand.* I speak English and also German.
• **aussi ... que** as ... as ◊ *aussi grand que moi* as big as me

aussitôt ADVERB
straight away ◊ *aussitôt après son retour* straight after his return
• **aussitôt que** as soon as ◊ *aussitôt que tu auras fini* as soon as you've finished

l' **Australie** FEM NOUN
Australia
• **en Australie (1)** in Australia
• **en Australie (2)** to Australia

australien ADJECTIVE, NOUN (FEM SING **australienne**)
Australian
• **un Australien** an Australian (*man*)
• **une Australienne** an Australian (*woman*)

autant ADVERB
• **autant de (1)** so much ◊ *Je ne veux pas autant de gâteau.* I don't want so much cake.
• **autant de (2)** so many ◊ *Je n'ai jamais vu autant de monde.* I've never seen so many people.
• **autant ... que (1)** as much ... as ◊ *J'ai autant d'argent que toi.* I've got as much money as you have.
• **autant ... que (2)** as many ... as ◊ *J'ai autant d'amis que lui.* I've got as many friends as he has.
• **d'autant plus que** all the more since ◊ *Elle est d'autant plus déçue qu'il le lui avait promis.* She's all the more disappointed since he had promised her.
• **d'autant moins que** even less since ◊ *C'est d'autant moins pratique pour lui qu'il doit changer deux fois de train.* It's even less convenient for him since he has to change trains twice.

l' **auteur** MASC NOUN
author

l' **auto** FEM NOUN
car

l' **autobus** MASC NOUN
bus ◊ *en autobus* by bus

l' **autocar** MASC NOUN
coach ◊ *en autocar* by coach

autocollant ADJECTIVE
see also **autocollant** NOUN
self-adhesive ◊ *une étiquette autocollante* a self-adhesive label
• **une enveloppe autocollante** a self-seal envelope

l' **autocollant** MASC NOUN
see also **autocollant** ADJECTIVE
sticker

l' **auto-école** FEM NOUN
driving school

automatique ADJECTIVE
automatic

l' **automne** MASC NOUN
autumn
• **en automne** in autumn

automobile ADJECTIVE
see also **automobile** NOUN
• **une course automobile** a motor race

l' **automobile** FEM NOUN
see also **automobile** ADJECTIVE

car

l'**automobiliste** MASC/FEM NOUN
motorist

l'**autoradio** MASC NOUN
car radio

l'**autorisation** FEM NOUN
[1] permission ◊ *Il m'a donné l'autorisation de sortir ce soir.* He's given me permission to go out tonight.
[2] permit ◊ *Il faut une autorisation pour camper ici.* You need a permit to camp here.

autoriser VERB
to give permission for ◊ *Il m'a autorisé à en parler.* He's given me permission to talk about it.

autoritaire ADJECTIVE
authoritarian

l'**autorité** FEM NOUN
authority

l'**autoroute** FEM NOUN
motorway

l'**auto-stop** MASC NOUN
♦**faire de l'auto-stop** to hitchhike

l'**auto-stoppeur** MASC NOUN
hitchhiker

l'**auto-stoppeuse** FEM NOUN
hitchhiker

autour ADVERB
around ◊ *autour de la maison* around the house

autre ADJECTIVE, PRONOUN
other ◊ *Je viendrai un autre jour.* I'll come some other day. ◊ *J'ai d'autres projets.* I've got other plans.
♦**autre chose** something else
♦**autre part** somewhere else
♦**un autre** another ◊ *Tu veux un autre morceau de gâteau?* Would you like another piece of cake?
♦**l'autre** the other ◊ *Non, pas celui-ci, l'autre.* No, not that one, the other one.
♦**d'autres** others ◊ *Je t'en apporterai d'autres.* I'll bring you some others.
♦**les autres** the others ◊ *Les autres sont arrivés plus tard.* The others arrived later.
♦**ni l'un ni l'autre** neither of them
♦**entre autres** among other things ◊ *Nous avons parlé, entre autres, de nos projets de vacances.* We talked about our holiday plans, among other things.

autrefois ADVERB
in the old days ◊ *Autrefois Saint-Tropez n'était qu'un village de pêcheurs.* In the old days Saint-Tropez was just a fishing village.

autrement ADVERB
[1] differently ◊ *Il l'a fait autrement.* He did it differently.
[2] otherwise ◊ *Je n'ai pas pu faire autrement.* I couldn't do otherwise.
♦**autrement dit** in other words

l'**Autriche** FEM NOUN
Austria
♦**en Autriche (1)** in Austria
♦**en Autriche (2)** to Austria

autrichien ADJECTIVE, NOUN (FEM SING **autrichienne**)
Austrian
♦**un Autrichien** an Austrian (*man*)
♦**une Autrichienne** an Austrian (*woman*)

l'**autruche** FEM NOUN
ostrich

aux PREPOSITION *see* **à**
> *aux is the contracted form of à + les.*
◊ *J'ai dit aux enfants d'aller jouer.* I told the children to go and play.

auxquelles PRONOUN
> *auxquelles is the contracted form of à + lesquelles.*
◊ *les revues auxquelles il est abonné* the magazines to which he subscribes

auxquels PRONOUN
> *auxquels is the contracted form of à + lesquels.*
◊ *les enfants auxquels il a parlé* the children he spoke to

l'**avalanche** FEM NOUN
avalanche

avaler VERB
to swallow

l'**avance** FEM NOUN
♦**être en avance** to be early
♦**à l'avance** beforehand ◊ *réserver longtemps à l'avance* to book well beforehand
♦**d'avance** in advance ◊ *payer d'avance* to pay in advance

avancé ADJECTIVE
advanced ◊ *à un niveau avancé* at an advanced level
♦**bien avancé** well under way ◊ *Les travaux sont déjà bien avancés.* The work is already well under way.

avancer VERB
[1] to move forward ◊ *Il avançait prudemment.* He was moving forward cautiously.
[2] to bring forward ◊ *La date de l'examen a été avancée.* The date of the exam has been brought forward.

☞

3 to put forward ◊ *Il a avancé sa montre d'une heure.* He put his watch forward an hour.

4 to be fast (*watch*) ◊ *Ma montre avance d'une heure.* My watch is an hour fast.

5 to lend ◊ *Peux-tu m'avancer cent francs?* Can you lend me 100 francs?

avant PREPOSITION, ADJECTIVE
> see also **avant** NOUN

1 before ◊ *avant qu'il ne pleuve* before it rains ◊ *avant de partir* before leaving

2 front ◊ *la roue avant* the front wheel ◊ *le siège avant* the front seat

♦ **avant tout** above all

l' **avant** MASC NOUN
> see also **avant** PREPOSITION

front ◊ *l'avant de la voiture* the front of the car

♦ **à l'avant** in front

♦ **en avant** forward ◊ *Il a fait un pas en avant.* He took a step forward.

l' **avantage** MASC NOUN
advantage

l' **avant-bras** MASC NOUN (PL les **avant-bras**)
forearm

avant-dernier ADJECTIVE (FEM **avant-dernière**, MASC PL **avant-derniers**)
last but one ◊ *l'avant-dernière page* the last page but one ◊ *Ils sont arrivés avant-derniers.* They arrived last but one.

avant-hier ADVERB
the day before yesterday ◊ *Il est arrivé avant-hier.* He arrived the day before yesterday.

avare ADJECTIVE
> see also **avare** NOUN

miserly

l' **avare** MASC/FEM NOUN
> see also **avare** ADJECTIVE

miser

avec PREPOSITION
with ◊ *avec mon père* with my father

♦ **Et avec ça?** Anything else? (*in shop*)

l' **avenir** MASC NOUN
future

♦ **à l'avenir** in future ◊ *À l'avenir, essayez d'être à l'heure.* Try to be on time in future.

♦ **dans un proche avenir** in the near future

l' **aventure** FEM NOUN
adventure

l' **avenue** FEM NOUN
avenue

l' **averse** FEM NOUN
shower (*of rain*)

avertir VERB
to warn

♦ **avertir quelqu'un de quelque chose** to warn somebody about something

l' **avertissement** MASC NOUN
warning

aveugle ADJECTIVE
blind

l' **avion** MASC NOUN
plane

♦ **aller en avion** to go by plane ◊ *Il est allé en Italie en avion.* He flew to Italy.

♦ **par avion** by airmail

l' **aviron** MASC NOUN
rowing

l' **avis** MASC NOUN

1 opinion ◊ *J'aimerais avoir ton avis.* I'd like to have your opinion.

♦ **à mon avis** in my opinion

2 notice ◊ *jusqu'à nouvel avis* until further notice

♦ **changer d'avis** to change one's mind ◊ *J'ai changé d'avis.* I've changed my mind.

l' **avocat** MASC NOUN

1 lawyer ◊ *Il est avocat.* He's a lawyer.

2 avocado

l' **avocate** FEM NOUN
lawyer ◊ *Elle est avocate.* She's a lawyer.

l' **avoine** FEM NOUN
oats ◊ *les flocons d'avoine* porridge oats

avoir VERB

Present tense:	
j'ai	nous avons
tu as	vous avez
il/elle a	ils/elles ont
Past participle:	
eu	

1 to have ◊ *Ils ont deux enfants.* They have two children. ◊ *Il a les yeux bleus.* He's got blue eyes. ◊ *J'ai déjà mangé.* I've already eaten. ◊ *Est-ce que tu as vu ce film?* Have you seen this film? ◊ *Je lui ai parlé hier.* I spoke to him yesterday.

♦ **On t'a bien eu!** (*informal*) You've been had!

2 to be ◊ *Il a trois ans.* He's three. ◊ *J'avais dix ans quand je l'ai rencontré.* I was ten when I met him.

♦ **il y a (1)** there is ◊ *Il y a quelqu'un à la porte.* There's somebody at the door.

- ◆**il y a (2)** there are ◊ *Il y a des chocolats sur la table.* There are some chocolates on the table.
- ◆**il y a (3)** ago ◊ *Je l'ai rencontré il y a deux ans.* I met him two years ago.
- ◆**Qu'est-ce qu'il y a?** What's the matter?
- ◆**Il n'y a qu'à partir plus tôt.** We'll just have to leave earlier.

l'**avortement** MASC NOUN
  abortion

avouer VERB
  to admit

avril MASC NOUN
  April
- ◆**en avril** in April

ayez, ayons VERB *see* **avoir**

B

le **baby-foot** NOUN
table football ◊ *jouer au baby-foot* to play table football

le **baby-sitting** NOUN
◆**faire du baby-sitting** to babysit

le **bac** NOUN = **baccalauréat**

le **baccalauréat** NOUN
A levels ◊ *Jacqueline a passé son baccalauréat l'année dernière.* Jacqueline did her A levels last year.

> ❶ The French **baccalauréat**, or **bac** for short, is taken at the age of 17 or 18. Students have to sit one of a variety of set subject combinations, rather than being able to choose any combination of subjects they want. If you pass you have the right to a place at university.

bâcler VERB
to botch up ◊ *Je déteste le travail bâclé!* I hate work that's not done properly!

le **bagage** NOUN
luggage
◆**faire ses bagages** to pack
◆**les bagages à main** hand luggage ◊ *un bagage à main* a piece of hand luggage

la **bagarre** NOUN
fight ◊ *Une bagarre a éclaté à la fermeture du pub.* A fight broke out when the pub closed.

se **bagarrer** VERB
to fight ◊ *Il s'est encore bagarré avec son frère.* He's been fighting with his brother again.

la **bagnole** NOUN (*informal*)
car

la **bague** NOUN
ring

la **baguette** NOUN
1 stick of French bread
2 chopstick ◊ *manger avec des baguettes* to eat with chopsticks
◆**une baguette magique** a magic wand

la **baie** NOUN
bay

la **baignade** NOUN
◆**"baignade interdite"** "no swimming"

se **baigner** VERB
to go swimming ◊ *Si on allait se baigner?* Shall we go swimming?

la **baignoire** NOUN
bath (*bathtub*)

bâiller VERB
to yawn

le **bain** NOUN
bath ◊ *prendre un bain* to take a bath ◊ *prendre un bain de soleil* to sunbathe

le **baiser** NOUN
kiss

la **baisse** NOUN
fall ◊ *La baisse du taux de chômage.* The fall in the unemployment rate.
◆**être en baisse** to be falling
◆**revoir les chiffres à la baisse** to revise figures downwards

baisser VERB
1 to turn down ◊ *Il fait moins froid, tu peux baisser le chauffage.* It's not so cold, you can turn down the heating.
2 to fall ◊ *Le prix des CD a baissé.* The price of CDs has fallen.
◆**se baisser** to bend down ◊ *Il s'est baissé pour ramasser son mouchoir.* He bent down to pick up his handkerchief.

le **bal** NOUN
dance ◊ *un bal populaire* a local dance

la **balade** NOUN (*informal*)
walk ◊ *faire une balade* to go for a walk

se **balader** VERB (*informal*)
to wander around ◊ *J'adore me balader dans les rues de Paris.* I love to wander around the streets of Paris.

le **baladeur** NOUN
personal stereo

le **balai** NOUN
broom ◊ *Je vais donner un coup de balai dans la cuisine.* I'm going to sweep the kitchen.

la **balance** NOUN
scales PL (*for weighing*)
◆**la Balance** Libra ◊ *Todd est Balance.* Todd is Libra.

se **balancer** VERB
to swing

la **balançoire** NOUN
swing

balayer VERB

1 to sweep ◊ *Jean-Pierre a balayé la cuisine.* Jean-Pierre swept the kitchen.
2 to sweep up ◊ *Va balayer les feuilles sur la terrasse.* Go and sweep up the leaves on the terrace.

le **balayeur** NOUN
roadsweeper

balbutier VERB
to stammer

le **balcon** NOUN
balcony

la **baleine** NOUN
whale

la **balle** NOUN
1 ball ◊ *une balle de tennis* a tennis ball
2 bullet

la **ballerine** NOUN
1 ballet dancer
2 ballet shoe ◊ *une paire de ballerines rouges* a pair of red ballet shoes

le **ballet** NOUN
ballet

le **ballon** NOUN
1 ball ◊ *lancer le ballon* to throw the ball
♦ *un ballon de football* a football
2 balloon

balnéaire ADJECTIVE
♦ *une station balnéaire* a seaside resort

banal ADJECTIVE (MASC PL **banaux**)
1 commonplace ◊ *La violence est devenue banale à la télévision.* Violence has become commonplace on television.
2 hackneyed ◊ *L'intrigue du film est très banale.* The plot of the film is very hackneyed.

la **banane** NOUN
1 banana ◊ *La banane est un fruit.* Banana is a fruit.
2 bumbag ◊ *Mes clés sont dans ma banane.* My keys are in my bumbag.

le **banc** NOUN
bench

bancaire ADJECTIVE
♦ *une carte bancaire* a bank card

le **bandage** NOUN
bandage

la **bande** NOUN
1 gang ◊ *une bande de voyous* a gang of louts
2 bunch ◊ *C'est une bande d'idiots!* They are a bunch of idiots!
3 bandage ◊ *une bande Velpeau* ® a crepe bandage

♦ *une bande dessinée* a comic strip

ℹ *Comic strips are very popular in France with people of all ages.*

♦ *une bande magnétique* a tape
♦ *la bande sonore* the sound track
♦ *Elle fait toujours bande à part.* She always keeps to herself.

le **bandeau** NOUN (PL les **bandeaux**)
headband

bander VERB
to bandage ◊ *L'infirmière lui a bandé la jambe.* The nurse bandaged his leg.

le **bandit** NOUN
bandit

la **banlieue** NOUN
suburbs ◊ *Christèle habite en banlieue.* Christèle lives in the suburbs.
♦ *les lignes de banlieue* suburban lines
♦ *les trains de banlieue* commuter trains

la **banque** NOUN
bank

le **banquet** NOUN
dinner ◊ *le banquet annuel de l'association* the club's annual dinner

la **banquette** NOUN
seat ◊ *la banquette arrière de la voiture* the back seat of the car

le **banquier** NOUN
banker

le **baptême** NOUN
christening ◊ *le baptême de notre fille* our daughter's christening
♦ *C'était mon baptême de l'air.* It was the first time I had flown.

le **baquet** NOUN
tub

le **bar** NOUN
bar

la **baraque** NOUN (*informal*)
house ◊ *Elle habite dans une belle baraque.* She lives in a beautiful house.

barbant ADJECTIVE (*informal*)
boring ◊ *Il est vraiment barbant!* He's so boring!

barbare ADJECTIVE
barbaric

la **barbe** NOUN
beard ◊ *Il porte la barbe.* He's got a beard.
♦ *Quelle barbe!* (*informal*) What a drag!
♦ *la barbe à papa* candyfloss

le **barbecue** NOUN

barbecue

barbouiller VERB
to daub ◊ *Les murs étaient barbouillés de graffitis.* The walls were daubed with graffiti.
◆ **J'ai l'estomac barbouillé.** (*informal*) I'm feeling queasy.

barbu ADJECTIVE
bearded ◊ *un grand barbu* a big, bearded man

barder VERB (*informal*)
◆ **Ça va barder!** There's going to be trouble!

le **baromètre** NOUN
barometer

la **barque** NOUN
rowing boat ◊ *Ils sont allés faire une promenade en barque.* They've gone for a row.

le **barrage** NOUN
dam
◆ **un barrage de police** a police roadblock

la **barre** NOUN
bar (*metal*) ◊ *une barre de fer* an iron bar

le **barreau** NOUN (PL les **barreaux**)
bar (*on window*) ◊ *Il s'est retrouvé derrière les barreaux.* He ended up behind bars.

barrer VERB
to block ◊ *Il y a un tronc d'arbre qui barre la route.* There's a tree trunk blocking the road.
◆ **se barrer** (*informal*) to clear off ◊ *Barre-toi!* Clear off!

la **barrette** NOUN
hair slide

la **barrière** NOUN
fence

le **bar-tabac** NOUN (PL les **bars-tabacs**)

> ❶ *A* **bar-tabac** *is a bar which also sells cigarettes and stamps; you can tell a* **bar-tabac** *by the red diamond-shaped sign outside it.*

le **bas** NOUN
see also **bas** ADJECTIVE
⓵ bottom ◊ *en bas de la page* at the bottom of the page ◊ *en bas de l'escalier* at the bottom of the stairs
⓶ stocking ◊ *une paire de bas* a pair of stockings

bas ADJECTIVE, ADVERB (FEM SING **basse**)
see also **bas** NOUN
low ◊ *parler à voix basse* to speak in a low voice

◆ **en bas (1)** down ◊ *Ça me donne le vertige de regarder en bas.* I get dizzy if I look down.
◆ **en bas (2)** (down) at the bottom ◊ *Son nom est tout en bas.* His name is down at the bottom. ◊ *Il y a un marchand de journaux en bas de la rue.* There's a newsagent's at the bottom of the street.
◆ **en bas (3)** downstairs ◊ *Elle habite en bas.* She lives downstairs.

le **bas-côté** NOUN
verge ◊ *Il s'est garé sur le bas-côté de la route.* He stopped his car on the verge.

la **bascule** NOUN
◆ **un fauteuil à bascule** a rocking chair

la **base** NOUN
base ◊ *la base de la pyramide* the base of the pyramid
◆ **de base** basic ◊ *Le pain et le lait sont des aliments de base.* Bread and milk are basic foods.
◆ **à base de** made from ◊ *des produits de beauté à base de plantes* cosmetics made from plants
◆ **une base de données** a database

le **basilic** NOUN
basil

le **basket** NOUN
basketball ◊ *jouer au basket* to play basketball

les **baskets** FEM NOUN
trainers ◊ *une paire de baskets* a pair of trainers

le/la **Basque** NOUN
Basque (*person, language*)

basque ADJECTIVE
Basque

basse ADJECTIVE see **bas**

la **basse-cour** NOUN (PL les **basses-cours**)
farmyard

le **bassin** NOUN
⓵ pond ◊ *Il y a un bassin à poissons rouges dans le parc.* There's a goldfish pond in the park.
⓶ pelvis ◊ *une fracture du bassin* a fractured pelvis

la **bassine** NOUN
bowl (*for washing*)

le **bas-ventre** NOUN
stomach ◊ *Elle se plaint de douleurs dans le bas-ventre.* She is complaining of pains in her stomach.

la **bataille** NOUN
battle

le **bateau** NOUN (PL les **bateaux**)
boat

B

le **bateau-mouche** NOUN (PL les **bateaux-mouches**)
pleasure boat

bâti ADJECTIVE
♦ **bien bâti** well-built

le **bâtiment** NOUN
building

bâtir VERB
to build

le **bâton** NOUN
stick ◊ *un coup de bâton* a blow with a stick

le **battement** NOUN
♦ **J'ai dix minutes de battement.** I've got ten minutes free.

la **batterie** NOUN
1 battery ◊ *La batterie est à plat.* The battery is flat.
2 drums ◊ *jouer de la batterie* to play drums
♦ **la batterie de cuisine** the pots and pans

le **batteur** NOUN
drummer

battre VERB
to beat ◊ *Quand je le vois, mon cœur bat plus vite.* When I see him, my heart beats faster.
♦ **se battre** to fight ◊ *Je me bats souvent avec mon frère.* I fight a lot with my brother.
♦ **battre les cartes** to shuffle the cards
♦ **battre les blancs en neige** beat the egg whites until stiff
♦ **battre son plein** to be in full swing ◊ *A minuit, la fête battait son plein.* At midnight, the party was in full swing.

bavard ADJECTIVE
talkative

bavarder VERB
to chat

baver VERB
to dribble

baveux ADJECTIVE (FEM SING **baveuse**)
runny ◊ *une omelette baveuse* a runny omelette

la **bavure** NOUN
blunder ◊ *une bavure policière* a police blunder

le **bazar** NOUN
general store
♦ **Quel bazar!** (*informal*) What a mess!

BCBG ADJECTIVE (= *bon chic bon genre*)
posh

la **BD** NOUN (= *bande dessinée*)
comic strip ◊ *Rose adore les BD.* Rose loves comic strips.

béant ADJECTIVE
gaping ◊ *un trou béant* a gaping hole

beau ADJECTIVE, ADVERB (MASC SING ALSO **bel**, FEM SING **belle**, MASC PL **beaux**)
beau changes to *bel* before a vowel and most words beginning with "h".
1 lovely ◊ *un bel été* a lovely summer ◊ *une belle journée* a fine day
2 beautiful ◊ *C'est une belle femme.* She is a beautiful woman.
3 good-looking ◊ *C'est un beau garçon.* He is a good-looking boy.
4 handsome ◊ *un bel homme* a handsome man
♦ **Il fait beau aujourd'hui.** It's a nice day today.
♦ **J'ai beau essayer, je n'y arrive pas.** However hard I try, I just can't do it.

beaucoup ADVERB
1 a lot ◊ *Il boit beaucoup.* He drinks a lot.
2 much ◊ *Elle n'a pas beaucoup d'argent.* She hasn't got much money. ◊ *Janet est beaucoup plus grande que moi.* Janet is much taller than me.
♦ **beaucoup de** a lot of ◊ *Il y avait beaucoup de monde au concert.* There were a lot of people at the concert. ◊ *Elle fait beaucoup de fautes.* She makes a lot of mistakes.
♦ **J'ai eu beaucoup de chance.** I was very lucky.

le **beau-fils** NOUN (PL les **beaux-fils**)
1 son-in-law
2 stepson

le **beau-frère** NOUN (PL les **beaux-frères**)
brother-in-law

le **beau-père** NOUN (PL les **beaux-pères**)
1 father-in-law
2 stepfather

la **beauté** NOUN
beauty

les **beaux-arts** MASC NOUN
fine arts

les **beaux-parents** MASC NOUN
in-laws

le **bébé** NOUN
baby

le **bec** NOUN
beak

la **bécane** NOUN (*informal*)
bike

la **bêche** NOUN
spade

bêcher VERB
to dig ◊ *Il bêchait son jardin.* He was digging the garden.

bégayer VERB
to stammer

beige ADJECTIVE
beige

le **beignet** NOUN
fritter ◊ *les beignets aux pommes* apple fritters

bel ADJECTIVE *see* **beau**

le/la **Belge** NOUN
Belgian

belge ADJECTIVE
Belgian

la **Belgique** NOUN
Belgium
+ **en Belgique (1)** in Belgium
+ **en Belgique (2)** to Belgium

le **bélier** MASC NOUN
ram
+ **le Bélier** Aries ◊ *Christine est Bélier.* Christine's Aries.

belle ADJECTIVE *see* **beau**

la **belle-famille** NOUN (PL les **belles-familles**)
in-laws

la **belle-fille** NOUN (PL les **belles-filles**)
1 daughter-in-law
2 stepdaughter

la **belle-mère** NOUN (PL les **belles-mères**)
1 mother-in-law
2 stepmother

la **belle-sœur** NOUN (PL les **belles-sœurs**)
sister-in-law

la **bénédiction** NOUN
blessing

le **bénéfice** NOUN
profit ◊ *La société réalise de gros bénéfices.* The company is making big profits.

bénévole ADJECTIVE
voluntary ◊ *du travail bénévole* voluntary work

bénir VERB
to bless

bénit ADJECTIVE
consecrated ◊ *l'eau bénite* holy water

la **béquille** NOUN
crutch ◊ *Gabriel marche avec des béquilles.* Gabriel walks on crutches.

le **berceau** NOUN (PL les **berceaux**)
cradle

bercer VERB
to rock

la **berceuse** NOUN
lullaby

le **béret** NOUN

beret

la **berge** NOUN
bank (*of river*)

le **berger** NOUN
shepherd

la **bergère** NOUN
shepherdess

le **besoin** NOUN
need
+ **avoir besoin de quelque chose** to need something ◊ *J'ai besoin d'argent.* I need some money. ◊ *J'ai besoin d'y réfléchir.* I need to think about it.
+ **une famille dans le besoin** a needy family

le **bétail** NOUN
livestock

la **bête** NOUN
see also **bête** ADJECTIVE
animal

bête ADJECTIVE
see also **bête** NOUN
stupid

la **bêtise** NOUN
+ **faire une bêtise** to do something stupid ◊ *Je crois que j'ai fait une bêtise.* I think I've done something stupid.
+ **dire des bêtises** to talk nonsense ◊ *Tu dis des bêtises!* You're talking nonsense!

le **béton** NOUN
concrete
+ **un alibi en béton** a cast-iron alibi

la **betterave** NOUN
beetroot ◊ *la salade de betterave* beetroot salad

le/la **beur** NOUN (*informal*)

🛈 A **beur** is a young person of North African origin born in France.

le **beurre** NOUN
butter ◊ *une sauce au beurre* a sauce made with butter

beurrer VERB
to butter

Beyrouth NOUN
Beirut

le **bibelot** NOUN
ornament

le **biberon** NOUN
baby's bottle

la **Bible** NOUN
Bible

le/la **bibliothécaire** NOUN
librarian

B

la **bibliothèque** NOUN
  1 library ◊ *emprunter un livre à la bibliothèque* to borrow a book from the library
  2 bookcase ◊ *une bibliothèque en chêne massif* a bookcase made of solid oak

le **bic** ® NOUN
  Biro ®

la **biche** NOUN
  doe

la **bicyclette** NOUN
  bicycle

le **bidet** NOUN
  bidet

le **bidon** NOUN
  see also **bidon** ADJECTIVE
  can ◊ *un bidon d'essence* a can of petrol

  bidon ADJECTIVE (*informal*)
  see also **bidon** NOUN
  phoney ◊ *Son histoire est complètement bidon.* His story is a complete load of rubbish.

le **bidonville** NOUN
  shanty town

la **Biélorussie** NOUN
  Belarus

le **bien** NOUN
  see also **bien** ADJECTIVE
  1 good ◊ *le bien et le mal* good and evil ◊ *Jean m'a dit beaucoup de bien de toi.* Jean told me a lot of good things about you. ◊ *C'est pour son bien.* It's for his own good.
  ◆ **faire du bien à quelqu'un** to do somebody good ◊ *Ses vacances lui ont fait beaucoup de bien.* His holiday has done him a lot of good.
  2 possession ◊ *son bien le plus précieux* his most treasured possession

  bien ADJECTIVE, ADVERB
  see also **bien** NOUN
  1 well ◊ *Daphne travaille bien.* Daphne works well. ◊ *Je me sens bien.* I feel fine. ◊ *Je ne me sens pas bien.* I don't feel well.
  2 good ◊ *Ce restaurant est vraiment bien.* This restaurant is really good.
  3 quite ◊ *bien assez* quite enough
  ◆ **Je veux bien le faire.** I'm quite willing to do it.
  ◆ **bien mieux** much better
  ◆ **J'espère bien y aller.** I very much hope to go.
  4 right ◊ *Ce n'est pas bien de dire du mal des gens.* It's not right to say nasty things about people. ◊ *Il croyait*

bien faire. He thought he was doing the right thing.
  ◆ **C'est bien fait pour lui!** It serves him right!

le **bien-être** NOUN
  well-being ◊ *une sensation de bien-être* a feeling of well-being

la **bienfaisance** NOUN
  charity
  ◆ **une œuvre de bienfaisance** a charity

  bien que CONJUNCTION
  although ◊ *Il fait assez chaud bien qu'il n'y ait pas de soleil.* It's quite warm although there's no sun.

  bien sûr ADVERB
  of course

  bientôt ADVERB
  soon ◊ *À bientôt!* See you soon!

le **bienvenu** NOUN
  ◆ **Vous êtes le bienvenu!** You're welcome! ◊ *Vous êtes tous les bienvenus!* You're all welcome!

la **bienvenue** NOUN
  welcome ◊ *Bienvenue à Paris!* Welcome to Paris! ◊ *Vous êtes la bienvenue!* You're welcome!

la **bière** NOUN
  beer
  ◆ **la bière blonde** lager
  ◆ **la bière brune** brown ale
  ◆ **la bière pression** draught beer

le **bifteck** NOUN
  steak

le **bigoudi** NOUN
  roller (*in hair*)

le **bijou** NOUN (PL les **bijoux**)
  jewel

la **bijouterie** NOUN
  jeweller's

le **bijoutier** NOUN
  jeweller

la **bijoutière** NOUN
  jeweller ◊ *Elle est bijoutière.* She's a jeweller.

le **bilan** NOUN
  ◆ **faire le bilan de quelque chose** to assess something ◊ *Il faut faire le bilan de la situation.* We need to assess the situation.

  bilingue ADJECTIVE
  bilingual

le **billard** NOUN
  billiards
  ◆ **le billard américain** pool

la **bille** NOUN
  marble (*toy*) ◊ *jouer aux billes* to play marbles

le **billet** NOUN

☞

1 <u>ticket</u> ◊ *un billet d'avion* a plane ticket

2 <u>banknote</u> ◊ *un billet de cent francs* a 100 franc note

le **billion** NOUN
<u>billion</u>

la **biographie** NOUN
<u>biography</u>

la **biologie** NOUN
<u>biology</u>

biologique ADJECTIVE
1 <u>organic</u> ◊ *des légumes biologiques* organic vegetables
2 <u>biological</u> ◊ *des armes biologiques* biological weapons

la **Birmanie** NOUN
<u>Burma</u>

bis ADVERB
| see also **bis** NOUN |
◊ *Il habite au douze bis rue des Fleurs.* He lives at 12A rue des Fleurs.

le **bis** NOUN
| see also **bis** ADVERB |
<u>encore</u>

la **biscotte** NOUN
<u>toasted bread</u> (*sold in packets*)

le **biscuit** NOUN
<u>biscuit</u>
♦ **un biscuit de Savoie** a sponge cake

la **bise** NOUN
<u>kiss</u> ◊ *Grosses bises de Bretagne.* Love and kisses from Brittany.
♦ **faire la bise à quelqu'un** (*informal*) to give somebody a peck on the cheek ◊ *Elle m'a fait la bise.* She gave me a peck on the cheek.

> *ⓘ Between girls and boys, and between girls, the normal French way of saying hello and goodbye is with kisses, usually one on each cheek. Boys shake hands with each other instead.*

le **bisou** NOUN (*informal*)
<u>kiss</u> ◊ *Viens faire un bisou à maman!* Come and give Mummy a little kiss!

bissextile ADJECTIVE
♦ **une année bissextile** a leap year

le **bistrot** NOUN (*informal*)
<u>café</u>

> *ⓘ Cafés in France sell both alcoholic and non-alcoholic drinks.*

bizarre ADJECTIVE
<u>strange</u>

la **blague** NOUN (*informal*)
1 <u>joke</u> ◊ *raconter une blague* to tell a joke
♦ **Sans blague!** No kidding!
2 <u>trick</u> ◊ *André nous a encore fait une blague!* André has played a trick on us again!

blaguer VERB (*informal*)
<u>to joke</u>

le **blaireau** NOUN (PL les **blaireaux**)
<u>shaving brush</u>

blâmer VERB
<u>to blame</u>

blanc ADJECTIVE (FEM SING **blanche**)
| see also **blanc** NOUN |
1 <u>white</u> ◊ *un chemisier blanc* a white blouse
2 <u>blank</u> ◊ *une page blanche* a blank page

le **blanc** NOUN
| see also **blanc** ADJECTIVE |
1 <u>white</u> ◊ *Colette est habillée tout en blanc.* Colette is dressed all in white.
2 <u>white wine</u> ◊ *un verre de blanc* a glass of white wine
♦ **un blanc d'œuf** an egg white
♦ **un blanc de poulet** a chicken breast

le **Blanc** NOUN
<u>white man</u>

la **Blanche** NOUN
<u>white woman</u>

blanche ADJECTIVE see **blanc**

la **blanchisserie** NOUN
<u>laundry</u>

le **blé** NOUN
<u>wheat</u>

blessé ADJECTIVE
| see also **blessé** NOUN |
<u>injured</u>

le **blessé** NOUN
| see also **blessé** ADJECTIVE |
<u>injured person</u> ◊ *L'accident a fait trois blessés.* Three people were injured in the accident.

la **blessée** NOUN
<u>injured person</u>

blesser VERB
1 <u>to injure</u> ◊ *Il a été blessé dans un accident de voiture.* He was injured in a car accident.
2 <u>to hurt</u> ◊ *Thérèse a fait exprès de le blesser.* Thérèse hurt him on purpose.
♦ **se blesser** to hurt oneself ◊ *Je me suis blessé au pied.* I've hurt my foot.

la **blessure** NOUN
<u>injury</u>

bleu ADJECTIVE

see also **bleu** NOUN

[1] blue ◊ *une veste bleue* a blue jacket
- **bleu marine** navy blue

[2] very rare (*steak*)

le **bleu** NOUN

see also **bleu** ADJECTIVE

[1] blue ◊ *Le bleu est ma couleur préférée.* Blue is my favourite colour.

[2] bruise ◊ *Il a un bleu au front.* He's got a bruise on his forehead.

le **bleuet** NOUN

cornflower

le **bloc** NOUN

pad ◊ *un bloc de papier à lettres* a pad of writing paper
- **le bloc opératoire** the operating theatre

le **bloc-notes** NOUN (PL les **blocs-notes**)

note pad

blond ADJECTIVE

blond
- **blond cendré** ash blond ◊ *Andrew a les cheveux blond cendré.* Andrew has ash blond hair.

bloquer VERB

to block ◊ *bloquer le passage* to block the way
- **être bloqué dans un embouteillage** to be stuck in a traffic jam

se **blottir** VERB

to huddle ◊ *Ils étaient blottis l'un contre l'autre.* They were huddled together.

la **blouse** NOUN

overall

le **blouson** NOUN

jacket ◊ *un blouson en cuir* a leather jacket

la **bobine** NOUN

reel ◊ *une bobine de fil* a reel of thread

le **bocal** NOUN (PL les **bocaux**)

jar

le **bœuf** NOUN

[1] ox

[2] beef ◊ *un rôti de bœuf* a joint of beef

bof EXCLAMATION (*informal*)
- **Le film t'a plu? - Bof! C'était pas terrible!** Did you like the film? – Well ... it wasn't that great!
- **Comment ça va? – Bof! Pas terrible.** How is it going? – Oh ... not too well actually.

le **bohémien** NOUN

gipsy

la **bohémienne** NOUN

gipsy

boire VERB

to drink
- **boire un coup** (*informal*) to have a drink

le **bois** NOUN

wood
- **en bois** wooden ◊ *une table en bois* a wooden table
- **avoir la gueule de bois** (*informal*) to have a hangover

la **boisson** NOUN

drink ◊ *une boisson chaude* a hot drink ◊ *une boisson non alcoolisée* a soft drink

la **boîte** NOUN

[1] box ◊ *une boîte d'allumettes* a box of matches
- **une boîte aux lettres** a letter box
- **une boîte postale** a PO Box

[2] tin ◊ *une boîte de sardines* a tin of sardines
- **une boîte de conserve** a tin
- **en boîte** tinned ◊ *des petits pois en boîte* tinned peas
- **une boîte de nuit** a night club
- **sortir en boîte** to go clubbing

boiter VERB

to limp

le **bol** NOUN

bowl
- **en avoir ras le bol** (*informal*) to be fed up ◊ *J'en ai ras le bol de ce boulot.* I'm fed up with this job.

bombarder VERB

to bomb

la **bombe** NOUN

[1] bomb ◊ *une bombe atomique* an atomic bomb

[2] aerosol ◊ *du déodorant en bombe aérosol* aerosol deodorant

bon ADJECTIVE, ADVERB (FEM SING **bonne**)

see also **bon** NOUN

[1] good ◊ *un bon restaurant* a good restaurant ◊ *Le tabac n'est pas bon pour la santé.* Smoking isn't good for you.
- **être bon en maths** to be good at maths
- **sentir bon** to smell nice
- **Bon courage!** Good luck!
- **Bon voyage!** Have a good trip!
- **Bon week-end!** Have a nice weekend!
- **Bonne chance!** Good luck!
- **Bonne journée!** Have a nice day!
- **Bonne nuit!** Good night!
- **Bon anniversaire!** Happy birthday!
- **Bonne année!** Happy New Year!

☞

2 right ◊ *Il est arrivé au bon moment.* He arrived at the right moment. ◊ *Ce n'est pas la bonne réponse.* That's not the right answer.
- ◆**Il fait bon aujourd'hui.** It's nice today.
- ◆**de bonne heure** early
- ◆**bon marché** cheap ◊ *Les fraises ne sont pas bon marché en hiver.* Strawberries aren't cheap in winter.
- ◆**Ah bon?** Really? ◊ *Je pars aux États-Unis la semaine prochaine. – Ah bon?* I'm going to the States next week. – Really?
- ◆**J'aimerais vraiment que tu viennes! – Bon, d'accord.** I'd really like you to come! – OK then, I will.
- ◆**Est-ce que ce yaourt est encore bon?** Is this yoghurt still OK?

le **bon** NOUN
> see also **bon** ADJECTIVE

voucher ◊ *un bon d'achat* a voucher
- ◆**pour de bon** for good ◊ *Cette fois, c'est pour de bon.* This time it's for good.

le **bonbon** NOUN
sweet

bondé ADJECTIVE
crowded

bondir VERB
to leap

le **bonheur** NOUN
happiness
- ◆**porter bonheur** to bring luck

le **bonhomme** NOUN (PL les **bonshommes**)
- ◆**un bonhomme de neige** a snowman

bonjour EXCLAMATION
1 Hello! ◊ *Donne le bonjour à tes parents de ma part.* Say hello to your parents for me.
2 Good morning!
3 Good afternoon!
*bonjour is used in the morning and afternoon; in the evening **bonsoir** is used instead.*
- ◆**C'est simple comme bonjour!** It's easy as pie!

bonne ADJECTIVE *see* **bon**

le **bonnet** NOUN
hat ◊ *un bonnet de laine* a woolly hat
- ◆**un bonnet de bain** a bathing cap

bonsoir EXCLAMATION
Good evening!

la **bonté** NOUN
kindness

le **bord** NOUN
1 edge ◊ *le bord de la table* the edge of the table

2 side ◊ *Jane a garé sa voiture au bord de la route.* Jane parked her car on the side of the road.
- ◆**au bord de la mer** at the seaside
- ◆**au bord de l'eau** by the water
- ◆**monter à bord** to go on board
- ◆**être au bord des larmes** to be on the verge of tears

le **bordeaux** NOUN
> see also **bordeaux** ADJECTIVE

Bordeaux wine
- ◆**du bordeaux rouge** claret

bordeaux ADJECTIVE
> see also **bordeaux** NOUN

maroon ◊ *une jupe bordeaux* a maroon skirt

le **bordel** NOUN
brothel ◊ *Quel bordel!* (*informal*) What a bloody mess!

border VERB
1 to line ◊ *une route bordée d'arbres* a tree-lined street
2 to trim ◊ *un col bordé de dentelle* a collar trimmed with lace
3 to tuck up ◊ *Sa mère vient la border tous les soirs.* Her mother comes and tucks her up every night.

la **bordure** NOUN
border
- ◆**une villa en bordure de mer** a villa right by the sea

la **borne** NOUN
terminal (*of computer*)

la **Bosnie** NOUN
Bosnia
- ◆**la Bosnie-Herzégovine** Bosnia-Herzegovina

la **bosse** NOUN
bump ◊ *Jacques a une grosse bosse au front.* Jacques has got a big bump on his forehead. ◊ *La route est pleine de bosses.* The road is very bumpy.

bosser VERB (*informal*)
to work
- ◆**bosser un examen** to study for an exam

le **bossu** NOUN
hunchback

la **bossue** NOUN
hunchback

botanique ADJECTIVE
> see also **botanique** NOUN

botanic ◊ *les jardins botaniques* the botanic gardens

la **botanique** NOUN
> see also **botanique** ADJECTIVE

botany

la **botte** NOUN

B

[1] boot ◇ *une paire de bottes* a pair of boots

◆ **les bottes de caoutchouc** wellington boots

[2] bunch ◇ *une botte de radis* a bunch of radishes

le **bottin** ® NOUN
phone book

le **bouc** NOUN
[1] goatee beard
[2] billy goat

◆ **un bouc émissaire** a scapegoat

la **bouche** NOUN
mouth

◆ **le bouche à bouche** the kiss of life
◆ **une bouche d'égout** a manhole
◆ **une bouche de métro** an entrance to the underground

la **bouchée** NOUN
mouthful

◆ **une bouchée à la reine** a chicken vol-au-vent

boucher VERB
see also **boucher** NOUN
[1] to fill ◇ *boucher un trou* to fill a hole
[2] to block ◇ *L'évier est bouché.* The sink is blocked. ◇ *J'ai le nez bouché.* My nose is blocked.

le **boucher** NOUN
see also **boucher** VERB
butcher ◇ *Il est boucher.* He's a butcher.

la **bouchère** NOUN
butcher ◇ *Elle est bouchère.* She's a butcher.

la **boucherie** NOUN
butcher's

le **bouchon** NOUN
[1] top (of plastic bottle)
[2] cork (of wine bottle)
[3] hold-up ◇ *Il y avait beaucoup de bouchons sur l'autoroute.* There were a lot of hold-ups on the motorway.

la **boucle** NOUN
curl (of hair)

◆ **une boucle d'oreille** an earring ◇ *une paire de boucles d'oreille* a pair of earrings

bouclé ADJECTIVE
curly

le **bouclier** NOUN
shield

le/la **bouddhiste** NOUN
Buddhist

bouder VERB
to sulk

le **boudin** NOUN
◆ **le boudin noir** black pudding

◆ **le boudin blanc** white pudding

la **boue** NOUN
mud

la **bouée** NOUN
buoy

◆ **une bouée de sauvetage** a life buoy

boueux ADJECTIVE (FEM SING **boueuse**)
muddy

la **bouffe** NOUN (*informal*)
food ◇ *La bouffe est infecte à la cantine.* The food in the canteen is revolting.

la **bouffée** NOUN
◆ **une bouffée d'air frais** a breath of fresh air

bouffer VERB (*informal*)
to eat

le **bougeoir** NOUN
candlestick

bouger VERB
to move

la **bougie** NOUN
candle

la **bouillabaisse** NOUN
fish soup

bouillant ADJECTIVE
[1] boiling ◇ *Faites cuire les pâtes à l'eau bouillante.* Cook the pasta in boiling water.
[2] piping hot ◇ *La soupe est servie bouillante.* The soup should be served piping hot.

bouillir VERB
to boil ◇ *L'eau bout.* The water's boiling.

◆ **Je bous d'impatience.** I'm bursting with impatience.

la **bouilloire** NOUN
kettle

le **bouillon** NOUN
stock ◇ *du bouillon de légumes* vegetable stock

la **bouillotte** NOUN
hot-water bottle

le **boulanger** NOUN
baker ◇ *Il est boulanger.* He's a baker.

la **boulangère** NOUN
baker ◇ *Elle est boulangère.* She's a baker.

la **boulangerie** NOUN
baker's

la **boule** NOUN
ball ◇ *une boule de cristal* a crystal ball

◆ **une boule de neige** a snowball
◆ **jouer aux boules** to play bowls

le **boulevard** NOUN

boulevard

bouleverser VERB
　1 to move deeply ◊ *Cette histoire déchirante m'a bouleversée.* This heartbreaking story moved me deeply.
　2 to shatter ◊ *La mort de son ami l'a bouleversé.* He was shattered by the death of his friend.
　3 to turn upside down ◊ *Cette rencontre a bouleversé sa vie.* This meeting turned his life upside down.

le **boulot** NOUN (*informal*)
　1 job ◊ *Anita a trouvé du boulot.* Anita has found a job.
　2 work ◊ *J'ai beaucoup de boulot en ce moment.* I've got a lot of work to do at the moment.

la **boum** NOUN (*informal*)
　party

le **bouquet** NOUN
　bunch of flowers ◊ *un bouquet de roses* a bunch of roses

le **bouquin** NOUN (*informal*)
　book

bouquiner VERB (*informal*)
　to read

bourdonner VERB
　to buzz

le **bourg** NOUN
　small market town

bourgeois ADJECTIVE
　middle-class ◊ *un quartier bourgeois* a posh area

le **bourgeon** NOUN
　bud

la **Bourgogne** NOUN
　Burgundy

bourré ADJECTIVE
　♦ bourré de stuffed with ◊ *un portefeuille bourré de billets* a wallet stuffed with banknotes
　♦ être bourré (*informal*) to be plastered ◊ *Il était complètement bourré.* He was completely plastered.

le **bourreau** NOUN (PL les **bourreaux**)
　executioner
　♦ C'est un véritable bourreau de travail. He's a real workaholic.

bourrer VERB
　to stuff ◊ *bourrer une valise de vêtements* to stuff clothes into a case

la **bourse** NOUN
　grant
　♦ la Bourse the Stock Exchange

bous VERB see **bouillir**

la **bousculade** NOUN
　crush ◊ *la bousculade dans les grands magasins au moment des soldes* the crush in the big stores at sale time

bousculer VERB
　1 to jostle ◊ *être bousculé par la foule* to be jostled by the crowd
　2 to rush ◊ *Je n'aime pas qu'on me bouscule.* I don't like to be rushed.

la **boussole** NOUN
　compass

bout VERB see **bouillir**

le **bout** NOUN
　1 end ◊ *Elle habite au bout de la rue.* She lives at the end of the street. ◊ *Jane est assise en bout de table.* Jane is sitting at the end of the table.
　2 tip ◊ *le bout du nez* the tip of the nose
　3 bit ◊ *un petit bout de fromage* a bit of cheese
　♦ un bout de papier a scrap of paper
　♦ au bout de after ◊ *Au bout d'un moment, il s'est endormi.* After a while he fell asleep.
　♦ Elle est à bout. She's at the end of her tether.

la **bouteille** NOUN
　bottle ◊ *une bouteille de vin rouge* a bottle of red wine
　♦ une bouteille de gaz a gas cylinder

la **boutique** NOUN
　shop

le **bouton** NOUN
　1 button
　2 spot (*on skin*) ◊ *J'ai un bouton sur le nez.* I've got a spot on my nose.
　3 bud ◊ *un bouton de rose* a rosebud
　♦ un bouton d'or a buttercup

le **bowling** NOUN
　1 tenpin bowling
　2 bowling alley

la **boxe** NOUN
　boxing

le **boxeur** NOUN
　boxer

le **bracelet** NOUN
　bracelet

le **bracelet-montre** NOUN (PL les **bracelets-montres**)
　wristwatch

le **brancard** NOUN
　stretcher

le **brancardier** NOUN
　stretcher-bearer

la **branche** NOUN
　branch

B

branché ADJECTIVE (*informal*)
 trendy ◊ *avoir un look branché* to look trendy

brancher VERB
 1 to connect ◊ *Le téléphone est branché?* Is the phone connected?
 2 to plug in ◊ *L'aspirateur n'est pas branché.* The hoover isn't plugged in.

le**bras** NOUN
 arm

la**brasse** NOUN
 breaststroke ◊ *nager la brasse* to do the breaststroke

la**brasserie** NOUN
 café-restaurant

brave ADJECTIVE
 nice ◊ *C'est un brave type.* He's a nice enough fellow.

bravo EXCLAMATION
 Bravo!

le**break** NOUN
 estate car

la**brebis** NOUN
 ewe
 ♦ **le fromage de brebis** sheep's cheese

bref ADJECTIVE, ADVERB (FEM SING **brève**)
 short ◊ *Sa lettre était brève.* His letter was short.
 ♦ **en bref** in brief ◊ *l'actualité en bref* the news in brief
 ♦ **... bref, ça s'est bien terminé.** ... to cut a long story short, it turned out all right in the end.

le**Brésil** NOUN
 Brazil

la**Bretagne** NOUN
 Brittany

la**bretelle** NOUN
 strap ◊ *La bretelle de son soutien-gorge dépasse.* Her bra strap is showing.
 ♦ **les bretelles** braces ◊ *Il porte des bretelles.* He's wearing braces.

breton ADJECTIVE, NOUN (FEM SING **bretonne**)
 Breton ◊ *Ils parlent breton.* They speak Breton.
 ♦ **un Breton** a Breton (*man*)
 ♦ **une Bretonne** a Breton (*woman*)
 ♦ **les Bretons** the Bretons

brève ADJECTIVE *see* **bref**

le**brevet** NOUN
 certificate

le**brevet des collèges** NOUN

> **ⓘ** The **brevet des collèges** is an exam you take at the end of **collège**, at the age of 15.

le**bricolage** NOUN
 do-it-yourself ◊ *Elle aime le bricolage.* She likes doing DIY.
 ◊ *un magasin de bricolage* a DIY shop

la**bricole** NOUN (*informal*)
 ♦ **J'ai acheté une bricole pour le bébé de Sabine.** I've bought a little something for Sabine's baby.
 ♦ **J'ai encore quelques bricoles à faire avant de partir.** I've still got a few things to do before I go.

bricoler VERB
 to do DIY ◊ *Pascal aime bricoler.* Pascal loves doing DIY.

le**bricoleur** NOUN
 DIY enthusiast

la**bricoleuse** NOUN
 DIY enthusiast

le**bridge** NOUN
 bridge (*game*) ◊ *Horst adore jouer au bridge.* Horst loves playing bridge.

brièvement ADVERB
 briefly ◊ *Expliquez-moi brièvement ce qui s'est passé.* Tell me briefly what happened.

la**brigade** NOUN
 squad (*of police*) ◊ *la brigade des stups* (*informal*) the drugs squad

brillamment ADVERB
 brilliantly ◊ *Il a réussi brillamment à son examen.* He did brilliantly in the exam.

brillant ADJECTIVE
 1 brilliant ◊ *une brillante carrière* a brilliant career ◊ *Ses notes ne sont pas brillantes.* His marks aren't brilliant.
 2 shiny ◊ *des cheveux brillants* shiny hair

briller VERB
 to shine

le**brin** NOUN
 ♦ **un brin d'herbe** a blade of grass
 ♦ **un brin de muguet** a sprig of lily of the valley

la**brindille** NOUN
 twig

la**brioche** NOUN
 brioche bun

la**brique** NOUN
 brick

le**briquet** NOUN
 cigarette lighter

la**brise** NOUN
 breeze

se **briser** VERB
to break ◊ *Le vase s'est brisé en mille morceaux.* The vase broke into a thousand pieces.

le/la **Britannique** NOUN
Briton
♦ **les Britanniques** the British

britannique ADJECTIVE
British

la **brocante** NOUN
junk ◊ *un magasin de brocante* a junk shop

le **brocanteur** NOUN
dealer in second-hand goods

la **brocanteuse** NOUN
dealer in second-hand goods

la **broche** NOUN
brooch ◊ *une broche en argent* a silver brooch
♦ **à la broche** spit-roasted ◊ *un poulet à la broche* a spit-roasted chicken

la **brochette** NOUN
skewer
♦ **les brochettes d'agneau** lamb kebabs

la **brochure** NOUN
brochure

broder VERB
to embroider

la **broderie** NOUN
embroidery

la **bronchite** NOUN
bronchitis ◊ *avoir une bronchite* to have bronchitis

le **bronze** NOUN
bronze ◊ *la médaille de bronze* the bronze medal

bronzer VERB
to get a tan ◊ *Il est bien bronzé.* He's got a good tan.
♦ **se bronzer** to sunbathe

la **brosse** NOUN
brush
♦ **une brosse à cheveux** a hairbrush
♦ **une brosse à dents** a toothbrush
♦ **Il est coiffé en brosse.** He's got a crew cut.

brosser VERB
to brush
♦ **se brosser les dents** to brush one's teeth ◊ *Je me brosse les dents tous les soirs.* I brush my teeth every night.

la **brouette** NOUN
wheelbarrow

le **brouillard** NOUN
fog ◊ *Il y a du brouillard.* It's foggy.

le **brouillon** NOUN

first draft ◊ *Ce n'est qu'un brouillon.* It's just a first draft.

les **broussailles** FEM NOUN
undergrowth SING

brouter VERB
to graze (*animals*)

broyer VERB
to crush
♦ **broyer du noir** to be down in the dumps

le **brugnon** NOUN
nectarine

le **bruit** NOUN
1 noise ◊ *J'ai entendu un bruit.* I heard a noise. ◊ *faire du bruit* to make a noise
♦ **sans bruit** without a sound
2 rumour ◊ *Des bruits circulent à son sujet.* There are rumours going round about him.

brûlant ADJECTIVE
1 blazing ◊ *un soleil brûlant* a blazing sun
2 boiling hot ◊ *Faith boit son café brûlant.* Faith drinks her coffee boiling hot.

le **brûlé** NOUN
smell of burning ◊ *Ça sent le brûlé.* There's a smell of burning.

brûler VERB
to burn
♦ **se brûler** to burn oneself

la **brûlure** NOUN
burn
♦ **des brûlures d'estomac** heartburn

la **brume** NOUN
mist

brun ADJECTIVE
brown
♦ **Catherine est brune.** Catherine's got dark hair.

le **brushing** NOUN
blow-dry ◊ *une coupe et un brushing* a cut and blow-dry

brusque ADJECTIVE
abrupt
♦ **d'un ton brusque** brusquely

brusquer VERB
to rush ◊ *Il ne faut pas la brusquer.* You mustn't rush her.

brut ADJECTIVE
♦ **le champagne brut** dry champagne
♦ **le pétrole brut** crude oil
♦ **son salaire brut** his gross salary

brutal ADJECTIVE (MASC PL **brutaux**)
brutal

brutaliser VERB

to knock about ◊ *Il a été brutalisé par la police.* He was treated roughly by the police.

Bruxelles NOUN
Brussels

bruyamment ADVERB
noisily

bruyant ADJECTIVE
noisy

la **bruyère** NOUN
heather

bu VERB *see* **boire**

la **bûche** NOUN
log
♦ **la bûche de Noël** the Yule log

> ❶ *This is what is usually eaten in France instead of Christmas pudding.*

le **bûcheron** NOUN
woodcutter

le **budget** NOUN
budget

le **buffet** NOUN
① sideboard ◊ *un buffet en chêne* an oak sideboard
② buffet ◊ *un buffet froid* a cold buffet ◊ *un buffet de gare* a station buffet

le **buisson** NOUN
bush

la **Bulgarie** NOUN
Bulgaria

la **bulle** NOUN
bubble ◊ *une bulle de savon* a soap bubble

le **bulletin** NOUN
① bulletin
♦ **le bulletin d'informations** the news bulletin
② report ◊ *Ton bulletin n'est pas fameux.* Your school report isn't very

good.
♦ **le bulletin météorologique** the weather report
♦ **le bulletin de salaire** pay slip
♦ **le bulletin de vote** the ballot paper

le **bureau** NOUN (PL les **bureaux**)
① desk ◊ *Posez le dossier sur mon bureau.* Put the file on my desk.
② office ◊ *Il vous attend dans son bureau.* He's waiting for you in his office.
♦ **un bureau de change** a bureau de change
♦ **le bureau de poste** the post office
♦ **le bureau de tabac** the tobacconist's
♦ **le bureau de vote** the polling station

bus VERB *see* **boire**

le **bus** NOUN
bus

le **buste** NOUN
bust

but VERB *see* **boire**

le **but** NOUN
① aim ◊ *Ils n'ont pas de but dans la vie.* They have no aim in life.
♦ **Quel est le but de votre visite?** What's the reason for your visit?
♦ **dans le but de** with the intention of ◊ *Je suis venue dans le but de vous aider.* I came to help you.
② goal ◊ *marquer un but* to score a goal

le **butane** NOUN
Calor gas ®

le **butin** NOUN
loot ◊ *Les cambrioleurs se sont partagé le butin.* The burglars shared the stolen goods.

buvais, buvait VERB *see* **boire**

le **buvard** NOUN
blotter

C

c' PRONOUN *see* **ce**

ça PRONOUN
> [1] this ◊ *Est-ce que vous pouvez me donner un peu de ça?* Can you give me a bit of this?
> [2] that ◊ *Est-ce que tu peux prendre ça, là-bas dans le coin?* Can you bring that from over there in the corner?
> [3] it ◊ *Ça ne fait rien.* It doesn't matter.
> ◆ **Comment ça va?** How are you?
> ◆ **Ça alors!** Well, well!
> ◆ **C'est ça.** That's right.
> ◆ **Ça y est!** That's it!

çà ADVERB
> ◆ **çà et là** here and there

la **cabane** NOUN
> hut

le **cabillaud** NOUN
> cod

la **cabine** NOUN
> cabin (*on a ship*)
> ◆ **une cabine d'essayage** a fitting room
> ◆ **une cabine téléphonique** a phone box

le **cabinet** NOUN
> surgery (*of doctor, of dentist*)
> ◆ **une chambre avec cabinet de toilette** a room with washing facilities

les **cabinets** MASC NOUN
> toilet SING

le **câble** NOUN
> cable

cabosser VERB
> to dent

la **cacahuète** NOUN
> peanut
> ◆ **le beurre de cacahuète** peanut butter

le **cacao** NOUN
> cocoa
> ◆ **le beurre de cacao** cocoa butter

cache-cache MASC NOUN
> ◆ **jouer à cache-cache** to play hide-and-seek

le **cachemire** NOUN
> cashmere ◊ *un pull en cachemire* a cashmere jumper

le **cache-nez** NOUN (PL les **cache-nez**)
> long woollen scarf

cacher VERB
> to hide ◊ *J'ai caché les cadeaux sous le lit.* I hid the presents under the bed. ◊ *Tu me caches quelque chose!* You're hiding something!

◆ **se cacher** to hide ◊ *Elle s'est cachée sous la table.* She's hiding under the table.

le **cachet** NOUN
> [1] tablet
> ◆ **un cachet d'aspirine** an aspirin
> [2] fee (*for performer*) ◊ *Il a touché un gros cachet pour ce concert.* He got a big fee for the concert.
> ◆ **le cachet de la poste** the postmark

la **cachette** NOUN
> hiding place
> ◆ **en cachette** on the sly ◊ *Il est sorti en cachette sans réveiller ses parents.* He crept out on the sly without waking his parents.

le **cachot** NOUN
> dungeon

le **cactus** NOUN
> cactus

le **cadavre** NOUN
> corpse

le **Caddie** ® NOUN
> supermarket trolley

le **cadeau** NOUN (PL les **cadeaux**)
> present ◊ *un cadeau d'anniversaire* a birthday present ◊ *un cadeau de Noël* a Christmas present
> ◆ **faire un cadeau à quelqu'un** to give somebody a present

le **cadenas** NOUN
> padlock

cadet ADJECTIVE (FEM SING **cadette**)
> | *see also* **cadet** NOUN |
> [1] younger (*brother, sister*) ◊ *ma sœur cadette* my younger sister
> [2] youngest (*son, daughter*) ◊ *son fils cadet* his youngest son

le **cadet** NOUN
> | *see also* **cadet** ADJECTIVE |
> youngest ◊ *C'est le cadet de la famille.* He's the youngest of the family.

la **cadette** NOUN
> youngest ◊ *C'est la cadette de la famille.* She's the youngest of the family.

le **cadre** NOUN
> [1] frame ◊ *un cadre en bois* a wooden frame
> [2] surroundings ◊ *L'hôtel est situé dans un très beau cadre.* The hotel is set in beautiful surroundings.
> [3] executive ◊ *un cadre supérieur* a senior executive

C

le **cafard** NOUN
cockroach
♦ **avoir le cafard** (*informal*) to be feeling down ◊ *J'ai le cafard.* I'm feeling down.

le **café** NOUN
1 coffee ◊ *un café au lait* a white coffee ◊ *un café crème* a strong white coffee
2 café

ⓘ *Cafés in France sell both alcoholic and non-alcoholic drinks.*

le **café-tabac** NOUN (PL les **cafés-tabacs**)

ⓘ *A café-tabac is a bar which also sells cigarettes and stamps; you can tell a café-tabac by the red diamond-shaped sign outside it.*

la **cafétéria** NOUN
cafeteria

la **cafetière** NOUN
1 coffee maker
2 coffee pot

la **cage** NOUN
cage
♦ **la cage d'escalier** the stairwell

la **cagoule** NOUN
balaclava

le **cahier** NOUN
exercise book ◊ *mon cahier de brouillon* my rough book

la **caille** NOUN
quail

le **caillou** NOUN (PL les **cailloux**)
pebble

la **caisse** NOUN
1 box ◊ *une caisse à outils* a tool box
2 till ◊ *le ticket de caisse* the till receipt
3 checkout ◊ *J'ai dû faire la queue à la caisse.* I had to queue at the checkout.

le **caissier** NOUN
cashier

la **caissière** NOUN
cashier

le **cake** NOUN
fruit cake

le **calcul** NOUN
1 calculation ◊ *Je me suis trompé dans mes calculs.* I made a mistake in my calculations.
2 arithmetic ◊ *Je ne suis pas très bon en calcul.* I'm not very good at arithmetic.

la **calculatrice** NOUN
calculator

calculer VERB
to work out ◊ *J'ai calculé combien ça allait coûter.* I worked out how much it was going to cost.

la **calculette** NOUN
pocket calculator

la **cale** NOUN
wedge

calé ADJECTIVE (*informal*)
♦ **Elle est calée en histoire.** She's really good at history.

le **caleçon** NOUN
1 boxer shorts
2 leggings

le **calendrier** NOUN
calendar

le **calepin** NOUN
notebook

caler VERB
to stall ◊ *La voiture a calé dans une côte.* The car stalled on a hill.

câlin ADJECTIVE
see also **câlin** NOUN
cuddly

le **câlin** NOUN
see also **câlin** ADJECTIVE
cuddle ◊ *faire un câlin à quelqu'un* to give somebody a cuddle

le **calmant** NOUN
tranquillizer

calme ADJECTIVE
see also **calme** NOUN
1 quiet ◊ *un endroit calme* a quiet place
2 calm ◊ *Caitlin est restée très calme.* Caitlin stayed very calm.

le **calme** NOUN
see also **calme** ADJECTIVE
peace and quiet ◊ *J'ai besoin de calme pour travailler.* I need peace and quiet to work.

calmer VERB
to soothe ◊ *Cette pommade calme les démangeaisons.* This ointment soothes itching.
♦ **se calmer** to calm down ◊ *Calme-toi!* Calm down!

la **calorie** NOUN
calorie

le/la **camarade** NOUN
friend
♦ **un camarade de classe** a school friend

le **cambriolage** NOUN
burglary

cambrioler VERB
  to burgle
le **cambrioleur** NOUN
  burglar
la **cambrioleuse** NOUN
  burglar
la **camelote** NOUN (*informal*)
  junk ◊ *C'est vraiment de la camelote.*
  It's absolute junk.
la **caméra** NOUN
  camera (*cinema, TV*)
  ◆ **une caméra numérique** a digital
  camera
le **caméscope** ® NOUN
  camcorder
le **camion** NOUN
  lorry
la **camionnette** NOUN
  van
le **camionneur** NOUN
  lorry driver
la **camomille** NOUN
  camomile tea
le **camp** NOUN
  camp ◊ *un camp de prisonniers* a
  prison camp ◊ *un camp de vacances*
  a holiday camp
la **campagne** NOUN
  [1] country
  ◆ **à la campagne** in the country ◊ *Nous*
  passons nos vacances à la
  campagne. We spend our holidays in
  the country.
  [2] campaign ◊ *une campagne de*
  marketing a marketing campaign
camper VERB
  to camp
le **campeur** NOUN
  camper
la **campeuse** NOUN
  camper
le **camping** NOUN
  camping ◊ *faire du camping* to go
  camping
  ◆ **un terrain de camping** a campsite
le **Canada** NOUN
  Canada
  ◆ **au Canada (1)** in Canada
  ◆ **au Canada (2)** to Canada
canadien ADJECTIVE, NOUN (FEM SING
  canadienne)
  Canadian
  ◆ **un Canadien** a Canadian (*man*)
  ◆ **une Canadienne** a Canadian (*woman*)
le **canal** NOUN (PL les **canaux**)
  canal
le **canapé** NOUN
  [1] sofa

  [2] open sandwich
le **canard** NOUN
  duck
le **canari** NOUN
  canary
le **cancer** NOUN
  cancer ◊ *le cancer du poumon* lung
  cancer
  ◆ **le Cancer** Cancer ◊ *Sabine est Cancer.*
  Sabine's Cancer.
le **candidat** NOUN
  [1] candidate (*in exam, election*)
  [2] applicant (*for job*)
la **candidate** NOUN
  [1] candidate (*in exam, election*)
  [2] applicant (*for job*)
la **candidature** NOUN
  ◆ **poser sa candidature à un poste** to
  apply for a job ◊ *Il a posé sa*
  candidature à des dizaines de postes.
  He has applied for dozens of jobs.
le **caneton** NOUN
  duckling
la **canette** NOUN
  ◆ **une canette de bière** a small bottle of
  beer
le **caniche** NOUN
  poodle
la **canicule** NOUN
  scorching heat
le **canif** NOUN
  penknife
le **caniveau** NOUN (PL les **caniveaux**)
  gutter
la **canne** NOUN
  walking stick
  ◆ **une canne à pêche** a fishing rod
la **cannelle** NOUN
  cinnamon
le **canoë** NOUN
  [1] canoe
  [2] canoeing ◊ *faire du canoë* to go
  canoeing
le **canon** NOUN
  [1] gun
  [2] cannon
le **canot** NOUN
  dinghy ◊ *un canot pneumatique* a
  rubber dinghy
  ◆ **un canot de sauvetage** a lifeboat
la **cantatrice** NOUN
  opera singer
la **cantine** NOUN
  canteen
le **caoutchouc** NOUN
  rubber
  ◆ **des bottes en caoutchouc** Wellington
  boots

le **cap** NOUN
cape

capable ADJECTIVE
♦ **Elle est capable de marcher pendant des heures.** She can walk for hours.
♦ **Il est capable de changer d'avis au dernier moment.** He's capable of changing his mind at the last minute.

la **cape** NOUN
cape

le **capitaine** NOUN
captain

la **capitale** NOUN
capital ◊ *la capitale de la France* the capital of France

le **capot** NOUN
bonnet (*of car*)

la **capote** NOUN (*informal*)
condom

la **câpre** NOUN
caper (*food*)

le **caprice** NOUN
♦ **faire des caprices** to make a fuss ◊ *Il n'aime pas les enfants qui font des caprices.* He doesn't like children who make a fuss.

capricieux ADJECTIVE (FEM SING **capricieuse**)
♦ **un enfant capricieux** an awkward child

le **Capricorne** NOUN
Capricorn ◊ *Helen est Capricorne.* Helen's Capricorn.

captivant ADJECTIVE
fascinating

la **captivité** NOUN
captivity ◊ *en captivité* in captivity

capturer VERB
to capture

la **capuche** NOUN
hood ◊ *un manteau à capuche* a coat with a hood

le **capuchon** NOUN
cap (*of pen*)

la **capucine** NOUN
nasturtium

le **car** NOUN
see also **car** CONJUNCTION
coach ◊ *un car scolaire* a school bus

car CONJUNCTION
see also **car** NOUN
because ◊ *Nous sommes inquiets car il n'est pas encore rentré.* We're worried because he isn't back yet.

la **carabine** NOUN
rifle

le **caractère** NOUN
personality ◊ *Il a le même caractère que son père.* He's got the same personality as his father.
♦ **Il a bon caractère.** He's good-natured.
♦ **Elle a mauvais caractère.** She's bad-tempered.
♦ **Il n'a pas un caractère facile.** He isn't easy to get on with.

caractéristique ADJECTIVE
see also **caractéristique** NOUN
characteristic

la **caractéristique** NOUN
see also **caractéristique** ADJECTIVE
characteristic

la **carafe** NOUN
jug ◊ *une carafe d'eau* a jug of water

les **Caraïbes** FEM NOUN
Caribbean Islands

le **caramel** NOUN
[1] caramel ◊ *la crème caramel* crème caramel
[2] toffee

la **caravane** NOUN
caravan

carbonique ADJECTIVE
♦ **le gaz carbonique** carbon dioxide

le **carburant** NOUN
fuel

cardiaque ADJECTIVE
♦ **une crise cardiaque** a heart attack
♦ **Ma tante est cardiaque.** My aunt has heart trouble.

le **cardigan** NOUN
cardigan

le/la **cardiologue** NOUN
heart specialist

le **carême** NOUN
Lent

la **caresse** NOUN
stroke ◊ *faire des caresses à un chat* to stroke a cat

caresser VERB
to stroke

la **carie** NOUN
tooth decay ◊ *J'ai une carie.* I've got a hole in my tooth.

caritatif ADJECTIVE (FEM SING **caritative**)
♦ **une organisation caritative** a charity

le **carnaval** NOUN
carnival

le **carnet** NOUN
[1] notebook
[2] book ◊ *un carnet d'adresses* an address book ◊ *un carnet de chèques* a cheque book ◊ *un carnet de*

☞

timbres a book of stamps ◊ *un carnet de tickets* a book of tickets

> ℹ In the Paris metro it is cheaper to buy tickets in a book of ten, known as a **carnet**.

♦ **mon carnet de notes** my school report

la **carotte** NOUN
carrot ◊ *les carottes râpées* grated carrots

carré ADJECTIVE

> see also **carré** NOUN

square
♦ **un mètre carré** a square metre

le **carré** NOUN

> see also **carré** ADJECTIVE

square

le **carreau** NOUN (PL les **carreaux**)
1 check ◊ *une chemise à carreaux* a checked shirt
2 tile (*on floor, wall*) ◊ *Je viens de laver les carreaux de la cuisine.* I've just washed the kitchen floor.
3 pane ◊ *Il a cassé un carreau.* He broke a windowpane.
4 diamonds (*cards*) ◊ *l'as de carreau* the ace of diamonds

le **carrefour** NOUN
junction

le **carrelage** NOUN
tiled floor

carrément ADVERB
1 completely ◊ *C'est carrément impossible.* It's completely impossible.
2 straight out ◊ *Dis-lui carrément ce que tu penses.* Tell him straight out what you think.

la **carrière** NOUN
career
♦ **un militaire de carrière** a professional soldier

la **carrure** NOUN
build ◊ *Il a une carrure d'athlète.* He has an athletic build.

le **cartable** NOUN
satchel

la **carte** NOUN
1 card
♦ **une carte d'anniversaire** a birthday card
♦ **une carte postale** a postcard
♦ **une carte de vœux** a Christmas card

> ℹ The French send greetings cards (**les cartes de vœux**) in January rather than at Christmas, with best wishes for the New Year.

♦ **une carte bancaire** a cash card
♦ **une carte bleue**

> ℹ **Carte bleue** is a major French debit card.

♦ **une carte de crédit** a credit card
♦ **une carte de fidélité** a loyalty card
♦ **une carte d'embarquement** a boarding card
♦ **une carte d'identité** an identity card
♦ **une carte de séjour** a residence permit
♦ **une carte téléphonique** a phonecard
♦ **un jeu de cartes (1)** a pack of cards
♦ **un jeu de cartes (2)** a card game
2 map ◊ *une carte de France* a map of France ◊ *une carte routière* a road map
3 menu ◊ *la carte des vins* the wine list
♦ **manger à la carte** to eat à la carte ◊ *Nous avons décidé de manger à la carte.* We decided to choose from the à la carte menu.

le **carton** NOUN
1 cardboard ◊ *un morceau de carton* a piece of cardboard
2 cardboard box ◊ *un carton à chaussures* a shoe box

la **cartouche** NOUN
cartridge
♦ **une cartouche de cigarettes** a carton of cigarettes

le **cas** NOUN (PL les **cas**)
case ◊ *plusieurs cas* several cases
♦ **ne faire aucun cas de** to take no notice of ◊ *Il ne fait aucun cas de ce qu'on lui dit.* He takes no notice of what people say to him.
♦ **en aucun cas** on no account
♦ **en tout cas** at any rate
♦ **au cas où** in case ◊ *Prends un sandwich au cas où la cantine serait fermée.* Take a sandwich in case the canteen's closed.
♦ **en cas de** in case of ◊ *En cas d'incendie, appelez ce numéro.* In case of fire, call this number.

la **cascade** NOUN
waterfall

le **cascadeur** NOUN
stuntman

la **caserne** NOUN
barracks

cash ADVERB
♦ **payer cash** to pay cash

le **casier** NOUN
locker

le **casque** NOUN

[1] helmet
[2] headphones

la **casquette** NOUN
cap

cassant ADJECTIVE
♦ **Il m'a parlé d'un ton cassant.** He spoke to me curtly.

le **casse-croûte** NOUN (PL les **casse-croûte**)
snack

le **casse-noix** NOUN (PL les **casse-noix**)
nutcrackers

casse-pieds ADJECTIVE (MASC, FEM, PL) (informal)
♦ **Il est vraiment casse-pieds!** He's a real pain in the neck!

casser VERB
to break ◊ J'ai cassé un verre. I've broken a glass.
♦ **se casser** to break ◊ Il s'est cassé la jambe au ski. He broke his leg when he was skiing.
♦ **se casser la tête** (informal) to go to a lot of trouble ◊ Je ne vais pas me casser la tête pour le dîner: je vais ouvrir une boîte de conserve. I'm not going to go to a whole lot of trouble over dinner: I'll just open a tin.

la **casserole** NOUN
saucepan

le **casse-tête** NOUN (PL les **casse-tête**)
♦ **C'est un vrai casse-tête!** It's a real headache!

la **cassette** NOUN
cassette

le **cassis** NOUN
blackcurrant

le **castor** NOUN
beaver

le **catalogue** NOUN
catalogue

la **catastrophe** NOUN
disaster

le **catch** NOUN
wrestling

le **catéchisme** NOUN
catechism

la **catégorie** NOUN
category

catégorique ADJECTIVE
firm ◊ un refus catégorique a flat refusal

la **cathédrale** NOUN
cathedral

catholique ADJECTIVE
see also **catholique** NOUN
Catholic

le/la **catholique** NOUN

see also **catholique** ADJECTIVE
Catholic

le **cauchemar** NOUN
nightmare ◊ faire un cauchemar to have a nightmare

la **cause** NOUN
cause
♦ **à cause de** because of ◊ Nous n'avons pas pu sortir à cause du mauvais temps. We couldn't go out because of the bad weather.

causer VERB
[1] to cause ◊ La tempête a causé beaucoup de dégâts. The storm caused a lot of damage.
[2] to chat ◊ Nous n'avons pas beaucoup eu le temps de causer. We didn't have much time to chat.

la **caution** NOUN
[1] bail
[2] deposit

le **cavalier** NOUN
[1] rider
[2] partner (at dance)

la **cavalière** NOUN
rider

la **cave** NOUN
cellar

la **caverne** NOUN
cave

le **CD** NOUN (PL les **CD**)
CD

le **CD-ROM** NOUN (PL les **CD-ROM**)
CD-ROM

ce ADJECTIVE (MASC SING **cet**, FEM SING **cette**, PL **ces**)
see also **ce** PRONOUN
*ce changes to **cet** before a vowel and most words beginning with "h".*
[1] this ◊ Tu peux prendre ce livre. You can take this book. ◊ cet après-midi this afternoon ◊ cet hiver this winter
♦ **ce livre-ci** this book
♦ **cette voiture-ci** this car
[2] that ◊ Je n'aime pas du tout ce film. I don't like that film at all.
♦ **ce livre-là** that book
♦ **cette voiture-là** that car

ce PRONOUN
see also **ce** ADJECTIVE
*ce changes to **c'** before the vowel in **est**, **était** and **étaient**.*
it ◊ Ce n'est pas facile. It's not easy.
♦ **c'est (1)** it is ◊ C'est vraiment trop cher. It's really too expensive.
◊ Ouvre, c'est moi! Open the door, it's me!

C

♦ **c'est (2)** he is ◊ *C'est un peintre du début du siècle.* He's a painter from the turn of the century.

♦ **c'est (3)** she is ◊ *C'est une actrice très célèbre.* She's a very famous actress.

♦ **ce sont** they are ◊ *Ce sont des amis à mes parents.* They're friends of my parents'.

♦ **Qui est-ce?** Who is it?

♦ **Qu'est-ce que c'est?** What is it?

♦ **ce qui** what ◊ *C'est ce qui compte.* That's what matters.

♦ **tout ce qui** everything that ◊ *J'ai rangé tout ce qui traînait par terre.* I've tidied up everything that was on the floor.

♦ **ce que** what ◊ *Je vais lui dire ce que je pense.* I'm going to tell him what I think.

♦ **tout ce que** everything ◊ *Tu peux avoir tout ce que tu veux.* You can have everything you want.

ceci PRONOUN
this ◊ *Prends ceci, tu en auras besoin.* Take this, you'll need it.

céder VERB
to give in ◊ *Elle a tellement insisté qu'il a fini par céder.* She went on so much that he eventually gave in.

♦ **céder à** to give in to ◊ *Je ne veux pas céder à ses caprices.* I'm not going to give in to her whims.

le **cédérom** NOUN
CD-ROM

la **cédille** NOUN
cedilla

la **ceinture** NOUN
belt ◊ *une ceinture en cuir* a leather belt

♦ **une ceinture de sauvetage** a lifebelt

♦ **votre ceinture de sécurité** your seatbelt

cela PRONOUN
1 it ◊ *Cela dépend.* It depends.
2 that ◊ *Je n'aime pas cela.* I don't like that.

♦ **C'est cela.** That's right.

♦ **à part cela** apart from that

célèbre ADJECTIVE
famous

célébrer VERB
to celebrate

le **céleri** NOUN
♦ **le céleri-rave** celeriac
♦ **le céleri en branche** celery

célibataire ADJECTIVE, NOUN
single

♦ **un célibataire** a bachelor

♦ **une célibataire** a single woman

celle PRONOUN see **celui**

celles PRONOUN see **ceux**

la **cellule** NOUN
cell

celui PRONOUN (FEM **celle**, MASC PL **ceux**, FEM PL **celles**)
the one ◊ *Prends celui que tu préfères.* Take the one you like best. ◊ *Je n'ai pas d'appareil photo mais je peux emprunter celui de ma sœur.* I haven't got a camera but I can borrow my sister's. ◊ *Je n'ai pas de platine laser mais je peux emprunter celle de mon frère.* I haven't got a CD player but I can borrow my brother's.

♦ **celui-ci** this one

♦ **celle-ci** this one

♦ **celui-là** that one

♦ **celle-là** that one

la **cendre** NOUN
ash

le **cendrier** NOUN
ashtray

censé ADJECTIVE
♦ **être censé faire quelque chose** to be supposed to do something ◊ *Vous êtes censé arriver à l'heure.* You're supposed to get here on time.

cent NUMBER
a hundred ◊ *cent francs* a hundred francs

cent is spelt with an -s when there are two or more hundreds, but not when it is followed by another number, as in "a hundred and two".

◊ *trois cents ans* three hundred years ◊ *cent deux kilomètres* a hundred and two kilometres ◊ *trois cent cinquante kilomètres* three hundred and fifty kilometres ◊ *trois cent mille kilomètres* three hundred thousand kilometres

le **cent** NOUN
cent (*currency*)

la **centaine** NOUN
about a hundred ◊ *Il y avait une centaine de personnes dans la salle.* There were about a hundred people in the hall.

♦ **des centaines de** hundreds of ◊ *Des centaines de réfugiés se sont présentés à l'ambassade.* Hundreds of refugees came to the embassy.

le **centenaire** NOUN
centenary

centième ADJECTIVE
hundredth

le **centilitre** NOUN
centilitre

le **centime** NOUN
centime

> *i* The franc is divided into 100 *centimes*.

◊ *une pièce de cinquante centimes* a 50-centime coin

le **centimètre** NOUN
centimetre

central ADJECTIVE (MASC PL **centraux**)
central

la **centrale** NOUN
power station ◊ *une centrale nucléaire* a nuclear power station

le **centre** NOUN
centre
♦ **un centre commercial** a shopping centre
♦ **un centre d'appels** a call centre

le **centre-ville** NOUN (PL les **centres-villes**)
town centre

cependant ADVERB
however

le **cercle** NOUN
circle ◊ *Entourez d'un cercle la bonne réponse.* Put a circle round the right answer.
♦ **un cercle vicieux** a vicious circle

le **cercueil** NOUN
coffin

la **céréale** NOUN
cereal ◊ *un bol de céréales* a bowl of cereal
♦ **un pain aux cinq céréales** a multigrain loaf

la **cérémonie** NOUN
ceremony

le **cerf** NOUN
stag

le **cerf-volant** NOUN (PL les **cerfs-volants**)
kite

la **cerise** NOUN
cherry

le **cerisier** NOUN
cherry tree

cerné ADJECTIVE
♦ **avoir les yeux cernés** to have shadows under one's eyes ◊ *Elle avait les yeux cernés.* She had shadows under her eyes.

cerner VERB
♦ **J'ai du mal à le cerner.** I can't figure him out.

certain ADJECTIVE
[1] certain ◊ *Je suis certain que je l'ai remis en place.* I'm certain that I put

it back. ◊ *Ce n'est pas certain.* It's not certain.
[2] some ◊ *Certaines personnes n'aiment pas la crème.* Some people don't like cream.
♦ **un certain temps** quite some time ◊ *J'ai mis un certain temps à comprendre ce qu'elle disait.* It took me quite some time to understand what she was saying.

certainement ADVERB
[1] definitely ◊ *C'est certainement le meilleur film que j'ai vu cette année.* It's definitely the best film I've seen this year.
[2] of course ◊ *Est-ce que je peux t'emprunter ton stylo? – Mais certainement!* Can I borrow your pen? – Of course!

certains PRONOUN
[1] some ◊ *certains de ses amis* some of his friends ◊ *certains d'entre vous* some of you
[2] some people ◊ *Certains pensent que le film est meilleur que le roman.* Some people think that the film is better than the novel.

certes ADVERB
certainly ◊ *Nous nous connaissons, certes, mais nous ne sommes pas amis.* We know each other, certainly, but we are not friends.

le **certificat** NOUN
certificate

le **cerveau** NOUN (PL les **cerveaux**)
brain

la **cervelle** NOUN
brain
♦ **se creuser la cervelle** (*informal*) to rack one's brains

le **CES** NOUN (= *Collège d'enseignement secondaire*)
secondary school

> *i* In France pupils go to a **CES** between the ages of 11 and 15, and then to a **lycée** until the age of 18.

ces ADJECTIVE
[1] these ◊ *Tu peux prendre ces photos si tu veux.* You can have these photos if you like.
♦ **ces photos-ci** these photos
[2] those ◊ *Ces montagnes sont dangereuses en hiver.* Those mountains are dangerous in winter.
♦ **ces livres-là** those books

cesse
♦ **sans cesse** ADVERB
continually

♦ **Elle me dérange sans cesse.** She keeps interrupting me.

cesser VERB
to stop ◊ *cesser de faire quelque chose* to stop doing something

le **cessez-le-feu** NOUN (PL les **cessez-le-feu**)
ceasefire

c'est-à-dire ADVERB
that is ◊ *Est-ce que tu peux venir lundi prochain, c'est-à-dire le quinze?* Can you come next Monday, that's the 15th?

cet ADJECTIVE (FEM SING **cette**)
*ce changes to **cet** before a vowel and most words beginning with "h".*
[1] this ◊ *cet après-midi* this afternoon ◊ *cet hiver* this winter ◊ *cette année* this year
♦ **cette semaine-ci** this week
[2] that ◊ *Est-ce que tu peux me passer cette assiette?* Could you pass me that plate?
♦ **cet homme-là** that man
♦ **cette nuit (1)** tonight ◊ *On prévoit de l'orage pour cette nuit.* A storm is forecast for tonight.
♦ **cette nuit (2)** last night ◊ *J'ai très mal dormi cette nuit.* I slept very badly last night.

cette PRONOUN *see* **ce**

ceux PRONOUN (FEM PL **celles**)
the ones ◊ *Prends ceux que tu préfères.* Take the ones you like best. ◊ *Je n'ai pas de skis mais je peux emprunter ceux de ma sœur.* I haven't got any skis but I can borrow my sister's. ◊ *Je n'ai pas de jumelles mais je peux emprunter celles de mon frère.* I haven't got any binoculars but I can borrow my brother's.
♦ **ceux-ci** these ones
♦ **celles-ci** these ones
♦ **ceux-là** those ones
♦ **celles-là** those ones

chacun PRONOUN
[1] each ◊ *Il nous a donné un cadeau à chacun.* He gave us each a present. ◊ *Nous avons chacun donné dix francs.* We each gave 10 francs.
[2] everyone ◊ *Chacun fait ce qu'il veut.* Everyone does what they like.

le **chagrin** NOUN
♦ **avoir du chagrin** to be very upset ◊ *Elle a eu beaucoup de chagrin à la mort de sa tante.* She was terribly upset by the death of her aunt.

le **chahut** NOUN

bedlam ◊ *Il y avait du chahut dans la classe.* There was bedlam in the classroom.

la **chaîne** NOUN
[1] chain ◊ *une chaîne en or* a gold chain
[2] channel (*on TV*) ◊ *Le film passe sur quelque chaîne?* Which channel is the film on?
♦ **une chaîne hi-fi** a hi-fi system
♦ **une chaîne laser** a CD player
♦ **une chaîne stéréo** a music centre
♦ **travailler à la chaîne** to work on an assembly line

la **chair** NOUN
flesh
♦ **en chair et en os** in the flesh ◊ *J'ai vu Mel Gibson en chair et en os.* I saw Mel Gibson in the flesh.
♦ **avoir la chair de poule** to have goose pimples

la **chaise** NOUN
chair
♦ **une chaise longue** a deckchair

le **châle** NOUN
shawl

la **chaleur** NOUN
[1] heat
[2] warmth

chaleureux ADJECTIVE (FEM SING **chaleureuse**)
warm ◊ *un accueil chaleureux* a warm welcome

se **chamailler** VERB (*informal*)
to squabble ◊ *Elle se chamaille sans cesse avec son frère.* She's always squabbling with her brother.

la **chambre** NOUN
room ◊ *C'est la chambre de Camille.* This is Camille's room.
♦ **une chambre à coucher** a bedroom
♦ **une chambre d'amis** a spare room
♦ **une chambre à un lit** a single room
♦ **une chambre pour une personne** a single room
♦ **une chambre pour deux personnes** a double room
♦ **"Chambres d'hôte"** "Bed and Breakfast"

le **chameau** NOUN (PL les **chameaux**)
camel

le **champ** NOUN
field

le **champagne** NOUN
champagne

le **champignon** NOUN
mushroom ◊ *une omelette aux champignons* a mushroom omelette

C

♦ **un champignon de Paris** a button mushroom

le **champion** NOUN
champion

le **championnat** NOUN
championship ◊ *le championnat du monde* the world championship

la **championne** NOUN
champion

la **chance** NOUN
1 luck
♦ **Bonne chance!** Good luck!
♦ **par chance** luckily
♦ **avoir de la chance** to be lucky ◊ *Tu as de la chance de partir au soleil!* You're lucky, going off to the sun!
2 chance ◊ *Il n'a aucune chance.* He's got no chance. ◊ *Il a des chances de réussir.* He's got a good chance of passing.

le **change** NOUN
exchange ◊ *le taux de change* the exchange rate

le **changement** NOUN
change ◊ *Il n'aime pas le changement.* He doesn't like changes.

changer VERB
to change ◊ *Il n'a pas beaucoup changé.* He hasn't changed much. ◊ *J'ai changé les draps ce matin.* I changed the sheets this morning. ◊ *J'ai changé trois cents francs.* I changed 300 francs.
♦ **se changer** to get changed ◊ *Je vais me changer avant de sortir.* I'm going to get changed before I go out.
♦ **changer de** to change ◊ *Je change de chaussures et j'arrive!* I'll change my shoes and then I'll be ready!
♦ **changer d'avis** to change one's mind ◊ *Appelle-moi si tu changes d'avis.* Give me a ring if you change your mind.
♦ **changer de chaîne** to change the channel

la **chanson** NOUN
song

le **chant** NOUN
singing ◊ *des cours de chant* singing lessons
♦ **un chant de Noël** a Christmas carol

le **chantage** NOUN
blackmail ◊ *faire du chantage à quelqu'un* to blackmail somebody

chanter VERB
to sing

le **chanteur** NOUN
singer

la **chanteuse** NOUN
singer

le **chantier** NOUN
building site

la **Chantilly** NOUN
whipped cream

chantonner VERB
to hum

le **chapeau** NOUN (PL les **chapeaux**)
hat

la **chapelle** NOUN
chapel

le **chapitre** NOUN
chapter

chaque ADJECTIVE
1 every ◊ *chaque année* every year
2 each ◊ *Ces verres coûtent cinquante francs chaque.* These glasses cost 50 francs each.

le **char** NOUN
tank (*military*)

le **charabia** NOUN (*informal*)
gibberish ◊ *Je n'y comprends rien: c'est du charabia.* I don't understand any of it: it's gibberish.

la **charade** NOUN
1 riddle
2 charade ◊ *jouer aux charades* to play charades

le **charbon** NOUN
coal
♦ **le charbon de bois** charcoal

la **charcuterie** NOUN
1 pork butcher's
2 cold meats

> ⓘ A **charcuterie** sells cuts of pork and pork products such as sausages, salami and pâté, as well as various cooked dishes and salads; **charcuterie** served at a meal is an assortment of ham, sausage and pâtés.

le **charcutier** NOUN
pork butcher

la **charcutière** NOUN
pork butcher

le **chardon** NOUN
thistle

charger VERB
to load
♦ **charger quelqu'un de faire quelque chose** to tell somebody to do something ◊ *Paul m'a chargé de vous dire que la clé est sous le paillasson.* Paul told me to tell you that the key's under the mat.

le **chariot** NOUN
   trolley (at supermarket)

charmant ADJECTIVE
   charming

le **charme** NOUN
   charm

charmer VERB
   to charm

la **charrue** NOUN
   plough

la **chasse** NOUN
   [1] hunting ◊ un chien de chasse a hunting dog
   [2] shooting ◊ la chasse au canard duck shooting
   ◆tirer la chasse d'eau to flush the toilet

le **chasse-neige** NOUN (PL les **chasse-neige**)
   snowplough

chasser VERB
   [1] to hunt ◊ Mon père chasse le lapin. My father hunts rabbits.
   [2] to chase away ◊ Ils ont chassé les cambrioleurs. They chased away the robbers.
   [3] to get rid of ◊ Ouvre donc la fenêtre pour chasser les odeurs de cuisine. Open the window to get rid of the cooking smells.

le **chasseur** NOUN
   hunter

le **chat** NOUN
   cat

la **châtaigne** NOUN
.   chestnut

le **châtaignier** NOUN
   chestnut tree

châtain ADJECTIVE (MASC, FEM, PL)
   brown ◊ J'ai les cheveux châtain. I've got brown hair.

le **château** NOUN (PL les **châteaux**)
   [1] castle
   ◆un château fort a castle
   [2] palace ◊ le château de Versailles the palace of Versailles

le **chaton** NOUN
   kitten

chatouiller VERB
   to tickle

chatouilleux ADJECTIVE (FEM SING **chatouilleuse**)
   ticklish

la **chatte** NOUN
   cat (female)

chaud ADJECTIVE
   [1] warm ◊ des vêtements chauds warm clothes
   ◆avoir chaud to be warm ◊ J'ai assez chaud. I'm warm enough.
   [2] hot ◊ Il fait chaud aujourd'hui. It's hot today. ◊ un plat chaud a hot dish ◊ Attention, c'est chaud! Mind, it's hot! ◊ J'ai trop chaud! I'm too hot!

le **chauffage** NOUN
   heating ◊ Le chauffage est en panne. The heating isn't working.
   ◆le chauffage central central heating

le **chauffe-eau** NOUN (PL les **chauffe-eau**)
   water heater

chauffer VERB
   to warm ◊ Je vais mettre de l'eau à chauffer pour faire du thé. I'm going to put some water on to make tea.

le **chauffeur** NOUN
   driver ◊ un chauffeur de taxi a taxi driver

le **chaume** NOUN
   ◆un toit de chaume a thatched roof

la **chaussée** NOUN
   road surface ◊ "Attention! Chaussée déformée" "Uneven road surface"

chausser VERB
   ◆Vous chaussez du combien? What size shoe do you take?

la **chaussette** NOUN
   sock

le **chausson** NOUN
   slipper
   ◆un chausson aux pommes an apple turnover

la **chaussure** NOUN
   shoe
   ◆les chaussures de ski ski boots

chauve ADJECTIVE
   bald

la **chauve-souris** NOUN (PL les **chauves-souris**)
   bat (animal)

le **chef** NOUN
   [1] head ◊ le chef de famille the head of the family
   ◆le chef de l'État the Head of State
   [2] boss ◊ Je dois demander la permission à mon chef. I have to get permission from my boss.
   ◆un chef d'entreprise a company director
   [3] chef ◊ la spécialité du chef the chef's speciality
   ◆un chef d'orchestre a conductor

le **chef-d'œuvre** NOUN (PL les **chefs-d'œuvre**)
   masterpiece

le **chemin** NOUN

C

[1] path ◊ *Je suis descendu à la plage par un petit chemin.* I went down a little path to the beach.
[2] way ◊ *Quel est le chemin le plus court pour aller à l'aéroport?* What's the quickest way to the airport?
♦ **en chemin** on the way ◊ *Je mangerai mon sandwich en chemin.* I'll eat my sandwich on the way.
♦ **les chemins de fer** the railways

la **cheminée** NOUN
[1] chimney
[2] fireplace

la **chemise** NOUN
[1] shirt ◊ *une chemise à carreaux* a checked shirt
♦ **une chemise de nuit** a nightdress
[2] folder ◊ *J'ai classé mes cours dans des chemises de couleurs différentes.* I've sorted my notes into different coloured folders.

le **chemisier** NOUN
blouse

le **chêne** NOUN
oak ◊ *une armoire en chêne* an oak wardrobe

le **chenil** NOUN
kennels

la **chenille** NOUN
caterpillar

le **chèque** NOUN
cheque
♦ **les chèques de voyage** traveller's cheques

le **chéquier** NOUN
cheque book

cher ADJECTIVE, ADVERB (FEM SING **chère**)
[1] dear ◊ *Chère Mélusine ...* Dear Mélusine ...
[2] expensive ◊ *C'est trop cher.* It's too expensive. ◊ *coûter cher* to be expensive

chercher VERB
[1] to look for ◊ *Je cherche mes clés.* I'm looking for my keys.
[2] to look up ◊ *chercher un mot dans le dictionnaire* to look up a word in the dictionary
♦ **aller chercher (1)** to go to get ◊ *Elle est allée chercher du pain pour ce midi.* She's gone to get some bread for lunch.
♦ **aller chercher (2)** to pick up ◊ *J'irai te chercher à la gare.* I'll pick you up at the station.

le **chercheur** NOUN
scientist

la **chercheuse** NOUN
scientist

chère ADJECTIVE *see* **cher**

chéri ADJECTIVE
see also **chéri** NOUN
darling ◊ *ma petite fille chérie* my darling daughter

le **chéri** NOUN
see also **chéri** ADJECTIVE
darling
♦ **mon chéri** darling

la **chérie** NOUN
darling
♦ **ma chérie** darling

le **cheval** NOUN (PL les **chevaux**)
horse ◊ *un cheval de course* a racehorse
♦ **à cheval** on horseback
♦ **faire du cheval** to go riding

le **chevalier** NOUN
knight

la **chevalière** NOUN
signet ring

chevalin ADJECTIVE
♦ **une boucherie chevaline** a horsemeat butcher's

les **chevaux** MASC NOUN *see* **cheval**

le **chevet** NOUN
♦ **une table de chevet** a bedside table
♦ **une lampe de chevet** a bedside lamp

les **cheveux** MASC NOUN
hair SING ◊ *Elle a les cheveux courts.* She's got short hair.

la **cheville** NOUN
ankle ◊ *se fouler la cheville* to sprain your ankle

la **chèvre** NOUN
goat
♦ **le fromage de chèvre** goat's cheese

le **chevreau** NOUN (PL les **chevreaux**)
kid (*animal, leather*)

le **chèvrefeuille** NOUN
honeysuckle

le **chevreuil** NOUN
[1] roe deer
[2] venison ◊ *un rôti de chevreuil* roast venison

le **chewing-gum** NOUN
chewing gum

chez PREPOSITION
♦ **chez Pierre (1)** at Pierre's house
♦ **chez Pierre (2)** to Pierre's house
♦ **chez moi (1)** at my house ◊ *Je suis resté chez moi ce week-end.* I stayed at home this weekend.
♦ **chez moi (2)** to my house ◊ *Je vais rentrer chez moi.* I'm going home.
♦ **chez le dentiste (1)** at the dentist's ◊ *J'ai rendez-vous chez le dentiste demain matin.* I've got an

☞

appointment at the dentist's tomorrow morning.
♦ **chez le dentiste (2)** to the dentist's ◊ *Je vais chez le dentiste.* I'm going to the dentist's.

chic ADJECTIVE
[1] smart ◊ *une tenue chic* a smart outfit
[2] nice ◊ *C'est chic de ta part de m'avoir invité.* (informal) It was nice of you to invite me.

la **chicorée** NOUN
endive

le **chien** NOUN
dog
♦ **"Attention, chien méchant"** "Beware of the dog"

la **chienne** NOUN
bitch (*dog*)

le **chiffon** NOUN
cloth

chiffonner VERB
to crease ◊ *Ma robe est toute chiffonnée.* My dress is all creased.

le **chiffre** NOUN
figure ◊ *en chiffres ronds* in round figures
♦ **les chiffres romains** Roman numerals

le **chignon** NOUN
bun (*in hair*) ◊ *Elle s'est fait un chignon.* She put her hair in a bun.

le **Chili** NOUN
Chile

la **chimie** NOUN
chemistry ◊ *un cours de chimie* a chemistry lesson

chimique ADJECTIVE
chemical ◊ *une réaction chimique* a chemical reaction
♦ **les produits chimiques** chemicals

la **Chine** NOUN
China

chinois ADJECTIVE, NOUN
Chinese ◊ *Il apprend le chinois.* He's learning Chinese.
♦ **un Chinois** a Chinese (*man*)
♦ **une Chinoise** a Chinese (*woman*)
♦ **les Chinois** the Chinese

le **chiot** NOUN
puppy

les **chips** FEM NOUN
crisps ◊ *un paquet de chips* a packet of crisps

chirurgical ADJECTIVE (MASC PL **chirurgicaux**)
♦ **une intervention chirurgicale** an operation

la **chirurgie** NOUN
surgery
♦ **la chirurgie esthétique** plastic surgery

le **chirurgien** NOUN
surgeon

le **choc** NOUN
shock ◊ *Ça m'a fait un sacré choc de le voir comme ça.* It gave me a hell of a shock to see him in that state.
♦ **Elle est encore sous le choc.** She's still in shock.

le **chocolat** NOUN
chocolate
♦ **un chocolat chaud** a hot chocolate
♦ **le chocolat à croquer** dark chocolate

le **chœur** NOUN
choir

choisir VERB
to choose

le **choix** NOUN
[1] choice
♦ **avoir le choix** to have the choice
[2] selection ◊ *Il n'y a pas beaucoup de choix dans ce magasin.* There's not a very wide selection of things in this shop.

le **chômage** NOUN
unemployment
♦ **être au chômage** to be unemployed

le **chômeur** NOUN
unemployed person ◊ *Il est chômeur.* He's unemployed.

la **chômeuse** NOUN
unemployed woman ◊ *Elle est chômeuse.* She's unemployed.

choquer VERB
to shock ◊ *Cette remarque m'a choqué.* I was shocked by that remark.

la **chorale** NOUN
choir

la **chose** NOUN
thing ◊ *J'ai fait des choses intéressantes pendant les vacances.* I did some interesting things during the holidays.
♦ **C'est peu de chose.** It's nothing really.

le **chou** NOUN (PL les **choux**)
cabbage
♦ **les choux de Bruxelles** Brussels sprouts
♦ **un chou à la crème** a choux bun

le **chouchou** NOUN (*informal*)
teacher's pet

la **chouchoute** NOUN (*informal*)
teacher's pet

la **choucroute** NOUN
sauerkraut (*with sausages and ham*)

la **chouette** NOUN
see also **chouette** ADJECTIVE
owl

chouette ADJECTIVE (*informal*)
see also **chouette** NOUN
brilliant ◊ *Chouette alors!* Brilliant!

le **chou-fleur** NOUN (PL les **choux-fleurs**)
cauliflower

chrétien ADJECTIVE (FEM SING **chrétienne**)
Christian ◊ *Il est chrétien.* He's a
Christian.

le **Christ** NOUN
Christ

chronologique ADJECTIVE
chronological

le **chronomètre** NOUN
stopwatch

chronométrer VERB
to time

le **chrysanthème** NOUN
chrysanthemum

> *ⓘ Chrysanthemums are strongly
> associated with funerals in France.*

chuchoter VERB
to whisper

chut EXCLAMATION
Shh!

la **chute** NOUN
fall
♦ **faire une chute** to fall
♦ **une chute d'eau** a waterfall

Chypre NOUN
Cyprus

-ci ADVERB
♦ **ce livre-ci** this book
♦ **ces bottes-ci** these boots

la **cible** NOUN
target

la **ciboulette** NOUN
chives

la **cicatrice** NOUN
scar

se **cicatriser** VERB
to heal up ◊ *Cette plaie s'est vite
cicatrisée.* This wound has healed up
quickly.

ci-contre ADVERB
opposite ◊ *la page ci-contre* the
opposite page

ci-dessous ADVERB
below ◊ *la photo ci-dessous* the
picture below

ci-dessus ADVERB
above

le **cidre** NOUN
cider

le **ciel** NOUN
① sky ◊ *un ciel nuageux* a cloudy
sky
② heaven ◊ *être au ciel* to be in
heaven

le **cierge** NOUN
candle (*in church*)

la **cigale** NOUN
cicada

le **cigare** NOUN
cigar ◊ *Il fume le cigare.* He smokes
cigars.

la **cigarette** NOUN
cigarette

la **cigogne** NOUN
stork

ci-joint ADVERB
enclosed ◊ *Veuillez trouver ci-joint
mon curriculum vitae.* Please find
enclosed my CV.

le **cil** NOUN
eyelash

le **ciment** NOUN
cement

le **cimetière** NOUN
cemetery

le/la **cinéaste** NOUN
film-maker

le **cinéma** NOUN
cinema

cinq NUMBER
five ◊ *Il est cinq heures du matin.* It's
five in the morning. ◊ *Il a cinq ans.*
He's five.
♦ **le cinq février** the fifth of February

la **cinquantaine** NOUN
about fifty ◊ *Il y avait une
cinquantaine de personnes.* There
were about fifty people there.
♦ **Il a la cinquantaine.** He's in his fifties.

cinquante NUMBER
fifty ◊ *Il a cinquante ans.* He's fifty.
♦ **cinquante et un** fifty-one
♦ **cinquante-deux** fifty-two

cinquième ADJECTIVE
see also **cinquième** NOUN
fifth ◊ *au cinquième étage* on the
fifth floor

la **cinquième** NOUN
see also **cinquième** ADJECTIVE
second year

> *ⓘ In French secondary schools,
> years are counted from the **sixième**
> (youngest) to **première** and **terminale**
> (oldest).*

☞

◊ *Mon frère est en cinquième.* My brother's in second year.

le **cintre** NOUN
coat hanger

le **cirage** NOUN
shoe polish

circonflexe ADJECTIVE
♦ **un accent circonflexe** a circumflex

la **circonstance** NOUN
circumstance ◊ *dans les circonstances actuelles* in the present circumstances

la **circulation** NOUN
1 traffic ◊ *Il y avait beaucoup de circulation.* There was a lot of traffic.
2 circulation ◊ *Elle a des problèmes de circulation.* She has bad circulation.

circuler VERB
to run ◊ *Il n'y a qu'un bus sur trois qui circule.* Only one bus in three is running.

la **cire** NOUN
wax

le **ciré** NOUN
oilskin jacket

cirer VERB
to polish (*shoes, floor*)

le **cirque** NOUN
circus

les **ciseaux** MASC NOUN
♦ **une paire de ciseaux** a pair of scissors

le **citadin** NOUN
city dweller

la **citation** NOUN
quotation

la **cité** NOUN
estate ◊ *J'habite dans une cité.* I live on an estate.
♦ **une cité universitaire** halls of residence
♦ **une cité-dortoir** a dormitory town

citer VERB
to quote

le **citoyen** NOUN
citizen

la **citoyenne** NOUN
citizen

la **citoyenneté** NOUN
citizenship

le **citron** NOUN
lemon
♦ **un citron vert** a lime
♦ **un citron pressé** a fresh lemon juice

la **citronnade** NOUN
still lemonade

la **citrouille** NOUN
pumpkin

le **civet** NOUN
stew ◊ *du civet de lapin* rabbit stew

civil ADJECTIVE
civilian
♦ **en civil** in civilian clothes

la **civilisation** NOUN
civilization

clair ADJECTIVE, ADVERB
1 light ◊ *vert clair* light green ◊ *C'est une pièce très claire.* It's a very light room.
2 clear (*water*)
♦ **voir clair** to see clearly
♦ **le clair de lune** moonlight

clairement ADVERB
clearly

la **clairière** NOUN
clearing

clandestin ADJECTIVE
♦ **un passager clandestin** a stowaway

la **claque** NOUN
slap ◊ *Elle m'a donné une claque.* She gave me a slap.

claquer VERB
1 to bang ◊ *On entend des volets qui claquent.* You can hear shutters banging.
2 to slam ◊ *Elle est partie en claquant la porte.* She left, slamming the door behind her.

les **claquettes** FEM NOUN
♦ **faire des claquettes** to tap-dance

la **clarinette** NOUN
clarinet ◊ *Gavin joue de la clarinette.* Gavin plays the clarinet.

la **classe** NOUN
1 class ◊ *C'est la meilleure élève de la classe.* She's the best pupil in the class. ◊ *voyager en première classe* to travel first class
2 classroom

classer VERB
to arrange ◊ *Les livres sont classés par ordre alphabétique.* The books are arranged in alphabetical order.

le **classeur** NOUN
ring binder

classique ADJECTIVE
1 classical ◊ *de la musique classique* classical music
2 classic ◊ *un style classique* a classic style

le **clavier** NOUN
keyboard (*of computer, typewriter*)

la **clé** NOUN

1 key ◊ *une clé de voiture* a car key
2 clef ◊ *la clé de sol* the treble clef
◊ *la clé de fa* the bass clef

la **clef** NOUN = **clé**

le **client** NOUN
customer

la **cliente** NOUN
customer

la **clientèle** NOUN
customers

cligner VERB
♦**cligner des yeux** to blink

le **clignotant** NOUN
indicator ◊ *Il a mis son clignotant à gauche.* He's indicating left.

le **climat** NOUN
climate

la **climatisation** NOUN
air conditioning

climatisé ADJECTIVE
air-conditioned ◊ *L'hôtel est climatisé.* The hotel is air-conditioned.

le **clin d'œil** NOUN (PL les **clins d'œil**)
wink
♦**en un clin d'œil** in a flash

la **clinique** NOUN
private hospital

cliquer VERB
to click ◊ *cliquer sur une icône* to click on an icon

le **clochard** NOUN
tramp

la **cloche** NOUN
bell

le **clocher** NOUN
1 church tower
2 steeple

le **clone** NOUN
clone

cloner VERB
to clone

le **clou** NOUN
nail
♦**un clou de girofle** a clove

le **clown** NOUN
clown

le **club** NOUN
club

le **cobaye** NOUN
guinea pig

le **coca** NOUN
Coke ®

la **cocaïne** NOUN
cocaine

la **coccinelle** NOUN
ladybird

cocher VERB
to tick ◊ *Cochez la bonne réponse.* Tick the right answer.

le **cochon** NOUN
| see also **cochon** ADJECTIVE |
pig
♦**un cochon d'Inde** a guinea pig

cochon ADJECTIVE (*informal*)
| see also **cochon** NOUN |
dirty ◊ *une histoire cochonne* a dirty story

le **cocktail** NOUN
1 cocktail
2 cocktail party

le **coco** NOUN
♦**une noix de coco** a coconut

cocorico EXCLAMATION
1 Cock-a-doodle-doo!
2 Three cheers for France!

> 🛈 The symbol of France is the cockerel and so *cocorico!* is sometimes used as an expression of French national pride.

la **cocotte** NOUN
casserole (*pan*)
♦**une cocotte-minute** ® a pressure cooker

le **code** NOUN
code
♦**le code de la route** the highway code
♦**le code postal** the postcode
♦**le code confidentiel** PIN number

le **cœur** NOUN
heart
♦**avoir bon cœur** to be kind-hearted
♦**la dame de cœur** the queen of hearts
♦**avoir mal au cœur** to feel sick
♦**par cœur** by heart ◊ *apprendre quelque chose par cœur* to learn something by heart

le **coffre** NOUN
1 boot (*of car*)
2 chest (*furniture*)

le **coffre-fort** NOUN (PL les **coffres-forts**)
safe

le **coffret** NOUN
♦**un coffret à bijoux** a jewellery box

le **cognac** NOUN
brandy

se **cogner** VERB
♦**se cogner à quelque chose** to bang into something ◊ *Je me suis cogné à la table.* I banged into the table. ◊ *Je me suis cogné la tête contre la porte du placard.* I banged my head on the cupboard door.

C

coiffé ADJECTIVE
♦ **Tu es bien coiffée.** Your hair looks nice.

coiffer VERB
♦ **se coiffer** to do one's hair

le **coiffeur** NOUN
  hairdresser

la **coiffeuse** NOUN
  hairdresser

la **coiffure** NOUN
  hairstyle ◇ *Cette coiffure te va bien.* That hairstyle suits you.
♦ **un salon de coiffure** a hairdresser's

le **coin** NOUN
  corner
♦ **au coin de la rue** on the corner of the street
♦ **Tu habites dans le coin?** Do you live near here?
♦ **Je ne suis pas du coin.** I'm not from here.
♦ **le bistrot du coin** the local pub

coincé ADJECTIVE
  [1] stuck ◇ *La clé est coincée dans la serrure.* The key is stuck in the keyhole.
  [2] stuffy ◇ *Il est un peu coincé.* (*informal*) He's a bit stuffy.

coincer VERB
  to jam ◇ *La porte est coincée.* The door's jammed.

la **coïncidence** NOUN
  coincidence

le **col** NOUN
  [1] collar
  [2] pass (*of mountain*)

la **colère** NOUN
  anger
♦ **Je suis en colère.** I'm angry.
♦ **se mettre en colère** to get angry

le **colin** NOUN
  hake

la **colique** NOUN
  diarrhoea

le **colis** NOUN
  parcel

collaborer VERB
  to collaborate

collant ADJECTIVE
  | *see also* **collant** NOUN |
  [1] sticky
  [2] clingy
♦ **Je le trouve un peu collant.** (*informal*) He's always hanging around me.

le **collant** NOUN
  | *see also* **collant** ADJECTIVE |
  tights ◇ *un collant en laine* woollen tights

la **colle** NOUN
  [1] glue ◇ *un tube de colle* a tube of glue
  [2] detention ◇ *J'ai une heure de colle samedi prochain.* (*informal*) I've got an hour's detention next Saturday.
♦ **Je n'en sais rien: tu me poses une colle.** (*informal*) I really don't know: you've got me there.

la **collecte** NOUN
  collection (*of money*) ◇ *On a fait une collecte au profit des victimes.* There was a collection for the victims.

la **collection** NOUN
  collection ◇ *une collection de timbres* a stamp collection

collectionner VERB
  to collect

le **collège** NOUN
  secondary school

> ❶ *In France pupils go to a **collège** between the ages of 11 and 15, and then to a **lycée** until the age of 18.*

le **collégien** NOUN
  schoolboy

la **collégienne** NOUN
  schoolgirl

le/la **collègue** NOUN
  colleague

coller VERB
  [1] to stick ◇ *Il y a un chewing-gum collé sous la chaise.* There's a bit of chewing gum stuck under the chair.
  [2] to be sticky ◇ *Ce timbre ne colle plus.* This stamp won't stick on.
  [3] to press ◇ *J'ai collé mon oreille au mur.* I pressed my ear against the wall.

le **collier** NOUN
  [1] necklace ◇ *un collier de perles* a pearl necklace
  [2] collar (*of dog, cat*)

la **colline** NOUN
  hill

la **collision** NOUN
  crash

la **colombe** NOUN
  dove

la **colonie** NOUN
♦ **aller en colonie de vacances** to go to summer camp

la **colonne** NOUN
  column
♦ **la colonne vertébrale** the spine

le **colorant** NOUN
  colouring

le **coloris** NOUN
colour

le **coma** NOUN
coma ◇ *être dans le coma* to be in a coma

le **combat** NOUN
fighting ◇ *Les combats ont repris ce matin.* Fighting started again this morning.
♦ **un combat de boxe** a boxing match

le **combattant** NOUN
♦ **un ancien combattant** a war veteran

combattre VERB
to fight

combien ADVERB
☐ how much ◇ *Vous en voulez combien? Un kilo?* How much do you want? One kilo?
♦ **C'est combien?** How much is that? ◇ *Combien est-ce que ça coûte?* How much does it cost? ◇ *Combien ça fait?* How much does it come to?
☐ how many ◇ *Tu en veux combien? Deux?* How many do you want? Two?
♦ **combien de (1)** how much ◇ *Combien de purée est-ce que je vous sers?* How much mashed potato shall I give you?
♦ **combien de (2)** how many ◇ *Combien de personnes as-tu invitées?* How many people have you invited?
♦ **combien de temps** how long ◇ *Combien de temps est-ce que tu seras absente?* How long will you be away?
♦ **Il y a combien de temps?** How long ago? ◇ *Il est parti il y a combien de temps?* How long ago did he leave?
♦ **On est le combien aujourd'hui? – On est le vingt.** What's the date today? – It's the 20th.

la **combinaison** NOUN
☐ combination ◇ *J'ai changé la combinaison de mon antivol.* I've changed the combination on my bike lock.
☐ slip (*petticoat*)
♦ **une combinaison de plongée** a wetsuit
♦ **une combinaison de ski** a ski suit

le **comble** NOUN
♦ **Alors ça, c'est le comble!** That's the last straw!

la **comédie** NOUN
comedy
♦ **une comédie musicale** a musical

le **comédien** NOUN
actor

la **comédienne** NOUN
actress

comestible ADJECTIVE
edible

comique ADJECTIVE
see also **comique** NOUN
comical

le **comique** NOUN
see also **comique** ADJECTIVE
comedian

le **comité** NOUN
committee

le **commandant** NOUN
captain (*of ship, plane*)

la **commande** NOUN
order ◇ *un bon de commande* an order form
♦ **être aux commandes** to be at the controls

commander VERB
☐ to order ◇ *J'ai commandé une robe par catalogue.* I've ordered a dress from a catalogue.
☐ to give orders ◇ *C'est moi qui commande ici, pas vous!* I give the orders here, not you!

comme CONJUNCTION, ADVERB
☐ like ◇ *Il est comme son père.* He's like his father. ◇ *Je voudrais un manteau comme celui de la photo.* I'd like a coat like the one in the picture.
☐ for ◇ *Qu'est-ce que tu veux comme dessert?* What would you like for pudding?
☐ as ◇ *J'ai travaillé comme serveuse cet été.* I worked as a waitress this summer. ◇ *Faites comme vous voulez.* Do as you like.
♦ **comme ça** like this ◇ *Ça se plie comme ça.* You fold it like this. ◇ *C'était un poisson grand comme ça.* The fish was this big.
♦ **comme il faut** properly ◇ *Mets le couvert comme il faut!* Set the table properly!
♦ **Comme tu as grandi!** How you've grown!
♦ **Regarde comme c'est beau!** Look, isn't it lovely!
♦ **comme ci comme ça** SO-SO ◇ *Comment est-ce que tu as trouvé le film? – Comme ci comme ça.* What did you think of the film? – So-so.

le **commencement** NOUN
beginning

commencer VERB
to start ◇ *Les cours commencent à huit heures.* Lessons start at 8 o'clock. ◇ *Il a commencé à pleuvoir.* It started raining. ◇ *J'ai commencé de*

C

réviser pour les examens. I've started revising for the exams.

comment ADVERB
how ◊ *Comment arrives-tu à travailler dans ce bruit?* How can you possibly work with this noise?
♦ **Comment allez-vous?** How are you?
♦ **Comment dit-on "pomme" en anglais?** How do you say "pomme" in English?
♦ **Comment s'appelle-t-il?** What's his name?
♦ **Comment?** What did you say?

le **commentaire** NOUN
comment

les **commérages** MASC NOUN
gossip SING

le **commerçant** NOUN
shopkeeper

le **commerce** NOUN
1 trade ◊ *le commerce extérieur* foreign trade
♦ **le commerce électronique** e-commerce
2 business ◊ *Il fait des études de commerce.* He's studying business.
3 shop ◊ *tenir un commerce* to have a shop
♦ **On trouve ça dans le commerce.** You can find it in the shops.

commercial ADJECTIVE (MASC PL **commerciaux**)
♦ **un centre commercial** a shopping centre

commettre VERB
to commit ◊ *Il a commis un crime grave.* He has committed a serious crime.

le **commissaire** NOUN
police superintendent

le **commissariat** NOUN
police station

les **commissions** FEM NOUN
shopping SING ◊ *J'ai quelques commissions à faire.* I've got some shopping to do.

commode ADJECTIVE
see also **commode** NOUN
handy ◊ *Ce sac est très commode pour les voyages.* This bag is very handy for travelling.
♦ **Son père n'est pas commode.** His father is a difficult character.

la **commode** NOUN
see also **commode** ADJECTIVE
chest of drawers

commun ADJECTIVE
shared ◊ *une salle de bain commune* a shared bathroom ◊ *Nous avons des*

intérêts communs. We have interests in common.
♦ **en commun** in common ◊ *Ils n'ont rien en commun.* They've got nothing in common.
♦ **les transports en commun** public transport
♦ **mettre quelque chose en commun** to share something ◊ *Nous mettons tous nos livres en commun.* We share all our books.

la **communauté** NOUN
community

la **communication** NOUN
communication
♦ **une communication téléphonique** a telephone call

la **communion** NOUN
communion ◊ *faire sa première communion* to make one's first communion

communiquer VERB
to communicate

communiste ADJECTIVE
communist ◊ *le Parti communiste* the Communist Party

compact ADJECTIVE
compact
♦ **un disque compact** a compact disc

la **compagne** NOUN
1 companion
2 partner (*living together*)

la **compagnie** NOUN
company ◊ *J'aime avoir de la compagnie.* I like to have company. ◊ *Je viendrai te tenir compagnie.* I'll come to keep you company.
♦ **une compagnie d'assurances** an insurance company
♦ **une compagnie aérienne** an airline

le **compagnon** NOUN
1 companion
2 partner (*living together*)

la **comparaison** NOUN
comparison ◊ *en comparaison de* in comparison with

comparer VERB
to compare

le **compartiment** NOUN
compartment (*on train*)

le **compas** NOUN
compass (*for drawing circles*)

compatible ADJECTIVE
compatible

la **compétence** NOUN
competence

compétent ADJECTIVE
competent

compétitif ADJECTIVE (FEM SING **compétitive**)
<u>competitive</u>

la **compétition** NOUN
<u>competition</u>
♦ **avoir l'esprit de compétition** to be competitive

complet ADJECTIVE (FEM SING **complète**)
| see also **complet** NOUN |
[1] <u>complete</u> ◊ *les œuvres complètes de Shakespeare* the complete works of Shakespeare
[2] <u>full</u> ◊ *L'hôtel est complet.* The hotel is full.
♦ **"complet"** "no vacancies"
♦ **le pain complet** wholemeal bread

le **complet** NOUN
| see also **complet** ADJECTIVE |
<u>suit</u> (*for man*)

complètement ADVERB
<u>completely</u> ◊ *J'avais complètement oublié que tu viendrais.* I'd completely forgotten that you were coming.

compléter VERB
<u>to complete</u> ◊ *Complétez les phrases suivantes.* Complete the following phrases.

complexe ADJECTIVE
<u>complex</u>

complexé ADJECTIVE
<u>screwed-up</u>

la **complication** NOUN
<u>complication</u>

le/la **complice** NOUN
<u>accomplice</u>

les **compliments** MASC NOUN
<u>compliment</u> SING
♦ **faire des compliments** to compliment ◊ *Il m'a fait des compliments sur ma robe.* He complimented me on my dress.

compliqué ADJECTIVE
<u>complicated</u> ◊ *C'est une histoire compliquée.* It's a complicated story.

le **complot** NOUN
<u>plot</u>

le **comportement** NOUN
<u>behaviour</u>

comporter VERB
[1] <u>to consist of</u> ◊ *Le château comporte trois parties.* The castle consists of three parts.
[2] <u>to have</u> ◊ *Ce modèle comporte un écran couleur.* This model has a colour screen.
♦ **se comporter** to behave ◊ *Il s'est comporté de façon odieuse.* He behaved atrociously.

composer VERB
<u>to compose</u> (*music, text*)
♦ **composer un numéro** to dial a number
♦ **se composer de** to consist of ◊ *L'uniforme se compose d'une veste, d'un pantalon et d'une cravate.* The uniform consists of a jacket, trousers and a tie.

le **compositeur** NOUN
<u>composer</u>

la **composition** NOUN
<u>test</u> ◊ *Nous avons une composition de français cet après-midi.* We've got a French test this afternoon.

la **compositrice** NOUN
<u>composer</u>

composter VERB
<u>to punch</u> ◊ *N'oublie pas de composter ton billet avant de monter dans le train.* Remember to punch your ticket before you get on the train.

> ⓘ *In France you have to punch your ticket on the platform to validate it before getting onto the train.*

la **compote** NOUN
<u>stewed fruit</u>
♦ **la compote de prunes** stewed plums

compréhensible ADJECTIVE
<u>understandable</u>

compréhensif ADJECTIVE (FEM SING **compréhensive**)
<u>understanding</u>
> *Be careful!* **compréhensif** *does not mean* **comprehensive**.

la **compréhension** NOUN
[1] <u>comprehension</u> ◊ *Il n'est pas très bon en compréhension orale.* She's not very good at listening comprehension.
[2] <u>sympathy</u>
♦ **Elle a fait preuve de beaucoup de compréhension à mon égard.** She was very sympathetic towards me.

comprendre VERB
[1] <u>to understand</u> ◊ *Je ne comprends pas ce que vous dites.* I don't understand what you're saying.
[2] <u>to include</u> ◊ *Le forfait ne comprend pas la location des skis.* The price doesn't include ski hire.

le **comprimé** NOUN
<u>tablet</u> ◊ *un comprimé d'aspirine* an aspirin

compris ADJECTIVE
<u>included</u> ◊ *Le service n'est pas compris.* Service is not included.

C

☞

♦ **y compris** including ◊ *Ils ont tout vendu, y compris leur voiture.* They sold everything, including their car.

♦ **non compris** excluding ◊ *un menu à cent francs, vin non compris* a set menu for 100 francs, excluding wine

♦ **cent francs tout compris** 100 francs all-inclusive

compromettre VERB
to compromise

le **compromis** NOUN
compromise ◊ *Ils sont parvenus à un compromis.* They came to a compromise.

la **comptabilité** NOUN
accounting ◊ *un cours de comptabilité* a course in accounting

le/la **comptable** NOUN
accountant ◊ *Il est comptable.* He's an accountant.

comptant ADVERB
♦ **payer comptant** to pay cash

le **compte** NOUN
account ◊ *J'ai déposé le chèque sur mon compte.* I've paid the cheque into my account.

♦ **Le compte est bon.** That's the right amount.

♦ **tenir compte de (1)** to take into account ◊ *Ils ont tenu compte de mon expérience.* They took my experience into account.

♦ **tenir compte de (2)** to take notice of ◊ *Il n'a pas tenu compte de mes conseils.* He took no notice of my advice.

♦ **travailler à son compte** to be self-employed

♦ **en fin de compte** all things considered ◊ *Le voyage ne s'est pas mal passé, en fin de compte.* The journey wasn't bad, all things considered.

compter VERB
to count

le **compte rendu** NOUN (PL les **comptes rendus**)
report

le **compteur** NOUN
meter

le **comptoir** NOUN
bar ◊ *au comptoir* at the bar

con ADJECTIVE (FEM SING **conne**) (*rude*)
bloody stupid

se **concentrer** VERB
to concentrate ◊ *J'ai du mal à me concentrer.* I find it hard to concentrate.

la **conception** NOUN
design

concernant PREPOSITION
regarding ◊ *Concernant notre nouveau projet, je voudrais ajouter que ...* Regarding our new project, I would like to add that ...

concerner VERB
to concern ◊ *en ce qui me concerne* as far as I'm concerned

♦ **Je ne me sens pas concerné.** I don't feel it's anything to do with me.

le **concert** NOUN
concert

le/la **concierge** NOUN
caretaker

conclure VERB
to conclude

la **conclusion** NOUN
conclusion

le **concombre** NOUN
cucumber

concorder VERB
to tally ◊ *Les dates concordent.* The dates tally.

le **concours** NOUN
☐1 competition ◊ *un concours de chant* a singing competition
☐2 competitive exam

concret ADJECTIVE (FEM SING **concrète**)
concrete

conçu VERB
designed ◊ *Ces appartements sont très mal conçus.* These flats are very badly designed.

la **concurrence** NOUN
competition ◊ *La concurrence est vive sur ce marché.* There's a lot of competition in this market.

le **concurrent** NOUN
competitor

la **concurrente** NOUN
competitor

condamner VERB
☐1 to sentence ◊ *Il a été condamné à deux ans de prison.* He was sentenced to two years in prison. ◊ *condamner à mort* to sentence to death
☐2 to condemn ◊ *Le gouvernement a condamné cette décision.* The government condemned this decision.

la **condition** NOUN
condition ◊ *Je le ferai à une condition ...* I'll do it, on one condition ...

♦ **à condition que** provided that ◊ *Je viendrai à condition qu'il me le*

C

demande. I'll come provided he asks
me to.
♦ **les conditions de travail** working
conditions

le **conditionnel** NOUN
conditional tense

le **conducteur** NOUN
driver

la **conductrice** NOUN
driver

conduire VERB
to drive ◊ *Est-ce que tu sais
conduire?* Can you drive? ◊ *Je te
conduirai chez le docteur.* I'll drive
you to the doctor's.
♦ **se conduire** to behave ◊ *Il s'est mal
conduit.* He behaved badly.

la **conduite** NOUN
behaviour

la **conférence** NOUN
[1] lecture ◊ *donner une conférence*
to give a lecture
[2] conference ◊ *une conférence
internationale* an international
conference

se **confesser** VERB
to go to confession

les **confettis** MASC NOUN
confetti

la **confiance** NOUN
[1] trust
♦ **avoir confiance en quelqu'un** to trust
somebody ◊ *Je n'ai pas confiance en
lui.* I don't trust him.
[2] confidence
♦ **Tu peux avoir confiance. Il sera à
l'heure.** You don't need to worry.
He'll be on time.
♦ **confiance en soi** self-confidence ◊ *Elle
manque de confiance en elle.* She
lacks self-confidence.

confiant ADJECTIVE
confident

les **confidences** FEM NOUN
♦ **faire des confidences à quelqu'un** to
confide in someone ◊ *Elle me fait
quelquefois des confidences.* She
sometimes confides in me.

confidentiel ADJECTIVE (FEM SING
confidentielle)
confidential

confier VERB
♦ **se confier à quelqu'un** to confide in
somebody ◊ *Elle s'est confiée à sa
meilleure amie.* She confided in her
best friend.

confirmer VERB
to confirm

la **confiserie** NOUN

sweet shop

confisquer VERB
to confiscate

confit ADJECTIVE
♦ **des fruits confits** crystallized fruits

la **confiture** NOUN
jam ◊ *la confiture de fraises*
strawberry jam
♦ **la confiture d'oranges** marmalade

le **conflit** NOUN
conflict

confondre VERB
to mix up ◊ *On le confond souvent
avec son frère.* People often mix him
up with his brother.

le **confort** NOUN
comfort
♦ **tout confort** with all mod cons ◊ *un
appartement tout confort* a flat with
all mod cons

confortable ADJECTIVE
comfortable ◊ *des chaussures
confortables* comfortable shoes

confus ADJECTIVE
[1] unclear ◊ *J'ai trouvé ses
explications confuses.* I thought his
explanation was unclear.
[2] embarrassed ◊ *Il avait l'air confus.*
He looked embarrassed.

la **confusion** NOUN
[1] confusion
[2] embarrassment ◊ *rougir de
confusion* to go red with
embarrassment

le **congé** NOUN
holiday ◊ *une semaine de congé* a
week's holiday
♦ **en congé** on holiday ◊ *Je serai en
congé la semaine prochaine.* I'll be
on holiday next week.
♦ **un congé de maladie** sick leave ◊ *Il
est en congé de maladie.* He's on
sick leave.

le **congélateur** NOUN
freezer

congeler VERB
to freeze

la **conjonction** NOUN
conjunction

la **conjonctivite** NOUN
conjunctivitis

la **conjugaison** NOUN
conjugation

la **connaissance** NOUN
[1] knowledge ◊ *... pour approfondir
vos connaissances ...* to increase your
knowledge

☞

2 acquaintance ◊ *Ce n'est pas vraiment une amie, juste une connaissance.* She's not really a friend, just an acquaintance.
♦ **perdre connaissance** to lose consciousness
♦ **faire la connaissance de quelqu'un** to meet somebody ◊ *J'ai fait la connaissance de son frère.* I met her brother.

connaître VERB
to know ◊ *Je ne connais pas du tout cette région.* I don't know this area at all. ◊ *Je le connais de vue.* I know him by sight.
♦ **Ils se sont connus à Nantes.** They first met in Nantes.
♦ **s'y connaître en quelque chose** to know about something ◊ *Je ne m'y connais pas beaucoup en musique classique.* I don't know much about classical music.

se connecter VERB
to log on ◊ *Je me suis connecté sur Internet il y a dix minutes.* I logged onto the internet ten minutes ago.

la **connerie** NOUN (*rude*)
bloody stupid thing ◊ *faire une connerie* to do something bloody stupid

connu ADJECTIVE
well-known ◊ *C'est un acteur connu.* He's a well-known actor.

conquérir VERB
to conquer

consacrer VERB
to devote ◊ *Il consacre beaucoup de temps à ses enfants.* He devotes a lot of time to his children. ◊ *Je suis désolé, je n'ai pas beaucoup de temps à vous consacrer.* I'm afraid I can't spare much time for you.

la **conscience** NOUN
conscience ◊ *avoir mauvaise conscience* to have a guilty conscience
♦ **prendre conscience de** to become aware of ◊ *Ils ont fini par prendre conscience de la gravité de la situation.* They eventually became aware of the seriousness of the situation.

consciencieux ADJECTIVE (FEM SING **consciencieuse**)
conscientious

conscient ADJECTIVE
conscious

consécutif ADJECTIVE (FEM SING **consécutive**)
consecutive

le **conseil** NOUN
advice ◊ *Est-ce que je peux te demander conseil?* Can I ask you for some advice?
♦ **un conseil** a piece of advice

conseiller VERB
see also **conseiller** NOUN
1 to advise ◊ *Il a été mal conseillé.* He has been badly advised.
2 to recommend ◊ *Il m'a conseillé ce livre.* He recommended this book to me.

le **conseiller** NOUN
see also **conseiller** VERB
1 councillor (*political*) ◊ *un conseiller municipal* a town councillor
2 adviser
♦ **le conseiller d'orientation** the careers adviser

le **consentement** NOUN
consent ◊ *le consentement des parents* the parents' consent

consentir VERB
to agree ◊ *consentir à quelque chose* to agree to something

la **conséquence** NOUN
consequence
♦ **en conséquence** consequently

conséquent ADJECTIVE
♦ **par conséquent** consequently

le **conservatoire** NOUN
school of music ◊ *Elle fait du piano au conservatoire.* She's learning the piano at the school of music.

la **conserve** NOUN
tin ◊ *Je vais ouvrir une conserve.* I'll open a tin.
♦ **une boîte de conserve** a tin
♦ **les conserves** tinned food ◊ *Il n'est pas bon de manger tous les jours des conserves.* It's not healthy to eat tinned food every day.
♦ **en conserve** tinned ◊ *des petits pois en conserve* tinned peas

conserver VERB
to keep ◊ *J'ai conservé toutes ses lettres.* I've kept all her letters.
♦ **se conserver** to keep ◊ *Ce pain se conserve plus d'une semaine.* This bread will keep for more than a week.

considérable ADJECTIVE
considerable ◊ *Il a fait des progrès considérables.* He's made considerable progress.

la **considération** NOUN
♦ **prendre quelque chose en considération** to take something into consideration

C

considérer VERB
- ◆**considérer que** to believe that ◊ *Je considère que le gouvernement devrait investir davantage dans l'éducation.* I believe that the government should invest more money in education.

la **consigne** NOUN
left-luggage office
- ◆**une consigne automatique** a left-luggage locker

consistant ADJECTIVE
substantial ◊ *un petit déjeuner consistant* a substantial breakfast

consister VERB
- ◆**consister à** to consist of ◊ *Mon travail consiste à répondre au téléphone et à recevoir les clients.* My job consists of answering the phone and welcoming the customers. ◊ *En quoi consiste votre travail?* What does your job involve?

la **console de jeu** NOUN
games console

consoler VERB
to console

le **consommateur** NOUN
1. consumer
2. customer (*in café*)

la **consommation** NOUN
1. consumption ◊ *la consommation d'électricité* electricity consumption
2. drink ◊ *Le billet d'entrée donne droit à une consommation gratuite.* The ticket entitles you to one free drink.

la **consommatrice** NOUN
1. consumer
2. customer (*in café*)

consommer VERB
1. to use ◊ *Ces grosses voitures consomment beaucoup d'essence.* These big cars use a lot of petrol.
2. to have a drink ◊ *Est-ce qu'on peut consommer à la terrasse?* Can we have drinks outside?

la **consonne** NOUN
consonant

constamment ADVERB
constantly ◊ *Elle se plaint constamment.* She's constantly complaining.

constant ADJECTIVE
constant

constater VERB
to notice

constipé ADJECTIVE
constipated

constitué ADJECTIVE

- ◆**être constitué de** to consist of

constituer VERB
to make up ◊ *les États qui constituent la Fédération russe* the states which make up the Russian Federation

la **construction** NOUN
building ◊ *des matériaux de construction* building materials
- ◆**une maison en construction** a house being built

construire VERB
to build ◊ *Ils font construire une maison neuve.* They're having a new house built.

le **consulat** NOUN
consulate ◊ *le consulat de France* the French consulate

la **consultation** NOUN
- ◆**les heures de consultation** surgery hours

consulter VERB
1. to consult ◊ *Tu devrais consulter un médecin.* You should see a doctor.
2. to see patients ◊ *Le docteur ne consulte pas le samedi.* The doctor doesn't see patients on Saturdays.

le **contact** NOUN
contact ◊ *les contacts humains* human contact
- ◆**Il a le contact facile.** He's very approachable.
- ◆**garder le contact avec quelqu'un** to keep in touch with somebody

contacter VERB
to get in touch with ◊ *Je te contacterai dès que j'aurai des nouvelles.* I'll get in touch with you as soon as I have some news.

contagieux ADJECTIVE (FEM SING **contagieuse**)
infectious ◊ *une maladie contagieuse* an infectious disease ◊ *Restez chez vous si vous êtes contagieux.* Stay at home if you've got something infectious.

contaminer VERB
to contaminate

le **conte de fées** NOUN (PL les **contes de fées**)
fairy tale

contempler VERB
to gaze at

contemporain ADJECTIVE
contemporary
- ◆**un auteur contemporain** a modern writer

contenir VERB

to contain ◊ *un portefeuille contenant de l'argent* a wallet containing money

content ADJECTIVE
glad ◊ *Je suis content que tu sois venu.* I'm glad you've come.
♦**content de** pleased with ◊ *Elle m'a dit qu'elle était contente de mon travail.* She told me she was pleased with my work.

contenter VERB
to please ◊ *Il est difficile à contenter.* He's hard to please.
♦**Je me contente de peu.** I can make do with very little.

contesté ADJECTIVE
controversial ◊ *Cette décision est très contestée.* This is a very controversial decision.

le **continent** NOUN
continent

continu ADJECTIVE
continuous
♦**faire la journée continue** to work without taking a full lunch break

continuellement ADVERB
constantly

continuer VERB
to carry on ◊ *Continuez sans moi!* Carry on without me! ◊ *Il ne veut pas continuer ses études.* He doesn't want to go on studying.
♦**continuer à faire quelque chose** to go on doing something ◊ *Ils ont continué à regarder la télé sans me dire bonjour.* They went on watching TV without saying hello to me.
♦**continuer de faire quelque chose** to go on doing something ◊ *Il continue de fumer malgré son asthme.* He keeps on smoking, despite his asthma.

contourner VERB
to go round ◊ *La route contourne la ville.* The road goes round the town.

le **contraceptif** NOUN
contraceptive

la **contraception** NOUN
contraception

le **contractuel** NOUN
traffic warden

la **contractuelle** NOUN
traffic warden

la **contradiction** NOUN
contradiction
♦**par esprit de contradiction** just to be awkward ◊ *Il a refusé de venir par esprit de contradiction.* He refused to come, just to be awkward.

le **contraire** NOUN
opposite ◊ *Il a fait le contraire de ce que je lui avais demandé.* He did the opposite of what I asked him.
♦**au contraire** on the contrary

contrarier VERB
1 to annoy ◊ *Il avait l'air contrarié.* He looked annoyed.
2 to upset ◊ *Est-ce que tu serais contrariée si je ne venais pas?* Would you be upset if I didn't come?

le **contraste** NOUN
contrast

le **contrat** NOUN
contract ◊ *un contrat de travail* an employment contract

la **contravention** NOUN
parking ticket

contre PREPOSITION
1 against ◊ *Ne mets pas ton vélo contre le mur.* Don't put your bike against the wall. ◊ *Tu es pour ou contre ce projet?* Are you for or against this plan?
2 for ◊ *échanger quelque chose contre quelque chose* to swap something for something
♦**par contre** on the other hand

la **contrebande** NOUN
smuggling
♦**des produits de contrebande** smuggled goods

la **contrebasse** NOUN
double bass

contrecœur
♦**à contrecœur** ADVERB
reluctantly ◊ *Il est venu à contrecœur.* He came reluctantly.

contredire VERB
to contradict ◊ *Il ne supporte pas d'être contredit.* He can't stand being contradicted.

la **contre-indication** NOUN
♦**"Contre-indication en cas d'eczéma"** "Should not be used by people with eczema"

le **contresens** NOUN
mistranslation

le **contretemps** NOUN
♦**Désolé d'être en retard: j'ai eu un contretemps.** Sorry I'm late: I was held up.

contribuer VERB
♦**contribuer à** to contribute to ◊ *Est-ce que tu veux contribuer au cadeau pour Marie?* Do you want to contribute to Marie's present?

le **contrôle** NOUN

1 control ◊ *le contrôle des passeports* passport control

2 check

◆ **un contrôle d'identité** an identity check

◆ **le contrôle des billets** ticket inspection

3 test ◊ *un contrôle antidopage* a drugs test

◆ **le contrôle continu** continuous assessment

contrôler VERB
to check ◊ *Personne n'a contrôlé mon billet.* Nobody checked my ticket.

le **contrôleur** NOUN
ticket inspector

la **contrôleuse** NOUN
ticket inspector

controversé ADJECTIVE
controversial

convaincre VERB

1 to persuade ◊ *Il a essayé de me convaincre de rester.* He tried to persuade me to stay.

2 to convince ◊ *Tu n'as pas l'air convaincu.* You don't look convinced.

la **convalescence** NOUN
convalescence

convenable ADJECTIVE
decent ◊ *un hôtel convenable* a decent hotel

◆ **Ce n'est pas convenable.** It's bad manners.

convenir VERB

◆ **convenir à** to suit ◊ *Est-ce que cette date te convient?* Does this date suit you? ◊ *J'espère que cela vous conviendra.* I hope this will suit you.

◆ **convenir de** to agree on ◊ *Nous avons convenu d'une date.* We've agreed on a date.

conventionné ADJECTIVE

◆ **un médecin conventionné** a Health Service doctor

> *ⓘ All doctors in France charge for treatment, but patients of Health Service doctors get their money refunded by the government.*

convenu ADJECTIVE
agreed ◊ *au moment convenu* at the agreed time

la **conversation** NOUN
conversation

la **convocation** NOUN
notification

convoquer VERB

◆ **convoquer quelqu'un à une réunion** to invite somebody to a meeting ◊ *Le directeur a convoqué tous les parents à la réunion.* The headmaster has invited all the parents to the meeting.

cool ADJECTIVE (*informal*)
cool

la **coopération** NOUN
co-operation

coopérer VERB
to co-operate

les **coordonnées** FEM NOUN
contact details ◊ *As-tu ses coordonnées?* Do you have his contact details?

le **copain** NOUN (*informal*)

1 friend ◊ *C'est un bon copain.* He's a good friend.

2 boyfriend ◊ *Je l'ai vue avec son copain hier soir.* I saw her with her boyfriend last night.

la **copie** NOUN

1 copy ◊ *Ce tableau n'est qu'une copie.* This picture is only a copy.

2 paper ◊ *Il a des copies à corriger ce week-end.* He's got some papers to mark this weekend.

copier VERB
to copy

◆ **copier-coller** to copy and paste

copieux ADJECTIVE (FEM SING **copieuse**)
hearty ◊ *un repas copieux* a hearty meal

la **copine** NOUN (*informal*)

1 friend ◊ *Je sors avec une copine ce soir.* I'm going out with a friend tonight.

2 girlfriend ◊ *Je ne savais pas qu'il avait une copine.* I didn't know he had a girlfriend.

le **coq** NOUN
cockerel

la **coque** NOUN
hull (*of boat*)

◆ **un œuf à la coque** a soft-boiled egg

le **coquelicot** NOUN
poppy

la **coqueluche** NOUN
whooping cough

le **coquillage** NOUN

1 shellfish

2 shell ◊ *Nous avons ramassé des coquillages sur la plage.* We picked up some shells on the beach.

la **coquille** NOUN
shell

◆ **une coquille d'œuf** an eggshell

◆ **une coquille Saint-Jacques** a scallop

coquin ADJECTIVE
cheeky ◊ *Il m'a regardé d'un air coquin.* He gave me a cheeky look.

le **cor** NOUN
horn ◊ *Je joue du cor.* I play the horn.

le **corbeau** NOUN (PL les **corbeaux**)
crow

la **corbeille** NOUN
basket ◊ *une corbeille de fruits* a basket of fruit
♦ **une corbeille à papier** a wastepaper basket

la **corde** NOUN
1 rope
2 string (*of violin, tennis racket*)
♦ **une corde à linge** a clothes line

la **cordonnerie** NOUN
shoe repair shop

le **cordonnier** NOUN
cobbler

coriace ADJECTIVE
tough

la **corne** NOUN
horn

la **cornemuse** NOUN
bagpipes ◊ *jouer de la cornemuse* to play the bagpipes

le **cornet** NOUN
♦ **un cornet de frites** a bag of chips
♦ **un cornet de glace** an ice cream cone

le **cornichon** NOUN
gherkin

la **Cornouailles** NOUN
Cornwall

le **corps** NOUN
body

correct ADJECTIVE
1 correct ◊ *Ce n'est pas tout à fait correct.* That's not quite correct.
2 reasonable ◊ *un salaire correct* a reasonable salary ◊ *Le repas était tout à fait correct.* The meal was quite reasonable.

la **correction** NOUN
correction

la **correspondance** NOUN
1 correspondence
♦ **un cours par correspondance** a correspondence course
2 connection (*train, plane*) ◊ *Il y a une correspondance pour Toulouse à dix heures.* There's a connection for Toulouse at ten o'clock.

le **correspondant** NOUN
penfriend

la **correspondante** NOUN
penfriend

correspondre VERB
to correspond

le **corridor** NOUN
corridor

corriger VERB
to mark ◊ *Le prof n'a pas encore corrigé nos copies.* The teacher hasn't marked our papers yet.

le **corsage** NOUN
blouse

corse ADJECTIVE, NOUN
Corsican
♦ **un Corse** a Corsican (*man*)
♦ **une Corse** a Corsican (*woman*)

la **Corse** NOUN
Corsica

la **corvée** NOUN
chore ◊ *Quelle corvée!* What a chore!

costaud ADJECTIVE
brawny

le **costume** NOUN
1 suit (*man's*) ◊ *Tu devrais mettre un costume et une cravate pour l'entretien.* You should wear a suit and tie for the interview.
2 costume (*theatre*) ◊ *Nous avons fait nous-mêmes tous les costumes pour la pièce.* We made all the costumes for the play ourselves.

la **côte** NOUN
1 coastline ◊ *La route longe la côte.* The road follows the coastline.
♦ **la Côte d'Azur** the French Riviera
2 hill ◊ *J'ai grimpé la côte.* I went up the hill.
3 rib ◊ *Il s'est cassé une côte en tombant.* He broke a rib when he fell.
4 chop ◊ *une côte de porc* a pork chop
♦ **une côte de bœuf** a rib of beef
♦ **côte à côte** side by side

le **côté** NOUN
side
♦ **à côté de (1)** next to ◊ *Le café est à côté du sucre.* The coffee's next to the sugar.
♦ **à côté de (2)** next door to ◊ *Il habite à côté de chez moi.* He lives next door to me.
♦ **de l'autre côté** on the other side ◊ *La pharmacie est de l'autre côté de la rue.* The chemist's is on the other side of the street.
♦ **De quel côté est-il parti?** Which way did he go?
♦ **mettre quelque chose de côté** to save something ◊ *J'ai mis de l'argent de côté.* I've saved some money.

la **côtelette** NOUN

chop ◊ *une côtelette d'agneau* a lamb chop

la **cotisation** NOUN

1 subscription (*to club, union*)
2 contributions (*to pension, national insurance*)

♦ **cotisations sociales** social security contributions

le **coton** NOUN

cotton ◊ *une chemise en coton* a cotton shirt

♦ **le coton hydrophile** cotton wool

le **cou** NOUN

neck

couchant ADJECTIVE

♦ **le soleil couchant** the setting sun

la **couche** NOUN

1 layer ◊ *la couche d'ozone* the ozone layer
2 coat (*of paint, varnish*)
3 nappy

couché ADJECTIVE

1 lying down ◊ *Il était couché sur le tapis.* He was lying on the carpet.
2 in bed ◊ *À huit heures, il était déjà couché.* He was already in bed at 8 o'clock.

le **coucher** NOUN

see also **coucher** VERB

♦ **un coucher de soleil** a sunset

se **coucher** VERB

see also **coucher** NOUN

1 to go to bed ◊ *Je me suis couché tard hier soir.* I went to bed late last night.
2 to set (*sun*)

la **couchette** NOUN

1 couchette (*on train*)
2 bunk (*on boat*)

le **coude** NOUN

elbow

coudre VERB

1 to sew ◊ *J'aime coudre.* I like sewing.
2 to sew on ◊ *Il ne sait même pas coudre un bouton.* He can't even sew a button on.

la **couette** NOUN

duvet

les **couettes** FEM NOUN

bunches ◊ *Quand j'étais petite, ma mère me faisait des couettes.* When I was little, my mother put my hair in bunches.

couler VERB

1 to run ◊ *Ne laissez pas couler les robinets.* Don't leave the taps running. ◊ *J'ai le nez qui coule.* My nose is running.

2 to flow ◊ *La rivière coulait lentement.* The river was flowing slowly.
3 to leak ◊ *Mon stylo coule.* My pen's leaking.
4 to sink ◊ *Un bateau a coulé pendant la tempête.* A boat sank during the storm.

la **couleur** NOUN

colour ◊ *De quelle couleur est leur voiture?* What colour is their car? ◊ *une pellicule couleur* a colour film

♦ **Tu as pris des couleurs.** You've got a tan.

la **couleuvre** NOUN

grass snake

les **coulisses** FEM NOUN

wings (*in theatre*)

♦ **dans les coulisses** behind the scenes

le **couloir** NOUN

corridor

le **coup** NOUN

1 knock ◊ *donner un coup à quelque chose* to give something a knock
2 blow

♦ **Il m'a donné un coup!** He hit me!
♦ **un coup de pied** a kick
♦ **un coup de poing** a punch

3 shock ◊ *Ça m'a fait un coup de le voir comme ça!* (*informal*) It gave me a shock to see him like that!

♦ **un coup de feu** a shot
♦ **un coup de fil** (*informal*) a ring ◊ *Je te donnerai un coup de fil dans la soirée.* I'll give you a ring this evening.
♦ **donner un coup de main à quelqu'un** to give somebody a hand ◊ *Je viendrai te donner un coup de main.* I'll come and give you a hand.
♦ **un coup d'œil** a quick look ◊ *jeter un coup d'œil* to have a quick look
♦ **attraper un coup de soleil** to get sunburnt
♦ **un coup de téléphone** a phone call
♦ **un coup de tonnerre** a clap of thunder
♦ **boire un coup** (*informal*) to have a drink
♦ **après coup** afterwards ◊ *Après coup j'ai regretté de m'être mis en colère.* Afterwards I was sorry I'd got angry.
♦ **à tous les coups** (*informal*) every time ◊ *Je me trompe de rue à tous les coups.* I get the street wrong every time.
♦ **du premier coup** first time ◊ *Il a été reçu au permis du premier coup.* He passed his driving test first time.

☞

♦ **sur le coup** at first ◊ *Sur le coup je ne l'ai pas reconnu.* I didn't recognize him at first.

coupable ADJECTIVE

see also **coupable** NOUN

guilty

le/la **coupable** NOUN

see also **coupable** ADJECTIVE

culprit

la **coupe** NOUN

cup (*sport*) ◊ *la coupe du monde* the World Cup
♦ **une coupe de cheveux** a haircut
♦ **une coupe de champagne** a glass of champagne

le **coupe-ongle** NOUN

nail-clippers

couper VERB

1 to cut
2 to turn off ◊ *couper le courant* to turn off the electricity
3 to take a short-cut ◊ *On peut couper par la forêt.* There's a short-cut through the woods.
♦ **couper l'appétit** to spoil one's appetite
♦ **se couper** to cut oneself ◊ *Je me suis coupé le doigt avec une boîte de conserve.* I cut my finger on a tin.
♦ **couper la parole à quelqu'un** to interrupt somebody

le **couple** NOUN

couple

le **couplet** NOUN

verse ◊ *le premier couplet* the first verse

la **coupure** NOUN

cut
♦ **une coupure de courant** a power cut

la **cour** NOUN

1 yard ◊ *la cour de l'école* the school yard
2 court ◊ *la cour de Louis XIV* the court of Louis XIV ◊ *la cour d'assises* the criminal court

le **courage** NOUN

courage

courageux ADJECTIVE (FEM SING **courageuse**)

brave

couramment ADVERB

1 fluently ◊ *Elle parle couramment japonais.* She speaks Japanese fluently.
2 commonly ◊ *C'est une expression que l'on emploie couramment.* It's a commonly used phrase.

courant ADJECTIVE

see also **courant** NOUN

1 common ◊ *C'est une erreur courante.* It's a common mistake.
2 standard ◊ *C'est un modèle courant.* It's a standard model.

le **courant** NOUN

see also **courant** ADJECTIVE

1 current (*of river*)
♦ **un courant d'air** a draught
2 power ◊ *une panne de courant* a power cut
♦ **Je le ferai dans le courant de la semaine.** I'll do it some time during the week.
♦ **être au courant de quelque chose** to know about something ◊ *Je ne suis pas au courant de ses projets pour l'été.* I don't know about her plans for the summer.
♦ **mettre quelqu'un au courant de quelque chose** to tell somebody about something
♦ **Tu es au courant?** Have you heard about it?
♦ **se tenir au courant de quelque chose** to keep up with something ◊ *J'essaie de me tenir au courant de l'actualité.* I try to keep up with the news.

le **coureur** NOUN

runner
♦ **un coureur à pied** a runner
♦ **un coureur cycliste** a racing cyclist
♦ **un coureur automobile** a racing driver

la **coureuse** NOUN

runner

la **courgette** NOUN

courgette

courir VERB

to run ◊ *Elle a traversé la rue en courant.* She ran across the street.
♦ **courir un risque** to run a risk

la **couronne** NOUN

crown

courons, courez VERB see **courir**

le **courrier** NOUN

mail ◊ *Est-ce qu'il y avait du courrier ce matin?* Was there any mail this morning?
♦ **N'oublie pas de poster le courrier.** Don't forget to post the letters.
♦ **le courrier électronique** email

Be careful! The French word **courrier** does not mean **courier**.

la **courroie** NOUN

♦ **la courroie du ventilateur** fan belt

le **cours** NOUN

1 lesson ◊ *un cours d'espagnol* a Spanish lesson ◊ *des cours particuliers* private lessons
2 course ◊ *un cours intensif* a crash course

C

③ rate ◊ *le cours du change* the exchange rate
♦ **au cours de** during ◊ *Il a été réveillé trois fois au cours de la nuit.* He was woken up three times during the night.

la **course** NOUN
① running ◊ *la course de fond* long-distance running
② race ◊ *une course hippique* a horse race
③ shopping ◊ *J'ai juste une course à faire.* I've just got a bit of shopping to do.
♦ **faire les courses** to go shopping ◊ *Elle est partie faire les courses de la semaine.* She's gone to do her weekly shopping.

court ADJECTIVE
see also **court** NOUN
short

le **court** NOUN
see also **court** ADJECTIVE
♦ **un court de tennis** a tennis court

couru VERB see **courir**

le **couscous** NOUN
couscous

> ❶ **couscous** is a spicy North African dish made with meat, vegetables and steamed semolina.

le **cousin** NOUN
cousin

la **cousine** NOUN
cousin

le **coussin** NOUN
cushion

le **coût** NOUN
cost ◊ *le coût de la vie* the cost of living

le **couteau** NOUN (PL les **couteaux**)
knife

coûter VERB
to cost ◊ *Est-ce que ça coûte cher?* Does it cost a lot?
♦ **Combien ça coûte?** How much is it?

coûteux ADJECTIVE (FEM SING **coûteuse**)
expensive

la **coutume** NOUN
custom

la **couture** NOUN
① sewing ◊ *Je n'aime pas la couture.* I don't like sewing.
♦ **faire de la couture** to sew
② seam ◊ *La couture de mon pantalon s'est défaite.* The seam of my trousers has come undone.

le **couturier** NOUN

fashion designer ◊ *un grand couturier* a top designer

la **couturière** NOUN
dressmaker

le **couvercle** NOUN
① lid (*of pan*)
② top (*of tube, jar, spray can*)

couvert VERB see **couvrir**

couvert ADJECTIVE
see also **couvert** NOUN
overcast (*sky*)
♦ **couvert de** covered with ◊ *Cet arbre est couvert de fleurs au printemps.* This tree is covered with blossom in spring.

le **couvert** NOUN
see also **couvert** ADJECTIVE
♦ **mettre le couvert** to lay the table

les **couverts** MASC NOUN
cutlery SING ◊ *Les couverts sont dans le tiroir de gauche.* The cutlery is in the left-hand drawer.

la **couverture** NOUN
blanket

le **couvre-lit** NOUN
bedspread

couvrir VERB
to cover ◊ *Le chien est revenu couvert de boue.* The dog came back covered with mud.
♦ **se couvrir (1)** to wrap up ◊ *Couvre-toi bien: il fait très froid dehors.* Wrap up well: it's very cold outside.
♦ **se couvrir (2)** to cloud over ◊ *Le ciel se couvre.* The sky's clouding over.

le **crabe** NOUN
crab

cracher VERB
to spit

le **crachin** NOUN
drizzle

la **craie** NOUN
chalk

craindre VERB
to fear ◊ *Tu n'as rien à craindre.* You've got nothing to fear.

la **crainte** NOUN
fear
♦ **de crainte de** for fear of ◊ *Il n'ose rien dire de crainte de la vexer.* He daren't say anything for fear of upsetting her.

craintif ADJECTIVE (FEM SING **craintive**)
timid

la **crampe** NOUN
cramp ◊ *J'ai une crampe au mollet.* I've got a cramp in my calf.

le **cran** NOUN
hole (*in belt*)

☞

♦avoir du cran (*informal*) to have guts

le **crâne** NOUN
  skull

  crâner VERB (*informal*)
  to show off

le **crapaud** NOUN
  toad

  craquer VERB
  ① to creak ◊ *Le plancher craque.* The floor creaks.
  ② to burst ◊ *Ma fermeture éclair a craqué.* My zip's burst.
  ③ to crack up ◊ *Je vais finir par craquer!* (*informal*) I'm going to crack up at this rate!
  ♦Quand j'ai vu cette robe, j'ai craqué! (*informal*) When I saw that dress, I couldn't resist it!

la **crasse** NOUN
  filth

la **cravate** NOUN
  tie

le **crawl** NOUN
  crawl ◊ *nager le crawl* to do the crawl

le **crayon** NOUN
  pencil ◊ *un crayon de couleur* a coloured pencil
  ♦un crayon feutre a felt-tip pen

la **création** NOUN
  creation

la **crèche** NOUN
  ① nursery ◊ *Elle dépose ses enfants à la crèche à huit heures.* She leaves her children at the nursery at 8 o'clock.
  ② nativity scene

le **crédit** NOUN
  credit

  créer VERB
  to create

la **crémaillère** NOUN
  ♦pendre la crémaillère to have a house-warming party

la **crème** NOUN
  see also **le crème**
  cream
  ♦la crème anglaise custard
  ♦la crème Chantilly whipped cream
  ♦la crème fouettée whipped cream
  ♦une crème caramel a crème caramel
  ♦une crème au chocolat a chocolate dessert

le **crème** NOUN
  see also **la crème**
  white coffee ◊ *un grand crème* a large white coffee

  crémeux ADJECTIVE (FEM SING **crémeuse**)

creamy

la **crêpe** NOUN
  pancake

la **crêperie** NOUN
  pancake restaurant

le **crépuscule** NOUN
  dusk

le **cresson** NOUN
  watercress

la **Crète** NOUN
  Crete

  creuser VERB
  to dig (*a hole*)
  ♦Ça creuse! That gives you a real appetite!
  ♦se creuser la cervelle (*informal*) to rack one's brains

  creux ADJECTIVE (FEM SING **creuse**)
  hollow

la **crevaison** NOUN
  puncture

  crevé ADJECTIVE
  ① punctured ◊ *un pneu crevé* a puncture
  ② knackered ◊ *Je suis complètement crevé!* (*informal*) I'm knackered!

  crever VERB
  ① to burst (*balloon*)
  ② to have a puncture (*motorist*) ◊ *J'ai crevé sur l'autoroute.* I had a puncture on the motorway.
  ♦Je crève de faim! (*informal*) I'm starving!
  ♦Je crève de froid! (*informal*) I'm freezing!

la **crevette** NOUN
  prawn
  ♦une crevette rose a prawn
  ♦une crevette grise a shrimp

le **cri** NOUN
  ① scream ◊ *J'ai entendu un cri.* I heard a scream. ◊ *pousser des cris de douleur* to scream with pain
  ② call ◊ *Il sait reconnaître les cris des oiseaux.* He can identify the calls of birds.
  ♦C'est le dernier cri. It's the latest fashion. ◊ *Ces chaussures sont du dernier cri.* These shoes are the latest fashion.

  criard ADJECTIVE
  garish (*colours*)

le **cric** NOUN
  jack (*for car*)

  crier VERB
  to shout
  ♦crier de douleur to scream with pain

le **crime** NOUN

C

1 crime ◊ *un crime de guerre* a war crime

2 murder ◊ *Un crime a été commis ici.* There was a murder here.

le **criminel** NOUN
1 criminal ◊ *un criminel de guerre* a war criminal
2 murderer

la **criminelle** NOUN
1 criminal
2 murderer

le **crin** NOUN
horsehair

la **crinière** NOUN
mane

le **criquet** NOUN
grasshopper

la **crise** NOUN
1 crisis
◆ **la crise économique** the recession
2 attack ◊ *une crise d'asthme* an asthma attack ◊ *une crise cardiaque* a heart attack
◆ **une crise de foie** an upset stomach
◆ **piquer une crise de nerfs** to go hysterical
◆ **avoir une crise de fou rire** to have a fit of the giggles

le **cristal** NOUN (PL les **cristaux**)
crystal ◊ *un verre en cristal* a crystal glass

le **critère** NOUN
criterion

critique ADJECTIVE
see also **critique** NOUN
critical

le **critique** NOUN
see also **la critique** AND **critique** ADJECTIVE
critic ◊ *un critique de cinéma* a film critic

la **critique** NOUN
see also **le critique** AND **critique** ADJECTIVE
1 criticism ◊ *Elle ne supporte pas les critiques.* She can't stand being criticized.
2 review ◊ *Le film a reçu de bonnes critiques.* The film's had good reviews.

critiquer VERB
to criticize

la **Croatie** NOUN
Croatia

le **crochet** NOUN
1 hook
2 detour ◊ *faire un crochet* to make a detour
3 crochet ◊ *un pull au crochet* a crocheted sweater

le **crocodile** NOUN
crocodile

croire VERB
to believe ◊ *Il croit tout ce qu'on lui raconte.* He believes everything he's told.
◆ **croire que** to think that ◊ *Tu crois qu'il fera meilleur demain?* Do you think the weather will be better tomorrow?
◆ **croire à quelque chose** to believe in something
◆ **croire en Dieu** to believe in God

crois VERB see **croire**

croîs VERB see **croître**

le **croisement** NOUN
crossroads ◊ *Tournez à gauche au croisement.* Turn left at the crossroads.

croiser VERB
◆ **J'ai croisé Anne-Laure dans la rue.** I bumped into Anne-Laure in the street.
◆ **croiser les bras** to fold one's arms
◆ **croiser les jambes** to cross one's legs
◆ **se croiser** to pass each other ◊ *Nous nous croisons dans l'escalier tous les matins.* We pass each other on the stairs every morning.

la **croisière** NOUN
cruise

la **croissance** NOUN
growth

le **croissant** NOUN
croissant ◊ *un croissant au beurre* a butter croissant

croit VERB see **croire**

croître VERB
to grow

la **croix** NOUN
cross
◆ **la Croix-Rouge** the Red Cross

le **croque-madame** NOUN (PL les **croque-madame**)
toasted ham and cheese sandwich with fried egg on top

le **croque-monsieur** NOUN (PL les **croque-monsieur**)
toasted ham and cheese sandwich

croquer VERB
to munch ◊ *croquer une pomme* to munch an apple
◆ **le chocolat à croquer** plain chocolate

le **croquis** NOUN
sketch

la **crotte** NOUN
◆ **une crotte de chien** dog dirt

le **crottin** NOUN

1 <u>manure</u> ◊ *du crottin de cheval* horse manure
2 <u>small goat's cheese</u>

croustillant ADJECTIVE
<u>crusty</u>

la **croûte** NOUN
1 <u>crust</u> (*of bread*)
◆ **en croûte** in pastry
2 <u>rind</u> (*of cheese*)
3 <u>scab</u> (*on skin*)

le **croûton** NOUN
1 <u>crust</u> (*end of loaf*)
2 <u>crouton</u> ◊ *des croûtons frottés d'ail* garlic croutons

croyons, croyez VERB *see* **croire**

les **CRS** MASC NOUN
<u>French riot police</u>

cru VERB *see* **croire**

cru ADJECTIVE
<u>raw</u> ◊ *la viande crue* raw meat
◆ **le jambon cru** Parma ham

crû VERB *see* **croître**

la **cruauté** NOUN
<u>cruelty</u>

la **cruche** NOUN
<u>jug</u>

les **crudités** FEM NOUN
<u>assorted raw vegetables</u>

cruel ADJECTIVE (FEM SING **cruelle**)
<u>cruel</u>

les **crustacés** MASC NOUN
<u>shellfish</u>

le **cube** NOUN
<u>cube</u>
◆ **un mètre cube** a cubic metre

la **cueillette** NOUN
<u>picking</u> ◊ *la cueillette des champignons* mushroom picking

cueillir VERB
<u>to pick</u> (*flowers, fruit*)

la **cuiller** NOUN
<u>spoon</u>
◆ **une cuiller à café** a teaspoon
◆ **une cuiller à soupe** a soup spoon

la **cuillère** NOUN
<u>spoon</u>
◆ **une cuillère à café** a teaspoon
◆ **une cuillère à soupe** a soup spoon

la **cuillerée** NOUN
<u>spoonful</u>

le **cuir** NOUN
<u>leather</u> ◊ *un sac en cuir* a leather bag
◆ **le cuir chevelu** the scalp

cuire VERB
<u>to cook</u> ◊ *cuire quelque chose à feu vif* to cook something on a high heat
◆ **cuire quelque chose au four** to bake something
◆ **cuire quelque chose à la vapeur** to steam something
◆ **faire cuire** to cook ◊ *"Faire cuire pendant une heure"* "Cook for one hour"
◆ **bien cuit** well done
◆ **trop cuit** overdone

la **cuisine** NOUN
1 <u>kitchen</u>
2 <u>cooking</u> ◊ *la cuisine française* French cooking
◆ **faire la cuisine** to cook

cuisiné ADJECTIVE
◆ **un plat cuisiné** a ready-made meal

cuisiner VERB
<u>to cook</u> ◊ *J'aime beaucoup cuisiner.* I love cooking.

le **cuisinier** NOUN
<u>cook</u>

la **cuisinière** NOUN
1 <u>cook</u>
2 <u>cooker</u> ◊ *une cuisinière à gaz* a gas cooker

la **cuisse** NOUN
<u>thigh</u>
◆ **une cuisse de poulet** a chicken leg

la **cuisson** NOUN
<u>cooking</u> ◊ *"une heure de cuisson"* "cooking time: one hour"

cuit VERB *see* **cuire**

le **cuivre** NOUN
<u>copper</u>

le **cul** NOUN (*rude*)
<u>bum</u>

le **culot** NOUN (*informal*)
<u>cheek</u> ◊ *Quel culot!* What a cheek! ◊ *Il a un sacré culot!* He's got a damn cheek!

la **culotte** NOUN
<u>knickers</u> PL

la **culpabilité** NOUN
<u>guilt</u>

le **cultivateur** NOUN
<u>farmer</u>

la **cultivatrice** NOUN
<u>farmer</u>

cultivé ADJECTIVE
<u>cultured</u> ◊ *Il est très cultivé.* He's very cultured.

cultiver VERB
<u>to grow</u> ◊ *Il cultive la vigne.* He grows grapes.
◆ **cultiver la terre** to farm the land

la **culture** NOUN
1 <u>farming</u> ◊ *les cultures intensives* intensive farming

2 education ◊ *Pour cet emploi, on demande une bonne culture générale.* For this job, a good general education is needed.

♦ **la culture physique** physical education

le **culturisme** NOUN
  body-building

le **curé** NOUN
  parish priest

le **cure-dent** NOUN
  toothpick

curieux ADJECTIVE (FEM SING **curieuse**)
  curious

la **curiosité** NOUN
  curiosity

le **curriculum vitae** NOUN
  CV

le **curseur** NOUN
  cursor

la **cuvette** NOUN
  bowl ◊ *une cuvette en plastique* a

plastic bowl

le **CV** NOUN (= *curriculum vitae*)
  CV

le **cybercafé** NOUN
  internet café

cyclable ADJECTIVE
♦ **une piste cyclable** a cycle track

le **cycle** NOUN
  cycle

le **cyclisme** NOUN
  cycling

le/la **cycliste** NOUN
  cyclist

le **cyclomoteur** NOUN
  moped

le **cyclone** NOUN
  hurricane

le **cygne** NOUN
  swan

C

D

---

d' PREPOSITION, ARTICLE *see* **de**

la **dactylo** NOUN

  1 typist ◊ *Elle est dactylo.* She's a typist.

  2 typing ◊ *Je prends des cours de dactylo.* I'm doing typing lessons.

le **daim** NOUN

  suede ◊ *une veste en daim* a suede jacket

la **dame** NOUN

  1 lady

  2 queen (*in cards, chess*)

les **dames** FEM NOUN

  draughts

le **Danemark** NOUN

  Denmark

le **danger** NOUN

  danger

  ♦ **être en danger** to be in danger

  ♦ **"Danger de mort"** "Extremely dangerous"

dangereux ADJECTIVE (FEM SING **dangereuse**)

  dangerous

danois ADJECTIVE, NOUN (FEM SING **danoise**)

  Danish ◊ *Il parle danois.* He speaks Danish.

  ♦ **un Danois** a Dane (*man*)

  ♦ **une Danoise** a Dane (*woman*)

  ♦ **les Danois** the Danish

dans PREPOSITION

  1 in ◊ *Il est dans sa chambre.* He's in his bedroom. ◊ *dans deux mois* in two months' time

  2 into ◊ *Il est entré dans mon bureau.* He came into my office.

  3 out of ◊ *On a bu dans des verres en plastique.* We drank out of plastic glasses.

la **danse** NOUN

  1 dance ◊ *la danse moderne* modern dance ◊ *des danses folkloriques* folk dances

  ♦ **la danse classique** ballet

  2 dancing ◊ *des cours de danse* dancing lessons

danser VERB

  to dance

le **danseur** NOUN

  dancer

la **danseuse** NOUN

  dancer

la **date** NOUN

  date ◊ *votre date de naissance* your date of birth ◊ *la date limite de vente* the sell-by date

  ♦ **un ami de longue date** an old friend

dater VERB

  ♦ **dater de** to date from ◊ *Cette coutume date du moyen âge.* This custom dates from the Middle Ages.

la **datte** NOUN

  date (*fruit*)

le **dauphin** NOUN

  dolphin

davantage ADVERB

  ♦ **davantage de** more ◊ *Il faudrait davantage de stages de formation.* There should be more training courses.

de PREPOSITION, ARTICLE

  *See also **du** (=de+le) and **des** (=de+les). de changes to **d'** before a vowel and most words beginning with "h".*

  1 of ◊ *le toit de la maison* the roof of the house ◊ *la voiture de Paul* Paul's car ◊ *la voiture de mes parents* my parents' car ◊ *la voiture d'Hélène* Hélène's car ◊ *deux bouteilles de vin* two bottles of wine ◊ *un litre d'essence* a litre of petrol

  ♦ **un bébé d'un an** a one-year-old baby

  ♦ **un billet de cinquante francs** a 50-franc note

  2 from ◊ *de Londres à Paris* from London to Paris ◊ *Il vient de Londres.* He comes from London. ◊ *une lettre de Victor* a letter from Victor

  3 by ◊ *augmenter de dix francs* to increase by ten francs

  *You use **de** to form expressions with the meaning of **some** and **any**.*

  ♦ **Je voudrais de l'eau.** I'd like some water. ◊ *du pain et de la confiture* bread and jam

  ♦ **Il n'a pas de famille.** He hasn't got any family.

  ♦ **Il n'y a plus de biscuits.** There aren't any more biscuits.

le **dé** NOUN

  1 dice

  2 thimble

le **dealer** NOUN (*informal*)

  drug-pusher

déballer VERB

  to unpack

le **débardeur** NOUN

tank top

débarquer VERB
to disembark ◊ *Nous avons dû débarquer à Marseille.* We had to disembark at Marseilles.
◆ **débarquer chez quelqu'un** (*informal*) to descend on somebody ◊ *Ils ont débarqué chez nous à dix heures du soir.* They descended on us at ten o'clock at night.

le **débarras** NOUN
junk room
◆ **Bon débarras!** Good riddance!

débarrasser VERB
to clear ◊ *Tu peux débarrasser la table, s'il te plaît?* Can you clear the table please?
◆ **se débarrasser de quelque chose** to get rid of something ◊ *Je me suis débarrassé de mon vieux frigo.* I got rid of my old fridge.

le **débat** NOUN
debate

se **débattre** VERB
to struggle

débile ADJECTIVE
crazy ◊ *C'est complètement débile!* (*informal*) That's totally crazy!

débordé ADJECTIVE
◆ **être débordé** to be snowed under

déborder VERB
to overflow (*river*)
◆ **déborder d'énergie** to be full of energy

le **débouché** NOUN
job prospect ◊ *Quels débouchés y a-t-il après ces études?* What sort of job does this course qualify you for?

déboucher VERB
1 to unblock (*sink, pipe*)
2 to open (*bottle*)
◆ **déboucher sur** to lead into ◊ *La rue débouche sur une place.* The street leads into a square.

debout ADVERB
1 standing up ◊ *Il a mangé ses céréales debout.* He ate his cereal standing up.
2 upright ◊ *Mets les livres debout sur l'étagère.* Put the books upright on the shelf.
3 up ◊ *Tu es déjà debout?* Are you up already?
◆ **Debout!** Get up!

déboutonner VERB
to unbutton

débraillé ADJECTIVE
sloppily dressed

débrancher VERB
to unplug

le **débris** NOUN
◆ **des débris de verre** bits of glass

débrouillard ADJECTIVE
streetwise

se **débrouiller** VERB
to manage ◊ *C'était difficile, mais je ne me suis pas trop mal débrouillé.* It was difficult, but I managed OK.
◆ **Débrouille-toi tout seul.** Sort things out for yourself.

le **début** NOUN
beginning ◊ *au début* at the beginning
◆ **début mai** in early May

le **débutant** NOUN
beginner

la **débutante** NOUN
beginner

débuter VERB
to start

décaféiné ADJECTIVE
decaffeinated

le **décalage horaire** NOUN
time difference (*between time zones*) ◊ *Il y a une heure de décalage horaire entre la France et la Grande-Bretagne.* There's an hour's time difference between France and Britain.

décalquer VERB
to trace

décapiter VERB
to behead

décapotable ADJECTIVE
convertible

décapsuler VERB
◆ **décapsuler une bouteille** to take the top off a bottle

le **décapsuleur** NOUN
bottle-opener

décéder VERB
to die ◊ *Son père est décédé il y a trois ans.* His father died three years ago.

décembre MASC NOUN
December
◆ **en décembre** in December

décemment ADVERB
decently

décent ADJECTIVE
decent

la **déception** NOUN
disappointment

décerner VERB
to award

le **décès** NOUN

death

décevant ADJECTIVE
disappointing ◊ *Ses résultats sont plutôt décevants.* His results are rather disappointing.

décevoir VERB
to disappoint

décharger VERB
to unload

se **déchausser** VERB
to take off one's shoes

les **déchets** MASC NOUN
waste SING ◊ *les déchets nucléaires* nuclear waste ◊ *les déchets toxiques* toxic waste

déchiffrer VERB
to decipher

déchirant ADJECTIVE
heart-rending

déchirer VERB
1 to tear (*clothes*)
2 to tear up ◊ *déchirer une lettre* to tear up a letter
3 to tear out ◊ *déchirer une page d'un livre* to tear a page out of a book
♦ **se déchirer** to tear ◊ *se déchirer un muscle* to tear a muscle

la **déchirure** NOUN
tear (*rip*)
♦ **une déchirure musculaire** a torn muscle

décidé ADJECTIVE
determined
♦ **C'est décidé.** It's decided.

décidément ADVERB
certainly ◊ *Décidément, je n'ai pas de chance aujourd'hui.* I'm certainly not having much luck today.

décider VERB
to decide
♦ **décider de faire quelque chose** to decide to do something ◊ *Ils ont décidé de passer leurs vacances en Normandie.* They decided to go to Normandy for their holiday.
♦ **se décider** to make up one's mind ◊ *Elle n'arrive pas à se décider.* She can't make up her mind.

décisif ADJECTIVE (FEM SING **décisive**)
decisive

la **décision** NOUN
decision

la **déclaration** NOUN
statement ◊ *Je n'ai aucune déclaration à faire.* I have no statement to make.
♦ **faire une déclaration de vol** to report something as stolen

déclarer VERB
to declare ◊ *déclarer la guerre à un pays* to declare war on a country
♦ **se déclarer** to break out ◊ *Le feu s'est déclaré dans la cantine.* The fire broke out in the canteen.

déclencher VERB
to set off (*alarm, explosion*)
♦ **se déclencher** to go off

le **déclic** NOUN
click

décoiffé ADJECTIVE
♦ **Elle était toute décoiffée.** Her hair was in a real mess.

le **décollage** NOUN
takeoff (*of plane*)

décollé ADJECTIVE
♦ **avoir les oreilles décollées** to have sticking-out ears

décoller VERB
1 to unstick ◊ *décoller une étiquette* to unstick a label
♦ **se décoller** to come unstuck
2 to take off ◊ *L'avion a décollé avec dix minutes de retard.* The plane took off ten minutes late.

décolleté ADJECTIVE
see also **décolleté** NOUN
low-cut

le **décolleté** NOUN
see also **décolleté** ADJECTIVE
♦ **un décolleté plongeant** a plunging neckline

se **décolorer** VERB
to fade ◊ *Ce T-shirt s'est décoloré au lavage.* This T-shirt has faded in the wash.
♦ **se faire décolorer les cheveux** to have one's hair bleached

les **décombres** MASC NOUN
rubble SING

se **décommander** VERB
to cry off ◊ *Elle devait venir mais elle s'est décommandée à la dernière minute.* She was supposed to be coming, but she cried off at the last minute.

déconcerté ADJECTIVE
disconcerted

décongeler VERB
to thaw

se **déconnecter** VERB
to log out

déconner VERB (*rude*)
to talk rubbish ◊ *Non mais, sans déconner, c'est vrai?* No kidding, is that true?

déconseiller VERB

D

◆**déconseiller à quelqu'un de faire quelque chose** to advise somebody not to do something ◊ *Je lui ai déconseillé d'y aller.* I advised him not to go.

◆**C'est déconseillé.** It's not recommended.

décontenancé ADJECTIVE
disconcerted

décontracté ADJECTIVE
relaxed
◆**s'habiller décontracté** to dress casually

se **décontracter** VERB
to relax ◊ *Il est allé faire du footing pour se décontracter.* He went jogging to relax.

le **décor** NOUN
décor

le **décorateur** NOUN
interior decorator

la **décoration** NOUN
decoration

la **décoratrice** NOUN
interior decorator

décorer VERB
to decorate

les **décors** MASC NOUN
1 scenery SING (*in play*)
2 set SING (*in film*)

décortiquer VERB
to shell
◆**des crevettes décortiquées** peeled shrimps

découdre VERB
to unpick
◆**se découdre** to come unstitched

découper VERB
1 to cut out ◊ *J'ai découpé cet article dans le journal.* I cut this article out of the paper.
2 to carve (*meat*)

décourageant ADJECTIVE
discouraging

décourager VERB
to discourage
◆**se décourager** to get discouraged ◊ *Ne te décourage pas!* Don't give up!

décousu ADJECTIVE
unstitched ◊ *L'ourlet est décousu.* The hem's come unstitched.

le **découvert** NOUN
overdraft

la **découverte** NOUN
discovery

découvrir VERB
to discover

décrire VERB
to describe

décrocher VERB
1 to take down ◊ *Tu peux m'aider à décrocher les rideaux?* Can you help me take down the curtains?
2 to pick up the phone ◊ *Il a décroché et a composé le numéro.* He picked up the phone and dialled the number.
◆**décrocher le téléphone** to take the phone off the hook

déçu VERB
disappointed

dédaigneux ADJECTIVE (FEM SING **dédaigneuse**)
disdainful ◊ *d'un air dédaigneux* disdainfully

le **dédain** NOUN
disdain ◊ *avec dédain* with disdain

dedans ADVERB
inside ◊ *C'est une jolie boîte: qu'est-ce qu'il y a dedans?* That's a nice box: what's in it?
◆**là-dedans (1)** in there ◊ *J'ai trouvé les clés là-dedans.* I found the keys in there.
◆**là-dedans (2)** in that ◊ *Il y a du vrai là-dedans.* There's some truth in that.

dédicacé ADJECTIVE
◆**un exemplaire dédicacé** a signed copy

dédier VERB
to dedicate

déduire VERB
to take off ◊ *Tu as déduit les vingt francs que je te devais?* Did you take off the twenty francs I owed you?
◆**déduire que** to deduce that ◊ *J'en déduis qu'il m'a menti.* That means he must have been lying.

défaire VERB
to undo
◆**défaire sa valise** to unpack
◆**se défaire** to come undone

la **défaite** NOUN
defeat

le **défaut** NOUN
fault

défavorable ADJECTIVE
unfavourable

défavorisé ADJECTIVE
underprivileged

défectueux ADJECTIVE (FEM SING **défectueuse**)
faulty

défendre VERB
1 to forbid
◆**défendre à quelqu'un de faire quelque chose** to forbid somebody to do

☞

something ◊ *Sa mère lui a défendu de le revoir.* Her mother forbade her to see him again.

[2] to defend ◊ *défendre ses idées* to defend your ideas ◊ *défendre quelqu'un* to defend somebody

défendu ADJECTIVE
forbidden ◊ *C'est défendu.* It's not allowed.

la **défense** NOUN
[1] defence ◊ *prendre la défense de quelqu'un* to back somebody up
♦ **"défense de fumer"** "no smoking"
[2] tusk (*of elephant*)

le **défi** NOUN
challenge
♦ **d'un air de défi** defiantly
♦ **sur un ton de défi** defiantly

défier VERB
[1] to challenge ◊ *Je te défie de trouver un meilleur exemple.* I challenge you to find a better example.
[2] to dare ◊ *Il m'a défié d'aller à l'école en pyjama.* He dared me to go to school in my pyjamas.

défigurer VERB
to disfigure

le **défilé** NOUN
[1] parade
♦ **un défilé de mode** a fashion show
[2] march

défiler VERB
to march

définir VERB
to define

définitif ADJECTIVE (FEM SING **définitive**)
final
♦ **en définitive** in the end ◊ *En définitive, ils ont décidé de rester.* In the end, they decided to stay.

définitivement ADVERB
for good ◊ *Elle s'est définitivement installée en Écosse en 1980.* She settled in Scotland for good in 1980.

déformer VERB
to stretch ◊ *Ne tire pas sur ton pull, tu vas le déformer.* Don't pull at your sweater, you'll stretch it.
♦ **se déformer** to stretch ◊ *Ce T-shirt s'est déformé au lavage.* This T-shirt has stretched in the wash.

se **défouler** VERB
to unwind ◊ *Je fais de l'aérobic pour me défouler.* I do aerobics to unwind.

dégagé ADJECTIVE
♦ **d'un air dégagé** casually
♦ **sur un ton dégagé** casually

dégager VERB

[1] to free ◊ *Ils ont mis une heure à dégager les victimes.* They took an hour to free the victims.
[2] to clear ◊ *des gouttes qui dégagent le nez* drops to clear your nose
♦ **Ça se dégage.** (*weather*) It's clearing up.

se **dégarnir** VERB
to go bald

les **dégâts** MASC NOUN
damage

le **dégel** NOUN
thaw

dégeler VERB
to thaw ◊ *faire dégeler un poulet congelé* to thaw out a frozen chicken

dégivrer VERB
[1] to defrost
[2] to de-ice

dégonfler VERB
to let down ◊ *Quelqu'un a dégonflé mes pneus.* Somebody let down my tyres.
♦ **se dégonfler** (*informal*) to chicken out

dégouliner VERB
to trickle

dégourdi ADJECTIVE
smart ◊ *Il n'est pas très dégourdi.* He's pretty clueless.

dégourdir VERB
♦ **se dégourdir les jambes** to stretch one's legs

le **dégoût** NOUN
disgust ◊ *une expression de dégoût* a disgusted expression
♦ **avec dégoût** disgustedly

dégoûtant ADJECTIVE
disgusting

dégoûté ADJECTIVE
disgusted
♦ **être dégoûté de tout** to be sick of everything

dégoûter VERB
to disgust ◊ *Ce genre de comportement me dégoûte.* That kind of behaviour makes me sick.
♦ **dégoûter quelqu'un de quelque chose** to put somebody off something ◊ *Ça m'a dégoûté de la viande.* That put me off meat.

se **dégrader** VERB
to deteriorate

le **degré** NOUN
degree
♦ **de l'alcool à 90 degrés** surgical spirit

dégringoler VERB

1 to rush down ◊ *Il a dégringolé l'escalier.* He rushed down the stairs.

2 to collapse

♦**Elle a fait dégringoler la pile de livres.** She knocked over the stack of books.

dégueulasse ADJECTIVE (*rude*)
disgusting

le **déguisement** NOUN
disguise

déguiser VERB

♦**se déguiser en quelque chose** to dress up as something ◊ *Elle s'était déguisée en vampire.* She was dressed up as a vampire.

la **dégustation** NOUN
tasting

déguster VERB

1 to taste (*food, wine*)

2 to enjoy

dehors ADVERB
outside ◊ *Je t'attends dehors.* I'll wait for you outside.

♦**jeter quelqu'un dehors** to throw somebody out

♦**en dehors de** apart from ◊ *En dehors de lui, tout le monde était content.* Apart from him, everybody was happy.

déjà ADVERB

1 already ◊ *J'ai déjà fini.* I've already finished.

2 before ◊ *Tu es déjà venu en France?* Have you been to France before?

déjeuner VERB

see also **déjeuner** NOUN

to have lunch

le **déjeuner** NOUN

see also **déjeuner** VERB

lunch

le **délai** NOUN

1 extension ◊ *J'ai demandé un délai d'une semaine.* I've asked for a week's extension.

2 time limit ◊ *être dans les délais* to be within the time limit

Be careful! délai does not mean delay.

délasser VERB
to relax ◊ *La lecture délasse.* Reading's relaxing.

♦**se délasser** to relax ◊ *J'ai pris un bain pour me délasser.* I had a bath to relax.

délavé ADJECTIVE
faded ◊ *un jean délavé* a pair of faded jeans

le **délégué** NOUN

representative ◊ *les délégués de classe* the class representatives

> 🛈 In French schools, each class elects two representatives or **délégués de classe**, one boy and one girl.

la **déléguée** NOUN
representative

déléguer VERB
to delegate

délibéré ADJECTIVE
deliberate

délicat ADJECTIVE

1 delicate ◊ *avoir la peau délicate* to have delicate skin

2 tricky ◊ *une situation délicate* a tricky situation

3 tactful ◊ *Il est toujours très délicat.* He's always very tactful.

4 thoughtful ◊ *C'est une attention délicate de sa part.* That was a kind thought on his part.

délicatement ADVERB

1 gently

2 tactfully

le **délice** NOUN
delight ◊ *Vivre ici est un vrai délice.* Living here is a real delight. ◊ *Ce gâteau est un vrai délice.* This cake's a real treat.

délicieux ADJECTIVE (FEM SING **délicieuse**)
delicious

la **délinquance** NOUN
crime ◊ *de nouvelles mesures pour combattre la délinquance juvénile* new measures to fight juvenile delinquency

le **délinquant** NOUN
criminal

la **délinquante** NOUN
criminal

délirer VERB

♦**Mais tu délires!** (*informal*) You're crazy!

le **délit** NOUN
criminal offence

délivrer VERB
to set free (*prisoner*)

le **deltaplane** NOUN
hang-glider

♦**faire du deltaplane** to go hang-gliding

demain ADVERB
tomorrow

♦**À demain!** See you tomorrow!

la **demande** NOUN
request

D

☞

♦ **une demande en mariage** an offer of marriage

♦ **"demandes d'emploi"** "situations wanted"

demandé ADJECTIVE

♦ **très demandé** very much in demand

demander VERB

1 to ask for ◊ *J'ai demandé la permission.* I've asked for permission. ◊ *Nous avons demandé notre chemin à un chauffeur de taxi.* We asked a taxi driver the way. ◊ *Je lui ai demandé de m'aider.* I asked him to help me.

2 to require ◊ *un travail qui demande beaucoup de temps* a job that requires a lot of time

♦ **se demander** to wonder ◊ *Je me demande à quelle heure il va venir.* I wonder what time he'll come.

*Be careful! **demander** does not mean to demand.*

le **demandeur d'asile** NOUN
asylum seeker

le **demandeur d'emploi** NOUN
job-seeker

la **demandeuse d'asile** NOUN
asylum seeker

la **demandeuse d'emploi** NOUN
job-seeker

la **démangeaison** NOUN
itching

démanger VERB
to itch ◊ *Ça me démange.* It itches.

le **démaquillant** NOUN
make-up remover

démaquiller VERB
♦ **se démaquiller** to remove one's make-up

la **démarche** NOUN
1 walk ◊ *Il a une drôle de démarche.* He's got a funny walk.
2 step ◊ *faire les démarches nécessaires pour obtenir quelque chose* to take the necessary steps to obtain something

démarrer VERB
to start (*car*)

démêler VERB
to untangle

le **déménagement** NOUN
move ◊ *C'était le jour de notre déménagement.* It was the day we moved house.

♦ **un camion de déménagement** a removal van

déménager VERB
to move house

le **déménageur** NOUN

removal man

dément ADJECTIVE
crazy

démentiel ADJECTIVE (FEM SING **démentielle**)
insane ◊ *un projet démentiel* an insane scheme

se **démerder** VERB (*rude*)
to get by ◊ *Ne t'inquiète pas, il saura se démerder.* Don't worry, he'll get by.

♦ **Démerde-toi tout seul.** Sort things out for yourself.

demi ADJECTIVE, ADVERB
see also **demi** NOUN
half ◊ *Il a trois ans et demi.* He's three and a half.

♦ **Il est trois heures et demie.** It's half past three.

♦ **Il est midi et demi.** It's half past twelve.

♦ **à demi endormi** half-asleep

le **demi** NOUN
see also **demi** ADJECTIVE
half pint of beer

♦ **Un demi, s'il vous plaît!** A beer please!

la **demi-baguette** NOUN
half a baguette

le **demi-cercle** NOUN
semicircle

la **demi-douzaine** NOUN
half-dozen ◊ *une demi-douzaine d'œufs* half a dozen eggs

la **demie** NOUN
half-hour ◊ *Le bus passe à la demie.* The bus comes by on the half-hour.

demi-écrémé ADJECTIVE
semi-skimmed

la **demi-finale** NOUN
semifinal

le **demi-frère** NOUN
half-brother

la **demi-heure** NOUN
half an hour ◊ *dans une demi-heure* in half an hour ◊ *toutes les demi-heures* every half an hour

la **demi-journée** NOUN
half-day ◊ *On peut louer un parasol à la demi-journée.* You can hire a sun umbrella for a half-day.

le **demi-litre** NOUN
half litre ◊ *un demi-litre de lait* half a litre of milk

la **demi-livre** NOUN
half-pound ◊ *une demi-livre de tomates* half a pound of tomatoes

la **demi-pension** NOUN

half board

♦**Cet hôtel propose des tarifs raisonnables en demi-pension.** This hotel has reasonable rates for half board.

demi-sel ADJECTIVE
♦**du beurre demi-sel** slightly salted butter

la **demi-sœur** NOUN
half-sister

la **démission** NOUN
resignation
♦**donner sa démission** to resign

démissionner VERB
to resign

le **demi-tarif** NOUN
1 half-price ◊ *un billet à demi-tarif* a half-price season ticket
2 half-fare ◊ *voyager à demi-tarif* to travel half-fare

le **demi-tour** NOUN
♦**faire demi-tour** to turn back ◊ *La nuit commence à tomber; il est temps de faire demi-tour.* It's getting dark; it's time we turned back.

la **démocratie** NOUN
democracy

démocratique ADJECTIVE
democratic

démodé ADJECTIVE
old-fashioned

la **demoiselle** NOUN
young lady
♦**une demoiselle d'honneur** a bridesmaid

démolir VERB
to demolish

le **démon** NOUN
devil

démonter VERB
1 to take down (*tent*)
2 to take apart (*machine*)

démontrer VERB
to show

dénoncer VERB
to denounce
♦**se dénoncer** to give oneself up ◊ *Il s'est dénoncé à la police.* He gave himself up to the police.

le **dénouement** NOUN
outcome

la **densité** NOUN
density

la **dent** NOUN
tooth ◊ *une dent de lait* a milk tooth ◊ *une dent de sagesse* a wisdom tooth

dentaire ADJECTIVE

dental

la **dentelle** NOUN
lace ◊ *un chemisier en dentelle* a lacy blouse

le **dentier** NOUN
denture

le **dentifrice** NOUN
toothpaste

le/la **dentiste** NOUN
dentist ◊ *Elle est dentiste.* She's a dentist.

le **déodorant** NOUN
deodorant

le **dépannage** NOUN
♦**un service de dépannage** a breakdown service

dépanner VERB
1 to fix ◊ *Il a dépanné la voiture en cinq minutes.* He fixed the car in five minutes.
2 to help out ◊ *Il m'a prêté cent francs pour me dépanner.* (*informal*) He lent me 100 francs to help me out.

la **dépanneuse** NOUN
breakdown lorry

le **départ** NOUN
departure ◊ *Le départ est à onze heures quinze.* The departure is at 11.15.
♦**Je lui téléphonerai la veille de son départ.** I'll phone him the day before he leaves.

le **département** NOUN
1 department ◊ *le département d'anglais à l'université* the English department at the university
2 administrative area

ⓘ France is divided into 96 **départements**, administrative areas rather like counties.

◊ *le département du Vaucluse* the Vaucluse region

dépasser VERB
1 to overtake ◊ *Il y a une voiture qui essaie de nous dépasser.* There's a car trying to overtake us.
2 to pass ◊ *Nous avons dépassé Dijon.* We've passed Dijon.
3 to exceed (*sum, limit*)

dépaysé ADJECTIVE
♦**se sentir un peu dépaysé** to feel a bit lost

se **dépêcher** VERB
to hurry ◊ *Dépêche-toi!* Hurry up!

dépendre VERB

◆**dépendre de** to depend on ◇ *Ça dépend du temps.* It depends on the weather.

◆**dépendre de quelqu'un** to be dependent on somebody

◆**Ça dépend.** It depends.

dépenser VERB
  to spend (*money*)

dépensier ADJECTIVE (FEM SING **dépensière**)

◆**Il est dépensier.** He's a big spender.

◆**Elle n'est pas dépensière.** She's not exactly extravagant.

dépilatoire ADJECTIVE

◆**une crème dépilatoire** a hair-removing cream

le **dépit** NOUN

◆**en dépit de** in spite of ◇ *Il y est allé en dépit de mes conseils.* He went in spite of my advice.

déplacé ADJECTIVE
  uncalled-for ◇ *C'était une remarque déplacée.* That remark was uncalled-for.

le **déplacement** NOUN
  trip ◇ *Ça vaut le déplacement.* It's worth the trip.

déplacer VERB
  1 to move ◇ *Tu peux m'aider à déplacer la table?* Can you help me move the table?
  2 to put off ◇ *déplacer un rendez-vous* to put off an appointment

◆**se déplacer (1)** to travel around ◇ *Il se déplace beaucoup pour son travail.* He travels around a lot for his work.

◆**se déplacer (2)** to get around ◇ *Il a du mal à se déplacer.* He has difficulty getting around.

◆**se déplacer une vertèbre** to slip a disc

déplaire VERB

◆**Cela me déplaît.** I dislike this.

déplaisant ADJECTIVE
  unpleasant

le **dépliant** NOUN
  leaflet

déplier VERB
  to unfold

déposer VERB
  1 to leave ◇ *J'ai déposé mon sac à la consigne.* I left my bag at the left luggage office.
  2 to put down ◇ *Déposez le paquet sur la table.* Put the parcel down on the table.

◆**déposer quelqu'un** to drop somebody off

dépourvu ADJECTIVE

◆**prendre quelqu'un au dépourvu** to take somebody by surprise ◇ *Sa question m'a pris au dépourvu.* His question took me by surprise.

la **dépression** NOUN
  depression

◆**faire de la dépression** to be suffering from depression

◆**faire une dépression** to have a breakdown

déprimant ADJECTIVE
  depressing

déprimer VERB
  to get depressed ◇ *Il déprime tout le temps.* He gets depressed all the time.

◆**Ce genre de temps me déprime.** This kind of weather makes me depressed.

depuis PREPOSITION, ADVERB
  1 since ◇ *Il habite Paris depuis 1983.* He's been living in Paris since 1983. ◇ *Je ne lui ai pas parlé depuis.* I haven't spoken to him since.

◆**depuis que** since ◇ *Il a plu tous les jours depuis qu'elle est arrivée.* It's rained every day since she arrived.
  2 for ◇ *Il habite Paris depuis cinq ans.* He's been living in Paris for five years.

◆**Depuis combien de temps?** How long? ◇ *Depuis combien de temps est-ce que vous le connaissez?* How long have you known him?

◆**Depuis quand?** How long? ◇ *Depuis quand est-ce que vous le connaissez?* How long have you known him?

le **député** NOUN
  Member of Parliament

la **députée** NOUN
  Member of Parliament

déraciner VERB
  to uproot

le **dérangement** NOUN

◆**en dérangement** out of order ◇ *Le téléphone est en dérangement.* The phone's out of order.

déranger VERB
  1 to bother ◇ *Excusez-moi de vous déranger.* I'm sorry to bother you.

◆**Ne vous dérangez pas, je vais répondre au téléphone.** You stay there, I'll answer the phone.
  2 to disorganize ◇ *Ne dérange pas mes livres, s'il te plaît.* Don't disorganize my books, please.

déraper VERB
  to skid

le/la **dermatologue** NOUN

dermatologist ◊ *Elle est dermatologue.* She's a dermatologist.

dernier ADJECTIVE (FEM SING **dernière**)
1. last ◊ *Il est arrivé dernier.* He arrived last. ◊ *la dernière fois* the last time
2. latest ◊ *le dernier film de Spielberg* Spielberg's latest film
♦ **en dernier** last ◊ *Ajoutez le lait en dernier.* Put the milk in last.

dernièrement ADVERB
recently

dérouler VERB
1. to unroll
2. to unwind
♦ **se dérouler** to take place ◊ *L'action se déroule dans les années vingt.* The action takes place in the 1920s.
♦ **Tout s'est déroulé comme prévu.** Everything went as planned.

derrière ADVERB, PREPOSITION
see also **derrière** NOUN
behind

le **derrière** NOUN
see also **derrière** ADVERB
1. back ◊ *la porte de derrière* the back door
2. backside ◊ *un coup de pied dans le derrière* a kick up the backside

des ARTICLE

des is the contracted form of de + les.

1. some ◊ *Tu veux des chips?* Would you like some crisps?

des is sometimes not translated.

◊ *J'ai des cousins en France.* I have cousins in France. ◊ *pendant des mois* for months
2. any ◊ *Tu as des frères?* Have you got any brothers?
3. of the ◊ *la fin des vacances* the end of the holidays ◊ *la voiture des Durand* the Durands' car
♦ **Il arrive des États-Unis.** He's arriving from the United States.

dès PREPOSITION
as early as ◊ *dès le mois de novembre* from November
♦ **dès le début** right from the start
♦ **Il vous appellera dès son retour.** He'll call you as soon as he gets back.
♦ **dès que** as soon as ◊ *Il m'a reconnu dès qu'il m'a vu.* He recognized me as soon as he saw me.

désabusé ADJECTIVE
disillusioned

le **désaccord** NOUN
disagreement

désagréable ADJECTIVE

unpleasant

désaltérer VERB
♦ **L'eau désaltère bien.** Water is very thirst-quenching.
♦ **se désaltérer** to quench one's thirst ◊ *Nous sommes allés dans un café pour nous désaltérer.* We went into a café to have a drink.

désapprobateur ADJECTIVE (FEM SING **désapprobatrice**)
disapproving ◊ *un regard désapprobateur* a disapproving look

le **désastre** NOUN
disaster

le **désavantage** NOUN
disadvantage

désavantager VERB
♦ **désavantager quelqu'un** to put somebody at a disadvantage ◊ *Cette nouvelle loi va désavantager les femmes.* The new law will put women at a disadvantage.

descendre VERB
1. to go down ◊ *Je suis tombé en descendant l'escalier.* I fell as I was going down the stairs.
2. to come down ◊ *Attends en bas; je descends!* Wait downstairs; I'm coming down!
3. to get down ◊ *Vous pouvez descendre ma valise, s'il vous plaît?* Can you get my suitcase down, please?
4. to get off ◊ *Nous descendons à la prochaine station.* We're getting off at the next station.

la **descente** NOUN
way down ◊ *Je t'attendrai au bas de la descente.* I'll wait for you at the bottom of the hill.
♦ **une descente de police** a police raid

la **description** NOUN
description

déséquilibré ADJECTIVE
unbalanced

déséquilibrer VERB
♦ **déséquilibrer quelqu'un** to throw somebody off balance ◊ *Le coup de poing l'a déséquilibré.* The punch threw him off balance.

désert ADJECTIVE
see also **désert** NOUN
deserted ◊ *Le dimanche, le centre commercial est désert.* On Sundays, the shopping centre is deserted.
♦ **une île déserte** a desert island

le **désert** NOUN
see also **désert** ADJECTIVE
desert

D

déserter VERB
to desert

désertique ADJECTIVE
desert ◊ *une région désertique* a
desert region

désespéré ADJECTIVE
desperate

désespérer VERB
to despair ◊ *Il ne faut pas
désespérer.* Don't despair.

le **désespoir** NOUN
despair

déshabiller VERB
to undress
♦ **se déshabiller** to get undressed

déshériter VERB
to disinherit
♦ **les déshérités** the underprivileged

déshydraté ADJECTIVE
dehydrated

désigner VERB
to choose ◊ *On l'a désignée pour
remettre le prix.* She was chosen to
present the prize.
♦ **désigner quelque chose du doigt** to
point at something

le **désinfectant** NOUN
disinfectant

désinfecter VERB
to disinfect

désintéressé ADJECTIVE
1 unselfish ◊ *un acte désintéressé*
an unselfish action
2 impartial ◊ *un conseil désintéressé*
impartial advice

désintéresser VERB
♦ **se désintéresser de quelque chose** to
lose interest in something

le **désir** NOUN
1 wish ◊ *Vos désirs sont des ordres.*
Your wish is my command.
2 will ◊ *le désir de réussir* the will
to succeed
3 desire ◊ *Ses yeux brillaient de
désir.* Her eyes were shining with
desire.

désirer VERB
to want ◊ *Vous désirez?* (*in shop*)
What would you like?

désobéir VERB
♦ **désobéir à quelqu'un** to disobey
somebody

désobéissant ADJECTIVE
disobedient

désobligeant ADJECTIVE
unpleasant ◊ *faire une remarque
désobligeante* to make an unpleasant
remark

le **désodorisant** NOUN
air freshener

désolé ADJECTIVE
sorry ◊ *Je suis vraiment désolé.* I'm
very sorry.
♦ **Désolé!** Sorry!

désopilant ADJECTIVE
hilarious

désordonné ADJECTIVE
untidy

le **désordre** NOUN
untidiness
♦ **Quel désordre!** What a mess!
♦ **en désordre** untidy ◊ *Sa chambre est
toujours en désordre.* His bedroom is
always untidy.

désormais ADVERB
from now on ◊ *Désormais, je boirai
de l'eau.* From now on I'll drink
water.

desquelles PRONOUN

> *desquelles is the contracted form of
> de + lesquelles.*

◊ *des négociations au cours
desquelles les patrons ont fait des
concessions* negotiations during
which the employers made
concessions

desquels PRONOUN

> *desquels is the contracted form of
> de + lesquels.*

◊ *les lacs au bord desquels nous
avons campé* the lakes on the banks
of which we camped

dessécher VERB
to dry out ◊ *Le soleil dessèche la
peau.* The sun dries your skin out.

desserrer VERB
to loosen

le **dessert** NOUN
pudding ◊ *Qu'est-ce que vous désirez
comme dessert?* What would you like
for pudding?

le **dessin** NOUN
drawing ◊ *C'est un dessin de ma
petite sœur.* It's a drawing my little
sister did.
♦ **un dessin animé** a cartoon (*film*)
♦ **un dessin humoristique** a cartoon
(*drawing*)

le **dessinateur** NOUN
♦ **un dessinateur industriel** a
draughtsman

dessiner VERB
to draw

dessous ADVERB
> see also **dessous** NOUN
underneath

◆ **en dessous** underneath ◊ *Soulève le pot de fleurs, la clé est en dessous.* Lift the flowerpot, the key's underneath.

◆ **par-dessous** underneath ◊ *Le grillage ne sert à rien, les lapins passent par-dessous.* The fence is useless, the rabbits get in underneath.

◆ **là-dessous** under there ◊ *Il s'est caché là-dessous.* He hid under there.

◆ **ci-dessous** below ◊ *Complétez les phrases ci-dessous.* Complete the sentences below.

◆ **au-dessous de** below ◊ *vingt degrés au-dessous de zéro* 20 degrees below zero

le **dessous** NOUN

see also **dessous** ADVERB

underneath

◆ **les voisins du dessous** the downstairs neighbours

◆ **avoir le dessus** to have the upper hand

◆ **les dessous** underwear ◊ *des dessous en soie* silk underwear

le **dessous-de-plat** NOUN (PL les **dessous-de-plat**)
tablemat

dessus ADVERB

see also **dessus** NOUN

on top ◊ *un gâteau avec des bougies dessus* a cake with candles on top

◆ **par-dessus** over ◊ *Nous avons sauté par-dessus la barrière.* We jumped over the gate.

◆ **au-dessus** above ◊ *la taille au-dessus* the size above ◊ *au-dessus du lit* above the bed

◆ **là-dessus (1)** on there ◊ *Tu peux écrire là-dessus.* You can write on there.

◆ **là-dessus (2)** with that ◊ *"Je démissionne!" Là-dessus, il est parti.* "I resign!" With that, he left.

◆ **ci-dessus** above ◊ *l'exemple ci-dessus* the example above

le **dessus** NOUN

see also **dessus** ADVERB

top

◆ **les voisins du dessus** the upstairs neighbours

le/la **destinataire** NOUN
addressee

la **destination** NOUN
destination

◆ **les passagers à destination de Paris** passengers travelling to Paris

destiné ADJECTIVE

intended for ◊ *Ce livre est destiné aux enfants.* This book is intended for children.

◆ **Elle était destinée à faire ce métier.** She was destined to go into that job.

la **destruction** NOUN
destruction

le **détachant** NOUN
stain remover

détacher VERB
to undo

◆ **se détacher de quelque chose (1)** to come off something ◊ *La poignée de la porte s'est détachée.* The door-handle came off.

◆ **se détacher de quelque chose (2)** to break away from something ◊ *Un wagon s'est détaché du reste du train.* A carriage broke away from the rest of the train.

le **détail** NOUN
detail

◆ **en détail** in detail

le **détective** NOUN
detective ◊ *un détective privé* a private detective

déteindre VERB
to fade (*in wash*)

détendre VERB
to relax ◊ *La lecture, ça me détend.* I find reading relaxing.

◆ **se détendre** to relax ◊ *Il est allé prendre un bain pour se détendre.* He's gone to have a bath to relax.

la **détente** NOUN
relaxation

le **détenu** NOUN
prisoner

la **détenue** NOUN
prisoner

se **détériorer** VERB
to deteriorate

déterminé ADJECTIVE
1 determined ◊ *C'est un homme déterminé.* He's a determined man.
2 specific ◊ *un but déterminé* a specific aim

détestable ADJECTIVE
horrible

détester VERB
to hate

la **détonation** NOUN
bang ◊ *J'ai entendu une détonation.* I heard a bang.

le **détour** NOUN
detour

◆ **Ça vaut le détour.** It's worth the trip.

le **détournement** NOUN

D

Français ~ Anglais

♦**un détournement d'avion** a hijacking

détrempé ADJECTIVE
  waterlogged

les **détritus** MASC NOUN
  litter SING

détruire VERB
  to destroy

la **dette** NOUN
  debt

le **deuil** NOUN
  ♦**être en deuil** to be in mourning

deux NUMBER
  two ◊ *Il était deux heures.* It was two
  o'clock. ◊ *Elle a deux ans.* She's two.
  ♦**deux fois** twice
  ♦**deux points** colon
  ♦**tous les deux** both ◊ *Nous y sommes
  allées toutes les deux.* We both went.
  ♦**le deux février** the second of February

deuxième ADJECTIVE
  second ◊ *au deuxième étage* on the
  second floor

deuxièmement ADVERB
  secondly

devais, devait, devaient VERB *see*
  devoir

dévaliser VERB
  to rob

devant ADVERB, PREPOSITION
  see also **devant** NOUN
  1 in front ◊ *Il marchait devant.* He
  was walking in front.
  2 in front of ◊ *Il était assis devant
  moi.* He was sitting in front of me.
  ♦**passer devant** to go past ◊ *Nous
  sommes passés devant chez toi.* We
  went past your house.

le **devant** NOUN
  see also **devant** ADVERB
  front ◊ *le devant de la maison* the
  front of the house
  ♦**les pattes de devant** the front legs

le **développement** NOUN
  development
  ♦**les pays en voie de développement**
  developing countries

développer VERB
  to develop ◊ *donner une pellicule à
  développer* to take a film to be
  developed
  ♦**se développer** to develop

devenir VERB
  to become

devez VERB *see* **devoir**

la **déviation** NOUN
  diversion

deviez VERB *see* **devoir**

deviner VERB
  to guess

la **devinette** NOUN
  riddle ◊ *poser une devinette à
  quelqu'un* to ask somebody a riddle

devions VERB *see* **devoir**

dévisager VERB
  ♦**dévisager quelqu'un** to stare at
  somebody

la **devise** NOUN
  currency ◊ *les devises étrangères*
  foreign currency

dévisser VERB
  to unscrew

dévoiler VERB
  to unveil

devoir VERB
  see also **devoir** NOUN

Present tense:	
je dois	nous devons
tu dois	vous devez
il/elle doit	ils/elles doivent
Past participle:	
dû	

  1 to have to ◊ *Je dois partir.* I've
  got to go.
  2 must ◊ *Tu dois être fatigué.* You
  must be tired.
  3 to be due to ◊ *Le nouveau centre
  commercial doit ouvrir en mai.* The
  new shopping centre is due to open
  in May.
  ♦**devoir quelque chose à quelqu'un** to
  owe somebody something ◊ *Combien
  est-ce que je vous dois?* How much
  do I owe you?

le **devoir** NOUN
  see also **devoir** VERB
  1 exercise
  ♦**les devoirs** homework
  ♦**un devoir sur table** a written test
  2 duty ◊ *Aller voter fait partie des
  devoirs du citoyen.* Voting is part of
  one's duty as a citizen.

devons VERB *see* **devoir**

dévorer VERB
  to devour

dévoué ADJECTIVE
  devoted

**devra, devrai, devras, devrez,
  devrons, devront** VERB *see* **devoir**

le **diabète** NOUN
  diabetes

diabétique ADJECTIVE
  diabetic ◊ *Je suis diabétique.* I'm
  diabetic.

le **diable** NOUN
  devil

D

le **diabolo** NOUN
    fruit cordial and lemonade
    ♦ **un diabolo menthe** a mint cordial and lemonade

diagonal ADJECTIVE (MASC PL **diagonaux**)
    diagonal

la **diagonale** NOUN
    diagonal
    ♦ **en diagonale** diagonally

le **diagramme** NOUN
    diagram

le **dialecte** NOUN
    dialect

le **dialogue** NOUN
    dialogue

le **diamant** NOUN
    diamond

le **diamètre** NOUN
    diameter

la **diapo** NOUN (*informal*)
    slide
    ♦ **une pellicule diapo** a slide film

la **diapositive** NOUN
    slide ◊ *projeter des diapositives* to show some slides

la **diarrhée** NOUN
    diarrhoea ◊ *avoir la diarrhée* to have diarrhoea

le **dictateur** NOUN
    dictator

la **dictature** NOUN
    dictatorship

la **dictée** NOUN
    dictation

dicter VERB
    to dictate

le **dictionnaire** NOUN
    dictionary

diététique ADJECTIVE
    ♦ **un magasin diététique** a health food shop

le **dieu** NOUN (PL les **dieux**)
    god ◊ *Dieu* God ◊ *Mon Dieu!* Oh my God!

la **différence** NOUN
    difference
    ♦ **la différence d'âge** the age difference
    ♦ **à la différence de** unlike

différent ADJECTIVE
    ① different ◊ *pour des raisons différentes* for different reasons
    ② various ◊ *pour différentes raisons* for various reasons
    ♦ **différent de** different to ◊ *Son point de vue est différent du mien.* His point of view is different to mine.

difficile ADJECTIVE

difficult ◊ *Son accent est difficile à comprendre.* His accent is difficult to understand.

difficilement ADVERB
    ♦ **faire quelque chose difficilement** to have trouble doing something ◊ *Ma grand-mère se déplace difficilement.* My grandmother has trouble getting around.
    ♦ **Je pouvais difficilement refuser.** It was difficult for me to refuse.

la **difficulté** NOUN
    difficulty ◊ *avec difficulté* with difficulty
    ♦ **être en difficulté** to be in difficulties

digérer VERB
    to digest

le **digestif** NOUN
    after-dinner liqueur

digne ADJECTIVE
    ♦ **digne de** worthy of ◊ *digne de confiance* trustworthy

la **dignité** NOUN
    dignity

le **dilemme** NOUN
    dilemma ◊ *être devant un dilemme* to be faced with a dilemma

diluer VERB
    to dilute

le **dimanche** NOUN
    ① Sunday ◊ *Aujourd'hui, nous sommes dimanche.* It's Sunday today.
    ② on Sunday ◊ *Dimanche, nous allons déjeuner chez mes grands-parents.* On Sunday we're having lunch at my grandparents'.
    ♦ **le dimanche** on Sundays ◊ *Le dimanche, je fais la grasse matinée.* I have a lie-in on Sundays.
    ♦ **tous les dimanches** every Sunday
    ♦ **dimanche dernier** last Sunday
    ♦ **dimanche prochain** next Sunday

diminuer VERB
    to decrease ◊ *Est-ce que tu peux diminuer le son?* Could you turn down the sound?

le **diminutif** NOUN
    pet name

la **diminution** NOUN
    ① reduction
    ② decrease

la **dinde** NOUN
    turkey ◊ *la dinde de Noël* the Christmas turkey

le **dindon** NOUN
    turkey

    *le **dindon** refers to a live turkey, whereas **la dinde** refers to the meat.*

le **dîner** NOUN
> see also **dîner** VERB

dinner (*evening meal*)

dîner VERB
> see also **dîner** NOUN

to have dinner (*evening meal*)

dingue ADJECTIVE (*informal*)
crazy

diplomate ADJECTIVE
> see also **diplomate** NOUN

diplomatic

le **diplomate** NOUN
> see also **diplomate** ADJECTIVE

diplomat

la **diplomatie** NOUN
diplomacy

le **diplôme** NOUN
qualification

diplômé ADJECTIVE
qualified

dire VERB
1 to say ◊ *Il a dit qu'il ne viendrait pas.* He said he wouldn't come.
♦ **on dit que ...** they say that ... ◊ *On dit que la nourriture est excellente là-bas.* They say that the food is excellent there.
2 to tell
♦ **dire quelque chose à quelqu'un** to tell somebody something ◊ *Elle m'a dit la vérité.* She told me the truth. ◊ *Il nous a dit de regarder cette émission.* He told us to watch this programme.
♦ **On dirait qu'il va pleuvoir.** It looks as if it's going to rain.
♦ **se dire quelque chose** ◊ *Quand je l'ai vu, je me suis dit qu'il avait vieilli.* When I saw him, I thought to myself that he'd aged.
♦ **Est-ce que ça se dit?** Can you say that?
♦ **Ça ne me dit rien.** That doesn't appeal to me.

direct ADJECTIVE
direct
♦ **en direct** live ◊ *une émission en direct* a live broadcast

directement ADVERB
straight ◊ *Il est rentré directement chez lui.* He went straight home.

le **directeur** NOUN
1 headteacher ◊ *Il est directeur.* He's a headteacher.
2 manager ◊ *Il est directeur du personnel.* He's a personnel manager.

la **direction** NOUN
1 management ◊ *la direction et les ouvriers* the management and the workers

2 direction ◊ *"toutes directions"* "all routes"

la **directrice** NOUN
1 headteacher ◊ *Elle est directrice.* She's a headteacher.
2 manager ◊ *Elle est directrice commerciale.* She's a sales manager.

dirent VERB see **dire**

le **dirigeant** NOUN
leader

la **dirigeante** NOUN
leader

diriger VERB
to manage ◊ *Il dirige une petite entreprise.* He manages a small company.
♦ **se diriger vers** to head for ◊ *Il se dirigeait vers la gare.* He was heading for the station.

dis VERB see **dire**
♦ **Dis-moi la vérité!** Tell me the truth!
♦ **dis donc** hey ◊ *Il a drôlement changé, dis donc!* Hey, he's really changed! ◊ *Dis donc, tu te souviens de Sam?* Hey, do you remember Sam?

disaient, disais, disait VERB see **dire**

la **discothèque** NOUN
disco (*club*)

le **discours** NOUN
speech

discret ADJECTIVE (FEM SING **discrète**)
discreet

la **discrimination** NOUN
discrimination ◊ *la discrimination raciale* racial discrimination ◊ *la discrimination sexuelle* sex discrimination

la **discussion** NOUN
discussion

discutable ADJECTIVE
debatable

discuter VERB
1 to talk ◊ *Nous avons discuté pendant des heures.* We talked for hours.
2 to argue ◊ *C'est ce que j'ai décidé, alors ne discutez pas!* That's what I've decided, so don't argue!

disent, disiez, disions VERB see **dire**

disons VERB see **dire**
let's say ◊ *C'est à, disons, une heure à pied.* It's an hour's walk, say.

disparaître VERB
to disappear
♦ **faire disparaître quelque chose (1)** to make something disappear ◊ *Il a fait disparaître le lapin dans son chapeau.*

He made the rabbit disappear in his hat.
- **faire disparaître quelque chose (2)** to get rid of something ◊ *Ils ont fait disparaître tous les documents compromettants.* They got rid of all the incriminating documents.

la **disparition** NOUN
    disappearance
- **une espèce en voie de disparition** an endangered species

disparu ADJECTIVE
- **être porté disparu** to be reported missing

le **dispensaire** NOUN
    community clinic

dispensé ADJECTIVE
- **être dispensé de quelque chose** to be excused something ◊ *Elle est dispensée de gymnastique.* She's excused gym.

disperser VERB
    to break up ◊ *La police a dispersé les manifestants.* The police broke up the demonstrators.
- **se disperser** to break up ◊ *Une fois l'ambulance partie, la foule s'est dispersée.* Once the ambulance had left, the crowd broke up.

disponible ADJECTIVE
    available

disposé ADJECTIVE
- **être disposé à faire quelque chose** to be willing to do something ◊ *Il était disposé à m'aider.* He was willing to help me.

disposer VERB
- **disposer de quelque chose** to have access to something ◊ *Je dispose d'un ordinateur.* I have access to a computer.

la **disposition** NOUN
- **prendre ses dispositions** to make arrangements ◊ *Est-ce que vous avez pris vos dispositions pour partir en France?* Have you made arrangements to go to France?
- **avoir quelque chose à sa disposition** to have something at one's disposal ◊ *J'ai une voiture à ma disposition pour la semaine.* I have a car at my disposal for the week.
- **Je suis à votre disposition.** I am at your service.
- **Je tiens ces livres à votre disposition.** The books are at your disposal.

la **dispute** NOUN
    argument

se **disputer** VERB

to argue

le **disquaire** NOUN
    record dealer

le **disque** NOUN
    record
- **un disque compact** a compact disc
- **le disque dur** hard disk

la **disquette** NOUN
    floppy disk

disséminé ADJECTIVE
    scattered

disséquer VERB
    to dissect

la **dissertation** NOUN
    essay

dissimuler VERB
    to conceal

se **dissiper** VERB
    to clear ◊ *Le brouillard va se dissiper dans l'après-midi.* The fog will clear during the afternoon.

le **dissolvant** NOUN
    nail polish remover

dissoudre VERB
    to dissolve
- **se dissoudre** to dissolve

dissuader VERB
- **dissuader quelqu'un de faire quelque chose** to dissuade somebody from doing something ◊ *Elle m'a dissuadé d'aller voir ce film.* She dissuaded me from going to see the film.

la **distance** NOUN
    distance

la **distillerie** NOUN
    distillery

distingué ADJECTIVE
    distinguished

distinguer VERB
    to distinguish

la **distraction** NOUN
    entertainment ◊ *Il lit beaucoup: c'est sa seule distraction.* He reads a lot: it's his only form of entertainment.

distraire VERB
- **Va voir un film, ça te distraira.** Go and see a film, it'll take your mind off things.

distrait ADJECTIVE
    absent-minded

distribuer VERB
    1 to give out ◊ *Distribue les livres, s'il te plaît.* Give out the books, please.
    2 to deal (*cards*)

le **distributeur** NOUN
- **un distributeur automatique** a vending machine

D

♦ **un distributeur de billets** a cash dispenser

dit VERB see **dire**

dit ADJECTIVE
known as ◊ *Pierre, dit Pierrot* Pierre, known as Pierrot

dites VERB see **dire**

♦ **Dites-moi ce que vous pensez.** Tell me what you think.

♦ **dites donc** hey ◊ *Dites donc, vous, là-bas!* Hey, you there!

divers ADJECTIVE
diverse

♦ **pour diverses raisons** for various reasons

se **divertir** VERB
to enjoy oneself

divin ADJECTIVE
divine

diviser VERB
to divide ◊ *Quatre divisé par deux égalent deux.* 4 divided by 2 equals 2.

le **divorcé** NOUN
divorcee

la **divorcée** NOUN
divorcee

divorcer VERB
to get divorced

dix NUMBER
ten ◊ *Elle a dix ans.* She's ten. ◊ *à dix heures* at ten o'clock

♦ **le dix février** the tenth of February

dix-huit NUMBER
eighteen ◊ *Elle a dix-huit ans.* She's eighteen. ◊ *à dix-huit heures* at 6 p.m.

dixième ADJECTIVE
tenth ◊ *au dixième étage* on the tenth floor

dix-neuf NUMBER
nineteen ◊ *Elle a dix-neuf ans.* She's nineteen. ◊ *à dix-neuf heures* at 7 p.m.

dix-sept NUMBER
seventeen ◊ *Elle a dix-sept ans.* She's seventeen. ◊ *à dix-sept heures* at 5 p.m.

la **dizaine** NOUN
about ten ◊ *une dizaine de jours* about ten days

le **do** NOUN
1 C ◊ *en do majeur* in C major
2 do ◊ *do, ré, mi ...* do, re, mi ...

le **docteur** NOUN
doctor ◊ *Elle est docteur.* She's a doctor.

le **document** NOUN
document

le **documentaire** NOUN
documentary

le/la **documentaliste** NOUN
librarian

la **documentation** NOUN
documentation

documenter VERB
♦ **se documenter sur quelque chose** to gather information on something

dodu ADJECTIVE
plump

le **doigt** NOUN
finger

♦ **les doigts de pied** the toes

dois, doit, doivent VERB see **devoir**

le **domaine** NOUN
1 estate ◊ *Il possède un immense domaine en Normandie.* He owns a huge estate in Normandy.
2 field ◊ *La chimie n'est pas mon domaine.* Chemistry's not my field.

domestique ADJECTIVE
see also **domestique** NOUN
domestic

♦ **les animaux domestiques** pets

le/la **domestique** NOUN
see also **domestique** ADJECTIVE
servant

le **domicile** NOUN
place of residence

♦ **à domicile** at home ◊ *Il travaille à domicile.* He works at home.

domicilié ADJECTIVE
♦ **"domicilié à: ..."** "address: ..."

dominer VERB
to dominate

♦ **se dominer** to control oneself

les **dominos** MASC NOUN
dominoes ◊ *jouer aux dominos* to play dominoes

le **dommage** NOUN
damage ◊ *La tempête a causé d'importants dommages.* The storm caused a lot of damage.

♦ **C'est dommage.** It's a shame. ◊ *C'est dommage que tu ne puisses pas venir.* It's a shame you can't come.

dompter VERB
to tame

le **dompteur** NOUN
animal tamer

la **dompteuse** NOUN
animal tamer

le **don** NOUN
1 donation
2 gift ◊ *avoir un don pour quelque chose* to have a gift for something

♦ **Elle a le don de m'énerver.** She's got a knack of getting on my nerves.

donc CONJUNCTION

so

le **donjon** NOUN

keep (of castle)

les **données** FEM NOUN

data

donner VERB

1 to give

♦ **donner quelque chose à quelqu'un** to give somebody something ◊ *Elle m'a donné son adresse.* She gave me her address.

♦ **Ça m'a donné faim.** That made me feel hungry.

2 to give away ◊ *Tu as toujours ta veste en daim? – Non, je l'ai donnée.* Have you still got your suede jacket? – No, I gave it away.

♦ **donner sur quelque chose** to overlook something ◊ *une fenêtre qui donne sur la mer* a window overlooking the sea

dont PRONOUN

1 of which ◊ *deux livres, dont l'un est en anglais* two books, one of which is in English ◊ *le prix dont il est si fier* the prize he's so proud of

2 of whom ◊ *dix blessés, dont deux grièvement* ten people injured, two of them seriously ◊ *la fille dont je t'ai parlé* the girl I told you about

doré ADJECTIVE

golden ◊ *une étoile dorée* a golden star

dorénavant ADVERB

from now on ◊ *Dorénavant, tu feras attention.* From now on, you'll be careful.

dorloter VERB

to pamper

dormir VERB

1 to sleep ◊ *Tu as bien dormi?* Did you sleep well?

2 to be asleep ◊ *Ne faites pas de bruit, il dort.* Don't make any noise, he's asleep.

le **dortoir** NOUN

dormitory

le **dos** NOUN

back ◊ *dos à dos* back to back

♦ **faire quelque chose dans le dos de quelqu'un** to do something behind somebody's back ◊ *Elle me critique dans mon dos.* She criticizes me behind my back.

♦ **de dos** from behind

♦ **nager le dos crawlé** to swim backstroke

♦ **"voir au dos"** "see over"

la **dose** NOUN

dose ◊ *Ne pas dépasser la dose prescrite.* Do not exceed the stated dose.

le **dossier** NOUN

1 file ◊ *une pile de dossiers* a stack of files

2 report ◊ *un bon dossier scolaire* a good school report

3 feature (in magazine)

4 back (of chair)

la **douane** NOUN

customs

le **douanier** NOUN

customs officer

le **double** NOUN

♦ **le double** twice as much ◊ *Il gagne le double.* He earns twice as much. ◊ *le double du prix normal* twice the normal price

♦ **en double** in duplicate ◊ *Garde cette photo, je l'ai en double.* Keep this photo, I've got a copy of it.

♦ **le double messieurs** the men's doubles (tennis)

double-cliquer VERB

to double-click ◊ *double-cliquer sur une icône* to double-click on an icon

doubler VERB

1 to double ◊ *Le prix a doublé en dix ans.* The price has doubled in 10 years.

2 to overtake ◊ *Il est dangereux de doubler sur cette route.* It's dangerous to overtake on this road.

♦ **un film doublé** a dubbed film

douce ADJECTIVE *see* **doux**

doucement ADVERB

1 gently ◊ *Il a frappé doucement à la porte.* He knocked gently at the door.

2 slowly ◊ *Roulez doucement!* Drive slowly! ◊ *Je ne comprends pas, parle plus doucement.* I don't understand, speak more slowly.

la **douceur** NOUN

1 softness ◊ *Cette crème maintient la douceur de votre peau.* This cream keeps your skin soft.

2 gentleness ◊ *parler avec douceur* to speak gently

♦ **L'avion a atterri en douceur.** The plane made a smooth landing.

la **douche** NOUN

shower

♦ **les douches** the shower room

♦ **prendre une douche** to have a shower

se **doucher** VERB

to have a shower

doué ADJECTIVE

talented
- **être doué en quelque chose** to be good at something ◊ *Il est doué en maths.* He's good at maths.

douillet ADJECTIVE (FEM SING **douillette**)
1. cosy ◊ *un anorak douillet* a cosy anorak
2. soft ◊ *Je ne supporte pas la douleur: je suis très douillette.* I can't stand pain: I'm a real softie.

la **douleur** NOUN
pain

douloureux ADJECTIVE (FEM SING **douloureuse**)
painful

le **doute** NOUN
doubt
- **sans doute** probably

douter VERB
to doubt
- **douter de quelque chose** to doubt something ◊ *Je doute de sa sincérité.* I have my doubts about his sincerity.
- **se douter de quelque chose** to suspect something ◊ *Je ne me doutais de rien.* I didn't suspect anything.
- **Je m'en doutais.** I suspected as much.

douteux ADJECTIVE (FEM SING **douteuse**)
1. dubious ◊ *une plaisanterie d'un goût douteux* a joke in dubious taste
2. suspicious-looking ◊ *un individu douteux* a suspicious-looking person

Douvres NOUN
Dover

doux ADJECTIVE (FEM SING **douce**, MASC PL **doux**)
1. soft ◊ *un tissu doux* soft material ◊ *les drogues douces* soft drugs
2. sweet ◊ *du cidre doux* sweet cider
3. mild ◊ *Il fait doux aujourd'hui.* It's mild today.
4. gentle ◊ *C'est quelqu'un de très doux.* He's a very gentle person.
- **en douce** on the quiet ◊ *Il m'a donné cinquante francs en douce.* He slipped me 50 francs on the quiet.

la **douzaine** NOUN
dozen ◊ *une douzaine d'œufs* a dozen eggs
- **une douzaine de personnes** about twelve people

douze NUMBER
twelve ◊ *Il a douze ans.* He's twelve.
- **le douze février** the twelfth of February

douzième ADJECTIVE

twelfth ◊ *au douzième étage* on the twelfth floor

la **dragée** NOUN
sugared almond

draguer VERB (*informal*)
- **draguer quelqu'un** to chat somebody up ◊ *Il est en train de la draguer.* He's chatting her up.
- **se faire draguer** to get chatted up ◊ *Marie-Claire aime se faire draguer.* Marie-Claire likes being chatted up.

le **dragueur** NOUN (*informal*)
flirt (*person*)

la **dragueuse** NOUN (*informal*)
flirt (*person*)

dramatique ADJECTIVE
tragic ◊ *une situation dramatique* a tragic situation
- **l'art dramatique** drama

le **drame** NOUN
drama (*incident*)
- **Ça n'est pas un drame si tu ne viens pas.** It's not the end of the world if you don't come.

le **drap** NOUN
sheet (*for bed*)

le **drapeau** NOUN (PL les **drapeaux**)
flag ◊ *le drapeau français* the French flag

dressé ADJECTIVE
trained ◊ *un chien bien dressé* a well-trained dog

dresser VERB
1. to draw up ◊ *dresser une liste* to draw up a list
2. to train ◊ *dresser un chien* to train a dog
- **dresser l'oreille** to prick up one's ears ◊ *Quand elle a dit ça, il a dressé l'oreille.* When she said that, he pricked up his ears.

la **drogue** NOUN
drug ◊ *le problème de la drogue* the drugs problem ◊ *la lutte contre la drogue* the war against drugs
- **les drogues douces** soft drugs
- **les drogues dures** hard drugs

le **drogué** NOUN
drug addict

la **droguée** NOUN
drug addict

droguer VERB
- **droguer quelqu'un** to drug somebody
- **se droguer** to take drugs

la **droguerie** NOUN
hardware shop

droit ADJECTIVE, ADVERB

see also **droit** NOUN

1 right ◊ *le bras droit* the right arm ◊ *le côté droit* the right-hand side

2 straight ◊ *une ligne droite* a straight line ◊ *Tiens-toi droite!* Stand up straight!

♦**tout droit** straight on

le **droit** NOUN

see also **droit** ADJECTIVE

1 right ◊ *les droits de l'homme* human rights

♦**avoir le droit de faire quelque chose** to be allowed to do something ◊ *On n'a pas le droit de fumer à l'école.* We're not allowed to smoke at school.

2 law ◊ *faire son droit* to study law ◊ *un étudiant en droit* a law student

la **droite** NOUN

see also **droit** ADJECTIVE

right ◊ *sur votre droite* on your right

♦**à droite (1)** on the right ◊ *la troisième rue à droite* the third street on the right

♦**à droite (2)** to the right ◊ *à droite de la fenêtre* to the right of the window ◊ *Tournez à droite.* Turn right.

♦**la voie de droite** the right-hand lane

♦**la droite** the right (*in politics*) ◊ *Elle est très à droite.* She's very right-wing.

droitier ADJECTIVE (FEM SING **droitière**)

right-handed ◊ *Elle est droitière.* She's right-handed.

drôle ADJECTIVE

funny ◊ *Ça n'est pas drôle.* It's not funny.

♦**un drôle de temps** funny weather

drôlement ADVERB (*informal*)

really ◊ *C'est drôlement bon.* It's really good.

du ARTICLE

du is the contracted form of de + le.

1 some ◊ *Tu veux du fromage?* Would you like some cheese?

2 any ◊ *Tu as du chocolat?* Have you got any chocolate?

3 of the ◊ *la porte du garage* the door of the garage ◊ *la femme du directeur* the headmaster's wife

dû VERB *see* **devoir**

see also **dû** ADJECTIVE

♦**Nous avons dû nous arrêter.** We had to stop.

dû ADJECTIVE (FEM **due,** MASC PL **dus**)

see also **dû** VERB

♦**dû à** due to ◊ *un retard dû au mauvais temps* a delay due to bad weather

le **duc** NOUN

duke

la **duchesse** NOUN

duchess

dupe ADJECTIVE

♦**Elle me ment mais je ne suis pas dupe.** She lies to me but I'm not taken in by that.

duquel PRONOUN (MASC PL **desquels,** FEM PL **desquelles**)

duquel is the contracted form of de + lequel.

◊ *l'homme duquel il parle* the man he is talking about

dur ADJECTIVE, ADVERB

hard ◊ *travailler dur* to work hard ◊ *être dur avec quelqu'un* to be hard on somebody

durant PREPOSITION

1 during ◊ *durant la nuit* during the night

2 for ◊ *durant des années* for years ◊ *des mois durant* for months

la **durée** NOUN

length ◊ *Quelle est la durée des études d'ingénieur?* How long does it take to train as an engineer?

♦**pour une durée de quinze jours** for a period of two weeks

♦**de courte durée** short ◊ *un séjour de courte durée* a short stay

♦**de longue durée** long ◊ *une absence de longue durée* a long absence

durement ADVERB

harshly

durer VERB

to last

la **dureté** NOUN

harshness ◊ *traiter quelqu'un avec dureté* to treat somebody harshly

le **DVD** NOUN

DVD

dynamique ADJECTIVE

dynamic

dyslexique ADJECTIVE

dyslexic

D

E

l' **eau** FEM NOUN (PL les **eaux**)
　　water
◆ **l'eau minérale** mineral water
◆ **l'eau plate** still water
◆ **tomber à l'eau** to fall through ◇ *Nos projets sont tombés à l'eau.* Our plans have fallen through.

ébahi ADJECTIVE
　　amazed

éblouir VERB
　　to dazzle

l' **éboueur** MASC NOUN
　　dustman

ébouillanter VERB
　　to scald

l' **écaille** FEM NOUN
　　scale (*of fish*)

s' **écailler** VERB
　　to flake

l' **écart** MASC NOUN
　　gap
◆ **à l'écart de** away from ◇ *Ils se sont assis à l'écart des autres.* They sat down away from the others.

écarté ADJECTIVE
　　remote
◆ **les bras écartés** arms outstretched
◆ **les jambes écartées** legs apart

écarter VERB
　　to open wide (*arms, legs*)
◆ **s'écarter** to move ◇ *Ils se sont écartés pour le laisser passer.* They moved to let him pass.

l' **échafaudage** MASC NOUN
　　scaffolding

l' **échalote** FEM NOUN
　　shallot

l' **échange** MASC NOUN
　　exchange ◇ *en échange de* in exchange for

échanger VERB
　　to swap ◇ *Je t'échange ce timbre contre celui-là.* I'll swap you this stamp for that one.

l' **échantillon** MASC NOUN
　　sample

échapper VERB
◆ **échapper à** to escape from ◇ *Le prisonnier a réussi à échapper à la police.* The prisoner managed to escape from the police.
◆ **s'échapper** to escape ◇ *Il s'est échappé de prison.* He escaped from prison.

◆ **l'échapper belle** to have a narrow escape ◇ *Nous l'avons échappé belle.* We had a narrow escape.

l' **écharde** FEM NOUN
　　splinter of wood

l' **écharpe** FEM NOUN
　　scarf

s' **échauffer** VERB
　　to warm up (*before exercise*)

l' **échec** MASC NOUN
　　failure

les **échecs** MASC NOUN
　　chess SING ◇ *jouer aux échecs* to play chess

l' **échelle** FEM NOUN
　　1 ladder
　　2 scale (*of map*)

échevelé ADJECTIVE
　　dishevelled

l' **écho** MASC NOUN
　　echo

échouer VERB
◆ **échouer à un examen** to fail an exam

éclabousser VERB
　　to splash

l' **éclair** MASC NOUN
　　flash of lightning
◆ **un éclair au chocolat** a chocolate éclair

l' **éclairage** MASC NOUN
　　lighting

l' **éclaircie** FEM NOUN
　　bright interval

éclairer VERB
◆ **Cette lampe éclaire bien.** This lamp gives a good light.

l' **éclat** MASC NOUN
　　1 fragment (*of glass*) ◇ *La vase a volé en éclats.* The vase smashed into pieces.
　　2 brightness (*of sun, colour*)
◆ **des éclats de rire** roars of laughter

éclatant ADJECTIVE
　　brilliant ◇ *des dents d'une blancheur éclatante* brilliant white teeth

éclater VERB
　　1 to burst (*tyre, balloon*)
◆ **éclater de rire** to burst out laughing
◆ **éclater en sanglots** to burst into tears
　　2 to break out ◇ *La Seconde Guerre mondiale a éclaté en 1939.* The Second World War broke out in 1939.

écœurant ADJECTIVE

sickly

écœurer VERB
- **Tous ces mensonges m'écœurent.** All these lies make me sick.

l'**école** FEM NOUN
school ◊ *aller à l'école* to go to school ◊ *une école privée* a private school ◊ *une école publique* a state school ◊ *une école maternelle* a nursery school

ⓘ *The **école maternelle** is a state school for 2-6 year-olds.*

l'**écolier** MASC NOUN
schoolboy

l'**écolière** FEM NOUN
schoolgirl

l'**écologie** FEM NOUN
ecology

écologique ADJECTIVE
ecological ◊ *une lessive écologique* an ecological washing powder

l'**économie** FEM NOUN
[1] economy ◊ *l'économie de la France* the French economy
[2] economics ◊ *un cours d'économie* an economics class

les **économies** FEM NOUN
savings
- **faire des économies** to save up ◊ *Je fais des économies pour partir en vacances.* I'm saving up for my holidays.

économique ADJECTIVE
[1] economic ◊ *une crise économique* an economic crisis
[2] economical ◊ *Il est plus économique d'acheter une grande boîte de lessive.* It's more economical to buy a large box of washing powder. ◊ *Cette petite voiture est économique.* This little car is cheap to run.

économiser VERB
to save

l'**économiseur d'écran** MASC NOUN
screen saver

l'**écorce** FEM NOUN
[1] bark (of tree)
[2] peel (of orange, lemon)

s'**écorcher** VERB
- **Je me suis écorché le genou.** I've grazed my knee.

écossais ADJECTIVE, NOUN (FEM SING **écossaise**)
[1] Scottish ◊ *Elle est écossaise.* She's Scottish.
- **un Écossais** a Scot (*man*)
- **une Écossaise** a Scot (*woman*)

- **les Écossais** the Scots
[2] tartan ◊ *une jupe écossaise* a tartan skirt

l'**Écosse** FEM NOUN
Scotland
- **en Écosse (1)** in Scotland ◊ *Il a passé une semaine en Écosse.* He spent a week in Scotland.
- **en Écosse (2)** to Scotland ◊ *Nous allons en Écosse l'été prochain.* We're going to Scotland next summer.

s'**écouler** VERB
[1] to flow out (*water*)
[2] to pass ◊ *Le temps s'écoule trop vite.* Time passes too quickly.

écouter VERB
to listen to ◊ *J'aime écouter de la musique.* I like listening to music.
- **Écoute-moi!** Listen!

l'**écouteur** MASC NOUN
earpiece (of phone)

l'**écran** MASC NOUN
screen
- **le petit écran** television
- **l'écran total** sunblock

écraser VERB
[1] to crush ◊ *Écrasez une gousse d'ail.* Crush a clove of garlic.
[2] to run over ◊ *Regarde bien avant de traverser, sinon tu vas te faire écraser.* Look carefully before you cross or you'll get run over.
- **s'écraser** to crash ◊ *L'avion s'est écrasé dans le désert.* The plane crashed in the desert.

écrémé ADJECTIVE
skimmed ◊ *le lait écrémé* skimmed milk

l'**écrevisse** FEM NOUN
crayfish

écrire VERB
to write ◊ *Nous nous écrivons régulièrement.* We write to each other regularly.
- **Ça s'écrit comment?** How do you spell that?

l'**écrit** MASC NOUN
written paper ◊ *L'écrit d'anglais a lieu la semaine prochaine.* The written paper in English is next week.
- **par écrit** in writing

l'**écriteau** MASC NOUN (PL les **écriteaux**)
notice

l'**écriture** FEM NOUN
writing ◊ *J'ai du mal à lire son écriture.* I can't read his writing.

l'**écrivain** MASC NOUN
writer ◊ *Elle est écrivain.* She's a writer.

E

Français ~ Anglais

l' **écrou** MASC NOUN
nut (*metal*)

s' **écrouler** VERB
to collapse

écru ADJECTIVE
off-white

l' **écureuil** MASC NOUN
squirrel

l' **écurie** FEM NOUN
stable

EDF FEM NOUN (= *Électricité de France*)
French electricity company

Édimbourg NOUN
Edinburgh

éditer VERB
to publish ◊ *On vient d'éditer un nouveau dictionnaire.* A new dictionary has just been published.

l' **éditeur** MASC NOUN
publisher

l' **édition** FEM NOUN
1 edition ◊ *une édition de poche* a paperback edition
2 publishing ◊ *Il travaille dans l'édition.* He works in publishing.

l' **édredon** MASC NOUN
eiderdown

l' **éducateur** MASC NOUN
teacher (*of people with special needs*)

éducatif ADJECTIVE (FEM SING **éducative**)
educational ◊ *un jeu éducatif* an educational game

l' **éducation** FEM NOUN
1 education ◊ *l'éducation physique* physical education ◊ *Il n'a pas beaucoup d'éducation.* He's not very well educated.
2 upbringing ◊ *Il a reçu une éducation très stricte.* He had a very strict upbringing.

l' **éducatrice** FEM NOUN
teacher (*of people with special needs*)

éduquer VERB
to educate

effacer VERB
to rub out

effarant ADJECTIVE
amazing ◊ *Il a mangé une quantité effarante de pain.* He ate an amazing amount of bread.

effectivement ADVERB
indeed ◊ *Il est effectivement plus rapide de passer par là.* It is indeed quicker to go this way. ◊ *Oui, effectivement.* Yes, indeed.
> Be careful! **effectivement** does not mean **effectively**.

effectuer VERB

1 to make ◊ *Ils ont effectué de nombreux changements.* They have made a lot of changes.
2 to do ◊ *On vient d'effectuer des travaux dans le bâtiment.* They have just done some work in the building.

effervescent ADJECTIVE
effervescent ◊ *un comprimé effervescent* an effervescent tablet

l' **effet** MASC NOUN
effect
♦ **faire de l'effet** to take effect ◊ *Ce médicament fait rapidement de l'effet.* This medicine takes effect quickly.
♦ **Ça m'a fait un drôle d'effet de le revoir.** It gave me a strange feeling to see him again.
♦ **en effet** yes indeed ◊ *Je ne me sens pas très bien. – En effet, tu as l'air pâle.* I don't feel very well. – Yes, you do look pale.

efficace ADJECTIVE
1 efficient ◊ *C'est une femme efficace.* She's an efficient woman.
2 effective ◊ *un médicament efficace* an effective medicine

s' **effondrer** VERB
to collapse

s' **efforcer** VERB
♦ **s'efforcer de faire quelque chose** to try hard to do something ◊ *Il s'efforce d'être aimable avec la clientèle.* He tries hard to be polite to the customers.

l' **effort** MASC NOUN
effort ◊ *faire un effort* to make an effort

effrayant ADJECTIVE
frightening

effrayer VERB
to frighten

effronté ADJECTIVE
cheeky ◊ *Ce gamin est vraiment effronté.* This kid's really cheeky.

effroyable ADJECTIVE
horrifying

égal ADJECTIVE (MASC PL **égaux**)
equal ◊ *une quantité égale de farine et de sucre* an equal quantity of flour and sugar
♦ **Ça m'est égal. (1)** I don't mind. ◊ *Tu préfères du riz ou des pâtes? – Ça m'est égal.* Would you rather have rice or pasta? – I don't mind.
♦ **Ça m'est égal. (2)** I don't care. ◊ *Fais ce que tu veux, ça m'est égal.* Do what you like, I don't care.

également ADVERB

also ◇ *On appelle également la France l'Hexagone à cause de sa forme.* France is also called the Hexagon because of its shape.

égaler VERB
to equal

l'**égalité** FEM NOUN
equality
♦**être à égalité** to be level ◇ *Maintenant les deux joueurs sont à égalité.* The two players are now level.

l'**égard** MASC NOUN
♦**à cet égard** in this respect

égarer VERB
to mislay ◇ *J'ai égaré mes clés.* I've mislaid my keys.
♦**s'égarer** to get lost ◇ *Ils se sont égarés dans la forêt.* They got lost in the forest.

l'**église** FEM NOUN
church ◇ *aller à l'église* to go to church

l'**égoïsme** MASC NOUN
selfishness

égoïste ADJECTIVE
selfish

l'**égout** MASC NOUN
sewer

l'**égratignure** FEM NOUN
scratch

l'**Égypte** FEM NOUN
Egypt

égyptien ADJECTIVE (FEM SING **égyptienne**)
Egyptian

l'**élan** MASC NOUN
♦**prendre de l'élan** to gather speed

s'**élancer** VERB
to hurl oneself

élargir VERB
to widen

l'**élastique** MASC NOUN
rubber band

l'**électeur** MASC NOUN
voter (*man*)

l'**élection** FEM NOUN
election ◇ *les élections présidentielles* the presidential election

l'**électrice** FEM NOUN
voter (*woman*)

l'**électricien** MASC NOUN
electrician

l'**électricité** FEM NOUN
electricity ◇ *une facture d'électricité* an electricity bill
♦**allumer l'électricité** to turn on the light
♦**éteindre l'électricité** to turn off the light

électrique ADJECTIVE
electric ◇ *le courant électrique* the electric current

l'**électronique** FEM NOUN
electronics

élégant ADJECTIVE
smart

élémentaire ADJECTIVE
elementary

l'**éléphant** MASC NOUN
elephant

l'**élevage** MASC NOUN
cattle rearing ◇ *faire de l'élevage* to rear cattle
♦**un élevage de porcs** a pig farm
♦**un élevage de poulets** a chicken farm
♦**les truites d'élevage** farmed trout

élevé ADJECTIVE
high ◇ *Le prix est trop élevé.* The price is too high.
♦**être bien élevé** to have good manners
♦**être mal élevé** to have bad manners

l'**élève** MASC/FEM NOUN
pupil

élever VERB
1 to bring up ◇ *Il a été élevé par sa grand-mère.* He was brought up by his grandmother.
2 to breed ◇ *Son oncle élève des chevaux.* His uncle breeds horses.
♦**élever la voix** to raise one's voice
♦**s'élever à** to come to ◇ *À combien s'élèvent les dégâts?* How much does the damage come to?

l'**éleveur** MASC NOUN
breeder

éliminatoire ADJECTIVE
♦**une note éliminatoire** a fail mark
♦**une épreuve éliminatoire** a qualifying round (*sport*)

éliminer VERB
to eliminate

élire VERB
to elect

elle PRONOUN
1 she ◇ *Elle est institutrice.* She is a primary school teacher.
2 her ◇ *Vous pouvez avoir confiance en elle.* You can trust her.
3 it ◇ *Prends cette chaise: elle est plus confortable.* Take this chair: it's more comfortable.
elle is also used for emphasis.
◇ *Elle, elle est toujours en retard!* Oh, SHE's always late!
♦**elle-même** herself ◇ *Elle l'a choisi elle-même.* She chose it herself.

elles PRONOUN

E

they ◇ *Où sont Anne et Rachel? – Elles sont allées au cinéma.* Where are Anne and Rachel? – They've gone to the cinema.
♦ **elles-mêmes** themselves

élogieux ADJECTIVE (FEM SING **élogieuse**)
  complimentary ◇ *Ton professeur a été très élogieux à propos de ton travail.* Your teacher was very complimentary about your work.

éloigné ADJECTIVE
  distant

s'**éloigner** VERB
  to go far away ◇ *Ne vous éloignez pas: le dîner est bientôt prêt!* Don't go far away: dinner will soon be ready!
♦ **Vous vous éloignez du sujet.** You are getting off the point.

l'**Élysée** MASC NOUN
  Elysée Palace

> ❶ The **Élysée** is the residence of the French president.

l'**e-mail** MASC NOUN
  email

l'**emballage** MASC NOUN
  ♦ **le papier d'emballage** wrapping paper

emballer VERB
  to wrap
  ♦ **s'emballer** (*informal*) to get excited ◇ *Il s'est emballé pour ce projet.* He got really excited about this plan.

l'**embarquement** MASC NOUN
  boarding ◇ *"embarquement immédiat"* "now boarding" ◇ *L'embarquement des passagers n'a pas encore été annoncé.* Passenger boarding has not been announced yet.

l'**embarras** MASC NOUN
  embarrassment ◇ *Votre question me met dans l'embarras.* It's difficult for me to answer your question.
  ♦ **Vous n'avez que l'embarras du choix.** The only problem is choosing.

embarrassant ADJECTIVE
  embarrassing

embarrasser VERB
  to embarrass ◇ *Cela m'embarrasse de vous demander encore un service.* I feel embarrassed to ask you to do something more for me.

embaucher VERB
  to take on ◇ *L'entreprise vient d'embaucher cinquante ouvriers.* The firm has just taken on fifty workers.

embêtant ADJECTIVE
  annoying

les **embêtements** MASC NOUN
  trouble SING

embêter VERB
  to bother
  ♦ **s'embêter** to be bored ◇ *Qu'est-ce qu'on s'embête ici!* Isn't it boring here!

l'**embouteillage** MASC NOUN
  traffic jam

embrasser VERB
  to kiss ◇ *Ils se sont embrassés.* They kissed each other.

s'**embrouiller** VERB
  to get confused ◇ *Il s'embrouille dans ses explications.* He gets confused when he explains things.

émerveiller VERB
  to dazzle

l'**émeute** FEM NOUN
  riot

émigrer VERB
  to emigrate

l'**émission** FEM NOUN
  programme ◇ *une émission de télévision* a TV programme

s'**emmêler** VERB
  to get tangled ◇ *Ma laine s'est emmêlée.* My wool has got tangled.

emménager VERB
  to move in ◇ *Nous venons d'emménager dans une nouvelle maison.* We've just moved into a new house.

emmener VERB
  to take ◇ *Ils m'ont emmené au cinéma pour mon anniversaire.* They took me to the cinema for my birthday.

emmerder VERB (*rude*)
  ♦ **Ça m'emmerde!** It pisses me off!
  ♦ **Je t'emmerde!** Piss off!
  ♦ **s'emmerder** to be bored stiff

l'**émoticon** MASC NOUN
  smiley (*computing*)

émotif ADJECTIVE (FEM SING **émotive**)
  emotional ◇ *Il est très émotif.* He's very emotional.

l'**émotion** FEM NOUN
  emotion

émouvoir VERB
  to move ◇ *Sa lettre l'a beaucoup émue.* She was deeply moved by his letter.

emparer VERB
  ♦ **s'emparer de** to grab ◇ *Il s'est emparé de ma valise.* He grabbed my case.

l'**empêchement** MASC NOUN
♦**Nous avons eu un empêchement de dernière minute.** We were held up at the last minute.

empêcher VERB
to prevent ◊ *Le café le soir m'empêche de dormir.* Coffee at night keeps me awake.
♦**Il n'a pas pu s'empêcher de rire.** He couldn't help laughing.

l'**empereur** MASC NOUN
emperor

s'**empiffrer** VERB (*informal*)
to stuff one's face ◊ *Arrête de t'empiffrer!* Stop stuffing your face!

empiler VERB
to pile up

empirer VERB
to worsen ◊ *La situation a encore empiré.* The situation got even worse.

l'**emplacement** MASC NOUN
site ◊ *Un panneau indique l'emplacement du château.* A sign shows the site of the castle.

l'**emploi** MASC NOUN
1 use ◊ *prêt à l'emploi* ready for use
♦**le mode d'emploi** directions for use
2 job ◊ *la création d'emplois* job creation
♦**un emploi du temps** a timetable

l'**employé** MASC NOUN
employee
♦**un employé de bureau** an office worker

l'**employée** FEM NOUN
employee
♦**une employée de banque** a bank clerk

employer VERB
1 to use ◊ *Quelle méthode employez-vous?* What method do you use?
2 to employ ◊ *L'entreprise emploie dix ingénieurs.* The firm employs ten engineers.

l'**employeur** MASC NOUN
employer

empoisonner VERB
to poison

emporter VERB
to take ◊ *N'emportez que le strict nécessaire.* Only take the bare minimum.
♦**plats à emporter** take-away meals
♦**s'emporter** to lose one's temper ◊ *Je m'emporte facilement et finis souvent par le regretter.* I'm quick to lose my

temper and I'm often sorry afterwards.

l'**empreinte** FEM NOUN
♦**une empreinte digitale** a fingerprint

s'**empresser** VERB
♦**s'empresser de faire quelque chose** to be quick to do something ◊ *Ils se sont empressés de nous annoncer la nouvelle.* They were quick to tell us the news.

emprisonner VERB
to imprison

l'**emprunt** MASC NOUN
loan

emprunter VERB
to borrow
♦**emprunter quelque chose à quelqu'un** to borrow something from somebody ◊ *Est-ce que je peux t'emprunter dix francs?* Can I borrow ten francs from you?

ému ADJECTIVE
touched ◊ *J'ai été très ému par sa gentillesse.* I was very touched by her kindness.

en PREPOSITION, PRONOUN
1 in ◊ *Il habite en France.* He lives in France. ◊ *La mariée est en blanc.* The bride is in white. ◊ *Je le verrai en mai.* I'll see him in May.
2 to ◊ *Je vais en France cet été.* I'm going to France this summer.
3 by ◊ *C'est plus rapide en voiture.* It's quicker by car.
4 made of ◊ *C'est en verre.* It's made of glass. ◊ *un collier en argent* a silver necklace
5 while ◊ *Il s'est coupé le doigt en ouvrant une boîte de conserve.* He cut his finger while opening a tin.
♦**Elle est sortie en courant.** She ran out.

When en is used with avoir and il y a, it is not translated in English.
◊ *Est-ce que tu as un dictionnaire? – Oui, j'en ai un.* Have you got a dictionary? – Yes, I've got one.
◊ *Combien d'élèves y a-t-il dans ta classe? – Il y en a trente.* How many pupils are there in your class? – There are 30.

en is also used with verbs and expressions normally followed by de to avoid repeating the same word.
◊ *Si tu as un problème, tu peux m'en parler.* If you've got a problem, you can talk about it with me. ◊ *Est-ce que tu peux me rendre ce livre? J'en ai besoin.* Can you give me back that book? I need it. ◊ *Il a un beau jardin*

et il en est très fier. He's got a beautiful garden and is very proud of it.

♦ **J'en ai assez.** I've had enough.

enceinte ADJECTIVE
pregnant ◊ *Elle est enceinte de six mois.* She's 6 months pregnant.

enchanté ADJECTIVE
delighted ◊ *Ma mère est enchantée de sa nouvelle voiture.* My mother's delighted with her new car.

♦ **Enchanté!** Pleased to meet you!

encombrant ADJECTIVE
bulky

encombrer VERB
to clutter

encore ADVERB
[1] still ◊ *Il est encore au travail.* He's still at work. ◊ *Il reste encore deux morceaux de gâteau.* There are two bits of cake left.
[2] even ◊ *C'est encore mieux.* That's even better.
[3] again ◊ *Il m'a encore demandé de l'argent.* He asked me for money again.

♦ **encore une fois** once again
♦ **pas encore** not yet ◊ *Je n'ai pas encore fini.* I haven't finished yet.

encourager VERB
to encourage

l' **encre** FEM NOUN
ink

l' **encyclopédie** FEM NOUN
encyclopaedia

l' **endive** FEM NOUN
chicory

endommager VERB
to damage

endormi ADJECTIVE
asleep

endormir VERB
to deaden ◊ *Cette piqûre sert à endormir le nerf.* This injection is to deaden the nerve.

♦ **s'endormir** to go to sleep

l' **endroit** MASC NOUN
place ◊ *C'est un endroit très tranquille.* It's a very quiet place.

♦ **à l'endroit (1)** the right way out
♦ **à l'endroit (2)** the right way up

endurant ADJECTIVE
tough (*person*)

endurcir VERB
to toughen up ◊ *Ces exercices servent à endurcir les soldats.* These exercises are to toughen up the soldiers.

♦ **s'endurcir** to become hardened

endurer VERB
to endure

l' **énergie** FEM NOUN
[1] energy ◊ *Je n'ai pas beaucoup d'énergie ce matin.* I haven't got much energy this morning.
[2] power ◊ *l'énergie nucléaire* nuclear power

♦ **avec énergie** vigorously ◊ *Il a protesté avec énergie.* He protested vigorously.

énergique ADJECTIVE
energetic ◊ *C'est une femme très énergique.* She's a very energetic woman.

♦ **des mesures énergiques** strong measures

énerver VERB
♦ **Il m'énerve!** He gets on my nerves!
♦ **Ce bruit m'énerve.** This noise gets on my nerves.
♦ **s'énerver** to get worked up
♦ **Ne t'énerve pas!** Take it easy!

l' **enfance** FEM NOUN
childhood

♦ **Je le connais depuis l'enfance.** I've known him since I was a child.

l' **enfant** MASC/FEM NOUN
child

l' **enfer** MASC NOUN
hell

s' **enfermer** VERB
♦ **Il s'est enfermé dans sa chambre.** He shut himself up in his bedroom.

enfiler VERB
[1] to put on ◊ *J'ai rapidement enfilé un pull avant de sortir.* I quickly put on a sweater before going out.
[2] to thread ◊ *J'ai du mal à enfiler cette aiguille.* I am having difficulty threading this needle.

enfin ADVERB
at last ◊ *J'ai enfin réussi à le joindre.* I have at last managed to contact him.

enflé ADJECTIVE
swollen

enfler VERB
to swell

enfoncer VERB
♦ **Il marchait, les mains enfoncées dans les poches.** He was walking with his hands thrust into his pockets.
♦ **s'enfoncer** to sink ◊ *Les roues de la voiture s'enfonçaient dans la boue.* The wheels of the car were sinking into the mud.

s' **enfuir** VERB
to run off

l' **engagement** MASC NOUN
  commitment

engager VERB
  to take on (*person*) ◊ *engager
  quelqu'un* to take somebody on

s' **engager** VERB
  to commit oneself ◊ *Le Premier
  ministre s'est engagé à combattre le
  chômage.* The Prime Minister has
  committed himself to fighting
  unemployment.
  ♦ **Il s'est engagé dans l'armée à dix-
  huit ans.** He joined the army when
  he was 18.

les **engelures** FEM NOUN
  chilblains

l' **engin** MASC NOUN
  device
  *Be careful! The French word **engin**
  does not mean **engine**.*

s' **engourdir** VERB
  to go numb ◊ *Mes doigts se sont
  engourdis avec le froid.* My fingers
  have gone numb with the cold.

engueuler VERB (*informal*)
  ♦ **engueuler quelqu'un** to tell somebody
  off ◊ *Tu vas te faire engueuler!*
  You're going to get a telling-off!

l' **énigme** FEM NOUN
  riddle

s' **enivrer** VERB
  to get drunk

enjamber VERB
  to stride over ◊ *enjamber une
  barrière* to stride over a fence

l' **enlèvement** MASC NOUN
  kidnapping

enlever VERB
  [1] to take off ◊ *Enlève donc ton
  manteau!* Take off your coat!
  [2] to kidnap ◊ *Un groupe terroriste a
  enlevé la femme de l'ambassadeur.* A
  terrorist group has kidnapped the
  ambassador's wife.

enneigé ADJECTIVE
  snowed up ◊ *Les routes sont encore
  enneigées.* The roads are still snowed
  up.

l' **ennemi** MASC NOUN
  enemy

l' **ennemie** FEM NOUN
  enemy

l' **ennui** MASC NOUN
  [1] boredom
  ♦ **C'est à mourir d'ennui.** It's enough to
  bore you to death.
  [2] problem ◊ *avoir des ennuis* to
  have problems

ennuyer VERB

  to bother ◊ *J'espère que cela ne
  vous ennuie pas trop.* I hope it
  doesn't bother you too much.
  ♦ **s'ennuyer** to be bored

ennuyeux ADJECTIVE (FEM SING **ennuyeuse**)
  [1] boring
  [2] awkward ◊ *Tu ne peux pas venir
  plus tôt? C'est bien ennuyeux.* You
  can't come any earlier? That's rather
  awkward.

énorme ADJECTIVE
  huge

énormément ADVERB
  ♦ **Il a énormément grossi.** He's got
  terribly fat.
  ♦ **Il y a énormément de neige.** There's
  an enormous amount of snow.

l' **enquête** FEM NOUN
  [1] investigation ◊ *La police a ouvert
  une enquête.* The police have begun
  an investigation.
  [2] survey ◊ *une enquête parmi les
  étudiants a montré que ...* a survey of
  students has shown that ...

enquêter VERB
  to investigate ◊ *La police enquête
  actuellement sur le crime.* The police
  are currently investigating the crime.

enrageant ADJECTIVE
  infuriating

enrager VERB
  to be furious ◊ *J'enrage de n'avoir
  pas pu profiter de cette occasion.* I'm
  furious I wasn't able to take
  advantage of this opportunity.

l' **enregistrement** MASC NOUN
  recording
  ♦ **l'enregistrement des bagages**
  baggage check-in

enregistrer VERB
  [1] to record ◊ *Ils viennent
  d'enregistrer un nouvel album.*
  They've just recorded a new album.
  [2] to check in ◊ *Vous pouvez
  enregistrer plusieurs valises.* You can
  check in several cases.

s' **enrhumer** VERB
  to catch a cold ◊ *Je suis enrhumé.*
  I've got a cold.

s' **enrichir** VERB
  to get rich

enrouler VERB
  to wind ◊ *Enroulez le fil autour de la
  bobine.* Wind the thread round the
  bobbin.

l' **enseignant** MASC NOUN
  teacher

l' **enseignante** FEM NOUN
  teacher

E

l' **enseignement** MASC NOUN
[1] education ◊ *les réformes de l'enseignement* education reforms
[2] teaching ◊ *l'enseignement des langues étrangères* the teaching of foreign languages

enseigner VERB
to teach ◊ *Mon père enseigne les maths dans un lycée.* My father teaches maths in a secondary school.

ensemble ADVERB
| *see also* **ensemble** NOUN |
together ◊ *tous ensemble* all together

l' **ensemble** MASC NOUN
| *see also* **ensemble** ADVERB |
outfit ◊ *Elle portait un ensemble vert.* She was wearing a green outfit.
♦ **l'ensemble de** the whole of ◊ *L'ensemble du personnel est en grève.* The whole workforce is on strike.
♦ **dans l'ensemble** on the whole

ensoleillé ADJECTIVE
sunny

ensuite ADVERB
then ◊ *Nous sommes allés au cinéma et ensuite au restaurant.* We went to the cinema and then to a restaurant.

entamer VERB
to start ◊ *Qui a entamé le gâteau?* Who's started the cake?

s' **entasser** VERB
to cram ◊ *Ils se sont tous entassés dans ma voiture.* They all crammed into my car.

entendre VERB
[1] to hear ◊ *Je ne t'entends pas.* I can't hear you.
♦ **J'ai entendu dire qu'il est dangereux de nager ici.** I've heard that it's dangerous to swim here.
[2] to mean ◊ *Qu'est-ce que tu entends par là?* What do you mean by that?
♦ **s'entendre** to get on ◊ *Il s'entend bien avec sa sœur.* He gets on well with his sister.

entendu ADJECTIVE
♦ **C'est entendu!** Agreed! ◊ *Je passerai te prendre à sept heures, c'est entendu.* That's agreed then, I'll pick you up at 7 o'clock.
♦ **bien entendu** of course ◊ *Il est bien entendu que je n'en parlerai à personne.* I won't tell anybody about it of course.

l' **enterrement** MASC NOUN
funeral (*burial*)

enterrer VERB

to bury

entêté ADJECTIVE
stubborn

s' **entêter** VERB
to persist ◊ *Il s'entête à refuser de voir le médecin.* He persists in refusing to go to the doctor.

l' **enthousiasme** MASC NOUN
enthusiasm

s' **enthousiasmer** VERB
to get enthusiastic ◊ *Il s'enthousiasme facilement.* He gets very enthusiastic about things.

entier ADJECTIVE (FEM SING **entière**)
whole ◊ *Il a mangé une quiche entière.* He ate a whole quiche. ◊ *Je n'ai pas lu le livre en entier.* I haven't read the whole book.
♦ **le lait entier** full fat milk

entièrement ADVERB
completely

l' **entorse** FEM NOUN
sprain ◊ *Il s'est fait une entorse à la cheville.* He's sprained his ankle.

entourer VERB
to surround ◊ *Le jardin est entouré d'un mur de pierres.* The garden is surrounded by a stone wall.

l' **entracte** MASC NOUN
interval

l' **entraînement** MASC NOUN
training

entraîner VERB
[1] to lead ◊ *Il se laisse facilement entraîner par les autres.* He's easily led.
[2] to train ◊ *Il entraîne l'équipe de France depuis cinq ans.* He's been training the French team for five years.
[3] to involve ◊ *Un mariage entraîne beaucoup de dépenses.* A wedding involves a lot of expense.
♦ **s'entraîner** to train ◊ *Il s'entraîne au foot tous les samedis matins.* He does football training every Saturday morning.

l' **entraîneur** MASC NOUN
trainer

entre PREPOSITION
between ◊ *Il est assis entre son père et son oncle.* He's sitting between his father and his uncle.
♦ **entre eux** among themselves
♦ **l'un d'entre eux** one of them

l' **entrecôte** FEM NOUN
rib steak

l' **entrée** FEM NOUN
[1] entrance

E

2 starter (*of meal*) ◊ *Qu'est ce que vous prenez comme entrée?* What would you like for the starter?

entreprendre VERB
to start on ◊ *Elle a entrepris des démarches pour adopter un enfant.* She's started on the procedures for adopting a child.

l' **entrepreneur** MASC NOUN
contractor

l' **entreprise** FEM NOUN
firm

entrer VERB
1 to come in ◊ *Entrez donc!* Come on in!
2 to go in ◊ *Ils sont tous entrés dans la maison.* They all went into the house.
♦ **entrer à l'hôpital** to go into hospital
♦ **entrer des données** to enter data ◊ *J'ai entré toutes les adresses de mon agenda sur mon ordinateur.* I've entered all the addresses in my diary onto my computer.

entre-temps ADVERB
meanwhile

l' **entretien** MASC NOUN
1 maintenance ◊ *un contrat d'entretien* a maintenance contract
2 interview ◊ *On m'a convoqué à un entretien pour un travail.* I've been called for a job interview.

l' **entrevue** FEM NOUN
interview ◊ *une entrevue avec le ministre* an interview with the minister

entrouvert ADJECTIVE
half-open ◊ *La porte était entrouverte.* The door was half open.

envahir VERB
to invade

l' **enveloppe** FEM NOUN
envelope

envelopper VERB
to wrap

envers PREPOSITION
see also **envers** NOUN
towards ◊ *Il est bien disposé envers elle.* He's well disposed towards her. ◊ *son attitude envers moi* his attitude to me

l' **envers** MASC NOUN
see also **envers** PREPOSITION
♦ **à l'envers** inside out ◊ *Je dois repasser ce chemisier à l'envers.* I have to iron this blouse inside out.

l' **envie** FEM NOUN
♦ **avoir envie de faire quelque chose** to feel like doing something ◊ *J'avais*

envie de pleurer. I felt like crying. ◊ *J'ai envie d'aller aux toilettes.* I want to go to the toilet.
♦ **Cette glace me fait envie.** I fancy some of that ice cream.

envier VERB
to envy

environ ADVERB
about ◊ *C'est à soixante kilomètres environ.* It's about 60 kilometres.

l' **environnement** MASC NOUN
environment

les **environs** MASC NOUN
area SING ◊ *les environs de Nantes* the Nantes area ◊ *Il y a beaucoup de choses intéressantes à voir dans les environs.* There are a lot of interesting things to see in the area.
♦ **aux environs de dix-neuf heures** around 7 p.m.

envisager VERB
to consider ◊ *Est-ce que vous envisagez de travailler à l'étranger?* Are you considering working abroad?

s' **envoler** VERB
1 to fly away ◊ *Le papillon s'est envolé.* The butterfly flew away.
2 to blow away ◊ *Toutes mes feuilles de cours se sont envolées.* All my lecture notes blew away.

envoyer VERB
to send ◊ *Ma tante m'a envoyé une carte pour mon anniversaire.* My aunt sent me a card for my birthday.
♦ **envoyer quelqu'un chercher quelque chose** to send somebody to get something ◊ *Sa mère l'a envoyé chercher du pain.* His mother sent him to get some bread.
♦ **envoyer un e-mail à quelqu'un** to send sb an email

épais ADJECTIVE (FEM SING **épaisse**)
thick

l' **épaisseur** FEM NOUN
thickness

épatant ADJECTIVE (*informal*)
great ◊ *C'est un type épatant.* He's a great guy.

l' **épaule** FEM NOUN
shoulder

l' **épée** FEM NOUN
sword

épeler VERB
to spell ◊ *Est-ce que vous pouvez épeler votre nom s'il vous plaît?* Can you spell your name please?

l' **épice** FEM NOUN
spice

épicé ADJECTIVE

☞

spicy ◊ *Ce n'est pas assez épicé pour moi: je trouve ça trop fade.* It's not spicy enough for me: I think it's too bland.

l'**épicerie** FEM NOUN
grocer's shop

l'**épicier** MASC NOUN
grocer

l'**épicière** FEM NOUN
grocer

l'**épidémie** FEM NOUN
epidemic

épiler VERB
◆**s'épiler les jambes** to shave one's legs
◆**s'épiler les sourcils** to pluck one's eyebrows

les **épinards** MASC NOUN
spinach SING

l'**épine** FEM NOUN
thorn

l'**épingle** FEM NOUN
pin
◆**une épingle de sûreté** a safety pin

l'**épisode** MASC NOUN
episode

éplucher VERB
to peel

l'**éponge** FEM NOUN
sponge

l'**époque** FEM NOUN
time ◊ *à cette époque de l'année* at this time of year
◆**à l'époque** at that time ◊ *À l'époque, beaucoup de gens n'avaient pas l'eau courante.* At that time a lot of people didn't have running water.

l'**épouse** FEM NOUN
wife

épouser VERB
to marry

épouvantable ADJECTIVE
awful

l'**épouvante** FEM NOUN
terror
◆**un film d'épouvante** a horror film

épouvanter VERB
to terrify

l'**époux** MASC NOUN
husband
◆**les nouveaux époux** the newly-weds

l'**épreuve** FEM NOUN
1 test ◊ *une épreuve orale* an oral test ◊ *une épreuve écrite* a written test
2 event (*sport*)

éprouver VERB
to feel ◊ *Qu'est-ce que vous avez éprouvé à ce moment-là?* What did you feel at that moment?

l'**EPS** FEM NOUN (= *éducation physique et sportive*)
PE (= physical education)

épuisé ADJECTIVE
exhausted

épuiser VERB
to wear out ◊ *Ce travail m'a complètement épuisé.* This job has completely worn me out.
◆**s'épuiser** to wear oneself out ◊ *Il s'épuise à garder un jardin impeccable.* He wears himself out keeping his garden immaculate.

l'**Équateur** MASC NOUN
Ecuador

l'**équateur** MASC NOUN
equator

l'**équation** FEM NOUN
equation

l'**équerre** FEM NOUN
set square

l'**équilibre** MASC NOUN
balance ◊ *J'ai failli perdre l'équilibre.* I nearly lost my balance.

équilibré ADJECTIVE
well-balanced

l'**équipage** MASC NOUN
crew

l'**équipe** FEM NOUN
team

équipé ADJECTIVE
◆**bien équipé** well-equipped

l'**équipement** MASC NOUN
equipment

les **équipements** MASC NOUN
facilities ◊ *les équipements sportifs* sports facilities

l'**équitation** FEM NOUN
riding ◊ *faire de l'équitation* to go riding

l'**équivalent** MASC NOUN
equivalent

l'**erreur** FEM NOUN
mistake
◆**faire erreur** to be mistaken

es VERB *see* **être**
◆**Tu es très gentille.** You're very kind.

l'**ESB** FEM NOUN (= *encéphalite spongiforme bovine*)
BSE

l'**escabeau** MASC NOUN (PL les **escabeaux**)
stepladder

l'**escalade** FEM NOUN
climbing ◊ *faire de l'escalade* to go climbing

escalader VERB
to climb

l' **escale** FEM NOUN
  ♦ **faire escale** to stop off

l' **escalier** MASC NOUN
  stairs
  ♦ **un escalier roulant** an escalator

l' **escargot** MASC NOUN
  snail

l' **esclavage** MASC NOUN
  slavery

l' **esclave** MASC/FEM NOUN
  slave

l' **escrime** FEM NOUN
  fencing

l' **escroc** MASC NOUN
  crook

l' **espace** MASC NOUN
  space
  ♦ **espace de travail** workspace

s' **espacer** VERB
  to become less frequent ◊ *Ses visites se sont peu à peu espacées.* His visits became less and less frequent.

l' **espadrille** FEM NOUN
  rope-soled sandal

l' **Espagne** FEM NOUN
  Spain
  ♦ **en Espagne (1)** in Spain
  ♦ **en Espagne (2)** to Spain

espagnol ADJECTIVE, NOUN
  Spanish ◊ *J'apprends l'espagnol.* I'm learning Spanish.
  ♦ **un Espagnol** a Spaniard (*man*)
  ♦ **une Espagnole** a Spaniard (*woman*)

l' **espèce** FEM NOUN
  [1] sort ◊ *Elle portait une espèce de cape en velours.* She was wearing a sort of velvet cloak.
  [2] species ◊ *une espèce en voie de disparition* an endangered species
  ♦ **Espèce d'idiot!** You idiot!

les **espèces** FEM NOUN
  cash SING ◊ *payer en espèces* to pay cash

espérer VERB
  to hope
  ♦ **J'espère bien.** I hope so. ◊ *Tu penses avoir réussi? – Oui, j'espère bien.* Do you think you've passed? – Yes, I hope so.

espiègle ADJECTIVE
  mischievous

l' **espion** MASC NOUN
  spy

l' **espionnage** MASC NOUN
  spying
  ♦ **un roman d'espionnage** a spy novel

l' **espionne** FEM NOUN
  spy

l' **espoir** MASC NOUN
  hope

l' **esprit** MASC NOUN
  mind ◊ *Ça ne m'est pas venu à l'esprit.* It didn't cross my mind.
  ♦ **avoir de l'esprit** to be witty ◊ *Il a beaucoup d'esprit.* He's very witty.

l' **esquimau** ® MASC NOUN (PL les **esquimaux**)
  ice lolly

l' **Esquimau** MASC NOUN (PL les **Esquimaux**)
  Eskimo

l' **Esquimaude** FEM NOUN
  Eskimo

l' **essai** MASC NOUN
  attempt ◊ *Ce n'est pas mal pour un coup d'essai.* It's not bad for a first attempt.
  ♦ **prendre quelqu'un à l'essai** to take somebody on for a trial period

essayer VERB
  [1] to try ◊ *Essaie de rentrer de bonne heure.* Try to come home early.
  [2] to try on ◊ *Essaie ce pull: il devrait bien t'aller.* Try this sweater on: it ought to look good on you.

l' **essence** FEM NOUN
  petrol

essentiel ADJECTIVE (FEM SING **essentielle**)
  essential
  ♦ **Tu es là: c'est l'essentiel.** You're here: that's the main thing.

s' **essouffler** VERB
  to get out of breath

l' **essuie-glace** MASC NOUN
  windscreen wiper

essuyer VERB
  to wipe
  ♦ **essuyer la vaisselle** to dry the dishes
  ♦ **s'essuyer** to dry oneself ◊ *Vous pouvez vous essuyer les mains avec cette serviette.* You can dry your hands on this towel.

est VERB *see* **être**
  see also **est** ADJECTIVE, NOUN
  ♦ **Elle est merveilleuse.** She's marvellous.

est ADJECTIVE
  see also **est** VERB, NOUN
  [1] east ◊ *la côte est des États-Unis* the east coast of the United States
  [2] eastern ◊ *dans la partie est du pays* in the eastern part of the country

l' **est** MASC NOUN
  see also **est** VERB, ADJECTIVE

E

☞

east ◊ *Je vis dans l'est de la France.* I live in the East of France.
♦ **vers l'est** eastwards
♦ **à l'est de Paris** east of Paris
♦ **l'Europe de l'Est** Eastern Europe
♦ **le vent d'est** the east wind

est-ce que ADVERB
♦ **Est-ce que c'est cher?** Is it expensive?
♦ **Quand est-ce qu'il part?** When is he leaving?

l' **esthéticienne** FEM NOUN
beautician

l' **estime** FEM NOUN
♦ **J'ai beaucoup d'estime pour elle.** I think a lot of her.

estimer VERB
♦ **estimer quelqu'un** to have great respect for somebody ◊ *Mon père l'estime beaucoup.* My father has a lot of respect for him.
♦ **estimer que** to consider that ◊ *J'estime que c'est de sa faute.* I consider that it's his fault.

l' **estivant** MASC NOUN
holiday-maker

l' **estivante** FEM NOUN
holiday-maker

l' **estomac** MASC NOUN
stomach

l' **Estonie** FEM NOUN
Estonia

l' **estrade** FEM NOUN
platform

et CONJUNCTION
and

établir VERB
to establish
♦ **s'établir à son compte** to set up in business

l' **établissement** MASC NOUN
establishment
♦ **un établissement scolaire** a school

l' **étage** MASC NOUN
floor ◊ *au premier étage* on the first floor
♦ **à l'étage** upstairs

l' **étagère** FEM NOUN
shelf

étaient VERB see **être**

l' **étain** MASC NOUN
tin

étais, était VERB see **être**
♦ **Il était très jeune.** He was very young.

l' **étalage** MASC NOUN
display

étaler VERB

to spread ◊ *Il a étalé la carte sur la table.* He spread the map on the table.

étanche ADJECTIVE
[1] watertight ◊ *Le toit n'est pas étanche.* The roof isn't watertight.
[2] waterproof (*watch*)

l' **étang** MASC NOUN
pond

étant VERB see **être**
♦ **Mes revenus étant limités** ... My income being limited ...

l' **étape** FEM NOUN
stage ◊ *une étape importante de la vie* an important stage in life
♦ **faire étape** to stop off

l' **État** MASC NOUN
state (*nation*) ◊ *un chef d'État* a head of state

l' **état** MASC NOUN
[1] state (*country*)
[2] condition ◊ *en bon état* in good condition ◊ *en mauvais état* in poor condition
♦ **remettre quelque chose en état** to repair something
♦ **le bureau d'état civil** the registry office

les **États-Unis** MASC NOUN
United States
♦ **aux États-Unis (1)** in the United States
♦ **aux États-Unis (2)** to the United States

été VERB see **être**
see also **été** NOUN
♦ **Il a été licencié.** He's been made redundant.

l' **été** MASC NOUN
see also **été** VERB
summer
♦ **en été** in the summer

éteindre VERB
[1] to switch off ◊ *N'oubliez pas d'éteindre la lumière en sortant.* Don't forget to switch off the light when you leave.
[2] to put out (*cigarette*)

étendre VERB
to spread ◊ *Elle a étendu une nappe propre sur la table.* She spread a clean cloth on the table.
♦ **étendre le linge** to hang out the washing
♦ **s'étendre** to lie down ◊ *Je vais m'étendre cinq minutes.* I'm going to lie down for five minutes.

l' **éternité** FEM NOUN

◆**J'ai attendu une éternité chez le médecin.** I waited for ages at the doctor's.

éternuer VERB
to sneeze

êtes VERB *see* **être**
◆**Vous êtes en retard.** You're late.

étiez VERB *see* **être**

étinceler VERB
to sparkle

étions VERB *see* **être**

l'**étiquette** FEM NOUN
label ◊ *L'étiquette du pot de confiture s'est décollée.* The label has come off the jam pot.

s'**étirer** VERB
to stretch ◊ *Elle s'est étirée paresseusement.* She stretched lazily.

l'**étoile** FEM NOUN
star
◆**une étoile de mer** a starfish
◆**une étoile filante** a shooting star
◆**dormir à la belle étoile** to sleep under the stars

étonnant ADJECTIVE
amazing

étonner VERB
to surprise ◊ *Cela m'étonnerait que le colis soit déjà arrivé.* I'd be surprised if the parcel had arrived yet.

étouffer VERB
◆**On étouffe ici: ouvre donc les fenêtres.** It's stifling in here: open the windows.
◆**s'étouffer** to choke ◊ *Ne mange pas si vite: tu vas t'étouffer!* Don't eat so fast: you'll choke!

l'**étourderie** FEM NOUN
absent-mindedness
◆**une erreur d'étourderie** a slip

étourdi ADJECTIVE
scatterbrained

l'**étourdissement** MASC NOUN
◆**avoir des étourdissements** to feel dizzy

étrange ADJECTIVE
strange

étranger ADJECTIVE (FEM SING **étrangère**)
see also **étranger** NOUN
foreign ◊ *un pays étranger* a foreign country
◆**une personne étrangère** a stranger

l'**étranger** MASC NOUN
see also **étranger** ADJECTIVE
1 foreigner
2 stranger
◆**à l'étranger** abroad

l'**étrangère** FEM NOUN
1 foreigner
2 stranger

étrangler VERB
to strangle
◆**s'étrangler** to choke ◊ *s'étrangler avec quelque chose* to choke on something

l'**être** MASC NOUN
see also **être** VERB
◆**un être humain** a human being

être VERB
see also **être** NOUN

Present tense:
je suis	nous sommes
tu es	vous êtes
il/elle est	ils/elles sont

Past participle:
été

1 to be ◊ *Je suis heureux.* I'm happy. ◊ *Mon père est instituteur.* My father's a primary school teacher. ◊ *Il est dix heures.* It's 10 o'clock.
2 to have ◊ *Il n'est pas encore arrivé.* He hasn't arrived yet.

les **étrennes** FEM NOUN
◆**Nous avons donné des étrennes à la gardienne.** We gave the caretaker a New Year gift.

étroit ADJECTIVE
narrow
◆**être à l'étroit** to be cramped ◊ *Nous sommes un peu à l'étroit dans cet appartement.* We're a bit cramped in this flat.

l'**étude** FEM NOUN
study ◊ *une étude de cas* a case study
◆**faire des études** to be studying ◊ *Il fait des études de droit.* He's studying law.

l'**étudiant** MASC NOUN
student

l'**étudiante** FEM NOUN
student

étudier VERB
to study

l'**étui** MASC NOUN
case ◊ *un étui à lunettes* a glasses case

eu VERB *see* **avoir**
◆**J'ai eu une bonne note.** I got a good mark.

euh EXCLAMATION
er ◊ *Euh ... je ne m'en souviens pas.* Er ... I can't remember.

l'**euro** MASC NOUN
euro (*currency*)

l'**Europe** FEM NOUN
Europe
♦ **en Europe (1)** in Europe
♦ **en Europe (2)** to Europe

européen ADJECTIVE (FEM SING **européenne**)
European

eux PRONOUN
them ◊ *Je pense souvent à eux.* I
often think of them.
eux is also used for emphasis.
◊ *Elle a accepté l'invitation, mais eux
ont refusé.* She accepted the
invitation, but THEY refused.

évacuer VERB
to evacuate

s'**évader** VERB
to escape

l'**évangile** MASC NOUN
gospel

s'**évanouir** VERB
to faint

s'**évaporer** VERB
to evaporate

évasif ADJECTIVE (FEM SING **évasive**)
evasive

l'**évasion** FEM NOUN
escape ◊ *Ils ont préparé leur évasion
pendant des mois.* They spent
months planning their escape.

éveillé ADJECTIVE
[1] awake ◊ *Il est resté éveillé toute la
nuit.* He stayed awake all night.
[2] bright ◊ *C'est un enfant très
éveillé pour son âge.* He's very bright
for his age.

s'**éveiller** VERB
to awaken

l'**événement** MASC NOUN
event

l'**éventail** MASC NOUN
fan (*hand-held*)
♦ **un large éventail de prix** a wide
range of prices

l'**éventualité** FEM NOUN
♦ **dans l'éventualité d'un retard** in the
event of a delay

éventuel ADJECTIVE (FEM SING **éventuelle**)
possible ◊ *une solution éventuelle* a
possible solution ◊ *les conséquences
éventuelles* the possible
consequences
Be careful! *éventuel does not mean*
eventual.

éventuellement ADVERB
possibly ◊ *Nous pourrions
éventuellement avoir besoin de vous.*
We may need you. ◊ *les difficultés
que vous pourriez éventuellement*
rencontrer the difficulties that you
may have
Be careful! *éventuellement does not*
mean eventually.

l'**évêque** MASC NOUN
bishop

évidemment ADVERB
[1] obviously ◊ *Les tomates sont
évidemment chères en cette saison.*
Tomatoes are obviously dear at this
time of year.
[2] of course ◊ *Est-ce que je peux
utiliser ton téléphone? – Évidemment,
tu n'as pas besoin de demander.* Can
I use your phone? – Of course, you
don't need to ask.

l'**évidence** FEM NOUN
♦ **C'est une évidence.** It's quite obvious.
♦ **de toute évidence** obviously ◊ *De
toute évidence, il ne veut pas nous
voir.* Obviously he doesn't want to
see us.
♦ **être en évidence** to be clearly visible
◊ *La lettre était en évidence sur la
table.* The letter was clearly visible on
the table.
♦ **mettre en évidence** to reveal

évident ADJECTIVE
obvious

l'**évier** MASC NOUN
sink

éviter VERB
to avoid

évolué ADJECTIVE
advanced

évoluer VERB
to progress ◊ *La chirurgie esthétique
a beaucoup évolué.* Plastic surgery
has progressed a great deal.
♦ **Il a beaucoup évolué.** He has come
on a great deal.

l'**évolution** FEM NOUN
[1] development ◊ *une évolution
rapide* rapid development
[2] evolution ◊ *la théorie de
l'évolution* the theory of evolution

évoquer VERB
to mention ◊ *Il a évoqué divers
problèmes dans son discours.* He
mentioned various problems in his
speech.

exact ADJECTIVE
[1] right ◊ *Avez-vous l'heure exacte?*
Have you got the time? ◊ *Votre
voiture est garée dehors, n'est-ce
pas? – C'est exact.* Your car's parked
outside, isn't it? – That's right.
[2] exact ◊ *Est-ce que vous pouvez
m'indiquer le prix exact du billet?*

Can you tell me the exact price of the ticket?

exactement ADVERB

exactly ◊ *C'est exactement ce que je cherchais.* That's exactly what I was looking for.

ex aequo ADJECTIVE

♦**Ils sont arrivés ex aequo.** They finished neck and neck.

exagérer VERB

1 to exaggerate ◊ *Vous exagérez!* You're exaggerating!

2 to go too far ◊ *Ça fait trois fois que tu arrives en retard: tu exagères!* That's three times you've been late: you really go too far sometimes!

l'**examen** MASC NOUN

exam ◊ *Nous allons passer l'examen d'anglais vendredi matin.* We're doing our English exam on Friday morning. ◊ *un examen de français* a French exam

♦**un examen médical** a medical

examiner VERB

to examine

exaspérant ADJECTIVE

infuriating

exaspérer VERB

to infuriate

l'**excédent** MASC NOUN

♦**l' excédent de bagages** excess baggage

excéder VERB

to exceed ◊ *un contrat dont la durée n'excède pas deux ans* a contract for a period not exceeding two years

♦**excéder quelqu'un** to drive somebody mad ◊ *Les cris des enfants l'excédaient.* The noise of the children was driving her mad.

excellent ADJECTIVE

excellent

excentrique ADJECTIVE

eccentric

excepté PREPOSITION

except ◊ *Toutes les chaussures excepté les sandales sont en solde.* All the shoes except sandals are reduced.

l'**exception** FEM NOUN

exception

♦**à l'exception de** except

exceptionnel ADJECTIVE (FEM SING **exceptionnelle**)

exceptional

l'**excès** MASC NOUN

♦**faire des excès** to overindulge ◊ *On fait souvent des excès aux environs de Noël.* People often overindulge around Christmas.

♦**les excès de vitesse** speeding

excessif ADJECTIVE (FEM SING **excessive**)

excessive

excitant ADJECTIVE

see also **excitant** NOUN

exciting

l'**excitant** MASC NOUN

see also **excitant** ADJECTIVE

stimulant ◊ *Le thé et le café sont des excitants.* Tea and coffee are stimulants.

l'**excitation** FEM NOUN

excitement

exciter VERB

to excite ◊ *Il était tout excité à l'idée de revoir ses cousins.* He was all excited about seeing his cousins again.

♦**s'exciter** (*informal*) to get excited ◊ *Ne t'excite pas trop vite: ça ne va peut-être pas marcher!* Don't get excited too soon: it may not work!

l'**exclamation** FEM NOUN

exclamation

exclu ADJECTIVE

♦**Il n'est pas exclu que ...** It's not impossible that ...

exclusif ADJECTIVE (FEM SING **exclusive**)

exclusive

l'**excursion** FEM NOUN

1 trip ◊ *faire une excursion* to go on a trip

2 walk ◊ *une excursion dans la montagne* a walk in the hills

l'**excuse** FEM NOUN

1 excuse ◊ *Il trouve toujours une bonne excuse pour ne pas faire la vaisselle.* He always finds a good excuse for not doing the washing-up.

2 apology ◊ *présenter ses excuses* to offer one's apologies

♦**un mot d'excuse** a note ◊ *Vous devez apporter un mot d'excuse signé par vos parents.* You have to bring a note signed by your parents.

excuser VERB

to excuse

♦**Excusez-moi. (1)** Sorry! ◊ *Excusez-moi, je ne vous avais pas vu.* Sorry, I didn't see you.

♦**Excusez-moi. (2)** Excuse me. ◊ *Excusez-moi, est-ce que vous avez l'heure?* Excuse me, have you got the time?

♦**s'excuser** to apologize ◊ *Il s'est excusé de son retard.* He apologized for being late.

exécuter VERB
  1 to execute ◊ *Le prisonnier a été exécuté à l'aube.* The prisoner was executed at dawn.
  2 to perform ◊ *Le pianiste va maintenant exécuter une valse de Chopin.* The pianist is now going to perform a waltz by Chopin.

l'**exemplaire** MASC NOUN
  copy

l'**exemple** MASC NOUN
  example ◊ *donner l'exemple* to set an example
  ♦ **par exemple** for example

s'**exercer** VERB
  to practise

l'**exercice** MASC NOUN
  exercise

exhiber VERB
  to show off ◊ *Il aime bien exhiber ses décorations.* He likes showing off his medals.
  ♦ **s'exhiber** to expose oneself

l'**exhibitionniste** MASC NOUN
  flasher

exigeant ADJECTIVE
  hard to please ◊ *Elle est vraiment exigeante.* She's really hard to please.

exiger VERB
  1 to demand ◊ *Le propriétaire exige d'être payé immédiatement.* The landlord is demanding to be paid immediately.
  2 to require ◊ *Ce travail exige beaucoup de patience.* This job requires a lot of patience.

l'**exil** MASC NOUN
  exile

exister VERB
  to exist ◊ *Ça n'existe pas.* It doesn't exist. ◊ *Ce manteau existe également en rose.* This coat's also available in pink.

exotique ADJECTIVE
  exotic ◊ *une plante exotique* an exotic plant ◊ *un yaourt aux fruits exotiques* a tropical fruit yoghurt

expédier VERB
  to send ◊ *expédier un colis* to send a parcel

l'**expéditeur** MASC NOUN
  sender

l'**expédition** FEM NOUN
  expedition
  ♦ **l'expédition du courrier** the dispatch of the mail

l'**expéditrice** FEM NOUN
  sender

l'**expérience** FEM NOUN
  1 experience ◊ *Elle a plusieurs années d'expérience.* She's got several years' experience.
  2 experiment ◊ *une expérience de chimie* a chemistry experiment

expérimenter VERB
  to test ◊ *Ces produits de beauté n'ont pas été expérimentés sur des animaux.* These cosmetics have not been tested on animals.

l'**expert** MASC NOUN
  expert

expirer VERB
  1 to expire (*document, passport*)
  2 to run out (*time allowed*)
  3 to breathe out (*person*)

l'**explication** FEM NOUN
  explanation
  ♦ **une explication de texte** a critical analysis (*of a text*)

expliquer VERB
  to explain ◊ *Il m'a expliqué comment faire.* He explained to me how to do it.
  ♦ **ça s'explique** it's understandable

l'**exploit** MASC NOUN
  achievement

l'**exploitation** FEM NOUN
  exploitation ◊ *Cet organisme lutte contre l'exploitation des femmes.* This organization fights against the exploitation of women.
  ♦ **une exploitation agricole** a farm

exploiter VERB
  to exploit ◊ *Il s'est fait exploiter par le patron du restaurant.* He was exploited by the owner of the restaurant.

explorer VERB
  to explore

exploser VERB
  to explode ◊ *La bombe a explosé en pleine rue.* The bomb exploded in the middle of the street.

l'**explosif** MASC NOUN
  explosive

l'**explosion** FEM NOUN
  explosion

l'**exportateur** MASC NOUN
  exporter

l'**exportation** FEM NOUN
  export

l'**exportatrice** FEM NOUN
  exporter

exporter VERB
  to export

l'**exposé** MASC NOUN

talk ◊ *On nous a demandé de faire un exposé sur l'environnement.* We were asked to give a talk on the environment.

exposer VERB
1 to show ◊ *Il expose ses peintures dans une galerie d'art.* He shows his paintings in a private art gallery.
2 to expose ◊ *N'exposez pas la pellicule à la lumière.* Do not expose the film to light.
3 to set out ◊ *Il nous a exposé les raisons de son départ.* He set out the reasons for his departure.
♦ s'exposer au soleil to stay out in the sun ◊ *Ne vous exposez pas trop longtemps au soleil.* Don't stay out too long in the sun.

l'**exposition** FEM NOUN
exhibition ◊ *une exposition de peinture* an exhibition of paintings

exprès ADVERB
1 on purpose ◊ *Je suis sûr qu'il l'a fait exprès.* I'm sure he did it on purpose.
2 specially ◊ *J'ai fait ce gâteau exprès pour toi.* I made this cake specially for you.

l'**express** MASC NOUN
1 espresso (*coffee*)
2 fast train ◊ *Il a décidé de prendre l'express de dix heures.* He decided to catch the fast train at 10 o'clock.

l'**expression** FEM NOUN
1 expression
2 phrase

exprimer VERB
to express
♦ s'exprimer to express oneself ◊ *Il s'exprime très bien pour un enfant de huit ans.* For a child of 8, he expresses himself very well.

exquis ADJECTIVE
exquisite

extérieur ADJECTIVE
see also **extérieur** NOUN
outside

l'**extérieur** MASC NOUN
see also **extérieur** ADJECTIVE
outside
♦ à l'extérieur outside ◊ *Les toilettes sont à l'extérieur.* The toilet is outside.

l'**externat** MASC NOUN
day school

l'**externe** MASC/FEM NOUN
day pupil

l'**extincteur** MASC NOUN
fire extinguisher

extra ADJECTIVE (MASC, FEM, PL)
excellent ◊ *Ce fromage est extra!* This cheese is excellent!

extraire VERB
to extract

l'**extrait** MASC NOUN
extract

extraordinaire ADJECTIVE
extraordinary

extravagant ADJECTIVE
extravagant

extrême ADJECTIVE
see also **extrême** NOUN
extreme ◊ *l'extrême droite et l'extrême gauche* the far right and the far left

l'**extrême** MASC NOUN
see also **extrême** ADJECTIVE
extreme

extrêmement ADVERB
extremely

l'**Extrême-Orient** MASC NOUN
the Far East

l'**extrémité** FEM NOUN
end ◊ *La gare est à l'autre extrémité de la ville.* The station is at the other end of the town.

E

F

F ABBREVIATION
franc

le **fa** NOUN
F

la **fabrication** NOUN
manufacture

fabriquer VERB
to make ◊ *fabriqué en France* made in France
♦ **Qu'est-ce qu'il fabrique?** (*informal*) What's he up to?

la **fac** NOUN (*informal*)
university
♦ **à la fac** at university

la **face** NOUN
♦ **face à face** face to face
♦ **en face de** opposite ◊ *Le bus s'arrête en face de chez moi.* The bus stops opposite my house.
♦ **faire face à quelque chose** to face something
♦ **Pile ou face? – Face.** Heads or tails? – Heads.

fâché ADJECTIVE
angry
♦ **être fâché contre quelqu'un** to be angry with somebody ◊ *Elle est fâchée contre moi.* She's angry with me.
♦ **être fâché avec quelqu'un** to be on bad terms with somebody ◊ *Elle est fâchée avec sa sœur.* She's on bad terms with her sister.

se **fâcher** VERB
♦ **se fâcher contre quelqu'un** to lose one's temper with somebody
♦ **se fâcher avec quelqu'un** to fall out with somebody ◊ *Il s'est fâché avec son frère.* He's fallen out with his brother.

facile ADJECTIVE
easy
♦ **facile à faire** easy to do

facilement ADVERB
easily

la **facilité** NOUN
♦ **un logiciel d'une grande facilité d'utilisation** a very user-friendly piece of software
♦ **Il a des facilités en langues.** He has a gift for languages.
*Be careful! **facilité** does not mean facility.*

la **façon** NOUN
way ◊ *De quelle façon?* In what way?

♦ **de toute façon** anyway

le **facteur** NOUN
postman ◊ *Il est facteur.* He's a postman.

la **facture** NOUN
bill ◊ *une facture de gaz* a gas bill

facultatif ADJECTIVE (FEM SING **facultative**)
optional

la **faculté** NOUN
faculty
♦ **avoir une grande faculté de concentration** to have great powers of concentration

fade ADJECTIVE
tasteless ◊ *La soupe est un peu fade.* The soup is a bit tasteless.

faible ADJECTIVE
weak ◊ *Je me sens encore faible.* I still feel a bit weak.
♦ **Il est faible en maths.** He's not very good at maths.

la **faiblesse** NOUN
weakness

la **faïence** NOUN
pottery

faillir VERB
♦ **J'ai failli tomber.** I nearly fell.

la **faillite** NOUN
bankruptcy
♦ **une entreprise en faillite** a bankrupt business
♦ **faire faillite** to go bankrupt

la **faim** NOUN
hunger
♦ **avoir faim** to be hungry

fainéant ADJECTIVE
lazy

faire VERB

Present tense:	
je fais	*nous faisons*
tu fais	*vous faites*
il/elle fait	*ils/elles font*
Past participle:	
fait	

[1] to make ◊ *Je vais faire un gâteau pour ce soir.* I'm going to make a cake for tonight. ◊ *Ils font trop de bruit.* They're making too much noise. ◊ *Je voudrais me faire de nouveaux amis.* I'd like to make new friends.
[2] to do ◊ *Qu'est-ce que tu fais?* What are you doing? ◊ *Il fait de l'italien.* He's doing Italian. ◊ *Qui veut*

F

bien faire la vaisselle? Who'll do the dishes?

③ to play ◊ *Il fait du piano.* He plays the piano.

④ to be ◊ *Qu'est-ce qu'il fait chaud!* Isn't it hot! ◊ *Espérons qu'il fera beau demain.* Let's hope it'll be nice weather tomorrow.

◆**Ça ne fait rien.** It doesn't matter.

◆**Ça fait cinquante-trois francs en tout.** That makes fify-three francs in all.

◆**Ça fait trois ans qu'ils habitent à Paris.** They've lived in Paris for three years.

◆**faire tomber** to knock over ◊ *Le chat a fait tomber le vase.* The cat knocked over the vase.

◆**faire faire quelque chose** to get something done ◊ *Je dois faire réparer ma voiture.* I've got to get my car repaired.

◆**Je vais me faire couper les cheveux.** I'm going to get my hair cut.

◆**Ne t'en fais pas!** Don't worry!

fais, faisaient, faisais, faisait VERB *see* **faire**

le **faisan** NOUN
pheasant

faisiez, faisions, faisons, fait VERB *see* **faire**

le **fait** NOUN
fact ◊ *Le fait que ...* The fact that ...

◆**un fait divers** a news item

◆**au fait** by the way ◊ *Au fait, est-ce que tu as aimé le film d'hier?* By the way, did you enjoy the film yesterday?

◆**en fait** actually ◊ *En fait je n'ai pas beaucoup de temps.* I haven't got much time actually.

faites VERB *see* **faire**

la **falaise** NOUN
cliff

falloir VERB *see* **faut, faudra, faudrait**

famé ADJECTIVE

◆**un quartier mal famé** a rough area

fameux ADJECTIVE (FEM SING **fameuse**)

◆**Ce n'est pas fameux.** It's not great.

familial ADJECTIVE (MASC PL **familiaux**)
family ◊ *une atmosphère familiale* a family atmosphere

◆**les allocations familiales** child benefit

familier ADJECTIVE (FEM SING **familière**)
familiar ◊ *C'est un nom qui m'est familier.* The name's familiar.

la **famille** NOUN

① family ◊ *une famille nombreuse* a big family ◊ *Nous passons Noël en famille.* We have a family Christmas.

② relatives ◊ *Il a de la famille à Paris.* He's got relatives in Paris.

la **famine** NOUN
famine

la **fanfare** NOUN
band

fantaisie ADJECTIVE

◆**des bijoux fantaisie** costume jewellery

fantastique ADJECTIVE
fantastic

le **fantôme** NOUN
ghost

la **farce** NOUN

① stuffing (*for chicken, turkey*)

② practical joke ◊ *André aime faire des farces.* André likes to play practical jokes.

farci ADJECTIVE
stuffed ◊ *des tomates farcies* stuffed tomatoes

la **farine** NOUN
flour

fascinant ADJECTIVE
fascinating

fasciner VERB
to fascinate

le **fascisme** NOUN
fascism

fasse, fassent, fasses, fassiez, fassions VERB *see* **faire**

◆**Pourvu qu'il fasse beau demain!** Let's hope it'll be fine tomorrow!

fatal ADJECTIVE
fatal

◆**C'était fatal.** It was bound to happen.

la **fatalité** NOUN
fate

fatigant ADJECTIVE
tiring

la **fatigue** NOUN
tiredness

fatigué ADJECTIVE
tired

se **fatiguer** VERB
to get tired

fauché ADJECTIVE (*informal*)
hard up

faudra VERB
faudra is the future tense of falloir.

◆**Il faudra qu'on soit plus rapide demain.** We'll have to be quicker tomorrow.

faudrait VERB
faudrait is the conditional tense of falloir.

◆**Il faudrait qu'on fasse attention.** We ought to be careful.

se **faufiler** VERB
- ◆ **Il s'est faufilé à travers la foule.** He made his way through the crowd.

la **faune** NOUN
wildlife

fausse ADJECTIVE see **faux**

faut VERB
faut is the present tense of falloir.
- ◆ **Il faut faire attention.** You've got to be careful.
- ◆ **Nous n'avons pas le choix, il faut y aller.** We've no choice, we've got to go.
- ◆ **Il faut que je parte.** I've got to go.
- ◆ **Il faut du courage pour faire ce métier.** It takes courage to do that job.

la **faute** NOUN
[1] mistake ◇ *faire une faute* to make a mistake
[2] fault ◇ *Ce n'est pas de ma faute.* It's not my fault.
- ◆ **sans faute** without fail ◇ *Je t'appellerai sans faute.* I'll phone you without fail.

le **fauteuil** NOUN
armchair
- ◆ **un fauteuil roulant** a wheelchair

faux ADJECTIVE, ADVERB (FEM SING **fausse**)
| see also **faux** NOUN |
untrue ◇ *C'est entièrement faux.* It's totally untrue.
- ◆ **faire un faux pas** to trip
- ◆ **Il chante faux.** He sings out of tune.

le **faux** NOUN
| see also **faux** ADJECTIVE |
fake ◇ *Ce tableau est un faux.* This painting is a fake.

la **faveur** NOUN
favour

favori ADJECTIVE (FEM SING **favorite**)
favourite

favoriser VERB
to favour ◇ *Ce système d'examen favorise ceux qui ont de la mémoire.* This exam system favours people with good memories.

le **fax** NOUN
fax

faxer VERB
to fax
- ◆ **faxer un document à quelqu'un** to fax somebody a document

la **fée** NOUN
fairy

feignant ADJECTIVE (*informal*)
lazy

les **félicitations** FEM NOUN
congratulations

féliciter VERB
to congratulate

la **femelle** NOUN
female (*animal*)

féminin ADJECTIVE
[1] female ◇ *les personnages féminins du roman* the female characters in the novel
[2] feminine ◇ *Elle est très féminine.* She's very feminine.
[3] women's ◇ *Elle joue dans l'équipe féminine de France.* She plays in the French women's team.

féministe ADJECTIVE
feminist

la **femme** NOUN
[1] woman
[2] wife ◇ *C'est la femme du directeur.* She's the headmaster's wife.
- ◆ **une femme au foyer** a housewife
- ◆ **une femme de ménage** a cleaning woman
- ◆ **une femme de chambre** a chambermaid

se **fendre** VERB
to crack

la **fenêtre** NOUN
window

le **fenouil** NOUN
fennel

la **fente** NOUN
slot

le **fer** NOUN
iron
- ◆ **un fer à cheval** a horseshoe
- ◆ **un fer à repasser** an iron

fera, ferai, feras, ferez VERB see **faire**

férié ADJECTIVE
- ◆ **un jour férié** a public holiday

feriez, ferions VERB see **faire**

ferme ADJECTIVE
| see also **ferme** NOUN |
firm ◇ *Elle s'est montrée très ferme à mon égard.* She was very firm with me.

la **ferme** NOUN
| see also **ferme** ADJECTIVE |
farm

fermé ADJECTIVE
[1] closed ◇ *La pharmacie est fermée.* The chemist's is closed.
[2] off ◇ *Est-ce que le gaz est fermé?* Is the gas off?

fermer VERB
[1] to close ◇ *N'oublie pas de fermer la fenêtre.* Don't forget to close the window.

[2] to turn off ◊ *As-tu bien fermé le robinet?* Have you turned the tap off?

♦**fermer à clef** to lock ◊ *N'oublie pas de fermer la porte à clef!* Don't forget to lock the door!

la**fermeture** NOUN
  ♦**les heures de fermeture** closing times
  ♦**une fermeture éclair** ® a zip

le**fermier** NOUN
  farmer

la**fermière** NOUN
  [1] woman farmer
  [2] farmer's wife

féroce ADJECTIVE
  fierce ◊ *un animal féroce* a fierce animal

ferons, feront VERB *see* **faire**

les**fesses** FEM NOUN
  buttocks

le**festival** NOUN
  festival

la**fête** NOUN
  [1] party ◊ *Nous organisons une petite fête pour son anniversaire.* We're having a little party for his birthday.
  ♦**faire la fête** to party
  [2] name day ◊ *C'est sa fête aujourd'hui.* It's his name day today.
  ♦**une fête foraine** a funfair
  ♦**la Fête Nationale** Bastille Day
  ♦**les fêtes de fin d'année** the festive season

fêter VERB
  to celebrate

le**feu** NOUN (PL les **feux**)
  [1] fire ◊ *prendre feu* to catch fire ◊ *faire du feu* to make a fire
  ♦**Au feu!** Fire!
  [2] traffic light ◊ *un feu rouge* a red light ◊ *le feu vert* the green light ◊ *Tournez à gauche aux feux.* Turn left at the lights.
  ♦**Avez-vous du feu?** Have you got a light?
  [3] heat ◊ *... mijoter à feu doux* ... simmer over a gentle heat
  ♦**un feu d'artifice** a firework display

le**feuillage** NOUN
  leaves

la**feuille** NOUN
  [1] leaf ◊ *des feuilles mortes* fallen leaves
  [2] sheet ◊ *une feuille de papier* a sheet of paper
  ♦**une feuille de maladie** a claim form for medical expenses

feuilleté ADJECTIVE

  ♦**de la pâte feuilletée** flaky pastry

feuilleter VERB
  to leaf through

le**feuilleton** NOUN
  serial

le**feutre** NOUN
  felt
  ♦**un stylo-feutre** a felt-tip pen

la**fève** NOUN
  broad bean

février MASC NOUN
  February
  ♦**en février** in February

fiable ADJECTIVE
  reliable

les**fiançailles** FEM NOUN
  engagement SING

fiancé ADJECTIVE
  ♦**être fiancé à quelqu'un** to be engaged to somebody

se**fiancer** VERB
  to get engaged

la**ficelle** NOUN
  [1] string ◊ *Passe-moi un bout de ficelle.* Give me a piece of string.
  [2] thin baguette (bread)

la**fiche** NOUN
  form ◊ *Remplissez cette fiche s'il vous plaît.* Fill in this form please.

se**ficher** VERB (*informal*)
  ♦**Je m'en fiche!** I don't care!
  ♦**Fiche-moi la paix!** Leave me alone!
  ♦**Quoi, tu n'as fait que ça? Tu te fiches de moi!** You've only done that much? You can't be serious!

le**fichier** NOUN
  file

fichu ADJECTIVE (*informal*)
  ♦**Ce parapluie est fichu.** This umbrella's knackered.

fidèle ADJECTIVE
  faithful

fier ADJECTIVE (FEM SING **fière**)
  proud

la**fierté** NOUN
  pride

la**fièvre** NOUN
  fever ◊ *J'ai de la fièvre.* I've got a temperature. ◊ *Il a trente-neuf de fièvre.* He's got a temperature of 39°C.

fiévreux ADJECTIVE (FEM SING **fiévreuse**)
  feverish

la**figue** NOUN
  fig

la**figure** NOUN

F

1 face ◊ *Il a reçu le ballon en pleine figure.* The ball hit him smack in the face.

2 figure (*illustration*) ◊ *Voir figure 2.1, page 32.* See figure 2.1, page 32.

le **fil** NOUN
thread ◊ *le fil à coudre* sewing thread
♦ **le fil de fer** wire
♦ **un coup de fil** a phone call

la **file** NOUN
line (*of people, objects*)
♦ **une file d'attente** a queue ◊ *se mettre à la file* to join the queue
♦ **à la file** one after the other
♦ **en file indienne** in single file

filer VERB
to speed along ◊ *Les voitures filent sur l'autoroute.* The cars are speeding along the motorway.
♦ **File dans ta chambre!** Off to your room with you!

le **filet** NOUN
net

la **fille** NOUN
1 girl ◊ *C'est une école de filles.* It's a girls' school.
2 daughter ◊ *C'est leur fille aînée.* She's their oldest daughter.

la **fillette** NOUN
little girl

le **filleul** NOUN
godson

la **filleule** NOUN
goddaughter

le **film** NOUN
film
♦ **un film policier** a thriller
♦ **un film d'aventures** an adventure film
♦ **un film d'épouvante** a horror film
♦ **le film alimentaire** Clingfilm ®

le **fils** NOUN
son

la **fin** NOUN
see also **fin** ADJECTIVE
end ◊ *Elle n'a pas regardé la fin du film.* She didn't watch the end of the film.
♦ **"Fin"** "The End"
♦ **À la fin, il a réussi à se décider.** In the end he managed to make up his mind.
♦ **Il sera en vacances fin juin.** He'll be on holiday at the end of June.
♦ **en fin de journée** at the end of the day
♦ **en fin de compte** when all's said and done
♦ **sans fin** endless

fin ADJECTIVE
see also **fin** NOUN
fine
♦ **des fines herbes** mixed herbs

la **finale** NOUN
final ◊ *les quarts de finale* the quarter finals

finalement ADVERB
1 at last ◊ *Nous sommes finalement arrivés.* At last we arrived.
2 after all ◊ *Finalement, tu avais raison.* You were right after all.

fini ADJECTIVE
finished

finir VERB
to finish ◊ *Le cours finit à onze heures.* The lesson finishes at 11 o'clock. ◊ *Je viens de finir ce livre.* I've just finished this book.
♦ **Il a fini par se décider.** He made up his mind in the end.

finlandais ADJECTIVE, NOUN
Finnish ◊ *Ils parlent finlandais.* They speak Finnish.
♦ **un Finlandais** a Finn (*man*)
♦ **une Finlandaise** a Finn (*woman*)
♦ **les Finlandais** the Finnish

la **Finlande** NOUN
Finland

la **firme** NOUN
firm

fis VERB *see* **faire**

la **fissure** NOUN
crack

fit VERB *see* **faire**

fixe ADJECTIVE
1 steady ◊ *Il n'a pas d'emploi fixe.* He hasn't got a steady job.
2 set ◊ *Il mange toujours à heures fixes.* He always eats at set times.
♦ **un menu à prix fixe** a set menu

fixer VERB
1 to fix ◊ *Les volets sont fixés avec des crochets.* The shutters are fixed with hooks. ◊ *Nous avons fixé une heure pour nous retrouver.* We fixed a time to meet.
2 to stare at ◊ *Ne fixe pas les gens comme ça!* Don't stare at people like that!

le **flacon** NOUN
bottle ◊ *un flacon de parfum* a bottle of perfume

le **flageolet** NOUN
small haricot bean

flamand ADJECTIVE, NOUN (FEM SING **flamande**)
1 Flemish ◊ *Il parle flamand chez lui.* He speaks Flemish at home.

2 **Fleming** (*Dutch-speaking Belgian*)
♦ **les Flamands** the Dutch-speaking Belgians

flambé ADJECTIVE
♦ **des bananes flambées** flambéed bananas

la **flamme** NOUN
flame
♦ **en flammes** on fire

le **flan** NOUN
baked custard

flâner VERB
to stroll

la **flaque** NOUN
puddle (*of water*)

le **flash** NOUN (PL les **flashes**)
flash (*of camera*)
♦ **un flash d'information** a newsflash

flatter VERB
to flatter

la **flèche** NOUN
arrow

les **fléchettes** FEM NOUN
darts ◊ *jouer aux fléchettes* to play darts

la **fleur** NOUN
flower

fleuri ADJECTIVE
1 full of flowers ◊ *Son jardin était très fleuri.* Her garden was full of flowers.
2 flowery ◊ *un papier peint fleuri* flowery wallpaper

fleurir VERB
to flower ◊ *Cette plante fleurit en automne.* This plant flowers in autumn.

le/la **fleuriste** NOUN
florist

le **fleuve** NOUN
river

le **flic** NOUN (*informal*)
cop

le **flipper** NOUN
pinball machine

flirter VERB
to flirt

le **flocon** NOUN
flake

flotter VERB
to float

flou ADJECTIVE
blurred

le **fluor** NOUN
♦ **le dentifrice au fluor** fluoride toothpaste

la **flûte** NOUN

flute ◊ *Je joue de la flûte.* I play the flute.
♦ **une flûte à bec** a recorder
♦ **Flûte!** (*informal*) Heck!

la **foi** NOUN
faith

le **foie** NOUN
liver
♦ **une crise de foie** a stomach upset

le **foin** NOUN
hay
♦ **un rhume des foins** hay fever

la **foire** NOUN
fair

la **fois** NOUN
time ◊ *la première fois* the first time ◊ *à chaque fois* each time ◊ *À chaque fois que je vais à la bibliothèque, j'oublie ma carte.* Every time I go to the library, I forget my card. ◊ *deux fois deux font quatre* two times two is four
♦ **une fois** once
♦ **deux fois** twice ◊ *deux fois plus de gens* twice as many people
♦ **une fois que** once ◊ *Tu te sentiras mieux une fois que tu auras mangé.* You'll feel better once you've had something to eat.
♦ **à la fois** at once ◊ *Je ne peux pas faire deux choses à la fois.* I can't do two things at once.

la **folie** NOUN
madness ◊ *C'est de la folie pure!* It's absolute madness!
♦ **faire une folie** to be extravagant

folklorique ADJECTIVE
folk ◊ *de la musique folklorique* folk music

folle ADJECTIVE (MASC SING **fou**)
mad

foncé ADJECTIVE
dark ◊ *bleu foncé* dark blue

foncer VERB (*informal*)
♦ **Je vais foncer à la boulangerie.** I'm just going to dash to the baker's.

la **fonction** NOUN
function
♦ **une voiture de fonction** a company car

le/la **fonctionnaire** NOUN
civil servant

fonctionner VERB
to work

le **fond** NOUN
1 bottom ◊ *Mon porte-monnaie est au fond de mon sac.* My purse is at the bottom of my bag.

F

2 end ◊ *Les toilettes sont au fond du couloir*. The toilets are at the end of the corridor.
◆**dans le fond** all things considered ◊ *Dans le fond, ce n'est pas si grave.* All things considered, it's not that bad.

fonder VERB
to found

fondre VERB
to melt ◊ *La tablette de chocolat a fondu dans ma poche.* The bar of chocolate melted in my pocket.
◆**fondre en larmes** to burst into tears

fondu ADJECTIVE
◆**du beurre fondu** melted butter

font VERB *see* **faire**

la **fontaine** NOUN
fountain

le **foot** NOUN (*informal*)
football

le **football** NOUN
football ◊ *jouer au football* to play football

le **footballeur** NOUN
footballer

le **footing** NOUN
jogging ◊ *faire du footing* to go jogging

forain ADJECTIVE
see also **forain** NOUN
◆**une fête foraine** a funfair

le **forain** NOUN
see also **forain** ADJECTIVE
fairground worker

la **force** NOUN
strength ◊ *Je n'ai pas beaucoup de force dans les bras.* I haven't got much strength in my arms.
◆**à force de** by ◊ *Il a grossi à force de manger autant.* He got fat by eating so much.
◆**de force** by force ◊ *Ils lui ont enlevé son pistolet de force.* They took the gun from him by force.

forcé ADJECTIVE
forced ◊ *un sourire forcé* a forced smile
◆**C'est forcé.** (*informal*) It's inevitable.

forcément ADVERB
◆**Ça devait forcément arriver.** That was bound to happen.
◆**pas forcément** not necessarily

la **forêt** NOUN
forest

le **forfait** NOUN
all-in price

◆**C'est compris dans le forfait**. It's included in the price.

le **forgeron** NOUN
blacksmith

la **formalité** NOUN
formality ◊ *Ce n'est qu'une simple formalité.* It's just a formality.

le **format** NOUN
size

la **formation** NOUN
training ◊ *la formation professionnelle* vocational training
◆**la formation continue** in-house training
◆**Il a une formation d'ingénieur.** He is a trained engineer.

la **forme** NOUN
shape
◆**être en forme** to be in good shape
◆**Je ne suis pas en forme aujourd'hui.** I'm not feeling too good today.
◆**Tu as l'air en forme.** You're looking well.

formellement ADVERB
strictly ◊ *Il est formellement interdit de fumer dans les couloirs.* It is strictly forbidden to smoke in the corridors.

former VERB
to form

formidable ADJECTIVE
great

le **formulaire** NOUN
form

fort ADJECTIVE, ADVERB
1 strong ◊ *Le café est trop fort.* The coffee's too strong.
2 good ◊ *Il est très fort en espagnol.* He's very good at Spanish.
3 loud ◊ *Est-ce vous pouvez parler plus fort?* Can you speak louder?
◆**frapper fort** to hit hard

le **fortifiant** NOUN
tonic (*medicine*)

la **fortune** NOUN
fortune
◆**de fortune** makeshift ◊ *Il a traversé la rivière sur un radeau de fortune.* He crossed the river on a makeshift raft.

le **forum de discussion** NOUN
chatroom

le **fossé** NOUN
ditch

fou ADJECTIVE (MASC SING ALSO **fol**, FEM SING **folle**)
mad
◆**Il y a un monde fou sur la plage!** (*informal*) There are loads of people on the beach!

♦ **attraper le fou rire** to get the giggles

la **foudre** NOUN

lightning ◊ *L'arbre a été frappé par la foudre.* The tree was struck by lightning.

foudroyant ADJECTIVE

instant ◊ *un succès foudroyant* an instant hit

le **fouet** NOUN

whisk

la **fougère** NOUN

fern

fouiller VERB

to rummage

le **fouillis** NOUN

mess ◊ *Il y a du fouillis dans sa chambre.* His bedroom is a mess.

le **foulard** NOUN

scarf ◊ *un foulard en soie* a silk scarf

la **foule** NOUN

crowd

♦ **une foule de** masses of ◊ *J'ai une foule de choses à faire demain.* I've got masses of things to do tomorrow.

le **four** NOUN

oven ◊ *un four à micro-ondes* a microwave oven

la **fourchette** NOUN

fork

la **fourmi** NOUN

ant

♦ **avoir des fourmis dans les jambes** to have pins and needles

le **fourneau** NOUN (PL les **fourneaux**)

stove

fourni ADJECTIVE

thick (*beard, hair*)

fournir VERB

to supply

le **fournisseur** NOUN

supplier

♦ **un fournisseur d'accès à Internet** an internet service provider

les **fournitures** FEM NOUN

♦ **les fournitures scolaires** school stationery

fourré ADJECTIVE

filled ◊ *un gâteau fourré à la confiture* a cake filled with jam

fourrer VERB (*informal*)

to put ◊ *Où est-ce que tu as fourré mon passeport?* Where have you put my passport?

le **fourre-tout** NOUN (PL les **fourre-tout**)

holdall

la **fourrure** NOUN

fur ◊ *un manteau de fourrure* a fur coat

foutre VERB (*rude*)

to do ◊ *Qu'est-ce qu'il fout?* What the hell is he doing?

♦ **Je n'en ai rien à foutre!** I don't give a damn!

foutu ADJECTIVE (*rude*)

1 knackered ◊ *Mon stylo est foutu.* My pen's knackered.

2 bloody ◊ *Qu'est-ce que j'ai fait de ce foutu stylo?* Where did I put that bloody pen?

le **foyer** NOUN

home ◊ *dans la plupart des foyers français* in most French homes

♦ **un foyer de jeunes** a youth club

la **fracture** NOUN

fracture

fragile ADJECTIVE

fragile ◊ *Attention, c'est fragile!* Be careful, it's fragile!

la **fragilité** NOUN

fragility

fraîche ADJECTIVE *see* **frais**

la **fraîcheur** NOUN

1 cool ◊ *la fraîcheur du soir* the cool of the evening

2 freshness ◊ *Je ne suis pas sûre de la fraîcheur du poisson.* I'm not sure about the freshness of the fish.

frais ADJECTIVE (FEM SING **fraîche**)

see also **frais** NOUN

1 fresh ◊ *des œufs frais* fresh eggs ◊ *Cette salade n'est pas très fraîche.* This lettuce isn't very fresh.

2 chilly ◊ *Il fait un peu frais ce soir.* It's a bit chilly this evening.

3 cool ◊ *des boissons fraîches* cool drinks

♦ **"servir frais"** "serve chilled"

♦ **mettre au frais** to put in a cool place

les **frais** MASC NOUN

see also **frais** ADJECTIVE

expenses

la **fraise** NOUN

strawberry

la **framboise** NOUN

raspberry

franc ADJECTIVE (FEM SING **franche**)

see also **franc** NOUN

frank

le **franc** NOUN

see also **franc** ADJECTIVE

franc

ⓘ *The* **franc** *is the unit of currency in France, Belgium, Switzerland and many former French colonies; it is divided into 100* **centimes**.

français ADJECTIVE, NOUN (FEM SING
française)
French ◊ *Il parle français
couramment.* He speaks French
fluently.
♦ **un Français** a Frenchman
♦ **une Française** a Frenchwoman
♦ **les Français** the French

la **France** NOUN
France
♦ **en France (1)** in France ◊ *Je suis né
en France.* I was born in France.
♦ **en France (2)** to France ◊ *Je pars en
France pour Noël.* I'm going to
France for Christmas.

franche ADJECTIVE *see* **franc**

franchement ADVERB
[1] frankly ◊ *Il m'a parlé franchement.*
He spoke to me frankly.
[2] really ◊ *C'est franchement
mauvais.* It's really bad.

franchir VERB
to get over

la **franchise** NOUN
frankness

francophone ADJECTIVE
French-speaking

la **frange** NOUN
fringe

la **frangipane** NOUN
almond cream

frapper VERB
to strike ◊ *Il l'a frappée au visage.*
He struck her in the face. ◊ *Son air
fatigué m'a frappé.* I was struck by
how tired she looked.

fredonner VERB
to hum

le **freezer** NOUN
freezing compartment

le **frein** NOUN
brake
♦ **le frein à main** handbrake

freiner VERB
to brake

frêle ADJECTIVE
frail

le **frelon** NOUN
hornet

frémir VERB
shudder ◊ *Cette idée me fait frémir.*
The idea makes me shudder.

fréquemment ADVERB
frequently

fréquent ADJECTIVE
frequent

fréquenté ADJECTIVE

busy ◊ *une rue très fréquentée* a
very busy street
♦ **un bar mal fréquenté** a rough
pub

fréquenter VERB
to see (*person*) ◊ *Je ne le fréquente
pas beaucoup.* I don't see him
often.

le **frère** NOUN
brother

le **friand** NOUN
♦ **un friand au fromage** a cheese
puff

la **friandise** NOUN
sweet

le **fric** NOUN (*informal*)
cash

le **frigidaire** ® NOUN
refrigerator

le **frigo** NOUN (*informal*)
fridge

frileux ADJECTIVE (FEM SING **frileuse**)
♦ **être frileux** to feel the cold ◊ *Elle est
très frileuse.* She really feels the
cold.

frimer VERB (*informal*)
to show off

les **fringues** FEM NOUN (*informal*)
clothes

fripé ADJECTIVE
crumpled

frire VERB
♦ **faire frire** to fry ◊ *Faites frire les
boulettes dans de l'huile très chaude.*
Fry the meatballs in very hot oil.

frisé ADJECTIVE
curly ◊ *Elle est très frisée.* She's got
very curly hair.

le **frisson** NOUN
shiver

frissonner VERB
to shiver

frit ADJECTIVE
fried ◊ *du poisson frit* fried fish

les **frites** FEM NOUN
chips

la **friture** NOUN
[1] fried food ◊ *On lui a conseillé
d'éviter les fritures.* He's been
advised to avoid fried food.
[2] fried fish ◊ *Nous allons faire une
friture ce soir.* We are going to have
fried fish tonight.

froid ADJECTIVE
see also **froid** NOUN
cold ◊ *Ça me laisse froid.* It leaves
me cold. ◊ *de la viande froide* cold
meat

le **froid** NOUN

> see also **froid** ADJECTIVE

cold

♦ **Il fait froid.** It's cold.

♦ **avoir froid** to be cold ◊ *Est-ce que tu as froid?* Are you cold?

se **froisser** VERB

> 1 to crease ◊ *Ce tissu se froisse très facilement.* This material creases very easily.
> 2 to take offence ◊ *Paul se froisse très facilement.* Paul's very quick to take offence.

♦ **se froisser un muscle** to strain a muscle

frôler VERB

> 1 to brush against ◊ *Le chat m'a frôlé au passage.* The cat brushed against me as it went past.
> 2 to narrowly avoid ◊ *Nous avons frôlé la catastrophe.* We narrowly avoided disaster.

le **fromage** NOUN

cheese

♦ **du fromage blanc** soft white cheese

le **froment** NOUN

wheat

♦ **une crêpe de froment** a pancake (*made with wheat flour*)

froncer VERB

♦ **froncer les sourcils** to frown

le **front** NOUN

forehead

la **frontière** NOUN

border

frotter VERB

to rub ◊ *se frotter les yeux* to rub one's eyes

♦ **frotter une allumette** to strike a match

le **fruit** NOUN

fruit

♦ **un fruit** a piece of fruit ◊ *Est-ce que vous voulez manger un fruit?* Would you like some fruit?

♦ **les fruits de mer** seafood

fruité ADJECTIVE

fruity

frustrer VERB

to frustrate

la **fugue** NOUN

♦ **faire une fugue** to run away

fuir VERB

> 1 to flee ◊ *fuir devant un danger* to flee from danger
> 2 to drip ◊ *Le robinet fuit.* The tap's dripping.

la **fuite** NOUN

> 1 leak ◊ *Il y a une fuite de gaz.* There is a gas leak.
> 2 flight (*escape*)

♦ **être en fuite** to be on the run

fumé ADJECTIVE

smoked ◊ *du saumon fumé* smoked salmon

la **fumée** NOUN

smoke

fumer VERB

to smoke

le **fumeur** NOUN

smoker

la **fumeuse** NOUN

smoker

fur

♦ **au fur et à mesure** ADVERB

as you go along ◊ *Je vérifie mon travail au fur et à mesure.* I check my work as I go along.

♦ **au fur et à mesure que** as ◊ *Je réponds à mon courrier au fur et à mesure que je le reçois.* I answer my mail as I receive it.

la **fureur** NOUN

fury

♦ **faire fureur** to be all the rage ◊ *Ce genre de sac fait fureur actuellement.* This sort of bag is all the rage at the moment.

furieux ADJECTIVE (FEM SING **furieuse**)

furious

le **furoncle** NOUN

boil (*on skin*)

fus VERB see **être**

le **fuseau** NOUN (PL les **fuseaux**)

ski pants

la **fusée** NOUN

rocket

le **fusil** NOUN

gun

fut VERB see **être**

futé ADJECTIVE

crafty

le **futur** NOUN

future

G

gâcher VERB
to waste ◇ *Je n'aime pas gâcher la nourriture.* I don't like to waste food.

le **gâchis** NOUN
waste

la **gaffe** NOUN
♦**faire une gaffe** to do something stupid
♦**Fais gaffe!** (*informal*) Watch out! ◇ *Fais gaffe: la peinture est encore humide!* Watch out: the paint's still wet!

le **gage** NOUN
forfeit (*in a game*) ◇ *recevoir un gage* to pay a forfeit

le **gagnant** NOUN
winner

la **gagnante** NOUN
winner

gagner VERB
to win ◇ *Qui a gagné?* Who won?
♦**gagner du temps** to gain time
♦**Il gagne bien sa vie.** He makes a good living.

gai ADJECTIVE
cheerful ◇ *Elle est très gaie.* She's very cheerful.

la **gaieté** NOUN
cheerfulness

la **galerie** NOUN
gallery ◇ *une galerie de peinture* an art gallery
♦**une galerie marchande** a shopping arcade
♦**une galerie de jeux d'arcade** an amusement arcade

le **galet** NOUN
pebble

la **galette** NOUN
⬚1 round flat cake ◇ *une galette de blé noir* a buckwheat pancake
⬚2 biscuit ◇ *des galettes pur beurre* shortbread biscuits
♦**la galette des Rois**

> ❶ *A **galette des Rois** is a cake eaten on Twelfth Night containing a figurine. The person who finds it is the king (or queen) and gets a paper crown. They then choose someone else to be their queen (or king).*

Galles FEM NOUN
♦**le pays de Galles** Wales
♦**le prince de Galles** the Prince of Wales

gallois ADJECTIVE, NOUN
Welsh ◇ *un peintre gallois* a Welsh painter
♦**un Gallois** a Welshman
♦**une Galloise** a Welshwoman
♦**les Gallois** the Welsh

le **galop** NOUN
gallop

galoper VERB
to gallop

le **gamin** NOUN (*informal*)
kid

la **gamine** NOUN (*informal*)
kid

la **gamme** NOUN
scale (*in music*) ◇ *Je dois faire des gammes tous les soirs.* I have to do my scales every night.
♦**une gamme de produits** a range of products

gammée ADJECTIVE
♦**la croix gammée** the swastika

le **gant** NOUN
glove ◇ *des gants en laine* woollen gloves
♦**un gant de toilette** a face cloth

le **garage** NOUN
garage

le/la **garagiste** NOUN
⬚1 garage owner
⬚2 mechanic

la **garantie** NOUN
guarantee

garantir VERB
to guarantee

le **garçon** NOUN
⬚1 boy
⬚2 waiter (*in a café*) ◇ *Garçon!* Waiter!
♦**un vieux garçon** a bachelor

le **garde** NOUN
see also **la garde**
⬚1 warder (*in prison*)
⬚2 security man
♦**un garde du corps** a bodyguard

la **garde** NOUN
see also **le garde**
⬚1 guarding ◇ *Il est chargé de la garde des prisonniers.* He's responsible for guarding the prisoners.
⬚2 guard ◇ *la relève de la garde* the changing of the guard
♦**être de garde** to be on duty ◇ *Mon père est de garde ce soir.* My father

is on duty tonight. ◊ *La pharmacie de garde ce week-end est ...* The duty chemist this weekend is ...

♦ **mettre en garde** to warn ◊ *Elle m'a mis en garde contre les pickpockets.* She warned me about pickpockets.

le **garde-côte** NOUN (PL les **garde-côtes**)
  coastguard

garder VERB
  ① to keep ◊ *Est-ce que tu as gardé toutes ses lettres?* Have you kept all his letters?
  ② to look after ◊ *Je garde ma nièce samedi après-midi.* I'm looking after my niece on Saturday afternoon.
  ③ to guard ◊ *Ils ont pris un gros chien pour garder la maison.* They got a big dog to guard the house.

♦ **se garder** to keep ◊ *Ces crêpes se gardent bien.* These pancakes keep well.

la **garderie** NOUN
  nursery

la **garde-robe** NOUN
  wardrobe (*clothes*) ◊ *Elle a une garde-robe bien fournie.* She's got an extensive wardrobe.

le **gardien** NOUN
  ① caretaker
  ② attendant (*in a museum*)

♦ **un gardien de but** a goalkeeper
♦ **un gardien de la paix** a police officer

la **gardienne** NOUN
  ① caretaker
  ② attendant (*in a museum*)

la **gare** NOUN
  see also **gare** EXCLAMATION
  station ◊ *la gare routière* the bus station

gare EXCLAMATION
  see also **gare** NOUN
♦ **Gare aux serpents!** Watch out for snakes!

garer VERB
  to park
♦ **se garer** to park ◊ *Où t'es-tu garé?* Where are you parked?

garni ADJECTIVE
♦ **un plat garni** a dish served with accompaniments (*vegetables, chips, rice etc*)

le **gars** NOUN (*informal*)
  guy

gaspiller VERB
  to waste

le **gâteau** NOUN (PL les **gâteaux**)
  cake
♦ **les gâteaux secs** biscuits

gâter VERB

to spoil ◊ *Il aime gâter ses petits enfants.* He likes to spoil his grandchildren.

♦ **se gâter** to go bad ◊ *Le temps va se gâter.* The weather's going to break.

gauche ADJECTIVE
  see also **gauche** NOUN
  left ◊ *le bras gauche* the left arm ◊ *le côté gauche* the left-hand side

la **gauche** NOUN
  see also **gauche** ADJECTIVE
  left ◊ *sur votre gauche* on your left
♦ **à gauche (1)** on the left ◊ *la deuxième rue à gauche* the second street on the left
♦ **à gauche (2)** to the left ◊ *à gauche de l'armoire* to the left of the cupboard ◊ *Tournez à gauche.* Turn left.
♦ **la voie de gauche** the left-hand lane
♦ **la gauche** the left (*in politics*) ◊ *Il est de gauche.* He's left-wing.

gaucher ADJECTIVE (FEM SING **gauchère**)
  left-handed

la **gaufre** NOUN
  waffle

la **gaufrette** NOUN
  wafer

le **Gaulois** NOUN
  Gaul ◊ *Astérix le Gaulois* Asterix the Gaul

gaulois ADJECTIVE
  Gallic

le **gaz** NOUN
  gas

gazeux ADJECTIVE (FEM SING **gazeuse**)
♦ **une boisson gazeuse** a fizzy drink
♦ **de l'eau gazeuse** sparkling water

le **gazole** NOUN
  diesel (*fuel*)

le **gazon** NOUN
  lawn

le **GDF** NOUN (= *Gaz de France*)
  French gas company

le **géant** NOUN
  giant

le **gel** NOUN
  frost

la **gelée** NOUN
  jelly

geler VERB
  to freeze ◊ *Il a gelé cette nuit.* There was a frost last night.

la **gélule** NOUN
  capsule (*containing medicine*)

les **Gémeaux** MASC NOUN
  Gemini ◊ *Henry est Gémeaux.* Henry's Gemini.

gémir VERB

G

to moan

gênant ADJECTIVE
awkward ◊ *un silence gênant* an awkward silence

la **gencive** NOUN
gum (*in mouth*)

le **gendarme** NOUN
policeman

la **gendarmerie** NOUN
[1] police force
[2] police station ◊ *Vous devriez porter plainte à la gendarmerie.* You should go to the police station and report it.

le **gendre** NOUN
son-in-law

gêné ADJECTIVE
embarrassed

gêner VERB
[1] to bother ◊ *Je ne voudrais pas vous gêner.* I don't want to bother you.
[2] to feel awkward ◊ *Son regard la gênait.* The way he was looking at her made her feel awkward.

général ADJECTIVE (MASC PL **généraux**)
see also **général** NOUN
general
♦ **en général** usually

le **général** NOUN (PL les **généraux**)
see also **général** ADJECTIVE
general

généralement ADVERB
generally

le/la **généraliste** NOUN
family doctor

la **génération** NOUN
generation

généreux ADJECTIVE (FEM SING **généreuse**)
generous

la **générosité** NOUN
generosity

le **genêt** NOUN
broom (*bush*)

la **génétique** NOUN
genetics

génétiquement ADVERB
genetically ◊ *génétiquement modifié* genetically-modified ◊ *les aliments génétiquement modifiés* GM foods ◊ *un organisme génétiquement modifié* a genetically-modified organism

Genève NOUN
Geneva

génial ADJECTIVE (MASC PL **géniaux**)
(*informal*)
great ◊ *Le film d'hier soir était génial.* The film last night was great.

le **genou** NOUN (PL les **genoux**)
knee ◊ *Elle est à genoux.* She's on her knees. ◊ *se mettre à genoux* to kneel down

le **genre** NOUN
kind ◊ *C'est un genre de gâteau à la crème.* It's a kind of cream cake.

les **gens** MASC NOUN
people

gentil ADJECTIVE (FEM SING **gentille**)
[1] nice ◊ *Nos voisins sont très gentils.* Our neighbours are very nice.
[2] kind ◊ *C'était très gentil de votre part.* It was very kind of you.

la **gentillesse** NOUN
kindness ◊ *Je l'ai remerciée de sa gentillesse.* I thanked her for her kindness. ◊ *C'est un homme d'une grande gentillesse.* He is a very nice man.

gentiment ADVERB
[1] nicely ◊ *Demande-le lui gentiment.* Ask him nicely.
[2] kindly ◊ *Ils nous ont gentiment proposé de rester dîner.* They kindly invited us to stay for dinner.

la **géographie** NOUN
geography

la **géométrie** NOUN
geometry

le **gérant** NOUN
manager

la **gérante** NOUN
manager

gérer VERB
to manage

germain ADJECTIVE
♦ **un cousin germain** a first cousin

le **geste** NOUN
gesture ◊ *Il a voulu faire un geste.* He wanted to make a gesture.
♦ **Ne faites pas un geste!** Don't move!

la **gestion** NOUN
management

le/la **gestionnaire de site** NOUN
webmaster

la **gifle** NOUN
slap across the face

gifler VERB
to slap across the face

gigantesque ADJECTIVE
gigantic

le **gigot** NOUN
leg of lamb

le **gilet** NOUN

1 waistcoat ◊ *un gilet en cuir* a leather waistcoat
2 cardigan ◊ *un gilet tricoté main* a hand-knitted cardigan
♦**un gilet de sauvetage** a life jacket

le **gingembre** NOUN
ginger

la **girafe** NOUN
giraffe

le **gitan** NOUN
gipsy

la **gitane** NOUN
gipsy

le **gîte** NOUN
♦**un gîte rural** a holiday house

la **glace** NOUN
1 ice ◊ *L'étang est recouvert de glace.* The pond is covered with ice.
2 ice cream ◊ *une glace à la fraise* a strawberry ice cream
3 mirror ◊ *Il se regarde souvent dans la glace.* He often looks at himself in the mirror.

glacé ADJECTIVE
1 icy ◊ *Il soufflait un vent glacé.* An icy wind was blowing.
2 iced ◊ *un thé glacé* an iced tea

glacial ADJECTIVE (MASC PL **glaciaux**)
icy

le **glaçon** NOUN
ice cube

glissant ADJECTIVE
slippery

glisser VERB
1 to slip ◊ *Il a glissé sur une peau de banane.* He slipped on a banana skin.
2 to be slippery ◊ *Attention, ça glisse!* Watch out, it's slippery!

global ADJECTIVE (MASC PL **globaux**)
total ◊ *la somme globale* the total amount

la **gloire** NOUN
glory

la **godasse** NOUN (*informal*)
shoe

le **goéland** NOUN
seagull

le **golf** NOUN
1 golf ◊ *Il joue au golf.* He plays golf.
2 golf course ◊ *un golf dix-huit trous* an 18-hole golf course

le **golfe** NOUN
gulf
♦**le golfe de Gascogne** the Bay of Biscay

la **gomme** NOUN
rubber

gommer VERB
to rub out

gonflé ADJECTIVE
1 swollen (*arm, finger, stomach*) ◊ *Elle a les pieds gonflés.* Her feet are swollen.
2 inflated (*ball, tyre*) ◊ *Le ballon de foot était mal gonflé.* The football wasn't properly inflated.
♦**Il est gonflé!** He's got a nerve!

gonfler VERB
1 to blow up ◊ *gonfler un ballon* to blow up a balloon
2 to pump up ◊ *Tu devrais gonfler ton pneu arrière.* You should pump up your back tyre.

la **gorge** NOUN
1 throat ◊ *J'ai mal à la gorge.* I've got a sore throat.
2 gorge ◊ *les gorges du Tarn* the Tarn gorges

la **gorgée** NOUN
sip ◊ *une gorgée d'eau* a sip of water

le **gorille** NOUN
gorilla

le/la **gosse** NOUN (*informal*)
kid

le **goudron** NOUN
tar

le **gouffre** NOUN
chasm
♦**Cette voiture est un vrai gouffre!** This car eats up money!

la **gourde** NOUN
water bottle

gourmand ADJECTIVE
greedy

la **gourmandise** NOUN
greed

la **gousse** NOUN
♦**une gousse d'ail** a clove of garlic

le **goût** NOUN
taste ◊ *Ça n'a pas de goût.* It's got no taste. ◊ *Elle a très bon goût.* She's got very good taste.

goûter VERB
see also **goûter** NOUN
1 to taste ◊ *Goûte donc ce fromage: tu verras comme il est bon!* Have a taste of this cheese: you'll see how nice it is!
2 to have a snack (*in the afternoon*) ◊ *Les enfants goûtent généralement vers quatre heures.* The children usually have a snack around 4 o'clock.

le **goûter** NOUN

see also **goûter** VERB
afternoon snack

la **goutte** NOUN
drop

le **gouvernement** NOUN
government

gouverner VERB
to govern

la **grâce** NOUN
♦ **grâce à** thanks to ◊ *Je suis arrivé à l'heure grâce à toi.* I arrived on time thanks to you.

gracieux ADJECTIVE (FEM SING **gracieuse**)
graceful

les **gradins** MASC NOUN
terraces (*in stadium*)

graduel ADJECTIVE (FEM SING **graduelle**)
gradual

les **grafitti** MASC NOUN
graffiti SING

le **grain** NOUN
grain ◊ *un grain de sable* a grain of sand
♦ **un grain de beauté** a beauty spot
♦ **un grain de café** a coffee bean
♦ **un grain de raisin** a grape

la **graine** NOUN
seed

la **graisse** NOUN
fat

la **grammaire** NOUN
grammar

le **gramme** NOUN
gramme

grand ADJECTIVE, ADVERB
1 tall ◊ *Il est grand pour son âge.* He's tall for his age.
2 big ◊ *une grande valise* a big suitcase ◊ *C'est sa grande sœur.* She's his big sister.
♦ **une grande personne** a grown-up
3 long ◊ *un grand voyage* a long journey
♦ **les grandes vacances** the summer holidays
4 great ◊ *C'est un grand ami à moi.* He's a great friend of mine.
♦ **un grand magasin** a department store
♦ **une grande surface** a hypermarket
♦ **les grandes écoles** top ranking colleges (*at university level*)
♦ **au grand air** out in the open air ◊ *Ça te fera beaucoup de bien d'être au grand air.* It'll be very good for you to be out in the open air.
♦ **grand ouvert** wide open

grand-chose NOUN
♦ **pas grand-chose** not much ◊ *Je n'ai pas acheté grand-chose au marché.* I

didn't buy much at the market.
◊ *Voici un petit cadeau: ce n'est pas grand-chose.* Here's a little present: it's nothing much.

la **Grande-Bretagne** NOUN
Britain

la **grandeur** NOUN
size

grandir VERB
to grow ◊ *Il a beaucoup grandi.* He's grown a lot.

la **grand-mère** NOUN (PL les **grands-mères**)
grandmother

grand-peine
♦ **à grand-peine** ADVERB
with great difficulty

le **grand-père** NOUN (PL les **grands-pères**)
grandfather

les **grands-parents** MASC NOUN
grandparents

la **grange** NOUN
barn

la **grappe** NOUN
♦ **une grappe de raisin** a bunch of grapes

gras ADJECTIVE (FEM SING **grasse**)
1 fatty (*food*) ◊ *Évitez les aliments gras.* Avoid fatty foods.
2 greasy ◊ *des cheveux gras* greasy hair
3 oily ◊ *une peau grasse* oily skin
♦ **faire la grasse matinée** to have a lie-in

gratis ADJECTIVE, ADVERB
free ◊ *J'ai eu ce stylo gratis.* I got this pen free.

le **gratte-ciel** NOUN (PL les **gratte-ciel**)
skyscraper

gratter VERB
1 to scratch ◊ *Ne gratte pas tes piqûres de moustiques!* Don't scratch your mosquito bites!
2 to be itchy ◊ *C'est épouvantable comme ça gratte!* It's terribly itchy!

gratuit ADJECTIVE
free ◊ *entrée gratuite* entrance free ◊ *J'ai deux places gratuites pour le film.* I've got two complimentary tickets for the film.

grave ADJECTIVE
1 serious ◊ *une maladie grave* a serious illness ◊ *Il avait l'air grave.* He was looking serious.
2 deep ◊ *Il a une voix grave.* He's got a deep voice.
♦ **Ce n'est pas grave.** It doesn't matter. ◊ *J'ai oublié ma clé. – Ce n'est pas grave, j'ai la mienne.* I've forgotten

my key. – It doesn't matter, I've got mine.

gravement ADVERB
<u>seriously</u> ◊ *Il a été gravement blessé.* He was seriously injured.

grec ADJECTIVE, NOUN (FEM SING **grecque**)
<u>Greek</u>
♦ **J'apprends le grec.** I'm learning Greek.
♦ **un Grec** a Greek (*man*)
♦ **une Grecque** a Greek (*woman*)
♦ **les Grecs** the Greeks

la **Grèce** NOUN
<u>Greece</u>
♦ **en Grèce (1)** in Greece
♦ **en Grèce (2)** to Greece

la **grêle** NOUN
<u>hail</u>

grêler VERB
♦ **Il grêle.** It's hailing.

grelotter VERB
<u>to shiver</u>

la **grenade** NOUN
1 <u>pomegranate</u>
2 <u>grenade</u>

le **grenier** NOUN
<u>attic</u>

la **grenouille** NOUN
<u>frog</u>

la **grève** NOUN
1 <u>strike</u>
♦ **en grève** on strike ◊ *Les ouvriers sont en grève depuis dix jours.* The workers have been on strike for ten days.
♦ **faire grève** to be on strike
2 <u>shore</u> ◊ *Nous nous sommes promenés le long de la grève.* We went for a walk along the shore.

le/la **gréviste** NOUN
<u>striker</u>

grièvement ADVERB
♦ **grièvement blessé** seriously injured

la **griffe** NOUN
1 <u>claw</u> ◊ *Le chat m'a donné un coup de griffe.* The cat scratched me.
2 <u>label</u> ◊ *la griffe d'un grand couturier* the label of a top designer

griffer VERB
<u>to scratch</u> ◊ *Le chat m'a griffé.* The cat scratched me.

grignoter VERB
<u>to nibble</u>

la **grillade** NOUN
<u>grilled food</u> ◊ *une grillade d'agneau* grilled lamb

la **grille** NOUN

1 <u>wire fence</u> ◊ *L'usine est entourée d'une haute grille.* The factory is surrounded by a high wire fence.
2 <u>metal gate</u> ◊ *Le facteur a sonné à la grille du jardin.* The postman rang at the garden gate.

le **grille-pain** NOUN (PL les **grille-pain**)
<u>toaster</u>

griller VERB
1 <u>to toast</u>
♦ **du pain grillé** toast
2 <u>to grill</u> ◊ *des saucisses grillées* grilled sausages

la **grimace** NOUN
♦ **faire des grimaces** to make faces

grimper VERB
<u>to climb</u>

grincer VERB
<u>to creak</u>

grincheux ADJECTIVE (FEM SING **grincheuse**)
<u>grumpy</u>

la **grippe** NOUN
<u>flu</u>
♦ **avoir la grippe** to have flu ◊ *J'ai eu une mauvaise grippe l'hiver dernier.* I had a bad attack of flu last winter.

grippé ADJECTIVE
♦ **être grippé** to have flu

gris ADJECTIVE
<u>grey</u>

le **Groenland** NOUN
<u>Greenland</u>

grogner VERB
1 <u>to growl</u> ◊ *Le chien a grogné quand je me suis approché de lui.* The dog growled when I went near it.
2 <u>to complain</u> ◊ *Arrête donc de grogner!* Stop complaining!

gronder VERB
♦ **se faire gronder** to get a telling off ◊ *Tu vas te faire gronder par ton père!* You're going to get a telling off from your father!

gros ADJECTIVE (FEM SING **grosse**)
1 <u>big</u> ◊ *une grosse pomme* a big apple
2 <u>fat</u> ◊ *Je suis trop grosse pour porter ça!* I'm too fat to wear that!

la **groseille** NOUN
♦ **la groseille rouge** redcurrant
♦ **la groseille à maquereau** gooseberry

la **grossesse** NOUN
<u>pregnancy</u>

grossier ADJECTIVE (FEM SING **grossière**)
<u>rude</u> ◊ *Ne sois pas si grossier!* Don't be so rude!
♦ **une erreur grossière** a bad mistake

grossir VERB

G

to put on weight ◊ *Il a beaucoup grossi.* He's put on a lot of weight.

grosso modo ADVERB
roughly ◊ *Dis-moi grosso modo ce que tu en penses.* Give me a rough idea what you think of it.

la **grotte** NOUN
cave

le **groupe** NOUN
group ◊ *votre groupe sanguin* your blood group

grouper VERB
to group ◊ *On nous a groupés dans différentes classes selon notre niveau.* We were grouped in different classes according to our level.
♦ **se grouper** to gather ◊ *Nous nous sommes groupés autour du feu.* We gathered round the fire.

le **guépard** NOUN
cheetah

la **guêpe** NOUN
wasp

guérir VERB
to recover ◊ *Il est maintenant complètement guéri.* He's now completely recovered.

la **guérison** NOUN
recovery

la **guerre** NOUN
war ◊ *en guerre* at war ◊ *une guerre civile* a civil war ◊ *la Deuxième Guerre mondiale* the Second World War

guetter VERB
to look out for ◊ *Elle guette l'arrivée du facteur tous les matins.* She looks out for the postman every morning.

la **gueule** NOUN

mouth (*rude when used for people*) ◊ *Le chat a ramené une souris dans sa gueule.* The cat brought in a mouse in its mouth.
♦ **Ta gueule!** (*rude*) Shut your face!
♦ **avoir la gueule de bois** (*informal*) to have a hangover

gueuler VERB (*informal*)
to bawl

le **guichet** NOUN
counter (*in bank, booking office*)

le **guide** NOUN
guide

guider VERB
to guide

le **guidon** NOUN
handlebars

les **guillemets** MASC NOUN
inverted commas ◊ *entre guillemets* in inverted commas

la **guirlande** NOUN
tinsel ◊ *Nous avons décoré le sapin de Noël avec des guirlandes.* We decorated the Christmas tree with tinsel.
♦ **des guirlandes en papier** paper chains

la **guitare** NOUN
guitar ◊ *Sais-tu jouer de la guitare?* Can you play the guitar?

la **gym** NOUN (*informal*)
PE

le **gymnase** NOUN
gym ◊ *Le lycée a un nouveau gymnase.* The school's got a new gym.

la **gymnastique** NOUN
gymnastics ◊ *faire de la gymnastique* to do one's exercises

H

habile ADJECTIVE
  skilful ◇ *Il est très habile de ses mains.*
  He is very clever with his hands.

habillé ADJECTIVE
  1 dressed ◇ *Il n'est pas encore habillé.* He's not dressed yet.
  2 smart ◇ *Cette robe fait très habillé.*
  This dress looks very smart.

s'**habiller** VERB
  1 to get dressed ◇ *Je me suis rapidement habillé.* I got dressed quickly.
  2 to dress up ◇ *Est-ce qu'il faut s'habiller pour la réception?* Do you have to dress up to go to the party?

l'**habitant** MASC NOUN
  inhabitant ◇ *Les habitants du quartier sont contre ce projet.* The local people are against this plan.

l'**habitante** FEM NOUN
  inhabitant

habiter VERB
  to live ◇ *Il habite à Montpellier.* He lives in Montpellier.

les **habits** MASC NOUN
  clothes

l'**habitude** FEM NOUN
  habit ◇ *une mauvaise habitude* a bad habit
  ◆ **avoir l'habitude de quelque chose** to be used to something ◇ *Elle a l'habitude des enfants.* She's used to children. ◇ *Je n'ai pas l'habitude de parler en public.* I'm not used to speaking in public.
  ◆ **d'habitude** usually
  ◆ **comme d'habitude** as usual

habituel ADJECTIVE (FEM SING **habituelle**)
  usual

s'**habituer** VERB
  ◆ **s'habituer à quelque chose** to get used to something ◇ *Il faudra que tu t'habitues à te lever tôt.* You'll have to get used to getting up early.

le **hachis** NOUN
  mince
  ◆ **le hachis Parmentier** shepherd's pie

la **haie** NOUN
  hedge

la **haine** NOUN
  hatred

haïr VERB
  to hate

l'**haleine** FEM NOUN

breath ◇ *avoir mauvaise haleine* to have bad breath ◇ *être hors d'haleine* to be out of breath

les **halles** FEM NOUN
  covered market SING

la **halte** NOUN
  stop ◇ *faire halte* to make a stop
  ◆ **Halte!** Stop!

l'**haltérophilie** FEM NOUN
  weightlifting

le **hamburger** NOUN
  hamburger

l'**hameçon** MASC NOUN
  fish hook

le **hamster** NOUN
  hamster

la **hanche** NOUN
  hip

le **handball** NOUN
  handball ◇ *jouer au handball* to play handball

le **handicapé** NOUN
  handicapped man

la **handicapée** NOUN
  handicapped woman

le **harcèlement** NOUN
  harassment ◇ *le harcèlement sexuel* sexual harassment

le **hareng** NOUN
  herring
  ◆ **un hareng saur** a kipper

le **haricot** NOUN
  bean
  ◆ **les haricots verts** runner beans
  ◆ **les haricots blancs** haricot beans

l'**harmonica** MASC NOUN
  mouth organ

la **harpe** NOUN
  harp

le **hasard** NOUN
  coincidence ◇ *C'était un pur hasard.*
  It was pure coincidence.
  ◆ **au hasard** at random ◇ *Choisis un numéro au hasard.* Choose a number at random.
  ◆ **par hasard** by chance ◇ *Je l'ai rencontrée tout à fait par hasard au supermarché.* I met her at the supermarket quite by chance.
  ◆ **à tout hasard (1)** just in case ◇ *Prends un parapluie à tout hasard.* Take an umbrella just in case.
  ◆ **à tout hasard (2)** on the off chance ◇ *Je ne sais pas s'il est chez lui, mais*

je vais l'appeler à tout hasard. I don't know if he's at home, but I'll phone on the off chance.

la **hâte** NOUN
- **à la hâte** hurriedly ◊ *Elle s'est habillée à la hâte.* She got dressed hurriedly.
- **J'ai hâte de te voir.** I can't wait to see you.

la **hausse** NOUN
  1 increase ◊ *la hausse des prix* price increase
  2 rise ◊ *On annonce une légère hausse de température.* The forecast is for a slight rise in temperature.

hausser VERB
- **hausser les épaules** to shrug one's shoulders

haut ADJECTIVE, ADVERB
  | see also **haut** NOUN |
  1 high ◊ *une haute montagne* a high mountain
  2 aloud ◊ *penser tout haut* to think aloud

le **haut** NOUN
  | see also **haut** ADJECTIVE |
  top
- **un mur de trois mètres de haut** a wall 3 metres high
- **en haut (1)** upstairs ◊ *La salle de bain est en haut.* The bathroom is upstairs.
- **en haut (2)** at the top ◊ *Le nid est tout en haut de l'arbre.* The nest is right at the top of the tree.

la **hauteur** NOUN
  height

le **haut-parleur** NOUN
  loudspeaker

l' **hebdomadaire** MASC NOUN
  weekly (*magazine*)

l' **hébergement** MASC NOUN
  accommodation

héberger VERB
  to put up ◊ *Mon cousin a dit qu'il nous hébergerait.* My cousin said he would put us up.

hein? INTERJECTION
  eh?
- **Hein? Qu'est-ce que tu dis?** Eh? What did you say?

hélas ADVERB
  unfortunately ◊ *Hélas, il ne restait plus de billets.* Unfortunately there were no tickets left.

l' **hélicoptère** MASC NOUN
  helicopter

l' **hémorragie** FEM NOUN
  haemorrhage

l' **herbe** FEM NOUN
  grass
- **les herbes de Provence** mixed herbs

le **hérisson** NOUN
  hedgehog

hériter VERB
  to inherit

l' **héritier** MASC NOUN
  heir

l' **héritière** FEM NOUN
  heiress

hermétique ADJECTIVE
  airtight

l' **héroïne** FEM NOUN
  1 heroine ◊ *l'héroïne du roman* the heroine of the novel
  2 heroin (*drug*)

le **héros** NOUN
  hero

l' **hésitation** FEM NOUN
  hesitation

hésiter VERB
  to hesitate ◊ *Il n'a pas hésité à nous aider.* He didn't hesitate to help us.
  ◊ *J'ai hésité entre le pull vert et le cardigan jaune.* I couldn't decide between the green pullover and the yellow cardigan. ◊ *Est-ce que tu viens ce soir? – J'hésite ...* Are you coming this evening? – I'm not sure ...
- **sans hésiter** without hesitating

l' **heure** FEM NOUN
  1 hour ◊ *Le trajet dure six heures.* The journey lasts six hours.
  2 time ◊ *Vous avez l'heure?* Have you got the time?
- **Quelle heure est-il?** What time is it?
- **À quelle heure?** What time? ◊ *À quelle heure arrivons-nous?* What time do we arrive?
- **deux heures du matin** 2 o'clock in the morning
- **être à l'heure** to be on time
- **une heure de français** a period of French

heureusement ADVERB
  luckily ◊ *Heureusement qu'il n'a pas été blessé.* Luckily he wasn't hurt.

heureux ADJECTIVE (FEM SING **heureuse**)
  happy

heurter VERB
  to hit

l' **hexagone** MASC NOUN
  hexagon
- **l'Hexagone** France

ⓘ *France is often referred to as l'Hexagone because of its six-sided shape.*

le **hibou** NOUN (PL les **hiboux**)
 owl

hier ADVERB
 yesterday
 ♦ **avant-hier** the day before yesterday

la **hi-fi** NOUN
 stereo
 ♦ **une chaîne hi-fi** a stereo system

hippique ADJECTIVE
 ♦ **un club hippique** a riding centre
 ♦ **un concours hippique** a horse show

l' **hippopotame** MASC NOUN
 hippopotamus

l' **hirondelle** FEM NOUN
 swallow (*bird*)

l' **histoire** FEM NOUN
 ① history ◊ *un cours d'histoire* a
 history lesson
 ② story ◊ *Ce roman raconte l'histoire
 de deux enfants.* This novel tells the
 story of two children.
 ♦ **Ne fais pas d'histoires!** Don't make a
 fuss!

historique ADJECTIVE
 historic ◊ *un monument historique* a
 historic monument

l' **hiver** MASC NOUN
 winter
 ♦ **en hiver** in winter

la **HLM** NOUN (= *habitation à loyer modéré*)
 council flat
 ♦ **des HLM** council housing

le **hockey** NOUN
 hockey
 ♦ **le hockey sur glace** ice hockey

hollandais ADJECTIVE, NOUN
 Dutch
 ♦ **J'apprends le hollandais.** I'm learning
 Dutch.
 ♦ **un Hollandais** a Dutch man
 ♦ **une Hollandaise** a Dutch woman
 ♦ **les Hollandais** the Dutch

la **Hollande** NOUN
 Holland
 ♦ **en Hollande (1)** in Holland
 ♦ **en Hollande (2)** to Holland

le **homard** NOUN
 lobster

homéopathique ADJECTIVE
 homeopathic

l' **hommage** MASC NOUN
 tribute

l' **homme** MASC NOUN
 man
 ♦ **un homme d'affaires** a businessman

homosexuel ADJECTIVE (FEM SING
 homosexuelle)
 homosexual

la **Hongrie** NOUN
 Hungary

hongrois ADJECTIVE
 Hungarian

honnête ADJECTIVE
 honest

l' **honnêteté** FEM NOUN
 honesty

l' **honneur** MASC NOUN
 honour

la **honte** NOUN
 shame ◊ *avoir honte de quelque
 chose* to be ashamed of something

l' **hôpital** MASC NOUN (PL les **hôpitaux**)
 hospital

le **hoquet** NOUN
 ♦ **avoir le hoquet** to have hiccups

l' **horaire** MASC NOUN
 timetable
 ♦ **les horaires de train** the train
 timetable

l' **horizon** MASC NOUN
 horizon

horizontal ADJECTIVE (MASC PL
 horizontaux)
 horizontal

l' **horloge** FEM NOUN
 clock

l' **horreur** FEM NOUN
 horror ◊ *un film d'horreur* a horror
 film
 ♦ **avoir horreur de** to hate ◊ *J'ai horreur
 du chou.* I hate cabbage.

horrible ADJECTIVE
 horrible

hors PREPOSITION
 ♦ **hors de** out of ◊ *Elle est hors de
 danger maintenant.* She's out of
 danger now.
 ♦ **hors taxes** duty-free

le **hors-d'œuvre** NOUN (PL les **hors-
 d'œuvre**)
 starter (*food*)

hospitalier ADJECTIVE (FEM SING
 hospitalière)
 hospitable ◊ *Ils sont très hospitaliers.*
 They're very hospitable.
 ♦ **les services hospitaliers** hospital
 services

l' **hospitalité** FEM NOUN
 hospitality

hostile ADJECTIVE
 hostile

l' **hôte** MASC/FEM NOUN
 ① host ◊ *N'oubliez pas de remercier
 vos hôtes.* Don't forget to thank your
 hosts.

H

2 guest ◊ *Cette ferme accueille des hôtes payants.* This farm takes paying guests.

l' **hôtel** MASC NOUN
hotel
♦ **l'hôtel de ville** the town hall

l' **hôtesse** FEM NOUN
hostess
♦ **une hôtesse de l'air** a stewardess

le **houx** NOUN
holly

l' **huile** FEM NOUN
oil
♦ **l'huile solaire** suntan oil

huit NUMBER
eight ◊ *Il est huit heures du matin.* It's eight in the morning. ◊ *Il a huit ans.* He's eight.
♦ **le huit février** the eighth of February
♦ **dans huit jours** in a week's time

la **huitaine** NOUN
♦ **une huitaine de jours** about a week ◊ *Nous serons de retour dans une huitaine de jours.* We'll be back in about a week.

huitième ADJECTIVE
eighth ◊ *au huitième étage* on the eighth floor

l' **huître** FEM NOUN
oyster

humain ADJECTIVE
see also **humain** NOUN
human

l' **humain** MASC NOUN
see also **humain** ADJECTIVE
human being

l' **humeur** FEM NOUN
mood ◊ *Il est de bonne humeur.* He's in a good mood. ◊ *Elle était de mauvaise humeur.* She was in a bad mood.

humide ADJECTIVE
damp ◊ *L'herbe est humide.* The grass is damp. ◊ *un climat humide* a damp climate

humilier VERB
to humiliate

humoristique ADJECTIVE
humorous
♦ **des dessins humoristiques** cartoons

l' **humour** MASC NOUN
humour ◊ *Il n'a pas beaucoup d'humour.* He hasn't got much sense of humour.

hurler VERB
to howl

la **hutte** NOUN
hut

hydratant ADJECTIVE
♦ **une crème hydratante** a moisturizing cream

hygiénique ADJECTIVE
hygienic
♦ **une serviette hygiénique** a sanitary towel
♦ **le papier hygiénique** toilet paper

l' **hymne** MASC NOUN
♦ **l'hymne national** the national anthem

l' **hypermarché** MASC NOUN
hypermarket

hypermétrope ADJECTIVE
long-sighted

hypocrite ADJECTIVE
hypocritical ◊ *Il est hypocrite.* He's a hypocrite.

l' **hypothèse** FEM NOUN
hypothesis

I

l' **iceberg** MASC NOUN
  iceberg

ici ADVERB
  here ◇ *Les assiettes sont ici.* The
  plates are here.
  ◆ **La mer monte parfois jusqu'ici.** The
  sea sometimes comes in as far as
  this.
  ◆ **Jusqu'ici nous n'avons eu aucun
  problème avec la voiture.** So far we
  haven't had any problems with the
  car.

l' **icône** FEM NOUN
  icon

idéal ADJECTIVE (MASC PL **idéaux**)
  ideal ◇ *C'est l'endroit idéal pour faire
  un pique-nique.* It's an ideal place to
  have a picnic.

l' **idée** FEM NOUN
  idea ◇ *C'est une bonne idée.* It's a
  good idea.

identifier VERB
  to identify ◇ *La police a identifié le
  meurtrier.* The police have identified
  the murderer.

identique ADJECTIVE
  identical ◇ *Ils ont obtenu des
  résultats identiques.* They obtained
  identical results.

l' **identité** FEM NOUN
  identity
  ◆ **une pièce d'identité** a form of
  identification ◇ *Avez-vous une pièce
  d'identité?* Have you got any form of
  identification?

idiot ADJECTIVE
  see also **idiot** NOUN
  1 stupid ◇ *une plaisanterie idiote* a
  stupid joke
  2 silly ◇ *Ne sois pas idiot!* Don't be
  silly!

l' **idiot** MASC NOUN
  see also **idiot** ADJECTIVE
  idiot

l' **idiote** FEM NOUN
  idiot

ignoble ADJECTIVE
  horrible ◇ *Il a été ignoble avec elle.*
  He was horrible to her.

ignorant ADJECTIVE
  ignorant

ignorer VERB
  1 not to know ◇ *J'ignore son nom.* I
  don't know his name.

  2 to ignore ◇ *Il m'a complètement
  ignoré.* He completely ignored me.

il PRONOUN
  1 he ◇ *Il est parti ce matin de bonne
  heure.* He left early this morning.
  2 it ◇ *Méfie-toi de ce chien: il mord.*
  Be careful of that dog: it bites. ◇ *Il
  pleut.* It's raining.

l' **île** FEM NOUN
  island
  ◆ **les îles Anglo-Normandes** the Channel
  Islands
  ◆ **les îles Britanniques** the British Isles
  ◆ **les îles Féroé** the Faroe Islands

illégal ADJECTIVE (MASC PL **illégaux**)
  illegal

illimité ADJECTIVE
  unlimited

illisible ADJECTIVE
  illegible ◇ *une écriture illisible*
  illegible handwriting

illuminer VERB
  to floodlight ◇ *Le château est
  illuminé tous les soirs pendant l'été.*
  The castle is floodlit every night in
  the summer.

l' **illusion** FEM NOUN
  illusion ◇ *Tu te fais des illusions!*
  You're deluding yourself!

l' **illustration** FEM NOUN
  illustration

illustré ADJECTIVE
  see also **illustré** NOUN
  illustrated

l' **illustré** MASC NOUN
  see also **illustré** ADJECTIVE
  comic

illustrer VERB
  to illustrate ◇ *Vous pouvez illustrer
  votre rédaction avec des exemples.*
  You may illustrate your essay with
  examples.

ils PRONOUN
  they ◇ *Ils nous ont appelés hier soir.*
  They phoned us last night.

l' **image** FEM NOUN
  picture ◇ *Les films donnent une
  fausse image de l'Amérique.* Films
  give a false picture of America.

l' **imagination** FEM NOUN
  imagination ◇ *Elle a beaucoup
  d'imagination.* She's got a vivid
  imagination.

imaginer VERB

☞

to imagine

l' **imbécile** MASC/FEM NOUN
idiot

l' **imitation** FEM NOUN
imitation

imiter VERB
to imitate

l' **immatriculation** FEM NOUN
♦ **une plaque d'immatriculation** a numberplate

l' **immédiat** MASC NOUN
♦ **dans l'immédiat** for the moment ◊ *Je n'ai pas besoin de ce livre dans l'immédiat.* I don't need this book for the moment.

immédiatement ADVERB
immediately

immense ADJECTIVE
1 huge ◊ *une immense fortune* a huge fortune
2 tremendous ◊ *un immense soulagement* a tremendous relief

l' **immeuble** MASC NOUN
block of flats

l' **immigration** FEM NOUN
immigration

l' **immigré** MASC NOUN
immigrant

l' **immigrée** FEM NOUN
immigrant

immobile ADJECTIVE
motionless

immobilier ADJECTIVE (FEM SING **immobilière**)
♦ **une agence immobilière** an estate agent's

immobiliser VERB
to immobilize

immunisé ADJECTIVE
immunized

l' **impact** MASC NOUN
impact

impair ADJECTIVE
odd ◊ *un nombre impair* an odd number

impardonnable ADJECTIVE
unforgivable

l' **impasse** FEM NOUN
cul-de-sac

l' **impatience** FEM NOUN
impatience

impatient ADJECTIVE
impatient

impeccable ADJECTIVE
1 immaculate ◊ *Elle est toujours impeccable.* She's always immaculate.
2 perfect ◊ *Il a fait un travail impeccable.* He's done a perfect job. ◊ *C'est impeccable!* That's perfect!

l' **imper** MASC NOUN (*informal*)
mac

l' **impératif** MASC NOUN
imperative

l' **impératrice** FEM NOUN
empress

l' **imperméable** MASC NOUN
raincoat

impertinent ADJECTIVE
cheeky ◊ *Ne sois pas impertinent!* Don't be cheeky!

impitoyable ADJECTIVE
merciless

impliquer VERB
to mean ◊ *Si tu vas à l'université, ça implique que tu vas devoir nous quitter.* If you go to university, it'll mean that you have to leave us.
♦ **être impliqué dans** to be involved in ◊ *Il est impliqué dans un scandale financier.* He's involved in a financial scandal.

impoli ADJECTIVE
rude

l' **importance** FEM NOUN
importance ◊ *C'est sans importance.* It doesn't matter.

important ADJECTIVE
1 important ◊ *un rôle important* an important role
2 considerable ◊ *une somme importante* a considerable sum

l' **importation** FEM NOUN
import ◊ *Les importations de pétrole ont baissé.* Oil imports have fallen.

importer VERB
see also **n'importe**
1 to import (*goods*)
2 to matter ◊ *Peu importe.* It doesn't matter.

imposant ADJECTIVE
imposing

imposer VERB
to impose
♦ **imposer quelque chose à quelqu'un** to make somebody do something

impossible ADJECTIVE
see also **impossible** NOUN
impossible

l' **impossible** MASC NOUN
see also **impossible** ADJECTIVE
♦ **Nous ferons l'impossible pour finir à temps.** We'll do our utmost to finish on time.

l' **impôt** MASC NOUN

tax

imprécis ADJECTIVE
imprecise

l' impression FEM NOUN
impression ◊ Il a fait bonne
impression à ma mère. He made a
good impression on my mother.

impressionnant ADJECTIVE
impressive

impressionner VERB
to impress

imprévisible ADJECTIVE
unpredictable

imprévu ADJECTIVE
unexpected

l' imprimante FEM NOUN
printer (for computer)

imprimé ADJECTIVE
printed ◊ un tissu imprimé a printed
fabric ◊ C'est imprimé en grandes
lettres. It's printed in large letters.

imprimer VERB
to print

impropre ADJECTIVE
♦impropre à la consommation unfit for
human consumption

improviser VERB
to improvise

improviste ADVERB
♦arriver à l'improviste to arrive
unexpectedly

l' imprudence FEM NOUN
carelessness
♦ Ne fais pas d'imprudences! Don't do
anything silly!

imprudent ADJECTIVE
[1] unwise ◊ Il serait imprudent de
prendre la voiture aujourd'hui. It
would be unwise to take the car
today.
[2] careless ◊ un conducteur
imprudent a careless driver

impuissant ADJECTIVE
helpless ◊ Elle se sentait
complètement impuissante. She felt
completely helpless.

impulsif ADJECTIVE (FEM SING impulsive)
impulsive

inabordable ADJECTIVE
prohibitive ◊ des prix inabordables
prohibitive prices

inaccessible ADJECTIVE
inaccessible ◊ Cette plage est
inaccessible par la route. This beach
is inaccessible by road.

inachevé ADJECTIVE
unfinished

inadmissible ADJECTIVE

intolerable ◊ Ce type de
comportement est inadmissible! This
sort of behaviour is intolerable!

inanimé ADJECTIVE
unconscious ◊ On l'a retrouvé
inanimé sur la route. He was found
unconscious on the road.

inaperçu ADJECTIVE
♦passer inaperçu to go unnoticed

inattendu ADJECTIVE
unexpected

l' inattention FEM NOUN
♦une faute d'inattention a careless
mistake

inaugurer VERB
to open (an exhibition)

incapable ADJECTIVE
incapable ◊ être incapable de faire
quelque chose to be incapable of
doing something

incassable ADJECTIVE
unbreakable

l' incendie MASC NOUN
fire ◊ un incendie de forêt a forest
fire

incertain ADJECTIVE
[1] uncertain ◊ Son avenir est encore
incertain. His future is still uncertain.
[2] unsettled ◊ Le temps est incertain.
The weather is unsettled.

l' incident MASC NOUN
incident

inciter VERB
♦inciter quelqu'un à faire quelque
chose to encourage somebody to do
something ◊ J'ai incité mes parents à
partir en voyage. I encouraged my
parents to go on a trip.

inclure VERB
to enclose ◊ Veuillez inclure une
enveloppe timbrée libellée à votre
adresse. Please enclose a stamped
addressed envelope.
♦jusqu'au dix mars inclus until 10th
March inclusive

incohérent ADJECTIVE
incoherent

incollable ADJECTIVE
♦être incollable sur quelque chose
(informal) to know everything there is
to know about something
♦le riz incollable non-stick rice

incolore ADJECTIVE
colourless

incompétent ADJECTIVE
incompetent

incompris ADJECTIVE
misunderstood

l'**inconnu** MASC NOUN
stranger ◊ *Ne parle pas à des inconnus.* Don't speak to strangers.
♦l'**inconnu** the unknown ◊ *la peur de l'inconnu* the fear of the unknown

l'**inconnue** FEM NOUN
stranger

inconsciemment ADVERB
unconsciously

inconscient ADJECTIVE
unconscious ◊ *Il est resté inconscient quelques minutes.* He was unconscious for several minutes.

incontestable ADJECTIVE
indisputable

incontournable ADJECTIVE
inevitable ◊ *l'incontournable petite robe noire* the inevitable little black dress

l'**inconvénient** MASC NOUN
disadvantage
♦**si vous n'y voyez pas d'inconvénient** if you have no objection

incorrect ADJECTIVE
1 incorrect ◊ *une réponse incorrecte* an incorrect answer
2 rude ◊ *Il a été incorrect avec la voisine.* He was rude to the woman next door.

incroyable ADJECTIVE
incredible

inculper VERB
♦**inculper de** to charge with ◊ *Il a été inculpé de meurtre.* He was charged with murder.

l'**Inde** FEM NOUN
India

indécis ADJECTIVE
1 indecisive ◊ *Il est constamment indécis.* He's always indecisive.
2 undecided ◊ *Je suis encore indécis.* I'm still undecided.

indéfiniment ADVERB
indefinitely

indélicat ADJECTIVE
tactless

indemne ADJECTIVE
unharmed ◊ *Il s'en est sorti indemne.* He escaped unharmed.

indemniser VERB
to compensate ◊ *Les victimes demandent maintenant à être indemnisées.* The victims are now demanding compensation.

indépendamment ADVERB
independently
♦**indépendamment de** irrespective of
◊ *Les allocations familiales sont versées indépendamment des revenus.* Child benefit is given irrespective of income.

l'**indépendance** FEM NOUN
independence

indépendant ADJECTIVE
independent

l'**index** MASC NOUN
1 index finger
2 index (*in book*)

indicatif ADJECTIVE (FEM SING **indicative**)
see also **indicatif** NOUN
♦**à titre indicatif** for your information

l'**indicatif** MASC NOUN
see also **indicatif** ADJECTIVE
1 dialling code
2 indicative (*of verb*)
3 theme tune (*of TV programme*)

les**indications** FEM NOUN
instructions ◊ *Il suffit de suivre les indications.* You just have to follow the instructions.

l'**indice** MASC NOUN
clue ◊ *La police cherche des indices.* The police are looking for clues.

indien ADJECTIVE, NOUN (FEM SING **indienne**)
Indian
♦**un Indien** an Indian (*man*)
♦**une Indienne** an Indian (*woman*)

l'**indifférence** FEM NOUN
indifference

indifférent ADJECTIVE
indifferent

l'**indigène** MASC/FEM NOUN
native

indigeste ADJECTIVE
indigestible

l'**indigestion** FEM NOUN
indigestion

indigne ADJECTIVE
unworthy

indigner VERB
♦**s'indigner de quelque chose** to get indignant about something

indiqué ADJECTIVE
advisable ◊ *Ce n'est pas très indiqué.* It's not really advisable.

indiquer VERB
to point out ◊ *Il m'a indiqué la mairie.* He pointed out the town hall.

indirect ADJECTIVE
indirect

indiscipliné ADJECTIVE
unruly

indiscret ADJECTIVE (FEM SING **indiscrète**)
indiscreet

indispensable ADJECTIVE

indispensable

indisposé ADJECTIVE
indisposed
♦ **être indisposée** to be having one's period

l'**individu** MASC NOUN
individual

individuel ADJECTIVE (FEM SING **individuelle**)
individual ◊ *servi en portions individuelles* served in individual portions
♦ **Vous aurez une chambre individuelle.** You'll have a room of your own.

indolore ADJECTIVE
painless

l'**Indonésie** FEM NOUN
Indonesia

indulgent ADJECTIVE
indulgent
♦ **Elle est trop indulgente avec son fils.** She's not firm enough with her son.

l'**industrie** FEM NOUN
industry

industriel ADJECTIVE (FEM SING **industrielle**)
see also **industriel** NOUN
industrial

l'**industriel** MASC NOUN
see also **industriel** ADJECTIVE
industrialist

inédit ADJECTIVE
unpublished

inefficace ADJECTIVE
[1] ineffective (*treatment*)
[2] inefficient ◊ *un service de transports publics inefficace* an inefficient public transport system

inégal ADJECTIVE (MASC PL **inégaux**)
[1] unequal ◊ *un combat inégal* an unequal struggle
[2] uneven ◊ *la qualité est inégale* the quality varies

inévitable ADJECTIVE
unavoidable
♦ **C'était inévitable!** That was bound to happen!

inexact ADJECTIVE
inaccurate

in extremis ADVERB
♦ **Il a réussi à attraper son train in extremis.** He just managed to catch his train.
♦ **Ils ont évité un accident in extremis.** They avoided an accident by the skin of their teeth.

l'**infarctus** MASC NOUN
coronary

infatigable ADJECTIVE

indefatigable ◊ *Il est infatigable.* He's indefatigable.

infect ADJECTIVE
revolting (*meal*)

s'**infecter** VERB
to go septic ◊ *La plaie s'est infectée.* The wound has gone septic.

l'**infection** FEM NOUN
infection

inférieur ADJECTIVE
lower ◊ *les membres inférieurs* the lower limbs ◊ *C'est moins cher, mais de qualité inférieure.* It's cheaper but of lower quality.

infernal ADJECTIVE (MASC PL **infernaux**)
terrible ◊ *Ils faisaient un bruit infernal.* They were making a terrible noise.

l'**infini** MASC NOUN
♦ **à l'infini** indefinitely ◊ *On pourrait en parler à l'infini.* We could discuss this indefinitely.

l'**infinitif** MASC NOUN
infinitive

l'**infirme** MASC/FEM NOUN
disabled person

l'**infirmerie** FEM NOUN
medical room ◊ *Elle est à l'infirmerie.* She's in the medical room.

l'**infirmier** MASC NOUN
nurse

l'**infirmière** FEM NOUN
nurse

inflammable ADJECTIVE
inflammable

l'**influence** FEM NOUN
influence

influencer VERB
to influence

l'**informaticien** MASC NOUN
computer scientist

l'**informaticienne** FEM NOUN
computer scientist

les **informations** FEM NOUN
[1] news (*on TV*) ◊ *les informations de vingt heures* the 8 o'clock news
[2] information ◊ *Je voudrais quelques informations, s'il vous plaît.* I'd like some information, please.
♦ **une information** a piece of information

l'**informatique** FEM NOUN
computing

informer VERB
to inform
♦ **s'informer** to find out ◊ *Je ne connais pas les heures de fermeture, mais je*

vais m'informer. I don't know when they close, but I'm going to find out.

infuser VERB
1 to brew (*tea*)
2 to infuse (*herbal tea*)

l'**infusion** FEM NOUN
herbal tea

l'**ingénieur** MASC NOUN
engineer

ingrat ADJECTIVE
ungrateful

l'**ingrédient** MASC NOUN
ingredient

inhabituel ADJECTIVE (FEM SING **inhabituelle**)
unusual

inhumain ADJECTIVE
inhuman

initial ADJECTIVE (MASC PL **initiaux**)
initial

l'**initiale** FEM NOUN
initial

l'**initiation** FEM NOUN
introduction ◊ *un stage d'initiation à la planche à voile* an introductory course in windsurfing

l'**initiative** FEM NOUN
initiative ◊ *avoir de l'initiative* to have initiative

injecter VERB
to inject

l'**injection** FEM NOUN
injection

l'**injure** FEM NOUN
1 insult ◊ *Il a pris ça comme une injure.* He took this as an insult.
2 abuse ◊ *lancer des injures à quelqu'un* to hurl abuse at somebody

injurier VERB
to insult

injurieux ADJECTIVE (FEM SING **injurieuse**)
abusive (*language*)

injuste ADJECTIVE
unfair

innocent ADJECTIVE
innocent

innombrable ADJECTIVE
innumerable

innover VERB
to break new ground

inoccupé ADJECTIVE
empty ◊ *un appartement inoccupé* an empty flat

inoffensif ADJECTIVE (FEM SING **inoffensive**)
harmless

l'**inondation** FEM NOUN
flood

inoubliable ADJECTIVE
unforgettable

inoxydable ADJECTIVE
♦*l'acier inoxydable* stainless steel

inquiet ADJECTIVE (FEM SING **inquiète**)
worried

inquiétant ADJECTIVE
worrying

s'**inquiéter** VERB
to worry ◊ *Ne t'inquiète pas!* Don't worry!

l'**inquiétude** FEM NOUN
anxiety

insatisfait ADJECTIVE
dissatisfied

l'**inscription** FEM NOUN
registration (*for school, course*)

s'**inscrire** VERB
♦*s'inscrire à* (1) to join ◊ *Je me suis inscrit au club de tennis.* I've joined the tennis club.
♦*s'inscrire à* (2) to register ◊ *N'attends pas trop pour t'inscrire à la fac.* Don't leave it too long to register at the university.

l'**insecte** MASC NOUN
insect

insensible ADJECTIVE
insensitive ◊ *Il la trouve insensible.* He thinks she's insensitive.

l'**insigne** MASC NOUN
badge

insignifiant ADJECTIVE
insignificant

insister VERB
to insist
♦**N'insiste pas!** Don't keep on!

l'**insolation** FEM NOUN
sunstroke

insolent ADJECTIVE
cheeky

insouciant ADJECTIVE
carefree

insoutenable ADJECTIVE
unbearable ◊ *une douleur insoutenable* an unbearable pain

inspecter VERB
to inspect

l'**inspecteur** MASC NOUN
inspector

l'**inspection** FEM NOUN
inspection

l'**inspectrice** FEM NOUN
inspector

inspirer VERB
1 to inspire

♦ **s'inspirer de** to take one's inspiration from ◊ *Le peintre s'est inspiré d'un poème.* The painter took his inspiration from a poem.
2 to breathe in ◊ *Inspirez! Expirez!* Breathe in! Breathe out!

instable ADJECTIVE
1 unsteady (*piece of furniture*)
2 unstable (*person*)

les **installations** FEM NOUN
facilities ◊ *Cet appartement est pourvu de toutes les installations modernes.* This flat has all modern facilities.

installer VERB
1 to put up (*shelves*)
2 to install (*gas, telephone*)
♦ **s'installer** to settle in ◊ *Nous nous sommes installés dans notre nouvel appartement.* We've settled into our new flat.
♦ **Installez-vous, je vous en prie.** Have a seat please.

l' **instant** MASC NOUN
moment ◊ *dans un instant* in a moment ◊ *Le dîner sera prêt dans un instant.* Dinner will be ready in a moment. ◊ *pour l'instant* for the moment

instantané ADJECTIVE
instant ◊ *du café instantané* instant coffee

l' **instinct** MASC NOUN
instinct

l' **institut** MASC NOUN
institute

l' **instituteur** MASC NOUN
primary school teacher

l' **institution** FEM NOUN
institution

l' **institutrice** FEM NOUN
primary school teacher

l' **instruction** FEM NOUN
1 instruction ◊ *J'ai suivi ses instructions.* I followed his instructions.
2 education ◊ *Il n'a pas beaucoup d'instruction.* He's not very well-educated.

s' **instruire** VERB
to educate oneself

instruit ADJECTIVE
educated

l' **instrument** MASC NOUN
instrument ◊ *un instrument de musique* a musical instrument

insuffisant ADJECTIVE
insufficient

♦ **"travail insuffisant"** (*on school report*) "must make more effort"

l' **insuline** FEM NOUN
insulin

insultant ADJECTIVE
insulting ◊ *Il s'est montré insultant avec elle.* He was insulting to her.

l' **insulte** FEM NOUN
insult

insulter VERB
to insult

insupportable ADJECTIVE
unbearable

intact ADJECTIVE
intact

intégral ADJECTIVE (MASC PL **intégraux**)
♦ **le texte intégral** unabridged version
♦ **un remboursement intégral** a full refund

l' **intégrisme** MASC NOUN
fundamentalism

l' **intelligence** FEM NOUN
intelligence

intelligent ADJECTIVE
intelligent

intense ADJECTIVE
intense

intensif ADJECTIVE (FEM SING **intensive**)
intensive
♦ **un cours intensif** a crash course

l' **intention** FEM NOUN
intention
♦ **avoir l'intention de faire quelque chose** to intend to do something ◊ *J'ai l'intention de lui en parler.* I intend to speak to him about it.

l' **interdiction** FEM NOUN
♦ **"interdiction de stationner"** "no parking"
♦ **"interdiction de fumer"** "no smoking"

interdire VERB
to forbid ◊ *Ses parents lui ont interdit de sortir.* His parents have forbidden him to go out.

interdit ADJECTIVE
forbidden ◊ *Il est interdit de fumer dans les couloirs.* Smoking in the corridors is forbidden.

intéressant ADJECTIVE
interesting ◊ *un livre intéressant* an interesting book
♦ **On lui a fait une offre intéressante.** They made him an attractive offer.
♦ **On trouve des CD à des prix très intéressants dans ce magasin.** You can get very cheap CDs in this shop.

intéresser VERB
to interest

◆ **s'intéresser à** to be interested in
◊ *Est-ce que vous vous intéressez à la politique?* Are you interested in politics?

l' **intérêt** MASC NOUN
interest
◆ **avoir intérêt à faire quelque chose** to do well to do something ◊ *Tu as intérêt à te dépêcher si tu veux prendre le train de dix heures.* You'd better hurry up if you want to catch the 10 o'clock train.

l' **intérieur** MASC NOUN
inside ◊ *Il fait plus frais à l'intérieur de la maison.* It's cooler inside the house.

l' **interlocuteur** MASC NOUN
◆ **son interlocuteur** the man he's speaking to

l' **interlocutrice** FEM NOUN
◆ **son interlocutrice** the woman he's speaking to

l' **intermédiaire** MASC NOUN
intermediary
◆ **par l'intermédiaire de** through ◊ *Je l'ai rencontré par l'intermédiaire de sa sœur.* I met him through his sister.

l' **internat** MASC NOUN
boarding school

international ADJECTIVE (MASC PL **internationaux**)
international

l' **internaute** MASC/FEM NOUN
internet user

l' **interne** MASC/FEM NOUN
boarder

l' **Internet** MASC NOUN
internet ◊ *sur Internet* on the internet

l' **interphone** MASC NOUN
intercom

l' **interprète** MASC/FEM NOUN
interpreter

interpréter VERB
to interpret

interrogatif ADJECTIVE (FEM SING **interrogative**)
interrogative

l' **interrogation** FEM NOUN
1 question
2 test ◊ *une interrogation écrite* a written test ◊ *une interrogation orale* an oral test

l' **interrogatoire** MASC NOUN
questioning
◆ **C'est un interrogatoire ou quoi?** Am I being cross-examined?

interroger VERB
to question

interrompre VERB
to interrupt

l' **interrupteur** MASC NOUN
switch

l' **interruption** FEM NOUN
interruption
◆ **sans interruption** without stopping ◊ *Il a parlé pendant deux heures sans interruption.* He spoke for two hours without stopping.

l' **intervalle** MASC NOUN
interval
◆ **dans l'intervalle** in the meantime

intervenir VERB
1 to intervene
2 to take action ◊ *La police est intervenue.* The police took action.

l' **intervention** FEM NOUN
intervention ◊ *une intervention militaire* a military intervention
◆ **une intervention chirurgicale** a surgical operation

l' **interview** FEM NOUN
interview (*on radio, TV*)

l' **intestin** MASC NOUN
intestine

intime ADJECTIVE
intimate
◆ **un journal intime** a diary

intimider VERB
to intimidate

l' **intimité** FEM NOUN
◆ **dans l'intimité** in private ◊ *Ce que vous faites dans l'intimité ne m'intéresse pas.* What you do in private doesn't interest me.
◆ **Le mariage a eu lieu dans l'intimité.** The wedding ceremony was private.

intitulé ADJECTIVE
entitled

intolérable ADJECTIVE
intolerable

l' **intoxication** FEM NOUN
◆ **une intoxication alimentaire** food poisoning

l' **Intranet** MASC NOUN
Intranet

intransigeant ADJECTIVE
uncompromising

l' **intrigue** FEM NOUN
plot (*of book, film*)

l' **introduction** FEM NOUN
introduction

introduire VERB
to introduce

l' **intuition** FEM NOUN
intuition

inusable ADJECTIVE

hard-wearing

inutile ADJECTIVE
useless

l'**invalide** MASC/FEM NOUN
disabled person

l'**invasion** FEM NOUN
invasion

inventer VERB
 1 to invent
 2 to make up ◊ *inventer une excuse*
to make up an excuse

l'**inventeur** MASC NOUN
inventor

l'**invention** FEM NOUN
invention

inverse ADJECTIVE
 see also **inverse** NOUN
♦**dans l'ordre inverse** in reverse order
♦**en sens inverse** in the opposite
direction

l'**inverse** MASC NOUN
 see also **inverse** ADJECTIVE
reverse
♦**Tu t'es trompé, c'est l'inverse.** You've
got it wrong, it's the other way
round.

l'**investissement** MASC NOUN
investment

invisible ADJECTIVE
invisible

l'**invitation** FEM NOUN
invitation

l'**invité** MASC NOUN
guest

l'**invitée** FEM NOUN
guest

inviter VERB
to invite

involontaire ADJECTIVE
unintentional ◊ *C'était tout à fait
involontaire.* It was quite
unintentional.

invraisemblable ADJECTIVE
unlikely ◊ *une histoire
invraisemblable* an implausible
story

ira, irai, iraient, irais VERB *see* **aller**
♦**J'irai demain au supermarché.** I'll go
to the supermarket tomorrow.

l'**Irak** MASC NOUN
Iraq

l'**Iran** MASC NOUN
Iran

iras, irez VERB *see* **aller**

irlandais ADJECTIVE, NOUN (FEM SING
irlandaise)
Irish

♦**un Irlandais** an Irishman
♦**une Irlandaise** an Irishwoman
♦**les Irlandais** the Irish

l'**Irlande** FEM NOUN
Ireland
♦**en Irlande (1)** in Ireland
♦**en Irlande (2)** to Ireland
♦**la République d'Irlande** the Irish
Republic
♦**l'Irlande du Nord** Northern Ireland

l'**ironie** FEM NOUN
irony

ironique ADJECTIVE
ironical

irons, iront VERB *see* **aller**
♦**Nous irons à la plage cet après-midi.**
We'll go to the beach this afternoon.

irrationnel ADJECTIVE (FEM SING
irrationnelle)
irrational

irréel ADJECTIVE (FEM SING **irréelle**)
unreal

irrégulier ADJECTIVE (FEM SING **irrégulière**)
irregular

irrésistible ADJECTIVE
irresistible

irritable ADJECTIVE
irritable

irriter VERB
to irritate

islamique ADJECTIVE
Islamic

l'**Islande** FEM NOUN
Iceland

isolé ADJECTIVE
isolated ◊ *une ferme isolée* an
isolated farm

Israël MASC NOUN
Israel

israélien ADJECTIVE, NOUN (FEM SING
israélienne)
Israeli
♦**un Israélien** an Israeli (*man*)
♦**une Israélienne** an Israeli (*woman*)
♦**les Israéliens** the Israelis

israélite ADJECTIVE
Jewish

l'**issue** FEM NOUN
♦**une voie sans issue** a dead end
♦**l'issue de secours** emergency exit

l'**Italie** FEM NOUN
Italy
♦**en Italie (1)** in Italy
♦**en Italie (2)** to Italy

italien ADJECTIVE, NOUN (FEM SING **italienne**)
Italian ◊ *J'apprends l'italien.* I'm
learning Italian.
♦**un Italien** an Italian (*man*)

☞

◆ **une Italienne** an Italian (*woman*)
◆ **les Italiens** the Italians

l' **itinéraire** MASC NOUN
  route

l' **IUT** MASC NOUN (= *Institut universitaire de technologie*)

institute of technology (*at university level*)

ivre ADJECTIVE
  drunk

l' **ivrogne** MASC/FEM NOUN
  drunkard

J

j' PRONOUN *see* **je**

la **jalousie** NOUN
jealousy

jaloux ADJECTIVE (FEM SING **jalouse**)
jealous

jamais ADVERB

[1] never ◇ *Est-ce que tu vas souvent au cinéma? – Non, jamais.* Do you go to the cinema often? – No, never. ◇ *Il ne boit jamais d'alcool.* He never drinks alcohol.

[2] ever

> *Phrases with **jamais** meaning **ever** are used with a verb in the subjunctive.*

◇ *C'est la plus belle chose que j'aie jamais vue.* It's the most beautiful thing I've ever seen.

la **jambe** NOUN
leg

le **jambon** NOUN
ham
♦ **le jambon cru** Parma ham

le **jambonneau** NOUN (PL les **jambonneaux**)
knuckle of ham

janvier MASC NOUN
January
♦ **en janvier** in January

le **Japon** NOUN
Japan
♦ **au Japon (1)** in Japan
♦ **au Japon (2)** to Japan

japonais ADJECTIVE, NOUN (FEM SING **japonaise**)
Japanese ◇ *Elle parle japonais.* She speaks Japanese.
♦ **un Japonais** a Japanese (*man*)
♦ **une Japonaise** a Japanese (*woman*)
♦ **les Japonais** the Japanese

le **jardin** NOUN
garden

le **jardinage** NOUN
gardening

le **jardinier** NOUN
gardener

la **jardinière** NOUN
gardener

jaune ADJECTIVE
| *see also* **jaune** NOUN |
yellow

le **jaune** NOUN
| *see also* **jaune** ADJECTIVE |
yellow
♦ **un jaune d'œuf** an egg yolk

jaunir VERB
to turn yellow

la **jaunisse** NOUN
jaundice

Javel NOUN
♦ **l'eau de Javel** bleach

le **jazz** NOUN
jazz

J.-C. ABBREVIATION (= *Jésus-Christ*)
♦ **44 avant J.-C.** 44 BC
♦ **115 après J.-C.** 115 AD

je PRONOUN

> ***je** changes to **j'** before a vowel and most words beginning with "h".*

I ◇ *Je t'appellerai ce soir.* I'll phone you this evening. ◇ *J'arrive!* I'm coming! ◇ *J'hésite.* I'm not sure.

le **jean** NOUN
jeans PL

la **jeannette** NOUN
Brownie ◇ *Elle est jeannette.* She's a Brownie.

Jésus-Christ MASC NOUN
Jesus Christ

le **jet** NOUN
[1] jet (*of water*)
[2] jet plane

jetable ADJECTIVE
disposable

la **jetée** NOUN
jetty

jeter VERB
[1] to throw ◇ *Il a jeté son manteau sur le lit.* He threw his coat onto the bed.
[2] to throw away ◇ *Mes parents ne jettent jamais rien.* My parents never throw anything away.
♦ **jeter un coup d'œil** to have a look

le **jeton** NOUN
counter (*in board game*)

le **jeu** NOUN (PL les **jeux**)
game ◇ *Je n'aime pas les jeux de société.* I don't like board games.
♦ **un jeu de cartes (1)** a pack of cards
♦ **un jeu de cartes (2)** a card game
♦ **un jeu de mots** a pun
♦ **un jeu électronique** an electronic game
♦ **les jeux vidéo** video games
♦ **en jeu** at stake ◇ *Des vies humaines sont en jeu.* Human lives are at stake.

le **jeudi** NOUN

☞

① Thursday ◇ *Aujourd'hui, nous sommes jeudi.* It's Thursday today.
② on Thursday ◇ *Il arrivera jeudi matin.* He's arriving on Thursday morning.
♦ **le jeudi** on Thursdays ◇ *Le musée est fermé le jeudi.* The museum is closed on Thursdays.
♦ **tous les jeudis** every Thursday
♦ **jeudi dernier** last Thursday
♦ **jeudi prochain** next Thursday

jeun
♦ **à jeun** ADVERB
on an empty stomach ◇ *à prendre à jeun* to be taken on an empty stomach ◇ *Il faut être à jeun pour la prise de sang.* You mustn't have eaten anything before giving a blood sample.

jeune ADJECTIVE
see also **jeune** NOUN
young ◇ *un jeune homme* a young man ◇ *une jeune femme* a young woman
♦ **une jeune fille** a girl

jeune NOUN
see also **jeune** ADJECTIVE
young person ◇ *les jeunes* young people

la **jeunesse** NOUN
youth

le **job** NOUN (*informal*)
job

le **jogging** NOUN
① jogging ◇ *Il fait du jogging.* He goes jogging.
② tracksuit ◇ *Je me suis acheté un jogging rose.* I bought myself a pink tracksuit.

la **joie** NOUN
joy

joindre VERB
① to put together ◇ *On va joindre les deux tables.* We're going to put the two tables together.
② to contact ◇ *Vous pouvez le joindre chez lui.* You can contact him at home.

joint ADJECTIVE
♦ **une pièce jointe** an enclosure (*in letter*)

joli ADJECTIVE
pretty

le **jonc** NOUN
rush

la **jonquille** NOUN
daffodil

la **joue** NOUN
cheek

jouer VERB
① to play ◇ *Elle est allée jouer avec les petits voisins.* She's gone to play with the children next door.
♦ **jouer de** to play (*instrument*) ◇ *Il joue de la guitare et du piano.* He plays the guitar and the piano.
♦ **jouer à** to play (*sport, game*) ◇ *Elle joue au tennis.* She plays tennis. ◇ *jouer aux cartes* to play cards
② to act ◇ *Je trouve qu'il joue très bien dans ce film.* I think he acts very well in this film.
♦ **On joue Hamlet au Théâtre de la Ville.** Hamlet is on at the Théâtre de la Ville.

le **jouet** NOUN
toy

le **joueur** NOUN
player
♦ **être mauvais joueur** to be a bad loser

la **joueuse** NOUN
player

le **jour** NOUN
day ◇ *J'ai passé trois jours chez mes cousins.* I stayed with my cousins for three days.
♦ **Il fait jour.** It's daylight.
♦ **mettre quelque chose à jour** to update something
♦ **le jour de l'An** New Year's Day
♦ **un jour de congé** a day off
♦ **un jour férié** a public holiday
♦ **dans huit jours** in a week
♦ **dans quinze jours** in a fortnight

le **journal** NOUN (PL les **journaux**)
① newspaper
♦ **le journal télévisé** the television news
② diary ◇ *Elle tient un journal depuis l'âge de douze ans.* She has been keeping a diary since she was 12.

journalier ADJECTIVE (FEM SING **journalière**)
daily

le **journalisme** NOUN
journalism

le/la **journaliste** NOUN
journalist ◇ *Elle est journaliste.* She's a journalist.

la **journée** NOUN
day

joyeux ADJECTIVE (FEM SING **joyeuse**)
happy
♦ **Joyeux anniversaire!** Happy birthday!
♦ **Joyeux Noël!** Merry Christmas!

le **judo** NOUN
judo

le **juge** NOUN
judge

juger VERB

to judge

juif ADJECTIVE (FEM SING **juive**)
Jewish ◊ *la cuisine juive* Jewish cooking
♦ **un juif** a Jew (*man*)
♦ **une juive** a Jew (*woman*)

juillet MASC NOUN
July
♦ **en juillet** in July

juin MASC NOUN
June
♦ **en juin** in June

le **jumeau** NOUN (PL les **jumeaux**)
twin

jumeler VERB
to twin ◊ *Saint-Brieuc est jumelée avec Aberystwyth.* Saint-Brieuc is twinned with Aberystwyth.

la **jumelle** NOUN
twin

les **jumelles** FEM NOUN
binoculars

la **jument** NOUN
mare

la **jungle** NOUN
jungle

la **jupe** NOUN
skirt

jurer VERB
to swear ◊ *Je jure que c'est vrai!* I swear it's true!

juridique ADJECTIVE
legal

le **jury** NOUN
jury

le **jus** NOUN
juice
♦ **un jus de fruit** a fruit juice

jusqu'à PREPOSITION
[1] as far as ◊ *Nous avons marché jusqu'au village.* We walked as far as the village.
[2] until ◊ *Il fait généralement chaud jusqu'à la mi-août.* It's usually hot until mid-August.
♦ **jusqu'à ce que** until ◊ *Tu peux rester ici jusqu'à ce qu'il cesse de pleuvoir.* You can stay here until it stops raining.
♦ **jusqu'à présent** so far

jusque PREPOSITION
as far as ◊ *Je l'ai raccompagnée jusque chez elle.* I went with her as far as her house. ◊ *Jusqu'ici nous n'avons pas eu de problèmes.* Up to now we've had no problems. ◊ *Jusqu'où es-tu allé?* How far did you go?

juste ADJECTIVE, ADVERB
[1] fair ◊ *Il est sévère, mais juste.* He's strict but fair.
[2] tight ◊ *Cette veste est un peu juste.* This jacket is a bit tight.
♦ **juste assez** just enough
♦ **chanter juste** to sing in tune

justement ADVERB
just ◊ *C'est justement pour cela qu'il est parti!* That's just the reason why he left!

la **justesse** NOUN
♦ **de justesse** only just ◊ *Il a eu son permis de justesse.* He only just passed his driving test.

la **justice** NOUN
justice

justifier VERB
to justify

juteux ADJECTIVE (FEM SING **juteuse**)
juicy

juvénile ADJECTIVE
youthful

J

K

la **K7** NOUN (= *cassette*)
cassette

kaki ADJECTIVE
khaki

le **kangourou** NOUN
kangaroo

le **karaté** NOUN
karate

la **kermesse** NOUN
fair

kidnapper VERB
to kidnap

le **kilo** NOUN
kilo

le **kilogramme** NOUN
kilogramme

le **kilomètre** NOUN
kilometre

le/la **kinésithérapeute** NOUN
physiotherapist

le **kiosque** NOUN
♦ **un kiosque à journaux** a news stand

le **klaxon** NOUN
horn (*of car*)

klaxonner VERB
to sound the horn

km ABBREVIATION (= *kilomètre*)
♦ **km/h** kph (= kilometres per hour)

KO ADJECTIVE
knocked out
♦ **mettre quelqu'un KO** to knock somebody out ◊ *Il l'a mis KO au troisième round.* He knocked him out in the third round.
♦ **Je suis complètement KO** (*informal*) I'm knackered.

le **K-way** ® NOUN
cagoule

L

l' ARTICLE, PRONOUN *see* **la, le**

la ARTICLE, PRONOUN

> *see also* **la** NOUN

> **la** *changes to* **l'** *before a vowel and most words beginning with "h".*

1 the ◊ *la maison* the house ◊ *l'actrice* the actress ◊ *l'herbe* the grass

2 her ◊ *Je la connais depuis longtemps.* I've known her for a long time. ◊ *C'est une femme intelligente: je l'admire beaucoup.* She's an intelligent woman: I admire her very much.

3 it ◊ *C'est une bonne émission: je la regarde toutes les semaines.* It's a good programme: I watch it every week.

4 one's

♦ **se mordre la langue** to bite one's tongue ◊ *Je me suis mordu la langue.* I've bitten my tongue.

♦ **dix francs la douzaine** 10 francs a dozen

le **la** NOUN

> *see also* **la** ARTICLE

1 A ◊ *en la bémol* in A flat

2 la ◊ *sol, la, si, do* so, la, ti, do

là ADVERB

1 there ◊ *Ton livre est là, sur la table.* Your book's there, on the table.

2 here ◊ *Elle n'est pas là.* She isn't here.

♦ **C'est là que ... (1)** That's where ... ◊ *C'est là que je suis né.* That's where I was born.

♦ **C'est là que ... (2)** That's when ... ◊ *C'est là que j'ai réalisé que je m'étais trompé.* That's when I realized that I had made a mistake.

là-bas ADVERB
over there

le **labo** NOUN (*informal*)
lab

le **laboratoire** NOUN
laboratory

labourer VERB
to plough

le **labyrinthe** NOUN
maze

le **lac** NOUN
lake

lacer VERB
to do up (*shoes*)

le **lacet** NOUN

lace

♦ **des chaussures à lacets** lace-up shoes

lâche ADJECTIVE

> *see also* **lâche** NOUN

1 loose ◊ *Le nœud est trop lâche.* The knot's too loose.

2 cowardly

♦ **Il est lâche.** He's a coward.

le **lâche** NOUN

> *see also* **lâche** ADJECTIVE

coward

lâcher VERB

1 to let go of ◊ *Il n'a pas lâché ma main de tout le film.* He didn't let go of my hand until the end of the film.

2 to drop ◊ *Il a été tellement surpris qu'il a lâché son verre.* He was so surprised that he dropped his glass.

3 to fail ◊ *Les freins ont lâché.* The brakes failed.

la **lâcheté** NOUN
cowardice

lacrymogène ADJECTIVE

♦ **le gaz lacrymogène** tear gas

la **lacune** NOUN
gap

là-dedans ADVERB
in there ◊ *Qu'est-ce qu'il y a là-dedans?* What's in there?

là-dessous ADVERB

1 under there ◊ *Mon carnet d'adresses est quelque part là-dessous.* My address book is under there somewhere.

2 behind it ◊ *Il y a quelque chose de louche là-dessous.* There's something fishy behind it.

là-dessus ADVERB
on there

là-haut ADVERB
up there

laid ADJECTIVE
ugly

la **laideur** NOUN
ugliness

le **lainage** NOUN
woollen garment

la **laine** NOUN
wool ◊ *un pull en laine* a wool jumper

laïque ADJECTIVE

♦ **une école laïque** a state school

la **laisse** NOUN

☞

lead ◊ *Tenez votre chien en laisse.*
Keep your dog on a lead.

laisser VERB
1 to leave ◊ *J'ai laissé mon
parapluie à la maison.* I've left my
umbrella at home.
2 to let ◊ *Laisse-le parler.* Let him
speak.
♦**Elle se laisse aller.** She's letting
herself go.

le **laisser-aller** NOUN
carelessness

le **lait** NOUN
milk
♦**un café au lait** a white coffee

la **laitue** NOUN
lettuce

les **lambeaux** MASC NOUN
♦**en lambeaux** tattered

la **lame** NOUN
blade ◊ *une lame de rasoir* a razor
blade

la **lamelle** NOUN
thin strip

lamentable ADJECTIVE
appalling

se **lamenter** VERB
to moan

le **lampadaire** NOUN
standard lamp

la **lampe** NOUN
lamp
♦**une lampe de poche** a torch

la **lance** NOUN
spear

le **lancement** NOUN
launch

lancer VERB
see also **lancer** NOUN
1 to throw ◊ *Lance-moi le ballon!*
Throw me the ball!
2 to launch ◊ *Ils viennent de lancer
un nouveau modèle.* They've just
launched a new model.
♦**se lancer dans** to embark on ◊ *Il s'est
lancé là-dedans sans bien réfléchir.*
He embarked on it without thinking
properly.

le **lancer** NOUN
see also **lancer** VERB
♦**le lancer de poids** putting the shot

lancinant ADJECTIVE
♦**une douleur lancinante** a shooting
pain

le **landau** NOUN
pram

la **lande** NOUN
moor

le **langage** NOUN
language

la **langouste** NOUN
crayfish

la **langue** NOUN
1 tongue ◊ *Un petit garçon m'a tiré
la langue.* A little boy stuck out his
tongue at me.
♦**sa langue maternelle** his mother
tongue
2 language ◊ *une langue étrangère*
a foreign language ◊ *une langue
vivante* a modern language

la **lanière** NOUN
strap

le **lapin** NOUN
rabbit

le **laps** NOUN
♦**un laps de temps** a space of time

la **laque** NOUN
hair spray

laquelle PRONOUN (PL **lesquelles**)
1 which ◊ *Laquelle de ces photos
préfères-tu?* Which of these photos
do you prefer? ◊ *À laquelle de tes
sœurs ressembles-tu?* Which of your
sisters do you look like?
2 whom ◊ *la personne à laquelle
vous faites référence* the person to
whom you are referring
*laquelle is often not translated in
English.*
◊ *la personne à laquelle je pense* the
person I'm thinking of

le **lard** NOUN
streaky bacon

les **lardons** MASC NOUN
chunks of bacon

large ADJECTIVE, ADVERB
see also **large** NOUN
wide
♦**voir large** to allow a bit extra
◊ *Achète un autre pain: il vaut mieux
voir large.* Buy another loaf of bread:
it's better to have a bit extra.

le **large** NOUN
see also **large** ADJECTIVE
♦**cinq mètres de large** 5 m wide
♦**le large** the open sea
♦**au large de** off the coast of ◊ *Le
bateau est actuellement au large du
Portugal.* The boat is off the coast of
Portugal at the moment.

largement ADVERB
♦**Vous avez largement le temps.** You
have plenty of time.
♦**C'est largement suffisant.** That's
ample.

la **largeur** NOUN

width

la **larme** NOUN
tear ◊ *être en larmes* to be in tears

la **laryngite** NOUN
laryngitis

le **laser** NOUN
laser
♦ **une chaîne laser** a compact disc player
♦ **un disque laser** a compact disc

lasser VERB
♦ **se lasser de** to get tired of ◊ *Il s'est lassé de la tapisserie à fleurs du salon.* He's got tired of the flowery wallpaper in the sitting room.

le **latin** NOUN
Latin

le **laurier** NOUN
laurel tree ◊ *une feuille de laurier* a bay leaf

lavable ADJECTIVE
washable

le **lavabo** NOUN
washbasin

le **lavage** NOUN
wash ◊ *Ce pull a rétréci au lavage.* This jumper has shrunk in the wash.

la **lavande** NOUN
lavender

le **lave-linge** NOUN (PL les **lave-linge**)
washing machine

laver VERB
to wash
♦ **se laver** to wash ◊ *se laver les mains* to wash one's hands

la **laverie** NOUN
♦ **une laverie automatique** a launderette

le **lave-vaisselle** NOUN (PL les **lave-vaisselle**)
dishwasher

le ARTICLE, PRONOUN
le changes to l' before a vowel and most words beginning with "h".
[1] the ◊ *le livre* the book ◊ *l'arbre* the tree ◊ *l'hélicoptère* the helicopter
[2] him ◊ *Daniel est un vieil ami: je le connais depuis plus de vingt ans.* Daniel is an old friend: I've known him for over 20 years.
[3] it ◊ *Où est mon stylo? Je ne le trouve plus.* Where's my pen? I can't find it. ◊ *Où est le fromage? – Je l'ai mis au frigo.* Where's the cheese? – I've put it in the fridge.
[4] one's
♦ **se laver le visage** to wash one's face ◊ *Évitez de vous laver le visage avec du savon.* Avoid washing your face with soap.

♦ **dix francs le kilo** 10 francs a kilo
♦ **Il est arrivé le douze mai.** He arrived on 12 May.

lécher VERB
to lick

le **lèche-vitrine** NOUN
♦ **faire du lèche-vitrine** to go window-shopping

la **leçon** NOUN
lesson

le **lecteur** NOUN
[1] reader
[2] foreign language assistant (*at a university*)
♦ **un lecteur de cassettes** a cassette player
♦ **un lecteur de CD** a CD player

la **lectrice** NOUN
[1] reader
[2] foreign language assistant (*at a university*)

la **lecture** NOUN
reading
> *Be careful! The French word lecture does not mean lecture.*

légal ADJECTIVE (MASC PL **légaux**)
legal

la **légende** NOUN
[1] legend
[2] key (*of map*)
[3] caption (*of picture*)

léger ADJECTIVE (FEM SING **légère**)
[1] light
[2] slight ◊ *un léger retard* a slight delay
♦ **à la légère** thoughtlessly ◊ *Il a agi à la légère.* He acted thoughtlessly.

légèrement ADVERB
[1] lightly ◊ *Habille-toi légèrement: il va faire chaud.* Wear light clothes: it's going to be hot.
[2] slightly ◊ *Il est légèrement plus grand que son frère.* He's slightly taller than his brother.

les **législatives** FEM NOUN
general election SING

le **légume** NOUN
vegetable

le **lendemain** NOUN
next day ◊ *le lendemain de son arrivée* the day after he arrived
♦ **le lendemain matin** the next morning

lent ADJECTIVE
slow

lentement ADVERB
slowly

la **lenteur** NOUN
slowness

L

la **lentille** NOUN

[1] contact lens ◊ *Est-ce que tu portes des lentilles?* Do you wear contact lenses?

[2] lentil ◊ *un rôti de porc aux lentilles* roast pork with lentils

le **léopard** NOUN

leopard

lequel PRONOUN (FEM SING **laquelle**, MASC PL **lesquels**, FEM PL **lesquelles**)

[1] which ◊ *Lequel de ces films as-tu préféré?* Which of the films did you prefer?

[2] whom ◊ *l'homme avec lequel elle a été vue pour la dernière fois* the man with whom she was last seen

lequel is often not translated in English.

◊ *le garçon avec lequel elle est sortie* the boy she went out with

les **ARTICLE, PRONOUN**

[1] the ◊ *les arbres* the trees

[2] them ◊ *Elle les a invités à dîner.* She invited them to dinner.

[3] one's

♦ **se brosser les dents** to brush one's teeth ◊ *Elle s'est brossé les dents.* She brushed her teeth.

♦ **dix francs les cinq** 10 francs for 5

la **lesbienne** NOUN

lesbian

lesquels PRONOUN (FEM **lesquelles**)

[1] which ◊ *Lesquelles de ces photos préfères-tu?* Which of the photos do you prefer?

[2] whom ◊ *les personnes avec lesquelles il est associé* the people with whom he is in partnership

lesquels is often not translated in English.

◊ *les gens chez lesquels nous avons dîné* the people we had dinner with

la **lessive** NOUN

[1] washing powder ◊ *une marque de lessive* a brand of washing powder

[2] wash ◊ *Est-ce que vous avez quelque chose à mettre à la lessive?* Have you got anything to go in the wash?

♦ **faire la lessive** to do the washing

leste ADJECTIVE

nimble

la **Lettonie** NOUN

Latvia

la **lettre** NOUN

letter ◊ *écrire une lettre* to write a lettre

les **lettres** FEM NOUN

arts ◊ *la faculté de lettres* the Faculty of Arts

leur ADJECTIVE, PRONOUN

[1] their ◊ *leur ami* their friend

[2] them ◊ *Je leur ai dit la vérité.* I told them the truth.

♦ **le leur** theirs ◊ *mon camion et le leur* my truck and theirs ◊ *Ma voiture est rouge, la leur est bleue.* My car's red, theirs is blue.

leurs ADJECTIVE, PRONOUN

their ◊ *leurs amis* their friends

♦ **les leurs** theirs ◊ *tes livres et les leurs* your books and theirs

levé ADJECTIVE

♦ **être levé** to be up ◊ *Est-ce qu'il est levé?* Is he up?

la **levée** NOUN

collection (*of mail*) ◊ *Prochaine levée: 17 heures* Next collection: 5 p.m.

lever VERB

see also **lever** NOUN

to raise ◊ *Levez vos verres!* Raise your glasses! ◊ *Levez la main si vous connaissez la réponse.* Put your hand up if you know the answer.

♦ **lever les yeux** to look up

♦ **se lever (1)** to get up ◊ *Il se lève tous les jours à six heures.* He gets up at 6 o'clock every day. ◊ *Lève-toi!* Get up!

♦ **se lever (2)** to rise ◊ *Le soleil se lève actuellement à cinq heures.* At the moment the sun rises at 5 o'clock.

♦ **se lever (3)** to stand up ◊ *Levez-vous!* Stand up!

le **lever** NOUN

see also **lever** VERB

♦ **le lever du soleil** sunrise

le **levier** NOUN

lever

la **lèvre** NOUN

lip

le **lévrier** NOUN

greyhound

la **levure** NOUN

yeast

♦ **la levure chimique** baking powder

le **lexique** NOUN

word list

le **lézard** NOUN

lizard

la **liaison** NOUN

affair ◊ *Ils ont eu une liaison dans leur jeunesse.* They had an affair when they were younger.

la **libellule** NOUN

dragonfly

libérer VERB

to free ◊ *Les otages ont été libérés hier soir.* The hostages were freed last night.

◆ **se libérer** to find time ◊ *J'essaierai de me libérer cet après-midi.* I'll try to find time this afternoon.

la **liberté** NOUN
freedom

◆ **mettre en liberté** to release ◊ *Il a été mis en liberté au bout d'un an de prison.* He was released after a year in prison.

le/la **libraire** NOUN
bookseller

la **librairie** NOUN
bookshop

Be careful! **librairie** does not mean **library**.

libre ADJECTIVE
[1] free ◊ *Tu es libre de faire ce que tu veux.* You are free to do as you wish. ◊ *Est-ce que cette place est libre?* Is this seat free?

◆ **Avez-vous une chambre de libre?** Have you got a free room?
[2] clear ◊ *La route est libre: vous pouvez traverser.* The road is clear: you can cross.

◆ **une école libre** a private school

le **libre-service** NOUN (PL les **libres-services**)
self-service store

la **Libye** NOUN
Libya

la **licence** NOUN
[1] degree ◊ *une licence de droit* a law degree
[2] licence ◊ *une licence d'exportation* an export licence

le **licencié** NOUN
graduate

la **licenciée** NOUN
graduate

licencier VERB
to make redundant ◊ *Ils viennent de licencier sept employés.* They've just made 7 employees redundant.

le **liège** NOUN
cork ◊ *des sets en liège* cork mats
◆ **un bouchon en liège** a cork (*for bottle*)

le **lien** NOUN
[1] connection ◊ *Il n'y aucun lien entre ces deux événements.* There's no connection between these two events.
◆ **un lien de parenté** a family tie
[2] link (*in computing*)

lier VERB

◆ **lier conversation avec quelqu'un** to get into conversation with somebody

◆ **se lier avec quelqu'un** to make friends with somebody ◊ *Je ne me lie pas facilement.* I don't make friends easily.

le **lierre** NOUN
ivy

le **lieu** NOUN (PL les **lieux**)
place ◊ *votre lieu de travail* your place of work
◆ **avoir lieu** to take place ◊ *La cérémonie a eu lieu dans la salle des fêtes.* The ceremony took place in the village hall.
◆ **au lieu de** instead of ◊ *J'aimerais une pomme au lieu de la glace.* I'd like an apple instead of ice cream.

le **lièvre** NOUN
hare

la **ligne** NOUN
[1] line (*phone, train*) ◊ *La ligne est mauvaise.* It's a bad line. ◊ *la ligne d'autobus numéro douze* the number 12 bus
◆ **en ligne** (*computing*) on-line
[2] figure ◊ *C'est mauvais pour la ligne.* It's bad for your figure.

ligoter VERB
to tie up

la **ligue** NOUN
league

le **lilas** NOUN
lilac

la **limace** NOUN
slug

la **lime** NOUN
◆ **une lime à ongles** a nail file

la **limitation** NOUN
◆ **la limitation de vitesse** the speed limit

la **limite** NOUN
[1] boundary (*of property, football pitch*)
[2] limit ◊ *Est-ce qu'il y a une limite d'âge?* Is there an age limit?
◆ **À la limite, on pourrait prendre le bus.** At a pinch we could go by bus.
◆ **la date limite** the deadline
◆ **la date limite de vente** the sell-by date

limiter VERB
to limit ◊ *Le nombre de billets est limité à deux par personne.* The number of tickets is limited to two per person.

la **limonade** NOUN
lemonade

le **lin** NOUN
linen ◊ *une veste en lin* a linen jacket

L

le **linge** NOUN
    [1] linen ◊ *le linge sale* dirty linen
    [2] washing ◊ *laver le linge* to do the
    washing
    ♦ **du linge de corps** underwear

la **lingerie** NOUN
    underwear (*women's*)

le **lion** NOUN
    lion
    ♦ **le Lion** Leo ◊ *Il est Lion.* He is Leo.

la **lionne** NOUN
    lioness

la **liqueur** NOUN
    liqueur

liquide ADJECTIVE
    see also **liquide** NOUN
    liquid

le **liquide** NOUN
    see also **liquide** ADJECTIVE
    liquid
    ♦ **payer quelque chose en liquide** to
    pay cash for something

lire VERB
    to read ◊ *Tu as lu "Madame Bovary"?*
    Have you read "Madame Bovary"?

lis, lisent, lisez VERB *see* **lire**
    ♦ **Je lis beaucoup.** I read a lot.

lisible ADJECTIVE
    legible

lisse ADJECTIVE
    smooth

la **liste** NOUN
    list
    ♦ **faire la liste de** to make a list of ◊ *J'ai*
    fait la liste de tout ce dont j'ai
    besoin. I've made a list of all the
    things I need.

lit VERB *see* **lire**
    see also **lit** NOUN

le **lit** NOUN
    see also **lit** VERB
    bed ◊ *un grand lit* a double bed
    ◊ *aller au lit* to go to bed
    ♦ **faire son lit** to make one's bed ◊ *Je*
    n'ai pas eu le temps de faire mon lit
    ce matin. I haven't had time to make
    my bed this morning.
    ♦ **un lit de camp** a campbed

la **literie** NOUN
    bedding

la **litière** NOUN
    [1] litter (*for cat*)
    [2] bedding (*of caged pet*)

le **litre** NOUN
    litre

littéraire ADJECTIVE
    ♦ **une œuvre littéraire** a work of
    literature

la **littérature** NOUN
    literature

le **littoral** NOUN (PL les **littoraux**)
    coast

la **Lituanie** NOUN
    Lithuania

la **livraison** NOUN
    delivery
    ♦ **la livraison des bagages** baggage
    reclaim

le **livre** NOUN
    see also **la livre**
    book
    ♦ **un livre de poche** a paperback

la **livre** NOUN
    see also **le livre**
    pound

    ⓘ *The French **livre** is 500 grams.*

    ◊ *une livre de beurre* a pound of butter
    ♦ **la livre sterling** the pound sterling
    ◊ *Le guide coûte trois livres.* The
    guide book costs £3.

livrer VERB
    to deliver

le **livret** NOUN
    booklet
    ♦ **le livret scolaire** the school report
    book

le **livreur** NOUN
    delivery man

local ADJECTIVE (MASC PL **locaux**)
    see also **local** NOUN
    local

le **local** NOUN (PL les **locaux**)
    see also **local** ADJECTIVE
    premises ◊ *Nous cherchons un local*
    pour les répétitions. We are looking
    for premises to rehearse in.

le/la **locataire** NOUN
    [1] tenant
    [2] lodger ◊ *Ils ont décidé de prendre*
    un locataire. They have decided to
    take a lodger.

la **location** NOUN
    ♦ **location de voitures** car rental
    ♦ **location de skis** ski hire
    *Be careful! The French word **location***
    *does not mean **location**.*

locaux ADJECTIVE, NOUN *see* **local**

la **locomotive** NOUN
    locomotive

la **loge** NOUN
    dressing room

le **logement** NOUN
    [1] housing
    [2] accommodation

loger VERB
to stay ◊ *Elle loge chez sa cousine quand elle revient dans la région.* She stays with her cousin when she comes back to the area.
♦ **trouver à se loger** to find somewhere to live ◊ *J'ai eu du mal à trouver à me loger.* I had difficulty finding somewhere to live.

le **logiciel** NOUN
software

logique ADJECTIVE
see also **logique** NOUN
logical

la **logique** NOUN
see also **logique** ADJECTIVE
logic

la **loi** NOUN
law

loin ADVERB
1 far ◊ *La gare n'est pas très loin d'ici.* The station is not very far from here.
2 far off ◊ *Noël n'est plus tellement loin.* Christmas isn't far off now.
3 a long time ago ◊ *Les vacances paraissent déjà tellement loin!* The holidays already seem such a long time ago!
♦ **au loin** in the distance ◊ *On aperçoit la mer au loin.* You can see the sea in the distance.
♦ **de loin (1)** from a long way away ◊ *On voit l'église de loin.* You can see the church from a long way away.
♦ **de loin (2)** by far ◊ *C'est de loin l'élève la plus brillante.* She is by far the brightest pupil.
♦ **C'est plus loin que la gare.** It's further on than the station.

lointain ADJECTIVE
see also **lointain** NOUN
distant ◊ *un pays lointain* a distant country ◊ *C'est un parent lointain de ma mère.* He's a distant relation of my mother.

le **lointain** NOUN
see also **lointain** ADJECTIVE
♦ **dans le lointain** in the distance

le **loir** NOUN
dormouse
♦ **dormir comme un loir** to sleep like a log

les **loisirs** MASC NOUN
1 free time SING ◊ *Qu'est-ce que vous faites pendant vos loisirs?* What do you do in your free time?

2 hobby ◊ *Le ski et l'équitation sont des loisirs coûteux.* Skiing and riding are expensive hobbies.

le **Londonien** NOUN
Londoner

la **Londonienne** NOUN
Londoner

Londres NOUN
London ◊ *le métro de Londres* the London underground
♦ **à Londres (1)** in London
♦ **à Londres (2)** to London

long ADJECTIVE (FEM SING **longue**)
see also **long** NOUN
long

le **long** NOUN
see also **long** ADJECTIVE
♦ **un bateau de trois mètres de long** a boat 3 m long
♦ **tout le long de** all along ◊ *Il y a des chemins de randonnée tout le long de la côte.* There are footpaths all along the coast.
♦ **marcher de long en large** to walk up and down

longer VERB
♦ **La route longe la forêt.** The road runs along the edge of the forest.
♦ **Nous avons longé la Seine à pied.** We walked along the Seine.

longtemps ADVERB
a long time ◊ *J'ai attendu longtemps chez le dentiste.* I waited a long time at the dentist's.
♦ **pendant longtemps** for a long time ◊ *On a cru pendant longtemps que la Terre était plate.* For a long time people thought the Earth was flat.
♦ **mettre longtemps à faire quelque chose** to take a long time to do something ◊ *Il a mis longtemps à répondre à ma lettre.* He took a long time to answer my letter.

longue ADJECTIVE see **long**

la **longue** NOUN
♦ **à la longue** in the end ◊ *Elle a fini par agacer tout le monde à la longue.* In the end she got on everybody's nerves.

longuement ADVERB
at length ◊ *Elle m'a longuement parlé de ses projets d'avenir.* She talked to me at length about her plans for the future.

la **longueur** NOUN
length
♦ **à longueur de journée** all day long ◊ *Elle mâche du chewing-gum à*

L

longueur de journée. She chews gum all day long.

le **look** NOUN
look ◊ *Il a un look d'enfer.* He looks so cool.

les **loques** FEM NOUN
♦**être en loques** to be torn to bits ◊ *Sa chemise était en loques.* His shirt was torn to bits.

lors de PREPOSITION
during ◊ *Je l'ai rencontré lors de mon stage en entreprise.* I met him during my work placement.

lorsque CONJUNCTION
when ◊ *J'allais composer ton numéro lorsque tu as appelé.* I was about to dial your number when you called.

le **lot** NOUN
prize
♦**le gros lot** the jackpot

la **loterie** NOUN
[1] lottery ◊ *la loterie nationale* the National Lottery
[2] raffle ◊ *J'ai gagné cet ours en peluche dans une loterie.* I won this teddy in a raffle.

la **lotion** NOUN
lotion ◊ *une bouteille de lotion solaire* a bottle of suntan lotion
♦**une lotion après-rasage** an aftershave
♦**une lotion démaquillante** cleansing milk

le **lotissement** NOUN
housing estate

le **loto** NOUN
lottery
♦**le loto sportif** the pools

le **loubard** NOUN (*informal*)
lout

louche ADJECTIVE
see also **louche** NOUN
fishy ◊ *une histoire louche* a fishy story

la **louche** NOUN
see also **louche** ADJECTIVE
ladle

loucher VERB
to squint

louer VERB
[1] to let ◊ *Ils louent des chambres à des étudiants.* They let rooms to students.
♦**"à louer"** "to let"
[2] to rent ◊ *Je loue un petit appartement au centre-ville.* I rent a little flat in the centre of town.
[3] to hire ◊ *Est-ce que vous louez des vélos?* Do you hire bikes? ◊ *Nous*

allons louer une voiture pour le week-end. We're going to hire a car for the weekend.
[4] to praise ◊ *Les journaux ont loué le courage des pompiers.* The newspapers praised the courage of the firefighters.

le **loup** NOUN
wolf

la **loupe** NOUN
magnifying glass

louper VERB (*informal*)
to miss ◊ *Dépêche-toi, tu vas louper ton train!* Hurry up, you'll miss your train!

lourd ADJECTIVE
see also **lourd** ADVERB
heavy ◊ *Mon sac est très lourd.* My bag's very heavy.

lourd ADVERB
see also **lourd** ADJECTIVE
close (*weather*) ◊ *Il fait très lourd aujourd'hui.* It's very close today.

la **loutre** NOUN
otter

la **loyauté** NOUN
loyalty

le **loyer** NOUN
rent

lu VERB see **lire**

la **lucarne** NOUN
skylight

la **luge** NOUN
sledge

lugubre ADJECTIVE
gloomy

lui PRONOUN
[1] him ◊ *Il a été très content du cadeau que je lui ai offert.* He was very pleased with the present I gave him. ◊ *C'est bien lui!* It's definitely him! ◊ *J'ai pensé à lui toute la journée.* I thought about him all day long.
[2] to him ◊ *Mon père est d'accord: je lui ai parlé ce matin.* My father said yes: I spoke to him this morning.
[3] her ◊ *Elle a été très contente du cadeau que je lui ai offert.* She was very pleased with the present I gave her.
[4] to her ◊ *Ma mère est d'accord: je lui ai parlé ce matin.* My mother said yes: I spoke to her this morning.
[5] it ◊ *Qu'est-ce que tu donnes à ton chat? – Je lui donne de la viande crue.* What do you give your cat? – I give it raw meat.

lui is also used for emphasis.
◊ *Lui, il est toujours en retard!* Oh him, he's always late!
◆**lui-même** himself ◊ *Il a construit son bateau lui-même.* He built his boat himself.

la **lumière** NOUN
light
◆**la lumière du jour** daylight

lumineux ADJECTIVE (FEM SING **lumineuse**)
◆**une enseigne lumineuse** a neon sign

lunatique ADJECTIVE
temperamental ◊ *Il est plutôt lunatique.* He's rather temperamental.

le **lundi** NOUN
1 Monday ◊ *Aujourd'hui, nous sommes lundi.* It's Monday today.
2 on Monday ◊ *Ils sont arrivés lundi.* They arrived on Monday.
◆**le lundi** on Mondays ◊ *Le lundi, je vais à la piscine.* I go swimming on Mondays.
◆**tous les lundis** every Monday
◆**lundi dernier** last Monday
◆**lundi prochain** next Monday
◆**le lundi de Pâques** Easter Monday

la **lune** NOUN
moon
◆**la lune de miel** honeymoon

les **lunettes** FEM NOUN
glasses
◆**des lunettes de soleil** sunglasses
◆**des lunettes de plongée** swimming goggles

la **lutte** NOUN
1 fight ◊ *la lutte contre le racisme* the fight against racism
2 wrestling ◊ *une épreuve de lutte* a wrestling bout

lutter VERB
to fight

le **luxe** NOUN
luxury
◆**de luxe** luxury ◊ *un hôtel de luxe* a luxury hotel

luxueux ADJECTIVE (FEM SING **luxueuse**)
luxurious

le **lycée** NOUN
secondary school
◆**lycée technique** technical college

> *i* *In France pupils go to a **collège** between the ages of 11 and 15, and then to a **lycée** until the age of 18.*

le **lycéen** NOUN
secondary school pupil

la **lycéenne** NOUN
secondary school pupil

L

M

M. ABBREVIATION (= *Monsieur*)
  <u>Mr</u> ◊ *M. Bernard* Mr Bernard

m' PRONOUN *see* **me**

ma ADJECTIVE
  <u>my</u> ◊ *ma mère* my mother ◊ *ma montre* my watch

les **macaronis** MASC NOUN
  <u>macaroni</u> SING

la **Macédoine** NOUN
  <u>Macedonia</u>

la **macédoine** NOUN
  ◆ **la macédoine de fruits** fruit salad
  ◆ **la macédoine de légumes** mixed vegetables

mâcher VERB
  <u>to chew</u>

le **machin** NOUN (*informal*)
  <u>thingy</u> ◊ *Passe-moi le machin pour râper les carottes.* Pass me the thingy for grating carrots. ◊ *Qu'est-ce que c'est que ce vieux machin?* What's this old thing?

machinalement ADVERB
  ◆ **Elle a regardé sa montre machinalement.** She looked at her watch without thinking.

la **machine** NOUN
  <u>machine</u>
  ◆ **une machine à laver** a washing machine
  ◆ **une machine à écrire** a typewriter
  ◆ **une machine à coudre** a sewing machine
  ◆ **une machine à sous** a fruit machine

le **machiste** NOUN
  <u>male chauvinist</u>

le **macho** NOUN (*informal*)
  <u>male chauvinist pig</u>

la **mâchoire** NOUN
  <u>jaw</u>

mâchonner VERB
  <u>to chew</u>

le **maçon** NOUN
  <u>bricklayer</u>

Madame FEM NOUN (PL **Mesdames**)
  1 <u>Mrs</u> ◊ *Madame Legall* Mrs Legall
  2 <u>lady</u> ◊ *Occupez-vous de Madame.* Could you look after this lady?
  3 <u>Madam</u> ◊ *Madame, ...* (*in letter*) ◊ *Madame! Vous avez oublié votre parapluie!* Excuse me! You've forgotten your umbrella!

Mademoiselle FEM NOUN (PL **Mesdemoiselles**)
  1 <u>Miss</u> ◊ *Mademoiselle Martin* Miss Martin
  2 <u>Madam</u> ◊ *Mademoiselle, ...* Dear Madam, ... (*in letter*)

le **magasin** NOUN
  <u>shop</u> ◊ *Les magasins ouvrent à huit heures.* The shops open at 8 o'clock.
  ◆ **faire les magasins** to go shopping

le **magazine** NOUN
  <u>magazine</u>

le **magicien** NOUN
  <u>magician</u>

la **magicienne** NOUN
  <u>magician</u>

la **magie** NOUN
  <u>magic</u> ◊ *un tour de magie* a magic trick

magique ADJECTIVE
  <u>magic</u> ◊ *une baguette magique* a magic wand

magistral ADJECTIVE (MASC PL **magistraux**)
  ◆ **un cours magistral** a lecture (*at university*)

magnétique ADJECTIVE
  <u>magnetic</u>

le **magnétophone** NOUN
  <u>tape recorder</u>
  ◆ **un magnétophone à cassettes** a cassette recorder

le **magnétoscope** NOUN
  <u>video recorder</u>

magnifique ADJECTIVE
  <u>superb</u>

mai MASC NOUN
  <u>May</u>
  ◆ **en mai** in May

maigre ADJECTIVE
  1 <u>skinny</u> ◊ *Ma mère me trouve trop maigre.* My mother says I'm too skinny.
  2 <u>lean</u> (*meat*)
  3 <u>low-fat</u> (*cheese, yoghurt*)

maigrir VERB
  <u>to lose weight</u> ◊ *Il fait un régime pour essayer de maigrir.* He's on a diet, to try to lose weight. ◊ *Elle a maigri de deux kilos en un mois.* She's lost two kilos in a month.

le **maillot de bain** NOUN
  1 <u>swimsuit</u>
  2 <u>swimming trunks</u>

la **main** NOUN
  <u>hand</u> ◊ *Donne-moi la main!* Give me your hand!

♦ **serrer la main à quelqu'un** to shake hands with somebody

♦ **se serrer la main** to shake hands ◊ *Les deux présidents se sont serré la main.* The two presidents shook hands.

♦ **sous la main** to hand ◊ *Est-ce que tu as son adresse sous la main?* Have you got his address to hand?

la **main-d'œuvre** NOUN
workforce ◊ *la main-d'œuvre de l'usine* the workforce of the factory

♦ **la main-d'œuvre immigrée** immigrant labour

maintenant ADVERB
1 now ◊ *Qu'est-ce que tu veux faire maintenant?* What do you want to do now? ◊ *C'est maintenant ou jamais.* It's now or never.
2 nowadays ◊ *Maintenant la plupart des gens font leurs courses au supermarché.* Nowadays most people do their shopping at the supermarket.

maintenir VERB
to maintain ◊ *Il maintient qu'il n'était pas là le jour du crime.* He maintains he wasn't there on the day of the crime.

♦ **se maintenir** to hold ◊ *Espérons que le beau temps va se maintenir pour le week-end!* Let's hope the good weather will hold over the weekend!

le **maire** NOUN
mayor

la **mairie** NOUN
town hall

mais CONJUNCTION
but ◊ *C'est cher mais de très bonne qualité.* It's expensive, but very good quality.

le **maïs** NOUN
1 maize
2 sweetcorn

la **maison** NOUN
see also **maison** ADJECTIVE
house ◊ *Ils habitent dans la maison qui est au bout de la rue.* They live in the house at the end of the street.

♦ **des maisons mitoyennes (1)** semi-detached houses

♦ **des maisons mitoyennes (2)** terraced houses

♦ **à la maison (1)** at home ◊ *Je serai à la maison cet après-midi.* I'll be at home this afternoon.

♦ **à la maison (2)** home ◊ *Elle est rentrée à la maison.* She's gone home.

maison ADJECTIVE (MASC, FEM, PL)

see also **maison** NOUN
home-made ◊ *Je préfère les tartes maison à celles qui sont achetées.* I prefer home-made pies to bought ones.

le **maître** NOUN
1 teacher (*in primary school*)
2 master (*of dog*)

♦ **un maître d'hôtel** a head waiter (*in restaurant*)

♦ **un maître nageur** a lifeguard

la **maîtresse** NOUN
1 teacher (*in primary school*)
2 mistress ◊ *Il paraît qu'il a une maîtresse.* They say he's got a mistress.

la **maîtrise** NOUN
master's degree ◊ *Elle a une maîtrise d'anglais.* She's got a master's degree in English.

♦ **la maîtrise de soi** self-control

maîtriser VERB

♦ **se maîtriser** to control oneself ◊ *Il se met facilement en colère et a du mal à se maîtriser.* He loses his temper easily and finds it hard to control himself.

majestueux ADJECTIVE (FEM SING **majestueuse**)
majestic

majeur ADJECTIVE

♦ **être majeur** to be 18 ◊ *Tu feras ce que tu voudras quand tu seras majeure.* You can do what you like once you're 18. ◊ *Elle sera majeure en août.* She comes of age in August.

♦ **la majeure partie** most ◊ *la majeure partie de mon salaire* most of my salary

la **majorité** NOUN
majority ◊ *dans la majorité des cas* in the majority of cases

♦ **la majorité et l'opposition** the government and the opposition

Majorque FEM NOUN
Majorca

la **majuscule** NOUN
capital letter ◊ *un M majuscule* a capital M

mal ADVERB, ADJECTIVE (MASC, FEM, PL)
see also **mal** NOUN
1 badly ◊ *Ce travail a été mal fait.* The work was badly done. ◊ *Il a mal compris.* He misunderstood.
2 wrong ◊ *C'est mal de mentir.* It's wrong to tell lies.

♦ **aller mal** to be ill ◊ *Son grand-père va très mal.* His grandfather is very ill.

☞

M

◆ **pas mal** quite good ◇ *Je te trouve pas mal sur cette photo.* I think you look quite good in this photo.

le **mal** NOUN (PL les **maux**)

> *see also* **mal** ADVERB

1 ache ◇ *J'ai mal à la tête.* I've got a headache. ◇ *J'ai mal aux dents.* I've got toothache. ◇ *J'ai mal au dos.* My back hurts. ◇ *Est-ce que vous avez mal à la gorge?* Have you got a sore throat?

◆ **Ça fait mal.** It hurts.

◆ **Où est-ce que tu as mal?** Where does it hurt?

◆ **faire mal à quelqu'un** to hurt somebody ◇ *Attention, tu me fais mal!* Be careful, you're hurting me!

◆ **se faire mal** to hurt oneself ◇ *Je me suis fait mal au bras.* I hurt my arm.

◆ **se donner du mal pour faire quelque chose** to go to a lot of trouble to do something ◇ *Il s'est donné beaucoup de mal pour que cette soirée soit réussie.* He went to a lot of trouble to make the party a success.

◆ **avoir le mal de mer** to be seasick

◆ **avoir le mal du pays** to be homesick

2 evil ◇ *le bien et le mal* good and evil

◆ **dire du mal de quelqu'un** to speak ill of somebody

malade ADJECTIVE

> *see also* **malade** NOUN

ill

◆ **tomber malade** to fall ill

le/la **malade** NOUN

> *see also* **malade** ADJECTIVE

patient

la **maladie** NOUN

illness

maladif ADJECTIVE (FEM SING **maladive**)

sickly ◇ *C'est un enfant maladif.* He's a sickly child.

la **maladresse** NOUN

clumsiness

maladroit ADJECTIVE

clumsy

le **malaise** NOUN

◆ **avoir un malaise** to feel faint ◇ *Elle a eu un malaise après le déjeuner.* She felt faint after lunch.

◆ **Son arrivée a créé un malaise parmi les invités.** Her arrival made the guests feel uncomfortable.

la **malchance** NOUN

bad luck

mâle ADJECTIVE

male

la **malédiction** NOUN

curse

mal en point ADJECTIVE (MASC, FEM, PL)

◆ **Il avait l'air mal en point quand je l'ai vu hier soir.** He didn't look too good when I saw him last night.

le **malentendu** NOUN

misunderstanding

le **malfaiteur** NOUN

criminal

mal famé ADJECTIVE (FEM **mal famée**, MASC PL **mal famés**)

◆ **un quartier mal famé** a seedy area

malgache ADJECTIVE

from Madagascar ◇ *Sa mère est malgache.* His mother's from Madagascar.

malgré PREPOSITION

in spite of ◇ *Il est toujours généreux malgré ses problèmes d'argent.* He's always generous in spite of his financial problems.

◆ **malgré tout** all the same ◇ *Il faisait mauvais mais nous sommes sortis malgré tout.* The weather was bad but we went out all the same.

le **malheur** NOUN

tragedy ◇ *Elle a eu beaucoup de malheurs dans sa vie.* She's had a lot of tragedy in her life.

◆ **faire un malheur** (*informal*) to be a smash hit ◇ *Leur dernier album a fait un malheur.* Their latest album was a smash hit.

malheureusement ADVERB

unfortunately

malheureux ADJECTIVE (FEM SING **malheureuse**)

miserable ◇ *Qu'est-ce que tu as? Tu as l'air malheureux.* What's wrong with you? You look miserable.

malhonnête ADJECTIVE

dishonest

la **malice** NOUN

mischief ◇ *Son regard était plein de malice.* His eyes were full of mischief.

malicieux ADJECTIVE (FEM SING **malicieuse**)

mischievous

> Be careful! *malicieux* does not mean *malicious*.

malin ADJECTIVE (FEM SING **maligne**)

crafty

◆ **C'est malin!** (*informal*) That's clever! ◇ *Ah c'est malin! Nous voilà enfermés à cause de toi!* That's clever! You've got us locked in!

la **malle** NOUN

trunk

malodorant ADJECTIVE

foul-smelling

malpropre ADJECTIVE
dirty

malsain ADJECTIVE
unhealthy

Malte MASC NOUN
Malta

maltraiter VERB
to ill-treat ◊ *Il maltraite son chien.* He ill-treats his dog.
♦ **des enfants maltraités** abused children

malveillant ADJECTIVE
malicious ◊ *des rumeurs malveillantes* malicious rumours

la **maman** NOUN
mum

la **mamie** NOUN
granny

le **mammifère** NOUN
mammal

la **manche** NOUN
see also **le manche**
1 sleeve (*of clothes*)
2 leg (*of game*) ◊ *Ils ont gagné la première manche du match.* They won the first leg of the match.
♦ **la Manche** the Channel

le **manche** NOUN
see also **la manche**
handle (*of pan*)

la **mandarine** NOUN
mandarin orange

le **manège** NOUN
merry-go-round

la **manette** NOUN
lever

mangeable ADJECTIVE
edible ◊ *C'est à peine mangeable!* It's practically inedible!

manger VERB
to eat

la **mangue** NOUN
mango

maniaque ADJECTIVE
fussy

la **manie** NOUN
1 obsession
♦ **avoir la manie de** to be obsessive about ◊ *Il a la manie du rangement.* He's obsessive about tidying up.
2 habit ◊ *J'essaie de respecter ses petites manies.* I try to go along with her little ways.

manier VERB
to handle

la **manière** NOUN
see also **les manières**
way

♦ **de manière à** so as to ◊ *Nous sommes partis tôt de manière à éviter la circulation.* We left early so as to avoid the traffic.
♦ **de toute manière** in any case ◊ *Je n'aurais pas pu venir de toute manière.* I couldn't have come in any case.

maniéré ADJECTIVE
affected

les **manières** FEM NOUN
see also **la manière**
1 manners ◊ *apprendre les bonnes manières* to learn good manners
2 fuss ◊ *Ne fais pas de manières: mange ta soupe!* Don't make a fuss: eat your soup!

le **manifestant** NOUN
demonstrator

la **manifestante** NOUN
demonstrator

la **manifestation** NOUN
demonstration ◊ *une manifestation pour la paix* a peace demonstration

manifester VERB
to demonstrate

manipuler VERB
1 to handle ◊ *Ce vase doit être manipulé avec soin.* This vase must be handled with care.
2 to manipulate ◊ *Tous les partis essaient de manipuler l'opinion publique.* All the parties are trying to manipulate public opinion.

le **mannequin** NOUN
model ◊ *Elle est mannequin.* She's a model.

manœuvrer VERB
to manœuvre

le **manque** NOUN
withdrawal ◊ *un drogué en état de manque* a drug addict suffering withdrawal symptoms
♦ **le manque de** lack of ◊ *Le manque de sommeil peut provoquer toutes sortes de troubles.* Lack of sleep can cause all sorts of problems.

manqué ADJECTIVE
♦ **un garçon manqué** a tomboy

manquer VERB
to miss ◊ *Tu n'as rien manqué: le film n'était pas très bon.* You didn't miss anything: the film wasn't very good. ◊ *Il manque des pages à ce livre.* There are some pages missing from this book.
♦ **Mes parents me manquent.** I miss my parents.

M

☞

♦ **Ma sœur me manque.** I miss my sister.

♦ **Il manque encore cent francs.** We are still 100 francs short.

♦ **manquer de** to lack ◊ *La quiche manque de sel.* The quiche hasn't got enough salt in it. ◊ *Je trouve qu'il a manqué de tact.* I don't think he was very tactful.

♦ **Il a manqué se tuer.** He nearly got killed.

le **manteau** NOUN (PL les **manteaux**)
coat

manuel ADJECTIVE (FEM SING **manuelle**)
see also **manuel** NOUN
manual

le **manuel** NOUN
see also **manuel** ADJECTIVE
1 textbook
2 handbook

le **maquereau** NOUN (PL les **maquereaux**)
mackerel

la **maquette** NOUN
model ◊ *une maquette de bateau* a model boat

le **maquillage** NOUN
make-up

se **maquiller** VERB
to put on one's make-up ◊ *Je vais me maquiller en vitesse.* I'll just quickly put on my make-up.

le **marais** NOUN
marsh

le **marbre** NOUN
marble ◊ *une statue en marbre* a marble statue

le **marchand** NOUN
1 shopkeeper
♦ **un marchand de journaux** a newsagent
2 stallholder (*in market*)

la **marchande** NOUN
1 shopkeeper
♦ **une marchande de fruits et de légumes** a greengrocer
2 stallholder (*in market*)

marchander VERB
to haggle

la **marchandise** NOUN
goods

la **marche** NOUN
1 step ◊ *Fais attention à la marche!* Mind the step!
2 walking ◊ *La marche me fait du bien.* Walking does me good.
♦ **être en état de marche** to be in working order ◊ *Cette voiture est en parfait état de marche.* This car is in perfect running order.

♦ **Ne montez jamais dans un train en marche.** Never try to get into a moving train.

♦ **mettre en marche** to start ◊ *Comment est-ce qu'on met la machine à laver en marche?* How do you start the washing machine?

♦ **la marche arrière** reverse gear

♦ **faire marche arrière** to reverse
3 march ◊ *une marche militaire* a military march

le **marché** NOUN
market
♦ **un marché aux puces** a flea market
♦ **le marché noir** the black market

marcher VERB
1 to walk ◊ *Elle marche cinq kilomètres par jour.* She walks 5 kilometres every day.
2 to run ◊ *Le métro marche normalement aujourd'hui.* The underground is running normally today.
3 to work ◊ *Est-ce que l'ascenseur marche?* Is the lift working?
4 to go well ◊ *Est-ce que les affaires marchent actuellement?* Is business going well at the moment?
♦ **Alors les études, ça marche?** (*informal*) How are you getting on at school?
♦ **faire marcher quelqu'un** to pull somebody's leg ◊ *Il essaie de te faire marcher.* He's pulling your leg.

le **marcheur** NOUN
walker

la **marcheuse** NOUN
walker

le **mardi** NOUN
1 Tuesday ◊ *Aujourd'hui, nous sommes mardi.* It's Tuesday today.
2 on Tuesday ◊ *Ils reviennent mardi.* They're coming back on Tuesday.
♦ **le mardi** on Tuesdays ◊ *Le mardi, je vais à la gym.* I go to the gym on Tuesdays.
♦ **tous les mardis** every Tuesday
♦ **mardi dernier** last Tuesday
♦ **mardi prochain** next Tuesday
♦ **Mardi gras** Shrove Tuesday

la **mare** NOUN
pond

le **marécage** NOUN
marsh

la **marée** NOUN
tide ◊ *la marée haute* high tide ◊ *la marée basse* low tide ◊ *la marée montante* the rising tide ◊ *la marée descendante* the ebb tide
♦ **une marée noire** an oil slick

la **margarine** NOUN
margarine

la **marge** NOUN
margin

le **mari** NOUN
husband ◊ *son mari* her husband

le **mariage** NOUN
[1] marriage
[2] wedding ◊ *un mariage civil* a
registry office wedding ◊ *un mariage
religieux* a church wedding

marié ADJECTIVE
see also **marié** NOUN
married

le **marié** NOUN
see also **marié** ADJECTIVE
bridegroom
♦ **les mariés** the bride and groom

la **mariée** NOUN
bride

se **marier** VERB
to marry ◊ *Elle s'est mariée avec un
ami d'enfance.* She married a
childhood friend.

marin ADJECTIVE
see also **marin** NOUN
sea ◊ *l'air marin* the sea air
♦ **un pull marin** a sailor's jersey

le **marin** NOUN
see also **marin** ADJECTIVE
sailor

marine ADJECTIVE (MASC, FEM, PL)
see also **marine** NOUN
♦ **bleu marine** navy-blue ◊ *un pull bleu
marine* a navy-blue sweater

la **marine** NOUN
see also **marine** ADJECTIVE
navy
♦ **la marine nationale** the French navy

la **marionnette** NOUN
puppet

le **marketing** NOUN
marketing

la **marmelade** NOUN
stewed fruit
♦ **la marmelade de pommes** stewed
apple
♦ **la marmelade d'oranges** marmalade

la **marmite** NOUN
cooking pot

marmonner VERB
to mumble

le **Maroc** NOUN
Morocco

marocain ADJECTIVE
Moroccan

la **maroquinerie** NOUN
leather goods shop

marquant ADJECTIVE
significant ◊ *un événement marquant*
a significant event

la **marque** NOUN
[1] mark ◊ *des marques de doigts*
fingermarks
[2] make ◊ *De quelle marque est ton
jean?* What make are your jeans?
[3] brand ◊ *une grande marque de
cognac* a well-known brand of cognac
♦ **l'image de marque** the public image
◊ *Le ministre tient à son image de
marque.* The minister cares about his
public image.
♦ **une marque déposée** a registered
trademark
♦ **A vos marques! prêts! partez!** Ready,
steady, go!

marquer VERB
[1] to mark ◊ *Peux-tu marquer sur la
carte où se trouve le village?* Can
you mark where the village is on the
map?
[2] to score ◊ *L'équipe irlandaise a
marqué dix points.* The Irish team
scored ten points.
[3] to celebrate ◊ *On va sortir au
restaurant pour marquer ton
anniversaire.* We'll eat out to
celebrate your birthday.

la **marraine** NOUN
godmother

marrant ADJECTIVE (*informal*)
funny

marre ADVERB (*informal*)
♦ **en avoir marre de quelque chose** to
be fed up with something ◊ *J'en ai
marre de faire la vaisselle.* I'm fed up
with doing the dishes.

se **marrer** VERB (*informal*)
to have a good laugh ◊ *On
s'est bien marrés.* We had a good
laugh.

le **marron** NOUN
see also **marron** ADJECTIVE
chestnut ◊ *la crème de marrons*
chestnut purée

marron ADJECTIVE (MASC, FEM, PL)
see also **marron** NOUN
brown ◊ *des chaussures marron*
brown shoes

le **marronnier** NOUN
chestnut tree

mars MASC NOUN
March
♦ **en mars** in March

le **marteau** NOUN (PL les **marteaux**)
hammer

M

martyriser VERB
to batter ◊ *des enfants martyrisés* battered children

masculin ADJECTIVE
[1] men's ◊ *la mode masculine* men's fashion
[2] masculine ◊ *"chat" est un nom masculin.* "chat" is a masculine noun. ◊ *Elle a une allure assez masculine.* She looks rather masculine.

le **masque** NOUN
mask

le **massacre** NOUN
massacre

massacrer VERB
to massacre

le **massage** NOUN
massage

la **masse** NOUN
◆**une masse de** (*informal*) masses of ◊ *J'ai une masse de choses à faire.* I've got masses of things to do.
◆**produire en masse** to mass-produce ◊ *Ces jouets sont produits en masse en Chine.* These toys are mass-produced in China.
◆**venir en masse** to come en masse ◊ *Les gens sont venus en masse pour accueillir Nelson Mandela.* People came en masse to welcome Nelson Mandela.

masser VERB
to massage
◆**se masser** to gather ◊ *Les manifestants se sont massés devant l'ambassade.* The demonstrators gathered in front of the embassy.

massif ADJECTIVE (FEM SING **massive**)
[1] solid (*gold, silver, wood*) ◊ *un bracelet en or massif* a solid gold bracelet
[2] massive ◊ *une dose massive d'antibiotiques* a massive dose of antibiotics
[3] mass ◊ *des départs massifs* a mass exodus

mat ADJECTIVE
matt ◊ *blanc mat* matt white ◊ *Je voudrais mes photos en mat.* I would like my photos matt.
◆**être mat** to be checkmate (*chess*)

le **match** NOUN
match ◊ *un match de football* a football match
◆**le match aller** the first leg
◆**le match retour** the second leg
◆**faire match nul** to draw

le **matelas** NOUN
mattress

◆**un matelas pneumatique** an air bed

matelassé ADJECTIVE
quilted ◊ *une veste matelassée* a quilted jacket

le **matelot** NOUN
sailor

les **matériaux** MASC NOUN
materials

le **matériel** NOUN
[1] equipment ◊ *du matériel de laboratoire* laboratory equipment
[2] gear ◊ *Il a pris tout son matériel de pêche avec lui.* He took all his fishing gear with him.

maternel ADJECTIVE (FEM SING **maternelle**)
motherly ◊ *Elle est très maternelle.* She's very motherly.
◆**ma grand-mère maternelle** my mother's mother
◆**mon oncle maternel** my mother's brother

la **maternelle** NOUN
nursery school

> **ⓘ** The **maternelle** is a state school for 2-6 year-olds.

la **maternité** NOUN
◆**le congé de maternité** maternity leave ◊ *Notre professeur de musique est en congé de maternité.* Our music teacher is on maternity leave.

les **mathématiques** FEM NOUN
mathematics

les **maths** FEM NOUN (*informal*)
maths

la **matière** NOUN
subject ◊ *Le latin est une matière facultative.* Latin is an optional subject.
◆**sans matières grasses** fat-free
◆**les matières premières** raw materials

le **matin** NOUN
morning ◊ *à trois heures du matin* at 3 o'clock in the morning ◊ *du matin au soir* from morning till night
◆**Je suis du matin.** I'm at my best in the morning.
◆**de bon matin** early in the morning

matinal ADJECTIVE (MASC PL **matinaux**)
morning ◊ *Je fais ma gymnastique matinale avant de déjeuner.* I do my morning exercises before breakfast.
◆**être matinal** to be up early ◊ *Tu es bien matinal aujourd'hui!* You're up early today!

la **matinée** NOUN
morning ◊ *Je t'appellerai demain dans la matinée.* I'll call you

sometime tomorrow morning. ◊ *en
début de matinée* early in the
morning

le **matou** NOUN
tomcat

matrimonial ADJECTIVE (MASC PL
matrimoniaux)
♦ **une agence matrimoniale** a marriage
bureau

maudire VERB
to curse

maudit ADJECTIVE (*informal*)
blasted ◊ *Où est passé ce maudit
parapluie?* Where's that blasted
umbrella got to?

maussade ADJECTIVE
sullen

mauvais ADJECTIVE, ADVERB
[1] bad ◊ *une mauvaise note* a bad
mark ◊ *Tu arrives au mauvais
moment.* You've come at a bad time.
♦ **Il fait mauvais.** The weather's bad.
♦ **être mauvais en** to be bad at ◊ *Je
suis mauvais en allemand.* I'm bad at
German.
[2] poor ◊ *J'ai trouvé que le film était
mauvais.* I thought the film was poor.
◊ *Il est en mauvaise santé.* His
health is poor.
♦ **Tu as mauvaise mine.** You don't look
well.
[3] wrong ◊ *Vous avez fait le mauvais
numéro.* You've dialled the wrong
number.
♦ **des mauvaises herbes** weeds
♦ **sentir mauvais** to smell

les **maux** MASC NOUN
♦ **des maux de ventre** stomachache SING
♦ **des maux de tête** headache SING

le **maximum** NOUN
maximum
♦ **au maximum (1)** as much as one can
◊ *Remplis le seau au maximum.* Fill
the bucket as full as you can.
♦ **au maximum (2)** at the very most
◊ *Ça va vous coûter deux cents
francs au maximum.* It'll cost you 200
francs at the very most.

la **mayonnaise** NOUN
mayonnaise

le **mazout** NOUN
fuel oil

me PRONOUN

*me changes to **m'** before a vowel
and most words beginning with "h".*
[1] me ◊ *Elle me téléphone tous les
jours.* She phones me every day. ◊ *Il
m'attend depuis une heure.* He's been
waiting for me for an hour.

[2] to me ◊ *Il me parle en allemand.*
He talks to me in German. ◊ *Elle m'a
expliqué la situation.* She explained
the situation to me.
[3] myself ◊ *Je vais me préparer
quelque chose à manger.* I'm going
to make myself something to eat.
*With reflexive verbs, **me** is often not
translated.*
◊ *Je me lève à sept heures tous les
matins.* I get up at 7 every morning.

le **mec** NOUN (*informal*)
guy

le **mécanicien** NOUN
mechanic

la **mécanicienne** NOUN
mechanic

la **mécanique** NOUN
[1] mechanics
[2] mechanism (*of watch, clock*)

le **mécanisme** NOUN
mechanism

méchamment ADVERB
nastily ◊ *Il lui a répondu
méchamment.* He answered him
nastily.

la **méchanceté** NOUN
nastiness

méchant ADJECTIVE
nasty ◊ *C'est un homme méchant.*
He's a nasty man. ◊ *Ne sois pas
méchant avec ton petit frère.* Don't
be nasty to your little brother.
♦ **"Attention, chien méchant"** "Beware
of the dog"

la **mèche** NOUN
lock (*of hair*)

mécontent ADJECTIVE
♦ **mécontent de** unhappy with ◊ *Elle est
mécontente de sa coupe de cheveux.*
She's unhappy with her haircut.

le **mécontentement** NOUN
displeasure ◊ *Il a exprimé son
mécontentement.* He expressed his
displeasure.

la **médaille** NOUN
medal

le **médecin** NOUN
doctor ◊ *aller chez le médecin* to go
to the doctor

la **médecine** NOUN
medicine (*subject*) ◊ *Il fait médecine.*
He's studying medicine.

les **médias** MASC NOUN
media SING

médical ADJECTIVE (MASC PL **médicaux**)
medical ◊ *la recherche médicale*
medical research

M

◆**passer une visite médicale** to have a medical

le **médicament** NOUN
medicine (*drug*)

médiéval ADJECTIVE (MASC PL **médiévaux**)
medieval

médiocre ADJECTIVE
poor ◊ *des notes médiocres* poor marks

méditer VERB
to meditate

la **Méditerranée** NOUN
Mediterranean

méditerranéen ADJECTIVE (FEM SING **méditerranéenne**)
Mediterranean

la **méduse** NOUN
jellyfish

la **méfiance** NOUN
mistrust

méfiant ADJECTIVE
mistrustful

se **méfier** VERB
◆**se méfier de quelqu'un** to distrust somebody ◊ *Si j'étais toi, je me méfierais de lui.* If I were you, I wouldn't trust him.

la **mégarde** NOUN
◆**par mégarde** by mistake ◊ *J'ai emporté son livre par mégarde.* I took his book by mistake.

le **mégot** NOUN
cigarette end

meilleur ADJECTIVE, ADVERB, NOUN
better ◊ *Ce serait meilleur avec du fromage râpé.* It would be better with grated cheese. ◊ *Il paraît que le film est meilleur que le livre.* They say that the film is better than the book.
◆**le meilleur** the best ◊ *C'est elle qui est la meilleure en sport.* She's the best at sport. ◊ *Je préfère garder le meilleur pour la fin.* I like to keep the best for last.
◆**le meilleur des deux** the better of the two
◆**meilleur marché** cheaper ◊ *La bière est meilleur marché en France.* Beer's cheaper in France.

mélancolique ADJECTIVE
melancholy

le **mélange** NOUN
mixture

mélanger VERB
1 to mix ◊ *Mélangez le tout.* Mix everything together.
2 to muddle up ◊ *Tu mélanges tout!* You're muddling everything up!

la **mêlée** NOUN
scrum

mêler VERB
◆**se mêler** to mix ◊ *Il ne cherche pas à se mêler aux autres.* He doesn't try to mix with the others.
◆**Mêle-toi de ce qui te regarde!** (*informal*) Mind your own business!

la **mélodie** NOUN
melody

le **melon** NOUN
melon

le **membre** NOUN
1 limb
2 member ◊ *un membre de la famille* a member of the family ◊ *les pays membres de l'Union européenne* the member countries of the European Union

la **mémé** NOUN (*informal*)
granny

même ADJECTIVE, ADVERB, PRONOUN
1 same ◊ *J'ai le même manteau.* I've got the same coat. ◊ *Tiens, c'est curieux j'ai le même!* That's strange, I've got the same one!
◆**en même temps** at the same time
◆**moi-même** myself ◊ *Je l'ai fait moi-même.* I did it myself.
◆**toi-même** yourself ◊ *Est-ce que tu vas faire les travaux toi-même?* Are you going to do the work yourself?
◆**eux-mêmes** themselves
2 even ◊ *Il n'a même pas pleuré.* He didn't even cry.

la **mémoire** NOUN
memory

la **menace** NOUN
threat

menacer VERB
to threaten

le **ménage** NOUN
housework ◊ *faire le ménage* to do the housework
◆**une femme de ménage** a cleaning woman

ménager ADJECTIVE (FEM SING **ménagère**)
◆**les travaux ménagers** housework

la **ménagère** NOUN
housewife

le **mendiant** NOUN
beggar

la **mendiante** NOUN
beggar

mendier VERB
to beg

mener VERB
to lead ◊ *Cette rue mène directement à la gare.* This street leads straight to the station.
♦**Cela ne vous mènera à rien!** That will get you nowhere!

la **méningite** NOUN
meningitis

les **menottes** FEM NOUN
handcuffs

le **mensonge** NOUN
lie

la **mensualité** NOUN
monthly payment ◊ *en dix mensualités* in ten monthly payments

mensuel ADJECTIVE (FEM SING **mensuelle**)
monthly

les **mensurations** FEM NOUN
measurements

la **mentalité** NOUN
mentality

le **menteur** NOUN
liar

la **menteuse** NOUN
liar

la **menthe** NOUN
mint

la **mention** NOUN
grade ◊ *Il a été reçu avec mention bien.* He got a grade B pass.

mentionner VERB
to mention

mentir VERB
to lie ◊ *Tu mens!* You're lying!

le **menton** NOUN
chin

menu ADJECTIVE, ADVERB
see also **menu** NOUN
[1] slim ◊ *Elle est menue.* She's slim. ◊ *Elle est petite et menue.* She's petite.
[2] very fine ◊ *Les oignons doivent être coupés menu.* The onions have to be cut up very fine.

le **menu** NOUN
see also **menu** ADJECTIVE
menu ◊ *le menu du jour* today's menu ◊ *le menu touristique* the tourist menu ◊ *le menu d'aide* the help menu

la **menuiserie** NOUN
woodwork

le **menuisier** NOUN
joiner

le **mépris** NOUN
contempt ◊ *Il nous a traités avec mépris.* He treated us with contempt.

méprisant ADJECTIVE

contemptuous

mépriser VERB
to despise

la **mer** NOUN
[1] sea ◊ *en mer* at sea
♦**au bord de la mer** at the seaside
♦**la mer du Nord** the North Sea
[2] tide ◊ *La mer est basse.* The tide is out. ◊ *La mer sera haute à sept heures.* It'll be high tide at 7 o'clock.

la **mercerie** NOUN
[1] haberdashery
[2] haberdasher's shop

merci EXCLAMATION
thank you ◊ *Merci de m'avoir raccompagné.* Thank you for taking me home.
♦**merci beaucoup** thank you very much

le **mercredi** NOUN
[1] Wednesday ◊ *Aujourd'hui, nous sommes mercredi.* It's Wednesday today.
[2] on Wednesday ◊ *Nous comptons partir mercredi.* We plan to leave on Wednesday.
♦**le mercredi** on Wednesdays ◊ *Le musée est fermé le mercredi.* The museum is shut on Wednesdays.
♦**tous les mercredis** every Wednesday
♦**mercredi dernier** last Wednesday
♦**mercredi prochain** next Wednesday

la **merde** NOUN (*rude*)
shit ◊ *Merde!* Shit!

la **mère** NOUN
mother

la **merguez** NOUN
spicy sausage

méridional ADJECTIVE (MASC PL **méridionaux**)
southern ◊ *Il a un accent méridional.* He's got a southern accent.

la **meringue** NOUN
meringue

mériter VERB
to deserve

le **merlan** NOUN
whiting

le **merle** NOUN
blackbird

la **merveille** NOUN
♦**Cet ordinateur est une vraie merveille!** This computer's really wonderful!
♦**à merveille** wonderfully ◊ *Elle se porte à merveille depuis son opération.* She's been wonderfully well since the operation.

merveilleux ADJECTIVE (FEM SING **merveilleuse**)

M

☞

marvellous

mes ADJECTIVE
my ◊ *mes parents* my parents

Mesdames FEM NOUN
ladies ◊ *Bonjour, Mesdames.* Good morning, ladies.

Mesdemoiselles FEM NOUN
ladies ◊ *Bonjour, Mesdemoiselles.* Good morning, ladies.

mesquin ADJECTIVE
mean

le **message** NOUN
message

la **messagerie** NOUN
◊ *une messagerie vocale* voice mail

la **messe** NOUN
mass ◊ *aller à la messe* to go to mass ◊ *la messe de minuit* midnight mass

messieurs MASC NOUN
gentlemen ◊ *Que puis-je faire pour vous, Messieurs?* What can I do for you, gentlemen?
♦ **Messieurs, ...** Dear Sirs, ... (*in letter*)

la **mesure** NOUN
[1] measurement ◊ *J'ai pris les mesures de la fenêtre.* I took the measurements of the window.
♦ **sur mesure** tailor-made ◊ *un costume sur mesure* a tailor-made suit
[2] measure ◊ *L'établissement a pris des mesures pour lutter contre le vandalisme.* The school has taken measures to combat vandalism.
♦ **au fur et à mesure** as one goes along ◊ *Quand je cuisine, je préfère faire la vaisselle au fur et à mesure.* When I'm cooking, I prefer to wash up as I go along.
♦ **être en mesure de faire quelque chose** to be in a position to do something ◊ *Nous ne sommes pas en mesure de vous renseigner.* We are not in a position to give you any information.

mesurer VERB
to measure ◊ *Mesurez la longueur et la largeur.* Measure the length and the width.
♦ **Il mesure un mètre quatre-vingts.** He's 1 m 80 tall.

met VERB *see* **mettre**

le **métal** NOUN (PL les **métaux**)
metal

métallique ADJECTIVE
metallic

la **météo** NOUN
weather forecast ◊ *Qu'est-ce que dit la météo pour cet après-midi?* What's the weather forecast for this afternoon?

la **méthode** NOUN
[1] method ◊ *des méthodes d'enseignement modernes* modern teaching methods
[2] tutor (*manual*) ◊ *une méthode de guitare* a guitar tutor

le **métier** NOUN
job ◊ *Quel métier est-ce que tu aimerais faire plus tard?* What job would you like to do when you're older?

le **mètre** NOUN
metre
♦ **un mètre ruban** a tape measure

le **métro** NOUN
underground ◊ *prendre le métro* to go by underground

mets VERB *see* **mettre**

le **metteur en scène** NOUN (PL les **metteurs en scène**)
[1] producer (*of play*)
[2] director (*of film*)

mettre VERB

Present tense:	
je mets	nous mettons
tu mets	vous mettez
il/elle met	ils/elles mettent
Past participle:	
mis	

[1] to put ◊ *Où est-ce que tu as mis les clés?* Where have you put the keys?
[2] to put on ◊ *Je mets mon manteau et j'arrive.* I'll put on my coat and then I'll be ready. ◊ *Il fait froid, je vais mettre le chauffage.* It's cold, I'm going to put the heating on.
[3] to wear ◊ *Marie-Claire ne met pas souvent de jupe.* Marie-Claire doesn't often wear a skirt. ◊ *Je n'ai rien à me mettre!* I've got nothing to wear!
[4] to take ◊ *Combien de temps as-tu mis pour aller à Lille?* How long did it take you to get to Lille? ◊ *Elle met des heures à se préparer.* She takes hours getting ready.
♦ **mettre en marche** to start ◊ *Comment met-on la machine à laver en marche?* How do you start the washing machine?
♦ **Vous pouvez vous mettre là.** You can sit there.
♦ **se mettre au lit** to get into bed
♦ **se mettre en maillot de bain** to put on one's swimsuit

◆**se mettre à** to start ◊ *Il s'est mis à la peinture à cinquante ans.* He started painting when he was 50. ◊ *Il est temps de se mettre au travail.* It's time to start work. ◊ *Elle s'est mise à pleurer.* She started crying.

le **meuble** NOUN
   piece of furniture ◊ *Je me suis cogné contre un meuble.* I bumped into a piece of furniture. ◊ *Ce magasin vend de beaux meubles.* This shop sells nice furniture.

le **meublé** NOUN
   ⓵ furnished flat
   ⓶ furnished room

meubler VERB
   to furnish

le **meurtre** NOUN
   murder

le **meurtrier** NOUN
   murderer

la **meurtrière** NOUN
   murderess

Mexico NOUN
   Mexico City

le **Mexique** NOUN
   Mexico

le **mi** NOUN
   ⓵ E ◊ *mi bémol* E flat
   ⓶ mi ◊ *do, ré, mi ...* do, re, mi ...

mi- PREFIX
   ⓵ half- ◊ *mi-clos* half-shut
   ⓶ mid- ◊ *à la mi-janvier* in mid-January

miauler VERB
   to mew

la **miche** NOUN
   loaf

mi-chemin
◆**à mi-chemin** ADVERB
   halfway

le **micro** NOUN
   microphone

le **microbe** NOUN
   germ

le **micro-ondes** NOUN
   microwave oven

le **micro-ordinateur** NOUN
   microcomputer

le **microscope** NOUN
   microscope

le **midi** NOUN
   ⓵ midday ◊ *à midi* at midday
◆**midi et demi** half past twelve
   ⓶ lunchtime ◊ *On a bien mangé à midi.* We had a good meal at lunchtime.
◆**le Midi** the South of France

la **mie** NOUN
   breadcrumbs

le **miel** NOUN
   honey

mien PRONOUN
◆**le mien** mine ◊ *Ce vélo-là, c'est le mien.* That bike's mine.

mienne PRONOUN
◆**la mienne** mine ◊ *Cette valise-là, c'est la mienne.* That case is mine.

miennes PRONOUN
◆**les miennes** mine ◊ *Heureusement que tu as tes clés: j'ai oublié les miennes.* It's lucky you've got your keys: I forgot mine.

miens PRONOUN
◆**les miens** mine ◊ *Ces CD-là, ce sont les miens.* Those CDs are mine.

la **miette** NOUN
   crumb (*of bread, cake*)

mieux ADVERB, ADJECTIVE, NOUN
   better ◊ *Je la connais mieux que son frère.* I know her better than her brother. ◊ *Elle va mieux.* She's better. ◊ *Les cheveux courts lui vont mieux.* She looks better with short hair.
◆**Il vaut mieux que tu appelles ta mère.** You'd better phone your mother.
◆**le mieux** the best ◊ *C'est la région que je connais le mieux.* It's the region I know best.
◆**faire de son mieux** to do one's best ◊ *Essaie de faire de ton mieux.* Try to do your best.
◆**de mieux en mieux** better and better
◆**au mieux** at best

mignon ADJECTIVE (FEM SING **mignonne**)
   sweet ◊ *Qu'est-ce qu'il est mignon!* Isn't he sweet!

la **migraine** NOUN
   migraine ◊ *J'ai la migraine.* I've got a migraine.

mijoter VERB
   to simmer

le **milieu** NOUN (PL les **milieux**)
   ⓵ middle
◆**au milieu de** in the middle of ◊ *Place le vase au milieu de la table.* Put the vase in the middle of the table.
◆**au beau milieu de** in the middle of ◊ *Quelqu'un a sonné à la porte au beau milieu de la nuit.* Somebody rang the bell in the middle of the night.
   ⓶ background ◊ *le milieu familial* the family background ◊ *Il vient d'un milieu modeste.* He comes from a modest background.

M

③ environment ◇ *le milieu marin* the marine environment

militaire ADJECTIVE
| *see also* **militaire** NOUN |
military ◇ *faire son service militaire* to do one's military service

le **militaire** NOUN
| *see also* **militaire** ADJECTIVE |
serviceman ◇ *Son père est militaire.* His father is in the services.
♦ *un militaire de carrière* a professional soldier

mille NUMBER
a thousand ◇ *mille francs* a thousand francs ◇ *deux mille personnes* two thousand people

le **millénaire** NOUN
millennium ◇ *le troisième millénaire* the third millennium

le **millefeuille** NOUN
vanilla slice

le **millénium** NOUN
millennium

le **milliard** NOUN
thousand million ◇ *cinq milliards de francs* five thousand million francs

le/la **milliardaire** NOUN
multimillionaire

le **millier** NOUN
thousand ◇ *des milliers de personnes* thousands of people
♦ *par milliers* by the thousand

le **milligramme** NOUN
milligramme

le **millimètre** NOUN
millimetre

le **million** NOUN
million ◇ *deux millions de personnes* two million people

le/la **millionnaire** NOUN
millionaire

le/la **mime** NOUN
mime artist

mimer VERB
to mimic

minable ADJECTIVE
① shabby ◇ *un imperméable minable* a shabby raincoat
② pathetic ◇ *Mon moniteur de ski était minable.* My skiing instructor was pathetic.

mince ADJECTIVE
① thin ◇ *une mince tranche de jambon* a thin slice of ham
② slim ◇ *Il est grand et mince.* He's tall and slim.
♦ **Mince alors!** (*informal*) Oh bother!

la **minceur** NOUN

① thinness ◇ *la minceur des murs* the thinness of the walls
② slimness ◇ *Elle enviait la minceur de sa sœur.* She envied her sister's slimness.

la **mine** NOUN
① expression
② look ◇ *Tu as bonne mine.* You look well. ◇ *Il a mauvaise mine.* He doesn't look well. ◇ *Elle avait une mine fatiguée.* She was looking tired.
③ appearance ◇ *Il ne faut pas juger les gens d'après leur mine.* You shouldn't judge people by their appearance.
④ lead (*of pencil*)
⑤ mine ◇ *une mine de charbon* a coal mine
♦ **faire mine de faire quelque chose** to pretend to do something ◇ *Elle a fait mine de le croire.* She pretended to believe him.
♦ **mine de rien** somehow or other ◇ *Elle a réussi mine de rien à le faire parler de lui.* Somehow or other she got him to talk about himself.

minéral ADJECTIVE (MASC PL **minéraux**)
mineral ◇ *l'eau minérale* mineral water

minéralogique ADJECTIVE
♦ **une plaque minéralogique** a number plate

le **minet** NOUN
pussycat

la **minette** NOUN
pussycat (*female*)

mineur ADJECTIVE
| *see also* **mineur** NOUN |
minor

le **mineur** NOUN
| *see also* **mineur** ADJECTIVE |
① boy under 18
♦ **les mineurs** the under-18s
② miner ◇ *Mon grand-père était mineur.* My grandfather was a miner.

la **mineure** NOUN
girl under 18

le **minidisque** NOUN
Minidisc ®

la **minijupe** NOUN
miniskirt

le **minimum** NOUN
minimum ◇ *Il en fait le minimum.* He does the absolute minimum.
♦ **au minimum** at the very least

le **ministère** NOUN
ministry ◇ *le ministère des Affaires étrangères* the Foreign Office

le **ministre** NOUN

<u>minister</u> ◊ *le ministre des Affaires étrangères* the Foreign Secretary

le **Minitel** ® NOUN

> ℹ️ *Minitel is France Telecom's online data service. You can use it instead of a phone directory, and to make bookings for transport, exhibitions etc.*

la **minorité** NOUN
<u>minority</u>

Minorque FEM NOUN
<u>Minorca</u>

le **minuit** NOUN
<u>midnight</u> ◊ *à minuit et quart* at a quarter past midnight

minuscule ADJECTIVE
> see also **minuscule** NOUN

<u>tiny</u>

la **minuscule** NOUN
> see also **minuscule** ADJECTIVE

<u>small letter</u>

la **minute** NOUN
<u>minute</u>
♦ **à la minute** just this minute ◊ *Je viens de l'appeler à la minute.* I've just this minute called him.

minutieux ADJECTIVE (FEM SING **minutieuse**)
<u>meticulous</u>
♦ **C'est un travail minutieux.** It's a fiddly job.

la **mirabelle** NOUN
<u>small yellow plum</u>

le **miracle** NOUN
<u>miracle</u>

le **miroir** NOUN
<u>mirror</u>

mis VERB *see* **mettre**

mis ADJECTIVE
♦ **bien mis** well turned out ◊ *Elle est toujours bien mise.* She's always well turned out.

miser VERB (*informal*)
<u>to bank on</u> ◊ *On ne peut pas miser là-dessus.* We can't bank on it.

misérable ADJECTIVE
<u>shabby-looking</u> ◊ *une femme d'aspect misérable* a shabby-looking woman

la **misère** NOUN
<u>extreme poverty</u>
♦ **un salaire de misère** starvation wages

le/la **missionnaire** NOUN
<u>missionary</u>

mit VERB *see* **mettre**

la **mi-temps** NOUN
> 1 <u>half</u> (*of match*) ◊ *la première mi-temps* the first half ◊ *la deuxième mi-temps* the second half
> 2 <u>half-time</u> ◊ *Je lui parlerai à la mi-temps.* I'll speak to him at half-time.

♦ **travailler à mi-temps** to work part-time

la **mitraillette** NOUN
<u>submachine gun</u>

mixte ADJECTIVE
♦ **une école mixte** a mixed school

Mlle ABBREVIATION (PL **Mlles**)
(= *Mademoiselle*)
<u>Miss</u> ◊ *Mlle Renoir* Miss Renoir

Mme ABBREVIATION (PL **Mmes**)
(= *Madame*)
<u>Mrs</u> ◊ *Mme Leroy* Mrs Leroy

le **mobile** NOUN
<u>motive</u> ◊ *Quel était le mobile du crime?* What was the motive for the crime?

le **mobilier** NOUN
<u>furniture</u>

la **mobylette** ® NOUN
<u>moped</u>

moche ADJECTIVE (*informal*)
> 1 <u>awful</u> ◊ *Cette couleur est vraiment moche.* That colour's really awful. ◊ *Je me trouve moche!* I think I look awful!
> 2 <u>rotten</u> ◊ *Il a la grippe, c'est moche pour lui.* He's got flu, that's rotten for him.

la **mode** NOUN
> see also **le mode**

<u>fashion</u> ◊ *être à la mode* to be fashionable

le **mode** NOUN
> see also **la mode**

♦ **le mode d'emploi** directions for use
♦ **le mode de vie** the way of life

le **modèle** NOUN
> 1 <u>model</u> ◊ *Le nouveau modèle sort en septembre.* The new model is coming out in September.
> 2 <u>style</u> (*of clothes*) ◊ *Est-ce que vous avez le même modèle en plus grand?* Have you got the same style in a bigger size?

modéré ADJECTIVE
<u>moderate</u>

moderne ADJECTIVE
<u>modern</u>

moderniser VERB
<u>to modernize</u>

modeste ADJECTIVE

M

☞

modest ◊ *Ne sois pas si modeste!* Don't be so modest!

la **modestie** NOUN
modesty

moelleux ADJECTIVE (FEM SING **moelleuse**)
soft ◊ *un coussin moelleux* a soft cushion

les **mœurs** FEM NOUN
social attitudes
◆*l'évolution des mœurs* changing attitudes

moi PRONOUN
me ◊ *Coucou, c'est moi!* Hello, it's me!
◆*Moi, je pense que tu as tort.* I personally think you're wrong.
◆*à moi* mine ◊ *Ce livre n'est pas à moi.* This book isn't mine. ◊ *un ami à moi* a friend of mine

moi-même PRONOUN
myself ◊ *J'ai tricoté ce pull moi-même.* I knitted this jumper myself.

moindre ADJECTIVE
◆*le moindre* the slightest ◊ *Il ne fait pas le moindre effort.* He doesn't make the slightest effort. ◊ *Je n'en ai pas la moindre idée.* I haven't the slightest idea.

le **moine** NOUN
monk

le **moineau** NOUN (PL les **moineaux**)
sparrow

moins ADVERB, PREPOSITION
1 less ◊ *Ça coûte moins de deux cents francs.* It costs less than 200 francs.
2 fewer ◊ *Il y a moins de gens aujourd'hui.* There are fewer people today.
◆*Il est cinq heures moins dix.* It's 10 to 5.
3 minus ◊ *quatre moins trois* 4 minus 3 ◊ *Il a fait moins cinq la nuit dernière.* It was minus five last night.
◆*le moins* the least ◊ *C'est le modèle le moins cher.* It's the least expensive model. ◊ *Ce sont les plages qui sont les moins polluées.* These are the least polluted beaches. ◊ *C'est l'album que j'aime le moins.* This is the album I like the least.
◆*de moins en moins* less and less ◊ *Il vient nous voir de moins en moins.* He comes to see us less and less often.
◆*Il a trois ans de moins que moi.* He's three years younger than me.
◆*au moins* at least ◊ *Ne te plains pas: au moins il ne pleut pas!* Don't complain: at least it's not raining!

◆**à moins que** unless
à moins que is followed by a verb in the subjunctive.
◊ *Je te retrouverai à dix heures à moins que le train n'ait du retard.* I'll meet you at 10 o'clock unless the train's late.

le **mois** NOUN
month

le **moisi** NOUN
◆*Ça sent le moisi.* It smells musty.

moisir VERB
to go mouldy ◊ *Le pain a moisi.* The bread's gone mouldy.

la **moisson** NOUN
harvest

moite ADJECTIVE
sweaty ◊ *J'ai toujours les mains moites.* My hands are always sweaty.

la **moitié** NOUN
half ◊ *Il a mangé la moitié du gâteau à lui seul.* He ate half the cake all by himself.
◆*la moitié du temps* half the time
◆*à la moitié de* halfway through ◊ *Elle est partie à la moitié du film.* She left halfway through the film.
◆*à moitié* half ◊ *Ton verre est encore à moitié plein.* Your glass is still half-full. ◊ *Ce sac était à moitié prix.* This bag was half-price.
◆*partager moitié moitié* to go halves ◊ *On partage moitié moitié, d'accord?* We'll go halves, OK?

la **molaire** NOUN
back tooth

la **Moldavie** NOUN
Moldova

molle ADJECTIVE
lethargic ◊ *Je la trouve un peu molle.* I find her a bit lethargic.

le **mollet** NOUN
see also **mollet** ADJECTIVE
calf (*of leg*)

mollet ADJECTIVE
see also **mollet** NOUN
◆*un œuf mollet* a soft-boiled egg

le/la **môme** NOUN (*informal*)
kid

le **moment** NOUN
moment
◆*en ce moment* at the moment ◊ *Nous avons beaucoup de travail en ce moment.* We have a lot of work at the moment.
◆*pour le moment* for the moment ◊ *Nous ne pensons pas déménager pour le moment.* We're not thinking of moving for the moment.

◆ **au moment où** just as ◊ *Il est arrivé au moment où j'allais partir.* He turned up just as I was leaving.

◆ **à ce moment-là (1)** at that point ◊ *À ce moment-là, on a vu arriver la police.* At that point, we saw the police coming.

◆ **à ce moment-là (2)** in that case ◊ *À ce moment-là, je devrai partir plus tôt.* In that case I'll have to leave earlier.

◆ **à tout moment (1)** at any moment ◊ *Elle peut arriver à tout moment.* She could arrive at any moment.

◆ **à tout moment (2)** constantly ◊ *Il nous dérange à tout moment pour des riens.* He's constantly bothering us about silly little things.

◆ **sur le moment** at the time ◊ *Sur le moment je n'ai rien dit.* At the time I didn't say anything.

◆ **par moments** at times ◊ *Elle se sent seule par moments.* She feels lonely at times.

momentané ADJECTIVE
　momentary

la **momie** NOUN
　mummy (*Egyptian*)

mon ADJECTIVE (FEM SING **ma**, PL **mes**)
　my ◊ *mon frère* my brother ◊ *mon ami* my friend

la **monarchie** NOUN
　monarchy

le **monastère** NOUN
　monastery

le **monde** NOUN
　world ◊ *faire le tour du monde* to go round the world
　◆ **Il y a du monde.** There are a lot of people.
　◆ **beaucoup de monde** a lot of people ◊ *Il y avait beaucoup de monde au concert.* There were a lot of people at the concert.
　◆ **peu de monde** not many people

mondial ADJECTIVE (MASC PL **mondiaux**)
　① world ◊ *la population mondiale* the world population
　② world-wide ◊ *une crise mondiale* a world-wide crisis

le **moniteur** NOUN
　① instructor ◊ *un moniteur de voile* a sailing instructor
　② monitor ◊ *le moniteur de mon ordinateur* my computer monitor

la **monitrice** NOUN
　instructor ◊ *une monitrice de ski* a ski instructor

la **monnaie** NOUN
　◆ **une pièce de monnaie** a coin

◆ **avoir de la monnaie** to have change ◊ *Est-ce que tu as de la monnaie?* Have you got any change? ◊ *Est-ce que vous avez la monnaie de cent francs?* Do you have change for 100 francs?

◆ **rendre la monnaie à quelqu'un** to give somebody their change

monotone ADJECTIVE
　monotonous

Monsieur MASC NOUN (PL **Messieurs**)
　① Mr ◊ *Monsieur Dupont* Mr Dupont
　② man ◊ *Il y a un monsieur qui veut te voir.* There's a man to see you.
　③ Sir ◊ *Monsieur, ...* Dear Sir, ... (*in letter*) ◊ *Monsieur! Vous avez oublié votre parapluie!* Excuse me! You've forgotten your umbrella!

le **monstre** NOUN
　see also **monstre** ADJECTIVE
　monster

monstre ADJECTIVE
　see also **monstre** NOUN
　◆ **Nous avons un travail monstre.** We've got a terrific amount of work.

le **mont** NOUN
　mount
　◆ **le mont Everest** Mount Everest
　◆ **le mont Blanc** Mont Blanc

la **montagne** NOUN
　mountain ◊ *de hautes montagnes* high mountains ◊ *Nous passons tous les ans un mois à la montagne.* We spend a month in the mountains every year.
　◆ **les montagnes russes** roller coaster

montagneux ADJECTIVE (FEM SING **montagneuse**)
　mountainous ◊ *une région montagneuse* a mountainous area

montant ADJECTIVE
　① rising ◊ *la marée montante* the rising tide
　② high ◊ *un pull à col montant* a high-necked jumper

monter VERB
　① to go up ◊ *Elle a du mal à monter les escaliers.* She has difficulty going upstairs. ◊ *Les prix ont encore monté.* Prices have gone up again.
　② to assemble ◊ *Est-ce que ces étagères sont difficiles à monter?* Are these shelves difficult to assemble?
　◆ **monter dans** to get on ◊ *Il est temps de monter dans l'avion.* It's time to get on the plane.
　◆ **monter sur** to stand on ◊ *Tu vas devoir monter sur une chaise pour changer l'ampoule.* You'll have to

M

☞

stand on a chair to change the light bulb.
♦ **monter à cheval** to ride

la **montre** NOUN
watch

montrer VERB
to show ◊ *Est-ce que vous pouvez me montrer la gare sur le plan?* Can you show me the station on the map?

la **monture** NOUN
frames (*of glasses*)

le **monument** NOUN
monument

se **moquer** VERB
♦ **se moquer de (1)** to make fun of ◊ *Ils se sont moqués de mes chaussures jaunes.* They made fun of my yellow shoes.
♦ **se moquer de (2)** (*informal*) not to care about ◊ *Il se moque complètement de la mode.* He couldn't care less about fashion.

la **moquette** NOUN
fitted carpet

moqueur ADJECTIVE (FEM SING **moqueuse**)
mocking

le **moral** NOUN
♦ **Elle a le moral.** She's in good spirits.
♦ **J'ai le moral à zéro.** I'm feeling really down.

la **morale** NOUN
moral ◊ *La morale de cette histoire est ...* The moral of the story is ...
♦ **faire la morale à quelqu'un** to lecture somebody

le **morceau** NOUN (PL les **morceaux**)
piece ◊ *un morceau de pain* a piece of bread

mordre VERB
to bite

mordu ADJECTIVE
♦ **Il est mordu de jazz.** (*informal*) He's crazy about jazz.

la **morgue** NOUN
mortuary

le **morse** NOUN
walrus

la **morsure** NOUN
bite

la **mort** NOUN
see also **mort** ADJECTIVE
death

mort ADJECTIVE
see also **mort** NOUN
dead ◊ *Nous avons trouvé un oiseau mort.* We found a dead bird.

◊ *Napoléon est mort en 1821.* Napoleon died in 1821.
♦ **Il était mort de peur.** He was scared to death.
♦ **Je suis morte de fatigue.** I'm dead tired.

mortel ADJECTIVE (FEM SING **mortelle**)
① deadly ◊ *un poison mortel* a deadly poison ◊ *Ces réunions de famille sont mortelles!* (*informal*) These family gatherings are deadly!
② fatal ◊ *une chute mortelle* a fatal fall

la **morue** NOUN
cod

Moscou NOUN
Moscow

la **mosquée** NOUN
mosque

le **mot** NOUN
① word ◊ *mot à mot* word for word
♦ **des mots croisés** a crossword
♦ **le mot de passe** the password
② note ◊ *Je vais lui écrire un mot pour lui dire qu'on arrive.* I'll write her a note to say we're coming.

le **motard** NOUN
① biker
② motorcycle cop (*informal*) ◊ *Il s'est fait arrêter par un motard pour excès de vitesse.* He was stopped for speeding by a motorcycle cop.

le **moteur** NOUN
engine
♦ **un bateau à moteur** a motor boat
♦ **un moteur de recherche** a search engine

le **motif** NOUN
pattern ◊ *des rideaux avec un motif d'oiseaux* curtains with a bird pattern
♦ **sans motif** for no reason ◊ *Il s'est fâché sans motif.* He got angry for no reason.

motivé ADJECTIVE
motivated

la **moto** NOUN
motorbike

le/la **motocycliste** NOUN
motorcyclist

mou ADJECTIVE (FEM SING **molle**)
① soft ◊ *Mon matelas est trop mou.* My mattress is too soft.
② lethargic ◊ *Je le trouve un peu mou.* I find him a bit lethargic.

la **mouche** NOUN
fly
♦ **prendre la mouche** to get into a huff

se **moucher** VERB
to blow one's nose

le **moucheron** NOUN
　midge

le **mouchoir** NOUN
　handkerchief
　♦ **un mouchoir en papier** a tissue

moudre VERB
　to grind

la **moue** NOUN
　pout
　♦ **faire la moue** to pout

la **mouette** NOUN
　seagull

la **moufle** NOUN
　mitt

mouillé ADJECTIVE
　wet

mouiller VERB
　to get wet ◊ *J'ai mouillé les manches de mon pull.* I got the sleeves of my jumper wet.
　♦ **se mouiller** to get wet ◊ *Attention, tu vas te mouiller!* Careful, you'll get wet!

moulant ADJECTIVE
　figure-hugging ◊ *une robe moulante* a figure-hugging dress

la **moule** NOUN
　see also **le moule**
　mussel

le **moule** NOUN
　see also **la moule**
　♦ **un moule à gâteaux** a cake tin

le **moulin** NOUN
　mill

moulu VERB see **moudre**

mourir VERB
　to die
　♦ **mourir de faim** to starve ◊ *Des centaines de personnes sont mortes de faim.* Hundreds of people starved to death.
　♦ **Je meurs de faim!** I'm starving!
　♦ **mourir de froid** to die of exposure
　♦ **Je meurs de froid!** I'm freezing!
　♦ **mourir d'envie de faire quelque chose** to be dying to do something ◊ *Je meurs d'envie d'aller me baigner.* I'm dying to go for a swim.

la **mousse** NOUN
　1 moss ◊ *un rocher recouvert de mousse* a rock covered with moss
　2 froth (*on beer*)
　3 lather (*of soap, shampoo*)
　4 mousse ◊ *une mousse au chocolat* a chocolate mousse ◊ *une mousse de poisson* a fish mousse
　♦ **la mousse à raser** shaving foam

mousseux ADJECTIVE (FEM SING **mousseuse**)
　♦ **un vin mousseux** a sparkling wine

la **moustache** NOUN
　moustache
　♦ **les moustaches** whiskers

le **moustique** NOUN
　mosquito

la **moutarde** NOUN
　mustard

le **mouton** NOUN
　1 sheep ◊ *une peau de mouton* a sheepskin
　2 mutton ◊ *un gigot de mouton* a leg of mutton

le **mouvement** NOUN
　movement

mouvementé ADJECTIVE
　eventful ◊ *des vacances mouvementées* eventful holidays

moyen ADJECTIVE (FEM SING **moyenne**)
　see also **moyen** NOUN
　1 average ◊ *Je suis plutôt moyenne en langues.* I'm just average at languages.
　2 medium ◊ *Elle est de taille moyenne.* She's of medium height.
　♦ **le moyen âge** the Middle Ages

le **moyen** NOUN
　see also **moyen** ADJECTIVE
　way ◊ *Quel est le meilleur moyen de le convaincre?* What's the best way of convincing him?
　♦ **Je n'en ai pas les moyens.** I can't afford it.
　♦ **Ils n'ont pas les moyens de s'acheter une voiture.** They can't afford to buy a car.
　♦ **un moyen de transport** a means of transport
　♦ **par tous les moyens** by every possible means

la **moyenne** NOUN
　♦ **avoir la moyenne** to get a pass mark ◊ *J'espère avoir la moyenne en maths.* I hope to get a pass mark in maths.
　♦ **en moyenne** on average
　♦ **la moyenne d'âge** the average age

le **Moyen-Orient** NOUN
　Middle East

muet ADJECTIVE (FEM SING **muette**)
　dumb
　♦ **un film muet** a silent film

le **muguet** NOUN
　lily of the valley

multiple ADJECTIVE
　numerous ◊ *en de multiples occasions* on numerous occasions

multiplier VERB
　to multiply

M

municipal ADJECTIVE (MASC PL **municipaux**)
♦ **la bibliothèque municipale** the public library

la **municipalité** NOUN
town council

les **munitions** FEM NOUN
ammunition SING

le **mur** NOUN
wall

mûr ADJECTIVE
1 ripe (*fruit*)
2 mature (*person*)

la **mûre** NOUN
bramble

mûrir VERB
1 to ripen ◊ *Les fraises ont mis du temps à mûrir.* The strawberries took a while to ripen.
2 to make mature ◊ *Cette expérience l'a beaucoup mûrie.* That experience has made her much more mature.

murmurer VERB
to whisper ◊ *Il m'a murmuré à l'oreille qu'il allait partir.* He whispered in my ear that he was going to go.

la **muscade** NOUN
nutmeg

le **muscat** NOUN
1 muscat grape
2 muscatel (*wine*) ◊ *un verre de muscat* a glass of muscatel

le **muscle** NOUN
muscle

musclé ADJECTIVE
muscular

le **museau** NOUN (PL les **museaux**)
muzzle

le **musée** NOUN
museum

musical ADJECTIVE (MASC PL **musicaux**)
musical
♦ **avoir l'oreille musicale** to be musical

le **music-hall** NOUN
variety ◊ *une chanteuse de music-hall* a variety singer

le **musicien** NOUN
musician

la **musicienne** NOUN
musician

la **musique** NOUN
music

musulman ADJECTIVE, NOUN
Muslim
♦ **un musulman** a Muslim (*man*)
♦ **une musulmane** a Muslim (*woman*)

la **mutation** NOUN
transfer ◊ *Il a demandé sa mutation à Paris.* He asked for a transfer to Paris.

myope ADJECTIVE
short-sighted

le **mystère** NOUN
mystery

mystérieux ADJECTIVE (FEM SING **mystérieuse**)
mysterious

le **mythe** NOUN
myth

N

n' PRONOUN see **ne**

la **nage** NOUN
- ♦**traverser une rivière à la nage** to swim across a river
- ♦**être en nage** to be sweating profusely

la **nageoire** NOUN
fin

nager VERB
to swim

le **nageur** NOUN
swimmer

la **nageuse** NOUN
swimmer

naïf ADJECTIVE (FEM SING **naïve**)
naïve

le **nain** NOUN
dwarf

la **naissance** NOUN
birth
- ♦**votre date de naissance** your date of birth

naître VERB
to be born
- ♦**Il est né en 1992.** He was born in 1992.

naïve ADJECTIVE see **naïf**

la **nana** NOUN (*informal*)
girl

la **nappe** NOUN
tablecloth

la **narine** NOUN
nostril

natal ADJECTIVE
native ◊ *mon pays natal* my native country

la **natation** NOUN
swimming ◊ *La natation est mon sport favori.* Swimming's my favourite sport.
- ♦**faire de la natation** to go swimming

la **nation** NOUN
nation
- ♦**les Nations unies** the United Nations

national ADJECTIVE (MASC PL **nationaux**)
national
- ♦**la fête nationale espagnole** the national day of Spain

la **nationale** NOUN
main road ◊ *En vélo, il vaut mieux éviter les nationales.* When on a bike it's better to avoid main roads.

la **nationalité** NOUN
nationality

la **natte** NOUN
plait ◊ *Cécile avait des nattes.* Cécile had plaits.

la **nature** NOUN
> see also **nature** ADJECTIVE

nature

nature ADJECTIVE
> see also **nature** NOUN

plain ◊ *un yaourt nature* a plain yoghurt

naturel ADJECTIVE (FEM SING **naturelle**)
natural

naturellement ADVERB
of course ◊ *Vous viendrez à notre fête? – Naturellement!* Are you coming to our party? – Of course! ◊ *Naturellement, il est encore en retard.* Of course, he's late again.

le **naufrage** NOUN
shipwreck

nautique ADJECTIVE
water
- ♦**les sports nautiques** water sports
- ♦**le ski nautique** water-skiing

le **navet** NOUN
turnip

la **navette** NOUN
shuttle ◊ *la navette entre la gare et l'aéroport* the shuttle between the station and the airport
- ♦**faire la navette** to commute ◊ *Je fais la navette entre Paris et Ivry.* I commute between Paris and Ivry.

le **navigateur** NOUN
browser (*on computer*)

la **navigation** NOUN
- ♦**La navigation est interdite ici.** Boats are not allowed here.

naviguer VERB
to sail

le **navire** NOUN
ship

ne ADVERB

> *ne* is combined with words such as *pas, personne, plus* and *jamais* to form negative phrases.
> ◊ *Je ne peux pas venir.* I can't come. ◊ *Ils ne vont jamais en boîte.* They never go to discos. ◊ *Je ne connais personne.* I don't know anyone.
> *ne* changes to *n'* before a vowel and most words beginning with "h".
> ◊ *Je n'ai pas d'argent.* I haven't got any money. ◊ *Il n'habite plus à Paris.* He doesn't live in Paris any more.

ne is sometimes not translated.
◊ *C'est plus loin que je ne le croyais.*
It's further than I thought.

né VERB *see* **naître**
born ◊ *Elle est née en 1990.* She was
born in 1990.

néanmoins ADVERB
nevertheless

nécessaire ADJECTIVE
necessary ◊ *Il est nécessaire de
réserver.* It's necessary to book.

le **nectar** NOUN
♦**le nectar d'abricot** apricot drink

néerlandais ADJECTIVE, NOUN (FEM SING
néerlandaise)
Dutch ◊ *Manon parle néerlandais.*
Manon speaks Dutch.
♦**un Néerlandais** a Dutchman
♦**une Néerlandaise** a Dutchwoman
♦**les Néerlandais** the Dutch

négatif ADJECTIVE (FEM SING **négative**)
  see also **négatif** NOUN
negative

le **négatif** NOUN
  see also **négatif** ADJECTIVE
negative (of photo)

négligé ADJECTIVE
scruffy ◊ *une tenue négligée* scruffy
clothes

négliger VERB
to neglect ◊ *Ces derniers temps il a
négligé son travail.* He's been
neglecting his work recently.

négocier VERB
to negotiate

la **neige** NOUN
snow
♦**un bonhomme de neige** a snowman

neiger VERB
to snow

le **nénuphar** NOUN
water lily

le **néon** NOUN
neon ◊ *une lampe au néon* a neon
light ◊ *La cuisine est éclairée au
néon.* The kitchen has a neon light.

néo-zélandais ADJECTIVE, NOUN (FEM SING
néo-zélandaise)
New Zealand ◊ *Le champion néo-
zélandais a gagné la course.* The New
Zealand champion won the race.
♦**un Néo-Zélandais** a New Zealander
(*man*)
♦**une Néo-Zélandaise** a New Zealander
(*woman*)

le **nerf** NOUN
nerve

♦**taper sur les nerfs de quelqu'un** to
get on somebody's nerves ◊ *Il me
tape sur les nerfs.* He's getting on my
nerves.

nerveux ADJECTIVE (FEM SING **nerveuse**)
nervous

la **nervosité** NOUN
nervousness

n'est-ce pas ADVERB
  *n'est-ce pas is used to check that
  something is true.*
◊ *Nous sommes le douze aujourd'hui,
n'est-ce pas?* It's the 12th today, isn't
it? ◊ *Ils sont venus l'an dernier,
n'est-ce pas?* They came last year,
didn't they? ◊ *Elle aura dix-huit ans
en octobre, n'est-ce pas?* She'll be 18
in October, won't she?

le **Net** NOUN
the Net

net ADJECTIVE, ADVERB (FEM SING **nette**)
  [1] clear ◊ *L'image n'est pas nette.*
The picture isn't very clear.
  [2] net ◊ *Poids net: 500 g.* Net weight:
500 g.
  [3] flatly ◊ *Il a refusé net de nous
aider.* He flatly refused to help us.
♦**s'arrêter net** to stop dead

nettement ADVERB
much ◊ *Ce magasin est nettement
plus cher.* This shop is much more
expensive.

le **nettoyage** NOUN
cleaning
♦**le nettoyage à sec** dry cleaning

nettoyer VERB
to clean

neuf NUMBER
  see also **neuf** ADJECTIVE
nine ◊ *Claire a neuf ans.* Claire's
nine. ◊ *Il est neuf heures du matin.*
It's nine in the morning.
♦**le neuf février** the ninth of February

neuf ADJECTIVE (FEM SING **neuve**)
  see also **neuf** NUMBER
new ◊ *des chaussures neuves* new
shoes

neutre ADJECTIVE
neutral

neuve ADJECTIVE *see* **neuf**

neuvième ADJECTIVE
ninth ◊ *au neuvième étage* on the
ninth floor

le **neveu** NOUN (PL les **neveux**)
nephew

le **nez** NOUN
nose

◆**se trouver nez à nez avec quelqu'un** to come face to face with somebody

ni CONJUNCTION

◆**ni ... ni ...** neither ... nor ... ◊ *Je n'aime ni les lentilles ni les épinards.* I like neither lentils nor spinach. ◊ *Elles ne sont venues ni l'une ni l'autre.* Neither of them came.

la **niche** NOUN
    kennel

le **nid** NOUN
    nest

la **nièce** NOUN
    niece

nier VERB
    to deny

n'importe ADVERB

◆**n'importe quel** any old ◊ *N'importe quel stylo fera l'affaire.* Any old pen will do.

◆**n'importe qui** anybody ◊ *N'ouvre pas la porte à n'importe qui.* Don't open the door to just anybody.

◆**n'importe quoi** anything ◊ *Je ferais n'importe quoi pour elle.* I'd do anything for her.

◆**Tu dis n'importe quoi.** You're talking rubbish.

◆**n'importe où** anywhere ◊ *On trouve ces fleurs n'importe où.* You can find these flowers anywhere.

◆**Ne laisse pas tes affaires n'importe où.** Don't leave your things lying everywhere.

◆**n'importe quand** any time ◊ *Tu peux venir n'importe quand.* You can come any time.

◆**n'importe comment** any old how ◊ *Ces livres sont rangés n'importe comment.* These books have been put away any old how.

le **niveau** NOUN (PL les **niveaux**)
    ☐1 level ◊ *le niveau de l'eau* the water level
    ☐2 standard ◊ *Ces deux enfants n'ont pas le même niveau.* These two children aren't at the same level.

◆**le niveau de vie** the standard of living

noble ADJECTIVE
    noble

la **noblesse** NOUN
    nobility

la **noce** NOUN
    wedding

◆**un repas de noce** a wedding reception

◆**Leurs noces d'or.** Their golden wedding anniversary.

nocif ADJECTIVE (FEM SING **nocive**)

harmful ◊ *une substance nocive* a harmful substance

nocturne ADJECTIVE
    see also **nocturne** NOUN
    ☐1 nocturnal ◊ *un oiseau nocturne* a nocturnal bird
    ☐2 by night ◊ *Découvrez le Paris nocturne!* Discover Paris by night!

la **nocturne** NOUN
    see also **nocturne** ADJECTIVE
    late-night opening ◊ *Nocturne le vendredi jusqu'à vingt-trois heures.* Late-night opening until 11 p.m. on Fridays.   ▲

le **Noël** NOUN
    Christmas ◊ *Qu'est-ce que tu as eu pour Noël?* What did you get for Christmas?

◆**Joyeux Noël!** Merry Christmas!

le **nœud** NOUN
    ☐1 knot ◊ *Il a fait un nœud à la corde.* He tied a knot in the rope.
    ☐2 bow ◊ *Janet avait un nœud dans les cheveux.* Janet had a bow in her hair.

◆**un nœud papillon** a bow tie

noir ADJECTIVE
    see also **noir** NOUN
    ☐1 black ◊ *Elle porte une robe noire.* She's wearing a black dress. ◊ *Elle est noire.* She's black.
    ☐2 dark ◊ *Il fait noir dehors.* It's dark outside.

le **noir** NOUN
    see also **noir** ADJECTIVE
    dark ◊ *J'ai peur du noir.* I'm afraid of the dark.

◆**le travail au noir** moonlighting

le **Noir** NOUN
    black man

◆**les Noirs** black people

la **Noire** NOUN
    black woman

la **noisette** NOUN
    hazelnut

la **noix** NOUN (PL les **noix**)
    walnut

◆**une noix de coco** a coconut

◆**les noix de cajou** cashew nuts

◆**une noix de beurre** a knob of butter

le **nom** NOUN
    ☐1 name ◊ *votre nom* your name

◆**mon nom de famille** my surname

◆**son nom de jeune fille** her maiden name

    ☐2 noun (in grammar) ◊ *un nom commun* a common noun ◊ *un nom propre* a proper noun

le **nombre** NOUN

N

number ◊ *Treize est un nombre impair.* Thirteen is an odd number. ◊ *un grand nombre d'amis* a large number of friends

nombreux ADJECTIVE (FEM SING **nombreuse**)

1 many ◊ *Il a gagné de nombreux matchs.* He's won many matches.

2 large ◊ *une famille nombreuse* a large family

♦ **peu nombreux** few ◊ *Nous étions peu nombreux à la réunion.* There were few of us at the meeting.

le **nombril** NOUN
navel

nommer VERB

1 to name ◊ *Il n'a voulu nommer personne.* He didn't want to name anybody.

2 to appoint ◊ *Il a été nommé directeur.* He was appointed director.

non ADVERB

no ◊ *Tu as vu Jean-Pierre? – Non.* Have you seen Jean-Pierre? – No.

♦ **non seulement** not only ◊ *Il est non seulement intelligent, mais aussi très gentil.* Not only is he intelligent, he's also very nice.

♦ **moi non plus** Neither do I. ◊ *Je n'aime pas les hamburgers. – Moi non plus.* I don't like hamburgers. – Neither do I. ◊ *Il n'y est pas allé et moi non plus.* He didn't go and neither did I.

non alcoolisé ADJECTIVE

non-alcoholic ◊ *les boissons non alcoolisées* non-alcoholic drinks

le **non-fumeur** NOUN

non-smoker ◊ *Gavin est un non-fumeur.* Gavin's a non-smoker.

♦ **une voiture non-fumeurs** a no-smoking carriage

le **nord** NOUN

> see also **nord** ADJECTIVE

north ◊ *Ils vivent dans le nord de l'île.* They live in the north of the island.

♦ **vers le nord** northwards

♦ **au nord de Paris** north of Paris

♦ **l'Afrique du Nord** North Africa

♦ **le vent du nord** the north wind

nord ADJECTIVE

> see also **nord** NOUN

1 north ◊ *la face nord du Mont-Blanc* the north face of Mont-Blanc

♦ **le pôle Nord** the North Pole

2 northern ◊ *Nous avons visité la partie nord de l'île.* We visited the northern part of the island.

le **nord-est** NOUN

north-east ◊ *les régions du nord-est* north-eastern regions

le **nord-ouest** NOUN
north-west

♦ **l'Europe du nord-ouest** north-west Europe

normal ADJECTIVE (MASC PL **normaux**)

1 normal ◊ *un bébé normal* a normal baby

2 natural ◊ *C'est tout à fait normal.* It's perfectly natural.

♦ **Vous trouvez que c'est normal?** Does that seem right to you?

normalement ADVERB

normally ◊ *Les aéroports fonctionnent tous normalement.* The airports are all working normally.

♦ **Normalement, elle doit arriver à huit heures.** She's supposed to arrive at 8 o'clock.

♦ **Tu es libre ce week-end? – Oui, normalement.** Are you free this weekend? – Yes, I should be.

normand ADJECTIVE

♦ **un village normand** a village in Normandy

♦ **la côte normande** the coast of Normandy

la **Normandie** NOUN
Normandy

la **Norvège** NOUN
Norway

norvégien ADJECTIVE, NOUN (FEM SING **norvégienne**)
Norwegian

♦ **Elle parle norvégien.** She speaks Norwegian.

♦ **un Norvégien** a Norwegian (*man*)

♦ **une Norvégienne** a Norwegian (*woman*)

nos ADJECTIVE

our ◊ *Où sont nos affaires?* Where are our things?

le **notaire** NOUN

solicitor ◊ *Son père est notaire.* His father's a solicitor.

la **note** NOUN

1 note ◊ *J'ai pris des notes pendant la conférence.* I took notes at the lecture. ◊ *Il a joué quelques notes au piano.* He played a few notes on the piano.

2 mark ◊ *Vincent a de bonnes notes en maths.* Vincent's got good marks in maths.

3 bill ◊ *Il n'a pas payé sa note.* He didn't pay his bill.

noter VERB

to make a note of ◊ *Tu as noté leur adresse? Did you make a note of their address?*

les **notions** FEM NOUN
basics ◊ *Il faut avoir des notions d'anglais.* You have to have some basic English. ◊ *Elle a des notions de comptabilité.* She knows the basics of accounting.

notre ADJECTIVE (PL **nos**)
our ◊ *Voici notre maison.* Here's our house.

nôtre PRONOUN
♦ **le nôtre** ours ◊ *À qui est ce chien? – C'est le nôtre.* Whose dog is it? – It's ours. ◊ *Leur voiture est rouge, la nôtre est bleue.* Their car is red, ours is blue.

nôtres PRONOUN
♦ **les nôtres** ours ◊ *Ces places-là sont les nôtres.* Those seats are ours.

nouer VERB
to tie

les **nouilles** FEM NOUN
noodles

nourrir VERB
to feed

la **nourriture** NOUN
food

nous PRONOUN
1 we ◊ *Nous avons deux enfants.* We have two children.
2 us ◊ *Viens avec nous.* Come with us.
♦ **nous-mêmes** ourselves

nouveau ADJECTIVE (MASC SING ALSO **nouvel**, FEM SING **nouvelle**, MASC PL **nouveaux**)
see also **nouveau** NOUN
new ◊ *Il me faut un nouveau pantalon.* I need some new trousers. ◊ *Elle a une nouvelle voiture.* She's got a new car.

*nouveau changes to **nouvel** before a vowel and most words beginning with "h".*

◊ *Il y a un nouvel élève dans ma classe.* There's a new boy in my class.
♦ **le nouvel an** New Year

le **nouveau** NOUN (PL les **nouveaux**)
see also **nouveau** ADJECTIVE
new pupil ◊ *Il y a plusieurs nouveaux dans la classe.* There are several new pupils in the class.
♦ **de nouveau** again ◊ *Il pleut de nouveau.* It's raining again.

le **nouveau-né** NOUN
newborn child

la **nouveauté** NOUN
novelty

nouvel, nouvelle ADJECTIVE *see* **nouveau**

la **nouvelle** NOUN
1 news ◊ *Tu connais la nouvelle? Teresa a gagné au loto.* Have you heard the news? Teresa won the lottery. ◊ *C'est une bonne nouvelle.* That's good news.
2 short story ◊ *une nouvelle de Maupassant* a short story by Maupassant
♦ **les nouvelles** the news ◊ *J'ai écouté les nouvelles à la radio.* I listened to the news on the radio.
♦ **avoir des nouvelles de quelqu'un** to hear from somebody ◊ *Je n'ai pas eu de nouvelles de lui.* I haven't heard from him.

la **Nouvelle-Zélande** NOUN
New Zealand

novembre MASC NOUN
November
♦ **en novembre** in November

le **noyau** NOUN (PL les **noyaux**)
stone (*of fruit*) ◊ *un noyau d'abricot* an apricot stone

le **noyer** NOUN
see also **noyer** VERB
walnut tree

se **noyer** VERB
see also **noyer** NOUN
to drown ◊ *Il s'est noyé dans la rivière.* He drowned in the river.

nu ADJECTIVE
1 naked ◊ *Ils se sont baignés nus.* They went for a swim naked. ◊ *tout nus* stark naked
2 bare ◊ *Elle avait les bras nus.* Her arms were bare. ◊ *Les murs étaient nus.* The walls were bare.

le **nuage** NOUN
cloud
♦ **un nuage de lait** a drop of milk

nuageux ADJECTIVE (FEM SING **nuageuse**)
cloudy

nucléaire ADJECTIVE
nuclear ◊ *l'énergie nucléaire* nuclear power

le/la **nudiste** NOUN
nudist

la **nuit** NOUN
night ◊ *Ils ont fait du bruit toute la nuit.* They were noisy all night.
♦ **Il fait nuit.** It's dark.
♦ **cette nuit** tonight ◊ *Il va rentrer cette nuit.* He'll be back tonight.
♦ **Bonne nuit!** Good night!
♦ **de nuit** by night

N

nul ADJECTIVE (FEM SING **nulle**)
  <u>rubbish</u>
• **Ce film est nul.** (*informal*) This film's rubbish.
• **être nul** to be no good ◊ *Je suis nul en maths.* I'm no good at maths.
• **un match nul** a draw (*in sport*) ◊ *Ils ont fait match nul.* It was a draw.
• **nulle part** nowhere ◊ *Je ne le vois nulle part.* I can't see it anywhere.

numérique ADJECTIVE
  <u>digital</u>

le **numéro** NOUN
  <u>number</u> ◊ *J'habite au numéro trois.* I live at number 3.
• **mon numéro de téléphone** my phone number
• **le numéro de compte** the account number

nu-pieds ADJECTIVE, ADVERB
  <u>barefoot</u> ◊ *Il se promenait nu-pieds.* He was walking barefoot.

la **nuque** NOUN
  <u>nape of the neck</u>

le **nylon** NOUN
  <u>nylon</u>

O

obéir VERB
to obey
* **obéir à quelqu'un** to obey somebody ◊ *Elle refuse d'obéir à ses parents.* She refuses to obey her parents.

obéissant ADJECTIVE
obedient

l' **objet** MASC NOUN
object
* **les objets de valeur** valuables
* **les objets trouvés** the lost property office

obligatoire ADJECTIVE
compulsory

obliger VERB
* **obliger quelqu'un à faire quelque chose** to force somebody to do something
* **Je suis bien obligé d'accepter.** I can't really refuse.

obscur ADJECTIVE
dark

l' **obscurité** FEM NOUN
darkness ◊ *dans l'obscurité* in the dark

l' **obsédé** MASC NOUN
sex maniac
* **un obsédé sexuel** a sex maniac

obséder VERB
to obsess ◊ *Il est obsédé par le travail.* He's obsessed by work.

l' **observation** FEM NOUN
comment ◊ *J'ai une ou deux observations à faire.* I've got one or two comments to make.

observer VERB
1. to watch ◊ *Il observait les canards sur le lac.* He watched the ducks on the lake.
2. to observe ◊ *Ils observent le règlement.* They observe the rules.

l' **obstacle** MASC NOUN
1. obstacle ◊ *surmonter un obstacle* to overcome an obstacle
2. fence (*in show jumping*)
* **une course d'obstacles** an obstacle race

obstiné ADJECTIVE
stubborn

obtenir VERB
1. to get ◊ *Ils ont obtenu cinquante pour cent des voix.* They got 50% of the votes.

2. to achieve ◊ *Nous avons obtenu de bons résultats.* We achieved good results.

l' **occasion** FEM NOUN
1. opportunity ◊ *C'est une occasion à ne pas manquer.* It's an opportunity not to be missed.
2. occasion ◊ *à l'occasion de son anniversaire* on the occasion of his birthday ◊ *à plusieurs occasions* on several occasions
3. bargain ◊ *Cet ordinateur est une bonne occasion.* This computer's a real bargain.
* **d'occasion** second-hand ◊ *une voiture d'occasion* a second-hand car

l' **Occident** MASC NOUN
West
* **en Occident** in the West

occidental ADJECTIVE (MASC PL **occidentaux**)
western
* **les pays occidentaux** the West

l' **occupation** FEM NOUN
occupation ◊ *la France sous l'Occupation* France during the Occupation

occupé ADJECTIVE
1. busy ◊ *Le directeur est très occupé.* The director's very busy.
2. taken ◊ *Est-ce que cette place est occupée?* Is this seat taken?
3. engaged ◊ *Les toilettes sont occupées.* The toilet's engaged. ◊ *La ligne est occupée.* The line's engaged.

occuper VERB
to occupy ◊ *Les enfants ne sont pas faciles à occuper quand il pleut.* Children aren't easy to keep occupied when it rains.
* **s'occuper de quelque chose (1)** to be in charge of something ◊ *Elle s'occupe d'un club de sport.* She's in charge of a sports club.
* **s'occuper de quelque chose (2)** to deal with something ◊ *Je vais m'occuper de ce dossier.* I'm going to deal with this file.
* **On s'occupe de vous?** (*in a shop*) Are you being attended to?

l' **océan** MASC NOUN
ocean ◊ *l'océan Indien* the Indian Ocean

octobre MASC NOUN

☞

October
- **en octobre** in October

l'**odeur** FEM NOUN
  smell ◇ *Il y a une drôle d'odeur ici.* There's a funny smell round here.

odieux ADJECTIVE (FEM SING **odieuse**)
  horrible ◇ *Elle a été odieuse avec nous.* She was horrible to us.

l'**œil** MASC NOUN (PL **les yeux**)
  eye ◇ *J'ai quelque chose dans l'œil.* I've got something in my eye.
- **à l'œil** (*informal*) for free ◇ *Il est entré à l'œil.* He got in for free.

l'**œillet** MASC NOUN
  carnation

l'**œuf** MASC NOUN
  egg
- **un œuf à la coque** a soft-boiled egg
- **un œuf dur** a hard-boiled egg
- **un œuf au plat** a fried egg
- **les œufs brouillés** scrambled eggs
- **un œuf de Pâques** an Easter egg

l'**œuvre** FEM NOUN
  work ◇ *J'étudie une œuvre de Molière.* I'm studying one of Molière's works.
- **une œuvre d'art** a work of art

offert VERB *see* **offrir**

l'**office** MASC NOUN
- **un office du tourisme** a tourist office

officiel ADJECTIVE (FEM SING **officielle**)
  official

l'**officier** MASC NOUN
  officer ◇ *Il est officier de marine.* He's a naval officer.

l'**offre** FEM NOUN
  offer ◇ *une offre spéciale* a special offer
- **"offres d'emploi"** "situations vacant"

offrir VERB
- **offrir quelque chose (1)** to offer something ◇ *On lui a offert un poste de secrétaire.* They offered her a secretarial post. ◇ *Elle lui a offert à boire.* She offered him a drink.
- **offrir quelque chose (2)** to give something ◇ *Il lui a offert des roses.* He gave her roses.
- **s'offrir quelque chose** to treat oneself to something ◇ *Je me suis offert une nouvelle paire de chaussures.* I treated myself to a new pair of shoes.

l'**oie** FEM NOUN
  goose

l'**oignon** MASC NOUN
  onion

l'**oiseau** MASC NOUN (PL **les oiseaux**)
  bird

l'**olive** FEM NOUN
  olive ◇ *l'huile d'olive* olive oil

olympique ADJECTIVE
- **les Jeux olympiques** the Olympic Games

l'**ombre** FEM NOUN
  [1] shade ◇ *Je vais me mettre à l'ombre.* I'm going to sit in the shade.
  [2] shadow
- **l'ombre à paupières** eye shadow

l'**omelette** FEM NOUN
  omelette

on PRONOUN
  [1] we ◇ *On va à la plage demain.* We're going to the beach tomorrow. ◇ *On a pensé que ça te ferait plaisir.* We thought you'd be pleased.
  [2] someone ◇ *On m'a volé mon porte-monnaie.* Someone has stolen my purse.
- **On m'a dit d'attendre.** I was told to wait.
- **On vous demande au téléphone.** There's a phone call for you.
  [3] you ◇ *On peut visiter le château en été.* You can visit the castle in the summer. ◇ *D'ici on peut voir la côte française.* From here you can see the French coast.

l'**oncle** MASC NOUN
  uncle

l'**onde** FEM NOUN
  wave (*on radio*) ◇ *sur les grandes ondes* on long wave

l'**ongle** MASC NOUN
  nail
- **se couper les ongles** to cut one's nails ◇ *Elle s'est coupé les ongles.* She cut her nails.

ont VERB *see* **avoir**
- **Ils ont beaucoup d'argent.** They've got lots of money.
- **Elles ont passé de bonnes vacances.** They had a good holiday.

l'**ONU** FEM NOUN (= *Organisation des Nations unies*)
  UN (= United Nations)

onze NUMBER
  eleven ◇ *Elle a onze ans.* She's eleven. ◇ *à onze heures* at eleven o'clock
- **le onze juin** the eleventh of June

onzième ADJECTIVE
  eleventh ◇ *au onzième étage* on the eleventh floor

l'**opéra** MASC NOUN
  opera

l'**opération** FEM NOUN
  operation

opérer VERB

to operate on ◊ *Elle a été opérée de l'appendicite.* She was operated on for appendicitis.

♦**se faire opérer** to have an operation ◊ *Elle s'est fait opérer.* She's had an operation.

l'**opinion** FEM NOUN

opinion

opposé ADJECTIVE

see also **opposé** NOUN

opposite ◊ *Elle est partie dans la direction opposée.* She went off in the opposite direction.

♦**être opposé à quelque chose** to be opposed to something

l'**opposé** MASC NOUN

see also **opposé** ADJECTIVE

the opposite

opposer VERB

♦**opposer quelqu'un à quelqu'un** to pit somebody against somebody ◊ *Ce match oppose les Français aux Allemands.* This match pits the French against the Germans.

♦**s'opposer** to conflict ◊ *Ces deux points de vue s'opposent.* These two points of view conflict.

♦**s'opposer à quelque chose** to oppose something ◊ *Son père s'oppose à son mariage.* Her father's against her marriage.

l'**opposition** FEM NOUN

opposition

♦**par opposition à** as opposed to ◊ *la littérature contemporaine par opposition à la littérature classique* modern literature, as opposed to classics

♦**faire opposition à un chèque** to stop a cheque

l'**opticien** MASC NOUN

optician ◊ *Il est opticien.* He's an optician.

l'**opticienne** FEM NOUN

optician ◊ *Elle est opticienne.* She's an optician.

optimiste ADJECTIVE

optimistic

l'**option** FEM NOUN

option

♦**une matière à option** an optional subject

l'**or** MASC NOUN

see also **or** CONJUNCTION

gold ◊ *un bracelet en or* a gold bracelet

or CONJUNCTION

see also **or** NOUN

and yet ◊ *Il était sûr de gagner, or il a perdu.* He was sure he would win, and yet he lost.

l'**orage** MASC NOUN

thunderstorm

orageux ADJECTIVE (FEM SING **orageuse**)

stormy

oral ADJECTIVE (MASC PL **oraux**)

see also **oral** NOUN

♦**une épreuve orale** an oral exam

♦**à prendre par voie orale** to be taken orally

l'**oral** MASC NOUN (PL les **oraux**)

see also **oral** ADJECTIVE

oral (*exam*) ◊ *un oral de français* a French oral

l'**orange** FEM NOUN

see also **orange** ADJECTIVE

orange (*fruit*)

orange ADJECTIVE (MASC, FEM, PL)

see also **orange** NOUN

orange (*in colour*) ◊ *des fleurs orange* orange flowers

l'**orchestre** MASC NOUN

1 orchestra ◊ *un orchestre symphonique* a symphony orchestra
2 band ◊ *un orchestre de jazz* a jazz band

l'**ordi** MASC NOUN (*informal*)

computer

ordinaire ADJECTIVE

see also **ordinaire** NOUN

1 ordinary ◊ *des gens ordinaires* ordinary people
2 standard ◊ *un format ordinaire* a standard size

l'**ordinaire** MASC NOUN

see also **ordinaire** ADJECTIVE

♦**sortir de l'ordinaire** to be out of the ordinary

l'**ordinateur** MASC NOUN

computer

l'**ordonnance** FEM NOUN

prescription

ordonné ADJECTIVE

tidy

ordonner VERB

♦**ordonner à quelqu'un de faire quelque chose** to order somebody to do something ◊ *Il m'a ordonné de sortir.* He ordered me to leave.

l'**ordre** MASC NOUN

order ◊ *par ordre alphabétique* in alphabetical order

♦**dans l'ordre** in order

♦**mettre en ordre** to tidy up

♦**jusqu'à nouvel ordre** until further notice

O

les **ordures** FEM NOUN
    rubbish SING
    ♦**jeter quelque chose aux ordures** to throw something in the bin

l' **oreille** FEM NOUN
    ear

l' **oreiller** MASC NOUN
    pillow

les **oreillons** MASC NOUN
    mumps

l' **organe** MASC NOUN
    organ (*in body*)

l' **organisateur** MASC NOUN
    organizer

l' **organisation** FEM NOUN
    organization

l' **organisatrice** FEM NOUN
    organizer

  organiser VERB
    to organize
    ♦**s'organiser** to get organized ◊ *Il ne sait pas s'organiser.* He can't get himself organized.

l' **organisme** MASC NOUN
    body (*organization*)

l' **orgue** MASC NOUN
    organ ◊ *Carl joue de l'orgue.* Carl plays the organ.

  orgueilleux ADJECTIVE (FEM SING **orgueilleuse**)
    proud

l' **Orient** MASC NOUN
    East
    ♦**en Orient** in the East

  oriental ADJECTIVE (MASC PL **orientaux**)
    1 oriental ◊ *un palais oriental* an oriental palace
    2 eastern ◊ *la frontière orientale de la Pologne* Poland's eastern border

l' **orientation** FEM NOUN
    orientation
    ♦**avoir le sens de l'orientation** to have a good sense of direction
    ♦**l'orientation professionnelle** careers advice

  originaire ADJECTIVE
    ♦**Elle est originaire de Paris.** She's from Paris.

  original ADJECTIVE (MASC PL **originaux**)
    see also **original** NOUN
    original ◊ *un film en version originale* a film in the original language

l' **original** MASC NOUN (PL les **originaux**)
    see also **original** ADJECTIVE
    original ◊ *L'original est au Louvre.* The original is in the Louvre.
    ♦**un vieil original** an old eccentric

l' **origine** FEM NOUN
    origin
    ♦**à l'origine** originally

l' **orphelin** MASC NOUN
    orphan

l' **orpheline** FEM NOUN
    orphan

l' **orteil** MASC NOUN
    toe

l' **orthographe** FEM NOUN
    spelling

l' **os** MASC NOUN
    bone

  oser VERB
    to dare
    ♦**oser faire quelque chose** to dare to do something

l' **otage** MASC NOUN
    hostage

  ôter VERB
    1 to take off ◊ *Elle a ôté son manteau.* She took off her coat.
    2 to take away

  ou CONJUNCTION
    or
    ♦**ou ... ou ...** either ... or ...
    ♦**ou bien** or else ◊ *On pourrait aller au cinéma ou bien rentrer directement.* We could go to the cinema or else go straight home.

  où PRONOUN, ADVERB
    1 where ◊ *Où est Nick?* Where's Nick? ◊ *Où allez-vous?* Where are you going? ◊ *Je sais où il est.* I know where he is. ◊ *C'est la maison où je suis né.* That's the house where I was born. ◊ *la ville d'où je viens* the town I come from
    2 that ◊ *Le jour où il est parti, tout le monde a pleuré.* The day that he left, everyone cried.
    ♦**Par où allons-nous passer?** Which way are we going to go?

l' **ouate** FEM NOUN
    cotton wool

  oublier VERB
    1 to forget ◊ *N'oublie pas de fermer la porte.* Don't forget to shut the door.
    2 to leave ◊ *J'ai oublié mon sac chez Sabine.* I left my bag at Sabine's.

l' **ouest** MASC NOUN
    see also **ouest** ADJECTIVE
    west ◊ *Elle vit dans l'ouest de l'Angleterre.* She lives in the West of England.
    ♦**à l'ouest de Paris** west of Paris
    ♦**vers l'ouest** westwards

♦ **l'Europe de l'Ouest** Western Europe
♦ **le vent d'ouest** the west wind

ouest ADJECTIVE (MASC, FEM, PL)

see also **ouest** NOUN

[1] west ◊ *la côte ouest de l'Écosse*
the west coast of Scotland
[2] western ◊ *la partie ouest du pays*
the western part of the country

ouf EXCLAMATION
phew!

oui ADVERB
yes

l'**ouragan** MASC NOUN
hurricane

l'**ourlet** MASC NOUN
seam

l'**ours** MASC NOUN
bear
♦ **un ours en peluche** a teddy bear

l'**outil** MASC NOUN
tool

outré ADJECTIVE
outraged ◊ *Il a été outré de son
insolence.* He was outraged at her
cheek.

ouvert VERB see **ouvrir**

ouvert ADJECTIVE
[1] open ◊ *Le magasin est ouvert.* The
shop's open.
[2] on ◊ *Il a laissé le robinet ouvert.*
He left the tap on.
♦ **avoir l'esprit ouvert** to be open-
minded

l'**ouverture** FEM NOUN
opening ◊ *les heures d'ouverture*
opening hours

l'**ouvre-boîte** MASC NOUN
tin opener

l'**ouvre-bouteille** MASC NOUN
bottle-opener

l'**ouvreuse** FEM NOUN
usherette

l'**ouvrier** MASC NOUN
worker ◊ *Son père est ouvrier dans
une usine.* His father's a factory
worker.

l'**ouvrière** FEM NOUN
worker

ouvrir VERB
to open ◊ *Ouvrez!* Open up! ◊ *Elle
a ouvert la porte.* She opened the
door.
♦ **s'ouvrir** to open ◊ *La porte s'est
ouverte.* The door opened.

ovale ADJECTIVE
oval

l'**ovni** MASC NOUN (= *objet volant non
identifié*)
UFO

l'**oxygène** MASC NOUN
oxygen

l'**ozone** MASC NOUN
ozone

O

P

le **Pacifique** NOUN
Pacific ◊ *l'océan Pacifique* the Pacific
Ocean

le **pacifiste** NOUN
pacifist

la **pagaille** NOUN
mess SING ◊ *Quelle pagaille!* What a
mess!

la **page** NOUN
page ◊ *Tournez la page.* Turn the
page.
  ◆ **la page d'accueil** the home page

la **paie** NOUN
wages

le **paiement** NOUN
payment

le **paillasson** NOUN
doormat

la **paille** NOUN
straw

le **pain** NOUN
  1 bread ◊ *un morceau de pain* a
  piece of bread ◊ *une tranche de pain*
  a slice of bread
  2 loaf ◊ *J'ai acheté un pain.* I
  bought a loaf of bread.
  ◆ **le pain complet** wholemeal bread
  ◆ **le pain d'épice** gingerbread
  ◆ **le pain de mie** sandwich loaf
  ◆ **le pain grillé** toast

pair ADJECTIVE
even ◊ *un nombre pair* an even
number
  ◆ **une jeune fille au pair** an au pair

la **paire** NOUN
pair ◊ *une paire de chaussures* a pair
of shoes

paisible ADJECTIVE
peaceful ◊ *un village paisible* a
peaceful village

la **paix** NOUN
peace
  ◆ **faire la paix (1)** to make peace ◊ *Les
  deux pays ont fait la paix.* The two
  countries have made peace with each
  other.
  ◆ **faire la paix (2)** to make it up ◊ *Laure
  a fait la paix avec son frère.* Laure
  made it up with her brother.
  ◆ **avoir la paix** to have peace and quiet
  ◊ *J'aimerais bien avoir la paix.* I'd like
  to have a bit of peace and quiet.
  ◆ **Fiche-lui la paix!** (*informal*) Leave him
  alone!

le **palais** NOUN
  1 palace ◊ *le palais de Buckingham*
  Buckingham Palace
  2 palate (*in mouth*)

pâle ADJECTIVE
pale ◊ *bleu pâle* pale blue

la **Palestine** NOUN
Palestine

la **pâleur** NOUN
paleness

le **palier** NOUN
landing ◊ *Il m'attendait sur le palier.*
He was waiting for me on the
landing.

pâlir VERB
to go pale

la **palme** NOUN
flipper (*for swimming*)

palmé ADJECTIVE
webbed ◊ *Les canards ont les pieds
palmés.* Ducks have webbed feet.

le **palmier** NOUN
palm tree

palpitant ADJECTIVE
thrilling ◊ *un roman palpitant* a
thrilling novel

le **pamplemousse** NOUN
grapefruit

le **panaché** NOUN
shandy

la **pancarte** NOUN
sign ◊ *Il y a une pancarte dans la
vitrine.* There's a sign in the window.

pané ADJECTIVE
fried in breadcrumbs ◊ *du poisson
pané* fish in breadcrumbs

le **panier** NOUN
basket

la **panique** NOUN
panic

paniquer VERB
to panic

la **panne** NOUN
breakdown
  ◆ **être en panne** to have broken down
  ◊ *L'ascenseur est en panne.* The lift's
  not working.
  ◆ **tomber en panne** to break down
  ◊ *Nous sommes tombés en panne
  sur l'autoroute.* We broke down on
  the motorway. ◊ *Nous sommes
  tombés en panne d'essence.* We've
  run out of petrol.
  ◆ **une panne de courant** a power cut

le **panneau** NOUN (PL les **panneaux**)
   sign ◊ *Ce panneau dit que la maison
   est à vendre.* This sign says that the
   house is for sale.
   ♦ **panneau d'affichage (1)** billboard
   ♦ **panneau d'affichage (2)** bulletin board
   (*on internet*)

le **panorama** NOUN
   panorama

le **pansement** NOUN
   [1] dressing (*bandage*)
   [2] sticking plaster

le **pantalon** NOUN
   trousers PL ◊ *Son pantalon est trop
   court.* His trousers are too short.
   ♦ **un pantalon de ski** a pair of ski pants

la **pantoufle** NOUN
   slipper

la **PAO** ABBREVIATION (= *publication assistée
   par ordinateur*)
   DTP (= desktop publishing)

le **paon** NOUN
   peacock

le **papa** NOUN
   dad

le **pape** NOUN
   pope

la **papeterie** NOUN
   stationer's

le **papi** NOUN (*informal*)
   granddad

le **papier** NOUN
   paper ◊ *une feuille de papier* a sheet
   of paper
   ♦ **Vos papiers, s'il vous plaît.** Your
   identity papers, please.
   ♦ **les papiers d'identité** identity papers
   ♦ **le papier à lettres** writing paper
   ♦ **le papier hygiénique** toilet paper
   ♦ **le papier peint** wallpaper

le **papillon** NOUN
   butterfly

le **paquebot** NOUN
   liner

la **pâquerette** NOUN
   daisy

Pâques MASC NOUN
   Easter ◊ *Je viendrai te voir à Pâques.*
   I'll come and see you at Easter.
   ♦ **les œufs de Pâques** Easter eggs

> ❶ In France, Easter eggs are said to
> be brought by the Easter bells or
> **cloches de Pâques** which fly from
> Rome and drop them in people's
> gardens.

le **paquet** NOUN
   [1] packet ◊ *Je voudrais un paquet de
   cigarettes.* I'd like a packet of
   cigarettes.
   [2] parcel ◊ *Sa mère lui a envoyé un
   paquet.* His mother sent him a
   parcel.

le **paquet-cadeau** NOUN (PL les **paquets-
   cadeaux**)
   gift-wrapped parcel ◊ *La vendeuse
   m'a fait un paquet-cadeau.* The
   shop assistant gift-wrapped it for
   me.

par PREPOSITION
   [1] by ◊ *L'Amérique a été découverte
   par Christophe Colomb.* America
   was discovered by Christopher
   Columbus.
   ♦ **deux par deux** two by two ◊ *Les
   élèves sont entrés deux par deux.*
   The pupils went in two by two.
   [2] with ◊ *Son nom commence par un
   H.* His name begins with H.
   [3] out of ◊ *Elle regardait par la
   fenêtre.* She was looking out of the
   window. ◊ *par habitude* out of
   habit
   [4] via ◊ *Nous sommes passés par
   Lyon pour aller à Grenoble.* We went
   via Lyons to Grenoble.
   [5] through ◊ *Il faut passer par la
   douane avant de prendre l'avion.* You
   have to go through customs before
   boarding the plane.
   [6] per ◊ *Prenez trois cachets par jour.*
   Take three tablets per day. ◊ *Le
   voyage coûte deux mille francs par
   personne.* The trip costs two
   thousand francs per person.
   ♦ **par ici (1)** this way ◊ *Il faut passer par
   ici pour y arriver.* You have to go this
   way to get there.
   ♦ **par ici (2)** round here ◊ *Il y a
   beaucoup de touristes par ici.* There
   are lots of tourists round here.
   ♦ **par-ci, par-là** here and there

le **parachute** NOUN
   parachute

le/la **parachutiste** NOUN
   parachutist

le **paradis** NOUN
   heaven

les **parages** MASC NOUN
   ♦ **dans les parages** in the area ◊ *Il n'y a
   pas d'hôtel dans les parages.* There
   are no hotels in the area.

le **paragraphe** NOUN
   paragraph

paraître VERB
   [1] to seem ◊ *Ça paraît incroyable.* It
   seems unbelievable.

P

☞

② to look ◊ *Elle paraît plus jeune que son frère.* She looks younger than her brother.

♦ **il paraît que** it seems that ◊ *Il paraît que c'est la faute de la direction.* It seems that it's the management's fault.

le **parallèle** NOUN

see also **la parallèle**

parallel ◊ *Il a fait un parallèle entre ces deux événements.* He drew a parallel between the two events.

la **parallèle** NOUN

see also **le parallèle**

parallel line

paralysé ADJECTIVE
paralysed

le **parapluie** NOUN
umbrella

le **parasol** NOUN
parasol

le **parc** NOUN

① park ◊ *Le dimanche, Chantal va se promener au parc.* On Sundays Chantal goes for a walk in the park.

♦ **un parc d'attractions** an amusement park

② grounds ◊ *Le château est situé au milieu d'un grand parc.* The castle is surrounded by extensive grounds.

parce que CONJUNCTION
because ◊ *Il n'est pas venu parce qu'il n'avait pas de voiture.* He didn't come because he didn't have a car.

le **parcmètre** NOUN
parking meter

parcourir VERB

① to cover ◊ *Gavin a parcouru cinquante kilomètres à vélo.* Gavin covered 50 kilometres on his bike.

② to glance through ◊ *J'ai parcouru le journal d'aujourd'hui.* I glanced through today's newspaper.

le **parcours** NOUN
journey

par-dessous ADVERB
underneath ◊ *Il portait un pull et une chemise par-dessous.* He was wearing a jumper with a shirt underneath.

le **pardessus** NOUN
overcoat

par-dessus ADVERB, PREPOSITION

① on top ◊ *Elle porte un chemisier et un pull rouge par-dessus.* She's wearing a blouse with a red jumper on top.

② over ◊ *Elle a sauté par-dessus le mur.* She jumped over the wall.

♦ **en avoir par-dessus la tête** to have had enough ◊ *J'en ai par-dessus la tête de tous ces problèmes.* I've had enough of all these problems.

le **pardon** NOUN

see also **pardon** EXCLAMATION

forgiveness

pardon EXCLAMATION

see also **pardon** NOUN

① sorry! ◊ *Oh, pardon! J'espère que je ne vous ai pas fait mal.* Oh, sorry! I hope I didn't hurt you.

♦ **demander pardon à quelqu'un** to apologize to somebody ◊ *Il leur a demandé pardon.* He apologized to them.

♦ **Je vous demande pardon.** I'm sorry.

② excuse me! ◊ *Pardon, madame! Pouvez-vous me dire où se trouve la poste?* Excuse me! Could you tell me where the post office is?

③ pardon? ◊ *Pardon? Je n'ai pas compris ce que vous avez dit.* Pardon? I didn't understand what you said.

pardonner VERB
to forgive ◊ *Nous lui avons pardonné de nous avoir menti.* We forgave him for lying to us.

le **pare-brise** NOUN (PL les **pare-brise**)
windscreen

le **pare-chocs** NOUN
bumper

pareil ADJECTIVE (FEM SING **pareille**)

① the same ◊ *Ces deux maisons ne sont pas pareilles.* These two houses aren't the same.

② like that ◊ *J'aime bien sa voiture. J'en voudrais une pareille.* I like his car. I'd like one like that.

③ such ◊ *Je refuse d'écouter des bêtises pareilles.* I won't listen to such nonsense.

♦ **sans pareil** unequalled ◊ *Il a joué cette symphonie avec un talent sans pareil.* He played this symphony with unequalled talent.

la **parenthèse** NOUN
bracket ◊ *entre parenthèses* in brackets

les **parents** MASC NOUN

① parents (*mother and father*)

② relatives ◊ *parents et amis* friends and relatives

la **paresse** NOUN
laziness

paresseux ADJECTIVE (FEM SING **paresseuse**)

lazy

parfait ADJECTIVE
perfect

parfaitement ADVERB
perfectly ◊ *Il parle parfaitement l'arabe.* He speaks perfect Arabic.

parfois ADVERB
sometimes

le parfum NOUN
1 perfume
2 flavour ◊ *Je voudrais une glace. – Quel parfum veux-tu?* I'd like an ice cream. – What flavour would you like?

parfumé ADJECTIVE
1 fragrant ◊ *une rose très parfumée* a very fragrant rose
2 flavoured ◊ *des biscuits parfumés au café* coffee-flavoured biscuits

la parfumerie NOUN
perfume shop

le pari NOUN
bet

parier VERB
to bet

Paris NOUN
Paris
♦ **à Paris (1)** in Paris
♦ **à Paris (2)** to Paris

parisien ADJECTIVE, NOUN (FEM SING **parisienne**)
1 Parisian ◊ *un célèbre couturier parisien* a famous Parisian designer
2 Paris ◊ *le métro parisien* the Paris metro
♦ **un Parisien** a Parisian (*man*)
♦ **une Parisienne** a Parisian (*woman*)

le parking NOUN
car park

> Be careful! The French word **parking** does not mean **parking**.

le parlement NOUN
parliament

parler VERB
1 to speak ◊ *Vous parlez français?* Do you speak French?
2 to talk ◊ *Nous étions en train de parler quand le directeur est entré.* We were talking when the headmaster came in.
♦ **parler de quelque chose à quelqu'un** to tell somebody about something ◊ *Il m'a parlé de sa nouvelle voiture.* He told me about his new car.

parmi PREPOSITION
among ◊ *Ils étaient parmi les meilleurs de la classe.* They were among the best pupils in the class.

la paroi NOUN

wall

la paroisse NOUN
parish

la parole NOUN
1 speech ◊ *l'usage de la parole* the power of speech
2 word ◊ *Il m'a donné sa parole.* He gave me his word. ◊ *Elle a tenu parole.* She kept her word.
♦ **les paroles** lyrics ◊ *J'aime les paroles de cette chanson.* I like the lyrics of this song.

le parquet NOUN
floor (*wooden*)

le parrain NOUN
godfather

parrainer VERB
to sponsor ◊ *Cette entreprise parraine notre équipe de rugby.* This firm is sponsoring our rugby team.

pars VERB *see* **partir**

la part NOUN
1 share ◊ *Vous n'avez pas eu votre part.* You haven't had your share.
2 piece ◊ *une part de gâteau* a piece of cake
♦ **prendre part à quelque chose** to take part in something ◊ *Il va prendre part à la réunion.* He's going to take part in the meeting.
♦ **de la part de (1)** on behalf of ◊ *Je dois vous remercier de la part de mon frère.* I must thank you on behalf of my brother.
♦ **de la part de (2)** from ◊ *C'est un cadeau pour toi, de la part de Françoise.* It's a present for you, from Françoise.
♦ **à part** except ◊ *Ils sont tous venus, à part Christian.* They all came, except Christian.

partager VERB
1 to share ◊ *Ils partagent un appartement.* They share a flat.
2 to divide ◊ *Janet a partagé le gâteau en quatre.* Janet divided the cake into four.

le/la partenaire NOUN
partner

le parti NOUN
party ◊ *le Parti socialiste* the Socialist Party

le participant NOUN
participant

la participante NOUN
participant

la participation NOUN
participation

le participe NOUN

P

participle
+ **le participe passé** the past participle
+ **le participe présent** the present
participle

participer VERB
+ **participer à quelque chose (1)** to take
part in something ◊ *André va
participer à la course.* André is going
to take part in the race.
+ **participer à quelque chose (2)** to
contribute to something ◊ *Je voudrais
participer aux frais.* I would like to
contribute to the cost.

la **particularité** NOUN
characteristic

particulier ADJECTIVE (FEM SING
particulière)
1 private ◊ *une maison particulière* a
private house
2 distinctive ◊ *Ce vin a un arôme
particulier.* This wine has a distinctive
flavour.
3 particular ◊ *Dans ce cas
particulier, je ne peux rien faire.* In
this particular case, I can't do
anything.
+ **en particulier (1)** particularly ◊ *J'aime
les fruits, en particulier les fraises.* I
like fruit, particularly strawberries.
+ **en particulier (2)** in private ◊ *Est-ce
que je peux vous parler en
particulier?* Can I speak to you in
private?

particulièrement ADVERB
particularly

la **partie** NOUN
1 part ◊ *Une partie du groupe
partira en Italie.* Part of the group will
go to Italy.
2 game ◊ *Nous avons fait une partie
de tennis.* We played a game of
tennis. ◊ *une partie de cartes* a game
of cards
+ **en partie** partly ◊ *Cela explique en
partie le problème.* That partly
explains the problem.
+ **en grande partie** largely ◊ *Son
histoire est en grande partie vraie.*
His story is largely true.
+ **faire partie de** to be part of ◊ *Ce
tableau fait partie d'une très belle
collection.* This picture is part of a
very beautiful collection.

partiel ADJECTIVE (FEM SING **partielle**)
partial

partir VERB
to go ◊ *Je lui ai téléphoné mais il
était déjà parti.* I phoned him but
he'd already gone.
+ **partir en vacances** to go on holiday

+ **partir de** to leave ◊ *Il est parti de Nice
à sept heures.* He left Nice at 7.
+ **à partir de** from ◊ *Je serai chez moi à
partir de huit heures.* I'll be at home
from eight o'clock onwards.

la **partition** NOUN
score (*in music*) ◊ *une partition de
piano* a piano score

partout ADVERB
everywhere

paru VERB *see* **paraître**

la **parution** NOUN
publication ◊ *Ce roman a eu
beaucoup de succès dès sa parution.*
This novel was very successful from
the moment it came out.

parvenir VERB
+ **parvenir à faire quelque chose** to
manage to do something ◊ *Elle est
finalement parvenue à ouvrir la porte.*
She finally managed to open the
door.
+ **faire parvenir quelque chose à
quelqu'un** to send something to
somebody ◊ *Je vous ferai parvenir le
colis avant lundi.* I'll send you the
parcel before Monday.

pas ADVERB
see also **pas** NOUN
+ **ne … pas** not ◊ *Il ne pleut pas.* It's not
raining. ◊ *Elle n'est pas venue.* She
didn't come. ◊ *Ils n'ont pas de
voiture.* They haven't got a car.
+ **Vous viendrez à notre soirée, n'est-ce
pas?** You're coming to our party,
aren't you?
+ **C'est Harry qui a gagné, n'est-ce pas?**
Harry won, didn't he?
+ **pas moi** not me ◊ *Elle veut aller au
cinéma, pas moi.* She wants to go to
the cinema, but I don't.
+ **pas du tout** not at all ◊ *Je n'aime pas
du tout ça.* I don't like that at all.
+ **pas mal** not bad ◊ *Ce n'est pas
mal pour un début.* That's not bad
for a first attempt. ◊ *Comment
allez-vous? – Pas mal.* How are you?
– Not bad.
+ **pas mal de** quite a lot of ◊ *Il y avait
pas mal de monde au concert.* There
were quite a lot of people at the
concert.

le **pas** NOUN
see also **pas** ADVERB
1 pace ◊ *Il marchait d'un pas rapide.*
He walked at a fast pace.
2 step ◊ *Faites trois pas en avant.*
Take three steps forward. ◊ *un pas en
arrière* a step backwards

3 footstep ◇ *J'entends des pas dans l'escalier.* I can hear footsteps on the stairs.

♦ **au pas** at walking pace ◇ *Le cheval est parti au pas.* The horse set off at walking pace.

♦ **faire les cent pas** to pace up and down ◇ *Il faisait les cent pas dans le corridor.* He was pacing up and down the corridor.

le **passage** NOUN

passage ◇ *J'ai traduit un passage de ce livre.* I translated a passage from this book.

♦ **Il a été éclaboussé au passage de la voiture.** He was soaked by a passing car.

♦ **de passage** passing through ◇ *Nous sommes de passage à Toulouse.* We're just passing through Toulouse.

♦ **un passage à niveau** a level crossing

♦ **un passage clouté** a pedestrian crossing

♦ **un passage protégé** a pedestrian crossing

♦ **un passage souterrain** a subway

passager ADJECTIVE (FEM SING **passagère**)

see also **passager** NOUN

temporary

le **passager** NOUN

see also **passager** ADJECTIVE

passenger

♦ **un passager clandestin** a stowaway

la **passagère** NOUN

passenger

le **passant** NOUN

passer-by

la **passante** NOUN

passer-by

passé ADJECTIVE

see also **passé** NOUN

1 last ◇ *Je l'ai vu la semaine passée.* I saw him last week.
2 past ◇ *Il est minuit passé.* It's past midnight.

le **passé** NOUN

see also **passé** ADJECTIVE

1 past ◇ *dans le passé* in the past
2 past tense ◇ *Mettez ce verbe au passé.* Put this verb into the past tense.

♦ **le passé composé** the perfect tense
♦ **le passé simple** the past historic

le **passeport** NOUN

passport

passer VERB

1 to cross ◇ *Nous avons passé la frontière belge.* We crossed the Belgian border.

2 to go through ◇ *Il faut passer la douane en sortant.* You have to go through customs on the way out.
3 to take ◇ *Gordon a passé ses examens la semaine dernière.* Gordon took his exams last week.

> *Be careful! passer un examen does not mean to pass an exam.*

4 to spend ◇ *Elle a passé la journée à ne rien faire.* She spent the day doing nothing. ◇ *Ils passent toujours leurs vacances au Danemark.* They always spend their holidays in Denmark.
5 to pass ◇ *Passe-moi le sel, s'il te plaît.* Pass me the salt, please.
6 to show ◇ *On passe "Le Kid" au cinéma cette semaine.* They're showing "The Kid" at the cinema this week.
7 to call in ◇ *Je passerai chez vous ce soir.* I'll call in this evening.

♦ **passer à la radio** to be on the radio ◇ *Mon père passe à la radio demain soir.* My father's on the radio tomorrow night.

♦ **passer à la télévision** to be on the television ◇ *"Titanic" passe à la télé ce soir.* "Titanic" is on TV tonight.

♦ **Ne quittez pas, je vous passe Madame Chevalier.** Hold on please, I'm putting you through to Mrs Chevalier.

♦ **passer par** to go through ◇ *Ils sont passés par Paris pour aller à Tours.* They went through Paris to get to Tours.

♦ **en passant** in passing ◇ *Je lui ai dit en passant que j'allais me marier.* I told him in passing that I was getting married.

♦ **laisser passer** to let through ◇ *Il m'a laissé passer.* He let me through.

♦ **se passer (1)** to take place ◇ *Cette histoire se passe au moyen âge.* This story takes place in the Middle Ages.

♦ **se passer (2)** to go ◇ *Comment se sont passés tes examens?* How did your exams go?

♦ **se passer (3)** to happen ◇ *Que s'est-il passé? Un accident?* What happened? Was there an accident?

♦ **Qu'est-ce qui se passe? Pourquoi est-ce qu'elle pleure?** What's the matter? Why is she crying?

♦ **se passer de** to do without ◇ *Je me passerai de café ce matin.* I'll do without coffee this morning.

la **passerelle** NOUN

1 footbridge (*over river*)
2 gangway (*onto plane, boat*)

P

le **passe-temps** NOUN
pastime

passif ADJECTIVE (FEM SING **passive**)
see also **passif** NOUN
passive

le **passif** NOUN
see also **passif** ADJECTIVE
passive ◊ _Mettez ce verbe au passif._
Put this verb into the passive.

la **passion** NOUN
passion

passionnant ADJECTIVE
fascinating

passionné ADJECTIVE
keen ◊ _Donald est un lecteur
passionné._ Donald is a keen reader.
♦ **Il est passionné de voile.** He's a
sailing fanatic.

passionner VERB
♦ **Son travail le passionne.** He's
passionate about his work.
♦ **se passionner pour quelque chose** to
have a passion for something ◊ _Harry
se passionne pour les perroquets._
Harry has a passion for parrots.

la **passoire** NOUN
sieve

la **pastèque** NOUN
watermelon

le **pasteur** NOUN
minister (_priest_)

la **pastille** NOUN
cough sweet

la **patate** NOUN (_informal_)
potato
♦ **une patate douce** a sweet potato

la **pâte** NOUN
1 pastry
2 dough
3 cake mixture
♦ **la pâte à crêpes** pancake batter
♦ **la pâte à modeler** Plasticine ®
♦ **la pâte d'amandes** marzipan

le **pâté** NOUN
pâté ◊ _Nous avons mangé du pâté
en entrée._ We had pâté as a starter.
♦ **un pâté de maisons** a block (_of
houses_)

paternel ADJECTIVE (FEM SING **paternelle**)
♦ **ma grand-mère paternelle** my father's
mother
♦ **mon oncle paternel** my father's
brother

les **pâtes** FEM NOUN
pasta SING

la **patience** NOUN
patience

patient ADJECTIVE
see also **patient** NOUN
patient

le **patient** NOUN
see also **patient** ADJECTIVE
patient

la **patiente** NOUN
patient

patienter VERB
to wait ◊ _Veuillez patienter un
instant, s'il vous plaît._ Please wait a
moment.

le **patin** NOUN
1 skate ◊ _Nic a enfilé ses patins._ Nic
put her skates on.
2 skating ◊ _Ils font du patin tous les
mercredis._ They go skating every
Wednesday.
♦ **les patins à glace** ice skates
♦ **les patins en ligne** Rollerblades ®
♦ **les patins à roulettes** roller skates

le **patinage** NOUN
skating
♦ **le patinage artistique** figure skating

patiner VERB
to skate

le **patineur** NOUN
skater

la **patineuse** NOUN
skater

la **patinoire** NOUN
ice rink

la **pâtisserie** NOUN
cake shop
♦ **faire de la pâtisserie** to bake
◊ _J'adore faire de la pâtisserie._ I love
baking.
♦ **les pâtisseries** cakes

le **pâtissier** NOUN
confectioner

la **pâtissière** NOUN
confectioner

la **patrie** NOUN
homeland

le **patron** NOUN
1 boss
2 pattern (_for dressmaking_)

la **patronne** NOUN
boss
♦ **Elle est patronne de café.** She runs a
café.

patronner VERB
to sponsor ◊ _Le festival est patronné
par des entreprises locales._ The
festival is sponsored by local
businesses.

la **patrouille** NOUN
patrol

la **patte** NOUN

1 paw (of dog, cat)
2 leg (of bird, animal)

paumer VERB (informal)
to lose ◊ J'ai paumé mes clefs. I've lost my keys.

la **paupière** NOUN
eyelid

la **pause** NOUN
1 break ◊ Ils font une pause. They're having a break. ◊ une pause de midi a lunch break
2 pause ◊ Il y a eu une pause dans la conversation. There was a pause in the conversation.

pauvre ADJECTIVE
poor ◊ Sa famille est pauvre. His family is poor. ◊ Pauvre Jean-Pierre! Il n'a pas eu de chance! Poor Jean-Pierre! He was unlucky!

la **pauvreté** NOUN
poverty

pavé ADJECTIVE
cobbled ◊ Les rues étaient pavées. The streets were cobbled.

le **pavillon** NOUN
house ◊ Ils habitent un pavillon de banlieue. They've got a house in the suburbs.

payant ADJECTIVE
paying ◊ Ce sont des hôtes payants. They're paying guests.
◆ **C'est payant.** You have to pay.
◊ L'entrée de la boîte est payante. You have to pay to get into the nightclub.

la **paye** NOUN
wages

payer VERB
1 to pay for ◊ Combien as-tu payé ta voiture? How much did you pay for your car?
◆ **J'ai payé ce T-shirt vingt francs.** I paid 20 francs for this T-shirt.
2 to pay ◊ Elle a été payée aujourd'hui. She got paid today.
◊ Son métier paye bien. His job pays good money. ◊ Elle est mal payée. She is badly paid.
◆ **faire payer quelque chose à quelqu'un** to charge somebody for something ◊ Il me l'a fait payer dix francs. He charged me 10 francs for it.
◆ **payer quelque chose à quelqu'un** to buy somebody something ◊ Allez, je vous paye un verre. Come on, I'll buy you a drink.

le **pays** NOUN
country

◆ **du pays** local ◊ le vin du pays the local wine

le **paysage** NOUN
landscape

le **paysan** NOUN
farmer

la **paysanne** NOUN
farmer

les **Pays-Bas** MASC NOUN
Netherlands
◆ **aux Pays-Bas (1)** in the Netherlands
◆ **aux Pays-Bas (2)** to the Netherlands

le **Pays de Galles** NOUN
Wales
◆ **au Pays de Galles (1)** in Wales
◊ Daphne habite au Pays de Galles. Daphne lives in Wales.
◆ **au Pays de Galles (2)** to Wales ◊ Elle part au Pays de Galles la semaine prochaine. She is going to Wales next week.

le **PC** NOUN
see also **PC** ABBREVIATION
PC (= personal computer) ◊ Il a tapé le rapport sur son PC. He typed the report on his PC.

PC ABBREVIATION (= Parti communiste)
see also **PC** NOUN
Communist Party

le **PDG** NOUN (= président-directeur général)
MD (= managing director)

le **péage** NOUN
1 toll ◊ Nous avons payé cinquante francs de péage. We paid a toll of 50 francs.
2 tollbooth ◊ Sabine s'est arrêtée au péage de l'autoroute. Sabine stopped at the motorway tollbooth.

ⓘ French motorways charge a toll.

la **peau** NOUN (PL les **peaux**)
skin ◊ Elle a la peau douce. She's got soft skin.

le/la **Peau-Rouge** NOUN (PL les **Peaux-Rouges**)
Red Indian

la **pêche** NOUN
1 peach
2 fishing
◆ **aller à la pêche** to go fishing
◆ **la pêche à la ligne** angling

le **péché** NOUN
sin

pêcher VERB
1 to fish for ◊ Ils sont partis pêcher la truite. They've gone fishing for trout.

P

☞

2 to catch ◊ *Jacques a pêché deux saumons.* Jacques caught two salmon.

le **pêcheur** NOUN
fisherman ◊ *Son père est pêcheur.* His father's a fisherman.
♦ **un pêcheur à la ligne** an angler

pédagogique ADJECTIVE
educational

la **pédale** NOUN
pedal

le **pédalo** NOUN
pedalo

pédestre ADJECTIVE
♦ **une randonnée pédestre** a ramble

le **peigne** NOUN
comb

peigner VERB
to comb ◊ *Elle peigne sa poupée.* She's combing her doll's hair.
♦ **se peigner** to comb one's hair ◊ *Il faut que je me peigne.* I must comb my hair.

le **peignoir** NOUN
dressing gown
♦ **un peignoir de bain** a bathrobe

peindre VERB
to paint

la **peine** NOUN
trouble
♦ **avoir de la peine à faire quelque chose** to have trouble doing something ◊ *J'ai eu beaucoup de peine à la convaincre.* I had a lot of trouble convincing her.
♦ **se donner de la peine** to make a real effort ◊ *Il s'est donné beaucoup de peine pour obtenir ces renseignements.* He made a real effort to get this information.
♦ **prendre la peine de faire quelque chose** to go to the trouble of doing something ◊ *Il a pris la peine de me rapporter ma valise.* He went to the trouble of returning my case to me.
♦ **faire de la peine à quelqu'un** to upset somebody ◊ *Ça me fait de la peine de la voir pleurer.* It upsets me to see her crying.
♦ **ce n'est pas la peine** there's no point ◊ *Ce n'est pas la peine de téléphoner.* There's no point in phoning.
♦ **à peine (1)** hardly ◊ *J'ai à peine eu le temps de me changer.* I hardly had time to get changed.
♦ **à peine (2)** only just ◊ *Elle vient à peine de se lever.* She's only just got up.

le **peintre** NOUN

painter

la **peinture** NOUN
1 painting ◊ *On expose des peintures de Gautier au musée.* There's an exhibition of Gautier's paintings at the museum.
2 paint ◊ *J'ai acheté de la peinture verte.* I bought some green paint.
♦ **"peinture fraîche"** "wet paint"

pêle-mêle ADVERB
higgledy-piggledy

peler VERB
to peel

la **pelle** NOUN
1 shovel
2 spade

la **pellicule** NOUN
film ◊ *une pellicule couleur* a colour film

les **pellicules** FEM NOUN
dandruff SING

la **pelote** NOUN
ball ◊ *une pelote de laine* a ball of wool

la **pelouse** NOUN
lawn

la **peluche** NOUN
♦ **un animal en peluche** a soft toy

le **penchant** NOUN
♦ **avoir un penchant pour quelque chose** to have a liking for something

pencher VERB
to tilt ◊ *Ce tableau penche vers la droite.* The picture's tilting to the right.
♦ **se pencher (1)** to lean over ◊ *Françoise s'est penchée sur son cahier.* Françoise leant over her exercise book.
♦ **se pencher (2)** to bend down ◊ *Il s'est penché pour ramasser sa casquette.* He bent down to pick his cap up.
♦ **se pencher (3)** to lean out ◊ *Annick s'est penchée par la fenêtre.* Annick leant out of the window.

pendant PREPOSITION
during ◊ *Ça s'est passé pendant l'été.* It happened during the summer.
♦ **pendant que** while ◊ *Christian a téléphoné pendant que Chantal prenait son bain.* Christian phoned while Chantal was having a bath.

le **pendentif** NOUN
pendant

la **penderie** NOUN
wardrobe (*for hanging clothes*)

pendre VERB

to hang ◊ *Il a pendu sa veste dans l'armoire.* He hung his jacket in the wardrobe.
♦ **pendre quelqu'un** to hang somebody ◊ *L'assassin a été pendu.* The murderer was hanged.

la **pendule** NOUN
clock

pénétrer VERB
[1] to enter ◊ *Ils ont pénétré dans la maison en passant par le jardin.* They entered the house through the garden.
[2] to penetrate ◊ *L'armée a pénétré sur le territoire ennemi.* The army penetrated enemy territory.

pénible ADJECTIVE
hard ◊ *Travailler sur un chantier est pénible.* Working on a building site is hard.
♦ **Il est vraiment pénible.** He's a real nuisance.

péniblement ADVERB
with difficulty

la **péniche** NOUN
barge

le **pénis** NOUN
penis

la **pénombre** NOUN
half-light

la **pensée** NOUN
thought ◊ *Il était perdu dans ses pensées.* He was lost in thought.

penser VERB
to think ◊ *Je pense que Yann a eu raison de partir.* I think Yann was right to leave.
♦ **penser à quelque chose** to think about something ◊ *Je pense à mes vacances.* I'm thinking about my holidays. ◊ *Pensez-y.* Think about it.
♦ **faire penser quelqu'un à quelque chose** to remind someone of something ◊ *Cette photo me fait penser à la Grèce.* This photo reminds me of Greece.
♦ **faire penser quelqu'un à faire quelque chose** to remind someone to do something ◊ *Fais-moi penser à téléphoner à Claire.* Remind me to phone Claire.
♦ **penser faire quelque chose** to be planning to do something ◊ *Ils pensent partir en Espagne en juillet.* They're planning to go to Spain in July.

la **pension** NOUN
[1] boarding school ◊ *Leur fille est en pension.* Their daughter is at boarding school.
[2] pension ◊ *Ma grand-mère reçoit sa pension tous les mois.* My grandma gets her pension every month.
[3] boarding house
♦ **la pension complète** full board

le/la **pensionnaire** NOUN
boarder

le **pensionnat** NOUN
boarding school

la **pente** NOUN
slope ◊ *une pente raide* a steep slope
♦ **en pente** sloping ◊ *Le toit de cette maison est en pente.* This house has a sloping roof.

la **Pentecôte** NOUN
Whitsun

le **pépin** NOUN
[1] pip ◊ *Cette orange est pleine de pépins.* This orange is full of pips.
[2] problem ◊ *avoir un pépin* (*informal*) to have a slight problem

perçant ADJECTIVE
[1] sharp ◊ *Il a une vue perçante.* He has very sharp eyes.
[2] piercing ◊ *un cri perçant* a piercing cry

percer VERB
to pierce ◊ *Christèle s'est fait percer les oreilles.* Christèle has had her ears pierced.

le **perdant** NOUN
loser

la **perdante** NOUN
loser

perdre VERB
to lose ◊ *Cécile a perdu ses clés.* Cécile's lost her keys.
♦ **J'ai perdu mon chemin.** I've lost my way.
♦ **perdre un match** to lose a match
♦ **perdre du temps** to waste time ◊ *J'ai perdu beaucoup de temps ce matin.* I've wasted a lot of time this morning. ◊ *Nous avons perdu notre temps à cette réunion.* That meeting was a waste of time.
♦ **se perdre** to get lost ◊ *Je me suis perdu en route.* I got lost on the way here.

perdu VERB see **perdre**

le **père** NOUN
father
♦ **le père Noël** Father Christmas

perfectionné ADJECTIVE
sophisticated

perfectionner VERB

P

to improve ◊ *Elle a besoin de perfectionner son anglais.* She needs to improve her English.

périmé ADJECTIVE
out-of-date ◊ *Mon passeport est périmé.* My passport's out of date.
♦**Ces yaourts sont périmés.** These yoghurts are past their use-by date.

la **période** NOUN
period

périodique ADJECTIVE
periodic

périphérique ADJECTIVE
see also **périphérique** NOUN
outlying ◊ *un quartier périphérique* an outlying district

le **périphérique** NOUN
see also **périphérique** ADJECTIVE
ring road

la **perle** NOUN
pearl

la **permanence** NOUN
♦**assurer une permanence** to operate a basic service ◊ *Ma banque assure une permanence le samedi matin.* My bank operates a basic service on Saturday mornings.
♦**être de permanence** to be on duty ◊ *Sophie ne peut pas venir, elle est de permanence ce soir.* Sophie can't come, she's on duty tonight.
♦**en permanence** permanently ◊ *Elle se plaint en permanence.* She's always complaining.

permanent ADJECTIVE
1 permanent ◊ *Il a un poste permanent.* He has a permanent job.
2 continuous ◊ *J'en ai assez de tes critiques permanentes.* I've had enough of your constant criticism.

la **permanente** NOUN
perm

permettre VERB
to allow
♦**permettre à quelqu'un de faire quelque chose** to allow somebody to do something ◊ *Sa mère lui permet de sortir le soir.* His mother allows him to go out at night.

le **permis** NOUN
permit ◊ *Il vous faut un permis pour camper ici.* You need a permit to camp here.
♦**le permis de conduire** driving licence
♦**un permis de séjour** a residence permit
♦**un permis de travail** a work permit

la **permission** NOUN

permission ◊ *Qui t'a donné la permission d'entrer?* Who gave you permission to come in?
♦**avoir la permission de faire quelque chose** to have permission to do something ◊ *J'ai la permission d'utiliser sa chaîne hi-fi.* I've got his permission to use his hi-fi.
♦**être en permission** to be on leave (*from the army*)

le **Pérou** NOUN
Peru

perpétuel ADJECTIVE (FEM SING **perpétuelle**)
perpetual

perplexe ADJECTIVE
puzzled ◊ *Ma question l'a laissé perplexe.* She was puzzled by my question.

le **perroquet** NOUN
parrot

la **perruche** NOUN
budgie

la **perruque** NOUN
wig

le **persil** NOUN
parsley

le **personnage** NOUN
1 figure ◊ *les grands personnages de l'histoire de France* the important figures in French history
2 character ◊ *le personnage principal du film* the main character in the film

la **personnalité** NOUN
1 personality ◊ *Ray a une personnalité forte.* Ray has a strong personality.
2 prominent figure ◊ *Il y avait beaucoup de personnalités politiques à ce dîner.* There were lots of prominent political figures at the dinner.

la **personne** NOUN
see also **personne** PRONOUN
person ◊ *Il y avait une trentaine de personnes dans la pièce.* There were about 30 people in the room. ◊ *une personne âgée* an elderly person
♦**en personne** in person

personne PRONOUN
see also **personne** NOUN
1 nobody ◊ *Il n'y a personne à la maison.* There's nobody at home. ◊ *Personne n'est venu le chercher.* Nobody came to fetch him.
2 anybody ◊ *Elle ne veut voir personne.* She doesn't want to see anybody.

personnel ADJECTIVE (FEM SING
personnelle)

see also **personnel** NOUN

personal

le **personnel** NOUN

see also **personnel** ADJECTIVE

staff ◊ *Il nous faut plus de personnel.*
We need more staff.
♦ **le service du personnel** the personnel
department

personnellement ADVERB
personally ◊ *Personnellement, je ne
suis pas d'accord.* Personally, I don't
agree.

la **perspective** NOUN
prospect ◊ *Les perspectives sont
bonnes.* The prospects are good.
♦ **perspectives d'avenir** prospects ◊ *Il y
a des perspectives d'avenir dans ce
métier.* This job has good prospects.
♦ **en perspective (1)** in prospect ◊ *Il y a
des changements en perspective.*
Changes are in prospect.
♦ **en perspective (2)** in perspective ◊ *Il a
dessiné la maison en perspective.* He
drew the house in perspective.

persuader VERB
to persuade
♦ **persuader quelqu'un de faire quelque
chose** to persuade somebody to do
something ◊ *Elle m'a persuadé de
l'accompagner.* She persuaded me to
go with her.

la **perte** NOUN
⑴ loss ◊ *des pertes d'emploi* job
losses
⑵ waste ◊ *Cette réunion a été une
perte de temps.* The meeting was a
waste of time.

perturber VERB
to disrupt ◊ *Un car en panne
perturbait la circulation.* A coach had
broken down and was disrupting the
traffic.

le **pèse-personne** NOUN
bathroom scales PL

peser VERB
to weigh ◊ *Elle pèse cent kilos.* She
weighs 100 kilos.

pessimiste ADJECTIVE
pessimistic

le **pétale** NOUN
petal

la **pétanque** NOUN

🛈 *pétanque* is a type of bowls
played in France, especially in the
south.

---

le **pétard** NOUN
firecracker

péter VERB (*rude*)
to fart

petit ADJECTIVE
⑴ small ◊ *Sonia habite une petite
ville.* Sonia lives in a small town.
⑵ little ◊ *Phyllis a une jolie petite
maison.* Phyllis has a nice little
house.
♦ **petit à petit** bit by bit
♦ **un petit ami** a boyfriend
♦ **une petite amie** a girlfriend
♦ **le petit déjeuner** breakfast ◊ *prendre
le petit déjeuner* to have breakfast
♦ **un petit pain** a bread roll
♦ **les petites annonces** the small ads
♦ **des petits pois** garden peas
♦ **les petits** young (*of animal*) ◊ *la lionne
et ses petits* the lioness and her
young

la **petite-fille** NOUN (PL les **petites-filles**)
granddaughter

le **petit-fils** NOUN (PL les **petits-fils**)
grandson

les **petits-enfants** MASC NOUN
grandchildren

le **pétrole** NOUN
oil ◊ *une lampe à pétrole* an oil lamp
Be careful! **pétrole** *does not mean*
petrol.

peu ADVERB, NOUN
not much ◊ *J'ai peu mangé à midi.* I
didn't eat much for lunch. ◊ *Il voyage
peu.* He doesn't travel much.
♦ **un peu** a bit ◊ *Elle est un peu timide.*
She's a bit shy. ◊ *un peu de gâteau* a
bit of cake
♦ **un petit peu** a little bit ◊ *un petit peu
de crème* a little bit of cream
♦ **peu de (1)** not many ◊ *Il y a peu de
bons films au cinéma.* There aren't
very many good films on at the
cinema. ◊ *Stéphanie a peu d'amis.*
Stéphanie hasn't got many
friends.
♦ **peu de (2)** not much ◊ *Il a peu
d'espoir de réussir.* He doesn't have
much hope of succeeding. ◊ *Il lui
reste peu d'argent.* He hasn't got
much money left.
♦ **à peu près (1)** more or less ◊ *J'ai à
peu près fini.* I've more or less
finished.
♦ **à peu près (2)** about ◊ *Le voyage
prend à peu près deux heures et
demie.* The journey takes about two
and a half hours.
♦ **peu à peu** little by little
♦ **peu avant** shortly before

P

☞

◆ **peu après** shortly afterwards

◆ **de peu** only just ◊ *Chantal a manqué son train de peu.* Chantal only just missed her train.

le **peuple** NOUN
people ◊ *le peuple français* the French people

la **peur** NOUN
fear

◆ **avoir peur de** to be afraid of ◊ *Il a peur du noir.* He's afraid of the dark.

◆ **avoir peur de faire quelque chose** to be frightened of doing something ◊ *Elle a peur d'y aller toute seule.* She's frightened of going on her own.

◆ **faire peur à quelqu'un** to frighten somebody ◊ *Cet homme-là me fait peur.* That man frightens me.

peureux ADJECTIVE (FEM SING **peureuse**)
fearful

peut VERB *see* **pouvoir**

◆ **Il ne peut pas venir.** He can't come.

peut-être ADVERB
perhaps ◊ *Je l'ai peut-être oublié à la maison.* Perhaps I've left it at home.

◆ **peut-être que** perhaps ◊ *Peut-être qu'elles n'ont pas pu téléphoner.* Perhaps they weren't able to phone.

peuvent, peux VERB *see* **pouvoir**

◆ **Je ne peux pas le faire.** I can't do it.

p. ex. ABBREVIATION (= *par exemple*)
e.g.

le **phare** NOUN
1 lighthouse ◊ *On voit le phare depuis le pont du bateau.* You can see the lighthouse from the ship's deck.
2 headlight ◊ *Il a laissé les phares de sa voiture allumés.* He left his headlights on.

la **pharmacie** NOUN
chemist's

> ⓘ *Chemist's shops in France are identified by a special green cross outside the shop.*

le **pharmacien** NOUN
pharmacist

la **pharmacienne** NOUN
pharmacist

le **phénomène** NOUN
phenomenon

la **philosophie** NOUN
philosophy

le **phoque** NOUN
seal (*animal*)

la **photo** NOUN
photograph ◊ *Elle a fait développer ses photos.* She's had her photographs developed.

◆ **en photo** in photographs ◊ *Je n'ai vu Venise qu'en photo.* I've only seen Venice in photographs.

◆ **prendre quelqu'un en photo** to take a photo of somebody ◊ *Claire nous a pris en photo.* Claire took a photo of us.

◆ **une photo d'identité** a passport photograph

la **photocopie** NOUN
photocopy

photocopier VERB
to photocopy

la **photocopieuse** NOUN
photocopier

le/la **photographe** NOUN
photographer

la **photographie** NOUN
1 photography
2 photograph

photographier VERB
to photograph

la **phrase** NOUN
sentence

physique ADJECTIVE
| *see also* **physique** NOUN |
physical

le **physique** NOUN
| *see also* **la physique**, **physique** ADJECTIVE |

◆ **Il a un physique agréable.** He's quite good-looking.

la **physique** NOUN
| *see also* **le physique**, **physique** ADJECTIVE |
physics ◊ *Graham est professeur de physique.* Graham is a physics teacher.

le/la **pianiste** NOUN
pianist ◊ *Elle est pianiste.* She's a pianist.

le **piano** NOUN
piano

le **pic** NOUN
peak ◊ *les pics enneigés des Pyrénées* the snowy peaks of the Pyrenees

◆ **à pic (1)** vertically ◊ *La falaise tombe à pic dans la mer.* The cliff drops vertically into the sea.

◆ **à pic (1)** just at the right time ◊ *Tu es arrivé à pic.* You arrived just at the right time.

la **pièce** NOUN
1 room ◊ *Mon lit est au centre de la pièce.* My bed is in the middle of the room.

◆ **un cinq-pièces** a five-roomed flat
2 play ◊ *On joue une pièce de Shakespeare au théâtre.* There's a play by Shakespeare on at the theatre.
3 part ◊ *Il faut changer une pièce du moteur.* There's an engine part which needs changing.
4 coin ◊ *des pièces d'un franc* some one-franc coins
◆ **cinquante francs pièce** 50 francs each ◊ *J'ai acheté ces T-shirts dix francs pièce.* I bought these T-shirts for ten francs each.
◆ **un maillot une pièce** a one-piece swimsuit
◆ **un maillot deux-pièces** a bikini
◆ **Avez-vous une pièce d'identité?** Have you got any identification?

le **pied** NOUN
foot ◊ *J'ai mal aux pieds.* My feet are hurting.
◆ **à pied** on foot
◆ **avoir pied** to be able to touch the bottom ◊ *Justine n'aime pas nager là où elle n'a pas pied.* Justine doesn't like swimming where she can't touch the bottom.

le **pied-noir** NOUN (PL les **pieds-noirs**)

> ℹ A **pied-noir** is a French person born in Algeria; most of them moved to France during the Algerian war in the 1950s.

◊ *Sa grand-mère est pied-noir.* His grandmother was born in Algeria.

le **piège** NOUN
trap
◆ **prendre quelqu'un au piège** to trap somebody

piéger VERB
to trap
◆ **un colis piégé** a parcel bomb
◆ **une voiture piégée** a car bomb

la **pierre** NOUN
stone
◆ **une pierre précieuse** a precious stone

le **piéton** NOUN
pedestrian

la **piétonne** NOUN
pedestrian

piétonnier ADJECTIVE (FEM SING **piétonnière**)
◆ **une rue piétonnière** a pedestrianized street
◆ **un quartier piétonnier** a pedestrianized area

la **pieuvre** NOUN

octopus

le **pigeon** NOUN
pigeon

piger VERB (*informal*)
to understand

la **pile** NOUN
see also **pile** ADVERB
1 pile ◊ *Il y a une pile de disques sur la table.* There's a pile of records on the table.
2 battery ◊ *Les piles de mon magnétophone sont usées.* The batteries in my tape recorder have run out.

pile ADVERB
see also **pile** NOUN
◆ **à deux heures pile** at two on the dot
◆ **jouer à pile ou face** to toss up
◆ **Pile ou face?** Heads or tails?

le **pilote** NOUN
pilot
◆ **un pilote de course** a racing driver
◆ **un pilote de ligne** an airline pilot

piloter VERB
to fly (*a plane*)

la **pilule** NOUN
pill
◆ **prendre la pilule** to be on the pill

le **piment** NOUN
chilli

le **pin** NOUN
pine

le **pinard** NOUN (*informal*)
wine

la **pince** NOUN
1 pliers PL (*tool*)
2 pincer (*of crab*)
◆ **une pince à épiler** tweezers
◆ **une pince à linge** a clothes peg

le **pinceau** NOUN (PL les **pinceaux**)
paintbrush

la **pincée** NOUN
◆ **une pincée de sel** a pinch of salt

pincer VERB
to pinch ◊ *Elle m'a pincé le bras.* She pinched my arm.

le **pingouin** NOUN
penguin

le **ping-pong** NOUN
table tennis ◊ *jouer au ping-pong* to play table tennis

la **pintade** NOUN
guinea fowl

le **pion** NOUN
1 pawn (*in chess*)
2 piece (*in draughts*)
3 supervisor (*man*)

P

☞

i In French secondary schools, the teachers are not responsible for supervising the pupils outside class. This job is done by people called **pions** or **surveillants**.

la **pionne** NOUN
   supervisor (woman)

la **pipe** NOUN
   pipe ◊ Mon grand-père fume la pipe. My granddad smokes a pipe.

   piquant ADJECTIVE
   1 prickly
   2 spicy

le **pique** NOUN
   see also **la pique**
   spades PL ◊ l'as de pique the ace of spades

la **pique** NOUN
   see also **le pique**
   cutting remark ◊ envoyer des piques à quelqu'un to make cutting remarks to somebody

le **pique-nique** NOUN
   picnic

   piquer VERB
   1 to bite ◊ Nous avons été piqués par les moustiques. We were bitten by mosquitoes.
   2 to burn ◊ Cette sauce me pique la langue. This sauce is burning my tongue.
   3 to steal ◊ On m'a piqué mon porte-monnaie. (informal) I've had my purse stolen.
   ◆ **se piquer** to prick oneself ◊ Il s'est piqué avec une aiguille. He pricked himself with a needle.

le **piquet** NOUN
   1 post ◊ Le chien est attaché à un piquet. The dog is tied to a post.
   2 peg ◊ Il nous manque un des piquets de la tente. One of our tent pegs is missing.

la **piqûre** NOUN
   1 injection ◊ Le médecin lui a fait une piqûre. The doctor gave him an injection.
   2 bite ◊ une piqûre de moustique a mosquito bite
   3 sting ◊ une piqûre d'abeille a bee sting

le **pirate** NOUN
   pirate
   ◆ **un pirate informatique** a hacker

   pire ADJECTIVE, NOUN
   worse ◊ C'est encore pire qu'avant. It's even worse than before.

◆ **le pire** the worst ◊ C'est la pire journée que j'aie jamais passée. That's the worst day I've ever had. ◊ Ce gamin est le pire de la bande. That boy is the worst in the group.
◆ **le pire de** the worst of ◊ Le pire de tout, c'est qu'on s'ennuie tout le temps. The worst of it is that we're always bored.

la **piscine** NOUN
   swimming pool

   pisser VERB (informal)
   to have a pee

la **pistache** NOUN
   pistachio ◊ une glace à la pistache a pistachio ice cream

la **piste** NOUN
   1 lead ◊ La police est sur une piste. The police are following a lead.
   2 runway ◊ L'avion s'est posé sur la piste. The plane landed on the runway.
   3 ski run ◊ Le skieur a descendu la piste. The skier came down the ski run.
   ◆ **une piste artificielle** a dry ski slope
   ◆ **la piste de danse** the dance floor
   ◆ **une piste cyclable** a cycle lane

le **pistolet** NOUN
   pistol

   pistonner VERB
   ◆ Il a été pistonné pour avoir ce travail. They pulled some strings to get him this job.

la **pitié** NOUN
   pity
   ◆ Il me fait pitié. I feel sorry for him.
   ◆ **avoir pitié de quelqu'un** to feel sorry for somebody

   pittoresque ADJECTIVE
   picturesque

la **pizza** NOUN
   pizza

le **placard** NOUN
   cupboard

la **place** NOUN
   1 place ◊ Vincent a eu la troisième place au concours. Vincent got third place in the competition.
   2 square ◊ la place du village the village square
   3 space ◊ Il ne reste plus de place pour se garer. There's no more space to park. ◊ Ça prend de la place. It takes up a lot of room.
   4 seat ◊ Toutes les places ont été vendues. All the seats have been sold.
   ◊ remettre quelque chose en place to put something back in its place

♦ **sur place** on the spot

♦ **à la place** instead ◊ *Il ne reste plus de tarte; désirez-vous quelque chose d'autre à la place?* There's no pie left; would you like something else instead?

♦ **à la place de** instead of

placer VERB

[1] to seat ◊ *Nous étions placés à côté du directeur.* We were seated next to the manager.

[2] to invest ◊ *Il a placé ses économies en Bourse.* He invested his money on the Stock Exchange.

le **plafond** NOUN
ceiling

la **plage** NOUN
beach

la **plaie** NOUN
wound

plaindre VERB

♦ **plaindre quelqu'un** to feel sorry for somebody ◊ *Je te plains.* I feel sorry for you.

♦ **se plaindre** to complain ◊ *Il n'arrête pas de se plaindre.* He never stops complaining.

♦ **se plaindre à quelqu'un** to complain to somebody ◊ *Ils se sont plaints au directeur.* They complained to the manager.

♦ **se plaindre de quelque chose** to complain about something ◊ *Elle s'est plainte du bruit.* She complained about the noise.

la **plaine** NOUN
plain (*level area*)

la **plainte** NOUN
complaint

♦ **porter plainte** to lodge a complaint

plaire VERB

♦ *Ce cadeau me plaît beaucoup.* I like this present a lot.

♦ *Ce film plaît beaucoup aux jeunes.* The film is very popular with young people.

♦ *Elle lui plaît.* He fancies her.

♦ **s'il te plaît** please

♦ **s'il vous plaît** please

plaisanter VERB
to joke

la **plaisanterie** NOUN
joke

le **plaisir** NOUN
pleasure

♦ **faire plaisir à quelqu'un** to please somebody ◊ *J'y suis allé pour lui faire plaisir.* I went there to please

him. ◊ *Ce cadeau me fait très plaisir.* I'm very pleased with this present.

plaît VERB *see* **plaire**

le **plan** NOUN
plan

♦ **un plan de la ville** a street map

♦ **au premier plan** in the foreground

la **planche** NOUN
plank

♦ **une planche à repasser** an ironing board

♦ **une planche à roulettes** a skateboard

♦ **une planche à voile** a sailboard

le **plancher** NOUN
floor

planer VERB

[1] to glide ◊ *L'avion planait dans le ciel.* The plane was gliding in the sky.

[2] to have one's head in the clouds ◊ *Ce garçon plane complètement.* (*informal*) He's not with us at all.

la **planète** NOUN
planet

la **plante** NOUN
plant

planter VERB

[1] to plant ◊ *Daphné a planté des tomates.* Daphne planted some tomatoes.

[2] to hammer in ◊ *Jean-Pierre a planté un clou dans le mur.* Jean-Pierre hammered a nail into the wall.

[3] to pitch ◊ *André a planté sa tente au bord du lac.* André pitched his tent next to the lake.

♦ **Ne reste pas planté là!** Don't just stand there!

♦ **se planter** (*informal*) to fail ◊ *Je me suis planté en maths.* I failed maths.

la **plaque** NOUN
(metal) plate

♦ **une plaque de verglas** a patch of ice

♦ **une plaque de chocolat** a bar of chocolate

♦ **une plaque d'immatriculation** a number plate (*of car*)

plaqué ADJECTIVE

♦ **plaqué or** gold-plated

♦ **plaqué argent** silver-plated

plaquer VERB (*informal*)

[1] to ditch ◊ *Elle a plaqué son copain.* She ditched her boyfriend.

[2] to pack in ◊ *Il a plaqué son boulot.* He packed in his job.

la **plaquette** NOUN

♦ **une plaquette de chocolat** a bar of chocolate

♦ **une plaquette de beurre** a pack of butter

P

le **plastique** NOUN
  plastic

plat ADJECTIVE
  see also **plat** NOUN
  flat
  ◆ **être à plat ventre** to be lying face down
  ◆ **l'eau plate** still water

le **plat** NOUN
  see also **plat** ADJECTIVE
  1 dish
  2 course ◇ *le plat principal* the main course
  ◆ **un plat cuisiné** a pre-cooked meal
  ◆ **le plat de résistance** the main course
  ◆ **le plat du jour** the dish of the day

le **platane** NOUN
  plane tree

le **plateau** NOUN (PL les **plateaux**)
  1 tray
  ◆ **un plateau de fromages** a selection of cheeses
  2 plateau

la **platine** NOUN
  see also **la platine**
  platinum

la **platine** NOUN
  see also **le platine**
  turntable (*of record player*)
  ◆ **une platine laser** a CD player

le **plâtre** NOUN
  plaster ◇ *une statue en plâtre* a statue made of plaster ◇ *avoir un bras dans le plâtre* to have an arm in plaster

plein ADJECTIVE
  see also **plein** NOUN
  full
  ◆ **à plein temps** full-time ◇ *Elle travaille à plein temps.* She works full-time.
  ◆ **plein de** (*informal*) lots of ◇ *un gâteau avec plein de crème* a cake with lots of cream
  ◆ **Il y a plein de gens dans la rue.** The street is full of people.
  ◆ **en plein air** in the open air
  ◆ **en pleine nuit** in the middle of the night
  ◆ **en plein jour** in broad daylight

le **plein** NOUN
  see also **plein** ADJECTIVE
  ◆ **faire le plein** to fill up (*petrol tank*) ◇ *Faites le plein, s'il vous plaît.* Fill it up, please.

pleurer VERB
  to cry

pleut VERB *see* **pleuvoir**

pleuvoir VERB
  to rain ◇ *Il pleut.* It's raining.

le **pli** NOUN
  1 fold
  2 pleat ◇ *Elle a repassé les plis de sa jupe.* She ironed the pleats of her skirt.
  3 crease ◇ *Il y a un pli sur la manche de ta chemise.* There's a crease in the sleeve of your shirt.

pliant ADJECTIVE
  folding ◇ *un lit pliant* a folding bed

plier VERB
  1 to fold ◇ *Elle a plié sa serviette.* She folded her towel.
  2 to bend ◇ *Elle a plié le bras.* She bent her arm.

le **plomb** NOUN
  1 lead ◇ *Ces jouets sont en plomb.* These toys are made of lead.
  2 fuse ◇ *Les plombs ont sauté.* The fuses have blown.
  ◆ **l'essence sans plomb** unleaded petrol

le **plombier** NOUN
  plumber
  ◆ **Il est plombier.** He's a plumber.

la **plongée** NOUN
  diving ◇ *faire de la plongée* to go diving

le **plongeoir** NOUN
  diving board

le **plongeon** NOUN
  dive

plonger VERB
  to dive ◇ *Jean a plongé dans la piscine.* Jean dived into the swimming pool.
  ◆ **J'ai plongé ma main dans l'eau.** I plunged my hand into the water.
  ◆ **être plongé dans son travail** to be absorbed in your work
  ◆ **se plonger dans un livre** to get absorbed in a book

plu VERB *see* **plaire**, **pleuvoir**

la **pluie** NOUN
  rain ◇ *sous la pluie* in the rain

la **plume** NOUN
  feather ◇ *une plume d'oiseau* a bird's feather
  ◆ **un stylo à plume** a fountain pen

plupart
  ◆ **la plupart** PRONOUN
  most (of them) ◇ *La plupart ont moins de quinze ans.* Most of them are under 15.
  ◆ **la plupart des** most ◇ *La plupart des gens ont vu ce film.* Most people have seen this film.
  ◆ **la plupart du temps** most of the time

le **pluriel** NOUN
  plural
  ◆ **au pluriel** in the plural

plus ADVERB, PREPOSITION

♦**ne ... plus (1)** not ... any more ◊ *Je ne veux plus le voir.* I don't want to see him any more.

♦**ne ... plus (2)** no longer ◊ *Il ne travaille plus ici.* He's no longer working here.

♦**Je n'ai plus de pain.** I've got no bread left.

♦**plus ... que** more ... than ◊ *Il est plus intelligent que son frère.* He's more intelligent than his brother. ◊ *Il travaille plus que moi.* He works more than me. ◊ *Elle est plus grande que moi.* She's bigger than me.

♦**C'est le plus grand de la famille.** He's the tallest in his family.

♦**plus ... plus ...** the more ... the more ... ◊ *Plus il gagne d'argent, plus il en veut.* The more money he earns, the more he wants.

♦**plus de (1)** more ◊ *Il nous faut plus de pain.* We need more bread.

♦**plus de (2)** more than ◊ *Il y avait plus de dix personnes.* There were more than 10 people.

♦**de plus** more ◊ *Il nous faut un joueur de plus.* We need one more player. ◊ *Le voyage a pris trois heures de plus que prévu.* The journey took 3 hours more than planned.

♦**en plus** more ◊ *J'ai apporté quelques gâteaux en plus.* I brought a few more cakes.

♦**de plus en plus** more and more ◊ *Il y a de plus en plus de touristes par ici.* There are more and more tourists round here. ◊ *Il fait de plus en plus chaud.* It's getting hotter and hotter.

♦**un peu plus difficile** a bit more difficult ◊ *Il fait un peu plus froid qu'hier.* It's a bit colder than yesterday.

♦**plus ou moins** more or less

♦**Quatre plus deux égalent six.** 4 plus 2 is 6.

plusieurs PRONOUN

several ◊ *Gaëlle a acheté plusieurs chemises.* Gaëlle bought several shirts. ◊ *Il y en a plusieurs.* There are several of them.

le **plus-que-parfait** NOUN

pluperfect

plutôt ADVERB

1 quite ◊ *Elle est plutôt jolie.* She's quite pretty.

2 rather ◊ *L'eau est plutôt froide.* The water's rather cold.

3 instead ◊ *Demande-leur plutôt de venir avec toi.* Ask them to come with you instead.

♦**plutôt que** rather than ◊ *Invite Marie plutôt que Nathalie.* Invite Marie rather than Nathalie.

pluvieux ADJECTIVE (FEM SING **pluvieuse**)

rainy

le **pneu** NOUN

tyre

la **pneumonie** NOUN

pneumonia

la **poche** NOUN

pocket

♦**l'argent de poche** pocket money

♦**un livre de poche** a paperback

la **poêle** NOUN

frying pan

♦**une poêle à frire** a frying pan

le **poème** NOUN

poem

la **poésie** NOUN

1 poetry

2 poem

le **poète** NOUN

poet

le **poids** NOUN

weight ◊ *vendre quelque chose au poids* to sell something by weight

♦**prendre du poids** to put on weight ◊ *Il a pris du poids.* He's put on weight.

♦**perdre du poids** to lose weight ◊ *Elle a perdu du poids.* She's lost weight.

♦**un poids lourd** a lorry

la **poignée** NOUN

1 handful ◊ *une poignée de sel* a handful of salt

2 handle ◊ *la poignée de la porte* the door handle

♦**une poignée de main** a handshake

le **poignet** NOUN

1 wrist ◊ *Je me suis fait mal au poignet.* I've hurt my wrist.

2 cuff (*of shirt*)

le **poil** NOUN

1 hair ◊ *Il y a des poils de chat partout sur la moquette.* There are cat hairs all over the carpet.

2 fur ◊ *Ton chien a un beau poil.* Your dog's got lovely fur.

♦**à poil** (*informal*) stark naked

poilu ADJECTIVE

hairy

poinçonner VERB

to punch ◊ *Le contrôleur a poinçonné les billets.* The conductor punched the tickets.

le **poing** NOUN

fist

♦**un coup de poing** a punch

P

le **point** NOUN

◻1 point ◊ *Je ne suis pas d'accord sur ce point.* I don't agree with this point. ◊ *Son point faible, c'est qu'elle est trop gentille.* Her weak point is she's too nice.

♦ **point de vue** point of view

◻2 full stop

♦ **être sur le point de faire quelque chose** to be just about to do something ◊ *J'étais sur le point de te téléphoner.* I was just about to phone you.

♦ **mettre au point** to finalize

♦ **Ce n'est pas encore au point.** It's not finalized yet.

♦ **à point** medium ◊ *Comment voulez-vous votre steak? – À point.* How would you like your steak? – Medium.

♦ **un point d'exclamation** an exclamation mark

♦ **un point d'interrogation** a question mark

♦ **un point noir** a blackhead

la **pointe** NOUN

point ◊ *la pointe d'un couteau* the point of a knife

♦ **être à la pointe du progrès** to be in the forefront of progress

♦ **sur la pointe des pieds** on tiptoe

♦ **les heures de pointe** peak hours

le **pointillé** NOUN

dotted line

pointu ADJECTIVE

pointed ◊ *un chapeau pointu* a pointed hat

la **pointure** NOUN

size (*of shoes*) ◊ *Quelle est votre pointure?* What size shoes do you take?

le **point-virgule** NOUN (PL **points-virgules**)

semicolon

la **poire** NOUN

pear

le **poireau** NOUN (PL les **poireaux**)

leek ◊ *la soupe aux poireaux* leek soup

le **pois** NOUN

pea

♦ **les petits pois** peas

♦ **les pois chiches** chickpeas

♦ **à pois** spotted ◊ *une robe à pois* a spotted dress

le **poison** NOUN

poison

le **poisson** NOUN

fish ◊ *Je n'aime pas le poisson.* I don't like fish. ◊ *André a pêché deux poissons.* André caught two fish.

♦ **les Poissons** Pisces ◊ *Monique est Poissons.* Monique is Pisces.

♦ **Poisson d'avril!** April fool!

i Pinning a paper fish to somebody's back is a traditional April fool joke in France.

♦ **un poisson rouge** a goldfish

la **poissonnerie** NOUN

fish shop

le **poissonnier** NOUN

fishmonger

la **poitrine** NOUN

◻1 chest ◊ *J'ai mal à la poitrine.* My chest hurts.

◻2 bust ◊ *Quel est votre tour de poitrine?* What's your bust size?

le **poivre** NOUN

pepper (*spice*)

le **poivron** NOUN

pepper (*vegetable*)

le **pôle** NOUN

pole

♦ **le pôle Nord** the North Pole

♦ **le pôle Sud** the South Pole

poli ADJECTIVE

polite

la **police** NOUN

police ◊ *La police recherche le voleur.* The police are looking for the thief.

♦ **police secours** emergency services ◊ *Ils ont appelé police secours.* They phoned the emergency services.

♦ **une police d'assurance** an insurance policy

policier ADJECTIVE (FEM SING **policière**)

see also **policier** NOUN

♦ **un roman policier** a detective novel

le **policier** NOUN

see also **policier** ADJECTIVE

policeman ◊ *Il est policier.* He's a policeman.

la **politesse** NOUN

politeness

la **politique** NOUN

politics ◊ *La politique ne l'intéresse pas du tout.* He's not at all interested in politics.

♦ **un homme politique** a politician

pollué ADJECTIVE

polluted

polluer VERB

to pollute

la **pollution** NOUN

pollution

le **polo** NOUN

polo shirt

la **Pologne** NOUN
　　Poland

polonais ADJECTIVE, NOUN (FEM SING
polonaise)
　　Polish ◇ *Elle parle polonais.* She
　　speaks Polish.
　　♦ **un Polonais** a Pole (*man*)
　　♦ **une Polonaise** a Pole (*woman*)
　　♦ **les Polonais** the Polish

la **Polynésie** NOUN
　　Polynesia

la **pommade** NOUN
　　ointment

la **pomme** NOUN
　　apple
　　♦ **les pommes de terre** potatoes
　　♦ **les pommes frites** chips
　　♦ **les pommes vapeur** boiled potatoes

la **pompe** NOUN
　　pump
　　♦ **une pompe à essence** a petrol pump
　　♦ **les pompes funèbres** undertakers

le **pompier** NOUN
　　fireman

le **pompiste** NOUN
　　petrol pump attendant

ponctuel ADJECTIVE (FEM SING **ponctuelle**)
　　①　punctual ◇ *Elle est toujours très
　　ponctuelle.* She's always very
　　punctual.
　　②　occasional ◇ *Nous avons
　　rencontré quelques problèmes
　　ponctuels.* We've had the occasional
　　problem.

pondre VERB
　　to lay (*eggs*)

le **poney** NOUN
　　pony

le **pont** NOUN
　　①　bridge
　　②　deck (*of ship*)
　　♦ **faire le pont** to take a long weekend
　　◇ *Nous faisons le pont pour la
　　Pentecôte.* We're taking a long
　　weekend for Whitsun.

populaire ADJECTIVE
　　①　popular ◇ *Ce chanteur est très
　　populaire en France.* This singer's
　　very popular in France.
　　②　working-class ◇ *un quartier
　　populaire de la ville* a working-class
　　area of town

la **population** NOUN
　　population

le **porc** NOUN
　　①　pig ◇ *Ils élèvent des porcs.* They
　　breed pigs.
　　②　pork ◇ *du rôti de porc* roast pork

la **porcelaine** NOUN
　　china ◇ *une tasse en porcelaine* a
　　china cup

le **port** NOUN
　　①　harbour
　　②　port

le **portable** NOUN
　　mobile phone ◇ *Je vais appeler
　　Marie sur mon portable.* I'll phone
　　Marie on my mobile.

le **portail** NOUN
　　gate

portatif ADJECTIVE (FEM SING **portative**)
　　portable

la **porte** NOUN
　　①　door ◇ *Ferme la porte, s'il te plaît.*
　　Close the door, please.
　　♦ **la porte d'entrée** the front door
　　②　gate ◇ *Vol 432 à destination de
　　Paris: porte numéro trois.* Flight 432
　　to Paris: gate 3.
　　♦ **mettre quelqu'un à la porte** to sack
　　somebody

le **porte-bagages** NOUN
　　luggage rack

le **porte-clés** NOUN
　　key ring

la **portée** NOUN
　　♦ **à portée de la main** within arm's
　　reach
　　♦ **hors de portée** out of reach

le **portefeuille** NOUN
　　wallet

le **portemanteau** NOUN (PL les
portemanteaux)
　　①　coat hanger
　　②　coat rack

le **porte-monnaie** NOUN (PL les **porte-
monnaie**)
　　purse

porter VERB
　　①　to carry ◇ *Il portait une valise.* He
　　was carrying a suitcase.
　　②　to wear ◇ *Elle porte une jolie robe
　　bleue.* She's wearing a lovely blue
　　dress.
　　♦ **se porter bien** to be well
　　♦ **se porter mal** to be unwell

la **portière** NOUN
　　door (*of car*)

la **portion** NOUN
　　portion

le **porto** NOUN
　　port (*wine*)

le **portrait** NOUN
　　portrait

portugais ADJECTIVE, NOUN (FEM SING
portugaise)

P

☞

Portuguese ◊ *Il parle portugais.* He speaks Portuguese.
- ◆ **un Portugais** a Portuguese (*man*)
- ◆ **une Portugaise** a Portuguese (*woman*)
- ◆ **les Portugais** the Portuguese

le **Portugal** NOUN
Portugal
- ◆ **au Portugal (1)** in Portugal
- ◆ **au Portugal (2)** to Portugal

poser VERB
1 to put down ◊ *J'ai posé la cafetière sur la table.* I put the coffee pot down on the table.
2 to pose ◊ *Cela pose un problème.* That poses a problem.
- ◆ **poser une question à quelqu'un** to ask somebody a question
- ◆ **se poser** to land ◊ *L'avion s'est posé à huit heures.* The plane landed at 8 o'clock.

positif ADJECTIVE (FEM SING **positive**)
positive

la **position** NOUN
position

posséder VERB
to own ◊ *Ils possèdent une jolie maison.* They own a lovely house.

la **possibilité** NOUN
possibility

possible ADJECTIVE
possible ◊ *Alain leur a dit que ce n'était pas possible.* Alain told them it wasn't possible.
- ◆ **le plus de gens possible** as many people as possible
- ◆ **le plus tôt possible** as early as possible
- ◆ **le moins d'argent possible** as little money as possible
- ◆ **Il travaille le moins possible.** He works as little as possible.
- ◆ **dès que possible** as soon as possible
- ◆ **faire son possible** to do all one can ◊ *Je ferai tout mon possible.* I'll do all I can.

la **poste** NOUN
see also **le poste**
1 post ◊ *Je vais l'envoyer par la poste.* I'm going to send it by post.
2 post office ◊ *Je vais à la poste pour acheter des timbres.* I'm going to the post office to buy some stamps.
- ◆ **mettre une lettre à la poste** to post a letter

le **poste** NOUN
see also **la poste**
1 post ◊ *Jean-Pierre a trouvé un poste de professeur.* Jean-Pierre has found a teaching post.

2 extension (*phone*) ◊ *Pouvez-vous me passer le poste de M. Salzedo?* Can you put me through to Mr Salzedo's extension?
3 set ◊ *un poste de radio* a radio set
- ◆ **un poste de police** a police station

poster VERB
see also **poster** NOUN
to post ◊ *Je vais poster ce colis.* I'm going to post this parcel.

le **poster** NOUN
see also **poster** VERB
poster ◊ *un poster de la Grèce* a poster of Greece

postérieur ADJECTIVE
1 later ◊ *Ce document est postérieur à 1314.* This document is from later than 1314.
2 back ◊ *la partie postérieure de ma jambe* the back of my leg

le **pot** NOUN
jar ◊ *J'ai fait trois pots de confiture.* I've made three jars of jam.
- ◆ **prendre un pot** (*informal*) to have a drink ◊ *On va prendre un pot ce soir.* We're going for a drink tonight.
- ◆ **un pot de fleurs** a plant pot

potable ADJECTIVE
- ◆ **eau potable** drinking water
- ◆ **"eau non potable"** "not drinking water"

le **potage** NOUN
soup

le **potager** NOUN
vegetable garden

le **pot-au-feu** NOUN (PL les **pot-au-feu**)
beef stew

le **pot-de-vin** NOUN (PL les **pots-de-vin**)
bribe

le **pote** NOUN (*informal*)
mate ◊ *Je sors avec mes potes ce soir.* I'm going out with my mates tonight.

le **poteau** NOUN (PL les **poteaux**)
post ◊ *Il s'est appuyé contre un poteau.* He leant against a post.
- ◆ **un poteau indicateur** a signpost

potentiel ADJECTIVE (FEM SING **potentielle**)
potential

la **poterie** NOUN
1 pottery ◊ *Elle fait de la poterie à l'école.* She does pottery at school.
2 piece of pottery ◊ *J'ai acheté deux poteries.* I bought two pieces of pottery.

le **potier** NOUN
potter

le **pou** NOUN (PL les **poux**)
louse

la **poubelle** NOUN
dustbin

le **pouce** NOUN
[1] thumb ◊ *Je me suis coincé le pouce dans la porte.* I trapped my thumb in the door.
[2] inch ◊ *Un pouce fait à peu près deux virgule cinq centimètres.* 1 inch equals roughly 2.5 centimetres.
♦ **manger sur le pouce** to have a quick snack

la **poudre** NOUN
[1] powder
[2] face powder
♦ **la poudre à laver** washing powder
♦ **le lait en poudre** powdered milk
♦ **le café en poudre** instant coffee

le **poulain** NOUN
foal

la **poule** NOUN
hen

le **poulet** NOUN
[1] chicken ◊ *J'adore le poulet.* I love chicken. ◊ *un poulet rôti* a roast chicken
[2] cop ◊ *Il s'est fait attraper par les poulets.* (*informal*) He got caught by the cops.

le **pouls** NOUN
pulse ◊ *Il m'a pris le pouls.* He took my pulse.

le **poumon** NOUN
lung

la **poupée** NOUN
doll

pour PREPOSITION
for ◊ *C'est un cadeau pour toi.* It's a present for you. ◊ *Qu'est-ce que tu veux pour ton petit déjeuner?* What would you like for breakfast?
♦ **pour faire quelque chose** to do something ◊ *Je lui ai téléphoné pour l'inviter.* I phoned him to invite him.
♦ **Pour aller à Strasbourg, s'il vous plaît?** Which way is it to Strasbourg, please?
♦ **pour que** so that
pour que is followed by a verb in the subjunctive.
◊ *Je lui ai prêté mon pull pour qu'elle n'ait pas froid.* I lent her my jumper so that she wouldn't be cold.
♦ **pour cent** per cent

le **pourboire** NOUN
tip ◊ *Il a donné un pourboire au garçon.* He gave the waiter a tip.

le **pourcentage** NOUN
percentage

pourquoi ADVERB, CONJUNCTION
why ◊ *Pourquoi est-ce qu'il ne vient pas avec nous?* Why isn't he coming with us? ◊ *Elle ne m'a pas dit pourquoi.* She didn't tell me why.

pourra, pourrai, pourras, pourrez VERB *see* **pouvoir**

pourri ADJECTIVE
rotten

pourrir VERB
to go bad ◊ *Ces poires ont pourri.* These pears have gone bad.

pourrons, pourront VERB *see* **pouvoir**

la **poursuite** NOUN
chase
♦ **se lancer à la poursuite de quelqu'un** to chase after somebody

poursuivre VERB
to carry on with ◊ *Ils ont poursuivi leur travail.* They carried on with their work.
♦ **se poursuivre** to go on ◊ *Le concert s'est poursuivi très tard.* The concert went on very late.

pourtant ADVERB
yet ◊ *Il a raté son examen. Pourtant, il n'est pas bête.* He failed his exam, yet he's not stupid.
♦ **C'est pourtant facile!** But it's easy!

pourvu ADJECTIVE
♦ **pourvu que ...** let's hope that ...
pourvu que is followed by a verb in the subjunctive.
◊ *Pourvu qu'il ne pleuve pas!* Let's hope it doesn't rain!

pousser VERB
[1] to push ◊ *Ils ont dû pousser la voiture.* They had to push the car.
[2] to grow ◊ *Mes cheveux poussent vite.* My hair grows quickly.
♦ **pousser un cri** to give a cry
♦ **se pousser** to move over ◊ *Pousse-toi, je ne vois rien.* Move over, I can't see a thing.

la **poussette** NOUN
pushchair

la **poussière** NOUN
[1] dust ◊ *La table est couverte de poussière.* The table's covered in dust.
[2] speck of dust ◊ *J'ai une poussière dans l'œil.* I've got a speck of dust in my eye.

poussiéreux ADJECTIVE (FEM SING **poussiéreuse**)
dusty

le **poussin** NOUN
chick

le **pouvoir** NOUN
see also **pouvoir** VERB

P

power ◊ *Le Premier ministre a beaucoup de pouvoir.* The Prime Minister has a lot of power.

pouvoir VERB

see also **pouvoir** NOUN

Present tense:	
je peux	nous pouvons
tu peux	vous pouvez
il/elle peut	ils/elles peuvent
Past participle:	
pu	

can ◊ *Je peux lui téléphoner si tu veux.* I can phone her if you want. ◊ *Puis-je venir vous voir samedi?* May I come and see you on Saturday? ◊ *Je ne pourrai pas venir samedi.* I can't come on Saturday. ◊ *J'ai fait tout ce que j'ai pu.* I did all I could.
♦ **Je n'en peux plus.** I'm exhausted.
♦ **Il se peut que ...** It's possible that ...

il se peut que is followed by a verb in the subjunctive.

◊ *Il se peut qu'elle ait déménagé.* It's possible that she's moved house. ◊ *Il se peut que j'y aille.* I might go.

la **prairie** NOUN
meadow

la **pratique** NOUN

see also **pratique** ADJECTIVE

practice ◊ *Je manque de pratique.* I'm out of practice.

pratique ADJECTIVE

see also **pratique** NOUN

practical ◊ *Ce sac est très pratique.* This bag's very practical.

pratiquement ADVERB
virtually ◊ *J'ai pratiquement fini.* I've virtually finished.

pratiquer VERB
to practise ◊ *Je dois pratiquer mon espagnol.* I need to practise my Spanish.
♦ **Pratiquez-vous un sport?** Do you do any sport?

le **pré** NOUN
meadow

la **précaution** NOUN
precaution ◊ *prendre ses précautions* to take precautions
♦ **par précaution** as a precaution ◊ *Il a pris une assurance par précaution.* He took out insurance as a precaution.
♦ **avec précaution** cautiously
♦ **"à manipuler avec précaution"** "handle with care"

précédemment ADVERB
previously

précédent ADJECTIVE
previous

précieux ADJECTIVE (FEM SING **précieuse**)
precious
♦ **une pierre précieuse** a precious stone
♦ **de précieux conseils** invaluable advice

le **précipice** NOUN
ravine ◊ *Leur voiture est tombée dans un précipice.* Their car fell into a ravine.

précipitamment ADVERB
hurriedly ◊ *Chantal est partie précipitamment.* Chantal left hurriedly.

la **précipitation** NOUN
haste ◊ *Il a agi avec précipitation.* He acted hastily.

se **précipiter** VERB
to rush

précis ADJECTIVE
precise
♦ **à huit heures précises** at exactly eight o'clock

précisément ADVERB
precisely

préciser VERB
1 to be more specific about ◊ *Pouvez-vous préciser ce que vous voulez dire?* Can you be more specific about what you want to say?
2 to specify ◊ *Pouvez-vous préciser les raisons de ce changement?* Can you specify the reasons for this change?

la **précision** NOUN
1 precision
2 detail ◊ *Je vais vous donner quelques précisions.* I'm going to give you some details.

la **préfecture** NOUN

🛈 A ***préfecture*** is the headquarters of a ***département***, one of the 96 administrative areas of France.

♦ **la préfecture de police** the police headquarters

préférable ADJECTIVE
preferable

préféré ADJECTIVE
favourite

la **préférence** NOUN
preference ◊ *Je n'ai pas de préférence.* I've no preference.
♦ **de préférence** preferably

préférer VERB
to prefer ◊ *Je préfère la cuisine de Teresa.* I prefer Teresa's cooking. ◊ *Je*

préfère manger à la cantine. I prefer
to eat in the canteen.
♦ **Je préférerais du thé.** I'd rather have
tea.
♦ **préférer quelqu'un à quelqu'un** to
prefer somebody to somebody ◊ *Je
le préfère à son frère.* I prefer him to
his brother.

préhistorique ADJECTIVE
prehistoric

le **préjugé** NOUN
prejudice ◊ *avoir des préjugés contre
quelqu'un* to be prejudiced against
somebody

premier ADJECTIVE (FEM SING **première**)
| see also **première** NOUN |

first ◊ *au premier étage* on the first
floor ◊ *C'est notre premier jour de
vacances.* It's the first day of our
holiday. ◊ *C'est la première fois que
je viens ici.* It's the first time I've
been here. ◊ *le premier mai* the first
of May ◊ *Il est arrivé premier.* He
came first.
♦ **le Premier ministre** the Prime Minister

la **première** NOUN
| see also **premier** ADJECTIVE |

1 first class ◊ *Nous avons voyagé
en première.* We travelled first class.
2 first gear ◊ *Passe en première
pour prendre ce virage.* Change into
first to go round this bend.
3 lower sixth form

ⓘ In French secondary schools,
years are counted from the **sixième**
(youngest) to **première** and **terminale**
(oldest).

◊ *Ma sœur est en première.* My
sister's in the lower sixth.

premièrement ADVERB
firstly

prendre VERB
to take ◊ *Prends tes affaires et viens
avec moi.* Take your things and come
with me.
♦ **prendre quelque chose à quelqu'un** to
take something from somebody ◊ *Il
m'a pris mon stylo!* He's taken my
pen!
♦ **Nous avons pris le train de huit
heures.** We took the eight o'clock train.
♦ **Je prends toujours le train pour aller
à Paris.** I always go to Paris by train.
♦ **passer prendre** to pick up ◊ *Je dois
passer prendre Richard.* I have to pick
up Richard.

♦ **prendre à gauche** to turn left ◊ *Prenez
à gauche en arrivant au rond-point.*
Turn left at the roundabout.
♦ **Il se prend pour Napoléon.** He thinks
he's Napoleon.
♦ **s'en prendre à quelqu'un** to lay into
somebody (*verbally*) ◊ *Il s'en est pris
à moi.* He laid into me.
♦ **s'y prendre** to set about it ◊ *Tu t'y
prends mal!* You're setting about it
the wrong way!

le **prénom** NOUN
first name ◊ *Quel est votre prénom?*
What's your first name?

préoccupé ADJECTIVE
worried

la **préparation** NOUN
preparation

préparer VERB
1 to prepare ◊ *Elle prépare le dîner.*
She's preparing dinner.
2 to make ◊ *Je vais préparer le
café.* I'm going to make the coffee.
3 to prepare for ◊ *Laure prépare
son examen d'économie.* Laure's
preparing for her economics exam.
♦ **se préparer** to get ready ◊ *Ils se
préparent à partir.* They're getting
ready to go.

la **préposition** NOUN
preposition

près ADVERB
♦ **tout près** nearby ◊ *J'habite tout près.*
I live nearby.
♦ **près de (1)** near (to) ◊ *Est-ce que c'est
près d'ici?* Is it near here?
♦ **près de (2)** next to ◊ *Assieds-toi près
de moi.* Sit down next to me.
♦ **près de (3)** nearly ◊ *Il y avait près de
cinq cents spectateurs.* There were
nearly 500 spectators.
♦ **de près** closely ◊ *Il a regardé la photo
de près.* He looked closely at the
photo.
♦ **à peu de chose près** more or less

la **présence** NOUN
1 presence ◊ *Sa présence est
rassurante.* His presence is
reassuring.
2 attendance ◊ *La présence aux
cours est obligatoire.* Attendance at
lessons is compulsory.

présent ADJECTIVE
| see also **présent** NOUN |
present

le **présent** NOUN
| see also **présent** ADJECTIVE |
present tense
♦ **à présent** now

P

la **présentation** NOUN
　presentation
♦ **faire les présentations** to do the introductions

présenter VERB
　to present ◊ *Il présentait le spectacle.* He presented the show.
♦ **présenter quelqu'un à quelqu'un** to introduce somebody to somebody ◊ *Il m'a présenté à sa sœur.* He introduced me to his sister.
♦ **Marc, je te présente Anaïs.** Marc, this is Anaïs.
♦ **se présenter (1)** to introduce oneself ◊ *Elle s'est présentée à ses collègues.* She introduced herself to her colleagues.
♦ **se présenter (2)** to arise ◊ *Si l'occasion se présente, nous irons en Écosse.* If the chance arises, we'll go to Scotland.
♦ **se présenter (3)** to stand ◊ *Monsieur Legros se présente encore aux élections.* Mr Legros is standing for election again.

le **préservatif** NOUN
　condom

préserver VERB
　to protect ◊ *préserver du froid* to protect from the cold

le **président** NOUN
　① president ◊ *le président des États-Unis* the president of the United States
　② chairman ◊ *le président du conseil d'administration* the chairman of the board of directors
♦ **le président directeur général** the chairman and managing director

présider VERB
　① to chair ◊ *Duncan a présidé la réunion.* Duncan chaired the meeting.
　② to be the guest of honour ◊ *Il présidait à table.* He was the guest of honour at the table.

presque ADVERB
　nearly ◊ *Il est presque six heures.* It's nearly 6 o'clock. ◊ *Nous sommes presque arrivés.* We're nearly there.
♦ **presque rien** hardly anything ◊ *Elle n'a presque rien mangé.* She's hardly eaten anything.
♦ **presque pas** hardly at all ◊ *Il ne dort presque pas.* He hardly sleeps at all.
♦ **presque pas de** hardly any ◊ *Il n'y a presque pas de place.* There's hardly any space.

la **presqu'île** NOUN
　peninsula

la **presse** NOUN

press ◊ *les représentants de la presse* representatives of the press

pressé ADJECTIVE
　① in a hurry ◊ *Je ne peux pas rester, je suis pressé.* I can't stay, I'm in a hurry.
　② urgent ◊ *Ce n'est pas très pressé.* It's not very urgent.
♦ **une orange pressée** a fresh orange juice

presser VERB
　① to squeeze ◊ *Tu peux me presser un citron?* Can you squeeze me a lemon?
　② to be urgent ◊ *Est-ce que ça presse?* Is it urgent?
♦ **se presser** to hurry up ◊ *Allez, presse-toi, on va être en retard!* Come on, hurry up, we're going to be late!
♦ **Rien ne presse.** There's no hurry.

le **pressing** NOUN
　dry-cleaner's

la **pression** NOUN
　① pressure
♦ **faire pression sur quelqu'un** to put pressure on somebody
　② draught beer (*informal*)

prêt ADJECTIVE
　see also **prêt** NOUN
　ready ◊ *Le déjeuner est prêt.* Lunch is ready. ◊ *Tu es prête?* Are you ready?

le **prêt** NOUN
　see also **prêt** ADJECTIVE
　loan

le **prêt-à-porter** NOUN
　ready-to-wear clothes PL

prétendre VERB
♦ **prétendre que** to claim that ◊ *Il prétend qu'il ne la connaît pas.* He claims he doesn't know her.
　Be careful! **prétendre** *does not mean to pretend.*

prétendu ADJECTIVE
　so-called ◊ *un prétendu expert* a so-called expert

prétentieux ADJECTIVE (FEM SING **prétentieuse**)
　pretentious

prêter VERB
♦ **prêter quelque chose à quelqu'un** to lend something to someone ◊ *Il m'a prêté sa voiture.* He lent me his car.
♦ **prêter attention à quelque chose** to pay attention to something

le **prétexte** NOUN

excuse ◊ *Il avait un prétexte pour ne pas venir.* He had an excuse for not coming.
◆ **sous aucun prétexte** on no account ◊ *Ne le dérangez sous aucun prétexte.* On no account must you disturb him.

prétexter VERB
to give as an excuse ◊ *Elle a prétexté une réunion.* She gave a meeting as her excuse. ◊ *Il a prétexté qu'il avait un rendez-vous.* He gave the excuse that he had an appointment.

le **prêtre** NOUN
priest

la **preuve** NOUN
[1] evidence ◊ *Il y a des preuves contre lui.* There's evidence against him.
[2] proof ◊ *Vous n'avez aucune preuve.* You haven't got any proof.
◆ **faire preuve de courage** to show courage
◆ **faire ses preuves** to prove oneself ◊ *Pour être embauché ici, il faut faire ses preuves.* To be employed here, you need to prove yourself.

prévenir VERB
◆ **prévenir quelqu'un** to warn somebody ◊ *Je te préviens, il est de mauvaise humeur.* I'm warning you, he's in a bad mood.

la **prévention** NOUN
prevention
◆ **des mesures de prévention** preventative measures
◆ **la prévention routière** road safety

la **prévision** NOUN
◆ **les prévisions météorologiques** the weather forecast
◆ **en prévision de quelque chose** in anticipation of something

prévoir VERB
[1] to plan ◊ *Nous prévoyons un pique-nique pour dimanche.* We're planning to have a picnic on Sunday.
◆ **Le départ est prévu pour dix heures.** The departure's scheduled for 10 o'clock.
[2] to allow ◊ *J'ai prévu assez à manger pour quatre.* I allowed enough food for four.
[3] to foresee ◊ *J'avais prévu qu'il serait en retard.* I'd foreseen that he'd be late.
◆ **Je prévois qu'il me faudra une heure de plus.** I reckon on it taking me another hour.

prier VERB

to pray to ◊ *Les Grecs priaient Dionysos.* The Greeks prayed to Dionysos.
◆ **prier quelqu'un de faire quelque chose** to ask somebody to do something ◊ *Elle l'a prié de sortir.* She asked him to leave.
◆ **je vous en prie (1)** please do ◊ *Je peux m'asseoir? – Je vous en prie.* May I sit down? – Please do.
◆ **je vous en prie (2)** please ◊ *Je vous en prie, ne me laissez pas seule.* Please, don't leave me alone.
◆ **je vous en prie (3)** don't mention it ◊ *Merci pour votre aide. – Je vous en prie.* Thanks for your help. – Don't mention it.

la **prière** NOUN
prayer ◊ *faire ses prières* to say one's prayers
◆ **"prière de ne pas fumer"** "no smoking please"

le **primaire** NOUN
primary education ◊ *Ses enfants sont encore en primaire.* His children are still in primary education.
◆ **l'école primaire** primary school

la **prime** NOUN
[1] bonus ◊ *Il a eu une prime en récompense de son travail.* He received a bonus for his work.
[2] free gift ◊ *J'ai eu ce stylo en prime avec l'agenda.* I got this pen as a free gift with the diary.
[3] premium ◊ *une prime d'assurance* an insurance premium

la **primevère** NOUN
primrose

le **prince** NOUN
prince ◊ *le prince Charles* Prince Charles

la **princesse** NOUN
princess ◊ *la princesse Diana* Princess Diana

principal ADJECTIVE (MASC PL **principaux**)
see also **principal** NOUN
main ◊ *le rôle principal* the main role

le **principal** NOUN (PL les **principaux**)
see also **principal** ADJECTIVE
[1] headmaster ◊ *le principal du collège* the headmaster of the school
[2] main thing ◊ *Personne n'a été blessé; c'est le principal.* Nobody was injured; that's the main thing.

le **principe** NOUN
principle
◆ **pour le principe** on principle

P

☞

◆**en principe (1)** as a rule ◊ *Il déjeune en principe à midi et demi.* As a rule he has lunch at 12.30.

◆**en principe (2)** in theory ◊ *En principe Anne doit arriver lundi.* In theory, Anne should arrive on Monday.

le **printemps** NOUN
　　spring

◆**au printemps** in spring

la **priorité** NOUN
　　① priority ◊ *C'est à faire en priorité.* It needs to be done as a priority.
　　② right of way ◊ *Tu n'as pas la priorité.* You haven't got right of way.

pris VERB *see* **prendre**

pris ADJECTIVE
　　① taken ◊ *Est-ce que cette place est prise?* Is this seat taken?
　　② busy ◊ *Je serai très pris la semaine prochaine.* I'll be very busy next week.

◆**avoir le nez pris** to have a stuffy nose

◆**être pris de panique** to be panic-stricken

la **prise** NOUN
　　① plug
　　② socket

◆**une prise de courant** a power point

◆**une prise multiple** an adaptor

◆**une prise de sang** a blood test

la **prison** NOUN
　　prison ◊ *aller en prison* to go to prison ◊ *être en prison* to be in prison

prisonnier ADJECTIVE
　　see also **prisonnier** NOUN
　　captive

le **prisonnier** NOUN
　　see also **prisonnier** ADJECTIVE
　　prisoner

la **prisonnière** NOUN
　　prisoner

prit VERB *see* **prendre**

privé ADJECTIVE
　　private ◊ *la propriété privée* private property ◊ *ma vie privée* my private life

◆**en privé** in private

priver VERB

◆**priver quelqu'un de quelque chose** to deprive somebody of something ◊ *Le prisonnier a été privé de nourriture.* The prisoner was deprived of food.

◆**Tu seras privé de dessert!** You won't get any pudding!

le **prix** NOUN
　　① price ◊ *Je n'arrive pas à lire le prix de ce livre.* I can't see the price of this book.
　　② prize ◊ *Cécile a eu le prix de la meilleure actrice.* Cécile got the prize for best actress.

◆**hors de prix** exorbitantly priced ◊ *Les repas sont hors de prix ici!* The price of meals here is exorbitant!

◆**à aucun prix** not at any price ◊ *Je n'irai là-bas à aucun prix.* I'm not going there, not at any price.

◆**à tout prix** at all costs ◊ *Je veux à tout prix voir ce film.* I want to see this film at all costs.

probable ADJECTIVE
　　likely ◊ *Il est probable qu'elle viendra.* It's likely she'll come.

◆**C'est peu probable.** That's unlikely.

probablement ADVERB
　　probably

le **problème** NOUN
　　problem

le **procédé** NOUN
　　process

le **procès** NOUN
　　trial ◊ *Le procès du meurtrier commence mardi.* The murder trial starts on Tuesday.

◆**Il est en procès avec son employeur.** He's involved in a lawsuit with his employer.

prochain ADJECTIVE
　　next ◊ *Nous descendons au prochain arrêt.* We're getting off at the next stop.

◆**la prochaine fois** next time

◆**la semaine prochaine** next week

◆**À la prochaine!** See you!

prochainement ADVERB
　　soon

proche ADJECTIVE
　　① near ◊ *Les magasins les plus proches étaient à trois kilomètres.* The nearest shops were 3 kilometres away. ◊ *dans un proche avenir* in the near future
　　② close ◊ *un ami proche* a close friend

◆**proche de** near to ◊ *La cathédrale est proche du château.* The cathedral is near the castle.

◆**le Proche-Orient** the Middle East

les **proches** MASC NOUN
　　close relatives

proclamer VERB
　　to proclaim

procurer VERB

◆**procurer quelque chose à quelqu'un** to get something for somebody ◊ *C'est lui qui m'a procuré ce travail.* He got me this job.

◆ **se procurer quelque chose** to get
something ◊ *Je me suis procuré leur
dernier catalogue.* I got their latest
catalogue.

le **producteur** NOUN
producer

la **production** NOUN
production

la **productrice** NOUN
producer

produire VERB
to produce
◆ **se produire** to take place ◊ *Ces
changements se sont produits l'an
dernier.* The changes took place last
year.

le **produit** NOUN
product ◊ *les produits de beauté*
beauty products

le **prof** NOUN (*informal*)
teacher ◊ *Elle est prof de maths.*
She's a maths teacher.

le **professeur** NOUN
⎡1⎤ teacher ◊ *Philippe est professeur
d'histoire.* Philippe's a history teacher.
⎡2⎤ professor ◊ *le professeur Dupont*
Professor Dupont
◆ **un professeur de faculté** a university
lecturer

la **profession** NOUN
profession ◊ *Quelle est votre
profession?* What's your profession?
◆ **"sans profession"** "unemployed"

professionnel ADJECTIVE (FEM SING
professionnelle)
professional

le **profil** NOUN
⎡1⎤ profile (*of person*) ◊ *de profil* in
profile
⎡2⎤ contours (*of object*)

le **profit** NOUN
profit ◊ *La société a fait des profits
importants.* The company made
significant profits.
◆ **tirer profit de quelque chose** to profit
from something
◆ **au profit de** in aid of ◊ *un spectacle
au profit de l'UNICEF* a show in aid
of UNICEF

profiter VERB
◆ **profiter de quelque chose** to take
advantage of something ◊ *Profitez du
beau temps pour aller faire du vélo.*
Take advantage of the good weather
and go cycling.
◆ **Profitez-en bien!** Make the most of it!

profond ADJECTIVE
deep

la **profondeur** NOUN

depth

le **programme** NOUN
⎡1⎤ programme ◊ *le programme du
festival* the festival programme
⎡2⎤ syllabus ◊ *le programme de
maths* the maths syllabus
⎡3⎤ program ◊ *un programme
informatique* a computer program

programmer VERB
⎡1⎤ to show ◊ *Ce film est programmé
dimanche soir.* The film is scheduled
for Sunday evening.
⎡2⎤ to program ◊ *Mon ordinateur
n'est pas programmé pour ça.* My
computer isn't programmed to do
that.

le **programmeur** NOUN
programmer ◊ *Marc est
programmeur.* Marc is a programmer.

la **programmeuse** NOUN
programmer ◊ *Elle est
programmeuse.* She's a programmer.

le **progrès** NOUN
progress ◊ *faire des progrès* to make
progress

progresser VERB
to progress

progressif ADJECTIVE (FEM SING
progressive)
progressive

le **projecteur** NOUN
⎡1⎤ projector ◊ *Le projecteur de
diapositives est en panne.* The slide
projector is broken.
⎡2⎤ spotlight ◊ *Elle était sous les
projecteurs.* She was under the
spotlight.

le **projet** NOUN
⎡1⎤ plan ◊ *des projets de vacances*
holiday plans
⎡2⎤ draft ◊ *le projet de construction
d'un musée* the draft for the
construction of a museum
◆ **un projet de loi** a bill (*in parliament*)

projeter VERB
⎡1⎤ to plan ◊ *Ils projettent d'acheter
une maison.* They're planning to buy
a house.
⎡2⎤ to cast ◊ *une ombre projetée sur
le mur* a shadow cast onto the wall
◆ **Elle a été projetée hors de la voiture.**
She was thrown out of the car.

prolonger VERB
⎡1⎤ to prolong ◊ *Je vais prolonger
mes vacances en Espagne.* I'm going
to prolong my holidays in Spain.
⎡2⎤ to extend ◊ *Je vais prolonger
mon abonnement.* I'm going to
extend my subscription.

☞

◆**se prolonger** to go on ◊ *La réunion s'est prolongée tard.* The meeting went on late.

la **promenade** NOUN
walk ◊ *Il y a de belles promenades par ici.* There are some nice walks round here.
◆**faire une promenade** to go for a walk
◆**faire une promenade en voiture** to go for a drive
◆**faire une promenade à vélo** to go for a bike ride

promener VERB
to take for a walk ◊ *Cordelia promène son chien tous les jours.* Cordelia takes her dog for a walk every day.
◆**se promener** to go for a walk ◊ *Chantal est partie se promener.* Chantal has gone for a walk.

la **promesse** NOUN
promise ◊ *faire une promesse* to make a promise ◊ *tenir sa promesse* to keep one's promise

promettre VERB
to promise ◊ *On m'a promis une augmentation.* They promised me a pay rise. ◊ *Elle m'a promis de me téléphoner.* She promised to phone me.

la **promotion** NOUN
promotion ◊ *Il espère avoir bientôt une promotion.* He's hoping to get promotion soon.
◆**être en promotion** to be on special offer ◊ *Les côtes de porc sont en promotion.* Pork chops are on special offer.

le **pronom** NOUN
pronoun

prononcer VERB
1 to pronounce ◊ *Le russe est difficile à prononcer.* Russian is difficult to pronounce.
2 to deliver ◊ *prononcer un discours* to deliver a speech
◆**se prononcer** to be pronounced ◊ *Le "e" final ne se prononce pas.* The final "e" isn't pronounced.

la **prononciation** NOUN
pronunciation

la **propagande** NOUN
propaganda

se **propager** VERB
to spread ◊ *Le feu s'est propagé rapidement.* The fire spread quickly.

la **proportion** NOUN
proportion

le **propos** NOUN

◆**à propos** by the way ◊ *À propos, quand est-ce que tu viens?* By the way, when are you coming?
◆**à propos de quelque chose** about something ◊ *C'est à propos de la soirée de vendredi.* It's about the party on Friday.

proposer VERB
◆**proposer quelque chose à quelqu'un (1)** to suggest something to somebody ◊ *Nous lui avons proposé une promenade en bateau.* We suggested going on a boat ride to him.
◆**proposer quelque chose à quelqu'un (2)** to offer somebody something ◊ *Ils m'ont proposé des chocolats.* They offered me some chocolates.

la **proposition** NOUN
offer ◊ *J'accepte ta proposition avec plaisir.* I'll be pleased to accept your offer.

propre ADJECTIVE
see also **propre** NOUN
1 clean ◊ *Ce mouchoir n'est pas propre.* This handkerchief isn't clean.
2 own ◊ *Gordon l'a fabriqué de ses propres mains.* Gordon made it with his own hands.
◆**propre à** characteristic of ◊ *C'est une coutume propre au Berry.* It's a custom you find in the Berry region.

le **propre** NOUN
see also **propre** ADJECTIVE
◆**recopier quelque chose au propre** to make a fair copy of something

proprement ADVERB
properly ◊ *Mange proprement!* Eat properly!
◆**le village proprement dit** the village itself
◆**à proprement parler** strictly speaking

la **propreté** NOUN
cleanliness

le **propriétaire** NOUN
see also **la propriétaire**
1 owner
2 landlord

la **propriétaire** NOUN
see also **le propriétaire**
1 owner
2 landlady

la **propriété** NOUN
property ◊ *la propriété privée* private property

le **prospectus** NOUN
leaflet

prospère ADJECTIVE
prosperous

la **prostituée** NOUN
prostitute

protecteur ADJECTIVE (FEM SING **protectrice**)
[1] protective ◊ *un vernis protecteur* a protective varnish
[2] patronizing ◊ *un ton protecteur* a patronizing tone

la **protection** NOUN
protection

protéger VERB
to protect

la **protéine** NOUN
protein

protestant ADJECTIVE (FEM SING **protestante**)
Protestant ◊ *une église protestante* a Protestant church
♦ **Robert est protestant.** Robert is a Protestant.

la **protestation** NOUN
protest

protester VERB
to protest ◊ *Ils protestent contre leurs conditions de travail.* They're protesting about their working conditions.

prouver VERB
to prove

la **provenance** NOUN
origin
♦ **un avion en provenance de Berlin** a plane arriving from Berlin

provenir VERB
♦ **provenir de (1)** to come from ◊ *Ces tomates proviennent d'Espagne.* These tomatoes come from Spain.
♦ **provenir de (2)** to be the result of ◊ *Cela provient d'un manque d'organisation.* This is the result of a lack of organization.

le **proverbe** NOUN
proverb

la **province** NOUN
province
♦ **en province** in the provinces ◊ *Ils habitent en province.* They live in the provinces.

le **proviseur** NOUN
headteacher (*of state secondary school*) ◊ *Elle est proviseur.* She's a headteacher.

la **provision** NOUN
supply ◊ *une provision de pommes de terre* a supply of potatoes

les **provisions** FEM NOUN
food ◊ *Nous n'avons plus beaucoup de provisions.* We haven't got much food left.

provisoire ADJECTIVE
temporary ◊ *un emploi provisoire* a temporary job

provoquer VERB
[1] to provoke ◊ *Il l'a provoquée en la traitant d'imbécile.* He provoked her by calling her stupid.
[2] to cause ◊ *Cet accident a provoqué la mort de quarante personnes.* The accident caused the death of 40 people.

la **proximité** NOUN
proximity
♦ **à proximité** nearby ◊ *Sabine habite à proximité.* Sabine lives nearby.

prudemment ADVERB
[1] carefully ◊ *Conduisez prudemment!* Drive carefully!
[2] wisely ◊ *Prudemment, il a fait des économies.* Wisely, he saved some money.
[3] cautiously ◊ *Le gouvernement a réagi prudemment.* The government reacted cautiously.

la **prudence** NOUN
caution
♦ **avec prudence** carefully ◊ *Ils ont conduit avec prudence.* They drove carefully.

prudent ADJECTIVE
[1] careful ◊ *Soyez prudents!* Be careful!
[2] wise ◊ *Laisse ton passeport à la maison, c'est plus prudent.* It would be wiser to leave your passport at home.

la **prune** NOUN
plum

le **pruneau** NOUN (PL les **pruneaux**)
prune

le/la **psychiatre** NOUN
psychiatrist

la **psychologie** NOUN
psychology

psychologique ADJECTIVE
psychological

le/la **psychologue** NOUN
psychologist

pu VERB see **pouvoir**
♦ **Je n'ai pas pu venir hier.** I couldn't come yesterday.

la **pub** NOUN (*informal*)
[1] advertising ◊ *Il y a trop de pub à la télé.* There's too much advertising on TV.
[2] adverts ◊ *Le film a été coupé par la pub.* The film was interrupted by adverts.

public ADJECTIVE (FEM SING **publique**)

P

☞

see also **public** NOUN

public ◊ *un jardin public* a public park
♦**une école publique** a state school

le**public** NOUN

see also **public** ADJECTIVE

1 public ◊ *Ce parc est ouvert au public.* The park's open to the public.
2 audience ◊ *Le public a applaudi le chanteur.* The audience applauded the singer.
♦**en public** in public ◊ *Je déteste parler en public.* I hate speaking in public.

publicitaire ADJECTIVE
♦**une agence publicitaire** an advertising agency
♦**un film publicitaire** a publicity film

la**publicité** NOUN

1 advertising ◊ *Muriel travaille dans la publicité.* Muriel works in advertising.
2 advert ◊ *Il y a trop de publicités dans ce journal.* There are too many adverts in this newspaper.
♦**faire de la publicité pour quelque chose** to publicize something

publier VERB
to publish ◊ *Bob vient de publier son nouveau roman.* Bob has just published his new novel.

publique ADJECTIVE *see* **public**

la**puce** NOUN

1 flea ◊ *Ce chien a des puces.* This dog has fleas.
2 chip ◊ *une puce électronique* a microchip
♦**une carte à puce** a smart card

les**puces** FEM NOUN
flea market SING

puer VERB
to stink ◊ *Ça pue le tabac ici!* It stinks of tobacco round here!

puéril ADJECTIVE
childish

puis VERB

see also **puis** ADVERB

see **pouvoir**
♦**Puis-je venir vous voir samedi?** May I come and see you on Saturday?

puis ADVERB

see also **puis** VERB

then ◊ *Faites dorer le poulet, puis ajoutez le vin blanc.* Fry the chicken till golden, then add white wine.

puisque CONJUNCTION
since ◊ *Puisque c'est si cher, nous irons manger ailleurs.* Since it's so expensive, we'll eat elsewhere.

la**puissance** NOUN
power

puissant ADJECTIVE
powerful

le**puits** NOUN
well ◊ *Il a un puits dans son jardin.* He's got a well in his garden.

le**pull** NOUN
jumper

le**pull-over** NOUN
jumper

le**pulvérisateur** NOUN
spray ◊ *un pulvérisateur de parfum* a perfume spray

pulvériser VERB

1 to pulverize ◊ *L'explosion a pulvérisé le bâtiment.* The explosion pulverized the building.
2 to spray ◊ *Il a pulvérisé de l'insecticide sur ses plantes.* He sprayed insecticide on his plants.

la**punaise** NOUN
drawing pin

punir VERB
to punish ◊ *Il a été puni pour avoir menti.* He was punished for lying.

la**punition** NOUN
punishment

le**pupitre** NOUN
desk (*for pupil*)

pur ADJECTIVE

1 pure ◊ *L'eau de cette source est très pure.* The water from this spring is very pure.
2 neat (*undiluted*) ◊ *du whisky pur* neat whisky ◊ *de l'eau de Javel pure* concentrated bleach
♦**c'est de la folie pure** it's sheer madness

la**purée** NOUN
mashed potatoes
♦**la purée de marrons** chestnut purée

la**putain** NOUN (*rude*)
whore

le**puzzle** NOUN
jigsaw puzzle

le**PV** NOUN (= *procès-verbal*)
parking ticket

le**pyjama** NOUN
pyjamas PL

la**pyramide** NOUN
pyramid

les**Pyrénées** FEM NOUN
Pyrenees
♦**dans les Pyrénées** in the Pyrenees

Q

le **QI** NOUN (= *quotient intellectuel*)
IQ

le **quai** NOUN

[1] quay ◊ *être à quai* to be alongside the quay

[2] platform ◊ *Le train partira du quai numéro quatre.* The train will leave from platform 4.

qualifier VERB

♦ **se qualifier** to qualify ◊ *Bob s'est qualifié pour la demi-finale.* Bob has qualified for the semifinal.

la **qualité** NOUN

quality ◊ *Ces outils sont de très bonne qualité.* These are very good quality tools.

quand CONJUNCTION, ADVERB

when ◊ *Quand est-ce que tu pars en vacances?* When are you going on holiday? ◊ *Quand je serai riche, j'achèterai une belle maison.* When I'm rich, I'll buy a nice house.

♦ **quand même** all the same ◊ *Je ne voulais pas de dessert, mais j'en ai mangé quand même.* I didn't want any dessert, but I had some all the same.

quant à PREPOSITION

regarding ◊ *Quant au problème de chauffage ...* Regarding the problem with the heating ... ◊ *Quant à moi, je n'arriverai qu'à dix heures.* As for me, I won't be arriving till 10 o'clock.

la **quantité** NOUN

amount

♦ **des quantités de** a great deal of ◊ *Ils ont invité des quantités de gens.* They invited a lot of people.

la **quarantaine** NOUN

about forty ◊ *une quarantaine de personnes* about forty people

♦ **Elle a la quarantaine.** She's in her forties.

quarante NUMBER

forty ◊ *Elle a quarante ans.* She's forty.

♦ **quarante et un** forty-one

♦ **quarante-deux** forty-two

le **quart** NOUN

quarter

♦ **le quart de** a quarter of ◊ *Elle a mangé le quart du gâteau.* She ate a quarter of the cake.

♦ **trois quarts** three quarters

♦ **un quart d'heure** a quarter of an hour

♦ **deux heures et quart** a quarter past two

♦ **dix heures moins le quart** a quarter to ten

♦ **Un quart d'eau minérale, s'il vous plaît.** A small bottle of mineral water, please.

le **quartier** NOUN

[1] area (*of town*) ◊ *un quartier tranquille* a quiet area

♦ **un cinéma de quartier** a local cinema

[2] piece ◊ *un quartier d'orange* a piece of orange

le **quartz** NOUN

♦ **une montre à quartz** a quartz watch

quasi ADVERB

nearly ◊ *La quasi-totalité des récoltes a été détruite.* Nearly all of the crop was destroyed.

quasiment ADVERB

nearly ◊ *Le film est quasiment fini.* The film's nearly finished.

♦ **quasiment jamais** hardly ever ◊ *Ils ne vont quasiment jamais en boîte.* They hardly ever go clubbing.

quatorze NUMBER

fourteen ◊ *Mon frère a quatorze ans.* My brother's fourteen. ◊ *à quatorze heures* at 2 p.m.

♦ **le quatorze février** the fourteenth of February

quatre NUMBER

four ◊ *Il est quatre heures du matin.* It's four in the morning. ◊ *Il a quatre ans.* He's four.

♦ **le quatre mars** the fourth of March

♦ **faire les quatre cents coups** to be a bit wild ◊ *Todd a fait les quatre cents coups dans sa jeunesse.* Todd was a bit wild in his youth.

quatre-vingts NUMBER

eighty

> **quatre-vingts** is spelt with an **-s** when it is followed by a noun, but not when it is followed by another number.

◊ *quatre-vingts francs* eighty francs ◊ *Elle a quatre-vingt-deux ans.* She's eighty-two.

♦ **quatre-vingt-dix** ninety

♦ **quatre-vingt-onze** ninety-one

♦ **quatre-vingt-quinze** ninety-five

♦ **quatre-vingt-dix-huit** ninety-eight

quatrième ADJECTIVE

see also **quatrième** NOUN

☞

fourth ◊ *au quatrième étage* on the fourth floor

la **quatrième** NOUN

> see also **quatrième** ADJECTIVE

third year

> ⓘ In French secondary schools, years are counted from the **sixième** (youngest) to **première** and **terminale** (oldest).

◊ *Mon frère est en quatrième.* My brother's in third year.

que CONJUNCTION, PRONOUN, ADVERB

1 that ◊ *Il sait que tu es là.* He knows that you're here. ◊ *la dame que j'ai rencontrée hier* the lady that I met yesterday ◊ *Le gâteau qu'elle a fait est délicieux.* The cake she's made is delicious.

♦ **Je veux que tu viennes.** I want you to come.

2 what ◊ *Que fais-tu?* What are you doing? ◊ *Que vas-tu lui dire?* What are you going to tell him?

♦ **Qu'est-ce que ...?** What ...? ◊ *Qu'est-ce que tu fais?* What are you doing? ◊ *Qu'est-ce que c'est?* What's that?

♦ **plus ... que** more ... than ◊ *C'est plus difficile que je ne le pensais.* It's more difficult than I thought. ◊ *Il est plus grand que moi.* He's bigger than me.

♦ **aussi ... que** as ... as ◊ *Elle est aussi jolie que sa sœur.* She's as pretty as her sister. ◊ *Le train est aussi cher que l'avion.* The train is as expensive as the plane.

♦ **ne ... que** only ◊ *Il ne boit que de l'eau.* He only drinks water. ◊ *Je ne l'ai vu qu'une fois.* I've only seen him once.

♦ **Qu'il est bête!** He's so silly!

quel ADJECTIVE (FEM SING **quelle**)

1 who ◊ *Quel est ton chanteur préféré?* Who's your favourite singer?

2 what ◊ *Quelle est ta couleur préférée?* What's your favourite colour? ◊ *Quelle heure est-il?* What time is it? ◊ *Quelle bonne surprise!* What a surprise!

3 which ◊ *Quel groupe préfères-tu?* Which band do you like best?

♦ **quel que soit (1)** whoever ◊ *quel que soit le coupable* whoever is guilty

♦ **quel que soit (2)** whatever ◊ *quel que soit votre avis* whatever your opinion

quelle ADJECTIVE see **quel**

quelque ADJECTIVE, ADVERB

1 some ◊ *Il a quelques amis à Paris.* He has some friends in Paris. ◊ *J'ai acheté quelques disques.* I bought some records.

2 a few ◊ *Il reste quelques bouteilles.* There are a few bottles left.

3 few ◊ *Ils ont fini les quelques bouteilles qui restaient.* They finished the few bottles that were left.

♦ **quelque chose (1)** something ◊ *J'ai quelque chose pour toi.* I've got something for you. ◊ *Je voudrais quelque chose de moins cher.* I'd like something cheaper.

♦ **quelque chose (2)** anything ◊ *Avez-vous quelque chose à déclarer?* Have you got anything to declare? ◊ *Tu as pensé à quelque chose d'autre?* Did you think of anything else?

♦ **quelque part (1)** somewhere ◊ *J'ai oublié mon sac quelque part.* I've left my umbrella somewhere.

♦ **quelque part (2)** anywhere ◊ *Vous allez quelque part ce week-end?* Are you going anywhere this weekend?

quelquefois ADVERB

sometimes

quelques-uns PRONOUN (FEM **quelques-unes**)

some ◊ *As-tu vu ses films? J'en ai vu quelques-uns.* Have you seen his films? I've seen some of them.

quelqu'un PRONOUN

1 somebody ◊ *Quelqu'un t'a appelé.* Somebody phoned you. ◊ *Il y a quelqu'un à la porte.* There's somebody at the door.

2 anybody ◊ *Est-ce que quelqu'un a vu mon parapluie?* Has anybody seen my umbrella? ◊ *Il y a quelqu'un?* Is there anybody there?

la **querelle** NOUN

quarrel

qu'est-ce que see **que**

qu'est-ce qui see **qui**

la **question** NOUN

1 question ◊ *Je t'ai posé une question.* I asked you a question.

2 matter ◊ *Ils se sont disputés pour des questions d'argent.* They argued over money matters.

♦ **Il n'en est pas question.** There's no question of it. ◊ *Il n'est pas question que je paye.* There's no question of me paying.

♦ **De quoi est-il question?** What's it about?

♦**Il est question de l'organisation du concert.** It's about the organization of the concert.

♦**hors de question** out of the question ◊ *Il est hors de question que nous restions ici.* It's out of the question that we stay here.

le **questionnaire** NOUN
    questionnaire

questionner VERB
    to question

la **queue** NOUN
    [1] tail ◊ *Le chien a agité la queue.* The dog wagged its tail.
    ♦**faire la queue** to queue
    ♦**une queue de cheval** a ponytail
    [2] rear ◊ *en queue du train* at the rear of the train
    [3] bottom ◊ *en queue de liste* at the bottom of the list
    [4] stalk (*of fruit, leaf*) ◊ *la queue d'une cerise* a cherry stalk

qui PRONOUN
    [1] who ◊ *Qui a téléphoné?* Who phoned? ◊ *Einstein était un génie.* Einstein was a genius.
    [2] whom ◊ *C'est la personne à qui j'ai parlé hier.* It's the person whom I spoke to yesterday.
    [3] that ◊ *Donne-moi la veste qui est sur la chaise.* Give me the jacket that's on the chair.
    ♦**Qui est-ce qui ...?** Who ...? ◊ *Qui est-ce qui t'emmène au spectacle?* Who's taking you to the show?
    ♦**Qui est-ce que ...?** Who ...? ◊ *Qui est-ce que tu as vu à cette soirée?* Who did you see at the party?
    ♦**Qu'est-ce qui ...?** What ...? ◊ *Qu'est-ce qui est sur la table?* What's on the table? ◊ *Qu'est-ce qui te prend?* What's the matter with you?
    ♦**À qui est ce sac?** Whose bag is this?
    ♦**À qui parlais-tu?** Who were you talking to?

la **quille** NOUN
    ♦**un jeu de quilles** skittles

la **quincaillerie** NOUN
    ironmonger's (shop)

la **quinzaine** NOUN
    about fifteen ◊ *Il y avait une quinzaine de personnes.* There were about fifteen people there.
    ♦**une quinzaine de jours** a fortnight

quinze NUMBER
    fifteen ◊ *Anaïs a quinze ans.* Anaïs is fifteen. ◊ *à quinze heures* at 3 p.m.
    ♦**le quinze février** the fifteenth of February
    ♦**dans quinze jours** in a fortnight's time

quitter VERB
    to leave ◊ *J'ai quitté la maison à huit heures.* I left the house at 8 o'clock.
    ♦**se quitter** to part ◊ *Les deux amis se sont quittés devant le café.* The two friends parted in front of the café.
    ♦**Ne quittez pas.** (*on telephone*) Hold the line. ◊ *Ne quittez pas, je vous passe Monsieur Divan.* Hold the line, I'll put you through to Monsieur Divan.

quoi PRONOUN
    what? ◊ *À quoi penses-tu?* What are you thinking about? ◊ *C'est quoi, ce truc?* What's this thing?
    ♦**Quoi de neuf?** What's new?
    ♦**As-tu de quoi écrire?** Have you got anything to write with?
    ♦**Je n'ai pas de quoi acheter une voiture.** I can't afford to buy a car.
    ♦**Quoi qu'il arrive.** Whatever happens.
    ♦**Il n'y a pas de quoi.** Don't mention it.
    ♦**Il n'y a pas de quoi s'énerver.** There's no reason for getting worked up.
    ♦**En quoi puis-je vous aider?** How may I help you?

quoique CONJUNCTION
    even though ◊ *Il va l'acheter quoique ce soit cher.* He's going to buy it even though it's expensive.

quotidien ADJECTIVE (FEM SING **quotidienne**)
    see also **quotidien** NOUN
    daily ◊ *Il est parti faire sa promenade quotidienne.* He's gone for his daily walk.
    ♦**la vie quotidienne** everyday life

le **quotidien** NOUN
    see also **quotidien** ADJECTIVE
    daily paper ◊ *"Le Monde" est un quotidien.* "Le Monde" is a daily paper.

Q

R

le **rab** NOUN (*informal*)
seconds (*of meal*) ◊ *Il y a du rab?* Are there any seconds?

le **rabais** NOUN
reduction (*in price*)
- **au rabais** at a discount

la **racaille** NOUN
riff-raff

raccompagner VERB
to take home ◊ *Tu peux me raccompagner?* Can you take me home?

le **raccourci** NOUN
shortcut

raccrocher VERB
to hang up (*telephone*)

la **race** NOUN
1 race ◊ *la race humaine* the human race
2 breed ◊ *De quelle race est ton chat?* What breed is your cat?
- **de race** pedigree ◊ *un chien de race* a pedigree dog

racheter VERB
1 to buy another ◊ *J'ai racheté un portefeuille.* I've bought another wallet. ◊ *racheter du lait* to buy more milk
2 to buy ◊ *Il m'a racheté ma moto.* He bought my bike from me.

la **racine** NOUN
root

le **racisme** NOUN
racism

raciste ADJECTIVE
racist

raconter VERB
- **raconter quelque chose à quelqu'un** to tell somebody about something ◊ *Raconte-moi ce qui s'est passé.* Tell me what happened. ◊ *Raconte-moi une histoire.* Tell me a story.
- **Qu'est-ce que tu racontes?** What are you talking about?

le **radar** NOUN
radar

le **radiateur** NOUN
radiator
- **un radiateur électrique** an electric heater

radin ADJECTIVE (*informal*)
stingy

la **radio** NOUN
1 radio ◊ *à la radio* on the radio
2 X-ray
- **passer une radio** to have an X-ray ◊ *Elle a passé une radio des poumons.* She had a chest X-ray.

le **radio-réveil** NOUN (PL les **radios-réveils**)
clock radio

le **radis** NOUN
radish

raffoler VERB
- **raffoler de** to be crazy about ◊ *Elle raffole de la tarte aux pommes.* She really loves apple tart.

rafraîchir VERB
to cool down
- **se rafraîchir (1)** to get cooler ◊ *Le temps se rafraîchit.* The weather's getting cooler.
- **se rafraîchir (2)** to freshen up ◊ *Il a pris une douche pour se rafraîchir.* He had a shower to freshen up.

rafraîchissant ADJECTIVE
refreshing

la **rage** NOUN
rabies
- **une rage de dents** raging toothache

le **ragoût** NOUN
stew

raide ADJECTIVE
1 steep ◊ *Cette pente est raide.* This is a steep slope.
2 straight ◊ *Laure a les cheveux raides.* Laure has straight hair.
3 stiff ◊ *Son bras est encore raide.* His arm's still stiff.
4 flat broke ◊ *Je suis raide ce mois-ci.* (*informal*) I'm flat broke this month.

la **raie** NOUN
1 skate (*fish*)
2 parting (*in hair*)

le **rail** NOUN
rail ◊ *par rail* by rail

le **raisin** NOUN
grapes ◊ *le raisin blanc* green grapes
- **des raisins secs** raisins

la **raison** NOUN
reason ◊ *sans raison* for no reason ◊ *Raison de plus pour y aller.* All the more reason for going.
- **Ce n'est pas une raison.** That's no excuse.
- **avoir raison** to be right ◊ *Tu as raison.* You're right.
- **en raison de** because of ◊ *en raison d'une grève* because of a strike

raisonnable ADJECTIVE
sensible ◊ *Elle est très raisonnable pour son âge.* She's very sensible for her age.

le **raisonnement** NOUN
reasoning ◊ *J'ai du mal à suivre son raisonnement.* I have difficulty following his reasoning.

rajouter VERB
to add

ralentir VERB
to slow down

râler VERB (*informal*)
to moan

le **ramassage** NOUN
♦ **le ramassage scolaire** the school bus service

ramasser VERB
[1] to pick up ◊ *Il a ramassé son crayon.* He picked up his pencil.
[2] to take in ◊ *Il a ramassé les copies.* He took in the exam papers.

la **rame** NOUN
[1] oar (*of boat*)
[2] train (*on the underground*)

le **rameau** NOUN (PL les **rameaux**)
branch
♦ **le dimanche des Rameaux** Palm Sunday

ramener VERB
[1] to bring back ◊ *Je t'ai ramené un souvenir de Grèce.* I've brought you back a present from Greece.
[2] to take home ◊ *Tu me ramènes?* Will you take me home?

ramer VERB
to row ◊ *C'est Jean-Pierre qui ramait.* Jean-Pierre was rowing.

la **rampe** NOUN
banister

la **rancune** NOUN
♦ **garder rancune à quelqu'un** to bear somebody a grudge
♦ **Sans rancune!** No hard feelings!

rancunier ADJECTIVE (FEM SING **rancunière**)
vindictive

la **randonnée** NOUN
♦ **une randonnée à vélo** a bike ride
♦ **une randonnée pédestre** a ramble
♦ **faire de la randonnée** to go hiking

le **randonneur** NOUN
hiker

la **randonneuse** NOUN
hiker

le **rang** NOUN
row (*line*) ◊ *au premier rang* in the front row ◊ *se mettre en rangs* to get into rows

la **rangée** NOUN
row (*line*) ◊ *une rangée de chaises* a row of chairs

ranger VERB
[1] to put away ◊ *J'ai rangé tes affaires.* I've put your things away.
[2] to tidy up ◊ *Va ranger ta chambre.* Go and tidy up your room.

le **rap** NOUN
rap ◊ *Robert est chanteur de rap.* Robert's a rap singer.

râper VERB
to grate ◊ *le fromage râpé* grated cheese

rapide ADJECTIVE
[1] fast ◊ *Cette voiture est très rapide.* This is a very fast car.
[2] quick ◊ *J'ai jeté un coup d'œil rapide sur ton travail.* I had a quick glance at your work.

rapidement ADVERB
quickly

le **rappel** NOUN
[1] booster (*vaccination*)
[2] curtain call

rappeler VERB
to call back ◊ *Je te rappelle dans cinq minutes.* I'll call you back in 5 minutes.
♦ **rappeler quelque chose à quelqu'un** to remind somebody of something ◊ *Cette odeur me rappelle mon enfance.* This smell reminds me of my childhood.
♦ **rappeler à quelqu'un de faire quelque chose** to remind somebody to do something ◊ *Rappelle-moi d'acheter des billets.* Remind me to get tickets.
♦ **se rappeler** to remember ◊ *Il s'est rappelé qu'il avait une course à faire.* He remembered he had some shopping to do.

le **rapport** NOUN
see also **les rapports**
[1] report ◊ *Il a écrit un rapport.* He wrote a report.
[2] connection ◊ *Je ne vois pas le rapport.* I can't see the connection.
♦ **par rapport à** in comparison with

rapporter VERB
to bring back ◊ *Je leur ai rapporté un cadeau.* I brought them back a present.

le **rapporteur** NOUN
telltale

la **rapporteuse** NOUN
telltale

les **rapports** MASC NOUN
see also **le rapport**

R

☞

relations ◊ *Leurs rapports avec leurs voisins se sont améliorés.* Their relations with their neighbours have improved.
♦ **les rapports sexuels** sexual intercourse

rapprocher VERB
1 to bring together ◊ *Cet accident a rapproché les deux frères.* The accident brought the two brothers together.
2 to bring closer ◊ *Il a rapproché le fauteuil de la télé.* He brought the armchair closer to the TV.
♦ **se rapprocher** to come closer
◊ *Rapproche-toi, tu verras mieux.* Come closer, you'll see better.

la **raquette** NOUN
1 racket (*tennis*)
2 bat (*table tennis*)

rare ADJECTIVE
rare ◊ *une plante rare* a rare plant

rarement ADVERB
rarely

ras ADJECTIVE, ADVERB
short ◊ *un chien à poil ras* a short-haired dog
♦ **à ras bords** to the brim ◊ *Il a rempli son verre à ras bords.* He filled his glass to the brim.
♦ **en avoir ras le bol de quelque chose** (*informal*) to be fed up with something
♦ **un pull ras du cou** a crew-neck jumper

raser VERB
to shave off ◊ *Ray a rasé sa barbe.* Ray has shaved off his beard.
♦ **se raser** to shave

le **rasoir** NOUN
see also **rasoir** ADJECTIVE
razor

rasoir ADJECTIVE (MASC, FEM, PL) (*informal*)
see also **rasoir** NOUN
dead boring

rassembler VERB
to assemble ◊ *Il a rassemblé les enfants dans la cour.* He assembled the children in the playground.
♦ **se rassembler** to gather together
◊ *Les passagers se sont rassemblés près du car.* The passengers gathered near the coach.

rassurer VERB
to reassure
♦ **Je suis rassuré.** I don't need to worry any more.
♦ **se rassurer** to be reassured
◊ *Rassure-toi!* Don't worry!

le **rat** NOUN
rat

raté ADJECTIVE
unsuccessful ◊ *Le gâteau est raté.* The cake's a failure.

le **râteau** NOUN (PL les **râteaux**)
rake

rater VERB
1 to miss ◊ *Chantal a raté son train.* Chantal missed her train.
2 to fail ◊ *J'ai raté mon examen de maths.* I failed my maths exam. ◊ *Elle a raté sa pizza.* Her pizza didn't turn out right.

la **RATP** NOUN
Paris transport authority

rattacher VERB
to tie up again ◊ *rattacher ses lacets* to tie up one's laces

rattraper VERB
1 to recapture ◊ *La police a rattrapé le voleur.* The police recaptured the thief.
2 to catch up with ◊ *Je vais rattraper Cécile.* I'll catch up with Cécile.
3 to make up for ◊ *Il faut rattraper le temps perdu.* We must make up for lost time.
♦ **se rattraper** to make up for it ◊ *Je n'ai pas le temps de sortir mais je me rattraperai après les examens.* I haven't got time to go out, but I'll make up for it after the exams.

la **rature** NOUN
correction ◊ *un texte sans ratures* a text with no corrections

ravi ADJECTIVE
♦ **être ravi** to be delighted ◊ *Ils étaient ravis de nous voir.* They were delighted to see us. ◊ *Je suis ravi que vous puissiez venir.* I'm delighted that you can come.

se **raviser** VERB
to change your mind ◊ *Il allait accepter, mais il s'est ravisé.* He was going to accept, but he changed his mind.

ravissant ADJECTIVE
lovely

rayé ADJECTIVE
striped ◊ *une chemise rayée* a striped shirt

rayer VERB
1 to scratch ◊ *Il a rayé la peinture de sa voiture.* He scratched the paintwork of his car.

[2] to cross off ◊ *Son nom a été rayé de la liste.* His name has been crossed off the list.

le **rayon** NOUN

[1] ray ◊ *un rayon de soleil* a ray of sunshine

[2] radius ◊ *le rayon d'un cercle* the radius of a circle

[3] shelf ◊ *les rayons d'une bibliothèque* the shelves of a bookcase

[4] department ◊ *le rayon hi-fi vidéo* the hi-fi and video department

♦ **les rayons X** X-rays

la **rayure** NOUN

stripe

le **ré** NOUN

[1] D ◊ *en ré majeur* in D major

[2] re ◊ *do, ré, mi ...* do, re, mi ...

la **réaction** NOUN

reaction

réagir VERB

to react

le **réalisateur** NOUN

director (*of film*) ◊ *Stephen Spielberg est réalisateur.* Stephen Spielberg is a film director.

la **réalisatrice** NOUN

director (*of film*) ◊ *Elle est réalisatrice.* She's a film director.

réaliser VERB

[1] to carry out ◊ *Ils ont réalisé leur projet.* They carried out their plan.

[2] to fulfil ◊ *Il a réalisé son rêve.* He has fulfilled his dream.

[3] to realize ◊ *Tu réalises ce que tu dis?* Do you realize what you're saying?

[4] to make ◊ *réaliser un film* to make a film

♦ **se réaliser** to come true ◊ *Mon rêve s'est réalisé.* My dream has come true.

réaliste ADJECTIVE

realistic

la **réalité** NOUN

reality

♦ **en réalité** in fact

le **rebelle** NOUN

rebel

rebondir VERB

to bounce

le **rebord** NOUN

edge ◊ *le rebord du lavabo* the edge of the washbasin

♦ **le rebord de la fenêtre** the window ledge

recaler VERB (*informal*)

♦ **J'ai été recalé en maths.** I failed maths.

récemment ADVERB

recently

récent ADJECTIVE

recent

le **récepteur** NOUN

receiver

la **réception** NOUN

reception desk

le/la **réceptionniste** NOUN

receptionist ◊ *Elle est réceptionniste.* She's a receptionist.

la **recette** NOUN

recipe

recevoir VERB

[1] to receive ◊ *J'ai reçu une lettre.* I received a letter.

[2] to see ◊ *Il a reçu trois clients ce matin.* He has seen three clients this morning.

[3] to have round ◊ *Je reçois des amis à dîner.* I'm having friends round for dinner.

♦ **être reçu à un examen** to pass an exam

le **rechange** NOUN

♦ **de rechange** spare (*battery, bulb*) ◊ *des vêtements de rechange* a change of clothes

la **recharge** NOUN

refill

le **réchaud** NOUN

stove

réchauffer VERB

[1] to reheat ◊ *Je vais réchauffer les légumes.* I'll reheat the vegetables.

[2] to warm up ◊ *Un bon café va te réchauffer.* A nice cup of coffee will warm you up.

♦ **se réchauffer** to warm oneself ◊ *Je vais me réchauffer près du feu.* I'll go and warm myself by the fire.

la **recherche** NOUN

research ◊ *Je voudrais faire de la recherche.* I'd like to do research.

♦ **être à la recherche de quelque chose** to be looking for something ◊ *Je suis à la recherche d'un emploi.* I'm looking for a job.

♦ **les recherches** search ◊ *La police a interrompu les recherches.* The police called off the search.

rechercher VERB

to look for ◊ *La police recherche l'assassin.* The police are looking for the killer.

la **rechute** NOUN

relapse

R

le **récipient** NOUN
container

le **récit** NOUN
story

réciter VERB
to recite

la **réclamation** NOUN
complaint ◊ *J'ai une réclamation à faire.* I want to make a complaint.
♦ **les réclamations** the complaints department

la **réclame** NOUN
advert ◊ *une réclame de lessive* an advert for washing powder
♦ **en réclame** on special offer ◊ *Le saumon était en réclame au supermarché.* Salmon was on special offer at the supermarket.

réclamer VERB
[1] to demand ◊ *Nous réclamons la semaine de trente heures.* We demand a 30-hour week.
[2] to complain ◊ *Elles sont toujours en train de réclamer.* They're always complaining about something.

reçois VERB *see* **recevoir**

la **récolte** NOUN
harvest

récolter VERB
[1] to harvest ◊ *Ils ont récolté le blé.* They harvested the wheat.
[2] to collect ◊ *Ils ont récolté deux mille francs.* They collected 2000 francs.
[3] to get ◊ *Il a récolté une amende.* (*informal*) He got a fine.

le **recommandé** NOUN
♦ **en recommandé** by registered mail ◊ *Je voudrais envoyer ce paquet en recommandé.* I'd like to send this parcel registered.

recommander VERB
to recommend ◊ *Je vous recommande ce restaurant.* I recommend this restaurant.

recommencer VERB
[1] to start again ◊ *Il a recommencé à pleuvoir.* It's started raining again.
[2] to do again ◊ *S'il n'est pas puni, il va recommencer.* If he's not punished he'll do it again.

la **récompense** NOUN
reward

récompenser VERB
to reward ◊ *Il m'a récompensée de mes efforts.* He rewarded me for my efforts.

réconcilier VERB

♦ **se réconcilier avec quelqu'un** to be make it up with somebody ◊ *Il s'est réconcilié avec sa sœur.* He has made it up with his sister.

reconnaissant ADJECTIVE
grateful

reconnaître VERB
[1] to recognize ◊ *Je ne l'ai pas reconnu.* I didn't recognize him.
[2] to admit ◊ *Je reconnais que j'ai eu tort.* I admit I was wrong.

reconstruire VERB
to rebuild

le **record** NOUN
record ◊ *battre un record* to break a record

recouvrir VERB
to cover ◊ *La neige recouvre le sol.* The ground is covered in snow.

la **récréation** NOUN
break ◊ *Les élèves sont en récréation.* The pupils are having their break.
♦ **la cour de récréation** the playground (*of school*)

le **rectangle** NOUN
rectangle

rectangulaire ADJECTIVE
rectangular

rectifier VERB
to correct

le **reçu** NOUN
see also **reçu** VERB
receipt

reçu VERB *see* **recevoir**
see also **reçu** NOUN
♦ **J'ai reçu un colis ce matin.** I received a parcel this morning.
♦ **être reçu à un examen** to pass an exam

reculer VERB
[1] to step back ◊ *Il a reculé pour la laisser entrer.* He stepped back to let her in.
[2] to reverse ◊ *J'ai reculé pour laisser passer le camion.* I reversed to let the lorry past.
[3] to postpone ◊ *Ils ont reculé la date du spectacle.* They postponed the show.

reculons
♦ **à reculons** ADVERB
backwards ◊ *Elle est entrée à reculons.* She came in backwards.

récupérer VERB
[1] to get back ◊ *Je vais récupérer ma voiture au garage.* I'm going to get my car back from the garage.

② to make up ◊ *J'ai des heures à récupérer.* I've got time to make up.
③ to recover ◊ *J'ai besoin de récupérer.* I need to recover.

recycler VERB
to recycle
♦ **se recycler** to retrain ◊ *Il a décidé de se recycler en informatique.* He decided to retrain as a computer programmer.

la **rédaction** NOUN
essay

redemander VERB
① to ask again for ◊ *Je vais lui redemander son adresse.* I'll ask him for his address again.
② to ask for more ◊ *Je vais redemander des carottes.* I'm going to ask for more carrots.

redescendre VERB
to go back down ◊ *Il est redescendu au premier étage.* He went back down to the first floor. ◊ *Elle a redescendu l'escalier.* She went back down the stairs.

rédiger VERB
to write (*an essay*)

redoubler VERB
to repeat a year ◊ *Il a raté son examen et doit redoubler.* He's failed his exam and will have to repeat the year.

la **réduction** NOUN
① reduction ◊ *une réduction du nombre des touristes* a reduction in the number of tourists
② discount ◊ *une réduction de cent francs* a 100 franc discount

réduire VERB
to cut ◊ *Ils ont réduit leurs prix.* They've cut their prices. ◊ *Il a réduit de moitié ses dépenses.* He has cut his spending by half.

réel ADJECTIVE (FEM SING **réelle**)
real

réellement ADVERB
really

refaire VERB
① to do again ◊ *Je dois refaire ce rapport.* I've got to do this report again.
② to take up again ◊ *Je voudrais refaire de la gym.* I'd like to take up gymnastics again.

le **réfectoire** NOUN
refectory

la **référence** NOUN
reference

♦ **faire référence à quelque chose** to refer to something
♦ **Ce n'est pas une référence!** That's no recommendation!

réfléchi ADJECTIVE
reflexive (*verb*)
♦ **C'est tout réfléchi.** My mind's made up.

réfléchir VERB
to think ◊ *Il est en train de réfléchir.* He's thinking.
♦ **réfléchir à quelque chose** to think about something ◊ *Je vais réfléchir à ta proposition.* I'll think about your suggestion.

le **reflet** NOUN
reflection ◊ *les reflets du soleil sur la mer* the reflection of the sun on the sea

refléter VERB
to reflect

le **réflexe** NOUN
reflex ◊ *avoir de bons réflexes* to have good reflexes

la **réflexion** NOUN
① thought ◊ *Elle est en pleine réflexion.* She's deep in thought.
② remark ◊ *faire des réflexions désagréables* to make nasty remarks
♦ **réflexion faite** on reflection

le **refrain** NOUN
chorus (*of song*)

le **réfrigérateur** NOUN
refrigerator

refroidir VERB
to cool ◊ *Laissez le gâteau refroidir.* Leave the cake to cool.
♦ **se refroidir** to get colder ◊ *Le temps se refroidit.* It's getting colder.

se **réfugier** VERB
to take shelter ◊ *Je me suis réfugié sous un arbre.* I took shelter under a tree.

le **refus** NOUN
refusal
♦ **Ce n'est pas de refus.** I wouldn't say no. ◊ *Voulez-vous une bière? – Ce n'est pas de refus.* Would you like a beer? – I wouldn't say no.

refuser VERB
to refuse ◊ *Il a refusé de payer sa part.* He refused to pay his share. ◊ *On lui a refusé une augmentation.* He was refused a pay rise.
♦ **Je refuse qu'on me parle ainsi!** I won't let anybody talk to me like that!

se **régaler** VERB

R

◆**Merci beaucoup: je me suis régalé!**
Thank you very much: it was
absolutely delicious!

le **regard** NOUN

look ◇ *Il lui a jeté un regard méfiant.*
He gave him a mistrustful look. ◇ *On
voyait à son regard qu'elle était
contrariée.* You could tell from the
look in her eyes that she was upset.

◆**Tous les regards se sont tournés vers
lui.** All eyes turned towards him.

regarder VERB

1 to look at ◇ *Il regardait ses photos
de vacances.* He was looking at his
holiday photos. ◇ *Regarde! J'ai
presque fini.* Look! I've nearly
finished.

2 to watch ◇ *Je regarde la
télévision.* I'm watching television.
◇ *Regarde où tu mets les pieds!*
Watch where you put your feet!

3 to concern ◇ *Ça ne nous regarde
pas.* It doesn't concern us.

◆**ne pas regarder à la dépense** to spare
no expense

le **régime** NOUN

1 régime (of a country)

2 diet ◇ *un régime sans sel* a salt-
free diet ◇ *se mettre au régime* to go
on a diet ◇ *suivre un régime* to be on
a diet

◆**un régime de bananes** a bunch of
bananas

la **région** NOUN

region

régional ADJECTIVE (MASC PL **régionaux**)

regional

le **registre** NOUN

register

la **règle** NOUN

1 ruler ◇ *Il a souligné son nom avec
une règle.* He underlined his name
with a ruler.

2 rule ◇ *C'est la règle.* That's the
rule. ◇ *en règle générale* as a general
rule

◆**être en règle** to be in order ◇ *Mes
papiers sont en règle.* My papers are
in order.

◆**les règles** period (*menstruation*)

le **règlement** NOUN

rules ◇ *Le règlement est affiché à
l'entrée.* The rules are up on the wall
by the entrance.

régler VERB

1 to adjust ◇ *Il faut que je règle
mon rétroviseur.* I'll have to adjust
my rear-view mirror.

2 to tune ◇ *J'ai réglé ma radio sur
476 FM.* I tuned my radio to 476 FM.

3 to set ◇ *J'ai réglé le thermostat à
vingt degrés.* I've set the thermostat
to 20 degrees.

4 to solve ◇ *Le problème est réglé.*
The problem's solved.

5 to settle ◇ *Elle a réglé sa facture.*
She's settled her bill. ◇ *J'ai réglé
Jean-Pierre pour l'essence.* I've
settled up with Jean-Pierre for the
petrol.

la **réglisse** NOUN

liquorice

le **règne** NOUN

reign ◇ *sous le règne de Henri IV* in
the reign of Henry IV

régner VERB

to reign

le **regret** NOUN

regret

◆**à regret** reluctantly

regretter VERB

1 to regret ◇ *Elle regrette ce qu'elle
a dit.* She regrets saying what she
did.

◆**Je regrette.** I'm sorry. ◇ *Je regrette, je
ne peux pas vous aider.* I'm sorry, I
can't help you.

2 to miss ◇ *Je regrette mon ancien
travail.* I miss my old job.

regrouper VERB

to group together ◇ *Nous avons
regroupé les enfants suivant leur âge.*
We grouped the children together
according to age.

◆**se regrouper** to gather together ◇ *Les
agriculteurs se sont regroupés pour
constituer un syndicat.* The farmers
joined together to form a union.

régulier ADJECTIVE (FEM SING **régulière**)

1 regular ◇ *des livraisons régulières*
regular deliveries ◇ *des bus réguliers*
a regular bus service

2 steady ◇ *à un rythme régulier* at a
steady rate

3 scheduled ◇ *des vols réguliers
pour Marseille* scheduled flights to
Marseilles

régulièrement ADVERB

regularly

le **rein** NOUN

kidney

◆**les reins** back (*of body*) ◇ *J'ai mal aux
reins.* My back hurts.

la **reine** NOUN

queen

rejoindre VERB

to go back to ◇ *J'ai rejoint mes
amis.* I went back to my friends.

♦**Je te rejoins au café.** I'll see you at the café.
♦**se rejoindre** to meet up ◊ *Elles se sont rejointes une heure après.* They met up an hour later.

relâcher VERB
to release (*prisoner, animal*)
♦**se relâcher** to get slack ◊ *Il se relâche dans son travail.* His work is getting careless.

le **relais** NOUN
relay race ◊ *le relais quatre fois cent mètres* the 4 x 100 metre relay
♦**prendre le relais** to take over

la **relation** NOUN
relationship
♦**les relations franco-britanniques** Anglo-French relations

se **relaxer** VERB
to relax

se **relayer** VERB
♦**se relayer pour faire quelque chose** to take it in turns to do something

le **relevé** NOUN
♦**un relevé de compte** a bank statement

relever VERB
[1] to collect ◊ *Je relève les copies dans cinq minutes.* I'll collect the papers in five minutes.
[2] to react to ◊ *Je n'ai pas relevé sa réflexion.* I didn't react to his remark.
♦**relever la tête** to look up
♦**se relever** to get up ◊ *Il est tombé mais s'est relevé aussitôt.* He fell, but got up immediately.

la **religieuse** NOUN
[1] nun ◊ *Marie est religieuse.* Marie is a nun.
[2] choux cream bun ◊ *des religieuses au chocolat* choux buns with chocolate cream and icing

religieux ADJECTIVE (FEM **religieuse**)
religious

la **religion** NOUN
religion

relire VERB
[1] to read over ◊ *Il a relu sa copie avant de la rendre.* He read his exam paper over before handing it in.
[2] to read again ◊ *Je voudrais relire ce roman.* I'd like to read this novel again.

remarquable ADJECTIVE
remarkable

la **remarque** NOUN
[1] remark ◊ *Il a fait une remarque désagréable.* He made a nasty remark.
[2] comment ◊ *Avez-vous des remarques à faire?* Have you any comments to make?

remarquer VERB
to notice ◊ *J'ai remarqué qu'elle avait l'air triste.* I noticed she was looking sad.
♦**faire remarquer quelque chose à quelqu'un** to point something out to somebody ◊ *Je lui ai fait remarquer que c'était un peu cher.* I pointed out to him that it was rather expensive.
♦**Remarquez, il n'est pas si bête que ça.** Mind you, he's not as stupid as all that.
♦**se remarquer** to be noticeable ◊ *David ne s'est pas rasé ce matin. Ça se remarque.* It's obvious David didn't shave this morning.
♦**se faire remarquer** to call attention to oneself

le **remboursement** NOUN
refund

rembourser VERB
to pay back ◊ *Bruno m'a remboursé l'argent qu'il me devait.* Bruno paid me back the money he owed me.
♦**"satisfait ou remboursé"** "satisfaction or your money back"

remercier VERB
to thank ◊ *Je te remercie pour ton cadeau.* Thank you for your present.
♦**remercier quelqu'un d'avoir fait quelque chose** to thank somebody for doing something ◊ *Je vous remercie de m'avoir invité.* Thank you for inviting me.

remettre VERB
[1] to put back on ◊ *Elle a remis son pull.* She put her sweater back on.
[2] to put back ◊ *Il a remis sa veste dans l'armoire.* He put his jacket back in the wardrobe.
[3] to put off ◊ *J'ai dû remettre mon rendez-vous.* I've had to put my appointment off.
♦**se remettre** to recover (*from illness*) ◊ *Mélusine s'est bien remise de son opération.* Mélusine has fully recovered from her operation.

le **remonte-pente** NOUN
ski-lift

remonter VERB
[1] to go back up ◊ *Il est remonté au premier étage.* He has gone back up to the first floor.
[2] to go up ◊ *Ils ont remonté la pente.* They went up the hill.

R

3 to buck up ◊ *Cette nouvelle m'a un peu remontée.* The news bucked me up a bit.
♦**remonter le moral à quelqu'un** to cheer somebody up

le**remords** NOUN
♦**avoir des remords** to feel remorse

la**remorque** NOUN
trailer (*of car*)

les**remparts** MASC NOUN
city walls

le**remplaçant** NOUN
supply teacher

la**remplaçante** NOUN
supply teacher

remplacer VERB
to replace ◊ *Il faut remplacer cette ampoule.* We need to replace this bulb. ◊ *Il remplace le prof de maths.* He's replacing the maths teacher.
♦**remplacer par** to replace with

rempli ADJECTIVE
busy ◊ *une journée bien remplie* a very busy day
♦**rempli de** full of ◊ *La salle était remplie de monde.* The room was full of people.

remplir VERB
1 to fill up ◊ *Elle a rempli son verre de vin.* She filled her glass with wine.
2 to fill in ◊ *Tu as rempli ton formulaire?* Have you filled in your form?
♦**se remplir** to fill up ◊ *La salle s'est remplie de monde.* The room filled up with people.

remuer VERB
1 to move ◊ *Elle a remué le bras.* She moved her arm.
2 to stir ◊ *Remuez la sauce pendant deux minutes.* Stir the sauce for two minutes.
♦**se remuer** (*informal*) to go to a lot of trouble ◊ *Ils se sont beaucoup remués pour organiser cette soirée.* They went to a lot of trouble organizing this party.

le**renard** NOUN
fox

la**rencontre** NOUN
♦**faire la rencontre de quelqu'un** to meet somebody ◊ *J'ai fait la rencontre de personnes intéressantes ce soir.* I met some interesting people this evening.
♦**aller à la rencontre de quelqu'un** to go and meet somebody ◊ *Je viendrai à ta rencontre.* I'll come and meet you.

rencontrer VERB
to meet
♦**se rencontrer** to meet ◊ *Ils se sont rencontrés il y a deux ans.* They met two years ago.

le**rendez-vous** NOUN
1 appointment ◊ *J'ai rendez-vous chez le coiffeur.* I've got an appointment at the hairdresser's. ◊ *prendre rendez-vous avec quelqu'un* to make an appointment with somebody
2 date ◊ *Tu sors ce soir? – Oui, j'ai un rendez-vous.* Are you going out tonight? – Yes, I've got a date.
♦**donner rendez-vous à quelqu'un** to arrange to meet somebody

rendre VERB
1 to give back ◊ *J'ai rendu ses disques à Christine.* I've given Christine her records back.
2 to take back ◊ *J'ai rendu mes livres à la bibliothèque.* I've taken my books back to the library.
♦**rendre quelqu'un célèbre** to make somebody famous
♦**se rendre** to give oneself up ◊ *Le meurtrier s'est rendu à la police.* The murderer gave himself up to the police.
♦**se rendre compte de quelque chose** to realize something

le**renfermé** NOUN
♦**sentir le renfermé** to smell stuffy

renifler VERB
to sniff

le**renne** NOUN
reindeer

renommé ADJECTIVE
renowned ◊ *La Bretagne est renommée pour ses plages.* Brittany is renowned for its beaches.

renoncer VERB
♦**renoncer à** to give up ◊ *Ils ont renoncé à leur projet.* They've given up their plan.
♦**renoncer à faire quelque chose** to give up the idea of doing something

renouveler VERB
to renew (*passport, contract*)
♦**se renouveler** to happen again ◊ *J'espère que ça ne se renouvellera pas.* I hope that won't happen again.

le**renseignement** NOUN
piece of information ◊ *Il me manque un renseignement.* There's one piece of information I still need.
♦**les renseignements (1)** information ◊ *Il m'a donné des renseignements.* He gave me some information.

♦ **les renseignements (2)** information desk

♦ **les renseignements (3)** directory inquiries

renseigner VERB

♦ **renseigner quelqu'un sur quelque chose** to give somebody information about something

♦ **Est-ce que je peux vous renseigner?** Can I help you?

♦ **se renseigner** to find out ◊ *Je vais me renseigner pour voir s'il n'y a pas un vol direct.* I'm going to find out if there's a direct flight.

rentable ADJECTIVE
profitable

la **rentrée** NOUN

♦ **la rentrée (des classes)** the start of the new school year

rentrer VERB

1 to come in ◊ *Rentre, tu vas prendre froid.* Come in, you'll catch cold.

2 to go in ◊ *Elle est rentrée dans le magasin.* She went into the shop.

3 to get home ◊ *Je suis rentré à sept heures hier soir.* I got home at 7 o'clock last night.

4 to put away ◊ *Tu as rentré la voiture?* Have you put the car away?

♦ **rentrer dans** to crash into ◊ *Sa voiture est rentrée dans un arbre.* He crashed into a tree.

♦ **rentrer dans l'ordre** to get back to normal

la **renverse** NOUN

♦ **tomber à la renverse** to fall backwards

renverser VERB

1 to knock over ◊ *J'ai renversé mon verre.* I knocked my glass over.

2 to knock down ◊ *Elle a été renversée par une voiture.* She was knocked down by a car.

3 to spill ◊ *Il a renversé de l'eau partout.* He has spilt water everywhere.

♦ **se renverser** to fall over (*glass, vase*)

renvoyer VERB

1 to send back ◊ *Je t'ai renvoyé ton courrier.* I've sent your mail back to you.

2 to dismiss ◊ *On a renvoyé deux employés.* Two employees have been dismissed.

répandu ADJECTIVE
common ◊ *C'est un préjugé très répandu.* It's a very common prejudice.

♦ **du vin répandu sur la table** wine spilt on the table

♦ **des papiers répandus sur le sol** papers scattered over the floor

la **réparation** NOUN
repair

réparer VERB
to repair

repartir VERB
to set off again ◊ *Il s'est arrêté pour déjeuner avant de repartir.* He stopped for lunch before setting off again. ◊ *Maree était là tout à l'heure, mais elle est repartie.* Maree was here a moment ago, but she's gone again.

♦ **repartir à zéro** to start again from scratch

le **repas** NOUN
meal

♦ **le repas de midi** lunch

♦ **le repas du soir** dinner

le **repassage** NOUN
ironing ◊ *Je déteste le repassage.* I hate ironing.

repasser VERB

1 to come back ◊ *Je repasserai demain.* I'll come back tomorrow.

2 to go back ◊ *Je dois repasser au magasin.* I've got to go back to the shop.

3 to iron ◊ *J'ai repassé ma chemise.* I've ironed my shirt.

4 to resit ◊ *Elle doit repasser son examen de maths.* She's got to resit her maths exam.

repérer VERB
to spot ◊ *J'ai repéré deux fautes.* I spotted two mistakes.

♦ **se repérer** to find one's way around ◊ *J'ai du mal à me repérer de nuit.* I have difficulty finding my way around when it's dark.

le **répertoire** NOUN
directory

répéter VERB

1 to repeat ◊ *Elle répète toujours la même chose.* She keeps repeating the same thing.

2 to rehearse ◊ *Les acteurs répètent une scène.* The actors are rehearsing a scene.

♦ **se répéter** to happen again ◊ *J'espère que cela ne se répétera pas!* I hope this won't happen again!

la **répétition** NOUN

1 repetition ◊ *Il y a beaucoup de répétitions dans ce texte.* There's a lot of repetition in this text.

R

◆ **des grèves à répétition** repeated strikes
2 rehearsal ◊ *Ils ont une répétition cet après-midi.* They've got a rehearsal this afternoon.
◆ **la répétition générale** the dress rehearsal

le **répondeur** NOUN
answering machine

répondre VERB
to answer ◊ *répondre à quelqu'un* to answer somebody

la **réponse** NOUN
answer ◊ *C'est la bonne réponse.* That's the right answer.

le **reportage** NOUN
1 report ◊ *J'ai vu ce reportage aux informations.* I saw that report on the news.
2 story ◊ *J'ai lu ce reportage dans "La Gazette".* I read that story in "La Gazette".

le **reporter** NOUN
reporter ◊ *Christian est reporter.* Christian is a reporter.

le **repos** NOUN
rest

reposer VERB
to put back down ◊ *Elle a reposé son verre sur la table.* She put her glass back down on the table.
◆ **se reposer** to have a rest ◊ *Tu pourras te reposer demain.* You'll be able to have a rest tomorrow.
◆ **se reposer sur quelqu'un** to rely on somebody

repousser VERB
1 to grow again ◊ *Ses cheveux ont repoussé.* Her hair has grown again.
2 to postpone ◊ *Le voyage est repoussé.* The trip's been postponed.

reprendre VERB
1 to take back ◊ *Il a repris son livre.* He's taken his book back.
2 to go back to ◊ *Elle a repris le travail.* She went back to work.
3 to start again ◊ *La réunion reprendra à deux heures.* The meeting will start again at 2 o'clock.
◆ **reprendre du pain** to take more bread
◆ **reprendre la route** to set off again
◆ **reprendre son souffle** to get one's breath back

le **représentant** NOUN
rep ◊ *Il est représentant chez Harper Collins.* He's a rep for Harper Collins.

la **représentante** NOUN
rep ◊ *Elle est représentante.* She's a sales rep.

la **représentation** NOUN
performance ◊ *la dernière représentation d'une pièce* the final performance of a play

représenter VERB
to show ◊ *Le tableau représente un enfant et un chat.* The picture shows a child with a cat.
◆ **se représenter** to arise again ◊ *Cette occasion ne se représentera pas.* This opportunity won't arise again.

le **reproche** NOUN
◆ **faire des reproches à quelqu'un** to reproach somebody

reprocher VERB
◆ **reprocher quelque chose à quelqu'un** to reproach somebody for something ◊ *Il m'a reproché mon retard.* He reproached me for being late.
◆ **Qu'est-ce que tu lui reproches?** What have you got against him?

la **reproduction** NOUN
reproduction

reproduire VERB
to reproduce
◆ **se reproduire** to happen again ◊ *Je te promets que ça ne se reproduira pas!* I promise it won't happen again!

républicain ADJECTIVE
republican

la **république** NOUN
republic ◊ *la République française* the French Republic

répugnant ADJECTIVE
repulsive

la **réputation** NOUN
reputation

le **requin** NOUN
shark

le **RER** NOUN
Greater Paris high-speed train service

le **réseau** NOUN (PL les **réseaux**)
network

la **réservation** NOUN
reservation

la **réserve** NOUN
stock ◊ *avoir quelque chose en réserve* to have a stock of something
◆ **mettre quelque chose en réserve** to put something aside

réservé ADJECTIVE
reserved ◊ *Cette table est réservée.* This table's reservee.

réserver VERB
1 to reserve ◊ *Cette table est réservée.* This table is reserved.

2 to book ◊ *Nous avons réservé une chambre.* We've booked a room.
3 to save ◊ *Je t'ai réservé une part de gâteau.* I've saved you a piece of cake.

le **réservoir** NOUN
   petrol tank

la **résidence** NOUN
   block of flats
   ♦ **une résidence secondaire** a second home

résistant ADJECTIVE
   1 hard-wearing ◊ *Ce tissu est résistant.* This fabric is hard-wearing.
   2 robust ◊ *Il est très résistant.* He's very robust.

résister VERB
   to resist

résolu ADJECTIVE
   ♦ **Le problème est résolu.** The problem's solved.

résoudre VERB
   to solve

le **respect** NOUN
   respect

respecter VERB
   to respect

la **respiration** NOUN
   breathing

respirer VERB
   to breathe

la **responsabilité** NOUN
   responsibility

responsable ADJECTIVE
   | see also **responsable** NOUN |
   responsible ◊ *être responsable de quelque chose* to be responsible for something

le/la **responsable** NOUN
   | see also **responsable** ADJECTIVE |
   1 person in charge ◊ *Je voudrais parler au responsable.* I'd like to speak to the person in charge.
   2 person responsible ◊ *Il faut punir les responsables.* Those responsible must be punished.

ressembler VERB
   ♦ **ressembler à (1)** to look like ◊ *Elle ne ressemble pas à sa sœur.* She doesn't look like her sister.
   ♦ **ressembler à (2)** to be like ◊ *Ça ressemble à un conte de fées.* It's like a fairy tale.
   ♦ **se ressembler (1)** to look alike ◊ *Les deux frères ne se ressemblent pas.* The two brothers don't look alike.
   ♦ **se rassembler (2)** to be alike ◊ *Ces deux pays ne se ressemblent pas.* These two countries aren't alike.

le **ressort** NOUN
   spring (metal) ◊ *Le ressort est cassé.* The spring is broken.

ressortir VERB
   to go out again

le **restaurant** NOUN
   restaurant

le **reste** NOUN
   rest
   ♦ **un reste de poulet** some left-over chicken
   ♦ **les restes** the left-overs

rester VERB
   1 to stay ◊ *Je reste à la maison ce week-end.* I'm staying at home this weekend.
   2 to be left ◊ *Il reste du pain.* There's some bread left. ◊ *Il me reste assez de temps.* I still have enough time.
   ♦ **Il ne me reste plus qu'à ...** I've just got to ... ◊ *Il ne me reste plus qu'à ranger mes affaires.* I've just got to put my things away.
   ♦ **Restons-en là.** Let's leave it at that.

le **résultat** NOUN
   result ◊ *le résultat des examens* the exam results

le **résumé** NOUN
   summary

résumer VERB
   to summarize
   Be careful! **résumer** does not mean **to resume**.

se **rétablir** VERB
   to get well

le **retard** NOUN
   delay ◊ *un retard de livraison* a delay in delivery
   ♦ **avoir du retard** to be late
   ♦ **être en retard de deux heures** to be two hours late
   ♦ **prendre du retard** to be delayed

retarder VERB
   1 to be slow ◊ *Ma montre retarde.* My watch is slow.
   2 to put back ◊ *Je dois retarder la pendule d'une heure.* I've got to put the clock back an hour.
   ♦ **être retardé** to be delayed ◊ *J'ai été retardé par un coup de téléphone.* I was held up by a phone call.

retenir VERB
   1 to remember ◊ *Tu as retenu leur adresse?* Do you remember their address?
   2 to book ◊ *J'ai retenu une chambre à l'hôtel.* I've booked a room at the hotel.

R

☞

♦ **retenir son souffle** to hold one's breath

retenu ADJECTIVE
1 reserved ◊ *Cette place est retenue.* This seat is reserved.
2 held up ◊ *J'ai été retenu par un coup de téléphone.* I was held up by a phone call.

la **retenue** NOUN
detention ◊ *Gerry est en retenue.* Gerry's in detention.

retirer VERB
1 to withdraw ◊ *Elle a retiré de l'argent.* She withdrew some money.
2 to take off ◊ *Il a retiré son pull.* He took off his sweater.

le **retour** NOUN
return
♦ **être de retour** to be back ◊ *Je serai de retour la semaine prochaine.* I'll be back next week.

retourner VERB
1 to go back ◊ *Est-ce que tu es retourné à Londres?* Have you been back to London?
2 to turn over ◊ *Elle a retourné la crêpe.* She turned the pancake over. ◊ *Il a retourné la poubelle.* He turned the bin upside down.
♦ **se retourner (1)** to turn round ◊ *Janet s'est retournée.* Janet turned round.
♦ **se retourner (2)** to turn over ◊ *La voiture s'est retournée.* The car turned over.

la **retraite** NOUN
♦ **être à la retraite** to be retired
♦ **prendre sa retraite** to retire

retraité ADJECTIVE
see also **retraité** NOUN
retired ◊ *Mon oncle est maintenant retraité.* My uncle's now retired.

le **retraité** NOUN
see also **retraité** ADJECTIVE
pensioner

la **retraitée** NOUN
pensioner

rétrécir VERB
to shrink ◊ *Son pull a rétréci au lavage.* Her sweater shrank in the wash.
♦ **se rétrécir** to get narrower ◊ *La rue se rétrécit.* The street gets narrower.

retrouver VERB
1 to find ◊ *J'ai retrouvé mon portefeuille.* I've found my wallet.
2 to meet up with ◊ *Je te retrouve au café à trois heures.* I'll meet you at the café at 3 o'clock.

♦ **se retrouver (1)** to meet up ◊ *Ils se sont retrouvés devant le cinéma.* They met up in front of the cinema.
♦ **se retrouver (2)** to find one's way around ◊ *Je n'arrive pas à me retrouver.* I can't find my way around.

le **rétroviseur** NOUN
rear-view mirror

la **réunion** NOUN
meeting

se **réunir** VERB
to meet ◊ *Ils se sont réunis à cinq heures.* They met at 5 o'clock.

réussi ADJECTIVE
successful ◊ *une soirée très réussie* a very successful party
♦ **être réussi** to be a success ◊ *Le repas était très réussi.* The meal was delicious.

réussir VERB
to be successful ◊ *Tous ses enfants ont très bien réussi.* All her children are very successful.
♦ **réussir à faire quelque chose** to succeed in doing something
♦ **réussir à un examen** to pass an exam

la **réussite** NOUN
success

la **revanche** NOUN
return match
♦ **prendre sa revanche** to get one's own back ◊ *Il a pris sa revanche en refusant de lui prêter son vélo.* He got his own back by refusing to lend him his bike.
♦ **en revanche** on the other hand ◊ *C'est cher mais en revanche c'est de la bonne qualité.* It is dear but on the other hand it's good quality.

le **rêve** NOUN
dream
♦ **de rêve** fantastic ◊ *des vacances de rêve* fantastic holidays

le **réveil** NOUN
alarm clock
♦ **mettre le réveil à huit heures** to set the alarm for eight o'clock

le **réveille-matin** NOUN (PL les **réveille-matin**)
alarm clock

réveiller VERB
to wake up ◊ *réveiller quelqu'un* to wake somebody up
♦ **se réveiller** to wake up

le **réveillon** NOUN
♦ **le réveillon du premier de l'an** New Year's Eve celebrations

♦ **le réveillon de Noël** Christmas Eve celebrations

réveillonner VERB
① to celebrate New Year's Eve
② to celebrate Christmas Eve

revenir VERB
to come back ◊ *Reviens vite!* Come back soon! ◊ *Son nom m'est revenu cinq minutes après.* His name came back to me five minutes later.
♦ **Ça revient au même.** It comes to the same thing.
♦ **Ça revient cher.** It costs a lot.
♦ **Je n'en reviens pas!** I can't get over it!
♦ **revenir sur ses pas** to retrace one's steps

le revenu NOUN
income

rêver VERB
to dream
♦ **rêver de quelque chose** to dream of something ◊ *J'ai rêvé de mes vacances cette nuit.* I dreamt about my holidays last night.

le réverbère NOUN
street lamp

le revers NOUN
① backhand ◊ *Becker a un excellent revers.* Becker has an excellent backhand.
② lapel (*of jacket*)
♦ **le revers de la médaille** the other side of the coin

revient VERB *see* **revenir**

réviser VERB
① to revise ◊ *Je dois réviser mon anglais.* I've got to revise my English.
② to service ◊ *Je dois faire réviser ma voiture.* I must get my car serviced.

la révision NOUN
revision

revoir VERB
① to see again ◊ *J'ai revu Sophie hier soir.* I saw Sophie again last night.
② to revise ◊ *Il est en train de revoir sa géographie.* He's revising his geography.
♦ **au revoir** goodbye

la révolution NOUN
revolution ◊ *la Révolution française* the French Revolution

le revolver NOUN
revolver

la revue NOUN
magazine

le rez-de-chaussée NOUN

ground floor ◊ *au rez-de-chaussée* on the ground floor

le Rhin NOUN
Rhine

le rhinocéros NOUN
rhinoceros

le Rhône NOUN
Rhone

la rhubarbe NOUN
rhubarb

le rhum NOUN
rum

le rhume NOUN
cold ◊ *J'ai attrapé un rhume.* I've caught a cold.
♦ **un rhume de cerveau** a head cold
♦ **le rhume des foins** hay fever

ri VERB *see* **rire**
♦ **Nous avons bien ri.** We had a good laugh.

riche ADJECTIVE
① well-off ◊ *Sa famille est très riche.* His family's very well-off.
② rich ◊ *riche en vitamines* rich in vitamins

le rideau NOUN (PL les **rideaux**)
curtain ◊ *tirer les rideaux* to draw the curtains

ridicule ADJECTIVE
ridiculous ◊ *Je trouve ça complètement ridicule.* I think that's absolutely ridiculous.

rien PRONOUN
see also **rien** NOUN
① nothing ◊ *Qu'est-ce que tu as acheté? – Rien.* What have you bought? – Nothing. ◊ *Ça n'a rien à voir.* It has nothing to do with it.
♦ **rien d'intéressant** nothing interesting
♦ **rien d'autre** nothing else
♦ **rien du tout** nothing at all
② anything ◊ *Il n'a rien dit.* He didn't say anything.
♦ **rien que (1)** just ◊ *rien que pour lui faire plaisir* just to please him ◊ *Rien que la voiture coûte un million.* The car alone costs a million.
♦ **rien que (2)** nothing but ◊ *rien que la vérité* nothing but the truth
♦ **De rien!** Not at all! ◊ *Merci beaucoup! – De rien!* Thank you very much! – Not at all!

le rien NOUN
see also **rien** PRONOUN
♦ **pour un rien** at the slightest thing ◊ *Il se met en colère pour un rien.* He loses his temper over the slightest thing.
♦ **en un rien de temps** in no time at all

R

rigoler VERB (*informal*)

 ① to laugh ◊ *Elle a rigolé en le voyant tomber.* She laughed when she saw him fall.

 ② to have fun ◊ *On a bien rigolé hier soir.* We had good fun last night.

 ③ to be joking ◊ *Ne te fâche pas, je rigolais.* Don't get upset, I was only joking.

 ♦ **pour rigoler** for a laugh

rigolo ADJECTIVE (FEM SING **rigolote**) (*informal*)

 funny

rincer VERB

 to rinse

rire VERB

 see also **rire** NOUN

 to laugh ◊ *Ce film m'a vraiment fait rire.* That film really made me laugh. ◊ *Nous avons bien ri.* We had a good laugh.

 ♦ **pour rire** for a laugh

le **rire** NOUN

 see also **rire** VERB

 laughter ◊ *Il a un rire bruyant.* He has a loud laugh.

le **risque** NOUN

 ① risk ◊ *prendre des risques* to take risks ◊ *à tes risques et périls* at your own risk

 ② danger ◊ *Il n'y a pas de risque qu'il l'apprenne.* There's no danger of him finding out.

risqué ADJECTIVE

 risky

risquer VERB

 to risk

 ♦ **Ça ne risque rien.** It's quite safe.

 ♦ **Il risque de se tuer.** He could get himself killed.

 ♦ **C'est ce qui risque de se passer.** That's what might well happen.

le **rivage** NOUN

 shore

la **rivière** NOUN

 river

le **riz** NOUN

 rice

le **RMI** NOUN

 Income Support ◊ *Il touche le RMI.* He's on Income Support.

la **RN** NOUN (= *route nationale*)

 A road

la **robe** NOUN

 dress

 ♦ **une robe de soirée** an evening dress

 ♦ **une robe de mariée** a wedding dress

 ♦ **une robe de chambre** a dressing gown

le **robinet** NOUN

 tap

le **robot** NOUN

 robot

la **roche** NOUN

 rock (*stone*)

le **rocher** NOUN

 rock

le **rock** NOUN

 rock (*music*) ◊ *un chanteur de rock* a rock singer

rôder VERB

 to loiter ◊ *Il y a un homme louche qui rôde autour de l'école.* There's a suspicious man loitering around the school.

les **rognons** MASC NOUN

 kidneys (*in cooking*)

le **roi** NOUN

 king

 ♦ **le jour des Rois** Twelfth Night

le **rôle** NOUN

 role

les **rollers** MASC NOUN

 Rollerblades ®

romain ADJECTIVE

 Roman ◊ *des ruines romaines* Roman remains

le **roman** NOUN

 novel

 ♦ **un roman policier** a detective story

 ♦ **un roman d'espionnage** a spy story

le **romancier** NOUN

 novelist

romantique ADJECTIVE

 romantic

rompre VERB

 ① to split up ◊ *Paul et Justine ont rompu.* Paul and Justine have split up.

 ② to break off ◊ *Ils ont rompu leurs fiançailles.* They've broken off their engagement.

les **ronces** FEM NOUN

 brambles

ronchonner VERB (*informal*)

 to grouse

rond ADJECTIVE

 see also **rond** NOUN

 ① round ◊ *La Terre est ronde.* The earth is round.

 ♦ **ouvrir des yeux ronds** to stare in amazement

 ② chubby ◊ *Il a les joues rondes.* He has chubby cheeks.

 ③ drunk ◊ *Il est complètement rond.* (*informal*) He's completely drunk.

le **rond** NOUN

 see also **rond** ADJECTIVE

circle ◊ *Elle a dessiné un rond sur le sable.* She drew a circle in the sand.
◆**en rond** in a circle ◊ *Ils se sont assis en rond.* They sat down in a circle.
◆**tourner en rond** to go round in circles
◆**Je n'ai plus un rond.** (*informal*) I haven't a penny left.

la **rondelle** NOUN
slice ◊ *une rondelle de citron* a slice of lemon

le **rond-point** NOUN (PL les **ronds-points**)
roundabout ◊ *La voiture s'est arrêtée au rond-point.* The car stopped at the roundabout.

ronfler VERB
to snore

le **rosbif** NOUN
roast beef

la **rose** NOUN
see also **rose** ADJECTIVE
rose

rose ADJECTIVE
see also **rose** NOUN
pink

le **rosé** NOUN
rosé (wine) ◊ *Je prendrai un verre de rosé.* I'll have a glass of rosé.

le **rosier** NOUN
rosebush

le **rôti** NOUN
roast meat
◆**un rôti de bœuf** a joint of beef

rôtir VERB
to roast ◊ *faire rôtir quelque chose* to roast something

la **roue** NOUN
wheel ◊ *une roue de secours* a spare wheel

rouge ADJECTIVE
see also **rouge** NOUN
red

le **rouge** NOUN
see also **rouge** ADJECTIVE
[1] red ◊ *Le rouge est ma couleur préférée.* Red is my favourite colour.
[2] red wine ◊ *un verre de rouge* a glass of red wine
◆**passer au rouge (1)** to change to red ◊ *Le feu est passé au rouge.* The light changed to red.
◆**passer au rouge (2)** to go through a red light ◊ *Jean-Pierre est passé au rouge.* Jean-Pierre went through a red light.
◆**un rouge à lèvres** a lipstick

la **rougeole** NOUN
measles

rougir VERB

[1] to blush ◊ *Il a rougi en me voyant.* He blushed when he saw me.
[2] to flush ◊ *Il a rougi de colère.* He flushed with anger.

la **rouille** NOUN
rust

rouillé ADJECTIVE
rusty

rouiller VERB
to go rusty

roulant ADJECTIVE
◆**un fauteuil roulant** a wheelchair
◆**une table roulante** a trolley

le **rouleau** NOUN (PL les **rouleaux**)
roll ◊ *un rouleau de papier peint* a roll of wallpaper
◆**un rouleau à pâtisserie** a rolling pin

rouler VERB
[1] to go ◊ *Le train roulait à 250 km/h.* The train was going at 250 km an hour.
[2] to drive ◊ *Il a roulé sans s'arrêter.* He drove without stopping.
[3] to roll ◊ *Gilles a roulé une cigarette.* Gilles rolled a cigarette.
[4] to roll up ◊ *Il a roulé le tapis.* He rolled the carpet up.
[5] to con ◊ *Ils se sont fait rouler.* (*informal*) They were conned.
◆**Alors, ça roule?** (*informal*) How's it going?

la **Roumanie** NOUN
Romania

le **rouquin** NOUN (*informal*)
redhead

la **rouquine** NOUN (*informal*)
redhead

rousse ADJECTIVE see **roux**

la **rousse** NOUN
redhead

la **route** NOUN
[1] road ◊ *au bord de la route* at the roadside
◆**une route nationale** an A road
[2] way ◊ *Je ne connais pas la route.* I don't know the way.
◆**Il y a trois heures de route.** It's a 3-hour journey.
◆**en route** on the way ◊ *Ils se sont arrêtés en route.* They stopped on the way.
◆**mettre en route** to start up ◊ *Il a mis le moteur en route.* He started the engine up.
◆**se mettre en route** to set off ◊ *Il s'est mis en route à cinq heures.* He set off at 5 o'clock.

le **routier** NOUN

R

☞

[1] <u>lorry driver</u> ◊ *Son père est routier.* His father's a lorry driver.
[2] <u>transport café</u> ◊ *Nous avons mangé dans un routier.* We ate in a transport café.

la **routine** NOUN
<u>routine</u>

roux ADJECTIVE (FEM SING **rousse**)
see also **roux** NOUN
[1] <u>red</u> ◊ *Harry a les cheveux roux.* Harry has red hair.
[2] <u>red-haired</u> ◊ *Isobel est rousse.* Isobel's red-haired.

le **roux** NOUN
see also **roux** ADJECTIVE
<u>redhead</u>

royal ADJECTIVE (MASC PL **royaux**)
<u>royal</u>

le **royaume** NOUN
<u>kingdom</u>
◆ **le Royaume-Uni** the United Kingdom

le **ruban** NOUN
<u>ribbon</u>
◆ **le ruban adhésif** adhesive tape

la **rubéole** NOUN
<u>German measles</u>

la **ruche** NOUN
<u>hive</u>

rudement ADVERB (*informal*)
<u>terribly</u> ◊ *C'était rudement bon.* It was terribly good.

la **rue** NOUN
<u>street</u>

la **ruelle** NOUN
<u>alley</u>

le **rugby** NOUN
<u>rugby</u> ◊ *Yann joue au rugby.* Yann plays rugby.

rugueux ADJECTIVE (FEM SING **rugueuse**)
<u>rough</u>

la **ruine** NOUN
<u>ruin</u> ◊ *les ruines de la cathédrale* the ruins of the cathedral

ruiner VERB
<u>to ruin</u>

le **ruisseau** NOUN (PL les **ruisseaux**)
<u>stream</u>

la **rumeur** NOUN
<u>rumour</u>

la **rupture** NOUN
<u>break-up</u>

la **ruse** NOUN
<u>trickery</u> ◊ *une ruse* a trick

rusé ADJECTIVE
<u>cunning</u>

russe ADJECTIVE, NOUN
<u>Russian</u> ◊ *Il parle russe.* He speaks Russian.
◆ **un Russe** a Russian (*man*)
◆ **une Russe** a Russian (*woman*)
◆ **les Russes** the Russians

la **Russie** NOUN
<u>Russia</u>

le **rythme** NOUN
[1] <u>rhythm</u> ◊ *J'aime le rythme de cette musique.* I like the beat of this music.
[2] <u>pace</u> ◊ *Il marche à un bon rythme.* He walks at a good pace.

S

s' PRONOUN see **se**

sa ADJECTIVE
[1] his ◊ *Paul est allé voir sa grand-mère.* Paul's gone to see his grandmother.
[2] her ◊ *Elle a embrassé sa mère.* She kissed her mother.

le **sable** NOUN
sand
♦ **des sables mouvants** quicksand

le **sablé** NOUN
shortbread biscuit

le **sabot** NOUN
[1] clog
[2] hoof (*of horse*)

le **sac** NOUN
bag
♦ **un sac de voyage** a travel bag
♦ **un sac de couchage** a sleeping bag
♦ **un sac à main** a handbag
♦ **un sac à dos** a rucksack
♦ **voyager sac au dos** to go backpacking

le **sachet** NOUN
sachet (*of sugar, coffee*)
♦ **du potage en sachet** packet soup
♦ **un sachet de thé** a tea bag

la **sacoche** NOUN
bag
♦ **une sacoche de bicyclette** a saddlebag

sacré ADJECTIVE
sacred

sage ADJECTIVE
[1] good (*well-behaved*) ◊ *Sois sage.* Be good.
[2] wise (*sensible*) ◊ *Il serait plus sage d'attendre.* It would be wiser to wait.

la **sagesse** NOUN
wisdom ◊ *Il a eu la sagesse de ne pas y aller.* He wisely didn't go.
♦ **une dent de sagesse** a wisdom tooth

le **Sagittaire** NOUN
Sagittarius ◊ *Michèle est Sagittaire.* Michèle is Sagittarius.

saignant ADJECTIVE
rare (*meat*)

saigner VERB
to bleed
♦ **saigner du nez** to have a nosebleed

sain ADJECTIVE
healthy
♦ **sain et sauf** safe and sound

saint ADJECTIVE
see also **saint** NOUN

holy ◊ *la semaine sainte* Holy Week
◊ *le Saint-Esprit* the Holy Spirit
♦ **la Sainte Vierge** the Blessed Virgin
♦ **le vendredi saint** Good Friday
♦ **la Saint-Sylvestre** New Year's Eve

le **saint** NOUN
see also **saint** ADJECTIVE
saint

la **sainte** NOUN
saint

sais VERB see **savoir**
♦ **Je ne sais pas.** I don't know.

saisir VERB
to take hold of
♦ **saisir l'occasion de faire quelque chose** to seize the opportunity to do something

la **saison** NOUN
season ◊ *Ce n'est pas la saison des fraises.* Strawberries are out of season. ◊ *un temps de saison* seasonable weather
♦ **la saison des vendanges** harvest time

sait VERB see **savoir**
♦ **Il sait que ...** He knows that ...
♦ **On ne sait jamais!** You never know!

la **salade** NOUN
[1] lettuce
[2] salad ◊ *une salade composée* a mixed salad ◊ *une salade de fruits* a fruit salad

le **saladier** NOUN
salad bowl

le **salaire** NOUN
salary

le **salami** NOUN
salami

le **salarié** NOUN
salaried employee

la **salariée** NOUN
salaried employee

le **salaud** NOUN (*rude*)
bastard

sale ADJECTIVE
dirty

salé ADJECTIVE
[1] salty ◊ *La soupe est trop salée.* The soup's too salty.
[2] salted ◊ *du beurre salé* salted butter
[3] savoury ◊ *des biscuits salés* savoury biscuits

saler VERB

to put salt in ◊ *J'ai oublié de saler la soupe.* I forgot to put salt in the soup.

la **saleté** NOUN

dirt ◊ *J'ai horreur de la saleté.* I hate dirt. ◊ *Il y a une saleté sur ta chemise.* There's some dirt on your shirt.

◆ **faire des saletés** to make a mess

salir VERB

◆ **salir quelque chose** to get something dirty

◆ **se salir** to get oneself dirty ◊ *Mets un tablier, sinon tu vas te salir.* Put on an apron or you'll get yourself dirty.

la **salle** NOUN

1. room

2. audience ◊ *Toute la salle l'a applaudi.* The whole audience applauded him.

3. ward (*in hospital*) ◊ *Il est à la salle douze.* He's in Ward 12.

◆ **la salle à manger** the dining room

◆ **la salle de séjour** the living room

◆ **la salle de bains** the bathroom

◆ **la salle d'attente** the waiting room

◆ **une salle de classe** a classroom

◆ **la salle des professeurs** the staffroom

◆ **une salle de concert** a concert hall

◆ **la salle d'embarquement** the departure lounge

le **salon** NOUN

lounge

◆ **un salon de thé** a tearoom

◆ **un salon de coiffure** a hair salon

◆ **un salon de beauté** a beauty salon

la **salope** NOUN (*rude*)

bitch

la **salopette** NOUN

1. dungarees

2. overalls

saluer VERB

◆ **saluer quelqu'un (1)** to say hello to somebody ◊ *Je l'ai croisé dans la rue et il m'a salué.* I met him in the street and he said hello.

◆ **saluer quelqu'un (2)** to say goodbye to somebody ◊ *Il nous a salués et il est parti.* He said goodbye and left.

salut EXCLAMATION (*informal*)

Hi!

le **samedi** NOUN

1. Saturday ◊ *Aujourd'hui, nous sommes samedi.* It's Saturday today.

2. on Saturday ◊ *Nous sommes allés au cinéma samedi.* We went to the cinema on Saturday.

◆ **le samedi** on Saturdays ◊ *Le magasin ferme à dix-huit heures le samedi.*

The shop closes at 6 p.m. on Saturdays.

◆ **tous les samedis** every Saturday

◆ **samedi dernier** last Saturday

◆ **samedi prochain** next Saturday

le **SAMU** NOUN

ambulance service

la **sandale** NOUN

sandal

le **sandwich** NOUN

sandwich

le **sang** NOUN

blood

◆ **en sang** covered in blood

le **sang-froid** NOUN

◆ **garder son sang-froid** to keep calm

◆ **perdre son sang-froid** to lose one's cool

◆ **faire quelque chose de sang-froid** to do something in cold blood

le **sanglier** NOUN

wild boar

le **sanglot** NOUN

◆ **éclater en sanglots** to burst into tears

la **Sanisette** ® NOUN

Superloo ®

sans PREPOSITION

without ◊ *Elle est venue sans son frère.* She came without her brother.

◆ **un pull sans manches** a sleeveless sweater

le/la **sans-abri** NOUN (PL les **sans-abri**)

homeless person ◊ *les sans-abri* the homeless

sans-gêne ADJECTIVE

inconsiderate

la **santé** NOUN

health ◊ *en bonne santé* in good health

◆ **Santé!** Cheers!

saoudien ADJECTIVE, NOUN (FEM SING **saoudienne**)

Saudi Arabian

◆ **un Saoudien** a Saudi Arabian (*man*)

◆ **une Saoudienne** a Saudi Arabian (*woman*)

le **sapeur-pompier** NOUN (PL les **sapeurs-pompiers**)

fireman

◆ **les sapeurs-pompiers** the fire brigade

le **sapin** NOUN

fir tree

◆ **un sapin de Noël** a Christmas tree

la **Sardaigne** NOUN

Sardinia

la **sardine** NOUN

sardine

le **satellite** NOUN

Français ~ Anglais

satellite

satisfaire VERB
to satisfy

satisfaisant ADJECTIVE
satisfactory

satisfait ADJECTIVE
satisfied ◊ *être satisfait de quelque chose* to be satisfied with something

la **sauce** NOUN
[1] sauce
[2] gravy

la **saucisse** NOUN
sausage

le **saucisson** NOUN
salami

sauf PREPOSITION
except ◊ *Tout le monde est venu sauf lui.* Everyone came except him.
♦ **sauf si** unless ◊ *Nous irons nous promener, sauf s'il fait mauvais.* We'll go for a walk, unless the weather's bad.
♦ **sauf que** except that ◊ *Tout s'est bien passé, sauf que nous sommes arrivés en retard.* Everything went OK, except that we arrived late.

le **saumon** NOUN
salmon

saur ADJECTIVE
♦ **un hareng saur** a kipper

le **saut** NOUN
jump
♦ **le saut en longueur** the long jump
♦ **le saut en hauteur** the high jump
♦ **le saut à la perche** the pole vault
♦ **le saut à l'élastique** bungee jumping
♦ **un saut périlleux** a somersault

sauter VERB
to jump ◊ *Nous avons sauté par-dessus la barrière.* We jumped over the gate.
♦ **sauter à la corde** to skip (*with a rope*)
♦ **faire sauter quelque chose** to blow something up ◊ *On a fait sauter le commissariat de police la nuit dernière.* The police station was blown up last night.

la **sauterelle** NOUN
grasshopper

sauvage ADJECTIVE
[1] wild ◊ *les animaux sauvages* wild animals ◊ *faire du camping sauvage* to camp in the wild
♦ **une région sauvage** an unspoiled area
[2] shy ◊ *Il est un peu sauvage.* He's a bit shy.

sauver VERB
to save

♦ **se sauver (1)** to run away ◊ *Il s'est sauvé à toutes jambes.* He ran away as fast as he could.
♦ **se sauver (2)** (*informal*) to be off ◊ *Allez, je me sauve!* Right, I'm off.

le **sauvetage** NOUN
rescue

le **sauveur** NOUN
saviour

savais, savait VERB *see* **savoir**
♦ **Je ne savais pas qu'il devait venir.** I didn't know he was going to come.

le **savant** NOUN
scientist

savent VERB *see* **savoir**
♦ **Ils ne savent pas ce qu'ils veulent.** They don't know what they want.

la **saveur** NOUN
flavour

savez VERB *see* **savoir**
♦ **Est-ce que vous savez où elle habite?** Do you know where she lives?

savoir VERB
to know ◊ *Je ne sais pas où il est allé.* I don't know where he's gone. ◊ *Nous ne savons pas s'il est bien arrivé.* We don't know if he's arrived safely. ◊ *Tu savais que Canberra était la capitale de l'Australie?* Did you know that Canberra was the capital of Australia? ◊ *Il ne sait pas ce qu'il va faire ce week-end.* He doesn't know what he's going to do this weekend.
♦ **Tu sais nager?** Can you swim?

le **savon** NOUN
soap

la **savonnette** NOUN
bar of soap

savons VERB *see* **savoir**

savoureux ADJECTIVE (FEM SING **savoureuse**)
tasty

le **saxo** NOUN (*informal*)
see also **la saxo**
[1] sax
[2] sax player

la **saxo** NOUN (*informal*)
see also **le saxo**
sax player

le **scandale** NOUN
scandal
♦ **faire scandale** to cause a scandal ◊ *Ce film a fait scandale.* The film caused a scandal.

scandaleux ADJECTIVE (FEM SING **scandaleuse**)
outrageous

S

le/la **Scandinave** NOUN
Scandinavian

scandinave ADJECTIVE
Scandinavian

la **Scandinavie** NOUN
Scandinavia

le **scarabée** NOUN
beetle

la **scène** NOUN
scene ◊ *une scène d'amour* a love
scene ◊ *la scène du crime* the scene
of the crime ◊ *Il m'a fait une scène.*
He made a scene.
♦ **une scène de ménage** a domestic row

sceptique ADJECTIVE
sceptical

le **schéma** NOUN
diagram

schématique ADJECTIVE
♦ **l'explication schématique d'une
théorie** the broad outline of a theory
♦ **Cette interprétation est un peu trop
schématique.** This interpretation is a
bit oversimplified.

la **scie** NOUN
saw
♦ **une scie à métaux** a hacksaw

la **science** NOUN
science
♦ **Elle est forte en sciences.** She is
good at science.
♦ **les sciences physiques** physics
♦ **les sciences naturelles** biology
♦ **les sciences économiques** economics
♦ **sciences po** (*informal*) politics ◊ *Mon
frère fait sciences po à Paris.* My
brother is studying politics in Paris.

la **science-fiction** NOUN
science fiction

scientifique ADJECTIVE
see also **scientifique** NOUN
scientific

le/la **scientifique** NOUN
see also **scientifique** ADJECTIVE
[1] scientist
[2] science student

scier VERB
to saw

scolaire ADJECTIVE
school ◊ *l'année scolaire* the school
year ◊ *les vacances scolaires* the
school holidays ◊ *mon livret scolaire*
my school report

le **Scorpion** NOUN
Scorpio ◊ *Catherine est Scorpion.*
Catherine is Scorpio.

le **Scotch** ® NOUN
adhesive tape

le **scrupule** NOUN
scruple

sculpter VERB
to sculpt

le **sculpteur** NOUN
sculptor

la **sculpture** NOUN
sculpture

le/la **SDF** NOUN (= *sans domicile fixe*)
homeless person
♦ **les SDF** the homeless

se PRONOUN
se forms part of reflexive
constructions.
[1] himself ◊ *Il se regarde dans la
glace.* He's looking at himself in the
mirror.
[2] herself ◊ *Elle se regarde dans la
glace.* She's looking at herself in the
mirror.
[3] itself ◊ *Le chien s'est fait mal.* The
dog hurt itself.
[4] oneself ◊ *se regarder dans une
glace* to look at oneself in a mirror
[5] themselves ◊ *Ils se sont regardés
dans la glace.* They looked at
themselves in the mirror.
se changes to *s'* before a vowel and
most words beginning with "h".
◊ *Elle s'admire dans sa nouvelle robe.*
She's admiring herself in her new
dress.
[6] each other ◊ *Ils s'aiment.* They
love each other.

la **séance** NOUN
[1] session ◊ *une séance de
rééducation* a physiotherapy session
[2] showing (*at the cinema*) ◊ *La
prochaine séance est à dix-neuf
heures.* The next showing is at 7 p.m.

le **seau** NOUN (PL les **seaux**)
bucket

sec ADJECTIVE (FEM SING **sèche**)
[1] dry ◊ *Mon jean n'est pas encore
sec.* My jeans aren't dry yet.
[2] dried ◊ *des figues sèches* dried
figs

le **sèche-cheveux** NOUN (PL les **sèche-
cheveux**)
hair dryer

le **sèche-linge** NOUN (PL les **sèche-linge**)
tumble dryer

sécher VERB
[1] to dry
[2] to be stumped ◊ *J'ai
complètement séché à l'interrogation
de maths.* (*informal*) I was completely
stumped in the maths test.

◆**se sécher** to dry oneself ◊ *Sèche-toi avec cette serviette.* Dry yourself with this towel.

la **sécheresse** NOUN
drought ◊ *une terrible sécheresse* a terrible drought

le **séchoir** NOUN
dryer

second ADJECTIVE
see also **second** NOUN
second ◊ *Il est arrivé second.* He came second.

le **second** NOUN
see also **second** ADJECTIVE
second floor ◊ *Elle habite au second.* She lives on the second floor.

secondaire ADJECTIVE
secondary ◊ *l'enseignement secondaire* secondary education
◆**des effets secondaires** side effects

la **seconde** NOUN
[1] second ◊ *Attends une seconde!* Wait a second!
[2] fifth year

> ⓘ In French secondary schools, years are counted from the **sixième** (youngest) to **première** and **terminale** (oldest).

◊ *Ma sœur est en seconde.* My sister's in fifth year.
[3] second class ◊ *voyager en seconde* to travel second-class

secouer VERB
to shake ◊ *secouer la tête* to shake one's head

secourir VERB
to rescue

le **secourisme** NOUN
first aid ◊ *J'ai un brevet de secourisme.* I've got a first aid qualification.

le **secours** NOUN
help ◊ *Il est allé chercher du secours.* He went to get help. ◊ *Au secours!* Help!
◆**les premiers secours** first aid
◆**une sortie de secours** an emergency exit
◆**la roue de secours** the spare wheel

le **secret** NOUN
see also **secret** ADJECTIVE
secret

secret ADJECTIVE (FEM SING **secrète**)
see also **secret** NOUN
secret

le **secrétaire** NOUN
see also **la secrétaire**

[1] secretary
[2] writing desk

la **secrétaire** NOUN
see also **le secrétaire**
secretary

le **secrétariat** NOUN
secretary's office

le **secteur** NOUN
sector ◊ *le secteur public* the public sector ◊ *le secteur privé* the private sector

la **section** NOUN
department (*of school*)

la **sécu** NOUN (*informal*)
Social Security

la **sécurité** NOUN
[1] safety
◆**être en sécurité** to be safe ◊ *On ne se sent pas en sécurité dans ce quartier.* You don't feel safe in this neighbourhood.
◆**la sécurité routière** road safety
◆**une ceinture de sécurité** a seatbelt
[2] security ◊ *par mesure de sécurité* as a security measure
◆**la sécurité sociale** Social Security
◆**la sécurité de l'emploi** job security

séduisant ADJECTIVE
attractive

le **seigle** NOUN
rye ◊ *un pain de seigle* a loaf of rye bread

le **seigneur** NOUN
lord
◆**le Seigneur** the Lord

le **sein** NOUN
breast
◆**au sein de** within ◊ *Chaque pays est autonome au sein de l'Europe.* Each country is independent within Europe.

seize NUMBER
sixteen ◊ *Elle a seize ans.* She's sixteen. ◊ *à seize heures* at 4 p.m.
◆**le seize février** the sixteenth of February

seizième ADJECTIVE
sixteenth

le **séjour** NOUN
stay ◊ *J'ai fait un séjour d'une semaine en Italie.* I stayed in Italy for a week.

le **sel** NOUN
salt

sélectionner VERB
to select

le **self** NOUN (*informal*)
self-service restaurant

le **self-service** NOUN

S

☞

self-service restaurant

la **selle** NOUN
saddle

selon PREPOSITION
according to ◊ *selon lui* according to him ◊ *selon mon humeur* according to what mood I'm in ◊ *Ils sont répartis selon leur âge.* They're divided up according to age.

la **semaine** NOUN
week
♦ **en semaine** on weekdays

semblable ADJECTIVE
similar

le **semblant** NOUN
♦ **faire semblant de faire quelque chose** to pretend to do something ◊ *Il fait semblant de dormir.* He's pretending to be asleep.

sembler VERB
to seem ◊ *Le temps semble s'améliorer.* The weather seems to be improving. ◊ *Il me semble inutile de s'en inquiéter.* It seems pointless to me to worry about it.

la **semelle** NOUN
1 sole
2 insole

la **semoule** NOUN
semolina

le **sens** NOUN
1 sense ◊ *avoir le sens de l'humour* to have a sense of humour ◊ *Je n'ai pas le sens de l'orientation.* I've got no sense of direction. ◊ *avoir le sens du rythme* to have a sense of rhythm ◊ *Ça n'a pas de sens.* It doesn't make sense.
♦ **le bon sens** common sense
2 direction ◊ *Tu tournes la poignée dans le mauvais sens.* You're turning the handle in the wrong direction.
♦ **sens dessus dessous** upside down
♦ **un sens interdit** a one-way street ◊ *J'ai failli prendre un sens interdit.* I nearly went the wrong way down a one-way street.
♦ **un sens unique** a one-way street

la **sensation** NOUN
feeling

sensé ADJECTIVE
sensible

sensible ADJECTIVE
1 sensitive ◊ *Elle est très sensible.* She's very sensitive.
2 visible ◊ *une amélioration sensible* a visible improvement

*Be careful! The French word **sensible** does not mean **sensible**.*

sensiblement ADVERB
1 visibly ◊ *Elle a sensiblement progressé.* She made visible progress.
2 approximately ◊ *Helen et Maree sont sensiblement de la même taille.* Helen and Maree are approximately the same height.

la **sentence** NOUN
sentence (*judgement*)

le **sentier** NOUN
path

le **sentiment** NOUN
feeling

sentimental ADJECTIVE (MASC PL **sentimentaux**)
sentimental

sentir VERB
1 to smell ◊ *Ça sent bon.* That smells good. ◊ *Ça sent mauvais.* It smells bad.
2 to smell of ◊ *Ça sent les frites ici.* It smells of chips in here.
3 to taste ◊ *Est-ce que tu sens l'ail dans le rôti?* Can you taste the garlic in the roast?
4 to feel ◊ *Ça t'a fait mal? – Non, je n'ai rien senti.* Did it hurt? – No, I didn't feel a thing. ◊ *Je ne me sens pas bien.* I don't feel well.
♦ **Il ne peut pas la sentir.** (*informal*) He can't stand her.

séparé ADJECTIVE
separated ◊ *Mes parents sont séparés.* My parents are separated.

séparément ADVERB
separately

séparer VERB
to separate ◊ *Séparez le blanc du jaune.* Separate the yolk from the white.
♦ **se séparer** to separate ◊ *Mes parents se sont séparés l'année dernière.* My parents separated last year.

sept NUMBER
seven ◊ *Il est arrivé à sept heures.* He arrived at seven o'clock. ◊ *Elle a sept ans.* She's seven.
♦ **le sept décembre** the seventh of December

septembre MASC NOUN
September
♦ **en septembre** in September

le **septennat** NOUN

> 🛈 **le septennat** is the seven-year term of office of the French President.

septième ADJECTIVE
seventh ◊ *au septième étage* on the seventh floor

sera, serai, seras, serez VERB *see* **être**
♦ **Je serai de retour à dix heures.** I'll be back at 10 o'clock.

la **série** NOUN
series

sérieusement ADVERB
seriously

sérieux ADJECTIVE (FEM SING **sérieuse**)
see also **sérieux** NOUN
[1] serious ◊ *Il plaisantait? – Non, il était sérieux.* Was he joking? – No, he was serious.
[2] responsible ◊ *C'est un employé très sérieux.* He's a very responsible employee.

le **sérieux** NOUN
see also **sérieux** ADJECTIVE
♦ **garder son sérieux** to keep a straight face ◊ *J'ai eu du mal à garder mon sérieux.* I had trouble keeping a straight face.
♦ **prendre quelque chose au sérieux** to take something seriously
♦ **prendre quelqu'un au sérieux** to take somebody seriously
♦ **Il manque un peu de sérieux.** He's not very responsible.

la **seringue** NOUN
syringe

séronégatif ADJECTIVE (FEM SING **séronégative**)
HIV-negative

serons, seront VERB *see* **être**

séropositif ADJECTIVE (FEM SING **séropositive**)
HIV-positive

le **serpent** NOUN
snake

la **serre** NOUN
greenhouse
♦ **l'effet de serre** the greenhouse effect

serré ADJECTIVE
[1] tight ◊ *Mon pantalon est trop serré.* My trousers are too tight.
[2] close-fought ◊ *Ça a été un match serré.* It was a close-fought game.

serrer VERB
♦ **Ce pantalon me serre trop.** These trousers are too tight for me.
♦ **serrer la main à quelqu'un** to shake hands with somebody
♦ **se serrer** to squeeze up ◊ *Serrez-vous un peu pour que je puisse m'asseoir.* Squeeze up a bit so I can sit down.

♦ **serrer quelqu'un dans ses bras** to hug somebody
♦ **"Serrer à droite"** "Keep right"

la **serrure** NOUN
lock

sers, sert VERB *see* **servir**

le **serveur** NOUN
[1] waiter (*in café*)
[2] server (*computer*)

la **serveuse** NOUN
waitress

serviable ADJECTIVE
helpful

le **service** NOUN
[1] service (*in restaurant*) ◊ *Le service est compris.* Service is included.
♦ **être de service** to be on duty
♦ **hors service** out of order
♦ **faire le service** to serve (*at table*) ◊ *Tu peux faire le service s'il te plaît?* Could you serve please?
[2] favour ◊ *rendre service à quelqu'un* to do somebody a favour ◊ *Est-ce que je peux te demander un service?* Can I ask you a favour?
[3] serve (*sport*) ◊ *Il a un bon service.* He's got a good serve.
♦ **le service militaire** military service
♦ **les services sociaux** the social services
♦ **les services secrets** the secret service

la **serviette** NOUN
[1] towel ◊ *une serviette de bain* a bath towel
♦ **une serviette hygiénique** a sanitary towel
[2] serviette (*napkin*)
[3] briefcase

servir VERB
to serve ◊ *On vous sert?* Are you being served?
♦ **À toi de servir.** (*tennis*) It's your serve.
♦ **se servir** to help oneself ◊ *Servez-vous.* Help yourself.
♦ **se servir de** to use ◊ *Tu te sers souvent de ton vélo?* Do you use your bike a lot?
♦ **servir à quelqu'un** to be of use to somebody ◊ *Ça m'a beaucoup servi.* It was very useful.
♦ **À quoi ça sert?** What's it for?
♦ **Ça ne sert à rien.** It's no use. ◊ *Ça ne sert à rien d'insister.* It's no use insisting.

ses ADJECTIVE
[1] his ◊ *Il est parti voir ses*

S

grands-parents. He's gone to see his grandparents.
2 her ◊ *Delphine a oublié ses baskets.* Delphine's forgotten her trainers.
3 its ◊ *la ville et ses alentours* the town and its surroundings

le **set** NOUN
1 tablemat *(on table)*
2 set *(in tennis)*

le **seuil** NOUN
doorstep

seul ADJECTIVE, ADVERB
1 alone ◊ *vivre seul* to live alone
2 by oneself ◊ *Elle est venue seule.* She came by herself.
♦ **faire quelque chose tout seul** to do something by oneself ◊ *Elle a fait ça toute seule?* Did she do it by herself?
♦ **se sentir seul** to feel lonely
♦ **un seul livre** one book only ◊ *Vous avez droit à un seul livre.* You're entitled to one book only.
♦ **Il reste une seule nectarine.** There's only one nectarine left.
♦ **le seul livre que ...** the only book that ... ◊ *C'est le seul Agatha Christie que je n'aie pas lu.* That's the only Agatha Christie I haven't read.
♦ **le seul** the only one ◊ *C'est la seule que je ne connaisse pas.* She's the only one I don't know.

seulement ADVERB
only
♦ **non seulement ... mais** not only ... but ◊ *Non seulement il a plu, mais en plus il a fait froid.* Not only did it rain, but it was cold as well.

sévère ADJECTIVE
strict ◊ *Mon prof de maths est très sévère.* My maths teacher is very strict.

sexuel ADJECTIVE (FEM SING **sexuelle**)
sexual ◊ *la discrimination sexuelle* sexual discrimination ◊ *l'éducation sexuelle* sex education

le **shampooing** NOUN
shampoo
♦ **se faire un shampooing** to wash one's hair

le **short** NOUN
shorts ◊ *Il était en short.* He was wearing shorts.

le **si** NOUN
see also **si** CONJUNCTION
1 B ◊ *en si bémol* in B flat
2 ti ◊ *la, si, do* la, ti, do

si CONJUNCTION, ADVERB
see also **si** NOUN

1 if ◊ *si tu veux* if you like ◊ *Je me demande si elle va venir.* I wonder if she'll come. ◊ *si seulement* if only
2 so ◊ *Elle est si gentille.* She's so kind. ◊ *Tout s'est passé si vite.* Everything happened so fast.
3 yes ◊ *Tu n'es pas allé à l'école habillé comme ça? – Si.* You didn't go to school dressed like that? – Yes I did.

la **Sicile** NOUN
Sicily

le **sida** NOUN
AIDS ◊ *Il a le sida.* He's got AIDS.

le **siècle** NOUN
century ◊ *le vingtième siècle* the twentieth century

le **siège** NOUN
1 seat *(in vehicle)*
2 head office

sien PRONOUN
♦ **le sien (1)** his ◊ *C'est le vélo de Paul? – Oui, c'est le sien.* Is this Paul's bike? – Yes, it's his.
♦ **le sien (2)** hers ◊ *C'est le vélo d'Isabelle? – Oui, c'est le sien.* Is this Isabelle's bike? – Yes, it's hers.

sienne PRONOUN
♦ **la sienne (1)** his ◊ *C'est la montre de Paul? – Oui, c'est la sienne.* Is this Paul's watch? – Yes, it's his.
♦ **la sienne (2)** hers ◊ *C'est la montre d'Isabelle? – Oui, c'est la sienne.* Is this Isabelle's watch? – Yes, it's hers.

siennes PRONOUN
♦ **les siennes (1)** his ◊ *Ce sont les cassettes de Christian? – Oui, ce sont les siennes.* Are these Christian's cassettes? – Yes, they're his.
♦ **les siennes (2)** hers ◊ *Ce sont les lunettes de Daphne? – Oui, ce sont les siennes.* Are these Daphne's glasses? – Yes, they're hers.

siens PRONOUN
♦ **les siens (1)** his ◊ *Ce sont les sandwichs de Pierre? – Oui, ce sont les siens.* Are these Pierre's sandwiches? – Yes, they're his.
♦ **les siens (2)** hers ◊ *Ce sont les sandwichs de Justine? – Oui, ce sont les siens.* Are these Justine's sandwiches? – Yes, they're hers.

la **sieste** NOUN
nap ◊ *faire la sieste* to have a nap

siffler VERB
to whistle

le **sifflet** NOUN
whistle

le **sigle** NOUN

acronym

le **signal** NOUN (PL les **signaux**)
signal

la **signature** NOUN
signature

le **signe** NOUN
sign
◆ **faire un signe de la main** to wave
◆ **faire signe à quelqu'un d'entrer** to beckon to somebody to come in
◆ **les signes du zodiaque** the signs of the zodiac

signer VERB
to sign

le **signet** NOUN
bookmark

la **signification** NOUN
meaning

signifier VERB
to mean ◊ *Que signifie ce mot?* What does this word mean?

le **silence** NOUN
silence
◆ **Silence!** Be quiet!

silencieux ADJECTIVE (FEM SING **silencieuse**)
[1] silent ◊ *Elle est restée silencieuse.* She remained silent.
[2] quiet ◊ *C'est très silencieux ici.* It's very quiet here.

la **silhouette** NOUN
figure ◊ *J'ai vu une silhouette dans le brouillard.* I saw a figure in the mist.

similaire ADJECTIVE
similar

le **simple** NOUN
see also **simple** ADJECTIVE
singles (*tennis*) ◊ *le simple messieurs* the men's singles ◊ *le simple dames* the ladies' singles

simple ADJECTIVE
see also **simple** NOUN
simple

simplement ADVERB
simply ◊ *C'est tout simplement inadmissible.* It's quite simply unacceptable.

simuler VERB
to simulate

simultané ADJECTIVE
simultaneous

sincère ADJECTIVE
sincere

sincèrement ADVERB
sincerely

la **sincérité** NOUN
sincerity

le **singe** NOUN
monkey

le **singulier** NOUN
singular ◊ *au féminin singulier* in the feminine singular

sinistre ADJECTIVE
sinister

sinon CONJUNCTION
otherwise ◊ *Dépêche-toi, sinon je pars sans toi.* Hurry up, otherwise I'll leave without you.

la **sirène** NOUN
mermaid
◆ **la sirène d'alarme** the fire alarm

le **sirop** NOUN
syrup
◆ **le sirop contre la toux** cough mixture

le **site** NOUN
setting ◊ *un site très sauvage* a totally unspoiled setting
◆ **un site pittoresque** a beauty spot
◆ **un site touristique** a tourist attraction
◆ **un site archéologique** an archaeological site
◆ **un site Web** a website

sitôt ADVERB
◆ **sitôt dit, sitôt fait** no sooner said than done
◆ **pas de sitôt** not for a long time ◊ *On ne le reverra pas de sitôt.* We won't see him again for a long time.

la **situation** NOUN
[1] situation
◆ **la situation de famille** marital status
[2] job ◊ *Il a une belle situation.* He's got a good job.

se **situer** VERB
to be situated ◊ *Versailles se situe à l'ouest de Paris.* Versailles is situated to the west of Paris.
◆ **bien situé** well situated

six NUMBER
six ◊ *Il est rentré à six heures.* He got back at six o'clock. ◊ *Il a six ans.* He's six.
◆ **le six février** the sixth of February

sixième ADJECTIVE
see also **sixième** NOUN
sixth ◊ *au sixième étage* on the sixth floor

la **sixième** NOUN
see also **sixième** ADJECTIVE
first year

> ⓘ In French secondary schools, years are counted from the **sixième** (youngest) to **première** and **terminale** (oldest).

S

◊ *Mon frère est en sixième.* My brother's in first year.

le **ski** NOUN
  [1] ski ◊ *J'ai loué des skis.* I hired skis.
  [2] skiing ◊ *J'adore le ski.* I love skiing. ◊ *faire du ski* to go skiing
  ◆ **le ski de fond** cross-country skiing
  ◆ **le ski nautique** water-skiing
  ◆ **le ski de piste** downhill skiing
  ◆ **le ski de randonnée** cross-country skiing

skier VERB
  to ski

le **skieur** NOUN
  skier

la **skieuse** NOUN
  skier

le **slip** NOUN
  pants
  ◆ **un slip de bain** swimming trunks

la **Slovaquie** NOUN
  Slovakia

la **Slovénie** NOUN
  Slovenia

le **SMIC** NOUN
  guaranteed minimum wage ◊ *Il touche le SMIC.* He's on the legal minimum wage.

le **smoking** NOUN
  dinner suit

la **SNCF** NOUN (= *Société nationale des chemins de fer français*)
  French railways

snob ADJECTIVE (FEM SING **snob**)
  snobbish

sobre ADJECTIVE
  [1] sober
  [2] plain ◊ *C'est une veste très sobre.* It's a very plain jacket.

social ADJECTIVE (MASC PL **sociaux**)
  social

le/la **socialiste** NOUN
  socialist

la **société** NOUN
  [1] society
  [2] company ◊ *une société d'ingénierie* an engineering company

la **sociologie** NOUN
  sociology

la **socquette** NOUN
  ankle sock

la **sœur** NOUN
  sister
  ◆ **une bonne sœur** (*informal*) a nun

soi PRONOUN

oneself ◊ *avoir confiance en soi* to have confidence in oneself
  ◆ **rester chez soi** to stay at home
  ◆ **Ça va de soi.** It goes without saying.

soi-disant ADVERB, ADJECTIVE
  supposedly ◊ *Il était soi-disant parti à Paris.* He had supposedly left for Paris.
  ◆ **un soi-disant poète** a so-called poet

la **soie** NOUN
  silk

la **soif** NOUN
  thirst
  ◆ **avoir soif** to be thirsty

soigner VERB
  to look after (*ill person, animal*) ◊ *Soigne-toi bien ce week-end!* Take good care of yourself this weekend!

soigneux ADJECTIVE (FEM SING **soigneuse**)
  careful ◊ *Tu devrais être plus soigneux avec tes livres.* You should be more careful with your books.

soi-même PRONOUN
  oneself ◊ *Il vaut mieux le faire soi-même.* It's better to do it oneself.

le **soin** NOUN
  care
  ◆ **prendre soin de quelque chose** to take care of something ◊ *Prends bien soin de ce livre.* Take good care of this book.

les **soins** MASC NOUN
  treatment SING
  ◆ **les premiers soins** first aid
  ◆ **"aux bons soins de Madame Martin"** (*on letter*) "c/o Mrs Martin"

le **soir** NOUN
  evening ◊ *ce soir* this evening
  ◆ **demain soir** tomorrow night
  ◆ **hier soir** last night

la **soirée** NOUN
  evening ◊ *en tenue de soirée* in evening dress

sois VERB see **être**
  ◆ **Sois tranquille!** Be quiet!

soit CONJUNCTION
  ◆ **soit ..., soit ...** either ... or ... ◊ *soit lundi, soit mardi* either Monday or Tuesday

la **soixantaine** NOUN
  about sixty ◊ *une soixantaine de personnes* about sixty people
  ◆ **Elle a la soixantaine.** She's in her sixties.

soixante NUMBER
  sixty ◊ *Il a soixante ans.* He's sixty.
  ◊ *soixante et un* sixty-one
  ◊ *soixante-deux* sixty-two

♦ **soixante et onze** seventy-one

♦ **soixante-quinze** seventy-five

soixante-dix NUMBER
seventy ◊ *Il a soixante-dix ans.* He's
seventy.

le **soja** NOUN
soya

♦ **des germes de soja** beansprouts

le **sol** NOUN
[1] floor ◊ *un sol carrelé* a tiled floor

♦ **à même le sol** on the floor
[2] soil ◊ *sur le sol français* on French
soil
[3] G ◊ *sol dièse* G sharp
[4] so ◊ *do, ré, mi, fa, sol ...* do, re,
mi, fa, so ...

solaire ADJECTIVE
solar ◊ *le système solaire* the solar
system

♦ **la crème solaire** sun cream

le **soldat** NOUN
soldier

le **solde** NOUN

♦ **être en solde** to be reduced ◊ *Les
chemisiers sont en solde.* The
blouses are reduced.

♦ **les soldes** the sales ◊ *faire les soldes*
to go round the sales ◊ *les soldes de
janvier* the January sales

soldé ADJECTIVE

♦ **être soldé** to be reduced ◊ *un article
soldé à dix francs* an item reduced to
10 francs

la **sole** NOUN
sole (*fish*)

le **soleil** NOUN
sun ◊ *au soleil* in the sun

♦ **Il y a du soleil.** It's sunny.

le **solfège** NOUN
musical theory ◊ *Il joue du violon
sans connaître le solfège.* He plays
the violin but he can't read music.

solidaire ADJECTIVE

♦ **être solidaire de quelqu'un** to back
somebody up

solide ADJECTIVE
[1] strong (*person*)
[2] solid (*object*)

solitaire ADJECTIVE
see also **solitaire** NOUN
solitary

le/la **solitaire** NOUN
see also **solitaire** ADJECTIVE
loner

la **solitude** NOUN
loneliness

la **solution** NOUN
solution

♦ **une solution de facilité** an easy way
out

sombre ADJECTIVE
dark

le **sommaire** NOUN
summary

la **somme** NOUN
see also **le somme**
sum

le **somme** NOUN
see also **la somme**
nap ◊ *faire un somme* to take a nap

le **sommeil** NOUN
sleep

♦ **avoir sommeil** to be sleepy

sommes VERB see **être**

♦ **Nous sommes en vacances.** We're on
holiday.

le **sommet** NOUN
summit

le **somnifère** NOUN
sleeping pill

somptueux ADJECTIVE (FEM SING
somptueuse)
sumptuous

son ADJECTIVE (FEM SING **sa**, PL **ses**)
see also **son** NOUN
[1] his ◊ *son père* his father ◊ *Il a
perdu son portefeuille.* He's lost his
wallet.
[2] her ◊ *son père* her father ◊ *Elle a
perdu son sac.* She's lost her bag.

le **son** NOUN
see also **son** ADJECTIVE
[1] sound ◊ *Le son n'est pas très bon.*
The sound's not very good. ◊ *baisser
le son* to turn the sound down
[2] bran

♦ **le pain de son** brown bread

le **sondage** NOUN
survey

♦ **un sondage d'opinion** an opinion poll

sonner VERB
to ring ◊ *On a sonné.* Somebody
rang the doorbell. ◊ *Le téléphone a
sonné.* The phone rang.

la **sonnerie** NOUN
bell (*electric*) ◊ *La sonnerie du
téléphone l'a réveillé.* He was woken
by the phone ringing.

la **sonnette** NOUN
bell ◊ *la sonnette d'alarme* the alarm
bell

la **sono** NOUN (*informal*)
sound system

sont VERB see **être**

♦ **Ils sont en vacances.** They're on
holiday.

S

sophistiqué ADJECTIVE
sophisticated

le **sort** NOUN
⬜1 spell ◊ *jeter un sort à quelqu'un* to cast a spell on somebody
♦ *un mauvais sort* a curse
⬜2 fate ◊ *abandonner quelqu'un à son triste sort* to leave somebody to their fate
♦ *tirer au sort* to draw lots

la **sorte** NOUN
sort ◊ *C'est une sorte de gâteau.* It's a sort of cake. ◊ *toutes sortes de choses* all sorts of things

la **sortie** NOUN
way out ◊ *Où est la sortie?* Where's the way out?
♦ *la sortie de secours* the emergency exit
♦ *Attends-moi à la sortie de l'école.* Meet me after school.

sortir VERB
⬜1 to go out ◊ *Il est sorti sans rien dire.* He went out without saying a word. ◊ *Il est sorti acheter un journal.* He's gone out to buy a newspaper. ◊ *J'aime sortir.* I like going out.
⬜2 to come out ◊ *Elle sort de l'hôpital demain.* She's coming out of hospital tomorrow. ◊ *Je l'ai rencontré en sortant de la pharmacie.* I met him coming out of the chemist's. ◊ *Ce modèle vient juste de sortir.* This model has just come out.
⬜3 to take out ◊ *Elle a sorti son porte-monnaie de son sac.* She took her purse out of her handbag. ◊ *Je vais sortir la voiture du garage.* I'll get the car out of the garage.
♦ *sortir avec quelqu'un* to be going out with somebody ◊ *Tu sors avec lui?* Are you going out with him?
♦ *s'en sortir* to manage ◊ *Ne t'en fais pas, tu t'en sortiras.* Don't worry, you'll manage OK.

la **sottise** NOUN
♦ *Ne fais pas de sottises.* Don't do anything silly.
♦ *Ne dis pas de sottises.* Don't talk nonsense.

le **sou** NOUN
♦ *une machine à sous* a fruit machine
♦ *Je n'ai pas un sou sur moi.* I haven't got a penny on me.
♦ *être près de ses sous* (*informal*) to be tight-fisted

le **souci** NOUN
worry
♦ *se faire du souci* to worry

soucieux ADJECTIVE (FEM SING **soucieuse**)

worried ◊ *Tu as l'air soucieux.* You look worried.

la **soucoupe** NOUN
saucer
♦ *une soucoupe volante* a flying saucer

soudain ADJECTIVE, ADVERB
⬜1 sudden ◊ *une douleur soudaine* a sudden pain
⬜2 suddenly ◊ *Soudain, il s'est fâché.* Suddenly, he got angry.

le **souffle** NOUN
breath
♦ *à bout de souffle* out of breath

le **soufflé** NOUN
soufflé ◊ *un soufflé au fromage* a cheese soufflé

souffler VERB
⬜1 to blow ◊ *Le vent soufflait fort.* The wind was blowing hard.
⬜2 to blow out ◊ *Souffle les bougies!* Blow out the candles!

la **souffrance** NOUN
suffering

souffrant ADJECTIVE
unwell

souffrir VERB
to be in pain ◊ *Il souffre beaucoup.* He's in a lot of pain.
♦ *Il ne peux pas la souffrir.* (*informal*) He can't stand her.

le **souhait** NOUN
wish ◊ *faire un souhait* to make a wish ◊ *Tous nos souhaits de réussite.* All our best wishes for your success. ◊ *les souhaits de bonne année* New Year's wishes
♦ *Atchoum! – À tes souhaits!* Atchoo! – Bless you!

souhaiter VERB
to wish ◊ *Il souhaite aller à l'université.* He wishes to go to university. ◊ *Nous vous souhaitons une bonne année.* We wish you a happy New Year.

soûl ADJECTIVE (*informal*)
drunk

soulager VERB
to relieve

soulever VERB
⬜1 to lift ◊ *Je n'arrive pas à soulever cette valise.* I can't lift this suitcase.
⬜2 to raise ◊ *Il faudra soulever la question lors de la réunion.* We'll have to raise the matter at the meeting.

le **soulier** NOUN
shoe

souligner VERB
to underline

le **soupçon** NOUN
suspicion
♦ **un soupçon de** a dash of ◊ *Ajoutez un soupçon de rhum.* Add a dash of rum.

soupçonner VERB
to suspect

la **soupe** NOUN
soup

le **soupir** NOUN
sigh

soupirer VERB
to sigh

souple ADJECTIVE
1 supple (*person*)
2 flexible (*system*)

la **source** NOUN
spring ◊ *l'eau de source* spring water

le **sourcil** NOUN
eyebrow

sourd ADJECTIVE
deaf

souriant ADJECTIVE
cheerful

le **sourire** NOUN
see also **sourire** VERB
smile

sourire VERB
see also **sourire** NOUN
to smile ◊ *sourire à quelqu'un* to smile at somebody

la **souris** NOUN
mouse

sournois ADJECTIVE
sly

sous PREPOSITION
under
♦ **sous terre** underground
♦ **sous la pluie** in the rain

sous-entendu ADJECTIVE
see also **sous-entendu** NOUN
implied

le **sous-entendu** NOUN
see also **sous-entendu** ADJECTIVE
insinuation

sous-marin ADJECTIVE
see also **sous-marin** NOUN
underwater

le **sous-marin** NOUN
see also **sous-marin** ADJECTIVE
submarine

le **sous-sol** NOUN
basement

le **sous-titre** NOUN
subtitle

sous-titré ADJECTIVE
with subtitles

la **soustraction** NOUN

subtraction

les **sous-vêtements** MASC NOUN
underwear SING

soutenir VERB
to support ◊ *Il m'a toujours soutenu contre elle.* He's always supported me against her.
♦ **soutenir que** to maintain that ◊ *Elle soutenait que c'était impossible.* She maintained that it was impossible.
♦ **soutenir l'allure** to keep up ◊ *Il marchait trop vite et je n'arrivais pas à soutenir l'allure.* He was walking too fast and I couldn't keep up.

souterrain ADJECTIVE
see also **souterrain** NOUN
underground

le **souterrain** NOUN
see also **souterrain** ADJECTIVE
underground passage

le **soutien** NOUN
support

le **soutien-gorge** NOUN (PL les **soutiens-gorge**)
bra

le **souvenir** NOUN
see also **se souvenir** VERB
1 memory ◊ *garder un bon souvenir de quelque chose* to have happy memories of something
2 souvenir ◊ *un souvenir de Lourdes* a souvenir of Lourdes
♦ **Garde ce livre en souvenir de moi.** Keep the book: it'll remind you of me.

se **souvenir** VERB
see also **souvenir** NOUN
♦ **se souvenir de quelque chose** to remember something ◊ *Je ne me souviens pas de son adresse.* I can't remember his address.
♦ **se souvenir que** to remember that ◊ *Je me souviens qu'il neigeait ce jour-là.* I remember it was snowing that day.

souvent ADVERB
often

soyez, soyons VERB see **être**
♦ **Soyons clairs!** Let's be clear about this!

la **SPA** NOUN (= *Société protectrice des animaux*)
RSPCA

spacieux ADJECTIVE (FEM SING **spacieuse**)
spacious

les **spaghettis** MASC NOUN
spaghetti SING

le **sparadrap** NOUN
sticking plaster

S

le **speaker** NOUN
announcer

la **speakerine** NOUN
announcer

spécial ADJECTIVE (MASC PL **spéciaux**)
[1] special ◊ *Qu'est-ce que tu fais ce week-end? – Rien de spécial.* What are you doing this weekend? – Nothing special.
♦ **les effets spéciaux** special effects
[2] peculiar ◊ *Elle a des goûts un peu spéciaux.* She has rather peculiar tastes.

spécialement ADVERB
[1] specially ◊ *Il est venu spécialement pour te parler.* He came specially to speak to you.
[2] particularly ◊ *Ce n'est pas spécialement difficile.* It's not particularly difficult.

se **spécialiser** VERB
♦ **se spécialiser dans quelque chose** to specialize in something ◊ *Je me suis spécialisé en histoire contemporaine.* I specialized in modern history.

le/la **spécialiste** NOUN
specialist

la **spécialité** NOUN
speciality

spécifier VERB
to specify

le **spectacle** NOUN
show

spectaculaire ADJECTIVE
spectacular

le **spectateur** NOUN
[1] member of the audience
[2] spectator

la **spectatrice** NOUN
[1] member of the audience
[2] spectator

la **spéléologie** NOUN
potholing

spirituel ADJECTIVE (FEM SING **spirituelle**)
[1] spiritual
[2] witty

splendide ADJECTIVE
magnificent

spontané ADJECTIVE
spontaneous

le **sport** NOUN
see also **sport** ADJECTIVE
sport ◊ *faire du sport* to do sport
♦ **les sports d'hiver** winter sports

sport ADJECTIVE (MASC, FEM, PL)
see also **sport** NOUN
casual ◊ *une veste sport* a casual jacket

sportif ADJECTIVE (FEM SING **sportive**)
see also **sportif** NOUN
[1] sporty ◊ *Elle est très sportive.* She's very sporty.
[2] sports ◊ *un club sportif* a sports club

le **sportif** NOUN
see also **sportif** ADJECTIVE
sportsman

la **sportive** NOUN
sportswoman

le **spot** NOUN
spotlight
♦ **un spot publicitaire** a commercial break

le **square** NOUN
public gardens

le **squelette** NOUN
skeleton

stable ADJECTIVE
stable
♦ **un emploi stable** a steady job

le **stade** NOUN
stadium

le **stage** NOUN
[1] training course ◊ *faire un stage de formation professionnelle* to go on a vocational training course
[2] work experience ◊ *Caroline a fait un stage chez Collins.* Caroline did work experience at Collins.
♦ **faire un stage en entreprise** to do a work placement
*Be careful! The French word **stage** does not mean stage.*

le/la **stagiaire** NOUN
see also **stagiaire** ADJECTIVE
trainee

stagiaire ADJECTIVE
see also **stagiaire** NOUN
trainee ◊ *un professeur stagiaire* a trainee teacher

le **stand** NOUN
[1] stand (at exhibition)
[2] stall (at fair)

le/la **standardiste** NOUN
operator

la **station** NOUN
♦ **une station de métro** an underground station
♦ **une station de taxis** a taxi rank
♦ **une station de ski** a ski resort

le **stationnement** NOUN
parking
♦ **"stationnement interdit"** "no parking"

stationner VERB
to park

la **station-service** NOUN (PL les **stations-service**)
service station

la **statistique** NOUN
statistic

le **steak** NOUN
steak
- **un steak frites** steak and chips
- **un steak haché** a hamburger

la **sténo** NOUN
shorthand ◇ *un cours de sténo* a shorthand course

la **sténodactylo** NOUN
shorthand typist

stérile ADJECTIVE
sterile

stimulant ADJECTIVE
stimulating

stimuler VERB
to stimulate

le **stop** NOUN
stop sign
- **faire du stop** to hitchhike

stopper VERB
to stop

le **store** NOUN
[1] blind (*on window*)
[2] awning

le **strapontin** NOUN
foldaway seat

la **stratégie** NOUN
strategy

stratégique ADJECTIVE
strategic

stressant ADJECTIVE
stressful

stressé ADJECTIVE
stressed out

strict ADJECTIVE
[1] strict (*person*) ◇ *Ma prof de français est très stricte.* My French teacher's very strict.
[2] severe (*clothes*) ◇ *une tenue très stricte* a very severe outfit
- **le strict minimum** the bare minimum

la **strophe** NOUN
stanza

studieux ADJECTIVE (FEM SING **studieuse**)
studious

le **studio** NOUN
[1] studio flat
[2] studio ◇ *un studio de télévision* a television studio

stupéfait ADJECTIVE
astonished

les **stupéfiants** MASC NOUN
narcotics

stupéfier VERB
to astonish ◇ *Sa réponse m'a stupéfié.* I was astonished by his answer.

stupide ADJECTIVE
stupid

le **style** NOUN
style

le/la **styliste** NOUN
designer

le **stylo** NOUN
pen
- **un stylo plume** a fountain pen
- **un stylo bille** a ballpoint pen
- **un stylo-feutre** a felt-tip pen

su VERB *see* **savoir**
- **Si j'avais su ...** If I'd known ...

subir VERB
to suffer (*defeat*)
- **subir une opération** to have an operation

subit ADJECTIVE
sudden

subitement ADVERB
suddenly

subjectif ADJECTIVE (FEM SING **subjective**)
subjective

le **subjonctif** NOUN
subjunctive

substituer VERB
to substitute ◇ *substituer un mot à un autre* to substitute one word for another

subtil ADJECTIVE
subtle

la **subvention** NOUN
subsidy

subventionner VERB
to subsidize

le **succès** NOUN
success ◇ *avoir du succès* to be successful

le **successeur** NOUN
successor

la **succursale** NOUN
branch (*of company*)

sucer VERB
to suck

la **sucette** NOUN
lollipop

le **sucre** NOUN
sugar
- **un sucre** a sugar-lump ◇ *Je prends deux sucres dans mon café.* I take two lumps of sugar in my coffee.
- **du sucre en morceaux** lump sugar
- **un sucre d'orge** a barley sugar
- **du sucre en poudre** caster sugar
- **du sucre glace** icing sugar

S

sucré ADJECTIVE
[1] sweet ◊ *Ce gâteau est un peu trop sucré.* This cake is a bit too sweet.
[2] sweetened ◊ *du lait concentré sucré* sweetened condensed milk

les **sucreries** FEM NOUN
sweet things

le **sucrier** NOUN
sugar bowl

le **sud** NOUN
see also **sud** ADJECTIVE
south ◊ *Ils vivent dans le sud de la France.* They live in the South of France.
♦ **vers le sud** southwards
♦ **au sud de Paris** south of Paris
♦ **l'Amérique du Sud** South America
♦ **le vent du sud** the south wind

sud ADJECTIVE
see also **sud** NOUN
[1] south ◊ *la côte sud de l'Espagne* the south coast of Spain
♦ **le pôle sud** the South Pole
[2] southern ◊ *Nous avons visité la partie sud du pays.* We visited the southern part of the country.

sud-africain ADJECTIVE
South African

sud-américain ADJECTIVE
South American

le **sud-est** NOUN
south-east ◊ *au sud-est* in the south-east

le **sud-ouest** NOUN
south-west ◊ *au sud-ouest* in the south-west

la **Suède** NOUN
Sweden

suédois ADJECTIVE, NOUN (FEM SING **suédoise**)
Swedish ◊ *Ils parlent suédois.* They speak Swedish.
♦ **un Suédois** a Swede (*man*)
♦ **une Suédoise** a Swede (*woman*)
♦ **les Suédois** the Swedes

suer VERB
to sweat

la **sueur** NOUN
sweat
♦ **en sueur** sweating

suffire VERB
to be enough ◊ *Tiens, voilà dix francs. Ça te suffit?* Here's 10 francs. Is that enough for you?
♦ **Ça suffit!** That's enough!

suffisamment ADVERB
enough ◊ *Ça n'est pas suffisamment grand.* It's not big enough. ◊ *Il n'y a*

pas suffisamment de chaises. There aren't enough chairs.

suffisant ADJECTIVE
[1] sufficient ◊ *Ça n'est pas une raison suffisante.* That's not sufficient reason.
[2] smug ◊ *Il est un peu trop suffisant.* He's rather smug.

suffoquer VERB
to suffocate

suggérer VERB
to suggest

se **suicider** VERB
to commit suicide

suis VERB see **être, suivre**
♦ **Je suis écossais.** I'm Scottish.
♦ **Suis-moi.** Follow me.

suisse ADJECTIVE, NOUN
see also **la Suisse**
Swiss ◊ *le franc suisse* the Swiss franc
♦ **un Suisse** a Swiss man
♦ **une Suisse** a Swiss woman
♦ **les Suisses** the Swiss

la **Suisse** NOUN
see also **suisse** ADJECTIVE
Switzerland ◊ *la Suisse allemande* German-speaking Switzerland ◊ *la Suisse romande* French-speaking Switzerland

la **suite** NOUN
[1] rest ◊ *Je vous raconterai la suite de l'histoire demain.* I'll tell you the rest of the story tomorrow.
[2] sequel (*to book, film*)
♦ **tout de suite** straightaway ◊ *J'y vais tout de suite.* I'll go straightaway.
♦ **de suite** in succession ◊ *Il a commis la même erreur trois fois de suite.* He made the same mistake three times in succession.
♦ **par la suite** subsequently ◊ *Il s'est avéré par la suite qu'il était coupable.* He subsequently turned out to be guilty.

suivant ADJECTIVE
following ◊ *le jour suivant* the following day ◊ *l'exercice suivant* the following exercise
♦ **Au suivant!** Next!

suivre VERB
[1] to follow ◊ *Il m'a suivie jusque chez moi.* He followed me home. ◊ *Vous me suivez ou est-ce que je parle trop vite?* Are you following me or am I speaking too fast?
[2] to do ◊ *Je suis un cours d'anglais à la fac.* I'm doing an English course at college.

⃞3 to keep up ◇ *Il n'arrive pas à suivre en maths.* He can't keep up in maths. ◇ *J'aime suivre l'actualité.* I like to keep up with the news.
♦**"à suivre"** "to be continued"
♦**suivre un régime** to be on a diet

sujet ADJECTIVE (FEM SING **sujette**)
  see also **sujet** NOUN
♦**être sujet à** to be prone to ◇ *Il est sujet au vertige.* He suffers from vertigo.

le **sujet** NOUN
  see also **sujet** ADJECTIVE
  subject
♦**au sujet de** about ◇ *C'est à quel sujet? – C'est au sujet de l'annonce parue dans "Le Monde" d'aujourd'hui.* What's it about? – It's about the advertisement in today's "Le Monde".
♦**un sujet de conversation** a topic of conversation
♦**un sujet d'examen** an examination question
♦**un sujet de plaisanterie** something to joke about

le **super** NOUN
  super (*petrol*)

superficiel ADJECTIVE (FEM SING **superficielle**)
  superficial

superflu ADJECTIVE
  superfluous

supérieur ADJECTIVE
  see also **supérieur** NOUN
  ⃞1 upper ◇ *la lèvre supérieure* the upper lip
  ⃞2 superior ◇ *qualité supérieure* superior quality ◇ *Il a toujours l'air tellement supérieur!* He always looks so superior!
♦**supérieur à** greater than ◇ *Choisissez un nombre supérieur à cent.* Choose a number greater than 100.

le **supérieur** NOUN
  see also **supérieur** ADJECTIVE
  superior ◇ *mon supérieur hiérarchique* my immediate superior

le **superlatif** NOUN
  superlative

le **supermarché** NOUN
  supermarket

superposé ADJECTIVE
♦**des lits superposés** bunk beds

superstitieux ADJECTIVE (FEM SING **superstitieuse**)
  superstitious

le **suppléant** NOUN
  supply teacher

la **suppléante** NOUN
  supply teacher

le **supplément** NOUN
♦**payer un supplément** to pay an additional charge
♦**Le vin est en supplément.** Wine is extra.
♦**un supplément de travail** extra work

supplémentaire ADJECTIVE
  additional ◇ *Voici quelques exercices supplémentaires.* Here are some additional exercises.
♦**faire des heures supplémentaires** to do overtime

le **supplice** NOUN
  torture ◇ *C'était un supplice.* It was torture.

supplier VERB
♦**supplier quelqu'un de faire quelque chose** to beg somebody to do something ◇ *Je t'en supplie!* I'm begging you!

supportable ADJECTIVE
  bearable

supporter VERB
  to stand (*tolerate*) ◇ *Je ne supporte pas l'hypocrisie.* I can't stand hypocrisy. ◇ *Elle ne supporte pas qu'on la critique.* She can't stand being criticized. ◇ *Je ne peux pas la supporter.* I can't stand her. ◇ *Je supporte mal la chaleur.* I can't stand hot weather.
  *Be careful! **supporter** does not mean **to support**.*

supposer VERB
  to suppose

supprimer VERB
  ⃞1 to cut ◇ *Deux mille emplois ont été supprimés dans le secteur public.* Two thousand jobs have been cut in the public sector.
  ⃞2 to cancel ◇ *Le train de Londres a été supprimé.* The train to London has been cancelled.
  ⃞3 to get rid of ◇ *Ils ont supprimé les témoins gênants.* They got rid of the awkward witnesses.

sur PREPOSITION
  ⃞1 on ◇ *Pose-le sur la table.* Put it down on the table. ◇ *Vous verrez l'hôpital sur votre droite.* You'll see the hospital on your right. ◇ *une conférence sur Balzac* a lecture on Balzac
  ⃞2 in ◇ *une personne sur dix* 1 person in 10
  ⃞3 out of ◇ *J'ai eu quatorze sur vingt en maths.* I got 14 out of 20 in maths.

S

☞

4 by ◊ *quatre mètres sur deux* 4 metres by 2

sûr ADJECTIVE
1 sure ◊ *Tu es sûr?* Are you sure?
♦ **sûr et certain** absolutely certain
2 reliable ◊ *C'est quelqu'un de très sûr.* He's a very reliable person.
3 safe ◊ *Ce quartier n'est pas très sûr la nuit.* This neighbourhood isn't very safe at night.
♦ **sûr de soi** self-confident ◊ *Elle est très sûre d'elle.* She's very self-confident.

sûrement ADVERB
certainly ◊ *Sûrement pas!* Certainly not! ◊ *Il est sûrement déjà parti.* He's sure to have already left.

la **sûreté** NOUN
♦ **mettre quelque chose en sûreté** to put something in a safe place

le **surf** NOUN
surfing

la **surface** NOUN
surface
♦ **les grandes surfaces** the supermarkets

surfer VERB
to go surfing
♦ **surfer sur le Net** to surf the Net

surgelé ADJECTIVE
frozen ◊ *des frites surgelées* frozen chips

les **surgelés** MASC NOUN
frozen food SING

surhumain ADJECTIVE
superhuman

sur-le-champ ADVERB
immediately

le **surlendemain** NOUN
♦ **le surlendemain de son arrivée** two days after he arrived
♦ **le surlendemain dans la matinée** two days later, in the morning

se **surmener** VERB
to work too hard ◊ *Ne te surmène pas trop pendant le week-end.* Don't work too hard over the weekend.

surmonter VERB
to overcome ◊ *Il nous reste de nombreux obstacles à surmonter.* We still have many obstacles to overcome.

surnaturel ADJECTIVE (FEM SING
surnaturelle)
supernatural

le **surnom** NOUN
nickname

surnommer NOUN
to nickname ◊ *On l'a surnommé "Kiki".* We nicknamed him "Kiki".

surpeuplé ADJECTIVE
overpopulated

surprenant ADJECTIVE
surprising

surprendre VERB
to surprise ◊ *Ça me surprendrait beaucoup qu'il arrive à l'heure.* I'd be very surprised if he arrived on time.
♦ **surprendre quelqu'un en train de faire quelque chose** to catch somebody doing something ◊ *Je l'ai surpris en train de fouiller dans mon placard.* I caught him rummaging in my cupboard.

surpris ADJECTIVE
surprised ◊ *Il était surpris de me voir.* He was surprised to see me.

la **surprise** NOUN
surprise ◊ *faire une surprise à quelqu'un* to give somebody a surprise

sursauter VERB
to jump ◊ *J'ai sursauté en entendant mon nom.* I jumped when I heard my name.

surtout ADVERB
1 especially ◊ *Il est assez timide, surtout avec les filles.* He's rather shy, especially with girls.
2 above all ◊ *Ce canapé est joli et surtout, il n'est pas salissant.* This sofa is pretty, and even more important, it doesn't show the dirt. ◊ *Surtout, ne répète pas ce que je t'ai dit!* Whatever you do, don't repeat what I told you!

le **surveillant** NOUN
supervisor (*man*)

> 🛈 In French secondary schools, the teachers are not responsible for supervising the pupils outside class. This job is done by people called **surveillants** or **pions**.

la **surveillante** NOUN
supervisor (*woman*)

surveiller VERB
1 to keep an eye on ◊ *Tu peux surveiller mes bagages?* Can you keep an eye on my luggage?
2 to keep a watch on ◊ *La police a surveillé la maison pendant une semaine.* The police kept the house under surveillance for a week.
3 to supervise ◊ *Nous sommes toujours surveillés pendant la récréation.* We're always supervised during break.

surveiller un examen to invigilate an exam
surveiller sa ligne to watch one's figure

le **survêtement** NOUN
tracksuit ◊ *un haut de survêtement* a tracksuit top ◊ *un pantalon de survêtement* tracksuit bottoms

la **survie** NOUN
survival

le **survivant** NOUN
survivor

la **survivante** NOUN
survivor

survivre VERB
to survive ◊ *survivre à un accident* to survive an accident

survoler VERB
to fly over

susceptible ADJECTIVE
touchy

suspect ADJECTIVE
suspicious ◊ *dans des circonstances suspectes* under suspicious circumstances

suspecter VERB
to suspect

le **suspense** NOUN
suspense
♦ **un film à suspense** a thriller

la **suture** NOUN
♦ **un point de suture** a stitch

svelte ADJECTIVE
slender

SVP ABBREVIATION (= *s'il vous plaît*)
please

le **sweat** NOUN
sweatshirt

la **syllabe** NOUN
syllable

le **symbole** NOUN
symbol

symbolique ADJECTIVE
symbolic

symboliser VERB

to symbolize

symétrique ADJECTIVE
symmetrical

sympa ADJECTIVE (*informal*)
nice ◊ *Elle est très sympa.* She's a really nice person.

la **sympathie** NOUN
♦ **J'ai beaucoup de sympathie pour lui.** I like him a lot.

sympathique ADJECTIVE
nice ◊ *Ce sont des gens très sympathiques.* They're very nice people.
Be careful! **sympathique** *does not mean* **sympathetic.**

sympathiser VERB
to get on well ◊ *Nous avons immédiatement sympathisé avec nos voisins.* We got on well with our neighbours straight away.

le **symptôme** NOUN
symptom

la **synagogue** NOUN
synagogue

le **syndicat** NOUN
trade union
♦ **le syndicat d'initiative** the tourist information office

synonyme ADJECTIVE
see also **synonyme** NOUN
synonymous ◊ *être synonyme de* to be synonymous with

le **synonyme** NOUN
see also **synonyme** ADJECTIVE
synonym

synthétique ADJECTIVE
synthetic

la **Syrie** NOUN
Syria

syrien ADJECTIVE (FEM SING **syrienne**)
Syrian

systématique ADJECTIVE
systematic

le **système** NOUN
system

S

T

t' PRONOUN *see* **te**

ta ADJECTIVE
> your ◊ *J'ai vu ta sœur hier.* I saw your sister yesterday.

le **tabac** NOUN
> [1] tobacco ◊ *le tabac blond* light tobacco ◊ *le tabac brun* dark tobacco
> [2] smoking ◊ *Le tabac est mauvais pour la santé.* Smoking is bad for you.

la **table** NOUN
> table
> ♦ **mettre la table** to lay the table
> ♦ **se mettre à table** to sit down to eat
> ♦ **À table!** Dinner's ready!
> ♦ **une table de nuit** a bedside table
> ♦ **"table des matières"** "contents"

le **tableau** NOUN (PL les **tableaux**)
> painting ◊ *un tableau de Monet* a painting by Monet
> ♦ **le tableau d'affichage** the notice board
> ♦ **le tableau noir** the blackboard

la **tablette** NOUN
> ♦ **une tablette de chocolat** a bar of chocolate

le **tableur** NOUN
> speadsheet

le **tablier** NOUN
> apron

le **tabouret** NOUN
> stool

la **tache** NOUN
> mark (*stain*)
> ♦ **des taches de rousseur** freckles

la **tâche** NOUN
> task

tacher VERB
> to leave a stain

tâcher VERB
> ♦ **tâcher de faire quelque chose** to try to do something ◊ *Tâche d'être à l'heure!* Try to be on time!

le **tact** NOUN
> tact ◊ *avoir du tact* to be tactful

la **tactique** NOUN
> tactics
> ♦ **changer de tactique** to try something different

la **taie** NOUN
> ♦ **une taie d'oreiller** a pillowcase

la **taille** NOUN
> [1] waist ◊ *Elle a la taille fine.* She has a slim waist.

> [2] height ◊ *un homme de taille moyenne* a man of average height
> [3] size ◊ *Avez-vous ma taille?* Have you got my size?

le **taille-crayon** NOUN
> pencil sharpener

le **tailleur** NOUN
> [1] tailor
> [2] suit (*lady's*)
> ♦ **Il est assis en tailleur.** He's sitting cross-legged.

se **taire** VERB
> to stop talking
> ♦ **Taisez-vous!** Be quiet!

le **talon** NOUN
> heel

le **tambour** NOUN
> drum

la **Tamise** NOUN
> Thames

le **tampon** NOUN
> pad ◊ *un tampon à récurer* a scouring pad
> ♦ **un tampon hygiénique** a tampon

tamponneuse ADJECTIVE
> ♦ **les autos tamponneuses** dodgems

tandis que CONJUNCTION
> while ◊ *Il a toujours de bonnes notes, tandis que les miennes sont mauvaises.* He always gets good marks, while mine are poor.

tant ADVERB
> so much ◊ *Je l'aime tant!* I love him so much!
> ♦ **tant de (1)** so much ◊ *tant de nourriture* so much food
> ♦ **tant de (2)** so many ◊ *tant de livres* so many books
> ♦ **tant que (1)** until ◊ *Tu ne sortiras pas tant que tu n'auras pas fini tes devoirs.* You're not going out until you've finished your homework.
> ♦ **tant que (2)** while ◊ *Profites-en tant que tu peux.* Make the most of it while you can.
> ♦ **tant mieux** so much the better
> ♦ **tant pis** never mind

la **tante** NOUN
> aunt

tantôt ADVERB
> sometimes ◊ *Nous venons tantôt à pied, tantôt en bus.* Sometimes we walk, sometimes we come by bus.

le **tapage** NOUN

[1] racket ◊ *Ils ont fait du tapage toute la nuit.* They made a racket all night long.

[2] fuss ◊ *On a fait beaucoup de tapage autour de cette affaire.* There was a lot of fuss about that business.

taper VERB
to beat down ◊ *Le soleil tape.* The sun's really beating down.
♦**taper quelqu'un** to hit somebody ◊ *Papa, il m'a tapé!* Dad, he hit me!
♦**taper sur quelque chose** to bang on something
♦**taper des pieds** to stamp one's feet
♦**taper des mains** to clap one's hands
♦**taper à la machine** to type ◊ *Tu sais taper à la machine?* Can you type? ◊ *Je vais taper cette lettre.* I'm going to type this letter.

le **tapis** NOUN
[1] carpet
♦**le tapis roulant (1)** the Travelator ® (*for people*)
♦**le tapis roulant (2)** the conveyor belt (*in factory*)
♦**le tapis roulant (3)** the carousel (*at baggage reclaim*)
♦**un tapis de souris** a mouse mat

tapisser VERB
to paper

la **tapisserie** NOUN
[1] wallpaper ◊ *Tu aimes la tapisserie de ma chambre?* Do you like the wallpaper in my bedroom?
[2] tapestry

taquiner VERB
to tease

tard ADVERB
late ◊ *Il est tard.* It's late.
♦**plus tard** later on
♦**au plus tard** at the latest

tardif ADJECTIVE (FEM SING **tardive**)
late ◊ *un déjeuner tardif* a late lunch

le **tarif** NOUN
♦**le tarif des consommations** the price list (*in café*)
♦**une communication à tarif réduit** an off-peak phone call
♦**un billet de train à tarif réduit** a concessionary train ticket
♦**un billet de train à plein tarif** a full-price train ticket
♦**Est-ce que vous faites un tarif de groupe?** Is there a reduction for groups?

la **tarte** NOUN
tart

la **tartine** NOUN

slice of bread ◊ *une tartine de confiture* a slice of bread and jam

tartiner VERB
to spread
♦**le fromage à tartiner** cheese spread

le **tas** NOUN
heap ◊ *un tas de charbon* a heap of coal
♦**un tas de** (*informal*) loads of ◊ *J'ai lu un tas de livres pendant les vacances.* I read loads of books in the holidays.

la **tasse** NOUN
cup

le **taureau** NOUN (PL les **taureaux**)
bull
♦**le Taureau** Taurus ◊ *Ils sont tous les deux Taureau.* They're both Taurus.

le **taux** NOUN
rate ◊ *le taux de change* the exchange rate

la **taxe** NOUN
tax
♦**la boutique hors taxes** the duty-free shop

le **taxi** NOUN
taxi

tchèque ADJECTIVE
Czech
♦**la République tchèque** the Czech Republic

te PRONOUN
te changes to t' before a vowel and most words beginning with "h".
[1] you ◊ *Je te vois.* I can see you. ◊ *Il t'a vu?* Did he see you?
[2] to you ◊ *Est-ce qu'il te parle en français?* Does he talk to you in French? ◊ *Elle t'a parlé?* Did she speak to you?
[3] yourself ◊ *Tu vas te rendre malade.* You'll make yourself sick.
With reflexive verbs, te is often not translated.
◊ *Comment tu t'appelles?* What's your name?

le **technicien** NOUN
technician

la **technicienne** NOUN
technician

technique ADJECTIVE
see also **technique** NOUN
technical

la **technique** NOUN
see also **technique** ADJECTIVE
technique

la **techno** NOUN
techno music

T

la **technologie** NOUN
technology

le **teint** NOUN
complexion ◇ *Elle a le teint clair.*
She's got a fair complexion.

la **teinte** NOUN
shade (*colour*)

le **teinturier** NOUN
dry cleaner's ◇ *Je vais porter ce
manteau chez le teinturier.* I'm going
to take this coat to the dry cleaner's.

tel ADJECTIVE (FEM SING **telle**)
◆**Il a un tel enthousiasme!** He's got
such enthusiasm!
◆**rien de tel** nothing like ◇ *Il n'y a rien
de tel qu'une bonne nuit de sommeil.*
There's nothing like a good night's
sleep.
◆**J'ai tout laissé tel quel.** I left
everything as it was.
◆**tel que** such as

la **télé** NOUN
telly ◇ *à la télé* on telly

la **télécarte** NOUN
phonecard

télécharger VERB
to download

la **télécommande** NOUN
remote control

la **téléconférence** NOUN
video conference

la **télécopie** NOUN
fax

le **télégramme** NOUN
telegram

le **téléphérique** NOUN
cable car

le **téléphone** NOUN
telephone ◇ *Elle est au téléphone.*
She's on the phone.

téléphoner VERB
to phone ◇ *Je vais téléphoner à
Claire.* I'll phone Claire. ◇ *Je peux
téléphoner?* Can I make a phone call?

le **télésiège** NOUN
chairlift

le **téléski** NOUN
ski-tow

le **téléspectateur** NOUN
viewer (*TV*)

la **téléspectatrice** NOUN
viewer (*TV*)

le **téléviseur** NOUN
television set

la **télévision** NOUN
television ◇ *à la télévision* on
television
◆**la télévision en circuit fermé** CCTV

◆**la télévision numérique** digital TV

telle ADJECTIVE
◆**Je n'ai jamais eu une telle peur.** I've
never had such a fright.
◆**telle que** such as

tellement ADVERB
1 so ◇ *Andrew est tellement gentil.*
Andrew's so nice. ◇ *Il travaille
tellement.* He works so hard.
2 so much ◇ *Il a tellement mangé
que ...* He ate so much that ...
3 so many ◇ *Il y avait tellement de
monde.* There were so many people.

telles ADJECTIVE
such ◇ *Je n'ai jamais entendu de
telles bêtises!* I've never heard such
nonsense!

tels ADJECTIVE
such ◇ *Nous n'avons pas de tels
orages chez nous.* We don't have
such storms back home.

le **témoignage** NOUN
testimony

témoigner VERB
to testify

le **témoin** NOUN
witness

la **température** NOUN
temperature ◇ *avoir de la
température* to have a temperature

la **tempête** NOUN
storm

le **temple** NOUN
1 church (*Protestant*)
2 temple (*Hindu, Sikh, Buddhist*)

temporaire ADJECTIVE
temporary

le **temps** NOUN
1 weather ◇ *Quel temps fait-il?*
What's the weather like?
2 time ◇ *Je n'ai pas le temps.* I
haven't got time. ◇ *Prends ton temps.*
Take your time. ◇ *Il est temps de
partir.* It's time to go.
◆**juste à temps** just in time
◆**de temps en temps** from time to time
◆**en même temps** at the same time
◆**à temps** in time ◇ *Il est arrivé à
temps pour le match.* He arrived in
time for the match.
◆**à plein temps** full time ◇ *Elle travaille
à plein temps.* She works full time.
◆**à temps complet** full time
◆**à temps partiel** part time ◇ *le travail à
temps partiel* part-time work
◆**dans le temps** at one time ◇ *Dans le
temps, on pouvait circuler en vélo
sans danger.* At one time, it was safe
to go around by bike.

[3] tense (*of verb*)

tenais, tenait VERB *see* **tenir**

la **tendance** NOUN
  ♦ **avoir tendance à faire quelque chose** to tend to do something ◊ *Il a tendance à exagérer.* He tends to exaggerate.

tendre ADJECTIVE
  see also **tendre** VERB
  tender

tendre VERB
  see also **tendre** ADJECTIVE
  to stretch out ◊ *Ils ont tendu une corde entre deux arbres.* They stretched out a rope between two trees.
  ♦ **tendre quelque chose à quelqu'un** to hold something out to somebody ◊ *Il lui a tendu les clés.* He held out the keys to her.
  ♦ **tendre la main** to hold out one's hand
  ♦ **tendre le bras** to reach out
  ♦ **tendre un piège à quelqu'un** to set a trap for someone

tendrement ADVERB
  tenderly

la **tendresse** NOUN
  tenderness

tendu ADJECTIVE
  tense ◊ *Il était très tendu aujourd'hui.* He was very tense today.

tenir VERB
  to hold ◊ *Tu peux tenir la lampe, s'il te plaît?* Can you hold the torch, please? ◊ *Il tenait un enfant par la main.* He was holding a child by the hand.
  ♦ **Tenez votre chien en laisse.** Keep your dog on the lead.
  ♦ **tenir à quelqu'un** to be attached to somebody ◊ *Il tient beaucoup à elle.* He's very attached to her.
  ♦ **tenir à faire quelque chose** to be determined to do something ◊ *Elle tient à y aller.* She's determined to go.
  ♦ **tenir de quelqu'un** to take after somebody ◊ *Il tient de son père.* He takes after his father.
  ♦ **Tiens, voilà un stylo.** Here's a pen.
  ♦ **Tiens, c'est Alain là-bas!** Look, that's Alain over there!
  ♦ **Tiens?** Really?
  ♦ **se tenir (1)** to stand ◊ *Il se tenait près de la porte.* He was standing by the door.
  ♦ **se tenir (2)** to be held ◊ *La foire va se tenir place du marché.* The fair will be held in the market place.
  ♦ **se tenir droit (1)** to stand up straight ◊ *Tiens-toi droit!* Stand up straight!

  ♦ **se tenir droit (2)** to sit up straight ◊ *Arrête de manger le nez dans ton assiette, tiens-toi droit.* Don't slouch while you're eating, sit up straight.
  ♦ **Tiens-toi bien!** Behave yourself!

le **tennis** NOUN
  [1] tennis ◊ *Elle joue au tennis.* She plays tennis.
  ♦ **le tennis de table** table tennis
  [2] tennis court ◊ *Il est au tennis.* He's at the tennis court.
  ♦ **les tennis** trainers

tentant ADJECTIVE
  tempting

la **tentation** NOUN
  temptation

la **tentative** NOUN
  attempt

la **tente** NOUN
  tent

tenter VERB
  to tempt ◊ *J'ai été tenté de tout abandonner.* I was tempted to give up. ◊ *Ça ne me tente vraiment pas d'aller à la piscine.* I don't really fancy going to the swimming pool.
  ♦ **tenter de faire quelque chose** to try to do something ◊ *Il a tenté plusieurs fois de s'évader.* He tried several times to escape.

tenu VERB *see* **tenir**

la **tenue** NOUN
  clothes
  ♦ **en tenue de soirée** in evening dress

le **terme** NOUN
  ♦ **à court terme** short-term
  ♦ **à long terme** long-term

la **terminale** NOUN
  upper sixth ◊ *Je suis en terminale.* I'm in upper sixth.

> ⓘ In French secondary schools, years are counted from the **sixième** (youngest) to **première** and **terminale** (oldest).

T

terminer VERB
  to finish
  ♦ **se terminer** to end ◊ *Les vacances se terminent demain.* The holidays end tomorrow.

le **terminus** NOUN
  terminus

le **terrain** NOUN
  land ◊ *Il veut acheter un terrain en Normandie.* He wants to buy some land in Normandy.
  ♦ **un terrain de camping** a campsite
  ♦ **un terrain de football** a football pitch

☞

◆ **un terrain de golf** a golf course
◆ **un terrain de jeu** a playground
◆ **un terrain de sport** a sports ground
◆ **un terrain vague** a piece of waste ground

la **terrasse** NOUN
terrace
◆ **Si on s'asseyait en terrasse?** Shall we sit outside? (*at café*)

la **terre** NOUN
earth
◆ **la Terre** the Earth
◆ **Elle s'est assise par terre.** She sat on the floor.
◆ **Il est tombé par terre.** He fell down.
◆ **la terre cuite** terracotta ◊ *un pot en terre cuite* a terracotta pot
◆ **la terre glaise** clay

terrible ADJECTIVE
terrible ◊ *Quelque chose de terrible est arrivé.* Something terrible has happened.
◆ **pas terrible** (*informal*) nothing special ◊ *Ce film n'est pas terrible.* The film's nothing special.

la **terrine** NOUN
pâté

le **territoire** NOUN
territory

terrorisé ADJECTIVE
terrified

le **terrorisme** NOUN
terrorism

le/la **terroriste** NOUN
terrorist

tes ADJECTIVE
your ◊ *J'aime bien tes baskets.* I like your trainers.

le **test** NOUN
test

le **testament** NOUN
will ◊ *Il est mort sans testament.* He died without leaving a will.

tester VERB
to test

le **tétanos** NOUN
tetanus

le **têtard** NOUN
tadpole

la **tête** NOUN
head ◊ *de la tête aux pieds* from head to foot
◆ **se laver la tête** to wash one's hair
◆ **la tête la première** headfirst
◆ **tenir tête à quelqu'un** to stand up to somebody
◆ **faire la tête** to sulk
◆ **en avoir par-dessus la tête** to be fed up

têtu ADJECTIVE
stubborn

le **texte** NOUN
text

le **TGV** NOUN (= *train à grande vitesse*)
high-speed train

le **thé** NOUN
tea ◊ *Je vous offre un thé?* Would you like a cup of tea? ◊ *un thé au lait* a white tea

le **théâtre** NOUN
theatre
◆ **faire du théâtre** to act ◊ *Est-ce que tu as déjà fait du théâtre?* Have you ever acted?

la **théière** NOUN
teapot

le **thème** NOUN
1 subject ◊ *Quel est le thème de l'émission?* What's the programme about?
2 prose (*translation into the foreign language*)

la **théorie** NOUN
theory

le **thermomètre** NOUN
thermometer

le **thon** NOUN
tuna

la **thune** NOUN (*informal*)
dosh

le **tibia** NOUN
1 shinbone ◊ *une fracture du tibia* a broken shinbone
2 shin ◊ *Il m'a donné un coup de pied dans le tibia.* He kicked me in the shin.

le **tic** NOUN
nervous twitch

le **ticket** NOUN
ticket ◊ *un ticket de métro* an underground ticket
◆ **le ticket de caisse** the till receipt

tiède ADJECTIVE
1 warm (*water, air*)
2 lukewarm (*food, drink*)

tien PRONOUN
◆ **le tien** yours ◊ *J'ai oublié mon stylo. Tu peux me prêter le tien?* I've forgotten my pen. Can you lend me yours?

tienne PRONOUN
◆ **la tienne** yours ◊ *Ce n'est pas ma raquette, c'est la tienne.* It's not my racket, it's yours.
◆ **À la tienne!** Cheers!

tiennes PRONOUN

◆**les tiennes** yours ◊ *J'ai pris mes baskets, mais j'ai oublié les tiennes.* I've brought my trainers, but I've forgotten yours.

tiens PRONOUN

◆**les tiens** yours ◊ *Je ne trouve pas mes feutres. Je peux utiliser les tiens?* I can't find my felt pens. Can I use yours?

tiens, tient VERB *see* **tenir**

le **tiers** NOUN

  third ◊ *Un tiers de la classe était pour.* A third of the class were in favour.

◆**le tiers monde** the Third World

la **tige** NOUN

  stem

le **tigre** NOUN

  tiger

le **tilleul** NOUN

  lime tea

le **timbre** NOUN

  stamp

le **timbre-poste** NOUN

  postage stamp

timide ADJECTIVE

  shy

timidement ADVERB

  shyly

la **timidité** NOUN

  shyness

le **tir** NOUN

  shooting

◆**le tir à l'arc** archery

le **tirage** NOUN

◆**par tirage au sort** by drawing lots ◊ *Les prix seront attribués par tirage au sort.* The prizes will be awarded by drawing lots.

le **tire-bouchon** NOUN

  corkscrew

la **tirelire** NOUN

  money box

tirer VERB

  1 to pull ◊ *Elle a tiré un mouchoir de son sac.* She pulled a handkerchief out of her bag. ◊ *Il m'a tiré les cheveux.* He pulled my hair. ◊ *"Tirer"* "Pull"

  2 to draw ◊ *tirer les rideaux* to draw the curtains ◊ *tirer un trait* to draw a line ◊ *tirer des conclusions* to draw conclusions

◆**tirer au sort** to draw lots

  3 to fire ◊ *Il a tiré plusieurs coups de feu.* He fired several shots. ◊ *Il a tiré sur les policiers.* He fired at the police.

◆**Tu t'en tires bien.** You're doing well.

le **tiret** NOUN

  dash (*hyphen*)

le **tiroir** NOUN

  drawer

la **tisane** NOUN

  herbal tea

tisser VERB

  to weave

le **tissu** NOUN

  material

◆**un sac en tissu** a cloth bag

le **titre** NOUN

  title

◆**les gros titres** the headlines

◆**un titre de transport** a travel ticket

tituber VERB

  to stagger

le **toast** NOUN

  1 piece of toast

  2 toast ◊ *porter un toast à quelqu'un* to drink a toast to somebody

le **toboggan** NOUN

  slide

toi PRONOUN

  you ◊ *Ça va? – Oui, et toi?* How are you? – Fine, and you? ◊ *J'ai faim, pas toi?* I'm hungry, aren't you?

◆**Assieds-toi.** Sit down.

◆**C'est à toi de jouer.** It's your turn to play.

◆**Est-ce que ce stylo est à toi?** Is this pen yours?

la **toile** NOUN

◆**un pantalon de toile** cotton trousers

◆**un sac de toile** a canvas bag

◆**une toile cirée** an oilcloth

◆**une toile d'araignée** a cobweb

la **toilette** NOUN

  1 wash ◊ *faire sa toilette* to have a wash

  2 outfit ◊ *une toilette élégante* an elegant outfit

les **toilettes** FEM NOUN

  toilet SING

toi-même PRONOUN

  yourself ◊ *Tu as fait ça toi-même?* Did you do it yourself?

le **toit** NOUN

  roof

◆**un toit ouvrant** a sunroof

tolérant ADJECTIVE

  tolerant

tolérer VERB

  to tolerate

la **tomate** NOUN

  tomato

la **tombe** NOUN

T

☞

grave

le **tombeau** NOUN (PL les **tombeaux**)
tomb

la **tombée** NOUN
♦ **à la tombée de la nuit** at nightfall

tomber VERB
to fall ◊ *Attention, tu vas tomber!* Be careful, you'll fall!
♦ **laisser tomber (1)** to drop ◊ *Elle a laissé tomber son stylo.* She dropped her pen.
♦ **laisser tomber (2)** to give up ◊ *Il a laissé tomber le piano.* He gave up the piano.
♦ **laisser tomber (3)** to let down ◊ *Il ne laisse jamais tomber ses amis.* He never lets his friends down.
♦ **tomber sur quelqu'un** to bump into someone ◊ *Je suis tombé sur lui en sortant de chez Pierre.* I bumped into him coming out of Pierre's place.
♦ **Ça tombe bien.** That's lucky.
♦ **Il tombe de sommeil.** He's asleep on his feet.

ton ADJECTIVE (FEM SING **ta**, PL **tes**)
see also **ton** NOUN
your ◊ *C'est ton stylo?* Is this your pen?

le **ton** NOUN
see also **ton** ADJECTIVE
1 tone of voice ◊ *Ne me parle pas sur ce ton.* Don't speak to me in that tone of voice.
2 colour ◊ *J'adore les tons pastel.* I love pastel colours.

la **tonalité** NOUN
dialling tone

la **tondeuse** NOUN
lawnmower

tondre VERB
to mow

tonique ADJECTIVE
fortifying

la **tonne** NOUN
tonne

le **tonneau** NOUN (PL les **tonneaux**)
barrel

le **tonnerre** NOUN
thunder

le **tonus** NOUN
♦ **avoir du tonus** to be energetic

le **torchon** NOUN
tea towel

tordre VERB
♦ **se tordre la cheville** to twist one's ankle

tordu ADJECTIVE

1 bent ◊ *Ce clou est un peu tordu.* This nail's a bit bent.
2 crazy ◊ *une histoire complètement tordue* a crazy story

le **torrent** NOUN
mountain stream

le **torse** NOUN
chest ◊ *Il était torse nu.* He was bare-chested.

le **tort** NOUN
♦ **avoir tort** to be wrong
♦ **donner tort à quelqu'un** to lay the blame on somebody

le **torticolis** NOUN
stiff neck ◊ *J'ai le torticolis.* I've got a stiff neck.

la **tortue** NOUN
tortoise

la **torture** NOUN
torture

torturer VERB
to torture

tôt ADVERB
early
♦ **au plus tôt** at the earliest
♦ **tôt ou tard** sooner or later

total ADJECTIVE (MASC PL **totaux**)
see also **total** NOUN
total

le **total** NOUN (PL les **totaux**)
see also **total** ADJECTIVE
total ◊ *faire le total* to work out the total
♦ **au total** in total

totalement ADVERB
totally

la **totalité** NOUN
♦ **la totalité des profs** all the teachers
♦ **la totalité du personnel** the entire staff

touchant ADJECTIVE
touching

toucher VERB
1 to touch ◊ *Ne touche pas à mes livres!* Don't touch my books!
♦ **Nos deux jardins se touchent.** Our gardens are next to each other.
2 to feel ◊ *Ce pull a l'air doux. Je peux toucher?* That sweater looks soft. Can I feel it?
3 to hit ◊ *La balle l'a touché en pleine poitrine.* The bullet hit him right in the chest.
4 to affect ◊ *Ces nouvelles réformes ne nous touchent pas.* The new reforms don't affect us.
5 to receive ◊ *Il a touché une grosse somme d'argent.* He received a large sum of money.

toujours ADVERB

  [1] <u>always</u> ◇ *Il est toujours très gentil.* He's always very nice.

  ◆ **pour toujours** forever

  [2] <u>still</u> ◇ *Quand nous sommes revenus, Pierre était toujours là.* When we got back Pierre was still there.

le **toupet** NOUN (*informal*)

  ◆ **avoir du toupet** to have a nerve

la **tour** NOUN

  | see also **le tour** |

  [1] <u>tower</u> ◇ *la Tour Eiffel* the Eiffel Tower

  [2] <u>tower block</u> ◇ *Il y a beaucoup de tours dans ce quartier.* There are a lot of tower blocks in this area.

le **tour** NOUN

  | see also **la tour** |

  <u>turn</u> ◇ *C'est ton tour de jouer.* It's your turn to play.

  ◆ **faire un tour** to go for a walk ◇ *Allons faire un tour dans le parc.* Let's go for a walk in the park.

  ◆ **faire un tour en voiture** to go for a drive

  ◆ **faire un tour à vélo** to go for a ride ◇ *Tu veux aller faire un tour à vélo?* Do you want to go for a bike ride?

  ◆ **faire le tour du monde** to travel round the world

  ◆ **à tour de rôle** alternately

le **tourbillon** NOUN

  <u>whirlpool</u>

le **tourisme** NOUN

  <u>tourism</u>

le/la **touriste** NOUN

  <u>tourist</u>

se **tourmenter** VERB

  <u>to fret</u> ◇ *Ne te tourmente pas, ça s'arrangera.* Don't fret about it, it'll be all right.

le **tournant** NOUN

  [1] <u>bend</u> ◇ *Il y a beaucoup de tournants dangereux sur cette route.* There are a lot of dangerous bends on this road.

  [2] <u>turning point</u> ◇ *Ça a été un tournant dans sa vie.* It was a turning point in his life.

la **tournée** NOUN

  [1] <u>round</u> ◇ *Le facteur commence sa tournée à sept heures du matin.* The postman starts his round at 7 o'clock in the morning. ◇ *Allez, qu'est-ce que vous voulez boire? C'est ma tournée.* Right, what are you drinking? It's my round.

  [2] <u>tour</u> ◇ *Il est en tournée aux États-Unis.* He's on tour in the United States.

tourner VERB

  [1] <u>to turn</u> ◇ *Tournez à droite au prochain feu.* Turn right at the lights. ◇ *Tourne-toi un peu plus vers moi, et souris!* Turn towards me a bit more, and smile!

  [2] <u>to go sour</u> ◇ *Le lait a tourné.* The milk's gone sour.

  ◆ **mal tourner** to go wrong ◇ *Ça a mal tourné.* It all went wrong.

  ◆ **tourner le dos à quelqu'un** to have one's back to somebody

  ◆ **tourner un film** to make a film

le **tournesol** NOUN

  <u>sunflower</u>

le **tournevis** NOUN

  <u>screwdriver</u>

le **tournoi** NOUN

  <u>tournament</u>

la **tourte** NOUN

  <u>pie</u> ◇ *une tourte aux poireaux* a leek pie

tous ADJECTIVE, PRONOUN *see* **tout**

la **Toussaint** NOUN

  <u>All Saints' Day</u>

tousser VERB

  <u>to cough</u>

tout ADJECTIVE, ADVERB, PRONOUN (MASC PL **tous**, FEM PL **toutes**)

  [1] <u>all</u> ◇ *tout le lait* all the milk ◇ *toute la nuit* all night ◇ *tous les livres* all the books ◇ *toutes les filles* all the girls ◇ *toute la journée* all day ◇ *tout le temps* all the time ◇ *C'est tout.* That's all. ◇ *Je les connais tous.* I know them all. ◇ *Nous y sommes toutes allées.* We all went. ◇ *Ça fait combien en tout?* How much is that all together?

  ◆ **Il est tout seul.** He's all alone.

  ◆ **pas du tout** not at all

  ◆ **tout de même** all the same

  [2] <u>every</u> ◇ *tous les jours* every day ◇ *tous les deux jours* every two days

  ◆ **tout le monde** everybody

  ◆ **tous les deux** both ◇ *Nous y sommes allés tous les deux.* We both went.

  ◆ **tous les trois** all three ◇ *Je les ai invités tous les trois.* I invited all three of them.

  [3] <u>everything</u> ◇ *Il a tout organisé.* He organized everything.

  [4] <u>very</u> ◇ *Elle habite tout près.* She lives very close.

  ◆ **tout en haut** right at the top

  ◆ **tout droit** straight ahead

  ◆ **tout d'abord** first of all

T

◆**tout à coup** suddenly

◆**tout à fait** absolutely

◆**tout à l'heure (1)** just now ◊ *Je l'ai vu tout à l'heure.* I saw him just now.

◆**tout à l'heure (2)** in a moment ◊ *Je finirai ça tout à l'heure.* I'll finish it in a moment.

◆**À tout à l'heure!** See you later!

◆**tout de suite** straight away

◆**Il a fait son travail tout en chantant.** He sang as he worked.

toutefois ADVERB
   however

toutes ADJECTIVE, PRONOUN *see* **tout**

la **toux** NOUN
   cough

le/la **toxicomane** NOUN
   drug addict

la **toxicomanie** NOUN
   drug addiction

le **TP** NOUN (= *travaux pratiques*)
   practical class ◊ *J'ai un TP de biologie à deux heures.* I've got a biology practical at two o'clock.

le **trac** NOUN
   ◆**avoir le trac** to be feeling nervous

tracasser VERB
   to worry ◊ *La santé de mon père me tracasse.* My dad's health worries me.
   ◆**se tracasser** to worry ◊ *Arrête de te tracasser pour rien!* Stop worrying about nothing!

la **trace** NOUN
   ① trace ◊ *Le voleur n'a pas laissé de traces.* The thief left no traces.
   ② mark ◊ *des traces de doigts* finger marks
   ◆**des traces de pas** footprints

tracer VERB
   to draw ◊ *tracer un trait* to draw a line

le **tracteur** NOUN
   tractor

la **tradition** NOUN
   tradition

traditionnel ADJECTIVE (FEM SING **traditionnelle**)
   traditional

le **traducteur** NOUN
   translator

la **traduction** NOUN
   translation

la **traductrice** NOUN
   translator

traduire VERB
   to translate

le **trafic** NOUN
   traffic

◆**le trafic de drogue** drug trafficking

le **trafiquant** NOUN
   ◆**un trafiquant de drogue** a drug trafficker

tragique ADJECTIVE
   tragic

trahir VERB
   to betray

la **trahison** NOUN
   betrayal

le **train** NOUN
   train
   ◆**un train électrique** a train set
   ◆**Il est en train de manger.** He's eating.

le **traîneau** NOUN (PL les **traîneaux**)
   sledge

traîner VERB
   ① to wander around ◊ *J'ai vu des jeunes qui traînaient en ville.* I saw some young people wandering around town.
   ② to hang about ◊ *Dépêche-toi, ne traîne pas!* Hurry up, don't hang about!
   ③ to drag on ◊ *La réunion a traîné jusqu'à midi.* The meeting dragged on till 12 o'clock.
   ◆**traîner des pieds** to drag one's feet
   ◆**laisser traîner qch** to leave sth lying around ◊ *Ne laisse pas traîner tes affaires.* Don't leave your things lying around.

le **train-train** NOUN
   humdrum routine

traire VERB
   to milk

le **trait** NOUN
   ① line ◊ *Tracez un trait.* Draw a line.
   ② feature ◊ *Elle a les traits fins.* She has delicate features.
   ◆**boire quelque chose d'un trait** to drink something down in one gulp
   ◆**un trait d'union** a hyphen

le **traitement** NOUN
   treatment
   ◆**le traitement de texte** word processing

traiter VERB
   to treat ◊ *Elle le traite comme un chien.* She treats him like a dog.
   ◆**Il m'a traité d'imbécile.** He called me an idiot.
   ◆**traiter de** to be about ◊ *Cet article traite des sans-abri.* This article is about the homeless.

le **traiteur** NOUN
   caterer

le **trajet** NOUN

1 journey ◊ *Il n'a pas arrêté de parler pendant tout le trajet.* He talked for the whole journey. ◊ *J'ai une heure de trajet pour aller au travail.* My journey to work takes an hour.

2 route ◊ *C'est le trajet le plus court.* It's the shortest route.

le **tramway** NOUN
tram

tranchant ADJECTIVE
sharp (*knife*)

la **tranche** NOUN
slice

tranquille ADJECTIVE
quiet ◊ *Cette rue est très tranquille.* This is a very quiet street.

♦ **Sois tranquille, il ne va rien lui arriver.** Don't worry, nothing will happen to him.

♦ **Tiens-toi tranquille!** Be quiet!

♦ **Laisse-moi tranquille.** Leave me alone.

♦ **Laisse ça tranquille.** Leave it alone.

tranquillement ADVERB
quietly ◊ *Nous étions tranquillement installés dans le salon.* We were just sitting quietly in the living room.

♦ **Est-ce que je peux travailler tranquillement cinq minutes?** Can I have five minutes to myself to work in peace?

la **tranquillité** NOUN
peace and quiet

transférer VERB
to transfer

transformer VERB
1 to transform ◊ *Son séjour en France l'a transformé.* His stay in France has transformed him.

2 to convert ◊ *Ils ont transformé la grange en garage.* They've converted the barn into a garage.

♦ **se transformer en** to turn into ◊ *La chenille se transforme en papillon.* The caterpillar turns into a butterfly.

la **transfusion** NOUN
♦ **une transfusion sanguine** a blood transfusion

transiger VERB
to compromise

transmettre VERB
♦ **transmettre quelque chose à quelqu'un** to pass something on to somebody

transpercer VERB
to go through ◊ *La pluie a transpercé mes vêtements.* The rain went through my clothes.

la **transpiration** NOUN

perspiration

transpirer VERB
to perspire

le **transport** NOUN
transport

♦ **les transports en commun** public transport

transporter VERB
1 to carry ◊ *Le train transportait des marchandises.* The train was carrying freight.

2 to move ◊ *Je ne sais pas comment je vais transporter mes affaires.* I don't know how I'm going to move my stuff.

traumatiser VERB
to traumatize

le **travail** NOUN (PL les **travaux**)
1 work ◊ *J'ai beaucoup de travail.* I've got a lot of work.

2 job ◊ *Il a un travail intéressant.* He's got an interesting job.

♦ **Il est sans travail depuis un an.** He has been out of work for a year.

♦ **le travail au noir** moonlighting

travailler VERB
to work

travailleur ADJECTIVE (FEM SING **travailleuse**)
| *see also* **travailleur** NOUN |
hard-working

le **travailleur** NOUN
| *see also* **travailleur** ADJECTIVE |
worker

la **travailleuse** NOUN
worker

les **travaillistes** MASC NOUN
the Labour Party SING

les **travaux** MASC NOUN
1 work SING ◊ *des travaux de construction* building work

2 roadworks ◊ *Il y a beaucoup de bruit à cause des travaux dans la rue.* There's a lot of noise from the roadworks.

♦ **être en travaux** to be undergoing alterations

♦ **les travaux dirigés** supervised practical work

♦ **les travaux manuels** handicrafts

♦ **les travaux ménagers** housework

le **travers** NOUN
♦ **en travers de** across ◊ *Il y avait un arbre en travers de la route.* There was a tree lying across the road.

♦ **de travers** crooked ◊ *Son chapeau était de travers.* His hat was crooked.

♦ **comprendre de travers** to misunderstand ◊ *Elle comprend*

T

☞

toujours tout de travers. She always gets the wrong idea.

♦ *J'ai avalé de travers.* Something went down the wrong way.

♦ **à travers** through ◊ *Cette vitre est tellement sale qu'on ne voit rien à travers.* This window is so dirty you can't see anything through it.

la **traversée** NOUN
　crossing

traverser VERB
　1 to cross ◊ *Traversez la rue.* Cross the street.
　2 to go through ◊ *Nous avons traversé la France pour aller en Espagne.* We went through France on the way to Spain. ◊ *La pluie a traversé mon manteau.* The rain went through my coat.

le **traversin** NOUN
　bolster

trébucher VERB
　to trip up

le **trèfle** NOUN
　1 clover
　2 clubs (*at cards*) ◊ *le roi de trèfle* the king of clubs

treize NUMBER
　thirteen ◊ *Il a treize ans.* He's thirteen. ◊ *à treize heures* at 1 p.m.
　♦ **le treize février** the thirteenth of February

treizième ADJECTIVE
　thirteenth

le **tréma** NOUN
　diaeresis

le **tremblement de terre** NOUN
　earthquake

trembler VERB
　to shake ◊ *trembler de peur* to shake with fear
　♦ **trembler de froid** to shiver

trempé ADJECTIVE
　soaking wet
　♦ **trempé jusqu'aux os** soaked to the skin

tremper VERB
　to soak
　♦ **tremper sa main dans l'eau** to dip one's hand in the water

le **tremplin** NOUN
　springboard

la **trentaine** NOUN
　about thirty ◊ *une trentaine de personnes* about thirty people
　♦ **Il a la trentaine.** He's in his thirties.

trente NUMBER
　thirty ◊ *Elle a trente ans.* She's thirty.

♦ **le trente janvier** the thirtieth of January
♦ **trente et un** thirty-one
♦ **trente-deux** thirty-two

trentième ADJECTIVE
　thirtieth

très ADVERB
　very

le **trésor** NOUN
　treasure

la **tresse** NOUN
　plait

le **triangle** NOUN
　triangle

la **tribu** NOUN
　tribe

le **tribunal** NOUN (PL les **tribunaux**)
　court

tricher VERB
　to cheat

tricolore ADJECTIVE
　three-coloured
　♦ **le drapeau tricolore** the French tricolour

> ❶ *le drapeau tricolore* is the French flag which is blue, white and red.

le **tricot** NOUN
　1 knitting ◊ *On fait du tricot à l'école.* We do knitting at school.
　2 sweater ◊ *Mets un tricot, il fait froid.* Put a sweater on, it's cold.

tricoter VERB
　to knit

trier VERB
　to sort out ◊ *Je vais trier mes papiers avant de partir en vacances.* I'm going to sort out my papers before I go on holiday.

le **trimestre** NOUN
　term

trinquer VERB
　to clink glasses

le **triomphe** NOUN
　triumph

triompher VERB
　to triumph

les **tripes** FEM NOUN
　tripe

le **triple** NOUN
　♦ **Ça m'a coûté le triple.** It cost me three times as much.
　♦ **Il gagne le triple de mon salaire.** He earns three times my salary.

tripler VERB
　to treble

les **triplés** MASC NOUN

triplets

triste ADJECTIVE
sad

la **tristesse** NOUN
sadness

le **trognon** NOUN
core ◊ *un trognon de pomme* an apple core

trois NUMBER
three ◊ *à trois heures du matin* at three in the morning ◊ *Elle a trois ans.* She's three. ◊ *trois fois* three times
♦ **le trois février** the third of February

troisième ADJECTIVE
see also **troisième** NOUN
third ◊ *au troisième étage* on the third floor

la **troisième** NOUN
see also **troisième** ADJECTIVE
fourth year

🛈 *In French secondary schools, years are counted from the **sixième** (youngest) to **première** and **terminale** (oldest).*

◊ *Mon frère est en troisième.* My brother's in fourth year.

les **trois-quarts** MASC NOUN
three-quarters ◊ *les trois-quarts de la classe* three-quarters of the class

le **trombone** NOUN
1 trombone ◊ *Il joue du trombone.* He plays the trombone.
2 paper clip

la **trompe** NOUN
trunk ◊ *la trompe d'un éléphant* an elephant's trunk

tromper VERB
to deceive
♦ **se tromper** to make a mistake ◊ *Tout le monde peut se tromper.* Anyone can make a mistake.
♦ **se tromper de jour** to get the wrong day
♦ **Vous vous êtes trompé de numéro.** You've got the wrong number.

la **trompette** NOUN
trumpet ◊ *Il joue de la trompette.* He plays the trumpet.
♦ **Il a le nez en trompette.** He's got a turned-up nose.

le **tronc** NOUN
trunk ◊ *un tronc d'arbre* a tree trunk

trop ADVERB
1 too ◊ *Il conduit trop vite.* He drives too fast.

2 too much ◊ *J'ai trop mangé.* I've eaten too much.
♦ **trop de (1)** too much ◊ *J'ai acheté trop de pain.* I bought too much bread. ◊ *trois francs de trop* 3 francs too much
♦ **trop de (2)** too many ◊ *J'ai apporté trop de vêtements.* I've brought too many clothes.
♦ **trois personnes de trop** 3 people too many

le **tropique** NOUN
tropic

le **trottoir** NOUN
pavement

le **trou** NOUN
hole
♦ **J'ai eu un trou de mémoire.** My mind went blank.

trouble ADJECTIVE, ADVERB
cloudy ◊ *L'eau est trouble.* The water's cloudy.
♦ **Sans mes lunettes je vois trouble.** Without my glasses I can't see properly.

les **troubles** MASC NOUN
♦ **une période de troubles politiques** a period of political instability

trouer VERB
to make a hole in ◊ *Il a troué la moquette avec sa cigarette.* He made a hole in the carpet with his cigarette.

la **trouille** NOUN
♦ **avoir la trouille** (*informal*) to be scared to death

la **troupe** NOUN
troop
♦ **une troupe de théâtre** a theatre company

le **troupeau** NOUN (PL les **troupeaux**)
♦ **un troupeau de moutons** a flock of sheep
♦ **un troupeau de vaches** a herd of cows

la **trousse** NOUN
pencil case
♦ **une trousse de toilette** a toilet bag

trouver VERB
1 to find ◊ *Je ne trouve pas mes lunettes.* I can't find my glasses.
2 to think ◊ *Je trouve que c'est bête.* I think it's stupid.
♦ **se trouver** to be ◊ *Où se trouve la poste?* Where is the post office? ◊ *Marseille se trouve dans le sud de la France.* Marseilles is in the South of France.
♦ **se trouver mal** to pass out

T

le **truc** NOUN (*informal*)
> 1 thing ◊ *un truc en plastique* a thing made of plastic ◊ *J'ai plein de trucs à faire ce week-end.* I've got loads of things to do this weekend.
> 2 trick ◊ *Je vais te montrer un truc qui réussit à tous les coups.* I'll show you a trick that never fails.

la **truite** NOUN
> trout

le **T-shirt** NOUN
> T-shirt

TSVP ABBREVIATION (= *tournez s'il vous plaît*)
> PTO (= please turn over)

tu PRONOUN
> you ◊ *Est-ce que tu as un animal familier?* Have you got a pet?

le **tuba** NOUN
> 1 tuba ◊ *Je joue du tuba.* I play the tuba.
> 2 snorkel

le **tube** NOUN
> 1 tube ◊ *un tube de dentifrice* a tube of toothpaste
> ◆ **un tube de rouge à lèvres** a lipstick
> 2 hit ◊ *Ça va être le tube de l'été.* It's going to be this summer's hit.

tuer VERB
> to kill
> ◆ **se tuer** to get killed ◊ *Il s'est tué dans un accident de voiture.* He got killed in a car accident.

tue-tête
> ◆ **à tue-tête** ADVERB
> at the top of one's voice ◊ *crier à tue-tête* to shout at the top of one's voice ◊ *Il chantait à tue-tête.* He was singing at the top of his voice.

la **tuile** NOUN
> tile ◊ *un toit en tuiles* a tiled roof

la **tunique** NOUN
> tunic

la **Tunisie** NOUN
> Tunisia

tunisien ADJECTIVE (FEM SING **tunisienne**)
> Tunisian

le **tunnel** NOUN
> tunnel
> ◆ **le tunnel sous la Manche** the Channel Tunnel

turbulent ADJECTIVE
> boisterous

turc ADJECTIVE, NOUN (FEM SING **turque**)
> Turkish ◊ *Il parle turc.* He speaks Turkish.
> ◆ **un Turc** a Turk (*man*)
> ◆ **une Turque** a Turk (*woman*)

la **Turquie** NOUN
> Turkey

tutoyer VERB
> ◆ **tutoyer quelqu'un** to address somebody as "tu"

> *i* **tutoyer quelqu'un** means to use **tu** when speaking to someone, rather than **vous**. Use **tu** only when talking to one person and when that person is someone of your own age or younger or whom you know well; use **vous** to everyone else. If in doubt use **vous**.

> ◆ **On se tutoie?** Shall we use "tu" to each other?

le **tuyau** NOUN (PL les **tuyaux**)
> 1 pipe
> ◆ **un tuyau d'arrosage** a hosepipe
> 2 tip ◊ *Il m'a donné un bon tuyau.* (*informal*) He gave me a handy tip.

la **TVA** NOUN (= *taxe sur la valeur ajoutée*)
> VAT

le **tympan** NOUN
> eardrum

le **type** NOUN (*informal*)
> guy ◊ *C'est un type formidable.* He's a great guy.

typique ADJECTIVE
> typical

le **tyran** NOUN
> tyrant ◊ *C'est un vrai tyran.* He's a real tyrant.

le/la **tzigane** NOUN
> gipsy

U

l' **UE** FEM NOUN (= *Union européenne*)
    the EU (= European Union)

un ARTICLE, PRONOUN, ADJECTIVE
    1 a ◊ *un garçon* a boy
    an ◊ *un œuf* an egg
    2 one ◊ *l'un des meilleurs* one of
    the best ◊ *un citron et deux oranges*
    one lemon and two oranges
    ◊ *Combien de timbres? – Un.* How
    many stamps? – One. ◊ *Elle a un an.*
    She's one year old.
  ♦ **l'un ..., l'autre ...** one ..., the other ...
    ◊ *L'un est grand, l'autre est petit.* One
    is tall, the other is short.
  ♦ **les uns ..., les autres ...** some ...,
    others ... ◊ *Les uns marchaient, les
    autres couraient.* Some were walking,
    others were running.
  ♦ **l'un ou l'autre** either of them ◊ *Prends
    l'un ou l'autre, ça m'est égal.* Take
    either of them, I don't mind.
  ♦ **un par un** one by one ◊ *Ils entraient
    un par un.* They went in one by one.

unanime ADJECTIVE
    unanimous

l' **unanimité** FEM NOUN
  ♦ **à l'unanimité** unanimously

une ARTICLE, PRONOUN, ADJECTIVE
    1 a ◊ *une fille* a girl
    an ◊ *une pomme* an apple
    2 one ◊ *une pomme et deux
    bananes* one apple and two bananas
    ◊ *Combien de cartes postales? – Une.*
    How many postcards? – One. ◊ *à une
    heure du matin* at one in the
    morning ◊ *l'une des meilleures* one
    of the best
  ♦ **l'une ..., l'autre ...** one ..., the other ...
    ◊ *L'une est grande, l'autre est petite.*
    One is tall, the other is short.
  ♦ **les unes..., les autres...** some ...,
    others ... ◊ *Les unes marchaient, les
    autres couraient.* Some were walking,
    others were running.
  ♦ **l'une ou l'autre** either of them
    ◊ *Prends l'une ou l'autre, ça m'est
    égal.* Take either of them, I don't
    mind.
  ♦ **une par une** one by one ◊ *Elles
    entraient une par une.* They went in
    one by one.

uni ADJECTIVE
    1 plain ◊ *un tissu uni* a plain fabric
    2 close-knit ◊ *une famille unie* a
    close-knit family

l' **uniforme** MASC NOUN
    uniform

l' **union** FEM NOUN
    union
  ♦ **l'Union européenne** the European
    Union
  ♦ **l'ex-Union soviétique** the former
    Soviet Union

unique ADJECTIVE
    unique ◊ *Tout individu a des
    empreintes uniques.* Everyone's
    fingerprints are unique. ◊ *C'est une
    occasion unique.* It's a unique
    opportunity.
  ♦ **Il est fils unique.** He's an only child.
  ♦ **Elle est fille unique.** She's an only
    child.

uniquement ADVERB
    only

l' **unité** FEM NOUN
    1 unity ◊ *l'unité européenne*
    European unity
    2 unit ◊ *une unité de mesure* a unit
    of measurement

l' **univers** MASC NOUN
    universe

universitaire ADJECTIVE
    university ◊ *un diplôme universitaire*
    a university degree
  ♦ **faire des études universitaires** to
    study at university

l' **université** FEM NOUN
    university ◊ *aller à l'université* to go
    to university

l' **urgence** FEM NOUN
  ♦ **C'est une urgence.** It's urgent.
  ♦ **Il n'y a pas urgence.** It's not urgent.
  ♦ **le service des urgences** the accident
    and emergency department
  ♦ **Il a été transporté d'urgence à
    l'hôpital.** He was rushed to hospital.
  ♦ **Téléphonez d'urgence.** Phone as soon
    as possible.

urgent ADJECTIVE
    urgent

l' **urine** FEM NOUN
    urine

les **USA** MASC NOUN
    USA
  ♦ **aux USA (1)** in the USA
  ♦ **aux USA (2)** to the USA

l' **usage** MASC NOUN
    use ◊ *à usage interne* for internal use
    ◊ *à usage externe* for external use
    only

◆**hors d'usage** out of action ◇ *Cet appareil est hors d'usage.* That machine's out of action.

usagé ADJECTIVE
1 old ◇ *un manteau usagé* an old coat
2 used ◇ *une seringue usagée* a used syringe

l'**usager** MASC NOUN
user ◇ *les usagers de la route* road users

usé ADJECTIVE
worn ◇ *Mon jean est un peu usé.* My jeans are a bit worn.

s'**user** VERB
to wear out ◇ *Mes baskets se sont usées en quinze jours.* My trainers wore out in two weeks.

l'**usine** FEM NOUN
factory ◇ *une usine de sardines* a sardine factory

l'**ustensile** MASC NOUN
◆**un ustensile de cuisine** a kitchen utensil

usuel ADJECTIVE (FEM SING **usuelle**)
everyday ◇ *la langue usuelle* everyday language

utile ADJECTIVE
useful

l'**utilisation** FEM NOUN
use ◇ *L'utilisation des calculatrices est interdite.* It is forbidden to use calculators.

utiliser VERB
to use

l'**utilité** FEM NOUN
use ◇ *Cet objet n'est pas d'une grande utilité.* This object isn't much use.

V

va VERB *see* **aller**

les **vacances** FEM NOUN
holidays ◊ *aller en vacances* to go on holiday ◊ *être en vacances* to be on holiday
- **les vacances de Noël** the Christmas holidays
- **les vacances de Pâques** the Easter holidays
- **les grandes vacances** the summer holidays

le **vacancier** NOUN
holiday-maker

la **vacancière** NOUN
holiday-maker

le **vacarme** NOUN
racket ◊ *Qu'est-ce que c'est que ce vacarme?* What's all this racket?

le **vaccin** NOUN
vaccination

la **vaccination** NOUN
vaccination ◊ *La vaccination est obligatoire.* Vaccination is compulsory.

vacciner VERB
to vaccinate ◊ *se faire vacciner contre la rubéole* to be vaccinated against German measles

la **vache** NOUN
~~see also~~ **vache** ADJECTIVE
cow

vache ADJECTIVE (*informal*)
~~see also~~ **vache** NOUN
mean ◊ *C'est vraiment vache, ce qu'il a dit.* What he said was really mean.
◊ *Il est vache.* He's a mean sod.

vachement ADVERB (*informal*)
really ◊ *Viens te baigner, l'eau est vachement chaude.* Come in the water, it's really warm.

le **vagabond** NOUN
tramp

le **vagin** NOUN
vagina

la **vague** NOUN
~~see also~~ **vague** ADJECTIVE
wave (*in sea*)
- **une vague de chaleur** a heat wave

vague ADJECTIVE
~~see also~~ **vague** NOUN
vague ◊ *J'ai un vague souvenir de lui.* I vaguely remember him.

vain ADJECTIVE
- **en vain** in vain

vaincre VERB
1 to defeat ◊ *L'armée a été vaincue.* The army was defeated.
2 to overcome ◊ *Il a réussi à vaincre sa timidité.* He managed to overcome his shyness.

le **vainqueur** NOUN
winner

vais VERB *see* **aller**
- **Je vais écrire à mes cousins.** I'm going to write to my cousins.

le **vaisseau** NOUN (PL les **vaisseaux**)
- **un vaisseau spatial** a spaceship
- **un vaisseau sanguin** a blood vessel

la **vaisselle** NOUN
1 washing-up ◊ *Je vais faire la vaisselle.* I'll do the washing-up.
2 dishes ◊ *Tu peux ranger la vaisselle s'il te plaît?* Can you put the dishes away please?

valable ADJECTIVE
valid ◊ *Ce billet d'avion est valable un an.* This plane ticket is valid for one year.

le **valet** NOUN
jack (*in card games*) ◊ *le valet de carreau* the jack of diamonds

la **valeur** NOUN
value ◊ *sans valeur* of no value
- **des objets de valeur** valuables ◊ *Ne laissez pas d'objets de valeur dans votre chambre.* Don't leave any valuables in your room.

valider VERB
to stamp ◊ *Vous devez faire valider votre billet avant votre départ.* You must get your ticket stamped before you leave.

la **valise** NOUN
suitcase
- **faire sa valise** to pack

la **vallée** NOUN
valley

valoir VERB
to be worth ◊ *Ça vaut combien?* How much is it worth? ◊ *Cette voiture vaut très cher.* This car's worth a lot of money.
- **Ça vaut mieux.** That would be better. ◊ *Il vaut mieux ne rien dire.* It would be better to say nothing.
- **valoir la peine** to be worth it ◊ *Ça vaudrait la peine d'essayer.* It would be worth a try.

le **vampire** NOUN

☞

vampire

le **vandalisme** NOUN
vandalism

la **vanille** NOUN
vanilla ◊ *une glace à la vanille* a vanilla ice cream

la **vanité** NOUN
vanity

vaniteux ADJECTIVE (FEM SING **vaniteuse**)
conceited

se **vanter** VERB
to boast

la **vapeur** NOUN
steam ◊ *des légumes cuits à la vapeur* steamed vegetables

la **varappe** NOUN
rock climbing ◊ *faire de la varappe* to go rock climbing

variable ADJECTIVE
changeable (*weather*)

la **varicelle** NOUN
chickenpox ◊ *Elle a la varicelle.* She's got chickenpox.

varié ADJECTIVE
varied ◊ *Son travail est très varié.* His job is very varied.

varier VERB
to vary
♦ **Le menu varie tous les jours.** The menu changes every day.

la **variété** NOUN
variety ◊ *Il n'y a pas beaucoup de variété.* There isn't much variety.
♦ **une émission de variétés** a television variety show

vas VERB *see* **aller**

le **vase** NOUN
see also **la vase**
vase

la **vase** NOUN
see also **le vase**
mud

vaste ADJECTIVE
vast

vaudrait, vaut VERB *see* **valoir**

le **vautour** NOUN
vulture

le **veau** NOUN (PL les **veaux**)
1 calf (*animal*)
2 veal (*meat*)

vécu VERB *see* **vivre**
♦ **Il a vécu à Paris pendant dix ans.** He lived in Paris for ten years.

la **vedette** NOUN
1 star ◊ *une vedette de cinéma* a film star
2 motor boat

♦ **une vedette de police** a police launch

végétal ADJECTIVE (MASC PL **végétaux**)
vegetable ◊ *l'huile végétale* vegetable oil

végétarien ADJECTIVE (FEM SING **végétarienne**)
vegetarian ◊ *Je suis végétarien.* I'm a vegetarian.

la **végétation** NOUN
vegetation

le **véhicule** NOUN
vehicle

la **veille** NOUN
the day before ◊ *la veille de son départ* the day before he left ◊ *la veille au soir* the previous evening
♦ **la veille de Noël** Christmas Eve
♦ **la veille du jour de l'An** New Year's Eve

veiller VERB
to stay up
♦ **veiller sur quelqu'un** to watch over somebody

veinard ADJECTIVE (*informal*)
♦ **Qu'est-ce qu'il est veinard!** He's such a lucky devil!

la **veine** NOUN
vein
♦ **avoir de la veine** (*informal*) to be lucky

le/la **véliplanchiste** NOUN
windsurfer

le **vélo** NOUN
bike ◊ *faire du vélo* to go cycling
♦ **un vélo tout-terrain** a mountain bike

le **vélomoteur** NOUN
moped

le **velours** NOUN
velvet ◊ *une robe en velours* a velvet dress
♦ **le velours côtelé** corduroy ◊ *un pantalon en velours côtelé* corduroy trousers

les **vendanges** FEM NOUN
grape harvest SING ◊ *On fait les vendanges en septembre.* The grape harvest is in September.

le **vendeur** NOUN
shop assistant

la **vendeuse** NOUN
shop assistant

vendre VERB
to sell
♦ **vendre quelque chose à quelqu'un** to sell somebody something ◊ *Il m'a vendu son vélo.* He sold me his bike.
♦ **"à vendre"** "for sale"

le **vendredi** NOUN

1 Friday ◇ *Aujourd'hui, nous sommes vendredi.* It's Friday today.
2 on Friday ◇ *Il est venu vendredi.* He came on Friday.
♦ **le vendredi** on Fridays ◇ *Je joue au foot le vendredi.* I play football on Fridays.
♦ **tous les vendredis** every Friday
♦ **vendredi dernier** last Friday
♦ **vendredi prochain** next Friday
♦ **le Vendredi saint** Good Friday

vénéneux ADJECTIVE (FEM SING **vénéneuse**)
poisonous (*plant*) ◇ *un champignon vénéneux* a poisonous mushroom

la **vengeance** NOUN
revenge

se **venger** VERB
to get revenge

venimeux ADJECTIVE (FEM SING **venimeuse**)
poisonous (*animal*) ◇ *un serpent venimeux* a poisonous snake

le **venin** NOUN
poison

venir VERB
to come ◇ *Il viendra demain.* He'll come tomorrow. ◇ *Il est venu nous voir.* He came to see us.
♦ **venir de** to have just ◇ *Je viens de le voir.* I've just seen him. ◇ *Je viens de lui téléphoner.* I've just phoned him.
♦ **faire venir quelqu'un** to call somebody out ◇ *faire venir le médecin* to call the doctor out

le **vent** NOUN
wind ◇ *Il y a du vent.* It's windy.

la **vente** NOUN
sale
♦ **en vente** on sale ◇ *Ce modèle est en vente dans les grands magasins.* This model is on sale in the department stores.
♦ **la vente par téléphone** telesales
♦ **une vente aux enchères** an auction

le **ventilateur** NOUN
fan (*for cooling*)

le **ventre** NOUN
stomach ◇ *avoir mal au ventre* to have stomachache

venu VERB see **venir**

le **ver** NOUN
worm
♦ **un ver de terre** an earthworm

le **verbe** NOUN
verb

le **verdict** NOUN
verdict

le **verger** NOUN
orchard

verglacé ADJECTIVE
icy ◇ *La route était verglacée.* The road was icy.

le **verglas** NOUN
black ice

véridique ADJECTIVE
truthful

la **vérification** NOUN
check ◇ *une vérification d'identité* an identity check

vérifier VERB
to check

véritable ADJECTIVE
real ◇ *C'était un véritable cauchemar.* It was a real nightmare.
♦ **en cuir véritable** made of real leather

la **vérité** NOUN
truth ◇ *dire la vérité* to tell the truth

verni ADJECTIVE
varnished
♦ **des chaussures vernies** patent leather shoes

vernir VERB
to varnish

le **vernis** NOUN
varnish ◇ *le vernis à ongles* nail varnish

verra, verrai, verras VERB see **voir**
♦ **on verra ...** we'll see ...

le **verre** NOUN
1 glass ◇ *une table en verre* a glass table ◇ *un verre d'eau* a glass of water
♦ **boire un verre** to have a drink
2 lens (*of spectacles*) ◇ *des verres de contact* contact lenses

verrez, verrons, verront VERB see **voir**

le **verrou** NOUN
bolt (*on door*)

verrouiller VERB
to bolt ◇ *N'oublie pas de verrouiller la porte du garage.* Don't forget to bolt the garage door.

la **verrue** NOUN
wart

le **vers** NOUN
see also **vers** PREPOSITION
line (*of poetry*) ◇ *au troisième vers* in the third line

vers PREPOSITION
see also **vers** NOUN
1 towards ◇ *Il allait vers la gare.* He was going towards the station.
2 at about ◇ *Il est rentré chez lui vers cinq heures.* He went home at about 5 o'clock.

verse
♦ **à verse** ADVERB

V

☞

◊ *Il pleut à verse.* It's pouring with rain.

le **Verseau** NOUN
Aquarius ◊ *Georges est Verseau.*
Georges is Aquarius.

le **versement** NOUN
instalment ◊ *en cinq versements* in 5 instalments

verser VERB
to pour ◊ *Est-ce que tu peux me verser un verre d'eau?* Could you pour me a glass of water?

la **version** NOUN
1 version
2 translation (*from the foreign language*)
♦ **un film en version originale** a film in the original language

le **verso** NOUN
back (*of sheet of paper*)
♦ **voir au verso** see overleaf

vert ADJECTIVE
green

la **vertèbre** NOUN
vertebra

vertical ADJECTIVE (MASC PL **verticaux**)
vertical

le **vertige** NOUN
vertigo ◊ *avoir le vertige* to have vertigo

la **verveine** NOUN
verbena tea

la **vessie** NOUN
bladder

la **veste** NOUN
jacket

le **vestiaire** NOUN
1 cloakroom (*in theatre, museum*)
2 changing room (*at sports ground*)

le **vestibule** NOUN
hall

le **vêtement** NOUN
garment
♦ **les vêtements** clothes

le/la **vétérinaire** NOUN
vet ◊ *Elle est vétérinaire.* She's a vet.

le **veuf** NOUN
widower ◊ *Il est veuf.* He's a widower.

veuille, veuillez, veuillons, veulent, veut VERB see **vouloir**
♦ **Veuillez fermer la porte en sortant.** Please shut the door when you go out.

la **veuve** NOUN
widow ◊ *Elle est veuve.* She's a widow.

veux VERB see **vouloir**

vexer VERB
♦ **vexer quelqu'un** to hurt somebody's feelings
♦ **se vexer** to be offended

la **viande** NOUN
meat
♦ **la viande hachée** mince

vibrer VERB
to vibrate

le **vice** NOUN
vice

vicieux ADJECTIVE (FEM SING **vicieuse**)
lecherous ◊ *Il est un peu vicieux.* He's a bit of a lecher.

la **victime** NOUN
victim

la **victoire** NOUN
victory

vide ADJECTIVE
see also **vide** NOUN
empty

le **vide** NOUN
see also **vide** ADJECTIVE
vacuum ◊ *emballé sous vide* vacuum-packed
♦ **avoir peur du vide** to be afraid of heights

la **vidéo** NOUN
see also **vidéo** ADJECTIVE
video

vidéo ADJECTIVE (MASC, FEM, PL)
see also **vidéo** NOUN
video ◊ *une cassette vidéo* a video cassette ◊ *un jeu vidéo* a video game ◊ *une caméra vidéo* a video camera

le **vidéoclip** NOUN
music video

le **vidéoclub** NOUN
video shop

vider VERB
to empty

la **vie** NOUN
life
♦ **être en vie** to be alive

vieil ADJECTIVE
vieil is used with a masculine singular noun in place of vieux when the noun begins with a vowel sound.
old ◊ *un vieil arbre* an old tree ◊ *un vieil homme* an old man

le **vieillard** NOUN
old man

vieille ADJECTIVE (MASC SING **vieux**)
see also **vieille** NOUN
old ◊ *une vieille dame* an old lady
♦ **une vieille fille** an old maid

la **vieille** NOUN
see also **vieille** ADJECTIVE

old woman
♦**Eh bien, ma vieille ...** (*informal*) Well, my dear ...

la **vieillesse** NOUN
old age

vieillir VERB
to age ◊ *Il a beaucoup vieilli depuis la dernière fois que je l'ai vu.* He's aged a lot since I last saw him.

viendrai, vienne, viens VERB *see* **venir**
♦**Je viendrai dès que possible.** I'll come as soon as possible.
♦**Je voudrais que tu viennes.** I'd like you to come.
♦**Viens ici!** Come here!

la **Vierge** NOUN
| *see also* **vierge** ADJECTIVE |
Virgo ◊ *Pascal est Vierge.* Pascal is Virgo.
♦**la Vierge** the Virgin Mary

vierge ADJECTIVE
| *see also* **Vierge** NOUN |
1 virgin ◊ *Il est vierge.* He's a virgin.
2 blank ◊ *une cassette vierge* a blank cassette

le **Viêt-Nam** NOUN
Vietnam

vietnamien ADJECTIVE, NOUN (FEM SING **vietnamienne**)
Vietnamese
♦**un Vietnamien** a Vietnamese (*man*)
♦**une Vietnamienne** a Vietnamese (*woman*)
♦**les Vietnamiens** the Vietnamese

vieux ADJECTIVE (FEM SING **vieille**)
| *see also* **vieux** NOUN |
old ◊ *Il fait plus vieux que son âge.* He looks older than he is.
♦**un vieux garçon** a bachelor

le **vieux** NOUN
| *see also* **vieux** ADJECTIVE |
old man ◊ *Eh bien, mon vieux ...* (*informal*) Well, my old mate ...
♦**les vieux** old people

vieux jeu ADJECTIVE (MASC, FEM, PL)
old-fashioned ◊ *Il est un peu vieux jeu.* He's a bit old-fashioned.

vif ADJECTIVE (FEM SING **vive**)
1 sharp (*mentally*) ◊ *Il est très vif.* He's very sharp.
♦**avoir l'esprit vif** to be quick-witted
2 crisp ◊ *L'air est plus vif à la campagne qu'en ville.* The air is crisper in the country than in the town.
3 bright (*colour*) ◊ *un bleu vif* a bright blue

la **vigne** NOUN
vine

♦**des champs de vigne** vineyards

le **vigneron** NOUN
wine grower

la **vignette** NOUN
tax disc

le **vignoble** NOUN
vineyard

vilain ADJECTIVE
1 naughty ◊ *C'est très vilain de dire des mensonges.* It's very naughty to tell lies.
2 ugly ◊ *Il n'est pas vilain.* He's not bad-looking.

la **villa** NOUN
villa ◊ *une villa en multipropriété* a time-share villa

le **village** NOUN
village

le **villageois** NOUN
villager

la **villageoise** NOUN
villager

la **ville** NOUN
town ◊ *Je vais en ville.* I'm going into town.
♦**une grande ville** a city

le **vin** NOUN
wine ◊ *le vin blanc* white wine ◊ *le vin rouge* red wine ◊ *le vin de pays* the local wine ◊ *le vin ordinaire* table wine

le **vinaigre** NOUN
vinegar

la **vinaigrette** NOUN
French dressing

vingt NUMBER
twenty ◊ *Elle a vingt ans.* She's twenty. ◊ *à vingt heures* at 8 p.m.
♦**le vingt février** the twentieth of February
♦**vingt et un** twenty-one
♦**vingt-deux** twenty-two

la **vingtaine** NOUN
about twenty ◊ *une vingtaine de personnes* about twenty people
♦**Il a une vingtaine d'années.** He's about twenty.

vingtième ADJECTIVE
twentieth

le **viol** NOUN
rape

violemment ADVERB
violently

la **violence** NOUN
violence

violent ADJECTIVE
violent

violer VERB

V

☞

to rape

violet ADJECTIVE (FEM SING **violette**)
purple

la **violette** NOUN
violet (*flower*)

le **violon** NOUN
violin ◊ *Je joue du violon.* I play the violin.

le **violoncelle** NOUN
cello ◊ *Elle joue du violoncelle.* She plays the cello.

le/la **violoniste** NOUN
violinist

la **vipère** NOUN
viper

le **virage** NOUN
bend ◊ *une route pleine de virages dangereux* a road full of dangerous bends

la **virgule** NOUN
1 comma
2 decimal point ◊ *trois virgule cinq* three point five

le **virus** NOUN
virus

vis VERB see **vivre**
see also **vis** NOUN
♦ *Je vis en Écosse.* I live in Scotland.

la **vis** NOUN
see also **vis** VERB
screw

le **visa** NOUN
visa

le **visage** NOUN
face ◊ *Elle a le visage rond.* She's got a round face.

vis-à-vis de PREPOSITION
with regard to ◊ *Ce n'est pas très juste vis-à-vis de lui.* It's not very fair to him.

viser VERB
to aim at ◊ *Il faut viser la cible.* You have to aim at the target.

la **visibilité** NOUN
visibility

visible ADJECTIVE
visible

la **visière** NOUN
peak (*of cap*)

la **visite** NOUN
visit
♦ **rendre visite à quelqu'un** to visit somebody ◊ *Je vais rendre visite à mon grand-père.* I'm going to visit my grandfather.
♦ **avoir de la visite** to have visitors ◊ *Nous avons de la visite aujourd'hui.* We've got visitors today.

♦ **une visite guidée** a guided tour
♦ **une visite médicale** a medical examination

visiter VERB
to visit

le **visiteur** NOUN
visitor

la **visiteuse** NOUN
visitor

le **vison** NOUN
mink (*fur*) ◊ *un manteau en vison* a mink coat

vit VERB see **vivre**
♦ **Il vit chez ses parents.** He lives with his parents.

vital ADJECTIVE (MASC PL **vitaux**)
vital ◊ *C'est une question vitale.* It's of vital importance.

la **vitamine** NOUN
vitamin

vite ADVERB
1 quick ◊ *Vite, ils arrivent!* Quick, they're coming! ◊ *Je peux aller dire au revoir à Claire? – Oui, mais fais vite!* Can I go and say goodbye to Claire? – Yes, but be quick! ◊ *Prenons la voiture, ça ira plus vite.* Let's take the car, it'll be quicker.
♦ **Le temps passe vite.** Time flies.
2 fast ◊ *Il roule trop vite.* He drives too fast.
3 soon ◊ *Il va vite oublier.* He'll soon forget.
♦ **Il a vite compris.** He understood immediately.

la **vitesse** NOUN
1 speed ◊ *à toute vitesse* at top speed ◊ *Nous sommes rentrés à toute vitesse.* We rushed back home.
2 gear ◊ *en première vitesse* in first gear

le **viticulteur** NOUN
wine grower ◊ *Mon oncle est viticulteur.* My uncle is a wine grower.

le **vitrail** NOUN (PL les **vitraux**)
stained-glass window

la **vitre** NOUN
window ◊ *Il a cassé une vitre.* He broke a window.

la **vitrine** NOUN
shop window

vivant ADJECTIVE
1 living ◊ *les êtres vivants* living creatures ◊ *les expériences sur les animaux vivants* experiments on live animals
2 lively ◊ *Elle est très vivante.* She's very lively.

vive ADJECTIVE (MASC SING **vif**)

see also **vive** EXCLAMATION

[1] sharp (*mentally*) ◊ *Elle est très vive.* She's very sharp.

[2] bright (*colour*)

♦**à vive allure** at a brisk pace

♦**de vive voix** in person ◊ *Je te le dirai de vive voix.* I'll tell you about it when I see you.

vive EXCLAMATION

see also **vive** ADJECTIVE

♦**Vive le roi!** Long live the king!

vivement EXCLAMATION

♦**Vivement les vacances!** Roll on the holidays!

vivre VERB

to live ◊ *J'aimerais vivre à l'étranger.* I'd like to live abroad. ◊ *Et ton grand-père? Il vit encore?* What about your grandfather? Is he still alive?

vlan EXCLAMATION

wham!

la **VO** NOUN

♦**un film en VO** a film in the original language

le **vocabulaire** NOUN

vocabulary

la **vocation** NOUN

vocation

le **vœu** NOUN (PL les **vœux**)

wish ◊ *faire un vœu* to make a wish ◊ *Meilleurs vœux de bonne année!* Best wishes for the New Year!

la **vogue** NOUN

fashion ◊ *C'est très en vogue en ce moment.* It's very fashionable at the moment.

voici PREPOSITION

[1] this is ◊ *Voici mon frère et voilà ma sœur.* This is my brother and that's my sister.

[2] here is ◊ *Tu as perdu ton stylo? Tiens, en voici un autre.* Have you lost your pen? Here's another one.

♦**Le voici!** Here he is! ◊ *Tu veux tes clés? Tiens, les voici!* You want your keys? Here you are!

la **voie** NOUN

lane ◊ *une route à trois voies* a 3-lane road

♦**par voie buccale** orally ◊ *à prendre par voie buccale* to be taken orally

♦**la voie ferrée** the railway track

voilà PREPOSITION

[1] there is ◊ *Tiens! Voilà Paul.* Look! There's Paul. ◊ *Tu as perdu ton stylo? Tiens, en voilà un autre.* Have you lost your pen? There's another one.

♦**Les voilà!** There they are!

[2] that is ◊ *Voilà ma sœur.* That's my sister.

le **voile** NOUN

see also **la voile**

veil ◊ *un voile de mariée* a wedding veil

la **voile** NOUN

see also **le voile**

[1] sail

[2] sailing ◊ *faire de la voile* to go sailing

♦**un bateau à voiles** a sailing boat

le **voilier** NOUN

sailing boat

voir VERB

Present tense:	
je vois	nous voyons
tu vois	vous voyez
il/elle voit	ils/elles voient
Past participle:	
vu	

to see ◊ *Venez me voir quand vous serez à Paris.* Come and see me when you're in Paris. ◊ *Je ne vois pas pourquoi il a fait ça.* I can't see why he did that.

♦**faire voir quelque chose à quelqu'un** to show somebody something ◊ *Il m'a fait voir sa collection de timbres.* He showed me his stamp collection.

♦**se voir** to be obvious ◊ *Est-ce que cette tache se voit?* Does that stain show? ◊ *Ça fait des années qu'elle n'a pas joué au tennis – Oui, ça se voit!* She hasn't played tennis for years – Yes, you can tell!

♦**avoir quelque chose à voir avec** to have something to do with ◊ *Ça n'a rien à voir avec lui, c'est entre toi et moi.* It's nothing to do with him, it's between you and me.

♦**Je ne peux vraiment pas la voir.** (*informal*) I really can't stand her.

le **voisin** NOUN

neighbour

le **voisinage** NOUN

♦**dans le voisinage** in the vicinity

la **voisine** NOUN

neighbour

la **voiture** NOUN

car ◊ *une voiture de sport* a sports car

la **voix** NOUN (PL les **voix**)

[1] voice ◊ *à voix basse* in a low voice

♦**à haute voix** aloud

2 vote ◊ *Il a obtenu cinquante pour cent des voix.* He got 50% of the votes.

le **vol** NOUN
1 flight
♦ **à vol d'oiseau** as the crow flies
♦ **le vol à voile** gliding
2 theft ◊ *un vol à main armée* an armed robbery

la **volaille** NOUN
poultry

le **volant** NOUN
1 steering wheel
2 shuttlecock

le **volcan** NOUN
volcano

la **volée** NOUN
volley (*in tennis*)
♦ **rattraper une balle à la volée** to catch a ball in mid-air

voler VERB
1 to fly ◊ *J'aimerais savoir voler.* I'd like to be able to fly.
2 to steal ◊ *On a volé mon appareil photo.* My camera's been stolen.
♦ **voler quelque chose à quelqu'un** to steal something from somebody ◊ *Ça n'est pas son stylo, il me l'a volé.* That's not his pen, he stole it from me.
♦ **voler quelqu'un** to rob somebody

le **volet** NOUN
shutter

le **voleur** NOUN
thief
♦ **Au voleur !** Stop thief!

la **voleuse** NOUN
thief

le **volley** NOUN
volleyball ◊ *jouer au volley* to play volleyball

le/la **volontaire** NOUN
volunteer

la **volonté** NOUN
willpower ◊ *Il a beaucoup de volonté.* He's got a lot of willpower.
♦ **la bonne volonté** goodwill
♦ **la mauvaise volonté** lack of goodwill

volontiers ADVERB
1 gladly ◊ *Je l'aiderais volontiers s'il me le demandais.* I'd gladly help him if he asked me.
2 please ◊ *Voulez-vous boire quelque chose? – Volontiers!* Would you like something to drink? – Yes, please!

le **volume** NOUN
volume ◊ *un dictionnaire en deux volumes* a two-volume dictionary

volumineux ADJECTIVE (FEM SING **volumineuse**)
bulky

vomir VERB
to vomit ◊ *Il a vomi toute la nuit.* He was vomiting all night.

vont VERB *see* **aller**

VOS ADJECTIVE
your ◊ *Rangez vos jouets, les enfants!* Children, put your toys away! ◊ *Merci pour vos fleurs, M. Durand.* Thanks for your flowers, Mr Durand.

le **vote** NOUN
vote

voter VERB
to vote

votre ADJECTIVE (PL **vos**)
your ◊ *C'est votre manteau?* Is this your coat?

vôtre PRONOUN
♦ **le vôtre** yours ◊ *J'aime bien notre prof de maths, mais le vôtre est plus patient.* I like our maths teacher, but yours is more patient. ◊ *À qui est cette écharpe? C'est la vôtre?* Whose is this scarf? Is it yours?
♦ **À la vôtre!** Cheers!

vôtres PRONOUN
♦ **les vôtres** yours ◊ *J'ai oublié mes lunettes de soleil. Vous avez apporté les vôtres?* I've forgotten my sunglasses. Have you brought yours?

voudra, voudrai, voudrais, voudras, voudrez, voudrons, voudront VERB
see **vouloir**
♦ **Je voudrais ...** I'd like ... ◊ *Je voudrais deux litres de lait, s'il vous plaît.* I'd like two litres of milk, please.

vouloir VERB

Present tense:	
je veux	nous voulons
tu veux	vous voulez
il/elle veut	ils/elles veulent
Past participle:	
voulu	

to want ◊ *Elle veut un vélo pour Noël.* She wants a bike for Christmas. ◊ *Je ne veux pas de dessert.* I don't want any pudding. ◊ *Il ne veut pas venir.* He doesn't want to come. ◊ *On va au cinéma? – Si tu veux.* Shall we go to the cinema? – If you like.
♦ **Je veux bien.** I'll be happy to. ◊ *Je veux bien le faire à ta place si ça t'arrange.* I don't mind doing it for you if you prefer.

♦ **Voulez-vous une tasse de thé? – Je veux bien.** Would you like a cup of tea? – Yes please.

♦ **sans le vouloir** without meaning to ◊ *Je l'ai vexé sans le vouloir.* I upset him without meaning to.

♦ **en vouloir à quelqu'un** to be angry at somebody ◊ *Il m'en veut de ne pas l'avoir invité à mon anniversaire.* He's angry at me for not inviting him to my birthday party.

♦ **vouloir dire** to mean ◊ *Qu'est-ce que ça veut dire?* What does that mean?

voulu VERB *see* **vouloir**

vous PRONOUN
[1] you ◊ *Vous aimez la pizza?* Do you like pizza?
[2] to you ◊ *Je vous écrirai bientôt.* I'll write to you soon.
[3] yourself ◊ *Vous vous êtes fait mal?* Have you hurt yourself?

♦ **vous-même** yourself ◊ *Vous l'avez fait vous-même?* Did you do it yourself?

vouvoyer VERB
♦ **vouvoyer quelqu'un** to address somebody as "vous"

> ❶ *vouvoyer quelqu'un* means to use *vous* when speaking to someone, rather than *tu*. Use *tu* only when talking to one person and when that person is someone of your own age or younger or whom you know well; use *vous* to everyone else. If in doubt use *vous*.

♦ **Est-ce que je dois vouvoyer ta sœur?** Should I use "vous" to your sister?

le **voyage** NOUN
journey ◊ *Avez-vous fait bon voyage?* Did you have a good journey?

♦ **Bon voyage!** Have a good trip!

voyager VERB
to travel

le **voyageur** NOUN
passenger

la **voyageuse** NOUN
passenger

voyaient, voyais, voyait VERB *see* **voir**

la **voyelle** NOUN
vowel

voyez, voyiez, voyions VERB *see* **voir**

voyons VERB *see* **voir**
[1] let's see ◊ *Voyons ce qu'on peut faire.* Let's see what we can do.
[2] come on ◊ *Voyons, sois raisonnable!* Come on, be reasonable!

le **voyou** NOUN
hooligan

vrac
♦ **en vrac** ADVERB
loose ◊ *du thé en vrac* loose tea

vrai ADJECTIVE
true ◊ *une histoire vraie* a true story ◊ *C'est vrai?* Is that true?

♦ **à vrai dire** to tell the truth

vraiment ADVERB
really

vraisemblable ADJECTIVE
likely ◊ *C'est peu vraisemblable.* That's not very likely. ◊ *Il va falloir trouver une excuse vraisemblable.* We'll have to find a convincing excuse.

le **VTT** NOUN (= *vélo tout-terrain*)
mountain bike

vu VERB *see* **voir**
♦ **être bien vu** to be popular (*person*) ◊ *Est-ce qu'il est bien vu à l'école?* Is he popular at school?

♦ **être mal vu** to be disapproved of ◊ *C'est mal vu de fumer ici.* They don't like people smoking here.

la **vue** NOUN
[1] eyesight ◊ *J'ai une mauvaise vue.* I've got bad eyesight.
[2] view ◊ *Il y a une belle vue d'ici.* There's a lovely view from here.

♦ **à vue d'œil** visibly ◊ *Elle grandit à vue d'œil.* Every time you see her, she's got taller.

vulgaire ADJECTIVE
vulgar ◊ *Ne dit pas ça, c'est très vulgaire.* Don't say that, it's very vulgar.

V

W

le **wagon** NOUN
railway carriage

le **wagon-lit** NOUN (PL les **wagons-lits**)
sleeper (*on train*)

le **wagon-restaurant** NOUN (PL les **wagons-restaurants**)
restaurant car

le **walkman** ® NOUN
Walkman ®

wallon ADJECTIVE, NOUN (FEM SING **wallonne**)
Walloon (*French-speaking Belgian*)
◆ **les Wallons** the French-speaking Belgians

la **Wallonie** NOUN
French-speaking Belgium

les **W.-C.** MASC NOUN
toilet SING

le **Web** NOUN
Web

le **webmaster** NOUN
webmaster

le **webzine** NOUN
webzine

le **week-end** NOUN
weekend

le **western** NOUN
western (*film*)

le **whisky** NOUN (PL les **whiskies**)
whisky

X

xénophobe ADJECTIVE
  prejudiced against foreigners
la **xénophobie** NOUN

  prejudice against foreigners
le **xylophone** NOUN
  xylophone

Y

y PRONOUN
  there ◊ *Nous y sommes allés l'été dernier.* We went there last summer. ◊ *Regarde dans le tiroir: je pense que les clés y sont.* Look in the drawer: I think the keys are in there.
  y replaces phrases with à in constructions like the ones below:
♦ **Je pensais à l'examen. – Mais arrête d'y penser!** I was thinking about the exam. – Well, stop thinking about it!
♦ **Je ne m'attendais pas à ça. – Moi, je m'y attendais.** I wasn't expecting that. – I was expecting it.
le **yaourt** NOUN
  yoghurt ◊ *un yaourt nature* a plain yoghurt ◊ *un yaourt aux fruits* a fruit

  yoghurt
les **yeux** MASC NOUN (SING **œil**)
  eyes ◊ *Elle a les yeux bleus.* She's got blue eyes.
le **yoga** NOUN
  yoga
le **yoghourt** NOUN
  yoghurt
la **Yougoslavie** NOUN
  Yugoslavia
♦ **l'ex-Yougoslavie** the former Yugoslavia
youpi EXCLAMATION
  Yippee!
le **yoyo** NOUN
  yo-yo

Z

zapper VERB
  to channel hop
le **zèbre** NOUN
  zebra
le **zéro** NOUN
  zero
♦ **Ils ont gagné trois à zéro.** They won three-nil.
zézayer VERB
  to lisp ◊ *Il zézaie.* He's got a lisp.

le **zigzag** NOUN
♦ **faire des zigzags** to zigzag
la **zone** NOUN
  zone
♦ **une zone industrielle** an industrial estate
le **zoo** NOUN
  zoo
zut EXCLAMATION
  Oh heck!

FRENCH IN ACTION

PUZZLES AND WORDGAMES

The puzzles and wordgames on the following pages have been designed to give you practice in using your dictionary. Make sure you read the "Dictionary Skills" section at the front of this book before you start. Don't worry, there are answers at the end of the wordgames in case you get really stuck!

WORDGAME 1

▶ CHOOSING THE RIGHT TRANSLATION ◀

Complete the crossword below by looking up the English words in the list and finding the correct French translations. There is a slight catch, however! All the English words have more than one French translation, but only one will fit correctly into each part of the crossword.

1. CLASS	7. CALF
2. THROW	8. PLACE
3. KNOW	9. DINNER
4. FIND	10. STAY
5. NUT	11. HARD
6. TAKE	12. LATE

WORDGAME 2

▶ PARTS OF SPEECH ◀

In each sentence below a word has been shaded. Put a tick in the appropriate box to show whether it's a **noun**, **adjective**, **adverb** or **verb** each time. Look in the section "Dictionary Skills" at the front of the book to remind you what nouns, adjectives, adverbs and verbs are. Remember, there may be more than one entry for each word.

SENTENCE	NOUN	ADJ	ADV	VERB
1. La **ferme** de mes parents est en Alsace.				
2. Il n'est pas **franc**.				
3. Le magasin **ferme** dans deux minutes.				
4. Le **dîner** est à 20 heures.				
5. Tu veux **goûter** ma mousse au chocolat?				
6. Je n'aime **pas** la bière.				
7. C'est un **faux** passeport.				
8. J'entends des **pas** dans l'escalier.				
9. Ce film nous a fait **rire**.				
10. Cette voiture est **mal** garée.				

295

▶ NOUNS ◀

a. This list contains the feminine form of some French nouns. Use your dictionary to find the **masculine** form. Remember, the masculine form usually appears in a separate entry.

b. Use your dictionary to find the **plural** of the following nouns. Remember, the plural form appears in brackets and in bold after the singular form.

MASCULINE	FEMININE
	danseuse
	boulangère
	Américaine
	animatrice
	avocate
	Parisienne
	libraire
	téléspectatrice
	pionne
	veuve

SINGULAR	PLURAL
chou	
canal	
bateau	
sapeur-pompier	
neveu	
travail	
vœu	
voix	
œil	
croque-monsieur	

WORDGAME 4

► ADJECTIVES ◄

Use the French-English side of your dictionary to find the **feminine singular** form of these adjectives. Remember, the feminine singular form appears in brackets and in bold after the masculine form.

MASCULINE	FEMININE
1. naturel	
2. beau	
3. heureux	
4. américain	
5. gros	
6. blanc	
7. faux	
8. sec	
9. favori	
10. frais	
11. bon	
12. fou	
13. public	
14. naïf	

WORDGAME 5

▶ VERB TENSES ◀

Use the verb tables on pages 316 to 329 to help you fill in the blanks in the table below.

INFINITIVE	PRESENT	IMPERFECT	FUTURE
faire		je	
se laver	il		
voir			nous
finir			elle
avoir		il	
aller	vous		
être	elles		
vouloir		ils	
devoir	tu		
mettre			je
dire		il	
pouvoir			nous

WORDGAME 6

► «MOTS CODÉS» ◄

In the boxes below, the letters of eight French words have been replaced by numbers. A number represents the same letter each time.

Try to crack the code and find the eight words. If you need help, use your dictionary.

Here is a clue: all the words you are looking for have something to do with CLOTHES.

1. P¹ | 2 | 3 | 4 | 2 | 5 | 6 | 3

2. 7 | 8 | P¹ | E⁹

3. 10 | 11 | 3 | 11 | 7 | 8 | P¹ | 9

4. 10 | 2 | 3 | 4 | 9 | 2 | 8

5. P¹ | 8 | 5 | 5

6. 12 | 13 | 2 | P¹ | 9 | 2 | 8

7. 12 | 13 | 2 | 8 | 14 | 14 | 9 | 4 | 4 | 9

8. 12 | 13 | 2 | 8 | 14 | 14 | 8 | 15 | 9

WORDGAME 7

▶ «MOTS CUISINÉS» ◀

Here is a list of French words for things you will find in the kitchen. Unfortunately, they have all been jumbled up. Try to work out what each word is and put the word in the boxes on the right. You will see there are five shaded boxes below. The five letters in the shaded boxes make up *another* French word for an object you can find in the kitchen.

1. féac   **Tu prends du sucre dans ton _____ ?**

2. rever   **Encore un _____ de vin?**

3. lesvisale   **je déteste faire la _____.**

4. rascosele   **Elle a fait cuire les pâtes dans une grande _____.**

5. grifo   **Le fromage est dans le _____.**

The word you are looking for is:

WORDGAME 1

1. classe
2. lancer
3. connaître
4. trouver
5. noisette
6. emmener
7. mollet
8. endroit
9. dîner
10. rester
11. dur
12. tard

WORDGAME 2

1. noun
2. adjective
3. verb
4. noun
5. verb
6. adverb
7. adjective
8. noun
9. verb
10. adverb

WORDGAME 3a

Masculine forms
1. danseur
2. boulanger
3. Américain
4. animateur
5. avocat
6. Parisien
7. libraire
8. téléspectateur
9. pion
10. veuf

WORDGAME 3b

Plural forms
1. choux
2. canaux
3. bateaux
4. sapeurs-pompiers
5. neveux
6. travaux
7. vœux
8. voix
9. yeux
10. croque-monsieur

WORDGAME 4

1. naturelle
2. belle
3. heureuse
4. américaine
5. grosse
6. blanche
7. fausse
8. sèche
9. favorite
10. fraîche
11. bonne
12. folle
13. publique
14. naïve

WORDGAME 5

1. je faisais
2. il se lave
3. nous verrons
4. elle finira
5. il avait
6. vous allez
7. elles sont
8. ils voulaient
9. tu dois
10. je mettrai
11. il disait
12. nous pourrons

WORDGAME 6

1. pantalon
2. jupe
3. minijupe
4. manteau
5. pull
6. chapeau
7. chaussette
8. chaussure

WORDGAME 7

1. café
2. verre
3. vaisselle
4. casserole
5. frigo

Missing word – évier

CORRESPONDENCE

▶ LETTER

Address of sender

Nathalie Leduc
18 rue des Tulipes
65004 Gervais

Place & Date

Gervais, le 14 février 2001

Chers Grand-maman et Grand-papa

Merci beaucoup pour les CD que vous m'avez envoyés. Vous avez vraiment bien choisi puisqu'il s'agit de mes deux chanteurs préférés: je n'arrête pas de les écouter!

Sinon, rien de nouveau ici. Je passe presque tout mon temps à préparer mes examens, qui commencent dans quinze jours. J'espère que je les réussirai tous, mais j'ai le trac pour mon examen de maths: c'est la matière que j'aime le moins.

Maman m'a dit que vous partiez en Crète la semaine prochaine. Je vous souhaite de très bonnes vacances, et je suis sûre que vous reviendrez tout bronzés.

Grosses bises

Nathalie

Or:
Affectueusement
Amicalement

STARTING A PERSONAL LETTER

Merci pour ta lettre.	*Thank you for your letter.*
Ça m'a fait plaisir d'avoir de tes nouvelles.	*It was lovely to hear from you.*
Je suis désolé de ne pas t'avoir écrit plus tôt.	*I'm sorry I didn't write sooner.*

ENDING A PERSONAL LETTER

Écris-moi bientôt!	*Write soon!*
Embrasse Sophie pour moi.	*Give my love to Sophie.*
Paul te fait ses amitiés.	*Paul sends his best wishes.*

CORRESPONDENCE

▶ EMAIL

> To give your email address to
> someone in French, say:
> **"Alice at n t net point co point f r"**

	Nouveau Message
A:	alice@ntnet.co.fr
De:	patrick@onemo.net
Objet:	show
Cc:	antoine@blt.com
Copie cachée:	

Fichier joint   Envoyer

Salut!

Je viens d'acheter le nouvel album de Rockstar. Il est génial!

J'ai trois billets gratuits pour leur show à Orléans samedi prochain, et j'espère que vous pourrez venir avec moi tous les deux!

À bientôt!

Nouveau message	New message
A	To
De	From
Objet	Subject
Cc	cc
Copie cachée	bcc
Fichier joint	Attachment
Envoyer	Send

TELEPHONE

▶ WHEN YOUR NUMBER ANSWERS

– **Bonjour! J'aimerais parler à Valérie.**
– Hello! Could I speak to Valérie, please?

– **Pourriez-vous lui demander de me rappeler, s'il vous plaît?**
– Would you ask him/her to call me back, please?

– **Je rappellerai dans une demi-heure.**
– I'll call back in half an hour.

▶ ANSWERING THE TELEPHONE

– **Bonjour! C'est Marc à l'appareil.**
– Hello! It's Marc speaking.

– **C'est moi.**
– Speaking.

– **Qui est à l'appareil?**
– Who's speaking?

▶ WHEN THE SWITCHBOARD ANSWERS

– **C'est de la part de qui?**
– Who shall I say is calling?

– **Je vous le/la passe.**
– I'm putting you through.

– **Ne quittez pas.**
– Please hold.

– **Voulez-vous laisser un message?**
– Would you like to leave a message?

▶ DIFFICULTIES

– **Je n'arrive pas à avoir le numéro.**
– I can't get through.

– **Je suis désolé, j'ai dû faire un faux numéro.**
– I'm sorry, I dialled the wrong number.

– **La ligne est très mauvaise.**
– This is a very bad line.

– **Leur téléphone est en dérangement.**
– Their phone is out of order.

NUMBERS

1	**un(e)**	13	**treize**	50	**cinquante**
2	**deux**	14	**quatorze**	60	**soixante**
3	**trois**	15	**quinze**	70	**soixante-dix**
4	**quatre**	16	**seize**	71	**soixante et onze**
5	**cinq**	17	**dix-sept**	72	**soixante-douze**
6	**six**	18	**dix-huit**	80	**quatre-vingts**
7	**sept**	19	**dix-neuf**	81	**quatre-vingt-un(e)**
8	**huit**	20	**vingt**	90	**quatre-vingt-dix**
9	**neuf**	21	**vingt et un(e)**	91	**quatre-vingt-onze**
10	**dix**	22	**vingt-deux**	100	**cent**
11	**onze**	30	**trente**		
12	**douze**	40	**quarante**		

101	**cent un(e)**	1,000	**mille**
300	**trois cents**	2,000	**deux mille**
301	**trois cent un(e)**	1,000,000	**un million**

▶ FRACTIONS *etc*

1/2	**un demi**
1/3	**un tiers**
2/3	**deux tiers**
1/4	**un quart**
1/5	**un cinquième**
0.5	**zéro virgule cinq (0,5)**
3.4	**trois virgule quatre (3,4)**
10%	**dix pour cent**
100%	**cent pour cent**

▶ EXAMPLES

il habite au dix	he lives at number ten
à la page dix-neuf	on page nineteen
au chapitre sept	in chapter seven

NUMBERS

1st	**premier (1ᵉʳ), première (1ʳᵉ)**	14th	**quatorzième (14ᵉ)**
2nd	**deuxième (2ᵉ)**	15th	**quinzième (15ᵉ)**
3rd	**troisième (3ᵉ)**	16th	**seizième (16ᵉ)**
4th	**quatrième (4ᵉ)**	17th	**dix-septième (17ᵉ)**
5th	**cinquième (5ᵉ)**	18th	**dix-huitième (18ᵉ)**
6th	**sixième (6ᵉ)**	19th	**dix-neuvième (19ᵉ)**
7th	**septième (7ᵉ)**	20th	**vingtième (20ᵉ)**
8th	**huitième (8ᵉ)**	21st	**vingt et unième (21ᵉ)**
9th	**neuvième (9ᵉ)**	22nd	**vingt-deuxième (22ᵉ)**
10th	**dixième (10ᵉ)**	30th	**trentième (30ᵉ)**
11th	**onzième (11ᵉ)**	100th	**centième (100ᵉ)**
12th	**douzième (12ᵉ)**	101st	**cent unième (101ᵉ)**
13th	**treizième (13ᵉ)**	1000th	**millième (1000ᵉ)**

Pierre est arrivé premier

► EXAMPLES

il habite au cinquième (étage)   he lives on the fifth floor
il est arrivé troisième   he came in third
échelle au vingt-cinq millième   scale one to twenty-five thousand

DATE

▶ LES JOURS DE LA SEMAINE

lundi
mardi
mercredi
jeudi
vendredi
samedi
dimanche

Quand?
lundi
le lundi
tous les lundis
mardi dernier
vendredi prochain
samedi en huit
samedi en quinze

▶ LES MOIS

janvier
février
mars
avril
mai
juin
juillet
août
septembre
octobre
novembre
décembre

Quand?
en février
le 1er décembre
le premier décembre
en 2001
en deux mille un

Quel jour sommes-nous?
Nous sommes le...
dimanche 1er octobre or
  dimanche premier octobre
lundi 26 février or
  lundi vingt-six février

▶ DAYS OF THE WEEK

Monday
Tuesday
Wednesday
Thursday
Friday
Saturday
Sunday

When?
on Monday
on Mondays
every Monday
last Tuesday
next Friday
a week on Saturday
two weeks on Saturday

▶ MONTHS OF THE YEAR

January
February
March
April
May
June
July
August
September
October
November
December

When?
in February
on 1 December
on the first of December
in 2001
in two thousand and one

What day is it?
It's...
Sunday, 1 October or
  Sunday, the first of October
Monday, 26 February or
  Monday, the twenty-sixth of February

TIME

Quelle heure est-il? What time is it?
Il est...   **It's...**

une heure

une heure dix

une heure et quart

une heure et demie

deux heures moins vingt

deux heures moins le quart

À quelle heure?   **At what time?**

à minuit

à midi

à une heure (de l'après-midi)

à huit heures (du soir)

> In France times are often given in the twenty-four hour clock.

à 11.15
or
onze heures quinze

à 20.45
or
vingt heures quarante-cinq

FALSE FRIENDS

French ≠ English

actuel ≠ actual

le système **actuel**	→	the **present** system
The film is based on **actual** events.	→	Le film repose sur des faits **réels**.

actuellement ≠ actually

Elle enseigne **actuellement** à Toulouse.	→	She is **currently** teaching in Toulouse.
Did it **actually** happen?	→	Est-ce que c'est **vraiment** arrivé?

agenda ≠ agenda

J'ai perdu mon **agenda**.	→	I've lost my **diary**.
on the **agenda**	→	à l'**ordre du jour**

attendre ≠ attend

J'**attends** d'avoir un appartement à moi.	→	I'm **waiting** until I've got a flat of my own.
They **attended** the meeting.	→	Ils ont **assisté à** la réunion.

compréhensif ≠ comprehensive

Mon patron s'est montré très **compréhensif**.	→	My boss was very **understanding**.
a **comprehensive** list	→	une liste **complète**

courrier ≠ courier

Est-ce qu'il y avait du **courrier** ce matin?	→	Was there any **post** this morning?
They sent it by **courier**.	→	Ils l'ont envoyé par **coursier**.

délai ≠ delay

J'ai demandé un **délai** d'une semaine. → I've asked for a week's **extension**.

There will be **delays** to trains on the London-Brighton line. → Il y aura des **retards** sur la ligne Londres-Brighton.

demander ≠ demand

J'ai **demandé** la permission. → I've **asked for** permission.

I **demand** to see your superior. → J'**exige de** voir votre chef.

effectivement ≠ effectively

Oui, **effectivement**. → Yes, **indeed**.

to use sth **effectively** → utiliser **efficacement** qch

engin ≠ engine

un **engin** thermonucléaire → a thermonuclear **device**

My car has a 1.6 litre **engine**. → Ma voiture a un **moteur** de 1,6 litres.

éventuel ≠ eventual

une solution **éventuelle** → a **possible** solution

The **eventual** winner of the election. → Le candidat **qui a finalement** remporté les élections.

éventuellement ≠ eventually

Nous pourrions **éventuelle-ment** y aller en voiture. → We could **possibly** go by car.

He **eventually** became Prime Minister. → Il est **finalement** devenu Premier ministre.

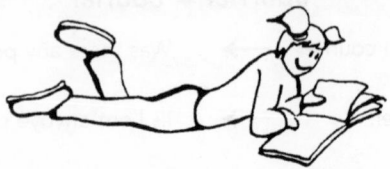

lecture ≠ lecture

La **lecture** est mon passe-temps favori. → **Reading** is my favourite hobby.

He's giving a **lecture** on crocodiles. → Il donne une **conférence** sur les crocodiles.

librairie ≠ library

On trouve cette BD dans la plupart des **librairies**. → You can buy this comic in most **bookshops**.

the public **library** → la **bibliothèque** municipale

location ≠ location

location de voitures → car **rental**

A hotel set in a beautiful **location**. → Un hôtel situé dans un **endroit** magnifique.

malicieux ≠ malicious

un sourire **malicieux** → a **mischievous** smile

a **malicious** rumour → une rumeur **malveillante**

parking ≠ parking

un **parking** souterrain → an underground **car park**

"no **parking**" → "**stationnement** interdit"

passer un examen ≠ to pass an exam

Je **passe** mon examen de maths demain. → I'm **sitting** my maths exam tomorrow.

I've **passed** my maths exam. → J'ai **réussi** mon examen de maths.

pétrole ≠ petrol

le **pétrole** de la mer du Nord → North Sea **oil**

This car uses too much **petrol**. → Cette voiture consomme trop d'**essence**.

résumer ≠ resume

Pouvez-vous **résumer** cet
article?
→
Could you **summarize** this article?

They've **resumed** work.
→
Ils ont **repris** le travail.

sensible ≠ sensible

Elle est très **sensible**
→
She's very **sensitive**.

Be **sensible**!
→
Sois **raisonnable**!

stage ≠ stage

Caroline a fait un **stage**
chez Collins.
→
Caroline did **work experience** at
Collins.

on **stage**
→
sur **scène**

the first **stage** of the operation
→
la première **phase** de l'opération

supporter ≠ support

Elle ne **supporte** pas
qu'on la critique.
→
She can't **stand** being criticized.

My mum has always
supported me.
→
Ma mère m'a toujours **soutenu**

sympathique ≠ sympathetic

Ce sont des gens très
sympathiques
→
They're very **nice** people.

She was very **sympathetic**
when I told her what
had happened.
→
Elle s'est montrée très **compatissante**
quand je lui ai expliqué ce qui
s'était passé.

312

FRENCH VERB TABLES

▶ CONTENTS

French Irregular Verb Forms

FRENCH VERB TABLES

This section contains fourteen important French verbs that you need to learn. All French verbs fall into two main categories – **regular** and **irregular** – and it is important to learn which verbs fall into which category.

The tables are arranged in the following order:

1. Regular verbs – **aimer**, **finir**, **attendre** and **se laver**
2. Very important irregular verbs – **avoir** and **être**
3. Other common irregular verbs – **aller**, **devoir**, **dire**, **faire**, **mettre**, **pouvoir**, **voir** and **vouloir**

At the top of each table you will find the infinitive, the imperative and the past participle. The lower section of the table shows you how to form six tenses of the verb:

PRESENT	e.g. je fais = **I do** or **I am doing**
PRESENT SUBJUNCTIVE*	e.g. je fasse = **I do**
IMPERFECT	e.g. je faisais = **I was doing** or **I did**
PERFECT	e.g. j'ai fait = **I did** or **I have done**
FUTURE	e.g. je ferai = **I will do**
CONDITIONAL	e.g. je ferais = **I would do**

*The French side of your dictionary will tell you which words must be followed by the subjunctive.

▶ REGULAR VERBS

There are three groups of regular verbs:

1. "-ER" verbs = verbs that end in -**er** like **aimer** on p316
2. "-IR" verbs = verbs that end in -**ir** like **finir** on p317
3. "-RE" verbs = verbs that end in -**re** like **attendre** on p318

They are called regular verbs because they follow one of three set patterns. When you have learnt these patterns, you will be able to form *any* regular verb.

HOW TO FORM A REGULAR VERB

i. a) To form the present, imperfect or present subjunctive tense, take the infinitive minus the last two letters. This is called the stem e.g. *aimer* → **aim-**, *finir* → **fin-**, and *attendre* → **attend-**

   b) To form the future or conditional tense, the stem is the whole infinitive for "-ER" and "-IR" verbs and the infinitive minus its final "E" for "-RE" verbs e.g. *aimer* → **aimer**, *finir* → **finir** and *attendre* → **attendr-**

ii. Next add the appropriate **ending**. You need to ask yourself three questions:

   a) **What sort of** verb am I using (-ER, -IR, -RE)?
   b) **Who** is doing the verb? (je, tu, il *etc*)?
   c) **When** are they doing it (in the present, the past or the future)?

Look at the verb tables for **aimer**, **finir** and **attendre**. The verb endings are underlined. These endings can be tagged onto the stem of *any* regular verb.

▶ AVOIR AND ÊTRE

Avoir (to have) and **être** (to be) are very important verbs which **must** be learnt. You use them when you want to say "**I have**" *etc* or "**I am**" *etc*. The present tense of **avoir** or **être** is also used to form the **perfect tense**. In most cases, **avoir** is used to form the perfect, but reflexive verbs like **se laver** (to wash oneself) and verbs of movement like **aller** (to go) and **venir** (to come) use **être** – e.g. the French for both "he's gone" and "he went" is **il est allé**, not **il a allé**. The following verbs use **être**:

aller	mourir	retourner
arriver	naître	revenir
descendre	partir	sortir
devenir	passer	tomber
entrer	rentrer	venir
monter	rester	

HOW TO FORM THE PERFECT TENSE

a) Take the infinitive of a French verb e.g. **donner**
b) Check if the verb uses **avoir** or **être** to form the perfect tense. e.g. **donner** uses **avoir**
c) If the person involved is **il** (he), take the appropriate present form of **avoir** – **il a**
d) Add the **past participle** – **il a donné**. The past participle is shown near the top of each verb table. If you want to form the past participle of *any* regular verb, simply take the infinitive of the verb, knock off the last two letters and add the following endings:

   "-ER" verbs add **é** – e.g. aimer → aim**é**
   "-IR" verbs add **i** – e.g. finir → fin**i**
   "-RE" verbs add **u** – e.g. attendre → attend**u**

e) **il a donné** means "he gave" or "he has given"

▶ IRREGULAR VERBS

Many French verbs are irregular and this means you have to learn them individually. There are tables of the most important irregular verbs such as **avoir** (to have), **être** (to be) and **faire** (to do) in this section. When you are translating from French and meet an unfamiliar verb form, you may be able to guess from the context that it comes from one of these verbs, and you can use the verb table to check. The most common irregular verb parts are listed on the French side of the dictionary, so you could also look there.

HOW TO USE THE VERB TABLES

You will find some useful example phrases at the top of each verb table, but if you can't find what you need to say or write in French there, use the verb table itself to help you. Imagine that you want to find the French for "he wants". Here's how to do it:

a) Look up **want** on the English-French side of the dictionary to find the French translation
b) French translation = **vouloir**
c) Turn to the verb tables section of your dictionary and find **vouloir**
d) When does he want it? He wants it **now**, so look for the heading *PRESENT*
e) Who wants it? **He** does. The French for "he" is **il** so look for **il** under the *PRESENT* heading
f) The French for "he wants" is "**il veut**"

▶ aimer

to like *or* to love

IMPERATIVE

aime
aimons
aimez

EXAMPLE PHRASES

*Tu **aimes** le chocolat?* Do you like chocolate?
*Je t'**aime**.* I love you.
*J'**aimerais** aller en Grèce.* I'd like to go to Greece.

PAST PARTICIPLE

aimé

PRESENT

j'	aime
tu	aimes
il	aime
nous	aimons
vous	aimez
ils	aiment

PERFECT

j'	ai aimé
tu	as aimé
il	a aimé
nous	avons aimé
vous	avez aimé
ils	ont aimé

FUTURE

j'	aimerai
tu	aimeras
il	aimera
nous	aimerons
vous	aimerez
ils	aimeront

PRESENT SUBJUNCTIVE

j'	aime
tu	aimes
il	aime
nous	aimions
vous	aimiez
ils	aiment

IMPERFECT

j'	aimais
tu	aimais
il	aimait
nous	aimions
vous	aimiez
ils	aimaient

CONDITIONAL

j'	aimerais
tu	aimerais
il	aimerait
nous	aimerions
vous	aimeriez
ils	aimeraient

FRENCH VERB TABLES

▶ finir

to finish

EXAMPLE PHRASES

Finis ta soupe! Finish your soup!
J'**ai fini!** I've finished!
Je **finirai** mes devoirs demain. I'll
  finish my homework tomorrow.

IMPERATIVE

finis
finissons
finissez

PAST PARTICIPLE

fini

PRESENT

je	finis
tu	finis
il	finit
nous	finissons
vous	finissez
ils	finissent

PERFECT

j'	ai fini
tu	as fini
il	a fini
nous	avons fini
vous	avez fini
ils	ont fini

FUTURE

je	finirai
tu	finiras
il	finira
nous	finirons
vous	finirez
ils	finiront

PRESENT SUBJUNCTIVE

je	finisse
tu	finisses
il	finisse
nous	finissions
vous	finissiez
ils	finissent

IMPERFECT

je	finissais
tu	finissais
il	finissait
nous	finissions
vous	finissiez
ils	finissaient

CONDITIONAL

je	finirais
tu	finirais
il	finirait
nous	finirions
vous	finiriez
ils	finiraient

FRENCH VERB TABLES

▶ attendre

to wait

IMPERATIVE

attends
attendons
attendez

EXAMPLE PHRASES

Attends-*moi!* Wait for me!
Tu **attends** *depuis longtemps?* Have you been waiting long?
*Je l'***ai attendu** *à la poste.* I waited for him at the post office.

PAST PARTICIPLE

attendu

PRESENT

j'	attends
tu	attends
il	attend
nous	attendons
vous	attendez
ils	attendent

PERFECT

j'	ai attendu
tu	as attendu
il	a attendu
nous	avons attendu
vous	avez attendu
ils	ont attendu

FUTURE

j'	attendrai
tu	attendras
il	attendra
nous	attendrons
vous	attendrez
ils	attendront

PRESENT SUBJUNCTIVE

j'	attende
tu	attendes
il	attende
nous	attendions
vous	attendiez
ils	attendent

IMPERFECT

j'	attendais
tu	attendais
il	attendait
nous	attendions
vous	attendiez
ils	attendaient

CONDITIONAL

j'	attendrais
tu	attendrais
il	attendrait
nous	attendrions
vous	attendriez
ils	attendraient

FRENCH VERB TABLES

▶ se laver

to wash (oneself)

EXAMPLE PHRASES

*Je **me lave** chaque matin.* I have a
  wash every morning.
*Il **s'est lavé** les mains.* He washed
  his hands.
*Elle va **se laver** les cheveux.* She's going
  to wash her hair.

IMPERATIVE

lave-toi
lavons-nous
lavez-vous

PAST PARTICIPLE

lavé

PRESENT

je	me lave
tu	te laves
il	se lave
nous	nous lavons
vous	vous lavez
ils	se lavent

PERFECT

je	me suis lavé
tu	t'es lavé
il	s'est lavé
nous	nous sommes lavés
vous	vous êtes lavés
ils	se sont lavés

FUTURE

je	me laverai
tu	te laveras
il	se lavera
nous	nous laverons
vous	vous laverez
ils	se laveront

PRESENT SUBJUNCTIVE

je	me lave
tu	te laves
il	se lave
nous	nous lavions
vous	vous laviez
ils	se lavent

IMPERFECT

je	me lavais
tu	te lavais
il	se lavait
nous	nous lavions
vous	vous laviez
ils	se lavaient

CONDITIONAL

je	me laverais
tu	te laverais
il	se laverait
nous	nous laverions
vous	vous laveriez
ils	se laveraient

FRENCH VERB TABLES

▶ avoir

to have

IMPERATIVE

aie
ayons
ayez

EXAMPLE PHRASES

Il **a** les yeux bleus. He's got blue eyes.
Quel âge **as**-tu? How old are you?
Il **a eu** un accident. He's had an
   accident.
J'**avais** faim. I was hungry.

PAST PARTICIPLE

eu

PRESENT

j' ai
tu as
il a
nous avons
vous avez
ils ont

PRESENT SUBJUNCTIVE

j' aie
tu aies
il ait
nous ayons
vous ayez
ils aient

PERFECT

j' ai eu
tu as eu
il a eu
nous avons eu
vous avez eu
ils ont eu

IMPERFECT

j' avais
tu avais
il avait
nous avions
vous aviez
ils avaient

FUTURE

j' aurai
tu auras
il aura
nous aurons
vous aurez
ils auront

CONDITIONAL

j' aurais
tu aurais
il aurait
nous aurions
vous auriez
ils auraient

FRENCH VERB TABLES

▶ être

to be

EXAMPLE PHRASES

Mon père est professeur. My father's a teacher.
Quelle heure est-il? Il est 10 heures. What time is it? – It's 10 o'clock
Ils ne sont pas encore arrivés. They haven't arrived yet.

IMPERATIVE

sois
soyons
soyez

PAST PARTICIPLE

été

PRESENT

je suis
tu es
il est
nous sommes
vous êtes
ils sont

PERFECT

j' ai été
tu as été
il a été
nous avons été
vous avez été
ils ont été

FUTURE

je serai
tu seras
il sera
nous serons
vous serez
ils seront

PRESENT SUBJUNCTIVE

je sois
tu sois
il soit
nous soyons
vous soyez
ils soient

IMPERFECT

j' étais
tu étais
il était
nous étions
vous étiez
ils étaient

CONDITIONAL

je serais
tu serais
il serait
nous serions
vous seriez
ils seraient

FRENCH VERB TABLES

▶ aller

to go

IMPERATIVE

va
allons
allez

EXAMPLE PHRASES

*Vous **allez** au cinéma?* Are you going to the cinema?
*Je **suis allé** à Londres.* I went to London.
*Est-ce que tu **es** déjà **allé** en Allemagne?* Have you ever been to Germany?

PAST PARTICIPLE

allé

PRESENT

je	vais
tu	vas
il	va
nous	allons
vous	allez
ils	vont

PERFECT

je	suis allé
tu	es allé
il	est allé
nous	sommes allés
vous	êtes allés
ils	sont allés

FUTURE

j'	irai
tu	iras
il	ira
nous	irons
vous	irez
ils	iront

PRESENT SUBJUNCTIVE

j'	aille
tu	ailles
il	aille
nous	allions
vous	alliez
ils	aillent

IMPERFECT

j'	allais
tu	allais
il	allait
nous	allions
vous	alliez
ils	allaient

CONDITIONAL

j'	irais
tu	irais
il	irait
nous	irions
vous	iriez
ils	iraient

FRENCH VERB TABLES

▶ devoir

to have to

EXAMPLE PHRASES

Je **dois** aller faire les courses ce matin.
  I have to do the shopping this morning.
Il **a dû** faire ses devoirs hier soir. He had
  to do his homework last night.
Il **devait** prendre le train pour aller
  travailler. He had to go to work by train.

IMPERATIVE

dois
devons
devez

PAST PARTICIPLE

dû, due, dus

PRESENT

je	dois
tu	dois
il	doit
nous	devons
vous	devez
ils	doivent

PERFECT

j'	ai dû
tu	as dû
il	a dû
nous	avons dû
vous	avez dû
ils	ont dû

FUTURE

je	devrai
tu	devras
il	devra
nous	devrons
vous	devrez
ils	devront

PRESENT SUBJUNCTIVE

je	doive
tu	doives
il	doive
nous	devions
vous	deviez
ils	doivent

IMPERFECT

je	devais
tu	devais
il	devait
nous	devions
vous	deviez
ils	devaient

CONDITIONAL

je	devrais
tu	devrais
il	devrait
nous	devrions
vous	devriez
ils	devraient

FRENCH VERB TABLES

▶ dire

to say

IMPERATIVE

dis
disons
dites

EXAMPLE PHRASES

*Qu'est-ce qu'elle **dit**?* What is she saying?
*"Bonjour!" **a**-t-il **dit**.* "Hello!" he said.
*Il m'**a dit** que le film était nul.* He told me that the film was rubbish.

PAST PARTICIPLE

dit

PRESENT

je	dis
tu	dis
il	dit
nous	disons
vous	dites
ils	disent

PERFECT

j'	ai dit
tu	as dit
il	a dit
nous	avons dit
vous	avez dit
ils	ont dit

FUTURE

je	dirai
tu	diras
il	dira
nous	dirons
vous	direz
ils	diront

PRESENT SUBJUNCTIVE

je	dise
tu	dises
il	dise
nous	disions
vous	disiez
ils	disent

IMPERFECT

je	disais
tu	disais
il	disait
nous	disions
vous	disiez
ils	disaient

CONDITIONAL

je	dirais
tu	dirais
il	dirait
nous	dirions
vous	diriez
ils	diraient

FRENCH VERB TABLES

▶ faire

to do *or* to make

EXAMPLE PHRASES

*Qu'est-ce que tu **fais**?* What are
you doing?
*Qu'est-ce qu'il **a fait**?* What has he
done? *or* What did he do?
*J'**ai fait** un gâteau.* I've made a cake *or*
I made a cake.

IMPERATIVE

fais
faisons
faites

PAST PARTICIPLE

fait

PRESENT

je	fais
tu	fais
il	fait
nous	faisons
vous	faites
ils	font

PERFECT

j'	ai fait
tu	as fait
il	a fait
nous	avons fait
vous	avez fait
ils	ont fait

FUTURE

je	ferai
tu	feras
il	fera
nous	ferons
vous	ferez
ils	feront

PRESENT SUBJUNCTIVE

je	fasse
tu	fasses
il	fasse
nous	fassions
vous	fassiez
ils	fassent

IMPERFECT

je	faisais
tu	faisais
il	faisait
nous	faisions
vous	faisiez
ils	faisaient

CONDITIONAL

je	ferais
tu	ferais
il	ferait
nous	ferions
vous	feriez
ils	feraient

FRENCH VERB TABLES

▶ mettre

to put

IMPERATIVE

mets
mettons
mettez

EXAMPLE PHRASES

Mets ton manteau! Put your coat on!
*Où est-ce que tu **as mis** les clés?*
  Where have you put the keys?
*J'**ai mis** le livre sur la table.* I put
  the book on the table.

PAST PARTICIPLE

mis

PRESENT

je	mets
tu	mets
il	met
nous	mettons
vous	mettez
ils	mettent

PERFECT

j'	ai mis
tu	as mis
il	a mis
nous	avons mis
vous	avez mis
ils	ont mis

FUTURE

je	mettrai
tu	mettras
il	mettra
nous	mettrons
vous	mettrez
ils	mettront

PRESENT SUBJUNCTIVE

je	mette
tu	mettes
il	mette
nous	mettions
vous	mettiez
ils	mettent

IMPERFECT

je	mettais
tu	mettais
il	mettait
nous	mettions
vous	mettiez
ils	mettaient

CONDITIONAL

je	mettrais
tu	mettrais
il	mettrait
nous	mettrions
vous	mettriez
ils	mettraient

FRENCH VERB TABLES

▶ pouvoir

to be able

EXAMPLE PHRASES

*Je **peux** t'aider, si tu veux.* I can help
  you if you like.
*J'ai fait tout ce que j'**ai pu**.* I did all I could.
*Je ne **pourrai** pas venir samedi.* I won't
  be able to come on Saturday.

IMPERATIVE

the imperative of **pouvoir**
is not used

PAST PARTICIPLE

pu

PRESENT

je	peux
tu	peux
il	peut
nous	pouvons
vous	pouvez
ils	peuvent

PERFECT

j'	ai pu
tu	as pu
il	a pu
nous	avons pu
vous	avez pu
ils	ont pu

FUTURE

je	pourrai
tu	pourras
il	pourra
nous	pourrons
vous	pourrez
ils	pourront

PRESENT SUBJUNCTIVE

je	puisse
tu	puisses
il	puisse
nous	puissions
vous	puissiez
ils	puissent

IMPERFECT

je	pouvais
tu	pouvais
il	pouvait
nous	pouvions
vous	pouviez
ils	pouvaient

CONDITIONAL

je	pourrais
tu	pourrais
il	pourrait
nous	pourrions
vous	pourriez
ils	pourraient

FRENCH VERB TABLES

▶ voir

to see

IMPERATIVE

vois
voyons
voyez

PAST PARTICIPLE

vu

EXAMPLE PHRASES

*Venez me **voir** quand vous serez à Paris.*
   Come and see me when you're in Paris.
*Je ne **vois** rien sans mes lunettes.*
   I can't see anything without my glasses.
*Est-ce que tu l'**as vu**? Did you see*
   him? *or* Have you seen him?

PRESENT

je	vois
tu	vois
il	voit
nous	voyons
vous	voyez
ils	voient

PERFECT

j'	ai vu
tu	as vu
il	a vu
nous	avons vu
vous	avez vu
ils	ont vu

FUTURE

je	verrai
tu	verras
il	verra
nous	verrons
vous	verrez
ils	verront

PRESENT SUBJUNCTIVE

je	voie
tu	voies
il	voie
nous	voyions
vous	voyiez
ils	voient

IMPERFECT

je	voyais
tu	voyais
il	voyait
nous	voyions
vous	voyiez
ils	voyaient

CONDITIONAL

je	verrais
tu	verrais
il	verrait
nous	verrions
vous	verriez
ils	verraient

FRENCH VERB TABLES

▶ vouloir

to want

EXAMPLE PHRASES

*Elle **veut** un vélo pour Noël.*
  She wants a bike for Christmas.
*Ils **voulaient** aller au cinéma.*
  They wanted to go to the cinema.
*Tu **voudrais** une tasse de thé?*
  Would you like a cup of tea?

IMPERATIVE

veuille
veuillons
veuillez

PAST PARTICIPLE

voulu

PRESENT

je	veux
tu	veux
il	veut
nous	voulons
vous	voulez
ils	veulent

PERFECT

j'	ai voulu
tu	as voulu
il	a voulu
nous	avons voulu
vous	avez voulu
ils	ont voulu

FUTURE

je	voudrai
tu	voudras
il	voudra
nous	voudrons
vous	voudrez
ils	voudront

PRESENT SUBJUNCTIVE

je	veuille
tu	veuilles
il	veuille
nous	voulions
vous	vouliez
ils	veuillent

IMPERFECT

je	voulais
tu	voulais
il	voulait
nous	voulions
vous	vouliez
ils	voulaient

CONDITIONAL

je	voudrais
tu	voudrais
il	voudrait
nous	voudrions
vous	voudriez
ils	voudraient

FRENCH IRREGULAR VERB FORMS

The following list is a summary of the main forms of other irregular verbs that you are likely to come across. For the present tense, all **je** and **nous** forms are shown. The **il**, **vous** and **ils** forms are also included wherever the part of the verb that goes with them follows an unusual pattern. For the imperfect, future and present subjunctive tenses, only the **je** form is given.

INFINITIVE	PRESENT	PAST PARTICIPLE	IMPERFECT	FUTURE	PRESENT SUBJUNCTIVE
acheter	j'achète nous achetons ils achètent	acheté	j'achetais	j'achèterai	j'achète
appeler	j'appelle il appelle nous appelons	appelé	j'appelais	j'appellerai	j'appelle
apprendre	j'apprends nous apprenons vous apprenez ils apprennent	appris	j'apprenais	j'apprendrai	j'apprenne
s'asseoir	je m'assieds nous nous asseyons vous vous asseyez ils s'asseyent	assis	je m'asseyais	je m'assiérai	je m'asseye
battre	je bats il bat nous battons	battu	je battais	je battrai	je batte
boire	je bois nous buvons ils boivent	bu	je buvais	je boirai	je boive
bouillir	je bous nous bouillons	bouilli	je bouillais	je bouillirai	je bouille
conclure	je conclus nous concluons	conclu	je concluais	je conclurai	je conclue
conduire	je conduis nous conduisons	conduit	je conduisais	je conduirai	je conduise
connaître	je connais il connaît nous connaissons	connu	je connaissais	je connaîtrai	je connaisse
coudre	je couds nous cousons vous cousez ils cousent	cousu	je cousais	je coudrai	je couse
courir	je cours nous courons	couru	je courais	je courrai	je coure
couvrir	je couvre nous couvrons	couvert	je couvrais	je couvrirai	je couvre
craindre	je crains nous craignons	craint	je craignais	je craindrai	je craigne

INFINITIVE	PRESENT	PAST PARTICIPLE	IMPERFECT	FUTURE	PRESENT SUBJUNCTIVE
créer	je crée nous créons	créé	je créais	je créerai	je crée
croire	je crois nous croyons ils croient	cru	je croyais	je croirai	je croie
croître	je croîs nous croissons	crû crue crus crues	je croissais	je croîtrai	je croisse
cueillir	je cueille nous cueillons	cueilli	je cueillais	je cueillerai	je cueille
cuire	je cuis nous cuisons ils cuisent	cuit	je cuisais	je cuirai	je cuise
dormir	je dors nous dormons	dormi	je dormais	je dormirai	je dorme
écrire	j'écris nous écrivons	écrit	j'écrivais	j'écrirai	j'écrive
falloir	il faut	fallu	il fallait	il faudra	il faille
fuir	je fuis nous fuyons ils fuient	fui	je fuyais	je fuirai	je fuie
haïr	je hais nous haïssons ils haïssent	haï	je haïssais	je haïrai	je haïsse
jeter	je jette nous jetons ils jettent	jeté	je jetais	je jetterai	je jette
joindre	je joins nous joignons	joint	je joignais	je joindrai	je joigne
lever	je lève nous levons ils lèvent	levé	je levais	je lèverai	je lève
lire	je lis nous lisons	lu	je lisais	je lirai	je lise
manger	je mange nous mangeons	mangé	je mangeais	je mangerai	je mange
mentir	je mens nous mentons	menti	je mentais	je mentirai	je mente
mourir	je meurs nous mourons ils meurent	mort	je mourais	je mourrai	je meure
naître	je nais il naît nous naissons	né	je naissais	je naîtrai	je naisse
offrir	j'offre nous offrons	offert	j'offrais	j'offrirai	j'offre

INFINITIVE	PRESENT	PAST PARTICIPLE	IMPERFECT	FUTURE	PRESENT SUBJUNCTIVE
paraître	je parais il paraît nous paraissons	paru	je paraissais	je paraîtrai	je paraisse
partir	je pars nous partons	parti	je partais	je partirai	je parte
plaire	je plais il plaît nous plaisons	plu	je plaisais	je plairai	je plaise
pleuvoir	il pleut	plu	il pleuvait	il pleuvra	il pleuve
prendre	je prends nous prenons ils prennent	pris	je prenais	je prendrai	je prenne
recevoir	je reçois il reçoit ils reçoivent	reçu	je recevais	je recevrai	je reçoive
rire	je ris nous rions	ri	je riais	je rirai	je rie
savoir	je sais nous savons ils savent	su	je savais	je saurai	je sache
servir	je sers nous servons	servi	je servais	je servirai	je serve
sortir	je sors nous sortons	sorti	je sortais	je sortirai	je sorte
souffrir	je souffre nous souffrons	souffert	je souffrais	je souffrirai	je souffre
suffire	je suffis nous suffisons	suffi	je suffisais	je suffirai	je suffise
suivre	je suis nous suivons	suivi	je suivais	je suivrai	je suive
se taire	je me tais nous nous taisons	tu	je me taisais	je me tairai	je me taise
tenir	je tiens nous tenons ils tiennent	tenu	je tenais	je tiendrai	je tienne
vaincre	je vaincs il vainc nous vainquons	vaincu	je vainquais	je vaincrai	je vainque
valoir	je vaux il vaut nous valons	valu	je valais	je vaudrai	je vaille
venir	je viens nous venons ils viennent	venu	je venais	je viendrai	je vienne
vivre	je vis nous vivons	vécu	je vivais	je vivrai	je vive

A

a ARTICLE

*Use **un** for masculine nouns, **une** for feminine nouns.*

un MASC ◊ *a book* un livre ◊ *a year ago* il y a un an

une FEM ◊ *an apple* une pomme

*You do not translate **a** when you want to describe somebody's job in French.*

◊ *He's a butcher.* Il est boucher.
◊ *She's a doctor.* Elle est médecin.

♦ **once a week** une fois par semaine
♦ **10 km an hour** dix kilomètres à l'heure
♦ **30 pence a kilo** trente pence le kilo
♦ **a hundred pounds** cent livres

AA NOUN (= Automobile Association)
la société de dépannage

aback ADVERB

♦ **to be taken aback** être décontenancé
◊ *I was taken aback by his reaction.* Sa réaction m'a décontenancé.

to **abandon** VERB
abandonner

abbey NOUN
l' abbaye FEM

abbreviation NOUN
l' abréviation FEM

ability NOUN

♦ **to have the ability to do something** être capable de faire quelque chose

able ADJECTIVE

♦ **to be able to do something** être capable de faire quelque chose

to **abolish** VERB
abolir

abortion NOUN
l' avortement MASC

♦ **She had an abortion.** Elle s'est fait avorter.

about PREPOSITION, ADVERB

[1] à propos de (*concerning*) ◊ *I'm phoning you about tomorrow's meeting.* Je vous appelle à propos de la réunion de demain.

[2] environ (*approximately*) ◊ *It takes about 10 hours.* Ça prend dix heures environ.

♦ **about a hundred pounds** une centaine de livres
♦ **at about 11 o'clock** vers onze heures

[3] dans (*around*) ◊ *to walk about the town* se promener dans la ville

[4] sur ◊ *a book about London* un livre sur Londres

♦ **to be about to do something** être sur le point de faire quelque chose ◊ *I was about to go out.* J'étais sur le point de sortir.

♦ **to talk about something** parler de quelque chose
♦ **What's it about?** De quoi s'agit-il?
♦ **How about going to the cinema?** Et si nous allions au cinéma?

above PREPOSITION, ADVERB

[1] au-dessus de (*higher than*) ◊ *He put his hands above his head.* Il a mis ses mains au-dessus de sa tête.

♦ **the flat above** l'appartement du dessus
♦ **mentioned above** mentionné ci-dessus
♦ **above all** par-dessus tout

[2] plus de (*more than*) ◊ *above 40 degrees* plus de quarante degrés

abroad ADVERB
à l'étranger ◊ *to go abroad* partir à l'étranger

abrupt ADJECTIVE
brusque ◊ *He was a bit abrupt with me.* Il s'est montré un peu brusque avec moi.

abruptly ADVERB
brusquement ◊ *He got up abruptly.* Il s'est levé brusquement.

absence NOUN
l' absence FEM

absent ADJECTIVE
absent

absent-minded ADJECTIVE
distrait ◊ *She's a bit absent-minded.* Elle est un peu distraite.

absolutely ADVERB

[1] tout à fait (*completely*) ◊ *Chantal's absolutely right.* Chantal a tout à fait raison.

[2] absolument ◊ *Do you think it's a good idea? – Absolutely!* Tu trouves que c'est une bonne idée? – Absolument!

absorbed ADJECTIVE

♦ **to be absorbed in something** être absorbé par quelque chose
♦ **to be absorbed in a book** être plongé dans un livre

absurd ADJECTIVE
absurde ◊ *That's absurd!* C'est absurde!

abuse NOUN

> see also **abuse** VERB

l' abus MASC (*misuse*)

♦ **to shout abuse at somebody** insulter quelqu'un
♦ **the issue of child abuse** la question des enfants maltraités
♦ **the problem of drug abuse** le problème de la drogue

to **abuse** VERB

> see also **abuse** NOUN

[1] maltraiter ◊ *abused children* les enfants maltraités MASC PL
♦ **to be abused** être maltraité (*child, woman*)
[2] injurier (*insult*)
♦ **to abuse drugs** se droguer

abusive ADJECTIVE
insultant (*insulting*) ◊ *abusive behaviour* un comportement insultant
♦ **When I refused, he became abusive.** Quand j'ai refusé, il s'est mis à m'injurier.
♦ **children with abusive parents** les enfants maltraités par leurs parents

academic ADJECTIVE
universitaire ◊ *the academic year* l'année universitaire FEM

academy NOUN
le collège ◊ *a military academy* un collège militaire

to **accelerate** VERB
accélérer

accelerator NOUN
l' accélérateur MASC

accent NOUN
l' accent MASC ◊ *He's got a French accent.* Il a l'accent français.

to **accept** VERB
accepter

acceptable ADJECTIVE
acceptable

access NOUN
[1] l' accès MASC ◊ *He has access to confidential information.* Il a accès à des renseignements confidentiels.
[2] le droit de visite ◊ *Her ex-husband has access to the children.* Son ex-mari a le droit de visite.

accessible ADJECTIVE
accessible

accessory NOUN
l' accessoire MASC ◊ *fashion accessories* les accessoires de mode

accident NOUN
l' accident MASC ◊ *to have an accident* avoir un accident
♦ **by accident (1)** (*by mistake*) accidentellement ◊ *The burglar killed him by accident.* Le cambrioleur l'a tué accidentellement.

♦ **by accident (2)** (*by chance*) par hasard ◊ *She met him by accident.* Elle l'a rencontré par hasard.

accidental ADJECTIVE
accidentel MASC
accidentelle FEM

to **accommodate** VERB
recevoir ◊ *The hotel can accommodate 50 people.* L'hôtel peut recevoir cinquante personnes.

accommodation NOUN
le logement

to **accompany** VERB
accompagner

accord NOUN
♦ **of his own accord** de son plein gré ◊ *He left of his own accord.* Il est parti de son plein gré.

accordingly ADVERB
en conséquence

according to PREPOSITION
selon ◊ *According to him, everyone had gone.* Selon lui, tout le monde était parti.

accordion NOUN
l' accordéon MASC

account NOUN
[1] le compte ◊ *a bank account* un compte en banque
♦ **to do the accounts** tenir la comptabilité
[2] (*report*)
le compte rendu
(PL les comptes rendus)
◊ *He gave a detailed account of what happened.* Il a donné un compte rendu détaillé des événements.
♦ **to take something into account** tenir compte de quelque chose
♦ **on account of** à cause de ◊ *We couldn't go out on account of the bad weather.* Nous n'avons pas pu sortir à cause du mauvais temps.

to **account for** VERB
expliquer ◊ *If she was ill, that would account for her poor results.* Si elle était malade, cela expliquerait ses résultats médiocres.

accountable ADJECTIVE
♦ **to be accountable to someone for something** être responsable de quelque chose devant quelqu'un

accountancy NOUN
la comptabilité

accountant NOUN
le/la comptable ◊ *She's an accountant.* Elle est comptable.

accuracy NOUN
l' exactitude FEM

A

accurate ADJECTIVE
    précis ◊ *accurate information* les
    renseignements précis MASC

accurately ADVERB
    avec précision

accusation NOUN
    l' accusation FEM

to **accuse** VERB
    ◆**to accuse somebody of something**
    accuser quelqu'un de quelque chose
    ◊ *The police are accusing her of
    murder.* La police l'accuse de
    meurtre.

ace NOUN
    l' as MASC ◊ *the ace of hearts* l'as de
    cœur

ache NOUN
    | *see also* **ache** VERB |
    la douleur

to **ache** VERB
    | *see also* **ache** NOUN |
    ◆**My leg's aching.** J'ai mal à la jambe.

to **achieve** VERB
    [1] atteindre (*an aim*)
    [2] remporter (*victory*)

achievement NOUN
    l' exploit MASC ◊ *That was quite an
    achievement.* C'était un véritable
    exploit.

acid NOUN
    l' acide MASC

acid rain NOUN
    les pluies acides FEM PL

acne NOUN
    l' acné FEM

acre NOUN
    le demi-hectare

    ⓘ *In France, land is measured in
    hectares. One acre is about 0.4
    hectares.*

acrobat NOUN
    l' acrobate MASC/FEM ◊ *He's an acrobat.*
    Il est acrobate.

across PREPOSITION, ADVERB
    de l'autre côté de ◊ *the shop across
    the road* la boutique de l'autre côté
    de la rue
    ◆**to walk across the road** traverser la
    rue
    ◆**to run across the road** traverser la
    rue en courant
    ◆**across from** (*opposite*) en face de ◊ *He
    sat down across from her.* Il s'est
    assis en face d'elle.

to **act** VERB
    | *see also* **act** NOUN |
    [1] jouer (*in play, film*) ◊ *He acts really
    well.* Il joue vraiment bien. ◊ *She's
    acting the part of Juliet.* Elle joue le
    rôle de Juliette.
    [2] agir (*take action*) ◊ *The police acted
    quickly.* La police a agi rapidement.
    ◆**She acts as his interpreter.** Elle lui
    sert d'interprète.

act NOUN
    | *see also* **act** VERB |
    l' acte MASC (*in play*) ◊ *in the first act*
    au premier acte

action NOUN
    l' action FEM ◊ *The film was full of
    action.* Il y avait beaucoup d'action
    dans le film.
    ◆**to take firm action against** prendre
    des mesures énergiques contre

active ADJECTIVE
    actif MASC
    active FEM
    ◊ *He's a very active person.* Il est très
    actif.
    ◆**an active volcano** un volcan en
    activité

activity NOUN
    l' activité FEM ◊ *outdoor activities* les
    activités de plein air

actor NOUN
    l' acteur MASC ◊ *Brad Pitt is a well-
    known actor.* Brad Pitt est un acteur
    connu.

actress NOUN
    l' actrice FEM ◊ *Julia Roberts is a well-
    known actress.* Julia Roberts est une
    actrice connue.

actual ADJECTIVE
    réel MASC
    réelle FEM
    ◊ *The film is based on actual events.*
    Le film repose sur des faits réels.
    ◆**What's the actual amount?** Quel est
    le montant exact?
    *Be careful not to translate **actual** by
    actuel.*

actually ADVERB
    [1] vraiment (*really*) ◊ *Did it actually
    happen?* Est-ce que c'est vraiment
    arrivé?
    [2] en fait (*in fact*) ◊ *Actually, I don't
    know him at all.* En fait, je ne le
    connais pas du tout.
    *Be careful not to translate **actually**
    by **actuellement**.*

acupuncture NOUN
    l' acuponcture FEM

ad NOUN
    [1] l' annonce FEM (*in paper*)
    [2] la pub (*on TV, radio*)

AD ABBREVIATION

☞

ap. J.-C. (= après Jésus-Christ) ◊ *in 800 AD* en huit cents après Jésus-Christ

to **adapt** VERB

adapter ◊ *His novel was adapted for television.* Son roman a été adapté pour la télévision.

♦**to adapt to something** (*get used to*) s'adapter à quelque chose ◊ *He adapted to his new school very quickly.* Il s'est adapté très vite à sa nouvelle école.

adaptor NOUN

l' adaptateur MASC

to **add** VERB

ajouter ◊ *Add two eggs to the mixture.* Ajoutez deux œufs au mélange.

♦**to add up** additionner ◊ *Add the figures up.* Additionnez les chiffres.

addict NOUN

(*drug addict*)

le drogué

la droguée

♦**Jean-Pierre's a football addict.** Jean-Pierre est un mordu de football.

addicted ADJECTIVE

♦**to be addicted to** (*drug*) s'adonner à ◊ *She's addicted to heroin.* Elle s'adonne à l'héroïne.

♦**She's addicted to soap operas.** C'est une mordue des soaps.

addition NOUN

♦**in addition** en plus ◊ *He's broken his leg and, in addition, he's caught a cold.* Il s'est cassé la jambe et en plus, il a attrapé un rhume.

♦**in addition to** en plus de ◊ *In addition to the price of the cassette, there's a charge for postage.* En plus du prix de la cassette, il y a des frais de port.

address NOUN

l' adresse FEM ◊ *What's your address?* Quelle est votre adresse?

adjective NOUN

l' adjectif MASC

to **adjust** VERB

régler ◊ *You can adjust the height of the chair.* Tu peux régler la hauteur de la chaise.

♦**to adjust to something** (*get used to*) s'adapter à quelque chose ◊ *He adjusted to his new school very quickly.* Il s'est adapté très vite à sa nouvelle école.

adjustable ADJECTIVE

réglable

administration NOUN

l' administration FEM

admiral NOUN

l' amiral MASC

to **admire** VERB

admirer

admission NOUN

l' entrée FEM ◊ *"admission free"* "entrée gratuite"

to **admit** VERB

1 admettre (*agree*) ◊ *I must admit that ...* Je dois admettre que ...

2 reconnaître (*confess*) ◊ *He admitted that he'd done it.* Il a reconnu qu'il l'avait fait.

admittance NOUN

♦**"no admittance"** "accès interdit"

adolescence NOUN

l' adolescence FEM

adolescent NOUN

l' adolescent MASC

l' adolescente FEM

to **adopt** VERB

adopter ◊ *Phil was adopted.* Phil a été adopté.

adopted ADJECTIVE

adoptif MASC

adoptive FEM

◊ *an adopted son* un fils adoptif

adoption NOUN

l' adoption FEM

to **adore** VERB

adorer

Adriatic Sea NOUN

la mer Adriatique

adult NOUN

l' adulte MASC/FEM

♦**adult education** l'enseignement pour adultes MASC

to **advance** VERB

see also **advance** NOUN

1 avancer (*move forward*) ◊ *The troops are advancing.* Les troupes avancent.

2 progresser (*progress*) ◊ *Technology has advanced a lot.* La technologie a beaucoup progressé.

advance NOUN

see also **advance** VERB

♦**in advance** à l'avance ◊ *They bought the tickets in advance.* Ils ont acheté les billets à l'avance.

advance booking NOUN

♦**Advance booking is essential.** Il est indispensable de réserver.

advanced ADJECTIVE

avancé

advantage NOUN

l' avantage MASC ◊ *Going to university has many advantages.* Aller à l'université présente de nombreux avantages.

♦**to take advantage of something** profiter de quelque chose ◊ *He took advantage of the good weather to go for a walk.* Il a profité du beau temps pour faire une promenade.

♦**to take advantage of somebody** exploiter quelqu'un ◊ *The company was taking advantage of its employees.* La société exploitait ses employés.

adventure NOUN
l' aventure FEM

adverb NOUN
l' adverbe MASC

advert, advertisement NOUN
1 la publicité (*on TV*)
2 l' annonce FEM (*in newspaper*)

to advertise VERB
faire de la publicité pour ◊ *They're advertising the new model.* Ils font de la publicité pour leur nouveau modèle.

♦**Jobs are advertised in the paper.** Le journal publie des annonces d'emplois.

advertising NOUN
la publicité

advice NOUN
les conseils MASC PL ◊ *to give somebody advice* donner des conseils à quelqu'un

♦**a piece of advice** un conseil ◊ *He gave me a good piece of advice.* Il m'a donné un bon conseil.

to advise VERB
conseiller ◊ *He advised me to wait.* Il m'a conseillé d'attendre. ◊ *He advised me not to go there.* Il m'a conseillé de ne pas y aller.

aerial NOUN
l' antenne FEM

aerobics PL NOUN
l' aérobic FEM SING ◊ *I'm going to aerobics tonight.* Je vais au cours d'aérobic ce soir.

aeroplane NOUN
l' avion MASC

aerosol NOUN
la bombe

affair NOUN
1 l' aventure FEM (*romantic*) ◊ *to have an affair with somebody* avoir une aventure avec quelqu'un
2 l' affaire FEM (*event*)

to affect VERB

affecter

affectionate ADJECTIVE
affectueux MASC
affectueuse FEM

to afford VERB
avoir les moyens d'acheter ◊ *I can't afford a new pair of jeans.* Je n'ai pas les moyens d'acheter un nouveau jean.

♦**We can't afford to go on holiday.** Nous n'avons pas les moyens de partir en vacances.

afraid ADJECTIVE
♦**to be afraid of something** avoir peur de quelque chose ◊ *I'm afraid of spiders.* J'ai peur des araignées.
♦**I'm afraid I can't come.** Je crains de ne pouvoir venir.
♦**I'm afraid so.** Hélas oui.
♦**I'm afraid not.** Hélas non.

Africa NOUN
l' Afrique FEM
♦**in Africa** en Afrique

African ADJECTIVE
see also **African** NOUN
africain MASC
africaine FEM

African NOUN
see also **African** ADJECTIVE
l' Africain MASC
l' Africaine FEM

after PREPOSITION, ADVERB, CONJUNCTION
après ◊ *after dinner* après le dîner ◊ *He ran after me.* Il a couru après moi. ◊ *soon after* peu après
♦**after I'd had a rest** après m'être reposé
♦**after having asked** après avoir demandé
♦**after all** après tout

afternoon NOUN
l' après-midi MASC/FEM ◊ *3 o'clock in the afternoon* trois heures de l'après-midi ◊ *this afternoon* cet après-midi ◊ *on Saturday afternoon* samedi après-midi

afters NOUN
le dessert

aftershave NOUN
l' après-rasage MASC

afterwards ADVERB
après ◊ *She left not long afterwards.* Elle est partie peu de temps après.

again ADVERB
1 de nouveau (*once more*) ◊ *They're friends again.* Ils sont de nouveau amis.

☞

② encore une fois (one more time) ◊ *Can you tell me again?* Tu peux me le dire encore une fois?

♦**not ... again** ne ... plus ◊ *I won't go there again.* Je n'y retournerai plus.

♦**Do it again!** Refais-le!

♦**again and again** à plusieurs reprises

against PREPOSITION
contre ◊ *He leant against the wall.* Il s'est appuyé contre le mur. ◊ *I'm against nuclear testing.* Je suis contre les essais nucléaires.

age NOUN
l' âge MASC ◊ *at the age of 16* à l'âge de seize ans ◊ *an age limit* une limite d'âge

♦**I haven't been to the cinema for ages.** Ça fait une éternité que je ne suis pas allé au cinéma.

aged ADJECTIVE
♦**aged 10** âgé de dix ans

agenda NOUN
l' ordre du jour MASC ◊ *on the agenda* à l'ordre du jour ◊ *the agenda for today's meeting* l'ordre du jour de la réunion d'aujourd'hui

Be careful not to translate **agenda** *by the French word* **agenda**.

agent NOUN
l' agent MASC ◊ *an estate agent* un agent immobilier ◊ *a travel agent* un agent de voyage

aggressive ADJECTIVE
agressif MASC
agressive FEM

ago ADVERB
♦**two days ago** il y a deux jours
♦**two years ago** il y a deux ans
♦**not long ago** il n'y a pas longtemps
♦**How long ago did it happen?** Il y a combien de temps que c'est arrivé?

agony NOUN
♦**to be in agony** souffrir le martyre ◊ *He was in agony.* Il souffrait le martyre.

to **agree** VERB
♦**to agree with** être d'accord avec ◊ *I agree with Carol.* Je suis d'accord avec Carol.

♦**to agree to do something** accepter de faire quelque chose ◊ *He agreed to go and pick her up.* Il a accepté d'aller la chercher.

♦**to agree that** ... admettre que ... ◊ *I agree that it's difficult.* J'admets que c'est difficile.

♦**Garlic doesn't agree with me.** Je ne supporte pas l'ail.

agreed ADJECTIVE

convenu ◊ *at the agreed time* au moment convenu

agreement NOUN
l' accord MASC
♦**to be in agreement** être d'accord ◊ *Everybody was in agreement with Ray.* Tout le monde était d'accord avec Ray.

agricultural ADJECTIVE
agricole

agriculture NOUN
l' agriculture FEM

ahead ADVERB
devant ◊ *She looked straight ahead.* Elle regardait droit devant elle.

♦**ahead of time** en avance
♦**to plan ahead** organiser à l'avance
♦**The French are 5 points ahead.** Les Français ont cinq points d'avance.
♦**Go ahead!** Allez-y!

aid NOUN
♦**in aid of charity** au profit d'associations caritatives

AIDS NOUN
le sida

to **aim** VERB
see also **aim** NOUN
♦**to aim at** braquer sur ◊ *He aimed a gun at me.* Il a braqué un revolver sur moi.

♦**The film is aimed at children.** Le film est destiné aux enfants.

♦**to aim to do something** avoir l'intention de faire quelque chose ◊ *Janice aimed to leave at 5 o'clock.* Janice avait l'intention de partir à cinq heures.

aim NOUN
see also **aim** VERB
l' objectif MASC ◊ *The aim of the festival is to raise money.* L'objectif du festival est de collecter des fonds.

air NOUN
l' air MASC ◊ *to get some fresh air* prendre l'air

♦**by air** en avion ◊ *I prefer to travel by air.* Je préfère voyager en avion.

air-conditioned ADJECTIVE
climatisé

air conditioning NOUN
la climatisation

Air Force NOUN
l' armée de l'air FEM

air hostess NOUN
l' hôtesse de l'air FEM ◊ *She's an air hostess.* Elle est hôtesse de l'air.

airline NOUN
la compagnie aérienne

airmail NOUN
♦**by airmail** par avion

airplane NOUN US
l' avion MASC

airport NOUN
l' aéroport MASC

aisle NOUN
l' allée centrale FEM

alarm NOUN
l' alarme FEM (*warning*)
♦**a fire alarm** un avertisseur d'incendie

alarm clock NOUN
le réveil

album NOUN
l' album MASC

alcohol NOUN
l' alcool MASC

alcoholic NOUN
see also **alcoholic** ADJECTIVE
l' alcoolique MASC/FEM ◊ *He's an alcoholic.* C'est un alcoolique.

alcoholic ADJECTIVE
see also **alcoholic** NOUN
alcoolisé ◊ *alcoholic drinks* des boissons alcoolisées

alert ADJECTIVE
[1] (*bright*)
vif MASC
vive FEM
◊ *He's a very alert baby.* C'est un bébé très vif.
[2] (*paying attention*)
vigilant ◊ *We must stay alert.* Nous devons rester vigilants.

A levels PL NOUN
le baccalauréat SING

ⓘ The baccalauréat (or bac for short) is taken at the age of 17 or 18. Students have to sit one of a variety of set subject combinations, rather than being able to choose any combination of subjects they want. If you pass you have the right to a place at university.

Algeria NOUN
l' Algérie FEM
♦**in Algeria** en Algérie

alike ADVERB
♦**to look alike** se ressembler ◊ *The two sisters look alike.* Les deux sœurs se ressemblent.

alive ADJECTIVE
vivant

all ADJECTIVE, PRONOUN, ADVERB
tout
(MASC PL tous)

◊ *all the time* tout le temps ◊ *I ate all of it.* J'ai tout mangé. ◊ *all day* toute la journée ◊ *all the books* tous les livres ◊ *all the apples* toutes les pommes
♦**All of us went.** Nous y sommes tous allés.
♦**after all** après tout ◊ *After all, nobody can make us go.* Après tout, personne ne peut nous obliger à y aller.
♦**all alone** tout seul ◊ *She's all alone.* Elle est toute seule.
♦**not at all** pas du tout ◊ *I'm not tired at all.* Je ne suis pas du tout fatigué.
♦**The score is 5 all.** Le score est de cinq partout.

allergic ADJECTIVE
allergique
♦**to be allergic to something** être allergique à quelque chose ◊ *I'm allergic to cats' hair.* Je suis allergique aux poils de chat.

alley NOUN
la ruelle

to **allow** VERB
♦**to be allowed to do something** être autorisé à faire quelque chose ◊ *He's not allowed to go out at night.* Il n'est pas autorisé à sortir le soir.
♦**to allow somebody to do something** permettre à quelqu'un de faire quelque chose ◊ *His mum allowed him to go out.* Sa mère lui a permis de sortir.

all right ADVERB
[1] bien (*okay*) ◊ *Everything turned out all right.* Tout s'est bien terminé.
♦**Are you all right?** Ça va?
[2] pas mal (*not bad*) ◊ *The film was all right.* Le film n'était pas mal.
[3] d'accord (*when agreeing*) ◊ *We'll talk about it later. – All right.* On en reparlera plus tard. – D'accord.
♦**Is that all right with you?** Tu es d'accord?

almond NOUN
l' amande FEM

almost ADVERB
presque ◊ *I've almost finished.* J'ai presque fini.

alone ADJECTIVE, ADVERB
seul ◊ *She lives alone.* Elle habite seule.
♦**to leave somebody alone** laisser quelqu'un tranquille ◊ *Leave her alone!* Laisse-la tranquille!
♦**to leave something alone** ne pas toucher à quelque chose ◊ *Leave my* ☞

things alone! Ne touche pas à mes affaires!

along PREPOSITION, ADVERB
le long de ◊ *Chris was walking along the beach.* Chris se promenait le long de la plage.
♦ **all along** depuis le début ◊ *He was lying to me all along.* Il m'a menti depuis le début.

aloud ADVERB
à haute voix ◊ *He read the poem aloud.* Il a lu le poème à haute voix.

alphabet NOUN
l' alphabet MASC

Alps PL NOUN
les Alpes FEM PL

already ADVERB
déjà ◊ *Liz had already gone.* Liz était déjà partie.

also ADVERB
aussi

altar NOUN
l' autel MASC

to **alter** VERB
changer

alternate ADJECTIVE
♦ **on alternate days** tous les deux jours

alternative NOUN
see also **alternative** ADJECTIVE
le choix ◊ *You have no alternative.* Tu n'as pas le choix.
♦ **Fruit is a healthy alternative to chocolate.** Les fruits sont plus sains que le chocolat.
♦ **There are several alternatives.** Il y a plusieurs possibilités.

alternative ADJECTIVE
see also **alternative** NOUN
autre ◊ *They made alternative plans.* Ils ont pris d'autres dispositions.
♦ **an alternative solution** une solution de rechange
♦ **alternative medicine** la médecine douce

alternatively ADVERB
♦ **Alternatively, we could just stay at home.** On pourrait aussi rester à la maison.

although CONJUNCTION
bien que
bien que has to be followed by a verb in the subjunctive.
◊ *Although she was tired, she stayed up late.* Bien qu'elle soit fatiguée, elle s'est couchée tard.

altogether ADVERB
[1] en tout (*in total*) ◊ *You owe me £20 altogether.* Tu me dois vingt livres en tout.

[2] tout à fait (*completely*) ◊ *I'm not altogether happy with your work.* Je ne suis pas tout à fait satisfait de votre travail.

aluminium NOUN (US **aluminum**)
l' aluminium MASC

always ADVERB
toujours ◊ *He's always moaning.* Il est toujours en train de ronchonner.

am VERB *see* be

a.m. ABBREVIATION
du matin ◊ *at 4 a.m.* à quatre heures du matin

amateur NOUN
l' amateur MASC

to **amaze** VERB
♦ **to be amazed** être stupéfait ◊ *I was amazed that I managed to do it.* J'étais stupéfait d'avoir réussi.

amazed ADJECTIVE
stupéfait ◊ *I was amazed that I managed to do it.* J'étais stupéfait d'y être arrivé.

amazing ADJECTIVE
[1] (*surprising*)
stupéfiant ◊ *That's amazing news!* C'est une nouvelle stupéfiante!
[2] (*excellent*)
exceptionnel MASC
exceptionnelle FEM
◊ *Vivian's an amazing cook.* Vivian est une cuisinière exceptionnelle.

ambassador NOUN
l' ambassadeur MASC
l' ambassadrice FEM

amber ADJECTIVE
♦ **an amber light** un feu orange

ambition NOUN
l' ambition FEM

ambitious ADJECTIVE
ambitieux MASC
ambitieuse FEM
◊ *She's very ambitious.* Elle est très ambitieuse.

ambulance NOUN
l' ambulance FEM

amenities PL NOUN
les aménagements MASC PL
♦ **The hotel has very good amenities.** L'hôtel est très bien aménagé.

America NOUN
l' Amérique FEM
♦ **in America** en Amérique
♦ **to America** en Amérique

American ADJECTIVE
see also **American** NOUN

A

américain ◇ *He's American.* Il est
américain. ◇ *She's American.* Elle est
américaine.

American NOUN
| see also **American** ADJECTIVE |
l' Américain MASC
l' Américaine FEM
♦ **the Americans** les Américains

among PREPOSITION
parmi ◇ *There were six children
among them.* Il y avait six enfants
parmi eux.
♦ **We were among friends.** Nous étions
entre amis.
♦ **among other things** entre autres

amount NOUN
⎡1⎤ la somme ◇ *a large amount of
money* une grosse somme d'argent
⎡2⎤ la quantité
♦ **a huge amount of rice** une énorme
quantité de riz

amp NOUN
⎡1⎤ l' ampère MASC (*of electricity*)
⎡2⎤ l' ampli MASC (*for hi-fi*)

amplifier NOUN
l' amplificateur MASC (*for hi-fi*)

to **amuse** VERB
amuser ◇ *He was most amused by
the story.* L'histoire l'a beaucoup
amusé.

amusement arcade NOUN
la salle de jeux électroniques

an ARTICLE *see* **a**

to **analyse** VERB
analyser

analysis NOUN
l' analyse FEM

to **analyze** VERB US
analyser

ancestor NOUN
l' ancêtre MASC/FEM

anchor NOUN
l' ancre FEM

ancient ADJECTIVE
⎡1⎤ (*civilization*)
antique ◇ *ancient Greece* la Grèce
antique
⎡2⎤ (*custom, building*)
ancien MASC
ancienne FEM
◇ *an ancient monument* un
monument ancien

and CONJUNCTION
et ◇ *you and me* toi et moi ◇ *2 and 2
are 4* deux et deux font quatre
♦ **Please try and come!** Essaie de venir!
♦ **He talked and talked.** Il n'a pas arrêté
de parler.
♦ **better and better** de mieux en mieux

angel NOUN
l' ange MASC

anger NOUN
la colère

angle NOUN
l' angle MASC

angler NOUN
le pêcheur à la ligne
la pêcheuse à la ligne

angling NOUN
la pêche à la ligne

angry ADJECTIVE
en colère ◇ *Dad looks very angry.*
Papa a l'air très en colère.
♦ **to be angry with somebody** être
furieux contre quelqu'un ◇ *Mum's
really angry with you.* Maman est
vraiment furieuse contre toi.
♦ **to get angry** se fâcher

animal NOUN
l' animal MASC
(PL les animaux)

ankle NOUN
la cheville

anniversary NOUN
l' anniversaire MASC ◇ *a wedding
anniversary* un anniversaire de
mariage

to **announce** VERB
annoncer

announcement NOUN
l' annonce FEM

to **annoy** VERB
agacer ◇ *He's really annoying me.* Il
m'agace vraiment.
♦ **to get annoyed** se fâcher ◇ *Don't get
so annoyed!* Ne vous fâchez pas!

annoying ADJECTIVE
agaçant ◇ *It's really annoying.* C'est
vraiment agaçant.

annual ADJECTIVE
annuel MASC
annuelle FEM
◇ *an annual meeting* une réunion
annuelle

anorak NOUN
l' anorak MASC

another ADJECTIVE
un autre
une autre
◇ *Would you like another piece of
cake?* Tu veux un autre morceau de
gâteau? ◇ *Have you got another skirt?*
Tu as une autre jupe?

to **answer** VERB
| see also **answer** NOUN |
répondre à ◇ *Can you answer my
question?* Peux-tu répondre à ma

☞

question? ◊ *to answer the phone* répondre au téléphone

♦**to answer the door** aller ouvrir ◊ *Can you answer the door please?* Tu peux aller ouvrir s'il te plaît?

answer NOUN

> see also **answer** VERB

[1] la ré**ponse** (*to question*)
[2] la **solution** (*to problem*)

answering machine NOUN
le ré**pondeur**

ant NOUN
la **fourmi**

to **antagonize** VERB
contrarier ◊ *He didn't want to antagonize her.* Il ne voulait pas la contrarier.

Antarctic NOUN
l' **Antarctique** FEM

anthem NOUN
♦**the national anthem** l'hymne national MASC

antibiotic NOUN
l' **antibiotique** MASC

antidepressant NOUN
l' **antidépresseur** MASC

antique NOUN
le **meuble ancien** (*furniture*)

antique shop NOUN
le **magasin d'antiquités**

antiseptic NOUN
l' **antiseptique** MASC

any ADJECTIVE, PRONOUN, ADVERB

> *Use **du, de la** or **des** to translate **any** according to the gender of the French noun that follows it. **du** and **de la** become **de l'** when they're followed by a noun starting with a vowel.*

[1] **du** ◊ *Would you like any bread?* Voulez-vous du pain?
de la ◊ *Would you like any beer?* Voulez-vous de la bière?
de l' ◊ *Have you got any mineral water?* Avez-vous de l'eau minérale?
des ◊ *Have you got any Blur CDs?* Avez-vous des CD de Blur?

> *If you want to say you haven't got any of something, use **de** whatever the gender of the following noun is. **de** becomes **d'** when it comes before a noun starting with a vowel.*

[2] **de** ◊ *I haven't got any books.* Je n'ai pas de livres.
d' ◊ *I haven't got any money.* Je n'ai pas d'argent.

> *Use **en** where there is no noun after **any**.*

[3] **en** ◊ *Sorry, I haven't got any.* Désolé, je n'en ai pas.

♦**any more (1)** (*additional*) encore de ◊ *Would you like any more coffee?* Est-ce que tu veux encore du café?

♦**any more (2)** (*no longer*) ne ... plus ◊ *I don't love him any more.* Je ne l'aime plus.

anybody PRONOUN
[1] **quelqu'un** (*in question*) ◊ *Has anybody got a pen?* Est-ce que quelqu'un a un stylo?
[2] **n'importe qui** (*no matter who*) ◊ *Anybody can learn to swim.* N'importe qui peut apprendre à nager.

> *Use **ne ... personne** in a negative sentence. **ne** comes before the verb, **personne** after it.*

[3] **ne ... personne** ◊ *I can't see anybody.* Je ne vois personne.

anyhow ADVERB
de toute façon ◊ *He doesn't want to go out and anyhow he's not allowed.* Il ne veut pas sortir et de toute façon il n'y est pas autorisé.

anyone PRONOUN
[1] **quelqu'un** (*in question*) ◊ *Has anyone got a pen?* Est-ce que quelqu'un a un stylo?
[2] **n'importe qui** (*no matter who*) ◊ *Anyone can learn to swim.* N'importe qui peut apprendre à nager.

> *Use **ne ... personne** in a negative sentence. **ne** comes before the verb, **personne** after it.*

[3] **ne ... personne** ◊ *I can't see anyone.* Je ne vois personne.

anything PRONOUN
[1] **quelque chose** (*in question*) ◊ *Would you like anything to eat?* Tu veux manger quelque chose?
[2] **n'importe quoi** (*no matter what*) ◊ *Anything could happen.* Il pourrait arriver n'importe quoi.

> *Use **ne ... rien** in a negative sentence. **ne** comes before the verb, **rien** after it.*

[3] **ne ... rien** ◊ *I can't hear anything.* Je n'entends rien.

anyway ADVERB
de toute façon ◊ *He doesn't want to go out and anyway he's not allowed.* Il ne veut pas sortir et de toute façon il n'y est pas autorisé.

anywhere ADVERB
[1] **quelque part** (*in question*) ◊ *Have you seen my coat anywhere?* Est-ce

que tu as vu mon manteau quelque
part?

2 n'importe où ◊ *You can buy
stamps almost anywhere.* On peut
acheter des timbres presque
n'importe où.

> *Use* **ne ... nulle part** *in a negative
sentence.* **ne** *comes before the verb,*
nulle part *after it.*

3 ne ... nulle part ◊ *I can't find it
anywhere.* Je ne le trouve nulle part.

apart ADVERB

♦**The two towns are 10 kilometres
apart.** Les deux villes sont à dix
kilomètres l'une de l'autre.

♦**apart from** à part ◊ *Apart from that,
everything's fine.* À part ça, tout va
bien.

apartment NOUN
l' appartement MASC

to **apologize** VERB
s'excuser ◊ *He apologized for being
late.* Il s'est excusé de son retard.

♦**I apologize!** Je vous prie de
m'excuser.

apology NOUN
les excuses FEM PL

apostrophe NOUN
l' apostrophe FEM

apparatus NOUN
1 le matériel (*in lab*)
2 les agrès MASC PL (*in gym*)

apparent ADJECTIVE
apparent

apparently ADVERB
apparemment

to **appeal** VERB

> see also **appeal** NOUN

lancer un appel ◊ *They appealed for
help.* Ils ont lancé un appel au
secours.

♦**Greece doesn't appeal to me.** Ça ne
me tente pas d'aller en Grèce.

♦**Does that appeal to you?** Ça te tente?

appeal NOUN

> see also **appeal** VERB

l' appel MASC ◊ *They have launched an
appeal.* Ils ont lancé un appel.

to **appear** VERB
1 apparaître (*come into view*) ◊ *The
bus appeared around the corner.* Le
bus est apparu au coin de la rue.

♦**to appear on TV** passer à la télé
2 paraître (*seem*) ◊ *She appeared to
be asleep.* Elle paraissait dormir.

appearance NOUN
l' apparence FEM (*looks*) ◊ *She takes
great care over her appearance.* Elle
prend grand soin de son apparence.

appendicitis NOUN
l' appendicite FEM

appetite NOUN
l' appétit MASC

to **applaud** VERB
applaudir

applause NOUN
les applaudissements MASC PL

apple NOUN
la pomme

♦**an apple tree** un pommier

applicant NOUN
le candidat
la candidate
◊ *There were a hundred applicants
for the job.* Il y avait cent candidats
pour ce poste.

application NOUN
♦**a job application** une candidature

application form NOUN
1 le dossier de candidature (*for job*)
2 le dossier d'inscription (*for
university*)

to **apply** VERB
♦**to apply for a job** poser sa
candidature à un poste

♦**to apply to** (*be relevant*) s'appliquer à
◊ *This rule doesn't apply to us.* Ce
règlement ne s'applique pas à nous.

appointment NOUN
le rendez-vous ◊ *I've got a dental
appointment.* J'ai rendez-vous chez le
dentiste.

to **appreciate** VERB
être reconnaissant de ◊ *I really
appreciate your help.* Je vous suis
extrêmement reconnaissant de votre
aide.

apprentice NOUN
l' apprenti MASC
l' apprentie FEM

to **approach** VERB
1 s'approcher de (*get nearer to*) ◊ *He
approached the house.* Il s'est
approché de la maison.
2 aborder (*tackle*) ◊ *to approach a
problem* aborder un problème

appropriate ADJECTIVE
approprié ◊ *That dress isn't very
appropriate for an interview.* Cette
robe n'est pas très appropriée pour
un entretien.

approval NOUN
l' approbation FEM

to **approve** VERB
♦**to approve of** approuver ◊ *I don't
approve of his choice.* Je n'approuve
pas son choix.

☞

♦**They didn't approve of his girlfriend.**
Sa copine ne leur a pas plu.

approximate ADJECTIVE
approximatif MASC
approximative FEM

apricot NOUN
l' **abricot** MASC

April NOUN
avril MASC
♦**in April** en avril
♦**April Fool's Day** le premier avril

apron NOUN
le **tablier**

Aquarius NOUN
le **Verseau** ◊ *I'm Aquarius.* Je suis
Verseau.

Arab ADJECTIVE
> see also **Arab** NOUN

arabe ◊ *the Arab countries* les pays
arabes

Arab NOUN
> see also **Arab** ADJECTIVE

l' **Arabe** MASC/FEM

Arabic NOUN
l' **arabe** MASC

arch NOUN
l' **arc** MASC

archaeologist NOUN
l' **archéologue** MASC/FEM ◊ *He's an
archaeologist.* Il est archéologue.

archaeology NOUN
l' **archéologie** FEM

archbishop NOUN
l' **archevêque** MASC

archeologist NOUN [US]
l' **archéologue** MASC/FEM ◊ *He's an
archeologist.* Il est archéologue.

archeology NOUN [US]
l' **archéologie** FEM

architect NOUN
l' **architecte** MASC/FEM ◊ *She's an
architect.* Elle est architecte.

architecture NOUN
l' **architecture** FEM

Arctic NOUN
l' **Arctique** MASC

are VERB *see* **be**

area NOUN
1 la **région** ◊ *She lives in the Paris
area.* Elle habite dans la région
parisienne.
2 le **quartier** ◊ *My favourite area of
Paris is Montmartre.* Montmartre est
le quartier de Paris que je préfère.
3 la **superficie** ◊ *The field has an
area of 1500m².* Le champ a une
superficie de mille cinq cent mètres
carrés.

Argentina NOUN
l' **Argentine** FEM
♦**in Argentina** en Argentine

Argentinian ADJECTIVE
argentin

to **argue** VERB
se disputer ◊ *They never stop
arguing.* Ils n'arrêtent pas de se
disputer.

argument NOUN
♦**to have an argument** se disputer
◊ *They had an argument.* Ils se sont
disputés.

Aries NOUN
le **Bélier** ◊ *I'm Aries.* Je suis Bélier.

arm NOUN
le **bras**

armchair NOUN
le **fauteuil**

armour NOUN (US **armor**)
l' **armure** FEM

army NOUN
l' **armée** FEM

around PREPOSITION, ADVERB
1 **autour de** ◊ *She wore a scarf
around her neck.* Elle portait une
écharpe autour du cou.
2 **environ** (*approximately*) ◊ *It costs
around £100.* Cela coûte environ cent
livres.
3 **vers** (*date, time*) ◊ *Let's meet at
around 8 p.m.* Retrouvons-nous vers
vingt heures.
♦**around here (1)** (*nearby*) près d'ici ◊ *Is
there a chemist's around here?* Est-ce
qu'il y a une pharmacie près d'ici?
♦**around here (2)** (*in this area*) dans les
parages ◊ *He lives around here.* Il
habite dans les parages.

to **arrange** VERB
♦**to arrange to do something** prévoir
de faire quelque chose ◊ *They
arranged to go out together on
Friday.* Ils ont prévu de sortir
ensemble vendredi.
♦**to arrange a meeting** convenir d'un
rendez-vous ◊ *Can we arrange a
meeting?* Pouvons-nous convenir d'un
rendez-vous?
♦**to arrange a party** organiser une fête

arrangement NOUN
l' **arrangement** MASC (*plan*)
♦**They made arrangements to go out
on Friday night.** Ils ont organisé une
sortie vendredi soir.

to **arrest** VERB
> see also **arrest** NOUN

arrêter ◊ *The police have arrested 5 people.* La police a arrêté cinq personnes.

arrest NOUN
see also **arrest** VERB
l' arrestation FEM ◊ *You're under arrest!* Vous êtes en état d'arrestation!

arrival NOUN
l' arrivée FEM

to **arrive** VERB
arriver ◊ *I arrived at 5 o'clock.* Je suis arrivé à cinq heures.

arrow NOUN
la flèche

art NOUN
l' art MASC

artery NOUN
l' artère FEM

art gallery NOUN
le musée

article NOUN
l' article MASC ◊ *a newspaper article* un article de journal

artificial ADJECTIVE
artificiel MASC
artificielle FEM

artist NOUN
l' artiste MASC/FEM ◊ *She's an artist.* C'est une artiste.

artistic ADJECTIVE
artistique

as CONJUNCTION, ADVERB
1 au moment où (*while*) ◊ *He came in as I was leaving.* Il est arrivé au moment où je partais.
2 puisque (*since*) ◊ *As it's Sunday, you can have a lie-in.* Tu peux faire la grasse matinée, puisque c'est dimanche.
◆ **as ... as** aussi ... que ◊ *Pierre's as tall as Michel.* Pierre est aussi grand que Michel.
◆ **twice as ... as** deux fois plus ... que ◊ *Her coat cost twice as much as mine.* Son manteau a coûté deux fois plus cher que le mien.
◆ **as much ... as** autant ... que ◊ *I haven't got as much money as you.* Je n'ai pas autant d'argent que toi.
◆ **as soon as possible** dès que possible ◊ *I'll do it as soon as possible.* Je le ferai dès que possible.
◆ **as from tomorrow** à partir de demain ◊ *As from tomorrow, the shop will stay open until 10 p.m.* À partir de demain, le magasin restera ouvert jusqu'à vingt-deux heures.

◆ **as though** comme si ◊ *She acted as though she hadn't seen me.* Elle a fait comme si elle ne m'avait pas vu.
◆ **as if** comme si
◆ **He works as a waiter in the holidays.** Il travaille comme serveur pendant les vacances.

asap ABBREVIATION (= *as soon as possible*)
dès que possible

ashamed ADJECTIVE
◆ **to be ashamed** avoir honte ◊ *You should be ashamed of yourself!* Tu devrais avoir honte!

ashtray NOUN
le cendrier

Asia NOUN
l' Asie FEM
◆ **in Asia** en Asie

Asian ADJECTIVE
see also **Asian** NOUN
asiatique ◊ *He's Asian.* C'est un Asiatique. ◊ *She's Asian.* C'est une Asiatique.

Asian NOUN
see also **Asian** ADJECTIVE
l' Asiatique MASC/FEM

to **ask** VERB
1 demander (*inquire, request*) ◊ *"Have you finished?" she asked.* "Tu as fini?" a-t-elle demandé.
◆ **to ask somebody something** demander quelque chose à quelqu'un ◊ *He asked her how old she was.* Il lui a demandé quel âge elle avait.
◆ **to ask for something** demander quelque chose ◊ *He asked for a cup of tea.* Il a demandé une tasse de thé.
◆ **to ask somebody to do something** demander à quelqu'un de faire quelque chose ◊ *She asked him to do the shopping.* Elle lui a demandé de faire les courses.
◆ **to ask about something** se renseigner sur quelque chose ◊ *I asked about train times to Leeds.* Je me suis renseigné sur les horaires des trains pour Leeds.
◆ **to ask somebody a question** poser une question à quelqu'un
2 inviter ◊ *Have you asked Matthew to the party?* Est-ce que tu as invité Matthew à la fête?
◆ **He asked her out.** (*on a date*) Il lui a demandé de sortir avec lui.

asleep ADJECTIVE
◆ **to be asleep** dormir ◊ *He's asleep.* Il dort.

♦ **to fall asleep** s'endormir ◊ *I fell asleep in front of the TV.* Je me suis endormi devant la télé.

asparagus NOUN
les asperges FEM PL

aspect NOUN
l' aspect MASC

aspirin NOUN
l' aspirine FEM

asset NOUN
l' atout MASC ◊ *Her experience will be an asset to the firm.* Son expérience sera un atout pour l'entreprise.

assignment NOUN
le devoir (*in school*)

assistance NOUN
l' aide FEM

assistant NOUN
1 (*in shop*)
le vendeur
la vendeuse
2 (*helper*)
l' assistant MASC
l' assistante FEM

association NOUN
l' association FEM

assortment NOUN
l' assortiment MASC

to **assume** VERB
supposer ◊ *I assume she won't be coming.* Je suppose qu'elle ne viendra pas.

to **assure** VERB
assurer ◊ *He assured me he was coming.* Il m'a assuré qu'il viendrait.

asthma NOUN
l' asthme MASC ◊ *I've got asthma.* J'ai de l'asthme.

to **astonish** VERB
étonner

astonished ADJECTIVE
étonné

astonishing ADJECTIVE
étonnant

astrology NOUN
l' astrologie FEM

astronaut NOUN
l' astronaute MASC/FEM

astronomy NOUN
l' astronomie FEM

asylum seeker NOUN
le demandeur d'asile
la demandeuse d'asile

at PREPOSITION
à + le becomes au, à + les becomes aux.
à ◊ *at 4 o'clock* à quatre heures ◊ *at Christmas* à Noël ◊ *at 50 km/h* à

cinquante km/h ◊ *at home* à la maison ◊ *two at a time* deux à la fois ◊ *at school* à l'école
au ◊ *at the office* au bureau
aux ◊ *at the races* aux courses
♦ **at night** la nuit
♦ **What are you doing at the weekend?** Qu'est-ce que tu fais ce week-end?

ate VERB *see* **eat**

Athens NOUN
Athènes
♦ **in Athens** à Athènes

athlete NOUN
l' athlète MASC/FEM

athletic ADJECTIVE
athlétique

athletics NOUN
l' athlétisme MASC ◊ *I like watching the athletics on TV.* J'aime bien regarder les épreuves d'athlétisme à la télé.

Atlantic NOUN
l' océan Atlantique MASC

atlas NOUN
l' atlas MASC

atmosphere NOUN
l' atmosphère FEM

atom NOUN
l' atome MASC

atomic ADJECTIVE
atomique ◊ *an atomic bomb* une bombe atomique

to **attach** VERB
fixer ◊ *They attached a rope to the car.* Ils ont fixé une corde à la voiture.
♦ **Please find attached ...** Veuillez trouver ci-joint ...

attached ADJECTIVE
♦ **to be attached to** être attaché à ◊ *He's very attached to his family.* Il est très attaché à sa famille.

to **attack** VERB
| *see also* **attack** NOUN |
attaquer ◊ *The dog attacked her.* Le chien l'a attaquée.

attack NOUN
| *see also* **attack** VERB |
l' attaque FEM

attempt NOUN
| *see also* **attempt** VERB |
la tentative ◊ *She gave up after several attempts.* Elle y a renoncé après plusieurs tentatives.

to **attempt** VERB
| *see also* **attempt** NOUN |
♦ **to attempt to do something** essayer de faire quelque chose ◊ *I attempted*

to write a song. J'ai essayé d'écrire une chanson.

to **attend** VERB
assister à ◊ to attend a meeting assister à une réunion
> Be careful not to translate **to attend** by **attendre**.

attention NOUN
l' attention FEM
♦**to pay attention to** faire attention à ◊ He didn't pay attention to what I was saying. Il ne faisait pas attention à ce que je disais.

attic NOUN
le grenier

attitude NOUN
l' attitude FEM (way of thinking) ◊ I really don't like your attitude! Je n'aime pas du tout ton attitude!

attorney NOUN [US]
l' avocat MASC
l' avocate FEM

to **attract** VERB
attirer ◊ The Lake District attracts lots of tourists. La région des lacs attire de nombreux touristes.

attraction NOUN
l' attraction FEM ◊ a tourist attraction une attraction touristique

attractive ADJECTIVE
séduisant ◊ She's very attractive. Elle est très séduisante.

aubergine NOUN
l' aubergine FEM

auction NOUN
la vente aux enchères

audience NOUN
les spectateurs MASC PL (in theatre)

audition NOUN
l' audition FEM

August NOUN
août MASC
♦**in August** en août

aunt, aunty NOUN
la tante ◊ my aunt ma tante

au pair NOUN
la jeune fille au pair ◊ She's an au pair. Elle est jeune fille au pair.

Australia NOUN
l' Australie FEM
♦**in Australia** en Australie
♦**to Australia** en Australie

Australian ADJECTIVE
see also **Australian** NOUN
australien MASC
australienne FEM
◊ He's Australian. Il est australien.

Australian NOUN

see also **Australian** ADJECTIVE
l' Australien MASC
l' Australienne FEM
♦**the Australians** les Australiens

Austria NOUN
l' Autriche FEM
♦**in Austria** en Autriche

Austrian ADJECTIVE
see also **Austrian** NOUN
autrichien MASC
autrichienne FEM
◊ She's Austrian. Elle est autrichienne.

Austrian NOUN
see also **Austrian** ADJECTIVE
l' Autrichien MASC
l' Autrichienne FEM
♦**the Austrians** les Autrichiens

author NOUN
l' auteur MASC ◊ She's a famous author. C'est un auteur connu.

autobiography NOUN
l' autobiographie FEM

autograph NOUN
l' autographe MASC

automatic ADJECTIVE
automatique ◊ an automatic door une porte automatique

automatically ADVERB
automatiquement

autumn NOUN
l' automne MASC
♦**in autumn** en automne

availability NOUN
la disponibilité

available ADJECTIVE
disponible ◊ Free brochures are available on request. Des brochures gratuites sont disponibles sur demande. ◊ Is Mr Cooke available today? Est-ce que Monsieur Cooke est disponible aujourd'hui?

avalanche NOUN
l' avalanche FEM

avenue NOUN
l' avenue FEM

average NOUN
see also **average** ADJECTIVE
la moyenne ◊ on average en moyenne

average ADJECTIVE
see also **average** NOUN
moyen MASC
moyenne FEM
◊ the average price le prix moyen

avocado NOUN
l' avocat MASC

to **avoid** VERB

☞

éviter ◊ *He avoids her when she's in a bad mood.* Il l'évite lorsqu'elle est de mauvaise humeur.

♦**to avoid doing something** éviter de faire quelque chose ◊ *Avoid going out on your own at night.* Évite de sortir seul le soir.

awake ADJECTIVE

♦**to be awake** être réveillé ◊ *Is she awake?* Elle est réveillée?

♦**He was still awake.** Il ne dormait pas encore.

award NOUN

le prix ◊ *He's won an award.* Il a remporté un prix. ◊ *the award for the best actor* le prix du meilleur acteur

aware ADJECTIVE

♦**to be aware of something** être conscient de quelque chose

away ADJECTIVE, ADVERB

absent (*not here*) ◊ *André's away today.* André est absent aujourd'hui.

♦**He's away for a week.** Il est parti pour une semaine.

♦**The town's 2 kilometres away.** La ville est à deux kilomètres d'ici.

♦**The coast is 2 hours away by car.** La côte est à deux heures de route.

♦**Go away!** Va-t'en!

♦**to put something away** ranger quelque chose ◊ *He put his toys away in the cupboard.* Il a rangé ses jouets dans le placard.

away match NOUN

le match à l'extérieur
(PL les matchs à l'extérieur)

awful ADJECTIVE

affreux MASC
affreuse FEM
◊ *That's awful!* C'est affreux!

♦**an awful lot of ...** énormément de ...

awfully ADVERB

♦**I'm awfully sorry.** Je suis vraiment désolé.

awkward ADJECTIVE

1 délicat (*difficult to deal with*) ◊ *an awkward situation* une situation délicate

2 gênant (*embarrassing*) ◊ *an awkward question* une question gênante

♦**It's a bit awkward for me to come and see you.** Ce n'est pas très pratique pour moi de venir vous voir.

axe NOUN

la hache

B

BA NOUN
la licence
♦ **a BA in French** une licence de français

baby NOUN
le bébé

baby carriage NOUN US
le landau

to **babysit** VERB
faire du baby-sitting

babysitter NOUN
le/la baby-sitter

babysitting NOUN
le baby-sitting

bachelor NOUN
le célibataire ◊ *He's a bachelor.* Il est célibataire.

back NOUN
see also **back** ADJECTIVE, VERB
1 le dos (*of person, horse, book*)
2 l' arrière MASC (*of car, house*) ◊ *in the back* à l'arrière
3 le verso (*of page*) ◊ *on the back* au verso
4 le fond (*of room, garden*) ◊ *at the back* au fond

back ADJECTIVE, ADVERB
see also **back** NOUN, VERB
arrière MASC, FEM, PL ◊ *the back seat* le siège arrière ◊ *the back wheel of my bike* la roue arrière de mon vélo
♦ **the back door** la porte de derrière
♦ **to get back** rentrer ◊ *What time did you get back?* À quelle heure est-ce que tu es rentré?
♦ **We went there by bus and walked back.** Nous y sommes allés en bus et nous sommes rentrés à pied.
♦ **He's not back yet.** Il n'est pas encore rentré.
♦ **to call somebody back** rappeler quelqu'un ◊ *I'll call back later.* Je rappellerai plus tard.

to **back** VERB
see also **back** NOUN, ADJECTIVE
soutenir (*support*) ◊ *I'm backing Tony Blair.* Je soutiens Tony Blair.
♦ **to back a horse** parier sur un cheval
♦ **to back out** se désister ◊ *They promised to help and then backed out.* Ils avaient promis de nous aider et ils se sont désistés.
♦ **to back somebody up** soutenir quelqu'un

backache NOUN

le mal au dos ◊ *to have backache* avoir mal au dos

backbone NOUN
la colonne vertébrale

to **backfire** VERB
échouer (*go wrong*)

background NOUN
1 (*of picture*)
l' arrière-plan MASC ◊ *a house in the background* une maison à l'arrière-plan
♦ **background noise** les bruits de fond MASC PL
2 le milieu
(les milieux PL)
◊ *his family background* son milieu familial

backhand NOUN
le revers

backing NOUN
le soutien (*support*)

backpack NOUN
le sac à dos

backpacker NOUN
1 (*globe-trotter*)
le routard
la routarde
2 (*hill-walker*)
le randonneur
la randonneuse

backpacking NOUN
♦ **to go backpacking** voyager sac au dos

back pain NOUN
le mal au dos ◊ *to have back pain* avoir mal au dos

backside NOUN
le derrière

backstroke NOUN
le dos crawlé

backup NOUN
le soutien (*support*)
♦ **a backup file** une sauvegarde

backwards ADVERB
en arrière ◊ *to take a step backwards* faire un pas en arrière
♦ **to fall backwards** tomber à la renverse

back yard NOUN
la cour

bacon NOUN
1 le lard (*French type*)
2 le bacon (*British type*) ◊ *bacon and eggs* des œufs au bacon

bad ADJECTIVE

[1] mauvais ◊ *a bad film* un mauvais film ◊ *the bad weather* le mauvais temps ◊ *to be in a bad mood* être de mauvaise humeur
♦**to be bad at something** être mauvais en quelque chose ◊ *I'm really bad at maths.* Je suis vraiment mauvais en maths.
[2] grave (*serious*) ◊ *a bad accident* un accident grave
[3] vilain (*naughty*) ◊ *You bad boy!* Vilain!
♦**to go bad** (*food*) se gâter
♦**I feel bad about it.** Ça m'ennuie.
♦**not bad** pas mal ◊ *That's not bad at all.* Ce n'est pas mal du tout.

badge NOUN
le badge

badly ADVERB
mal ◊ *badly paid* mal payé
♦**badly wounded** grièvement blessé
♦**He badly needs a rest.** Il a sérieusement besoin de se reposer.

badminton NOUN
le badminton ◊ *to play badminton* jouer au badminton

bad-tempered ADJECTIVE
♦**to be bad-tempered (1)** (*by nature*) avoir mauvais caractère ◊ *He's a really bad-tempered person.* Il a vraiment mauvais caractère.
♦**to be bad-tempered (2)** (*temporarily*) être de mauvaise humeur ◊ *He was really bad-tempered yesterday.* Il était vraiment de mauvaise humeur hier.

baffled ADJECTIVE
déconcerté

bag NOUN
le sac
♦**an old bag** (*person*) une vieille peau

baggage NOUN
les bagages MASC PL

baggage reclaim NOUN
la livraison des bagages

baggy ADJECTIVE
ample

bagpipes PL NOUN
la cornemuse SING ◊ *Ed plays the bagpipes.* Ed joue de la cornemuse.

to **bake** VERB
♦**to bake a cake** faire un gâteau

baked ADJECTIVE
cuit au four MASC
cuite au four FEM
◊ *baked potatoes* les pommes de terre cuites au four FEM
♦**baked beans** les haricots blancs à la sauce tomate MASC

baker NOUN
le boulanger
la boulangère
◊ *He's a baker.* Il est boulanger.

bakery NOUN
la boulangerie

baking ADJECTIVE
♦**It's baking in here!** Il fait une chaleur torride ici!

balance NOUN
l' équilibre MASC ◊ *to lose one's balance* perdre l'équilibre

balanced ADJECTIVE
équilibré

balcony NOUN
le balcon

bald ADJECTIVE
chauve

ball NOUN
[1] la balle (*tennis, golf, cricket*)
[2] le ballon (*football, rugby*)

ballet NOUN
le ballet ◊ *We went to a ballet.* Nous sommes allés voir un ballet.
♦**ballet lessons** les cours de danse MASC

ballet dancer NOUN
le danseur classique
la danseuse classique

ballet shoes PL NOUN
les chaussons de danse MASC PL

balloon NOUN
le ballon (*for parties*)
♦**a hot-air balloon** une montgolfière

ballpoint pen NOUN
le stylo à bille

ballroom dancing NOUN
la danse de salon

ban NOUN
see also **ban** VERB
l' interdiction FEM

to **ban** VERB
see also **ban** NOUN
interdire

banana NOUN
la banane ◊ *a banana skin* une peau de banane

band NOUN
[1] le groupe (*rock band*)
[2] la fanfare (*brass band*)

bandage NOUN
see also **bandage** VERB
le bandage

to **bandage** VERB
see also **bandage** NOUN
mettre un bandage à ◊ *The nurse bandaged his arm.* L'infirmière lui a mis un bandage au bras.

Band-Aid ® NOUN [US]
le pansement adhésif

bandit NOUN
le bandit

bang NOUN
| see also **bang** VERB |
[1] la détonation ◊ *I heard a loud bang.* J'ai entendu une forte détonation.
[2] le coup ◊ *a bang on the head* un coup sur la tête
♦**Bang!** Pan!

to **bang** VERB
| see also **bang** NOUN |
se cogner (*part of body*) ◊ *I banged my head.* Je me suis cogné la tête.
♦**to bang the door** claquer la porte
♦**to bang on the door** cogner à la porte

banger NOUN
[1] le tacot (*old car*) ◊ *His car's an old banger.* Sa voiture est un vieux tacot.
[2] la saucisse (*sausage*) ◊ *bangers and mash* les saucisses à la purée

Bangladesh NOUN
le Bangladesh
♦**from Bangladesh** du Bangladesh

bank NOUN
[1] la banque (*financial*)
[2] le bord (*of river, lake*)

bank account NOUN
le compte en banque

banker NOUN
le banquier

bank holiday NOUN
le jour férié

banknote NOUN
le billet de banque

banned ADJECTIVE
interdit

bar NOUN
[1] le bar (*pub*)
[2] le comptoir (*counter*)
♦**a bar of chocolate** une tablette de chocolat
♦**a bar of soap** une savonnette

barbaric ADJECTIVE
barbare

barbecue NOUN
le barbecue

barber NOUN
le coiffeur pour hommes

bare ADJECTIVE
nu

barefoot ADJECTIVE, ADVERB
nu-pieds MASC, FEM, PL ◊ *The children go around barefoot.* Les enfants se promènent nu-pieds.

♦**to be barefoot** avoir les pieds nus ◊ *She was barefoot.* Elle avait les pieds nus.

barely ADVERB
à peine ◊ *I could barely hear what she was saying.* J'entendais à peine ce qu'elle disait.

bargain NOUN
l' affaire FEM ◊ *It was a bargain!* C'était une affaire!

barge NOUN
la péniche

to **bark** VERB
aboyer

barmaid NOUN
la barmaid ◊ *She's a barmaid.* Elle est barmaid.

barman NOUN
le barman ◊ *He's a barman.* Il est barman.

barn NOUN
la grange

barrel NOUN
le tonneau
(les tonneaux PL)

barrier NOUN
la barrière

bartender NOUN [US]
le barman ◊ *He's a bartender.* Il est barman.

base NOUN
la base

baseball NOUN
le base-ball
♦**a baseball cap** une casquette de base-ball

based ADJECTIVE
♦**based on** fondé sur

basement NOUN
le sous-sol

to **bash** VERB
| see also **bash** NOUN |
♦**to bash something** taper sur quelque chose

bash NOUN
| see also **bash** VERB |
♦**I'll have a bash.** Je vais essayer.

basic ADJECTIVE
[1] de base ◊ *It's a basic model.* C'est un modèle de base.
[2] rudimentaire ◊ *The accommodation is pretty basic.* Le logement est plutôt rudimentaire.

basically ADVERB
tout simplement ◊ *Basically, I just don't like him.* Tout simplement, je ne l'aime pas.

basics PL NOUN

B

☞

les **rudiments** MASC PL

basil NOUN
le **basilic**

basin NOUN
le **lavabo** (*washbasin*)

basis NOUN
♦ **on a daily basis** quotidiennement
♦ **on a regular basis** régulièrement

basket NOUN
le **panier**

basketball NOUN
le **basket**

bass NOUN
[1] la **basse** (*guitar, singer*) ◊ *He plays the bass.* Il joue de la basse. ◊ *He's a bass.* Il est basse.
♦ **a bass guitar** une guitare basse
♦ **a double bass** une contrebasse
[2] les **graves** MASC PL (*on hi-fi*)

bass drum NOUN
la **grosse caisse**

bassoon NOUN
le **basson** ◊ *I play the bassoon.* Je joue du basson.

bastard NOUN
le **salaud** (*rude*) ◊ *You bastard!* Salaud!

bat NOUN
[1] (*for cricket, rounders*)
la **batte**
[2] (*for table tennis*)
la **raquette**
[3] (*animal*)
la **chauve-souris**
(les **chauves-souris** PL)

bath NOUN
[1] le **bain** ◊ *to have a bath* prendre un bain
♦ **a hot bath** un bain chaud
[2] la **baignoire** (*bathtub*) ◊ *There's a spider in the bath.* Il y a une araignée dans la baignoire.

to **bathe** VERB
se **baigner**

bathing suit NOUN US
le **maillot de bain**

bathroom NOUN
la **salle de bains**

baths PL NOUN
la **piscine** SING

bath towel NOUN
la **serviette de bain**

batter NOUN
la **pâte à frire**

battery NOUN
[1] la **pile** (*for torch, toy*)
[2] la **batterie** (*of car*)

battle NOUN

la **bataille** ◊ *the Battle of Hastings* la bataille de Hastings
♦ **It was a battle, but we managed in the end.** Il a fallu se battre, mais on a fini par y arriver.

battleship NOUN
le **cuirassé**

bay NOUN
la **baie**

BC ABBREVIATION (= *before Christ*)
av. J.-C. (= *avant Jésus-Christ*) ◊ *in 200 BC* en deux cents avant Jésus-Christ

to **be** VERB
être ◊ *I'm tired.* Je suis fatigué. ◊ *You're late.* Tu es en retard. ◊ *She's English.* Elle est anglaise. ◊ *Edinburgh is in Scotland.* Édimbourg est en Écosse. ◊ *It's 4 o'clock.* Il est quatre heures. ◊ *We are all happy.* Nous sommes tous heureux. ◊ *They are in Paris at the moment.* Ils sont à Paris en ce moment. ◊ *I've been ill.* J'ai été malade.
♦ **It's the 28th of October today.** Nous sommes le vingt-huit octobre.
♦ **Have you been to Greece before?** Est-ce que tu es déjà allé en Grèce?
♦ **I've never been to Paris.** Je ne suis jamais allé à Paris.
♦ **to be killed** être tué
When you are saying what somebody's occupation is, you leave out the "a" in French.
◊ *She's a doctor.* Elle est médecin.
◊ *He's a student.* Il est étudiant.
With certain adjectives, such as "cold", "hot", "hungry" and "thirsty", use avoir instead of être.
♦ **I'm cold.** J'ai froid.
♦ **I'm hungry.** J'ai faim.
When saying how old somebody is, use avoir not être.
♦ **I'm fourteen.** J'ai quatorze ans.
♦ **How old are you?** Quel âge as-tu?
When referring to the weather, use faire.
♦ **It's cold.** Il fait froid.
♦ **It's too hot.** Il fait trop chaud.
♦ **It's a nice day.** Il fait beau.

beach NOUN
la **plage**

bead NOUN
la **perle**

beak NOUN
le **bec**

beam NOUN
le **rayon**

beans PL NOUN
[1] les **haricots** MASC PL

[2] les haricots blancs à la sauce tomate MASC PL (*baked beans*) ◊ *I had beans on toast.* J'ai mangé des haricots blancs à la sauce tomate sur du pain grillé.
+**broad beans** les fèves FEM
+**green beans** les haricots verts MASC
+**kidney beans** les haricots rouges MASC

bear NOUN
> see also **bear** VERB

l' ours MASC

to **bear** VERB
> see also **bear** NOUN

+**I can't bear it!** C'est insupportable!
+**to bear up** tenir le coup
+**Bear up!** Tiens bon!

beard NOUN
la barbe
+**He's got a beard.** Il est barbu.
+**a man with a beard** un barbu

bearded ADJECTIVE
barbu

beat NOUN
> see also **beat** VERB

le rythme

to **beat** VERB
> see also **beat** NOUN

battre ◊ *We beat them 3-0.* On les a battus trois à zéro.
+**Beat it!** Fiche le camp! (*informal*)
+**to beat somebody up** tabasser quelqu'un (*informal*)

beautiful ADJECTIVE
beau MASC
belle FEM
(beaux MASC PL)

beautifully ADVERB
admirablement

beauty NOUN
la beauté

beauty spot NOUN
le site pittoresque

became VERB *see* **become**

because CONJUNCTION
parce que ◊ *I did it because ...* Je l'ai fait parce que ...
+**because of** à cause de ◊ *because of the weather* à cause du temps

to **become** VERB
devenir ◊ *He became a famous writer.* Il est devenu un grand écrivain.

bed NOUN
le lit ◊ *in bed* au lit
+**to go to bed** aller se coucher
+**to go to bed with somebody** coucher avec quelqu'un

bed and breakfast NOUN

la chambre d'hôte ◊ *We stayed in a bed and breakfast.* Nous avons logé dans une chambre d'hôte.
+**How much is it for bed and breakfast?** C'est combien pour la chambre et le petit déjeuner?

bedclothes PL NOUN
les draps et les couvertures MASC PL

bedding NOUN
la literie

bedroom NOUN
la chambre

bedsit NOUN
la chambre meublée

bedspread NOUN
le dessus-de-lit
(les dessus-de-lit PL)

bedtime NOUN
+**Ten o'clock is my usual bedtime.** Je me couche généralement à dix heures.
+**Bedtime!** Au lit!

bee NOUN
l' abeille FEM

beef NOUN
le bœuf
+**roast beef** le rosbif

beefburger NOUN
le hamburger

been VERB *see* **be**

beer NOUN
la bière

beetle NOUN
le scarabée

beetroot NOUN
la betterave rouge

before PREPOSITION, CONJUNCTION, ADVERB
[1] avant ◊ *before Tuesday* avant mardi
[2] avant de ◊ *before going* avant de partir ◊ *Before opening the packet, read the instructions.* Avant d'ouvrir le paquet, lisez le mode d'emploi. ◊ *I'll phone before I leave.* J'appellerai avant de partir.
[3] déjà (*already*) ◊ *I've seen this film before.* J'ai déjà vu ce film. ◊ *Have you been to Scotland before?* Vous êtes déjà venu en Écosse?
+**the day before** la veille
+**the week before** la semaine précédente

beforehand ADVERB
à l'avance

to **beg** VERB
[1] mendier (*for money*)
[2] supplier ◊ *He begged me to stop.* Il m'a supplié d'arrêter.

began VERB *see* **begin**

beggar NOUN
le mendiant
la mendiante

to **begin** VERB
commencer
♦**to begin doing something** commencer
à faire quelque chose

beginner NOUN
le débutant
la débutante
◊ *I'm just a beginner.* Je ne suis
qu'un débutant.

beginning NOUN
le début ◊ *in the beginning* au début

begun VERB *see* **begin**

behalf NOUN
♦**on behalf of somebody** pour
quelqu'un

to **behave** VERB
se comporter ◊ *He behaved like an
idiot.* Il s'est comporté comme un
idiot. ◊ *She behaved very badly.* Elle
s'est très mal comportée.
♦**to behave oneself** être sage ◊ *Did the
children behave themselves?* Est-ce
que les enfants ont été sages?
♦**Behave!** Sois sage!

behaviour NOUN (US **behavior**)
le comportement

behind PREPOSITION, ADVERB
see also **behind** NOUN
derrière ◊ *behind the television*
derrière la télévision
♦**to be behind** (*late*) avoir du retard
◊ *I'm behind with my revision.* J'ai
du retard dans mes révisions.

behind NOUN
see also **behind** PREPOSITION, ADVERB
le derrière

beige ADJECTIVE
beige

Belgian ADJECTIVE
see also **Belgian** NOUN
belge ◊ *Belgian chocolate* le chocolat
belge ◊ *She's Belgian.* Elle est belge.

Belgian NOUN
see also **Belgian** ADJECTIVE
le/la Belge
♦**the Belgians** les Belges

Belgium NOUN
la Belgique
♦**in Belgium** en Belgique

to **believe** VERB
croire ◊ *I don't believe you.* Je ne te
crois pas.

♦**to believe in something** croire à
quelque chose ◊ *Do you believe in
ghosts?* Tu crois aux fantômes?
♦**to believe in God** croire en Dieu

bell NOUN
1 la sonnette (*doorbell*)
♦**to ring the bell** sonner à la porte
2 la cloche (*in church*)
3 la sonnerie (*in school*)
4 la clochette ◊ *Our cat has a bell
on its neck.* Notre chat a une
clochette sur son collier.

belly NOUN
le ventre

to **belong** VERB
♦**to belong to somebody** être à
quelqu'un ◊ *Who does it belong to?*
C'est à qui? ◊ *That belongs to me.*
C'est à moi.
♦**Do you belong to any clubs?** Est-ce
que tu es membre d'un club?
♦**Where does this belong?** Où est-ce
que ça va?

belongings PL NOUN
les affaires FEM PL

below PREPOSITION, ADVERB
1 au-dessous de ◊ *below the castle*
au-dessous du château
2 en dessous ◊ *on the floor below* à
l'étage en dessous
♦**10 degrees below freezing** moins dix

belt NOUN
la ceinture

beltway NOUN US
le périphérique

bench NOUN
1 le banc (*seat*)
2 l' établi MASC (*for woodwork*)

bend NOUN
see also **bend** VERB
1 le virage (*in road*)
2 le coude (*in river*)

to **bend** VERB
see also **bend** NOUN
1 courber (*back*)
2 plier (*leg, arm*) ◊ *I can't bend my
arm.* Je n'arrive pas à plier le bras.
♦**"do not bend"** "ne pas plier"
3 tordre (*object*) ◊ *You've bent it.* Tu
l'as tordu.
4 se tordre ◊ *It bends easily.* Ça
tord facilement.
♦**to bend down** se baisser
♦**to bend over** se pencher

beneath PREPOSITION
sous

benefit NOUN
see also **benefit** VERB
l' avantage MASC (*advantage*)

B

♦**unemployment benefit** les allocations de chômage FEM PL

to **benefit** VERB

see also **benefit** NOUN

♦**He'll benefit from the change.** Le changement lui fera du bien.

bent VERB see **bend**

bent ADJECTIVE
    tordu ◊ *a bent fork* une fourchette tordue

beret NOUN
    le béret

berserk ADJECTIVE
♦**to go berserk** devenir fou furieux ◊ *She went berserk.* Elle est devenue folle furieuse.

berth NOUN
    la couchette

beside PREPOSITION
    à côté de ◊ *beside the television* à côté de la télévision
♦**He was beside himself.** Il était hors de lui.
♦**That's beside the point.** Cela n'a rien à voir.

besides ADVERB
    en plus ◊ *Besides, it's too expensive.* En plus, c'est trop cher.

best ADJECTIVE, ADVERB
    [1] meilleur ◊ *He's the best player in the team.* Il est le meilleur joueur de l'équipe. ◊ *Janet's the best at maths.* Janet est la meilleure en maths.
    [2] le mieux ◊ *Emma sings best.* C'est Emma qui chante le mieux. ◊ *That's the best I can do.* Je ne peux pas faire mieux.
♦**to do one's best** faire de son mieux ◊ *It's not perfect, but I did my best.* Ça n'est pas parfait, mais j'ai fait de mon mieux.
♦**to make the best of it** s'en contenter ◊ *We'll have to make the best of it.* Il va falloir nous en contenter.

best man NOUN
    le garçon d'honneur

bet NOUN
    see also **bet** VERB
    le pari ◊ *to make a bet* faire un pari

to **bet** VERB
    see also **bet** NOUN
    parier ◊ *I bet you he won't come.* Je te parie qu'il ne viendra pas. ◊ *I bet he forgot.* Je parie qu'il a oublié.

to **betray** VERB
    trahir

better ADJECTIVE, ADVERB
    [1] meilleur ◊ *This one's better than that one.* Celui-ci est meilleur que celui-là. ◊ *a better way to do it* une meilleure façon de le faire
    [2] mieux ◊ *That's better!* C'est mieux comme ça.
♦**better still** encore mieux ◊ *Go and see her tomorrow, or better still, go today.* Va la voir demain, ou encore mieux, vas-y aujourd'hui.
♦**to get better (1)** (*improve*) s'améliorer ◊ *I hope the weather gets better soon.* J'espère que le temps va s'améliorer bientôt. ◊ *My French is getting better.* Mon français s'améliore.
♦**to get better (2)** (*from illness*) se remettre ◊ *I hope you get better soon.* J'espère que tu vas vite te remettre.
♦**to feel better** se sentir mieux ◊ *Are you feeling better now?* Tu te sens mieux maintenant?
♦**You'd better do it straight away.** Vous feriez mieux de le faire immédiatement.
♦**I'd better go home.** Je ferais mieux de rentrer.

betting shop NOUN
    le bureau de paris

between PREPOSITION
    entre ◊ *Stroud is between Oxford and Bristol.* Stroud est entre Oxford et Bristol. ◊ *between 15 and 20 minutes* entre quinze et vingt minutes.

bewildered ADJECTIVE
♦**He looked bewildered.** Il avait l'air perplexe.

beyond PREPOSITION
    au-delà de ◊ *There was a lake beyond the mountain.* Il y avait un lac au-delà de la montagne.
♦**beyond belief** incroyable
♦**beyond repair** irréparable

biased ADJECTIVE
    partial

Bible NOUN
    la Bible

bicycle NOUN
    le vélo

bifocals PL NOUN
    les verres à double foyer MASC PL

big ADJECTIVE
    [1] grand ◊ *a big house* une grande maison ◊ *my big brother* mon grand frère ◊ *her big sister* sa grande sœur
♦**He's a big guy.** C'est un grand gaillard.
    [2] (*car, animal, book, parcel*)
    gros MASC
    grosse FEM

☞

◊ *a big car* une grosse voiture

bigheaded ADJECTIVE
♦**to be bigheaded** avoir la grosse tête

bike NOUN
le vélo ◊ *by bike* en vélo

bikini NOUN
le bikini

bilingual ADJECTIVE
bilingue

bill NOUN
[1] l' addition FEM (*in restaurant*) ◊ *Can we have the bill, please?* L'addition, s'il vous plaît.
[2] la facture (*for gas, electricity, telephone*)
[3] le billet US ◊ *a five-dollar bill* un billet de cinq dollars

billiards NOUN
le billard ◊ *to play billiards* jouer au billard

billion NOUN
le milliard

bin NOUN
la poubelle

bingo NOUN
le bingo

binoculars PL NOUN
les jumelles FEM PL
♦**a pair of binoculars** des jumelles

biochemistry NOUN
la biochimie

biography NOUN
la biographie

biology NOUN
la biologie

bird NOUN
l' oiseau MASC
(les oiseaux PL)

birdwatching NOUN
♦**My hobby's birdwatching.** Mon passe-temps favori est d'observer les oiseaux.
♦**to go birdwatching** aller observer les oiseaux

Biro ® NOUN
le bic ®

birth NOUN
la naissance ◊ *date of birth* la date de naissance

birth certificate NOUN
l' acte de naissance MASC

birth control NOUN
la contraception

birthday NOUN
l' anniversaire MASC ◊ *When's your birthday?* Quelle est la date de ton anniversaire?

♦**a birthday cake** un gâteau d'anniversaire
♦**I'm going to have a birthday party.** Je vais faire une fête pour mon anniversaire.

biscuit NOUN
le gâteau sec

bishop NOUN
l' évêque MASC

bit VERB *see* **bite**

bit NOUN
le morceau
(les morceaux PL)
◊ *Would you like another bit?* Est-ce que tu en veux un autre morceau?
♦**a bit of (1)** (*piece of*) un morceau de ◊ *a bit of cake* un morceau de gâteau
♦**a bit of (2)** (*a little*) un peu de ◊ *a bit of music* un peu de musique
♦**It's a bit of a nuisance.** C'est ennuyeux.
♦**a bit** un peu ◊ *He's a bit mad.* Il est un peu fou. ◊ *a bit too hot* un peu trop chaud ◊ *Wait a bit!* Attends un peu! ◊ *Do you play football? – A bit.* Tu joues au football? – Un peu.
♦**to fall to bits** se désintégrer
♦**to take something to bits** démonter quelque chose
♦**bit by bit** petit à petit

bitch NOUN
[1] la garce (*person*)
[2] la chienne (*female dog*)

to **bite** VERB
see also **bite** NOUN
[1] mordre (*person, dog*)
[2] piquer (*insect*) ◊ *I got bitten by mosquitoes.* Je me suis fait piquer par des moustiques.
♦**to bite one's nails** se ronger les ongles

bite NOUN
see also **bite** VERB
[1] la piqûre (*insect bite*)
[2] la morsure (*animal bite*)
♦**to have a bite to eat** manger un morceau

bitten VERB *see* **bite**

bitter ADJECTIVE
see also **bitter** NOUN
[1] amer MASC
amère FEM
[2] (*weather, wind*)
glacial
(glaciaux MASC PL)
◊ *It's bitter today.* Il fait glacial aujourd'hui.

B

bitter NOUN
see also **bitter** ADJECTIVE
la bière brune

black ADJECTIVE
noir ◇ *a black jacket* une veste noire
◇ *She's black.* Elle est noire.

blackberry NOUN
la mûre

blackbird NOUN
le merle

blackboard NOUN
le tableau noir

black coffee NOUN
le café

blackcurrant NOUN
le cassis

blackmail NOUN
see also **blackmail** VERB
le chantage ◇ *That's blackmail!* C'est
du chantage!

to **blackmail** VERB
see also **blackmail** NOUN
♦**to blackmail somebody** faire chanter
quelqu'un ◇ *He blackmailed her.* Il l'a
fait chanter.

blackout NOUN
la panne d'électricité (*power cut*)
♦**to have a blackout** (*faint*) s'évanouir

black pudding NOUN
le boudin

blade NOUN
la lame

to **blame** VERB
♦**Don't blame me!** Ça n'est pas ma
faute!
♦**I blame the police.** À mon avis, c'est
la faute de la police.
♦**He blamed it on my sister.** Il a dit
que c'était la faute de ma sœur.

blank ADJECTIVE
see also **blank** NOUN
1 (*paper*)
blanc MASC
blanche FEM
2 (*cassette, video, page*)
vierge
♦**My mind went blank.** J'ai eu un trou.

blank NOUN
see also **blank** ADJECTIVE
le blanc ◇ *Fill in the blanks.*
Remplissez les blancs.

blank cheque NOUN
le chèque en blanc

blanket NOUN
la couverture

blast NOUN
♦**a bomb blast** une explosion

blatant ADJECTIVE
flagrant

blaze NOUN
l' incendie MASC

blazer NOUN
le blazer

bleach NOUN
l' eau de Javel FEM

bleached ADJECTIVE
décoloré ◇ *bleached hair* les cheveux
décolorés MASC PL

bleak ADJECTIVE
désolé (*place*)
♦**The future looks bleak.** L'avenir
semble peu prometteur.

to **bleed** VERB
saigner ◇ *My nose is bleeding.* Je
saigne du nez.

bleeper NOUN
le bip

blender NOUN
le mixer

to **bless** VERB
bénir (*religiously*)
♦**Bless you!** (*after sneezing*) À tes
souhaits!

blew VERB see **blow**

blind ADJECTIVE
see also **blind** NOUN
aveugle

blind NOUN
see also **blind** ADJECTIVE
le store (*for window*)

blindfold NOUN
see also **blindfold** VERB
le bandeau
(les bandeaux PL)

to **blindfold** VERB
see also **blindfold** NOUN
♦**to blindfold somebody** bander les
yeux à quelqu'un

to **blink** VERB
cligner des yeux

bliss NOUN
♦**It was bliss!** C'était merveilleux!

blister NOUN
l' ampoule FEM

blizzard NOUN
la tempête de neige

blob NOUN
la goutte ◇ *a blob of glue* une goutte
de colle

block NOUN
see also **block** VERB
l' immeuble MASC ◇ *He lives in our
block.* Il habite dans notre immeuble.
♦**a block of flats** un immeuble

to **block** VERB

☞

see also **block** NOUN
bloquer

blockage NOUN
l' obstruction FEM

bloke NOUN
le mec (*informal*)

blonde ADJECTIVE
blond ◊ *She's got blonde hair.* Elle a
les cheveux blonds.

blood NOUN
le sang

blood pressure NOUN
♦**to have high blood pressure** faire de
la tension

blood sports NOUN
les sports sanguinaires MASC PL

blood test NOUN
la prise de sang

bloody ADJECTIVE
♦**bloody difficult** sacrément difficile
♦**that bloody television** cette putain de
télévision
♦**Bloody hell!** Merde!

blouse NOUN
le chemisier

blow NOUN
see also **blow** VERB
le coup

to **blow** VERB
see also **blow** NOUN
souffler (*wind, person*)
♦**to blow one's nose** se moucher
♦**to blow a whistle** siffler
♦**to blow out a candle** éteindre une
bougie
♦**to blow up (1)** faire sauter ◊ *The
terrorists blew up a police station.*
Les terroristes ont fait sauter un
commissariat de police.
♦**to blow up (2)** gonfler ◊ *to blow up a
balloon* gonfler un ballon
♦**The house blew up.** La maison a
sauté.

blow-dry NOUN
le brushing
♦**A cut and blow-dry, please.** Une
coupe brushing, s'il vous plaît.

blown VERB *see* **blow**

blue ADJECTIVE
bleu ◊ *a blue dress* une robe bleue
♦**a blue film** un film pornographique
♦**It came out of the blue.** C'était
complètement inattendu.

blues PL NOUN
le blues SING

to **bluff** VERB
see also **bluff** NOUN
bluffer

bluff NOUN
see also **bluff** VERB
le bluff ◊ *It's just a bluff.* C'est du
bluff.

blunder NOUN
la gaffe

blunt ADJECTIVE
1 brusque (*person*)
2 émoussé (*knife*)

to **blush** VERB
rougir

board NOUN
1 (*wooden*)
la planche
2 (*blackboard*)
le tableau
(les tableaux PL)
◊ *on the board* au tableau
3 (*noticeboard*)
le panneau
(les panneaux PL)
4 (*for board games*)
le jeu
(les jeux PL)
5 (*for chess*)
l' échiquier MASC
♦**on board** à bord
♦**"full board"** "pension complète"

boarder NOUN
l' interne MASC/FEM

board game NOUN
le jeu de société
(les jeux de société PL)

boarding card NOUN
la carte d'embarquement

boarding school NOUN
le pensionnat
♦**I go to boarding school.** Je suis
interne.

to **boast** VERB
se vanter ◊ *Stop boasting!* Arrête de
te vanter!
♦**to boast about something** se vanter
de quelque chose

boat NOUN
le bateau
(les bateaux PL)

body NOUN
le corps

bodybuilding NOUN
le culturisme

bodyguard NOUN
le garde du corps

bog NOUN
la tourbière (*marsh*)

boil NOUN
see also **boil** VERB
le furoncle

to **boil** VERB

B

see also **boil** NOUN
1 faire bouillir ◇ *to boil some water* faire bouillir de l'eau
♦**to boil an egg** faire cuire un œuf
2 bouillir ◇ *The water's boiling.* L'eau bout. ◇ *The water's boiled.* L'eau a bouilli.
♦**to boil over** déborder

boiled ADJECTIVE
à l'eau ◇ *boiled potatoes* des pommes de terre à l'eau
♦**a boiled egg** un œuf à la coque

boiling ADJECTIVE
♦**It's boiling in here!** Il fait une chaleur torride ici!
♦**boiling hot** torride ◇ *a boiling hot day* une journée torride

bolt NOUN
1 le verrou (*on door*)
2 le boulon (*with nut*)

bomb NOUN
see also **bomb** VERB
la bombe

to **bomb** VERB
see also **bomb** NOUN
bombarder

bomber NOUN
le bombardier

bombing NOUN
l' attentat à la bombe MASC

bond NOUN
le lien

bone NOUN
1 l' os MASC (*of human, animal*)
2 l' arête FEM (*of fish*)

bone dry ADJECTIVE
complètement sec MASC
complètement sèche FEM

bonfire NOUN
le feu
(les feux PL)

bonnet NOUN
le capot (*of car*)

bonus NOUN
1 la prime (*extra payment*)
2 le plus (*added advantage*)

book NOUN
see also **book** VERB
le livre

to **book** VERB
see also **book** NOUN
réserver ◇ *We haven't booked.* Nous n'avons pas réservé.

bookcase NOUN
la bibliothèque

booklet NOUN
la brochure

bookmark NOUN

le signet (*computing*)

bookshelf NOUN
l' étagère à livres FEM

bookshop NOUN
la librairie

to **boost** VERB
stimuler ◇ *to boost the economy* stimuler l'économie
♦**The win boosted the team's morale.** La victoire a remonté le moral de l'équipe.

boot NOUN
1 le coffre (*of car*)
2 la botte (*fashion boot*)
3 la chaussure de marche (*for hiking*)
♦**football boots** des chaussures de foot

booze NOUN
l' alcool MASC

border NOUN
la frontière

bore VERB *see* **bear**

bored ADJECTIVE
♦**to be bored** s'ennuyer ◇ *I was bored.* Je m'ennuyais.
♦**to get bored** s'ennuyer

boredom NOUN
l' ennui MASC

boring ADJECTIVE
ennuyeux MASC
ennuyeuse FEM

born ADJECTIVE
♦**to be born** naître ◇ *I was born in 1982.* Je suis né en mille neuf cent quatre-vingt-deux.

to **borrow** VERB
emprunter ◇ *Can I borrow your pen?* Je peux emprunter ton stylo?
♦**to borrow something from somebody** emprunter quelque chose à quelqu'un ◇ *I borrowed some money from a friend.* J'ai emprunté de l'argent à un ami.

Bosnia NOUN
la Bosnie

Bosnian ADJECTIVE
bosniaque

boss NOUN
le patron
la patronne

to **boss around** VERB
♦**to boss somebody around** donner des ordres à quelqu'un

bossy ADJECTIVE
autoritaire

both ADJECTIVE, PRONOUN
tous les deux MASC PL
toutes les deux FEM PL

☞

◊ *We both went.* Nous y sommes allés tous les deux. ◊ *Emma and Jane both went.* Emma et Jane y sont allées toutes les deux. ◊ *Both of your answers are wrong.* Vos réponses sont toutes les deux mauvaises. ◊ *Both of them have left.* Ils sont partis tous les deux. ◊ *Both of us went.* Nous y sommes allés tous les deux. ◊ *Both Maggie and John are against it.* Maggie et John sont tous les deux contre.

♦**He speaks both German and Italian.** Il parle allemand et italien.

to **bother** VERB
 1 tracasser (*worry*) ◊ *What's bothering you?* Qu'est-ce qui te tracasse?
 2 déranger (*disturb*) ◊ *I'm sorry to bother you.* Je suis désolé de vous déranger.
♦**no bother** aucun problème
♦**Don't bother!** Ça n'est pas la peine!
♦**to bother to do something** prendre la peine de faire quelque chose ◊ *He didn't bother to tell me about it.* Il n'a pas pris la peine de m'en parler.

bottle NOUN
 la bouteille

bottle bank NOUN
 le conteneur à verre

bottle-opener NOUN
 l' ouvre-bouteille MASC

bottom NOUN
 see also **bottom** ADJECTIVE
 1 le fond (*of container, bag, sea*)
 2 le derrière (*buttocks*)
 3 le bas (*of page, list*)

bottom ADJECTIVE
 see also **bottom** NOUN
 inférieur ◊ *the bottom shelf* l'étagère inférieure
♦**the bottom sheet** le drap de dessous

bought VERB *see* **buy**

to **bounce** VERB
 rebondir

bouncer NOUN
 le videur

bound ADJECTIVE
♦**He's bound to fail.** Il va sûrement échouer.

boundary NOUN
 la frontière

bow NOUN
 see also **bow** VERB
 1 le nœud (*knot*) ◊ *to tie a bow* faire un nœud
 2 l' arc MASC ◊ *a bow and arrows* un arc et des flèches

to **bow** VERB
 see also **bow** NOUN
 faire une révérence

bowels PL NOUN
 les intestins MASC PL

bowl NOUN
 see also **bowl** VERB
 le bol (*for soup, cereal*)

to **bowl** VERB
 see also **bowl** NOUN
 lancer la balle (*in cricket*)

bowler NOUN
 le lanceur (*in cricket*)

bowling NOUN
 le bowling
♦**to go bowling** jouer au bowling
♦**a bowling alley** un bowling

bowls NOUN
 les boules FEM PL ◊ *to play bowls* jouer aux boules

bow tie NOUN
 le nœud papillon

box NOUN
 la boîte ◊ *a box of matches* une boîte d'allumettes
♦**a cardboard box** un carton

boxer NOUN
 le boxeur

boxer shorts PL NOUN
 le caleçon SING

boxing NOUN
 la boxe

Boxing Day NOUN
 le lendemain de Noël ◊ *on Boxing Day* le lendemain de Noël

boy NOUN
 le garçon

boyfriend NOUN
 le copain ◊ *Have you got a boyfriend?* Est-ce que tu as un copain?

bra NOUN
 le soutien-gorge
 (les soutiens-gorge PL)

brace NOUN
 l' appareil MASC (*on teeth*) ◊ *She wears a brace.* Elle a un appareil.

bracelet NOUN
 le bracelet

brackets PL NOUN
♦**in brackets** entre parenthèses

brain NOUN
 le cerveau
 (les cerveaux PL)

brainy ADJECTIVE
 intelligent

brake NOUN
 see also **brake** VERB

le <u>frein</u>

to **brake** VERB
> see also **brake** NOUN
<u>freiner</u>

branch NOUN
1 la <u>branche</u> (*of tree*)
2 l' <u>agence</u> FEM (*of bank*)

brand NOUN
la <u>marque</u> ◊ *a well-known brand of coffee* une marque de café bien connue

brand name NOUN
la <u>marque</u>

brand-new ADJECTIVE
<u>tout neuf</u> MASC
<u>toute neuve</u> FEM

brandy NOUN
le <u>cognac</u>

brass NOUN
le <u>cuivre</u>
♦ **the brass section** les cuivres

brass band NOUN
la <u>fanfare</u>

brat NOUN
♦ **He's a spoiled brat.** C'est un enfant gâté.

brave ADJECTIVE
<u>courageux</u> MASC
<u>courageuse</u> FEM

Brazil NOUN
le <u>Brésil</u>
♦ **in Brazil** au Brésil

bread NOUN
le <u>pain</u> ◊ *brown bread* le pain complet ◊ *white bread* le pain blanc
♦ **bread and butter** les tartines de pain beurrées FEM PL

break NOUN
> see also **break** VERB
1 la <u>pause</u> (*rest*) ◊ *to take a break* faire une pause
2 la <u>récréation</u> (*at school*) ◊ *during morning break* pendant la récréation du matin
♦ **the Christmas break** les vacances de Noël FEM PL
♦ **Give me a break!** Laisse-moi tranquille!

to **break** VERB
> see also **break** NOUN
1 <u>casser</u> ◊ *Careful, you'll break something!* Attention, tu vas casser quelque chose!
2 <u>se casser</u> (*get broken*) ◊ *Careful, it'll break!* Attention, ça va se casser!
♦ **to break one's leg** se casser la jambe
◊ *I broke my leg.* Je me suis cassé la jambe.

♦ **He broke his arm.** Il s'est cassé le bras.
♦ **to break a promise** rompre une promesse
♦ **to break a record** battre un record
♦ **to break the law** violer la loi

to **break down** VERB
<u>tomber en panne</u> ◊ *The car broke down.* La voiture est tombée en panne.

to **break in** VERB
<u>entrer par effraction</u>

to **break off** VERB
1 <u>casser</u> ◊ *He broke off a piece of chocolate.* Il a cassé un bout de chocolat.
2 <u>se casser</u> ◊ *The branch broke off when she sat on it.* La branche s'est cassée quand elle s'est assise dessus.

to **break open** VERB
<u>forcer</u> (*door, cupboard*)

to **break out** VERB
1 <u>se déclarer</u> (*fire*)
2 <u>éclater</u> (*war*)
3 <u>s'évader</u> (*prisoner*)
♦ **to break out in a rash** être couvert de boutons

to **break up** VERB
1 <u>se disperser</u> (*crowd*)
2 <u>se terminer</u> (*meeting, party*)
3 <u>se séparer</u> (*couple*)
♦ **to break up a fight** mettre fin à une bagarre
♦ **We break up next Wednesday.** Nos vacances commencent mercredi.

breakdown NOUN
1 la <u>panne</u> (*in vehicle*) ◊ *to have a breakdown* tomber en panne
2 la <u>dépression</u> (*mental*) ◊ *to have a breakdown* faire une dépression

breakdown van NOUN
la <u>dépanneuse</u>

breakfast NOUN
le <u>petit déjeuner</u> ◊ *What would you like for breakfast?* Qu'est-ce vous voulez pour le petit déjeuner?

break-in NOUN
le <u>cambriolage</u>

breast NOUN
le <u>sein</u> (*of woman*)
♦ **chicken breast** le blanc de poulet

to **breast-feed** VERB
<u>allaiter</u>

breaststroke NOUN
la <u>brasse</u>

breath NOUN
l' <u>haleine</u> FEM ◊ *to have bad breath* avoir mauvaise haleine
♦ **to be out of breath** être essoufflé

♦ **to get one's breath back** reprendre son souffle

to **breathe** VERB
respirer

to **breathe in** VERB
inspirer

to **breathe out** VERB
expirer

to **breed** VERB
> see also **breed** NOUN
se reproduire (*reproduce*)
♦ **to breed dogs** faire de l'élevage de chiens

breed NOUN
> see also **breed** VERB
la race

breeze NOUN
la brise

brewery NOUN
la brasserie

to **bribe** VERB
soudoyer

brick NOUN
la brique
♦ **a brick wall** un mur en brique

bricklayer NOUN
le maçon

bride NOUN
la mariée

bridegroom NOUN
le marié

bridesmaid NOUN
la demoiselle d'honneur

bridge NOUN
1 le pont ◊ *a suspension bridge* un pont suspendu
2 le bridge ◊ *to play bridge* jouer au bridge

brief ADJECTIVE
bref MASC
brève FEM

briefcase NOUN
la serviette

briefly ADVERB
brièvement

briefs PL NOUN
le slip SING
♦ **a pair of briefs** un slip

bright ADJECTIVE
1 (*colour, light*)
vif MASC
vive FEM
◊ *a bright colour* une couleur vive
♦ **bright blue** bleu vif ◊ *a bright blue car* une voiture bleu vif
2 intelligent ◊ *He's not very bright.* Il n'est pas très intelligent.

brilliant ADJECTIVE
1 (*wonderful*)
génial
(géniaux MASC PL)
◊ *Brilliant!* Génial!
2 (*clever*)
brillant ◊ *a brilliant scientist* un savant brillant

to **bring** VERB
1 apporter ◊ *Bring warm clothes.* Apportez des vêtements chauds. ◊ *Could you bring me my trainers?* Tu peux m'apporter mes baskets?
2 amener (*person*) ◊ *Can I bring a friend?* Est-ce que je peux amener un ami?

to **bring about** VERB
provoquer ◊ *The war brought about a change in people's attitudes.* La guerre a provoqué un changement dans l'attitude des gens.

to **bring back** VERB
rapporter

to **bring forward** VERB
avancer ◊ *The meeting was brought forward.* On a avancé la réunion.

to **bring up** VERB
élever ◊ *She brought up 5 children on her own.* Elle a élevé cinq enfants toute seule.

Britain NOUN
la Grande-Bretagne
♦ **in Britain** en Grande-Bretagne
♦ **to Britain** en Grande-Bretagne
♦ **I'm from Britain.** Je suis britannique.
♦ **Great Britain** la Grande-Bretagne

British ADJECTIVE
britannique
♦ **the British** les Britanniques MASC PL
♦ **the British Isles** les îles Britanniques FEM PL

Brittany NOUN
la Bretagne
♦ **in Brittany** en Bretagne
♦ **to Brittany** en Bretagne
♦ **She's from Brittany.** Elle est bretonne.

broad ADJECTIVE
large (*wide*)
♦ **in broad daylight** en plein jour

broadcast NOUN
> see also **broadcast** VERB
l' émission FEM

to **broadcast** VERB
> see also **broadcast** NOUN
diffuser ◊ *The interview was broadcast all over the world.* L'interview a été diffusé dans le monde entier.
♦ **to broadcast live** retransmettre en direct

broad-minded ADJECTIVE
large d'esprit

broccoli NOUN
les brocolis MASC PL

brochure NOUN
la brochure

to **broil** VERB US
♦**to broil something** faire griller
quelque chose

broke VERB see **break**

broke ADJECTIVE
♦**to be broke** (without money) être fauché

broken ADJECTIVE
cassé ◊ It's broken. C'est cassé. ◊ a
broken leg une jambe cassée ◊ He's
got a broken arm. Il a le bras cassé.

bronchitis NOUN
la bronchite

bronze NOUN
le bronze ◊ the bronze medal la
médaille de bronze

brooch NOUN
la broche

broom NOUN
le balai

brother NOUN
le frère ◊ my brother mon frère ◊ my
big brother mon grand frère

brother-in-law NOUN
le beau-frère
(les beaux-frères PL)

brought VERB see **bring**

brown ADJECTIVE
[1] (clothes)
marron MASC, FEM, PL
[2] (hair)
brun
[3] (tanned)
bronzé
♦**brown bread** le pain complet

Brownie NOUN
la jeannette

to **browse** VERB
parcourir le Net (on internet)

browser NOUN
le navigateur (for internet)

bruise NOUN
le bleu

brush NOUN
see also **brush** VERB
[1] la brosse
[2] (paintbrush)
le pinceau
(les pinceaux PL)

to **brush** VERB
see also **brush** NOUN
brosser

♦**to brush one's hair** se brosser les
cheveux ◊ I brushed my hair. Je me
suis brossé les cheveux.
♦**to brush one's teeth** se brosser les
dents ◊ I brush my teeth every night.
Je me brosse les dents tous les soirs.

Brussels NOUN
Bruxelles
♦**in Brussels** à Bruxelles
♦**to Brussels** à Bruxelles

Brussels sprouts PL NOUN
les choux de Bruxelles MASC PL

brutal ADJECTIVE
brutal
(brutaux MASC PL)

BSc NOUN (= Bachelor of Science)
la licence
♦**a BSc in Mathematics** une licence de
mathématiques

BSE NOUN (= bovine spongiform
encephalopathy)
l' ESB FEM (= l'encéphalite
spongiforme bovine)

bubble NOUN
la bulle

bubble bath NOUN
le bain moussant

bubble gum NOUN
le chewing-gum

bucket NOUN
le seau
(les seaux PL)

buckle NOUN
la boucle (on belt, watch, shoe)

Buddhism NOUN
le bouddhisme

Buddhist ADJECTIVE
bouddhiste

buddy NOUN US
le copain
la copine

budget NOUN
le budget

budgie NOUN
la perruche

buffet NOUN
le buffet

buffet car NOUN
la voiture-bar

bug NOUN
[1] l' insecte MASC (insect)
[2] le microbe (infection) ◊ There's a
bug going round. Il y a un microbe
qui traîne.
♦**a stomach bug** une gastroentérite
[3] le bug (in computer)

bugged ADJECTIVE

B

sur écoute ◊ *The room was bugged.*
La pièce était sur écoute.

to **build** VERB
construire ◊ *They're going to build houses here.* On va construire des maisons ici.
♦**to build up** (*increase*) s'accumuler

builder NOUN
1 l' entrepreneur MASC (*owner of firm*)
2 le maçon (*worker*)

building NOUN
le bâtiment

built VERB see **build**

bulb NOUN
l' ampoule FEM (*electric*)

Bulgaria NOUN
la Bulgarie

bull NOUN
le taureau
(les taureaux PL)

bullet NOUN
la balle

bulletin board NOUN
le panneau d'affichage électronique
(*computer*)

bullfighting NOUN
la tauromachie

bully NOUN
see also **bully** VERB
la brute ◊ *He's a big bully.* C'est une brute.

to **bully** VERB
see also **bully** NOUN
tyranniser

bum NOUN
le derrière (*bottom*)

bum bag NOUN
la banane

bump NOUN
see also **bump** VERB
1 la bosse (*lump*)
2 l' accrochage MASC (*minor accident*)
◊ *We had a bump.* Nous avons eu un accrochage.

to **bump** VERB
see also **bump** NOUN
♦**to bump into something** rentrer dans quelque chose ◊ *We bumped into his car.* Nous sommes rentrés dans sa voiture.
♦**to bump into somebody (1)** (*literally*) rentrer dans quelqu'un ◊ *He stopped suddenly and I bumped into him.* Il s'est arrêté subitement et je lui suis rentré dedans.
♦**to bump into somebody (2)** (*meet by chance*) rencontrer par hasard

♦**I bumped into Jane in the supermarket.** J'ai rencontré Jane par hasard au supermarché.

bumper NOUN
le pare-chocs
(les pare-chocs PL)

bumpy ADJECTIVE
cahoteux MASC
cahoteuse FEM

bun NOUN
le petit pain au lait

bunch NOUN
♦**a bunch of flowers** un bouquet de fleurs
♦**a bunch of grapes** une grappe de raisin
♦**a bunch of keys** un trousseau de clés

bunches PL NOUN
les couettes FEM PL ◊ *She has her hair in bunches.* Elle a des couettes.

bungalow NOUN
le bungalow

bunk NOUN
la couchette

burger NOUN
le hamburger

burglar NOUN
le cambrioleur
la cambrioleuse

to **burglarize** VERB US
cambrioler

burglary NOUN
le cambriolage

to **burgle** VERB
cambrioler ◊ *Her house was burgled.* Sa maison a été cambriolée.

burn NOUN
see also **burn** VERB
la brûlure

to **burn** VERB
see also **burn** NOUN
1 brûler (*rubbish, documents*)
2 faire brûler (*food*) ◊ *I burned the cake.* J'ai fait brûler le gâteau.
♦**to burn oneself** se brûler ◊ *I burned myself on the oven door.* Je me suis brûlé sur la porte du four.
♦**I've burned my hand.** Je me suis brûlé la main.
♦**to burn down** brûler ◊ *The factory burned down.* L'usine a brûlé.

to **burst** VERB
éclater ◊ *The balloon burst.* Le ballon a éclaté.
♦**to burst a balloon** faire éclater un ballon
♦**to burst out laughing** éclater de rire
♦**to burst into flames** prendre feu
♦**to burst into tears** fondre en larmes

to **bury** VERB
   enterrer
bus NOUN
   l' autobus MASC ◊ *the bus driver* le
   conducteur d'autobus ◊ *a bus stop* un
   arrêt d'autobus
   ♦ **the school bus** le car scolaire
   ♦ **a bus pass** une carte d'abonnement
   pour le bus
   ♦ **a bus station** une gare routière
   ♦ **a bus ticket** un ticket de bus
bush NOUN
   le buisson
business NOUN
   [1] l' entreprise FEM (*firm*) ◊ *He's got
   his own business.* Il a sa propre
   entreprise.
   [2] les affaires FEM PL (*commerce*) ◊ *He's
   away on business.* Il est en voyage
   d'affaires.
   ♦ **a business trip** un voyage d'affaires
   ♦ **It's none of my business.** Ça ne me
   regarde pas.
businessman NOUN
   l' homme d'affaires MASC
businesswoman NOUN
   la femme d'affaires
busker NOUN
   le musicien de rue
   la musicienne de rue
bust NOUN
   la poitrine (*chest*)
busy ADJECTIVE
   [1] occupé (*person, phone line*)
   [2] chargé (*day, schedule*)
   [3] très fréquenté (*shop, street*)
busy signal NOUN [US]
   la tonalité "occupé"
but CONJUNCTION
   mais ◊ *I'd like to come, but I'm busy.*
   J'aimerais venir mais je suis occupé.
butcher NOUN
   le boucher ◊ *He's a butcher.* Il est
   boucher.
butcher's NOUN
   la boucherie
butter NOUN
   le beurre
butterfly NOUN

   le papillon
buttocks PL NOUN
   les fesses FEM PL
button NOUN
   le bouton
to **buy** VERB
   see also **buy** NOUN
   acheter ◊ *He bought me an ice
   cream.* Il m'a acheté une glace. ◊ *I
   bought him an ice cream.* Je lui ai
   acheté une glace.
   ♦ **to buy something from somebody**
   acheter quelque chose à quelqu'un
   ◊ *I bought a watch from him.* Je lui
   ai acheté une montre.
buy NOUN
   see also **buy** VERB
   ♦ **It was a good buy.** C'était une bonne
   affaire.
by PREPOSITION
   [1] par ◊ *The thieves were caught by
   the police.* Les voleurs ont été arrêtés
   par la police.
   [2] de ◊ *a painting by Picasso* un
   tableau de Picasso ◊ *a book by Balzac*
   un livre de Balzac
   [3] en ◊ *by car* en voiture ◊ *by train*
   en train ◊ *by bus* en autobus
   [4] à côté de (*close to*) ◊ *Where's the
   bank? – It's by the post office.* Où est
   la banque? – Elle est à côté de la
   poste.
   [5] avant (*not later than*) ◊ *We have to
   be there by 4 o'clock.* Nous devons y
   être avant quatre heures.
   ♦ **by the time ... quand ...** ◊ *By the time
   I got there it was too late.* Quand je
   suis arrivé il était déjà trop tard. ◊ *It'll
   be ready by the time you get back.*
   Ça sera prêt quand vous reviendrez.
   ♦ **That's fine by me.** Ça me va.
   ♦ **all by himself** tout seul
   ♦ **all by herself** toute seule
   ♦ **I did it all by myself.** Je l'ai fait tout
   seul.
   ♦ **by the way** au fait
bye EXCLAMATION
   salut!
bypass NOUN
   la route de contournement

C

cab NOUN
le <u>taxi</u>

cabbage NOUN
le <u>chou</u>
(les <u>choux</u> PL)

cabin NOUN
la <u>cabine</u> (on ship)

cabinet NOUN
- **a bathroom cabinet** une armoire de salle de bain
- **a drinks cabinet** un bar

cable NOUN
le <u>câble</u>

cable car NOUN
le <u>téléphérique</u>

cable television NOUN
la <u>télévision par câble</u>

cactus NOUN
le <u>cactus</u>

cadet NOUN
- **a police cadet** un élève policier
- **a cadet officer** un élève officier

café NOUN
le <u>café</u>

> **🛈** Cafés in France sell both alcoholic and non-alcoholic drinks.

cafeteria NOUN
la <u>cafétéria</u>

cage NOUN
la <u>cage</u>

cagoule NOUN
le <u>K-way</u> ®

cake NOUN
le <u>gâteau</u>
(les <u>gâteaux</u> PL)

to **calculate** VERB
<u>calculer</u>

calculation NOUN
le <u>calcul</u>

calculator NOUN
la <u>machine à calculer</u>

calendar NOUN
le <u>calendrier</u>

calf NOUN
① (of cow)
le <u>veau</u>
(les <u>veaux</u> PL)
② (of leg)
le <u>mollet</u>

call NOUN
see also **call** VERB

l' <u>appel</u> MASC (by phone) ◊ Thanks for your call. Merci de votre appel.
- **a phone call** un coup de téléphone
- **to be on call** (doctor) être de permanence ◊ He's on call this evening. Il est de permanence ce soir.

to **call** VERB
see also **call** NOUN

<u>appeler</u> ◊ I'll tell him you called. Je lui dirai que vous avez appelé. ◊ This is the number to call. C'est le numéro à appeler. ◊ We called the police. Nous avons appelé la police. ◊ Everyone calls him Jimmy. Tout le monde l'appelle Jimmy.
- **to be called** s'appeler ◊ He's called Fluffy. Il s'appelle Fluffy. ◊ What's she called? Elle s'appelle comment?
- **to call somebody names** insulter quelqu'un
- **He called me an idiot.** Il m'a traité d'idiot.

to **call back** VERB
<u>rappeler</u> (phone again) ◊ I'll call back at 6 o'clock. Je rappellerai à six heures.

to **call for** VERB
<u>passer prendre</u> ◊ I'll call for you at 2.30. Je passerai te prendre à deux heures et demie.

to **call off** VERB
<u>annuler</u> ◊ The match was called off. Le match a été annulé.

call box NOUN
la <u>cabine téléphonique</u>

call centre NOUN
le <u>centre d'appels</u>

calm ADJECTIVE
<u>calme</u>

to **calm down** VERB
<u>se calmer</u> ◊ Calm down! Calme-toi!

Calor gas ® NOUN
le <u>butane</u>

calorie NOUN
la <u>calorie</u>

calves PL NOUN see **calf**

Cambodia NOUN
le <u>Cambodge</u>
- **in Cambodia** au Cambodge

camcorder NOUN
le <u>caméscope</u>

came VERB see **come**

camel NOUN

le chameau
(les chameaux PL)

camera NOUN
1 (for photos)
l' appareil photo MASC
(les appareils photo PL)
2 (for filming, TV)
la caméra

cameraman NOUN
le caméraman

to **camp** VERB

see also **camp** NOUN

camper

camp NOUN

see also **camp** VERB

le camp
♦ **a camp bed** un lit de camp

campaign NOUN
la campagne

camper NOUN
1 (person)
le campeur
la campeuse
2 (van)
le camping-car

camping NOUN
le camping
♦ **to go camping** faire du camping ◇ We
went camping in Cornwall. Nous
avons fait du camping en
Cornouailles.

camping gas ® NOUN
le butane

campsite NOUN
le terrain de camping

campus NOUN
le campus

can NOUN

see also **can** VERB

1 la boîte (tin) ◇ a can of sweetcorn
une boîte de maïs ◇ a can of beer
une boîte de bière
2 le bidon (jerry can) ◇ a can of
petrol un bidon d'essence

can VERB

see also **can** NOUN

1 pouvoir (be able to, be allowed to)
◇ I can't come. Je ne peux pas venir.
◇ Can I help you? Est-ce que je peux
vous aider? ◇ Can I use your phone?
Est-ce que je peux me servir de votre
téléphone? ◇ You could hire a bike.
Tu pourrais louer un vélo. ◇ I couldn't
sleep because of the noise. Je ne
pouvais pas dormir à cause du bruit.
can is sometimes not translated.
◇ I can't hear you. Je ne t'entends
pas. ◇ I can't remember. Je ne m'en

souviens pas. ◇ Can you speak
French? Parlez-vous français?
2 savoir (have learnt how to) ◇ I can
swim. Je sais nager. ◇ He can't drive.
Il ne sait pas conduire.
♦ **That can't be true!** Ce n'est pas
possible!
♦ **You could be right.** Vous avez peut-
être raison.

Canada NOUN
le Canada
♦ **in Canada** au Canada
♦ **to Canada** au Canada

Canadian ADJECTIVE

see also **Canadian** NOUN

canadien MASC
canadienne FEM

Canadian NOUN

see also **Canadian** ADJECTIVE

le Canadien
la Canadienne

canal NOUN
le canal
(les canaux PL)

Canaries PL NOUN
♦ **the Canaries** les îles Canaries FEM PL

canary NOUN
le canari

to **cancel** VERB
annuler ◇ The match was cancelled.
Le match a été annulé.

cancellation NOUN
l' annulation FEM

cancer NOUN
1 le cancer ◇ He's got cancer. Il a le
cancer.
2 le Cancer ◇ I'm Cancer. Je suis
Cancer.

candidate NOUN
le candidat
la candidate

candle NOUN
la bougie

candy NOUN US
les bonbons MASC PL
♦ **a candy** un bonbon

candyfloss NOUN
la barbe à papa

cannabis NOUN
le cannabis

canned ADJECTIVE
en conserve (food)

cannot VERB see **can**

canoe NOUN
le canoë

canoeing NOUN

♦**to go canoeing** faire du canoë ◊ *We went canoeing.* Nous avons fait du canoë.

can-opener NOUN
l' ouvre-boîte MASC

can't VERB *see* **can**

canteen NOUN
la cantine

to **canter** VERB
aller au petit galop

canvas NOUN
la toile

cap NOUN
[1] la casquette (*hat*)
[2] le bouchon (*of bottle, tube*)

capable ADJECTIVE
capable

capacity NOUN
la capacité

capital NOUN
[1] la capitale ◊ *Cardiff is the capital of Wales.* Cardiff est la capitale du pays de Galles.
[2] la majuscule (*letter*) ◊ *Write your address in capitals.* Écris ton adresse en majuscules.

capitalism NOUN
le capitalisme

capital punishment NOUN
la peine capitale

Capricorn NOUN
le Capricorne ◊ *I'm Capricorn.* Je suis Capricorne.

to **capsize** VERB
chavirer

captain NOUN
le capitaine ◊ *She's captain of the hockey team.* Elle est capitaine de l'équipe de hockey.

caption NOUN
la légende

to **capture** VERB
capturer

car NOUN
la voiture
♦**to go by car** aller en voiture ◊ *We went by car.* Nous y sommes allés en voiture.
♦**a car crash** un accident de voiture

caramel NOUN
le caramel

caravan NOUN
la caravane ◊ *a caravan site* un camping pour caravanes

card NOUN
la carte
♦**a card game** un jeu de cartes

cardboard NOUN
le carton

cardigan NOUN
le cardigan

cardphone NOUN
le téléphone à carte

care NOUN
see also **care** VERB
le soin ◊ *with care* avec soin
♦**to take care of** s'occuper de ◊ *I take care of the children on Saturdays.* Le samedi, je m'occupe des enfants.
♦**Take care! (1)** (*Be careful!*) Fais attention!
♦**Take care! (2)** (*Look after yourself!*) Prends bien soin de toi!

to **care** VERB
see also **care** NOUN
♦**to care about** se soucier de ◊ *They don't care about their image.* Ils se soucient peu de leur image.
♦**I don't care!** Ça m'est égal! ◊ *She doesn't care.* Ça lui est égal.
♦**to care for somebody** (*patients, old people*) s'occuper de quelqu'un

career NOUN
la carrière
♦**a careers adviser** un conseiller d'orientation

careful ADJECTIVE
♦**Be careful!** Fais attention!

carefully ADVERB
[1] soigneusement ◊ *She carefully avoided talking about it.* Elle évitait soigneusement d'en parler.
[2] prudemment (*safely*) ◊ *Drive carefully!* Conduisez prudemment!
♦**Think carefully!** Réfléchis bien!

careless ADJECTIVE
[1] (*work*)
peu soigné
♦**a careless mistake** une faute d'inattention
[2] (*person*)
peu soigneux MASC
peu soigneuse FEM
◊ *She's very careless.* Elle est bien peu soigneuse.
[3] imprudent ◊ *a careless driver* un conducteur imprudent

caretaker NOUN
le gardien
la gardienne

car-ferry NOUN
le ferry

cargo NOUN
la cargaison

car hire NOUN
la location de voitures

Caribbean ADJECTIVE
see also **Caribbean** NOUN
antillais ◇ *Caribbean food* la cuisine
antillaise

Caribbean NOUN
see also **Caribbean** ADJECTIVE
[1] les Caraïbes FEM PL (*islands*) ◇ *We're
going to the Caribbean.* Nous allons
aux Caraïbes.
◆ **He's from the Caribbean.** Il est
antillais.
[2] la mer des Caraïbes (*sea*)

caring ADJECTIVE
◆ **She's a very caring teacher.** C'est un
professeur qui se préoccupe du bien-
être de ses élèves.
◆ **She has very caring parents.** Ses
parents sont très affectueux.

carnation NOUN
l' œillet MASC

carnival NOUN
le carnaval

carol NOUN
◆ **a Christmas carol** un chant de Noël

car park NOUN
le parking

carpenter NOUN
le charpentier ◇ *He's a carpenter.* Il
est charpentier.

carpentry NOUN
la menuiserie

carpet NOUN
[1] le tapis ◇ *a Persian carpet* un
tapis persan
[2] la moquette (*fitted*)

car phone NOUN
le téléphone de voiture

car rental NOUN [US]
la location de voitures

carriage NOUN
la voiture

carrier bag NOUN
le sac en plastique

carrot NOUN
la carotte

to **carry** VERB
[1] porter ◇ *I'll carry your bag.* Je vais
porter ton sac.
[2] transporter ◇ *a plane carrying 100
passengers* un avion transportant
cent passagers

to **carry on** VERB
continuer ◇ *Carry on!* Continue!
◇ *She carried on talking.* Elle a
continué à parler.

to **carry out** VERB
exécuter (*orders*)

carrycot NOUN
le porte-bébé

cart NOUN
la charrette

carton NOUN
la brique (*of milk, juice*)

cartoon NOUN
[1] le dessin animé (*film*)
[2] le dessin humoristique (*in
newspaper*)
◆ **a strip cartoon** une bande dessinée

cartridge NOUN
la cartouche

to **carve** VERB
découper (*meat*)

case NOUN
[1] la valise ◇ *I've packed my case.*
J'ai fait ma valise.
[2] le cas
(les cas PL)
◇ *in some cases* dans certains cas
◆ **in that case** dans ce cas ◇ *I don't
want it. – In that case, I'll take it.* Je
n'en veux pas. – Dans ce cas, je le
prends.
◆ **in case** au cas où ◇ *in case it rains* au
cas où il pleuvrait
◆ **just in case** à tout hasard ◇ *Take
some money, just in case.* Prends de
l'argent à tout hasard.

cash NOUN
l' argent MASC ◇ *I'm a bit short of
cash.* Je suis un peu à court d'argent.
◆ **in cash** en liquide ◇ *£2000 in cash*
deux mille livres en liquide
◆ **to pay cash** payer comptant
◆ **a cash card** une carte de retrait
◆ **the cash desk** la caisse
◆ **a cash dispenser** un distributeur
automatique de billets
◆ **a cash register** une caisse

cashew NOUN
la noix de cajou

cashier NOUN
le caissier
la caissière

cashmere NOUN
le cachemire ◇ *a cashmere sweater*
un pull en cachemire

casino NOUN
le casino

casserole NOUN
le ragoût ◇ *I'm going to make a
casserole.* Je vais faire un ragoût.
◆ **a casserole dish** une cocotte

cassette NOUN
la cassette
◆ **a cassette player** un lecteur de
cassettes
◆ **a cassette recorder** un magnétophone

C

cast NOUN
les acteurs MASC PL ◊ *After the play, we met the cast.* Après la représentation, nous avons rencontré les acteurs.

castle NOUN
le château
(les châteaux PL)

casual ADJECTIVE
1 décontracté ◊ *I prefer casual clothes.* Je préfère les vêtements décontractés.
2 désinvolte ◊ *a casual attitude* une attitude désinvolte
3 en passant ◊ *It was just a casual remark.* C'était juste une remarque en passant.

casually ADVERB
♦ **to dress casually** s'habiller de façon décontractée

casualty NOUN
les urgences FEM PL (*in hospital*)

cat NOUN
le chat
la chatte
◊ *Have you got a cat?* Est-ce que tu as un chat?

catalogue NOUN
le catalogue

catalytic converter NOUN
le catalyseur

catarrh NOUN
le rhume chronique

catastrophe NOUN
la catastrophe

to **catch** VERB
1 attraper ◊ *to catch a thief* attraper un voleur ◊ *My cat catches birds.* Mon chat attrape des oiseaux.
♦ **to catch somebody doing something** attraper quelqu'un en train de faire quelque chose ◊ *If they catch you smoking ...* S'ils t'attrapent en train de fumer ...
♦ **to catch a cold** attraper un rhume
2 prendre (*bus, train*) ◊ *We caught the last bus.* Nous avons pris le dernier bus.
3 saisir (*hear*) ◊ *I didn't catch his name.* Je n'ai pas saisi son nom.
♦ **to catch up** rattraper son retard ◊ *I've got to catch up: I was away last week.* Je dois rattraper mon retard: j'étais absent la semaine dernière.

catching ADJECTIVE
contagieux MASC
contagieuse FEM
◊ *It's not catching.* Ce n'est pas contagieux.

catering NOUN
la restauration

cathedral NOUN
la cathédrale

Catholic ADJECTIVE
see also **Catholic** NOUN
catholique

Catholic NOUN
see also **Catholic** ADJECTIVE
le/la catholique ◊ *I'm a Catholic.* Je suis catholique.

cattle PL NOUN
le bétail SING

caught VERB see **catch**

cauliflower NOUN
le chou-fleur
(les choux-fleurs PL)

cause NOUN
see also **cause** VERB
la cause

to **cause** VERB
see also **cause** NOUN
provoquer ◊ *to cause an accident* provoquer un accident

cautious ADJECTIVE
prudent

cautiously ADVERB
avec précaution ◊ *She cautiously opened the door.* Elle a ouvert la porte avec précaution.
♦ **He reacted cautiously.** Il a réagi prudemment.

cave NOUN
la grotte

CCTV (= *closed-circuit television*) NOUN
la télévision en circuit fermé

CD NOUN
le CD
(les CD PL)

CD player NOUN
la platine laser

CD-ROM NOUN
le CD-ROM
(les CD-ROM PL)

ceasefire NOUN
le cessez-le-feu
(les cessez-le-feu PL)

ceiling NOUN
le plafond

to **celebrate** VERB
fêter (*birthday*)

celebration NOUN
la fête

celebrity NOUN
la célébrité

celery NOUN
le céleri

cell NOUN
la cellule

cellar NOUN
la cave ◊ *a wine cellar* une cave à vins

cello NOUN
le violoncelle ◊ *I play the cello.* Je joue du violoncelle.

cement NOUN
le ciment

cemetery NOUN
le cimetière

cent NOUN
le cent ◊ *twenty cents* vingt cents

centenary NOUN
le centenaire

center NOUN US
le centre

centigrade ADJECTIVE
centigrade ◊ *20 degrees centigrade* vingt degrés centigrade

centimetre NOUN (US **centimeter**)
le centimètre

central ADJECTIVE
central
(centraux MASC PL)

central heating NOUN
le chauffage central

centre NOUN
le centre ◊ *a sports centre* un centre sportif

century NOUN
le siècle ◊ *the 20th century* le vingtième siècle ◊ *the 21st century* le vingt et unième siècle

cereal NOUN
les céréales FEM PL ◊ *I have cereal for breakfast.* Je prends des céréales au petit déjeuner.

ceremony NOUN
la cérémonie

certain ADJECTIVE
certain ◊ *a certain person* une certaine personne ◊ *I'm absolutely certain it was him.* Je suis absolument certain que c'était lui.
♦**I don't know for certain.** Je n'en suis pas certain.
♦**to make certain** s'assurer ◊ *I made certain the door was locked.* Je me suis assuré que la porte était fermée à clé.

certainly ADVERB
vraiment ◊ *I certainly expected something better.* Je m'attendais vraiment à quelque chose de mieux.
♦**Certainly not!** Certainement pas!
♦**So it was a surprise? – It certainly was!** C'était donc une surprise? – Ça oui alors!

certificate NOUN
le certificat

CFCs PL NOUN
les CFC MASC PL

chain NOUN
la chaîne

chair NOUN
⒈ la chaise ◊ *a table and 4 chairs* une table et quatre chaises
⒉ le fauteuil (*armchair*)

chairlift NOUN
le télésiège

chairman NOUN
le président

chalet NOUN
le chalet

chalk NOUN
la craie

challenge NOUN
see also **challenge** VERB
le défi

to **challenge** VERB
see also **challenge** NOUN
♦**She challenged me to a race.** Elle m'a proposé de faire la course avec elle.

challenging ADJECTIVE
stimulant ◊ *a challenging job* un travail stimulant

chambermaid NOUN
la femme de chambre

champagne NOUN
le champagne

champion NOUN
le champion
la championne

championship NOUN
le championnat

chance NOUN
⒈ la chance ◊ *Do you think I've got any chance?* Tu crois que j'ai une chance? ◊ *Their chances of winning are very good.* Ils ont de fortes chances de gagner.
♦**No chance!** Pas question!
⒉ l' occasion FEM ◊ *I'd like to have a chance to travel.* J'aimerais avoir l'occasion de voyager.
♦**I'll write when I get the chance.** J'écrirai quand j'aurai un moment.
♦**by chance** par hasard ◊ *We met by chance.* Nous nous sommes rencontrés par hasard.
♦**to take a chance** prendre un risque ◊ *I'm taking no chances!* Je ne veux prendre aucun risque!

Chancellor of the Exchequer NOUN
le chancelier de l'Échiquier

to **change** VERB

see also **change** NOUN

1 changer ◊ *The town has changed a lot.* La ville a beaucoup changé. ◊ *I'd like to change £50.* Je voudrais changer cinquante livres.

Use **changer de** when you change one thing for another.

2 changer de ◊ *You have to change trains in Paris.* Il faut changer de train à Paris. ◊ *I'm going to change my shoes.* Je vais changer de chaussures. ◊ *He wants to change his job.* Il veut changer d'emploi.

♦ **to change one's mind** changer d'avis ◊ *I've changed my mind.* J'ai changé d'avis.

♦ **to change gear** changer de vitesse

3 se changer ◊ *She's changing to go out.* Elle est en train de se changer pour sortir.

♦ **to get changed** se changer ◊ *I'm going to get changed.* Je vais me changer.

4 échanger (*swap*) ◊ *Can I change this sweater? It's too small.* Est-ce que je peux échanger ce pull? Il est trop petit.

change NOUN

see also **change** VERB

1 le changement ◊ *There's been a change of plan.* Il y a eu un changement de programme.

2 la monnaie (*money*) ◊ *I haven't got any change.* Je n'ai pas de monnaie.

♦ **a change of clothes** des vêtements de rechange

♦ **for a change** pour changer ◊ *Let's play tennis for a change.* Si on jouait au tennis pour changer?

changeable ADJECTIVE
variable

changing room NOUN
1 le salon d'essayage (*in shop*)
2 le vestiaire (*for sport*)

channel NOUN
la chaîne (*TV*) ◊ *There's football on the other channel.* Il y a du football sur l'autre chaîne.

♦ **the Channel** la Manche

♦ **the Channel Islands** les îles Anglo-Normandes FEM PL

♦ **the Channel Tunnel** le tunnel sous la Manche

chaos NOUN
le chaos

chap NOUN
le type ◊ *He's a nice chap.* C'est un type sympa.

chapel NOUN

la chapelle (*part of church*)

chapter NOUN
le chapitre

character NOUN
1 le caractère ◊ *Give me some idea of his character.* Décris-moi un peu son caractère.

♦ **She's quite a character.** C'est un drôle de numéro.

2 le personnage (*in play, film*) ◊ *The character played by Depardieu ...* Le personnage joué par Depardieu ...

characteristic NOUN
la caractéristique

charcoal NOUN
le charbon de bois

charge NOUN

see also **charge** VERB

les frais MASC PL ◊ *Is there a charge for delivery?* Est-ce qu'il y a des frais de livraison?

♦ **an extra charge** un supplément

♦ **free of charge** gratuit

♦ **to reverse the charges** appeler en P.C.V. ◊ *I'd like to reverse the charges.* Je voudrais appeler en P.C.V.

♦ **to be on a charge** être inculpé ◊ *He's on a charge of murder.* Il est inculpé de meurtre.

♦ **to be in charge** être responsable ◊ *Mrs Munday was in charge of the group.* Madame Munday était responsable du groupe.

to **charge** VERB

see also **charge** NOUN

1 prendre (*money*) ◊ *How much did he charge you?* Combien est-ce qu'il vous a pris? ◊ *They charge £10 an hour.* Ils prennent dix livres de l'heure.

2 inculper (*with crime*) ◊ *The police have charged him with murder.* La police l'a inculpé de meurtre.

charity NOUN
l' association caritative FEM ◊ *He gave the money to charity.* Il a donné l'argent à une association caritative.

charm NOUN
le charme ◊ *He's got a lot of charm.* Il a beaucoup de charme.

charming ADJECTIVE
charmant

chart NOUN
le tableau
(les tableaux PL)
◊ *The chart shows the rise of unemployment.* Le tableau indique la progression du chômage.

♦the charts le hit-parade ◊ *This album is number one in the charts.* Cet album est numéro un au hit-parade.

charter flight NOUN
le charter

to **chase** VERB
> see also **chase** NOUN
pourchasser

chase NOUN
> see also **chase** VERB
la poursuite ◊ *a car chase* une poursuite en voiture

chat NOUN
> see also **chat** VERB
♦to have a chat bavarder

to **chat** VERB
> see also **chat** NOUN
bavarder
♦to chat somebody up draguer quelqu'un (*informal*) ◊ *Gabriel's not very good at chatting up girls.* Gabriel n'est pas très doué pour draguer les filles.

chatroom NOUN
le forum de discussion

chat show NOUN
le talk-show

chauvinist NOUN
♦a male chauvinist un machiste

cheap ADJECTIVE
bon marché MASC, FEM, PL
◊ *a cheap T-shirt* un T-shirt bon marché

cheaper ADJECTIVE
moins cher MASC
moins chère FEM
◊ *It's cheaper by bus.* C'est moins cher en bus.

to **cheat** VERB
> see also **cheat** NOUN
tricher ◊ *You're cheating!* Tu triches!

cheat NOUN
> see also **cheat** VERB
le tricheur
la tricheuse

check NOUN
> see also **check** VERB
[1] le contrôle ◊ *a security check* un contrôle de sécurité
[2] le chèque US ◊ *to write a check* faire un chèque
[3] l' addition FEM US ◊ *Can we have the check, please?* L'addition, s'il vous plaît.

to **check** VERB
> see also **check** NOUN
vérifier ◊ *I'll check the time of the train.* Je vais vérifier l'heure du train.

◊ *Could you check the oil, please?* Pourriez-vous vérifier le niveau d'huile, s'il vous plaît?

♦to check in (1) (*at airport*) se présenter à l'enregistrement ◊ *What time do I have to check in?* À quelle heure est-ce que je dois me présenter à l'enregistrement?

♦to check in (2) (*in hotel*) se présenter à la réception

♦to check out (*from hotel*) régler sa note

checked ADJECTIVE
à carreaux (*fabric*)

checkers NOUN US
les dames FEM PL ◊ *to play checkers* jouer aux dames

check-in NOUN
l' enregistrement MASC

checking account NOUN US
le compte courant

checkout NOUN
la caisse

check-up NOUN
l' examen de routine MASC

cheek NOUN
[1] la joue ◊ *He kissed her on the cheek.* Il l'a embrassée sur la joue.
[2] le culot ◊ *What a cheek!* Quel culot!

cheeky ADJECTIVE
effronté ◊ *Don't be cheeky!* Ne sois pas effronté!
♦a cheeky smile un sourire malicieux

cheer NOUN
> see also **cheer** VERB
les hourras MASC PL
♦to give a cheer pousser des hourras
♦Cheers! (1) (*good health*) À la vôtre!
♦Cheers! (2) (*thanks*) Merci!

to **cheer** VERB
> see also **cheer** NOUN
applaudir
♦to cheer somebody up remonter le moral à quelqu'un ◊ *I was trying to cheer him up.* J'essayais de lui remonter le moral.
♦Cheer up! Ne te laisse pas abattre!

cheerful ADJECTIVE
gai

cheerio EXCLAMATION
salut!

cheese NOUN
le fromage

chef NOUN
le chef

chemical NOUN
le produit chimique

C

chemist NOUN
[1] (dispenser)
le pharmacien
la pharmacienne
[2] (shop)
la pharmacie ◊ You get it from the chemist. C'est vendu en pharmacie.

> *ⓘ* Chemist's shops in France are identified by a special green cross outside the shop.

[3] (scientist)
le/la chimiste

chemistry NOUN
la chimie ◊ the chemistry lab le laboratoire de chimie

cheque NOUN
le chèque ◊ to write a cheque faire un chèque ◊ to pay by cheque payer par chèque

chequebook NOUN
le carnet de chèques

cherry NOUN
la cerise

chess NOUN
les échecs MASC PL ◊ to play chess jouer aux échecs

chessboard NOUN
l' échiquier MASC

chest NOUN
la poitrine (of person) ◊ his chest measurement son tour de poitrine
♦ **a chest of drawers** une commode

chestnut NOUN
le marron ◊ We have turkey with chestnuts. Nous mangeons de la dinde aux marrons.

to **chew** VERB
mâcher

chewing gum NOUN
le chewing-gum

chick NOUN
le poussin ◊ a hen and her chicks une poule et ses poussins

chicken NOUN
le poulet

chickenpox NOUN
la varicelle

chickpeas PL NOUN
les pois chiches MASC PL

chief NOUN
see also **chief** ADJECTIVE
le chef ◊ the chief of security le chef de la sécurité

chief ADJECTIVE
see also **chief** NOUN

principal ◊ His chief reason for resigning was the low pay. La principale raison de sa démission était son mauvais salaire.

child NOUN
l' enfant MASC/FEM ◊ all the children tous les enfants

childish ADJECTIVE
puéril

child minder NOUN
la nourrice

children PL NOUN see **child**

Chile NOUN
le Chili
♦ **in Chile** au Chili

to **chill** VERB
mettre au frais ◊ Put the wine in the fridge to chill. Mets le vin au frais dans le réfrigérateur.

chilli NOUN
le piment

chilly ADJECTIVE
froid

chimney NOUN
la cheminée

chin NOUN
le menton

china NOUN
la porcelaine ◊ a china plate une assiette en porcelaine

China NOUN
la Chine
♦ **in China** en Chine

Chinese ADJECTIVE
see also **Chinese** NOUN
chinois ◊ a Chinese restaurant un restaurant chinois
♦ **a Chinese man** un Chinois
♦ **a Chinese woman** une Chinoise

Chinese NOUN
see also **Chinese** ADJECTIVE
le chinois (language)
♦ **the Chinese** (people) les Chinois

chip NOUN
[1] la frite (food) ◊ We bought some chips. Nous avons acheté des frites.
[2] la puce (in computer)

chiropodist NOUN
le/la pédicure ◊ He's a chiropodist. Il est pédicure.

chives PL NOUN
la ciboulette SING

chocolate NOUN
le chocolat ◊ a chocolate cake un gâteau au chocolat
♦ **hot chocolate** le chocolat chaud

choice NOUN

le <u>choix</u> ◇ *I had no choice.* Je n'avais pas le choix.

choir NOUN
la <u>chorale</u> ◇ *I sing in the school choir.* Je chante dans la chorale de l'école.

to **choke** VERB
s'<u>étrangler</u>
◆ **He choked on a fishbone.** Il s'est étranglé avec une arête de poisson.

to **choose** VERB
<u>choisir</u> ◇ *It's difficult to choose.* C'est difficile de choisir.

to **chop** VERB
see also **chop** NOUN
<u>émincer</u> ◇ *Chop the onions.* Émincez les oignons.

chop NOUN
see also **chop** VERB
la <u>côte</u> ◇ *a pork chop* une côte de porc

chopsticks PL NOUN
les <u>baguettes</u> FEM PL

chose, chosen VERB *see* **choose**

Christ NOUN
le <u>Christ</u>

christening NOUN
le <u>baptême</u>

Christian NOUN
see also **Christian** ADJECTIVE
le <u>chrétien</u>
la <u>chrétienne</u>

Christian ADJECTIVE
see also **Christian** NOUN
<u>chrétien</u> MASC
<u>chrétienne</u> FEM

Christian name NOUN
le <u>prénom</u>

Christmas NOUN
<u>Noël</u> MASC ◇ *Happy Christmas!* Joyeux Noël!
◆ **Christmas Day** le jour de Noël
◆ **Christmas Eve** la veille de Noël
◆ **a Christmas tree** un arbre de Noël
◆ **a Christmas card** une carte de Noël

> ❶ *The French more often send greetings cards (une carte de vœux) in January rather than at Christmas, with best wishes for the New Year.*

◆ **Christmas dinner** le repas de Noël

> ❶ *Most French people have their Christmas meal (réveillon de Noël) on the evening of Christmas Eve, though some have a repas de Noël on Christmas Day.*

◆ **Christmas pudding**

> ❶ *The French usually have a Yule log (une bûche de Noël) for pudding at the Christmas meal. You could explain what Christmas pudding is using the example given.*

◇ *Christmas pudding is made with dried fruit and spices, and steamed.* Le "Christmas pudding" est un gâteau avec des raisins secs, parfumé avec des épices et cuit à la vapeur.

chunk NOUN
le <u>gros morceau</u>
(les gros morceaux PL)
◇ *Cut the meat into chunks.* Coupez la viande en gros morceaux.

church NOUN
l' <u>église</u> FEM ◇ *James doesn't go to church every Sunday.* James ne va pas à l'église tous les dimanches.
◆ **the Church of England** l'Église anglicane

cider NOUN
le <u>cidre</u>

cigar NOUN
le <u>cigare</u>

cigarette NOUN
la <u>cigarette</u>

cigarette lighter NOUN
le <u>briquet</u>

cinema NOUN
le <u>cinéma</u> ◇ *I'm going to the cinema this evening.* Je vais au cinéma ce soir.

cinnamon NOUN
la <u>cannelle</u>

circle NOUN
le <u>cercle</u> ◇ *to stand in a circle* faire cercle.

circular ADJECTIVE
<u>circulaire</u>

circulation NOUN
1 la <u>circulation</u> (*of blood*)
2 le <u>tirage</u> (*of newspaper*)

circumflex NOUN
l' <u>accent circonflexe</u> MASC

circumstances PL NOUN
les <u>circonstances</u> FEM PL

circus NOUN
le <u>cirque</u>

citizen NOUN
le <u>citoyen</u>
la <u>citoyenne</u>
◇ *a French citizen* un citoyen français

citizenship NOUN

la citoyenneté

City NOUN
♦the City la City de Londres

city NOUN
la ville
♦the city centre le centre-ville ◊ It's in the city centre. C'est au centre-ville.

city technology college NOUN
le collège technique

civilization NOUN
la civilisation

civil servant NOUN
le/la fonctionnaire ◊ Jenny is a civil servant. Jenny est fonctionnaire.

civil war NOUN
la guerre civile

to **claim** VERB
see also **claim** NOUN
[1] prétendre ◊ He claims to have found the money. Il prétend avoir trouvé l'argent.
[2] percevoir (receive) ◊ She's claiming unemployment benefit. Elle perçoit des allocations chômage.
♦She can't claim unemployment benefit. Elle n'a pas droit aux allocations chômage.
♦to claim on one's insurance se faire rembourser par son assurance ◊ We claimed on our insurance. Nous nous sommes fait rembourser par notre assurance.

claim NOUN
see also **claim** VERB
la demande d'indemnité (on insurance policy) ◊ to make a claim faire une demande d'indemnité

to **clap** VERB
applaudir (applaud)
♦to clap one's hands frapper dans ses mains ◊ I've trained my dog to sit when I clap my hands. J'ai dressé mon chien à s'asseoir quand je frappe dans mes mains.

clarinet NOUN
la clarinette ◊ I play the clarinet. Je joue de la clarinette.

to **clash** VERB
[1] jurer (colours) ◊ These two colours clash. Ces deux couleurs jurent.
[2] tomber en même temps (events) ◊ The concert clashes with Ann's party. Le concert tombe en même temps que la soirée d'Ann.

clasp NOUN
le fermoir (of necklace)

class NOUN

[1] la classe (group) ◊ We're in the same class. Nous sommes dans la même classe.
[2] le cours (lesson) ◊ I go to dancing classes. Je vais à des cours de danse.

classic ADJECTIVE
see also **classic** NOUN
classique ◊ a classic example un cas classique

classic NOUN
see also **classic** ADJECTIVE
le classique (book, film)

classical ADJECTIVE
classique ◊ I like classical music. J'aime la musique classique.

classmate NOUN
le camarade de classe
la camarade de classe

classroom NOUN
la classe

claw NOUN
[1] la griffe (of cat, dog)
[2] la serre (of bird)
[3] la pince (of crab, lobster)

clean ADJECTIVE
see also **clean** VERB
propre ◊ a clean shirt une chemise propre

to **clean** VERB
see also **clean** ADJECTIVE
nettoyer

cleaner NOUN
[1] la femme de ménage (woman)
[2] l' agent d'entretien MASC (man)

cleaner's NOUN
la teinturerie

cleaning lady NOUN
la femme de ménage

cleansing lotion NOUN
la lotion démaquillante

clear ADJECTIVE
see also **clear** VERB
[1] clair ◊ a clear explanation une explication claire ◊ It's clear you don't believe me. Il est clair que tu ne me crois pas.
[2] libre (road, way) ◊ The road's clear now. La route est libre maintenant.

to **clear** VERB
see also **clear** ADJECTIVE
[1] dégager ◊ The police are clearing the road after the accident. La police dégage la route après l'accident.
[2] se dissiper (fog, mist) ◊ The mist soon cleared. La brume s'est vite dissipée.
♦to be cleared of a crime être reconnu non coupable d'un crime ◊ She was

cleared of murder. Elle a été reconnue non coupable du meurtre.
◆**to clear the table** débarrasser la table ◇ *I'll clear the table.* Je vais débarrasser la table.
◆**to clear up** ranger ◇ *Who's going to clear all this up?* Qui va ranger tout ça?
◆**I think it's going to clear up.** (*weather*) Je pense que le temps va se lever.

to **clear off** VERB
filer ◇ *Clear off and leave me alone!* File et laisse-moi tranquille!

clearly ADVERB
1 clairement ◇ *She explained it very clearly.* Elle l'a expliqué très clairement.
2 nettement ◇ *The French coast was clearly visible.* On distinguait nettement la côte française.
3 distinctement ◇ *to speak clearly* parler distinctement

clementine NOUN
la clémentine

clever ADJECTIVE
1 intelligent ◇ *She's very clever.* Elle est très intelligente.
2 (*ingenious*)
astucieux MASC
astucieuse FEM
◇ *a clever system* un système astucieux
◆**What a clever idea!** Quelle bonne idée!

click NOUN
see also **click** VERB
le petit bruit (*of door, camera*)

to **click** VERB
see also **click** NOUN
cliquer (*with mouse*)
◆**to click on an icon** cliquer sur une icône

client NOUN
le client
la cliente

cliff NOUN
la falaise

climate NOUN
le climat

to **climb** VERB
1 escalader ◇ *We're going to climb Snowdon.* Nous allons escalader le Snowdon.
2 monter (*stairs*)

climber NOUN
le grimpeur
la grimpeuse

climbing NOUN
l' escalade FEM

◆**to go climbing** faire de l'escalade ◇ *We're going climbing in Scotland.* Nous allons faire de l'escalade en Écosse.

Clingfilm ® NOUN
le film alimentaire

clinic NOUN
le centre médical
(les centres médicaux PL)

clip NOUN
1 la barrette (*for hair*)
2 le court extrait (*film*) ◇ *some clips from Kevin Costner's latest film* quelques courts extraits du dernier film de Kevin Costner

clippers PL NOUN
◆**nail clippers** le coupe-ongle SING
(les coupe-ongles PL)

cloakroom NOUN
1 le vestiaire (*for coats*)
2 les toilettes FEM PL (*toilet*)

clock NOUN
1 l' horloge FEM ◇ *the church clock* l'horloge de l'église
2 la pendule (*smaller*)
◆**an alarm clock** un réveil
◆**a clock-radio** un radio-réveil

clockwork NOUN
◆**Everything went like clockwork.** Tout a marché comme sur des roulettes.

clog NOUN
le sabot

clone NOUN
see also **clone** VERB
le clone (*animal, plant*)

to **clone** VERB
see also **clone** NOUN
cloner ◇ *a cloned sheep* un mouton cloné

close ADJECTIVE, ADVERB
see also **close** VERB
1 près (*near*) ◇ *The shops are very close.* Les magasins sont tout près.
◆**close to** près de ◇ *The youth hostel is close to the station.* L'auberge de jeunesse est près de la gare.
◆**Come closer.** Rapproche-toi.
2 proche (*in relationship*) ◇ *We're just inviting close relations.* Nous n'invitons que les parents proches. ◇ *She's a close friend of mine.* C'est une proche amie. ◇ *I'm very close to my sister.* Je suis très proche de ma sœur.
3 très serré (*contest*) ◇ *It's going to be very close.* Ça va être très serré.
4 lourd (*weather*) ◇ *It's close this afternoon.* Il fait lourd cet après-midi.

to **close** VERB

☞

see also **close** ADJECTIVE

1 fermer ◊ *What time does the pool close?* La piscine ferme à quelle heure? ◊ *The shops close at 5.30.* Les magasins ferment à cinq heures et demie. ◊ *Please close the door.* Fermez la porte, s'il vous plaît.
2 se fermer ◊ *The doors close automatically.* Les portes se ferment automatiquement.

closed ADJECTIVE
fermé ◊ *The bank's closed.* La banque est fermée.

closely ADVERB
de près (*look, examine*)

cloth NOUN
le tissu (*material*)
♦a cloth un chiffon ◊ *Wipe it with a damp cloth.* Nettoyez-le avec un chiffon humide.

clothes PL NOUN
les vêtements MASC PL ◊ *new clothes* des vêtements neufs
♦a clothes line un fil à linge
♦a clothes peg une pince à linge

cloud NOUN
le nuage

cloudy ADJECTIVE
nuageux MASC
nuageuse FEM

clove NOUN
♦a clove of garlic une gousse d'ail

clown NOUN
le clown

club NOUN
le club ◊ *a golf club* (*society and for playing golf*) un club de golf
♦the youth club la maison des jeunes
♦clubs (*in cards*) le trèfle ◊ *the ace of clubs* l'as de trèfle

to **club together** VERB
se cotiser ◊ *We clubbed together to buy her a present.* Nous nous sommes cotisés pour lui acheter un cadeau.

clubbing NOUN
♦to go clubbing sortir en boîte

clue NOUN
l' indice MASC ◊ *an important clue* un indice important
♦I haven't a clue. Je n'en ai pas la moindre idée.

clumsy ADJECTIVE
maladroit

clutch NOUN
la pédale d'embrayage (*of car*)

clutter NOUN
le désordre ◊ *There's too much clutter in here.* Il y a trop de désordre ici.

coach NOUN
1 le car MASC ◊ *We went there by coach.* Nous y sommes allés en car.
♦the coach station la gare routière
♦a coach trip une excursion en car
2 l' entraîneur MASC (*trainer*) ◊ *the French coach* l'entraîneur de l'équipe de France

coal NOUN
le charbon
♦a coal mine une mine de charbon
♦a coal miner un mineur

coarse ADJECTIVE
1 (*surface, fabric*)
rugueux MASC
rugueuse FEM
◊ *The bag was made of coarse cloth.* Le sac était fait d'un tissu rugueux.
2 (*vulgar*)
grossier MASC
grossière FEM
◊ *coarse language* un langage grossier

coast NOUN
la côte ◊ *It's on the west coast of Scotland.* C'est sur la côte ouest de l'Écosse.

coastguard NOUN
le garde-côte
(les garde-côtes PL)

coat NOUN
le manteau
(les manteaux PL)
◊ *a warm coat* un manteau chaud
♦a coat of paint une couche de peinture

coat hanger NOUN
le cintre

cobweb NOUN
la toile d'araignée

cocaine NOUN
la cocaïne

cock NOUN
le coq (*cockerel*)

cockerel NOUN
le coq

cockney NOUN
le cockney ◊ *I'm a cockney.* Je suis cockney.

cocoa NOUN
le cacao ◊ *a cup of cocoa* une tasse de cacao

coconut NOUN
la noix de coco

cod NOUN
le cabillaud

C

code NOUN
le code

coffee NOUN
le café
♦ **A cup of coffee, please.** Un café, s'il vous plaît.

coffeepot NOUN
la cafetière

coffee table NOUN
la table basse

coffin NOUN
le cercueil

coin NOUN
la pièce de monnaie
♦ **a 5 franc coin** une pièce de cinq francs

coincidence NOUN
la coïncidence

coinphone NOUN
le téléphone à pièces

Coke ® NOUN
le coca ◊ *a can of Coke* ® une boîte de coca

colander NOUN
la passoire

cold ADJECTIVE
see also **cold** NOUN
froid ◊ *The water's cold.* L'eau est froide.
♦ **It's cold today.** Il fait froid aujourd'hui.
♦ **to be cold** (*person*) avoir froid ◊ *I'm cold.* J'ai froid. ◊ *Are you cold?* Est-ce que tu as froid?

cold NOUN
see also **cold** ADJECTIVE
[1] le froid ◊ *I can't stand the cold.* Je ne supporte pas le froid.
[2] le rhume ◊ *to catch a cold* attraper un rhume
♦ **to have a cold** avoir un rhume ◊ *I've got a bad cold.* J'ai un gros rhume.
♦ **a cold sore** un bouton de fièvre

coleslaw NOUN
la salade de chou cru à la mayonnaise

to **collapse** VERB
s'effondrer ◊ *He collapsed.* Il s'est effondré.

collar NOUN
[1] le col (*of coat, shirt*)
[2] le collier (*for animal*)

collarbone NOUN
la clavicule ◊ *I broke my collarbone.* Je me suis cassé la clavicule.

colleague NOUN
le/la collègue

to **collect** VERB

[1] ramasser ◊ *The teacher collected the exercise books.* Le professeur a ramassé les cahiers. ◊ *They collect the rubbish twice a week.* Ils ramassent les ordures deux fois par semaine.
[2] faire collection de ◊ *I collect stamps.* Je fais collection de timbres.
[3] aller chercher ◊ *Their mother collects them from school.* Leur mère va les chercher à l'école.
[4] faire une collecte ◊ *They're collecting for charity.* Ils font une collecte pour une association caritative.

collect call NOUN US
la communication en PCV

collection NOUN
[1] la collection ◊ *my CD collection* ma collection de CD
[2] la collecte ◊ *a collection for charity* une collecte pour une association caritative
[3] la levée (*of mail*) ◊ *Next collection: 5 p.m.* Prochaine levée: 17 heures

collector NOUN
le collectionneur
la collectionneuse

college NOUN
le collège ◊ *a technical college* un collège d'enseignement technique

to **collide** VERB
entrer en collision

collie NOUN
le colley

colliery NOUN
la houillère

collision NOUN
la collision

colon NOUN
les deux points MASC PL (*punctuation mark*)

colonel NOUN
le colonel

colour NOUN (US **color**)
la couleur ◊ *What colour is it?* C'est de quelle couleur?
♦ **a colour film** (*for camera*) une pellicule en couleur

colourful ADJECTIVE (US **colorful**)
coloré

colouring NOUN (US **coloring**)
le colorant (*for food*)

comb NOUN
see also **comb** VERB
le peigne

to **comb** VERB
see also **comb** NOUN

◆**to comb one's hair** se peigner ◊ *You haven't combed your hair.* Tu ne t'es pas peigné.

combination NOUN
la combinaison

to **combine** VERB
☐1 allier ◊ *The film combines humour with suspense.* Le film allie l'humour au suspense.
☐2 concilier ◊ *It's difficult to combine a career with a family.* Il est difficile de concilier carrière et vie de famille.

to **come** VERB
☐1 venir ◊ *Can I come too?* Est-ce que je peux venir aussi? ◊ *Some friends came to see us.* Quelques amis sont venus nous voir. ◊ *I'll come with you.* Je viens avec toi.
☐2 arriver (*arrive*) ◊ *I'm coming!* J'arrive! ◊ *They came late.* Ils sont arrivés en retard. ◊ *The letter came this morning.* La lettre est arrivée ce matin.
◆**to come back** revenir ◊ *Come back!* Reviens!
◆**to come down (1)** (*person, lift*) descendre
◆**to come down (2)** (*prices*) baisser
◆**to come from** venir de ◊ *Where do you come from?* Tu viens d'où?
◆**to come in** entrer ◊ *Come in!* Entrez!
◆**Come on!** Allez!
◆**to come out** sortir ◊ *when we came out of the cinema* quand nous sommes sortis du cinéma ◊ *It's just come out on video.* Ça vient de sortir en vidéo.
◆**None of my photos came out.** Mes photos n'ont rien donné.
◆**to come round** reprendre connaissance (*after faint, operation*)
◆**to come up** monter ◊ *Come up here!* Monte!
◆**to come up to somebody (1)** s'approcher de quelqu'un ◊ *She came up to me and kissed me.* Elle s'est approchée de moi et m'a embrassé.
◆**to come up to somebody (2)** (*to speak to them*) aborder quelqu'un ◊ *A man came up to me and said ...* Un homme m'a abordé et m'a dit ...

comedian NOUN
le comique

comedy NOUN
la comédie

comfortable ADJECTIVE
☐1 confortable (*bed, chair*)
☐2 à l'aise (*person*) ◊ *I'm very comfortable, thanks.* Je suis parfaitement à l'aise, merci.

comic NOUN
l' illustré MASC (*magazine*)

comic strip NOUN
la bande dessinée

coming ADJECTIVE
prochain ◊ *in the coming months* au cours des prochains mois

comma NOUN
la virgule

command NOUN
l' ordre MASC

comment NOUN
see also **comment** VERB
le commentaire ◊ *He made no comment.* Il n'a fait aucun commentaire.
◆**No comment!** Je n'ai rien à dire!

to **comment** VERB
see also **comment** NOUN
◆**to comment on something** faire des commentaires sur quelque chose

commentary NOUN
le reportage en direct (*on TV, radio*)

commentator NOUN
le commentateur sportif
la commentatrice sportive

commercial NOUN
le spot publicitaire

commission NOUN
la commission ◊ *Salesmen work on commission.* Les représentants travaillent à la commission.

to **commit** VERB
◆**to commit a crime** commettre un crime
◆**to commit oneself** s'engager ◊ *I don't want to commit myself.* Je ne veux pas m'engager.
◆**to commit suicide** se suicider ◊ *He committed suicide.* Il s'est suicidé.

committee NOUN
le comité

common ADJECTIVE
see also **common** NOUN
courant ◊ *"Smith" is a very common surname.* "Smith" est un nom de famille très courant.
◆**in common** en commun ◊ *We've got a lot in common.* Nous avons beaucoup de choses en commun.

common NOUN
see also **common** ADJECTIVE
le terrain communal ◊ *We went for a walk on the common.* Nous sommes allés nous promener sur le terrain communal.

Commons PL NOUN

English ~ French

♦**the House of Commons** la Chambre des communes

common sense NOUN
le <u>bon sens</u> ◊ *Use your common sense!* Sers-toi de ton bon sens!

to **communicate** VERB
<u>communiquer</u>

communication NOUN
la <u>communication</u>

communion NOUN
la <u>communion</u> ◊ *my First Communion* ma première communion

communism NOUN
le <u>communisme</u>

communist NOUN
| see also **communist** ADJECTIVE |
le/la <u>communiste</u>

communist ADJECTIVE
| see also **communist** NOUN |
<u>communiste</u>
♦**the Communist Party** le Parti communiste

community NOUN
la <u>communauté</u>

to **commute** VERB
<u>faire la navette</u> ◊ *She commutes between Liss and London.* Elle fait la navette entre Liss et Londres.

compact disc NOUN
le <u>disque compact</u>
♦**a compact disc player** une platine laser

companion NOUN
le <u>compagnon</u>
la <u>compagne</u>

company NOUN
1 la <u>société</u> ◊ *He works for a big company.* Il travaille pour une grosse société.
2 la <u>compagnie</u> ◊ *an insurance company* une compagnie d'assurance ◊ *a theatre company* une compagnie théâtrale
♦**to keep somebody company** tenir compagnie à quelqu'un ◊ *I'll keep you company.* Je vais te tenir compagnie.

comparatively ADVERB
<u>relativement</u>

to **compare** VERB
<u>comparer</u> ◊ *People always compare him with his brother.* On le compare toujours à son frère.
♦**compared with** en comparaison de ◊ *Oxford is small compared with London.* Oxford est une petite ville en comparaison de Londres.

comparison NOUN
la <u>comparaison</u>

compartment NOUN
le <u>compartiment</u>

compass NOUN
la <u>boussole</u>

compelling ADJECTIVE
<u>fascinant</u> (*gripping*) ◊ *It's a violent yet compelling film.* C'est un film violent mais fascinant.

compensation NOUN
l' <u>indemnité</u> FEM ◊ *They got £2000 compensation.* Ils ont reçu une indemnité de deux mille livres.

compere NOUN
l' <u>animateur</u> MASC
l' <u>animatrice</u> FEM

to **compete** VERB
<u>participer</u> ◊ *I'm competing in the marathon.* Je participe au marathon.
♦**to compete for something** se disputer quelque chose ◊ *There are 50 students competing for 6 places.* Ils sont cinquante étudiants à se disputer six places.

competent ADJECTIVE
<u>compétent</u>

competition NOUN
le <u>concours</u> ◊ *a singing competition* un concours de chant

competitive ADJECTIVE
<u>compétitif</u> MASC
<u>compétitive</u> FEM
◊ *a very competitive price* un prix très compétitif
♦**to be competitive** (*person*) avoir l'esprit de compétition ◊ *He's a very competitive person.* Il a vraiment l'esprit de compétition.

competitor NOUN
le <u>concurrent</u>
la <u>concurrente</u>

to **complain** VERB
<u>se plaindre</u> ◊ *I'm going to complain to the manager.* Je vais me plaindre au directeur. ◊ *We complained about the noise.* Nous nous sommes plaints du bruit.

complaint NOUN
la <u>plainte</u> ◊ *There were lots of complaints about the food.* Il y a eu beaucoup de plaintes à propos de la nourriture.

complete ADJECTIVE
<u>complet</u> MASC
<u>complète</u> FEM

completely ADVERB
<u>complètement</u>

complexion NOUN

☞

le teint

complicated ADJECTIVE
compliqué

compliment NOUN
see also **compliment** VERB
le compliment

to **compliment** VERB
see also **compliment** NOUN
complimenter ◇ _They complimented me on my French._ Ils m'ont complimenté sur mon français.

complimentary ADJECTIVE
⊡ élogieux _(flattering)_ ◇ _He was very complimentary about my garden._ Il a été très élogieux à propos de mon jardin.
⊡ gratuit _(free)_
♦**I've got two complimentary tickets for tonight.** J'ai deux places gratuites pour ce soir.

composer NOUN
le compositeur
la compositrice

comprehension NOUN
⊡ la compréhension _(understanding)_
⊡ l' exercice de compréhension FEM _(school exercise)_

comprehensive ADJECTIVE
complet MASC
complète FEM
◇ _a comprehensive guide_ un guide complet
Be careful not to translate
**comprehensive** by **compréhensif**.

comprehensive school NOUN
⊡ le collège
⊡ le lycée

> ℹ _In France pupils go to a **collège** between the ages of 11 and 15, and then to a **lycée** until the age of 18._

compromise NOUN
see also **compromise** VERB
le compromis ◇ _We reached a compromise._ Nous sommes parvenus à un compromis.

to **compromise** VERB
see also **compromise** NOUN
♦**Let's compromise.** Essayons de trouver un compromis.

compulsory ADJECTIVE
obligatoire

computer NOUN
l' ordinateur MASC

computer game NOUN
le jeu électronique
(les jeux électroniques PL)

computer programmer NOUN

le programmeur
la programmeuse
◇ _She's a computer programmer._ Elle est programmeuse.

computer science NOUN
l' informatique FEM ◇ _a degree in computer science_ un diplôme d'informatique

computing NOUN
l' informatique FEM

to **concentrate** VERB
se concentrer ◇ _I couldn't concentrate._ Je n'arrivais pas à me concentrer.

concentration NOUN
la concentration

concern NOUN
l' inquiétude FEM _(preoccupation)_
◇ _They expressed concern about the image of the school._ Ils ont exprimé leur inquiétude concernant l'image de l'école.

concerned ADJECTIVE
♦**to be concerned** s'inquiéter ◇ _His mother is concerned about him._ Sa mère s'inquiète à son sujet.
♦**as far as I'm concerned** en ce qui me concerne

concerning PREPOSITION
concernant ◇ _For further information concerning the job, contact Mr Ross Hutchison._ Pour plus d'informations concernant cet emploi, contacter M. Ross Hutchinson.

concert NOUN
le concert

concrete NOUN
le béton

to **condemn** VERB
condamner ◇ _The government has condemned the decision._ Le gouvernement a condamné cette décision.

condition NOUN
⊡ la condition ◇ _I'll do it, on one condition ..._ Je veux bien le faire, à une condition ...
⊡ l' état MASC ◇ _in bad condition_ en mauvais état ◇ _in good condition_ en bon état

conditional NOUN
le conditionnel

conditioner NOUN
le baume démêlant _(for hair)_

condom NOUN
le préservatif

to **conduct** VERB
diriger _(orchestra)_

C

conductor NOUN
le chef d'orchestre

cone NOUN
le cornet ◊ *an ice-cream cone* un
cornet de glace

conference NOUN
la conférence

to **confess** VERB
avouer ◊ *He finally confessed.* Il a
fini par avouer. ◊ *He confessed to the
murder.* Il a avoué avoir commis le
meurtre.

confession NOUN
la confession

confetti NOUN
les confettis MASC PL

confidence NOUN
[1] la confiance ◊ *I've got confidence
in you.* J'ai confiance en toi.
[2] l' assurance FEM ◊ *She lacks
confidence.* Elle manque d'assurance.

confident ADJECTIVE
sûr ◊ *I'm confident everything will be
okay.* Je suis sûr que tout ira bien.
◆**She's seems quite confident.** Elle a
l'air sûre d'elle.

confidential ADJECTIVE
confidentiel MASC
confidentielle FEM

to **confirm** VERB
confirmer (*booking*)

confirmation NOUN
la confirmation

conflict NOUN
le conflit

to **confuse** VERB
◆**to confuse somebody** embrouiller les
idées de quelqu'un ◊ *Don't confuse
me!* Ne m'embrouille pas les idées!

confused ADJECTIVE
désorienté

confusing ADJECTIVE
◆**The traffic signs are confusing.** Les
panneaux de signalisation ne sont
pas clairs.

confusion NOUN
la confusion

to **congratulate** VERB
féliciter ◊ *My friends congratulated
me on passing the test.* Mes amis
m'ont félicité d'avoir réussi à
l'examen.

congratulations PL NOUN
les félicitations FEM PL
◊ *Congratulations on your new job!*
Félicitations pour votre nouveau
poste!

conjunction NOUN

la conjonction

conjurer NOUN
le prestidigitateur

connection NOUN
[1] le rapport ◊ *There's no connection
between the two events.* Il n'y a
aucun rapport entre les deux
événements.
[2] le contact (*electrical*) ◊ *There's a
loose connection.* Il y a un mauvais
contact.
[3] la correspondance (*of trains,
planes*) ◊ *We missed our connection.*
Nous avons raté la correspondance.

to **conquer** VERB
conquérir

conscience NOUN
la conscience

conscious ADJECTIVE
conscient

consciousness NOUN
la connaissance
◆**to lose consciousness** perdre
connaissance ◊ *I lost consciousness.*
J'ai perdu connaissance.

consequence NOUN
la conséquence ◊ *What are the
consequences for the environment?*
Quelles sont les conséquences pour
l'environnement?
◆**as a consequence** en conséquence

consequently ADVERB
par conséquent

conservation NOUN
la protection

conservative ADJECTIVE
see also **conservative** NOUN
conservateur MASC
conservatrice FEM
◆**the Conservative Party** le Parti
conservateur

Conservative NOUN
see also **conservative** ADJECTIVE
le conservateur
la conservatrice
◆**to vote Conservative** voter
conservateur
◆**the Conservatives** les conservateurs

conservatory NOUN
le jardin d'hiver

to **consider** VERB
[1] considérer ◊ *He considers it a
waste of time.* Il considère que c'est
une perte de temps.
[2] envisager ◊ *We considered
cancelling our holiday.* Nous avons
envisagé d'annuler nos vacances.
◆**I'm considering the idea.** J'y songe.

considerate ADJECTIVE

☞

délicat

considering PREPOSITION
[1] étant donné ◇ *Considering we were there for a month ...* Étant donné que nous étions là pour un mois ...
[2] tout compte fait ◇ *I got a good mark, considering.* J'ai eu une bonne note, tout compte fait.

to **consist** VERB
♦ **to consist of** être composé de ◇ *The band consists of three guitarists, a saxophonist and a drummer.* Le groupe est composé de trois guitaristes, un saxophoniste et un batteur.

consonant NOUN
la consonne

constant ADJECTIVE
constant

constantly ADVERB
constamment

constipated ADJECTIVE
constipé

to **construct** VERB
construire

construction NOUN
la construction

to **consult** VERB
consulter

consumer NOUN
le consommateur
la consommatrice

contact NOUN
| see also **contact** VERB |
le contact ◇ *I'm in contact with her.* Je suis en contact avec elle.

to **contact** VERB
| see also **contact** NOUN |
joindre ◇ *Where can we contact you?* Où pouvons-nous vous joindre?

contact lenses PL NOUN
les verres de contact MASC PL

to **contain** VERB
contenir

container NOUN
le récipient

contempt NOUN
le mépris

contents PL NOUN
[1] le contenu SING (*of container*)
[2] la table des matières SING (*of book*)

contest NOUN
le concours

contestant NOUN
le concurrent
la concurrente

context NOUN
le contexte

continent NOUN
le continent ◇ *How many continents are there?* Combien y a-t-il de continents?
♦ **the Continent** l'Europe FEM ◇ *I've never been to the Continent.* Je ne suis jamais allé en Europe.

continental breakfast NOUN
le petit déjeuner à la française

to **continue** VERB
[1] continuer ◇ *She continued talking to her friend.* Elle a continué à parler à son amie.
[2] reprendre (*after interruption*) ◇ *We continued working after lunch.* Nous avons repris le travail après le déjeuner.

continuous ADJECTIVE
continu
♦ **continuous assessment** le contrôle continu

contraceptive NOUN
le contraceptif

contract NOUN
le contrat

to **contradict** VERB
contredire

contrary NOUN
le contraire
♦ **on the contrary** au contraire

contrast NOUN
le contraste

to **contribute** VERB
[1] contribuer (*to success, achievement*) ◇ *The treaty will contribute to world peace.* Le traité va contribuer à la paix dans le monde.
[2] participer (*share in*) ◇ *He didn't contribute to the discussion.* Il n'a pas participé à la discussion.
[3] donner (*give*) ◇ *She contributed £10.* Elle a donné dix livres.

contribution NOUN
[1] la contribution
[2] la cotisation (*to pension, national insurance*)

control NOUN
| see also **control** VERB |
le contrôle
♦ **to lose control** (*of vehicle*) perdre le contrôle ◇ *He lost control of the car.* Il a perdu le contrôle de son véhicule.
♦ **the controls** les commandes FEM (*of machine*)
♦ **to be in control** être maître de la situation
♦ **to keep control** (*of people*) se faire obéir ◇ *He can't keep control of the*

class. Il n'arrive pas à se faire obéir de sa classe.

◆ **out of control** (*child, class*) déchaîné

to **control** VERB

> *see also* **control** NOUN
>
> 1 diriger (*country, organization*)
> 2 se faire obéir de ◊ *He can't control the class.* Il n'arrive pas à se faire obéir de sa classe.
> 3 maîtriser ◊ *I couldn't control the horse.* Je ne suis pas arrivé à maîtriser le cheval.

◆ **to control oneself** se contrôler

controversial ADJECTIVE

controversé ◊ *a controversial book* un livre controversé

convenient ADJECTIVE

bien situé (*place*) ◊ *The hotel's convenient for the airport.* L'hôtel est bien situé par rapport à l'aéroport.

◆ **It's not a convenient time for me.** C'est une heure qui ne m'arrange pas.

◆ **Would Monday be convenient for you?** Est-ce que lundi vous conviendrait?

conventional ADJECTIVE

conventionnel MASC
conventionnelle FEM

convent school NOUN

le couvent ◊ *She goes to convent school.* Elle va au couvent.

conversation NOUN

la conversation ◊ *a French conversation class* un cours de conversation française

to **convert** VERB

transformer ◊ *We've converted the loft into a spare room.* Nous avons transformé le grenier en chambre d'amis.

to **convict** VERB

reconnaître coupable ◊ *He was convicted of the murder.* Il a été reconnu coupable du meurtre.

to **convince** VERB

persuader ◊ *I'm not convinced.* Je n'en suis pas persuadé.

to **cook** VERB

> *see also* **cook** NOUN
>
> 1 faire la cuisine ◊ *I can't cook.* Je ne sais pas faire la cuisine.
> 2 préparer ◊ *She's cooking lunch.* Elle est en train de préparer le déjeuner.
> 3 faire cuire ◊ *Cook the pasta for 10 minutes.* Faites cuire les pâtes pendant dix minutes.

◆ **to be cooked** être cuit ◊ *When the potatoes are cooked ...* Lorsque les pommes de terre sont cuites ...

cook NOUN

> *see also* **cook** VERB
>
> le cuisinier
> la cuisinière
> ◊ *Matthew's an excellent cook.* Matthew est un excellent cuisinier.

cookbook NOUN

le livre de cuisine

cooker NOUN

la cuisinière ◊ *a gas cooker* une cuisinière à gaz

cookery NOUN

la cuisine

cookie NOUN US

le gâteau sec

cooking NOUN

la cuisine ◊ *I like cooking.* J'aime bien faire la cuisine.

cool ADJECTIVE

frais MASC
fraîche FEM
◊ *a cool place* un endroit frais

◆ **to stay cool** (*keep calm*) garder son calme ◊ *He stayed cool.* Il a gardé son calme.

◆ **keep cool!** du calme!

cooperation NOUN

la coopération

cop NOUN

le flic (*informal*)

to **cope** VERB

se débrouiller ◊ *It was hard, but we coped.* C'était dur, mais nous nous sommes débrouillés.

◆ **to cope with** faire face à ◊ *She's got a lot of problems to cope with.* Elle doit faire face à de nombreux problèmes.

copper NOUN

> 1 le cuivre ◊ *a copper bracelet* un bracelet en cuivre
> 2 le flic (*informal: policeman*)

copy NOUN

> *see also* **copy** VERB
>
> 1 la copie (*of letter, document*)
> 2 l' exemplaire MASC (*of book*)

to **copy** VERB

> *see also* **copy** NOUN
>
> copier ◊ *The teacher accused him of copying.* Le professeur l'a accusé d'avoir copié.

◆ **to copy and paste** copier-coller

core NOUN

le trognon (*of fruit*) ◊ *an apple core* un trognon de pomme

cork NOUN
1 le bouchon (of bottle)
2 le liège (material) ◊ a cork table mat un set de table en liège

corkscrew NOUN
le tire-bouchon

corn NOUN
1 le blé (wheat)
2 le maïs (sweetcorn)
♦ **corn on the cob** l'épi de maïs MASC

corner NOUN
1 le coin ◊ in a corner of the room dans un coin de la pièce
♦ **the shop on the corner** la boutique au coin de la rue
♦ **He lives just round the corner.** Il habite tout près d'ici.
2 le corner (in football)

cornet NOUN
1 le cornet à pistons ◊ He plays the cornet. Il joue du cornet à pistons.
2 le cornet (ice cream)

cornflakes PL NOUN
les corn-flakes MASC PL

cornstarch NOUN US
la farine de maïs

Cornwall NOUN
la Cornouailles
♦ **in Cornwall** en Cornouailles

corporal NOUN
le caporal

corporal punishment NOUN
le châtiment corporel

corpse NOUN
le cadavre

correct ADJECTIVE
see also **correct** VERB
exact ◊ That's correct. C'est exact.
♦ **the correct choice** le bon choix
♦ **the correct answer** la bonne réponse

to **correct** VERB
see also **correct** ADJECTIVE
corriger

correction NOUN
la correction

correctly ADVERB
correctement

correspondent NOUN
le correspondant
la correspondante
◊ our foreign correspondent notre correspondant à l'étranger

corridor NOUN
le couloir

corruption NOUN
la corruption

Corsica NOUN
la Corse

♦ **in Corsica** en Corse

cosmetics PL NOUN
les produits de beauté MASC PL

cosmetic surgery NOUN
la chirurgie esthétique

to **cost** VERB
see also **cost** NOUN
coûter ◊ The meal costs a hundred francs. Le repas coûte cent francs.
◊ How much does it cost? Combien est-ce que ça coûte? ◊ It costs too much. Ça coûte trop cher.

cost NOUN
see also **cost** VERB
le coût
♦ **the cost of living** le coût de la vie
♦ **at all costs** à tout prix

costume NOUN
le costume

cosy ADJECTIVE
douillet MASC
douillette FEM

cot NOUN
le lit d'enfant

cottage NOUN
le cottage
♦ **a thatched cottage** une chaumière

cottage cheese NOUN
le cottage cheese

cotton NOUN
le coton ◊ a cotton shirt une chemise en coton
♦ **cotton wool** le coton hydrophile

couch NOUN
le canapé

couchette NOUN
la couchette

to **cough** VERB
see also **cough** NOUN
tousser

cough NOUN
see also **cough** VERB
la toux ◊ a bad cough une mauvaise toux
♦ **I've got a cough.** Je tousse.
♦ **a cough sweet** une pastille

could VERB see **can**

council NOUN
le conseil

> ⓘ The nearest French equivalent of a local council would be a **conseil municipal**, which administers a **commune**.

♦ **He's on the council.** Il fait partie du conseil municipal.
♦ **a council estate** une cité HLM

C

♦**a council house** une HLM

> **ℹ** **HLM** stands for **habitation à loyer modéré** which means "low-rent home".

councillor NOUN
♦**She's a local councillor.** Elle fait partie du conseil municipal.

to **count** VERB
compter
♦**to count on** compter sur ◊ *You can count on me.* Tu peux compter sur moi.

counter NOUN
[1] le comptoir (*in shop*)
[2] le guichet (*in post office, bank*)
[3] le jeton (*in game*)

country NOUN
[1] le pays ◊ *the border between the two countries* la frontière entre les deux pays
[2] la campagne ◊ *I live in the country.* J'habite à la campagne.
♦**country dancing** la danse folklorique

countryside NOUN
la campagne

county NOUN
le comté

> **ℹ** The nearest French equivalent of a county would be a **département**.

♦**the county council**

> **ℹ** The nearest French equivalent of a county council would be a **conseil général**, which administers a **département**.

couple NOUN
le couple ◊ *the couple who live next door* le couple qui habite à côté
♦**a couple** deux ◊ *a couple of hours* deux heures
♦**Could you wait a couple of minutes?** Pourriez-vous attendre quelques minutes?

courage NOUN
le courage

courgette NOUN
la courgette

courier NOUN
[1] (*for tourists*)
l' accompagnateur MASC
l' accompagnatrice FEM
[2] (*delivery service*)
le coursier ◊ *They sent it by courier.* Ils l'ont envoyé par coursier.

> Be careful not to translate **courier** by the French word **courrier**.

course NOUN
[1] le cours ◊ *a French course* un cours de français ◊ *to go on a course* suivre un cours
[2] le plat ◊ *the main course* le plat principal
♦**the first course** l'entrée FEM
[3] le terrain ◊ *a golf course* un terrain de golf
♦**of course** bien sûr ◊ *Do you love me? – Of course I do!* Tu m'aimes? – Bien sûr que oui!

court NOUN
[1] (*of law*)
le tribunal
(les tribunaux PL)
◊ *He was in court last week.* Il est passé devant le tribunal la semaine dernière.
[2] (*tennis*)
le court ◊ *There are tennis and squash courts.* Il y a des courts de tennis et de squash.

courtyard NOUN
la cour

cousin NOUN
le cousin
la cousine

cover NOUN
see also **cover** VERB
[1] la couverture (*of book*)
[2] la housse (*of duvet*)

to **cover** VERB
see also **cover** NOUN
[1] couvrir ◊ *My face was covered with mosquito bites.* J'avais le visage couvert de piqûres de moustique.
[2] prendre en charge ◊ *Our insurance didn't cover it.* Notre assurance ne l'a pas pris en charge.
♦**to cover up a scandal** étouffer un scandale

cow NOUN
la vache

coward NOUN
le lâche ◊ *She's a coward.* Elle est lâche.

cowardly ADJECTIVE
lâche

cowboy NOUN
le cow-boy

crab NOUN
le crabe

crack NOUN
see also **crack** VERB
[1] la fissure (*in wall*)
[2] la fêlure (*in cup, window*)

☞

3 le crack (drug)
♦**I'll have a crack at it.** Je vais tenter le coup.

to **crack** VERB
see also **crack** NOUN
casser (nut, egg)
♦**to crack a joke** sortir une blague

to **crack down on** VERB
être ferme avec ◇ The police are cracking down on motorists who drive too fast. La police va être ferme avec les automobilistes qui roulent trop vite.

cracked ADJECTIVE
fêlé (cup, window)

cracker NOUN
1 le cracker (biscuit)
2 le diablotin (Christmas cracker)

cradle NOUN
le berceau
(les berceaux PL)

craft NOUN
les travaux manuels MASC PL ◇ We do craft at school. Nous avons des cours de travaux manuels à l'école.
♦**a craft centre** un centre artisanal

craftsman NOUN
l' artisan MASC

to **cram** VERB
1 entasser ◇ We crammed our stuff into the boot. Nous avons entassé nos affaires dans le coffre.
2 bachoter (for exams)

crammed ADJECTIVE
♦**crammed with** bourré de ◇ Her bag was crammed with books. Son sac était bourré de livres.

crane NOUN
la grue (machine)

to **crash** VERB
see also **crash** NOUN
avoir un accident ◇ He's crashed his car. Il a eu un accident de voiture.
♦**The plane crashed.** L'avion s'est écrasé.

crash NOUN
see also **crash** VERB
1 la collision (of car)
2 l' accident MASC (of plane)
♦**a crash helmet** un casque
♦**a crash course** un cours intensif

to **crawl** VERB
see also **crawl** NOUN
marcher à quatre pattes (baby)

crawl NOUN
see also **crawl** VERB
le crawl ◇ to do the crawl nager le crawl

crazy ADJECTIVE

fou MASC
folle FEM

cream ADJECTIVE
see also **cream** NOUN
crème MASC, FEM, PL (colour)

cream NOUN
see also **cream** ADJECTIVE
la crème ◇ strawberries and cream les fraises à la crème
♦**a cream cake** un gâteau à la crème
♦**cream cheese** le fromage à la crème
♦**sun cream** la crème solaire

crease NOUN
le pli

creased ADJECTIVE
froissé

to **create** VERB
créer

creation NOUN
la création

creative ADJECTIVE
créatif MASC
créative FEM

creature NOUN
la créature

crèche NOUN
la crèche

credit NOUN
le crédit ◇ on credit à crédit

credit card NOUN
la carte de crédit

creeps PL NOUN
♦**It gives me the creeps.** Ça me donne la chair de poule.

to **creep up** VERB
s'approcher à pas de loup
♦**to creep up on somebody** s'approcher de quelqu'un à pas de loup

crept VERB see **creep up**

cress NOUN
le cresson

crew NOUN
1 l' équipage MASC (of ship, plane)
2 l' équipe FEM ◇ a film crew une équipe de tournage

crew cut NOUN
les cheveux en brosse MASC PL

cricket NOUN
1 le cricket ◇ I play cricket. Je joue au cricket.
♦**a cricket bat** une batte de cricket
2 le grillon (insect)

crime NOUN
1 le délit ◇ Murder is a crime. Le meurtre est un délit.
2 la criminalité (lawlessness)
♦**Crime is rising.** La criminalité augmente.

criminal NOUN
see also **criminal** ADJECTIVE
le criminel
la criminelle

criminal ADJECTIVE
see also **criminal** NOUN
criminel MASC
criminelle FEM
◊ It's criminal! C'est criminel!
♦ It's a criminal offence. C'est un crime puni par la loi.
♦ to have a criminal record avoir un casier judiciaire

crisis NOUN
la crise

crisp ADJECTIVE
croquant (food)

crisps PL NOUN
les chips FEM PL ◊ a bag of crisps un paquet de chips

criterion NOUN
le critère

critic NOUN
le critique

critical ADJECTIVE
critique
♦ a critical remark une critique

criticism NOUN
la critique

to **criticize** VERB
critiquer

Croatia NOUN
la Croatie
♦ in Croatia en Croatie

to **crochet** VERB
crocheter

crocodile NOUN
le crocodile

crook NOUN
l' escroc MASC (criminal)

crop NOUN
la récolte ◊ a good crop of apples une bonne récolte de pommes

cross NOUN
see also **cross** ADJECTIVE, VERB
la croix

cross ADJECTIVE
see also **cross** NOUN, VERB
fâché ◊ to be cross about something être fâché à propos de quelque chose

to **cross** VERB
see also **cross** ADJECTIVE, NOUN
traverser (street, bridge)
♦ to cross out barrer
♦ to cross over traverser

cross-country NOUN
le cross (race)

♦ cross-country skiing le ski de fond

crossing NOUN
① la traversée (by boat) ◊ the crossing from Dover to Calais la traversée de Douvres à Calais
② le passage clouté (for pedestrians)

crossroads NOUN
le carrefour

crossword NOUN
les mots croisés MASC PL ◊ I like doing crosswords. J'aime faire les mots croisés.

to **crouch down** VERB
s'accroupir

crow NOUN
le corbeau
(les corbeaux PL)

crowd NOUN
la foule
♦ the crowd (at sports match) les spectateurs MASC PL

crowded ADJECTIVE
bondé

crown NOUN
la couronne

crucifix NOUN
le crucifix

crude ADJECTIVE (vulgar)
grossier MASC
grossière FEM

cruel ADJECTIVE
cruel MASC
cruelle FEM

cruise NOUN
la croisière ◊ to go on a cruise faire une croisière

crumb NOUN
la miette

to **crush** VERB
écraser

crutch NOUN
la béquille

cry NOUN
see also **cry** VERB
le cri ◊ He gave a cry of surprise. Il a poussé un cri de surprise.
♦ Go on, have a good cry! Vas-y, pleure un bon coup!

to **cry** VERB
see also **cry** NOUN
pleurer ◊ The baby's crying. Le bébé pleure.

crystal NOUN
le cristal
(les cristaux PL)

CTC NOUN (= city technology college)
le collège technique

cub NOUN

C

[1] (*animal*)
le <u>petit</u>
[2] (*scout*)
le <u>louveteau</u>
(les louveteaux PL)

cube NOUN
le <u>cube</u>

cubic ADJECTIVE
♦ **a cubic metre** un mètre cube

cucumber NOUN
le <u>concombre</u>

cuddle NOUN
le <u>câlin</u> ◊ *Come and give me a cuddle.* Viens me faire un câlin.

cue NOUN
la <u>queue de billard</u> (*for snooker, pool*)

culottes PL NOUN
la <u>jupe-culotte</u> SING

culture NOUN
la <u>culture</u>

cunning ADJECTIVE
[1] (*person*)
<u>rusé</u>
[2] (*plan, idea*)
<u>astucieux</u> MASC
<u>astucieuse</u> FEM

cup NOUN
[1] la <u>tasse</u> ◊ *a china cup* une tasse en porcelaine
♦ **a cup of coffee** un café
[2] la <u>coupe</u> (*trophy*)

cupboard NOUN
le <u>placard</u>

to **cure** VERB
see also **cure** NOUN
<u>guérir</u>

cure NOUN
see also **cure** VERB
le <u>remède</u>

curious ADJECTIVE
<u>curieux</u> MASC
<u>curieuse</u> FEM

curl NOUN
la <u>boucle</u> (*in hair*)

curly ADJECTIVE
[1] <u>bouclé</u> (*loosely curled*)
[2] <u>frisé</u> (*tightly curled*)

currant NOUN
le <u>raisin de Corinthe</u> (*dried fruit*)

currency NOUN
la <u>devise</u> ◊ *foreign currency* les devises étrangères FEM PL

current NOUN
see also **current** ADJECTIVE
le <u>courant</u> ◊ *The current is very strong.* Le courant est très fort.

current ADJECTIVE
see also **current** NOUN
<u>actuel</u> MASC
<u>actuelle</u> FEM
◊ *the current situation* la situation actuelle

current account NOUN
le <u>compte courant</u>

current affairs PL NOUN
l' <u>actualité</u> FEM SING

curriculum NOUN
le <u>programme</u>

curriculum vitae NOUN
le <u>curriculum vitae</u>

curry NOUN
le <u>curry</u>

curse NOUN
la <u>malédiction</u> (*spell*)

curtain NOUN
le <u>rideau</u>
(les rideaux PL)
♦ **to draw the curtains** tirer les rideaux

cushion NOUN
le <u>coussin</u>

custard NOUN
la <u>crème anglaise</u> (*for pouring*)

custody NOUN
la <u>garde</u> (*of child*)

custom NOUN
la <u>coutume</u> MASC ◊ *It's an old custom.* C'est une ancienne coutume.

customer NOUN
le <u>client</u>
la <u>cliente</u>

customs PL NOUN
la <u>douane</u> SING

customs officer NOUN
le <u>douanier</u>
la <u>douanière</u>

cut NOUN
see also **cut** VERB
[1] la <u>coupure</u> ◊ *He's got a cut on his forehead.* Il a une coupure au front.
[2] la <u>coupe</u> ◊ *a cut and blow-dry* une coupe brushing
[3] la <u>réduction</u> (*in price, spending*)

to **cut** VERB
see also **cut** NOUN
[1] <u>couper</u> ◊ *I'll cut some bread.* Je vais couper du pain.
♦ **to cut oneself** se couper ◊ *I cut my foot on a piece of glass.* Je me suis coupé au pied avec un morceau de verre.
[2] <u>réduire</u> (*price, spending*)
♦ **to cut down** abattre (*tree*)
♦ **to cut off** couper ◊ *The electricity was cut off.* L'électricité a été coupée.
♦ **to cut up** hacher (*vegetables, meat*)

cutback NOUN

la <u>réduction</u> ◊ *staff cutbacks* des
réductions de personnel

cute ADJECTIVE
<u>mignon</u>

cutlery NOUN
les <u>couverts</u> MASC PL

cutting NOUN
la <u>coupure de presse</u> (*from
newspaper*)

CV NOUN
le <u>C.V.</u>

cybercafé NOUN
le <u>cybercafé</u>

to **cycle** VERB

see also **cycle** NOUN

<u>faire de la bicyclette</u> ◊ *I like cycling.*
J'aime faire de la bicyclette.
◆**I cycle to school.** Je vais à l'école à
bicyclette.

cycle NOUN

see also **cycle** VERB

la <u>bicyclette</u>
◆**a cycle ride** une promenade à
bicyclette

◆**a cycle lane** une piste cyclable

cycling NOUN
le <u>cyclisme</u>

cyclist NOUN
le/la <u>cycliste</u>

cylinder NOUN
le <u>cylindre</u>

Cyprus NOUN
<u>Chypre</u>
◆**in Cyprus** à Chypre
◆**We went to Cyprus.** Nous sommes
allés à Chypre.

Czech ADJECTIVE

see also **Czech** NOUN

<u>tchèque</u>
◆**the Czech Republic** la République
tchèque

Czech NOUN

see also **Czech** ADJECTIVE

1 le/la <u>Tchèque</u> (*person*)
2 le <u>tchèque</u> (*language*)

D

dad NOUN
1 le père ◊ *my dad* mon père ◊ *his dad* son père
2 le papa

Use papa only when you are talking to your father or using it as his name; otherwise use père.

♦**Dad!** Papa! ◊ *I'll ask Dad.* Je vais demander à papa.

daddy NOUN
le papa ◊ *Say hello to your daddy!* Dis bonjour à ton papa! ◊ *Hello Daddy!* Bonjour Papa!

daffodil NOUN
la jonquille

daft ADJECTIVE
idiot

daily ADJECTIVE, ADVERB
1 quotidien MASC
quotidienne FEM
◊ *It's part of my daily routine.* Ça fait partie de mes occupations quotidiennes.
2 tous les jours ◊ *The pool is open daily from 9 a.m. to 6 p.m.* La piscine est ouverte tous les jours de neuf heures à dix-huit heures.

dairy NOUN
la crémerie (*shop*)

dairy products PL NOUN
les produits laitiers MASC PL

daisy NOUN
la pâquerette

dam NOUN
le barrage

damage NOUN
see also **damage** VERB
les dégâts MASC PL ◊ *The storm did a lot of damage.* La tempête a fait beaucoup de dégâts.

to **damage** VERB
see also **damage** NOUN
endommager

damn NOUN
see also **damn** ADJECTIVE
♦**I don't give a damn!** Je m'en fiche! (*informal*)
♦**Damn!** Zut! (*informal*)

damn ADJECTIVE, ADVERB
see also **damn** NOUN
♦**It's a damn nuisance!** Quelle barbe!

damp ADJECTIVE
humide

dance NOUN

see also **dance** VERB
1 la danse ◊ *The last dance was a waltz.* La dernière danse était une valse.
2 le bal ◊ *Are you going to the dance tonight?* Tu vas au bal ce soir?

to **dance** VERB
see also **dance** NOUN
danser
♦**to go dancing** aller danser ◊ *Let's go dancing!* Si on allait danser?

dancer NOUN
le danseur
la danseuse

dandruff NOUN
les pellicules FEM PL

Dane NOUN
le Danois
la Danoise

danger NOUN
le danger
♦**in danger** en danger ◊ *His life is in danger.* Sa vie est en danger.
♦**to be in danger of** risquer de ◊ *We were in danger of missing the plane.* Nous risquions de rater l'avion.

dangerous ADJECTIVE
dangereux MASC
dangereuse FEM

Danish ADJECTIVE
see also **Danish** NOUN
danois

Danish NOUN
see also **Danish** ADJECTIVE
le danois (*language*)

to **dare** VERB
oser
♦**to dare to do something** oser faire quelque chose ◊ *I didn't dare to tell my parents.* Je n'ai pas osé le dire à mes parents.
♦**I dare say it'll be okay.** Je suppose que ça va aller.

daring ADJECTIVE
audacieux MASC
audacieuse FEM

dark ADJECTIVE
see also **dark** NOUN
1 sombre (*room*) ◊ *It's dark.* (*inside*) Il fait sombre.
♦**It's dark outside.** Il fait nuit dehors.
♦**It's getting dark.** La nuit tombe.
2 foncé (*colour*) ◊ *She's got dark hair.* Elle a les cheveux foncés. ◊ *a dark green sweater* un pull vert foncé

dark NOUN
see also **dark** ADJECTIVE
le noir ◊ *I'm afraid of the dark.* J'ai peur du noir.
♦ **after dark** après la tombée de la nuit

darkness NOUN
l' obscurité FEM ◊ *The room was in darkness.* La chambre était dans l'obscurité.

darling NOUN
le chéri
la chérie
◊ *Thank you, darling!* Merci, chéri!

dart NOUN
la fléchette ◊ *to play darts* jouer aux fléchettes

to **dash** VERB
see also **dash** NOUN
se précipiter ◊ *Everyone dashed to the window to look.* Tout le monde s'est précipité vers la fenêtre pour regarder.
♦ **I must dash!** Il faut que je me sauve!

dash NOUN
see also **dash** VERB
le tiret (*punctuation mark*)

data PL NOUN
les données FEM PL

database NOUN
la base de données (*on computer*)

date NOUN
[1] la date ◊ *my date of birth* ma date de naissance
♦ **What's the date today?** Quel jour sommes-nous?
♦ **to have a date with somebody** sortir avec quelqu'un ◊ *She's got a date with Ian tonight.* Elle sort avec Ian ce soir.
♦ **out of date (1)** (*passport*) périmé
♦ **out of date (2)** (*technology*) dépassé
♦ **out of date (3)** (*clothes*) démodé
[2] la datte (*fruit*)

daughter NOUN
la fille

daughter-in-law NOUN
la belle-fille
(les belles-filles PL)

dawn NOUN
l' aube FEM ◊ *at dawn* à l'aube

day NOUN
*Use **jour** to refer to the whole 24-hour period. **journée** only refers to the time when you are awake.*
[1] le jour ◊ *We stayed in Nice for three days.* Nous sommes restés trois jours à Nice.
♦ **every day** tous les jours

[2] la journée ◊ *during the day* dans la journée ◊ *I stayed at home all day.* Je suis resté à la maison toute la journée.
♦ **the day before** la veille ◊ *the day before my birthday* la veille de mon anniversaire
♦ **the day after** le lendemain
♦ **the day after tomorrow** après-demain ◊ *We're leaving the day after tomorrow.* Nous partons après-demain.
♦ **the day before yesterday** avant-hier ◊ *He arrived the day before yesterday.* Il est arrivé avant-hier.

dead ADJECTIVE, ADVERB
[1] mort ◊ *He was already dead when the doctor came.* Il était déjà mort quand le docteur est arrivé.
♦ **He was shot dead.** Il a été abattu.
[2] absolument (*totally*) ◊ *You're dead right!* Tu as absolument raison!
♦ **dead on time** à l'heure pile ◊ *The train arrived dead on time.* Le train est arrivé à l'heure pile.

dead end NOUN
l' impasse FEM

deadline NOUN
la date limite ◊ *The deadline for entries is May 2nd.* La date limite d'inscription est le deux mai.

deaf ADJECTIVE
sourd

deafening ADJECTIVE
assourdissant

deal NOUN
see also **deal** VERB
le marché
♦ **It's a deal!** Marché conclu!
♦ **a great deal** beaucoup ◊ *a great deal of money* beaucoup d'argent

to **deal** VERB
see also **deal** NOUN
donner (*cards*) ◊ *It's your turn to deal.* C'est à toi de donner.
♦ **to deal with something** s'occuper de quelque chose ◊ *He promised to deal with it immediately.* Il a promis de s'en occuper immédiatement.

dealer NOUN
[1] (*of goods*)
le marchand
la marchande
[2] (*of drugs*)
le dealer

dealt VERB *see* **deal**

dear ADJECTIVE
[1] cher MASC
chère FEM

D

◊ *Dear Mrs Duval* Chère Madame Duval

♦ **Dear Sir/Madam** (*in a circular*) Madame, Monsieur
[2] (*expensive*)
coûteux MASC
coûteuse FEM

death NOUN
la mort ◊ *after his death* après sa mort

♦ **I was bored to death.** Je me suis ennuyé à mourir.

debate NOUN
see also **debate** VERB
le débat

to **debate** VERB
see also **debate** NOUN
débattre

debt NOUN
la dette ◊ *He's got a lot of debts.* Il a beaucoup de dettes.

♦ **to be in debt** avoir des dettes

decade NOUN
la décennie

decaffeinated ADJECTIVE
décaféiné

to **decay** VERB
se délabrer (*building*) ◊ *a decaying mansion* un manoir qui se délabre

to **deceive** VERB
tromper

December NOUN
décembre MASC

♦ **in December** en décembre

decent ADJECTIVE
convenable ◊ *a decent education* une éducation convenable

to **decide** VERB
[1] décider ◊ *I decided to write to her.* J'ai décidé de lui écrire. ◊ *I decided not to go.* J'ai décidé de ne pas y aller.
[2] se décider ◊ *I can't decide.* Je n'arrive pas à me décider. ◊ *Haven't you decided yet?* Tu ne t'es pas encore décidé?

♦ **to decide on something** se mettre d'accord sur quelque chose ◊ *They haven't decided on a name yet.* Ils ne se sont pas encore mis d'accord sur un nom.

decimal ADJECTIVE
décimal ◊ *the decimal system* le système décimal

decision NOUN
la décision

♦ **to make a decision** prendre une décision

decisive ADJECTIVE

décidé (*person*)

deck NOUN
[1] (*of ship*)
le pont

♦ **on deck** sur le pont
[2] (*of cards*)
le jeu
(les jeux PL)

deckchair NOUN
la chaise longue

to **declare** VERB
déclarer

to **decorate** VERB
[1] décorer ◊ *I decorated the cake with glacé cherries.* J'ai décoré le gâteau avec des cerises confites.
[2] peindre (*paint*)
[3] tapisser (*wallpaper*)

decorations PL NOUN
les décorations FEM PL

decrease NOUN
see also **decrease** VERB
la diminution ◊ *a decrease in the number of unemployed people* une diminution du nombre de chômeurs

to **decrease** VERB
see also **decrease** NOUN
diminuer

dedicated ADJECTIVE
dévoué ◊ *a very dedicated teacher* un professeur très dévoué

♦ **dedicated to (1)** consacré à ◊ *a museum dedicated to Napoleon* un musée consacré à Napoléon

♦ **dedicated to (2)** dédicacé à ◊ *The book is dedicated "to Emma, with love from Harry".* Le livre est dédicacé "à Emma, avec tout mon amour, Harry".

dedication NOUN
[1] le dévouement (*commitment*)
[2] la dédicace (*in book, on radio*)

to **deduct** VERB
déduire

deep ADJECTIVE
[1] (*water, hole, cut*)
profond ◊ *Is it deep?* Est-ce que c'est profond?

♦ **How deep is the lake?** Quelle est la profondeur du lac?

♦ **a hole 4 metres deep** un trou de quatre mètres de profondeur
[2] (*layer*)
épais MASC
épaisse FEM
◊ *a deep layer of snow* une épaisse couche de neige ◊ *The snow was really deep.* Il y avait une épaisse couche de neige.

◆**He's got a deep voice.** Il a la voix grave.

◆**to take a deep breath** respirer à fond

deeply ADVERB
　profondément (*depressed*)

deer NOUN
　[1] le cerf (*red deer*)
　[2] le daim (*fallow deer*)
　[3] le chevreuil (*roe deer*)

defeat NOUN
　see also **defeat** VERB
　la défaite

to **defeat** VERB
　see also **defeat** NOUN
　battre

defect NOUN
　le défaut

defence NOUN
　la défense

to **defend** VERB
　défendre

defender NOUN
　le défenseur

to **define** VERB
　définir

definite ADJECTIVE
　[1] précis ◊ *I haven't got any definite plans.* Je n'ai pas de projets précis.
　[2] net MASC
　nette FEM
　◊ *It's a definite improvement.* Cela constitue une nette amélioration.
　[3] sûr ◊ *Perhaps we'll go to Spain, but it's not definite.* Nous irons peut-être en Espagne, mais ce n'est pas sûr.

◆**He was definite about it.** Il a été catégorique.

definitely ADVERB
　vraiment ◊ *He's definitely the best player.* C'est vraiment lui le meilleur joueur.

◆**He's the best player. – Definitely!** C'est le meilleur joueur. – C'est sûr!

◆**I definitely think he'll come.** Je suis sûr qu'il va venir.

definition NOUN
　la définition

degree NOUN
　[1] le degré ◊ *a temperature of 30 degrees* une température de trente degrés
　[2] la licence ◊ *a degree in English* une licence d'anglais

to **delay** VERB
　see also **delay** NOUN
　[1] retarder ◊ *We decided to delay our departure.* Nous avons décidé de retarder notre départ.

　[2] tarder ◊ *Don't delay!* Ne tarde pas!

◆**to be delayed** être retardé ◊ *Our flight was delayed.* Notre vol a été retardé.

delay NOUN
　see also **delay** VERB
　le retard ◊ *There will be delays to trains on the London-Brighton line.* Il y aura des retards sur la ligne Londres-Brighton.
　*Be careful not to translate **delay** by délai.*

to **delete** VERB
　effacer (*on computer, tape*)

deliberate ADJECTIVE
　délibéré

deliberately ADVERB
　exprès ◊ *She did it deliberately.* Elle l'a fait exprès.

delicate ADJECTIVE
　délicat

delicatessen NOUN
　l' épicerie fine FEM

delicious ADJECTIVE
　délicieux MASC
　délicieuse FEM

delight NOUN
◆**to her delight** à sa plus grande joie

delighted ADJECTIVE
　ravi ◊ *He'll be delighted to see you.* Il sera ravi de vous voir.

delightful ADJECTIVE
　(*meal, evening*)
　délicieux MASC
　délicieuse FEM

to **deliver** VERB
　[1] livrer ◊ *I deliver newspapers.* Je livre les journaux.
　[2] distribuer (*mail*)

delivery NOUN
　la livraison

to **demand** VERB
　see also **demand** NOUN
　exiger
　*Be careful not to translate **to demand** by **demander**.*

demand NOUN
　see also **demand** VERB
　la demande (*for product*)

demanding ADJECTIVE
　astreignant ◊ *It's a very demanding job.* C'est un travail très astreignant.

demo NOUN
　la manif (*protest*)

democracy NOUN
　la démocratie

democratic ADJECTIVE
　démocratique

to **demolish** VERB
démolir

to **demonstrate** VERB
[1] faire une démonstration de (show) ◇ She demonstrated the technique. Elle a fait une démonstration de la technique.
[2] manifester (protest)
♦**to demonstrate against something** manifester contre quelque chose

demonstration NOUN
[1] la démonstration (of method, technique)
[2] la manifestation (protest)

demonstrator NOUN
(protester)
le manifestant
la manifestante

denim NOUN
le jean ◇ a denim jacket une veste en jean

denims PL NOUN
le jean SING (jeans)

Denmark NOUN
le Danemark
♦**in Denmark** au Danemark
♦**to Denmark** au Danemark

dense ADJECTIVE
[1] (crowd, fog)
dense
[2] (smoke)
épais MASC
épaisse FEM
♦**He's so dense!** Il est vraiment bouché!

dent NOUN
see also **dent** VERB
la bosse

to **dent** VERB
see also **dent** NOUN
cabosser

dental ADJECTIVE
dentaire
♦**dental floss** le fil dentaire

dentist NOUN
le/la dentiste ◇ Catherine is a dentist. Catherine est dentiste.

to **deny** VERB
nier ◇ She denied everything. Elle a tout nié.

deodorant NOUN
le déodorant

to **depart** VERB
partir

department NOUN
[1] le rayon (in shop) ◇ the shoe department le rayon chaussures
[2] le département (university, school) ◇ the English department le département d'anglais

department store NOUN
le grand magasin

departure NOUN
le départ

departure lounge NOUN
le hall des départs

to **depend** VERB
♦**to depend on** dépendre de ◇ The price depends on the quality. Le prix dépend de la qualité.
♦**depending on the weather** selon le temps
♦**It depends.** Ça dépend.

to **deport** VERB
expulser

deposit NOUN
[1] les arrhes FEM PL (part payment) ◇ You have to pay a deposit when you book. Il faut verser des arrhes lors de la réservation.
[2] la caution (when hiring something) ◇ You get the deposit back when you return the bike. On vous remboursera la caution quand vous ramènerez le vélo.
[3] la consigne (on bottle)

depressed ADJECTIVE
déprimé ◇ I'm feeling depressed. Je suis déprimé.

depressing ADJECTIVE
déprimant

depth NOUN
la profondeur

deputy head NOUN
le directeur adjoint
la directrice adjointe

to **descend** VERB
descendre

to **describe** VERB
décrire

description NOUN
la description

desert NOUN
le désert

desert island NOUN
l' île déserte FEM

to **deserve** VERB
mériter

design NOUN
see also **design** VERB
[1] la conception ◇ It's a completely new design. C'est une conception entièrement nouvelle.
[2] le motif ◇ a geometric design un motif géométrique

◆**fashion design** le stylisme

to **design** VERB
> see also **design** NOUN

dessiner (clothes, furniture)

designer NOUN
le/la styliste (of clothes)
◆**designer clothes** les vêtements griffés MASC

desire NOUN
> see also **desire** VERB

le désir

to **desire** VERB
> see also **desire** NOUN

désirer

desk NOUN
[1] (in office)
le bureau
(les bureaux PL)
[2] (for pupil)
le pupitre
[3] (in hotel)
la réception
[4] (at airport)
le comptoir

despair NOUN
le désespoir
◆**I was in despair.** J'étais désespéré.

desperate ADJECTIVE
désespéré ◊ a desperate situation une situation désespérée
◆**to get desperate** désespérer ◊ I was getting desperate. Je commençais à désespérer.

desperately ADVERB
[1] terriblement ◊ We're desperately worried. Nous sommes terriblement inquiets.
[2] désespérément ◊ He was desperately trying to persuade her. Il essayait désespérément de la persuader.

to **despise** VERB
mépriser

despite PREPOSITION
malgré

dessert NOUN
le dessert ◊ for dessert comme dessert

destination NOUN
la destination

to **destroy** VERB
détruire

destruction NOUN
la destruction

detached house NOUN
le pavillon

detail NOUN
le détail ◊ in detail en détail

detailed ADJECTIVE
détaillé

detective NOUN
l' inspecteur de police MASC
◆**a private detective** un détective privé
◆**a detective story** un roman policier

detention NOUN
◆**to get a detention** être consigné

detergent NOUN
[1] le détergent
[2] la lessive [US]

determined ADJECTIVE
déterminé
◆**to be determined to do something** être déterminé à faire quelque chose ◊ She's determined to succeed. Elle est déterminée à réussir.

detour NOUN
le détour

devaluation NOUN
la dévaluation

devastated ADJECTIVE
anéanti ◊ I was devastated. J'étais anéanti.

devastating ADJECTIVE
[1] (upsetting)
accablant
[2] (flood, storm)
dévastateur MASC
dévastatrice FEM

to **develop** VERB
[1] développer ◊ to get a film developed faire développer un film
[2] se développer ◊ Girls develop faster than boys. Les filles se développent plus vite que les garçons.
◆**to develop into** se transformer en ◊ The argument developed into a fight. La dispute s'est transformée en bagarre.
◆**a developing country** un pays en voie de développement

development NOUN
le développement ◊ the latest developments les derniers développements

device NOUN
l' appareil MASC

devil NOUN
le diable ◊ Poor devil! Pauvre diable!

to **devise** VERB
concevoir

devoted ADJECTIVE
dévoué ◊ He's completely devoted to her. Il lui est très dévoué.

diabetes NOUN
le diabète

diabetic NOUN

☞

le/la <u>diabétique</u> ◊ *I'm a diabetic.* Je suis diabétique.

diagonal ADJECTIVE
<u>diagonal</u>
(<u>diagonaux</u> MASC PL)

diagram NOUN
le <u>diagramme</u>

to **dial** VERB
<u>composer</u> (*number*)

dialling tone NOUN
la <u>tonalité</u>

dialogue NOUN
le <u>dialogue</u>

diamond NOUN
le <u>diamant</u> ◊ *a diamond ring* une bague en diamant
♦ **diamonds** (*at cards*) le <u>carreau</u> SING

diaper NOUN US
la <u>couche</u>

diarrhoea NOUN
la <u>diarrhée</u> ◊ *I've got diarrhoea.* J'ai la diarrhée.

diary NOUN
1 l' <u>agenda</u> MASC ◊ *I've got her phone number in my diary.* J'ai son numéro de téléphone dans mon agenda.
2 le <u>journal</u>
(les journaux PL)
◊ *I keep a diary.* Je tiens un journal.

dice NOUN
le <u>dé</u>

dictation NOUN
la <u>dictée</u>

dictionary NOUN
le <u>dictionnaire</u>

did VERB *see* **do**

to **die** VERB
<u>mourir</u> ◊ *He died last year.* Il est mort l'année dernière.
♦ **to be dying to do something** mourir d'envie de faire quelque chose ◊ *I'm dying to see you.* Je meurs d'envie de te voir.

diesel NOUN
1 le <u>gazole</u> (*fuel*) ◊ *30 litres of diesel, please.* Trente litres de gazole, s'il vous plaît.
2 la <u>voiture diesel</u> (*car*) ◊ *Our car's a diesel.* Nous avons une voiture diesel.

diet NOUN
see also **diet** VERB
1 l' <u>alimentation</u> FEM ◊ *a healthy diet* une alimentation saine
2 le <u>régime</u> (*for slimming*) ◊ *I'm on a diet.* Je suis au régime.

to **diet** VERB
see also **diet** NOUN

<u>faire un régime</u> ◊ *I've been dieting for two months.* Je fais un régime depuis deux mois.

difference NOUN
la <u>différence</u> ◊ *There's not much difference in age between us.* Il n'y a pas une grande différence d'âge entre nous.
♦ **It makes no difference.** Ça revient au même.

different ADJECTIVE
<u>différent</u> ◊ *We are very different.* Nous sommes très différents. ◊ *Paris is different from London.* Paris est différent de Londres.

difficult ADJECTIVE
<u>difficile</u> ◊ *It's difficult to choose.* C'est difficile de choisir.

difficulty NOUN
la <u>difficulté</u> ◊ *without difficulty* sans difficulté
♦ **to have difficulty doing something** avoir du mal à faire quelque chose

to **dig** VERB
1 <u>creuser</u> (*hole*)
2 <u>bêcher</u> (*garden*)
♦ **to dig something up** déterrer quelque chose

digestion NOUN
la <u>digestion</u>

digger NOUN
la <u>pelleteuse</u> (*machine*)

digital television NOUN
la <u>télévision numérique</u>

digital watch NOUN
la <u>montre à affichage numérique</u>

dim ADJECTIVE
1 <u>faible</u> (*light*)
2 <u>limité</u> (*stupid*)

dimension NOUN
la <u>dimension</u>

to **diminish** VERB
<u>diminuer</u>

din NOUN
le <u>vacarme</u>

diner NOUN US
le <u>snack</u>

dinghy NOUN
♦ **a rubber dinghy** un canot pneumatique
♦ **a sailing dinghy** un dériveur

dining car NOUN
le <u>wagon-restaurant</u>
(les wagons-restaurants PL)

dining room NOUN
la <u>salle à manger</u>

dinner NOUN
1 le <u>déjeuner</u> (*at midday*)

2 le dîner (*in the evening*)

dinner jacket NOUN
le smoking

dinner party NOUN
le dîner

dinner time NOUN
1 l' heure du déjeuner FEM (*midday*)
2 l' heure du dîner FEM (*in the evening*)

dinosaur NOUN
le dinosaure

dip NOUN

see also **dip** VERB

♦to go for a dip aller se baigner

to **dip** VERB

see also **dip** NOUN

tremper ◊ *He dipped a biscuit into his tea.* Il a trempé un biscuit dans son thé.

diploma NOUN
le diplôme ◊ *a diploma in social work* un diplôme d'assistante sociale

diplomat NOUN
le/la diplomate

diplomatic ADJECTIVE
diplomatique

direct ADJECTIVE, ADVERB

see also **direct** VERB

direct ◊ *the most direct route* le chemin le plus direct ◊ *You can't fly to Marseilles direct from Manchester.* Il n'y a pas de vols directs de Manchester à Marseille.

to **direct** VERB

see also **direct** ADJECTIVE

1 réaliser (*film, programme*)
2 mettre en scène (*play, show*)

direction NOUN
la direction ◊ *We're going in the wrong direction.* Nous allons dans la mauvaise direction.

♦to ask somebody for directions demander son chemin à quelqu'un

director NOUN
1 (*of company*)
le directeur
la directrice
2 (*of play*)
le metteur en scène
(les metteurs en scène PL)
3 (*of film, programme*)
le réalisateur
la réalisatrice

directory NOUN
1 l' annuaire MASC (*phone book*)
2 le répertoire (*computing*)

dirt NOUN
la saleté

dirty ADJECTIVE
sale

♦to get dirty se salir
♦to get something dirty salir quelque chose

disabled ADJECTIVE
handicapé

♦the disabled les handicapés

disadvantage NOUN
le désavantage

to **disagree** VERB
♦We always disagree. Nous ne sommes jamais d'accord.
♦I disagree! Je ne suis pas d'accord!
♦He disagrees with me. Il n'est pas d'accord avec moi.

disagreement NOUN
le désaccord

to **disappear** VERB
disparaître

disappearance NOUN
la disparition

disappointed ADJECTIVE
déçu

disappointing ADJECTIVE
décevant

disappointment NOUN
la déception

disaster NOUN
le désastre

disastrous ADJECTIVE
désastreux MASC
désastreuse FEM

disc NOUN
le disque

discipline NOUN
la discipline

disc jockey NOUN
le disc-jockey

disco NOUN
la soirée disco ◊ *There's a disco at the school tonight.* Il y a une soirée disco à l'école ce soir.

to **disconnect** VERB
1 débrancher (*electrical equipment*)
2 couper (*telephone, water supply*)

discount NOUN
la réduction ◊ *a discount for students* une réduction pour les étudiants

to **discourage** VERB
décourager

♦to get discouraged se décourager ◊ *Don't get discouraged!* Ne te décourage pas!

to **discover** VERB
découvrir

discrimination NOUN

☞

la <u>discrimination</u> ◊ *racial discrimination* la discrimination raciale

to **discuss** VERB

[1] <u>discuter de</u> ◊ *I'll discuss it with my parents.* Je vais en discuter avec mes parents.

[2] <u>discuter sur</u> (*topic*) ◊ *We discussed the problem of pollution.* Nous avons discuté du problème de la pollution.

discussion NOUN
la <u>discussion</u>

disease NOUN
la <u>maladie</u>

disgraceful ADJECTIVE
<u>scandaleux</u> MASC
<u>scandaleuse</u> FEM

to **disguise** VERB
<u>déguiser</u> ◊ *He was disguised as a policeman.* Il était déguisé en policier.

disgusted ADJECTIVE
<u>dégoûté</u> ◊ *I was absolutely disgusted.* J'étais complètement dégoûté.

disgusting ADJECTIVE
[1] <u>dégoûtant</u> (*food, smell*) ◊ *It looks disgusting.* Ça a l'air dégoûtant.
[2] <u>honteux</u> (*disgraceful*) ◊ *That's disgusting!* C'est honteux!

dish NOUN
le <u>plat</u> ◊ *a china dish* un plat en porcelaine ◊ *a vegetarian dish* un plat végétarien
◆**to do the dishes** faire la vaisselle
◊ *He never does the dishes.* Il ne fait jamais la vaisselle.

dishonest ADJECTIVE
<u>malhonnête</u>

dish soap NOUN [US]
le <u>produit à vaisselle</u>

dish towel NOUN [US]
le <u>torchon</u>

dishwasher NOUN
le <u>lave-vaisselle</u>
(les lave-vaisselle PL)

disinfectant NOUN
le <u>désinfectant</u>

disk NOUN
le <u>disque</u>
◆**a floppy disk** une disquette
◆**the hard disk** le disque dur

diskette NOUN
la <u>disquette</u>

to **dislike** VERB
see also **dislike** NOUN
<u>ne pas aimer</u> ◊ *I really dislike cabbage.* Je n'aime vraiment pas le chou.

dislike NOUN
see also **dislike** VERB
◆**my likes and dislikes** ce que j'aime et ce que je n'aime pas

dismal ADJECTIVE
<u>lugubre</u>

to **dismiss** VERB
<u>renvoyer</u> (*employee*)

disobedient ADJECTIVE
<u>désobéissant</u>

display NOUN
see also **display** VERB
l' <u>étalage</u> MASC ◊ *There was a lovely display of fruit in the window.* Il y avait un superbe étalage de fruits en vitrine.
◆**to be on display** être exposé ◊ *Her best paintings were on display.* Ses meilleurs tableaux étaient exposés.
◆**a firework display** un feu d'artifice

to **display** VERB
see also **display** NOUN
[1] <u>montrer</u> ◊ *She proudly displayed her medal.* Elle a montré sa médaille avec fierté.
[2] <u>exposer</u> (*in shop window*)

disposable ADJECTIVE
<u>jetable</u>

to **disqualify** VERB
<u>disqualifier</u>
◆**to be disqualified** être disqualifié ◊ *He was disqualified.* Il a été disqualifié.

to **disrupt** VERB
<u>perturber</u> ◊ *Protesters disrupted the meeting.* Des manifestants ont perturbé la réunion. ◊ *Train services are being disrupted by the strike.* Les horaires de train sont perturbés par la grève.

dissatisfied ADJECTIVE
◆**We were dissatisfied with the service.** Nous n'étions pas satisfaits du service.

to **dissolve** VERB
<u>dissoudre</u>

distance NOUN
la <u>distance</u> ◊ *a distance of 40 kilometres* une distance de quarante kilomètres
◆**It's within walking distance.** On peut y aller à pied.
◆**in the distance** au loin

distant ADJECTIVE
<u>lointain</u> ◊ *in the distant future* dans un avenir lointain

distillery NOUN
la <u>distillerie</u> ◊ *a whisky distillery* une distillerie de whisky

distinction NOUN

[1] la distinction ◊ *to make a distinction between ...* faire la distinction entre ...
[2] la mention très bien ◊ *I got a distinction in my piano exam.* J'ai eu la mention très bien à mon examen de piano.

distinctive ADJECTIVE
distinctif MASC
distinctive FEM

to **distract** VERB
distraire

to **distribute** VERB
distribuer

district NOUN
[1] le quartier (*of town*)
[2] la région (*of country*)

to **disturb** VERB
déranger ◊ *I'm sorry to disturb you.* Je suis désolé de vous déranger.

ditch NOUN
see also **ditch** VERB
le fossé

to **ditch** VERB
see also **ditch** NOUN
plaquer (*informal*) ◊ *She's just ditched her boyfriend.* Elle vient de plaquer son copain.

dive NOUN
see also **dive** VERB
le plongeon

to **dive** VERB
see also **dive** NOUN
plonger

diver NOUN
le plongeur
la plongeuse

diversion NOUN
la déviation (*for traffic*)

to **divide** VERB
[1] diviser ◊ *Divide the pastry in half.* Divisez la pâte en deux. ◊ *12 divided by 3 is 4.* Douze divisé par trois égalent quatre.
[2] se diviser ◊ *We divided into two groups.* Nous nous sommes divisés en deux groupes.

diving NOUN
la plongée
♦ **a diving board** un plongeoir

division NOUN
la division

divorce NOUN
le divorce

divorced ADJECTIVE
divorcé ◊ *My parents are divorced.* Mes parents sont divorcés.

DIY NOUN

le bricolage ◊ *to do DIY* faire du bricolage ◊ *a DIY shop* un magasin de bricolage

dizzy ADJECTIVE
♦ **to feel dizzy** avoir la tête qui tourne ◊ *I feel dizzy.* J'ai la tête qui tourne.

DJ NOUN
le disc-jockey

to **do** VERB
[1] faire ◊ *What are you doing this evening?* Qu'est-ce que tu fais ce soir? ◊ *I do a lot of cycling.* Je fais beaucoup de vélo. ◊ *I haven't done my homework.* Je n'ai pas fait mes devoirs. ◊ *She did it by herself.* Elle l'a fait toute seule. ◊ *I'll do my best.* Je ferai de mon mieux.
♦ **to do well** marcher bien ◊ *The firm is doing well.* L'entreprise marche bien. ◊ *She's doing well at school.* Ses études marchent bien.
[2] aller (*be enough*) ◊ *It's not very good, but it'll do.* Ce n'est pas très bon, mais ça ira.
♦ **That'll do, thanks.** Ça ira, merci.

*In English **do** is used to make questions. In French questions are made either with **est-ce que** or by reversing the order of verb and subject.*

◊ *Do you like French food?* Est-ce que vous aimez la cuisine française? ◊ *Where does he live?* Où est-ce qu'il habite? ◊ *Do you speak English?* Parlez-vous anglais? ◊ *What do you do in your free time?* Qu'est-ce que vous faites pendant vos loisirs? ◊ *Where did you go for your holidays?* Où es-tu allé pendant tes vacances?

*Use **ne ... pas** in negative sentences for **don't**.*

◊ *I don't understand.* Je ne comprends pas. ◊ *Why didn't you come?* Pourquoi n'êtes-vous pas venus?

***do** is not translated when it is used in place of another verb.*

◊ *I hate maths. – So do I.* Je déteste les maths. – Moi aussi. ◊ *I didn't like the film. – Neither did I.* Je n'ai pas aimé le film. – Moi non plus. ◊ *Do you like horses? – No I don't.* Est-ce que tu aimes les chevaux? – Non.

*Use **n'est-ce pas** to check information.*

◊ *You go swimming on Fridays, don't you?* Tu fais de la natation le vendredi, n'est-ce pas? ◊ *The bus stops at the youth hostel, doesn't it?*

English ~ French

Le bus s'arrête à l'auberge de jeunesse, n'est-ce pas?
♦ **How do you do!** Enchanté!
♦ **to do up (1)** (shoes) lacer ◊ Do up your shoes! Lace tes chaussures!
♦ **to do up (2)** (renovate) retaper ◊ They're doing up an old cottage. Ils retapent une vieille maison.
♦ **to do up (3)** (shirt, cardigan) boutonner
♦ **Do up your zip!** (on trousers) Ferme ta braguette!
♦ **to do without** se passer de ◊ I couldn't do without my computer. Je ne pourrais pas me passer de mon ordinateur.

dock NOUN
le dock (for ships)

doctor NOUN
le médecin ◊ She's a doctor. Elle est médecin. ◊ I'd like to be a doctor. Je voudrais être médecin.

document NOUN
le document

documentary NOUN
le documentaire

to **dodge** VERB
échapper à (attacker)

dodgems PL NOUN
les autos tamponneuses FEM PL ◊ to go on the dodgems aller faire un tour d'autos tamponneuses

does VERB see **do**

doesn't = **does not**

dog NOUN
le chien
la chienne
◊ Have you got a dog? Est-ce que tu as un chien?

do-it-yourself NOUN
le bricolage

dole NOUN
les allocations chômage FEM PL
♦ **to be on the dole** toucher le chômage ◊ A lot of people are on the dole. Beaucoup de gens touchent le chômage.
♦ **to go on the dole** s'inscrire au chômage

doll NOUN
la poupée

dollar NOUN
le dollar

dolphin NOUN
le dauphin

domestic ADJECTIVE
♦ **a domestic flight** un vol intérieur

dominoes PL NOUN

♦ **to have a game of dominoes** faire une partie de dominos

to **donate** VERB
donner

done VERB see **do**

donkey NOUN
l' âne MASC

donor NOUN
[1] (to charity)
le donateur
la donatrice
[2] (of blood, organ for transplant)
le donneur
la donneuse

don't = **do not**

door NOUN
[1] la porte ◊ the first door on the right la première porte à droite
[2] la portière (of car, train)

doorbell NOUN
la sonnette
♦ **to ring the doorbell** sonner
♦ **Suddenly the doorbell rang.** Soudain, on a sonné.

doorman NOUN
le portier

doorstep NOUN
le pas de la porte

dormitory NOUN
le dortoir

dose NOUN
la dose

dosh NOUN
le fric (informal: money)

dot NOUN
le point (on letter "i", in email address)
♦ **on the dot** à l'heure pile ◊ He arrived at 9 o'clock on the dot. Il est arrivé à neuf heures pile.

to **double** VERB
see also **double** ADJECTIVE
doubler ◊ The number of attacks has doubled. Le nombre d'agressions a doublé.

double ADJECTIVE, ADVERB
see also **double** VERB
double ◊ a double helping une double portion
♦ **to cost double** coûter le double ◊ First-class tickets cost double. Les billets de première classe coûtent le double.
♦ **a double bed** un grand lit
♦ **a double room** une chambre pour deux personnes
♦ **a double-decker bus** un autobus à impériale

double bass NOUN

la <u>contrebasse</u> ◊ *I play the double bass.* Je joue de la contrebasse.

to **double-click** VERB
<u>double-cliquer</u> ◊ *to double-click on an icon* double-cliquer sur une icône

double glazing NOUN
le <u>double vitrage</u>

doubles PL NOUN
le <u>double</u> SING (*in tennis*) ◊ *to play mixed doubles* jouer en double mixte

doubt NOUN
see also **doubt** VERB
le <u>doute</u> ◊ *I have my doubts.* J'ai des doutes.

to **doubt** VERB
see also **doubt** NOUN
<u>douter de</u>
◆ **I doubt it.** J'en doute.
◆ **to doubt that** douter que
   douter que has to be followed by a verb in the subjunctive.
   ◊ *I doubt he'll agree.* Je doute qu'il soit d'accord.

doubtful ADJECTIVE
◆ **to be doubtful about doing something** hésiter à faire quelque chose ◊ *I'm doubtful about going by myself.* J'hésite à y aller tout seul.
◆ **It's doubtful.** Ce n'est pas sûr.
◆ **You sound doubtful.** Tu n'as pas l'air sûr.

dough NOUN
la <u>pâte</u>

doughnut NOUN
le <u>beignet</u> ◊ *a jam doughnut* un beignet à la confiture

Dover NOUN
<u>Douvres</u> ◊ *We went from Dover to Boulogne.* Nous sommes allés de Douvres à Boulogne.
◆ **in Dover** à Douvres

down ADVERB, ADJECTIVE, PREPOSITION
[1] <u>en bas</u> (*below*) ◊ *His office is down on the first floor.* Son bureau est en bas, au premier étage. ◊ *It's down there.* C'est là-bas.
[2] <u>à terre</u> (*to the ground*) ◊ *He threw down his racket.* Il a jeté sa raquette à terre.
◆ **They live just down the road.** Ils habitent tout à côté.
◆ **to come down** descendre ◊ *Come down here!* Descends!
◆ **to go down** descendre ◊ *The rabbit went down the hole.* Le lapin est descendu dans le terrier.
◆ **to sit down** s'asseoir ◊ *Sit down!* Asseyez-vous!

◆ **to feel down** avoir le cafard ◊ *I'm feeling a bit down.* J'ai un peu le cafard.
◆ **The computer's down.** L'ordinateur est en panne.

to **download** VERB
<u>télécharger</u> ◊ *to download a file* télécharger un fichier

downpour NOUN
la <u>pluie torrentielle</u> ◊ *a sudden downpour* une pluie soudaine et torrentielle

downstairs ADVERB, ADJECTIVE
[1] <u>au rez-de-chaussée</u> ◊ *The bathroom's downstairs.* La salle de bain est au rez-de-chaussée.
[2] <u>du rez-de-chaussée</u> ◊ *the downstairs bathroom* la salle de bain du rez-de-chaussée
◆ **the people downstairs** les voisins du dessous

downtown ADJECTIVE [US]
<u>dans le centre</u>

to **doze** VERB
<u>sommeiller</u>
◆ **to doze off** s'assoupir

dozen NOUN
la <u>douzaine</u> ◊ *two dozen* deux douzaines ◊ *a dozen eggs* une douzaine d'œufs
◆ **I've told you that dozens of times.** Je t'ai dit ça des centaines de fois.

drab ADJECTIVE
<u>terne</u> (*clothes*)

draft NOUN [US]
le <u>courant d'air</u>

to **drag** VERB
see also **drag** NOUN
<u>traîner</u> (*thing, person*)

drag NOUN
see also **drag** VERB
◆ **It's a real drag!** C'est la barbe! (*informal*)
◆ **in drag** travesti ◊ *He was in drag.* Il était travesti.

dragon NOUN
le <u>dragon</u>

drain NOUN
see also **drain** VERB
l' <u>égout</u> MASC ◊ *The drains are blocked.* Les égouts sont bouchés.

to **drain** VERB
see also **drain** NOUN
<u>égoutter</u> (*vegetables, pasta*)

draining board NOUN
l' <u>égouttoir</u> MASC

drainpipe NOUN
le <u>tuyau d'écoulement</u>

drama NOUN
l' art dramatique MASC ◊ *Drama is my favourite subject.* L'art dramatique est ma matière préférée.
- **drama school** l'école d'art dramatique ◊ *I'd like to go to drama school.* J'aimerais entrer dans une école d'art dramatique.
- **Greek drama** le théâtre grec

dramatic ADJECTIVE
spectaculaire ◊ *It was really dramatic!* C'était vraiment spectaculaire! ◊ *a dramatic improvement* une amélioration spectaculaire
- **dramatic news** une nouvelle extraordinaire

drank VERB *see* **drink**

drapes PL NOUN US
les rideaux MASC PL

drastic ADJECTIVE
(*change*)
radical
(radicaux MASC PL)
- **to take drastic action** prendre des mesures énergiques

draught NOUN
le courant d'air

draughts NOUN
les dames FEM PL ◊ *to play draughts* jouer aux dames

to **draw** VERB
see also **draw** NOUN
[1] dessiner ◊ *He's good at drawing.* Il dessine bien.
- **to draw a picture** faire un dessin
- **to draw a picture of somebody** faire le portrait de quelqu'un
- **to draw a line** tirer un trait
[2] faire match nul (*sport*) ◊ *We drew 2-2.* Nous avons fait match nul deux à deux.
- **to draw the curtains** tirer les rideaux
- **to draw lots** tirer au sort

draw NOUN
see also **draw** VERB
[1] le match nul (*sport*) ◊ *The game ended in a draw.* La partie s'est soldée par un match nul.
[2] le tirage au sort (*in lottery*) ◊ *The draw takes place on Saturday.* Le tirage au sort a lieu samedi.

drawback NOUN
l' inconvénient MASC

drawer NOUN
le tiroir

drawing NOUN
le dessin

drawing pin NOUN

la punaise

drawn VERB *see* **draw**

dreadful ADJECTIVE
[1] terrible ◊ *a dreadful mistake* une terrible erreur
[2] affreux MASC
affreuse FEM
◊ *The weather was dreadful.* Il a fait un temps affreux.
- **I feel dreadful.** Je ne me sens vraiment pas bien.
- **You look dreadful.** (*ill*) Tu as une mine affreuse.

to **dream** VERB
see also **dream** NOUN
rêver ◊ *I dreamed I was in Belgium.* J'ai rêvé que j'étais en Belgique.

dream NOUN
see also **dream** VERB
le rêve ◊ *It was just a dream.* Ce n'était qu'un rêve.
- **a bad dream** un cauchemar

to **drench** VERB
- **to get drenched** se faire tremper ◊ *We got drenched.* Nous nous sommes fait tremper.

dress NOUN
see also **dress** VERB
la robe

to **dress** VERB
see also **dress** NOUN
s'habiller ◊ *I got up, dressed, and went downstairs.* Je me suis levé, je me suis habillé et je suis descendu.
- **to dress somebody** habiller quelqu'un ◊ *She dressed the children.* Elle a habillé les enfants.
- **to get dressed** s'habiller ◊ *I got dressed quickly.* Je me suis habillé rapidement.
- **to dress up** se déguiser ◊ *I dressed up as a ghost.* Je me suis déguisé en fantôme.

dressed ADJECTIVE
habillé ◊ *I'm not dressed yet.* Je ne suis pas encore habillé. ◊ *How was she dressed?* Comment est-ce qu'elle était habillée?
- **She was dressed in a green sweater and jeans.** Elle portait un pull vert et un jean.

dresser NOUN
le vaisselier (*furniture*)

dressing gown NOUN
la robe de chambre

dressing table NOUN
la coiffeuse

drew VERB *see* **draw**

dried VERB *see* **dry**

drier NOUN
le séchoir

drift NOUN
see also **drift** VERB
♦a snow drift une congère

to **drift** VERB
see also **drift** NOUN
1 aller à la dérive (boat)
2 s'amonceler (snow)

drill NOUN
see also **drill** VERB
la perceuse

to **drill** VERB
see also **drill** NOUN
percer

to **drink** VERB
see also **drink** NOUN
boire ◊ What would you like to drink? Qu'est-ce que voulez boire? ◊ She drank three cups of tea. Elle a bu trois tasses de thé. ◊ He'd been drinking. Il avait bu.
♦I don't drink. Je ne bois pas d'alcool.

drink NOUN
see also **drink** VERB
1 la boisson ◊ a cold drink une boisson fraîche ◊ a hot drink une boisson chaude
2 le verre (alcoholic) ◊ They've gone out for a drink. Ils sont allés prendre un verre.
♦to have a drink prendre un verre

drinking water NOUN
l' eau potable FEM

drive NOUN
see also **drive** VERB
1 le tour en voiture
♦to go for a drive aller faire un tour en voiture ◊ We went for a drive in the country. Nous sommes allés faire un tour à la campagne.
♦We've got a long drive tomorrow. Nous avons une longue route à faire demain.
2 l' allée FEM (of house) ◊ He parked his car in the drive. Il a garé sa voiture dans l'allée.

to **drive** VERB
see also **drive** NOUN
1 conduire (a car) ◊ She's learning to drive. Elle apprend à conduire. ◊ Can you drive? Tu sais conduire?
2 aller en voiture (go by car) ◊ Did you go by train? – No, we drove. Vous êtes partis en train? – Non, nous y sommes allés en voiture.
3 emmener en voiture ◊ My mother drives me to school. Ma mère m'emmène à l'école en voiture.

♦to drive somebody home raccompagner quelqu'un ◊ He offered to drive me home. Il m'a proposé de me raccompagner.
♦to drive somebody mad rendre quelqu'un fou ◊ He drives her mad. Il la rend folle.

driver NOUN
1 le conducteur
la conductrice
◊ She's an excellent driver. C'est une excellente conductrice.
2 (of taxi, bus)
le chauffeur ◊ He's a bus driver. Il est chauffeur d'autobus.

driver's license NOUN US
le permis de conduire

driving instructor NOUN
le moniteur d'auto-école ◊ He's a driving instructor. Il est moniteur d'auto-école.

driving lesson NOUN
la leçon de conduite

driving licence NOUN
le permis de conduire

driving test NOUN
♦to take one's driving test passer son permis de conduire ◊ He's taking his driving test tomorrow. Il passe son permis de conduire demain.
♦She's just passed her driving test. Elle vient d'avoir son permis.

drizzle NOUN
la bruine

drop NOUN
see also **drop** VERB
la goutte ◊ a drop of water une goutte d'eau.

to **drop** VERB
see also **drop** NOUN
1 laisser tomber ◊ I dropped the glass and it broke. J'ai laissé tomber le verre et il s'est cassé. ◊ I'm going to drop chemistry. Je vais laisser tomber la chimie.
2 déposer ◊ Could you drop me at the station? Pouvez-vous me déposer à la gare?

drought NOUN
la sécheresse

drove VERB see **drive**

to **drown** VERB
se noyer ◊ A boy drowned here yesterday. Un jeune garçon s'est noyé ici hier.

drug NOUN
1 le médicament (medicine) ◊ They need food and drugs. Ils ont besoin de nourriture et de médicaments.

☞

2 la drogue (*illegal*) ◊ *hard drugs* les drogues dures ◊ *soft drugs* les drogues douces
- **to take drugs** se droguer
- **a drug addict** un drogué ◊ *She's a drug addict.* C'est une droguée.
- **a drug pusher** un dealer
- **a drug smuggler** un trafiquant de drogue
- **the drugs squad** la brigade antidrogue

drugstore NOUN US
le drugstore

drum NOUN
le tambour ◊ *an African drum* un tambour africain
- **a drum kit** une batterie
- **drums** la batterie SING ◊ *I play drums.* Je joue de la batterie.

drummer NOUN
(*in rock group*)
le batteur
la batteuse

drunk ADJECTIVE
see also **drunk** NOUN
ivre ◊ *He was drunk.* Il était ivre.

drunk NOUN
see also **drunk** ADJECTIVE
l' ivrogne MASC/FEM ◊ *The streets were full of drunks.* Les rues étaient pleines d'ivrognes.

dry ADJECTIVE
see also **dry** VERB
1 sec MASC
sèche FEM
◊ *The paint isn't dry yet.* La peinture n'est pas encore sèche.
2 (*weather*)
sans pluie ◊ *a long dry period* une longue période sans pluie

to **dry** VERB
see also **dry** ADJECTIVE
1 sécher ◊ *The washing will dry quickly in the sun.* Le linge va sécher vite au soleil. ◊ *some dried flowers* des fleurs séchées
- **to dry one's hair** se sécher les cheveux ◊ *I haven't dried my hair yet.* Je ne me suis pas encore séché les cheveux.
2 faire sécher (*clothes*) ◊ *There's nowhere to dry clothes here.* Il n'y a pas d'endroit où faire sécher les vêtements ici.
- **to dry the dishes** essuyer la vaisselle

dry-cleaner's NOUN
la teinturerie

dryer NOUN
le séchoir (*for clothes*)

- **a tumble dryer** un séchoir à linge
- **a hair dryer** un sèche-cheveux

DTP NOUN (= *desktop publishing*)
la PAO (= *publication assistée par ordinateur*)

dubbed ADJECTIVE
doublé ◊ *The film was dubbed into French.* Le film était doublé en français.

dubious ADJECTIVE
réticent ◊ *My parents were a bit dubious about it.* Mes parents étaient un peu réticents à ce sujet.

duck NOUN
le canard

due ADJECTIVE, ADVERB
- **to be due to do something** devoir faire quelque chose ◊ *He's due to arrive tomorrow.* Il doit arriver demain.
- **The plane's due in half an hour.** L'avion doit arriver dans une demi-heure.
- **When's the baby due?** Le bébé est prévu pour quand?
- **due to** à cause de ◊ *The trip was cancelled due to bad weather.* Le voyage a été annulé à cause du mauvais temps.

dug VERB see **dig**

dull ADJECTIVE
1 ennuyeux MASC
ennuyeuse FEM
◊ *He's nice, but a bit dull.* Il est sympathique, mais un peu ennuyeux.
2 (*weather, day*)
maussade

dumb ADJECTIVE
1 muet MASC
muette FEM
- **She's deaf and dumb.** Elle est sourde-muette.
2 (*stupid*)
bête ◊ *That was a really dumb thing I did!* C'était vraiment bête de ma part!

dummy NOUN
la tétine (*for baby*)

dump NOUN
see also **dump** VERB
- **It's a real dump!** C'est un endroit minable!
- **a rubbish dump** une décharge

to **dump** VERB
see also **dump** NOUN
1 déposer (*waste*) ◊ *"no dumping"* "défense de déposer des ordures"
2 plaquer (*informal*) ◊ *He's just dumped his girlfriend.* Il vient de plaquer sa copine.

dungarees PL NOUN
la salopette SING

dungeon NOUN
le cachot

duration NOUN
la durée

during PREPOSITION
pendant ◊ *during the day* pendant la journée

dusk NOUN
le crépuscule ◊ *at dusk* au crépuscule

dust NOUN
see also **dust** VERB
la poussière

to **dust** VERB
see also **dust** NOUN
épousseter ◊ *I dusted the shelves.* J'ai épousseté les étagères.
♦**I hate dusting!** Je déteste faire les poussières.

dustbin NOUN
la poubelle

dustman NOUN
l' éboueur MASC ◊ *He's a dustman.* Il est éboueur.

dusty ADJECTIVE
poussiéreux MASC
poussiéreuse FEM

Dutch ADJECTIVE
see also **Dutch** NOUN
hollandais ◊ *She's Dutch.* Elle est hollandaise.

Dutch NOUN
see also **Dutch** ADJECTIVE
le hollandais (*language*)
♦**the Dutch** les Hollandais

Dutchman NOUN
le Hollandais

Dutchwoman NOUN
la Hollandaise

duty NOUN
le devoir ◊ *It was his duty to tell the police.* C'était son devoir de prévenir la police.
♦**to be on duty (1)** (*policeman*) être de service
♦**to be on duty (2)** (*doctor, nurse*) être de garde

duty-free ADJECTIVE
hors taxes MASC, FEM, PL
♦**the duty-free shop** la boutique hors taxes

duvet NOUN
la couette

DVD NOUN
le DVD ◊ *I've got that film on DVD.* J'ai ce film en DVD.

dwarf NOUN
le nain
la naine

dying VERB *see* **die**

dynamic ADJECTIVE
dynamique

dyslexia NOUN
la dyslexie

E

each ADJECTIVE, PRONOUN

1 chaque ◇ *each day* chaque jour
◇ *Each house in our street has its
own garden.* Chaque maison dans
notre rue a son propre jardin.
2 chacun MASC
chacune FEM
◇ *The girls each have their own
bedroom.* Les filles ont chacune leur
chambre. ◇ *They have 10 points each.*
Ils ont dix points chacun. ◇ *The
plates cost £5 each.* Les assiettes coûtent
cinq livres chacune. ◇ *He gave each
of us £10.* Il nous a donné dix livres
à chacun.

*Use a reflexive verb to translate
each other.*

♦ **They hate each other.** Ils se détestent.
♦ **We wrote to each other.** Nous nous
sommes écrit.
♦ **They don't know each other.** Ils ne se
connaissent pas.

eager ADJECTIVE

♦ **to be eager to do something** être
impatient de faire quelque chose

ear NOUN
l' oreille FEM

earache NOUN

♦ **to have earache** avoir mal aux oreilles

earlier ADVERB

1 tout à l'heure ◇ *I saw him earlier.*
Je l'ai vu tout à l'heure.
2 plus tôt (*in the morning*) ◇ *I ought
to get up earlier.* Je devrais me lever
plus tôt.

early ADVERB, ADJECTIVE

1 tôt (*early in the day*) ◇ *I have to get
up early.* Je dois me lever tôt.
♦ **to have an early night** se coucher tôt
2 en avance (*ahead of time*) ◇ *I came
early to get a good seat.* Je suis venu
en avance pour avoir une bonne
place.

to **earn** VERB
gagner ◇ *She earns £5 an hour.* Elle
gagne cinq livres de l'heure.

earnings PL NOUN
le salaire SING

earring NOUN
la boucle d'oreille

earth NOUN
la terre

earthquake NOUN
le tremblement de terre

easily ADVERB

facilement

east ADJECTIVE, ADVERB

see also **east** NOUN

1 est MASC, FEM, PL ◇ *the east coast* la
côte est
♦ **an east wind** un vent d'est
♦ **east of** à l'est de ◇ *It's east of
London.* C'est à l'est de Londres.
2 vers l'est ◇ *We were travelling
east.* Nous allions vers l'est.

east NOUN

see also **east** ADJECTIVE

l' est MASC ◇ *in the east* dans l'est

eastbound ADJECTIVE

♦ **The car was eastbound on the M25.**
Le voiture se trouvait sur la M25 en
direction de l'est.
♦ **Eastbound traffic is moving very
slowly.** La circulation vers l'est
avance très lentement.

Easter NOUN
Pâques FEM ◇ *at Easter* à Pâques ◇ *We
went to my grandparents' for Easter.*
Nous sommes allés chez mes
grands-parents à Pâques.

Easter egg NOUN
l' œuf de Pâques MASC

eastern ADJECTIVE

♦ **the eastern part of the island** la partie
est de l'île
♦ **Eastern Europe** l'Europe de l'Est

easy ADJECTIVE
facile

easy chair NOUN
le fauteuil

easy-going ADJECTIVE
facile à vivre
(faciles à vivre PL)
◇ *She's very easy-going.* Elle est très
facile à vivre.

to **eat** VERB
manger
♦ **Would you like something to eat?**
Est-ce que tu veux manger quelque
chose?

EC NOUN (= *European Community*)
la CE (= Communauté européenne)

eccentric ADJECTIVE
excentrique

echo NOUN
l' écho MASC

eco-friendly ADJECTIVE
respectueux de l'environnement
MASC

respectueuse de l'environnement
FEM

ecological ADJECTIVE
écologique

ecology NOUN
l' écologie FEM

e-commerce NOUN
le commerce électronique

economic ADJECTIVE
rentable (*profitable*)

economical ADJECTIVE
1 économe (*person*)
2 économique (*method, car*)

economics NOUN
l' économie FEM
◆**He's studying economics.** Il étudie les sciences économiques.

to **economize** VERB
faire des économies ◇ *to economize on something* faire des économies sur quelque chose

economy NOUN
l' économie FEM

ecstasy NOUN
l' ecstasy FEM (*drug*)
◆ **to be in ecstasy** s'extasier

ecu NOUN (= *European Currency Unit*)
l' écu MASC

eczema NOUN
l' eczéma MASC

edge NOUN
le bord

edgy ADJECTIVE
tendu

Edinburgh NOUN
Édimbourg

editor NOUN
(*of newspaper*)
le rédacteur en chef
la rédactrice en chef

educated ADJECTIVE
cultivé

education NOUN
1 l' éducation FEM ◇ *There should be more investment in education.* On devrait investir plus dans l'éducation.
2 l' enseignement MASC (*teaching*)
◇ *She works in education.* Elle travaille dans l'enseignement.

educational ADJECTIVE
(*experience, toy*)
éducatif MASC
éducative FEM
◇ *It was very educational.* C'était très éducatif.

effect NOUN
l' effet MASC ◇ *special effects* les effets spéciaux

effective ADJECTIVE
efficace

effectively ADVERB
efficacement
　　*Be careful not to translate **effectively** by **effectivement**.*

efficient ADJECTIVE
efficace

effort NOUN
l' effort MASC

e.g. ABBREVIATION
p. ex. (= *par exemple*)

egg NOUN
l' œuf MASC ◇ *a hard-boiled egg* un œuf dur ◇ *a soft-boiled egg* un œuf à la coque ◇ *a fried egg* un œuf sur le plat
◆ **scrambled eggs** les œufs brouillés

egg cup NOUN
le coquetier

eggplant NOUN US
l' aubergine FEM

Egypt NOUN
l' Égypte FEM
◆ **in Egypt** en Égypte

Eiffel Tower NOUN
la tour Eiffel

eight NUMBER
huit ◇ *She's eight.* Elle a huit ans.

eighteen NUMBER
dix-huit ◇ *She's eighteen.* Elle a dix-huit ans.

eighteenth ADJECTIVE
dix-huitième ◇ *her eighteenth birthday* son dix-huitième anniversaire ◇ *the eighteenth floor* le dix-huitième étage
◆ **the eighteenth of August** le dix-huit août

eighth ADJECTIVE
huitième ◇ *the eighth floor* le huitième étage
◆ **the eighth of August** le huit août

eighty NUMBER
quatre-vingts

Eire NOUN
la République d'Irlande
◆ **in Eire** en République d'Irlande

either ADVERB, CONJUNCTION, PRONOUN
non plus ◇ *I don't like milk, and I don't like eggs either.* Je n'aime pas le lait, et je n'aime pas les œufs non plus. ◇ *I've never been to Spain. – I haven't either.* Je ne suis jamais allé en Espagne. – Moi non plus.
◆ **either ... or ...** soit ... soit ... ◇ *You can have either ice cream or yoghurt.* Tu peux prendre soit une glace soit un yaourt.

☞

♦ **either of them** l'un ou l'autre ◇ *Take either of them.* Prends l'un ou l'autre.

♦ **I don't like either of them.** Je n'aime ni l'un ni l'autre.

elastic NOUN
l' élastique MASC

elastic band NOUN
l' élastique MASC

elbow NOUN
le coude

elder ADJECTIVE
aîné ◇ *my elder sister* ma sœur aînée

elderly ADJECTIVE
âgé

♦ **the elderly** les personnes âgées FEM

eldest ADJECTIVE
aîné ◇ *my eldest sister* ma sœur aînée ◇ *He's the eldest.* C'est l'aîné.

to **elect** VERB
élire

election NOUN
l' élection FEM

electric ADJECTIVE
électrique ◇ *an electric fire* un radiateur électrique ◇ *an electric guitar* une guitare électrique

♦ **an electric blanket** une couverture chauffante

electrical ADJECTIVE
électrique

♦ **an electrical engineer** un ingénieur électricien

electrician NOUN
l' électricien MASC ◇ *He's an electrician.* Il est électricien.

electricity NOUN
l' électricité FEM

electronic ADJECTIVE
électronique

electronics NOUN
l' électronique FEM ◇ *My hobby is electronics.* Ma passion, c'est l'électronique.

elegant ADJECTIVE
élégant

elementary school NOUN US
l' école primaire FEM

elephant NOUN
l' éléphant MASC

elevator NOUN US
l' ascenseur MASC

eleven NUMBER
onze ◇ *She's eleven.* Elle a onze ans.

eleventh ADJECTIVE
onzième ◇ *the eleventh floor* le onzième étage ◇ *the eleventh of August* le onze août

else ADVERB
d'autre ◇ *somebody else* quelqu'un d'autre ◇ *nobody else* personne d'autre ◇ *nothing else* rien d'autre

♦ **something else** autre chose

♦ **anything else** autre chose ◇ *Would you like anything else?* Désirez-vous autre chose?

♦ **I don't want anything else.** Je ne veux rien d'autre.

♦ **somewhere else** ailleurs

♦ **anywhere else** autre part

email NOUN
see also **email** VERB
le courrier électronique

♦ **email address** l'adresse e-mail FEM ◇ *My email address is: ...* Mon adresse e-mail, c'est: ...

to **email** VERB
see also **email** NOUN

♦ **to email somebody** envoyer un e-mail à quelqu'un

embankment NOUN
le talus

embarrassed ADJECTIVE
gêné ◇ *I was really embarrassed.* J'étais vraiment gêné.

embarrassing ADJECTIVE
gênant ◇ *It was so embarrassing.* C'était tellement gênant.

embassy NOUN
l' ambassade FEM ◇ *the British Embassy* l'ambassade de Grande-Bretagne ◇ *the French Embassy* l'ambassade de France

to **embroider** VERB
broder

embroidery NOUN
la broderie ◇ *I do embroidery.* Je fais de la broderie.

emergency NOUN
l' urgence FEM ◇ *This is an emergency!* C'est une urgence!

♦ **in an emergency** en cas d'urgence

♦ **an emergency exit** une sortie de secours

♦ **an emergency landing** un atterrissage forcé

♦ **the emergency services** les services d'urgence MASC

to **emigrate** VERB
émigrer

emotion NOUN
l' émotion FEM

emotional ADJECTIVE
(*person*)
émotif MASC
émotive FEM

emperor NOUN

l' empereur MASC

to **emphasize** VERB
- ♦to emphasize something insister sur quelque chose
- ♦to emphasize that ... souligner que ...

empire NOUN
l' empire MASC

to **employ** VERB
employer ◊ *The factory employs 600 people.* L'usine emploie six cents personnes.

employee NOUN
l' employé MASC
l' employée FEM

employer NOUN
l' employeur MASC

employment NOUN
l' emploi MASC

empty ADJECTIVE
see also **empty** VERB
vide

to **empty** VERB
see also **empty** ADJECTIVE
vider
- ♦to empty something out vider quelque chose

to **encourage** VERB
encourager
- ♦to encourage somebody to do something encourager quelqu'un à faire quelque chose

encouragement NOUN
l' encouragement MASC

encyclopedia NOUN
l' encyclopédie FEM

end NOUN
see also **end** VERB
1 la fin ◊ *the end of the film* la fin du film ◊ *the end of the holidays* la fin des vacances
- ♦in the end en fin de compte ◊ *In the end I decided to stay at home.* En fin de compte j'ai décidé de rester à la maison.
- ♦It turned out all right in the end. Ça s'est bien terminé.
2 le bout ◊ *at the end of the street* au bout de la rue ◊ *at the other end of the table* à l'autre bout de la table
- ♦for hours on end des heures entières

to **end** VERB
see also **end** NOUN
finir ◊ *What time does the film end?* À quelle heure est-ce que le film finit?
- ♦to end up doing something finir par faire quelque chose ◊ *I ended up walking home.* J'ai fini par rentrer chez moi à pied.

ending NOUN
la fin ◊ *It was an exciting film, especially the ending.* C'était un film passionnant, surtout la fin.

endless ADJECTIVE
interminable ◊ *The journey seemed endless.* Le voyage a paru interminable.

enemy NOUN
l' ennemi MASC
l' ennemie FEM

energetic ADJECTIVE
énergique (*person*)

energy NOUN
l' énergie FEM

engaged ADJECTIVE
1 occupé (*busy, in use*) ◊ *I phoned, but it was engaged.* J'ai téléphoné, mais c'était occupé.
2 fiancé (*to be married*) ◊ *She's engaged to Brian.* Elle est fiancée à Brian.
- ♦to get engaged se fiancer

engaged tone NOUN
la tonalité "occupé"

engagement NOUN
les fiançailles FEM PL ◊ *an engagement ring* une bague de fiançailles

engine NOUN
le moteur
> Be careful not to translate **engine** by the French word **engin**.

engineer NOUN
l' ingénieur MASC ◊ *He's an engineer.* Il est ingénieur.

engineering NOUN
l' ingénierie FEM

England NOUN
l' Angleterre FEM
- ♦in England en Angleterre
- ♦to England en Angleterre
- ♦I'm from England. Je suis anglais.

English ADJECTIVE
see also **English** NOUN
anglais ◊ *I'm English.* Je suis anglais.
- ♦English people les Anglais

English NOUN
see also **English** ADJECTIVE
l' anglais MASC (*language*) ◊ *Do you speak English?* Est-ce que vous parlez anglais?
- ♦the English les Anglais

Englishman NOUN
l' Anglais MASC

Englishwoman NOUN
l' Anglaise FEM

to **enjoy** VERB

☞

aimer ◊ Did you enjoy the film? Est-ce que vous avez aimé le film?
- **to enjoy oneself** s'amuser ◊ I really enjoyed myself. Je me suis vraiment bien amusé. ◊ Did you enjoy yourselves at the party? Est-ce vous vous êtes bien amusés à la fête?

enjoyable ADJECTIVE
agréable

enlargement NOUN
l' agrandissement MASC (of photo)

enormous ADJECTIVE
énorme

enough PRONOUN, ADJECTIVE
assez de ◊ enough time assez de temps ◊ I didn't have enough money. Je n'avais pas assez d'argent. ◊ Have you got enough? Tu en as assez? ◊ I've had enough! J'en ai assez!
- **big enough** suffisamment grand
- **warm enough** suffisamment chaud
- **That's enough.** Ça suffit.

to **enquire** VERB
- **to enquire about something** se renseigner sur quelque chose ◊ I am going to enquire about train times. Je vais me renseigner sur les horaires de trains.

enquiry NOUN
- **to make enquiries (about something)** se renseigner (sur quelque chose)
- **"enquiries"** "renseignements"

to **enter** VERB
entrer
- **to enter a room** entrer dans une pièce
- **to enter a competition** s'inscrire à une compétition

to **entertain** VERB
recevoir (guests)

entertainer NOUN
l' artiste de variétés MASC/FEM

entertaining ADJECTIVE
amusant

enthusiasm NOUN
l' enthousiasme MASC

enthusiast NOUN
- **a railway enthusiast** un passionné des trains
- **She's a DIY enthusiast.** C'est une passionnée de bricolage.

enthusiastic ADJECTIVE
enthousiaste

entire ADJECTIVE
entier MASC
entière FEM
◊ the entire world le monde entier

entirely ADVERB
entièrement

entrance NOUN
l' entrée FEM
- **an entrance exam** un concours d'entrée
- **entrance fee** le prix d'entrée

entry NOUN
l' entrée FEM
- **"no entry" (1)** (on door) "défense d'entrer"
- **"no entry" (2)** (on road sign) "sens interdit"
- **an entry form** une feuille d'inscription

entry phone NOUN
l' interphone MASC

envelope NOUN
l' enveloppe FEM

envious ADJECTIVE
envieux MASC
envieuse FEM

environment NOUN
l' environnement MASC

environmental ADJECTIVE
écologique

environment-friendly ADJECTIVE
écologique

envy NOUN
see also **envy** VERB
l' envie FEM

to **envy** VERB
see also **envy** NOUN
envier ◊ I don't envy you! Je ne t'envie pas!

epileptic NOUN
l' épileptique MASC/FEM

episode NOUN
l' épisode MASC (of TV programme, story)

equal ADJECTIVE
see also **equal** VERB
égal
(égaux MASC PL)

to **equal** VERB
see also **equal** ADJECTIVE
égaler

equality NOUN
l' égalité FEM

to **equalize** VERB
égaliser (in sport)

equator NOUN
l' équateur MASC

equipment NOUN
l' équipement MASC ◊ fishing equipment l'équipement de pêche ◊ skiing equipment l'équipement de ski

equipped ADJECTIVE
- **equipped with** équipé de
- **to be well equipped** être bien équipé

equivalent NOUN
l' équivalent MASC
◆**equivalent to** équivalent à

error NOUN
l' erreur FEM

escalator NOUN
l' escalier roulant MASC

escape NOUN
> see also **escape** VERB

l' évasion FEM (*from prison*)

to **escape** VERB
> see also **escape** NOUN

s'échapper ◇ *A lion has escaped.* Un lion s'est échappé.
◆**to escape from prison** s'évader de prison

escort NOUN
l' escorte FEM ◇ *a police escort* une escorte de police

Eskimo NOUN
l' Esquimau MASC
l' Esquimaude FEM
◆**the Eskimos** les Esquimaux

especially ADVERB
surtout ◇ *It's very hot there, especially in the summer.* Il fait très chaud là-bas, surtout en été.

essay NOUN
la dissertation ◇ *a history essay* une dissertation d'histoire

essential ADJECTIVE
essentiel MASC
essentielle FEM
◇ *It's essential to bring warm clothes.* Il est essentiel d'apporter des vêtements chauds.

estate NOUN
la cité (*housing estate*) ◇ *I live on an estate.* J'habite dans une cité.

estate agent NOUN
l' agent immobilier MASC

estate car NOUN
le break

to **estimate** VERB
estimer ◇ *They estimated it would take three weeks.* Ils ont estimé que cela prendrait trois semaines.

etc ABBREVIATION (= *et cetera*)
etc.

Ethiopia NOUN
l' Éthiopie FEM
◆**in Ethiopia** en Éthiopie

ethnic ADJECTIVE
1 ethnique (*racial*) ◇ *an ethnic minority* une minorité ethnique
2 folklorique (*clothes, music*)

EU NOUN (= *European Union*)
l' Union européenne FEM

euro NOUN
l' euro MASC ◇ *50 euros* 50 euros

Eurocheque NOUN
l' eurochèque MASC

Europe NOUN
l' Europe FEM
◆**in Europe** en Europe
◆**to Europe** en Europe

European ADJECTIVE
> see also **European** NOUN

européen MASC
européenne FEM

European NOUN
> see also **European** ADJECTIVE

(*person*)
l' Européen MASC
l' Européenne FEM

to **evacuate** VERB
évacuer

eve NOUN
◆**Christmas Eve** la veille de Noël
◆**New Year's Eve** la Saint-Sylvestre

even ADVERB
> see also **even** ADJECTIVE

même ◇ *I like all animals, even snakes.* J'aime tous les animaux, même les serpents.
◆**even if** même si ◇ *I'd never do that, even if you asked me.* Je ne ferais jamais ça, même si tu me le demandais.
◆**not even** même pas ◇ *He never stops working, not even at the weekend.* Il n'arrête jamais de travailler, même pas le week-end.
◆**even though** bien que
> **bien que** has to be followed by a verb in the subjunctive.

◇ *He's never got any money, even though his parents are quite rich.* Il n'a jamais d'argent, bien que ses parents soient assez riches.
◆**even more** encore plus ◇ *I liked Boulogne even more than Paris.* J'ai encore plus aimé Boulogne que Paris.

even ADJECTIVE
> see also **even** ADVERB

régulier MASC
régulière FEM
◇ *an even layer of snow* une couche régulière de neige
◆**an even number** un nombre pair
◆**to get even with somebody** prendre sa revanche sur quelqu'un ◇ *He wanted to get even with her.* Il voulait prendre sa revanche sur elle.

evening NOUN
le soir ◇ *in the evening* le soir
◇ *yesterday evening* hier soir
◇ *tomorrow evening* demain soir

☞

♦ **all evening** toute la soirée
♦ **Good evening!** Bonsoir!

evening class NOUN
le cours du soir
(les cours du soir PL)

event NOUN
l' événement MASC
♦ **a sporting event** une épreuve sportive

eventful ADJECTIVE
mouvementé

eventual ADJECTIVE
final
> *Be careful not to translate **eventual** by **éventuel**.*

eventually ADVERB
finalement
> *Be careful not to translate **eventually** by **éventuellement**.*

ever ADVERB
♦ **Have you ever been to Germany?** Est-ce que tu es déjà allé en Allemagne?
♦ **Have you ever seen her?** Vous l'avez déjà vue?
♦ **I haven't ever done that.** Je ne l'ai jamais fait.
♦ **the best I've ever seen** le meilleur que j'aie jamais vu
♦ **for the first time ever** pour la première fois
♦ **ever since** depuis que ◊ *ever since I met him* depuis que je l'ai rencontré
♦ **ever since then** depuis ce moment-là

every ADJECTIVE
chaque ◊ *every pupil* chaque élève
♦ **every time** chaque fois ◊ *Every time I see him he's depressed.* Chaque fois que je le vois il est déprimé.
♦ **every day** tous les jours
♦ **every week** toutes les semaines
♦ **every now and then** de temps en temps

everybody PRONOUN
tout le monde ◊ *Everybody had a good time.* Tout le monde s'est bien amusé. ◊ *Everybody makes mistakes.* Tout le monde peut se tromper.

everyone PRONOUN
tout le monde ◊ *Everyone opened their presents.* Tout le monde a ouvert ses cadeaux. ◊ *Everyone should have a hobby.* Tout le monde devrait avoir un passe-temps.

everything PRONOUN
tout ◊ *You've thought of everything!* Tu as pensé à tout!
♦ **Have you remembered everything?** Est-ce que tu n'as rien oublié?
♦ **Money isn't everything.** L'argent ne fait pas le bonheur.

everywhere ADVERB
partout ◊ *I looked everywhere, but I couldn't find it.* J'ai regardé partout, mais je n'ai pas pu le trouver.
◊ *There were policemen everywhere.* Il y avait des policiers partout.

evil ADJECTIVE
mauvais

ex- PREFIX
ex- ◊ *his ex-wife* son ex-femme

exact ADJECTIVE
exact

exactly ADVERB
exactement ◊ *exactly the same* exactement le même ◊ *not exactly* pas exactement
♦ **It's exactly 10 o'clock.** Il est dix heures précises.

to **exaggerate** VERB
exagérer

exaggeration NOUN
l' exagération FEM

exam NOUN
l' examen MASC ◊ *a French exam* un examen de français ◊ *the exam results* les résultats des examens MASC

examination NOUN
l' examen MASC

to **examine** VERB
examiner ◊ *He examined her passport.* Il a examiné son passeport.
◊ *The doctor examined him.* Le docteur l'a examiné.

examiner NOUN
l' examinateur MASC
l' examinatrice FEM

example NOUN
l' exemple MASC
♦ **for example** par exemple

excellent ADJECTIVE
excellent ◊ *Her results were excellent.* Elle a eu d'excellents résultats.
♦ **It was excellent fun.** C'était vraiment super.

except PREPOSITION
sauf ◊ *everyone except me* tout le monde sauf moi
♦ **except for** sauf
♦ **except that** sauf que ◊ *The weather was great, except that it was a bit cold.* Il a fait un temps superbe, sauf qu'il a fait un peu froid.

exception NOUN
l' exception FEM
♦ **to make an exception** faire une exception

exceptional ADJECTIVE
exceptionnel MASC

exceptionnelle FEM

excess baggage NOUN
l' excédent de bagages MASC

to **exchange** VERB
échanger ◇ *I exchanged the book for a video.* J'ai échangé le livre contre une vidéo.

exchange rate NOUN
le taux de change

excited ADJECTIVE
excité

exciting ADJECTIVE
passionnant

exclamation mark NOUN
le point d'exclamation

excuse NOUN
see also **excuse** VERB
l' excuse FEM

to **excuse** VERB
see also **excuse** NOUN
♦**Excuse me!** Pardon!

ex-directory ADJECTIVE
♦**to be ex-directory** être sur liste rouge
♦**to go ex-directory** se mettre sur liste rouge

to **execute** VERB
exécuter

execution NOUN
l' exécution FEM

executive NOUN
le cadre (*in business*) ◇ *He's an executive.* Il est cadre.

exercise NOUN
l' exercice MASC
♦**an exercise bike** un vélo d'appartement
♦**an exercise book** un cahier

exhausted ADJECTIVE
épuisé

exhaust fumes PL NOUN
les gaz d'échappement MASC PL

exhaust pipe NOUN
le tuyau d'échappement

exhibition NOUN
l' exposition FEM

ex-husband NOUN
l' ex-mari MASC

to **exist** VERB
exister

exit NOUN
la sortie

exotic ADJECTIVE
exotique

to **expect** VERB
[1] attendre ◇ *I'm expecting him for dinner.* Je l'attends pour dîner.

◇ *She's expecting a baby.* Elle attend un enfant.
[2] s'attendre à ◇ *I was expecting the worst.* Je m'attendais au pire.
[3] supposer ◇ *I expect it's a mistake.* Je suppose qu'il s'agit d'une erreur.

expedition NOUN
l' expédition FEM

to **expel** VERB
♦**to get expelled** (*from school*) se faire renvoyer

expenses PL NOUN
les frais MASC PL

expensive ADJECTIVE
cher MASC
chère FEM

experience NOUN
l' expérience FEM

experienced ADJECTIVE
expérimenté

experiment NOUN
l' expérience FEM

expert NOUN
le/la spécialiste ◇ *He's a computer expert.* C'est un spécialiste en informatique.
♦**He's an expert cook.** Il cuisine très bien.

to **expire** VERB
expirer

to **explain** VERB
expliquer

explanation NOUN
l' explication FEM

to **explode** VERB
exploser

to **exploit** VERB
exploiter

exploitation NOUN
l' exploitation FEM

to **explore** VERB
explorer (*place*)

explorer NOUN
l' explorateur MASC
l' exploratrice FEM

explosion NOUN
l' explosion FEM

explosive ADJECTIVE
see also **explosive** NOUN
explosif MASC
explosive FEM

explosive NOUN
see also **explosive** ADJECTIVE
l' explosif MASC

to **express** VERB
exprimer
♦**to express oneself** s'exprimer ◇ *It's not easy to express oneself in a*

☞

foreign language. Ce n'est pas facile de s'exprimer dans une langue étrangère.

expression NOUN
l' expression FEM ◊ *It's an English expression.* C'est une expression anglaise.

expressway NOUN [US]
l' autoroute urbaine FEM

extension NOUN
1 l' annexe FEM (*of building*)
2 le poste (*telephone*)
In France phone numbers are broken into groups of two digits where possible.
♦**Extension 3137, please.** Poste trente et un trente-sept, s'il vous plaît.

extensive ADJECTIVE
1 vaste (*knowledge, range*) ◊ *The castle is set in extensive grounds.* Le château est situé au cœur d'un vaste domaine.
2 considérable (*damage, alterations*) ◊ *The earthquake caused extensive damage.* Le tremblement de terre a causé des dommages considérables.

extensively ADVERB
♦**He has travelled extensively in Europe.** Il a beaucoup voyagé en Europe.
♦**The building was extensively renovated last year.** Le bâtiment a été entièrement rénové l'année dernière.

extent NOUN
♦**to some extent** dans une certaine mesure

exterior ADJECTIVE
extérieur

extinct ADJECTIVE
♦**to become extinct** disparaître
♦**to be extinct** avoir disparu ◊ *The species is almost extinct.* Cette espèce a presque disparu.

extinguisher NOUN
l' extincteur MASC (*fire extinguisher*)

extortionate ADJECTIVE
exorbitant

extra ADJECTIVE, ADVERB
supplémentaire ◊ *an extra blanket* une couverture supplémentaire
♦**to pay extra** payer un supplément
♦**Breakfast is extra.** Il y a un supplément pour le petit déjeuner.
♦**It costs extra.** Il y a un supplément.

extraordinary ADJECTIVE
extraordinaire

extravagant ADJECTIVE
(*person*)
dépensier MASC
dépensière FEM

extreme ADJECTIVE
extrême

extremely ADVERB
extrêmement

extremist NOUN
l' extrémiste MASC/FEM

eye NOUN
l' œil MASC
(les yeux PL)
◊ *I've got green eyes.* J'ai les yeux verts.
♦**to keep an eye on something** surveiller quelque chose

eyebrow NOUN
le sourcil

eyelash NOUN
le cil

eyelid NOUN
la paupière

eyeliner NOUN
l' eye-liner MASC

eye shadow NOUN
l' ombre à paupières FEM

eyesight NOUN
la vue

F

fabric NOUN
le <u>tissu</u>

fabulous ADJECTIVE
<u>formidable</u> ◊ *The show was fabulous.* Le spectacle était formidable.

face NOUN
see also **face** VERB
1. le <u>visage</u> (*of person*)
2. le <u>cadran</u> (*of clock*)
3. la <u>paroi</u> (*of cliff*)
♦ **on the face of it** à première vue
♦ **in the face of these difficulties** face à ces difficultés
♦ **face to face** face à face
♦ **a face cloth** un gant de toilette

to **face** VERB
see also **face** NOUN
<u>faire face à</u> (*place, problem*)
♦ **to face up to something** faire face à quelque chose ◊ *You must face up to your responsibilities.* Vous devez faire face à vos responsabilités.

face cloth NOUN
le <u>gant de toilette</u>

> ⓘ *The French traditionally wash with a towelling glove rather than a flannel.*

facilities PL NOUN
l' <u>équipement</u> MASC SING ◊ *This school has excellent facilities.* Cette école dispose d'un excellent équipement.
♦ **toilet facilities** les toilettes FEM
♦ **cooking facilities** la cuisine équipée SING

fact NOUN
le <u>fait</u>
♦ **in fact** en fait

factory NOUN
l' <u>usine</u> FEM

to **fade** VERB
1. <u>passer</u> (*colour*) ◊ *The colour has faded in the sun.* La couleur a passé au soleil.
♦ **My jeans have faded.** Mon jean est délavé.
2. <u>baisser</u> ◊ *The light was fading fast.* La lumière baissait rapidement.
3. <u>diminuer</u> ◊ *The noise gradually faded.* Le bruit a diminué peu à peu.

fag NOUN
la <u>clope</u> (*cigarette*)

to **fail** VERB

see also **fail** NOUN
1. <u>rater</u> ◊ *I failed the history exam.* J'ai raté l'examen d'histoire.
2. <u>échouer</u> ◊ *In our class, no one failed.* Dans notre classe, personne n'a échoué.
3. <u>lâcher</u> ◊ *My brakes failed.* Mes freins ont lâché.
♦ **to fail to do something** ne pas faire quelque chose ◊ *She failed to return her library books.* Elle n'a pas rendu ses livres à la bibliothèque.

fail NOUN
see also **fail** VERB
♦ **without fail** sans faute

failure NOUN
1. l' <u>échec</u> MASC ◊ *feelings of failure* un sentiment d'échec SING
2. le <u>raté</u>
la <u>ratée</u>
◊ *He's a failure.* C'est un raté.
3. la <u>défaillance</u> ◊ *a mechanical failure* une défaillance mécanique

faint ADJECTIVE
see also **faint** VERB
<u>faible</u> ◊ *His voice was very faint.* Sa voix était très faible.
♦ **to feel faint** se trouver mal

to **faint** VERB
see also **faint** ADJECTIVE
<u>s'évanouir</u> ◊ *All of a sudden she fainted.* Tout à coup elle s'est évanouie.

fair ADJECTIVE
see also **fair** NOUN
1. <u>juste</u> ◊ *That's not fair.* Ce n'est pas juste.
2. (*hair*)
<u>blond</u> ◊ *He's got fair hair.* Il a les cheveux blonds.
3. (*skin*)
<u>clair</u> ◊ *people with fair skin* les gens qui ont la peau claire
4. (*weather*)
<u>beau</u> MASC
<u>belle</u> FEM
◊ *The weather was fair.* Il faisait beau.
5. (*good enough*)
<u>assez bon</u> MASC
<u>assez bonne</u> FEM
◊ *I have a fair chance of winning.* J'ai d'assez bonnes chances de gagner.
6. (*sizeable*)
<u>considérable</u> ◊ *That's a fair distance.* Ça représente une distance considérable.

fair NOUN

> see also **fair** ADJECTIVE

la foire ◊ *They went to the fair.* Ils sont allés à la foire.

♦**a trade fair** une foire commerciale

fairground NOUN
le champ de foire

fair-haired ADJECTIVE
♦**My mother is fair-haired.** Ma mère a les cheveux blonds.

fairly ADVERB
1 équitablement ◊ *The cake was divided fairly.* Le gâteau a été partagé équitablement.
2 assez (*quite*) ◊ *That's fairly good.* C'est assez bien.

fairness NOUN
la justice

fairy NOUN
la fée

fairy tale NOUN
le conte de fées
(les contes de fées PL)

faith NOUN
1 la foi ◊ *the Catholic faith* la foi catholique
2 la confiance ◊ *People have lost faith in the government.* Les gens ont perdu confiance dans le gouvernement.

faithful ADJECTIVE
fidèle

faithfully ADVERB
♦**Yours faithfully ...** (*in letter*) Veuillez agréer mes salutations distinguées ...

fake NOUN

> see also **fake** ADJECTIVE

le faux ◊ *The painting was a fake.* Le tableau était un faux.

fake ADJECTIVE

> see also **fake** NOUN

faux MASC
fausse FEM
◊ *She wore fake fur.* Elle portait une fausse fourrure.

fall NOUN

> see also **fall** VERB

1 la chute ◊ *a fall of snow* une chute de neige ◊ *She had a nasty fall.* Elle a fait une mauvaise chute.
♦**the Niagara Falls** les chutes du Niagara
2 l' automne MASC (*autumn*) US

to **fall** VERB

> see also **fall** NOUN

1 tomber ◊ *He tripped and fell.* Il a trébuché et il est tombé.
2 baisser ◊ *Prices are falling.* Les prix baissent.

♦**to fall down (1)** (*person*) tomber ◊ *She's fallen down.* Elle est tombée.
♦**to fall down (2)** (*building*) s'écrouler ◊ *The house is slowly falling down.* La maison est en train de s'écrouler.
♦**to fall for (1)** se laisser prendre à ◊ *They fell for it.* Ils s'y sont laissé prendre.
♦**to fall for (2)** tomber amoureux de ◊ *She's falling for him.* Elle est en train de tomber amoureuse de lui.
♦**to fall off** tomber de ◊ *The book fell off the shelf.* Le livre est tombé de l'étagère.
♦**to fall out with somebody** se fâcher avec quelqu'un ◊ *Sarah's fallen out with her boyfriend.* Sarah s'est fâchée avec son copain.
♦**to fall through** tomber à l'eau ◊ *Our plans have fallen through.* Nos projets sont tombés à l'eau.

fallen VERB *see* **fall**

false ADJECTIVE
faux MASC
fausse FEM
♦**a false alarm** une fausse alerte
♦**false teeth** les fausses dents FEM

fame NOUN
la renommée

familiar ADJECTIVE
familier MASC
familière FEM
◊ *a familiar face* un visage familier
♦**to be familiar with something** bien connaître quelque chose ◊ *I'm familiar with his work.* Je connais bien ses œuvres.

family NOUN
la famille
♦**the Cooke family** la famille Cooke

famine NOUN
la famine

famous ADJECTIVE
célèbre

fan NOUN
1 l' éventail MASC (*hand-held*)
2 le ventilateur (*electric*)
3 le/la fan (*of person, band*) ◊ *I'm a fan of Take That.* Je suis une fan de Take That.
4 le/la supporter (*of sport*) ◊ *football fans* les supporters de football

fanatic NOUN
le/la fanatique

to **fancy** VERB
♦**to fancy something** avoir envie de quelque chose ◊ *I fancy an ice cream.* J'ai envie d'une glace.
♦**to fancy doing something** avoir envie de faire quelque chose

♦He fancies her. Elle lui plaît.

fancy dress NOUN
le <u>déguisement</u> ◊ *He was wearing fancy dress.* Il portait un déguisement.
♦a fancy-dress ball un bal costumé

fantastic ADJECTIVE
<u>fantastique</u>

far ADJECTIVE, ADVERB
<u>loin</u> ◊ *Is it far?* Est-ce que c'est loin?
♦far from loin de ◊ *It's not far from London.* Ce n'est pas loin de Londres. ◊ *It's far from easy.* C'est loin d'être facile.
♦How far is it? C'est à quelle distance?
♦How far is it to Geneva? Combien y a-t-il jusqu'à Genève?
♦How far have you got? (*with a task*) Où en êtes-vous?
♦at the far end à l'autre bout ◊ *at the far end of the room* à l'autre bout de la pièce
♦far better beaucoup mieux
♦as far as I know pour autant que je sache

fare NOUN
① le <u>prix du billet</u> (*on trains, buses*)
② le <u>prix de la course</u> (*in taxi*)
♦half fare le demi-tarif
♦full fare le plein tarif

Far East NOUN
l' <u>Extrême-Orient</u> MASC
♦in the Far East en Extrême-Orient

farm NOUN
la <u>ferme</u>

farmer NOUN
l' <u>agriculteur</u> MASC
l' <u>agricultrice</u> FEM
◊ *He's a farmer.* Il est agriculteur.

farmhouse NOUN
la <u>ferme</u>

farming NOUN
l' <u>agriculture</u> FEM
♦dairy farming l'industrie laitière

fascinating ADJECTIVE
<u>fascinant</u>

fashion NOUN
la <u>mode</u>
♦in fashion à la mode

fashionable ADJECTIVE
<u>à la mode</u> ◊ *Jane wears very fashionable clothes.* Jane porte des vêtements très à la mode. ◊ *a fashionable restaurant* un restaurant à la mode

fast ADJECTIVE, ADVERB
① <u>vite</u> ◊ *He can run fast.* Il sait courir vite.
② <u>rapide</u> ◊ *a fast car* une voiture rapide
♦That clock's fast. Cette pendule avance.
♦He's fast asleep. Il est profondément endormi.

fat ADJECTIVE
┌─────────────────────┐
│ *see also* **fat** NOUN │
└─────────────────────┘
<u>gros</u> MASC
<u>grosse</u> FEM

fat NOUN
┌──────────────────────────┐
│ *see also* **fat** ADJECTIVE │
└──────────────────────────┘
① le <u>gras</u> (*on meat, in food*) ◊ *It's very high in fat.* C'est très gras.
② la <u>matière grasse</u> (*for cooking*)

fatal ADJECTIVE
① (*causing death*)
<u>mortel</u> MASC
<u>mortelle</u> FEM
◊ *a fatal accident* un accident mortel
② (*disastrous*)
<u>fatal</u> ◊ *He made a fatal mistake.* Il a fait une erreur fatale.

father NOUN
le <u>père</u> ◊ *my father* mon père

father-in-law NOUN
le <u>beau-père</u>
(les beaux-pères PL)

faucet NOUN US
le <u>robinet</u>

fault NOUN
① la <u>faute</u> (*mistake*) ◊ *It's my fault.* C'est de ma faute.
② le <u>défaut</u> (*defect*) ◊ *There's a fault in this material.* Ce tissu a un défaut.
♦a mechanical fault une défaillance mécanique

faulty ADJECTIVE
<u>défectueux</u> MASC
<u>défectueuse</u> FEM
◊ *This machine is faulty.* Cette machine est défectueuse.

favour NOUN (US **favor**)
le <u>service</u>
♦to do somebody a favour rendre service à quelqu'un ◊ *Could you do me a favour?* Tu peux me rendre service?
♦to be in favour of something être pour quelque chose ◊ *I'm in favour of nuclear disarmament.* Je suis pour le désarmament nucléaire.

favourite ADJECTIVE (US **favorite**)
┌────────────────────────────┐
│ *see also* **favourite** NOUN │
└────────────────────────────┘
<u>favori</u> MASC
<u>favorite</u> FEM
◊ *Blue's my favourite colour.* Le bleu est ma couleur favorite.

favourite NOUN (US **favorite**)

F

see also **favourite** ADJECTIVE
le favori
la favorite ◊ *Liverpool are favourites to win the Cup.* L'équipe de Liverpool est favorite pour la coupe.

fax NOUN
see also **fax** VERB
le fax
◆**to send somebody a fax** envoyer un fax à quelqu'un

to **fax** VERB
see also **fax** NOUN
◆**to fax somebody** envoyer un fax à quelqu'un

fear NOUN
see also **fear** VERB
la peur

to **fear** VERB
see also **fear** NOUN
craindre ◊ *You have nothing to fear.* Vous n'avez rien à craindre.

feather NOUN
la plume

feature NOUN
la caractéristique (*of person, object*) ◊ *an important feature* une caractéristique essentielle

February NOUN
février MASC
◆**in February** en février

fed VERB *see* **feed**

fed up ADJECTIVE
◆**to be fed up with something** en avoir marre de quelque chose ◊ *I'm fed up of waiting for him.* J'en ai marre de l'attendre.

to **feed** VERB
donner à manger à ◊ *Have you fed the cat?* Est-ce que tu as donné à manger au chat?
◆**He worked hard to feed his family.** Il travaillait dur pour nourrir sa famille.

to **feel** VERB
1 se sentir ◊ *I don't feel well.* Je ne me sens pas bien. ◊ *I feel a bit lonely.* Je me sens un peu seul.
2 sentir ◊ *I didn't feel much pain.* Je n'ai presque rien senti.
3 toucher ◊ *The doctor felt his forehead.* Le docteur lui a touché le front.
◆**I was feeling hungry.** J'avais faim.
◆**I was feeling cold, so I went inside.** J'avais froid, alors je suis rentré.
◆**I feel like ...** (*want*) J'ai envie de ... ◊ *Do you feel like an ice cream?* Tu as envie d'une glace?

feeling NOUN

1 la sensation (*physical*) ◊ *a burning feeling* une sensation de brûlure
2 le sentiment (*emotional*) ◊ *a feeling of satisfaction* un sentiment de satisfaction

feet PL NOUN *see* **foot**

fell VERB *see* **fall**

felt VERB *see* **feel**

felt-tip pen NOUN
le stylo-feutre

female ADJECTIVE
see also **female** NOUN
1 femelle ◊ *a female animal* un animal femelle
2 féminin ◊ *the female sex* le sexe féminin

female NOUN
see also **female** ADJECTIVE
la femelle (*animal*)

feminine ADJECTIVE
féminin

feminist NOUN
le/la féministe

fence NOUN
la barrière

fern NOUN
la fougère

ferocious ADJECTIVE
féroce

ferry NOUN
le ferry

fertile ADJECTIVE
fertile

fertilizer NOUN
l' engrais MASC

festival NOUN
le festival ◊ *a jazz festival* un festival de jazz

to **fetch** VERB
1 aller chercher ◊ *Fetch the bucket.* Va chercher le seau.
2 se vendre (*sell for*) ◊ *His painting fetched £5000.* Son tableau s'est vendu cinq mille livres.

fever NOUN
la fièvre (*temperature*)

few ADJECTIVE, PRONOUN
peu de (*not many*) ◊ *few books* peu de livres
◆**a few (1)** quelques ◊ *a few hours* quelques heures
◆**a few (2)** quelques-uns ◊ *How many apples do you want? – A few.* Tu veux combien de pommes? – Quelques-unes.
◆**quite a few people** pas mal de monde

fewer ADJECTIVE

moins de ◊ *There are fewer people
than there were yesterday.* Il y a
moins de monde qu'hier. ◊ *There are
fewer pupils in this class.* Il y a
moins d'élèves dans cette classe.

fiancé NOUN
le fiancé ◊ *He's my fiancé.* C'est
mon fiancé.

fiancée NOUN
la fiancée ◊ *She's my fiancée.* C'est
ma fiancée.

fiction NOUN
les romans MASC PL (*novels*)

field NOUN
[1] le champ (*in countryside*) ◊ *a field
of wheat* un champ de blé
[2] le terrain (*for sport*) ◊ *a football
field* un terrain de football
[3] le domaine (*subject*) ◊ *He's an
expert in his field.* C'est un expert
dans son domaine.

fierce ADJECTIVE
[1] féroce ◊ *The dog looked very
fierce.* Le chien avait l'air très féroce.
[2] violent ◊ *The wind was very
fierce.* Le vent était très violent. ◊ *a
fierce attack* une attaque violente

fifteen NUMBER
quinze ◊ *I'm fifteen.* J'ai quinze ans.

fifteenth ADJECTIVE
quinzième ◊ *the fifteenth floor* le
quinzième étage
♦ **the fifteenth of August** le quinze août

fifth ADJECTIVE
cinquième ◊ *the fifth floor* le
cinquième étage
♦ **the fifth of August** le cinq août

fifty NUMBER
cinquante ◊ *He's fifty.* Il a cinquante
ans.

fifty-fifty ADJECTIVE, ADVERB
moitié-moitié ◊ *They split the prize
money fifty-fifty.* Ils ont partagé
l'argent du prix moitié-moitié.
♦ **a fifty-fifty chance** une chance sur
deux

fight NOUN
see also **fight** VERB
[1] la bagarre ◊ *There was a fight in
the pub.* Il y a eu une bagarre au
pub.
[2] la lutte ◊ *the fight against cancer*
la lutte contre le cancer

to **fight** VERB
see also **fight** NOUN
[1] se battre ◊ *They were fighting.* Ils
se battaient.
[2] lutter contre ◊ *The doctors tried
to fight the disease.* Les médecins

ont essayé de lutter contre la
maladie. ◊ *He fought against the urge
to smoke.* Il a lutté contre son envie
de fumer.

fighting NOUN
les bagarres FEM PL ◊ *Fighting broke
out outside the pub.* Des bagarres
ont éclaté devant le pub.

figure NOUN
[1] le chiffre (*number*) ◊ *Can you give
me the exact figures?* Pouvez-vous
me donner les chiffres exacts?
[2] la silhouette (*outline of person*)
◊ *Hélène saw the figure of a man on
the bridge.* Hélène a vu la silhouette
d'un homme sur le pont.
♦ **She's got a good figure.** Elle est bien
faite.
♦ **I have to watch my figure.** Je dois
faire attention à ma ligne.
[3] le personnage (*personality*) ◊ *She's
an important political figure.* C'est un
personnage politique important.

to **figure out** VERB
[1] calculer ◊ *I'll try to figure out how
much it'll cost.* Je vais essayer de
calculer combien ça va coûter.
[2] voir ◊ *I couldn't figure out what it
meant.* Je n'arrivais pas à voir ce que
ça voulait dire.
[3] cerner ◊ *I can't figure him out at
all.* Je n'arrive pas du tout à le
cerner.

file NOUN
see also **file** VERB
[1] le dossier (*document*) ◊ *Have we
got a file on the suspect?* Est-ce que
nous avons un dossier sur le
suspect?
[2] la chemise (*folder*) ◊ *She keeps all
her letters in a cardboard file.* Elle
garde toutes ses lettres dans une
chemise en carton.
[3] le classeur (*ring binder*)
[4] le fichier (*on computer*)
[5] la lime (*for nails, metal*)

to **file** VERB
see also **file** NOUN
[1] classer (*papers*)
[2] limer (*nails, metal*) ◊ *to file one's
nails* se limer les ongles

to **fill** VERB
remplir ◊ *She filled the glass with
water.* Elle a rempli le verre
d'eau.
♦ **to fill in (1)** remplir ◊ *Can you fill this
form in please?* Est-ce que vous
pouvez remplir ce formulaire s'il vous
plaît?

☞

- **to fill in** (2) boucher ◊ *He filled the hole in with soil.* Il a bouché le trou avec de la terre.
- **to fill up** remplir ◊ *He filled the cup up to the brim.* Il a rempli la tasse à ras bords.
- **Fill it up, please.** (*at petrol station*) Le plein, s'il vous plaît.

film NOUN
1 le film (*movie*)
2 la pellicule (*for camera*)

film star NOUN
la vedette de cinéma ◊ *He's a film star.* C'est une vedette de cinéma.

filthy ADJECTIVE
dégoûtant

final ADJECTIVE
see also **final** NOUN
1 (*last*)
dernier MASC
dernière FEM
◊ *our final farewells* nos derniers adieux
2 (*definite*)
définitif MASC
définitive FEM
◊ *a final decision* une décision définitive
- **I'm not going and that's final.** Je n'y vais pas, un point c'est tout.

final NOUN
see also **final** ADJECTIVE
la finale ◊ *Boris Becker is in the final.* Boris Becker va disputer la finale.

finally ADVERB
1 enfin (*lastly*) ◊ *Finally, I would like to say ...* Enfin, je voudrais dire ...
2 finalement (*eventually*) ◊ *They finally decided to leave on Saturday instead of Friday.* Ils ont finalement décidé de partir samedi au lieu de vendredi.

to **find** VERB
1 trouver ◊ *I can't find the exit.* Je ne trouve pas la sortie.
2 retrouver (*something lost*) ◊ *Did you find your pen?* Est-ce que tu as retrouvé ton crayon?
- **to find something out** découvrir quelque chose ◊ *I'm determined to find out the truth.* Je suis décidé à découvrir la vérité.
- **to find out about** (1) (*make enquiries*) se renseigner sur ◊ *Try to find out about the cost of a hotel.* Essaye de te renseigner sur le prix d'un hôtel.
- **to find out about** (2) (*by chance*) apprendre ◊ *I found out about their affair.* J'ai appris leur liaison.

fine ADJECTIVE, ADVERB
see also **fine** NOUN
1 excellent (*very good*) ◊ *He's a fine musician.* C'est un excellent musicien.
- **to be fine** aller bien ◊ *How are you? – I'm fine.* Comment ça va? – Ça va bien.
- **I feel fine.** Je me sens bien.
- **The weather is fine today.** Il fait beau aujourd'hui.
2 fin (*not coarse*) ◊ *She's got very fine hair.* Elle a les cheveux très fins.

fine NOUN
see also **fine** ADJECTIVE
1 l' amende FEM ◊ *She got a £50 fine.* Elle a eu une amende de cinquante livres.
2 la contravention (*for traffic offence*) ◊ *I got a fine for driving through a red light.* J'ai eu une contravention pour avoir grillé un feu rouge.

finger NOUN
le doigt
- **my little finger** mon petit doigt

fingernail NOUN
l' ongle MASC

finish NOUN
see also **finish** VERB
l' arrivée FEM (*of race*) ◊ *We saw the finish of the London Marathon.* Nous avons vu l'arrivée du marathon de Londres.

to **finish** VERB
see also **finish** NOUN
1 finir ◊ *I've finished!* J'ai fini!
- **to finish doing something** finir de faire quelque chose
2 terminer ◊ *I've finished the book.* J'ai terminé ce livre. ◊ *The film has finished.* Le film est terminé.

Finland NOUN
la Finlande
- **in Finland** en Finlande
- **to Finland** en Finlande

Finn NOUN
le Finlandais
la Finlandaise

Finnish ADJECTIVE
see also **Finnish** NOUN
finlandais

Finnish NOUN
see also **Finnish** ADJECTIVE
le finnois (*language*)

fire NOUN
see also **fire** VERB
1 le feu
(les feux PL)
◊ *He made a fire to warm himself up.* Il a fait du feu pour se réchauffer.

♦ **to be on fire** être en feu
2 (*accidental*)
l' incendie MASC ◇ *The house was destroyed by fire.* La maison a été détruite par un incendie.
3 (*heater*)
le radiateur ◇ *Turn the fire on.* Allume le radiateur.
♦ **the fire brigade** les pompiers MASC PL
♦ **a fire alarm** un avertisseur d'incendie
♦ **a fire engine** une voiture de pompiers
♦ **a fire escape** un escalier de secours
♦ **a fire extinguisher** un extincteur
♦ **a fire station** une caserne de pompiers

to **fire** VERB
see also **fire** NOUN
tirer (*shoot*) ◇ *She fired twice.* Elle a tiré deux fois.
♦ **to fire at somebody** tirer sur quelqu'un ◇ *The terrorist fired at the crowd.* Le terroriste a tiré sur la foule.
♦ **to fire a gun** tirer un coup de feu
♦ **to fire somebody** mettre quelqu'un à la porte ◇ *He was fired from his job.* Il a été mis à la porte.

fireman NOUN
le pompier ◇ *He's a fireman.* Il est pompier.

fireplace NOUN
la cheminée

fire station NOUN
la caserne de pompiers

fireworks PL NOUN
le feu d'artifice SING ◇ *Are you going to see the fireworks?* Est-ce que tu vas voir le feu d'artifice?

firm ADJECTIVE
see also **firm** NOUN
ferme ◇ *to be firm with somebody* se montrer ferme avec quelqu'un

firm NOUN
see also **firm** ADJECTIVE
l' entreprise FEM ◇ *He works for a large firm in London.* Il travaille pour une grande entreprise à Londres.

first ADJECTIVE, ADVERB
see also **first** NOUN
1 premier MASC
première FEM
◇ *the first of September* le premier septembre ◇ *the first time* la première fois
♦ **to come first** (*in exam, race*) arriver premier ◇ *Rachel came first.* Rachel est arrivée première.
2 d'abord ◇ *I want to get a job, but first I have to pass my exams.* Je

veux trouver du travail, mais d'abord je dois réussir à mes examens.
♦ **first of all** tout d'abord

first NOUN
see also **first** ADJECTIVE
le premier
la première
◇ *She was the first to arrive.* Elle est arrivée la première.
♦ **at first** au début

first aid NOUN
les premiers secours MASC PL
♦ **a first aid kit** une trousse de secours

first-class ADJECTIVE
1 de première classe ◇ *She has booked a first-class ticket.* Elle a réservé un billet de première classe.
2 excellent ◇ *a first-class meal* un excellent repas
♦ **a first-class stamp**

> ⓘ *In France there is no first-class or second-class postage. However letters cost more to send than postcards, so you have to remember to say what you are sending when buying stamps.*

firstly ADVERB
premièrement ◇ *Firstly, let's see what the book is about.* Premièrement, voyons de quoi parle ce livre.

fir tree NOUN
le sapin

fish NOUN
see also **fish** VERB
le poisson ◇ *I caught three fish.* J'ai pêché trois poissons. ◇ *I don't like fish.* Je n'aime pas le poisson.

to **fish** VERB
see also **fish** NOUN
pêcher
♦ **to go fishing** aller à la pêche ◇ *We went fishing in the River Dee.* Nous sommes allés à la pêche sur la Dee.

fisherman NOUN
le pêcheur ◇ *He's a fisherman.* Il est pêcheur.

fish fingers PL NOUN
les bâtonnets de poisson MASC PL

fishing NOUN
la pêche ◇ *My hobby is fishing.* La pêche est mon passe-temps favori.

fishing boat NOUN
le bateau de pêche

fishing rod NOUN
la canne à pêche

fishing tackle NOUN

F

le matériel de pêche

fish sticks PL NOUN US
les bâtonnets de poisson MASC PL

fist NOUN
le poing

to **fit** VERB
> see also **fit** ADJECTIVE, NOUN

[1] être la bonne taille (be the right size) ◊ Does it fit? Est-ce que c'est la bonne taille?

In French you usually specify whether something is too big, small, tight etc.

♦ **These trousers don't fit me. (1)** (too big) Ce pantalon est trop grand pour moi.

♦ **These trousers don't fit me. (2)** (too small) Ce pantalon est trop petit pour moi.

[2] installer (fix up) ◊ He fitted an alarm in his car. Il a installé une alarme dans sa voiture.

[3] adapter (attach) ◊ She fitted a plug to the hair dryer. Elle a adapté une prise au sèche-cheveux.

♦ **to fit in (1)** (match up) correspondre ◊ That story doesn't fit in with what he told us. Cette histoire ne correspond pas à ce qu'il nous a dit.

♦ **to fit in (2)** (person) s'adapter ◊ She fitted in well at her new school. Elle s'est bien adaptée à sa nouvelle école.

fit ADJECTIVE
> see also **fit** VERB, NOUN

en forme (in condition) ◊ He felt relaxed and fit after his holiday. Il se sentait détendu et en forme après ses vacances.

fit NOUN
> see also **fit** ADJECTIVE, VERB

♦ **to have a fit (1)** (epileptic) avoir une crise d'épilepsie

♦ **to have a fit (2)** (be angry) piquer une crise de nerfs ◊ My Mum will have a fit when she sees the carpet! Ma mère va piquer une crise de nerfs quand elle va voir la moquette!

fitted carpet NOUN
la moquette

fitted kitchen NOUN
la cuisine aménagée

fitting room NOUN
la cabine d'essayage

five NUMBER
cinq ◊ He's five. Il a cinq ans.

to **fix** VERB

[1] réparer (mend) ◊ Can you fix my bike? Est-ce que tu peux réparer mon vélo?

[2] fixer (decide) ◊ Let's fix a date for the party. Fixons une date pour la soirée. ◊ They fixed a price for the car. Ils ont fixé un prix pour la voiture.

[3] préparer ◊ Janice fixed some food for us. Janice nous a préparé à manger.

fixed ADJECTIVE
fixe ◊ at a fixed time à une heure fixe ◊ at a fixed price à un prix fixe ◊ a fixed-price menu un menu à prix fixe

♦ **My parents have very fixed ideas.** Mes parents ont des idées très arrêtées.

fizzy ADJECTIVE
gazeux MASC
gazeuse FEM
◊ I don't like fizzy drinks. Je n'aime pas les boissons gazeuses.

flabby ADJECTIVE
flasque

flag NOUN
le drapeau
(les drapeaux PL)

flame NOUN
la flamme

flamingo NOUN
le flamant rose

flan NOUN
[1] la tarte (sweet) ◊ a raspberry flan une tarte aux framboises
[2] la quiche (savoury) ◊ a cheese and onion flan une quiche au fromage et aux oignons

flannel NOUN
le gant de toilette (for face)

to **flap** VERB
battre de ◊ The bird flapped its wings. L'oiseau battait des ailes.

flash NOUN
> see also **flash** VERB

le flash
(les flashes PL)
◊ Has your camera got a flash? Est-ce que ton appareil photo a un flash?

♦ **a flash of lightning** un éclair

♦ **in a flash** en un clin d'œil

to **flash** VERB
> see also **flash** NOUN

[1] clignoter ◊ The police car's blue light was flashing. Le gyrophare de la voiture de police clignotait.

[2] <u>projeter</u> ◇ *They flashed a torch in his face.* Ils lui ont projeté la lumière d'une torche en plein visage.
♦**She flashed her headlights.** Elle a fait un appel de phares.

flask NOUN
le <u>thermos</u> (*vacuum flask*)

flat ADJECTIVE
see also **flat** NOUN
[1] <u>plat</u> ◇ *a flat roof* un toit plat ◇ *flat shoes* des chaussures plates
[2] <u>crevé</u> (*tyre*) ◇ *I've got a flat tyre.* J'ai un pneu crevé.

flat NOUN
see also **flat** ADJECTIVE
l' <u>appartement</u> MASC ◇ *She lives in a flat.* Elle habite un appartement.

to **flatter** VERB
<u>flatter</u>

flattered ADJECTIVE
<u>flatté</u>

flavour NOUN
[1] le <u>goût</u> (*taste*) ◇ *This cheese has a very strong flavour.* Ce fromage a un goût très fort.
[2] le <u>parfum</u> (*variety*) ◇ *Which flavour of ice cream would you like?* Quel parfum de glace est-ce que tu veux?

flavouring NOUN
le <u>parfum</u>

flew VERB *see* **fly**

flexible ADJECTIVE
<u>flexible</u> ◇ *flexible working hours* les horaires flexibles MASC

to **flick** VERB
<u>appuyer sur</u> ◇ *She flicked the switch to turn the light on.* Elle a appuyé sur le bouton pour allumer la lumière.
♦**to flick through a book** feuilleter un livre

to **flicker** VERB
<u>trembloter</u> ◇ *The light flickered.* La lumière a trembloté.

flight NOUN
le <u>vol</u> ◇ *What time is the flight to Paris?* À quelle heure est le vol pour Paris?
♦**a flight of stairs** un escalier

flight attendant NOUN
[1] l' <u>hôtesse de l'air</u> FEM (*woman*)
[2] le <u>steward</u> (*man*)

to **fling** VERB
<u>jeter</u> ◇ *He flung the dictionary onto the floor.* Il a jeté le dictionnaire par terre.

to **float** VERB
<u>flotter</u> ◇ *A leaf was floating on the water.* Une feuille flottait sur l'eau.

flock NOUN
♦**a flock of sheep** un troupeau de moutons
♦**a flock of birds** un vol d'oiseaux

flood NOUN
see also **flood** VERB
[1] l' <u>inondation</u> FEM ◇ *The rain has caused many floods.* La pluie a provoqué de nombreuses inondations.
[2] le <u>flot</u> ◇ *He received a flood of letters.* Il a reçu un flot de lettres.

to **flood** VERB
see also **flood** NOUN
<u>inonder</u> ◇ *The river has flooded the village.* La rivière a inondé le village.

flooding NOUN
les <u>inondations</u> FEM PL

floor NOUN
[1] le <u>sol</u> ◇ *a tiled floor* un sol carrelé
♦**on the floor** par terre
[2] l' <u>étage</u> MASC (*storey*) ◇ *the first floor* le premier étage
♦**the ground floor** le rez-de-chaussée
♦**on the third floor** au troisième étage

flop NOUN
le <u>fiasco</u> ◇ *The film was a flop.* Le film a été un fiasco.

floppy disk NOUN
la <u>disquette</u>

florist NOUN
le/la <u>fleuriste</u>

flour NOUN
la <u>farine</u>

to **flow** VERB
[1] <u>couler</u> (*river*)
[2] <u>s'écouler</u> (*flow out*) ◇ *Water was flowing from the pipe.* De l'eau s'écoulait du tuyau.

flower NOUN
see also **flower** VERB
la <u>fleur</u>

to **flower** VERB
see also **flower** NOUN
<u>fleurir</u>

flown VERB *see* **fly**

flu NOUN
la <u>grippe</u> ◇ *She's got flu.* Elle a la grippe.

fluent ADJECTIVE
♦**He speaks fluent French.** Il parle couramment le français.

flung VERB *see* **fling**

flush NOUN
see also **flush** VERB
la <u>chasse d'eau</u> (*of toilet*)

to **flush** VERB
see also **flush** NOUN

F

♦**to flush the toilet** tirer la chasse

flute NOUN
la flûte ◊ *I play the flute.* Je joue de la flûte.

fly NOUN
see also **fly** VERB
la mouche (*insect*)

to **fly** VERB
see also **fly** NOUN
1 voler ◊ *The plane flies at a speed of 400 km per hour.* L'avion vole à quatre cents kilomètres à l'heure.
2 aller en avion (*passenger*) ◊ *He flew from Paris to New York.* Il est allé de Paris à New York en avion.
♦**to fly away** s'envoler ◊ *The bird flew away.* L'oiseau s'est envolé.

foal NOUN
le poulain

focus NOUN
see also **focus** VERB
♦**to be out of focus** être flou ◊ *The house is out of focus in this photo.* La maison est floue sur cette photo.

to **focus** VERB
see also **focus** NOUN
mettre au point ◊ *Try to focus the binoculars.* Essaye de mettre les jumelles au point.
♦**to focus on something (1)** (*with camera, telescope*) régler la mise au point sur quelque chose ◊ *The cameraman focused on the bird.* Le caméraman a réglé la mise au point sur l'oiseau.
♦**to focus on something (2)** (*concentrate*) se concentrer sur quelque chose ◊ *Let's focus on the plot of the play.* Concentrons-nous sur l'intrigue de la pièce.

fog NOUN
le brouillard

foggy ADJECTIVE
♦**It's foggy.** Il y a du brouillard.
♦**a foggy day** un jour de brouillard

foil NOUN
le papier d'aluminium (*kitchen foil*)
◊ *She wrapped the meat in foil.* Elle a enveloppé la viande dans du papier d'aluminium.

fold NOUN
see also **fold** VERB
le pli

to **fold** VERB
see also **fold** NOUN
plier ◊ *He folded the newspaper in half.* Il a plié le journal en deux.
♦**to fold something up** plier quelque chose

♦**to fold one's arms** croiser ses bras
◊ *She folded her arms.* Elle a croisé les bras.

folder NOUN
1 la chemise ◊ *She kept all her letters in a folder.* Elle gardait toutes ses lettres dans une chemise.
2 le classeur (*ring binder*)

folding ADJECTIVE
♦**a folding chair** une chaise pliante
♦**a folding bed** un lit pliant

to **follow** VERB
suivre ◊ *She followed him.* Elle l'a suivi. ◊ *You go first and I'll follow.* Va devant, je te suis.

following ADJECTIVE
suivant ◊ *the following day* le jour suivant

fond ADJECTIVE
♦**to be fond of somebody** aimer beaucoup quelqu'un ◊ *I'm very fond of her.* Je l'aime beaucoup.

food NOUN
la nourriture
♦**We need to buy some food.** Nous devons acheter à manger.
♦**cat food** la nourriture pour chat
♦**dog food** la nourriture pour chien

food processor NOUN
le robot

fool NOUN
l' idiot MASC
l' idiote FEM

foot NOUN
1 le pied (*of person*) ◊ *My feet are aching.* J'ai mal aux pieds.
2 la patte (*of animal*) ◊ *The dog's foot was injured.* Le chien était blessé à la patte.
♦**on foot** à pied
3 le pied (*12 inches*)

> ⓘ In France measurements are in metres and centimetres rather than feet and inches. A foot is about 30 centimetres.

♦**Dave is 6 foot tall.** Dave mesure un mètre quatre-vingt.
♦**That mountain is 5000 feet high.** Cette montagne fait mille six cents mètres de haut.

football NOUN
1 le football (*game*) ◊ *I like playing football.* J'aime jouer au football.
2 le ballon (*ball*) ◊ *Paul threw the football over the fence.* Paul a envoyé le ballon par dessus la clôture.

footballer NOUN

le <u>footballeur</u>
la <u>footballeuse</u>

football player NOUN
le <u>joueur de football</u>
la <u>joueuse de football</u>
◊ *He's a famous football player.* C'est un joueur de football célèbre.

footie NOUN
le <u>foot</u>

footpath NOUN
le <u>sentier</u> ◊ *Jane followed the footpath through the forest.* Jane a suivi le sentier à travers la forêt.

footprint NOUN
la <u>trace de pas</u> ◊ *He saw some footprints in the sand.* Il a vu des traces de pas sur le sable.

footstep NOUN
le <u>pas</u> ◊ *I can hear footsteps on the stairs.* J'entends des pas dans l'escalier.

for PREPOSITION

There are several ways of translating for. Scan the examples to find one that is similar to what you want to say.

[1] <u>pour</u> ◊ *a present for me* un cadeau pour moi ◊ *the train for London* le train pour Londres ◊ *He works for the government.* Il travaille pour le gouvernement. ◊ *I'll do it for you.* Je vais le faire pour toi. ◊ *Can you do it for tomorrow?* Est-ce que vous pouvez le faire pour demain? ◊ *Are you for or against the idea?* Êtes-vous pour ou contre cette idée? ◊ *Oxford is famous for its university.* Oxford est célèbre pour son université.

*When referring to periods of time, use **pendant** for the future and completed actions in the past, and **depuis** (with the French verb in the present tense) for something that started in the past and is still going on.*

[2] <u>pendant</u> ◊ *He worked in France for two years.* Il a travaillé en France pendant deux ans. ◊ *She will be away for a month.* Elle sera absente pendant un mois. ◊ *There are road works for three kilometres.* Il y a des travaux pendant trois kilomètres.

[3] <u>depuis</u> ◊ *He's been learning French for two years.* Il apprend le français depuis deux ans. ◊ *She's been away for a month.* Elle est absente depuis un mois.

When talking about amounts of money, you do not translate for.

◊ *I sold it for £5.* Je l'ai vendu cinq livres. ◊ *He paid fifty pence for his ticket.* Il a payé son billet cinquante pence.
♦ **What's the French for "lion"?** Comment dit-on "lion" en français?
♦ **It's time for lunch.** C'est l'heure du déjeuner.
♦ **What for?** Pour quoi faire? ◊ *Give me some money! – What for?* Donne-moi de l'argent! – Pour quoi faire?
♦ **What's it for?** Ça sert à quoi?
♦ **for sale** à vendre ◊ *The factory's for sale.* L'usine est en vente.

to **forbid** VERB
<u>défendre</u>
♦ **to forbid somebody to do something** défendre à quelqu'un de faire quelque chose ◊ *I forbid you to go out tonight!* Je te défends de sortir ce soir.

forbidden ADJECTIVE
<u>défendu</u> ◊ *Smoking is strictly forbidden.* Il est strictement défendu de fumer.

force NOUN
see also **force** VERB
la <u>force</u> ◊ *the force of the explosion* la force de l'explosion
♦ **in force** en vigueur ◊ *No-smoking rules are now in force.* Un règlement qui interdit de fumer est maintenant en vigueur.

to **force** VERB
see also **force** NOUN
<u>forcer</u> ◊ *They forced him to open the safe.* Ils l'ont obligé à ouvrir le coffre-fort.

forecast NOUN
♦ **the weather forecast** la météo

foreground NOUN
le <u>premier plan</u> ◊ *in the foreground* au premier plan

forehead NOUN
le <u>front</u>

foreign ADJECTIVE
<u>étranger</u> MASC
<u>étrangère</u> FEM

foreigner NOUN
l' <u>étranger</u> MASC
l' <u>étrangère</u> FEM

to **foresee** VERB
<u>prévoir</u> ◊ *He had foreseen the problem.* Il avait prévu ce problème.

forest NOUN
la <u>forêt</u>

forever ADVERB
[1] <u>pour toujours</u> ◊ *He's gone forever.* Il est parti pour toujours.

F

2 toujours (*always*) ◊ *She's forever complaining.* Elle est toujours en train de se plaindre.

forgave VERB *see* **forgive**

to **forge** VERB
contrefaire ◊ *She tried to forge his signature.* Elle a essayé de contrefaire sa signature.

forged ADJECTIVE
faux MASC
fausse FEM
◊ *forged banknotes* des faux billets

to **forget** VERB
oublier ◊ *I've forgotten his name.* J'ai oublié son nom. ◊ *I'm sorry, I completely forgot!* Je suis désolé, j'ai complètement oublié!

to **forgive** VERB
♦ **to forgive somebody** pardonner à quelqu'un ◊ *I forgive you.* Je te pardonne.
♦ **to forgive somebody for doing something** pardonner à quelqu'un d'avoir fait quelque chose ◊ *She forgave him for forgetting her birthday.* Elle lui a pardonné d'avoir oublié son anniversaire.

forgot, forgotten VERB *see* **forget**

fork NOUN
1 la fourchette (*for eating*)
2 la fourche (*for gardening*)
3 la bifurcation (*in road*)

form NOUN
1 le formulaire (*paper*) ◊ *to fill in a form* remplir un formulaire
2 la forme (*type*) ◊ *I'm against hunting in any form.* Je suis contre la chasse sous toutes ses formes.
♦ **in top form** en pleine forme
♦ **She's in the fourth form.** Elle est en troisième.

formal ADJECTIVE
1 (*occasion*)
officiel MASC
officielle FEM
◊ *a formal dinner* un dîner officiel
2 (*person*)
guindé
3 (*language*)
soutenu ◊ *In English, "residence" is a formal term.* En anglais, "residence" est un terme soutenu.
♦ **formal clothes** une tenue habillée
♦ **He's got no formal education.** Il n'a pas fait beaucoup d'études.

former ADJECTIVE
ancien MASC
ancienne FEM

◊ *a former pupil* un ancien élève
◊ *the former Prime Minister* l'ancien Premier ministre

formerly ADVERB
autrefois

fort NOUN
le fort

forth ADVERB
♦ **to go back and forth** aller et venir
♦ **and so forth** et ainsi de suite

fortnight NOUN
♦ **a fortnight** quinze jours ◊ *I'm going on holiday for a fortnight.* Je pars en vacances pendant quinze jours.

fortunate ADJECTIVE
♦ **to be fortunate** avoir de la chance ◊ *He was extremely fortunate to survive.* Il a eu énormément de chance de survivre.
♦ **It's fortunate that I remembered the map.** C'est une chance que j'aie pris la carte.

fortunately ADVERB
heureusement ◊ *Fortunately, it didn't rain.* Heureusement, il n'a pas plu.

fortune NOUN
la fortune ◊ *Kate earns a fortune!* Kate gagne une fortune!
♦ **to tell somebody's fortune** dire la bonne aventure à quelqu'un

forty NUMBER
quarante ◊ *He's forty.* Il a quarante ans.

forward ADVERB
see also **forward** VERB
♦ **to move forward** avancer

to **forward** VERB
see also **forward** ADVERB
faire suivre ◊ *He forwarded all Janette's letters.* Il a fait suivre toutes les lettres de Janette.

forward slash NOUN
la barre oblique

to **foster** VERB
♦ **She has fostered more than fifteen children.** Plus de quinze enfants ont été placés chez elle.

foster child NOUN
l' enfant adoptif MASC
l' enfant adoptive FEM

fought VERB *see* **fight**

foul ADJECTIVE
see also **foul** NOUN
infect ◊ *The weather was foul.* Le temps était infect. ◊ *What a foul smell!* Quelle odeur infecte!

foul NOUN
see also **foul** ADJECTIVE

la <u>faute</u> ◊ *Ferguson committed a foul.* Ferguson a fait une faute.

found VERB *see* **find**

to **found** VERB
<u>fonder</u> ◊ *Baden Powell founded the Scout Movement.* Baden Powell a fondé le mouvement scout.

foundations PL NOUN
les <u>fondations</u> FEM PL

fountain NOUN
la <u>fontaine</u>

fountain pen NOUN
le <u>stylo à encre</u>

four NUMBER
<u>quatre</u> ◊ *She's four.* Elle a quatre ans.

fourteen NUMBER
<u>quatorze</u> ◊ *I'm fourteen.* J'ai quatorze ans.

fourteenth ADJECTIVE
<u>quatorzième</u> ◊ *the fourteenth floor* le quatorzième étage
♦**the fourteenth of August** le quatorze août

fourth ADJECTIVE
<u>quatrième</u> ◊ *the fourth floor* le quatrième étage
♦**the fourth of July** le quatre juillet

fox NOUN
le <u>renard</u>

fragile ADJECTIVE
<u>fragile</u>

frame NOUN
le <u>cadre</u> (*for picture*)

France NOUN
la <u>France</u>
♦**in France** en France
♦**to France** en France
♦**He's from France.** Il est français.

frantic ADJECTIVE
♦**I was going frantic.** J'étais dans tous mes états.
♦**to be frantic with worry** être folle d'inquiétude

fraud NOUN
☐1 la <u>fraude</u> (*crime*) ◊ *He was jailed for fraud.* On l'a mis en prison pour fraude.
☐2 l' <u>imposteur</u> MASC (*person*) ◊ *He's not a real doctor, he's a fraud.* Ce n'est pas un vrai médecin, c'est un imposteur.

freckles PL NOUN
les <u>taches de rousseur</u> FEM PL

free ADJECTIVE
see also **free** VERB
☐1 <u>gratuit</u> (*free of charge*) ◊ *a free brochure* une brochure gratuite

☐2 <u>libre</u> (*not busy, not taken*) ◊ *Is this seat free?* Est-ce que cette place est libre? ◊ *Are you free after school?* Tu es libre après l'école?

to **free** VERB
see also **free** ADJECTIVE
<u>libérer</u>

freedom NOUN
la <u>liberté</u>

freeway NOUN US
l' <u>autoroute</u> FEM

to **freeze** VERB
☐1 <u>geler</u> ◊ *The water had frozen.* L'eau avait gelé.
☐2 <u>congeler</u> (*food*) ◊ *She froze the rest of the raspberries.* Elle a congelé le reste des framboises.

freezer NOUN
le <u>congélateur</u>

freezing ADJECTIVE
♦**It's freezing!** Il fait un froid de canard! (*informal*)
♦**I'm freezing!** Je suis gelé! (*informal*)
♦**3 degrees below freezing** moins trois

freight NOUN
la <u>cargaison</u> (*goods*)
♦**a freight train** un train de marchandises

French ADJECTIVE
see also **French** NOUN
<u>français</u> ◊ *He's French.* Il est français. ◊ *She's French.* Elle est française.

French NOUN
see also **French** ADJECTIVE
le <u>français</u> (*language*) ◊ *Do you speak French?* Est-ce que tu parles français?
♦**the French** (*people*) les Français

French beans PL NOUN
les <u>haricots verts</u> MASC PL

French fries PL NOUN
les <u>frites</u> FEM PL

French horn NOUN
le <u>cor (d'harmonie)</u> ◊ *I play the French horn.* Je joue du cor.

French kiss NOUN
le <u>baiser profond</u>

French loaf NOUN
la <u>baguette</u>

Frenchman NOUN
le <u>Français</u>

French windows PL NOUN
la <u>porte-fenêtre</u> SING
(les portes-fenêtres PL)

Frenchwoman NOUN
la <u>Française</u>

frequent ADJECTIVE
<u>fréquent</u> ◊ *frequent showers* des averses fréquentes

☞

F

◆**There are frequent buses to the town centre.** Il y a beaucoup de bus pour le centre ville.

fresh ADJECTIVE
frais MASC
fraîche FEM

◆**I need some fresh air.** J'ai besoin de prendre l'air.

to**freshen up** VERB
faire un brin de toilette ◊ *I'd like to go and freshen up.* Je voudrais faire un brin de toilette.

to**fret** VERB
se tracasser ◊ *Philip was fretting about his exams.* Philip se tracassait au sujet de ses examens.

Friday NOUN
le vendredi ◊ *on Friday* vendredi ◊ *on Fridays* le vendredi ◊ *every Friday* tous les vendredis ◊ *last Friday* vendredi dernier ◊ *next Friday* vendredi prochain

fridge NOUN
le frigo

fried ADJECTIVE
frit ◊ *fried vegetables* des légumes frits

◆**a fried egg** un œuf sur le plat

friend NOUN
l' ami MASC
l' amie FEM

friendly ADJECTIVE
1 gentil MASC
gentille FEM
◊ *She's really friendly.* Elle est vraiment gentille.
2 accueillant ◊ *Liverpool is a very friendly city.* Liverpool est une ville très accueillante.

friendship NOUN
l' amitié FEM

fright NOUN
la peur ◊ *I got a terrible fright!* Ça m'a fait une peur terrible!

to**frighten** VERB
faire peur à ◊ *Horror films frighten him.* Les films d'horreur lui font peur.

frightened ADJECTIVE
◆**to be frightened** avoir peur ◊ *I'm frightened!* J'ai peur!
◆**to be frightened of something** avoir peur de quelque chose ◊ *Anna's frightened of spiders.* Anna a peur des araignées.

frightening ADJECTIVE
effrayant

fringe NOUN
la frange (*of hair*) ◊ *She's got a fringe.* Elle a une frange.

Frisbee ® NOUN
le Frisbee ® ◊ *to play Frisbee* jouer au Frisbee

fro ADVERB
◆**to go to and fro** aller et venir

frog NOUN
la grenouille
◆**frogs' legs** les cuisses de grenouille FEM

from PREPOSITION
de ◊ *Where do you come from?* D'où venez-vous? ◊ *I come from Perth.* Je viens de Perth. ◊ *a letter from my sister* une lettre de ma sœur ◊ *The hotel is one kilometre from the beach.* L'hôtel est à un kilomètre de la plage.
◆**from ... to ...** de ... à ... ◊ *He flew from London to Paris.* Il a pris l'avion de Londres à Paris. ◊ *from 1 o'clock to 2* d'une heure à deux heures ◊ *The price was reduced from £10 to £5.* Ils ont réduit le prix de dix livres à cinq.
◆**from ... onwards** à partir de ... ◊ *We'll be at home from 7 o'clock onwards.* Nous serons chez nous à partir de sept heures.

front NOUN
see also **front** ADJECTIVE
le devant ◊ *the front of the house* le devant de la maison
◆**in front** devant ◊ *a house with a car in front* une maison avec une voiture devant ◊ *the car in front* la voiture de devant
◆**in front of** devant ◊ *in front of the house* devant la maison ◊ *the car in front of us* la voiture devant nous
◆**in the front** (*of car*) à l'avant ◊ *I was sitting in the front.* J'étais assis à l'avant.
◆**at the front of the train** à l'avant du train

front ADJECTIVE
see also **front** NOUN
1 de devant ◊ *the front row* la rangée de devant
2 avant ◊ *the front seats of the car* les sièges avant de la voiture
◆**the front door** la porte d'entrée

frontier NOUN
la frontière

frost NOUN
le gel

frosting NOUN US
le glaçage (*on cake*)

frosty ADJECTIVE
◆**It's frosty today.** Il gèle aujourd'hui.

to**frown** VERB

froncer les sourcils ◊ *He frowned.* Il a froncé les sourcils.

froze VERB *see* **freeze**

frozen ADJECTIVE
see also **freeze**
surgelé (*food*) ◊ *frozen chips* des frites surgelées

fruit NOUN
le fruit
♦ **fruit juice** le jus de fruits
♦ **a fruit salad** une salade de fruits

fruit machine NOUN
la machine à sous

frustrated ADJECTIVE
frustré

to **fry** VERB
faire frire ◊ *Fry the onions for 5 minutes.* Faites frire les oignons pendant cinq minutes.

frying pan NOUN
la poêle

fuel NOUN
le carburant (*for car, aeroplane*) ◊ *to run out of fuel* avoir une panne de carburant

to **fulfil** VERB
réaliser ◊ *Robert fulfilled his dream to visit China.* Robert a réalisé son rêve de visiter la Chine.

full ADJECTIVE, ADVERB
1 plein ◊ *The tank's full.* Le réservoir est plein.
2 complet MASC
complète FEM
◊ *He asked for full information on the job.* Il a demandé des renseignements complets sur le poste.
♦ **your full name** vos nom et prénoms ◊ *My full name is Ian John Marr.* Je m'appelle Ian John Marr.
♦ **I'm full.** (*after meal*) J'ai bien mangé.
♦ **at full speed** à toute vitesse ◊ *He drove at full speed.* Il conduisait à toute vitesse.
♦ **There was a full moon.** C'était la pleine lune.

full stop NOUN
le point

full-time ADJECTIVE, ADVERB
à plein temps ◊ *Gillian has got a full-time job.* Gillian a un travail à plein temps. ◊ *Gillian works full-time.* Gillian travaille à plein temps.

fully ADVERB
complètement ◊ *He hasn't fully recovered from his illness.* Il n'est pas complètement remis de sa maladie.

fumes PL NOUN
les fumées FEM PL ◊ *The factory gave out dangerous fumes.* L'usine rejetait des fumées dangereuses.
♦ **exhaust fumes** les gaz d'échappement MASC

fun ADJECTIVE
see also **fun** NOUN
marrant ◊ *She's a fun person.* Elle est marrante.

fun NOUN
see also **fun** ADJECTIVE
♦ **to have fun** s'amuser ◊ *We had great fun playing in the snow.* Nous nous sommes bien amusés à jouer dans la neige.
♦ **for fun** pour rire ◊ *He entered the competition just for fun.* Il a participé à la compétition juste pour rire.
♦ **to make fun of somebody** se moquer de quelqu'un ◊ *They made fun of him.* Ils se sont moqués de lui.
♦ **It's fun!** C'est chouette!
♦ **Have fun!** Amuse-toi bien!

funds PL NOUN
les fonds MASC PL ◊ *to raise funds* collecter des fonds

funeral NOUN
l' enterrement MASC

funfair NOUN
la fête foraine

funny ADJECTIVE
1 drôle (*amusing*) ◊ *It was really funny.* C'était vraiment drôle.
2 bizarre (*strange*) ◊ *There's something funny about him.* Il est un peu bizarre.

fur NOUN
1 la fourrure ◊ *a fur coat* un manteau de fourrure
2 le poil ◊ *the dog's fur* le poil du chien

furious ADJECTIVE
furieux MASC
furieuse FEM
◊ *Dad was furious with me.* Papa était furieux contre moi.

furniture NOUN
les meubles MASC PL ◊ *a piece of furniture* un meuble

further ADVERB, ADJECTIVE
plus loin ◊ *London is further from Manchester than Leeds is.* Londres est plus loin de Manchester que Leeds.
♦ **How much further is it?** C'est encore loin?

further education NOUN
l' enseignement postscolaire MASC

F

fuse NOUN
le <u>fusible</u> ◊ *The fuse has blown.* Le fusible a sauté.

fuss NOUN
l' <u>agitation</u> FEM ◊ *What's all the fuss about?* Qu'est-ce que c'est que toute cette agitation?
♦ **to make a fuss** faire des histoires ◊ *He's always making a fuss about nothing.* Il fait toujours des histoires pour rien.

fussy ADJECTIVE

<u>difficile</u> ◊ *She is very fussy about her food.* Elle est très difficile sur la nourriture.

future NOUN
[1] l' <u>avenir</u> MASC ◊ *What are your plans for the future?* Quels sont vos projets pour l'avenir?
♦ **in future** à l'avenir ◊ *Be more careful in future.* Sois plus prudent à l'avenir.
[2] le <u>futur</u> (*in grammar*) ◊ *Put this sentence into the future.* Mettez cette phrase au futur.

G

to **gain** VERB
- ◆**to gain weight** prendre du poids
- ◆**to gain speed** prendre de la vitesse

gallery NOUN
le <u>musée</u> ◊ *an art gallery* un musée d'art

to **gamble** VERB
<u>jouer</u> ◊ *He gambled £100 at the casino.* Il a joué cent livres au casino.

gambler NOUN
le <u>joueur</u>

gambling NOUN
le <u>jeu</u> ◊ *He likes gambling.* Il aime le jeu.

game NOUN
1 le <u>jeu</u>
(les jeux PL)
◊ *The children were playing a game.* Les enfants jouaient à un jeu.
2 (*sport*)
le <u>match</u> ◊ *a game of football* un match de football
- ◆**a game of cards** une partie de cartes

gang NOUN
la <u>bande</u>

gangster NOUN
le <u>gangster</u>

gap NOUN
1 le <u>trou</u> ◊ *There's a gap in the hedge.* Il y a un trou dans la haie.
2 l' <u>intervalle</u> MASC ◊ *a gap of four years* un intervalle de quatre ans

garage NOUN
le <u>garage</u>

garbage NOUN
les <u>ordures</u> FEM PL

garden NOUN
le <u>jardin</u>

gardener NOUN
le <u>jardinier</u> ◊ *He's a gardener.* Il est jardinier.

gardening NOUN
le <u>jardinage</u> ◊ *Margaret loves gardening.* Margaret aime le jardinage.

gardens PL NOUN
le <u>jardin public</u> SING

garlic NOUN
l' <u>ail</u> MASC

garment NOUN
le <u>vêtement</u>

gas NOUN
1 le <u>gaz</u>
- ◆**a gas cooker** une cuisinière à gaz

- ◆**a gas cylinder** une bouteille de gaz
- ◆**a gas fire** un radiateur à gaz
- ◆**a gas leak** une fuite de gaz
2 l' <u>essence</u> FEM (*petrol*) US

gasoline NOUN US
l' <u>essence</u> FEM

gate NOUN
1 le <u>portail</u> (*of garden*)
2 la <u>barrière</u> (*of field*)
3 la <u>porte</u> (*at airport*)

gateau NOUN
le <u>gâteau à la crème</u>

to **gather** VERB
se <u>rassembler</u> (*assemble*) ◊ *People gathered in front of Buckingham Palace.* Les gens se sont rassemblés devant Buckingham Palace.
- ◆**to gather speed** prendre de la vitesse ◊ *The train gathered speed.* Le train a pris de la vitesse.

gave VERB *see* **give**

gay ADJECTIVE
<u>homosexuel</u> MASC
<u>homosexuelle</u> FEM

to **gaze** VERB
- ◆**to gaze at something** fixer quelque chose du regard ◊ *He gazed at her.* Il l'a fixée du regard.

GCSE NOUN
le <u>brevet des collèges</u>

gear NOUN
1 la <u>vitesse</u> (*in car*) ◊ *in first gear* en première vitesse ◊ *to change gear* changer de vitesse
2 le <u>matériel</u> ◊ *camping gear* le matériel de camping
- ◆**your sports gear** (*clothes*) tes affaires de sport

gear lever NOUN
le <u>levier de vitesse</u>

gearshift NOUN US
le <u>levier de vitesse</u>

geese PL NOUN *see* **goose**

gel NOUN
le <u>gel</u>
- ◆**hair gel** le gel pour les cheveux

gem NOUN
la <u>pierre précieuse</u>

Gemini NOUN
les <u>Gémeaux</u> MASC PL ◊ *I'm Gemini.* Je suis Gémeaux.

gender NOUN
1 le <u>sexe</u> (*of person*)
2 le <u>genre</u> (*of noun*)

gene NOUN
le gène

general NOUN
see also **general** ADJECTIVE
le général
(les généraux PL)

general ADJECTIVE
see also **general** NOUN
général
(généraux MASC PL)
♦ **in general** en général

general election NOUN
les élections législatives FEM PL

general knowledge NOUN
les connaissances générales FEM PL

generally ADVERB
généralement ◊ I generally go shopping on Saturday. Généralement, je fais mes courses le samedi.

generation NOUN
la génération ◊ the younger generation la nouvelle génération

generator NOUN
le générateur

generous ADJECTIVE
généreux MASC
généreuse FEM
◊ That's very generous of you. C'est très généreux de votre part.

genetic ADJECTIVE
génétique

genetically-modified ADJECTIVE
génétiquement modifié

genetics NOUN
la génétique

Geneva NOUN
Genève
♦ **in Geneva** à Genève
♦ **to Geneva** à Genève
♦ **Lake Geneva** le lac Léman

genius NOUN
le génie ◊ She's a genius! C'est un génie!

gentle ADJECTIVE
doux MASC
douce FEM

gentleman NOUN
le monsieur
(les messieurs PL)
◊ Good morning, gentlemen. Bonjour messieurs.

gently ADVERB
doucement

gents NOUN
les toilettes pour hommes FEM PL
◊ Can you tell me where the gents is, please? Pouvez-vous me dire où sont les toilettes, s'il vous plaît?

♦ **"gents"** (on sign) "messieurs"

genuine ADJECTIVE
1 véritable (real) ◊ These are genuine diamonds. Ce sont de véritables diamants.
2 sincère (sincere) ◊ She's a very genuine person. C'est quelqu'un de très sincère.

geography NOUN
la géographie

germ NOUN
le microbe

German ADJECTIVE
see also **German** NOUN
allemand

German NOUN
see also **German** ADJECTIVE
1 (person)
l' Allemand MASC
l' Allemande FEM
2 (language)
l' allemand ◊ Do you speak German? Parlez-vous allemand?

German measles NOUN
la rubéole

Germany NOUN
l' Allemagne FEM
♦ **in Germany** en Allemagne
♦ **to Germany** en Allemagne

gesture NOUN
le geste

to **get** VERB
There are several ways of translating get. Scan the examples to find one that is similar to what you want to say.
1 avoir (have, receive) ◊ I got lots of presents. J'ai eu beaucoup de cadeaux. ◊ He got first prize. Il a eu le premier prix. ◊ Jackie got good exam results. Jackie a eu de bons résultats aux examens. ◊ How many have you got? Combien en avez-vous?
2 aller chercher (fetch) ◊ Quick, get help! Allez vite chercher de l'aide!
3 attraper (catch) ◊ They've got the thief. Ils ont attrapé le voleur.
4 prendre (train, bus) ◊ I'm getting the bus into town. Je prends le bus pour aller en ville.
5 comprendre (understand) ◊ I don't get the joke. Je ne comprends pas cette blague.
6 aller (go) ◊ How do you get to the castle? Comment est-ce qu'on va au château?
7 arriver (arrive) ◊ He should get here soon. Il devrait arriver bientôt.

8 devenir (become) ◊ to get old
devenir vieux

♦**to something done** faire faire
quelque chose ◊ to get one's hair cut
se faire couper les cheveux

♦**to get something for somebody**
trouver quelque chose pour
quelqu'un ◊ The librarian got the
book for me. Le bibliothécaire m'a
trouvé le livre.

♦**to have got to do something** devoir
faire quelque chose ◊ I've got to tell
him. Je dois le lui dire.

♦**to get away** s'échapper ◊ One of the
burglars got away. L'un des
cambrioleurs s'est échappé.

♦**to get back (1)** rentrer ◊ What time
did you get back? Tu es rentré à
quelle heure?

♦**to get back (2)** récupérer ◊ He got his
money back. Il a récupéré son argent.

♦**to get in** rentrer ◊ What time did you
get in last night? Tu es rentré à
quelle heure hier soir?

♦**to get into** monter dans ◊ Sharon got
into the car. Sharon est montée dans
la voiture.

♦**to get off** descendre de (vehicle, bike)
◊ Isobel got off the train. Isobel est
descendue du train.

♦**to get on (1)** (vehicle) monter dans
◊ Phyllis got on the bus. Phyllis est
montée dans le bus.

♦**to get on (2)** (bike) enfourcher ◊ Carol
got on her bike. Carol a enfourché
son vélo.

♦**to get on with somebody** s'entendre
avec quelqu'un ◊ He doesn't get on
with his parents. Il ne s'entend pas
avec ses parents. ◊ We got on really
well. Nous nous sommes très bien
entendus.

♦**to get out** sortir ◊ Hélène got out of
the car. Hélène est sortie de la
voiture. ◊ Get out! Sortez!

♦**to get something out** sortir quelque
chose ◊ She got the map out. Elle a
sorti la carte.

♦**to get over (1)** se remettre ◊ It took
her a long time to get over the
illness. Il lui a fallu longtemps pour
se remettre de sa maladie.

♦**to get over (2)** surmonter ◊ He
managed to get over the problem. Il
a réussi à résoudre le problème.

♦**to get together** se retrouver ◊ Could
we get together this evening?
Pourrait-on se retrouver ce soir?

♦**to get up** se lever ◊ What time do
you get up? Tu te lèves à quelle
heure?

ghetto blaster NOUN
le radiocassette portable

ghost NOUN
le fantôme

giant ADJECTIVE
see also **giant** NOUN
énorme ◊ They ate a giant meal. Ils
ont mangé un énorme repas.

giant NOUN
see also **giant** ADJECTIVE
le géant
la géante

gift NOUN
1 (present)
le cadeau
(les cadeaux PL)
2 (talent)
le don

♦**to have a gift for something** être
doué pour quelque chose ◊ Dave has
a gift for painting. Dave est doué
pour la peinture.

gifted ADJECTIVE
doué ◊ Janice is a gifted dancer.
Janice est douée pour la danse.

gift shop NOUN
la boutique de cadeaux

gigantic ADJECTIVE
gigantesque

gin NOUN
le gin

ginger NOUN
see also **ginger** ADJECTIVE
le gingembre ◊ Add a teaspoon of
ginger. Ajoutez une cuillère à café de
gingembre.

ginger ADJECTIVE
see also **ginger** NOUN
roux MASC
rousse FEM
◊ Chris has ginger hair. Chris a les
cheveux roux.

giraffe NOUN
la girafe

girl NOUN
1 la fille ◊ They've got a girl and
two boys. Ils ont une fille et deux
garçons.
2 la petite fille (young) ◊ a five-
year-old girl une petite fille de cinq
ans
3 la jeune fille (older) ◊ a sixteen-
year-old girl une jeune fille de seize
ans ◊ an English girl une jeune
Anglaise

girlfriend NOUN
1 la copine (lover) ◊ Damon's
girlfriend is called Justine. La copine
de Damon s'appelle Justine.

G

2 l' amie FEM (friend) ◊ She often
went out with her girlfriends. Elle
sortait souvent avec ses amies.

to **give** VERB
donner
♦**to give something to somebody**
donner quelque chose à quelqu'un
◊ He gave me £10. Il m'a donné dix
livres.
♦**to give something back to somebody**
rendre quelque chose à quelqu'un ◊ I
gave the book back to him. Je lui ai
rendu le livre.
♦**to give something out** distribuer
quelque chose ◊ The teacher gave
out the books. Le professeur a
distribué les livres.
♦**to give in** céder ◊ His Mum gave in
and let him go out. Sa mère a cédé
et l'a laissé sortir.
♦**to give out** distribuer ◊ He gave out
the exam papers. Il a distribué les
sujets d'examen.
♦**to give up** laisser tomber ◊ I couldn't
do it, so I gave up. Je n'arrivais pas
à le faire, alors j'ai laissé tomber.
♦**to give up doing something** arrêter
de faire quelque chose ◊ He gave up
smoking. Il a arrêté de fumer.
♦**to give oneself up** se rendre ◊ The
thief gave himself up. Le voleur s'est
rendu.
♦**to give way** céder la priorité (in traffic)

glad ADJECTIVE
content ◊ She's glad she's done it.
Elle est contente de l'avoir fait.

glamorous ADJECTIVE
1 (person)
glamour MASC, FEM, PL ◊ She's very
glamourous. Elle est très glamour.
2 (job)
prestigieux MASC
prestigieuse FEM
♦**to have a glamorous lifestyle** vivre
comme une star

to **glance** VERB
| see also **glance** NOUN |
♦**to glance at something** jeter un coup
d'œil à quelque chose ◊ Peter
glanced at his watch. Peter a jeté un
coup d'œil à sa montre.

glance NOUN
| see also **glance** VERB |
le coup d'œil ◊ at first glance au
premier coup d'œil

to **glare** VERB
♦**to glare at somebody** lancer un
regard furieux à quelqu'un ◊ He
glared at me. Il m'a lancé un regard
furieux.

glaring ADJECTIVE
♦**a glaring mistake** une erreur qui
saute aux yeux

glass NOUN
le verre ◊ a glass of milk un verre de
lait

glasses PL NOUN
les lunettes FEM PL ◊ Jean-Pierre wears
glasses. Jean-Pierre porte des
lunettes.

glider NOUN
le planeur

gliding NOUN
le vol à voile ◊ My hobby is gliding.
Je fais du vol à voile.

global ADJECTIVE
mondial
(mondiaux MASC PL)
♦**on a global scale** à l'échelle mondiale

global warming NOUN
le réchauffement de la planète

globe NOUN
le globe

gloomy ADJECTIVE
1 morose ◊ She's been feeling very
gloomy recently. Elle se sent très
morose ces derniers temps.
2 lugubre ◊ He lives in a small
gloomy flat. Il habite un petit
appartement lugubre.

glorious ADJECTIVE
magnifique

glove NOUN
le gant

glove compartment NOUN
la boîte à gants

glue NOUN
| see also **glue** VERB |
la colle

to **glue** VERB
| see also **glue** NOUN |
coller

GM ADJECTIVE (= genetically modified)
génétiquement modifié ◊ GM foods
les aliments génétiquement modifiés
MASC

GMO ABBREVIATION (= genetically-
modified organism)
l' OGM MASC (= l'organisme
génétiquement modifié)

go NOUN
| see also **go** VERB |
♦**to have a go at doing something**
essayer de faire quelque chose ◊ He
had a go at making a cake. Il a
essayé de faire un gâteau.
♦**Whose go is it?** À qui le tour?

to **go** VERB

see also **go** NOUN

1 aller ◊ *I'm going to the cinema tonight.* Je vais au cinéma ce soir.

2 partir (*leave*) ◊ *Where's Pierre? – He's gone.* Où est Pierre? – Il est parti.

3 s'en aller (*go away*) ◊ *I'm going now.* Je m'en vais.

4 marcher (*vehicle*) ◊ *My car won't go.* Ma voiture ne marche pas.

♦ **to go home** rentrer à la maison ◊ *I go home at about 4 o'clock.* Je rentre à la maison vers quatre heures.

♦ **to go for a walk** aller se promener ◊ *Shall we go for a walk?* Si on allait se promener?

♦ **How did it go?** Comment est-ce que ça s'est passé?

♦ **I'm going to do it tomorrow.** Je vais le faire demain.

♦ **It's going to be difficult.** Ça va être difficile.

to **go after** VERB

suivre ◊ *Quick, go after them!* Vite, suivez-les!

to **go ahead** VERB

♦ **The meeting will go ahead as planned.** La réunion aura bien lieu comme prévu.

♦ **We'll go ahead with your plan.** Nous allons mettre votre projet à exécution.

♦ **Go ahead!** Vas-y!

to **go away** VERB

s'en aller ◊ *Go away!* Allez-vous-en!

to **go back** VERB

*Use **rentrer** only when you are entering a building, usually your home; otherwise use **retourner**.*

1 retourner ◊ *We went back to the same place.* Nous sommes retournés au même endroit.

2 rentrer ◊ *Is he still here? – No, he's gone back home.* Est-ce qu'il est encore là? – Non, il est rentré chez lui.

to **go by** VERB

passer ◊ *Two policemen went by.* Deux policiers sont passés.

to **go down** VERB

1 descendre (*person*) ◊ *to go down the stairs* descendre l'escalier

2 baisser (*decrease*) ◊ *The price of computers has gone down.* Le prix des ordinateurs a baissé.

3 se dégonfler (*deflate*) ◊ *My airbed kept going down.* Mon matelas pneumatique se dégonflait constamment.

♦ **My brother's gone down with flu.** Mon frère a attrapé la grippe.

to **go for** VERB

attaquer (*attack*) ◊ *Suddenly the dog went for me.* Soudain, le chien m'a attaqué.

♦ **Go for it!** (*go on!*) Vas-y, fonce!

to **go in** VERB

entrer ◊ *He knocked on the door and went in.* Il a frappé à la porte et il est entré.

to **go off** VERB

1 exploser (*bomb*) ◊ *The bomb went off.* La bombe a explosé.

2 se déclencher (*alarm, gun*) ◊ *The fire alarm went off.* L'avertisseur d'incendie s'est déclenché.

3 sonner (*alarm clock*) ◊ *My alarm clock goes off at seven every morning.* Mon réveil sonne à sept heures tous les matins.

4 tourner (*food*) ◊ *The milk's gone off.* Le lait a tourné.

5 partir (*go away*) ◊ *Patrick went off in a huff.* Patrick est parti de mauvaise humeur.

to **go on** VERB

1 se passer (*happen*) ◊ *What's going on?* Qu'est-ce qui se passe?

2 continuer (*carry on*) ◊ *The concert went on until 11 o'clock at night.* Le concert a continué jusqu'à onze heures du soir.

♦ **to go on doing something** continuer à faire quelque chose ◊ *He went on reading.* Il a continué à lire.

♦ **to go on at somebody** être sur le dos de quelqu'un ◊ *My parents always go on at me.* Mes parents sont toujours sur mon dos.

♦ **Go on!** Allez! ◊ *Go on, tell me what the problem is!* Allez, dis-moi quel est le problème!

to **go out** VERB

1 sortir (*person*) ◊ *Are you going out tonight?* Tu sors ce soir?

♦ **to go out with somebody** sortir avec quelqu'un ◊ *Are you going out with him?* Est-ce que tu sors avec lui?

2 s'éteindre (*light, fire, candle*) ◊ *Suddenly the lights went out.* Soudain, les lumières se sont éteintes.

to **go past** VERB

♦ **to go past something** passer devant quelque chose ◊ *He went past the shop.* Il est passé devant la boutique.

to **go round** VERB

♦ **to go round a corner** prendre un tournant

♦ **to go round to somebody's house** aller chez quelqu'un

G

♦**to go round a museum** visiter un musée

♦**to go round the shops** faire les boutiques

♦**There's a bug going round.** Il y a un microbe qui circule.

to **go through** VERB
traverser ◊ *We went through Paris to get to Rennes.* Nous avons traversé Paris pour aller à Rennes.

to **go up** VERB
1 monter (*person*) ◊ *to go up the stairs* monter l'escalier
2 augmenter (*increase*) ◊ *The price has gone up.* Le prix a augmenté.

♦**to go up in flames** s'embraser ◊ *The whole factory went up in flames.* L'usine toute entière s'est embrasée.

to **go with** VERB
aller avec ◊ *Does this blouse go with that skirt?* Est-ce que ce chemisier va avec cette jupe?

goal NOUN
le but ◊ *to score a goal* marquer un but ◊ *His goal is to become the world champion.* Son but est de devenir champion du monde.

goalkeeper NOUN
le gardien de but

goat NOUN
la chèvre

♦**goat's cheese** le fromage de chèvre

god NOUN
le dieu
(les dieux PL)
◊ *I believe in God.* Je crois en Dieu.

goddaughter NOUN
la filleule

godfather NOUN
le parrain

godmother NOUN
la marraine

godson NOUN
le filleul

goggles PL NOUN
1 les lunettes de protection FEM PL
(*of welder, mechanic etc*)
2 les lunettes de plongée FEM PL (*of swimmer*)

gold NOUN
l' or MASC ◊ *They found some gold.* Ils ont trouvé de l'or. ◊ *a gold necklace* un collier en or

goldfish NOUN
le poisson rouge ◊ *I've got five goldfish.* J'ai cinq poissons rouges.

gold-plated ADJECTIVE
plaqué or MASC
plaquée or FEM

golf NOUN
le golf ◊ *My dad plays golf.* Mon père joue au golf.

♦**a golf club** un club de golf

golf course NOUN
le terrain de golf

gone VERB *see* go

good ADJECTIVE
1 bon MASC
bonne FEM
◊ *It's a very good film.* C'est un très bon film. ◊ *Vegetables are good for you.* Les légumes sont bons pour la santé.

♦**to be good at something** être bon en quelque chose ◊ *Jane's very good at maths.* Jane est très bonne en maths.
2 (*kind*)
gentil MASC
gentille FEM
◊ *They were very good to me.* Ils ont été très gentils avec moi. ◊ *That's very good of you.* C'est très gentil de votre part.
3 (*not naughty*)
sage ◊ *Be good!* Sois sage!

♦**for good** pour de bon ◊ *One day he left for good.* Un jour il est parti pour de bon.

♦**Good morning!** Bonjour!

♦**Good afternoon!** Bonjour!

♦**Good evening!** Bonsoir!

♦**Good night!** Bonne nuit!

♦**It's no good complaining.** Cela ne sert à rien de se plaindre.

goodbye EXCLAMATION
au revoir!

Good Friday NOUN
le Vendredi saint

good-looking ADJECTIVE
beau MASC
belle FEM
(beaux MASC PL)
◊ *He's very good-looking.* Il est très beau.

good-natured ADJECTIVE
facile à vivre (*person*)

goods PL NOUN
les marchandises FEM PL (*in shop*)

♦**a goods train** un train de marchandises

goose NOUN
l' oie FEM

gooseberry NOUN
la groseille à maquereau

gorgeous ADJECTIVE
1 superbe ◊ *She's gorgeous!* Elle est superbe!

2 splendide ◊ *The weather was gorgeous.* Il a fait un temps splendide.

gorilla NOUN
le gorille

gospel NOUN
le gospel (*music*)

gossip NOUN

see also **gossip** VERB

1 les cancans MASC PL (*rumours*) ◊ *Tell me the gossip!* Raconte-moi les cancans!

2 la commère (*woman*) ◊ *She's such a gossip!* C'est une vraie commère!

3 le bavard (*man*) ◊ *What a gossip!* Quel bavard!

to **gossip** VERB

see also **gossip** NOUN

1 bavarder (*chat*) ◊ *They were always gossiping.* Elles étaient tout le temps en train de bavarder.

2 faire des commérages (*about somebody*) ◊ *They gossiped about her.* Elles faisaient des commérages à son sujet.

got VERB *see* **get**

gotten VERB US *see* **get**

government NOUN
le gouvernement

GP NOUN
le médecin généraliste

to **grab** VERB
saisir

graceful ADJECTIVE
élégant

grade NOUN
la note (*at school*) ◊ *He got good grades in his exams this year.* Il a eu de bonnes notes à ses examens cette année.

grade school NOUN US
l'école primaire FEM

gradual ADJECTIVE
progressif MASC
progressive FEM

gradually ADVERB
peu à peu ◊ *We gradually got used to it.* Nous nous y sommes habitués peu à peu.

graduate NOUN
1 (*from university*)
le diplômé
la diplômée
2 (*from US high school*)
le bachelier
la bachelière

graffiti PL NOUN
les graffiti MASC PL

grain NOUN
le grain

gram NOUN
le gramme

grammar NOUN
la grammaire

grammar school NOUN
1 le collège
2 le lycée

ⓘ *In France pupils go to a **collège** between the ages of 11 and 15, and then to a **lycée** until the age of 18. French schools are mostly non-selective.*

grammatical ADJECTIVE
grammatical
(grammaticaux MASC PL)

gramme NOUN
le gramme ◊ *500 grammes of cheese* cinq cents grammes de fromage

grand ADJECTIVE
somptueux MASC
somptueuse FEM
◊ *Samantha lives in a very grand house.* Samantha habite une maison somptueuse.

grandchild NOUN
le petit-fils
la petite-fille
♦ **my grandchildren** mes petits-enfants MASC

granddad NOUN
le papi ◊ *my granddad* mon papi

granddaughter NOUN
la petite-fille
(les petites-filles PL)

grandfather NOUN
le grand-père
(les grands-pères PL)
◊ *my grandfather* mon grand-père

grandma NOUN
la mamie ◊ *my grandma* ma mamie

grandmother NOUN
la grand-mère
(les grands-mères PL)
◊ *my grandmother* ma grand-mère

grandpa NOUN
le papi ◊ *my grandpa* mon papi

grandparents PL NOUN
les grands-parents MASC PL ◊ *my grandparents* mes grands-parents

grandson NOUN
le petit-fils
(les petits-fils PL)

granny NOUN
la mamie ◊ *my granny* ma mamie

grant NOUN

G

☞

la bourse

grape NOUN
le raisin

grapefruit NOUN
le pamplemousse

graph NOUN
le graphique

graphics PL NOUN
les images de synthèse FEM PL ◊ *I designed the graphics, she wrote the text.* J'ai conçu les images de synthèse, elle a écrit le texte.
♦ **He works in computer graphics.** Il fait de l'infographie.

to **grasp** VERB
saisir

grass NOUN
l' herbe FEM ◊ *The grass is long.* L'herbe est haute.
♦ **to cut the grass** tondre le gazon

grasshopper NOUN
la sauterelle

to **grate** VERB
râper ◊ *to grate some cheese* râper du fromage

grateful ADJECTIVE
reconnaissant

grave NOUN
la tombe

gravel NOUN
le gravier

graveyard NOUN
le cimetière

gravy NOUN
la sauce au jus de viande

grease NOUN
le lubrifiant

greasy ADJECTIVE
gras MASC
grasse FEM
◊ *He has greasy hair.* Il a les cheveux gras. ◊ *The food was very greasy.* la nourriture était très grasse.

great ADJECTIVE
1 génial
(géniaux MASC PL)
◊ *That's great!* C'est génial!
2 grand ◊ *a great mansion* un grand manoir

Great Britain NOUN
la Grande-Bretagne
♦ **in Great Britain** en Grande-Bretagne
♦ **to Great Britain** en Grande-Bretagne
♦ **I'm from Great Britain.** Je suis britannique.

great-grandfather NOUN
l' arrière-grand-père MASC
(les arrière-grands-pères PL)

great-grandmother NOUN
l' arrière-grand-mère FEM
(les arrière-grands-mères PL)

Greece NOUN
la Grèce
♦ **in Greece** en Grèce
♦ **to Greece** en Grèce

greedy ADJECTIVE
1 gourmand (*for food*) ◊ *I want some more cake. – Don't be so greedy!* Je veux encore du gâteau. – Ne sois pas si gourmand!
2 avide (*for money*)

Greek ADJECTIVE
see also **Greek** NOUN
grec MASC
grecque FEM
◊ *Dionysis is Greek.* Dionysis est grec.
◊ *She's Greek.* Elle est grecque.

Greek NOUN
see also **Greek** ADJECTIVE
1 (*person*)
le Grec
la Grecque
2 (*language*)
le grec

green ADJECTIVE
see also **green** NOUN
1 vert ◊ *a green car* une voiture verte ◊ *a green light* un feu vert ◊ *a green salad* une salade verte
2 écologiste (*movement, candidate*)
◊ *the Green Party* le parti écologiste

green NOUN
see also **green** ADJECTIVE
le vert ◊ *a dark green* un vert foncé
♦ **greens** (*vegetables*) les légumes verts MASC
♦ **the Greens** (*party*) les Verts MASC

greengrocer's NOUN
le marchand de fruits et légumes

greenhouse NOUN
la serre
♦ **the greenhouse effect** l'effet de serre MASC

Greenland NOUN
le Groenland

to **greet** VERB
accueillir ◊ *He greeted me with a kiss.* Il m'a accueillie en me donnant un baiser.

greeting NOUN
♦ **Greetings from Bangor!** Bonjour de Bangor!
♦ **"Season's greetings"** "Meilleurs vœux pour les fêtes de fin d'année"

greetings card NOUN
la carte de vœux

grew VERB *see* **grow**

grey ADJECTIVE
<u>gris</u> ◊ *She's got grey hair.* Elle a les cheveux gris.
♦He's going grey. Il grisonne.

grey-haired ADJECTIVE
<u>grisonnant</u>

grid NOUN
[1] (*in road*)
la <u>grille</u>
[2] (*of electricity*)
le <u>réseau</u>
(les réseaux PL)

grief NOUN
le <u>chagrin</u>

grill NOUN
see also **grill** VERB
le <u>gril</u> (*of cooker*)
♦a mixed grill les grillades FEM PL

to **grill** VERB
see also **grill** NOUN
♦to grill something faire griller quelque chose

grim ADJECTIVE
<u>sinistre</u>

to **grin** VERB
see also **grin** NOUN
<u>sourire</u> ◊ *Dave grinned at me.* Dave m'a souri.

grin NOUN
see also **grin** VERB
le <u>large sourire</u>

to **grind** VERB
<u>moudre</u> (*coffee, pepper*)

to **grip** VERB
<u>saisir</u>

gripping ADJECTIVE
<u>palpitant</u> (*exciting*)

grit NOUN
le <u>gravillon</u>

to **groan** VERB
see also **groan** NOUN
<u>gémir</u> ◊ *He groaned with pain.* Il a gémi sous l'effet de la douleur.

groan NOUN
see also **groan** VERB
le <u>gémissement</u> (*of pain*)

grocer NOUN
l' <u>épicier</u> MASC ◊ *He's a grocer.* Il est épicier.

groceries PL NOUN
les <u>provisions</u> FEM PL

grocer's (shop) NOUN
l' <u>épicerie</u> FEM

grocery store NOUN US
l' <u>épicerie</u> FEM

groom NOUN

le <u>marié</u> (*bridegroom*) ◊ *the groom and his best man* le marié et son témoin

to **grope** VERB
♦to grope for something chercher quelque chose à tâtons ◊ *He groped for the light switch.* Il a cherché à tâtons l'interrupteur.

gross ADJECTIVE
<u>dégoûtant</u> (*revolting*) ◊ *It was really gross!* C'était vraiment dégoûtant!

grossly ADVERB
<u>largement</u> ◊ *We're grossly underpaid.* Nous sommes largement sous-payés.

ground NOUN
see also **ground** VERB
[1] le <u>sol</u> (*earth*) ◊ *The ground's wet.* Le sol est mouillé.
[2] le <u>terrain</u> (*for sport*) ◊ *a football ground* un terrain de football
[3] la <u>raison</u> (*reason*) ◊ *We've got grounds for complaint.* Nous avons des raisons de nous plaindre.
♦on the ground par terre ◊ *We sat on the ground.* Nous nous sommes assis par terre.

ground VERB see **grind**
see also **ground** NOUN
♦ground coffee le café moulu

ground floor NOUN
le <u>rez-de-chaussée</u>
♦on the ground floor au rez-de-chaussée

group NOUN
le <u>groupe</u>

to **grow** VERB
[1] <u>pousser</u> (*plant*) ◊ *Grass grows quickly.* L'herbe pousse vite.
[2] <u>grandir</u> (*person, animal*) ◊ *Haven't you grown!* Comme tu as grandi!
[3] <u>augmenter</u> (*increase*) ◊ *The number of unemployed people has grown.* Le nombre de chômeurs a augmenté.
[4] <u>faire pousser</u> (*cultivate*) ◊ *My Dad grows potatoes.* Mon père fait pousser des pommes de terre.
♦to grow a beard se laisser pousser la barbe
♦to grow up grandir ◊ *Oh, grow up!* Ne fais pas l'enfant!
♦He's grown out of his jacket. Sa veste est devenue trop petite pour lui.

to **growl** VERB
<u>grogner</u>

grown VERB see **grow**

growth NOUN

G

la croissance ◊ *economic growth* la
croissance économique

grub NOUN
la bouffe (*informal*)

grudge NOUN
la rancune
♦ **to bear a grudge against somebody**
garder rancune à quelqu'un

gruesome ADJECTIVE
horrible

guarantee NOUN
see also **guarantee** VERB
la garantie
♦ **a five-year guarantee** une garantie de
cinq ans

to **guarantee** VERB
see also **guarantee** NOUN
garantir ◊ *I can't guarantee he'll
come.* Je ne peux pas garantir qu'il
viendra.

to **guard** VERB
see also **guard** NOUN
garder ◊ *They guarded the palace.* Ils
gardaient le palais.
♦ **to guard against something** protéger
contre quelque chose

guard NOUN
see also **guard** VERB
le chef de train (*of train*)
♦ **a security guard** un vigile
♦ **a guard dog** un chien de garde

to **guess** VERB
see also **guess** NOUN
deviner ◊ *Can you guess what it is?*
Devine ce que c'est!
♦ **to guess wrong** se tromper ◊ *Janice
guessed wrong.* Janice s'est trompée.

guess NOUN
see also **guess** VERB
la supposition ◊ *It's just a guess.*
C'est une simple supposition.
♦ **Have a guess!** Devine!

guest NOUN
[1] l' invité MASC
l' invitée FEM
◊ *We have guests staying with us.*
Nous avons des invités.
[2] (*of hotel*)
le client
la cliente

guesthouse NOUN

le petit hôtel

guide NOUN
[1] le guide (*book, person*) ◊ *We
bought a guide to Paris.* Nous avons
acheté un guide sur Paris. ◊ *The
guide showed us round the castle.* Le
guide nous a fait visiter le château.
[2] l' éclaireuse FEM (*girl guide*)
♦ **the Guides** les Éclaireuses

guidebook NOUN
le guide

guide dog NOUN
le chien d'aveugle

guilty ADJECTIVE
coupable ◊ *to feel guilty* se sentir
coupable ◊ *She was found guilty.* Elle
a été reconnue coupable.

guinea pig NOUN
le cobaye

guitar NOUN
la guitare ◊ *I play the guitar.* Je joue
de la guitare.

gum NOUN
le chewing-gum (*sweet*)
♦ **gums** (*in mouth*) les gencives FEM

gun NOUN
[1] le revolver (*small*)
[2] le fusil (*rifle*)

gunpoint NOUN
♦ **at gunpoint** sous la menace d'une
arme

gust NOUN
♦ **a gust of wind** une rafale de vent

guy NOUN
le type ◊ *Who's that guy?* C'est qui
ce type? ◊ *He's a nice guy.* C'est un
type sympa.

gym NOUN
la gym ◊ *Emma goes to the gym
every day.* Emma va tous les jours à
la gym.
♦ **gym classes** les cours de gym MASC

gymnast NOUN
le/la gymnaste ◊ *She's a gymnast.*
Elle est gymnaste.

gymnastics NOUN
la gymnastique ◊ *to do gymnastics*
faire de la gymnastique

gypsy NOUN
le/la Tzigane

H

habit NOUN
l' habitude FEM ◊ *a bad habit* une mauvaise habitude

to **hack** VERB
◆**to hack into a system** s'introduire dans un système

hacker NOUN
le/la pirate informatique

had VERB *see* **have**

haddock NOUN
l' églefin MASC

hadn't = **had not**

hail NOUN

> *see also* **hail** VERB

la grêle

to **hail** VERB

> *see also* **hail** NOUN

grêler ◊ *It's hailing.* Il grêle.

hair NOUN
1 les cheveux MASC PL ◊ *She's got long hair.* Elle a les cheveux longs. ◊ *He's got black hair.* Il a les cheveux noirs. ◊ *He's losing his hair.* Il perd ses cheveux.
◆**to brush one's hair** se brosser les cheveux ◊ *I brush my hair every morning.* Je me brosse les cheveux tous les matins.
◆**to wash one's hair** se laver les cheveux ◊ *I need to wash my hair.* Il faut que je me lave les cheveux.
◆**to have one's hair cut** se faire couper les cheveux ◊ *I've just had my hair cut.* Je viens de me faire couper les cheveux.
◆**a hair (1)** (*from head*) un cheveu
◆**a hair (2)** (*from body*) un poil
2 le pelage (*fur of animal*)

hairbrush NOUN
la brosse à cheveux

haircut NOUN
la coupe
◆**to have a haircut** se faire couper les cheveux ◊ *I've just had a haircut.* Je viens de me faire couper les cheveux.

hairdresser NOUN
le coiffeur
la coiffeuse
◊ *He's a hairdresser.* Il est coiffeur.

hairdresser's NOUN
le coiffeur ◊ *at the hairdresser's* chez le coiffeur

hair dryer NOUN
le sèche-cheveux

(les sèche-cheveux PL)

hair gel NOUN
le gel pour les cheveux

hairgrip NOUN
la pince à cheveux

hair spray NOUN
la laque

hairstyle NOUN
la coiffure

hairy ADJECTIVE
poilu ◊ *He's got hairy legs.* Il a les jambes poilues.

half NOUN

> *see also* **half** ADJECTIVE

1 la moitié ◊ *half of the cake* la moitié du gâteau
2 le billet demi-tarif (*ticket*) ◊ *A half to York, please.* Un billet demi-tarif pour York, s'il vous plaît.
◆**two and a half** deux et demi
◆**half an hour** une demi-heure
◆**half past ten** dix heures et demie
◆**half a kilo** cinq cents grammes
◆**to cut something in half** couper quelque chose en deux

half ADJECTIVE, ADVERB

> *see also* **half** NOUN

1 demi ◊ *a half chicken* un demi-poulet
2 à moitié ◊ *He was half asleep.* Il était à moitié endormi.

half-hour NOUN
la demi-heure

half-price ADJECTIVE, ADVERB
◆**at half-price** à moitié prix

half-term NOUN
les petites vacances FEM PL
◆**What are you planning to do at half-term?** Qu'as-tu prévu de faire pendant les petites vacances ?

half-time NOUN
la mi-temps

halfway ADVERB
1 à mi-chemin ◊ *halfway between Oxford and London* à mi-chemin entre Oxford et Londres
2 à la moitié ◊ *halfway through the chapter* à la moitié du chapitre

hall NOUN
1 l' entrée FEM (*in house*)
2 la salle ◊ *the village hall* la salle des fêtes

Hallowe'en NOUN
la veille de la Toussaint

hallway NOUN
le vestibule

halt NOUN
◆ **to come to a halt** s'arrêter

ham NOUN
le jambon
◆ **a ham sandwich** un sandwich au jambon

hamburger NOUN
le hamburger

hammer NOUN
le marteau
(les marteaux PL)

hamster NOUN
le hamster

hand NOUN
see also **hand** VERB
1 la main (of person)
◆ **to give somebody a hand** donner un coup de main à quelqu'un ◇ Can you give me a hand? Tu peux me donner un coup de main?
◆ **on the one hand ..., on the other hand ...** d'une part ..., d'autre part ...
2 l' aiguille FEM (of clock)

to **hand** VERB
see also **hand** NOUN
passer ◇ He handed me the book. Il m'a passé le livre.
◆ **to hand something in** rendre quelque chose ◇ Martin handed his exam paper in. Martin a rendu sa copie d'examen.
◆ **to hand something out** distribuer quelque chose ◇ The teacher handed out the books. Le professeur a distribué les livres.
◆ **to hand something over** remettre quelque chose ◇ She handed the keys over to me. Elle m'a remis les clés.

handbag NOUN
le sac à main
(les sacs à main PL)

handball NOUN
le handball (game)
◆ **to play handball** jouer au handball

handbook NOUN
le manuel

handcuffs PL NOUN
les menottes FEM PL

handkerchief NOUN
le mouchoir

handle NOUN
see also **handle** VERB
1 la poignée (of door)
2 l' anse FEM (of cup)
3 le manche (of knife)
4 la queue (of saucepan)

to **handle** VERB
see also **handle** NOUN
◆ **He handled it well.** Il s'en est bien tiré.
◆ **Kath handled the travel arrangements.** Kath s'est occupée de l'organisation du voyage.
◆ **She's good at handling children.** Elle sait s'y prendre bien avec les enfants.

handlebars PL NOUN
le guidon SING

handmade ADJECTIVE
fait à la main

handsome ADJECTIVE
beau MASC
belle FEM
◇ He's very handsome. Il est très beau.

handwriting NOUN
l' écriture FEM

handy ADJECTIVE
1 pratique ◇ This knife's very handy. Ce couteau est très pratique.
2 sous la main ◇ Have you got a pen handy? Est-ce que tu as un stylo sous la main?

to **hang** VERB
1 accrocher ◇ Mike hung the painting on the wall. Mike a accroché le tableau au mur.
2 pendre ◇ They hanged the criminal. Ils ont pendu le criminel.
◆ **to hang around** traîner ◇ On Saturdays we hang around in the park. Le samedi nous traînons dans le parc.
◆ **to hang on** patienter ◇ Hang on a minute please. Patientez une minute s'il vous plaît.
◆ **to hang up (1)** (clothes) accrocher ◇ Hang your jacket up on the hook. Accrochez votre veste au portemanteau.
◆ **to hang up (2)** (phone) raccrocher ◇ I tried to phone him but he hung up on me. J'ai essayé de l'appeler, mais il m'a raccroché au nez.

hanger NOUN
le cintre (coat hanger)

hang-gliding NOUN
le deltaplane
◆ **to go hang-gliding** faire du deltaplane

hangover NOUN
la gueule de bois ◇ to have a hangover avoir la gueule de bois

to **happen** VERB
se passer ◇ What's happened? Qu'est-ce qui s'est passé?

◆**as it happens** justement ◊ *As it happens, I don't want to go.* Justement, je ne veux pas y aller.

happily ADVERB
  [1] joyeusement ◊ *"Don't worry!" he said happily.* "Ne te fais pas de souci!" dit-il joyeusement.
  [2] heureusement (*fortunately*) ◊ *Happily, everything went well.* Heureusement, tout s'est bien passé.

happiness NOUN
  le bonheur

happy ADJECTIVE
  heureux MASC
  heureuse FEM
  ◊ *Janet looks happy.* Janet a l'air heureuse.
◆**I'm very happy with your work.** Je suis très satisfait de ton travail.
◆**Happy birthday!** Bon anniversaire!

harassment NOUN
  le harcèlement ◊ *police harassment* le harcèlement policier

harbour NOUN (US **harbor**)
  le port

hard ADJECTIVE, ADVERB
  [1] dur ◊ *This cheese is very hard.* Ce fromage est très dur. ◊ *He's worked very hard.* Il a travaillé très dur.
  [2] difficile ◊ *This question's too hard for me.* Cette question est trop difficile pour moi.

hard disk NOUN
  le disque dur (*of computer*)

hardly ADVERB
◆**I've hardly got any money.** Je n'ai presque pas d'argent.
◆**I hardly know you.** Je te connais à peine.
◆**hardly ever** presque jamais

hard up ADJECTIVE
  fauché

hardware NOUN
  le hardware (*computing*)

hare NOUN
  le lièvre

to **harm** VERB
◆**to harm somebody** faire du mal à quelqu'un ◊ *I didn't mean to harm you.* Je ne voulais pas te faire de mal.
◆**to harm something** nuire à quelque chose ◊ *Chemicals harm the environment.* Les produits chimiques nuisent à l'environnement.

harmful ADJECTIVE
  nuisible ◊ *harmful chemicals* des produits chimiques nuisibles

harmless ADJECTIVE
  inoffensif MASC
  inoffensive FEM
  ◊ *Most spiders are harmless.* La plupart des araignées sont inoffensives.

harsh ADJECTIVE
  dur

has VERB *see* **have**

hasn't = **has not**

hat NOUN
  le chapeau
  (les chapeaux PL)

to **hate** VERB
  détester ◊ *I hate maths.* Je déteste les maths.

hatred NOUN
  la haine

haunted ADJECTIVE
  hanté
◆**a haunted house** une maison hantée

to **have** VERB
  [1] avoir ◊ *Have you got a sister?* Tu as une sœur? ◊ *He's got blue eyes.* Il a les yeux bleus. ◊ *I've got a cold.* J'ai un rhume. ◊ *He's done it, hasn't he?* Il l'a fait, non? ◊ *Have you got any money? – No, I haven't!* Est-ce que tu as de l'argent? – Non, je n'en ai pas!
  The perfect tense of some verbs is formed with être.
  [2] être ◊ *They have arrived.* Ils sont arrivés. ◊ *Has he gone?* Est-ce qu'il est parti?
  [3] prendre ◊ *He had his breakfast.* Il a pris son petit déjeuner. ◊ *to have a shower* prendre une douche
◆**to have got to do something** devoir faire quelque chose ◊ *She's got to do it.* Elle doit le faire.
◆**to have a party** faire une fête
◆**to have one's hair cut** se faire couper les cheveux

haven't = **have not**

hay NOUN
  le foin

hay fever NOUN
  le rhume des foins ◊ *Do you get hay fever?* Est-ce que vous êtes sujet au rhume des foins?

hazelnut NOUN
  la noisette

he PRONOUN
  il ◊ *He loves dogs.* Il aime les chiens.

head NOUN
  see also **head** VERB
  [1] (*of person*)
  la tête ◊ *The wine went to my head.* Le vin m'est monté à la tête.

H

2 (of private or primary school)
le <u>directeur</u>
la <u>directrice</u>
3 (of state secondary school)
le <u>proviseur</u>
4 (leader)
le <u>chef</u> ◇ a head of state un chef
d'État
♦ **to have a head for figures** être doué
pour les chiffres
♦ **Heads or tails? – Heads.** Pile ou face? –
Face.

to **head** VERB

see also **head** NOUN

♦ **to head for something** se diriger vers
quelque chose ◇ They headed for the
church. Ils se sont dirigés vers
l'église.

headache NOUN
♦ **I've got a headache.** J'ai mal à la
tête.

headlight NOUN
le <u>phare</u>

headline NOUN
le <u>titre</u>

headmaster NOUN
1 le <u>directeur</u> (of private or primary
school)
2 le <u>proviseur</u> (of state secondary
school)

headmistress NOUN
1 la <u>directrice</u> (of private or primary
school)
2 le <u>proviseur</u> (of state secondary
school)

headphones PL NOUN
les <u>écouteurs</u> MASC PL

headquarters PL NOUN
le <u>siège</u> SING (of organization)

headteacher NOUN
1 (of private or primary school)
le <u>directeur</u>
la <u>directrice</u>
2 (of state secondary school)
le <u>proviseur</u>
◇ She's a headteacher. Elle est
proviseur.

to **heal** VERB
<u>cicatriser</u> ◇ The wound soon healed.
La blessure a vite cicatrisé.

health NOUN
la <u>santé</u>

healthy ADJECTIVE
1 <u>en bonne santé</u> (person) ◇ Lesley's
a healthy person. Lesley est en
bonne santé.
2 <u>sain</u> (climate, food) ◇ a healthy diet
une alimentation saine

heap NOUN

le <u>tas</u> ◇ a rubbish heap un tas
d'ordures

to **hear** VERB
1 <u>entendre</u> ◇ He heard the dog bark.
Il a entendu le chien aboyer. ◇ She
can't hear very well. Elle entend mal.
◇ I heard that she was ill. J'ai
entendu dire qu'elle était malade.
♦ **to hear about something** entendre
parler de quelque chose
2 <u>apprendre</u> (news) ◇ Did you hear
the good news? Est-ce que tu as
appris la bonne nouvelle?
♦ **to hear from somebody** avoir des
nouvelles de quelqu'un ◇ I haven't
heard from him recently. Je n'ai pas
eu de ses nouvelles récemment.

heart NOUN
le <u>cœur</u>
♦ **to learn something by heart**
apprendre quelque chose par cœur
♦ **the ace of hearts** l'as de cœur

heart attack NOUN
la <u>crise cardiaque</u>

heartbroken ADJECTIVE
♦ **to be heartbroken** avoir le cœur brisé

heat NOUN

see also **heat** VERB

la <u>chaleur</u>

to **heat** VERB

see also **heat** NOUN

<u>faire chauffer</u> ◇ Heat gently for 5
minutes. Faire chauffer à feu doux
pendant cinq minutes.
♦ **to heat up (1)** (cooked food) faire
réchauffer ◇ He heated the soup up. Il
a fait réchauffer la soupe.
♦ **to heat up (2)** (water, oven) chauffer
◇ The water is heating up. L'eau
chauffe.

heater NOUN
le <u>radiateur</u> ◇ an electric heater un
radiateur électrique

heather NOUN
la <u>bruyère</u>

heating NOUN
le <u>chauffage</u>

heaven NOUN
le <u>paradis</u>

heavily ADVERB
<u>lourdement</u> ◇ The car was heavily
loaded. La voiture était lourdement
chargée.
♦ **He drinks heavily.** C'est un gros
buveur.

heavy ADJECTIVE
1 <u>lourd</u> ◇ This bag's very heavy. Ce
sac est très lourd.
♦ **heavy rain** une grosse averse

2 **chargé** (*busy*) ◊ *I've got a very heavy week ahead.* Je vais avoir une semaine très chargée.

♦**to be a heavy drinker** être un gros buveur

he'd = **he would**, = **he had**

hedge NOUN
la haie

hedgehog NOUN
le hérisson

heel NOUN
le talon

height NOUN
1 la taille (*of person*)
2 la hauteur (*of object*)
3 l' altitude FEM (*of mountain*)

heir NOUN
l' héritier MASC

heiress NOUN
l' héritière FEM

held VERB *see* hold

helicopter NOUN
l' hélicoptère MASC

hell NOUN
l' enfer MASC
♦**Hell!** merde! (*rude*)

he'll = **he will**, = **he shall**

hello EXCLAMATION
bonjour!

helmet NOUN
le casque

to **help** VERB
  see also **help** NOUN
aider ◊ *Can you help me?* Est-ce que vous pouvez m'aider?
♦**Help!** Au secours!
♦**Help yourself!** Servez-vous!
♦**He can't help it.** Il n'y peut rien.

help NOUN
  see also **help** VERB
l' aide FEM ◊ *Do you need any help?* Vous avez besoin d'aide?

helpful ADJECTIVE
serviable ◊ *He was very helpful.* Il a été très serviable.

hen NOUN
la poule

her ADJECTIVE
  see also **her** PRONOUN
son MASC ◊ *her father* son père
sa FEM ◊ *her mother* sa mère
ses PL ◊ *her parents* ses parents
sa becomes son before a vowel sound.
♦**her friend (1)** (*male*) son ami
♦**her friend (2)** (*female*) son amie
Do not use son/sa/ses with parts of the body.

◊ *She's going to wash her hair.* Elle va se laver les cheveux. ◊ *She's cleaning her teeth.* Elle se brosse les dents. ◊ *She's hurt her foot.* Elle s'est fait mal au pied.

her PRONOUN
  see also **her** ADJECTIVE
la becomes l' before a vowel sound.
1 la ◊ *I can see her.* Je la vois.
◊ *Look at her!* Regarde-la!
l' ◊ *I saw her.* Je l'ai vue.
Use lui when her means to her.
2 lui ◊ *I gave her a book.* Je lui ai donné un livre. ◊ *I told her the truth.* Je lui ai dit la vérité.
Use elle after prepositions.
3 elle ◊ *I'm going with her.* Je vais avec elle. ◊ *He sat next to her.* Il s'est assis à côté d'elle.
elle is also used in comparisons.
◊ *I'm older than her.* Je suis plus âgé qu'elle.

herb NOUN
l' herbe FEM
♦**herbs** les fines herbes ◊ *What herbs do you use in this sauce?* Quelles fines herbes utilise-t-on pour cette sauce?

here ADVERB
ici ◊ *I live here.* J'habite ici.
♦**here is ...** voici ... ◊ *Here's Helen.* Voici Helen. ◊ *Here he is!* Le voici!
♦**here are ...** voici ... ◊ *Here are the books.* Voici les livres.

heritage NOUN
le patrimoine

hero NOUN
le héros ◊ *He's a real hero!* C'est un véritable héros!

heroin NOUN
l' héroïne FEM ◊ *Heroin is a hard drug.* L'héroïne est une drogue dure.
♦**a heroin addict** un héroïnomane ◊ *She's a heroin addict.* C'est une héroïnomane.

heroine NOUN
l' héroïne FEM ◊ *the heroine of the novel* l'héroïne du roman

hers PRONOUN
le sien + MASC NOUN ◊ *Is this her coat? – No, hers is black.* C'est son manteau? – Non, le sien est noir.
la sienne + FEM NOUN ◊ *Is this her car? – No, hers is white.* C'est sa voiture? – Non, la sienne est blanche.
les siens + MASC PL NOUN ◊ *my parents and hers* mes parents et les siens
les siennes + FEM PL NOUN ◊ *my reasons and hers* mes raisons et les siennes

H

☞

♦**Is this hers?** C'est à elle? ◊ *This book is hers.* Ce livre est à elle. ◊ *Whose is this? – It's hers.* C'est à qui? – À elle.

herself PRONOUN
1 se ◊ *She's hurt herself.* Elle s'est blessée.
2 elle (*after preposition*) ◊ *She talked mainly about herself.* Elle a surtout parlé d'elle.
3 elle-même ◊ *She did it herself.* Elle l'a fait elle-même.
♦**by herself** toute seule ◊ *She doesn't like travelling by herself.* Elle n'aime pas voyager toute seule.

he's = **he is,** = **he has**

to **hesitate** VERB
hésiter

heterosexual ADJECTIVE
hétérosexuel MASC
hétérosexuelle FEM

hi EXCLAMATION
salut!

hiccups PL NOUN
♦**to have hiccups** avoir le hoquet

to **hide** VERB
se cacher ◊ *He hid behind a bush.* Il s'est caché derrière un buisson.
♦**to hide something** cacher quelque chose ◊ *Paula hid the present.* Paula a caché le cadeau.

hide-and-seek NOUN
♦**to play hide-and-seek** jouer à cache-cache

hideous ADJECTIVE
hideux MASC
hideuse FEM

hi-fi NOUN
la chaîne hi-fi
(les chaînes hi-fi PL)

high ADJECTIVE, ADVERB
1 haut ◊ *It's too high.* C'est trop haut.
♦**How high is the wall?** Quelle est la hauteur du mur?
♦**The wall's 2 metres high.** Le mur fait deux mètres de haut.
2 élevé ◊ *a high price* un prix élevé ◊ *a high temperature* une température élevée
♦**at high speed** à grande vitesse
♦**It's very high in fat.** C'est très gras.
♦**She's got a very high voice.** Elle a la voix très aiguë.
♦**to be high** (*on drugs*) être défoncé (*informal*)
♦**to get high** se défoncer (*informal*) ◊ *to get high on crack* se défoncer au crack

higher education NOUN

l' enseignement supérieur MASC

high-heeled ADJECTIVE
à hauts talons
♦**high-heeled shoes** des chaussures à hauts talons

high jump NOUN
le saut en hauteur (*sport*)

highlight NOUN
see also **highlight** VERB
le clou ◊ *the highlight of the evening* le clou de la soirée

to **highlight** VERB
see also **highlight** NOUN
1 souligner (*underline*)
2 surligner (*with highlighter pen*)

highlighter NOUN
le surligneur

high-rise NOUN
la tour ◊ *I live in a high-rise.* J'habite dans une tour.

high school NOUN
le lycée

to **hijack** VERB
détourner

hijacker NOUN
le pirate de l'air

hike NOUN
la randonnée

hiking NOUN
♦**to go hiking** faire une randonnée

hilarious ADJECTIVE
hilarant ◊ *It was hilarious!* C'était hilarant!

hill NOUN
la colline ◊ *She walked up the hill.* Elle a gravi la colline.

hill-walking NOUN
la randonnée de basse montagne ◊ *to go hill-walking* faire de la randonnée de basse montagne

him PRONOUN
le becomes l' before a vowel sound.
1 le ◊ *I can see him.* Je le vois.
◊ *Look at him!* Regarde-le!
l' ◊ *I saw him.* Je l'ai vu.
*Use **lui** when **him** means **to him,** and after prepositions.*
2 lui ◊ *I gave him a book.* Je lui ai donné un livre. ◊ *I told him the truth.* Je lui ai dit la vérité. ◊ *I'm going with him.* Je vais avec lui. ◊ *She sat next to him.* Elle s'est assise à côté de lui.
lui is also used in comparisons.
◊ *I'm older than him.* Je suis plus âgé que lui.

himself PRONOUN

[1] se ◇ *He's hurt himself.* Il s'est
blessé.
[2] lui ◇ *He talked mainly about
himself.* Il a surtout parlé de lui.
[3] lui-même ◇ *He did it himself.* Il l'a
fait lui-même.
♦**by himself** tout seul ◇ *He was
travelling by himself.* Il voyageait tout
seul.

Hindu ADJECTIVE
hindou ◇ *a Hindu temple* un temple
hindou

hint NOUN
see also **hint** VERB
l' allusion FEM
♦**to drop a hint** faire une allusion

to **hint** VERB
see also **hint** NOUN
laisser entendre ◇ *He hinted that I
had a good chance of getting the job.*
Il m'a laissé entendre que j'avais de
grandes chances d'avoir ce travail.
♦**What are you hinting at?** Qu'est-ce
que vous voulez dire par là ?

hip NOUN
la hanche

hippie NOUN
le hippie
la hippie

hippo NOUN
l' hippopotame MASC

to **hire** VERB
see also **hire** NOUN
[1] louer ◇ *to hire a car* louer une
voiture
[2] engager (*person*) ◇ *They hired a
cleaner.* Ils ont engagé une femme de
ménage.

hire NOUN
see also **hire** VERB
la location
♦**car hire** location de voitures
♦**for hire** à louer

hire car NOUN
la voiture de location

his ADJECTIVE
see also **his** PRONOUN
son MASC ◇ *his father* son père
sa FEM SING ◇ *his mother* sa mère
ses PL ◇ *his parents* ses parents
*sa becomes son before a vowel
sound.*
♦**his friend (1)** (*male*) son ami
♦**his friend (2)** (*female*) son amie
*Do not use son/sa/ses with parts of
the body.*
◇ *He's going to wash his hair.* Il va se
laver les cheveux. ◇ *He's cleaning his*

teeth. Il se brosse les dents. ◇ *He's
hurt his foot.* Il s'est fait mal au pied.

his PRONOUN
see also **his** ADJECTIVE
le sien + MASC NOUN ◇ *Is this his coat? –
No, his is black.* C'est son manteau? –
Non, le sien est noir.
la sienne + FEM NOUN ◇ *Is this his car? –
No, his is white.* C'est sa voiture? –
Non, la sienne est blanche.
les siens + MASC PL NOUN ◇ *my parents
and his* mes parents et les siens
les siennes + FEM PL NOUN ◇ *my reasons
and his* mes raisons et les siennes
♦**Is this his?** C'est à lui? ◇ *This book is
his.* Ce livre est à lui. ◇ *Whose is
this? – It's his.* C'est à qui? – À lui.

history NOUN
l' histoire FEM

to **hit** VERB
see also **hit** NOUN
[1] frapper ◇ *Andrew hit him.* Andrew
l'a frappé.
[2] renverser ◇ *He was hit by a car.* Il
a été renversé par une voiture.
[3] toucher ◇ *The arrow hit the target.*
La flèche a touché la cible.
♦**to hit it off with somebody** bien
s'entendre avec quelqu'un ◇ *She hit it
off with his parents.* Elle s'est bien
entendue avec ses parents.

hit NOUN
see also **hit** VERB
[1] le tube (*song*) ◇ *Blur's latest hit* le
dernier tube de Blur
[2] le succès (*success*) ◇ *The film was
a massive hit.* Le film a eu un
immense succès.

hitch NOUN
le contretemps ◇ *There's been a
slight hitch.* Il y a eu un léger
contretemps.

to **hitchhike** VERB
faire de l'auto-stop

hitchhiker NOUN
l' auto-stoppeur MASC
l' auto-stoppeuse FEM

hitchhiking NOUN
l' auto-stop MASC ◇ *Hitchhiking can be
dangerous.* Il peut être dangereux de
faire de l'auto-stop.

hit man NOUN
le tueur à gages

HIV-negative ADJECTIVE
séronégatif MASC
séronégative FEM

HIV-positive ADJECTIVE
séropositif MASC
séropositive FEM

H

hobby NOUN
le passe-temps favori ◊ *What are your hobbies?* Quels sont tes passe-temps favoris?

hockey NOUN
le hockey ◊ *I play hockey.* Je joue au hockey.

to **hold** VERB
[1] tenir (*hold on to*) ◊ *She held the baby.* Elle tenait le bébé.
[2] contenir (*contain*) ◊ *This bottle holds one litre.* Cette bouteille contient un litre.
♦ **to hold a meeting** avoir une réunion
♦ **Hold the line!** (*on telephone*) Ne quittez pas!
♦ **Hold it!** (*wait*) Attends!
♦ **to get hold of something** (*obtain*) trouver quelque chose ◊ *I couldn't get hold of it.* Je n'ai pas réussi à en trouver.

to **hold on** VERB
[1] tenir bon (*keep hold*) ◊ *The cliff was slippery but he managed to hold on.* La falaise était glissante, mais il est parvenu à tenir bon.
♦ **to hold on to something** se cramponner à quelque chose ◊ *He held on to the chair.* Il se cramponnait à la chaise.
[2] attendre (*wait*) ◊ *Hold on, I'm coming!* Attends, je viens!
♦ **Hold on!** (*on telephone*) Ne quittez pas!

to **hold up** VERB
♦ **to hold up one's hand** lever la main ◊ *Pierre held up his hand.* Pierre a levé la main.
♦ **to hold somebody up** (*delay*) retenir quelqu'un ◊ *I was held up at the office.* J'ai été retenu au bureau.
♦ **to hold up a bank** (*rob*) braquer une banque (*informal*)

hold-up NOUN
[1] le hold-up (*at bank*)
[2] le retard (*delay*)
[3] le bouchon (*traffic jam*)

hole NOUN
le trou

holiday NOUN
[1] les vacances FEM PL ◊ *Did you have a good holiday?* Tu as passé de bonnes vacances? ◊ *our holidays in France* nos vacances en France
♦ **on holiday** en vacances ◊ *to go on holiday* partir en vacances ◊ *We are on holiday.* Nous sommes en vacances.
♦ **the school holidays** les vacances scolaires

[2] le jour férié (*public holiday*) ◊ *Next Wednesday is a holiday.* Mercredi prochain est un jour férié.
[3] le jour de congé (*day off*) ◊ *He took a day's holiday.* Il a pris un jour de congé.
♦ **a holiday camp** un camp de vacances

Holland NOUN
la Hollande
♦ **in Holland** en Hollande
♦ **to Holland** en Hollande

hollow ADJECTIVE
creux MASC
creuse FEM

holly NOUN
le houx ◊ *a sprig of holly* un brin de houx

holy ADJECTIVE
saint

home NOUN
see also **home** ADVERB
la maison
♦ **at home** à la maison
♦ **Make yourself at home.** Faites comme chez vous.

home ADVERB
see also **home** NOUN
à la maison ◊ *I'll be home at 5 o'clock.* Je serai à la maison à cinq heures.
♦ **to get home** rentrer ◊ *What time did he get home?* Il est rentré à quelle heure?

home address NOUN
l' adresse FEM ◊ *What's your home address?* Quelle est votre adresse?

homeland NOUN
la patrie

homeless ADJECTIVE
sans abri MASC, FEM, PL
♦ **the homeless** les sans-abri

home match NOUN
le match à domicile

homeopathy NOUN
l' homéopathie FEM

home page NOUN
la page d'accueil

homesick ADJECTIVE
♦ **to be homesick** avoir le mal du pays

homework NOUN
les devoirs MASC PL ◊ *Have you done your homework?* Est-ce que tu as fait tes devoirs? ◊ *my geography homework* mes devoirs de géographie

homosexual ADJECTIVE
see also **homosexual** NOUN
homosexuel MASC

homosexuelle FEM

homosexual NOUN
see also **homosexual** ADJECTIVE
l' homosexuel MASC
l' homosexuelle FEM

honest ADJECTIVE
[1] (*trustworthy*)
honnête ◊ *She's a very honest person.* Elle est très honnête.
[2] (*sincere*)
franc MASC
franche FEM
◊ *He was very honest with her.* Il a été très franc avec elle.

honestly ADVERB
franchement ◊ *I honestly don't know.* Franchement, je n'en sais rien.

honesty NOUN
l' honnêteté FEM

honey NOUN
le miel

honeymoon NOUN
la lune de miel

honour NOUN (US **honor**)
l' honneur MASC

hood NOUN
[1] la capuche (*on coat*)
[2] le capot (*of car*) US

hook NOUN
le crochet ◊ *He hung the painting on the hook.* Il a suspendu le tableau au crochet.
♦**to take the phone off the hook** décrocher le téléphone
♦**a fish-hook** un hameçon

hooligan NOUN
le voyou
(les voyoux PL)

hooray EXCLAMATION
hourra!

Hoover ® NOUN
l' aspirateur MASC

to **hoover** VERB
passer l'aspirateur ◊ *to hoover the lounge* passer l'aspirateur dans le salon

to **hope** VERB
see also **hope** NOUN
espérer ◊ *I hope he comes.* J'espère qu'il va venir. ◊ *I'm hoping for good results.* J'espère avoir de bons résultats.
♦**I hope so.** Je l'espère.
♦**I hope not.** J'espère que non.

hope NOUN
see also **hope** VERB
l' espoir MASC

♦**to give up hope** perdre espoir ◊ *Don't give up hope!* Ne perds pas espoir!

hopeful ADJECTIVE
[1] plein d'espoir ◊ *I'm hopeful.* Je suis plein d'espoir.
♦**He's hopeful of winning.** Il a bon espoir de gagner.
[2] (*situation*)
prometteur MASC
prometteuse FEM
◊ *The prospects look hopeful.* Les perspectives semblent prometteuses.

hopefully ADVERB
avec un peu de chance ◊ *Hopefully he'll make it in time.* Avec un peu de chance, il arrivera à temps.

hopeless ADJECTIVE
nul MASC
nulle FEM
◊ *I'm hopeless at maths.* Je suis nul en maths.

horizon NOUN
l' horizon MASC

horizontal ADJECTIVE
horizontal
(horizontaux MASC PL)

horn NOUN
[1] le klaxon ◊ *He sounded his horn.* Il a klaxonné.
[2] le cor ◊ *I play the horn.* Je joue du cor.

horoscope NOUN
l' horoscope MASC

horrible ADJECTIVE
horrible ◊ *What a horrible dress!* Quelle robe horrible!

horrifying ADJECTIVE
effrayant

horror NOUN
l' horreur FEM

horror film NOUN
le film d'horreur

horse NOUN
le cheval
(les chevaux PL)

horse-racing NOUN
les courses de chevaux FEM PL

horseshoe NOUN
le fer à cheval

hose NOUN
le tuyau
(les tuyaux PL)
◊ *a garden hose* un tuyau d'arrosage

hosepipe NOUN
le tuyau d'arrosage

hospital NOUN
l' hôpital MASC
(les hôpitaux PL)

H

☞

◊ *Take me to the hospital!* Emmenez-moi à l'hôpital! ◊ *in hospital* à l'hôpital

hospitality NOUN
l' hospitalité FEM

host NOUN
l' hôte MASC
l' hôtesse FEM
◊ *Don't forget to write and thank your hosts.* N'oublie pas d'écrire à tes hôtes pour les remercier.

hostage NOUN
l' otage MASC
♦ **to take somebody hostage** prendre quelqu'un en otage

hostel NOUN
le foyer (*for refugees, homeless people*)
♦ **a youth hostel** une auberge de jeunesse

hostile ADJECTIVE
hostile

hot ADJECTIVE
1 chaud (*warm*) ◊ *a hot bath* un bain chaud ◊ *a hot country* un pays chaud
*When you are talking about a person being hot, you use **avoir chaud**.*
◊ *I'm hot.* J'ai chaud. ◊ *I'm too hot.* J'ai trop chaud.
*When you mean that the weather is hot, you use **faire chaud**.*
◊ *It's hot.* Il fait chaud. ◊ *It's very hot today.* Il fait très chaud aujourd'hui.
2 épicé (*spicy*) ◊ *a very hot curry* un curry très épicé

hot dog NOUN
le hot-dog

hotel NOUN
l' hôtel MASC ◊ *We stayed in a hotel.* Nous avons logé à l'hôtel.

hour NOUN
l' heure FEM ◊ *She always takes hours to get ready.* Elle passe toujours des heures à se préparer.
♦ **a quarter of an hour** un quart d'heure
♦ **half an hour** une demi-heure
♦ **two and a half hours** deux heures et demie

hourly ADJECTIVE, ADVERB
toutes les heures ◊ *There are hourly buses.* Il y a des bus toutes les heures.
♦ **to be paid hourly** être payé à l'heure

house NOUN
la maison
♦ **at his house** chez lui
♦ **We stayed at their house.** Nous avons séjourné chez eux.

housewife NOUN
la femme au foyer ◊ *She's a housewife.* Elle est femme au foyer.

housework NOUN
le ménage
♦ **to do the housework** faire le ménage

hovercraft NOUN
l' aéroglisseur MASC

how ADVERB
comment ◊ *How are you?* Comment allez-vous?
♦ **How many?** Combien?
♦ **How many ...?** Combien de ...? ◊ *How many pupils are there in the class?* Combien d'élèves y a-t-il dans la classe?
♦ **How much?** Combien?
♦ **How much ...?** Combien de ...? ◊ *How much sugar do you want?* Combien de sucres voulez-vous?
♦ **How old are you?** Quel âge as-tu?
♦ **How far is it to Edinburgh?** Combien y a-t-il de kilomètres d'ici à Édimbourg?
♦ **How long have you been here?** Depuis combien de temps êtes-vous là?
♦ **How do you say "apple" in French?** Comment dit-on "apple" en français?

however CONJUNCTION
pourtant ◊ *This, however, isn't true.* Pourtant, ce n'est pas vrai.

to **howl** VERB
hurler

HTML NOUN
le langage HTML ◊ *an HTML document* un document en langage HTML

to **hug** VERB
see also **hug** NOUN
serrer dans ses bras ◊ *He hugged her.* Il l'a serrée dans ses bras.

hug NOUN
see also **hug** VERB
♦ **to give somebody a hug** serrer quelqu'un dans ses bras ◊ *She gave them a hug.* Elle les a serrés dans ses bras.

huge ADJECTIVE
immense

to **hum** VERB
fredonner

human ADJECTIVE
humain ◊ *the human body* le corps humain

human being NOUN
l' être humain MASC

humble ADJECTIVE
humble

humour NOUN (US **humor**)
l' humour MASC

♦**to have a sense of humour** avoir le sens de l'humour

hundred NUMBER
♦**a hundred** cent ◊ *a hundred francs* cent francs
♦**five hundred** cinq cents
♦**five hundred and one** cinq cent un
♦**hundreds of people** des centaines de personnes

hung VERB *see* **hang**

Hungarian NOUN

see also **Hungarian** ADJECTIVE

1 (*person*)
le Hongrois
la Hongroise
2 (*language*)
le hongrois

Hungarian ADJECTIVE

see also **Hungarian** NOUN

hongrois ◊ *She's Hungarian.* Elle est hongroise.

Hungary NOUN
la Hongrie
♦**in Hungary** en Hongrie
♦**to Hungary** en Hongrie

hunger NOUN
la faim

hungry ADJECTIVE
♦**to be hungry** avoir faim ◊ *I'm hungry.* J'ai faim.

to **hunt** VERB
1 chasser (*animal*) ◊ *People used to hunt wild boar.* On chassait le sanglier autrefois.
♦**to go hunting** aller à la chasse
2 pourchasser (*criminal*) ◊ *The police are hunting the killer.* La police pourchasse le criminel.
♦**to hunt for something** (*search*) chercher quelque chose partout ◊ *I hunted everywhere for that book.* J'ai cherché ce livre partout.

hunting NOUN
la chasse ◊ *I'm against hunting.* Je suis contre la chasse.
♦**fox-hunting** la chasse au renard

hurdle NOUN
l' obstacle MASC

hurricane NOUN

l' ouragan MASC

to **hurry** VERB

see also **hurry** NOUN

se dépêcher ◊ *Sharon hurried back home.* Sharon s'est dépêchée de rentrer chez elle.
♦**Hurry up!** Dépêche-toi!

hurry NOUN

see also **hurry** VERB

♦**to be in a hurry** être pressé
♦**to do something in a hurry** faire quelque chose en vitesse
♦**There's no hurry.** Rien ne presse.

to **hurt** VERB

see also **hurt** ADJECTIVE

♦**to hurt somebody (1)** (*physically*) faire mal à quelqu'un ◊ *You're hurting me!* Tu me fais mal!
♦**to hurt somebody (2)** (*emotionally*) blesser quelqu'un ◊ *His remarks really hurt me.* Ses remarques m'ont vraiment blessé.
♦**to hurt oneself** se faire mal ◊ *I fell over and hurt myself.* Je me suis fait mal en tombant.
♦**That hurts.** Ça fait mal. ◊ *It hurts to have a tooth out.* Ça fait mal de se faire arracher une dent.
♦**My leg hurts.** J'ai mal à la jambe.

hurt ADJECTIVE

see also **hurt** VERB

blessé ◊ *Is he badly hurt?* Est-ce qu'il est grièvement blessé? ◊ *He was hurt in the leg.* Il a été blessé à la jambe. ◊ *I was hurt by what he said.* J'ai été blessé par ce qu'il a dit.
♦**Luckily, nobody got hurt.** Heureusement, il n'y a pas eu de blessés.

husband NOUN
le mari

hut NOUN
la hutte

hymn NOUN
le cantique

hypermarket NOUN
l' hypermarché MASC

hyphen NOUN
le trait d'union

H

I

I PRONOUN
1 je ◇ *I speak French.* Je parle français.
je changes to j' before a vowel and most words beginning with "h".
◇ *I love cats.* J'aime les chats.
2 moi ◇ *Ann and I* Ann et moi

ice NOUN
1 la glace ◇ *There was ice on the lake.* Il y avait de la glace sur le lac.
2 le verglas (*on road*)

iceberg NOUN
l' iceberg MASC

icebox NOUN [US]
le frigo

ice cream NOUN
la glace ◇ *vanilla ice cream* la glace à la vanille

ice cube NOUN
le glaçon

ice hockey NOUN
le hockey sur glace

Iceland NOUN
l' Islande FEM
♦ **in Iceland** en Islande
♦ **to Iceland** en Islande

ice lolly NOUN
la glace à l'eau

ice rink NOUN
la patinoire

ice-skating NOUN
le patinage sur glace
♦ **to go ice-skating** faire du patin à glace

icing NOUN
le glaçage (*on cake*)
♦ **icing sugar** le sucre glace

icon NOUN
l' icône FEM

icy ADJECTIVE
glacial
(glaciaux MASC PL)
◇ *There was an icy wind.* Il y avait un vent glacial.
♦ **The roads are icy.** Il y a du verglas sur les routes.

I'd = **I had,** = **I would**

idea NOUN
l' idée FEM ◇ *Good idea!* Bonne idée!

ideal ADJECTIVE
idéal
(idéaux MASC PL)

identical ADJECTIVE
identique

identification NOUN
l' identification FEM

to **identify** VERB
identifier

identity card NOUN
la carte d'identité

idiom NOUN
l' expression idiomatique FEM

idiot NOUN
l' idiot MASC
l' idiote FEM

idiotic ADJECTIVE
stupide

idle ADJECTIVE
fainéant (*lazy*)

i.e. ABBREVIATION
c.-à-d. (= c'est-à-dire)

if CONJUNCTION
si ◇ *You can have it if you like.* Tu peux le prendre si tu veux.
si changes to s' before il and ils.
◇ *Do you know if he's there?* Savez-vous s'il est là?
♦ **if only** si seulement ◇ *If only I had more money!* Si seulement j'avais plus d'argent!
♦ **if not** sinon ◇ *Are you coming? If not, I'll go with Mark.* Est-ce que tu viens? Sinon, j'irai avec Mark.

ignorant ADJECTIVE
ignorant

to **ignore** VERB
♦ **to ignore something** ne tenir aucun compte de quelque chose ◇ *She ignored my advice.* Elle n'a tenu aucun compte de mes conseils.
♦ **to ignore somebody** ignorer quelqu'un ◇ *She saw me, but she ignored me.* Elle m'a vu, mais elle m'a ignoré.
♦ **Just ignore him!** Ne fais pas attention à lui!

ill ADJECTIVE
malade (*sick*)
♦ **to be taken ill** tomber malade ◇ *She was taken ill while on holiday.* Elle est tombée malade pendant qu'elle était en vacances.

I'll = **I will**

illegal ADJECTIVE
illégal
(illégaux MASC PL)

illegible ADJECTIVE
illisible

illness NOUN
la maladie

to **ill-treat** VERB
maltraiter

illusion NOUN
l' illusion FEM

illustration NOUN
l' illustration FEM

image NOUN
l' image FEM ◊ *The company has changed its image.* La société a changé d'image.

imagination NOUN
l' imagination FEM

to **imagine** VERB
imaginer ◊ *You can imagine how I felt!* Tu peux imaginer ce que j'ai ressenti! ◊ *Is he angry? – I imagine so.* Est-ce qu'il est en colère? – J'imagine que oui.

to **imitate** VERB
imiter

imitation NOUN
l' imitation FEM

immediate ADJECTIVE
immédiat

immediately ADVERB
immédiatement ◊ *I'll do it immediately.* Je vais le faire immédiatement.

immigrant NOUN
l' immigré MASC
l' immigrée FEM

immigration NOUN
l' immigration FEM

immoral ADJECTIVE
immoral
(immoraux MASC PL)

impartial ADJECTIVE
impartial
(impartiaux MASC PL)

impatience NOUN
l' impatience FEM

impatient ADJECTIVE
impatient
♦ **to get impatient** s'impatienter
◊ *People are getting impatient.* Les gens commencent à s'impatienter.

impatiently ADVERB
avec impatience ◊ *We waited impatiently.* Nous avons attendu avec impatience.

impersonal ADJECTIVE
impersonnel MASC
impersonnelle FEM

importance NOUN
l' importance FEM

important ADJECTIVE

important

impossible ADJECTIVE
impossible

to **impress** VERB
impressionner ◊ *She's trying to impress you.* Elle essaie de t'impressionner.

impressed ADJECTIVE
impressionné ◊ *I'm very impressed!* Je suis très impressionné!

impression NOUN
l' impression FEM ◊ *I was under the impression that ...* J'avais l'impression que ...

impressive ADJECTIVE
impressionnant

to **improve** VERB
[1] améliorer (*make better*) ◊ *They have improved the service.* Ils ont amélioré le service.
[2] s'améliorer (*get better*) ◊ *The weather is improving.* Le temps s'améliore. ◊ *My French has improved.* Mon français s'est amélioré.

improvement NOUN
[1] l' amélioration FEM (*of condition*) ◊ *It's a great improvement.* C'est une nette amélioration.
[2] le progrès (*of learner*) ◊ *There's been an improvement in his French.* Il a fait des progrès en français.

in PREPOSITION, ADVERB

There are several ways of translating in. Scan the examples to find one that is similar to what you want to say. For other expressions with in, see the verbs go, come, get, give etc.

[1] dans ◊ *in the house* dans la maison ◊ *in my bag* dans mon sac ◊ *in the sixties* dans les années soixante ◊ *I'll see you in three weeks.* Je te verrai dans trois semaines.
[2] à ◊ *in the country* à la campagne ◊ *in school* à l'école ◊ *in hospital* à l'hôpital ◊ *in London* à Londres ◊ *in spring* au printemps ◊ *in the sun* au soleil ◊ *in the shade* à l'ombre ◊ *in a loud voice* à voix haute ◊ *the boy in the blue shirt* le garçon à la chemise bleue ◊ *It was written in pencil.* C'était écrit au crayon.
[3] en ◊ *in French* en français ◊ *in summer* en été ◊ *in May* en mai ◊ *in 1996* en dix-neuf cent quatre-vingt seize ◊ *I did it in 3 hours.* Je l'ai fait en trois heures. ◊ *in town* en ville ◊ *in prison* en prison ◊ *in tears* en

larmes ◊ *in good condition* en bon état

*When **in** refers to a country which is feminine, use **en**; when the country is masculine, use **au**; when the country is plural, use **aux**.*

◊ *in France* en France ◊ *in Portugal* au Portugal ◊ *in the United States* aux États-Unis

[4] de ◊ *the best pupil in the class* le meilleur élève de la classe ◊ *the best team in the world* la meilleure équipe du monde ◊ *the tallest person in the family* le plus grand de la famille ◊ *at 4 o'clock in the afternoon* à quatre heures de l'après-midi ◊ *at 6 in the morning* à six heures du matin

♦ **in the afternoon** l'après-midi
♦ **You look good in that dress.** Tu es jolie avec cette robe.
♦ **in time** à temps ◊ *We arrived in time for dinner.* Nous sommes arrivés à temps pour le dîner.
♦ **in here** ici ◊ *It's hot in here.* Il fait chaud ici.
♦ **in the rain** sous la pluie
♦ **one person in ten** une personne sur dix
♦ **to be in** (*at home, work*) être là ◊ *He wasn't in.* Il n'était pas là.
♦ **to ask somebody in** inviter quelqu'un à entrer

inaccurate ADJECTIVE
inexact

inadequate ADJECTIVE
inadéquat (*measures, resources*)
♦ **I felt completely inadequate.** Je ne me sentais absolument pas à la hauteur.

incentive NOUN
♦ **There is no incentive to work.** Il n'y a rien qui incite à travailler.

inch NOUN
le pouce

> *In France measurements are in metres and centimetres rather than feet and inches. An inch is about 2.5 centimetres.*

♦ **6 inches** quinze centimètres

incident NOUN
l' incident MASC

inclined ADJECTIVE
♦ **to be inclined to do something** avoir tendance à faire quelque chose ◊ *He's inclined to arrive late.* Il a tendance à arriver en retard.

to **include** VERB

comprendre ◊ *Service is not included.* Le service n'est pas compris.

including PREPOSITION
compris ◊ *It will be 200 francs, including tax.* Ça coûtera deux cents francs, toutes taxes comprises.

inclusive ADJECTIVE
compris ◊ *The inclusive price is 200 francs.* Ça coûte deux cents francs tout compris.
♦ **inclusive of tax** taxes comprises

income NOUN
le revenu

income tax NOUN
l' impôt sur le revenu MASC

incompetent ADJECTIVE
incompétent

incomplete ADJECTIVE
incomplet MASC
incomplète FEM

inconsistent ADJECTIVE
incohérent

inconvenience NOUN
♦ **I don't want to cause any inconvenience.** Je ne veux pas vous déranger.

inconvenient ADJECTIVE
♦ **That's very inconvenient for me.** Ça ne m'arrange pas du tout.

incorrect ADJECTIVE
incorrect

increase NOUN
see also **increase** VERB
l' augmentation FEM ◊ *an increase in road accidents* une augmentation des accidents de la route

to **increase** VERB
see also **increase** NOUN
augmenter

incredible ADJECTIVE
incroyable

indecisive ADJECTIVE
indécis (*person*)

indeed ADVERB
vraiment ◊ *It's very hard indeed.* C'est vraiment très difficile.
♦ **Know what I mean? – Indeed I do.** Tu vois ce que je veux dire? – Oui, tout à fait.
♦ **Thank you very much indeed!** Merci beaucoup!

independence NOUN
l' indépendance FEM

independent ADJECTIVE
indépendant
♦ **an independent school** une école privée

index NOUN
l' index MASC (*in book*)

index finger NOUN
l' index MASC

India NOUN
l' Inde FEM
♦**in India** en Inde
♦**to India** en Inde

Indian ADJECTIVE
see also **Indian** NOUN
indien MASC
indienne FEM

Indian NOUN
see also **Indian** ADJECTIVE
(*person*)
l' Indien MASC
l' Indienne FEM
♦**an American Indian** un Indien
d'Amérique

to **indicate** VERB
indiquer

indicator NOUN
le clignotant (*on car*) ◊ *Put your
indicators on.* Mets tes clignotants.

indigestion NOUN
l' indigestion FEM
♦**I've got indigestion.** J'ai une
indigestion.

individual ADJECTIVE
individuel MASC
individuelle FEM

indoor ADJECTIVE
♦**an indoor swimming pool** une piscine
couverte

indoors ADVERB
à l'intérieur ◊ *They're indoors.* Ils
sont à l'intérieur.
♦**to go indoors** rentrer ◊ *We'd better
go indoors.* Nous ferions mieux de
rentrer.

industrial ADJECTIVE
industriel MASC
industrielle FEM

industrial estate NOUN
la zone industrielle

industry NOUN
l' industrie FEM ◊ *the tourist industry*
l'industrie du tourisme ◊ *the oil
industry* l'industrie pétrolière ◊ *I'd like
to work in industry.* J'aimerais
travailler dans l'industrie.

inefficient ADJECTIVE
inefficace

inevitable ADJECTIVE
inévitable

inexpensive ADJECTIVE
bon marché MASC, FEM, PL ◊ *an
inexpensive hotel* un hôtel bon

marché ◊ *inexpensive holidays* des
vacances bon marché

inexperienced ADJECTIVE
inexpérimenté

infant school NOUN

> **ⓘ** CP (*cours préparatoire*) is the
> equivalent of first-year infants, and
> CE1 (*cours élémentaire première
> année*) the equivalent of second-year
> infants.

◊ *He's just started at infant school.* Il
vient d'entrer au cours préparatoire.

infection NOUN
l' infection FEM ◊ *an ear infection* une
infection de l'oreille
♦**a throat infection** une angine

infectious ADJECTIVE
contagieux MASC
contagieuse FEM
◊ *It's not infectious.* Ce n'est pas
contagieux.

infinitive NOUN
l' infinitif MASC

infirmary NOUN
l' hôpital MASC
(les hôpitaux PL)

inflatable ADJECTIVE
gonflable (*mattress, dinghy*)

inflation NOUN
l' inflation FEM

influence NOUN
see also **influence** VERB
l' influence FEM ◊ *He's a bad influence
on her.* Il a mauvaise influence sur
elle.

to **influence** VERB
see also **influence** NOUN
influencer

influenza NOUN
la grippe

to **inform** VERB
informer
♦**to inform somebody of something**
informer quelqu'un de quelque chose
◊ *Nobody informed me of the new
plan.* Personne ne m'a informé de ce
nouveau projet.

informal ADJECTIVE
1 (*person, party*)
décontracté ◊ *"informal dress"* "tenue
décontractée"
2 (*colloquial*)
familier MASC
familière FEM
◊ *informal language* le langage
familier

I

☞

♦ **an informal visit** une visite non officielle

information NOUN
les <u>renseignements</u> MASC PL
◊ *important information* les renseignements importants
♦ **a piece of information** un renseignement
♦ **Could you give me some information about trains to Paris?** Pourriez-vous me renseigner sur les trains pour Paris?

information office NOUN
le <u>bureau des renseignements</u>

infuriating ADJECTIVE
<u>exaspérant</u>

ingenious ADJECTIVE
<u>ingénieux</u> MASC
<u>ingénieuse</u> FEM

ingredient NOUN
l' <u>ingrédient</u> MASC

inhabitant NOUN
l' <u>habitant</u> MASC
l' <u>habitante</u> FEM

to **inherit** VERB
<u>hériter de</u> ◊ *She inherited her father's house.* Elle a hérité de la maison de son père.

initials PL NOUN
les <u>initiales</u> FEM PL ◊ *Her initials are CDT.* Ses initiales sont CDT.

initiative NOUN
l' <u>initiative</u> FEM

to **inject** VERB
<u>injecter</u> (*drug*)

injection NOUN
la <u>piqûre</u>

to **injure** VERB
<u>blesser</u>

injured ADJECTIVE
<u>blessé</u>

injury NOUN
la <u>blessure</u>

injury time NOUN
les <u>arrêts de jeu</u> MASC PL

injustice NOUN
l' <u>injustice</u> FEM

ink NOUN
l' <u>encre</u> FEM

in-laws PL NOUN
les <u>beaux-parents</u> MASC PL

inn NOUN
l' <u>auberge</u> FEM

inner ADJECTIVE
<u>intérieur</u>
♦ **the inner city** les quartiers déshérités du centre ville MASC PL

inner tube NOUN
la <u>chambre à air</u>

innocent ADJECTIVE
<u>innocent</u>

inquest NOUN
l' <u>enquête</u> FEM

to **inquire** VERB
♦ **to inquire about something** se renseigner sur quelque chose ◊ *I'm going to inquire about train times.* Je vais me renseigner sur les horaires des trains.

inquiries office NOUN
le <u>bureau des renseignements</u>

inquiry NOUN
♦ **to make inquiries about something** faire des demandes de renseignement ◊ *"inquiries"* "renseignements"

inquisitive ADJECTIVE
<u>curieux</u> MASC
<u>curieuse</u> FEM

insane ADJECTIVE
<u>fou</u> MASC
<u>folle</u> FEM

inscription NOUN
l' <u>inscription</u> FEM

insect NOUN
l' <u>insecte</u> MASC

insect repellent NOUN
l' <u>insectifuge</u> MASC

insensitive ADJECTIVE
<u>indélicat</u> ◊ *That was a bit insensitive of you.* C'était un peu indélicat de ta part.

inside NOUN
see also **inside** ADVERB
l' <u>intérieur</u> MASC

inside ADVERB, PREPOSITION
see also **inside** NOUN
à l'intérieur ◊ *They're inside.* Ils sont à l'intérieur. ◊ *inside the house* à l'intérieur de la maison
♦ **to go inside** rentrer
♦ **Come inside!** Rentrez!

insincere ADJECTIVE
<u>peu sincère</u>

to **insist** VERB
<u>insister</u> ◊ *I didn't want to, but he insisted.* Je ne voulais pas, mais il a insisté.
♦ **to insist on doing something** insister pour faire quelque chose ◊ *She insisted on paying.* Elle a insisté pour payer.
♦ **He insisted he was innocent.** Il affirmait qu'il était innocent.

to **inspect** VERB
<u>inspecter</u>

inspector NOUN
l' inspecteur MASC (*police*) ◊ *Inspector Jill Brown* l'inspecteur Jill Brown
♦**ticket inspector** (*on buses*) le contrôleur

instalment NOUN
1 le versement (*payment*) ◊ *to pay in instalments* payer en plusieurs versements
2 l' épisode MASC (*episode*)

instance NOUN
♦**for instance** par exemple

instant ADJECTIVE
immédiat ◊ *It was an instant success.* Ça a été un succès immédiat.
♦**instant coffee** le café instantané

instantly ADVERB
tout de suite

instead ADVERB
♦**instead of (1)** (*followed by noun*) à la place de ◊ *He went instead of Peter.* Il y est allé à la place de Peter.
♦**instead of (2)** (*followed by verb*) au lieu de ◊ *We played tennis instead of going swimming.* Nous avons joué au tennis au lieu d'aller nager.
♦**The pool was closed, so we played tennis instead.** La piscine était fermée, alors nous avons joué au tennis.

instinct NOUN
l' instinct MASC

institute NOUN
l' institut MASC

institution NOUN
l' institution FEM

to **instruct** VERB
♦**to instruct somebody to do something** donner l'ordre à quelqu'un de faire quelque chose ◊ *She instructed us to wait outside.* Elle nous a donné l'ordre d'attendre dehors.

instructions PL NOUN
1 les instructions FEM PL ◊ *Follow the instructions carefully.* Suivez soigneusement les instructions.
2 le mode d'emploi SING (*booklet*) ◊ *Where are the instructions?* Où est le mode d'emploi?

instructor NOUN
le moniteur
la monitrice
◊ *a skiing instructor* un moniteur de ski ◊ *a driving instructor* un moniteur d'auto-école

instrument NOUN
l' instrument MASC ◊ *Do you play an instrument?* Est-ce que tu joues d'un instrument?

insufficient ADJECTIVE
insuffisant

insulin NOUN
l' insuline FEM

insult NOUN
see also **insult** VERB
l' insulte FEM

to **insult** VERB
see also **insult** NOUN
insulter

insurance NOUN
l' assurance FEM ◊ *his car insurance* son assurance automobile
♦**an insurance policy** une police d'assurance

intelligent ADJECTIVE
intelligent

to **intend** VERB
♦**to intend to do something** avoir l'intention de faire quelque chose ◊ *I intend to do French at university.* J'ai l'intention d'étudier le français à l'université.

intense ADJECTIVE
intense

intensive ADJECTIVE
intensif MASC
intensive FEM

intention NOUN
l' intention FEM

intercom NOUN
l' interphone MASC

interest NOUN
see also **interest** VERB
l' intérêt MASC ◊ *to show an interest in something* manifester de l'intérêt pour quelque chose
♦**What interests do you have?** Quels sont tes centres d'intérêt?
♦**My main interest is music.** Ce qui m'intéresse le plus c'est la musique.

to **interest** VERB
see also **interest** NOUN
intéresser ◊ *It doesn't interest me.* Ça ne m'intéresse pas.
♦**to be interested in something** s'intéresser à quelque chose ◊ *I'm not interested in politics.* Je ne m'intéresse pas à la politique.

interesting ADJECTIVE
intéressant

interior NOUN
l' intérieur MASC

interior designer NOUN
le/la designer

intermediate ADJECTIVE
(*course, level*)
moyen MASC
moyenne FEM

internal ADJECTIVE
interne

international ADJECTIVE
international
(internationaux MASC PL)

internet NOUN
l' Internet MASC ◊ *on the internet* sur Internet

internet café NOUN
le cybercafé

internet user NOUN
l' internaute MASC/FEM

to **interpret** VERB
servir d'interprète ◊ *Steve couldn't speak French, so his friend interpreted.* Comme Steve ne savait pas le français, son ami a servi d'interprète.

interpreter NOUN
l' interprète MASC/FEM

to **interrupt** VERB
interrompre

interruption NOUN
l' interruption FEM

interval NOUN
l' entracte MASC (*in play, concert*)

interview NOUN
see also **interview** VERB
1 l' interview FEM (*on TV, radio*)
2 l' entretien MASC (*for job*)

to **interview** VERB
see also **interview** NOUN
interviewer (*on TV, radio*) ◊ *I was interviewed on the radio.* J'ai été interviewé à la radio.

interviewer NOUN
l' interviewer MASC (*on TV, radio*)

intimate ADJECTIVE
intime

into PREPOSITION
1 dans ◊ *He got into the car.* Il est monté dans la voiture.
2 en ◊ *I'm going into town.* Je vais en ville. ◊ *Translate it into French.* Traduisez ça en français. ◊ *Divide into two groups.* Répartissez-vous en deux groupes.

to **introduce** VERB
présenter ◊ *I'd like to introduce Michelle Davies.* Je vous présente Michelle Davies. ◊ *He introduced me to his parents.* Il m'a présenté à ses parents.

introduction NOUN

l' introduction FEM (*in book*)

intruder NOUN
l' intrus MASC
l' intruse FEM

intuition NOUN
l' intuition FEM

to **invade** VERB
envahir

invalid NOUN
le/la malade

to **invent** VERB
inventer

invention NOUN
l' invention FEM

inventor NOUN
l' inventeur MASC
l' inventrice FEM

investigation NOUN
l' enquête FEM (*police*)

investment NOUN
l' investissement MASC ◊ *The railway system is suffering from a lack of investment.* Le réseau ferroviaire souffre d'un manque d'investissement.

invigilator NOUN
le surveillant
la surveillante

invisible ADJECTIVE
invisible

invitation NOUN
l' invitation FEM

to **invite** VERB
inviter ◊ *He's not invited.* Il n'est pas invité.
◆ **to invite somebody to a party** inviter quelqu'un à une fête

to **involve** VERB
nécessiter ◊ *His job involves a lot of travelling.* Son travail nécessite de nombreux déplacements.
◆ **to be involved in something** (*crime, drugs*) être impliqué dans quelque chose
◆ **to be involved with somebody** (*in relationship*) avoir une relation avec quelqu'un

IQ NOUN (= *intelligence quotient*)
le Q.I. (= quotient intellectuel)

Iran NOUN
l' Iran MASC
◆ **in Iran** en Iran

Iraq NOUN
l' Iraq MASC
◆ **in Iraq** en Iraq

Iraqi ADJECTIVE
see also **Iraqi** NOUN
irakien MASC

irakienne FEM
◊ *the Iraqi government* le
gouvernement irakien

Iraqi NOUN
see also **Iraqi** ADJECTIVE
l' Irakien MASC
l' Irakienne FEM
♦**the Iraqis** les Irakiens

Ireland NOUN
l' Irlande FEM
♦**in Ireland** en Irlande
♦**to Ireland** en Irlande
♦**I'm from Ireland.** Je suis irlandais.

Irish ADJECTIVE
see also **Irish** NOUN
irlandais ◊ *Irish music* la musique
irlandaise

Irish NOUN
see also **Irish** ADJECTIVE
l' irlandais MASC (*language*)
♦**the Irish** (*people*) les Irlandais

Irishman NOUN
l' Irlandais MASC

Irishwoman NOUN
l' Irlandaise FEM

iron NOUN
see also **iron** VERB
1 le fer (*metal*)
2 le fer à repasser (*for clothes*)

to **iron** VERB
see also **iron** NOUN
repasser

ironic ADJECTIVE
ironique

ironing NOUN
le repassage ◊ *to do the ironing*
faire le repassage

ironing board NOUN
la planche à repasser

ironmonger's (shop) NOUN
la quincaillerie

irrelevant ADJECTIVE
hors de propos ◊ *That's irrelevant.*
C'est hors de propos.

irresponsible ADJECTIVE
irresponsable (*person*) ◊ *That was
irresponsible of him.* C'était
irresponsable de sa part.

irritating ADJECTIVE
irritant

is VERB see **be**

Islam NOUN
l' Islam MASC

Islamic ADJECTIVE
islamique ◊ *Islamic law* la loi
islamique
♦**Islamic fundamentalists** les intégristes
musulmans MASC

island NOUN
l' île FEM

isle NOUN
♦**the Isle of Man** l'île de Man
♦**the Isle of Wight** l'île de Wight

isolated ADJECTIVE
isolé

ISP NOUN (= *internet service provider*)
le fournisseur d'accès à Internet

Israel NOUN
Israël MASC
♦**in Israel** en Israël

Israeli ADJECTIVE
see also **Israeli** NOUN
israélien MASC
israélienne FEM

Israeli NOUN
see also **Israeli** ADJECTIVE
l' Israélien MASC
l' Israélienne FEM

issue NOUN
see also **issue** VERB
1 la question (*matter*) ◊ *a
controversial issue* une question
controversée
2 le numéro (*of magazine*)

to **issue** VERB
see also **issue** NOUN
distribuer (*equipment, supplies*)

it PRONOUN
*Remember to check if **it** stands for a
masculine or feminine noun.*
1 il ◊ *Where's my book? – It's on the
table.* Où est mon livre? – Il est sur la
table.
elle ◊ *When does the pool close? – It
closes at 8.* La piscine ferme à quelle
heure? – Elle ferme à vingt heures.
*Use **le** or **la** when **it** is the object of
the sentence. **le** and **la** change to **l'**
before a vowel and most words
beginning with "h".*
2 le ◊ *There's a croissant left. Do
you want it?* Il reste un croissant. Tu
le veux?
l' ◊ *It's a good film. Did you see it?*
C'est un bon film. L'as-tu vu?
la ◊ *I don't want this apple. Take it.*
Je ne veux pas de cette pomme.
Prends-la.
l' ◊ *He's got a new car. – Yes, I saw
it.* Il a une nouvelle voiture. – Oui, je
l'ai vue.
♦**It's raining.** Il pleut.
♦**It's 6 o'clock.** Il est six heures.
♦**It's Friday tomorrow.** Demain c'est
vendredi.
♦**Who is it? – It's me.** Qui est-ce? –
C'est moi.
♦**It's expensive.** C'est cher.

Italian ADJECTIVE

> see also **Italian** NOUN

italien MASC
italienne FEM

Italian NOUN

> see also **Italian** ADJECTIVE

1 (*person*)
l' Italien MASC
l' Italienne FEM
2 (*language*)
l' italien MASC

Italy NOUN
l' Italie FEM
♦ **in Italy** en Italie
♦ **to Italy** en Italie

to **itch** VERB
♦ **It itches.** Ça me démange.
♦ **My head's itching.** J'ai des démangeaisons à la tête.

itchy ADJECTIVE
♦ **My arm is itchy.** J'ai des fourmis dans le bras.

it'd = **it had**, = **it would**

item NOUN
l' article MASC (*object*)

itinerary NOUN
l' itinéraire MASC

it'll = **it will**

its ADJECTIVE

> *Remember to check if **its** refers to a masculine, feminine or plural noun.*

son MASC ◊ *What's its name?* Quel est son nom?
sa FEM ◊ *Every thing in its place.* Chaque chose à sa place.
ses PL ◊ *The dog is losing its hair.* Le chien perd ses poils.

it's = **it is**, = **it has**

itself PRONOUN
se

> *se* changes to *s'* before a vowel and most words beginning with "h".

◊ *The heating switches itself off.* Le chauffage s'arrête automatiquement.

I've = **I have**

J

jab NOUN
la <u>piqûre</u> (*injection*)

jack NOUN
1 le <u>cric</u> (*for car*)
2 le <u>valet</u> (*playing card*)

jacket NOUN
la <u>veste</u>
- **jacket potatoes** les pommes de terre en robe des champs FEM

jackpot NOUN
le <u>gros lot</u>
- **to win the jackpot** gagner le gros lot

jail NOUN
see also **jail** VERB
la <u>prison</u>
- **to go to jail** aller en prison

to **jail** VERB
see also **jail** NOUN
<u>emprisonner</u>

jam NOUN
la <u>confiture</u> ◊ *strawberry jam* la confiture de fraises
- **a traffic jam** un embouteillage

jam jar NOUN
le <u>pot à confiture</u>

jammed ADJECTIVE
<u>coincé</u> ◊ *The window's jammed.* La fenêtre est coincée.

jam-packed ADJECTIVE
<u>bondé</u> ◊ *The room was jam-packed.* La salle était bondée.

janitor NOUN
le <u>concierge</u> ◊ *He's a janitor.* Il est concierge.

January NOUN
<u>janvier</u> MASC
- **in January** en janvier

Japan NOUN
le <u>Japon</u>
- **in Japan** au Japon
- **from Japan** du Japon

Japanese ADJECTIVE
see also **Japanese** NOUN
<u>japonais</u>

Japanese NOUN
see also **Japanese** ADJECTIVE
1 (*person*)
le <u>Japonais</u>
la <u>Japonaise</u>
- **the Japanese** les Japonais
2 (*language*)
le <u>japonais</u>

jar NOUN
le <u>bocal</u>

(les bocaux PL)
◊ *an empty jar* un bocal vide
- **a jar of honey** un pot de miel

jaundice NOUN
la <u>jaunisse</u>

javelin NOUN
le <u>javelot</u>

jaw NOUN
la <u>mâchoire</u>

jazz NOUN
le <u>jazz</u>

jealous ADJECTIVE
<u>jaloux</u> MASC
<u>jalouse</u> FEM

jeans PL NOUN
le <u>jean</u> SING

Jehovah's Witness NOUN
le <u>témoin de Jéhovah</u> ◊ *She's a Jehovah's Witness.* Elle est témoin de Jéhovah.

Jello ® NOUN US
la <u>gelée</u>

jelly NOUN
la <u>gelée</u>

jellyfish NOUN
la <u>méduse</u>

jersey NOUN
le <u>pull-over</u> (*pullover*)

Jesus NOUN
<u>Jésus</u> MASC

jet NOUN
le <u>jet</u> (*plane*)

jetlag NOUN
- **to be suffering from jetlag** être sous le coup du décalage horaire

jetty NOUN
la <u>jetée</u>

Jew NOUN
le <u>Juif</u>
la <u>Juive</u>

jewel NOUN
le <u>bijou</u>
(les bijoux PL)

jeweller NOUN (US **jeweler**)
le <u>bijoutier</u>
la <u>bijoutière</u>
◊ *He's a jeweller.* Il est bijoutier.

jeweller's shop NOUN (US **jeweler's shop**)
la <u>bijouterie</u>

jewellery NOUN (US **jewelry**)
les <u>bijoux</u> MASC PL

Jewish ADJECTIVE

juif MASC
juive FEM

jigsaw NOUN
le puzzle

job NOUN
1 l' emploi MASC ◊ *He's lost his job.* Il a perdu son emploi.
♦ **I've got a Saturday job.** Je travaille le samedi.
2 (*chore, task*)
le travail
(les travaux PL)
◊ *That was a difficult job.* C'était un travail difficile.

job centre NOUN
l' agence pour l'emploi FEM

jobless ADJECTIVE
sans emploi

jockey NOUN
le jockey

to jog VERB
faire du jogging

jogging NOUN
le jogging
♦ **to go jogging** faire du jogging

john NOUN US
les toilettes FEM PL

to join VERB
1 s'inscrire à (*become member of*)
◊ *I'm going to join the ski club.* Je vais m'inscrire au club de ski.
2 se joindre à ◊ *Do you mind if I join you?* Puis-je me joindre à vous?

joiner NOUN
le menuisier ◊ *He's a joiner.* Il est menuisier.

joint NOUN
1 l' articulation FEM (*in body*)
2 le rôti (*of meat*)
3 le joint (*drugs*)

joke NOUN
see also **joke** VERB
la plaisanterie
♦ **to tell a joke** raconter une plaisanterie

to joke VERB
see also **joke** NOUN
plaisanter ◊ *I'm only joking.* Je plaisante.

jolly ADJECTIVE
jovial
(joviaux MASC PL)

Jordan NOUN
la Jordanie (*country*)
♦ **in Jordan** en Jordanie

to jot down VERB
noter

jotter NOUN
(*pad*)

le bloc-notes
(les blocs-notes PL)

journalism NOUN
le journalisme

journalist NOUN
le/la journaliste ◊ *She's a journalist.* Elle est journaliste.

journey NOUN
1 le voyage ◊ *I don't like long journeys.* Je n'aime pas les longs voyages.
♦ **to go on a journey** faire un voyage
2 le trajet (*to school, work*) ◊ *The journey to school takes about half an hour.* Il y a une demi-heure de trajet pour aller à l'école.
♦ **a bus journey** un trajet en autobus

joy NOUN
la joie

joystick NOUN
le manette de jeu (*for computer game*)

judge NOUN
see also **judge** VERB
le juge ◊ *She's a judge.* Elle est juge.

to judge VERB
see also **judge** NOUN
juger

judo NOUN
le judo ◊ *My hobby is judo.* Je fais du judo.

jug NOUN
le pot

juggler NOUN
le jongleur
la jongleuse

juice NOUN
le jus ◊ *orange juice* le jus d'orange

July NOUN
juillet MASC
♦ **in July** en juillet

jumble sale NOUN
la vente de charité

to jump VERB
sauter
♦ **to jump over something** sauter par-dessus quelque chose
♦ **to jump out of the window** sauter par la fenêtre
♦ **to jump off the roof** sauter du toit

jumper NOUN
le pull-over (*pullover*)

junction NOUN
le carrefour (*of roads*)

June NOUN
juin MASC
♦ **in June** en juin

jungle NOUN

la <u>jungle</u>

junior NOUN
♦ **the juniors** (*in school*) les élèves des petites classes

junior school NOUN
l' <u>école primaire</u> FEM

junk NOUN
le <u>bric-à-brac</u> NO PL (*old things*) ◊ *The attic's full of junk.* Le grenier est rempli de bric-à-brac.
♦ **to eat junk food** manger n'importe comment
♦ **a junk shop** un magasin de brocante

jury NOUN
le <u>jury</u>

just ADVERB

<u>juste</u> ◊ *just after Christmas* juste après Noël ◊ *We had just enough money.* Nous avions juste assez d'argent. ◊ *just in time* juste à temps
♦ **just here** ici
♦ **I'm rather busy just now.** Je suis assez occupé en ce moment.
♦ **I did it just now.** Je viens de le faire.
♦ **He's just arrived.** Il vient d'arriver.
♦ **I'm just coming!** J'arrive!
♦ **It's just a suggestion.** Ce n'est qu'une suggestion.

justice NOUN
la <u>justice</u>

to **justify** VERB
<u>justifier</u>

J

K

kangaroo NOUN
le <u>kangourou</u>

karaoke NOUN
le <u>karaoké</u>

karate NOUN
le <u>karaté</u>

kebab NOUN
1 la <u>brochette</u> (*shish kebab*)
2 le <u>doner kebab</u> (*doner kebab*)

keen ADJECTIVE
<u>enthousiaste</u> ◊ *He doesn't seem very keen.* Il n'a pas l'air très enthousiaste.
♦**She's a keen student.** C'est une étudiante assidue.
♦**to be keen on something** aimer quelque chose ◊ *I'm keen on maths.* J'aime les maths. ◊ *I'm not very keen on maths.* Je n'aime pas trop les maths.
♦**to be keen on somebody** (*fancy them*) être très attiré par quelqu'un ◊ *He's keen on her.* Il est très attiré par elle.
♦**to be keen on doing something** avoir très envie de faire quelque chose ◊ *I'm not very keen on going.* Je n'ai pas très envie d'y aller.

to **keep** VERB
1 <u>garder</u> (*retain*) ◊ *You can keep it.* Tu peux le garder.
2 <u>rester</u> (*remain*) ◊ *Keep still!* Reste tranquille!
♦**Keep quiet!** Tais-toi!
♦**I keep forgetting my keys.** J'oublie tout le temps mes clés.
♦**to keep on doing something (1)** (*continue*) continuer à faire quelque chose ◊ *He kept on reading.* Il a continué à lire.
♦**to keep on doing something (2)** (*repeatedly*) ne pas arrêter de faire quelque chose ◊ *The car keeps on breaking down.* La voiture n'arrête pas de tomber en panne.
♦**"keep out"** "défense d'entrer"

to **keep up** VERB
<u>se maintenir à la hauteur de quelqu'un</u> ◊ *Matthew walks so fast I can't keep up.* Matthew marche tellement vite que je n'arrive pas à me maintenir à sa hauteur.
♦**I can't keep up with the rest of the class.** Je n'arrive pas à suivre le reste de la classe.

keep-fit NOUN
la <u>gymnastique d'entretien</u>

♦**I go to keep-fit classes.** Je vais à des cours de gymnastique.

kennel NOUN
la <u>niche</u>

kept VERB *see* **keep**

kerosene NOUN US
le <u>pétrole</u>

kettle NOUN
la <u>bouilloire</u>

key NOUN
la <u>clé</u>

keyboard NOUN
le <u>clavier</u> ◊ *... with Mike Moran on keyboards* ... avec Mike Moran aux claviers

keyring NOUN
le <u>porte-clés</u>

kick NOUN
see also **kick** VERB
le <u>coup de pied</u>

to **kick** VERB
see also **kick** NOUN
♦**to kick somebody** donner un coup de pied à quelqu'un ◊ *He kicked me.* Il m'a donné un coup de pied. ◊ *He kicked the ball hard.* Il a donné un bon coup de pied dans le ballon.
♦**to kick off** (*in football*) donner le coup d'envoi

kick-off NOUN
le <u>coup d'envoi</u> ◊ *The kick-off is at 10 o'clock.* Le coup d'envoi sera donné à dix heures.

kid NOUN
see also **kid** VERB
le/la <u>gosse</u> (*child*)

to **kid** VERB
see also **kid** NOUN
<u>plaisanter</u> ◊ *I'm just kidding.* Je plaisante.

to **kidnap** VERB
<u>kidnapper</u>

kidney NOUN
1 le <u>rein</u> (*human*) ◊ *He's got kidney trouble.* Il a des problèmes de reins.
2 le <u>rognon</u> (*to eat*) ◊ *I don't like kidneys.* Je n'aime pas les rognons.

to **kill** VERB
<u>tuer</u> ◊ *He was killed in a car accident.* Il a été tué dans un accident de voiture.
♦**Luckily, nobody was killed.** Il n'y a heureusement pas eu de victimes.

◆**Six people were killed in the accident.** L'accident a fait six morts.
◆**to kill oneself** se suicider ◊ *He killed himself.* Il s'est suicidé.

killer NOUN
[1] (*murderer*)
le meurtrier
la meurtrière
◊ *The police are searching for the killer.* La police recherche le meurtrier.
[2] (*hit man*)
le tueur
la tueuse
◊ *a hired killer* un tueur à gages
◆**Meningitis can be a killer.** La méningite peut être mortelle.

kilo NOUN
le kilo ◊ *10 francs a kilo* dix francs le kilo

kilometre NOUN (US **kilometer**)
le kilomètre

kilt NOUN
le kilt

kind ADJECTIVE
see also **kind** NOUN
gentil MASC
gentille FEM
◆**to be kind to somebody** être gentil avec quelqu'un
◆**Thank you for being so kind.** Merci pour votre gentillesse.

kind NOUN
see also **kind** ADJECTIVE
la sorte ◊ *It's a kind of sausage.* C'est une sorte de saucisse.

kindergarten NOUN
l' école maternelle FEM

kindly ADVERB
gentiment ◊ *"Don't worry," she said kindly.* "Ne t'en fais pas", m'a-t-elle dit gentiment.
◆**Kindly refrain from smoking.** Veuillez vous abstenir de fumer.

kindness NOUN
la gentillesse

king NOUN
le roi

kingdom NOUN
le royaume

kiosk NOUN
la cabine téléphonique (*phone box*)

kipper NOUN
le hareng fumé

kiss NOUN
see also **kiss** VERB
le baiser ◊ *a passionate kiss* un baiser passionné

to **kiss** VERB
see also **kiss** NOUN
[1] embrasser ◊ *He kissed her passionately.* Il l'a embrassée passionnément.
[2] s'embrasser ◊ *They kissed.* Ils se sont embrassés.

kit NOUN
[1] les affaires FEM PL (*clothes for sport*)
◊ *I've forgotten my gym kit.* J'ai oublié mes affaires de gym.
[2] la trousse ◊ *a tool kit* une trousse à outils ◊ *a first aid kit* une trousse de secours ◊ *a puncture repair kit* une trousse de réparations
◆**a drum kit** une batterie
◆**a sewing kit** un nécessaire à couture

kitchen NOUN
la cuisine ◊ *a fitted kitchen* une cuisine aménagée
◆**the kitchen units** les éléments de cuisine MASC
◆**a kitchen knife** un couteau de cuisine

kite NOUN
le cerf-volant
(les cerfs-volants PL)

kitten NOUN
le chaton

knee NOUN
le genou
(les genoux PL)
◆**He was on his knees.** Il était à genoux.

to **kneel (down)** VERB
s'agenouiller

knew VERB see **know**

knickers PL NOUN
la culotte SING
◆**a pair of knickers** une culotte

knife NOUN
le couteau
(les couteaux PL)
◆**a kitchen knife** un couteau de cuisine
◆**a sheath knife** un couteau à gaine
◆**a penknife** un canif

to **knit** VERB
tricoter

knitting NOUN
le tricot ◊ *I like knitting.* J'aime faire du tricot.

knives PL NOUN see **knife**

knob NOUN
le bouton (*on door, radio, TV, radiator*)

to **knock** VERB
see also **knock** NOUN
frapper ◊ *Someone's knocking at the door.* Quelqu'un frappe à la porte.
◆**to knock somebody down** renverser quelqu'un ◊ *She was knocked down*

K

by a car. Elle a été renversée par une voiture.

♦to knock somebody out (1) (defeat) éliminer ◊ They were knocked out early in the tournament. Ils ont été éliminés au début du tournoi.

♦to knock somebody out (2) (stun) assommer ◊ They knocked out the watchman. Ils ont assommé le gardien.

knock NOUN
> see also **knock** VERB
le <u>coup</u>

knot NOUN
le <u>nœud</u>

♦to tie a knot in something faire un nœud à quelque chose

to **know** VERB

> *Use savoir for knowing facts, connaître for knowing people and places.*

1 <u>savoir</u> ◊ It's a long way. – Yes, I know. C'est loin. – Oui, je sais. ◊ I don't know. Je ne sais pas. ◊ I don't know what to do. Je ne sais pas quoi faire. ◊ I don't know how to do it. Je ne sais pas comment faire.

2 <u>connaître</u> ◊ I know her. Je la connais. ◊ I know Paris well. Je connais bien Paris.

♦I don't know any German. Je ne parle pas du tout allemand.

♦to know that ... savoir que ... ◊ I know that you like chocolate. Je sais que tu aimes le chocolat. ◊ I didn't know that your Dad was a policeman. Je ne savais pas que ton père était policier.

♦to know about something (1) (be aware of) être au courant de quelque chose ◊ Do you know about the meeting this afternoon? Tu es au courant de la réunion de cet après-midi?

♦to know about something (2) (be knowledgeable about) s'y connaître en quelque chose ◊ He knows a lot about cars. Il s'y connaît en voitures. ◊ I don't know much about computers. Je ne m'y connais pas bien en informatique.

♦to get to know somebody apprendre à connaître quelqu'un

♦How should I know? (I don't know!) Comment veux-tu que je le sache?

♦You never know! On ne sait jamais!

know-all NOUN
le/la <u>je-sais-tout</u> ◊ He's such a know-all! C'est Monsieur je-sais-tout!

know-how NOUN
le <u>savoir-faire</u>

knowledge NOUN
la <u>connaissance</u>

knowledgeable ADJECTIVE
♦to be knowledgeable about something s'y connaître en quelque chose ◊ She's very knowledgeable about computers. Elle s'y connaît bien en informatique.

known VERB see **know**

Koran NOUN
le <u>Coran</u>

Korea NOUN
la <u>Corée</u>
♦in Korea en Corée

kosher ADJECTIVE
<u>kascher</u> MASC, FEM, PL

L

lab NOUN (= *laboratory*)
le <u>labo</u>
♦ **a lab technician** un laborantin

label NOUN
l' <u>étiquette</u> FEM

labor NOUN US
♦ **to be in labor** être en train
d'accoucher
♦ **the labor market** le marché du travail
♦ **a labor union** un syndicat

laboratory NOUN
le <u>laboratoire</u>

Labour NOUN
les <u>travaillistes</u> MASC PL ◊ *My parents
vote Labour.* Mes parents votent pour
les travaillistes.
♦ **the Labour Party** le parti travailliste

labour NOUN
♦ **to be in labour** être en train
d'accoucher
♦ **the labour market** le marché du
travail

labourer NOUN
le <u>manœuvre</u>
♦ **a farm labourer** un ouvrier agricole

lace NOUN
1 le <u>lacet</u> (*of shoe*)
2 la <u>dentelle</u> ◊ *a lace collar* un col
en dentelle

lack NOUN
le <u>manque</u> ◊ *He got the job despite
his lack of experience.* Il a obtenu le
poste en dépit de son manque
d'expérience.
♦ **There was no lack of volunteers.** Les
volontaires ne manquaient pas.

lacquer NOUN
la <u>laque</u>

lad NOUN
le <u>gars</u>

ladder NOUN
l' <u>échelle</u> FEM

lady NOUN
la <u>dame</u>
♦ **a young lady** une jeune fille
♦ **Ladies and gentlemen ...** Mesdames,
Messieurs ...
♦ **the ladies'** les toilettes pour dames FEM

ladybird NOUN
la <u>coccinelle</u>

to **lag behind** VERB
<u>rester en arrière</u>

lager NOUN
la <u>bière blonde</u>

laid VERB *see* **lay**

laid-back ADJECTIVE
<u>relaxe</u>

lain VERB *see* **lie**

lake NOUN
le <u>lac</u>
♦ **Lake Geneva** le lac Léman

lamb NOUN
l' <u>agneau</u> MASC
(les agneaux PL)
♦ **a lamb chop** une côtelette d'agneau

lame ADJECTIVE
<u>boiteux</u> ◊ *My pony is lame.* Mon
poney boîte.

lamp NOUN
la <u>lampe</u>

lamppost NOUN
le <u>réverbère</u>

lampshade NOUN
l' <u>abat-jour</u> MASC
(les abat-jour PL)

land NOUN
see also **land** VERB
la <u>terre</u>
♦ **a piece of land** un terrain

to **land** VERB
see also **land** NOUN
<u>atterrir</u> (*plane, passenger*)

landing NOUN
1 l' <u>atterrissage</u> MASC (*of plane*)
2 le <u>palier</u> (*of staircase*)

landlady NOUN
la <u>propriétaire</u>

landlord NOUN
le <u>propriétaire</u>

landmark NOUN
le <u>point de repère</u> (*for finding your
way*)
♦ **Big Ben is one of London's most
famous landmarks.** Big Ben est l'un
des sites les plus célèbres du paysage
londonien.

landowner NOUN
le <u>propriétaire terrien</u>

landscape NOUN
le <u>paysage</u>

lane NOUN
1 le <u>chemin</u> (*in country*)
2 la <u>voie</u> (*on motorway*)

language NOUN
la <u>langue</u> ◊ *French isn't a difficult
language.* Le français n'est pas une
langue difficile.

☞

♦**to use bad language** dire des grossièretés

language laboratory NOUN
le laboratoire de langues

lap NOUN
le tour de piste (*sport*) ◊ *I ran ten laps.* J'ai fait dix tours de piste en courant.
♦**on my lap** sur mes genoux

laptop NOUN
le portable (*computer*)

larder NOUN
le garde-manger
(les garde-manger PL)

large ADJECTIVE
① grand ◊ *a large house* une grande maison
② (*person, animal*)
gros MASC
grosse FEM
◊ *a large dog* un gros chien

largely ADVERB
en grande partie ◊ *It's largely the fault of the government.* C'est en grande partie la faute du gouvernement.

laser NOUN
le laser

lass NOUN
la jeune fille

last ADJECTIVE, ADVERB
see also **last** VERB
① dernier MASC
dernière FEM
◊ *last Friday* vendredi dernier ◊ *last week* la semaine dernière ◊ *last summer* l'été dernier
② en dernier ◊ *He arrived last.* Il est arrivé en dernier.
③ pour la dernière fois ◊ *I've lost my bag. – When did you see it last?* J'ai perdu mon sac. – Quand est-ce que tu l'as vu pour la dernière fois? ◊ *When I last saw him, he was wearing a blue shirt.* La dernière fois que je l'ai vu, il portait une chemise bleue.
♦**the last time** la dernière fois ◊ *the last time I saw her* la dernière fois que je l'ai vue ◊ *That's the last time I take your advice!* C'est la dernière fois que je suis tes conseils!
♦**last night (1)** (*evening*) hier soir ◊ *I got home at midnight last night.* Je suis rentré à minuit hier soir.
♦**last night (2)** (*sleeping hours*) la nuit dernière ◊ *I couldn't sleep last night.* J'ai eu du mal à dormir la nuit dernière.
♦**at last** enfin

to last VERB
see also **last** ADJECTIVE
durer ◊ *The concert lasts two hours.* Le concert dure deux heures.

lastly ADVERB
finalement ◊ *Lastly, what time do you arrive?* Finalement, à quelle heure arrives-tu?

late ADJECTIVE, ADVERB
① en retard ◊ *Hurry up or you'll be late!* Dépêche-toi, sinon tu vas être en retard! ◊ *I'm often late for school.* J'arrive souvent en retard à l'école.
♦**to arrive late** arriver en retard ◊ *She arrived late.* Elle est arrivée en retard.
② tard ◊ *I went to bed late.* Je me suis couché tard.
♦**in the late afternoon** en fin d'après-midi
♦**in late May** fin mai

lately ADVERB
ces derniers temps ◊ *I haven't seen him lately.* Je ne l'ai pas vu ces derniers temps.

later ADVERB
plus tard ◊ *I'll do it later.* Je ferai ça plus tard.
♦**See you later!** À tout à l'heure!

latest ADJECTIVE
dernier MASC
dernière FEM
◊ *their latest album* leur dernier album
♦**at the latest** au plus tard ◊ *by 10 o'clock at the latest* à dix heures au plus tard

Latin NOUN
le latin ◊ *I do Latin.* Je fais du latin.

Latin America NOUN
l' Amérique latine FEM
♦**in Latin America** en Amérique latine

Latin American ADJECTIVE
latino-américain

latter NOUN
le second
la seconde
♦**the former ..., the latter ...** le premier ..., le second ... ◊ *The former lives in the US, the latter in Australia.* Le premier habite aux États-Unis, le second en Australie.
♦**The latter is the more expensive of the two systems.** Ce dernier système est le plus coûteux des deux.

laugh NOUN
see also **laugh** VERB
le rire
♦**It was a good laugh.** (*it was fun*) On s'est bien amusés.

to **laugh** VERB
see also **laugh** NOUN
rire
♦ **to laugh at something** se moquer de
quelque chose ◊ *They laughed at her.*
Ils se sont moqués d'elle.

to **launch** VERB
lancer (*product, rocket, boat*) ◊ *They're
going to launch a new model.* Ils
vont lancer un nouveau modèle.

Launderette ® NOUN
la laverie

Laundromat ® NOUN US
la laverie

laundry NOUN
le linge (*clothes*)

lavatory NOUN
les toilettes FEM PL

lavender NOUN
la lavande

law NOUN
[1] la loi ◊ *The laws are very strict.*
Les lois sont très sévères.
♦ **It's against the law.** C'est illégal.
[2] le droit (*subject*) ◊ *My sister's
studying law.* Ma sœur fait des
études de droit.

lawn NOUN
la pelouse

lawnmower NOUN
la tondeuse à gazon

law school NOUN US
la faculté de droit

lawyer NOUN
l' avocat MASC
l' avocate FEM
◊ *My mother's a lawyer.* Ma mère est
avocate.

to **lay** VERB
*lay is also a form of **lie** VERB.*
mettre ◊ *She laid the baby in her
cot.* Elle a mis le bébé dans son lit.
♦ **to lay the table** mettre la table
♦ **to lay something on (1)** (*provide*)
organiser quelque chose ◊ *They laid
on extra buses.* Ils ont organisé un
service de bus supplémentaire.
♦ **to lay something on (2)** (*prepare*)
préparer quelque chose ◊ *They laid
on a special meal.* Ils ont préparé un
repas soigné.

to **lay off** VERB
licencier ◊ *My father's been laid off.*
Mon père a été licencié.

lay-by NOUN
l' aire de stationnement FEM

layer NOUN

la couche ◊ *the ozone layer* la
couche d'ozone

layout NOUN
[1] la mise en page (*of newspaper
article*)
[2] la disposition (*of house, buildings*)
◊ *It took me some time to get
familiar with the layout of the school.*
J'ai mis un certain temps à me
familiariser avec la disposition de
l'école.

lazy ADJECTIVE
paresseux MASC
paresseuse FEM

lead NOUN
*This word has two pronunciations.
Make sure you choose the right
translation.*
see also **lead** VERB
[1] le fil (*cable*)
[2] la laisse (*for dog*)
♦ **to be in the lead** être en tête ◊ *Our
team is in the lead.* Notre équipe est
en tête.
[3] le plomb (*metal*)

to **lead** VERB
see also **lead** NOUN
mener ◊ *the street that leads to the
station* la rue qui mène à la gare
♦ **to lead the way** montrer le chemin
♦ **to lead somebody away** emmener
quelqu'un ◊ *The police led the man
away.* La police a emmené l'homme.

leaded petrol NOUN
l' essence au plomb FEM

leader NOUN
[1] (*of expedition, gang*)
le chef
[2] (*of political party*)
le dirigeant
la dirigeante

lead-free ADJECTIVE
♦ **lead-free petrol** de l'essence sans
plomb

lead singer NOUN
le chanteur principal
la chanteuse principale

leaf NOUN
la feuille

leaflet NOUN
la brochure

league NOUN
le championnat ◊ *They are at the
top of the league.* Ils sont en tête du
championnat.
♦ **the Premier League** la première
division

leak NOUN
see also **leak** VERB

L

la <u>fuite</u> ◊ *a gas leak* une fuite de gaz

to **leak** VERB

> see also **leak** NOUN

<u>fuir</u> (*pipe, water, gas*)

to **lean** VERB

<u>se pencher</u> ◊ *Don't lean over too far.* Ne te penche pas trop. ◊ *She leant out of the window.* Elle s'est penchée par la fenêtre.

♦ **to lean forward** se pencher en avant
♦ **to lean on something** s'appuyer contre quelque chose ◊ *He leant on the wall.* Il s'est appuyé contre le mur.
♦ **to be leaning against something** être appuyé contre quelque chose ◊ *The ladder was leaning against the wall.* L'échelle était appuyée contre le mur.
♦ **to lean something against a wall** appuyer quelque chose contre un mur ◊ *He leant his bike against the wall.* Il a appuyé son vélo contre le mur.

to **lean out** VERB

<u>se pencher au dehors</u>

♦ **She leant out of the window.** Elle s'est penché par la fenêtre.

to **lean over** VERB

<u>se pencher</u> ◊ *Don't lean over too far.* Ne te penche pas trop loin.

to **leap** VERB

<u>sauter</u> ◊ *They lept over the stream.* Ils ont sauté pour traverser la rivière.

♦ **He leapt out of his chair when his team scored.** Il s'est levé d'un bond lorsque son équipe a marqué.

leap year NOUN

l' <u>année bissextile</u> FEM

to **learn** VERB

<u>apprendre</u> ◊ *I'm learning to ski.* J'apprends à skier.

learner NOUN

♦ **She's a quick learner.** Elle apprend vite.
♦ **French learners** (*people learning French*) ceux qui apprennent le français

learner driver NOUN

le <u>conducteur débutant</u>
la <u>conductrice débutante</u>

learnt VERB *see* **learn**

least ADVERB, ADJECTIVE, PRONOUN

♦ **the least (1)** (*followed by noun*) le moins de ◊ *It takes the least time.* C'est ce qui prend le moins de temps.
♦ **the least (2)** (*after a verb*) le moins ◊ *Maths is the subject I like the least.* Les maths sont la matière que j'aime le moins.

*When **least** is followed by an adjective, the translation depends on whether the noun referred to is masculine, feminine or plural.*

♦ **the least ... (1)** le moins ... ◊ *the least expensive hotel* l'hôtel le moins cher
♦ **the least ... (2)** la moins ... ◊ *the least expensive seat* la place la moins chère
♦ **the least ... (3)** les moins ... ◊ *the least expensive hotels* les hôtels les moins chers ◊ *the least expensive seats* les places les moins chères
♦ **It's the least I can do.** C'est le moins que je puisse faire.
♦ **at least (1)** au moins ◊ *It'll cost at least £200.* Ça va coûter au moins deux cents livres.
♦ **at least (2)** du moins ◊ *... but at least nobody was hurt.* ... mais du moins personne n'a été blessé. ◊ *It's totally unfair – at least, that's my opinion.* C'est vraiment injuste – du moins c'est ce que je pense.

leather NOUN

le <u>cuir</u> ◊ *a black leather jacket* un blouson en cuir noir

leave NOUN

> see also **leave** VERB

① le <u>congé</u> (*from job*)
② la <u>permission</u> (*from army*) ◊ *He is on leave for a week.* Il est en permission pendant une semaine.

to **leave** VERB

> see also **leave** NOUN

① <u>laisser</u> (*deliberately*) ◊ *Don't leave your camera in the car.* Ne laisse pas ton appareil-photo dans la voiture.
② <u>oublier</u> (*by mistake*) ◊ *I've left my book at home.* J'ai oublié mon livre à la maison. ◊ *Make sure you haven't left anything behind.* Vérifiez bien que vous n'avez rien oublié.
③ <u>partir</u> (*go*) ◊ *The bus leaves at 8.* Le car part à huit heures. ◊ *She's just left.* Elle vient de partir.
④ <u>quitter</u> (*go away from*) ◊ *We leave London at six o'clock.* Nous quittons Londres à six heures. ◊ *My sister left home last year.* Ma sœur a quitté la maison l'an dernier.

♦ **to leave somebody alone** laisser quelqu'un tranquille ◊ *Leave me alone!* Laisse-moi tranquille!

to **leave out** VERB

<u>mettre à l'écart</u> ◊ *Not knowing the language I felt really left out.* Comme je ne connaissais pas la langue, je me suis vraiment senti à l'écart.

leaves PL NOUN *see* **leaf**

Lebanon NOUN

le <u>Liban</u>
- **in Lebanon** au Liban

lecture NOUN

> *see also* **lecture** VERB

[1] (*public*)
la <u>conférence</u>
[2] (*at university*)
le <u>cours magistral</u>
(les cours magistraux PL)

> *Be careful not to translate* **lecture** *by the French word* **lecture**.

to **lecture** VERB

> *see also* **lecture** NOUN

[1] <u>enseigner</u> ◊ *She lectures at the technical college.* Elle enseigne au collège technique.
[2] <u>faire la morale</u> ◊ *He's always lecturing us.* Il n'arrête pas de nous faire la morale.

lecturer NOUN

le <u>professeur d'université</u> ◊ *She's a lecturer.* Elle est professeur d'université.

led VERB *see* **lead**

leek NOUN

le <u>poireau</u>
(les poireaux PL)

left VERB *see* **leave**

left ADJECTIVE, ADVERB

> *see also* **left** NOUN

[1] <u>gauche</u> (*not right*) ◊ *my left hand* ma main gauche ◊ *on the left side of the road* sur le côté gauche de la route
[2] <u>à gauche</u> ◊ *Turn left at the traffic lights.* Tournez à gauche aux prochains feux.
- **I haven't got any money left.** Il ne me reste plus d'argent.

left NOUN

> *see also* **left** ADJECTIVE

la <u>gauche</u>
- **on the left** à gauche ◊ *Remember to drive on the left.* N'oubliez pas de conduire à gauche.

left-hand ADJECTIVE

- **the left-hand side** la gauche ◊ *It's on the left-hand side.* C'est à gauche.

left-handed ADJECTIVE

<u>gaucher</u> MASC
<u>gauchère</u> FEM

left-luggage office NOUN

la <u>consigne</u>

leg NOUN

la <u>jambe</u> ◊ *She's broken her leg.* Elle s'est cassé la jambe.
- **a chicken leg** une cuisse de poulet
- **a leg of lamb** un gigot d'agneau

legal ADJECTIVE

<u>légal</u>

(légaux MASC PL)

leggings NOUN

le <u>caleçon</u> SING

leisure NOUN

les <u>loisirs</u> MASC PL ◊ *What do you do in your leisure time?* Qu'est-ce que tu fais pendant tes loisirs?

leisure centre NOUN

le <u>centre de loisirs</u>

lemon NOUN

le <u>citron</u>

lemonade NOUN

la <u>limonade</u>

to **lend** VERB

<u>prêter</u> ◊ *I can lend you some money.* Je peux te prêter de l'argent.

length NOUN

la <u>longueur</u>
- **It's about a metre in length.** Ça fait environ un mètre de long.

lens NOUN

[1] la <u>lentille</u> (*contact lens*)
[2] le <u>verre</u> (*of spectacles*)
[3] l' <u>objectif</u> MASC (*of camera*)

Lent NOUN

le <u>carême</u>

lent VERB *see* **lend**

lentil NOUN

la <u>lentille</u>

Leo NOUN

le <u>Lion</u> ◊ *I'm Leo.* Je suis Lion.

leotard NOUN

le <u>justaucorps</u>

lesbian NOUN

la <u>lesbienne</u>

less PRONOUN, ADVERB, ADJECTIVE

[1] <u>moins</u> ◊ *He's less intelligent than her.* Il est moins intelligent qu'elle. ◊ *A bit less, please.* Un peu moins, s'il vous plaît.
[2] <u>moins de</u> ◊ *I've got less time for hobbies now.* J'ai moins de temps pour les loisirs maintenant.
- **less than (1)** (*with amounts*) moins de ◊ *It's less than a kilometre from here.* C'est à moins d'un kilomètre d'ici. ◊ *It costs less than 100 francs.* Ça coûte moins de cent francs. ◊ *less than half* moins de la moitié
- **less than (2)** (*in comparisons*) moins que ◊ *He spent less than me.* Il a dépensé moins que moi. ◊ *I've got less than you.* J'en ai moins que toi. ◊ *It cost less than we thought.* Ça a coûté moins cher que nous ne le pensions.

lesson NOUN

[1] la <u>leçon</u> ◊ *a French lesson* une leçon de français

L

☞

2 le cours (*class*) ◊ *The lessons last forty minutes each.* Chaque cours dure quarante minutes.

to **let** VERB

1 laisser (*allow*)

♦ **to let somebody do something** laisser quelqu'un faire quelque chose ◊ *Let me have a look.* Laisse-moi voir. ◊ *My parents won't let me stay out that late.* Mes parents ne me laissent pas sortir aussi tard.

♦ **to let somebody know** faire savoir à quelqu'un ◊ *I'll let you know as soon as possible.* Je vous le ferai savoir dès que possible.

♦ **to let down** décevoir ◊ *I won't let you down.* Je ne vous décevrai pas.

♦ **to let somebody go** lâcher quelqu'un ◊ *Let me go!* Lâche-moi!

♦ **to let in** laisser entrer ◊ *They wouldn't let me in because I was under 18.* Ils ne m'ont pas laissé entrer parce que j'avais moins de dix-huit ans.

> *To make suggestions using **let's**, you can ask questions beginning **si on**.* ◊ *Let's go to the cinema!* Si on allait au cinéma?

♦ **Let's go!** Allons-y!

2 louer (*hire out*) ◊ "*to let*" "à louer"

letter NOUN
la lettre

letterbox NOUN
la boîte à lettres

lettuce NOUN
la salade

leukaemia NOUN
la leucémie

level ADJECTIVE

see also **level** NOUN

plan ◊ *A snooker table must be perfectly level.* Un billard doit être parfaitement plan.

level NOUN

see also **level** ADJECTIVE

le niveau
(les niveaux PL)
◊ *The level of the river is rising.* Le niveau de la rivière monte.

♦ **"A" levels** le baccalauréat

> ❶ *The French **baccalauréat** (or **bac** for short) is taken at the age of 17 or 18. Students have to sit one of a variety of set subject combinations, rather than being able to choose any combination of subjects they want. If you pass you have the right to a place at university.*

level crossing NOUN
le passage à niveau

lever NOUN
le levier

liable ADJECTIVE

♦ **He's liable to lose his temper.** Il se met facilement en colère.

liar NOUN
le menteur
la menteuse

liberal ADJECTIVE
(*opinions*)
libéral
(libéraux MASC PL)

♦ **the Liberal Democrats** le parti libéral-démocrate

liberation NOUN
la libération

liberty NOUN
la liberté

Libra NOUN
la Balance ◊ *I'm Libra.* Je suis Balance.

librarian NOUN
le/la bibliothécaire ◊ *My mother is a librarian.* Ma mère est bibliothécaire.

library NOUN
la bibliothèque

♦ **a library book** un livre de bibliothèque

> *Be careful not to translate **library** by **librairie**.*

Libya NOUN
la Libye

♦ **in Libya** en Libye

licence NOUN (US **license**)
le permis

♦ **a driving licence** un permis de conduire

to **lick** VERB
lécher

lid NOUN
le couvercle

to **lie** VERB

see also **lie** NOUN

mentir (*not tell the truth*) ◊ *I know she's lying.* Je sais qu'elle ment.

♦ **to lie down** s'allonger

♦ **to be lying down** être allongé ◊ *He was lying on the sofa.* Il était allongé sur le canapé. ◊ *When I'm on holiday I lie on the beach all day.* Quand je suis en vacances, je reste allongé sur la plage toute la journée.

lie NOUN

see also **lie** VERB

le mensonge

♦ **to tell a lie** mentir

♦**That's a lie!** Ce n'est pas vrai!

lie-in NOUN
♦**to have a lie-in** faire la grasse matinée ◊ *I have a lie-in on Sundays.* Je fais la grasse matinée le dimanche.

lieutenant NOUN
le <u>lieutenant</u>

life NOUN
la <u>vie</u>

lifebelt NOUN
la <u>bouée de sauvetage</u>

lifeboat NOUN
le <u>canot de sauvetage</u>

lifeguard NOUN
le <u>maître nageur</u>

life jacket NOUN
le <u>gilet de sauvetage</u>

life-saving NOUN
le <u>sauvetage</u> ◊ *I've done a course in life-saving.* J'ai pris des cours de sauvetage.

lifestyle NOUN
le <u>style de vie</u>

to **lift** VERB
see also **lift** NOUN
<u>soulever</u> ◊ *It's too heavy, I can't lift it.* C'est trop lourd, je ne peux pas le soulever.

lift NOUN
see also **lift** VERB
l' <u>ascenseur</u> MASC ◊ *The lift isn't working.* L'ascenseur est en panne.
♦**He gave me a lift to the cinema.** Il m'a emmené au cinéma en voiture.
♦**Would you like a lift?** Est-ce que je peux vous déposer quelque part?

light ADJECTIVE
see also **light** NOUN, VERB
1 (*not heavy*)
<u>léger</u> MASC
<u>légère</u> FEM
◊ *a light jacket* une veste légère ◊ *a light meal* un repas léger
2 (*colour*)
<u>clair</u> ◊ *a light blue sweater* un pull bleu clair

light NOUN
see also **light** ADJECTIVE, VERB
1 la <u>lumière</u> ◊ *to switch on the light* allumer la lumière ◊ *to switch off the light* éteindre la lumière
2 la <u>lampe</u> ◊ *There's a light by my bed.* Il y a une lampe près de mon lit.
♦**the traffic lights** les feux MASC
♦**Have you got a light?** (*for cigarette*) Avez-vous du feu?

to **light** VERB
see also **light** ADJECTIVE, NOUN
<u>allumer</u> (*candle, cigarette, fire*)

light bulb NOUN
l' <u>ampoule</u> FEM

lighter NOUN
le <u>briquet</u> (*for cigarettes*)

lighthouse NOUN
le <u>phare</u>

lightning NOUN
les <u>éclairs</u> MASC PL
♦**a flash of lightning** un éclair

to **like** VERB
see also **like** PREPOSITION
1 <u>aimer</u> ◊ *I don't like mustard.* Je n'aime pas la moutarde. ◊ *I like riding.* J'aime monter à cheval.
*Note that **aimer** also means to love, so make sure you use **aimer bien** for just liking somebody.*
2 <u>aimer bien</u> ◊ *I like Paul, but I don't want to go out with him.* J'aime bien Paul, mais je ne veux pas sortir avec lui.
♦**I'd like ...** Je voudrais ... ◊ *I'd like an orange juice, please.* Je voudrais un jus d'orange, s'il vous plaît. ◊ *Would you like some coffee?* Voulez-vous du café?
♦**I'd like to ...** J'aimerais ... ◊ *I'd like to go to Russia one day.* J'aimerais aller en Russie un jour. ◊ *I'd like to wash my hands.* J'aimerais me laver les mains.
♦**Would you like to go for a walk?** Tu veux aller faire une promenade?
♦**... if you like ...** si tu veux

like PREPOSITION
see also **like** VERB
<u>comme</u> ◊ *It's fine like that.* C'est bien comme ça. ◊ *Do it like this.* Fais-le comme ça. ◊ *a city like Paris* une ville comme Paris ◊ *It's a bit like salmon.* C'est un peu comme du saumon.
♦**What's the weather like?** Quel temps fait-il?
♦**to look like somebody** ressembler à quelqu'un ◊ *You look like my brother.* Tu ressembles à mon frère.

likely ADJECTIVE
<u>probable</u> ◊ *That's not very likely.* C'est peu probable.
♦**She's likely to come.** Elle viendra probablement.
♦**She's not likely to come.** Elle ne viendra probablement pas.

Lilo ® NOUN
le <u>matelas pneumatique</u>

lily of the valley NOUN
le <u>muguet</u>

L

lime NOUN
le citron vert (*fruit*)

limit NOUN
la limite ◊ *The speed limit is 70 mph.*
La vitesse est limitée à cent dix
kilomètres à l'heure.

limousine NOUN
la limousine

to **limp** VERB
boiter

line NOUN
1 la ligne ◊ *a straight line* une ligne
droite
2 le trait (*to divide, cancel*) ◊ *Draw a
line under each answer.* Tirez un trait
après chaque réponse.
3 la voie (*railway track*)
♦ **Hold the line, please.** Ne quittez pas.
♦ **It's a very bad line.** La ligne est très
mauvaise.
♦ **on line** (*computing*) en ligne

linen NOUN
le lin ◊ *a linen jacket* une veste en lin

liner NOUN
le paquebot (*ship*)

linguist NOUN
♦ **to be a good linguist** être doué pour
les langues ◊ *She's a good linguist.*
Elle est douée pour les langues.

lining NOUN
la doublure (*of jacket, skirt etc*)

link NOUN
see also **link** VERB
1 le rapport ◊ *the link between
smoking and cancer* le rapport entre
le tabagisme et le cancer
2 le lien (*computing*)

to **link** VERB
see also **link** NOUN
relier

lino NOUN
le linoléum

lion NOUN
le lion

lioness NOUN
la lionne

lip NOUN
la lèvre

to **lip-read** VERB
lire sur les lèvres

lip salve NOUN
la pommade pour les lèvres

lipstick NOUN
le rouge à lèvres

liqueur NOUN
la liqueur

liquid NOUN
le liquide

liquidizer NOUN
le mixer

list NOUN
see also **list** VERB
la liste

to **list** VERB
see also **list** NOUN
faire une liste de ◊ *List your
hobbies!* Fais une liste de tes
hobbies!

to **listen** VERB
écouter ◊ *Listen to this!* Écoutez ceci!
◊ *Listen to me!* Écoutez-moi!

listener NOUN
l' auditeur MASC
l' auditrice FEM

lit VERB *see* **light**

liter NOUN US
le litre

literally ADVERB
vraiment (*completely*) ◊ *It was literally
impossible to find a seat.* Il était
vraiment impossible de trouver une
place.
♦ **to translate literally** faire une
traduction littérale

literature NOUN
la littérature ◊ *I'm studying English
Literature.* J'étudie la littérature
anglaise.

litre NOUN
le litre

litter NOUN
les ordures FEM PL

litter bin NOUN
la poubelle

little ADJECTIVE
petit ◊ *a little girl* une petite fille
♦ **a little** un peu ◊ *How much would
you like? – Just a little.* Combien en
voulez-vous? – Juste un peu.
♦ **very little** très peu ◊ *We've got very
little time.* Nous avons très peu de
temps.
♦ **little by little** petit à petit

live ADJECTIVE
see also **live** VERB
1 vivant (*animal*)
2 en direct (*broadcast*)
♦ **There's live music on Fridays.** Il y a
des musiciens qui jouent le vendredi.

to **live** VERB
see also **live** ADJECTIVE
1 vivre ◊ *I live with my
grandmother.* Je vis avec ma
grand-mère.
♦ **to live on something** vivre de
quelque chose ◊ *He lives on benefit.*
Il vit de ses indemnités.

[2] habiter (*reside*) ◊ *Where do you live? Où est-ce que tu habites?* ◊ *I live in Edinburgh.* J'habite à Édimbourg.
♦ **She's living with two Greek students.** Elle partage un appartement avec deux étudiants grecs.
♦ **to live together** vivre ensemble ◊ *My parents aren't living together any more.* Mes parents ne vivent plus ensemble.
♦ **They're not married, they're living together.** Ils ne sont pas mariés, ils vivent en concubinage.

lively ADJECTIVE
animé ◊ *It was a lively party.* C'était une soirée animée.
♦ **She's got a lively personality.** Elle est pleine de vitalité.

liver NOUN
le foie

lives PL NOUN
les vies FEM PL

living NOUN
♦ **to make a living** gagner sa vie
♦ **What does she do for a living?** Qu'est-ce qu'elle fait dans la vie?

living room NOUN
la salle de séjour

lizard NOUN
le lézard

load NOUN
see also **load** VERB
♦ **loads of** un tas de ◊ *loads of people* un tas de gens ◊ *loads of money* un tas d'argent
♦ **You're talking a load of rubbish!** Tu ne dis que des bêtises!

to **load** VERB
see also **load** NOUN
charger ◊ *a trolley loaded with luggage* un chariot chargé de bagages

loaf NOUN
le pain
♦ **a loaf of bread** un pain

loan NOUN
see also **loan** VERB
le prêt

to **loan** VERB
see also **loan** NOUN
prêter

to **loathe** VERB
détester ◊ *I loathe her.* Je la déteste.

loaves PL NOUN see **loaf**

lobster NOUN
le homard

local ADJECTIVE

local
(locaux MASC PL)
◊ *the local paper* le journal local
♦ **a local call** une communication urbaine

location NOUN
l' endroit MASC ◊ *A hotel set in a beautiful location.* Un hôtel situé dans un endroit magnifique.
*Be careful not to translate **location** by the French word **location**.*

loch NOUN
le loch

lock NOUN
see also **lock** VERB
la serrure ◊ *The lock is broken.* La serrure est cassée.

to **lock** VERB
see also **lock** NOUN
fermer à clé ◊ *Make sure you lock your door.* N'oubliez pas de fermer votre porte à clé.

to **lock out** VERB
♦ **The door slammed and I was locked out.** La porte a claqué et je me suis retrouvé à la porte.

locker NOUN
le casier
♦ **the locker room** le vestiaire
♦ **the left-luggage lockers** la consigne automatique

locket NOUN
le médaillon

lodger NOUN
le/la locataire

loft NOUN
le grenier

log NOUN
la bûche (*of wood*)

to **log in** VERB
se connecter

to **log off** NOUN
se déconnecter

to **log on** VERB
se connecter

to **log out** VERB
se déconnecter

logical ADJECTIVE
logique

lollipop NOUN
la sucette

lolly NOUN
la glace à l'eau (*ice lolly*)

London NOUN
Londres
♦ **in London** à Londres
♦ **to London** à Londres
♦ **I'm from London.** Je suis de Londres.

L

Londoner NOUN
le <u>Londonien</u>
la <u>Londonienne</u>

loneliness NOUN
la <u>solitude</u>

lonely ADJECTIVE
<u>seul</u>
♦ **to feel lonely** se sentir seul ◇ *She feels a bit lonely.* Elle se sent un peu seule.

lonesome ADJECTIVE
♦ **to feel lonesome** se sentir seul

long ADJECTIVE, ADVERB
see also **long** VERB
<u>long</u> MASC
<u>longue</u> FEM
◇ *She's got long hair.* Elle a les cheveux longs. ◇ *The room is 6 metres long.* La pièce fait six mètres de long.
♦ **how long?** (*time*) combien de temps? ◇ *How long did you stay there?* Combien de temps êtes-vous resté là-bas? ◇ *How long have you been here?* Depuis combien de temps êtes-vous ici? ◇ *How long is the flight?* Combien de temps dure le vol?
♦ **I've been waiting a long time.** J'attends depuis longtemps.
♦ **It takes a long time.** Ça prend du temps.
♦ **as long as** si ◇ *I'll come as long as it's not too expensive.* Je viendrai si ce n'est pas trop cher.

to **long** VERB
see also **long** ADJECTIVE
♦ **to long to do something** attendre avec impatience de faire quelque chose
♦ **I'm longing to see my boyfriend again.** J'attends avec impatience de revoir mon copain.

long-distance ADJECTIVE
♦ **a long-distance call** une communication interurbaine

longer ADVERB
see also **long** ADJECTIVE
♦ **They're no longer going out together.** Ils ne sortent plus ensemble.
♦ **I can't stand it any longer.** Je ne peux plus le supporter.

long jump NOUN
le <u>saut en longueur</u>

loo NOUN
les <u>toilettes</u> FEM PL ◇ *Where's the loo?* Où sont les toilettes?

look NOUN
see also **look** VERB
♦ **to have a look** regarder ◇ *Have a look at this!* Regardez ceci!
♦ **I don't like the look of it.** Ça ne me dit rien.

to **look** VERB
see also **look** NOUN
1 <u>regarder</u> ◇ *Look!* Regardez!
♦ **to look at something** regarder quelque chose ◇ *Look at the picture.* Regardez cette image.
2 <u>avoir l'air</u> (*seem*) ◇ *She looks surprised.* Elle a l'air surprise. ◇ *That cake looks nice.* Ce gâteau a l'air bon. ◇ *It looks fine.* Ça a l'air bien.
♦ **to look like somebody** ressembler à quelqu'un ◇ *He looks like his brother.* Il ressemble à son frère.
♦ **What does she look like?** Comment est-elle physiquement?
♦ **Look out!** Attention!
♦ **to look after** s'occuper de ◇ *I look after my little sister.* Je m'occupe de ma petite sœur.
♦ **to look for** chercher ◇ *I'm looking for my passport.* Je cherche mon passeport.
♦ **to look forward to something** attendre quelque chose avec impatience ◇ *I'm looking forward to the holidays.* J'attends les vacances avec impatience.
♦ **Looking forward to hearing from you.** J'espère avoir bientôt de tes nouvelles.
♦ **to look round (1)** (*look behind*) se retourner ◇ *I shouted and he looked round.* J'ai crié et il s'est retourné.
♦ **to look round (2)** (*have a look*) jeter un coup d'œil ◇ *I'm just looking round.* Je jette simplement un coup d'œil.
♦ **to look round a museum** visiter un musée
♦ **I like looking round the shops.** J'aime faire les boutiques.
♦ **to look up** (*word, name*) chercher ◇ *If you don't know a word, look it up in the dictionary.* Si vous ne connaissez pas un mot, cherchez-le dans le dictionnaire.

loose ADJECTIVE
<u>ample</u> (*clothes*)
♦ **loose change** la petite monnaie

lord NOUN
le <u>seigneur</u> (*feudal*)
♦ **the House of Lords** la Chambre des lords
♦ **good Lord!** mon Dieu!

lorry NOUN
le <u>camion</u>

lorry driver NOUN

le <u>routier</u> ◊ *He's a lorry driver.* Il est
routier.
to **lose** VERB
<u>perdre</u> ◊ *I've lost my purse.* J'ai
perdu mon porte-monnaie.
♦**to get lost** se perdre ◊ *I was afraid of
getting lost.* J'avais peur de me
perdre.
loser NOUN
[1] le <u>perdant</u>
la <u>perdante</u>
♦**to be a bad loser** être mauvais
perdant
[2] (*pathetic person*)
le <u>loser</u> ◊ *He's such a loser!* C'est un
vrai loser!
loss NOUN
la <u>perte</u>
lost VERB *see* **lose**
lost ADJECTIVE
<u>perdu</u>
lost-and-found NOUN `US`
les <u>objets trouvés</u> MASC PL
lost property office NOUN
les <u>objets trouvés</u> MASC PL
lot NOUN
♦**a lot** beaucoup
♦**a lot of** beaucoup de ◊ *We saw a lot
of interesting things.* Nous avons vu
beaucoup de choses intéressantes.
♦**lots of** un tas de ◊ *She's got lots of
money.* Elle a un tas d'argent. ◊ *He's
got lots of friends.* Il a un tas d'amis.
♦**What did you do at the weekend? –
Not a lot.** Qu'as-tu fait ce week-end?
– Pas grand-chose.
♦**Do you like football? – Not a lot.** Tu
aimes le football? – Pas tellement.
♦**That's the lot.** C'est tout.
lottery NOUN
la <u>loterie</u>
♦**to win the lottery** gagner à la loterie
loud ADJECTIVE
<u>fort</u> ◊ *The television is too loud.* La
télévision est trop forte.
loudly ADVERB
<u>fort</u>
loudspeaker NOUN
le <u>haut-parleur</u>
lounge NOUN
le <u>salon</u>
lousy ADJECTIVE
<u>infect</u> ◊ *The food in the canteen is
lousy.* La nourriture de la cantine est
infecte.
♦**I feel lousy.** Je suis mal fichu.
(*informal*)
love NOUN
| *see also* **love** VERB |

l' <u>amour</u> MASC
♦**to be in love** être amoureux ◊ *She's
in love with Paul.* Elle est amoureuse
de Paul.
♦**to make love** faire l'amour
♦**Give Delphine my love.** Embrasse
Delphine pour moi.
♦**Love, Rosemary.** Amitiés, Rosemary.
to **love** VERB
| *see also* **love** NOUN |

[1] <u>aimer</u> (*be in love with*) ◊ *I love you.*
Je t'aime.
[2] <u>aimer beaucoup</u> (*like a lot*)
◊ *Everybody loves her.* Tout le
monde l'aime beaucoup. ◊ *I'd love to
come.* J'aimerais beaucoup venir.
[3] <u>adorer</u> (*things*) ◊ *I love chocolate.*
J'adore le chocolat. ◊ *I love skiing.*
J'adore le ski.
lovely ADJECTIVE
<u>charmant</u> ◊ *What a lovely surprise!*
Quelle charmante surprise! ◊ *She's a
lovely person.* Elle est charmante.
♦**It's a lovely day.** Il fait très beau
aujourd'hui.
♦**Is your meal OK? – Yes, it's lovely.**
Est-ce que c'est bon? – Oui, c'est
délicieux.
♦**They've got a lovely house.** Ils ont
une très belle maison.
♦**Have a lovely time!** Amusez-vous
bien!
lover NOUN
[1] (*in relationship*)
l' <u>amant</u> MASC
la <u>maîtresse</u>
[2] (*of hobby, wine*)
l' <u>amateur</u> MASC ◊ *an art lover* un
amateur d'art ◊ *She is a lover of
good food.* Elle est amateur de bonne
cuisine.
low ADJECTIVE, ADVERB
(*price, level*)
<u>bas</u> MASC
<u>basse</u> FEM
◊ *That plane is flying very low.* Cet
avion vole très bas.
♦**the low season** la basse saison ◊ *in
the low season* en basse saison
lower ADJECTIVE
| *see also* **lower** VERB |
<u>inférieur</u> ◊ *on the lower floor* a
l'étage inférieur
to **lower** VERB
| *see also* **lower** ADJECTIVE |
<u>baisser</u>
lower sixth NOUN
la <u>première</u> ◊ *He's in the lower sixth.*
Il est en première.
low-fat ADJECTIVE

`L`

☞

allégé ◊ *a low-fat yoghurt* un yaourt allégé

loyalty NOUN
la fidélité

loyalty card NOUN
la carte de fidélité

lozenge NOUN
la pastille (*sweet*)

L-plates PL NOUN
les plaques de conducteur débutant FEM PL

luck NOUN
la chance ◊ *She hasn't had much luck.* Elle n'a pas eu beaucoup de chance.
♦**Good luck!** Bonne chance!
♦**Bad luck!** Pas de chance!

luckily ADVERB
heureusement

lucky ADJECTIVE
♦**to be lucky (1)** (*be fortunate*) avoir de la chance ◊ *He's lucky, he's got a job.* Il a de la chance, il a un emploi. ◊ *He wasn't hurt. – That was lucky!* Il n'a pas été blessé. – C'est une chance!
♦**to be lucky (2)** (*bring luck*) porter bonheur ◊ *Black cats are lucky in Britain.* Les chats noirs portent bonheur en Grande-Bretagne.
♦**a lucky horseshoe** un fer à cheval porte-bonheur

luggage NOUN
les bagages MASC PL

lukewarm ADJECTIVE
tiède (*water, food*)
♦**The response was lukewarm.** Sa réaction a été peu enthousiaste.

lump NOUN
1 le morceau
(les morceaux PL)
◊ *a lump of butter* un morceau de beurre

2 (*swelling*)
la bosse ◊ *He's got a lump on his forehead.* Il a une bosse sur le front.

lunatic NOUN
le fou
la folle
◊ *He's an absolute lunatic.* Il est complètement fou.

lunch NOUN
le déjeuner
♦**to have lunch** déjeuner ◊ *We have lunch at 12.30.* Nous déjeunons à midi et demie.

luncheon voucher NOUN
le ticket-restaurant

lung NOUN
le poumon
♦**lung cancer** le cancer du poumon

luscious ADJECTIVE
délicieux MASC
délicieuse FEM

lush ADJECTIVE
luxuriant

lust NOUN
le désir

Luxembourg NOUN
1 le Luxembourg (*country*)
♦**in Luxembourg** au Luxembourg
♦**to Luxembourg** au Luxembourg
2 Luxembourg (*city*)
♦**in Luxembourg** à Luxembourg

luxurious ADJECTIVE
luxueux MASC
luxueuse FEM

luxury NOUN
le luxe ◊ *It was luxury!* C'était un vrai luxe!
♦**a luxury hotel** un hôtel de luxe

lying VERB *see* **lie**

lyrics PL NOUN
les paroles FEM PL (*of song*)

M

mac NOUN
l' imper MASC

macaroni NOUN
les macaronis MASC PL

machine NOUN
la machine

machine gun NOUN
la mitrailleuse

machinery NOUN
les machines FEM PL

mackerel NOUN
le maquereau
(les maquereaux PL)

mad ADJECTIVE
1 (insane)
fou MASC
folle FEM
◊ You're mad! Tu es fou!
2 (angry)
furieux MASC
furieuse FEM
◊ She'll be mad when she finds out.
Elle sera furieuse quand elle va s'en
apercevoir.
♦ to be mad about (1) (sport, activity)
être enragé de ◊ He's mad about
football. Il est enragé de foot.
♦ to be mad about (2) (person, animal)
adorer ◊ She's mad about horses.
Elle adore les chevaux.

madam NOUN
madame FEM ◊ Would you like to
order, Madam? Désirez-vous
commander, Madame?

made VERB see **make**

madly ADVERB
♦ They're madly in love. Ils sont
éperdument amoureux.

madman NOUN
le fou

madness NOUN
la folie ◊ It's absolute madness. C'est
de la pure folie.

magazine NOUN
le magazine

maggot NOUN
l' asticot MASC

magic ADJECTIVE
see also **magic** NOUN
1 magique (magical) ◊ a magic wand
une baguette magique
2 super (brilliant)
♦ It was magic! C'était super!

magic NOUN

see also **magic** ADJECTIVE
la magie
♦ a magic trick un tour de magie
♦ My hobby is magic. Je fais des tours
de magie.

magician NOUN
le prestidigitateur (conjurer)

magnet NOUN
l' aimant MASC

magnificent ADJECTIVE
1 magnifique (beautiful) ◊ a
magnificent view une vue magnifique
2 superbe (outstanding) ◊ It was a
magnificent effort. Ils ont fait un
superbe effort.

magnifying glass NOUN
la loupe

maid NOUN
la domestique (servant)
♦ an old maid (spinster) une vieille fille

maiden name NOUN
le nom de jeune fille

mail NOUN
le courrier ◊ Here's your mail. Voici
ton courrier.
♦ email (electronic mail) le courrier
électronique
♦ by mail par la poste

mailbox NOUN US
la boîte à lettres

mailing list NOUN
la liste d'adresses

mailman NOUN US
le facteur

main ADJECTIVE
principal
(principaux MASC PL)
◊ the main problem le principal
problème
♦ the main thing is to ... l'essentiel est
de ...

mainly ADVERB
principalement

main road NOUN
la grande route ◊ I don't like cycling
on main roads. Je n'aime pas faire
du vélo sur les grandes routes.

to **maintain** VERB
entretenir (machine, building)

maintenance NOUN
l' entretien MASC (of machine, building)

maize NOUN
le maïs

majesty NOUN

la majesté
♦ **Your Majesty** Votre Majesté

major ADJECTIVE
majeur ◊ *a major problem* un problème majeur
♦ **in C major** en do majeur

Majorca NOUN
Majorque FEM ◊ *We went to Majorca in August.* Nous sommes allés à Majorque en août.

majority NOUN
la majorité

make NOUN
| see also **make** VERB |

la marque ◊ *What make is that car?* De quelle marque est cette voiture?

to **make** VERB
| see also **make** NOUN |

[1] faire ◊ *I'm going to make a cake.* Je vais faire un gâteau. ◊ *He made it himself.* Il l'a fait lui-même. ◊ *I make my bed every morning.* Je fais mon lit tous les matins. ◊ *2 and 2 make 4.* Deux et deux font quatre.
[2] fabriquer (*manufacture*) ◊ *made in France* fabriqué en France
[3] gagner (*earn*) ◊ *He makes a lot of money.* Il gagne beaucoup d'argent.
♦ **to make somebody do something** obliger quelqu'un à faire quelque chose ◊ *My mother makes me do my homework.* Ma mère m'oblige à faire mes devoirs.
♦ **to make lunch** préparer le repas ◊ *She's making lunch.* Elle prépare le repas.
♦ **to make a phone call** donner un coup de téléphone ◊ *I'd like to make a phone call.* J'aimerais donner un coup de téléphone.
♦ **to make fun of somebody** se moquer de quelqu'un ◊ *They made fun of him.* Ils se sont moqués de lui.
♦ **What time do you make it?** Quelle heure avez-vous?

to **make out** VERB
[1] déchiffrer (*read*) ◊ *I can't make out the address on the label.* Je n'arrive pas à déchiffrer l'adresse sur l'étiquette.
[2] comprendre (*understand*) ◊ *I can't make her out at all.* Je n'arrive pas du tout à la comprendre.
[3] prétendre (*claim, pretend*) ◊ *They're making out it was my fault.* Ils prétendent que c'était ma faute.
♦ **to make a cheque out to somebody** libeller un chèque à l'ordre de quelqu'un

to **make up** VERB

[1] inventer (*invent*) ◊ *He made up the whole story.* Il a inventé cette histoire de toutes pièces.
[2] se réconcilier (*after argument*) ◊ *They had a quarrel, but soon made up.* Ils se sont disputés, mais se sont vite réconciliés.
♦ **to make oneself up** se maquiller ◊ *She spends hours making herself up.* Elle passe des heures à se maquiller.

maker NOUN
le fabricant ◊ *Europe's biggest car manufacturer* le plus grand fabriquant de voitures d'Europe
♦ **a film maker** un cinéaste

make-up NOUN
le maquillage

Malaysia NOUN
la Malaisie
♦ **in Malaysia** en Malaisie

male ADJECTIVE
[1] mâle (*animals, plants*) ◊ *a male kitten* un chaton mâle
[2] masculin (*person, on official forms*) ◊ *Sex: male.* Sexe : masculin.
♦ **Most football players are male.** La plupart des joueurs de football sont des hommes.
♦ **a male chauvinist** un macho
♦ **a male nurse** un infirmier

malicious ADJECTIVE
malveillant ◊ *a malicious rumour* une rumeur malveillante
> Be careful not to translate **malicious** by **malicieux**.

mall NOUN
le centre commercial

Malta NOUN
Malte
♦ **in Malta** à Malte
♦ **to Malta** à Malte

mammoth NOUN
| see also **mammoth** ADJECTIVE |
le mammouth

mammoth ADJECTIVE
| see also **mammoth** NOUN |
monstre ◊ *a mammoth task* un travail monstre

man NOUN
l' homme MASC ◊ *an old man* un vieil homme

to **manage** VERB
[1] gérer (*be in charge of*) ◊ *She manages a big store.* Elle dirige un grand magasin. ◊ *He manages our football team.* Il dirige notre équipe de foot.

[2] se débrouiller (*get by*) ◊ *We haven't got much money, but we manage.* Nous n'avons pas beaucoup d'argent, mais nous nous débrouillons. ◊ *It's okay, I can manage.* Ça va, je me débrouille.
◆**Can you manage okay?** Tu y arrives?
◆**to manage to do something** réussir à faire quelque chose ◊ *Luckily I managed to pass the exam.* J'ai heureusement réussi à avoir mon examen.
◆**I can't manage all that.** (*food*) C'est trop pour moi.

manageable ADJECTIVE
faisable (*task*)

management NOUN
[1] la gestion (*organization*) ◊ *He's responsible for the management of the company.* Il est responsable de la gestion de la société.
[2] la direction (*people in charge*) ◊ *"under new management"* "changement de direction"

manager NOUN
[1] (*of company*)
le directeur
la directrice
[2] (*of shop, restaurant*)
le gérant
la gérante
[3] (*of team, performer*)
le manager

manageress NOUN
la gérante

mandarin NOUN
la mandarine (*fruit*)

mango NOUN
la mangue

mania NOUN
la manie

maniac NOUN
le fou
la folle
◊ *He drives like a maniac.* Il conduit comme un fou.
◆**a religious maniac** un fanatique religieux

to **manipulate** VERB
manipuler

mankind NOUN
l' humanité FEM

man-made ADJECTIVE
synthétique (*fibre*)

manner NOUN
la façon
◆**She behaves in an odd manner.** Elle se comporte de façon étrange.

◆**He has a confident manner.** Il a de l'assurance.

manners PL NOUN
les manières FEM PL ◊ *good manners* les bonnes manières ◊ *Her manners are appalling.* Elle a de très mauvaises manières.
◆**It's bad manners to speak with your mouth full.** Ce n'est pas poli de parler la bouche pleine.

manpower NOUN
la main-d'œuvre

mansion NOUN
le manoir

mantelpiece NOUN
la cheminée

manual NOUN
le manuel

to **manufacture** VERB
fabriquer

manufacturer NOUN
le fabricant

manure NOUN
le fumier

manuscript NOUN
le manuscrit

many ADJECTIVE, PRONOUN
beaucoup de ◊ *The film has many special effects.* Le film a beaucoup d'effets spéciaux. ◊ *He hasn't got many friends.* Il n'a pas beaucoup d'amis. ◊ *Were there many people at the concert?* Est-ce qu'il y avait beaucoup de gens au concert?
◆**very many** beaucoup de ◊ *I haven't got very many CDs.* Je n'ai pas beaucoup de CD.
◆**not many** pas beaucoup
◆**How many?** Combien? ◊ *How many do you want?* Combien en veux-tu?
◆**how many ...?** combien de ...? ◊ *How many francs do you get for £1?* Combien de francs a-t-on pour une livre?
◆**too many** trop ◊ *That's too many.* C'est trop.
◆**too many ...** trop de ... ◊ *She makes too many mistakes.* Elle fait trop d'erreurs.
◆**so many** autant ◊ *I didn't know there would be so many.* Je ne pensais pas qu'il y en aurait autant.
◆**so many ...** autant de ... ◊ *I've never seen so many policemen.* Je n'ai jamais vu autant de policiers.

map NOUN
[1] la carte (*of country, area*)
[2] le plan (*of town*)

marathon NOUN

M

le marathon ◊ *the London marathon* le marathon de Londres

marble NOUN
le marbre ◊ *a marble statue* une statue en marbre
♦ **to play marbles** jouer aux billes

March NOUN
mars MASC
♦ **in March** en mars

march NOUN
see also **march** VERB
la manifestation (*demonstration*)

to **march** VERB
see also **march** NOUN
1 marcher au pas (*soldiers*)
2 défiler (*protesters*)

mare NOUN
la jument

margarine NOUN
la margarine

margin NOUN
la marge ◊ *Write notes in the margin.* Écrivez vos notes dans la marge.

marijuana NOUN
la marijuana

marina NOUN
la marina

marital status NOUN
la situation de famille

mark NOUN
see also **mark** VERB
1 la note (*in school*) ◊ *I get good marks for French.* J'ai de bonnes notes en français.
2 la tache (*stain*) ◊ *You've got a mark on your skirt.* Tu as une tache sur ta jupe.
3 le mark (*German currency*)

to **mark** VERB
see also **mark** NOUN
corriger ◊ *The teacher hasn't marked my homework yet.* Le professeur n'a pas encore corrigé mon devoir.

market NOUN
le marché

marketing NOUN
le marketing

marketplace NOUN
la place du marché

marmalade NOUN
la confiture d'oranges

maroon ADJECTIVE
bordeaux MASC, FEM, PL (*colour*)

marriage NOUN
le mariage

married ADJECTIVE

marié ◊ *They are not married.* Ils ne sont pas mariés. ◊ *They have been married for 15 years.* Ils sont mariés depuis quinze ans. ◊ *a married couple* un couple marié

marrow NOUN
la courge (*vegetable*)
♦ **bone marrow** la moelle

to **marry** VERB
épouser ◊ *He wants to marry her.* Il veut l'épouser.
♦ **to get married** se marier ◊ *My sister's getting married in June.* Ma sœur se marie en juin.

marvellous ADJECTIVE (US **marvelous**)
1 excellent ◊ *She's a marvellous cook.* C'est une excellente cuisinière.
2 superbe ◊ *The weather was marvellous.* Il a fait un temps superbe.

marzipan NOUN
la pâte d'amandes

mascara NOUN
le mascara

masculine ADJECTIVE
masculin

mashed potatoes PL NOUN
la purée ◊ *sausages and mashed potatoes* des saucisses avec de la purée

mask NOUN
le masque

masked ADJECTIVE
masqué

mass NOUN
1 la multitude ◊ *a mass of books and papers* une multitude de livres et de papiers
2 la messe (*in church*) ◊ *We go to mass on Sunday.* Nous allons à la messe le dimanche.
♦ **the mass media** les médias MASC PL

massage NOUN
le massage

massive ADJECTIVE
énorme

to **master** VERB
maîtriser

masterpiece NOUN
le chef-d'œuvre
(les chefs-d'œuvre PL)

mat NOUN
le paillasson (*doormat*)
♦ **a table mat** un set de table
♦ **a beach mat** un tapis de plage

match NOUN
see also **match** VERB
1 l' allumette FEM ◊ *a box of matches* une boîte d'allumettes

2 (sport)
le match
(les matchs PL)
◊ a football match un match de foot

to **match** VERB

see also **match** NOUN

être assorti à ◊ The jacket matches
the trousers. La veste est assortie au
pantalon.
• **These colours don't match.** Ces
couleurs ne vont pas ensemble.

matching ADJECTIVE
assorti ◊ My bedroom has matching
wallpaper and curtains. Ma chambre
a du papier peint et des rideaux
assortis.

mate NOUN
le pote (informal) ◊ On Friday night I
go out with my mates. Vendredi soir,
je sors avec mes potes.

material NOUN
1 le tissu (cloth)
2 la documentation (information,
data) ◊ I'm collecting material for
my project. Je rassemble une
documentation pour mon dossier.
• **raw materials** les matières premières
FEM

mathematics NOUN
les mathématiques FEM PL

maths NOUN
les maths FEM PL

matron NOUN
l' infirmière-chef FEM (in hospital)

matter NOUN

see also **matter** VERB

la question ◊ It's a matter of life and
death. C'est une question de vie ou
de mort.
• **What's the matter?** Qu'est-ce qui ne
va pas?
• **as a matter of fact** en fait

to **matter** VERB

see also **matter** NOUN

• **it doesn't matter (1)** (I don't mind) ça
ne fait rien ◊ I can't give you the
money today. – It doesn't matter. Je
ne peux pas te donner l'argent
aujourd'hui. – Ça ne fait rien.
• **it doesn't matter (2)** (it makes no
difference) ça n'a pas d'importance
◊ Shall I phone today or tomorrow? –
Whenever, it doesn't matter. Est-ce
que j'appelle aujourd'hui ou demain?
– Quand tu veux, ça n'a pas
d'importance.
• **It matters a lot to me.** C'est très
important pour moi.

mattress NOUN
le matelas

mature ADJECTIVE
mûr ◊ She's quite mature for her
age. Elle est très mûre pour son âge.

maximum NOUN

see also **maximum** ADJECTIVE

le maximum

maximum ADJECTIVE

see also **maximum** NOUN

maximum MASC, FEM, PL ◊ The maximum
speed is 100 km/h. La vitesse
maximum autorisée est de cent
kilomètres à l'heure.
• **the maximum amount** le maximum

May NOUN
mai MASC
• **in May** en mai
• **May Day** le Premier Mai

may VERB
• **He may come.** Il va peut-être venir.
◊ It may rain. Il va peut-être pleuvoir.
• **Are you going to the party? – I don't
know, I may.** Est-ce que tu vas à la
soirée? – Je ne sais pas, peut-être.
• **May I smoke?** Est-ce que je peux
fumer?

maybe ADVERB
peut-être ◊ maybe not peut-être pas
◊ a bit boring, maybe peut-être un
peu ennuyeux ◊ Maybe she's at
home. Elle est peut-être chez elle.
◊ Maybe he'll change his mind. Il va
peut-être changer d'avis.

mayonnaise NOUN
la mayonnaise

mayor NOUN
le maire

maze NOUN
le labyrinthe

me PRONOUN

*me becomes m' before a vowel
sound.*

1 me ◊ Could you lend me your
pen? Est-ce que tu peux me prêter
ton stylo?
m' ◊ Can you tell me the way to the
station? Est-ce que vous pouvez
m'indiquer le chemin de la gare?
◊ Can you help me? Est-ce que tu
peux m'aider? ◊ He heard me. Il m'a
entendu.

moi is used in exclamations.

2 moi ◊ Me too! Moi aussi! ◊ Excuse
me! Excusez-moi! ◊ Look at me!
Regarde-moi! ◊ Wait for me!
Attends-moi! ◊ Come with me!
Suivez-moi!

*moi is also used after prepositions
and in comparisons.*

M

◊ *You're after me.* Tu es après moi.
◊ *Is it for me?* C'est pour moi?
◊ *She's older than me.* Elle est plus âgée que moi.

meal NOUN
le repas

mealtime NOUN
♦ **at mealtimes** aux heures des repas

to **mean** VERB
| see also **mean** ADJECTIVE AND **means** NOUN |
vouloir dire ◊ *What does "complet" mean?* Qu'est-ce que "complet" veut dire? ◊ *I don't know what it means.* Je ne sais pas ce que ça veut dire. ◊ *What do you mean?* Qu'est que vous voulez dire? ◊ *That's not what I meant.* Ce n'est pas ce que je voulais dire.
♦ **Which one do you mean?** Duquel veux-tu parler?
♦ **Do you really mean it?** Tu es sérieux?
♦ **to mean to do something** avoir l'intention de faire quelque chose ◊ *I didn't mean to offend you.* Je n'avais pas l'intention de vous blesser.

mean ADJECTIVE
| see also **mean** VERB AND **means** NOUN |
[1] radin (*with money*) ◊ *He's too mean to buy Christmas presents.* Il est trop radin pour acheter des cadeaux de Noël.
[2] méchant (*unkind*) ◊ *You're being mean to me.* Tu es méchant avec moi.
♦ **That's a really mean thing to say!** Ce n'est vraiment pas gentil de dire ça!

meaning NOUN
le sens

means NOUN
| see also **mean** VERB AND ADJECTIVE |
le moyen ◊ *He'll do it by any possible means.* Il le fera par tous les moyens. ◊ *a means of transport* un moyen de transport
♦ **by means of** au moyen de ◊ *He got in by means of a stolen key.* Il est entré au moyen d'une clé volée.
♦ **by all means** bien sûr ◊ *Can I come? – By all means!* Est-ce que je peux venir? – Bien sûr!

meant VERB *see* **mean**

meanwhile ADVERB
pendant ce temps

measles NOUN
la rougeole

to **measure** VERB
[1] mesurer ◊ *I measured the page.* J'ai mesuré la page.

[2] faire ◊ *The room measures 3 metres by 4.* La pièce fait trois mètres sur quatre.

measurements PL NOUN
[1] les dimensions FEM PL (*of object*)
◊ *What are the measurements of the room?* Quelles sont les dimensions de la pièce?
[2] les mensurations FEM PL (*of body*)
◊ *What are your measurements?* Quelles sont tes mensurations?
♦ **my waist measurement** mon tour de taille
♦ **What's your neck measurement?** Quel est votre tour de cou?

meat NOUN
la viande ◊ *I don't eat meat.* Je ne mange pas de viande.

Mecca NOUN
La Mecque

mechanic NOUN
le mécanicien ◊ *He's a mechanic.* Il est mécanicien.

mechanical ADJECTIVE
mécanique

medal NOUN
la médaille
♦ **the gold medal** la médaille d'or

medallion NOUN
le médaillon

media PL NOUN
les médias MASC PL

median strip NOUN US
le terre-plein central

medical ADJECTIVE
| see also **medical** NOUN |
médical
(médicaux MASC PL)
◊ *medical treatment* les soins médicaux
♦ **medical insurance** l'assurance maladie FEM
♦ **to have medical problems** avoir des problèmes de santé
♦ **She's a medical student.** Elle est étudiante en médecine.

medical NOUN
| see also **medical** ADJECTIVE |
♦ **to have a medical** passer une visite médicale

medicine NOUN
[1] la médecine (*subject*) ◊ *I want to study medicine.* Je veux faire médecine.
♦ **alternative medicine** la médecine douce
[2] le médicament (*medication*) ◊ *I need some medicine.* J'ai besoin d'un médicament.

Mediterranean ADJECTIVE
méditerranéen MASC
méditerranéenne FEM
♦**the Mediterranean** la Méditerranée

medium ADJECTIVE
moyen MASC
moyenne FEM
◊ *a man of medium height* un homme de taille moyenne

medium-sized ADJECTIVE
de taille moyenne ◊ *a medium-sized town* une ville de taille moyenne

to **meet** VERB
[1] rencontrer (*by chance*) ◊ *I met Paul when I was walking the dog.* J'ai rencontré Paul alors que je promenais mon chien. ◊ *Have you met him before?* Est-ce que tu l'as déjà rencontré?
[2] se rencontrer ◊ *We met by chance in the shopping centre.* Nous nous sommes rencontrés par hasard dans le centre commercial.
[3] retrouver (*by arrangement*) ◊ *I'm going to meet my friends.* Je vais retrouver mes amis.
[4] se retrouver ◊ *Let's meet in front of the tourist office.* Retrouvons-nous devant l'office de tourisme.
♦**I like meeting new people.** J'aime faire de nouvelles connaissances.
[5] aller chercher (*pick up*) ◊ *I'll meet you at the station.* J'irai te chercher à la gare.

meeting NOUN
[1] la réunion (*for work*) ◊ *a business meeting* une réunion d'affaires
[2] la rencontre (*socially*) ◊ *their first meeting* leur première rencontre

mega ADJECTIVE
♦**He's mega rich.** Il est hyper-riche. (*informal*)

melody NOUN
la mélodie

melon NOUN
le melon

to **melt** VERB
fondre ◊ *The snow is melting.* La neige est en train de fondre.

member NOUN
le membre
♦**a Member of Parliament** un député

membership NOUN
l' adhésion FEM (*of party, union*) ◊ *I'm going to apply for membership of the club.* Je vais faire une demande d'adhésion au club.

membership card NOUN
la carte de membre

memento NOUN
le souvenir

memorial NOUN
le monument ◊ *a war memorial* un monument aux morts

to **memorize** VERB
apprendre par cœur

memory NOUN
[1] la mémoire (*also for computer*) ◊ *I haven't got a good memory.* Je n'ai pas une bonne mémoire.
[2] le souvenir (*recollection*) ◊ *to bring back memories* rappeler des souvenirs

men PL NOUN *see* **man**
les hommes MASC PL

to **mend** VERB
réparer

meningitis NOUN
la méningite

mental ADJECTIVE
[1] mental (mentaux MASC PL) ◊ *a mental illness* une maladie mentale
[2] (*mad*) fou MASC folle FEM ◊ *You're mental!* Tu es fou!
♦**a mental hospital** un hôpital psychiatrique

mentality NOUN
la mentalité

to **mention** VERB
mentionner
♦**Thank you! – Don't mention it!** Merci! – Il n'y a pas de quoi!

menu NOUN
le menu ◊ *Could I have the menu please?* Est-ce que je pourrais avoir le menu s'il vous plaît?

merchant NOUN
le marchand ◊ *a wine merchant* un marchand de vin

mercy NOUN
la pitié

mere ADJECTIVE
♦**a mere five percent** à peine cinq pour cent
♦**It's a mere formality.** C'est une simple formalité.
♦**the merest hint of criticism** la moindre petite critique

meringue NOUN
la meringue

merry ADJECTIVE
♦**Merry Christmas!** Joyeux Noël!

merry-go-round NOUN

M

le manège

mess NOUN
le fouillis ◊ *My bedroom's usually in a mess.* Il y a généralement du fouillis dans ma chambre.

to **mess about** VERB
♦**to mess about with something** (*interfere with*) tripoter quelque chose ◊ *Stop messing about with my computer!* Arrête de tripoter mon ordinateur!
♦**Don't mess about with my things!** Ne touche pas à mes affaires!

to **mess up** VERB
♦**to mess something up** mettre la pagaille dans quelque chose ◊ *My little brother has messed up my cassettes.* Mon petit frère a mis la pagaille dans mes cassettes.

message NOUN
le message

messenger NOUN
le messager

messy ADJECTIVE
1 salissant (*dirty*) ◊ *a messy job* un travail salissant
2 en désordre (*untidy*) ◊ *Your desk is really messy.* Ton bureau est vraiment en désordre.
3 désordonnée (*person*) ◊ *She's so messy!* Elle est tellement désordonnée!
♦**My writing is terribly messy.** J'ai une écriture de cochon.

met VERB *see* **meet**

metal NOUN
le métal
(les métaux PL)

meter NOUN
1 le compteur (*for gas, electricity, taxi*)
2 le parcmètre (*parking meter*)
3 le mètre (*unit of measurement*) US

method NOUN
la méthode

Methodist NOUN
le/la méthodiste ◊ *I'm a Methodist.* Je suis méthodiste.

metre NOUN
le mètre

metric ADJECTIVE
métrique

Mexico NOUN
le Mexique
♦**in Mexico** au Mexique
♦**to Mexico** au Mexique

to **miaow** VERB
miauler

mice PL NOUN *see* **mouse**

microchip NOUN
la puce

microphone NOUN
le microphone

microscope NOUN
le microscope

microwave oven NOUN
le four à micro-ondes

mid ADJECTIVE
♦**in mid May** à la mi-mai

midday NOUN
le midi
♦**at midday** à midi

middle NOUN
le milieu ◊ *in the middle of the road* au milieu de la route ◊ *in the middle of the night* au milieu de la nuit ◊ *the middle seat* la place du milieu

middle-aged ADJECTIVE
d'un certain âge ◊ *a middle-aged man* un homme d'un certain âge
♦**to be middle-aged** avoir la cinquantaine
♦**She's middle-aged.** Elle a la cinquantaine.

Middle Ages PL NOUN
♦**the Middle Ages** le Moyen Âge SING

middle-class ADJECTIVE
de la classe moyenne ◊ *a middle-class family* une famille de la classe moyenne

Middle East NOUN
le Moyen-Orient
♦**in the Middle East** au Moyen-Orient

middle name NOUN
le deuxième nom

midge NOUN
le moucheron

midnight NOUN
minuit MASC
♦**at midnight** à minuit

midwife NOUN
la sage-femme
(les sages-femmes PL)
◊ *She's a midwife.* Elle est sage-femme.

might VERB
Use **peut-être** *to express possibility.*
◊ *He might come later.* Il va peut-être venir plus tard. ◊ *We might go to Spain next year.* Nous irons peut-être en Espagne l'an prochain. ◊ *She might not have understood.* Elle n'a peut-être pas compris.

migraine NOUN
la migraine ◊ *I've got a migraine.* J'ai la migraine.

mike NOUN

le <u>micro</u>

mild ADJECTIVE
<u>doux</u> MASC
<u>douce</u> FEM
◊ *The winters are quite mild.* Les hivers sont assez doux.

mile NOUN
le <u>mille</u>

> *ⓘ In France distances are expressed in kilometres. A mile is about 1.6 kilometres.*

◊ *It's 5 miles from here.* C'est à huit kilomètres d'ici.
♦ **We walked miles!** Nous avons fait des kilomètres à pied!

military ADJECTIVE
<u>militaire</u>

milk NOUN
see also **milk** VERB
le <u>lait</u> ◊ *tea with milk* du thé au lait

to **milk** VERB
see also **milk** NOUN
<u>traire</u>

milk chocolate NOUN
le <u>chocolat au lait</u>

milkman NOUN

> *ⓘ In France milk is not delivered to people's homes.*

◊ *He's a milkman.* Il livre le lait à domicile.

milk shake NOUN
le <u>milk-shake</u>

mill NOUN
le <u>moulin</u> (*for grain*)

millennium NOUN
le <u>millénaire</u> ◊ *the third millennium* le troisième millénaire
♦ **the millennium** le millénium

millimetre NOUN (US **millimeter**)
le <u>millimètre</u>

million NOUN
le <u>million</u>

millionaire NOUN
le <u>millionnaire</u>

to **mimic** VERB
<u>imiter</u>

mince NOUN
la <u>viande hachée</u>

mince pie NOUN
la <u>tartelette de Noël</u>

to **mind** VERB
see also **mind** NOUN

① <u>garder</u> ◊ *Could you mind the baby this afternoon?* Est-ce que tu pourrais garder le bébé cet après-midi?
② <u>surveiller</u> (*keep an eye on*) ◊ *Could you mind my bags for a few minutes?* Est-ce que vous pourriez surveiller mes bagages pendant quelques minutes?
♦ **Do you mind if I open the window?** Est-ce que je pourrais ouvrir la fenêtre?
♦ **I don't mind.** Ça ne me dérange pas. ◊ *I don't mind the noise.* Le bruit ne me dérange pas.
♦ **Never mind!** Ça ne fait rien!
♦ **Mind that bike!** Attention au vélo!
♦ **Mind the step!** Attention à la marche!

mind NOUN
see also **mind** VERB
♦ **to make up one's mind** se décider ◊ *I haven't made up my mind yet.* Je ne me suis pas encore décidé.
♦ **to change one's mind** changer d'avis ◊ *He's changed his mind.* Il a changé d'avis.
♦ **Are you out of your mind?** Tu as perdu la tête?

mine PRONOUN
see also **mine** NOUN
le <u>mien</u> + MASC NOUN ◊ *Is this your coat? – No, mine's black.* C'est ton manteau? – Non, le mien est noir.
la <u>mienne</u> + FEM NOUN ◊ *Is this your car? – No, mine's green.* C'est ta voiture? – Non, la mienne est verte.
les <u>miens</u> + MASC PL NOUN ◊ *her parents and mine* ses parents et les miens
les <u>miennes</u> + FEM PL NOUN ◊ *Your hands are dirty, mine are clean.* Tes mains sont sales, les miennes sont propres.
♦ **It's mine.** C'est à moi. ◊ *This book is mine.* Ce livre est à moi. ◊ *Whose is this? – It's mine.* C'est à qui? – À moi.

mine NOUN
see also **mine** PRONOUN
la <u>mine</u> ◊ *a coal mine* une mine de charbon ◊ *a land mine* une mine terrestre

miner NOUN
le <u>mineur</u>

mineral water NOUN
l' <u>eau minérale</u> FEM

miniature ADJECTIVE
see also **miniature** NOUN
<u>miniature</u> ◊ *a miniature version* une version miniature

miniature NOUN
see also **miniature** ADJECTIVE
la <u>miniature</u>

M

minibus NOUN
le minibus

minicab NOUN
le taxi

> ❶ In France the distinction between black taxis and minicabs does not exist.

Minidisc ® NOUN
le minidisque

minimum NOUN
> see also **minimum** ADJECTIVE

le minimum

minimum ADJECTIVE
> see also **minimum** NOUN

minimum MASC, FEM, PL ◊ The minimum wage in Britain is .... Le salaire minimum en Grande-Bretagne est ... ◊ The minimum age for driving is 17. L'âge minimum pour conduire est dix-sept ans.
♦ **the minimum amount** le minimum

miniskirt NOUN
la mini-jupe

minister NOUN
1 le ministre (in government)
2 le pasteur (of church)

ministry NOUN
le ministère (in government) ◊ The Ministry of Culture Le Ministère de la Culture

mink NOUN
le vison ◊ a mink coat un manteau en vison

minor ADJECTIVE
mineur ◊ a minor problem un problème mineur
♦ **in D minor** en ré mineur
♦ **a minor operation** une opération bénigne

minority NOUN
la minorité

mint NOUN
1 la menthe (plant) ◊ mint sauce la sauce à la menthe
2 le bonbon à la menthe (sweet)

minus PREPOSITION
moins ◊ 16 minus 3 is 13. Seize moins trois égale treize. ◊ It's minus two degrees outside. Il fait moins deux dehors. ◊ I got a B minus. J'ai eu un B moins.

minute NOUN
> see also **minute** ADJECTIVE

la minute ◊ Wait a minute! Attends une minute!

minute ADJECTIVE
> see also **minute** NOUN

minuscule ◊ Her flat is minute. Son appartement est minuscule.

miracle NOUN
le miracle

mirror NOUN
1 la glace (on wall)
2 le rétroviseur (in car)

to **misbehave** VERB
se conduire mal

miscellaneous ADJECTIVE
divers

mischief NOUN
les bêtises FEM PL ◊ My little sister's always up to mischief. Ma petite sœur fait constamment des bêtises.

mischievous ADJECTIVE
coquin

miser NOUN
l' avare MASC/FEM

miserable ADJECTIVE
1 (person)
malheureux MASC
malheureuse FEM
◊ You're looking miserable. Tu as l'air malheureux.
2 (weather)
épouvantable ◊ The weather was miserable. Il faisait un temps épouvantable.
♦ **to feel miserable** ne pas avoir le moral ◊ I'm feeling miserable. Je n'ai pas le moral.

misery NOUN
1 (unhappiness)
la tristesse ◊ All that money brought nothing but misery. Tout cet argent n'a apporté que de la tristesse.
2 (unhappy person)
le pleurnicheur
la pleurnicheuse
◊ She's a real misery. C'est une vraie pleurnicheuse.

misfortune NOUN
le malheur

mishap NOUN
la mésaventure

to **misjudge** VERB
mal juger (person) ◊ I've misjudged her. Je l'ai mal jugée.
♦ **He misjudged the bend.** Il a mal pris le virage.

to **mislay** VERB
égarer ◊ I've mislaid my passport. J'ai égaré mon passeport.

misleading ADJECTIVE
trompeur MASC
trompeuse FEM

Miss NOUN
1 Mademoiselle

(Mesdemoiselles PL)
2 (*in address*)
Mlle
(Mlles PL)

to **miss** VERB
1 rater ◊ *Hurry or you'll miss the bus.* Dépêche-toi ou tu vas rater le bus. ◊ *He missed the target.* Il a raté la cible.
2 manquer ◊ *to miss an opportunity* manquer une occasion
♦ **I miss you.** Tu me manques. ◊ *I'm missing my family.* Ma famille me manque. ◊ *I miss him.* Il me manque. ◊ *I miss them.* Ils me manquent.

missing ADJECTIVE
manquant ◊ *the missing part* la pièce manquante
♦ **to be missing** avoir disparu ◊ *My rucksack is missing.* Mon sac à dos a disparu. ◊ *Two members of the group are missing.* Deux membres du groupe ont disparu.

missionary NOUN
le/la missionnaire

mist NOUN
la brume

mistake NOUN
see also **mistake** VERB
1 la faute (*slip*) ◊ *a spelling mistake* une faute d'orthographe
♦ **to make a mistake (1)** (*in writing, speaking*) faire une faute
♦ **to make a mistake (2)** (*get mixed up*) se tromper ◊ *I'm sorry, I made a mistake.* Je suis désolé, je me suis trompé.
2 l' erreur FEM (*misjudgement*) ◊ *It was a mistake to buy those yellow shoes.* J'ai fait une erreur en achetant ces chaussures jaunes.
♦ **by mistake** par erreur ◊ *I took his bag by mistake.* J'ai pris son sac par erreur.

to **mistake** VERB
see also **mistake** NOUN
♦ **He mistook me for my sister.** Il m'a prise pour ma sœur.

mistaken ADJECTIVE
♦ **to be mistaken** se tromper ◊ *If you think I'm going to get up at 6 o'clock, you're mistaken.* Si tu penses que je vais me lever à six heures, tu te trompes.

mistakenly ADVERB
à tort

mistletoe NOUN
le gui

mistook VERB see **mistake**

mistress NOUN
1 le professeur (*teacher*) ◊ *our French mistress* notre professeur de français
2 la maîtresse (*lover*) ◊ *He's got a mistress.* Il a une maîtresse.

to **mistrust** VERB
se méfier de

misty ADJECTIVE
brumeux MASC
brumeuse FEM
◊ *a misty morning* un matin brumeux

to **misunderstand** VERB
mal comprendre ◊ *Sorry, I misunderstood you.* Je suis désolé, je t'avais mal compris.

misunderstanding NOUN
le malentendu

misunderstood VERB see **misunderstand**

mix NOUN
see also **mix** VERB
le mélange ◊ *It's a mix of science fiction and comedy.* C'est un mélange de science-fiction et de comédie.
♦ **a cake mix** une préparation pour gâteau

to **mix** VERB
see also **mix** NOUN
1 mélanger ◊ *Mix the flour with the sugar.* Mélangez la farine au sucre.
2 combiner ◊ *He's mixing business with pleasure.* Il combine les affaires et le plaisir.
♦ **to mix with somebody** (*associate*) fréquenter quelqu'un
♦ **He doesn't mix much.** Il se tient à l'écart.
♦ **to mix up** (*people*) confondre ◊ *He always mixes me up with my sister.* Il me confond toujours avec ma sœur.
♦ **The travel agent mixed up the bookings.** L'agence de voyage s'est embrouillée dans les réservations.
♦ **I'm getting mixed up.** Je ne m'y retrouve plus.

mixed ADJECTIVE
♦ **a mixed salad** une salade composée
♦ **a mixed school** une école mixte
♦ **a mixed grill** un assortiment de grillades

mixer NOUN
♦ **She's a good mixer.** Elle est très sociable.

mixture NOUN
le mélange ◊ *a mixture of spices* un mélange d'épices
♦ **cough mixture** le sirop pour la toux

M

mix-up NOUN
la <u>confusion</u>

to **moan** VERB
<u>râler</u> ◊ *She's always moaning.* Elle est toujours en train de râler.

mobile home NOUN
le <u>mobile home</u>

mobile phone NOUN
le <u>portable</u>

to **mock** VERB
> see also **mock** ADJECTIVE

<u>ridiculiser</u>

mock ADJECTIVE
> see also **mock** VERB

♦ a mock exam un examen blanc

mod cons PL NOUN
♦ "all mod cons" "tout confort"

model NOUN
> see also **model** ADJECTIVE

[1] le <u>modèle</u> (*type*) ◊ *His car is the latest model.* Sa voiture est le tout dernier modèle.
[2] la <u>maquette</u> (*mock-up*) ◊ *a model of the castle* une maquette du château
[3] le <u>mannequin</u> (*fashion*) ◊ *She's a famous model.* C'est un mannequin célèbre.

model ADJECTIVE
> see also **model** NOUN

♦ a model plane un modèle réduit d'avion
♦ a model railway un modèle réduit de voie ferrée
♦ He's a model pupil. C'est un élève modèle.

to **model** VERB
> see also **model** NOUN

♦ She was modelling a Lorna Bailey outfit. Elle présentait une tenue de la collection Lorna Bailey.

modem NOUN
le <u>modem</u>

moderate ADJECTIVE
<u>modéré</u> ◊ *His views are quite moderate.* Ses opinions sont assez modérées.

♦ a moderate amount of un peu de
♦ a moderate price un prix raisonnable

modern ADJECTIVE
<u>moderne</u>

to **modernize** VERB
<u>moderniser</u>

modest ADJECTIVE
<u>modeste</u>

to **modify** VERB
<u>modifier</u>

moist ADJECTIVE

<u>humide</u> (*skin, soil*) ◊ *Make sure the soil is moist.* Assurez-vous que la terre est humide.

moisture NOUN
l' <u>humidité</u> FEM

moisturizer NOUN
[1] la <u>crème hydratante</u> (*cream*)
[2] le <u>lait hydratant</u> (*lotion*)

moldy ADJECTIVE [US]
<u>moisi</u>

mole NOUN
[1] la <u>taupe</u> (*animal*)
[2] le <u>grain de beauté</u> (*on skin*)

moment NOUN
l' <u>instant</u> MASC ◊ *Could you wait a moment?* Pouvez-vous attendre un instant? ◊ *in a moment* dans un instant ◊ *Just a moment!* Un instant!

♦ at the moment en ce moment
♦ any moment now d'un moment à l'autre ◊ *They'll be arriving any moment now.* Ils vont arriver d'un moment à l'autre.

momentous ADJECTIVE
<u>capital</u> (*event*)

Monaco NOUN
<u>Monaco</u>

♦ in Monaco à Monaco

monarch NOUN
le <u>monarque</u>

monarchy NOUN
la <u>monarchie</u>

monastery NOUN
le <u>monastère</u>

Monday NOUN
le <u>lundi</u> ◊ *on Monday* lundi ◊ *on Mondays* le lundi ◊ *every Monday* tous les lundis ◊ *last Monday* lundi dernier ◊ *next Monday* lundi prochain

money NOUN
l' <u>argent</u> MASC ◊ *I need to change some money.* J'ai besoin de changer de l'argent.

♦ to make money gagner de l'argent

mongrel NOUN
le <u>bâtard</u> ◊ *My dog's a mongrel.* Mon chien est un bâtard.

monitor NOUN
le <u>moniteur</u> (*of computer*)

monk NOUN
le <u>moine</u>

monkey NOUN
le <u>singe</u>

monotonous ADJECTIVE
<u>monotone</u>

monster NOUN
le <u>monstre</u>

month NOUN

le <u>mois</u> ◊ *this month* ce mois-ci
◊ *next month* le mois prochain ◊ *last
month* le mois dernier ◊ *every month*
tous les mois ◊ *at the end of the
month* à la fin du mois

monthly ADJECTIVE
<u>mensuel</u> MASC
<u>mensuelle</u> FEM

monument NOUN
le <u>monument</u>

mood NOUN
l' <u>humeur</u> FEM
◆**to be in a bad mood** être de mauvaise
humeur
◆**to be in a good mood** être de bonne
humeur

moody ADJECTIVE
1 <u>lunatique</u> (*temperamental*)
2 <u>maussade</u> (*in a bad mood*)

moon NOUN
la <u>lune</u> ◊ *There's a full moon tonight.*
Il y a pleine lune ce soir.
◆**to be over the moon** (*happy*) être aux
anges

moor NOUN
see also **moor** VERB
la <u>lande</u>

to **moor** VERB
see also **moor** NOUN
<u>amarrer</u> (*boat*)

mop NOUN
le <u>balai laveur</u> (*for floor*)

moped NOUN
le <u>cyclomoteur</u>

moral ADJECTIVE
see also **moral** NOUN
<u>moral</u>
(moraux MASC PL)

moral NOUN
see also **moral** ADJECTIVE
la <u>morale</u> ◊ *the moral of the story* la
morale de l'histoire
◆**morals** la moralité

morale NOUN
le <u>moral</u> ◊ *Their morale is very low.*
Leur moral est très bas.

more ADJECTIVE, PRONOUN, ADVERB
*When comparing one amount with
another, you usually use **plus**.*
1 <u>plus</u> ◊ *Beer is more expensive in
Britain.* La bière est plus chère en
Grande-Bretagne. ◊ *Could you speak
more slowly?* Est-ce que vous
pourriez parler plus lentement? ◊ *a
bit more* un peu plus ◊ *There isn't
any more.* Il n'y en a plus.
◆**more ... than** plus ... que ◊ *He's more
intelligent than me.* Il est plus
intelligent que moi. ◊ *She practises*

more than I do. Elle s'entraîne plus
que moi. ◊ *More girls than boys do
French.* Il y a plus de filles que de
garçons qui font du français.
2 <u>plus de</u> (*followed by noun*) ◊ *There
are more girls in the class.* Il y a plus
de filles dans la classe. ◊ *I get more
homework than you do.* J'ai plus de
devoirs que toi. ◊ *I spent more than
500 francs.* J'ai dépensé plus de cinq
cents francs.
*When referring to an additional
amount, more than there is already,
you usually use **encore**.*
3 <u>encore</u> ◊ *Is there any more?* Est-ce
qu'il y en a encore? ◊ *Would you like
some more?* Vous en voulez encore?
◊ *It'll take a few more days.* Ça
prendra encore quelques jours.
4 <u>encore de</u> (*followed by noun*)
◊ *Could I have some more chips?*
Est-ce que je pourrais avoir encore
des frites? ◊ *Do you want some more
tea?* Voulez-vous encore du thé?
◆**more or less** plus ou moins
◆**more than ever** plus que jamais

moreover ADVERB
en <u>outre</u>

morning NOUN
le <u>matin</u> ◊ *this morning* ce matin
◊ *tomorrow morning* demain matin
◊ *every morning* tous les matins
◆**in the morning** le matin ◊ *at 7 o'clock
in the morning* à sept heures du
matin
◆**a morning paper** un journal du matin

Morocco NOUN
le <u>Maroc</u>
◆**in Morocco** au Maroc

Moscow NOUN
<u>Moscou</u>
◆**in Moscow** à Moscou

Moslem NOUN
le <u>musulman</u>
la <u>musulmane</u>
◊ *He's a Moslem.* Il est musulman.

mosque NOUN
la <u>mosquée</u>

mosquito NOUN
le <u>moustique</u>
◆**a mosquito bite** une piqûre de
moustique

most ADVERB, ADJECTIVE, PRONOUN
*Use **la plupart de** when **most (of)** is
followed by a plural noun and **la
majeure partie (de)** when **most (of)**
is followed by a singular noun.*
1 <u>la plupart de</u> ◊ *most of my
friends* la plupart de mes amis
◊ *most people* la plupart des gens

M

☞

◊ *Most cats are affectionate.* La plupart des chats sont affectueux.
♦ **most of them** la plupart d'entre eux
♦ **most of the time** la plupart du temps
2 la majeure partie de ◊ *most of the work* la majeure partie du travail ◊ *most of the class* la majeure partie de la classe ◊ *most of the night* la majeure partie de la nuit
♦ **the most** le plus ◊ *He's the one who talks the most.* C'est lui qui parle le plus.

When **most** *is followed by adjective, the translation depends on whether the noun referred to is masculine, feminine or plural.*

♦ **the most ... (1)** le plus ... ◊ *the most expensive restaurant* le restaurant le plus cher
♦ **the most ... (2)** la plus ... ◊ *the most expensive seat* la place la plus chère
♦ **the most ... (3)** les plus ... ◊ *the most expensive restaurants* les restaurants les plus chers ◊ *the most expensive seats* les places les plus chères
♦ **to make the most of something** profiter au maximum de quelque chose
♦ **at the most** au maximum ◊ *Two hours at the most.* Deux heures au maximum.

mostly ADVERB
♦ **The teachers are mostly quite nice.** La plupart des professeurs sont assez gentils.

MOT NOUN
le contrôle technique ◊ *Her car failed its MOT.* Sa voiture n'a pas obtenu le certificat du contrôle technique.

motel NOUN
le motel

moth NOUN
le papillon de nuit

mother NOUN
la mère ◊ *my mother* ma mère
♦ **mother tongue** la langue maternelle

mother-in-law NOUN
la belle-mère
(les belles-mères PL)

Mother's Day NOUN
la fête des Mères

ℹ *Mother's Day is usually on the last Sunday of May in France.*

motionless ADJECTIVE
immobile

motivated ADJECTIVE

motivé ◊ *He is highly motivated.* Il est très motivé.

motivation NOUN
la motivation

motive NOUN
le mobile ◊ *the motive for the killing* le mobile du crime

motor NOUN
le moteur ◊ *The boat has a motor.* Le bateau a un moteur.

motorbike NOUN
la moto

motorboat NOUN
le bateau à moteur

motorcycle NOUN
le vélomoteur

motorcyclist NOUN
le motard

motorist NOUN
l' automobiliste MASC/FEM

motor mechanic NOUN
le mécanicien garagiste

motor racing NOUN
la course automobile

motorway NOUN
l' autoroute FEM ◊ *on the motorway* sur l'autoroute

mouldy ADJECTIVE
moisi

to **mount** VERB
1 monter ◊ *They're mounting a publicity campaign.* Ils montent une campagne publicitaire.
2 augmenter ◊ *Tension is mounting.* La tension augmente.

to **mount up** VERB
1 s'accumuler ◊ *Letters had mounted up while we were on holiday.* Les lettres s'étaient accumulées pendant que nous étions en vacances.
2 augmenter ◊ *My savings are mounting up gradually.* Mes économies augmentent progressivement.

mountain NOUN
la montagne
♦ **a mountain bike** un VTT (= vélo tout-terrain)

mountaineer NOUN
l' alpiniste MASC/FEM

mountaineering NOUN
l' alpinisme MASC ◊ *I go mountaineering.* Je fais de l'alpinisme.

mountainous ADJECTIVE
montagneux MASC
montagneuse FEM

mouse NOUN
la <u>souris</u> (*also for computer*) ◇ *white mice* des souris blanches

mouse mat NOUN
le <u>tapis de souris</u>

mousse NOUN
[1] la <u>mousse</u> (*food*) ◇ *chocolate mousse* la mousse au chocolat
[2] la <u>mousse coiffante</u> (*for hair*)

moustache NOUN
la <u>moustache</u> ◇ *He's got a moustache.* Il a une moustache.
♦ **a man with a moustache** un moustachu

mouth NOUN
la <u>bouche</u>

mouthful NOUN
la <u>bouchée</u>

mouth organ NOUN
l' <u>harmonica</u> MASC ◇ *I play the mouth organ.* Je joue de l'harmonica.

mouthwash NOUN
le <u>bain de bouche</u>

move NOUN
see also **move** VERB
[1] le <u>tour</u> ◇ *It's your move.* C'est ton tour.
[2] le <u>déménagement</u> ◇ *Our move from Oxford to Luton ...* Notre déménagement d'Oxford à Luton ...
♦ **to get a move on** se remuer ◇ *Get a move on!* Remue-toi!

to **move** VERB
see also **move** NOUN
[1] <u>bouger</u> ◇ *Don't move!* Ne bouge pas! ◇ *Could you move your stuff please?* Est-ce que tu peux bouger tes affaires s'il te plaît?
[2] <u>avancer</u> ◇ *The car was moving very slowly.* La voiture avançait très lentement.
[3] <u>émouvoir</u> ◇ *I was very moved by the film.* J'ai été très émue par ce film.
♦ **to move house** déménager ◇ *We're moving in July.* Nous allons déménager en juillet.
♦ **to move forward** avancer
♦ **to move in** emménager ◇ *They're moving in next week.* Ils emménagent la semaine prochaine.
♦ **to move over** se pousser ◇ *Could you move over a bit?* Est-ce que vous pouvez vous pousser un peu?

movement NOUN
le <u>mouvement</u>

movie NOUN
le <u>film</u>

♦ **the movies** le cinéma ◇ *Let's go to the movies!* Si on allait au cinéma?

moving ADJECTIVE
[1] <u>en marche</u> (*not stationary*) ◇ *a moving bus* un bus en marche
[2] <u>touchant</u> (*touching*) ◇ *a moving story* une histoire touchante

to **mow** VERB
<u>tondre</u>
♦ **to mow the lawn** tondre le gazon

mower NOUN
la <u>tondeuse à gazon</u>

mown VERB *see* **mow**

MP NOUN
le <u>député</u> ◇ *She's an MP.* Elle est député.

mph ABBREVIATION (= *miles per hour*)
<u>km/h</u> (= *kilomètres-heure*) ◇ *to drive at 50 mph* rouler à 80 km/h

> ❶ *In France, speed is expressed in kilometres per hour. 50 mph is about 80 km/h.*

Mr NOUN
[1] <u>Monsieur</u>
(Messieurs PL)
[2] (*in address*)
<u>M.</u>
(MM. PL)

Mrs NOUN
[1] <u>Madame</u>
(Mesdames PL)
[2] (*in address*)
<u>Mme</u>
(Mmes PL)

MS NOUN (= *multiple sclerosis*)
la <u>sclérose en plaques</u> ◇ *She's got MS.* Elle a la sclérose en plaques.

Ms NOUN
[1] <u>Madame</u>
(Mesdames PL)
[2] (*in address*)
<u>Mme</u>
(Mmes PL)

> ❶ *There isn't a direct equivalent of **Ms** in French. If you are writing to somebody and don't know whether she is married, use **Madame**.*

much ADJECTIVE, ADVERB, PRONOUN
[1] <u>beaucoup</u> (*with verb*) ◇ *Do you go out much?* Tu sors beaucoup? ◇ *I don't like sport much.* Je n'aime pas beaucoup le sport. ◇ *I feel much better now.* Je me sens beaucoup mieux maintenant.
[2] <u>beaucoup de</u> (*followed by noun*) ◇ *I haven't got much money.* Je n'ai pas

M

☞

beaucoup d'argent. ◊ *I don't want much rice.* Je ne veux pas beaucoup de riz.

♦**very much (1)** *(with verb)* beaucoup ◊ *I enjoyed the film very much.* J'ai beaucoup apprécié le film. ◊ *Thank you very much.* Merci beaucoup.

♦**very much (2)** *(followed by noun)* beaucoup de ◊ *I haven't got very much money.* Je n'ai pas beaucoup d'argent.

♦**not much (1)** pas beaucoup ◊ *Have you got a lot of luggage? – No, not much.* As-tu beaucoup de bagages? – Non, pas beaucoup.

♦**not much (2)** pas grand-chose ◊ *What's on TV? – Not much.* Qu'est-ce qu'il y a à la télé? – Pas grand-chose. ◊ *What did you think of it? – Not much.* Qu'est-ce que tu en as pensé? – Pas grand-chose.

♦**How much?** Combien? ◊ *How much do you want?* Tu en veux combien? ◊ *How much time have you got?* Tu as combien de temps? ◊ *How much is it?* *(cost)* Combien est-ce que ça coûte?

♦**too much** trop ◊ *That's too much!* C'est trop! ◊ *It costs too much.* Ça coûte trop cher. ◊ *They give us too much homework.* Ils nous donnent trop de devoirs.

♦**so much** autant ◊ *I didn't think it would cost so much.* Je ne pensais pas que ça coûterait autant. ◊ *I've never seen so much traffic.* Je n'ai jamais vu autant de circulation.

mud NOUN
la <u>boue</u>

muddle NOUN
le <u>désordre</u> ◊ *The photos are in a muddle.* Les photos sont en désordre.

to **muddle up** VERB
<u>confondre</u> *(people)* ◊ *He muddles me up with my sister.* Il me confond avec ma sœur.

♦**to get muddled up** s'embrouiller ◊ *I'm getting muddled up.* Je m'embrouille.

muddy ADJECTIVE
<u>boueux</u> MASC
<u>boueuse</u> FEM

muesli NOUN
le <u>muesli</u>

muffler NOUN [US]
le <u>silencieux</u>

mug NOUN
| *see also* **mug** VERB |

la <u>grande tasse</u> ◊ *Do you want a cup or a mug?* Est-ce que vous voulez une tasse normale ou une grande tasse?

♦**a beer mug** une chope à bière

to **mug** VERB
| *see also* **mug** NOUN |

<u>agresser</u> ◊ *He was mugged in the city centre.* Il s'est fait agresser au centre-ville.

mugger NOUN
l' <u>agresseur</u> MASC

mugging NOUN
l' <u>agression</u> FEM

muggy ADJECTIVE
<u>lourd</u> ◊ *It's muggy today.* Il fait lourd aujourd'hui.

multiple choice test NOUN
le <u>QCM</u> (= questionnaire à choix multiples)

multiple sclerosis NOUN
la <u>sclérose en plaques</u> ◊ *She's got multiple sclerosis.* Elle a la sclérose en plaques.

multiplication NOUN
la <u>multiplication</u>

to **multiply** VERB
<u>multiplier</u> ◊ *to multiply 6 by 3* multiplier six par trois

multi-storey car park NOUN
le <u>parking à plusieurs étages</u>

mum NOUN
> *You use **maman** only when you are talking to your mother or using it as her name; otherwise use **mère**.*

1 la <u>mère</u> ◊ *my mum* ma mère ◊ *her mum* sa mère
2 la <u>maman</u> ◊ *Mum!* Maman! ◊ *I'll ask Mum.* Je vais demander à maman.

mummy NOUN
1 la <u>maman</u> *(mum)* ◊ *Mummy says I can go.* Maman dit que je peux y aller.
2 la <u>momie</u> *(Egyptian)*

mumps NOUN
les <u>oreillons</u> MASC PL

murder NOUN
| *see also* **murder** VERB |

le <u>meurtre</u>

to **murder** VERB
| *see also* **murder** NOUN |

<u>assassiner</u> ◊ *He was murdered.* Il a été assassiné.

murderer NOUN
l' <u>assassin</u> MASC

muscle NOUN
le <u>muscle</u>

muscular ADJECTIVE
<u>musclé</u>

museum NOUN
  le musée

mushroom NOUN
  le champignon ◊ *mushroom
  omelette* l'omelette aux champignons

music NOUN
  la musique

musical ADJECTIVE
  | see also **musical** NOUN |
  doué pour la musique ◊ *I'm not
  musical.* Je ne suis pas doué pour la
  musique.
  ♦ **a musical instrument** un instrument
  de musique

musical NOUN
  | see also **musical** ADJECTIVE |
  la comédie musicale

music centre NOUN
  la chaîne stéréo

musician NOUN
  le musicien
  la musicienne

Muslim NOUN
  le musulman
  la musulmane
  ◊ *He's a Muslim.* Il est musulman.

mussel NOUN
  la moule

must VERB
  *When **must** means that you assume
  or suppose something, use **devoir**;
  when it means it's necessary to do
  something, eg **I must buy some
  presents**, use **il faut que ...**, which
  comes from the verb f**alloir** and is
  followed by a verb in the
  subjunctive.*
  [1] devoir (*I suppose*) ◊ *You must be
  tired.* Tu dois être fatigué. ◊ *They
  must have plenty of money.* Ils
  doivent avoir beaucoup d'argent.
  ◊ *There must be some problem.* Il
  doit y avoir un problème.
  [2] il faut que ◊ *I must buy some
  presents.* Il faut que j'achète des
  cadeaux. ◊ *I really must go now.* Il
  faut que j'y aille.
  ♦ **You mustn't forget to send her a
  card.** N'oublie surtout pas de lui
  envoyer une carte.
  ♦ **You must come and see us.**
  (*invitation*) Venez donc nous voir.

mustard NOUN
  la moutarde

mustn't VERB = **must not**

to **mutter** VERB
  marmonner

mutton NOUN
  le mouton

my ADJECTIVE
  mon MASC ◊ *my father* mon père
  ma FEM ◊ *my aunt* ma tante
  mes PL ◊ *my parents* mes parents
  *ma becomes **mon** before a vowel
  sound.*
  ♦ **my friend (1)** (*male*) mon ami
  ♦ **my friend (2)** (*female*) mon amie
  *Do not use **mon/ma/mes** with parts
  of the body.*
  ◊ *I want to wash my hair.* Je voudrais
  me laver les cheveux. ◊ *I'm going to
  clean my teeth.* Je vais me brosser les
  dents. ◊ *I've hurt my foot.* Je me suis
  fait mal au pied.

myself PRONOUN
  [1] me ◊ *I've hurt myself.* Je me suis
  fait mal. ◊ *I really enjoyed myself.* Je
  me suis vraiment bien amusé.
  ◊ *...when I look at myself in the
  mirror.* ...quand je me regarde dans
  la glace.
  [2] moi ◊ *I don't like talking about
  myself.* Je n'aime pas parler de moi.
  [3] moi-même ◊ *I made it myself.* Je
  l'ai fait moi-même.
  ♦ **by myself** tout seul ◊ *I don't like
  travelling by myself.* Je n'aime pas
  voyager tout seul.

mysterious ADJECTIVE
  mystérieux MASC
  mystérieuse FEM

mystery NOUN
  le mystère
  ♦ **a murder mystery** (*novel*) un roman
  policier

myth NOUN
  [1] le mythe (*legend*) ◊ *a Greek myth*
  un mythe grec
  [2] l' idée reçue FEM (*untrue idea*)
  ◊ *That's a myth.* C'est une idée reçue.

mythology NOUN
  la mythologie

M

N

naff ADJECTIVE
nul MASC
nulle FEM

to **nag** VERB
harceler (scold) ◊ She's always nagging me. Elle me harcèle constamment.

nail NOUN
[1] l' ongle MASC (on finger, toe) ◊ Don't bite your nails! Ne te ronge pas les ongles!
[2] le clou (made of metal)

nailbrush NOUN
la brosse à ongles

nailfile NOUN
la lime à ongles

nail scissors PL NOUN
les ciseaux à ongles MASC PL

nail varnish NOUN
le vernis à ongles
♦ **nail varnish remover** le dissolvant

naked ADJECTIVE
nu

name NOUN
le nom
♦ **What's your name?** Comment vous appelez-vous?

nanny NOUN
la garde d'enfants ◊ She's a nanny. C'est une garde d'enfants.

nap NOUN
le petit somme
♦ **to have a nap** faire un petit somme

napkin NOUN
la serviette

nappy NOUN
la couche

narrow ADJECTIVE
étroit

narrow-minded ADJECTIVE
borné

nasty ADJECTIVE
[1] mauvais (bad) ◊ a nasty cold un mauvais rhume ◊ a nasty smell une mauvaise odeur
[2] méchant (unfriendly) ◊ He gave me a nasty look. Il m'a regardé d'un air méchant.

nation NOUN
la nation

national ADJECTIVE
national
(nationaux MASC PL)

◊ He's the national champion. C'est le champion national.
♦ **the national elections** les élections législatives FEM

national anthem NOUN
l' hymne national MASC

National Health Service NOUN
la Sécurité sociale

> ❶ In France you have to pay for medical treatment when you receive it, and then claim it back from the **Sécurité sociale**.

nationalism NOUN
le nationalisme ◊ Scottish nationalism le nationalisme écossais

nationalist NOUN
le/la nationaliste

nationality NOUN
la nationalité

National Lottery NOUN
la Loterie nationale

national park NOUN
le parc national
(les parcs nationaux PL)

native ADJECTIVE
natal ◊ my native country mon pays natal
♦ **native language** la langue maternelle ◊ English is not their native language. L'anglais n'est pas leur langue maternelle.

natural ADJECTIVE
naturel MASC
naturelle FEM

naturalist NOUN
le naturaliste

naturally ADVERB
naturellement ◊ Naturally, we were very disappointed. Nous avons naturellement été très déçus.

nature NOUN
la nature

naughty ADJECTIVE
vilain ◊ Naughty girl! Vilaine! ◊ Don't be naughty! Ne fais pas le vilain!

navy NOUN
la marine ◊ He's in the navy. Il est dans la marine.

navy-blue ADJECTIVE
bleu marine MASC, FEM, PL ◊ a navy-blue skirt une jupe bleu marine

Nazi NOUN

le Nazi
la Nazie
◊ *the Nazis* les Nazis

near ADJECTIVE

see also **near** PREPOSITION

proche ◊ *It's fairly near.* C'est assez proche.
♦ **It's near enough to walk.** On peut facilement y aller à pied.
♦ **the nearest** le plus proche ◊ *Where's the nearest service station?* Où est la station-service la plus proche? ◊ *The nearest shops were three kilometres away.* Les magasins les plus proches étaient à trois kilomètres.

near PREPOSITION, ADVERB

see also **near** ADJECTIVE

près de ◊ *I live near Liverpool.* J'habite près de Liverpool. ◊ *near my house* près de chez moi
♦ **near here** près d'ici ◊ *Is there a bank near here?* Est-ce qu'il y a une banque près d'ici?
♦ **near to** près de ◊ *It's very near to the school.* C'est tout près de l'école.

nearby ADVERB

see also **nearby** ADJECTIVE

à proximité ◊ *There's a supermarket nearby.* Il y a un supermarché à proximité.

nearby ADJECTIVE

see also **nearby** ADVERB

1 proche (*close*) ◊ *a nearby garage* un garage proche
2 voisin (*neighbouring*) ◊ *We went to the nearby village of Torrance.* Nous sommes allés à Torrance, le village voisin.

nearly ADVERB

presque ◊ *Dinner's nearly ready.* Le dîner est presque prêt. ◊ *I'm nearly 15.* J'ai presque quinze ans.
♦ **I nearly missed the train.** J'ai failli rater le train.

neat ADJECTIVE

soigné ◊ *She has very neat writing.* Elle a une écriture très soignée.
♦ **a neat whisky** un whisky sec

neatly ADVERB

soigneusement ◊ *neatly folded* soigneusement plié
♦ **neatly dressed** impeccable

necessarily ADVERB
♦ **not necessarily** pas forcément

necessary ADJECTIVE

nécessaire

necessity NOUN

la chose nécessaire ◊ *A car is a necessity, not a luxury.* Une voiture est une chose nécessaire et non pas un luxe.

neck NOUN

1 le cou (*of body*)
♦ **a stiff neck** un torticolis
2 l' encolure FEM (*of garment*) ◊ *a V-neck sweater* un pull avec une encolure en V

necklace NOUN

le collier

to **need** VERB

see also **need** NOUN

avoir besoin de ◊ *I need a bigger size.* J'ai besoin d'une plus grande taille.
♦ **to need to do something** avoir besoin de faire quelque chose ◊ *I need to change some money.* J'ai besoin de changer de l'argent.

need NOUN

see also **need** VERB

♦ **There's no need to book.** Il n'est pas nécessaire de réserver.

needle NOUN

l' aiguille FEM

needlework NOUN

la couture ◊ *We have needlework lessons at school.* Nous avons des cours de couture à l'école.

negative NOUN

see also **negative** ADJECTIVE

le négatif (*photo*)

negative ADJECTIVE

see also **negative** NOUN

négatif MASC
négative FEM
◊ *He's got a very negative attitude.* Il a une attitude très négative.

neglected ADJECTIVE

mal tenu (*untidy*) ◊ *The garden is neglected.* Le jardin est mal tenu.

negligee NOUN

le déshabillé

to **negotiate** VERB

négocier

negotiations PL NOUN

les négociations FEM PL

neighbour NOUN (US **neighbor**)

le voisin
la voisine
◊ *the neighbours' garden* le jardin des voisins

neighbourhood NOUN (US **neighborhood**)

le quartier

neither PRONOUN, CONJUNCTION, ADVERB

aucun des deux
aucune des deux

N

◊ *Carrots or peas? – Neither, thanks.*
Des carottes ou des petits pois? –
Aucun des deux merci. ◊ *Neither of
them is coming.* Aucun des deux ne
vient.
♦**neither ... nor ...** ni ... ni ... ◊ *Neither
Sarah nor Tamsin is coming to the
party.* Ni Sarah ni Tamsin ne vient à
la soirée.
♦**Neither do I.** Moi non plus. ◊ *I don't
like him. – Neither do I!* Je ne l'aime
pas. – Moi non plus!
♦**Neither have I.** Moi non plus. ◊ *I've
never been to Spain. – Neither
have I.* Je ne suis jamais allé en
Espagne. – Moi non plus.

neon NOUN
le <u>néon</u>
♦**a neon light** une lampe au néon

nephew NOUN
le <u>neveu</u>
(les neveux PL)
◊ *my nephew* mon neveu

nerve NOUN
1 le <u>nerf</u> ◊ *She sometimes gets on
my nerves.* Elle me tape quelquefois
sur les nerfs.
2 le <u>toupet</u> (*cheek*) ◊ *He's got a
nerve!* Il a du toupet!

nerve-racking ADJECTIVE
<u>angoissant</u>

nervous ADJECTIVE
<u>tendu</u> (*tense*) ◊ *I bite my nails when
I'm nervous.* Je me ronge les ongles
quand je suis tendu.
♦**to be nervous about something**
appréhender de faire quelque chose
◊ *I'm a bit nervous about flying to
Paris by myself.* J'appréhende un peu
d'aller toute seule en avion à Paris.

nest NOUN
le <u>nid</u>

Net NOUN
le <u>Net</u> ◊ *to surf the Net* surfer sur le
Net

net NOUN
le <u>filet</u> ◊ *a fishing net* un filet de
pêche

netball NOUN

> ❶ Netball is not played in France.
> Both sexes play basketball or
> volleyball instead.

♦**Netball is a bit like basketball, but
it's normally played by girls.** Le
netball ressemble un peu au basket,
mais est généralement pratiqué par
les filles.

Netherlands PL NOUN

les <u>Pays-Bas</u> MASC PL
♦**in the Netherlands** aux Pays-Bas

network NOUN
le <u>réseau</u>
(les réseaux PL)

neurotic ADJECTIVE
<u>névrosé</u>

never ADVERB
1 <u>jamais</u> ◊ *Have you ever been to
Germany? – No, never.* Est-ce que tu
es déjà allé en Allemagne? – Non,
jamais. ◊ *When are you going to
phone him? – Never!* Quand est-ce
que tu vas l'appeler? – Jamais!
*Add ne if the sentence contains a
verb.*
2 <u>ne ... jamais</u> ◊ *I never write
letters.* Je n'écris jamais. ◊ *I have
never been camping.* Je n'ai jamais
fait de camping. ◊ *Never leave
valuables in your car.* Ne laissez
jamais d'objets de valeur dans votre
voiture.
♦**Never again!** Plus jamais!
♦**Never mind.** Ça ne fait rien.

new ADJECTIVE
1 <u>nouveau</u> MASC
<u>nouvelle</u> FEM
(nouveaux MASC PL)
◊ *her new boyfriend* son nouveau
copain ◊ *I need a new dress.* J'ai
besoin d'une nouvelle robe.
2 (*brand new*)
<u>neuf</u> MASC
<u>neuve</u> FEM
◊ *They've got a new car.* Ils ont une
voiture neuve.

newborn ADJECTIVE
♦**a newborn baby** un nouveau-né

newcomer NOUN
le <u>nouveau venu</u>
la <u>nouvelle venue</u>
(les nouveaux venus MASC PL)

news NOUN
1 les <u>nouvelles</u> FEM PL ◊ *good news*
de bonnes nouvelles ◊ *I've had some
bad news.* J'ai reçu de mauvaises
nouvelles. ◊ *It was nice to have your
news.* J'ai été content d'avoir de tes
nouvelles.
2 la <u>nouvelle</u> (*single piece of news*)
◊ *That's wonderful news!* Quelle
bonne nouvelle!
3 le <u>journal télévisé</u> (*on TV*) ◊ *I
watch the news every evening.* Je
regarde le journal télévisé tous les
soirs.
4 les <u>informations</u> FEM PL (*on radio*) ◊ *I
listen to the news every morning.*

J'écoute les informations tous les
matins.

newsagent NOUN
le marchand de journaux

newsdealer NOUN US
le marchand de journaux

newspaper NOUN
le journal
(les journaux PL)
◊ *I deliver newspapers.* Je distribue
des journaux.

newsreader NOUN
le présentateur
la présentatrice

New Year NOUN
le Nouvel An ◊ *to celebrate New
Year* fêter le Nouvel An
♦**Happy New Year!** Bonne Année!
♦**New Year's Day** le premier de l'An
♦**New Year's Eve** la Saint-Sylvestre ◊ *a
New Year's Eve party* un réveillon du
premier de l'An

New Zealand NOUN
la Nouvelle-Zélande
♦**in New Zealand** en Nouvelle-Zélande

New Zealander NOUN
le Néo-Zélandais
la Néo-Zélandaise

next ADJECTIVE, ADVERB, PREPOSITION
[1] prochain (*in time*) ◊ *next Saturday*
samedi prochain ◊ *next year* l'année
prochaine ◊ *next summer* l'été
prochain
[2] suivant (*in sequence*) ◊ *the next train*
le train suivant ◊ *Next please!* Au
suivant!
[3] ensuite (*afterwards*) ◊ *What shall I
do next?* Qu'est-ce que je fais ensuite?
◊ *What happened next?* Qu'est-ce qui
s'est passé ensuite?
♦**next to** à côté de ◊ *next to the bank* à
côté de la banque
♦**the next day** le lendemain ◊ *The next
day we visited Dublin.* Le lendemain
nous avons visité Dublin.
♦**the next time** la prochaine fois ◊ *the
next time you see her* la prochaine
fois que tu la verras
♦**next door** à côté ◊ *They live next
door.* Ils habitent à côté. ◊ *the people
next door* les gens d'à côté
♦**the next room** la pièce d'à côté

NHS NOUN
la Sécurité sociale

> ⓘ *In France you have to pay for
> medical treatment when you receive
> it, and then claim it back from the
> **Sécurité sociale**.*

nice ADJECTIVE
[1] (*kind*)
gentil MASC
gentille FEM
◊ *Your parents are very nice.* Tes
parents sont très gentils. ◊ *It was
nice of you to remember my
birthday.* C'était gentil de ta part de
te souvenir de mon anniversaire.
♦**to be nice to somebody** être gentil
avec quelqu'un
[2] (*pretty*)
joli ◊ *That's a nice dress!* Qu'est-ce
qu'elle est jolie, cette robe! ◊ *Avignon
is a nice town.* Avignon est une jolie
ville.
[3] (*food*)
bon MASC
bonne FEM
◊ *It's very nice.* C'est très bon. ◊ *a
nice cup of coffee* une bonne tasse
de café
♦**Have a nice time!** Amuse-toi bien!
♦**nice weather** le beau temps
♦**It's a nice day.** Il fait beau.

nickname NOUN
le surnom

niece NOUN
la nièce ◊ *my niece* ma nièce

Nigeria NOUN
le Nigéria
♦**in Nigeria** au Nigéria

night NOUN
[1] la nuit ◊ *I want a single room for
two nights.* Je veux une chambre à
un lit pour deux nuits.
♦**My mother works nights.** Ma mère
travaille de nuit.
♦**at night** la nuit
♦**all night** toute la nuit
♦**Goodnight!** Bonne nuit!
♦**a night club** une boîte de nuit
[2] le soir (*evening*) ◊ *last night* hier
soir

nightdress NOUN
la chemise de nuit

nightie NOUN
la chemise de nuit

nightlife NOUN
♦**There's plenty of nightlife.** Il y a plein
de choses à faire le soir.

nightmare NOUN
le cauchemar ◊ *It was a real
nightmare!* Ça a été un vrai
cauchemar!
♦**to have a nightmare** faire un
cauchemar

nightshirt NOUN
la chemise de nuit

nil NOUN

N

☞

le <u>zéro</u> ◊ *We won one-nil.* Nous avons gagné un à zéro.

nine NUMBER
<u>neuf</u> MASC
<u>neuve</u> FEM
◊ *She's nine.* Elle a neuf ans.

nineteen NUMBER
<u>dix-neuf</u> ◊ *She's nineteen.* Elle a dix-neuf ans.

nineteenth NOUN
<u>dix-neuvième</u> ◊ *her nineteenth birthday* son dix-neuvième anniversaire ◊ *the nineteenth floor* le dix-neuvième étage
♦ **the nineteenth of August** le dix-neuf août

ninety NUMBER
<u>quatre-vingt-dix</u>

ninth ADJECTIVE
<u>neuvième</u> ◊ *the ninth floor* le neuvième étage
♦ **the ninth of August** le neuf août

no ADVERB, ADJECTIVE
[1] <u>non</u> ◊ *Are you coming? – No.* Est-ce que vous venez? – Non. ◊ *Would you like some more? – No thank you.* Vous en voulez encore? – Non merci.
[2] <u>pas de</u> (*not any*) ◊ *There's no hot water.* Il n'y a pas d'eau chaude.
◊ *There are no trains on Sundays.* Il n'y a pas de trains le dimanche. ◊ *No problem.* Pas de problème.
♦ **I've got no idea.** Je n'en ai aucune idée.
♦ **No way!** Pas question!
♦ **"no smoking"** "défense de fumer"

nobody PRONOUN
[1] <u>personne</u> ◊ *Who's going with you? – Nobody.* Qui t'accompagne? – Personne.
*Add **ne** if the sentence contains a verb.*
[2] <u>ne ... personne</u> ◊ *There was nobody in the office.* Il n'y avait personne au bureau.
♦ **Nobody likes him.** Personne ne l'aime.

to **nod** VERB
<u>acquiescer d'un signe de tête</u> (*in agreement*)
♦ **to nod at somebody** saluer quelqu'un d'un signe de tête (*as greeting*)

noise NOUN
le <u>bruit</u> ◊ *Please make less noise.* Faites moins de bruit s'il vous plaît.

noisy ADJECTIVE
<u>bruyant</u>

to **nominate** VERB

[1] <u>nommer</u> (*appoint*) ◊ *She was nominated as director.* Elle a été nommée directrice.
[2] <u>proposer</u> (*propose*) ◊ *I nominate Ian Alexander as president of the society.* Je propose Ian Alexander comme président de la société.
♦ **He was nominated for an Oscar.** Il a été nominé pour un Oscar.

none PRONOUN
[1] <u>aucun</u> MASC
<u>aucune</u> FEM
◊ *How many sisters have you got? – None.* Tu as combien de sœurs? – Aucune. ◊ *What sports do you do? – None.* Qu'est-ce que tu fais comme sport? – Je n'en fais aucun.
*Add **ne** if the sentence contains a verb.*
[2] <u>aucun ... ne</u> ◊ *None of my friends wanted to come.* Aucun de mes amis n'a voulu venir.
♦ **There's none left.** Il n'y en a plus.
♦ **There are none left.** Il n'y en a plus.

nonsense NOUN
les <u>bêtises</u> FEM PL ◊ *She talks a lot of nonsense.* Elle dit beaucoup de bêtises. ◊ *Nonsense!* Ne dis pas de bêtises!

non-smoker NOUN
le <u>non-fumeur</u> ◊ *He's a non-smoker.* Il est non-fumeur.

non-smoking ADJECTIVE
<u>non-fumeur</u> ◊ *a non-smoking carriage* une voiture non-fumeurs

non-stop ADJECTIVE, ADVERB
[1] <u>direct</u> ◊ *a non-stop flight* un vol direct
[2] <u>sans arrêt</u> ◊ *He talks non-stop.* Il parle sans arrêt.

noodles PL NOUN
les <u>nouilles</u> FEM PL

noon NOUN
<u>midi</u> ◊ *at noon* à midi

no one PRONOUN
[1] <u>personne</u> ◊ *Who's going with you? – No one.* Qui t'accompagne? – Personne.
*Add **ne** if the sentence contains a verb.*
[2] <u>ne ... personne</u> ◊ *There was no one in the office.* Il n'y avait personne au bureau.
♦ **No one likes him.** Personne ne l'aime.

nor CONJUNCTION
♦ **neither ... nor** ni ... ni ◊ *neither the cinema nor the swimming pool* ni le cinéma, ni la piscine

♦**Nor do I.** Moi non plus. ◊ *I didn't like the film. – Nor did I.* Je n'ai pas aimé le film. – Moi non plus.
♦**Nor have I.** Moi non plus. ◊ *I haven't seen him. – Nor have I.* Je ne l'ai pas vu. – Moi non plus.

normal ADJECTIVE
  [1] (*usual*)
  habituel MASC
  habituelle FEM
  ◊ *at the normal time* à l'heure habituelle
  [2] (*standard*)
  normal
  (normaux MASC PL)
  ◊ *a normal car* une voiture normale

normally ADVERB
  [1] généralement (*usually*) ◊ *I normally arrive at nine o'clock.* J'arrive généralement à neuf heures.
  [2] normalement (*as normal*) ◊ *In spite of the strike, the airports are working normally.* Malgré la grève, les aéroports fonctionnent normalement.

Normandy NOUN
  la Normandie
♦**in Normandy** en Normandie
♦**to Normandy** en Normandie

north ADJECTIVE, ADVERB
  see also **north** NOUN
  [1] nord MASC, FEM, PL ◊ *the north coast* la côte nord
♦**a north wind** un vent du nord
  [2] vers le nord ◊ *We were travelling north.* Nous allions vers le nord.
♦**north of** au nord de ◊ *It's north of London.* C'est au nord de Londres.

north NOUN
  see also **north** ADJECTIVE
  le nord ◊ *in the north* dans le nord

North America NOUN
  l' Amérique du Nord FEM

northbound ADJECTIVE
  ◊ *The truck was northbound on the M5.* Le camion se trouvait sur la M5 en direction du nord.
♦**Northbound traffic is moving very slowly.** La circulation vers le nord avance très lentement.

northeast NOUN
  le nord-est ◊ *in the northeast* au nord-est

northern ADJECTIVE
♦**the northern part of the island** la partie nord de l'île
♦**Northern Europe** l'Europe du Nord

Northern Ireland NOUN
  l' Irlande du Nord FEM

♦**in Northern Ireland** en Irlande du Nord
♦**to Northern Ireland** en Irlande du Nord
♦**I'm from Northern Ireland.** Je viens d'Irlande du Nord.

North Pole NOUN
  le pôle Nord

North Sea NOUN
  la mer du Nord

northwest NOUN
  le nord-ouest ◊ *in the northwest* au nord-ouest

Norway NOUN
  la Norvège
♦**in Norway** en Norvège

Norwegian ADJECTIVE
  see also **Norwegian** NOUN
  norvégien MASC
  norvégienne FEM

Norwegian NOUN
  see also **Norwegian** ADJECTIVE
  [1] (*person*)
  le Norvégien
  la Norvégienne
  [2] (*language*)
  le norvégien

nose NOUN
  le nez
  (les nez PL)

nosebleed NOUN
♦**to have a nosebleed** saigner du nez
  ◊ *I often get nosebleeds.* Je saigne souvent du nez.

nosy ADJECTIVE
  fouineur MASC
  fouineuse FEM

not ADVERB
  [1] pas ◊ *Are you coming or not?* Est-ce que tu viens ou pas?
♦**not really** pas vraiment
♦**not at all** pas du tout
♦**not yet** pas encore ◊ *Have you finished? – Not yet.* As-tu fini? – Pas encore.
  Add ***ne*** *before a verb.*
  [2] ne ... pas ◊ *I'm not sure.* Je ne suis pas sûr. ◊ *It's not raining.* Il ne pleut pas. ◊ *You shouldn't do that.* Tu ne devrais pas faire ça. ◊ *They haven't arrived yet.* Ils ne sont pas encore arrivés.
  [3] non ◊ *I hope not.* J'espère que non. ◊ *Can you lend me £10? – I'm afraid not.* Est-ce que tu peux me prêter dix livres? – Non, désolé.

note NOUN
  [1] la note ◊ *to take notes* prendre des notes

N

☞

2 le mot (letter) ◊ I'll write her a note. Je vais lui écrire un mot.

3 le billet (banknote) ◊ a £5 note un billet de cinq livres

to **note down** VERB
noter

notebook NOUN
le carnet

notepad NOUN
le bloc-notes
(les blocs-notes PL)

notepaper NOUN
le papier à lettres

nothing NOUN
1 rien ◊ What's wrong? – Nothing. Qu'est-ce qui ne va pas? – Rien.
◊ nothing special rien de particulier
*Add **ne** if the sentence contains a verb.*
2 ne ... rien ◊ He does nothing. Il ne fait rien. ◊ He ate nothing for breakfast. Il n'a rien mangé au petit-déjeuner.
♦ **Nothing is open on Sundays.** Rien n'est ouvert le dimanche.

notice NOUN
see also **notice** VERB
(sign)
le panneau
(les panneaux PL)
♦ **to put up a notice** mettre un panneau
♦ **a warning notice** un avertissement
♦ **Don't take any notice of him!** Ne fais pas attention à lui!

to **notice** VERB
see also **notice** NOUN
remarquer

notice board NOUN
le panneau d'affichage
(les panneaux d'affichage PL)

nought NOUN
le zéro

noun NOUN
le nom

novel NOUN
le roman

novelist NOUN
le romancier
la romancière

November NOUN
novembre MASC
♦ **in November** en novembre

now ADVERB, CONJUNCTION
maintenant ◊ What are you doing now? Qu'est-ce que tu fais maintenant?

♦ **just now** en ce moment ◊ I'm rather busy just now. Je suis très occupé en ce moment.
♦ **I did it just now.** Je viens de le faire.
♦ **He should be there by now.** Il doit être arrivé à l'heure qu'il est.
♦ **It should be ready by now.** Ça devrait être déjà prêt.
♦ **now and then** de temps en temps

nowhere ADVERB
nulle part ◊ nowhere else nulle part ailleurs

nuclear ADJECTIVE
nucléaire ◊ nuclear power l'énergie nucléaire ◊ a nuclear power station une centrale nucléaire

nude ADJECTIVE
see also **nude** NOUN
nu
♦ **to sunbathe nude** faire du bronzage intégral

nude NOUN
see also **nude** ADJECTIVE
♦ **in the nude** nu

nudist NOUN
le/la nudiste

nuisance NOUN
♦ **It's a nuisance.** C'est très embêtant.
♦ **Sorry to be a nuisance.** Désolé de vous déranger.

numb ADJECTIVE
engourdi ◊ My legs have gone numb. J'ai les jambes engourdies.
◊ numb with cold engourdi par le froid

number NOUN
1 le nombre (total amount) ◊ a large number of people un grand nombre de gens
2 le numéro (of house, telephone, bank account) ◊ They live at number 5. Ils habitent au numéro cinq. ◊ What's your phone number? Quel est votre numéro de téléphone? ◊ You've got the wrong number. Vous vous êtes trompé de numéro.
3 le chiffre (figure, digit) ◊ I can't read the second number. Je n'arrive pas à lire le deuxième chiffre.

number plate NOUN
la plaque d'immatriculation

nun NOUN
la religieuse ◊ She's a nun. Elle est religieuse.

nurse NOUN
l' infirmier MASC
l' infirmière FEM
◊ She's a nurse. Elle est infirmière.

nursery NOUN
    1 la crèche (*for children*)
    2 la pépinière (*for plants*)

nursery school NOUN
    l' école maternelle FEM

> ⓘ The **école maternelle** is a state
> school for 2-6 year-olds.

nursery slope NOUN
    la piste pour débutants

nut NOUN
    1 (*peanut*)
    la cacahuète
    2 (*hazelnut*)
    la noisette
    3 (*walnut*)
    la noix
    (les noix PL)
    4 (*made of metal*)
    l' écrou MASC

nutmeg NOUN
    la noix de muscade

nutritious ADJECTIVE
    nourrissant

nuts ADJECTIVE
♦**He's nuts.** Il est dingue.

nutter NOUN
♦**He's a nutter.** Il est complètement
    cinglé. (*informal*)

nylon NOUN
    le nylon

N

O

oak NOUN
le chêne ◊ *an oak table* une table en chêne

oar NOUN
l' aviron MASC

oats NOUN
l' avoine FEM

obedient ADJECTIVE
obéissant

to obey VERB
◆to obey the rules respecter le règlement

object NOUN
l' objet MASC ◊ *a familiar object* un objet familier

objection NOUN
l' objection FEM

objective NOUN
l' objectif MASC

oblong ADJECTIVE
rectangulaire

oboe NOUN
le hautbois ◊ *I play the oboe.* Je joue du hautbois.

obscene ADJECTIVE
obscène

observant ADJECTIVE
observateur MASC
observatrice FEM

to observe VERB
observer

obsessed ADJECTIVE
obsédé ◊ *He's obsessed with trains.* Il est obsédé par les trains.

obsession NOUN
l' obsession FEM ◊ *It's getting to be an obsession with you.* Ça devient une obsession chez toi.
◆Football's an obsession of mine. Le football est une de mes passions.

obsolete ADJECTIVE
dépassé

obstacle NOUN
l' obstacle MASC

obstinate ADJECTIVE
obstiné

to obstruct VERB
bloquer ◊ *A lorry was obstructing the traffic.* Un camion bloquait la circulation.

to obtain VERB
obtenir

obvious ADJECTIVE
évident

obviously ADVERB
[1] évidemment (*of course*) ◊ *Do you want to pass the exam? – Obviously!* Tu veux être reçu à l'examen? – Évidemment!
◆Obviously not! Bien sûr que non!
[2] manifestement (*visibly*) ◊ *She was obviously exhausted.* Elle était manifestement épuisée.

occasion NOUN
l' occasion FEM ◊ *a special occasion* une occasion spéciale
◆on several occasions à plusieurs reprises

occasionally ADVERB
de temps en temps

occupation NOUN
la profession

to occupy VERB
occuper ◊ *That seat is occupied.* Cette place est occupée.

to occur VERB
avoir lieu (*happen*) ◊ *The accident occurred yesterday.* L'accident a eu lieu hier.
◆It suddenly occurred to me that ... Il m'est soudain venu à l'esprit que ...

ocean NOUN
l' océan MASC

o'clock ADVERB
◆at four o'clock à quatre heures
◆It's five o'clock. Il est cinq heures.

October NOUN
octobre MASC
◆in October en octobre

octopus NOUN
la pieuvre

odd ADJECTIVE
[1] bizarre ◊ *That's odd!* C'est bizarre!
[2] impair ◊ *an odd number* un chiffre impair

of PREPOSITION
[1] de ◊ *some photos of my holiday* des photos de mes vacances ◊ *a boy of ten* un garçon de dix ans
de changes to d' before a vowel and most words beginning with "h".
d' ◊ *a kilo of oranges* un kilo d'oranges
de + le changes to du, and de + les changes to des.
du ◊ *the end of the film* la fin du film
des ◊ *the end of the holidays* la fin des vacances

2 (*with quantity, amount*)
en ◊ *He's got four sisters. I've met two of them.* Il a quatre sœurs. J'en ai rencontré deux. ◊ *Can I have half of that?* Je peux en avoir la moitié?
♦ **three of us** trois d'entre nous
♦ **a friend of mine** un de mes amis
♦ **the 14th of September** le quatorze septembre
♦ **That's very kind of you.** C'est très gentil de votre part.
♦ **It's made of wood.** C'est en bois.

off ADVERB, PREPOSITION, ADJECTIVE
*For other expressions with **off**, see the verbs **get, take, turn** etc.*
1 éteint (*heater, light, TV*) ◊ *All the lights are off.* Toutes les lumières sont éteintes.
2 fermé (*tap, gas*) ◊ *Are you sure the tap is off?* Tu es sûr que le robinet est fermé?
3 annulé (*cancelled*) ◊ *The match is off.* Le match est annulé.
♦ **to be off sick** être malade
♦ **a day off** un jour de congé ◊ *to take a day off work* prendre un jour de congé
♦ **She's off school today.** Elle n'est pas à l'école aujourd'hui.
♦ **I must be off now.** Je dois m'en aller maintenant.
♦ **I'm off.** Je m'en vais.

offence NOUN (US **offense**)
le délit (*crime*)

offensive ADJECTIVE
choquant

offer NOUN
see also **offer** VERB
la proposition ◊ *a good offer* une proposition intéressante
♦ **"on special offer"** "en promotion"

to **offer** VERB
see also **offer** NOUN
proposer ◊ *He offered to help me.* Il m'a proposé de m'aider. ◊ *I offered to go with them.* Je leur ai proposé de les accompagner.

office NOUN
le bureau
(les bureaux PL)
◊ *She works in an office.* Elle travaille dans un bureau.

officer NOUN
l' officier MASC

official ADJECTIVE
officiel MASC
officielle FEM

off-licence NOUN
le marchand de vins et spiritueux

off-peak ADVERB
hors saison (*off-season*) ◊ *It's cheaper to go on holiday off-peak.* C'est moins cher de partir en vacances hors saison.
♦ **to phone off-peak** appeler pendant les heures creuses

offside ADJECTIVE
hors jeu (*in football*)

often ADVERB
souvent ◊ *It often rains.* Il pleut souvent. ◊ *How often do you go to the gym?* Tu vas souvent à la gym? ◊ *I'd like to go skiing more often.* J'aimerais aller skier plus souvent.

oil NOUN
see also **oil** VERB
1 l' huile FEM (*for lubrication, cooking*)
♦ **an oil painting** une peinture à l'huile
2 le pétrole (*crude oil*) ◊ *North Sea oil* le pétrole de la mer du Nord

to **oil** VERB
see also **oil** NOUN
graisser

oil rig NOUN
la plateforme pétrolière ◊ *He works on an oil rig.* Il travaille sur une plateforme pétrolière.

oil slick NOUN
la marée noire

oil well NOUN
le puits de pétrole
(les puits de pétrole PL)

ointment NOUN
la pommade MASC

okay EXCLAMATION, ADJECTIVE
d'accord (*agreed*) ◊ *Could you call back later? – Okay!* Tu peux rappeler plus tard? – D'accord! ◊ *I'll meet you at six o'clock, okay?* Je te retrouve à six heures, d'accord? ◊ *Is that okay?* C'est d'accord?
♦ **I'll do it tomorrow, if that's okay with you.** Je le ferai demain, si tu es d'accord.
♦ **Are you okay?** Ça va?
♦ **How was your holiday? – It was okay.** C'était comment tes vacances? – Pas mal.
♦ **What's your teacher like? – He's okay.** Il est comment ton prof? – Il est sympa. (*informal*)

old ADJECTIVE
1 vieux MASC
vieille FEM
◊ *an old dog* un vieux chien ◊ *an old house* une vieille maison
vieux changes to vieil before a vowel and most words beginning with "h".

O

vieil ◊ *an old man* un vieil homme
*When talking about people it is more
polite to use **âgé** instead of **vieux**.*
âgé ◊ *old people* les personnes âgées
2 (*former*)
ancien MASC
ancienne FEM
◊ *my old English teacher* mon ancien
professeur d'anglais
◆ **How old are you?** Quel âge as-tu?
◆ **He's ten years old.** Il a dix ans.
◆ **my older brother** mon frère aîné ◊ *my
older sister* ma sœur aînée
◆ **She's two years older than me.** Elle a
deux ans de plus que moi.
◆ **I'm the oldest in the family.** Je suis
l'aîné de la famille.

old age pensioner NOUN
le retraité
la retraitée
◊ *She's an old age pensioner.* Elle est
retraitée.

old-fashioned ADJECTIVE
1 démodé ◊ *She wears old-
fashioned clothes.* Elle porte des
vêtements démodés.
2 (*person*)
vieux jeu MASC, FEM, PL ◊ *My parents are
rather old-fashioned.* Mes parents
sont plutôt vieux jeu.

olive NOUN
l' olive FEM

olive oil NOUN
l' huile d'olive FEM

olive tree NOUN
l' olivier MASC

Olympic ADJECTIVE
olympique
◆ **the Olympics** les Jeux olympiques
MASC

omelette NOUN
l' omelette FEM

on PREPOSITION, ADVERB
see also **on** ADJECTIVE
*There are several ways of translating
on. Scan the examples to find one
that is similar to what you want to
say. For other expressions with **on**,
see the verbs **go**, **put**, **turn** etc.*
1 sur ◊ *on the table* sur la table ◊ *on
an island* sur une île
2 à ◊ *on the left* à gauche ◊ *on the
2nd floor* au deuxième étage ◊ *I go
to school on my bike.* Je vais à
l'école à vélo.
◆ **on TV** à la télé ◊ *What's on TV?*
Qu'est-ce qu'il y a à la télé?
◆ **on the radio** à la radio ◊ *I heard it on
the radio.* Je l'ai entendu à la radio.

◆ **on the bus (1)** (*by bus*) en bus ◊ *I go
into town on the bus.* Je vais en ville
en bus.
◆ **on the bus (2)** (*inside*) dans le bus
◊ *There were no empty seats on the
bus.* Il n'y avait pas de places libres
dans le bus.
◆ **on holiday** en vacances ◊ *They're on
holiday.* Ils sont en vacances.
◆ **on strike** en grève
*With days and dates **on** is not
translated.*
◊ *on Friday* vendredi ◊ *on Fridays* le
vendredi ◊ *on Christmas Day* le jour
de Noël ◊ *on June 20th* le vingt juin
◊ *on my birthday* le jour de mon
anniversaire

on ADJECTIVE
see also **on** PREPOSITION
1 allumé (*heater, light, TV*) ◊ *I think I
left the light on.* Je crois que j'ai
laissé la lumière allumée.
2 ouvert (*tap, gas*) ◊ *Leave the tap
on.* Laisse le robinet ouvert.
3 en marche (*machine*) ◊ *Is the
dishwasher on?* Est-ce que le
lave-vaisselle est en marche?
◆ **What's on at the cinema?** Qu'est-ce
qui passe au cinéma?

once ADVERB
une fois ◊ *once a week* une fois par
semaine ◊ *once more* encore une fois
◊ *I've been to France once before.*
J'ai déjà été une fois en France.
◆ **Once upon a time ...** Il était une
fois ...
◆ **at once** tout de suite
◆ **once in a while** de temps en temps
◆ **once and for all** une fois pour toutes

one NUMBER, PRONOUN
*Use **un** for masculine nouns and **une**
for feminine nouns.*
1 un ◊ *one day* un jour ◊ *Do you
need a stamp? – No thanks, I've got
one.* Est-ce que tu as besoin d'un
timbre? – Non merci, j'en ai un.
une ◊ *one minute* une minute ◊ *I've
got one brother and one sister.* J'ai
un frère et une sœur.
2 on (*impersonal*) ◊ *One never
knows.* On ne sait jamais.
◆ **this one (1)** celui-ci (*masculine*)
◊ *Which foot is hurting? – This one.*
Quel pied te fait mal? – Celui-ci.
◆ **this one (2)** celle-ci (*feminine*) ◊ *Which
is the best photo? – This one.* Quelle
est la meilleure photo? – Celle-ci.
◆ **that one (1)** celui-là (*masculine*)
◊ *Which bag is yours? – That one.*
Lequel est ton sac? – Celui-là.

♦**that one (2)** celle-là (*feminine*) ◊ *Which seat do you want? – That one.* Quelle place voulez-vous? – Celle-là.

oneself PRONOUN
1 se ◊ *to hurt oneself* se faire mal
2 soi-même ◊ *It's quicker to do it oneself.* C'est plus rapide de le faire soi-même.

one-way ADJECTIVE
♦**a one-way street** une impasse

onion NOUN
l' oignon MASC ◊ *onion soup* la soupe à l'oignon

only ADVERB, ADJECTIVE, CONJUNCTION
1 seul ◊ *Monday is the only day I'm free.* Le lundi est le seul jour où je suis libre. ◊ *French is the only subject I like.* Le français est la seule matière que j'aime.
2 seulement ◊ *How much was it? – Only 10 francs.* Combien c'était? – Seulement dix francs.
3 ne ... que ◊ *We only want to stay for one night.* Nous ne voulons rester qu'une nuit. ◊ *These cassettes are only 30 francs.* Ces cassettes ne coûtent que trente francs.
4 mais ◊ *I'd like the same sweater, only in black.* Je voudrais le même pull, mais en noir.
♦**an only child** un enfant unique

onwards ADVERB
à partir de ◊ *from July onwards* à partir de juillet

open ADJECTIVE
see also **open** VERB
ouvert ◊ *The baker's is open on Sunday morning.* La boulangerie est ouverte le dimanche matin.
♦**in the open air** en plein air

to **open** VERB
see also **open** ADJECTIVE
1 ouvrir ◊ *Can I open the window?* Est-ce que je peux ouvrir la fenêtre? ◊ *What time do the shops open?* Les magasins ouvrent à quelle heure?
2 s'ouvrir ◊ *The door opens automatically.* La porte s'ouvre automatiquement. ◊ *The door opened and in came the teacher.* La porte s'est ouverte et le professeur est entré.

opening hours PL NOUN
les heures d'ouverture FEM PL

opera NOUN
l' opéra MASC

to **operate** VERB
1 fonctionner ◊ *I don't know how the electoral system operates in*

France. Je ne sais pas comment fonctionne le système électoral en France.
2 faire fonctionner ◊ *How do you operate the video?* Comment fait-on fonctionner le magnétoscope?
3 opérer (*medically*)
♦**to operate on someone** opérer quelqu'un

operation NOUN
l' opération FEM ◊ *a major operation* une grave opération
♦**to have an operation** se faire opérer ◊ *I have never had an operation.* Je ne me suis jamais fait opérer.

operator NOUN
le/la standardiste (*on telephone*)

opinion NOUN
l' avis MASC ◊ *in my opinion* à mon avis ◊ *He asked me my opinion.* Il m'a demandé mon avis.
♦**What's your opinion?** Qu'est-ce vous en pensez?

opinion poll NOUN
le sondage

opponent NOUN
l' adversaire MASC/FEM

opportunity NOUN
l' occasion FEM
♦**to have the opportunity to do something** avoir l'occasion de faire quelque chose ◊ *I've never had the opportunity to go to France.* Je n'ai jamais eu l'occasion d'aller en France.

opposed ADJECTIVE
◊ *I've always been opposed to violence.* J'ai toujours été contre la violence.
♦**as opposed to** par opposition à

opposing ADJECTIVE
opposé (*team*)

opposite ADJECTIVE, ADVERB, PREPOSITION
1 opposé ◊ *It's in the opposite direction.* C'est dans la direction opposée.
2 en face ◊ *They live opposite.* Ils habitent en face.
3 en face de ◊ *the girl sitting opposite me* la fille assise en face de moi
♦**the opposite sex** l'autre sexe

opposition NOUN
l' opposition FEM

optician NOUN
l' opticien MASC
l' opticienne FEM
◊ *She's an optician.* Elle est opticienne.

optimist NOUN
l' optimiste MASC/FEM

optimistic ADJECTIVE
optimiste

option NOUN
[1] le choix (*choice*) ◊ *I've got no option.* Je n'ai pas le choix.
[2] la matière à option (*optional subject*) ◊ *I'm doing geology as my option.* La géologie est ma matière à option.

optional ADJECTIVE
facultatif MASC
facultative FEM

or CONJUNCTION
[1] ou ◊ *Would you like tea or coffee?* Est-ce que tu veux du thé ou du café?
Use ni … ni in negative sentences.
◊ *I don't eat meat or fish.* Je ne mange ni viande, ni poisson.
[2] sinon (*otherwise*) ◊ *Hurry up or you'll miss the bus.* Dépêche-toi, sinon tu vas rater le bus.
♦ **Give me the money, or else!** Donne-moi l'argent, sinon tu vas le regretter!

oral ADJECTIVE
see also **oral** NOUN
oral
(oraux MASC PL)
♦ **an oral exam** un oral

oral NOUN
see also **oral** ADJECTIVE
l' oral MASC
(les oraux PL)
◊ *I've got my French oral soon.* Je vais bientôt passer mon oral de français.

orange NOUN
see also **orange** ADJECTIVE
l' orange FEM
♦ **an orange juice** un jus d'orange

orange ADJECTIVE
see also **orange** NOUN
orange MASC, FEM, PL

orchard NOUN
le verger

orchestra NOUN
l' orchestre MASC ◊ *I play in the school orchestra.* Je joue dans l'orchestre de l'école.

order NOUN
see also **order** VERB
[1] l' ordre MASC (*sequence*) ◊ *in alphabetical order* dans l'ordre alphabétique

[2] la commande (*instruction*) ◊ *The waiter took our order.* Le garçon a pris notre commande.
♦ **in order to** pour ◊ *He does it in order to earn money.* Il le fait pour gagner de l'argent.
♦ **"out of order"** "en panne"

to **order** VERB
see also **order** NOUN
commander ◊ *We ordered steak and chips.* Nous avons commandé un steak frites. ◊ *Are you ready to order?* Vous êtes prêt à commander?
♦ **to order somebody about** donner des ordres à quelqu'un ◊ *She was fed up with being ordered about.* Elle en avait marre qu'on lui donne des ordres en permanence.

ordinary ADJECTIVE
[1] ordinaire ◊ *an ordinary day* une journée ordinaire
[2] comme les autres (*people*) ◊ *an ordinary family* une famille comme les autres ◊ *He's just an ordinary guy.* C'est un type comme les autres.

organ NOUN
l' orgue MASC (*instrument*) ◊ *I play the organ.* Je joue de l'orgue.

organic ADJECTIVE
biologique (*vegetables, fruit*)

organization NOUN
l' organisation FEM

to **organize** VERB
organiser

origin NOUN
l' origine FEM

original ADJECTIVE
original
(originaux MASC PL)
◊ *It's a very original idea.* C'est une idée très originale.
♦ **Our original plan was to go camping.** A l'origine nous avions l'intention de faire du camping.

originally ADVERB
à l'origine

Orkneys PL NOUN
les Orcades FEM PL
♦ **in the Orkneys** dans les Orcades

ornament NOUN
le bibelot

orphan NOUN
l' orphelin MASC
l' orpheline FEM

ostrich NOUN
l' autruche FEM

other ADJECTIVE, PRONOUN
autre ◊ *Have you got these jeans in other colours?* Est-ce que vous avez

ce jean dans d'autres couleurs? ◊ *on the other side of the street* de l'autre côté de la rue ◊ *the other day* l'autre jour

♦ **the other one** l'autre ◊ *This one? – No, the other one.* Celui-ci? – Non, l'autre.

♦ **the others** les autres ◊ *The others are going but I'm not.* Les autres y vont mais pas moi.

otherwise ADVERB, CONJUNCTION

1 sinon *(if not)* ◊ *Note down the number, otherwise you'll forget it.* Note le numéro, sinon tu vas l'oublier. ◊ *Put some sunscreen on, you'll get burned otherwise.* Mets une crème solaire, sinon tu vas attraper des coups de soleil.

2 à part ça *(in other ways)* ◊ *I'm tired, but otherwise I'm fine.* Je suis fatigué, mais à part ça, ça va.

ought VERB

*To translate **ought to** use the conditional tense of **devoir**.*

◊ *I ought to phone my parents.* Je devrais appeler mes parents. ◊ *You ought not to do that.* Tu ne devrais pas faire ça. ◊ *He ought to win.* Il devrait gagner.

ounce NOUN

l' once FEM

ℹ️ *In France measurements are in grammes and kilogrammes. One ounce is about 30 grammes.*

◊ *8 ounces of cheese* 250 grammes de fromage

our ADJECTIVE

notre ◊ *Our house is quite big.* Notre maison est plutôt grande.

nos PL ◊ *Our neighbours are very nice.* Nos voisins sont très gentils.

ours PRONOUN

le nôtre + MASC NOUN ◊ *Your garden is very big, ours is much smaller.* Votre jardin est très grand, le nôtre est beaucoup plus petit.

la nôtre + FEM NOUN ◊ *Your school is very different from ours.* Votre école est très différente de la nôtre.

les nôtres + PL NOUN ◊ *Our teachers are strict. – Ours are too.* Nos professeurs sont sévères. – Les nôtres aussi.

♦ **Is this ours?** C'est à nous? ◊ *This car is ours.* Cette voiture est à nous. ◊ *Whose is this? – It's ours.* C'est à qui? – À nous.

ourselves PRONOUN

1 nous ◊ *We really enjoyed ourselves.* Nous nous sommes vraiment bien amusés.

2 nous-mêmes ◊ *We built our garage ourselves.* Nous avons construit notre garage nous-mêmes.

out ADVERB

*There are several ways of translating **out**. Scan the examples to find one that is similar to what you want to say. For other expressions with **out**, see the verbs **go**, **put**, **turn** etc.*

1 dehors *(outside)* ◊ *It's cold out.* Il fait froid dehors.

2 éteint *(light, fire)* ◊ *All the lights are out.* Toutes les lumières sont éteintes.

♦ **She's out.** Elle est sortie.

♦ **She's out shopping.** Elle est sortie faire des courses.

♦ **She's out for the afternoon.** Elle ne sera pas là de tout l'après-midi.

♦ **out there** dehors ◊ *It's cold out there.* Il fait froid dehors.

♦ **to go out** sortir ◊ *I'm going out tonight.* Je sors ce soir.

♦ **to go out with somebody** sortir avec quelqu'un ◊ *I've been going out with him for two months.* Je sors avec lui depuis deux mois.

♦ **out of (1)** dans ◊ *to drink out of a glass* boire dans un verre

♦ **out of (2)** sur ◊ *in 9 cases out of 10* dans neuf cas sur dix

♦ **out of (3)** en dehors de ◊ *He lives out of town.* Il habite en dehors de la ville.

♦ **3 km out of town** à trois kilomètres de la ville

♦ **out of curiosity** par curiosité

♦ **out of work** sans emploi

♦ **That is out of the question.** C'est hors de question.

♦ **You're out!** *(in game)* Tu es éliminé!

♦ **"way out"** "sortie"

outbreak NOUN

1 l' accès MASC *(of disease)* ◊ *a salmonella outbreak* un accès de salmonelle

2 le début ◊ *the outbreak of war* le début de la guerre

outcome NOUN

l' issue FEM ◊ *What was the outcome of the negotiations?* Quelle a été l'issue des négociations?

outdoor ADJECTIVE

en plein air ◊ *an outdoor swimming pool* une piscine en plein air

♦ **outdoor activities** les activités de plein air FEM

outdoors ADVERB
au grand air

outfit NOUN
la tenue ◊ *She bought a new outfit for the wedding.* Elle a acheté une nouvelle tenue pour le mariage.
♦ **a cowboy outfit** une panoplie de cowboy

outgoing ADJECTIVE
extraverti ◊ *She's very outgoing.* Elle est très extravertie.

outing NOUN
la sortie ◊ *to go on an outing* faire une sortie

outline NOUN
1 les grandes lignes FEM PL (*summary*) ◊ *This is an outline of the plan.* Voici les grandes lignes du projet.
2 les contours MASC PL (*shape*) ◊ *We could see the outline of the mountain in the mist.* Nous distinguions les contours de la montagne dans la brume.

outlook NOUN
1 l' attitude FEM (*attitude*) ◊ *my outlook on life* mon attitude face à la vie
2 les perspectives FEM PL (*prospects*) ◊ *the economic outlook* les perspectives économiques
♦ **The outlook is poor.** Les choses s'annoncent mal.

outrageous ADJECTIVE
1 (*behaviour*)
scandaleux MASC
scandaleuse FEM
2 (*price*)
exorbitant

outset NOUN
le début ◊ *at the outset* dès le début

outside NOUN
see also **outside** ADJECTIVE
l' extérieur MASC

outside ADJECTIVE, ADVERB, PREPOSITION
see also **outside** NOUN
1 extérieur ◊ *the outside walls* les murs extérieurs
2 dehors ◊ *It's very cold outside.* Il fait très froid dehors.
3 en dehors de ◊ *outside the school* en dehors de l'école ◊ *outside school hours* en dehors des heures de cours

outsize ADJECTIVE
énorme

outskirts PL NOUN
la banlieue ◊ *on the outskirts of the town* dans les banlieues de la ville

outstanding ADJECTIVE
remarquable

oval ADJECTIVE
ovale

oven NOUN
le four

over PREPOSITION, ADVERB, ADJECTIVE
*When there is movement over something, use **par-dessus**; when something is located above something, use **au-dessus de**.*
1 par-dessus ◊ *The ball went over the wall.* Le ballon est passé par-dessus le mur.
2 au-dessus de ◊ *There's a mirror over the washbasin.* Il y a une glace au-dessus du lavabo.
3 plus de (*more than*) ◊ *It's over twenty kilos.* Ça pèse plus de vingt kilos. ◊ *The temperature was over thirty degrees.* Il faisait une température de plus de trente degrés.
4 pendant (*during*) ◊ *over the holidays* pendant les vacances ◊ *over Christmas* pendant les fêtes de Noël
5 terminé (*finished*) ◊ *I'll be happy when the exams are over.* Je serai content quand les examens seront terminés.
♦ **over here** ici
♦ **over there** là-bas
♦ **all over Scotland** dans toute l'Écosse
♦ **The baker's is over the road.** La boulangerie est de l'autre côté de la rue.
♦ **I spilled coffee over my shirt.** J'ai renversé du café sur ma chemise.

overall ADVERB
dans l'ensemble (*generally*) ◊ *My results were quite good overall.* Mes résultats étaient assez bons dans l'ensemble.

overalls PL NOUN
les bleus de travail MASC PL

overcast ADJECTIVE
couvert ◊ *The sky was overcast.* Le ciel était couvert.

to **overcharge** VERB
♦ **He overcharged me.** Il m'a fait payer trop cher.
♦ **They overcharged us for the meal.** Ils nous ont fait payer de trop pour le repas.

overcoat NOUN
le pardessus

overdone ADJECTIVE
trop cuit (*food*)

overdose NOUN
l' overdose FEM (*of drugs*) ◊ *to take an overdose* prendre une overdose

overdraft NOUN
le découvert

♦ **to have an overdraft** être à découvert

to **overestimate** VERB
  surestimer

overhead projector NOUN
  le rétroprojecteur

to **overlook** VERB
  ☐1 donner sur (*have view of*) ◊ *The hotel overlooked the beach.* L'hôtel donnait sur la plage.
  ☐2 négliger (*forget about*) ◊ *He had overlooked one important problem.* Il avait négligé un problème important.

overseas ADVERB
  à l'étranger ◊ *I'd like to work overseas.* J'aimerais travailler à l'étranger.

oversight NOUN
  l' oubli MASC

to **oversleep** VERB
  se réveiller en retard ◊ *I overslept this morning.* Je me suis réveillé en retard ce matin.

to **overtake** VERB
  dépasser

overtime NOUN
  les heures supplémentaires FEM PL
  ◊ *to work overtime* faire des heures supplémentaires

overtook VERB *see* **overtake**

overweight ADJECTIVE
  trop gros MASC
  trop grosse FEM

to **owe** VERB
  devoir
  ♦ **to owe somebody something** devoir quelque chose à quelqu'un ◊ *I owe you 50 francs.* Je te dois cinquante francs.

owing to PREPOSITION
  en raison de ◊ *owing to bad weather* en raison du mauvais temps

owl NOUN
  le hibou
  (les hiboux PL)

to **own** VERB
  $\boxed{see\ also\ \textbf{own}\ ADJECTIVE}$
  posséder

own ADJECTIVE
  $\boxed{see\ also\ \textbf{own}\ VERB}$
  propre ◊ *I've got my own bathroom.* J'ai ma propre salle de bains.
  ♦ **I'd like a room of my own.** J'aimerais avoir une chambre à moi.
  ♦ **on his own** tout seul ◊ *on her own* toute seule ◊ *on our own* tout seuls

to **own** VERB
  $\boxed{see\ also\ \textbf{own}\ ADJECTIVE}$
  posséder

to **own up** VERB
  avouer
  ♦ **to own up to something** admettre quelque chose

owner NOUN
  le/la propriétaire

oxygen NOUN
  l' oxygène MASC

oyster NOUN
  l' huître FEM

ozone NOUN
  l' ozone FEM

ozone layer NOUN
  la couche d'ozone

O

P

PA NOUN
la <u>secrétaire de direction</u> (*personal assistant*) ◊ *She's a PA.* Elle est secrétaire de direction.
♦ **the PA system** (*public address*) les haut-parleurs MASC PL

pace NOUN
l' <u>allure</u> FEM (*speed*) ◊ *He was walking at a brisk pace.* Il marchait à vive allure.

Pacific NOUN
le <u>Pacifique</u>

pacifier NOUN [US]
la <u>tétine</u>

to **pack** VERB
| see also **pack** NOUN |
<u>faire ses bagages</u> ◊ *I'll help you pack.* Je vais t'aider à faire tes bagages.
♦ **I've already packed my case.** J'ai déjà fait ma valise.
♦ **Pack it in!** (*stop it*) Laisse tomber!

pack NOUN
| see also **pack** VERB |
1 le <u>paquet</u> (*packet*) ◊ *a pack of cigarettes* un paquet de cigarettes
2 le <u>pack</u> (*of yoghurts, cans*) ◊ *a six-pack* un pack de six
♦ **a pack of cards** un jeu de cartes

package NOUN
le <u>paquet</u>
♦ **a package holiday** un voyage organisé

packed ADJECTIVE
<u>bondé</u> ◊ *The cinema was packed.* Le cinéma était bondé.

packed lunch NOUN
le <u>repas froid</u> ◊ *I take a packed lunch to school.* J'apporte un repas froid à l'école.

packet NOUN
le <u>paquet</u> ◊ *a packet of cigarettes* un paquet de cigarettes

pad NOUN
(*notepad*)
le <u>bloc-notes</u>
(les blocs-notes PL)

to **paddle** VERB
| see also **paddle** NOUN |
1 <u>pagayer</u> (*canoe*)
2 <u>faire trempette</u> (*in water*)

paddle NOUN
| see also **paddle** VERB |
la <u>pagaie</u> (*for canoe*)
♦ **to go for a paddle** faire trempette

padlock NOUN
le <u>cadenas</u>

paedophile NOUN
le <u>pédophile</u>

page NOUN
| see also **page** VERB |
la <u>page</u> (*of book*)

to **page** VERB
| see also **page** NOUN |
♦ **to page somebody** faire appeler quelqu'un

pager NOUN
le <u>récepteur d'appel</u>

paid VERB *see* **pay**

paid ADJECTIVE
1 <u>rémunéré</u> (*work*)
2 <u>payé</u> ◊ *3 weeks' paid holiday* trois semaines de congés payés

pail NOUN
le <u>seau</u>
(les seaux PL)

pain NOUN
la <u>douleur</u> ◊ *a terrible pain* une douleur insupportable
♦ **I've got a pain in my stomach.** J'ai mal à l'estomac.
♦ **to be in pain** souffrir ◊ *She's in a lot of pain.* Elle souffre beaucoup.
♦ **He's a real pain.** Il est vraiment pénible.

painful ADJECTIVE
<u>douloureux</u> MASC
<u>douloureuse</u> FEM
◊ *to suffer from painful periods* souffrir de règles douloureuses
♦ **Is it painful?** Ça te fait mal?

painkiller NOUN
l' <u>analgésique</u> MASC

paint NOUN
| see also **paint** VERB |
la <u>peinture</u>

to **paint** VERB
| see also **paint** NOUN |
<u>peindre</u> ◊ *to paint something green* peindre quelque chose en vert

paintbrush NOUN
le <u>pinceau</u>
(les pinceaux PL)

painter NOUN
le <u>peintre</u>

painting NOUN
1 la <u>peinture</u> ◊ *My hobby is painting.* Je fais de la peinture.
2 (*picture*)

le tableau
(les tableaux PL)
◊ *a painting by Picasso* un tableau de Picasso

pair NOUN
la paire ◊ *a pair of shoes* une paire de chaussures ◊ *a pair of scissors* une paire de ciseaux
♦ **a pair of trousers** un pantalon
♦ **a pair of jeans** un jean
♦ **a pair of pants (1)** (*briefs*) un slip
♦ **a pair of pants (2)** (*boxer shorts*) un caleçon
♦ **in pairs** deux par deux ◊ *We work in pairs.* Nous travaillons deux par deux.

pajamas PL NOUN US
le pyjama SING ◊ *my pajamas* mon pyjama
♦ **a pair of pajamas** un pyjama
♦ **a pajama top** une veste de pyjama

Pakistan NOUN
le Pakistan
♦ **in Pakistan** au Pakistan
♦ **to Pakistan** au Pakistan
♦ **He's from Pakistan.** Il est pakistanais.

Pakistani NOUN
see also **Pakistani** ADJECTIVE
le Pakistanais
la Pakistanaise

Pakistani ADJECTIVE
see also **Pakistani** NOUN
pakistanais MASC
pakistanaise FEM

pal NOUN
le copain
la copine

palace NOUN
le palais

pale ADJECTIVE
pâle ◊ *a pale blue shirt* une chemise bleu pâle

Palestine NOUN
la Palestine
♦ **in Palestine** en Palestine

Palestinian ADJECTIVE
see also **Palestinian** NOUN
palestinien MASC
palestinienne FEM

Palestinian NOUN
see also **Palestinian** ADJECTIVE
le Palestinien
la Palestinienne

palm NOUN
la paume (*of hand*)
♦ **a palm tree** un palmier

pamphlet NOUN
la brochure

pan NOUN

[1] la casserole (*saucepan*)
[2] la poêle (*frying pan*)

pancake NOUN
la crêpe

panic NOUN
see also **panic** VERB
la panique

to **panic** VERB
see also **panic** NOUN
s'affoler ◊ *Don't panic!* Pas de panique!

panther NOUN
la panthère

panties PL NOUN
le slip SING

pantomime NOUN
le spectacle de Noël pour enfants

pants PL NOUN
[1] le slip SING (*briefs*) ◊ *a pair of pants* un slip
[2] le caleçon SING (*boxer shorts*) ◊ *a pair of pants* un caleçon
[3] le pantalon SING (*trousers*) US ◊ *a pair of pants* un pantalon

pantyhose PL NOUN US
le collant SING

paper NOUN
[1] le papier ◊ *a piece of paper* un morceau de papier ◊ *a paper towel* une serviette en papier
[2] (*newspaper*)
le journal
(les journaux PL)
◊ *I saw an advert in the paper.* J'ai vu une annonce dans le journal.
♦ **an exam paper** une épreuve écrite

paperback NOUN
le livre de poche

paper boy NOUN
le livreur de journaux

paper clip NOUN
le trombone

paper girl NOUN
la livreuse de journaux

paper round NOUN
la tournée de distribution de journaux

paperweight NOUN
le presse-papiers

paperwork NOUN
la paperasse ◊ *He had a lot of paperwork to do.* Il avait beaucoup de paperasse à faire.

parachute NOUN
le parachute

parade NOUN
le défilé

paradise NOUN

P

☞

le paradis

paraffin NOUN
le pétrole ◊ *a paraffin lamp* une lampe à pétrole

paragraph NOUN
le paragraphe

parallel ADJECTIVE
parallèle

paralysed ADJECTIVE
paralysé

paramedic NOUN
l' auxiliaire médical MASC
l' auxiliaire médicale FEM

parcel NOUN
le colis

pardon NOUN
♦**Pardon?** Pardon?

parent NOUN
1 le père (*father*)
2 la mère (*mother*)
♦ **my parents** mes parents MASC

Paris NOUN
Paris FEM
♦**in Paris** à Paris
♦**to Paris** à Paris
♦**She's from Paris.** Elle est parisienne.

Parisian ADJECTIVE
see also **Parisian** NOUN
parisien MASC
parisienne FEM

Parisian NOUN
see also **Parisian** ADJECTIVE
le Parisien
la Parisienne

park NOUN
see also **park** VERB
le parc
♦ **a national park** un parc national
♦ **a theme park** un parc à thème
♦ **a car park** un parking

to **park** VERB
see also **park** NOUN
1 garer ◊ *Where can I park my car?* Où est-ce que je peux garer ma voiture?
2 se garer ◊ *We couldn't find anywhere to park.* Nous avons eu du mal à nous garer.

parking NOUN
le stationnement ◊ *"no parking"* "stationnement interdit"
Be careful not to translate parking by the French word parking.

parking lot NOUN US
le parking

parking meter NOUN
le parcmètre

parking ticket NOUN
le p.-v. (*informal*)

parliament NOUN
le parlement

parole NOUN
♦**on parole** en liberté conditionnelle

parrot NOUN
le perroquet

parsley NOUN
le persil

part NOUN
1 la partie (*section*) ◊ *The first part of the film was boring.* La première partie du film était ennuyeuse.
2 la pièce (*component*) ◊ *spare parts* les pièces de rechange
3 le rôle (*in play, film*)
♦ **to take part in something** participer à quelque chose ◊ *A lot of people took part in the demonstration.* Beaucoup de gens ont participé à la manifestation.

to **part with** VERB
♦**to part with something** se défaire de quelque chose

particular ADJECTIVE
particulier MASC
particulière FEM
◊ *Are you looking for anything particular?* Est-ce que vous voulez quelque chose de particulier?
♦**nothing in particular** rien de particulier

particularly ADVERB
particulièrement
♦ **not particularly** pas particulièrement

parting NOUN
la raie (*in hair*)

partly ADVERB
en partie

partner NOUN
1 (*in game*)
le/la partenaire
2 (*in business*)
l' associé MASC
l' associée FEM
3 (*in dance*)
le cavalier
la cavalière
4 le compagnon (*boyfriend*)
la compagne (*girlfriend*)

part-time ADJECTIVE, ADVERB
à temps partiel ◊ *a part-time job* un travail à temps partiel ◊ *She works part-time.* Elle travaille à temps partiel.

party NOUN
1 la fête ◊ *a birthday party* une fête d'anniversaire ◊ *a Christmas party*

une fête de Noël ◊ *a New Year party*
une fête du Nouvel An
[2] la soirée (*more formal*) ◊ *I'm going to a party on Saturday.* Je vais à une soirée samedi.
[3] le parti (*political*) ◊ *the Conservative Party* le Parti conservateur
[4] le groupe (*group*) ◊ *a party of tourists* un groupe de touristes

pass NOUN
see also **pass** VERB
[1] le col (*in mountains*) ◊ *The pass was blocked with snow.* Le col était enneigé.
[2] la passe (*in football*)
♦ **to get a pass** (*in exam*) être reçu ◊ *She got a pass in her piano exam.* Elle a été reçue à son examen de piano. ◊ *I got six passes.* J'ai été reçu dans six matières.
♦ **a bus pass** une carte de bus

to **pass** VERB
see also **pass** NOUN
[1] être reçu (*exam*) ◊ *to pass an exam* être reçu à un examen ◊ *I hope I'll pass the exam.* J'espère que je serai reçu à l'examen. ◊ *Did you pass?* Tu as été reçu?
[2] passer ◊ *Could you pass me the salt, please?* Est-ce que vous pourriez me passer le sel, s'il vous plaît? ◊ *The time has passed quickly.* Le temps a passé rapidement.
[3] passer devant ◊ *I pass his house on my way to school.* Je passe devant chez lui en allant à l'école.
Be careful not to translate **to pass an exam** *by* **passer un examen.**

to **pass out** VERB
s'évanouir (*faint*)

passage NOUN
[1] le passage (*piece of writing*) ◊ *Read the passage carefully.* Lisez attentivement le passage.
[2] le couloir (*corridor*)

passenger NOUN
le passager
la passagère

passion NOUN
la passion

passive ADJECTIVE
passif MASC
passive FEM
♦ **passive smoking** le tabagisme passif

Passover NOUN
la Pâque juive ◊ *at Passover* à la Pâque juive

passport NOUN

le passeport ◊ *passport control* le contrôle des passeports

password NOUN
le mot de passe

past ADVERB, PREPOSITION
see also **past** NOUN
après (*beyond*) ◊ *It's on the right, just past the station.* C'est sur la droite, juste après la gare.
♦ **to go past (1)** passer ◊ *The bus went past without stopping.* Le bus est passé sans s'arrêter.
♦ **to go past (2)** passer devant ◊ *The bus goes past our house.* Le bus passe devant notre maison.
♦ **It's half past ten.** Il est dix heures et demie.
♦ **It's quarter past nine.** Il est neuf heures et quart.
♦ **It's ten past eight.** Il est huit heures dix.
♦ **It's past midnight.** Il est minuit passé.

past NOUN
see also **past** ADVERB
le passé ◊ *She lives in the past.* Elle vit dans le passé.
♦ **in the past** (*previously*) autrefois ◊ *This was common in the past.* C'était courant autrefois.

pasta NOUN
les pâtes FEM PL ◊ *Pasta is easy to cook.* Les pâtes sont faciles à préparer.

paste NOUN
la colle (*glue*)

pasteurized ADJECTIVE
pasteurisé

pastime NOUN
le passe-temps
(les passe-temps PL)
◊ *Her favourite pastime is knitting.* Son passe-temps favori est le tricot.

pastry NOUN
la pâte
♦ **pastries** les pâtisseries FEM

patch NOUN
[1] la pièce ◊ *a patch of material* une pièce de tissu
[2] la rustine (*for flat tyre*)
♦ **He's got a bald patch.** Il a le crâne dégarni.

patched ADJECTIVE
rapiécé ◊ *a pair of patched jeans* un jean rapiécé

pâté NOUN
le pâté

path NOUN
[1] le chemin (*footpath*)
[2] l' allée FEM (*in garden, park*)

P

pathetic ADJECTIVE
lamentable ◊ *Our team was pathetic.*
Notre équipe a été lamentable.

patience NOUN
1 la patience ◊ *He hasn't got much
patience.* Il n'a pas beaucoup de
patience.
2 la réussite (*card game*) ◊ *to play
patience* faire une réussite

patient NOUN

> see also **patient** ADJECTIVE

le patient
la patiente

patient ADJECTIVE

> see also **patient** NOUN

patient

patio NOUN
le patio

patriotic ADJECTIVE
patriote

patrol NOUN
la patrouille

patrol car NOUN
la voiture de police

pattern NOUN
le motif ◊ *a geometric pattern* un
motif géométrique
♦ **a sewing pattern** un patron

pause NOUN
la pause

pavement NOUN
le trottoir

pavilion NOUN
le pavillon

paw NOUN
la patte

pay NOUN

> see also **pay** VERB

le salaire

to **pay** VERB

> see also **pay** NOUN

1 payer ◊ *They pay me more on
Sundays.* Je suis payé davantage le
dimanche.
2 régler ◊ *to pay by cheque* régler
par chèque ◊ *to pay by credit card*
régler par carte de crédit
♦ **to pay for something** payer quelque
chose ◊ *I paid for my ticket.* J'ai payé
mon billet. ◊ *I paid 50 francs for it.*
Je l'ai payé cinquante francs.
♦ **to pay extra for something** payer un
supplément pour quelque chose
◊ *You have to pay extra for parking.*
Il faut payer un supplément pour le
parking.

♦ **to pay attention** faire attention
◊ *Don't pay any attention to him!* Ne
fais pas attention à lui!
♦ **to pay somebody a visit** rendre visite à
quelqu'un ◊ *Paul paid us a visit last
night.* Paul nous a rendu visite hier soir.
♦ **to pay somebody back** rembourser
quelqu'un ◊ *I'll pay you back
tomorrow.* Je te rembourserai demain.

payable ADJECTIVE
♦ **Make the cheque payable to "ABC
Ltd".** Libellez le chèque à l'ordre de
"ABC Ltd".

payment NOUN
le paiement

payphone NOUN
le téléphone public

PC NOUN (= *personal computer*)
le PC ◊ *She typed the report on her
PC.* Elle a tapé le rapport sur son PC.

PE NOUN
l' EPS FEM ◊ *We do PE twice a week.*
Nous avons EPS deux fois par
semaine.

pea NOUN
le petit pois

peace NOUN
1 la paix (*after war*)
2 le calme (*quietness*)

peaceful ADJECTIVE
1 paisible (*calm*) ◊ *a peaceful
afternoon* un après-midi paisible
2 pacifique (*not violent*) ◊ *a peaceful
protest* une manifestation pacifique

peach NOUN
la pêche

peacock NOUN
le paon

peak NOUN
la cime (*of mountain*)
♦ **the peak rate** le plein tarif ◊ *You pay
the peak rate for calls at this time of
day.* On paie le plein tarif quand on
appelle à cette heure-ci.
♦ **in peak season** en haute saison

peanut NOUN
la cacahuète ◊ *a packet of peanuts*
un paquet de cacahuètes

peanut butter NOUN
le beurre de cacahuètes ◊ *a
peanut-butter sandwich* un sandwich
au beurre de cacahuètes

pear NOUN
la poire

pearl NOUN
la perle

pebble NOUN
le galet ◊ *a pebble beach* une plage
de galets

peckish ADJECTIVE
♦**to feel a bit peckish** avoir un petit creux

peculiar ADJECTIVE
bizarre ◊ *He's a peculiar person.* Il est bizarre. ◊ *It tastes peculiar.* Ça a un goût bizarre.

pedal NOUN
la pédale

pedestrian NOUN
le piéton

pedestrian crossing NOUN
le passage pour piétons

pedestrianized ADJECTIVE
♦**a pedestrianized street** une rue piétonne

pedigree ADJECTIVE
de race (*animal*) ◊ *a pedigree dog* un chien de race ◊ *a pedigree labrador.* un labrador de pure race.

pee NOUN
♦**to have a pee** faire pipi

peek NOUN
♦**to have a peek at something** jeter un coup d'œil à quelque chose
♦**No peeking!** On ne regarde pas!

peel NOUN
see also **peel** VERB
l' écorce FEM (*of orange*)

to **peel** VERB
see also **peel** NOUN
1 éplucher ◊ *Shall I peel the potatoes?* J'épluche les pommes de terre?
2 peler ◊ *My nose is peeling.* Mon nez pèle.

peg NOUN
1 (*for coats*)
le portemanteau
(les portemanteaux PL)
2 (*clothes peg*)
la pince à linge
3 (*tent peg*)
le piquet

Pekinese NOUN
le pékinois

pelican crossing NOUN
le passage pour piétons

pellet NOUN
le plomb (*for gun*)

pelvis NOUN
le bassin

pen NOUN
le stylo

to **penalize** VERB
pénaliser

penalty NOUN
1 la peine (*punishment*)

♦**the death penalty** la peine de mort
2 le penalty (*in football*)
3 la pénalité (*in rugby*)
♦**a penalty shoot-out** les tirs au but MASC PL

pence PL NOUN
les pence MASC PL

pencil NOUN
le crayon
♦**in pencil** au crayon

pencil case NOUN
la trousse

pencil sharpener NOUN
le taille-crayon

pendant NOUN
le pendentif

penfriend NOUN
le correspondant
la correspondante

penguin NOUN
le pingouin

penicillin NOUN
la pénicilline

penis NOUN
le pénis

penitentiary NOUN US
la prison

penknife NOUN
le canif

penny NOUN
le penny
(les pence PL)

pension NOUN
la retraite

pensioner NOUN
le retraité
la retraitée

pentathlon NOUN
le pentathlon

people PL NOUN
1 les gens MASC PL ◊ *The people were nice.* Les gens étaient sympathiques. ◊ *a lot of people* beaucoup de gens
2 les personnes FEM PL (*individuals*) ◊ *six people* six personnes ◊ *several people* plusieurs personnes
♦**How many people are there in your family?** Vous êtes combien dans votre famille?
♦**French people** les Français
♦**black people** les Noirs
♦**People say that** ... On dit que ...

pepper NOUN
1 le poivre (*spice*) ◊ *Pass the pepper, please.* Passez-moi le poivre, s'il vous plaît.
2 le poivron (*vegetable*) ◊ *a green pepper* un poivron vert

P

peppermill NOUN
le moulin à poivre

peppermint NOUN
la pastille de menthe (*sweet*)

♦**peppermint chewing gum** le chewing-gum à la menthe

per PREPOSITION
par ◊ *per day* par jour ◊ *per week* par semaine

♦**30 miles per hour** trente miles à l'heure

per cent ADVERB
pour cent ◊ *fifty per cent* cinquante pour cent

percentage NOUN
le pourcentage

percolator NOUN
la cafetière électrique

percussion NOUN
la percussion ◊ *I play percussion.* Je joue des percussions.

perfect ADJECTIVE
parfait ◊ *Chantal speaks perfect English.* Chantal parle un anglais parfait.

perfectly ADVERB
parfaitement

to **perform** VERB
jouer (*act, play*)

performance NOUN
[1] le spectacle (*show*) ◊ *The performance lasts two hours.* Le spectacle dure deux heures.
[2] l' interprétation FEM (*acting*) ◊ *his performance as Hamlet* son interprétation d'Hamlet
[3] la performance (*results*) ◊ *the team's poor performance* la médiocre performance de l'équipe

perfume NOUN
le parfum

perhaps ADVERB
peut-être ◊ *a bit boring, perhaps* peut-être un peu ennuyeux ◊ *Perhaps he's ill.* Il est peut-être malade.

♦**perhaps not** peut-être pas

period NOUN
[1] la période ◊ *for a limited period* pour une période limitée
[2] l' époque FEM (*in history*) ◊ *the Victorian period* l'époque victorienne
[3] les règles FEM PL (*menstruation*) ◊ *I'm having my period.* J'ai mes règles.
[4] le cours (*lesson time*) ◊ *Each period lasts forty minutes.* Chaque cours dure quarante minutes.

perm NOUN
la permanente ◊ *She's got a perm.* Elle a une permanente.

♦**to have a perm** se faire faire une permanente

permanent ADJECTIVE
permanent

permission NOUN
la permission ◊ *Could I have permission to leave early?* Pourrais-je avoir la permission de partir plus tôt?

permit NOUN
le permis ◊ *a fishing permit* un permis de pêche

to **persecute** VERB
persécuter

Persian ADJECTIVE
♦**a Persian cat** un chat persan

persistent ADJECTIVE
tenace (*person*)

person NOUN
la personne ◊ *She's a very nice person.* C'est une personne très sympathique.

♦**in person** en personne

personal ADJECTIVE
personnel MASC
personnelle FEM

♦**personal column** les annonces personnelles FEM PL

personality NOUN
la personnalité

personally ADVERB
personnellement ◊ *I don't know him personally.* Je ne le connais pas personnellement. ◊ *Personally I don't agree.* Personnellement, je ne suis pas d'accord.

personal stereo NOUN
le walkman ®

personnel NOUN
le personnel

perspiration NOUN
la transpiration

to **persuade** VERB
persuader

♦**to persuade somebody to do something** persuader quelqu'un de faire quelque chose ◊ *She persuaded me to go with her.* Elle m'a persuadé de l'accompagner.

pessimist NOUN
le/la pessimiste ◊ *I'm a pessimist.* Je suis pessimiste.

pessimistic ADJECTIVE
pessimiste

pest NOUN
le/la casse-pieds (*person*) ◊ *He's a real pest!* C'est un vrai casse-pieds!

to **pester** VERB
importuner

pet NOUN
l' animal familier MASC ◊ *Have you got a pet?* Est-ce que tu as un animal familier?
♦**She's the teacher's pet.** C'est la chouchoute de la maîtresse.

petition NOUN
la pétition

petrified ADJECTIVE
pétrifié

petrol NOUN
l' essence FEM
♦**unleaded petrol** l'essence sans plomb
*Be careful not to translate **petrol** by pétrole.*

petrol station NOUN
la station-service
(les stations-service PL)

petrol tank NOUN
le réservoir d'essence

phantom NOUN
le fantôme

pharmacy NOUN
la pharmacie

> ❶ *Pharmacies in France are identified by a special green cross outside the shop.*

pheasant NOUN
le faisan

philosophy NOUN
la philosophie

phobia NOUN
la phobie

phone NOUN
> see also **phone** VERB

le téléphone ◊ *Where's the phone?* Où est le téléphone? ◊ *Is there a phone here?* Est-ce qu'il y a un téléphone ici?
♦**by phone** par téléphone
♦**to be on the phone** être au téléphone ◊ *She's on the phone at the moment.* Elle est au téléphone en ce moment.
♦**Can I use the phone, please?** Est-ce que je peux téléphoner, s'il vous plaît?

to phone VERB
> see also **phone** NOUN

appeler ◊ *I'll phone the station.* Je vais appeler la gare.

phone bill NOUN
la facture de téléphone

phone book NOUN
l' annuaire MASC

phone box NOUN
la cabine téléphonique

phone call NOUN
l' appel MASC ◊ *There's a phone call for you.* Il y a un appel pour vous.
♦**to make a phone call** téléphoner ◊ *Can I make a phone call?* Est-ce que je peux téléphoner?

phonecard NOUN
la carte de téléphone

phone number NOUN
le numéro de téléphone

photo NOUN
la photo
♦**to take a photo** prendre une photo
♦**to take a photo of somebody** prendre quelqu'un en photo

photocopier NOUN
la photocopieuse

photocopy NOUN
> see also **photocopy** VERB

la photocopie

to photocopy VERB
> see also **photocopy** NOUN

photocopier

photograph NOUN
> see also **photograph** VERB

la photo
♦**to take a photograph** prendre une photo
♦**to take a photograph of somebody** prendre quelqu'un en photo

to photograph VERB
> see also **photograph** NOUN

photographier

photographer NOUN
le/la photographe ◊ *She's a photographer.* Elle est photographe.

photography NOUN
la photo ◊ *My hobby is photography.* Je fais de la photo.

phrase NOUN
l' expression FEM

phrase book NOUN
le guide de conversation

physical ADJECTIVE
> see also **physical** NOUN

physique

physical NOUN US
> see also **physical** ADJECTIVE

l' examen médical MASC

physicist NOUN
le physicien
la physicienne
◊ *He's a physicist.* Il est physicien.

physics NOUN
la physique ◊ *She teaches physics.* Elle enseigne la physique.

physiotherapist NOUN
le/la kinésithérapeute

physiotherapy NOUN

P

☞

la kinésithérapie

pianist NOUN
le/la pianiste

piano NOUN
le piano ◊ *I play the piano.* Je joue
du piano. ◊ *I have piano lessons.* Je
prends des leçons de piano.

pick NOUN

> see also **pick** VERB

♦ **Take your pick!** Faites votre choix!

to **pick** VERB

> see also **pick** NOUN

☐1 choisir (*choose*) ◊ *I picked the
biggest piece.* J'ai choisi le plus gros
morceau.
☐2 sélectionner (*for team*) ◊ *I've been
picked for the team.* J'ai été
sélectionné pour faire partie de
l'équipe.
☐3 cueillir (*fruit, flowers*)
♦ **to pick on somebody** harceler
quelqu'un ◊ *She's always picking on
me.* Elle me harcèle constamment.
♦ **to pick out** choisir ◊ *I like them all –
it's difficult to pick one out.* Ils me
plaisent tous – c'est difficile d'en
choisir un.
♦ **to pick up (1)** (*collect*) venir chercher
◊ *We'll come to the airport to pick
you up.* Nous irons vous chercher à
l'aéroport.
♦ **to pick up (2)** (*from floor*) ramasser
◊ *Could you help me pick up the
toys?* Tu peux m'aider à ramasser les
jouets?
♦ **to pick up (3)** (*learn*) apprendre ◊ *I
picked up some Spanish during my
holiday.* J'ai appris quelques mots
d'espagnol pendant mes vacances.

pickpocket NOUN
le pickpocket

picnic NOUN
le pique-nique
♦ **to have a picnic** pique-niquer ◊ *We
had a picnic on the beach.* Nous
avons pique-niqué sur la plage.

picture NOUN
☐1 l' illustration FEM ◊ *Children's books
have lots of pictures.* Il y a beaucoup
d'illustrations dans les livres pour
enfants.
☐2 la photo ◊ *My picture was in the
paper.* Ma photo était dans le journal.
☐3 (*painting*)
le tableau
(les tableaux PL)
◊ *a famous picture* un tableau célèbre
♦ **to paint a picture of something**
peindre quelque chose
☐4 (*drawing*)

le dessin
♦ **to draw a picture of something**
dessiner quelque chose
♦ **the pictures** (*cinema*) le cinéma ◊ *Shall
we go to the pictures?* On va au
cinéma?

picturesque ADJECTIVE
pittoresque

pie NOUN
la tourte ◊ *an apple pie* une tourte
aux pommes

piece NOUN
le morceau
(les morceaux PL)
◊ *A small piece, please.* Un petit
morceau, s'il vous plaît.
♦ **a piece of furniture** un meuble
♦ **a piece of advice** un conseil

pier NOUN
la jetée

to **pierce** VERB
percer ◊ *She's going to have her
ears pierced.* Elle va se faire percer
les oreilles.

pierced ADJECTIVE
percé ◊ *I've got pierced ears.* J'ai les
oreilles percées.

piercing NOUN
le piercing ◊ *She has several
piercings.* Elle a plusieurs piercings.

pig NOUN
le cochon

pigeon NOUN
le pigeon

piggyback NOUN
♦ **to give somebody a piggyback** porter
quelqu'un sur son dos ◊ *I can't give
you a piggyback, you're too heavy.*
Je ne peux pas te porter sur mon
dos, tu es trop lourd.

piggy·bank NOUN
la tirelire

pigtail NOUN
la natte

pile NOUN
☐1 le tas (*untidy heap*)
☐2 la pile (*tidy stack*)

piles PL NOUN
les hémorroïdes FEM PL ◊ *to suffer
from piles* avoir des hémorroïdes

pile-up NOUN
le carambolage

pill NOUN
la pilule
♦ **to be on the pill** prendre la pilule

pillar NOUN
le pilier

pillar box NOUN

la <u>boîte aux lettres</u>

pillow NOUN
l' <u>oreiller</u> MASC

pilot NOUN
le <u>pilote</u> ◊ *He's a pilot.* Il est pilote.

pimple NOUN
le <u>bouton</u>

pin NOUN
l' <u>épingle</u> FEM
♦**I've got pins and needles.** J'ai des fourmis.

PIN NOUN (= *personal identification number*)
le <u>code confidentiel</u>

pinafore NOUN
le <u>tablier</u>

pinball NOUN
le <u>flipper</u> ◊ *to play pinball* jouer au flipper
♦**a pinball machine** un flipper

to **pinch** VERB
[1] <u>pincer</u> ◊ *He pinched me!* Il m'a pincé!
[2] <u>piquer</u> (*informal: steal*) ◊ *Who's pinched my pen?* Qui est-ce qui m'a piqué mon stylo?

pine NOUN
le <u>pin</u> ◊ *a pine table* une table en pin

pineapple NOUN
l' <u>ananas</u> MASC

pink ADJECTIVE
<u>rose</u>

pint NOUN
la <u>pinte</u>

> ⓘ *In France measurements are in litres and centilitres. A pint is about 0.6 litres.*

♦**to have a pint** boire une bière ◊ *He's gone out for a pint.* Il est parti boire une bière.
♦**a pint of milk** un demi-litre de lait

pipe NOUN
[1] la <u>conduite</u> (*for water, gas*) ◊ *The pipes froze.* Les conduites d'eau ont gelé.
[2] la <u>pipe</u> (*for smoking*) ◊ *He smokes a pipe.* Il fume la pipe.
♦**the pipes** (*bagpipes*) la cornemuse ◊ *He plays the pipes.* Il joue de la cornemuse.

pirate NOUN
le <u>pirate</u>

pirated ADJECTIVE
<u>pirate</u> ◊ *a pirated video* une vidéo pirate

Pisces NOUN

les <u>Poissons</u> MASC PL ◊ *I'm Pisces.* Je suis Poissons.

pissed ADJECTIVE
<u>bourré</u> (*informal*)

pistol NOUN
le <u>pistolet</u>

pitch NOUN
> *see also* **pitch** VERB

le <u>terrain</u> ◊ *a football pitch* un terrain de football

to **pitch** VERB
> *see also* **pitch** NOUN

<u>dresser</u> (*tent*) ◊ *We pitched our tent near the beach.* Nous avons dressé notre tente près de la plage.

pity NOUN
> *see also* **pity** VERB

la <u>pitié</u>
♦**What a pity!** Quel dommage!

to **pity** VERB
> *see also* **pity** NOUN

<u>plaindre</u>

pizza NOUN
la <u>pizza</u>

place NOUN
> *see also* **place** VERB

[1] l' <u>endroit</u> MASC (*location*) ◊ *It's a quiet place.* C'est un endroit tranquille. ◊ *There are a lot of interesting places to visit.* Il y a beaucoup d'endroits intéressants à visiter.
[2] la <u>place</u> (*space*) ◊ *a parking place* une place de parking ◊ *a university place* une place à l'université
♦**to change places** changer de place ◊ *Tamsin, change places with Delphine!* Tamsin, change de place avec Delphine!
♦**to take place** avoir lieu
♦**at your place** chez toi ◊ *Shall we meet at your place?* On se retrouve chez toi?
♦**to my place** chez moi ◊ *Do you want to come round to my place?* Tu veux venir chez moi?

to **place** VERB
> *see also* **place** NOUN

[1] <u>poser</u> ◊ *He placed his hand on hers.* Il a posé la main sur la sienne.
[2] <u>classer</u> (*in competition, contest*)

placement NOUN
le <u>stage</u>
♦**to do a work placement** faire un stage en entreprise

plaid ADJECTIVE
<u>écossais</u> ◊ *a plaid shirt* une chemise écossaise

plain NOUN

P

see also **plain** ADJECTIVE
la plaine

plain ADJECTIVE, ADVERB
see also **plain** NOUN
1 uni (*not patterned*) ◊ *a plain carpet* un tapis uni
2 simple (*not fancy*) ◊ *a plain white blouse* un simple chemisier blanc

plain chocolate NOUN
le chocolat à croquer

plait NOUN
la natte ◊ *She wears her hair in a plait.* Elle a une natte.

plan NOUN
see also **plan** VERB
1 le projet ◊ *What are your plans for the holidays?* Quels sont tes projets pour les vacances? ◊ *to make plans* faire des projets
♦ **Everything went according to plan.** Tout s'est passé comme prévu.
2 le plan (*map*) ◊ *a plan of the campsite* un plan du terrain de camping
♦ **my essay plan** le plan de ma dissertation

to **plan** VERB
see also **plan** NOUN
1 préparer (*make plans for*) ◊ *We're planning a trip to France.* Nous préparons un voyage en France.
2 planifier (*make schedule for*) ◊ *Plan your revision carefully.* Planifiez vos révisions avec soin.
♦ **to plan to do something** avoir l'intention de faire quelque chose ◊ *I'm planning to get a job in the holidays.* J'ai l'intention de trouver un job pour les vacances.

plane NOUN
l' avion MASC ◊ *by plane* en avion

planet NOUN
la planète

planning NOUN
la préparation ◊ *The trip needs careful planning.* Le voyage nécessite une préparation méticuleuse.
♦ **family planning** le planning familial

plant NOUN
see also **plant** VERB
1 la plante ◊ *to water the plants* arroser les plantes
2 l' usine FEM (*factory*)

to **plant** VERB
see also **plant** NOUN
planter

plant pot NOUN
le pot de fleurs

plaque NOUN
la plaque (*on wall*)

plaster NOUN
1 le pansement adhésif (*sticking plaster*) ◊ *Have you got a plaster, by any chance?* Vous n'auriez pas un pansement adhésif, par hasard?
2 le plâtre (*for fracture*) ◊ *Her leg's in plaster.* Elle a la jambe dans le plâtre.

plastic NOUN
see also **plastic** ADJECTIVE
le plastique ◊ *It's made of plastic.* C'est en plastique.

plastic ADJECTIVE
see also **plastic** NOUN
en plastique ◊ *a plastic bag* un sac en plastique ◊ *a plastic mac* un imperméable en plastique

plate NOUN
l' assiette FEM (*for food*)

platform NOUN
1 le quai (*at station*) ◊ *on platform 7* sur le quai numéro sept
2 l' estrade FEM (*for performers*)

play NOUN
see also **play** VERB
la pièce ◊ *a play by Shakespeare* une pièce de Shakespeare
♦ **to put on a play** monter une pièce

to **play** VERB
see also **play** NOUN
1 jouer ◊ *He's playing with his friends.* Il joue avec ses amis. ◊ *What sort of music do they play?* Quel genre de musique jouent-ils?
2 jouer contre (*against person, team*) ◊ *France will play Scotland next month.* La France jouera contre l'Écosse le mois prochain.
3 jouer à (*sport, game*) ◊ *I play hockey.* Je joue au hockey. ◊ *Can you play pool?* Tu sais jouer au billard américain?
4 jouer de (*instrument*) ◊ *I play the guitar.* Je joue de la guitare.
5 écouter (*record, cassette, music*) ◊ *She's always playing that record.* Elle écoute tout le temps ce disque.

to **play down** VERB
dédramatiser ◊ *He tried to play down his illness.* Il a essayé de dédramatiser sa maladie.

player NOUN
1 (*of sport*)
le joueur
l joueuse
◊ *a football player* un joueur de football
2 (*of instrument*)
le musicien
la musicienne

♦ **a piano player** un pianiste
♦ **a saxophone player** un saxophoniste

playful ADJECTIVE
espiègle

playground NOUN
[1] la cour de récréation (at school)
[2] l' aire de jeux FEM (in park)

playgroup NOUN
la garderie

playing card NOUN
la carte à jouer
(les cartes à jouer PL)

playing field NOUN
le terrain de sport

playtime NOUN
la récréation

playwright NOUN
le dramaturge

pleasant ADJECTIVE
agréable

please EXCLAMATION
[1] s'il vous plaît (polite form) ◊ Two
coffees, please. Deux cafés, s'il vous
plaît.
[2] s'il te plaît (familiar form) ◊ Please
write back soon. Réponds vite, s'il te
plaît.

pleased ADJECTIVE
content ◊ My mother's not going to
be very pleased. Ma mère ne va pas
être contente du tout. ◊ It's beautiful:
she'll be pleased with it. C'est beau:
elle va être contente.
♦ **Pleased to meet you!** Enchanté!

pleasure NOUN
le plaisir ◊ I read for pleasure. Je lis
pour le plaisir.

plenty NOUN
largement assez ◊ I've got plenty.
J'en ai largement assez. ◊ That's
plenty, thanks. Ça suffit largement,
merci.
♦ **plenty of (1)** (a lot) beaucoup de ◊ I've
got plenty to do. J'ai beaucoup de
choses à faire.
♦ **plenty of (2)** (enough) largement assez
de ◊ I've got plenty of money. J'ai
largement assez d'argent. ◊ We've
got plenty of time. Nous avons
largement le temps.

pliers PL NOUN
la pince SING
♦ **a pair of pliers** une pince

plot NOUN
see also **plot** VERB
[1] l' intrigue FEM (of story, play)
[2] la conspiration (against somebody)
◊ a plot against the president une
conspiration contre le président

[3] le carré (of land) ◊ a vegetable plot
un carré de légumes

to **plot** VERB
see also **plot** NOUN
comploter ◊ They were plotting to
kill him. Ils complotaient de le tuer.

plough NOUN
see also **plough** VERB
la charrue

to **plough** VERB
see also **plough** NOUN
labourer

plug NOUN
[1] la prise de courant (electrical)
◊ The plug is faulty. La prise est
défectueuse.
[2] le bouchon (for sink)

to **plug in** VERB
brancher ◊ Is it plugged in? Est-ce
que c'est branché?

plum NOUN
la prune ◊ plum jam la confiture de
prunes

plumber NOUN
le plombier ◊ He's a plumber. Il est
plombier.

plump ADJECTIVE
dodu

to **plunge** VERB
plonger

plural NOUN
le pluriel

plus PREPOSITION, ADJECTIVE
plus ◊ 4 plus 3 equals 7. Quatre plus
trois égalent sept. ◊ three children
plus a dog trois enfants plus un
chien
♦ **I got a B plus.** J'ai eu un Bien.

p.m. ABBREVIATION
♦ **at 8 p.m.** à huit heures du soir

*❶ In France times are often given
using the 24-hour clock.*

♦ **at 2 p.m.** à quatorze heures

pneumonia NOUN
la pneumonie

poached ADJECTIVE
poché ◊ a poached egg un œuf
poché

pocket NOUN
la poche
♦ **pocket money** l'argent de poche MASC
◊ £8 a week pocket money huit livres
d'argent de poche par semaine

pocket calculator NOUN
la calculette

poem NOUN

P

le poème

poet NOUN
le poète

poetry NOUN
la poésie

point NOUN
see also **point** VERB
1 le point (*spot, score*) ◊ *a point on the horizon* un point à l'horizon ◊ *They scored 5 points.* Ils ont marqué cinq points.
2 la remarque (*comment*) ◊ *He made some interesting points.* Il a fait quelque remarques intéressantes.
3 la pointe (*tip*) ◊ *a pencil with a sharp point* un crayon à la pointe aiguisée
4 le moment (*in time*) ◊ *At that point, we decided to leave.* À ce moment-là, nous avons décidé de partir.
♦ **a point of view** un point de vue
♦ **to get the point** comprendre ◊ *Sorry, I don't get the point.* Désolé, je ne comprends pas.
♦ **That's a good point!** C'est vrai!
♦ **There's no point.** Cela ne sert à rien. ◊ *There's no point in waiting.* Cela ne sert à rien d'attendre.
♦ **What's the point?** À quoi bon? ◊ *What's the point of leaving so early?* À quoi bon partir si tôt?
♦ **Punctuality isn't my strong point.** La ponctualité n'est pas mon fort.
♦ **two point five (2.5)** deux virgule cinq (2,5)

to point VERB
see also **point** NOUN
montrer du doigt ◊ *Don't point!* Ne montre pas du doigt!
♦ **to point at somebody** montrer quelqu'un du doigt ◊ *She pointed at Anne.* Elle a montré Anne du doigt.
♦ **to point a gun at somebody** braquer un revolver sur quelqu'un
♦ **to point something out (1)** (*show*) montrer quelque chose ◊ *The guide pointed out Notre-Dame to us.* Le guide nous a montré Notre-Dame.
♦ **to point something out (2)** (*mention*) signaler quelque chose ◊ *I should point out that ...* Je dois vous signaler que ...

pointless ADJECTIVE
inutile ◊ *It's pointless to argue.* Il est inutile de discuter.

poison NOUN
see also **poison** VERB
le poison

to poison VERB

see also **poison** NOUN
empoisonner

poisonous ADJECTIVE
1 (*snake*)
venimeux MASC
venimeuse FEM
2 (*plant, mushroom*)
vénéneux MASC
vénéneuse FEM
3 (*gas*)
toxique

to poke VERB
♦ **He poked the ground with his stick.** Il tapotait le sol avec sa canne.
♦ **She poked me in the ribs.** Elle m'a enfoncé le doigt dans les côtes.

poker NOUN
le poker ◊ *I play poker.* Je joue au poker.

Poland NOUN
la Pologne
♦ **in Poland** en Pologne
♦ **to Poland** en Pologne

polar bear NOUN
l' ours blanc MASC

Pole NOUN
(*Polish person*)
le Polonais
la Polonaise

pole NOUN
le poteau
(les poteaux PL)
◊ *a telegraph pole* un poteau télégraphique
♦ **a tent pole** un montant de tente
♦ **a ski pole** un bâton de ski
♦ **the North Pole** le pôle Nord
♦ **the South Pole** le pôle Sud

pole vault NOUN
le saut à la perche

police PL NOUN
la police ◊ *We called the police.* Nous avons appelé la police.
♦ **a police car** une voiture de police
♦ **a police station** un commissariat de police

policeman NOUN
le policier ◊ *He's a policeman.* Il est policier.

policewoman NOUN
la femme policier ◊ *She's a policewoman.* Elle est femme policier.

polio NOUN
la polio

Polish ADJECTIVE
see also **Polish** NOUN
polonais

Polish NOUN
see also **Polish** ADJECTIVE

le <u>polonais</u> (*language*)

polish NOUN

> see also **polish** VERB

[1] le <u>cirage</u> (*for shoes*)
[2] la <u>cire</u> (*for furniture*)

to **polish** VERB

> see also **polish** NOUN

[1] <u>cirer</u> (*shoes, furniture*)
[2] <u>faire briller</u> (*glass*)

polite ADJECTIVE
<u>poli</u>

politely ADVERB
<u>poliment</u>

politeness NOUN
la <u>politesse</u>

political ADJECTIVE
<u>politique</u>

politician NOUN
le <u>politicien</u>
la <u>politicienne</u>

politics PL NOUN
la <u>politique</u> SING ◊ *I'm not interested in politics.* La politique ne m'intéresse pas.

poll NOUN
le <u>sondage</u> ◊ *A recent poll revealed that ...* Un sondage récent a révélé que ...

pollen NOUN
le <u>pollen</u>

to **pollute** VERB
<u>polluer</u>

polluted ADJECTIVE
<u>pollué</u>

pollution NOUN
la <u>pollution</u>

polo-necked sweater NOUN
le <u>pull à col roulé</u>

polo shirt NOUN
le <u>polo</u>

polythene bag NOUN
le <u>sac en plastique</u>

pond NOUN
[1] l' <u>étang</u> MASC (*big*)
[2] la <u>mare</u> (*smaller*)
[3] le <u>bassin</u> ◊ *We've got a pond in our garden.* Nous avons un bassin dans notre jardin.

pony NOUN
le <u>poney</u>

ponytail NOUN
la <u>queue de cheval</u> ◊ *He's got a ponytail.* Il a une queue de cheval.

pony trekking NOUN
♦ **to go pony trekking** faire une randonnée à dos de poney

poodle NOUN

le <u>caniche</u>

pool NOUN
[1] la <u>flaque</u> (*puddle*)
[2] l' <u>étang</u> MASC (*pond*)
[3] la <u>piscine</u> (*for swimming*)
[4] le <u>billard américain</u> (*game*) ◊ *Shall we have a game of pool?* Si on jouait au billard américain?
♦ **the pools** (*football*) le loto sportif ◊ *to do the pools* jouer au loto sportif

poor ADJECTIVE
[1] <u>pauvre</u> ◊ *a poor family* une famille pauvre ◊ *Poor David, he's very unlucky!* Le pauvre David, il n'a vraiment pas de chance!
♦ **the poor** les pauvres MASC
[2] <u>médiocre</u> (*bad*) ◊ *a poor mark* une note médiocre

poorly ADJECTIVE
<u>souffrant</u> ◊ *She's poorly.* Elle est souffrante.

pop ADJECTIVE
<u>pop</u> ◊ *pop music* la musique pop ◊ *a pop star* une pop star ◊ *a pop group* un groupe pop ◊ *a pop song* une chanson pop

to **pop in** VERB
<u>passer</u> ◊ *I just popped in to say hello.* Je suis juste passé dire bonjour. ◊ *I need to pop in to the supermarket for some milk.* Je dois passer au supermarché pour chercher du lait.

to **pop out** VERB
<u>sortir</u> ◊ *He's just popped out to the supermarket.* Il vient de sortir pour aller au supermarché.

to **pop round** VERB
<u>passer</u> ◊ *I'm just popping round to John's.* Je vais juste passer chez John.

popcorn NOUN
le <u>pop-corn</u>

pope NOUN
le <u>pape</u>

poppy NOUN
le <u>coquelicot</u>

Popsicle ® NOUN US
la <u>glace à l'eau</u>

popular ADJECTIVE
<u>populaire</u> ◊ *She's a very popular girl.* C'est une fille très populaire. ◊ *This is a very popular style.* C'est un style très populaire.

population NOUN
la <u>population</u>

porch NOUN
le <u>porche</u>

pork NOUN

P

☞

le porc ◊ *a pork chop* une côtelette de porc ◊ *I don't eat pork.* Je ne mange pas de porc.

porn NOUN
> see also **porn** ADJECTIVE

le porno

porn ADJECTIVE
> see also **porn** NOUN

porno MASC, FEM, PL ◊ *a porn film* un film porno ◊ *a porn mag* un magazine porno

pornographic ADJECTIVE
pornographique ◊ *a pornographic magazine* un magazine pornographique

pornography NOUN
la pornographie

porridge NOUN
le porridge

port NOUN
1 le port (*harbour*)
2 le porto (*wine*) ◊ *a glass of port* un verre de porto

portable ADJECTIVE
portable ◊ *a portable TV* un téléviseur portable

porter NOUN
1 le portier (*in hotel*)
2 le porteur (*at station*)

portion NOUN
la portion ◊ *a large portion of chips* une grosse portion de frites

portrait NOUN
le portrait

Portugal NOUN
le Portugal
♦ **in Portugal** au Portugal
♦ **We went to Portugal.** Nous sommes allés au Portugal.

Portuguese ADJECTIVE
> see also **Portuguese** NOUN

portugais

Portuguese NOUN
> see also **Portuguese** ADJECTIVE

1 (*person*)
le Portugais
la Portugaise
2 (*language*)
le portugais

posh ADJECTIVE
chic MASC, FEM, PL ◊ *a posh hotel* un hôtel chic

position NOUN
la position ◊ *an uncomfortable position* une position inconfortable

positive ADJECTIVE
1 (*good*)
positif MASC

positive FEM
◊ *a positive attitude* une attitude positive
2 (*sure*)
certain ◊ *I'm positive.* J'en suis certain.

to **possess** VERB
posséder

possession NOUN
♦ **Have you got all your possessions?** Est-ce tu as toutes tes affaires?

possibility NOUN
♦ **It's a possibility.** C'est possible.

possible ADJECTIVE
possible ◊ *as soon as possible* aussitôt que possible

possibly ADVERB
peut-être (*perhaps*) ◊ *Are you coming to the party? – Possibly.* Est-ce que tu viens à la soirée? – Peut-être.
♦ **... if you possibly can** ... si cela vous est possible
♦ **I can't possibly come.** Je ne peux vraiment pas venir.

post NOUN
> see also **post** VERB

1 (*letters*)
le courrier ◊ *Is there any post for me?* Est-ce qu'il y a du courrier pour moi?
2 (*pole*)
le poteau
(les poteaux PL)
◊ *The ball hit the post.* Le ballon a heurté le poteau.

to **post** VERB
> see also **post** NOUN

poster ◊ *I've got some cards to post.* J'ai quelques cartes à poster.

postage NOUN
l' affranchissement MASC

postbox NOUN
la boîte aux lettres

postcard NOUN
la carte postale

postcode NOUN
le code postal

poster NOUN
1 le poster ◊ *I've got posters on my bedroom walls.* J'ai des posters sur les murs de ma chambre.
2 l' affiche FEM (*advertising*) ◊ *There are posters all over town.* Il y a des affiches dans toute la ville.

postman NOUN
le facteur ◊ *He's a postman.* Il est facteur.

postmark NOUN
le cachet de la poste

post office NOUN
la <u>poste</u> ◊ *Where's the post office, please?* Où est la poste, s'il vous plaît? ◊ *She works for the post office.* Elle travaille à la poste.

to **postpone** VERB
<u>remettre à plus tard</u> ◊ *The match has been postponed.* Le match a été remis à plus tard.

postwoman NOUN
la <u>factrice</u> ◊ *She's a postwoman.* Elle est factrice.

pot NOUN
[1] le <u>pot</u> ◊ *a pot of jam* un pot de confiture
[2] la <u>théière</u> (*teapot*)
[3] la <u>cafetière</u> (*coffeepot*)
[4] l' <u>herbe</u> FEM (*marijuana*) ◊ *to smoke pot* fumer de l'herbe
♦**the pots and pans** les casseroles FEM

potato NOUN
la <u>pomme de terre</u> ◊ *potato salad* la salade de pommes de terre
♦**mashed potatoes** la purée
♦**boiled potatoes** les pommes vapeur
♦**a baked potato** une pomme de terre en robe des champs

potential NOUN
see also **potential** ADJECTIVE
♦**He has great potential.** Il a de l'avenir.

potential ADJECTIVE
see also **potential** NOUN
<u>possible</u> ◊ *a potential problem* un problème possible

pothole NOUN
le <u>nid de poule</u> (*in road*)

pot plant NOUN
la <u>plante en pot</u>

pottery NOUN
la <u>poterie</u>

pound NOUN
see also **pound** VERB
la <u>livre</u> (*weight, money*) ◊ *How many francs do you get for a pound?* Combien de francs a-t-on pour une livre? ◊ *a pound coin* une pièce d'une livre

> ❶ *In France measurements are in grammes and kilogrammes. One pound is about 450 grammes.*

◊ *a pound of carrots* un demi-kilo de carottes

to **pound** VERB
see also **pound** NOUN
<u>battre</u> ◊ *My heart was pounding.* J'avais le cœur qui battait.

to **pour** VERB
[1] <u>verser</u> (*liquid*) ◊ *She poured some water into the pan.* Elle a versé de l'eau dans la casserole.
♦**She poured him a drink.** Elle lui a servi à boire.
♦**Shall I pour you a cup of tea?** Je vous sers une tasse de thé?
[2] <u>pleuvoir à verse</u> (*rain*) ◊ *It's pouring.* Il pleut à verse.
♦**in the pouring rain** sous une pluie torrentielle

poverty NOUN
la <u>pauvreté</u>

powder NOUN
la <u>poudre</u>

power NOUN
[1] le <u>courant</u> (*electricity*) ◊ *The power's off.* Le courant est coupé.
♦**a power cut** une coupure de courant
♦**a power point** une prise de courant
♦**a power station** une centrale électrique
[2] l' <u>énergie</u> FEM (*energy*) ◊ *nuclear power* l'énergie nucléaire ◊ *solar power* l'énergie solaire
[3] le <u>pouvoir</u> (*authority*) ◊ *to be in power* être au pouvoir

powerful ADJECTIVE
<u>puissant</u>

practical ADJECTIVE
<u>pratique</u> ◊ *a practical suggestion* un conseil pratique
♦**She's very practical.** Elle a l'esprit pratique.

practically ADVERB
<u>pratiquement</u> ◊ *It's practically impossible.* C'est pratiquement impossible.

practice NOUN
l' <u>entraînement</u> MASC (*for sport*) ◊ *football practice* l'entraînement de foot
♦**I've got to do my piano practice.** Je dois travailler mon piano.
♦**It's normal practice in our school.** C'est ce qui se fait dans notre école.
♦**in practice** en pratique
♦**a medical practice** un cabinet médical

to **practise** VERB (US **practice**)
[1] <u>s'exercer</u> (*music, hobby*) ◊ *I ought to practise more.* Je devrais m'exercer davantage.
[2] <u>travailler</u> (*instrument*) ◊ *I practise the flute every evening.* Je travaille ma flûte tous les soirs.
[3] <u>pratiquer</u> (*language*) ◊ *I practised my French when we were on holiday.* J'ai pratiqué mon français pendant les vacances.

P

4 s'entraîner (*sport*) ◊ *The team practises on Thursdays.* L'équipe s'entraîne le jeudi. ◊ *I don't practise enough.* Je ne m'entraîne pas assez.

practising ADJECTIVE
pratiquant ◊ *She's a practising Catholic.* Elle est catholique pratiquante.

to **praise** VERB
faire l'éloge de ◊ *Everyone praises her cooking.* Tout le monde fait l'éloge de sa cuisine. ◊ *The teachers praised our work.* Les professeurs ont fait l'éloge de notre travail.

pram NOUN
le landau

prawn NOUN
la crevette

prawn cocktail NOUN
le cocktail de crevettes

to **pray** VERB
prier ◊ *to pray for something* prier pour quelque chose

prayer NOUN
la prière

precaution NOUN
la précaution
◆ **to take precautions** prendre ses précautions

preceding ADJECTIVE
précédent

precinct NOUN
◆ **a shopping precinct** un centre commercial
◆ **a pedestrian precinct** une zone piétonnière

precious ADJECTIVE
précieux MASC
précieuse FEM

precise ADJECTIVE
précis ◊ *at that precise moment* à cet instant précis

precisely ADVERB
précisément ◊ *Precisely!* Précisément!
◆ **at 10 a.m. precisely** à dix heures précises

to **predict** VERB
prédire

predictable ADJECTIVE
prévisible

prefect NOUN

> *i* French schools do not have prefects. You could explain what a prefect is using the example given.

◆ **My sister's a prefect.** Ma sœur est en dernière année et est chargée de maintenir la discipline.

to **prefer** VERB
préférer ◊ *Which would you prefer?* Lequel préfères-tu? ◊ *I prefer French to chemistry.* Je préfère le français à la chimie.

preference NOUN
la préférence

pregnant ADJECTIVE
enceinte ◊ *She's six months pregnant.* Elle est enceinte de six mois.

prehistoric ADJECTIVE
préhistorique

prejudice NOUN
1 le préjugé ◊ *That's just a prejudice.* C'est un préjugé.
2 les préjugés MASC PL ◊ *There's a lot of racial prejudice.* Il y a beaucoup de préjugés raciaux.

prejudiced ADJECTIVE
◆ **to be prejudiced against somebody** avoir des préjugés contre quelqu'un

premature ADJECTIVE
prématuré
◆ **a premature baby** un prématuré

Premier League NOUN
la première division ◊ *in the Premier League* en première division

premises PL NOUN
les locaux MASC PL ◊ *They're moving to new premises.* Ils vont occuper de nouveaux locaux.

premonition NOUN
la prémonition

preoccupied ADJECTIVE
préoccupé

prep NOUN
les devoirs MASC PL (*homework*)
◊ *history prep* les devoirs d'histoire

preparation NOUN
la préparation

to **prepare** VERB
préparer ◊ *She has to prepare lessons in the evening.* Elle doit préparer ses cours le soir.
◆ **to prepare for something** se préparer pour quelque chose ◊ *We're preparing for our skiing holiday.* Nous nous préparons pour nos vacances à la neige.

prepared ADJECTIVE
◆ **to be prepared to do something** être prêt à faire quelque chose ◊ *I'm prepared to help you.* Je suis prêt à t'aider.

prep school NOUN
l' école primaire privée FEM

Presbyterian NOUN
see also **Presbyterian** ADJECTIVE
le presbytérien
la presbytérienne

Presbyterian ADJECTIVE
see also **Presbyterian** NOUN
presbytérien MASC
presbytérienne FEM

to **prescribe** VERB
prescrire

prescription NOUN
l' ordonnance FEM ◇ *You can't get it without a prescription.* On ne peut pas se le procurer sans ordonnance.

presence NOUN
la présence
• **presence of mind** présence d'esprit

present ADJECTIVE
see also **present** NOUN, VERB
1 (*in attendance*)
présent ◇ *He wasn't present at the meeting.* Il n'était pas présent à la réunion.
2 (*current*)
actuel MASC
actuelle FEM
◇ *the present situation* la situation actuelle
• **the present tense** le présent

present NOUN
see also **present** ADJECTIVE, VERB
1 (*gift*)
le cadeau
(les cadeaux PL)
◇ *I'm going to buy presents.* Je vais acheter des cadeaux.
• **to give somebody a present** offrir un cadeau à quelqu'un
2 (*time*)
le présent ◇ *up to the present* jusqu'à présent
• **for the present** pour l'instant
• **at present** en ce moment

to **present** VERB
see also **present** ADJECTIVE, NOUN
• **to present somebody with something** (*prize, medal*) remettre quelque chose à quelqu'un

presenter NOUN
(*on TV*)
le présentateur
la présentatrice

presently ADVERB
1 bientôt (*soon*) ◇ *You'll feel better presently.* Tu vas bientôt te sentir mieux.

2 actuellement (*at present*) ◇ *They're presently on tour.* Ils sont actuellement en tournée.

president NOUN
le président
la présidente

press NOUN
see also **press** VERB
la presse
• **a press conference** une conférence de presse

to **press** VERB
see also **press** NOUN
1 appuyer ◇ *Don't press too hard!* N'appuie pas trop fort!
2 appuyer sur ◇ *He pressed the accelerator.* Il a appuyé sur l'accélérateur.

pressed ADJECTIVE
• **We are pressed for time.** Le temps nous manque.

press-up NOUN
• **to do press-ups** faire des pompes ◇ *I do twenty press-ups every morning.* Je fais vingt pompes tous les matins.

pressure NOUN
see also **pressure** VERB
la pression ◇ *He's under a lot of pressure at work.* Il est sous pression au travail.
• **a pressure group** un groupe de pression

to **pressure** VERB
see also **pressure** NOUN
faire pression sur ◇ *My parents are pressuring me.* Mes parents font pression sur moi.

to **pressurize** VERB
• **to pressurize somebody to do something** faire pression sur quelqu'un pour qu'il fasse quelque chose ◇ *My parents are pressurizing me to stay on at school.* Mes parents font pression sur moi pour que je reste à l'école.

prestige NOUN
le prestige

prestigious ADJECTIVE
prestigieux MASC
prestigieuse FEM

presumably ADVERB
vraisemblablement

to **presume** VERB
supposer ◇ *I presume so.* Je suppose que oui.

to **pretend** VERB
• **to pretend to do something** faire semblant de faire quelque chose ◇ *He*

P

pretended to be asleep. Il faisait semblant de dormir.

*Be careful not to translate **to pretend** by **prétendre**.*

pretty ADJECTIVE, ADVERB
1 joli ◊ *She's very pretty.* Elle est très jolie.
2 plutôt (*rather*) ◊ *That film was pretty bad.* Ce film était plutôt mauvais.
♦**The weather was pretty awful.** Il faisait un temps minable.
♦**It's pretty much the same.** C'est pratiquement la même chose.

to **prevent** VERB
empêcher
♦**to prevent somebody from doing something** empêcher quelqu'un de faire quelque chose ◊ *They try to prevent us from smoking.* Ils essaient de nous empêcher de fumer.

previous ADJECTIVE
précédent

previously ADVERB
auparavant

prey NOUN
la proie ◊ *a bird of prey* un oiseau de proie

price NOUN
le prix

price list NOUN
la liste des prix

to **prick** VERB
piquer ◊ *I've pricked my finger.* Je me suis piqué le doigt.

pride NOUN
la fierté

priest NOUN
le prêtre ◊ *He's a priest.* Il est prêtre.

primarily ADVERB
principalement

primary ADJECTIVE
principal
(principaux MASC PL)

primary school NOUN
l' école primaire FEM ◊ *She's still at primary school.* Elle est encore à l'école primaire.

prime minister NOUN
le Premier ministre

primitive ADJECTIVE
primitif MASC
primitive FEM

prince NOUN
le prince ◊ *the Prince of Wales* le prince de Galles

princess NOUN
la princesse ◊ *Princess Anne* la princesse Anne

principal ADJECTIVE
see also **principal** NOUN
principal
(principaux MASC PL)

principal NOUN
see also **principal** ADJECTIVE
le principal (*of college*)

principle NOUN
le principe
(les principaux PL)
♦**on principle** par principe

print NOUN
1 le tirage (*photo*) ◊ *colour prints* des tirages en couleur
2 les caractères MASC PL (*letters*) ◊ *in small print* en petits caractères
3 l' empreinte digitale FEM (*fingerprint*)
4 la gravure (*picture*) ◊ *a framed print* une gravure encadrée

printer NOUN
l' imprimante FEM (*machine*)

printout NOUN
le tirage

priority NOUN
la priorité

prison NOUN
la prison
♦**in prison** en prison

prisoner NOUN
le prisonnier
la prisonnière

prison officer NOUN
le gardien de prison
la gardienne de prison

privacy NOUN
l' intimité FEM

private ADJECTIVE
privé ◊ *a private school* une école privée
♦**private property** la propriété privée
♦**"private"** (*on envelope*) "personnel"
♦**a private bathroom** une salle de bain individuelle
♦**I have private lessons.** Je prends des cours particuliers.

to **privatize** VERB
privatiser

privilege NOUN
le privilège

prize NOUN
le prix ◊ *to win a prize* gagner un prix

prize-giving NOUN
la distribution des prix

prizewinner NOUN
le gagnant
la gagnante

pro NOUN
+ **the pros and cons** le pour et le contre
◇ *We weighed up the pros and cons.*
Nous avons pesé le pour et le contre.

probability NOUN
la probabilité

probable ADJECTIVE
probable

probably ADVERB
probablement ◇ *probably not*
probablement pas

problem NOUN
le problème ◇ *No problem!* Pas de
problème!

proceeds PL NOUN
la recette SING

process NOUN
le processus ◇ *the peace process* le
processus de paix
+ **to be in the process of doing
something** être en train de faire
quelque chose ◇ *We're in the process
of painting the kitchen.* Nous sommes
en train de peindre la cuisine.

procession NOUN
la procession (*religious*)

to **produce** VERB
1 produire (*manufacture*)
2 monter (*play, show*)

producer NOUN
(*of play, show*)
le metteur en scène
(les metteurs en scène PL)

product NOUN
le produit

production NOUN
1 la production ◇ *They're increasing
production of luxury models.* Ils
augmentent la production des
modèles de luxe.
2 la mise en scène (*play, show*) ◇ *a
production of "Hamlet"* une mise en
scène de "Hamlet"

profession NOUN
la profession

professional NOUN
see also **professional** ADJECTIVE
le professionnel
la professionnelle

professional ADJECTIVE
see also **professional** NOUN
(*player*)
professionnel MASC
professionnelle FEM
◇ *a professional musician* un musicien
professionnel
+ **a very professional piece of work** un
vrai travail de professionnel

professionally ADVERB

+ **She sings professionally.** C'est une
chanteuse professionnelle.

professor NOUN
le professeur d'université
+ **He's the French professor.** Il est
titulaire de la chaire de français.

profit NOUN
le bénéfice

profitable ADJECTIVE
rentable

program NOUN
see also **program** VERB
le programme ◇ *a computer
program* un programme informatique
+ **a TV program** US une émission de
télévision

to **program** VERB
see also **program** NOUN
programmer (*computer*)

programme NOUN
1 l' émission FEM (*on TV, radio*)
2 le programme (*of events*)

programmer NOUN
le programmeur
la programmeuse
◇ *She's a programmer.* Elle est
programmeuse.

programming NOUN
la programmation

progress NOUN
le progrès ◇ *You're making progress!*
Vous faites des progrès!

to **prohibit** VERB
interdire ◇ *Smoking is prohibited.* Il
est interdit de fumer.

project NOUN
1 le projet (*plan*) ◇ *a development
project* un projet de développement
2 le dossier (*research*) ◇ *I'm doing a
project on education in France.* Je
prépare un dossier sur l'éducation en
France.

projector NOUN
le projecteur

promenade NOUN
le front de mer

promise NOUN
see also **promise** VERB
la promesse ◇ *He made me a
promise.* Il m'a fait une promesse.
+ **That's a promise!** C'est promis!

to **promise** VERB
see also **promise** NOUN
promettre ◇ *She promised to write.*
Elle a promis d'écrire. ◇ *I'll write, I
promise!* J'écrirai, c'est promis!

promising ADJECTIVE

P

♦**a promising player** un joueur qui a de l'avenir

to **promote** VERB
♦**to be promoted** être promu ◊ *She was promoted after six months.* Elle a été promue au bout de six mois.

promotion NOUN
la promotion

prompt ADJECTIVE, ADVERB
rapide ◊ *a prompt reply* une réponse rapide
♦**at eight o'clock prompt** à huit heures précises

promptly ADVERB
♦**We left promptly at seven.** Nous sommes partis à sept heures précises.

pronoun NOUN
le pronom

to **pronounce** VERB
prononcer ◊ *How do you pronounce that word?* Comment est-ce qu'on prononce ce mot?

pronunciation NOUN
la prononciation

proof NOUN
la preuve

proper ADJECTIVE
[1] vrai (*genuine*) ◊ *proper French bread* du vrai pain français ◊ *We didn't have a proper lunch, just sandwiches.* Nous n'avons pas pris de vrai repas, juste des sandwichs.
♦**It's difficult to get a proper job.** Il est difficile de trouver un travail correct.
[2] adéquat ◊ *You have to have the proper equipment.* Il faut avoir l'équipement adéquat. ◊ *We need proper training.* Il nous faut une formation adéquate.
♦**If you had come at the proper time** ... Si tu étais venu à l'heure dite ...

properly ADVERB
[1] comme il faut (*correctly*) ◊ *You're not doing it properly.* Tu ne t'y prends pas comme il faut.
[2] convenablement (*appropriately*) ◊ *Dress properly for your interview.* Habille-toi convenablement pour ton entretien.

property NOUN
la propriété
♦**"private property"** "propriété privée"
♦**stolen property** les objets volés MASC PL

proportional ADJECTIVE
proportionnel MASC
proportionnelle FEM

◊ *proportional representation* la représentation proportionnelle

proposal NOUN
la proposition (*suggestion*)

to **propose** VERB
proposer ◊ *I propose a new plan.* Je propose un changement de programme.
♦**to propose to do something** avoir l'intention de faire quelque chose ◊ *What do you propose to do?* Qu'est-ce que tu as l'intention de faire?
♦**to propose to somebody** (*for marriage*) demander quelqu'un en mariage ◊ *He proposed to her at the restaurant.* Il l'a demandée en mariage au restaurant.

to **prosecute** VERB
poursuivre en justice ◊ *They were prosecuted for murder.* Ils ont été poursuivis en justice pour meutre.
♦**"Trespassers will be prosecuted"** "Défense d'entrer sous peine de poursuites"

prospect NOUN
la perspective ◊ *It'll improve my career prospects.* Ça va améliorer mes perspectives d'avenir.

prospectus NOUN
le prospectus

prostitute NOUN
la prostituée
♦**a male prostitute** un prostitué

to **protect** VERB
protéger

protection NOUN
la protection

protein NOUN
la protéine

protest NOUN
see also **protest** VERB
la protestation ◊ *He ignored their protests.* Il a ignoré leurs protestations.
♦**a protest march** une manifestation

to **protest** VERB
see also **protest** NOUN
protester

Protestant NOUN
see also **Protestant** ADJECTIVE
le protestant
la protestante
◊ *I'm a Protestant.* Je suis protestant.

Protestant ADJECTIVE
see also **Protestant** NOUN
protestant ◊ *a Protestant church* une église protestante

protester NOUN

le <u>manifestant</u>
la <u>manifestante</u>

proud ADJECTIVE
<u>fier</u> MASC
<u>fière</u> FEM
◊ *Her parents are proud of her.* Ses parents sont fiers d'elle.

to **prove** VERB
<u>prouver</u> ◊ *The police couldn't prove it.* La police n'a pas pu le prouver.

proverb NOUN
le <u>proverbe</u>

to **provide** VERB
<u>fournir</u>
♦ **to provide somebody with something** fournir quelque chose à quelqu'un ◊ *They provided us with maps.* Ils nous ont fourni des cartes.

to **provide for** VERB
<u>subvenir aux besoins de</u> ◊ *He can't provide for his family any more.* Il ne peut plus subvenir aux besoins de sa famille.

provided CONJUNCTION
<u>à condition que</u>
à condition que has to be followed by the subjunctive.
◊ *He'll play in the next match provided he's fit.* Il jouera dans le prochain match, à condition qu'il soit en forme.

provisional ADJECTIVE
<u>provisoire</u>

prowler NOUN
le <u>rôdeur</u>
la <u>rôdeuse</u>

prune NOUN
le <u>pruneau</u>
(les pruneaux PL)

to **pry** VERB
♦ **He's always prying into other people's affairs.** Il met toujours son nez dans les affaires des autres.

pseudonym NOUN
le <u>pseudonyme</u>

psychiatrist NOUN
le/la <u>psychiatre</u> ◊ *She's a psychiatrist.* Elle est psychiatre.

psychoanalyst NOUN
le/la <u>psychanalyste</u>

psychological ADJECTIVE
<u>psychologique</u>

psychologist NOUN
le/la <u>psychologue</u> ◊ *He's a psychologist.* Il est psychologue.

psychology NOUN
la <u>psychologie</u>

PTO ABBREVIATION (= *please turn over*)
<u>T.S.V.P.</u> (= *tournez, s'il vous plaît*)

pub NOUN
le <u>pub</u>

public NOUN
see also **public** ADJECTIVE
le <u>public</u> ◊ *open to the public* ouvert au public
♦ **in public** en public

public ADJECTIVE
see also **public** NOUN
<u>public</u> MASC
<u>publique</u> FEM
♦ **a public holiday** un jour férié
♦ **public opinion** l'opinion publique FEM
♦ **the public address system** les <u>haut-parleurs</u> MASC PL

publican NOUN
le <u>patron de pub</u>
la <u>patronne de pub</u>
♦ **My uncle's a publican.** Mon oncle tient un pub.

publicity NOUN
la <u>publicité</u>

public school NOUN
l' <u>école privée</u> FEM

public transport NOUN
les <u>transports en commun</u> MASC PL

to **publish** VERB
<u>publier</u>

publisher NOUN
l' <u>éditeur</u> MASC

pudding NOUN
le <u>dessert</u> ◊ *What's for pudding?* Qu'est-ce qu'il y a comme dessert?
♦ **rice pudding** le riz au lait
♦ **black pudding** le boudin noir

puddle NOUN
la <u>flaque</u>

puff pastry NOUN
la <u>pâte feuilletée</u>

to **pull** VERB
<u>tirer</u> ◊ *Pull!* Tirez!
♦ **He pulled the trigger.** Il a appuyé sur la gâchette.
♦ **to pull a muscle** se froisser un muscle ◊ *I pulled a muscle when I was training.* Je me suis froissé un muscle à l'entraînement.
♦ **You're pulling my leg!** Tu me fais marcher!
♦ **to pull down** démolir
♦ **to pull out (1)** arracher (*tooth, weed*)
♦ **to pull out (2)** déboîter (*car*) ◊ *The car pulled out to overtake.* La voiture a déboîté pour doubler.
♦ **to pull out (3)** se retirer (*withdraw*) ◊ *She pulled out of the tournament.* Elle s'est retirée du tournoi.

P

♦ **to pull through** s'en sortir ◊ *They think he'll pull through.* Ils pensent qu'il va s'en sortir.

♦ **to pull up** s'arrêter (*car*) ◊ *A black car pulled up beside me.* Une voiture noire s'est arrêtée à côté de moi.

pullover NOUN
le pull-over

pulse NOUN
le pouls ◊ *The nurse felt his pulse.* L'infirmière a pris son pouls.

pulses PL NOUN
les légumes secs MASC PL

pump NOUN
see also **pump** VERB
1 la pompe ◊ *a bicycle pump* une pompe à vélo ◊ *a petrol pump* une pompe à essence
2 la chaussure de sport (*shoe*)

to **pump** VERB
see also **pump** NOUN
pomper
♦ **to pump up** gonfler (*tyre*)

pumpkin NOUN
le potiron

punch NOUN
see also **punch** VERB
1 le coup de poing (*blow*) ◊ *He gave me a punch.* Il m'a donné un coup de poing.
2 le punch (*drink*)

to **punch** VERB
see also **punch** NOUN
1 donner un coup de poing à (*hit*) ◊ *He punched me!* Il m'a donné un coup de poing!
2 composter (*in ticket machine*) ◊ *Punch your ticket before you get on the train.* Compostez votre billet avant de monter dans le train.
3 poinçonner (*by hand*) ◊ *He forgot to punch my ticket.* Il a oublié de poinçonner mon billet.

punch-up NOUN
la bagarre (*informal*)

punctual ADJECTIVE
ponctuel MASC
ponctuelle FEM

punctuation NOUN
la ponctuation

puncture NOUN
la crevaison ◊ *I had to mend a puncture.* J'ai dû réparer une crevaison.
♦ **to have a puncture** crever ◊ *I had a puncture on the motorway.* J'ai crevé sur l'autoroute.

to **punish** VERB
punir

♦ **to punish somebody for something** punir quelqu'un de quelque chose
♦ **to punish somebody for doing something** punir quelqu'un d'avoir fait quelque chose

punishment NOUN
la punition

punk NOUN
le/la punk (*person*)
♦ **a punk rock band** un groupe de punk rock

pupil NOUN
l' élève MASC/FEM

puppet NOUN
la marionnette

puppy NOUN
le chiot

to **purchase** VERB
acheter

pure ADJECTIVE
pur ◊ *pure orange juice* du pur jus d'orange ◊ *He's doing pure maths.* Il fait des maths pures.

purple ADJECTIVE
violet MASC
violette FEM

purpose NOUN
le but ◊ *What is the purpose of these changes?* Quel est le but de ces changements? ◊ *his purpose in life* son but dans la vie
♦ **on purpose** exprès ◊ *He did it on purpose.* Il l'a fait exprès.

to **purr** VERB
ronronner

purse NOUN
1 le porte-monnaie (les porte-monnaie PL)
2 (*handbag*) US le sac à main (les sacs à main PL)

to **pursue** VERB
poursuivre

pursuit NOUN
l' activité FEM ◊ *outdoor pursuits* les activités de plein air

push NOUN
see also **push** VERB
♦ **to give somebody a push** pousser quelqu'un ◊ *He gave me a push.* Il m'a poussé.

to **push** VERB
see also **push** NOUN
1 pousser ◊ *Don't push!* Arrêtez de pousser!
2 appuyer sur (*button*)
♦ **to push somebody to do something** pousser quelqu'un à faire quelque

chose ◊ *My parents are pushing me to go to university.* Mes parents me poussent à entrer à l'université.
♦**to push drugs** revendre de la drogue
♦**Push off!** Dégage!

to **push around** VERB
bousculer ◊ *He likes pushing people around.* Il aime bien bousculer les gens.

to **push through** VERB
se frayer un passage ◊ *The ambulancemen pushed through the crowd.* Les ambulanciers se sont frayé un passage dans la foule.
♦**I pushed my way through.** Je me suis frayé un passage.

pushchair NOUN
la poussette

pusher NOUN
(*of drugs*)
le revendeur
la revendeuse

push-up NOUN
la pompe
♦**to do push-ups** faire des pompes

to **put** VERB
[1] mettre (*place*) ◊ *Where shall I put my things?* Où est-ce que je peux mettre mes affaires? ◊ *She's putting the baby to bed.* Elle met le bébé au lit.
[2] écrire (*write*) ◊ *Don't forget to put your name on the paper.* N'oubliez pas d'écrire votre nom sur la feuille.

to **put across** VERB
communiquer ◊ *He finds it hard to put his ideas across.* Il a du mal à communiquer ses idées.

to **put aside** VERB
mettre de côté ◊ *Can you put this aside for me till tomorrow?* Est-ce que vous pouvez mettre ça de côté pour moi jusqu'à demain?

to **put away** VERB
ranger ◊ *Can you put away the dishes, please?* Tu peux ranger la vaisselle, s'il te plaît?

to **put back** VERB
remettre en place (*replace*) ◊ *Put it back when you've finished with it.* Remets-le en place une fois que tu auras fini.

to **put down** VERB
[1] poser ◊ *I'll put these bags down for a minute.* Je vais poser ces sacs une minute.
[2] noter (*in writing*) ◊ *I've put down a few ideas.* J'ai noté quelques idées.

♦**to have an animal put down** faire piquer un animal ◊ *We had to have our old dog put down.* Nous avons dû faire piquer notre vieux chien.

to **put forward** VERB
[1] avancer (*clock*) ◊ *Next week it'll be time to put the clocks forward an hour.* La semaine prochaine, il sera temps d'avancer les montres d'une heure.
[2] proposer (*idea, argument*) ◊ *to put forward a suggestion* proposer une suggestion

to **put in** VERB
installer (*install*) ◊ *We're going to get central heating put in.* Nous allons faire installer le chauffage central.
♦**He has put in a lot of work on this project.** Il a fourni beaucoup de travail pour ce projet.

to **put off** VERB
[1] éteindre (*switch off*) ◊ *Shall I put the light off?* Est-ce que j'éteins la lumière?
[2] remettre à plus tard (*postpone*) ◊ *I keep putting it off.* Je n'arrête pas de remettre ça à plus tard.
[3] déranger (*distract*) ◊ *Stop putting me off!* Arrête de me déranger!
[4] décourager (*discourage*) ◊ *He's not easily put off.* Il ne se laisse pas facilement décourager.

to **put on** VERB
[1] mettre (*clothes, lipstick, record*) ◊ *I'll put my coat on.* Je vais mettre mon manteau.
[2] allumer (*light, heater, telly*) ◊ *Shall I put the heater on?* J'allume le chauffage?
[3] monter (*play, show*) ◊ *We're putting on "Bugsy Malone".* Nous sommes en train de monter "Bugsy Malone".
[4] mettre à cuire ◊ *I'll put the potatoes on.* Je vais mettre les pommes de terre à cuire.
♦**to put on weight** grossir ◊ *He's put on a lot of weight.* Il a beaucoup grossi.

to **put out** VERB
éteindre (*light, cigarette, fire*) ◊ *It took them five hours to put out the fire.* Ils ont mis cinq heures à éteindre l'incendie.

to **put through** VERB
passer ◊ *Can you put me through to the manager?* Est-ce que vous pouvez me passer le directeur?
♦**I'm putting you through.** Je vous passe la communication.

P

to **put up** VERB

⓵ mettre (*pin up*) ◊ *The poster's great. I'll put it up on my wall.* Le poster est super. Je vais le mettre au mur.

⓶ monter (*tent*) ◊ *We put up our tent in a field.* Nous avons monté la tente dans un champ.

⓷ augmenter (*price*) ◊ *They've put up the price.* Ils ont augmenté le prix.

⓸ héberger (*accommodate*) ◊ *My friend will put me up for the night.* Mon ami va m'héberger pour la nuit.

♦ **to put one's hand up** lever la main ◊ *If you have any questions, put up your hand.* Si vous avez une question, levez la main.

♦ **to put up with something** supporter quelque chose ◊ *I'm not going to put up with it any longer.* Je ne vais pas supporter ça plus longtemps.

puzzle NOUN
le puzzle (*jigsaw*)

puzzled ADJECTIVE
perplexe ◊ *You look puzzled!* Tu as l'air perplexe!

puzzling ADJECTIVE
déconcertant

pyjamas PL NOUN
le pyjama SING ◊ *my pyjamas* mon pyjama
♦ **a pair of pyjamas** un pyjama
♦ **a pyjama top** un haut de pyjama

pyramid NOUN
la pyramide

Pyrenees PL NOUN
les Pyrénées FEM PL
♦ **in the Pyrenees** dans les Pyrénées
♦ **We went to the Pyrenees.** Nous sommes allés dans les Pyrénées.

Q

quaint ADJECTIVE
pittoresque (*house, village*)

qualification NOUN
le diplôme ◊ *to leave school without any qualifications* quitter l'école sans aucun diplôme
♦ **vocational qualifications** des qualifications professionnelles

qualified ADJECTIVE
⟦1⟧ qualifié (*trained*) ◊ *a qualified driving instructor* un moniteur d'auto-école qualifié
⟦2⟧ diplômé (*nurse, teacher*) ◊ *a qualified nurse* une infirmière diplômée

to **qualify** VERB
⟦1⟧ obtenir son diplôme (*for job*) ◊ *She qualified as a teacher last year.* Elle a obtenu son diplôme de professeur l'année dernière.
⟦2⟧ se qualifier (*in competition*) ◊ *Our team didn't qualify.* Notre équipe ne s'est pas qualifiée.

quality NOUN
la qualité ◊ *a good quality of life* une bonne qualité de vie ◊ *good-quality ingredients* des ingrédients de bonne qualité ◊ *She's got lots of good qualities.* Elle a beaucoup de qualités.

quantity NOUN
la quantité

quarantine NOUN
la quarantaine ◊ *in quarantine* en quarantaine

quarrel NOUN
see also **quarrel** VERB
la dispute

to **quarrel** VERB
see also **quarrel** NOUN
se disputer

quarry NOUN
la carrière (*for stone*)

quarter NOUN
le quart
♦ **three quarters** trois quarts
♦ **a quarter of an hour** un quart d'heure ◊ *three quarters of an hour* trois quarts d'heure
♦ **a quarter past ten** dix heures et quart
♦ **a quarter to eleven** onze heures moins le quart

quarter final NOUN
le quart de finale

quartet NOUN

le quatuor ◊ *a string quartet* un quatuor à cordes

quay NOUN
le quai

queasy ADJECTIVE
♦ **to feel queasy** avoir mal au cœur ◊ *I'm feeling queasy.* J'ai mal au cœur.

queen NOUN
⟦1⟧ la reine ◊ *Queen Victoria* la reine Victoria
⟦2⟧ la dame (*playing card*) ◊ *the queen of hearts* la dame de cœur
♦ **the Queen Mother** la reine mère

query NOUN
see also **query** VERB
la question

to **query** VERB
see also **query** NOUN
mettre en question ◊ *No one queried my decision.* Personne n'a mis en question ma décision.

question NOUN
see also **question** VERB
la question ◊ *Can I ask a question?* Est-ce que je peux poser une question? ◊ *That's a difficult question.* C'est une question difficile.
♦ **It's out of the question.** C'est hors de question.

to **question** VERB
see also **question** NOUN
interroger ◊ *He was questioned by the police.* Il a été interrogé par la police.

question mark NOUN
le point d'interrogation

questionnaire NOUN
le questionnaire

queue NOUN
see also **queue** VERB
la queue

to **queue** VERB
see also **queue** NOUN
faire la queue
♦ **to queue for something** faire la queue pour avoir quelque chose ◊ *We had to queue for tickets.* Nous avons dû faire la queue pour avoir les billets.

quick ADJECTIVE, ADVERB
rapide ◊ *a quick lunch* un déjeuner rapide ◊ *It's quicker by train.* C'est plus rapide en train.
♦ **Be quick!** Dépêche-toi!

☞

♦**She's a quick learner.** Elle apprend vite.

♦**Quick, phone the police!** Téléphonez vite à la police!

quickly ADVERB
vite ◊ *It was all over very quickly.* Ça s'est passé très vite.

quiet ADJECTIVE
[1] (*not talkative or noisy*)
silencieux MASC
silencieuse FEM
◊ *You're very quiet today.* Tu es bien silencieux aujourd'hui. ◊ *The engine's very quiet.* Le moteur est très silencieux.
[2] (*peaceful*)
tranquille ◊ *a quiet little town* une petite ville tranquille ◊ *a quiet weekend* un week-end tranquille

♦**Be quiet!** Tais-toi!

♦**Quiet!** Silence!

quietly ADVERB
[1] doucement (*speak*) ◊ *"She's dead,"* he said quietly. "Elle est morte" dit-il doucement.
[2] silencieusement (*move*) ◊ *He quietly opened the door.* Il a ouvert la porte sans faire de bruit.

quilt NOUN
la couette (*duvet*)

to **quit** VERB
quitter (*place, premises, job*) ◊ *She's decided to quit her job.* Elle a décidé de quitter son emploi.

♦**I quit!** J'abandonne!

quite ADVERB
[1] assez (*rather*) ◊ *It's quite warm*

today. Il fait assez bon aujourd'hui.
◊ *I quite liked the film, but...* J'ai trouvé le film assez bon, mais...
[2] tout à fait (*entirely*) ◊ *I'm not quite sure.* Je n'en suis pas tout à fait sûr.
◊ *It's not quite the same.* Ce n'est pas tout à fait la même chose.

♦**quite good** pas mal

♦**I've been there quite a lot.** J'y suis allé pas mal de fois.

♦**quite a lot of money** pas mal d'argent

♦**It costs quite a lot to go abroad.** Ça coûte assez cher d'aller à l'étranger.

♦**It's quite a long way.** C'est assez loin.

♦**It was quite a shock.** Ça a été un sacré choc.

♦**There were quite a few people there.** Il y avait pas mal de gens.

quiz NOUN
le jeu-concours

quota NOUN
le quota

quotation NOUN
la citation ◊ *a quotation from Shakespeare* une citation de Shakespeare

quote NOUN
see also **quote** VERB
la citation ◊ *a Shakespeare quote* une citation de Shakespeare

♦**quotes** (*quotation marks*) les guillemets MASC ◊ *in quotes* entre guillemets

to **quote** VERB
see also **quote** NOUN
citer ◊ *He's always quoting Shakespeare.* Il n'arrête pas de citer Shakespeare.

R

rabbi NOUN
le rabbin

rabbit NOUN
le lapin
♦ **a rabbit hutch** un clapier

rabies NOUN
la rage
♦ **a dog with rabies** un chien enragé

race NOUN
see also **race** VERB
1 la course (*sport*) ◊ *a cycle race* une course cycliste
2 la race (*species*) ◊ *the human race* la race humaine
♦ **race relations** les relations interraciales FEM

to **race** VERB
see also **race** NOUN
1 courir ◊ *We raced to catch the bus.* Nous avons couru pour attraper le bus.
2 faire la course (*have a race*)
♦ **I'll race you!** On fait la course!

racecourse NOUN
le champ de courses

racehorse NOUN
le cheval de course
(les chevaux de course PL)

racer NOUN
le vélo de course (*bike*)

racetrack NOUN
la piste

racial ADJECTIVE
racial
(raciaux MASC PL)
◊ *racial discrimination* la discrimination raciale

racing car NOUN
la voiture de course

racing driver NOUN
le pilote de course

racism NOUN
le racisme

racist ADJECTIVE
see also **racist** NOUN
raciste

racist NOUN
see also **racist** ADJECTIVE
le/la raciste

rack NOUN
(*for luggage*)
le porte-bagages
(les porte-bagages PL)

racket NOUN

1 la raquette (*for sport*) ◊ *my tennis racket* ma raquette de tennis
2 le boucan (*noise*) ◊ *They're making a terrible racket.* Ils font un boucan de tous les diables. (*informal*)

racquet NOUN
la raquette

radar NOUN
le radar

radiation NOUN
la radiation

radiator NOUN
le radiateur

radio NOUN
la radio
♦ **on the radio** à la radio
♦ **a radio station** une station de radio

radioactive ADJECTIVE
radioactif MASC
radioactive FEM

radio cassette NOUN
le radiocassette

radio-controlled ADJECTIVE
téléguidé (*model plane, car*)

radish NOUN
le radis

RAF NOUN (= *Royal Air Force*)
la R.A.F. ◊ *He's in the RAF.* Il est dans la R.A.F.

raffle NOUN
la tombola ◊ *a raffle ticket* un billet de tombola

raft NOUN
le radeau
(les radeaux PL)

rag NOUN
le chiffon ◊ *a piece of rag* un chiffon
♦ **dressed in rags** en haillons

rage NOUN
la rage ◊ *mad with rage* fou de rage
♦ **to be in a rage** être furieux ◊ *She was in a rage.* Elle était furieuse.
♦ **It's all the rage.** Ça fait fureur.

raid NOUN
see also **raid** VERB
1 (*burglary*)
le hold-up
(les hold-up PL)
◊ *There was a bank raid near my house.* Il y a eu un hold-up dans une banque près de chez moi.
2 la descente ◊ *a police raid* une descente de police

to **raid** VERB

☞

see also **raid** NOUN
faire une descente dans (*police*)
◊ *The police raided a club in Soho.*
La police a fait une descente dans un
club de Soho.

rail NOUN
1 la rampe (*on stairs*)
2 la balustrade (*on bridge, balcony*)
◊ *Don't lean over the rail!* Ne vous
penchez pas sur la balustrade!
3 le rail (*on railway line*)
♦ **by rail** en train

railcard NOUN
la carte de chemin de fer ◊ *a young
person's railcard* une carte de chemin
de fer tarif jeune

railroad NOUN US
le chemin de fer
♦ **a railroad line** une ligne de chemin de
fer
♦ **a railroad station** une gare

railway NOUN
le chemin de fer ◊ *the privatization
of the railways* la privatisation des
chemins de fer
♦ **a railway line** une ligne de chemin de
fer
♦ **a railway station** une gare

rain NOUN
see also **rain** VERB
la pluie ◊ *in the rain* sous la pluie

to **rain** VERB
see also **rain** NOUN
pleuvoir ◊ *It rains a lot here.* Il pleut
beaucoup par ici.
♦ **It's raining.** Il pleut.

rainbow NOUN
l' arc-en-ciel MASC
(les arcs-en-ciel PL)

raincoat NOUN
l' imperméable MASC

rainforest NOUN
la forêt tropicale humide

rainy ADJECTIVE
pluvieux MASC
pluvieuse FEM

to **raise** VERB
1 lever (*lift*) ◊ *He raised his hand.* Il
a levé la main.
2 améliorer (*improve*) ◊ *They want to
raise standards in schools.* Ils veulent
améliorer le niveau dans les écoles.
♦ **to raise money** collecter des fonds
◊ *The school is raising money for a
new gym.* L'école collecte des fonds
pour un nouveau gymnase.

raisin NOUN
le raisin sec

rake NOUN

le râteau
(les râteaux PL)

rally NOUN
1 le rassemblement (*of people*)
2 le rallye (*sport*) ◊ *a rally driver* un
pilote de rallye
3 l' échange MASC (*in tennis*)

ram NOUN
see also **ram** VERB
le bélier (*sheep*)

to **ram** VERB
see also **ram** NOUN
emboutir (*vehicle*) ◊ *The thieves
rammed a police car.* Les voleurs ont
embouti une voiture de police.

ramble NOUN
la randonnée ◊ *to go for a ramble*
faire une randonnée

rambler NOUN
le randonneur
la randonneuse

ramp NOUN
la rampe d'accès (*for wheelchairs*)

ran VERB *see* **run**

ranch NOUN
le ranch

random ADJECTIVE
♦ **a random selection** une sélection
effectuée au hasard
♦ **at random** au hasard ◊ *We picked the
number at random.* Nous avons
choisi le numéro au hasard.

rang VERB *see* **ring**

range NOUN
see also **range** VERB
le choix ◊ *There's a wide range of
colours.* Il y a un grand choix de
coloris.
♦ **a range of subjects** diverses matières
◊ *We study a range of subjects.* Nous
étudions diverses matières.
♦ **a mountain range** une chaîne de
montagnes

to **range** VERB
see also **range** NOUN
♦ **to range from ... to** se situer entre ...
et ◊ *Temperatures in summer range
from 20 to 35 degrees.* Les
températures estivales se situent
entre vingt et trente-cinq degrés.
♦ **Tickets range from £2 to £20.** Les
billets coûtent entre deux et vingt
livres.

rank NOUN
see also **rank** VERB
♦ **a taxi rank** une station de taxis

to **rank** VERB
see also **rank** NOUN

♦He's ranked third in the United
States. Il est classé troisième aux
Etats-Unis.

ransom NOUN
la rançon

rap NOUN
le rap (music)

rape NOUN
see also **rape** VERB
le viol

to **rape** VERB
see also **rape** NOUN
violer

rapids PL NOUN
les rapides MASC PL

rapist NOUN
le violeur

rare ADJECTIVE
[1] rare (unusual) ◊ a rare plant une
plante rare
[2] saignant (steak)

rash NOUN
l' éruption de boutons FEM ◊ I've got
a rash on my chest. J'ai une éruption
de boutons sur la poitrine.

rasher NOUN
la tranche ◊ an egg and two rashers
of bacon un œuf et deux tranches de
bacon

raspberry NOUN
la framboise ◊ raspberry jam la
confiture de framboises

rat NOUN
le rat

rate NOUN
see also **rate** VERB
[1] le tarif (price) ◊ There are reduced
rates for students. Il y a des tarifs
réduits pour les étudiants.
[2] le taux (level) ◊ the divorce rate le
taux de divorce ◊ a high rate of
interest un taux d'intérêt élevé

to **rate** VERB
see also **rate** NOUN
considérer comme
♦He is rated the best. Il est considéré
comme le meilleur.
♦How do you rate him? Qu'est-ce que
vous pensez de lui?

rather ADVERB
plutôt ◊ I was rather disappointed.
J'étais plutôt déçu. ◊ £20! That's
rather a lot! Vingt livres! C'est plutôt
cher!
♦rather a lot of pas mal de ◊ I've got
rather a lot of homework to do. J'ai
pas mal de devoirs à faire.
♦rather than plutôt que ◊ We decided
to camp, rather than stay at a hotel.

Nous avons décidé de camper plutôt
que d'aller à l'hôtel.
♦I'd rather ... J'aimerais mieux ... ◊ I'd
rather stay in tonight. J'aimerais
mieux rester à la maison ce soir.
◊ Would you like a sweet? – I'd rather
have an apple. Tu veux un bonbon?
– J'aimerais mieux une pomme.

rattle NOUN
le hochet (for baby)

rattlesnake NOUN
le serpent à sonnette

to **rave** VERB
see also **rave** NOUN
s'extasier ◊ They raved about the
film. Ils se sont extasiés sur le film.

rave NOUN
see also **rave** VERB
la rave (party)
♦rave music le rave

raven NOUN
le corbeau
(les corbeaux PL)

ravenous ADJECTIVE
♦to be ravenous avoir une faim de
loup ◊ I'm ravenous! J'ai une faim de
loup!

raving ADJECTIVE
♦raving mad fou à lier ◊ She's raving
mad! Elle est folle à lier.

raw ADJECTIVE
cru (food)
♦raw materials les matières premières
FEM

razor NOUN
le rasoir ◊ some disposable razors
des rasoirs jetables
♦a razor blade une lame de rasoir

RE NOUN
l' éducation religieuse FEM

reach NOUN
see also **reach** VERB
♦out of reach hors de portée ◊ The
light switch was out of reach.
L'interrupteur était hors de portée.
♦within easy reach of à proximité de
◊ The hotel is within easy reach of
the town centre. L'hôtel se trouve à
proximité du centre-ville.

to **reach** VERB
see also **reach** NOUN
[1] arriver à ◊ We reached the hotel
at 7 p.m. Nous sommes arrivés à
l'hôtel à sept heures du soir.
♦We hope to reach the final. Nous
espérons aller en finale.
[2] parvenir à (decision) ◊ Eventually
they reached a decision. Ils sont
finalement parvenus à une décision.

R

♦**He reached for his gun.** Il a tendu la main pour prendre son revolver.

to **react** VERB
réagir

reaction NOUN
la réaction

reactor NOUN
le réacteur ◊ *a nuclear reactor* un réacteur nucléaire

to **read** VERB
lire ◊ *I don't read much.* Je ne lis pas beaucoup. ◊ *Have you read "Animal Farm"?* Est-ce que tu as lu "La ferme des animaux"? ◊ *Read the text out loud.* Lis le texte à haute voix.

to **read out** VERB
lire ◊ *He read out the article to me.* Il m'a lu l'article.
♦**to read out the results** annoncer les résultats

reader NOUN
(*person*)
le lecteur
la lectrice

readily ADVERB
volontiers ◊ *She readily agreed.* Elle a accepté volontiers.

reading NOUN
la lecture ◊ *Reading is one of my hobbies.* La lecture est l'une de mes activités favorites.

ready ADJECTIVE
prêt ◊ *She's nearly ready.* Elle est presque prête. ◊ *He's always ready to help.* Il est toujours prêt à rendre service.
♦**a ready meal** un plat cuisiné
♦**to get ready** se préparer ◊ *She's getting ready to go out.* Elle est en train de se préparer pour sortir.
♦**to get something ready** préparer quelque chose ◊ *He's getting the dinner ready.* Il est en train de préparer le dîner.

real ADJECTIVE
[1] vrai ◊ *He wasn't a real policeman.* Ce n'était pas un vrai policier. ◊ *Her real name is Cordelia.* Son vrai nom est Cordelia.
[2] véritable ◊ *It's real leather.* C'est du cuir véritable. ◊ *It was a real nightmare.* C'était un véritable cauchemar.
♦**in real life** dans la réalité

realistic ADJECTIVE
réaliste

reality NOUN
la réalité

to **realize** VERB

♦**to realize that ...** se rendre compte que ... ◊ *We realized that something was wrong.* Nous nous sommes rendu compte que quelque chose n'allait pas.

really ADVERB
vraiment ◊ *She's really nice.* Elle est vraiment sympathique. ◊ *Do you want to go? – Not really.* Tu veux y aller? – Pas vraiment.
♦**I'm learning German. – Really?** J'apprends l'allemand. – Ah bon?
♦**Do you really think so?** Tu es sûr?

realtor NOUN [US]
l' agent immobilier MASC

rear ADJECTIVE
see also **rear** NOUN
arrière MASC, FEM, PL ◊ *a rear wheel* une roue arrière

rear NOUN
see also **rear** ADJECTIVE
l' arrière MASC ◊ *at the rear of the train* à l'arrière du train

reason NOUN
la raison ◊ *There's no reason to think that ...* Il n'y a aucune raison de penser que ...
♦**for security reasons** pour des raisons de sécurité
♦**That was the main reason I went.** C'est surtout pour ça que j'y suis allé.

reasonable ADJECTIVE
[1] raisonnable (*sensible*) ◊ *Be reasonable!* Sois raisonnable!
[2] correct (*not bad*) ◊ *He wrote a reasonable essay.* Sa dissertation était correcte.

reasonably ADVERB
raisonnablement ◊ *The team played reasonably well.* L'équipe a joué raisonnablement bien.
♦**reasonably priced accommodation** un logement à un prix raisonnable

to **reassure** VERB
rassurer

reassuring ADJECTIVE
rassurant

rebellious ADJECTIVE
rebelle

receipt NOUN
le reçu

to **receive** VERB
recevoir

receiver NOUN
le combiné (*of phone*)
♦**to pick up the receiver** décrocher

recent ADJECTIVE
récent

recently ADVERB
ces derniers temps ◊ *I've been doing a lot of training recently.* Je me suis beaucoup entraîné ces derniers temps.

reception NOUN
la réception ◊ *Please leave your key at reception.* Merci de laisser votre clé à la réception. ◊ *The reception will be at a big hotel.* La réception aura lieu dans un grand hôtel.

receptionist NOUN
le/la réceptionniste

recession NOUN
la récession

recipe NOUN
la recette

to **reckon** VERB
penser ◊ *What do you reckon?* Qu'est-ce que tu en penses?

reclining ADJECTIVE
♦ a reclining seat un siège inclinable

recognizable ADJECTIVE
reconnaissable

to **recognize** VERB
reconnaître ◊ *You'll recognize me by my red hair.* Vous me reconnaîtrez à mes cheveux roux.

to **recommend** VERB
conseiller ◊ *What do you recommend?* Qu'est-ce que vous me conseillez?

to **reconsider** VERB
reconsidérer

record NOUN
see also **record** VERB
1 le disque (*recording*) ◊ *my favourite record* mon disque préféré
2 le record (*sport*) ◊ *the world record* le record du monde
♦ in record time en un temps record ◊ *She finished the job in record time.* Elle a terminé le travail en un temps record.
♦ a criminal record un casier judiciaire ◊ *He's got a criminal record.* Il a un casier judiciaire.
♦ records (*of police, hospital*) les archives FEM ◊ *I'll check in the records.* Je vais vérifier dans les archives.
♦ There is no record of your booking. Il n'y a aucune trace de votre réservation.

to **record** VERB
see also **record** NOUN
enregistrer (*on film, tape*) ◊ *They've just recorded their new album.* Ils viennent d'enregistrer leur nouveau disque.

recorded delivery NOUN
♦ to send something recorded delivery envoyer quelque chose en recommandé

recorder NOUN
la flûte à bec (*instrument*) ◊ *She plays the recorder.* Elle joue de la flûte à bec.
♦ a cassette recorder un magnétophone à cassettes
♦ a video recorder un magnétoscope

recording NOUN
l' enregistrement MASC

record player NOUN
le tourne-disque

to **recover** VERB
se remettre ◊ *He's recovering from a knee injury.* Il se remet d'une blessure au genou.

recovery NOUN
le rétablissement
♦ Best wishes for a speedy recovery! Meilleurs vœux de prompt rétablissement!

rectangle NOUN
le rectangle

rectangular ADJECTIVE
rectangulaire

to **recycle** VERB
recycler

recycling NOUN
le recyclage

red ADJECTIVE
1 rouge ◊ *a red rose* une rose rouge ◊ *red meat* la viande rouge
♦ a red light (*traffic light*) un feu rouge ◊ *to go through a red light* brûler un feu rouge
2 (*hair*)
roux MASC
rousse FEM
◊ *Tamsin's got red hair.* Tamsin a les cheveux roux.

Red Cross NOUN
la Croix-Rouge

redcurrant NOUN
la groseille

to **redecorate** VERB
1 retapisser (*with wallpaper*)
2 refaire les peintures (*with paint*)

red-haired ADJECTIVE
roux MASC
rousse FEM

red-handed ADJECTIVE
♦ to catch somebody red-handed prendre quelqu'un la main dans le sac ◊ *He was caught red-handed.* Il a été pris la main dans le sac.

R

redhead NOUN
le <u>roux</u>
la <u>rousse</u>

to **redo** VERB
<u>refaire</u>

to **reduce** VERB
<u>réduire</u> ◊ *at a reduced price* à prix réduit
♦ **"reduce speed now"** "ralentir"

reduction NOUN
la <u>réduction</u> ◊ *a 5% reduction* une réduction de cinq pour cent
♦ **"huge reductions!"** "prix sacrifiés!"

redundancy NOUN
le <u>licenciement</u> ◊ *There were fifty redundancies.* Il y a eu cinquante licenciements.
♦ **his redundancy payment** ses indemnités de licenciement

redundant ADJECTIVE
♦ **to be made redundant** être licencié ◊ *He was made redundant yesterday.* Il a été licencié hier.

reed NOUN
(*plant*)
le <u>roseau</u>
(les roseaux PL)

reel NOUN
la <u>bobine</u> (*of thread*)

to **refer** VERB
♦ **to refer to** faire allusion à ◊ *What are you referring to?* À quoi faites-vous allusion?

referee NOUN
l' <u>arbitre</u> MASC

reference NOUN
[1] l' <u>allusion</u> FEM ◊ *He made no reference to the murder.* Il n'a fait aucune allusion au meurtre.
[2] les <u>références</u> FEM PL (*for job application*) ◊ *Would you please give me a reference?* Pouvez-vous me fournir des références?
♦ **a reference book** un ouvrage de référence

to **refill** VERB
<u>remplir à nouveau</u> ◊ *He refilled my glass.* Il a rempli mon verre à nouveau.

refinery NOUN
la <u>raffinerie</u>

to **reflect** VERB
<u>refléter</u> (*light, image*)

reflection NOUN
le <u>reflet</u> (*in mirror*)

reflex NOUN
le <u>réflexe</u>

reflexive ADJECTIVE
<u>réfléchi</u> ◊ *a reflexive verb* un verbe réfléchi

refresher course NOUN
le <u>cours de recyclage</u>

refreshing ADJECTIVE
<u>rafraîchissant</u>

refreshments PL NOUN
les <u>rafraîchissements</u> MASC PL

refrigerator NOUN
le <u>réfrigérateur</u>

to **refuel** VERB
<u>se ravitailler en carburant</u> ◊ *The plane stops in Boston to refuel.* L'avion s'arrête à Boston pour se ravitailler en carburant.

refuge NOUN
le <u>refuge</u>

refugee NOUN
le <u>réfugié</u>
la <u>réfugiée</u>

refund NOUN
see also **refund** VERB
le <u>remboursement</u>

to **refund** VERB
see also **refund** NOUN
<u>rembourser</u>

refusal NOUN
le <u>refus</u>

to **refuse** VERB
see also **refuse** NOUN
<u>refuser</u>

refuse NOUN
see also **refuse** VERB
les <u>ordures</u> FEM PL
♦ **refuse collection** le ramassage des ordures

to **regain** VERB
♦ **to regain consciousness** reprendre connaissance

regard NOUN
see also **regard** VERB
♦ **Give my regards to Alice.** Transmettez mon bon souvenir à Alice.
♦ **Louis sends his regards.** Vous avez le bonjour de Louis.
♦ **"with kind regards"** "bien cordialement"

to **regard** VERB
see also **regard** NOUN
♦ **to regard something as** considérer quelque chose comme
♦ **as regards ...** concernant ...

regarding PREPOSITION
<u>relatif à</u> MASC
<u>relative à</u> FEM
◊ *the laws regarding the export of animals* les lois relatives à l'exportation des animaux

◆**Regarding John, ...** Quant à John, ...

regardless ADVERB
◆**regardless of the weather** peu importe le temps
◆**regardless of the consequences** peu importent les conséquences

regiment NOUN
le régiment

region NOUN
la région

regional ADJECTIVE
régional
(régionaux PL)

register NOUN
see also **register** VERB
le registre d'absences (in school)

to **register** VERB
see also **register** NOUN
s'inscrire (at school, college)

registered ADJECTIVE
◆**a registered letter** une lettre recommandée

registration NOUN
[1] l' appel MASC (roll call)
[2] le numéro d'immatriculation (of car)

regret NOUN
see also **regret** VERB
le regret
◆**I've got no regrets.** Je ne regrette rien.

to **regret** VERB
see also **regret** NOUN
regretter ◊ Give me the money or you'll regret it! Donne-moi l'argent, sinon tu vas le regretter!
◆**to regret doing something** regretter d'avoir fait quelque chose ◊ I regret saying that. Je regrette d'avoir dit ça.

regular ADJECTIVE
[1] régulier MASC
régulière FEM
◊ at regular intervals à intervalles réguliers ◊ a regular verb un verbe régulier
◆**to take regular exercise** faire régulièrement de l'exercice
[2] (average)
normal
(normaux PL)
◊ a regular portion of fries une portion de frites normale

regularly ADVERB
régulièrement

regulation NOUN
le règlement

rehearsal NOUN
la répétition

to **rehearse** VERB
répéter

rein NOUN
la rêne ◊ the reins les rênes

reindeer NOUN
le renne

to **reject** VERB
rejeter (idea, suggestion) ◊ We rejected that idea straight away. Nous avons immédiatement rejeté cette idée.
◆**I applied but they rejected me.** J'ai posé ma candidature mais ils l'ont rejetée.

relapse NOUN
la rechute ◊ to have a relapse faire une rechute

related ADJECTIVE
apparenté (people) ◊ We're related. Nous sommes apparentés.
◆**The two events were not related.** Il n'y avait aucun rapport entre les deux événements.

relation NOUN
[1] (person)
le parent
la parente
◊ He's a distant relation. C'est un parent éloigné. ◊ my close relations mes parents proches
◆**my relations** ma famille
◆**I've got relations in London.** J'ai de la famille à Londres.
[2] (connection)
le rapport ◊ It has no relation to reality. Cela n'a aucun rapport avec la réalité.
◆**in relation to** par rapport à

relationship NOUN
les relations FEM PL ◊ We have a good relationship. Nous avons de bonnes relations.
◆**I'm not in a relationship at the moment.** Je ne sors avec personne en ce moment.

relative NOUN
le parent
la parente
◊ my close relatives mes proches parents
◆**all her relatives** toute sa famille

relatively ADVERB
relativement

to **relax** VERB
se détendre ◊ I relax listening to music. Je me détends en écoutant de la musique.
◆**Relax! Everything's fine.** Ne t'en fais pas! Tout va bien.

relaxation NOUN

R

☞

la <u>détente</u> ◊ *I don't have much time for relaxation.* Je n'ai pas beaucoup de moments de détente.

relaxed ADJECTIVE
<u>détendu</u>

relaxing ADJECTIVE
<u>reposant</u>
♦ **I find cooking relaxing.** Cela me détend de faire la cuisine.

relay NOUN
♦ **a relay race** une course de relais

to **release** VERB
> see also **release** NOUN
[1] <u>libérer</u> (*prisoner*)
[2] <u>divulguer</u> (*report, news*)
[3] <u>sortir</u> (*record, video*)

release NOUN
> see also **release** VERB
la <u>libération</u> (*from prison*) ◊ *the release of Nelson Mandela* la libération de Nelson Mandela
♦ **the band's latest release** le dernier disque du groupe

relegated ADJECTIVE
<u>déclassé</u> (*sport*)

relevant ADJECTIVE
<u>approprié</u> (*documents*)
♦ **That's not relevant.** Ça n'a aucun rapport.
♦ **to be relevant to something** être en rapport avec quelque chose
◊ *Education should be relevant to real life.* L'enseignement devrait être en rapport avec la réalité.

reliable ADJECTIVE
<u>fiable</u> ◊ *a reliable car* une voiture fiable ◊ *He's not very reliable.* Il n'est pas très fiable.

relief NOUN
le <u>soulagement</u> ◊ *That's a relief!* Quel soulagement!

to **relieve** VERB
<u>soulager</u> ◊ *This injection will relieve the pain.* Cette piqûre va soulager la douleur.

relieved ADJECTIVE
<u>soulagé</u> ◊ *I was relieved to hear ...* J'ai été soulagé d'apprendre ...

religion NOUN
la <u>religion</u> ◊ *What religion are you?* Quelle est votre religion?

religious ADJECTIVE
[1] <u>religieux</u> MASC
<u>religieuse</u> FEM
◊ *my religious beliefs* mes croyances religieuses
[2] <u>croyant</u> ◊ *I'm not religious.* Je ne suis pas croyant.

reluctant ADJECTIVE

♦ **to be reluctant to do something** être peu disposé à faire quelque chose
◊ *They were reluctant to help us.* Ils étaient peu disposés à nous aider.

reluctantly ADVERB
<u>à contrecœur</u> ◊ *She reluctantly accepted.* Elle a accepté à contrecœur.

to **rely on** VERB
<u>compter sur</u> ◊ *I'm relying on you.* Je compte sur toi.

to **remain** VERB
<u>rester</u>
♦ **to remain silent** garder le silence

remaining ADJECTIVE
le <u>reste de</u> ◊ *the remaining ingredients* le reste des ingrédients

remains PL NOUN
les <u>restes</u> MASC PL ◊ *the remains of the picnic* les restes du pique-nique
◊ *human remains* des restes humains
♦ **Roman remains** les vestiges romains
MASC

remake NOUN
le <u>remake</u> (*of film*)

remark NOUN
la <u>remarque</u>

remarkable ADJECTIVE
<u>remarquable</u>

remarkably ADVERB
<u>remarquablement</u>

to **remarry** VERB
<u>se remarier</u> ◊ *She remarried three years ago.* Elle s'est remariée il y a trois ans.

remedy NOUN
le <u>remède</u> ◊ *a good remedy for a sore throat* un bon remède contre le mal de gorge

to **remember** VERB
<u>se souvenir de</u> ◊ *I can't remember his name.* Je ne me souviens pas de son nom. ◊ *I don't remember.* Je ne m'en souviens pas.
> In French you often say "don't forget" instead of **remember**.
◊ *Remember your passport!* N'oublie pas ton passeport! ◊ *Remember to write your name on the form.* N'oubliez pas d'écrire votre nom sur le formulaire.

Remembrance Day NOUN
le <u>jour de l'Armistice</u> ◊ *on Remembrance Day* le jour de l'Armistice

to **remind** VERB
<u>rappeler</u> ◊ *It reminds me of Scotland.* Cela me rappelle l'Écosse. ◊ *I'll remind you tomorrow.* Je te le

rappellerai demain. ◊ *Remind me to
speak to Daniel.* Rappelle-moi de
parler à Daniel.

remorse NOUN
le remords ◊ *He showed no remorse.*
Il a manifesté aucun remords.

remote ADJECTIVE
isolé ◊ *a remote village* un village
isolé

remote control NOUN
la télécommande

remotely ADVERB
◆ **I'm not remotely interested.** Je ne
suis absolument pas intéressé.
◆ **Do you think it would be remotely
possible?** Pensez-vous que cela serait
éventuellement possible?

removable ADJECTIVE
amovible

removal NOUN
le déménagement (*from house*)
◆ **a removal van** un camion de
déménagement

to **remove** VERB
1 enlever ◊ *Please remove your bag
from my seat.* Est-ce que vous
pouvez enlever votre sac de mon
siège?
2 faire partir (*stain*) ◊ *Did you
remove the stain?* Est-ce que tu as
fait partir la tache?

rendezvous NOUN
le rendez-vous
(les rendez-vous PL)

to **renew** VERB
renouveler (*passport, licence*)

renewable ADJECTIVE
renouvelable (*energy, resource*)

to **renovate** VERB
rénover ◊ *The building's been
renovated.* Le bâtiment a été rénové.

renowned ADJECTIVE
renommé

rent NOUN
see also **rent** VERB
le loyer

to **rent** VERB
see also **rent** NOUN
louer ◊ *We rented a car.* Nous avons
loué une voiture.

rental NOUN
la location ◊ *Car rental is included in
the price.* Le prix comprend la
location d'une voiture.

rental car NOUN
la voiture de location

to **reorganize** VERB
réorganiser

rep NOUN (= *representative*)
le représentant
la représentante

repaid VERB *see* **repay**

to **repair** VERB
see also **repair** NOUN
réparer
◆ **to get something repaired** faire
réparer quelque chose ◊ *I got the
washing machine repaired.* J'ai fait
réparer la machine à laver.

repair NOUN
see also **repair** VERB
la réparation

to **repay** VERB
rembourser (*money*)

repayment NOUN
le remboursement

to **repeat** VERB
see also **repeat** NOUN
répéter

repeat NOUN
see also **repeat** VERB
la reprise ◊ *There are too many
repeats on TV.* Il y a trop de reprises
à la télé.

repeatedly ADVERB
à plusieurs reprises

repellent NOUN
◆ **insect repellent** l'insectifuge MASC

repetitive ADJECTIVE
(*movement, work*)
répétitif MASC
répétitive FEM

to **replace** VERB
remplacer

replay NOUN
see also **replay** VERB
◆ **There will be a replay on Friday.** Le
match sera rejoué vendredi.

to **replay** VERB
see also **replay** NOUN
rejouer (*match*)

replica NOUN
la réplique

reply NOUN
see also **reply** VERB
la réponse

to **reply** VERB
see also **reply** NOUN
répondre

report NOUN
see also **report** VERB
1 (*of event*)
le compte rendu
(les comptes rendus PL)
2 (*news report*)

R

☞

le reportage ◇ *a report in the paper*
un reportage dans le journal
[3] (*at school*)
le bulletin scolaire ◇ *I got a good
report this term.* J'ai un bon bulletin
scolaire ce trimestre.

to **report** VERB

see also **report** NOUN

[1] signaler ◇ *I reported the theft to
the police.* J'ai signalé le vol au
commissariat.

[2] se présenter ◇ *Report to reception
when you arrive.* Présentez-vous à la
réception à votre arrivée.

reporter NOUN

le reporter ◇ *Charlotte would like to
be a reporter.* Charlotte aimerait être
reporter.

to **represent** VERB

représenter

representative ADJECTIVE

représentatif MASC
représentative FEM

reproduction NOUN

la reproduction

reptile NOUN

le reptile

republic NOUN

la république

repulsive ADJECTIVE

repoussant

reputable ADJECTIVE

de bonne réputation

reputation NOUN

la réputation

request NOUN

see also **request** VERB

la demande

to **request** VERB

see also **request** NOUN

demander

to **require** VERB

exiger ◇ *The job requires a sound
knowledge of classical music.* Cet
emploi exige une bonne connaissance
de la musique classique.

♦ **What qualifications are required?**
Quelles sont les diplômes requis?

requirement NOUN

la condition requise

♦ **What are the requirements for the
job?** Quelles sont les conditions
requises pour le poste?

♦ **entry requirements** (*for university*) les
critères d'entrée MASC

to **rescue** VERB

see also **rescue** NOUN

sauver

rescue NOUN

see also **rescue** VERB

[1] le sauvetage ◇ *a rescue operation*
une opération de sauvetage

♦ **a mountain rescue team** une équipe
de sauvetage en montagne

[2] le secours ◇ *the rescue services*
les services de secours

♦ **to come to somebody's rescue** venir
au secours de quelqu'un ◇ *He came
to my rescue.* Il est venu à mon
secours.

research NOUN

[1] la recherche (*experimental*) ◇ *He's
doing research.* Il fait de la recherche.

[2] les recherches FEM PL (*theoretical*)
◇ *She's doing some research in the
library.* Elle fait des recherches à la
bibliothèque.

resemblance NOUN

la ressemblance

to **resent** VERB

être contrarié par ◇ *I really resented
your criticism.* J'ai été vraiment
contrarié par tes critiques.

resentful ADJECTIVE

plein de ressentiment

♦ **to feel resentful towards somebody**
en vouloir à quelqu'un

reservation NOUN

la réservation (*booking*) ◇ *I've got a
reservation for two nights.* J'ai une
réservation pour deux nuits. ◇ *I'd like
to make a reservation for this evening.*
J'aimerais faire une réservation pour
ce soir.

reserve NOUN

see also **reserve** VERB

[1] (*place*)
la réserve ◇ *a nature reserve* une
réserve naturelle

[2] (*person*)
le remplaçant
la remplaçante
◇ *I was reserve in the game last
Saturday.* J'étais remplaçant dans le
match de samedi dernier.

to **reserve** VERB

see also **reserve** NOUN

réserver ◇ *I'd like to reserve a table
for tomorrow evening.* J'aimerais
réserver une table pour demain soir.

reserved ADJECTIVE

réservé ◇ *a reserved seat* une place
réservée ◇ *He's quite reserved.* Il est
assez réservé.

reservoir NOUN

le réservoir

resident NOUN

le <u>résident</u>
la <u>résidente</u>

residential ADJECTIVE
<u>résidentiel</u> MASC
<u>résidentielle</u> FEM
◊ *a residential area* un quartier résidentiel

to **resign** VERB
<u>donner sa démission</u>

resistance NOUN
♦**He was in the resistance.** Il faisait de la résistance.
♦**the French Resistance** la Résistance

to **resit** VERB
<u>repasser</u> ◊ *I'm resitting the exam in December.* Je vais repasser l'examen en décembre.

resolution NOUN
la <u>résolution</u>
♦**Have you made any new year's resolutions?** Tu as pris de bonnes résolutions pour l'année nouvelle?

resort NOUN
la <u>station balnéaire</u> (*at seaside*) ◊ *It's a resort on the Costa del Sol.* C'est une station balnéaire sur la Costa del Sol.
♦**a ski resort** une station de ski
♦**as a last resort** en dernier recours

resource NOUN
la <u>ressource</u>

respect NOUN
see also **respect** VERB
le <u>respect</u>

to **respect** VERB
see also **respect** NOUN
<u>respecter</u>

respectable ADJECTIVE
1 <u>respectable</u>
2 <u>correct</u> (*standard, marks*)

respectively ADVERB
<u>respectivement</u>

responsibility NOUN
la <u>responsabilité</u>

responsible ADJECTIVE
1 (*in charge*)
<u>responsable</u>
♦**to be responsible for something** être responsable de quelque chose ◊ *He's responsible for booking the tickets.* Il est responsable de la réservation des billets.
♦**It's a responsible job.** C'est un poste à responsabilités.
2 (*mature*)
<u>sérieux</u> MASC
<u>sérieuse</u> FEM
◊ *You should be more responsible.* Tu devrais être un peu plus sérieux.

rest NOUN
see also **rest** VERB
1 le <u>repos</u> (*relaxation*) ◊ *five minutes' rest* cinq minutes de repos
♦**to have a rest** se reposer ◊ *We stopped to have a rest.* Nous nous sommes arrêtés pour nous reposer.
2 le <u>reste</u> (*remainder*) ◊ *I'll do the rest.* Je ferai le reste. ◊ *the rest of the money* le reste de l'argent
♦**the rest of them** les autres ◊ *The rest of them went swimming.* Les autres sont allés nager.

to **rest** VERB
see also **rest** NOUN
1 <u>se reposer</u> (*relax*) ◊ *She's resting in her room.* Elle se repose dans sa chambre.
2 <u>ménager</u> (*not overstrain*) ◊ *He has to rest his knee.* Il doit ménager son genou.
3 <u>appuyer</u> (*lean*) ◊ *I rested my bike against the window.* J'ai appuyé mon vélo contre la fenêtre.

restaurant NOUN
le <u>restaurant</u> ◊ *We don't often go to restaurants.* Nous n'allons pas souvent au restaurant.
♦**a restaurant car** un wagon-restaurant

restful ADJECTIVE
<u>reposant</u>

restless ADJECTIVE
<u>agité</u>

restoration NOUN
la <u>restauration</u>

to **restore** VERB
<u>restaurer</u> (*building, picture*)

to **restrict** VERB
<u>limiter</u>

rest room NOUN US
les <u>toilettes</u> FEM PL

result NOUN
see also **result** VERB
le <u>résultat</u> ◊ *my exam results* mes résultats d'examen ◊ *What was the result? – One-nil.* Quel a été le résultat? – Un à zéro.

to **result** VERB
see also **result** NOUN
♦**to result in** entraîner

to **resume** VERB
<u>reprendre</u> ◊ *They've resumed work.* Ils ont repris le travail.
Be careful not to translate **to resume** by **résumer**.

résumé NOUN US
le <u>curriculum vitae</u>

to **retire** VERB

R

☞

prendre sa retraite ◊ *He retired last year.* Il a pris sa retraite l'an dernier.

retired ADJECTIVE
retraité ◊ *She's retired.* Elle est retraitée.
◆ **a retired teacher** un professeur à la retraite

retirement NOUN
la retraite

to **retrace** VERB
◆ **to retrace one's steps** revenir sur ses pas ◊ *I retraced my steps.* Je suis revenu sur mes pas.

return NOUN
see also **return** VERB
1 le retour ◊ *after our return* à notre retour
◆ **the return journey** le voyage de retour
◆ **a return match** un match retour
2 l' aller retour MASC (*ticket*) ◊ *A return to Avignon, please.* Un aller retour pour Avignon, s'il vous plaît.
◆ **in return** en échange ◊ *... and I help her in return* ... et je l'aide en échange
◆ **in return for** en échange de
◆ **Many happy returns!** Bon anniversaire!

to **return** VERB
see also **return** NOUN
1 revenir (*come back*) ◊ *I've just returned from holiday.* Je viens de revenir de vacances.
◆ **to return home** rentrer à la maison
2 retourner (*go back*) ◊ *He returned to France the following year.* Il est retourné en France l'année suivante.
3 rendre (*give back*) ◊ *She borrows my things and doesn't return them.* Elle m'emprunte mes affaires et ne me les rend pas.

reunion NOUN
la réunion

to **reuse** VERB
réutiliser

to **reveal** VERB
révéler

revenge NOUN
la vengeance ◊ *in revenge* par vengeance
◆ **to take revenge** se venger ◊ *They planned to take revenge on him.* Ils voulaient se venger de lui.

to **reverse** VERB
see also **reverse** ADJECTIVE
faire marche arrière (*car*) ◊ *He reversed without looking.* Il a fait marche arrière sans regarder.

◆ **to reverse the charges** (*telephone*) appeler en PCV

> ℹ *In France, reversing the charges is only possible for international calls.*

◊ *I'd like to make a reverse charge call to Britain.* Je voudrais appeler la Grande-Bretagne en PCV.

reverse ADJECTIVE
see also **reverse** VERB
inverse ◊ *in reverse order* dans l'ordre inverse
◆ **in reverse gear** en marche arrière

review NOUN
la critique (*of book, film, programme*) ◊ *The book had good reviews.* Ce livre a eu de bonnes critiques.

to **revise** VERB
réviser ◊ *I haven't started revising yet.* Je n'ai pas encore commencé à réviser.
◆ **I've revised my opinion.** J'ai changé d'opinion.

revision NOUN
les révisions FEM PL ◊ *Have you done a lot of revision?* Est-ce que tu as fait beaucoup de révisions?

to **revive** VERB
ranimer ◊ *The nurses tried to revive him.* Les infirmières ont essayé de le ranimer.

revolting ADJECTIVE
dégoûtant

revolution NOUN
la révolution
◆ **the French Revolution** la Révolution française

revolutionary ADJECTIVE
révolutionnaire

revolver NOUN
le revolver

reward NOUN
la récompense

rewarding ADJECTIVE
gratifiant ◊ *a rewarding job* un travail gratifiant

to **rewind** VERB
rembobiner ◊ *to rewind a cassette* rembobiner une cassette

rheumatism NOUN
le rhumatisme

Rhine NOUN
le Rhin

rhinoceros NOUN
le rhinocéros

Rhone NOUN
le Rhône

rhubarb NOUN
la rhubarbe ◊ *a rhubarb tart* une tarte à la rhubarbe

rhythm NOUN
le rythme

rib NOUN
la côte

ribbon NOUN
le ruban

rice NOUN
le riz
♦ **rice pudding** le riz au lait

rich ADJECTIVE
riche
♦ **the rich** les riches MASC

to **rid** VERB
♦ **to get rid of** se débarrasser de ◊ *I want to get rid of some old clothes.* Je veux me débarrasser de vieux vêtements.

ridden VERB *see* **ride**

ride NOUN
see also **ride** VERB
♦ **to go for a ride (1)** (*on horse*) monter à cheval
♦ **to go for a ride (2)** (*on bike*) faire un tour en vélo ◊ *We went for a bike ride.* Nous sommes allés faire un tour en vélo.
♦ **It's a short bus ride to the town centre.** Ce n'est pas loin du centre-ville en bus.

to **ride** VERB
see also **ride** NOUN
monter à cheval (*on horse*) ◊ *I'm learning to ride.* J'apprends à monter à cheval.
♦ **to ride a bike** faire du vélo ◊ *Can you ride a bike?* Tu sais faire du vélo?

rider NOUN
[1] (*on horse*)
le cavalier
la cavalière
◊ *She's a good rider.* C'est une bonne cavalière.
[2] (*on bike*)
le/la cycliste

ridiculous ADJECTIVE
ridicule ◊ *Don't be ridiculous!* Ne sois pas ridicule!

riding NOUN
l' équitation FEM
♦ **to go riding** faire de l'équitation
♦ **a riding school** une école d'équitation

rifle NOUN
le fusil ◊ *a hunting rifle* un fusil de chasse

rig NOUN
♦ **an oil rig** une plate-forme pétrolière

right ADJECTIVE, ADVERB
see also **right** NOUN

*There are several ways of translating **right**. Scan the examples to find one that is similar to what you want to say.*

[1] (*factually correct, suitable*)
bon MASC
bonne FEM
◊ *the right answer* la bonne réponse
◊ *It isn't the right size.* Ce n'est pas la bonne taille. ◊ *We're on the right train.* Nous sommes dans le bon train.
♦ **Is this the right road for Arles?** Est-ce que c'est bien la route pour aller à Arles?
[2] (*correctly*)
correctement ◊ *Am I pronouncing it right?* Est-ce que je prononce ça correctement?
♦ **to be right (1)** (*person*) avoir raison ◊ *You were right!* Tu avais raison!
♦ **to be right (2)** (*statement, opinion*) être vrai ◊ *That's right!* C'est vrai!
[3] (*accurate*)
juste ◊ *Do you have the right time?* Est-ce que vous avez l'heure juste?
[4] (*morally correct*)
bien ◊ *It's not right to behave like that.* Ce n'est pas bien d'agir comme ça.
♦ **I think you did the right thing.** Je pense que tu as bien fait.
[5] (*not left*)
droit ◊ *my right hand* ma main droite
[6] (*turn, look*)
à droite ◊ *Turn right at the traffic lights.* Tournez à droite aux prochains feux.
♦ **Right! Let's get started.** Bon! On commence.
♦ **right away** tout de suite ◊ *I'll do it right away.* Je vais le faire tout de suite.

right NOUN
see also **right** ADJECTIVE
[1] le droit
♦ **You've got no right to do that.** Vous n'avez pas le droit de faire ça.
[2] la droite (*not left*)
♦ **on the right** à droite ◊ *Remember to drive on the right.* N'oubliez pas de conduire à droite.
♦ **right of way** la priorité ◊ *It was our right of way.* Nous avions la priorité.

right-hand ADJECTIVE
♦ **the right-hand side** la droite ◊ *It's on the right-hand side.* C'est à droite.

right-handed ADJECTIVE
droitier MASC

R

droitière FEM

rightly ADVERB
avec raison ◊ *She rightly decided not to go.* Elle a décidé, avec raison, de ne pas y aller.
♦ **if I remember rightly** si je me souviens bien

rim NOUN
la monture ◊ *glasses with wire rims* des lunettes avec une monture métallique

ring NOUN
see also **ring** VERB
1 l' anneau MASC
(les anneaux PL)
◊ *a gold ring* un anneau en or
2 (*with stones*)
la bague ◊ *a diamond ring* une bague de diamants
♦ **a wedding ring** une alliance
3 (*circle*)
le cercle ◊ *to stand in a ring* se mettre en cercle
4 (*of bell*)
le coup de sonnette ◊ *I was woken by a ring at the door.* J'ai été réveillé par un coup de sonnette.
♦ **to give somebody a ring** appeler quelqu'un ◊ *I'll give you a ring this evening.* Je t'appellerai ce soir.

to **ring** VERB
see also **ring** NOUN
1 téléphoner ◊ *Your mother rang this morning.* Ta mère a téléphoné ce matin.
♦ **to ring somebody** appeler quelqu'un
◊ *I'll ring you tomorrow morning.* Je t'appellerai demain matin.
♦ **to ring somebody up** donner un coup de fil à quelqu'un
2 sonner ◊ *The phone's ringing.* Le téléphone sonne.
♦ **to ring the bell** (*doorbell*) sonner à la porte ◊ *I rang the bell three times.* J'ai sonné trois fois à la porte.
♦ **to ring back** rappeler ◊ *I'll ring back later.* Je rappellerai plus tard.

ring binder NOUN
le classeur

ring road NOUN
1 la rocade (*ordinary road*)
2 le périphérique (*motorway*)

rink NOUN
1 la patinoire (*for ice-skating*)
2 la piste (*for roller-skating*)

to **rinse** VERB
rincer

riot NOUN
see also **riot** VERB

l' émeute FEM

to **riot** VERB
see also **riot** NOUN
faire une émeute

to **rip** VERB
1 déchirer ◊ *I've ripped my jeans.* J'ai déchiré mon jean.
2 se déchirer ◊ *My skirt's ripped.* Ma jupe s'est déchirée.

to **rip off** VERB
arnaquer ◊ *The hotel ripped us off.* L'hôtel nous a arnaqués.

to **rip up** VERB
déchirer ◊ *He read the note and then ripped it up.* Il a lu le mot, puis l'a déchiré.

ripe ADJECTIVE
mûr

rip-off NOUN
♦ **It's a rip-off!** C'est de l'arnaque! (*informal*)

rise NOUN
see also **rise** VERB
1 la hausse (*in prices, temperature*)
◊ *a sudden rise in temperature* une hausse subite de température
2 l' augmentation FEM (*pay rise*)

to **rise** VERB
see also **rise** NOUN
1 augmenter (*increase*) ◊ *Prices are rising.* Les prix augmentent.
2 se lever ◊ *The sun rises early in June.* Le soleil se lève tôt en juin.

riser NOUN
♦ **to be an early riser** être matinal

risk NOUN
see also **risk** VERB
le risque
♦ **to take risks** prendre des risques
♦ **It's at your own risk.** C'est à vos risques et périls.

to **risk** VERB
see also **risk** NOUN
risquer ◊ *You risk getting a fine.* Vous risquez de recevoir une amende.
♦ **I wouldn't risk it if I were you.** À votre place, je ne prendrais pas ce risque.

risky ADJECTIVE
risqué

rival NOUN
see also **rival** ADJECTIVE
le rival
(les rivaux PL)
la rivale

rival ADJECTIVE
see also **rival** NOUN

rival
　1 rival ◇ *a rival gang* une bande rivale
　2 concurrent ◇ *a rival company* une société concurrente

rivalry NOUN
　la rivalité (*between towns, schools*)

river NOUN
　1 la rivière ◇ *The river runs alongside the canal.* La rivière longe le canal.
　2 le fleuve (*major*) ◇ *the rivers of France* les fleuves de France
　♦ **the river Seine** la Seine

Riviera NOUN
　♦ **the French Riviera** la Côte d'Azur
　♦ **the Italian Riviera** la Riviera italienne

road NOUN
　1 la route ◇ *There's a lot of traffic on the roads.* Il y a beaucoup de circulation sur les routes.
　2 la rue (*street*) ◇ *They live across the road.* Ils habitent de l'autre côté de la rue.

road map NOUN
　la carte routière

road rage NOUN
　l' agressivité au volant FEM

road sign NOUN
　le panneau de signalisation
　(les panneaux de signalisation PL)

roadworks PL NOUN
　les travaux MASC PL

roast ADJECTIVE
　rôti ◇ *roast chicken* le poulet rôti
　◇ *roast potatoes* les pommes de terre rôties
　♦ **roast pork** le rôti de porc
　♦ **roast beef** le rôti de bœuf

to **rob** VERB
　♦ **to rob somebody** voler quelqu'un ◇ *I've been robbed.* On m'a volé.
　♦ **to rob somebody of something** voler quelque chose à quelqu'un ◇ *He was robbed of his wallet.* On lui a volé son portefeuille.
　♦ **to rob a bank** dévaliser une banque

robber NOUN
　le voleur
　♦ **a bank-robber** un cambrioleur de banques

robbery NOUN
　le vol
　♦ **a bank robbery** un hold-up
　♦ **armed robbery** le vol à main armée

robin NOUN
　le rouge-gorge

robot NOUN
　le robot

rock NOUN

see also **rock** VERB
　1 la roche (*substance*) ◇ *They tunnelled through the rock.* Ils ont creusé un tunnel dans la roche.
　2 le rocher (*boulder*) ◇ *I sat on a rock.* Je me suis assis sur un rocher.
　3 la pierre (*stone*) ◇ *The crowd started to throw rocks.* La foule s'est mise à lancer des pierres.
　4 le rock (*music*) ◇ *a rock concert* un concert de rock ◇ *He's a rock star.* C'est une rock star.
　5 le sucre d'orge (*sweet*) ◇ *a stick of rock* un bâton de sucre d'orge
　♦ **rock and roll** le rock'n'roll

to **rock** VERB
see also **rock** NOUN
　ébranler ◇ *The explosion rocked the building.* L'explosion a ébranlé le bâtiment.

rockery NOUN
　la rocaille

rocket NOUN
　la fusée (*firework, spacecraft*)

rocking chair NOUN
　le rocking-chair

rocking horse NOUN
　le cheval à bascule

rod NOUN
　la canne à pêche (*for fishing*)

rode VERB *see* **ride**

role NOUN
　le rôle

role play NOUN
　le jeu de rôle
　(les jeux de rôles PL)
　◇ *to do a role play* faire un jeu de rôle

roll NOUN
see also **roll** VERB
　1 le rouleau
　(les rouleaux PL)
　◇ *a roll of tape* un rouleau de ruban adhésif ◇ *a toilet roll* un rouleau de papier hygiénique
　2 (*bread*)
　le petit pain

to **roll** VERB
see also **roll** NOUN
　rouler
　♦ **to roll out the pastry** abaisser la pâte

roll call NOUN
　l' appel MASC

roller NOUN
　le rouleau
　(les rouleaux PL)

Rollerblade ® NOUN
　le roller ◇ *a pair of Rollerblades* une paire de rollers

rollercoaster NOUN

R

English ~ French

les montagnes russes FEM PL

roller skates PL NOUN
les patins à roulettes MASC PL

roller-skating NOUN
le patin à roulettes
♦ **to go roller-skating** faire du patin à roulettes

rolling pin NOUN
le rouleau à pâtisserie

Roman ADJECTIVE, NOUN
romain (*ancient*) ◊ *a Roman villa* une villa romaine ◊ *the Roman empire* l'empire romain
♦ **the Romans** les Romains

Roman Catholic NOUN
le/la catholique ◊ *He's a Roman Catholic.* Il est catholique.

romance NOUN
[1] les romans d'amour MASC PL (*novels*) ◊ *I read a lot of romance.* Je lis beaucoup de romans d'amour.
[2] le charme (*glamour*) ◊ *the romance of Paris* le charme de Paris
♦ **a holiday romance** une idylle de vacances

Romania NOUN
la Roumanie
♦ **in Romania** en Roumanie

Romanian ADJECTIVE
roumain

romantic ADJECTIVE
romantique

roof NOUN
le toit

roof rack NOUN
la galerie

room NOUN
[1] la pièce ◊ *the biggest room in the house* la plus grande pièce de la maison
[2] la chambre (*bedroom*) ◊ *She's in her room.* Elle est dans sa chambre.
♦ **a single room** une chambre pour une personne
♦ **a double room** une chambre pour deux personnes
[3] la salle (*in school*) ◊ *the music room* la salle de musique
[4] la place (*space*) ◊ *There's no room for that box.* Il n'y a pas de place pour cette boîte.

roommate NOUN
le/la camarade de chambre

root NOUN
la racine

to **root around** VERB
fouiller ◊ *She started rooting around in her handbag.* Elle a commencé à fouiller dans son sac à main.

to **root out** VERB
traquer ◊ *They are determined to root out corruption.* Ils sont déterminés à traquer la corruption.

rope NOUN
la corde

to **rope in** VERB
enrôler ◊ *I was roped in to help with the refreshments.* J'ai été enrôlé pour servir les rafraîchissements.

rose VERB *see* **rise**

rose NOUN
la rose (*flower*)

to **rot** NOUN
VERB
pourrir

rotten ADJECTIVE
pourri (*decayed*) ◊ *a rotten apple* une pomme pourrie
♦ **rotten weather** un temps pourri
♦ **That's a rotten thing to do.** Ce n'est vraiment pas gentil.
♦ **to feel rotten** être mal fichu (*informal*)

rough ADJECTIVE
[1] (*surface*)
rêche ◊ *My hands are rough.* J'ai les mains rêches.
[2] (*game*)
violent ◊ *Rugby's a rough sport.* Le rugby est un sport violent.
[3] (*place*)
difficile ◊ *It's a rough area.* C'est un quartier difficile.
[4] (*water*)
houleux MASC
houleuse FEM
◊ *The sea was rough.* La mer était houleuse.
[5] approximatif MASC
approximative FEM
♦ **I've got a rough idea.** J'en ai une idée approximative.
♦ **to feel rough** ne pas être dans son assiette ◊ *I feel rough.* Je ne suis pas dans mon assiette.

roughly ADVERB
à peu près ◊ *It weighs roughly 20 kilos.* Ça pèse à peu près vingt kilos.

round ADJECTIVE, ADVERB, PREPOSITION
see also **round** NOUN
[1] rond ◊ *a round table* une table ronde
[2] autour de (*around*) ◊ *We were sitting round the table.* Nous étions assis autour de la table. ◊ *She wore a scarf round her neck.* Elle portait une écharpe autour du cou.
♦ **It's just round the corner.** (*very near*) C'est tout près.

♦ **to go round to somebody's house**
aller chez quelqu'un ◊ *I went round
to my friend's house.* Je suis allé
chez mon ami.

♦ **to have a look round** faire un tour
◊ *We're going to have a look round.*
Nous allons faire un tour.

♦ **to go round a museum** visiter un
musée

♦ **round here** près d'ici ◊ *Is there a
chemist's round here?* Est-ce qu'il y a
une pharmacie près d'ici?

♦ **He lives round here.** Il habite dans les
parages.

♦ **all round** partout ◊ *There were
vineyards all round.* Il y avait des
vignobles partout.

♦ **all year round** toute l'année

♦ **round about** (*roughly*) environ ◊ *It
costs round about £100.* Cela coûte
environ cent livres. ◊ *round about 8
o'clock* à huit heures environ

round NOUN

see also **round** ADJECTIVE

1 la manche (*of tournament*)
2 le round (*of boxing match*)

♦ **a round of golf** une partie de golf

♦ **a round of drinks** une tournée ◊ *He
bought a round of drinks.* Il a offert
une tournée.

to **round off** VERB
terminer ◊ *They rounded off the
meal with liqueurs.* Ils ont terminé le
repas par des liqueurs.

to **round up** VERB
1 rassembler (*sheep, cattle, suspects*)
2 arrondir (*figure*)

roundabout NOUN
1 (*at junction*)
le rond-point
(les ronds-points PL)
2 (*at funfair*)
le manège

rounders NOUN

> 🛈 *Rounders is not played in France.*

♦ **Rounders is a bit like baseball, but
it's mostly played by children.** Le
"rounders" ressemble un peu au
base-ball, mais est surtout pratiqué
par les enfants.

round trip NOUN US
l' aller et retour MASC

♦ **a round-trip ticket** un billet de
aller-retour

route NOUN
1 l' itinéraire MASC ◊ *We're planning
our route.* Nous établissons notre
itinéraire.

2 le parcours (*of bus*)

routine NOUN

♦ **my daily routine** mes occupations
quotidiennes

row NOUN

> *This word has two pronunciations.
> Make sure you choose the right
> translation.*

see also **row** VERB

1 la rangée ◊ *a row of houses* une
rangée de maisons
2 le rang (*of seats*) ◊ *Our seats are
in the front row.* Nos places se
trouvent au premier rang.

♦ **five times in a row** cinq fois d'affilée

3 le vacarme (*noise*) ◊ *What's that
terrible row?* qu'est-ce que c'est que
ce vacarme?

4 la dispute (*quarrel*)

♦ **to have a row** se disputer ◊ *They've
had a row.* Ils se sont disputés.

to **row** VERB

see also **row** NOUN

1 ramer ◊ *We took turns to row.*
Nous avons ramé à tour de rôle.
2 faire de l'aviron (*as sport*)

rowboat NOUN US
le bateau à rames

rowing NOUN
l' aviron MASC (*sport*) ◊ *My hobby is
rowing.* Je fais de l'aviron.

♦ **a rowing boat** un bateau à rames

royal ADJECTIVE
royal
(royaux MASC PL)

♦ **the royal family** la famille royale

to **rub** VERB
1 frotter (*stain*)
2 se frotter (*part of body*) ◊ *Don't rub
your eyes!* Ne te frotte pas les yeux!

♦ **to rub something out** effacer quelque
chose

rubber NOUN
1 le caoutchouc ◊ *rubber soles* des
semelles en caoutchouc
2 la gomme (*eraser*) ◊ *Can I borrow
your rubber?* Je peux emprunter ta
gomme?

♦ **a rubber band** un élastique

rubbish NOUN

see also **rubbish** ADJECTIVE

1 les ordures FEM PL (*refuse*) ◊ *When
do they collect the rubbish?* Quand
est-ce qu'ils ramassent les ordures?
2 la camelote (*junk*) ◊ *They sell a lot
of rubbish at the market.* Ils vendent
beaucoup de camelote au marché.
3 les bêtises FEM PL (*nonsense*) ◊ *Don't
talk rubbish!* Ne dis pas de bêtises!

☞

♦ **That's a load of rubbish!** C'est vraiment n'importe quoi! (*informal*)
♦ **a rubbish bin** une poubelle
♦ **a rubbish dump** une décharge

rubbish ADJECTIVE

see also **rubbish** NOUN

nul MASC
nulle FEM
◊ *They're a rubbish team!* Cette équipe est nulle!

rucksack NOUN
le sac à dos

rude ADJECTIVE
1 (*impolite*)
impoli ◊ *It's rude to interrupt.* C'est impoli de couper la parole aux gens.
2 (*offensive*)
grossier MASC
grossière FEM
◊ *a rude joke* une plaisanterie grossière ◊ *He was very rude to me.* Il a été très grossier avec moi.
♦ **a rude word** un gros mot

rug NOUN
1 le tapis ◊ *a Persian rug* un tapis persan
2 la couverture (*blanket*) ◊ *a tartan rug* une couverture écossaise

rugby NOUN
le rugby ◊ *I play rugby.* Je joue au rugby.

ruin NOUN

see also **ruin** VERB

la ruine ◊ *the ruins of the castle* les ruines du château
♦ **in ruins** en ruine

to **ruin** VERB

see also **ruin** NOUN

1 abîmer ◊ *You'll ruin your shoes.* Tu vas abîmer tes chaussures.
2 gâcher ◊ *It ruined our holiday.* Ça a gâché nos vacances.
3 ruiner (*financially*)

rule NOUN
1 la règle ◊ *the rules of grammar* les règles de grammaire
♦ **as a rule** en règle générale
2 le règlement (*regulation*) ◊ *It's against the rules.* C'est contre le règlement.

to **rule out** VERB
écarter (*possibility*) ◊ *I'm not ruling anything out.* Je n'écarte aucune possibilité.

ruler NOUN
la règle ◊ *Can I borrow your ruler?* Je peux emprunter ta règle?

rum NOUN
le rhum

rumour NOUN (US **rumor**)
la rumeur ◊ *It's just a rumour.* Ce n'est qu'une rumeur.

rump steak NOUN
le romsteak

run NOUN

see also **run** VERB

le point (*in cricket*) ◊ *to score a run* marquer un point
♦ **to go for a run** courir ◊ *I go for a run every morning.* Je cours tous les matins.
♦ **I did a ten-kilometre run.** J'ai couru dix kilomètres.
♦ **on the run** en fuite ◊ *The criminals are still on the run.* Les criminels sont toujours en fuite.
♦ **in the long run** à long terme

to **run** VERB

see also **run** NOUN

1 courir ◊ *I ran five kilometres.* J'ai couru cinq kilomètres.
♦ **to run a marathon** participer à un marathon
2 diriger (*manage*) ◊ *He runs a large company.* Il dirige une grosse société.
3 organiser (*organize*) ◊ *They run music courses in the holidays.* Ils organisent des cours de musique pendant les vacances.
4 couler (*water*) ◊ *Don't leave the tap running.* Ne laisse pas couler le robinet.
♦ **to run a bath** faire couler un bain
5 conduire (*by car*) ◊ *I can run you to the station.* Je peux te conduire à la gare.
♦ **to run away** s'enfuir ◊ *They ran away before the police came.* Ils se sont enfuis avant l'arrivée de la police.
♦ **Time is running out.** Il ne reste plus beaucoup de temps.
♦ **to run out of something** se trouver à court de quelque chose ◊ *We ran out of money.* Nous nous sommes trouvés à court d'argent.
♦ **to run somebody over** écraser quelqu'un
♦ **to get run over** se faire écraser ◊ *Be careful, or you'll get run over!* Fais attention, sinon tu vas te faire écraser!

rung VERB see **ring**

runner NOUN
le coureur
la coureuse

runner beans PL NOUN
les haricots verts MASC PL

runner-up NOUN
le second

la seconde

running NOUN
la course ◊ *Running is my favourite sport.* La course est mon sport préféré.

run-up NOUN
♦**in the run-up to Christmas** pendant la période de préparation de Noël

runway NOUN
la piste

rural ADJECTIVE
rural
(ruraux MASC PL)

rush NOUN
| see also **rush** VERB |
la hâte
♦**in a rush.** à la hâte

to **rush** VERB
| see also **rush** NOUN |
1 se précipiter (*run*) ◊ *Everyone rushed outside.* Tout le monde s'est précipité dehors.
2 se dépêcher (*hurry*) ◊ *There's no need to rush.* Ce n'est pas la peine de se dépêcher.

rush hour NOUN
les heures de pointe FEM PL ◊ *in the*

rush hour aux heures de pointe

rusk NOUN
la biscotte

Russia NOUN
la Russie
♦**in Russia** en Russie
♦**to Russia** en Russie

Russian ADJECTIVE
| see also **Russian** NOUN |
russe

Russian NOUN
| see also **Russian** ADJECTIVE |
1 le/la Russe (*person*)
2 le russe (*language*)

rust NOUN
la rouille

rusty ADJECTIVE
rouillé ◊ *a rusty bike* un vélo rouillé ◊ *My French is very rusty.* Mon français est très rouillé.

ruthless ADJECTIVE
sans pitié

rye NOUN
le seigle
♦**rye bread** le pain de seigle

R

S

Sabbath NOUN
1. le dimanche (*Christian*)
2. le sabbat (*Jewish*)

sack NOUN
see also **sack** VERB
le sac
♦ **to get the sack** être mis à la porte

to **sack** VERB
see also **sack** NOUN
♦ **to sack somebody** mettre quelqu'un à la porte ◊ *He was sacked.* On l'a mis à la porte.

sacred ADJECTIVE
sacré

sacrifice NOUN
le sacrifice

sad ADJECTIVE
triste

saddle NOUN
la selle

saddlebag NOUN
la sacoche

sadly ADVERB
1. tristement ◊ *"She's gone," he said sadly.* "Elle est partie," a-t-il dit tristement.
2. malheureusement (*unfortunately*) ◊ *Sadly, it was too late.* Malheureusement, il était trop tard.

safe NOUN
see also **safe** ADJECTIVE
le coffre-fort
(les coffres-forts PL)
◊ *She put the money in the safe.* Elle a mis l'argent dans le coffre-fort.

safe ADJECTIVE
see also **safe** NOUN
1. sans danger ◊ *Don't worry, it's perfectly safe.* Ne vous inquiétez pas, c'est absolument sans danger.
♦ **Is it safe?** Ça n'est pas dangereux?
2. sûr (*machine, ladder*) ◊ *This car isn't safe.* Cette voiture n'est pas sûre.
3. hors de danger (*out of danger*)
◊ *You're safe now.* Vous êtes hors de danger maintenant.
♦ **to feel safe** se sentir en sécurité
♦ **safe sex** le sexe sans risques

safety NOUN
la sécurité
♦ **a safety belt** une ceinture de sécurité
♦ **a safety pin** une épingle de nourrice

Sagittarius NOUN

le/la Sagittaire ◊ *I'm Sagittarius.* Je suis Sagittaire.

Sahara NOUN
♦ **the Sahara Desert** le Sahara

said VERB *see* **say**

sail NOUN
see also **sail** VERB
la voile

to **sail** VERB
see also **sail** NOUN
1. naviguer (*travel*)
2. prendre la mer (*set off*) ◊ *The boat sails at eight o'clock.* Le bateau prend la mer à huit heures.

sailing NOUN
la voile ◊ *His hobby is sailing.* Son passe-temps, c'est la voile.
♦ **to go sailing** faire de la voile
♦ **a sailing boat** un voilier
♦ **a sailing ship** un grand voilier

sailor NOUN
le marin ◊ *He's a sailor.* Il est marin.

saint NOUN
le saint
la sainte

sake NOUN
♦ **for the sake of** dans l'intérêt de

salad NOUN
la salade
♦ **salad cream** la mayonnaise
♦ **salad dressing** la vinaigrette

salami NOUN
le salami

salary NOUN
le salaire

sale NOUN
les soldes MASC PL (*reductions*)
◊ *There's a sale on at Harrods.* Ce sont les soldes chez Harrods.
♦ **on sale** en vente
♦ **The factory's for sale.** L'usine est en vente.
♦ **"for sale"** "à vendre"

sales assistant NOUN
le vendeur
la vendeuse
◊ *She's a sales assistant.* Elle est vendeuse.

salesman NOUN
1. le représentant (*sales rep*) ◊ *He's a salesman.* Il est représentant.
♦ **a double-glazing salesman** un représentant en doubles vitrages
2. le vendeur (*sales assistant*)

sales rep NOUN
le représentant
la représentante

saleswoman NOUN
[1] la représentante (sales rep)
◊ She's a saleswoman. Elle est représentante.
[2] la vendeuse (sales assistant)

salmon NOUN
le saumon

salon NOUN
le salon ◊ a hair salon un salon de coiffure ◊ a beauty salon un salon de beauté

saloon car NOUN
la berline

salt NOUN
le sel

salty ADJECTIVE
salé

to **salute** VERB
saluer

Salvation Army NOUN
l' armée du Salut FEM

same ADJECTIVE
même ◊ the same model le même modèle ◊ at the same time en même temps
♦They're exactly the same. Ils sont exactement pareils.
♦It's not the same. Ça n'est pas pareil.

sample NOUN
l' échantillon MASC

sand NOUN
le sable

sandal NOUN
la sandale ◊ a pair of sandals une paire de sandales

sand castle NOUN
le château de sable
(les châteaux de sable PL)

sandwich NOUN
le sandwich ◊ a cheese sandwich un sandwich au fromage

sandwich course NOUN
le cours avec stage pratique

sang VERB see **sing**

sanitary napkin NOUN US
la serviette hygiénique

sanitary towel NOUN
la serviette hygiénique

sank VERB see **sink**

Santa Claus NOUN
le père Noël

sarcastic ADJECTIVE
sarcastique

sardine NOUN
la sardine

sat VERB see **sit**

satchel NOUN
le cartable

satellite NOUN
le satellite
♦a satellite dish une antenne parabolique
♦satellite television la télévision par satellite

satisfactory ADJECTIVE
satisfaisant

satisfied ADJECTIVE
satisfait

Saturday NOUN
le samedi ◊ on Saturday samedi ◊ on Saturdays le samedi ◊ every Saturday tous les samedis ◊ last Saturday samedi dernier ◊ next Saturday samedi prochain
♦I've got a Saturday job. Je travaille le samedi.

sauce NOUN
la sauce

saucepan NOUN
la casserole

saucer NOUN
la soucoupe

Saudi Arabia NOUN
l' Arabie Saoudite FEM
♦in Saudi Arabia en Arabie Saoudite

sauna NOUN
le sauna

sausage NOUN
[1] la saucisse
[2] le saucisson (salami)
♦a sausage roll un friand à la saucisse

to **save** VERB
[1] mettre de côté (save up money)
◊ I've saved £50 already. J'ai déjà mis cinquante livres de côté.
[2] économiser (spend less) ◊ I saved £20 by waiting for the sales. J'ai économisé vingt livres en attendant les soldes.
♦to save time gagner du temps ◊ We took a taxi to save time. Nous avons pris un taxi pour gagner du temps. ◊ It saved us time. Ça nous a fait gagner du temps.
[3] sauver (rescue) ◊ Luckily, all the passengers were saved. Heureusement, tous les passagers ont été sauvés.
[4] sauvegarder (on computer) ◊ I saved the file onto a diskette. J'ai sauvegardé le fichier sur disquette.
♦to save up mettre de l'argent de côté ◊ I'm saving up for a new bike. Je

S

☞

mets de l'argent à côté pour un nouveau vélo.

savings PL NOUN
les économies FEM PL ◊ *She spent all her savings on a computer.* Elle a dépensé toutes ses économies en achetant un ordinateur.

savoury ADJECTIVE
salé ◊ *Is it sweet or savoury?* C'est sucré ou salé?

saw VERB *see* **see**

saw NOUN
la scie

sax NOUN
le saxo (*informal*) ◊ *I play the sax.* Je joue du saxo.

saxophone NOUN
le saxophone ◊ *I play the saxophone.* Je joue du saxophone.

to **say** VERB
dire ◊ *What did he say?* Qu'est-ce qu'il a dit? ◊ *Did you hear what she said?* Tu as entendu ce qu'elle a dit?
♦ **Could you say that again?** Pourriez-vous répéter s'il vous plaît?
♦ **That goes without saying.** Cela va sans dire.

saying NOUN
le dicton ◊ *It's just a saying.* C'est juste un dicton.

scale NOUN
1 l' échelle FEM (*of map*) ◊ *a large-scale map* une carte à grande échelle
2 l' ampleur FEM (*size, extent*) ◊ *a disaster on a massive scale* un désastre d'une ampleur incroyable
3 la gamme (*in music*)

scales PL NOUN
la balance SING (*in kitchen, shop*)
♦ **bathroom scales** le pèse-personne SING

scampi PL NOUN
les scampi MASC PL

scandal NOUN
1 le scandale (*outrage*) ◊ *It caused a scandal.* Ça a fait scandale.
2 les ragots MASC PL (*gossip*) ◊ *It's just scandal.* Ce ne sont que des ragots.

Scandinavia NOUN
la Scandinavie
♦ **in Scandinavia** en Scandinavie

Scandinavian ADJECTIVE
scandinave

scar NOUN
la cicatrice

scarce ADJECTIVE
limité ◊ *scarce resources* des ressources limitées

♦ **Jobs are scarce these days.** Il y a peu de travail ces temps-ci.

scarcely ADVERB
à peine ◊ *I scarcely knew him.* Je le connaissais à peine.

scare NOUN
see also **scare** VERB
la panique
♦ **a bomb scare** une alerte à la bombe

to **scare** VERB
see also **scare** NOUN
♦ **to scare somebody** faire peur à quelqu'un ◊ *He scares me.* Il me fait peur.

scarecrow NOUN
l' épouvantail MASC

scared ADJECTIVE
♦ **to be scared** avoir peur ◊ *I was scared stiff.* J'avais terriblement peur.
♦ **to be scared of** avoir peur de ◊ *Are you scared of him?* Est-ce que tu as peur de lui?

scarf NOUN
1 l' écharpe FEM (*long*)
2 le foulard (*square*)

scary ADJECTIVE
effrayant ◊ *It was really scary.* C'était vraiment effrayant.

scene NOUN
1 les lieux MASC PL (*place*) ◊ *The police were soon on the scene.* La police est vite arrivée sur les lieux. ◊ *the scene of the crime* les lieux du crime
2 le spectacle (*event, sight*) ◊ *It was an amazing scene.* C'était un spectacle étonnant.
♦ **to make a scene** faire une scène

scenery NOUN
le paysage (*landscape*)

scent NOUN
le parfum (*perfume*)

schedule NOUN
le programme ◊ *a busy schedule* un programme chargé
♦ **on schedule** comme prévu
♦ **to be behind schedule** avoir du retard

scheduled flight NOUN
le vol régulier

scheme NOUN
1 le truc (*idea*) ◊ *a crazy scheme he dreamed up* un truc farfelu qu'il a inventé
2 le projet (*project*) ◊ *a council road-widening scheme* un projet municipal d'élargissement des routes

scholarship NOUN
la bourse

school NOUN

l' école FEM
+**to go to school** aller à l'école

schoolbook NOUN
le livre scolaire

schoolboy NOUN
l' écolier MASC

schoolchildren PL NOUN
les écoliers MASC PL

schoolgirl NOUN
l' écolière FEM

science NOUN
la science

science fiction NOUN
la science-fiction

scientific ADJECTIVE
scientifique

scientist NOUN
(*doing research*)
le chercheur
la chercheuse
◊ *She's a scientist.* Elle est
chercheuse.
+**He trained as a scientist.** Il a une
formation scientifique.

scissors PL NOUN
les ciseaux MASC PL ◊ *a pair of scissors*
une paire de ciseaux

to **scoff** VERB
bouffer (*eat*) ◊ *My brother scoffed all
the sandwiches.* Mon frère a bouffé
tous les sandwichs.

scone NOUN
le scone

scooter NOUN
1 le scooter
2 la trottinette (*child's toy*)

score NOUN
see also **score** VERB
le score ◊ *The score was three nil.*
Le score était trois à zéro.

to **score** VERB
see also **score** NOUN
1 marquer (*goal, point*) ◊ *to score a
goal* marquer un but
+**to score 6 out of 10** obtenir un score
de six sur dix
2 compter les points (*keep score*)
◊ *Who's going to score?* Qui va
compter les points?

Scorpio NOUN
le Scorpion ◊ *I'm Scorpio.* Je suis
Scorpion.

Scot NOUN
l' Écossais MASC
l' Écossaise FEM

Scotch tape ® NOUN US
le scotch ®

Scotland NOUN

l' Écosse FEM
+**in Scotland** en Écosse
+**to Scotland** en Écosse
+**I'm from Scotland.** Je suis écossais.

Scots ADJECTIVE
écossais ◊ *a Scots accent* un accent
écossais

Scotsman NOUN
l' Écossais MASC

Scotswoman NOUN
l' Écossaise FEM

Scottish ADJECTIVE
écossais ◊ *a Scottish accent* un
accent écossais

scout NOUN
le scout ◊ *I'm in the Scouts.* Je suis
scout.

scrambled eggs PL NOUN
les œufs brouillés MASC PL

scrap NOUN
see also **scrap** VERB
1 le bout ◊ *a scrap of paper* un bout
de papier
2 la bagarre (*fight*)
+**scrap iron** la ferraille

to **scrap** VERB
see also **scrap** NOUN
abandonner (*plan, idea*) ◊ *In the end
the plan was scrapped.* Finalement le
projet a été abandonné.

scrapbook NOUN
l' album MASC

to **scratch** VERB
see also **scratch** NOUN
se gratter ◊ *Stop scratching!* Arrête
de te gratter!

scratch NOUN
see also **scratch** VERB
l' égratignure FEM (*on skin*)
+**to start from scratch** partir de zéro

scream NOUN
see also **scream** VERB
le hurlement

to **scream** VERB
see also **scream** NOUN
hurler

screen NOUN
l' écran MASC

screen-saver NOUN
l' économiseur d'écran MASC

screw NOUN
la vis

screwdriver NOUN
le tournevis

to **scribble** VERB
griffonner

to **scrub** VERB

S

récurer ◊ *to scrub a pan* récurer une casserole

sculpture NOUN
la sculpture

sea NOUN
la mer

seafood NOUN
les fruits de mer MASC PL ◊ *I don't like seafood.* Je n'aime pas les fruits de mer.

seagull NOUN
la mouette

seal NOUN
| see also **seal** VERB |
1 le phoque (*animal*)
2 le cachet (*on letter*)

to **seal** VERB
| see also **seal** NOUN |
1 sceller (*document*)
2 coller (*letter*)

seaman NOUN
le marin

to **search** VERB
| see also **search** NOUN |
fouiller ◊ *They searched the woods for her.* Ils ont fouillé les bois pour la trouver.
♦ **to search for something** chercher quelque chose ◊ *He searched for evidence.* Il cherchait des preuves.

search NOUN
| see also **search** VERB |
la fouille

search engine NOUN
le moteur de recherche

search party NOUN
l' expédition de secours FEM

seashore NOUN
le bord de la mer ◊ *on the seashore* au bord de la mer

seasick ADJECTIVE
♦ **to be seasick** avoir le mal de mer

seaside NOUN
le bord de la mer ◊ *at the seaside* au bord de la mer

season NOUN
la saison ◊ *What's your favourite season?* Quelle est ta saison préférée?
♦ **out of season** hors saison ◊ *It's cheaper to go there out of season.* C'est moins cher d'y aller hors saison.
♦ **during the holiday season** en période de vacances
♦ **a season ticket** une carte d'abonnement

seat NOUN

le siège

seat belt NOUN
la ceinture de sécurité

sea water NOUN
l' eau de mer FEM

seaweed NOUN
les algues FEM PL

second ADJECTIVE
| see also **second** NOUN |
deuxième ◊ *on the second page* à la deuxième page
♦ **to come second** (*in race*) arriver deuxième
♦ **to travel second class** voyager en seconde
♦ **the second of March** le deux mars

second NOUN
| see also **second** ADJECTIVE |
la seconde ◊ *It'll only take a second.* Ça va prendre juste une seconde.

secondary school NOUN
1 le collège
2 le lycée

ⓘ In France pupils go to a **collège** between the ages of 11 and 15, and then to a **lycée** until the age of 18.

second-class ADJECTIVE, ADVERB
1 de seconde classe (*ticket, compartment*)
♦ **to travel second-class** voyager en seconde
2 à tarif réduit (*stamp, letter*) ◊ *to send something second-class* envoyer quelque chose à tarif réduit

secondhand ADJECTIVE
d'occasion ◊ *a secondhand car* une voiture d'occasion

secondly ADVERB
deuxièmement
♦ **firstly ... secondly ...** d'abord ... ensuite ... ◊ *Firstly, it's too expensive. Secondly, it wouldn't work anyway.* D'abord, c'est trop cher. Ensuite, ça ne marcherait quand même pas.

secret ADJECTIVE
| see also **secret** NOUN |
secret MASC
secrète FEM
◊ *a secret mission* une mission secrète

secret NOUN
| see also **secret** ADJECTIVE |
le secret ◊ *It's a secret.* C'est un secret. ◊ *Can you keep a secret?* Tu sais garder un secret?
♦ **in secret** en secret

secretary NOUN

le/la secrétaire ◊ *She's a secretary.*
Elle est secrétaire.

secretly NOUN
secrètement

section NOUN
la section

security NOUN
1 la sécurité ◊ *a feeling of security*
un sentiment de sécurité ◊ *a
campaign to improve airport security*
une campagne visant à améliorer la
sécurité dans les aéroports
◆**job security** la sécurité de l'emploi

security guard NOUN
1 le vigile (*on guard*)
2 le convoyeur de fonds
(*transporting money*)

sedan NOUN US
la berline

to **see** VERB
voir ◊ *I can't see.* Je n'y vois rien. ◊ *I
saw him yesterday.* Je l'ai vu hier.
◊ *Have you seen him?* Est-ce que tu
l'as vu?
◆**See you!** Salut!
◆**See you soon!** À bientôt!
◆**to see to something** s'occuper de
quelque chose ◊ *The window's stuck
again. Can you see to it please?* La
fenêtre est encore coincée. Tu peux
t'en occuper s'il te plaît?

seed NOUN
la graine ◊ *sunflower seeds* des
graines de tournesol

to **seek** VERB
chercher
◆**to seek help** chercher de l'aide

to **seem** VERB
avoir l'air ◊ *She seems tired.* Elle a
l'air fatiguée. ◊ *The shop seemed to
be closed.* Le magasin avait l'air
d'être fermé.
◆**That seems like a good idea.** Ce n'est
pas une mauvaise idée.
◆**It seems that ...** Il paraît que ... ◊ *It
seems she's getting married.* Il paraît
qu'elle va se marier.
◆**There seems to be a problem.** Il
semble y avoir un problème.

seen VERB *see* **see**

seesaw NOUN
le tapecul

see-through ADJECTIVE
transparent

seldom ADVERB
rarement

to **select** VERB
sélectionner

selection NOUN

la sélection

self-assured ADJECTIVE
sûr de soi ◊ *He's very self-assured.* Il
est très sûr de lui.

self-catering ADJECTIVE
◆**a self-catering apartment** un
appartement de vacances

self-centred ADJECTIVE (US **self-centered**)
égocentrique

self-confidence NOUN
la confiance en soi ◊ *He hasn't got
much self-confidence.* Il n'a pas très
confiance en lui.

self-conscious ADJECTIVE
◆**to be self-conscious (1)** (*embarrassed*)
être mal à l'aise ◊ *She was really
self-conscious at first.* Elle était
vraiment mal à l'aise au début.
◆**to be self-conscious (2)** (*shy*) manquer
d'assurance ◊ *He's always been
rather self-conscious.* Il a toujours
manqué un peu d'assurance.

self-contained ADJECTIVE
◆**a self-contained flat** un appartement
indépendant

self-control NOUN
le sang-froid

self-defence NOUN (US *self-defence*)
l'autodéfense FEM ◊ *self-defence
classes* les cours d'autodéfense
◆**She killed him in self-defence.** Elle l'a
tué en légitime défense.

self-discipline NOUN
l'autodiscipline FEM

self-disciplined ADJECTIVE
◆**he is self-disciplined** il fait preuve
d'autodiscipline

self-employed ADJECTIVE
◆**to be self-employed** travailler à son
compte ◊ *He's self-employed.* Il
travaille à son compte.
◆**the self-employed** les travailleurs
indépendants MASC PL

selfish ADJECTIVE
égoïste ◊ *Don't be so selfish.* Ne sois
pas si égoïste.

self-respect NOUN
l'amour-propre MASC

self-service ADJECTIVE
◆**It's self-service.** (*café, shop*) C'est un
self-service.
◆**a self-service restaurant** un restaurant
self-service

to **sell** VERB
vendre ◊ *He sold it to me.* Il me l'a
vendu.

sell off VERB
liquider

S

to **sell out** VERB
se vendre ◊ *The tickets sold out in three hours.* Les billets se sont tous vendus en trois heures. ◊ *The show didn't quite sell out.* Ce spectacle ne s'est pas très bien vendu.
♦ **The tickets are all sold out.** Il ne reste plus de billets.

to **sell-by date** NOUN
la date limite de vente

selling price NOUN
le prix de vente

Sellotape ® NOUN
le scotch ®

semi NOUN
la maison jumelée ◊ *We live in a semi.* Nous habitons dans une maison jumelée.

semicircle NOUN
le demi-cercle

semicolon NOUN
le point-virgule

semi-detached house NOUN
la maison jumelée ◊ *We live in a semi-detached house.* Nous habitons dans une maison jumelée.

semi-final NOUN
la demi-finale

semi-skimmed milk NOUN
le lait demi-écrémé

to **send** VERB
envoyer ◊ *She sent me a birthday card.* Elle m'a envoyé une carte d'anniversaire.
♦ **to send back** renvoyer
♦ **to send off (1)** (*goods, letter*) envoyer
♦ **to send off (2)** (*in sports match*) renvoyer du terrain ◊ *He was sent off.* On l'a renvoyé du terrain.
♦ **to send off for something (1)** (*free*) se faire envoyer quelque chose ◊ *I've sent off for a brochure.* Je me suis fait envoyer une brochure.
♦ **to send off for something (2)** (*paid for*) commander quelque chose par correspondance ◊ *She sent off for a book.* Elle a commandé un livre par correspondance.
♦ **to send out** envoyer
♦ **to send out for** commander par téléphone ◊ *Shall we send out for a pizza?* Et si on commandait une pizza par téléphone?

sender NOUN
l' expéditeur MASC
l' expéditrice FEM

senior ADJECTIVE
haut placé

♦ **senior management** les cadres supérieurs MASC PL
♦ **senior school** le lycée
♦ **senior pupils** les grandes classes FEM PL

senior citizen NOUN
la personne du troisième âge
(les personnes du troisième âge PL)

sensational ADJECTIVE
sensationnel MASC
sensationnelle FEM

sense NOUN
1 le bon sens (*wisdom*) ◊ *Use your common sense!* Un peu de bon sens, voyons!
♦ **It makes sense.** C'est logique.
♦ **It doesn't make sense.** Ça n'a pas de sens.
2 le sens (*faculty*) ◊ *the five senses* les cinq sens
♦ **the sense of touch** le toucher
♦ **the sense of smell** l'odorat MASC
♦ **the sixth sense** le sixième sens
♦ **sense of humour** le sens de l'humour ◊ *He's got no sense of humour.* Il n'a aucun sens de l'humour.

senseless ADJECTIVE
insensé

sensible ADJECTIVE
raisonnable ◊ *Be sensible!* Sois raisonnable!
*Be careful not to translate **sensible** by the French word **sensible**.*

sensitive ADJECTIVE
sensible ◊ *She's very sensitive.* Elle est très sensible.

sensuous ADJECTIVE
sensuel MASC
sensuelle FEM

sent VERB *see* **send**

sentence NOUN
see also **sentence** VERB
1 la phrase ◊ *What does this sentence mean?* Que veut dire cette phrase?
2 la condamnation (*judgment*)
3 la peine (*punishment*) ◊ *the death sentence* la peine de mort
♦ **He got a life sentence.** Il a été condamné à la réclusion à perpétuité.

to **sentence** VERB
see also **sentence** NOUN
♦ **to sentence somebody to life imprisonment** condamner quelqu'un à la réclusion à perpétuité
♦ **to sentence somebody to death** condamner quelqu'un à mort

sentimental ADJECTIVE
sentimental
(sentimentaux MASC PL)

separate ADJECTIVE

see also **separate** VERB

séparé ◊ *I wrote it on a separate sheet.* Je l'ai écrit sur une feuille séparée.

♦ **The children have separate rooms.** Les enfants ont chacun leur chambre.

♦ **on separate occasions** à différentes reprises

to **separate** VERB

see also **separate** ADJECTIVE

1 séparer
2 se séparer (*married couple*)

separately ADVERB
séparément

separation NOUN
la séparation

September NOUN
septembre MASC
♦ **in September** en septembre

sequel NOUN
la suite (*book, film*)

sequence NOUN
1 l' ordre MASC
♦ **in sequence** par ordre
♦ **a sequence of events** une succession d'événements
2 la séquence (*in film*)

sergeant NOUN
1 le sergent (*army*)
2 le brigadier (*police*)

serial NOUN
le feuilleton

series NOUN
1 la série ◊ *a TV series* une série télévisée
2 la suite (*of numbers*)

serious ADJECTIVE
1 sérieux MASC
sérieuse FEM
◊ *You look very serious.* Tu as l'air sérieux.
♦ **Are you serious?** Sérieusement?
2 (*illness, mistake*)
grave

seriously ADVERB
sérieusement ◊ *No, but seriously ...* Non, mais sérieusement ...
♦ **to take somebody seriously** prendre quelqu'un au sérieux
♦ **seriously injured** gravement blessé
♦ **Seriously?** Vraiment?

sermon NOUN
le sermon

servant NOUN
le/la domestique

to **serve** VERB

see also **serve** NOUN

1 servir ◊ *Dinner is served.* Le dîner est servi. ◊ *It's Agassi's turn to serve.* C'est à Agassi de servir.
2 purger (*prison sentence*)
♦ **to serve time** être en prison
♦ **It serves you right.** C'est bien fait pour toi.

serve NOUN

see also **serve** VERB

le service (*tennis*)
♦ **It's your serve.** C'est à toi de servir.

server NOUN
le serveur (*computing*)

to **service** VERB

see also **service** NOUN

réviser (*car, washing machine*)

service NOUN

see also **service** VERB

1 le service ◊ *Service is included.* Le service est compris.
2 la révision (*of car*)
3 l' office MASC (*church service*)
♦ **the Fire Service** les sapeurs-pompiers MASC PL
♦ **the armed services** les forces armées FEM

service area NOUN
l' aire de service FEM

service charge NOUN
le service ◊ *There's no service charge.* Le service est compris.

serviceman NOUN
le militaire ◊ *He's a serviceman.* Il est militaire.

service station NOUN
la station-service
(les stations-service PL)

serviette NOUN
la serviette

session NOUN
la séance

set NOUN

see also **set** VERB

1 le jeu
(les jeux PL)
◊ *a set of keys* un jeu de clés ◊ *a chess set* un jeu d'échecs
♦ **a train set** un train électrique
2 (*in tennis*)
le set

to **set** VERB

see also **set** NOUN

1 mettre à sonner (*alarm clock*) ◊ *I set the alarm for 7 o'clock.* J'ai mis le réveil à sept heures.
2 établir (*record*) ◊ *The world record was set last year.* Le record du monde a été établi l'année dernière.

S

☞

3 se coucher (sun) ◊ *The sun was setting.* Le soleil se couchait.
- **The film is set in Morocco.** L'action du film se déroule au Maroc.
- **to set off** partir ◊ *We set off for London at 9 o'clock.* Nous sommes partis pour Londres à neuf heures.
- **to set out** partir ◊ *We set out for London at 9 o'clock.* Nous sommes partis pour Londres à neuf heures.
- **to set sail** prendre la mer
- **to set the table** mettre le couvert

settee NOUN
le canapé

to **settle** VERB
1 résoudre (*problem*)
2 régler (*argument, account*)
- **to settle down** (*calm down*) se calmer
- **Settle down!** Du calme!
- **to settle in** s'installer
- **to settle on something** opter pour quelque chose

seven NUMBER
sept ◊ *She's seven.* Elle a sept ans.

seventeen NUMBER
dix-sept ◊ *He's seventeen.* Il a dix-sept ans.

seventeenth ADJECTIVE
dix-septième ◊ *her seventeenth birthday* son dix-septième anniversaire ◊ *the seventeenth floor* le dix-septième étage
- **the seventeenth of August** le dix-sept août

seventh ADJECTIVE
septième ◊ *the seventh floor* le septième étage
- **the seventh of August** le sept août

seventy NUMBER
soixante-dix

several ADJECTIVE, PRONOUN
plusieurs ◊ *several schools* plusieurs écoles
- **several of them** plusieurs ◊ *I've seen several of them.* J'en ai vu plusieurs.

to **sew** VERB
coudre
- **to sew up** (*tear*) recoudre

sewing NOUN
la couture ◊ *I like sewing.* J'aime faire de la couture.
- **a sewing machine** une machine à coudre

sewn VERB see **sew**

sex NOUN
le sexe
- **to have sex with somebody** coucher avec quelqu'un
- **sex education** l'éducation sexuelle FEM

sexism NOUN
le sexisme

sexist ADJECTIVE
sexiste

sexual ADJECTIVE
sexuel MASC
sexuelle FEM
◊ *sexual discrimination* la discrimination sexuelle ◊ *sexual harassment* le harcèlement sexuel

sexuality NOUN
la sexualité

sexy ADJECTIVE
sexy MASC, FEM, PL

shabby ADJECTIVE
miteux MASC
miteuse FEM

shade NOUN
1 l' ombre FEM
- **in the shade** à l'ombre ◊ *It was 35 degrees in the shade.* Il faisait trente-cinq à l'ombre.
2 la nuance (*colour*) ◊ *a shade of blue* une nuance de bleu

shadow NOUN
l' ombre FEM

to **shake** VERB
1 secouer ◊ *She shook the rug.* Elle a secoué le tapis.
2 trembler (*tremble*) ◊ *He was shaking with cold.* Il tremblait de froid.
- **to shake one's head** (*in refusal*) faire non de la tête
- **to shake hands with somebody** serrer la main à quelqu'un ◊ *They shook hands.* Ils se sont serré la main.

shaken ADJECTIVE
secoué ◊ *I was feeling a bit shaken.* J'étais un peu secoué.

shaky ADJECTIVE
tremblant (*hand, voice*)

shall VERB
- **Shall I shut the window?** Vous voulez que je ferme la fenêtre?
- **Shall we ask him to come with us?** Si on lui demandait de venir avec nous?

shallow ADJECTIVE
peu profond (*water, pool*)

shambles NOUN
la pagaille ◊ *It's a complete shambles.* C'est la pagaille complète.

shame NOUN
la honte ◊ *The shame of it!* Quelle honte!
- **What a shame!** Quel dommage!
- **It's a shame that ...** c'est dommage que ...

c'est dommage que has to be
followed by a verb in the
subjunctive.
◊ *It's a shame he isn't here.* C'est
dommage qu'il ne soit pas ici.

shampoo NOUN
le shampooing ◊ *a bottle of*
shampoo une bouteille de
shampooing

shandy NOUN
le panaché

shan't = shall not

shape NOUN
la forme

share NOUN
see also **share** VERB
1 l' action FEM (*in company*) ◊ *They've*
got shares in British Gas. Ils ont des
actions de British Gas.
2 la part ◊ *Everybody pays their*
share. Tout le monde paie sa part.

to **share** VERB
see also **share** NOUN
partager ◊ *to share a room with*
somebody partager une chambre
avec quelqu'un
♦ **to share out** distribuer ◊ *They shared*
the sweets out among the children.
Ils ont distribué les bonbons aux
enfants.

shark NOUN
le requin

sharp ADJECTIVE
1 tranchant (*razor, knife*)
2 pointu (*spike, point*)
3 intelligent (*clever*) ◊ *She's very*
sharp. Elle est très intelligente.
♦ **at two o'clock sharp** à deux heures
pile

to **shave** VERB
se raser (*have a shave*)
♦ **to shave one's legs** se raser les
jambes

shaver NOUN
♦ **an electric shaver** un rasoir électrique

shaving cream NOUN
la crème à raser

shaving foam NOUN
la mousse à raser

she PRONOUN
elle ◊ *She's very nice.* Elle est très
gentille.

shed NOUN
la remise

she'd = she had, = she would

sheep NOUN
le mouton

sheepdog NOUN

le chien de berger
(les chiens de berger PL)

sheer ADJECTIVE
pur ◊ *It's sheer greed.* C'est de
l'avidité pure.

sheet NOUN
le drap (*on bed*)
♦ **a sheet of paper** une feuille de papier

shelf NOUN
1 l' étagère FEM (*in house*)
2 le rayon (*in shop*)

shell NOUN
1 le coquillage (*on beach*)
2 la coquille (*of egg, nut*)
3 l' obus MASC (*explosive*)

she'll = she will

shellfish NOUN
les fruits de mer MASC PL

shell suit NOUN
le survêtement

shelter NOUN
♦ **to take shelter** se mettre à l'abri
♦ **a bus shelter** un arrêt d'autobus

shelves PL NOUN see **shelf**

shepherd NOUN
le berger

sheriff NOUN
le shérif

sherry NOUN
le xérès

she's = she is, = she has

Shetland Islands PL NOUN
les îles Shetland FEM PL

shield NOUN
le bouclier

shift NOUN
see also **shift** VERB
le service ◊ *His shift starts at 8*
o'clock. Il prend son service à huit
heures. ◊ *the night shift* le service de
nuit
♦ **to do shift work** faire les trois-huit

to **shift** VERB
see also **shift** NOUN
déplacer (*move*) ◊ *I couldn't shift the*
wardrobe on my own. Je n'ai pas pu
déplacer l'armoire tout seul.
♦ **Shift yourself!** Pousse-toi de là!
(*informal*)

shifty ADJECTIVE
1 louche (*person*) ◊ *He looked shifty.*
Il avait l'air louche.
2 fuyant (*eyes*)

shin NOUN
le tibia

to **shine** VERB
briller ◊ *The sun was shining.* Le
soleil brillait.

S

shiny ADJECTIVE
brillant

ship NOUN
[1] le bateau
(les bateaux PL)
[2] (warship)
le navire

shipbuilding NOUN
la construction navale

shipwreck NOUN
le naufrage

shipwrecked ADJECTIVE
♦ to be shipwrecked faire naufrage

shipyard NOUN
le chantier naval

shirt NOUN
[1] la chemise (man's)
[2] le chemisier (woman's)

shit EXCLAMATION
Merde! (rude)

to **shiver** VERB
frissonner

shock NOUN
see also **shock** VERB
le choc
♦ to get a shock (1) (surprise) avoir un choc
♦ to get a shock (2) (electric) recevoir une décharge
♦ an electric shock une décharge

to **shock** VERB
see also **shock** NOUN
[1] bouleverser (upset) ◊ They were shocked by the tragedy. Ils ont été bouleversés par la tragédie.
[2] choquer (scandalize) ◊ I was rather shocked by her attitude. J'ai été assez choqué par son attitude.

shocked ADJECTIVE
choqué ◊ He'll be shocked if you say that. Tu vas le choquer si tu dis ça.

shocking ADJECTIVE
choquant ◊ It's shocking! C'est choquant!
♦ a shocking waste un gaspillage épouvantable

shoe NOUN
la chaussure

shoelace NOUN
le lacet

shoe polish NOUN
le cirage

shoe shop NOUN
le magasin de chaussures

shone VERB see **shine**

shook VERB see **shake**

to **shoot** VERB

[1] abattre (kill) ◊ He was shot by a sniper. Il a été abattu par un franc-tireur.
[2] fusiller (execute) ◊ He was shot at dawn. Il a été fusillé à l'aube.
[3] tirer (gun) ◊ Don't shoot! Ne tirez pas!
♦ to shoot at somebody tirer sur quelqu'un
♦ He shot himself with a revolver. (dead) Il s'est suicidé d'un coup de revolver.
♦ He was shot in the leg. (wounded) Il a reçu une balle dans la jambe.
♦ to shoot an arrow envoyer une flèche
[4] tourner (film) ◊ The film was shot in Prague. Le film a été tourné à Prague.
[5] shooter (in football)

shooting NOUN
[1] les coups de feu MASC PL ◊ They heard shooting. Ils ont entendu des coups de feu.
♦ a shooting une fusillade
[2] la chasse (hunting) ◊ to go shooting aller à la chasse

shop NOUN
le magasin ◊ a sports shop un magasin de sports

shop assistant NOUN
le vendeur
la vendeuse
◊ She's a shop assistant. Elle est vendeuse.

shopkeeper NOUN
le commerçant
la commerçante
◊ He's a shopkeeper. Il est commerçant.

shoplifting NOUN
le vol à l'étalage

shopping NOUN
les courses FEM PL (purchases) ◊ Can you get the shopping from the car? Tu peux aller chercher les courses dans la voiture?
♦ I love shopping. J'adore faire du shopping.
♦ to go shopping (1) (for food) faire des courses
♦ to go shopping (2) (for pleasure) faire du shopping
♦ a shopping bag un sac à provisions
♦ a shopping centre un centre commercial

shop window NOUN
la vitrine

shore NOUN
le rivage
♦ on shore à terre

short ADJECTIVE

[1] <u>court</u> ◊ *a short skirt* une jupe
courte ◊ *short hair* les cheveux courts

♦**too short** trop court ◊ *It was a great
holiday, but too short.* C'étaient des
vacances super, mais trop courtes.

[2] <u>petit</u> (*person, period of time*) ◊ *She's
quite short.* Elle est assez petite. ◊ *a
short break* une petite pause ◊ *a
short walk* une petite promenade

♦**to be short of something** être à court
de quelque chose ◊ *I'm short of
money.* Je suis à court d'argent.

♦**at short notice** au dernier moment

♦**In short, the answer's no.** Bref, la
réponse est non.

shortage NOUN
la <u>pénurie</u> ◊ *a water shortage* une
pénurie d'eau

short cut NOUN
le <u>raccourci</u> ◊ *I took a short cut.* J'ai
pris un raccourci.

shorthand NOUN
la <u>sténo</u>

shortly ADVERB
<u>bientôt</u>

shorts PL NOUN
le <u>short</u> SING

♦**a pair of shorts** un short

short-sighted ADJECTIVE
<u>myope</u>

short story NOUN
la <u>nouvelle</u>

shot VERB *see* **shoot**

shot NOUN

[1] (*gunshot*)
le <u>coup de feu</u>
(les coups de feu PL)

[2] (*photo*)
la <u>photo</u> ◊ *a shot of Edinburgh
Castle* une photo du château
d'Édimbourg

[3] (*vaccination*)
le <u>vaccin</u>

shotgun NOUN
le <u>fusil de chasse</u>
(les fusils de chasse PL)

should VERB

*When **should** means "ought to", use
devoir.*

<u>devoir</u> ◊ *You should take more
exercise.* Vous devriez faire plus
d'exercice. ◊ *He should be there by
now.* Il devrait être arrivé maintenant.
◊ *That shouldn't be too hard.* Ça ne
devrait pas être trop difficile.

♦**should have** avoir dû ◊ *I should have
told you before.* J'aurais dû te le dire
avant.

*When **should** means "would", use
the conditional tense.*

♦**I should go if I were you.** Si j'étais
vous, j'irais.

♦**I should be so lucky!** Ça serait trop
beau!

shoulder NOUN
l' <u>épaule</u> FEM

♦**a shoulder bag** un sac à bandoulière

shouldn't = **should not**

to **shout** VERB

see also **shout** NOUN

<u>crier</u> ◊ *Don't shout!* Ne criez pas!
◊ *"Go away!" he shouted.* "Allez-
vous-en!" a-t-il crié.

shout NOUN

see also **shout** VERB

le <u>cri</u>

shovel NOUN
la <u>pelle</u>

show NOUN

see also **show** VERB

[1] le <u>spectacle</u> (*performance*)
[2] l' <u>émission</u> FEM (*programme*)
[3] le <u>salon</u> (*exhibition*)

to **show** VERB

see also **show** NOUN

[1] <u>montrer</u>

♦**to show somebody something**
montrer quelque chose à quelqu'un
◊ *Have I shown you my new trainers?*
Je t'ai montré mes nouvelles
baskets?

[2] <u>faire preuve de</u> ◊ *She showed
great courage.* Elle a fait preuve de
beaucoup de courage.

♦**It shows.** Ça se voit. ◊ *I've never
been riding before. – It shows.* Je n'ai
jamais fait de cheval. – Ça se voit.

♦**to show off** frimer (*informal*)

♦**to show up** (*turn up*) se pointer ◊ *He
showed up late as usual.* Il s'est
pointé en retard comme d'habitude.

shower NOUN

[1] la <u>douche</u>

♦**to have a shower** prendre une
douche

[2] l' <u>averse</u> FEM (*of rain*)

showerproof ADJECTIVE
<u>imperméabilisé</u>

showing NOUN
la <u>projection</u> (*of film*)

shown VERB *see* **show**

show-off NOUN
le <u>frimeur</u>
la <u>frimeuse</u>

shrank VERB *see* **shrink**

to **shriek** VERB
<u>hurler</u>

S

shrimps PL NOUN
les crevettes FEM PL

to **shrink** VERB
rétrécir (clothes, fabric)

Shrove Tuesday NOUN
le mardi gras

to **shrug** VERB
♦ **to shrug one's shoulders** hausser les épaules

shrunk VERB see **shrink**

to **shudder** VERB
frissonner

to **shuffle** VERB
♦ **to shuffle the cards** battre les cartes

to **shut** VERB
fermer ◊ What time do you shut? À quelle heure est-ce que vous fermez? ◊ What time do the shops shut? À quelle heure est-ce que les magasins ferment?
♦ **to shut down** fermer ◊ The cinema shut down last year. Le cinéma a fermé l'année dernière.
♦ **to shut up (1)** (close) fermer
♦ **to shut up (2)** (be quiet) se taire ◊ Shut up! Tais-toi!

shutters PL NOUN
les volets MASC PL

shuttle NOUN
la navette

shuttlecock NOUN
le volant (badminton)

shy ADJECTIVE
timide

Sicily NOUN
la Sicile
♦ **in Sicily** en Sicile
♦ **to Sicily** en Sicile

sick ADJECTIVE
1 malade (ill) ◊ He was sick for four days. Il a été malade pendant quatre jours.
2 de mauvais goût (joke, humour) ◊ That's really sick! C'est vraiment de mauvais goût!
♦ **to be sick** (vomit) vomir ◊ I feel sick. J'ai envie de vomir.
♦ **to be sick of something** en avoir assez de quelque chose ◊ I'm sick of your jokes. J'en ai assez de tes plaisanteries.

sickening ADJECTIVE
écœurant

sick leave NOUN
le congé de maladie

sickness NOUN
la maladie

sick note NOUN

1 le mot d'absence (from parents)
2 le certificat médical (from doctor)

sick pay NOUN
l' indemnité de maladie FEM

side NOUN
1 le côté (of object, building, car) ◊ He was driving on the wrong side of the road. Il roulait du mauvais côté de la route.
2 le bord (of pool, river, road) ◊ by the side of the lake au bord du lac
3 le flanc (of hill)
4 l' équipe FEM (team)
♦ **He's on my side. (1)** (on my team) Il est dans mon équipe.
♦ **He's on my side. (2)** (supporting me) Il est de mon côté.
♦ **side by side** côte à côte
♦ **the side entrance** l'entrée latérale
♦ **to take sides** prendre parti ◊ She always takes his side. Elle prend toujours son parti.

sideboard NOUN
le buffet

side-effect NOUN
l' effet secondaire MASC

side street NOUN
la petite rue transversale

sidewalk NOUN US
le trottoir

sideways ADVERB
1 de côté (look, be facing)
2 de travers (move)
♦ **sideways on** de profil

sieve NOUN
la passoire

sigh NOUN
see also **sigh** VERB
le soupir

to **sigh** VERB
see also **sigh** NOUN
soupirer

sight NOUN
1 la vue ◊ to have poor sight avoir une mauvaise vue
♦ **to know somebody by sight** connaître quelqu'un de vue
2 le spectacle ◊ It was an amazing sight. C'était un spectacle étonnant.
♦ **in sight** visible
♦ **out of sight** hors de vue
♦ **the sights** (tourist spots) les attractions touristiques FEM
♦ **to see the sights of London** visiter Londres

sightseeing NOUN
le tourisme
♦ **to go sightseeing** faire du tourisme

sign NOUN

see also **sign** VERB

1 (*notice*)

le panneau

(les panneaux PL)

◊ *There was a big sign saying "private".* Il y avait un grand panneau indiquant "privé".

♦ **a road sign** un panneau

2 (*gesture, indication*)

le signe ◊ *There's no sign of improvement.* Il n'y a aucun signe d'amélioration.

♦ **What sign are you?** (*star sign*) Tu es de quel signe?

to **sign** VERB

see also **sign** NOUN

signer

♦ **to sign on (1)** (*as unemployed*) s'inscrire au chômage

♦ **to sign on (2)** (*for course*) s'inscrire

signal NOUN

see also **signal** VERB

le signal

(les signaux PL)

to **signal** VERB

see also **signal** NOUN

♦ **to signal to somebody** faire un signe à quelqu'un

signalman NOUN

l' aiguilleur MASC

signature NOUN

la signature

significance NOUN

l' importance FEM

significant ADJECTIVE

important

sign language NOUN

le langage par signes

signpost NOUN

le poteau indicateur

silence NOUN

le silence

silencer NOUN

le silencieux

silent ADJECTIVE

silencieux MASC

silencieuse FEM

silicon chip NOUN

la puce électronique

silk NOUN

see also **silk** ADJECTIVE

la soie

silk ADJECTIVE

see also **silk** NOUN

en soie ◊ *a silk scarf* un foulard en soie

silky ADJECTIVE

soyeux MASC

soyeuse FEM

silly ADJECTIVE

bête

silver NOUN

l' argent MASC ◊ *a silver medal* une médaille d'argent

similar ADJECTIVE

semblable

♦ **similar to** semblable à

simple ADJECTIVE

1 simple ◊ *It's very simple.* C'est très simple.

2 (*simple-minded*)

simplet MASC

simplette FEM

◊ *He's a bit simple.* Il est un peu simplet.

simply ADVERB

simplement ◊ *It's simply not possible.* Ça n'est tout simplement pas possible.

simultaneous ADJECTIVE

simultané

sin NOUN

see also **sin** VERB

le péché

to **sin** VERB

see also **sin** NOUN

pécher

since PREPOSITION, ADVERB, CONJUNCTION

1 depuis ◊ *since Christmas* depuis Noël ◊ *since then* depuis ce moment-là ◊ *I haven't seen him since.* Je ne l'ai pas vu depuis.

♦ **ever since** depuis ce moment-là

2 depuis que ◊ *I haven't seen her since she left.* Je ne l'ai pas vue depuis qu'elle est partie.

3 puisque (*because*) ◊ *Since you're tired, let's stay at home.* Puisque tu es fatigué, restons à la maison.

sincere ADJECTIVE

sincère

sincerely ADVERB

♦ **Yours sincerely ... (1)** (*in business letter*) Veuillez agréer l'expression de mes sentiments les meilleurs ...

♦ **Yours sincerely ... (2)** (*in personal letter*) Cordialement ...

to **sing** VERB

chanter ◊ *He sang out of tune.* Il chantait faux. ◊ *Have you ever sung this tune before?* Vous avez déjà chanté cet air-là?

singer NOUN

le chanteur

la chanteuse

singing NOUN

le chant

S

single ADJECTIVE

see also **single** NOUN

célibataire (*unmarried*)

♦ **a single room** une chambre pour une personne

♦ **not a single thing** rien du tout

single NOUN

see also **single** ADJECTIVE

1 l' aller simple MASC (*ticket*) ◊ *A single to Toulouse, please.* Un aller simple pour Toulouse, s'il vous plaît.

2 le 45 tours (*record*)

♦ **a CD single** un CD single

single parent NOUN

♦ **She's a single parent.** Elle élève ses enfants toute seule.

♦ **a single parent family** une famille monoparentale

singles PL NOUN

le simple SING (*in tennis*) ◊ *the women's singles* le simple dames

singular NOUN

le singulier ◊ *in the singular* au singulier

sinister ADJECTIVE

sinistre

sink NOUN

see also **sink** VERB

l' évier MASC

to **sink** VERB

see also **sink** NOUN

couler

sir NOUN

monsieur MASC

♦ **Yes sir.** Oui, Monsieur.

siren NOUN

la sirène

sister NOUN

1 la sœur ◊ *my little sister* ma petite sœur

2 l' infirmière en chef FEM (*nurse*)

sister-in-law NOUN

la belle-sœur

(les belles-sœurs PL)

to **sit** VERB

s'asseoir

♦ **to sit on something** s'asseoir sur quelque chose ◊ *She sat on the chair.* Elle s'est assise sur la chaise.

♦ **to sit down** s'asseoir

♦ **to be sitting** être assis

♦ **to sit an exam** passer un examen

sitcom NOUN

la comédie de situation

(les comédies de situation PL)

site NOUN

1 le site ◊ *an archaeological site* un site archéologique

♦ **the site of the accident** le lieu de l'accident

2 le camping (*campsite*)

♦ **a building site** un chantier

sitting room NOUN

le salon

situated ADJECTIVE

♦ **to be situated** être situé ◊ *The village is situated on the side of a hill.* Le village est situé sur le flanc d'une colline.

situation NOUN

la situation

six NUMBER

six ◊ *He's six.* Il a six ans.

sixteen NUMBER

seize ◊ *He's sixteen.* Il a seize ans.

sixteenth ADJECTIVE

seizième ◊ *her sixteenth birthday* son seizième anniversaire ◊ *the sixteenth floor* le seizième étage

♦ **the sixteenth of August** le seize août

sixth ADJECTIVE

sixième ◊ *the sixth floor* le sixième étage

♦ **the sixth of August** le six août

sixty NUMBER

soixante

size NOUN

> ℹ *France uses the European system to show clothing and shoe sizes.*

1 la taille (*of object, clothing*) ◊ *What size do you take?* Quelle taille est-ce que vous faites?

♦ **I'm a size ten.** Je fais du trente-huit.

2 la pointure (*of shoes*)

♦ **I take size six.** Je fais du trente-neuf.

to **skate** VERB

1 faire du patin à glace (*ice-skate*)

2 faire du patin à roulettes (*roller-skate*)

skateboard NOUN

le skateboard

skateboarding NOUN

le skateboard ◊ *to go skateboarding* faire du skateboard

skates PL NOUN

les patins MASC PL

skating NOUN

le patin à glace ◊ *to go skating* faire du patin à glace

♦ **a skating rink** une patinoire

skeleton NOUN

le squelette

sketch NOUN

see also **sketch** VERB

le <u>croquis</u> (*drawing*)

to **sketch** VERB
| *see also* **sketch** NOUN |
♦ **to sketch something** faire un croquis de quelque chose

ski NOUN
| *see also* **ski** VERB |
le <u>ski</u>
♦ **ski boots** les chaussures de ski FEM
♦ **a ski lift** un remonte-pente
♦ **ski pants** le fuseau SING
♦ **a ski pole** un bâton de ski
♦ **a ski slope** une piste de ski
♦ **a ski suit** une combinaison de ski

to **ski** VERB
| *see also* **ski** NOUN |
<u>skier</u> ◊ *Can you ski?* Tu sais skier?

to **skid** VERB
<u>déraper</u>

skier NOUN
le <u>skieur</u>
la <u>skieuse</u>

skiing NOUN
le <u>ski</u> ◊ *to go skiing* faire du ski
♦ **to go on a skiing holiday** aller aux sports d'hiver

skilful ADJECTIVE
<u>adroit</u>

skill NOUN
le <u>talent</u> ◊ *He played with great skill.* Il a joué avec beaucoup de talent.

skilled ADJECTIVE
♦ **a skilled worker** un ouvrier spécialisé

skimmed milk NOUN
le <u>lait écrémé</u>

skimpy ADJECTIVE
① <u>minuscule</u> (*clothes*)
② <u>maigre</u> (*meal*)

skin NOUN
la <u>peau</u>
(les peaux PL)
♦ **skin cancer** le cancer de la peau

skinhead NOUN
le/la <u>skinhead</u>

skinny ADJECTIVE
<u>maigre</u>

skin-tight ADJECTIVE
<u>collant</u>

skip NOUN
| *see also* **skip** VERB |
la <u>benne</u> (*container*)

to **skip** VERB
| *see also* **skip** NOUN |
<u>sauter</u> ◊ *to skip a meal* sauter un repas
♦ **to skip a lesson** sécher un cours

skirt NOUN
la <u>jupe</u>

skittles NOUN
les <u>quilles</u> FEM PL ◊ *to play skittles* jouer aux quilles

to **skive** VERB
<u>tirer au flanc</u> (*be lazy*)
♦ **to skive off** sécher (*informal*) ◊ *to skive off school* sécher les cours

skull NOUN
le <u>crâne</u>

sky NOUN
le <u>ciel</u>

skyscraper NOUN
le <u>gratte-ciel</u>
(les gratte-ciel PL)

slack ADJECTIVE
① <u>lâche</u> (*rope*)
② <u>négligent</u> (*person*)

to **slag off** VERB
♦ **to slag somebody off** dire du mal de quelqu'un

to **slam** VERB
<u>claquer</u> ◊ *The door slammed.* La porte a claqué. ◊ *She slammed the door.* Elle a claqué la porte.

slang NOUN
l' <u>argot</u> MASC

slap NOUN
| *see also* **slap** VERB |
la <u>claque</u>

to **slap** VERB
| *see also* **slap** NOUN |
♦ **to slap somebody** donner une claque à quelqu'un

slate NOUN
l' <u>ardoise</u> FEM

sledge NOUN
la <u>luge</u>

sledging NOUN
♦ **to go sledging** faire de la luge

sleep NOUN
| *see also* **sleep** VERB |
le <u>sommeil</u>
♦ **I need some sleep.** J'ai besoin de dormir.
♦ **to go to sleep** s'endormir

to **sleep** VERB
| *see also* **sleep** NOUN |
<u>dormir</u> ◊ *I couldn't sleep last night.* J'ai mal dormi la nuit dernière.
♦ **to sleep with somebody** coucher avec quelqu'un
♦ **to sleep together** coucher ensemble

to **sleep around** VERB
<u>coucher à droite et à gauche</u>

to **sleep in** VERB
① <u>ne pas se réveiller</u> (*accidentally*)
◊ *I'm sorry I'm late, I slept in.* Désolé

S

☞

d'être en retard: je ne me suis pas
réveillé.
2 faire la grasse matinée (*on
purpose*)

sleeping bag NOUN
le sac de couchage
(les sacs de couchage PL)

sleeping car NOUN
le wagon-lit
(les wagons-lits PL)

sleeping pill NOUN
le somnifère

sleepy ADJECTIVE
♦**to feel sleepy** avoir sommeil ◊ *I was
feeling sleepy.* J'avais sommeil.
♦**a sleepy little village** un petit village
tranquille

sleet NOUN
see also **sleet** VERB
la neige fondue

to **sleet** VERB
see also **sleet** NOUN
♦**It's sleeting**. Il tombe de la neige
fondue.

sleeve NOUN
1 la manche ◊ *long sleeves* les
manches longues ◊ *short sleeves* les
manches courtes
2 la pochette (*record sleeve*)

sleigh NOUN
le traîneau
(les traîneaux PL)

slept VERB *see* **sleep**

slice NOUN
see also **slice** VERB
la tranche

to **slice** VERB
see also **slice** NOUN
couper en tranches

slick NOUN
♦**an oil slick** une marée noire

slide NOUN
see also **slide** VERB
1 le toboggan (*in playground*)
2 la diapositive (*photo*)
3 la barrette (*hair slide*)

to **slide** VERB
see also **slide** NOUN
glisser

slight ADJECTIVE
léger MASC
légère FEM
◊ *a slight problem* un léger problème
◊ *a slight improvement* une légère
amélioration

slightly ADVERB
légèrement

slim ADJECTIVE
see also **slim** VERB

mince

to **slim** VERB
see also **slim** ADJECTIVE
faire un régime (*be on a diet*) ◊ *I'm
slimming.* Je fais un régime.

sling NOUN
l' écharpe FEM ◊ *She had her arm in a
sling.* Elle avait le bras en écharpe.

slip NOUN
see also **slip** VERB
1 l' erreur FEM (*mistake*)
2 le jupon (*underskirt*)
3 la combinaison (*full-length
underskirt*)
♦**a slip of paper** un bout de papier
♦**a slip of the tongue** un lapsus

to **slip** VERB
see also **slip** NOUN
glisser ◊ *He slipped on the ice.* Il a
glissé sur le verglas.
♦**to slip up** faire une erreur (*make a
mistake*)

slipper NOUN
le chausson
♦**a pair of slippers** des chaussons

slippery ADJECTIVE
glissant

slip-up NOUN
l' erreur FEM

slope NOUN
la pente

sloppy ADJECTIVE
1 bâclé (*work*)
2 négligé (*person, appearance*)

slot NOUN
la fente

slot machine NOUN
1 la machine à sous (*for gambling*)
2 le distributeur automatique
(*vending machine*)

slow ADJECTIVE, ADVERB
1 lent ◊ *He's a bit slow.* Il est un
peu lent.
2 lentement ◊ *to go slow* (*person,
car*) aller lentement ◊ *Drive slower!*
Conduisez plus lentement!
♦**My watch is slow.** Ma montre
retarde.

to **slow down** VERB
ralentir

slowly ADVERB
lentement

slug NOUN
la limace

slum NOUN
1 le quartier insalubre (*area*)
2 le taudis (*house*)

slush NOUN

la <u>neige fondue</u>

sly ADJECTIVE
<u>rusé</u> (*person*)
♦ **a sly smile** un sourire sournois

smack NOUN
see also **smack** VERB
la <u>tape</u>

to **smack** VERB
see also **smack** NOUN
♦ **to smack somebody** donner une tape
à quelqu'un

small ADJECTIVE
<u>petit</u>
♦ **small change** la petite monnaie

smart ADJECTIVE
1 (*elegant*)
<u>chic</u> MASC, FEM, PL
2 (*clever*)
<u>intelligent</u>
♦ **a smart idea** une idée astucieuse

smash NOUN
see also **smash** VERB
l' <u>accident</u> MASC

to **smash** VERB
see also **smash** NOUN
1 <u>casser</u> (*break*) ◊ *I've smashed my watch.* J'ai cassé ma montre.
2 <u>se briser</u> (*get broken*) ◊ *The glass smashed into tiny pieces.* Le verre s'est brisé en mille morceaux.

smashing ADJECTIVE
<u>formidable</u> ◊ *I think he's smashing.* Je le trouve formidable.

smell NOUN
see also **smell** VERB
l' <u>odeur</u> FEM
♦ **the sense of smell** l'odorat MASC

to **smell** VERB
see also **smell** NOUN
1 <u>sentir mauvais</u> ◊ *That old dog really smells!* Qu'est-ce qu'il sent mauvais, ce vieux chien!
♦ **to smell of something** sentir quelque chose ◊ *It smells of petrol.* Ça sent l'essence.
2 <u>sentir</u> (*detect*) ◊ *I can't smell anything.* Je ne sens rien.

smelly ADJECTIVE
<u>qui sent mauvais</u> ◊ *He's got smelly feet.* Il a les pieds qui sentent mauvais.

smelt VERB *see* **smell**

smile NOUN
see also **smile** VERB
le <u>sourire</u>

to **smile** VERB
see also **smile** NOUN
<u>sourire</u>

smiley NOUN
l' <u>émoticon</u> MASC

smoke NOUN
see also **smoke** VERB
la <u>fumée</u>

to **smoke** VERB
see also **smoke** NOUN
<u>fumer</u> ◊ *I don't smoke.* Je ne fume pas. ◊ *He smokes cigars.* Il fume le cigare.

smoker NOUN
le <u>fumeur</u>
la <u>fumeuse</u>

smoking NOUN
♦ **to give up smoking** arrêter de fumer
♦ **Smoking is bad for you.** Le tabac est mauvais pour la santé.
♦ **"no smoking"** "défense de fumer"

smooth ADJECTIVE
1 (*surface*)
<u>lisse</u>
2 (*person*)
<u>mielleux</u> MASC
<u>mielleuse</u> FEM

smudge NOUN
la <u>bavure</u>

smug ADJECTIVE
<u>suffisant</u>

to **smuggle** VERB
1 <u>passer en fraude</u> (*goods*) ◊ *to smuggle cigarettes into a country* faire passer des cigarettes en fraude dans un pays
2 <u>faire passer clandestinement</u> (*people*)
♦ **They managed to smuggle him out of prison.** Ils ont réussi à le faire sortir de prison clandestinement.

smuggler NOUN
le <u>contrebandier</u>
la <u>contrebandière</u>

smuggling NOUN
la <u>contrebande</u>

smutty ADJECTIVE
<u>cochon</u> MASC
<u>cochonne</u> FEM
◊ *a smutty story* une histoire cochonne

snack NOUN
l' <u>en-cas</u> MASC
(les en-cas PL)
♦ **to have a snack** prendre un en-cas

snack bar NOUN
le <u>snack-bar</u>

snail NOUN
l' <u>escargot</u> MASC

snake NOUN
le <u>serpent</u>

S

to **snap** VERB
casser net (*break*) ◊ *The branch
snapped.* La branche a cassé net.
♦**to snap one's fingers** faire claquer ses
doigts

snap fastener NOUN
le bouton-pression
(les boutons-pression PL)

snapshot NOUN
la photo

to **snarl** VERB
gronder (*animal*)

to **snatch** VERB
♦**to snatch something from somebody**
arracher quelque chose à quelqu'un
◊ *He snatched the keys from my
hand.* Il m'a arraché les clés des
mains.
♦**My bag was snatched.** On m'a
arraché mon sac.

to **sneak** VERB
♦**to sneak in** entrer furtivement
♦**to sneak out** sortir furtivement
♦**to sneak up on somebody**
s'approcher de quelqu'un sans faire
de bruit

to **sneeze** VERB
éternuer

to **sniff** VERB
[1] renifler ◊ *Stop sniffing!* Arrête de
renifler!
[2] flairer ◊ *The dog sniffed my hand.*
Le chien m'a flairé la main.
♦**to sniff glue** sniffer de la colle

snob NOUN
le/la snob

snooker NOUN
le billard ◊ *to play snooker* jouer au
billard

snooze NOUN
le petit somme ◊ *to have a snooze*
faire un petit somme

to **snore** VERB
ronfler

snow NOUN
see also **snow** VERB
la neige

to **snow** VERB
see also **snow** NOUN
neiger ◊ *It's snowing.* Il neige.

snowball NOUN
la boule de neige
(les boules de neige PL)

snowflake NOUN
le flocon de neige
(les flocons de neige PL)

snowman NOUN
le bonhomme de neige
(les bonshommes de neige PL)

◊ *to build a snowman* faire un
bonhomme de neige

SO CONJUNCTION, ADVERB
[1] alors ◊ *The shop was closed, so I
went home.* Le magasin était fermé,
alors je suis rentré chez moi. ◊ *So,
have you always lived in London?*
Alors, vous avez toujours vécu à
Londres?
♦**So what?** Et alors?
[2] donc (*so that*) ◊ *It rained, so I got
wet.* Il pleuvait, donc j'ai été mouillé.
[3] tellement (*very*) ◊ *It was so heavy!*
C'était tellement lourd! ◊ *He was
talking so fast I couldn't understand.*
Il parlait tellement vite que je ne
comprenais pas.
♦**It's not so heavy!** Ça n'est pas si
lourd que ça!
♦**How's your father? – Not so good.**
Comment va ton père? – Pas très
bien.
♦**so much** (*a lot*) tellement ◊ *I love you
so much.* Je t'aime tellement.
♦**so much ..., so many ...** tellement
de ... ◊ *I've got so much work.* J'ai
tellement de travail. ◊ *I've got so
many things to do today.* J'ai
tellement de choses à faire
aujourd'hui.
[4] aussi (*in comparisons*) ◊ *He's like
his sister but not so clever.* Il est
comme sa sœur mais pas aussi
intelligent.
♦**so do I** moi aussi ◊ *I love horses. –
So do I.* J'aime les chevaux. – Moi
aussi.
♦**so have we** nous aussi ◊ *I've been to
France twice. – So have we.* Je suis
allé en France deux fois. – Nous
aussi.
♦**I think so.** Je crois.
♦**I hope so.** J'espère bien.
♦**That's not so.** Ça n'est pas le cas.
♦**so far** jusqu'à présent ◊ *It's been easy
so far.* Ça a été facile jusqu'à présent.
♦**so far so good** jusqu'ici ça va
♦**ten or so people** environ dix
personnes
♦**at five o'clock or so** à environ cinq
heures

to **soak** VERB
tremper

soaked ADJECTIVE
trempé ◊ *By the time we got back
we were soaked.* Nous sommes
rentrés trempés.

soaking ADJECTIVE
trempé ◊ *By the time we got back
we were soaking.* Nous sommes
rentrés trempés.

◆ **soaking wet** trempé ◇ *Your shoes are soaking wet.* Tes chaussures sont trempées.

soap NOUN
le savon

soap opera NOUN
le feuilleton à l'eau de rose
(les feuilletons à l'eau de rose PL)

soap powder NOUN
la lessive

to **sob** VERB
sangloter ◇ *She was sobbing.* Elle sanglotait.

sober ADJECTIVE
sobre

to **sober up** VERB
dessoûler

soccer NOUN
le football ◇ *to play soccer* jouer au football
◆ **a soccer player** un joueur de football

social ADJECTIVE
social
(sociaux MASC PL)
◇ *a social class* une classe sociale
◆ **I have a good social life.** Je vois beaucoup de monde.

socialism NOUN
le socialisme

socialist ADJECTIVE
see also **socialist** NOUN
socialiste

socialist NOUN
see also **socialist** ADJECTIVE
le/la socialiste

social security NOUN
1 l' aide sociale FEM (*money*)
◆ **to be on social security** recevoir de l'aide sociale
2 la sécurité sociale (*organization*)

social worker NOUN
1 (*woman*)
l' assistante sociale FEM ◇ *She's a social worker.* Elle est assistante sociale.
2 (*man*)
le travailleur social
(les travailleurs sociaux PL)
◇ *He's a social worker.* Il est travailleur social.

society NOUN
1 la société ◇ *We live in a multicultural society.* Nous vivons dans une société multiculturelle.
2 le club ◇ *a drama society* un club de théâtre

sociology NOUN
la sociologie

sock NOUN
la chaussette

socket NOUN
la prise de courant
(les prises de courant PL)

soda NOUN
le soda (*soda water*)

soda pop NOUN US
le soda

sofa NOUN
le canapé

soft ADJECTIVE
1 (*fabric, texture*)
doux MASC
douce FEM
2 (*pillow, bed*)
mou MASC
molle FEM
◆ **soft cheeses** les fromages à pâte molle MASC
3 (*hair*)
fin
◆ **to be soft on somebody** (*be kind to*) être indulgent avec quelqu'un
◆ **a soft drink** une boisson non alcoolisée
◆ **soft drugs** les drogues douces FEM
◆ **a soft option** une solution de facilité

software NOUN
le logiciel

soggy ADJECTIVE
1 (*soaked*)
trempé ◇ *a soggy tissue* un mouchoir trempé
2 (*not crisp*)
mou MASC
molle FEM
◇ *soggy chips* des frites molles

soil NOUN
la terre

solar ADJECTIVE
solaire
◆ **solar panel** le panneau solaire

solar power NOUN
l' énergie solaire FEM

sold VERB see **sell**

soldier NOUN
le soldat ◇ *He's a soldier.* Il est soldat.

solicitor NOUN
1 (*for lawsuits*)
l' avocat MASC
l' avocate FEM
◇ *He's a solicitor.* Il est avocat.
2 (*for wills, property*)
le/la notaire
◇ *She's a solicitor.* Elle est notaire.

solid ADJECTIVE
1 (*not hollow*)

S

☞

massif MASC
massive FEM
◊ *solid gold* l'or massif
[2] solide ◊ *a solid wall* un mur solide
♦**for three hours solid** pendant trois
heures entières

solo NOUN
le solo ◊ *a guitar solo* un solo de
guitare

solution NOUN
la solution

to **solve** VERB
résoudre

SOME ADJECTIVE, PRONOUN

*When **some** means "a certain
amount of", use **du**, **de la** or **des**
according to the gender of the
French noun that follows it. **du** and
de la become **de l'** when they are
followed by a noun starting with a
vowel.*

[1] du ◊ *Would you like some bread?*
Voulez-vous du pain?
de la ◊ *Would you like some beer?*
Voulez-vous de la bière?
de l' ◊ *Have you got some mineral
water?* Avez-vous de l'eau minérale?
des ◊ *I've got some Blur albums.* J'ai
des albums de Blur.
♦**Some people say that ...** Il y a des
gens qui disent que ...
♦**some day** un de ces jours
♦**some day next week** un jour la
semaine prochaine
[2] (*some but not all*)
certains ◊ *Are these mushrooms
poisonous? – Only some.* Est-ce que
ces champignons sont vénéneux? –
Certains le sont.
♦**some of them** quelques-uns ◊ *I only
sold some of them.* J'en ai seulement
vendu quelques-uns.
♦**I only took some of it.** J'en ai
seulement pris un peu.
♦**I'm going to buy some stamps. Do
you want some too?** Je vais acheter
des timbres. Tu en veux aussi?
♦**Would you like some coffee? – No
thanks, I've got some.** Tu veux du
café? – Non merci, j'en ai déjà.

somebody PRONOUN
quelqu'un ◊ *Somebody stole my
bag.* Quelqu'un a volé mon sac.

somehow ADVERB
♦**I'll do it somehow.** Je trouverai le
moyen de le faire.
♦**Somehow I don't think he believed
me.** Quelque chose me dit qu'il ne
m'a pas cru.

someone PRONOUN

quelqu'un ◊ *Someone stole my bag.*
Quelqu'un a volé mon sac.

someplace ADVERB US
quelque part

something PRONOUN
quelque chose ◊ *something special*
quelque chose de spécial ◊ *Wear
something warm.* Mets quelque
chose de chaud. ◊ *That's really
something!* C'est vraiment quelque
chose! ◊ *It cost £100, or something
like that.* Ça a coûté cent livres, ou
quelque chose comme ça.
♦**His name is Pierre or something.** Il
s'appelle Pierre, ou quelque chose
comme ça.

sometime ADVERB
un de ces jours ◊ *You must come
and see us sometime.* Passez donc
nous voir un de ces jours.
♦**sometime last month** dans le courant
du mois dernier

sometimes ADVERB
quelquefois ◊ *Sometimes I think
she hates me.* Quelquefois j'ai
l'impression qu'elle me déteste.

somewhere ADVERB
quelque part ◊ *I left my keys
somewhere.* J'ai laissé mes clés
quelque part. ◊ *I'd like to go on
holiday, somewhere sunny.*
J'aimerais aller en vacances, quelque
part où il fait du soleil.

son NOUN
le fils

song NOUN
la chanson

son-in-law NOUN
le gendre

soon ADVERB
bientôt ◊ *very soon* très bientôt
♦**soon afterwards** peu après
♦**as soon as possible** aussitôt que
possible

sooner ADVERB
plus tôt ◊ *Can't you come a bit
sooner?* Tu ne peux pas venir un peu
plus tôt?
♦**sooner or later** tôt ou tard

soot NOUN
la suie

soppy ADJECTIVE
sentimental
(sentimentaux MASC PL)

soprano NOUN
le/la soprano (*singer*)

sorcerer NOUN
le sorcier

sore ADJECTIVE

see also **sore** NOUN

♦**My feet are sore.** J'ai mal aux pieds.
♦**It's sore.** Ça fait mal.
♦**That's a sore point.** C'est un point sensible.

sore NOUN
see also **sore** ADJECTIVE
la plaie

sorry ADJECTIVE
désolé ◊ *I'm really sorry.* Je suis vraiment désolé. ◊ *I'm sorry, I haven't got any change.* Je suis désolé, je n'ai pas de monnaie. ◊ *I'm sorry I'm late.* Je suis désolé d'être en retard.
♦**sorry!** pardon!
♦**sorry?** pardon?
♦**I'm sorry about the noise.** Je m'excuse pour le bruit.
♦**You'll be sorry!** Tu le regretteras!
♦**to feel sorry for somebody** plaindre quelqu'un

sort NOUN
la sorte ◊ *What sort of bike have you got?* Quelle sorte de vélo as-tu?

to **sort out** VERB
[1] ranger (*objects*)
[2] résoudre (*problems*)

so-so ADVERB
comme ci comme ça ◊ *How are you feeling? – So-so.* Comment est-ce que tu te sens? – Comme ci comme ça.

sought VERB *see* **to seek**

soul NOUN
[1] l' âme FEM (*spirit*)
[2] la soul (*music*)

sound NOUN
see also **sound** VERB, ADJECTIVE
[1] le bruit (*noise*) ◊ *Don't make a sound!* Pas un bruit! ◊ *the sound of footsteps* des bruits de pas
[2] le son ◊ *Can I turn the sound down?* Je peux baisser le son?

to **sound** VERB
see also **sound** NOUN, ADJECTIVE
♦**That sounds interesting.** Ça a l'air intéressant.
♦**It sounds as if she's doing well at school.** Elle a l'air de bien travailler à l'école.
♦**That sounds like a good idea.** C'est une bonne idée.

sound ADJECTIVE, ADVERB
see also **sound** NOUN, VERB
bon MASC
bonne FEM
◊ *That's sound advice.* C'est un bon conseil.
♦**sound asleep** profondément endormi

soundtrack NOUN
la bande sonore

soup NOUN
la soupe ◊ *vegetable soup* la soupe aux légumes

sour ADJECTIVE
aigre

south ADJECTIVE, ADVERB
see also **south** NOUN
[1] sud MASC, FEM, PL ◊ *the south coast* la côte sud
[2] vers le sud ◊ *We were travelling south.* Nous allions vers le sud.
♦**south of** au sud de ◊ *It's south of London.* C'est au sud de Londres.

south NOUN
see also **south** ADJECTIVE
le sud ◊ *in the south* dans le sud ◊ *the South of France* le sud de la France

South Africa NOUN
l' Afrique du Sud FEM
♦**in South Africa** en Afrique du Sud
♦**to South Africa** en Afrique du Sud

South America NOUN
l' Amérique du Sud FEM
♦**in South America** en Amérique du Sud
♦**to South America** en Amérique du Sud

South American ADJECTIVE
see also **South American** NOUN
sud-américain

South American NOUN
see also **South American** ADJECTIVE
le Sud-Américain
la Sud-Américaine

southbound ADJECTIVE
♦**The southbound carriageway is blocked.** La route est bloquée en direction du sud.
♦**The suspect vehicle was southbound on the M1.** Le véhicule suspect se trouvait sur la M1 en direction du sud.

southeast NOUN
le sud-est ◊ *southeast England* le sud-est de l'Angleterre

southern ADJECTIVE
♦**the southern part of the island** la partie sud de l'île
♦**Southern England** le sud de l'Angleterre

South Pole NOUN
le pôle Sud

South Wales NOUN
le sud du Pays de Galles

southwest NOUN

S

☞

le <u>sud-ouest</u> ◇ *southwest France* le sud-ouest de la France

souvenir NOUN
le <u>souvenir</u>
♦ **a souvenir shop** une boutique de souvenirs

Soviet ADJECTIVE
♦ **the former Soviet Union** l'ex-Union Soviétique FEM

soya NOUN
le <u>soja</u>

soy sauce NOUN
la <u>sauce de soja</u>

space NOUN
1 la <u>place</u> ◇ *There isn't enough space.* Il n'y a pas suffisamment de place.
♦ **a parking space** une place de parking
2 l' <u>espace</u> MASC (*universe, gap*) ◇ *Leave a space after your answer.* Laissez un espace après votre réponse.

spacecraft NOUN
l' <u>engin spatial</u> MASC

spade NOUN
la <u>pelle</u>
♦ **spades** (*in cards*) le pique SING ◇ *the ace of spades* l'as de pique

Spain NOUN
l' <u>Espagne</u> FEM
♦ **in Spain** en Espagne
♦ **to Spain** en Espagne

Spaniard NOUN
l' <u>Espagnol</u> MASC
l' <u>Espagnole</u> FEM

spaniel NOUN
l' <u>épagneul</u> MASC

Spanish ADJECTIVE
see also **Spanish** NOUN
<u>espagnol</u> ◇ *She's Spanish.* Elle est espagnole.

Spanish NOUN
see also **Spanish** ADJECTIVE
l' <u>espagnol</u> MASC (*language*)
♦ **the Spanish** les Espagnols

to **spank** VERB
♦ **to spank somebody** donner une fessée à quelqu'un

spanner NOUN
la <u>clé anglaise</u>

spare ADJECTIVE
see also **spare** VERB, NOUN
<u>de rechange</u> ◇ *spare batteries* des piles de rechange ◇ *a spare part* une pièce de rechange
♦ **a spare room** une chambre d'amis

♦ **spare time** le temps libre ◇ *What do you do in your spare time?* Qu'est-ce que tu fais pendant ton temps libre?
♦ **spare wheel** une roue de secours

to **spare** VERB
see also **spare** ADJECTIVE, NOUN
♦ **Can you spare a moment?** Vous pouvez m'accorder un instant?
♦ **I can't spare the time.** Je n'ai pas le temps.
♦ **There's no room to spare.** Il n'y a plus de place.
♦ **We arrived with time to spare.** Nous sommes arrivés en avance.

spare NOUN
see also **spare** ADJECTIVE, VERB
♦ **a spare** un autre ◇ *I've lost my key. – Have you got a spare?* J'ai perdu ma clé. – Tu en as une autre?

sparkling ADJECTIVE
<u>pétillant</u> (*water*)
♦ **sparkling wine** le mousseux

sparrow NOUN
le <u>moineau</u>
(les moineaux PL)

spat VERB see **spit**

to **speak** VERB
<u>parler</u> ◇ *Do you speak English?* Est-ce que vous parlez anglais?
♦ **to speak to somebody** parler à quelqu'un ◇ *Have you spoken to him?* Tu lui as parlé? ◇ *She spoke to him about it.* Elle lui en a parlé.
♦ **spoken French** le français parlé

to **speak up** VERB
<u>parler plus fort</u> ◇ *Speak up, we can't hear you.* Parle plus fort, nous ne t'entendons pas.

speaker NOUN
1 l' <u>enceinte</u> FEM (*loudspeaker*)
2 l' <u>intervenant</u> MASC (*in debate*)

special ADJECTIVE
<u>spécial</u>
(spéciaux MASC PL)

specialist NOUN
le/la <u>spécialiste</u>

speciality NOUN
la <u>spécialité</u>

to **specialize** VERB
<u>se spécialiser</u> ◇ *We specialize in skiing equipment.* Nous nous spécialisons dans les articles de ski.

specially ADVERB
1 <u>spécialement</u> ◇ *It's specially designed for teenagers.* C'est spécialement conçu pour les adolescents.

♦ **not specially** pas spécialement ◊ *Do you like opera? – Not specially.* Tu aimes l'opéra? – Pas spécialement.
  2 surtout ◊ *It can be very cold here, specially in winter.* Il peut faire très froid ici, surtout en hiver.

species NOUN
  l' espèce FEM

specific ADJECTIVE
  1 (*particular*)
  particulier MASC
  particulière FEM
  ◊ *certain specific issues* certains problèmes particuliers
  2 (*precise*)
  précis ◊ *Could you be more specific?* Est-ce que vous pourriez être plus précis?

specifically ADVERB
  1 spécialement ◊ *It's specifically designed for teenagers.* C'est spécialement conçu pour les adolescents.
  2 particulièrement ◊ *in Britain, or more specifically in England* en Grande-Bretagne, ou plus particulièrement en Angleterre
  ♦ **I specifically said that ...** J'ai clairement dit que ...

specs, spectacles PL NOUN
  les lunettes FEM PL

spectacular ADJECTIVE
  spectaculaire

spectator NOUN
  le spectateur
  la spectatrice

speech NOUN
  le discours ◊ *to make a speech* faire un discours

speechless ADJECTIVE
  muet MASC
  muette FEM
  ◊ *speechless with admiration* muet d'admiration
  ♦ **I was speechless.** Je suis resté sans voix.

speed NOUN
  la vitesse ◊ *a three-speed bike* un vélo à trois vitesses ◊ *at top speed* à toute vitesse

to **speed up** VERB
  accélérer

speedboat NOUN
  la vedette

speeding NOUN
  l' excès de vitesse MASC ◊ *He was fined for speeding.* Il a reçu une contravention pour excès de vitesse.

speed limit NOUN

  la limitation de vitesse
  ♦ **to break the speed limit** faire un excès de vitesse

speedometer NOUN
  le compteur

to **spell** VERB
  | see also **spell** NOUN |
  1 écrire (*in writing*) ◊ *How do you spell that?* Comment est-ce que ça s'écrit?
  2 épeler (*out loud*) ◊ *Can you spell that please?* Est-ce que vous pouvez épeler, s'il vous plaît?
  ♦ **I can't spell.** Je fais des fautes d'orthographe.

spell NOUN
  | see also **spell** VERB |
  ♦ **to cast a spell on somebody** jeter un sort à quelqu'un
  ♦ **to be under somebody's spell** être sous le charme de quelqu'un

spelling NOUN
  l' orthographe FEM ◊ *My spelling is terrible.* Je fais beaucoup de fautes d'orthographe.
  ♦ **a spelling mistake** une faute d'orthographe

spelt VERB see **spell**

to **spend** VERB
  1 dépenser (*money*)
  2 passer (*time*) ◊ *He spent a month in France.* Il a passé un mois en France.

spice NOUN
  l' épice FEM

spicy ADJECTIVE
  épicé

spider NOUN
  l' araignée FEM

to **spill** VERB
  1 renverser (*tip over*) ◊ *He spilled his coffee over his trousers.* Il a renversé son café sur son pantalon.
  2 se répandre (*get spilt*) ◊ *The soup spilled all over the table.* La soupe s'est répandue sur la table.

spinach NOUN
  les épinards MASC PL

spin drier NOUN
  l' essoreuse FEM

spine NOUN
  la colonne vertébrale

spinster NOUN
  la célibataire

spire NOUN
  la flèche

spirit NOUN
  1 le courage (*courage*)

S

☞

♦ **to be in good spirits** être de bonne humeur

2 l' **énergie** FEM (*energy*)

spirits PL NOUN
les **alcools forts** MASC PL ◊ *I don't drink spirits.* Je ne bois pas d'alcools forts.

spiritual ADJECTIVE
religieux MASC
religieuse FEM
◊ *the spiritual leader of Tibet* le chef religieux du Tibet

spit NOUN
see also **spit** VERB
la **salive**

to **spit** VERB
see also **spit** NOUN
cracher
♦ **to spit something out** cracher quelque chose

spite NOUN
see also **spite** VERB
♦ **in spite of** malgré
♦ **out of spite** par méchanceté

to **spite** VERB
see also **spite** NOUN
contrarier ◊ *He just did it to spite me.* Il a fait ça juste pour me contrarier.

spiteful ADJECTIVE
1 (*action*)
méchant
2 (*person*)
rancunier MASC
rancunière FEM

to **splash** VERB
see also **splash** NOUN
éclabousser ◊ *Careful! Don't splash me!* Attention! Ne m'éclabousse pas!

splash NOUN
see also **splash** VERB
le **plouf** ◊ *I heard a splash.* J'ai entendu un plouf.
♦ **a splash of colour** une touche de couleur

splendid ADJECTIVE
splendide

splint NOUN
l' **attelle** FEM

splinter NOUN
l' **écharde** FEM

to **split** VERB
1 **fendre** (*break apart*) ◊ *He split the wood with an axe.* Il a fendu le bois avec une hache.
2 **se fendre** ◊ *The ship hit a rock and split in two.* Le bateau a percuté un rocher et s'est fendu en deux.

3 **partager** (*divide up*) ◊ *They decided to split the profits.* Ils ont décidé de partager les bénéfices.
♦ **to split up (1)** (*couple*) rompre
♦ **to split up (2)** (*group*) se disperser

to **spoil** VERB
1 **abîmer** (*object*)
2 **gâcher** (*occasion*)
3 **gâter** (*child*)

spoiled ADJECTIVE
gâté ◊ *a spoiled child* un enfant gâté

spoilsport NOUN
le/la **trouble-fête**

spoilt ADJECTIVE
gâté ◊ *a spoilt child* un enfant gâté

spoilt VERB see **spoil**

spoke VERB see **speak**

spoke NOUN
le **rayon** (*of wheel*)

spoken VERB see **speak**

spokesman NOUN
le **porte-parole**
(les porte-parole PL)

spokeswoman NOUN
le **porte-parole**
(les porte-parole PL)

sponge NOUN
l' **éponge** FEM
♦ **a sponge bag** une trousse de toilette
♦ **a sponge cake** un biscuit de Savoie

sponsor NOUN
see also **sponsor** VERB
le **donateur**
la **donatrice**

to **sponsor** VERB
see also **sponsor** NOUN
parrainer ◊ *The festival was sponsored by ...* Le festival a été parrainé par ...

spontaneous ADJECTIVE
spontané

spooky ADJECTIVE
1 **sinistre** (*eerie*)
♦ **a spooky story** une histoire qui fait froid dans le dos
2 **étrange** (*strange*) ◊ *a spooky coincidence* une étrange coïncidence

spoon NOUN
la **cuiller**
♦ **a spoonful** une cuillerée

sport NOUN
le **sport** ◊ *What's your favourite sport?* Quel est ton sport préféré?
♦ **a sports bag** un sac de sport
♦ **a sports car** une voiture de sport
♦ **a sports jacket** une veste sport
♦ **Go on, be a sport!** Allez, sois sympa!

sportsman NOUN

le <u>sportif</u>

sportswear NOUN
les <u>vêtements de sport</u> MASC PL

sportswoman NOUN
la <u>sportive</u>

sporty ADJECTIVE
<u>sportif</u> MASC
<u>sportive</u> FEM
◊ *I'm not very sporty.* Je ne suis pas très sportif.

spot NOUN
see also **spot** VERB
⓵ la <u>tache</u> (*mark*) ◊ *There's a spot on your shirt.* Il y a une tache sur ta chemise.
⓶ le <u>pois</u> (*in pattern*) ◊ *a red dress with white spots* une robe rouge à pois blancs
⓷ le <u>bouton</u> (*pimple*) ◊ *He's covered in spots.* Il est couvert de boutons.
⓸ le <u>coin</u> (*place*) ◊ *It's a lovely spot for a picnic.* C'est un coin agréable pour un pique-nique.
♦ **on the spot** (1) (*immediately*) sur-le-champ ◊ *They gave her the job on the spot.* Ils lui ont offert le poste sur-le-champ.
♦ **on the spot** (2) (*at the same place*) sur place ◊ *Luckily they were able to mend the car on the spot.* Heureusement ils ont pu réparer la voiture sur place.

to **spot** VERB
see also **spot** NOUN
<u>repérer</u> ◊ *I spotted a mistake.* J'ai repéré une faute.

spotless ADJECTIVE
<u>immaculé</u>

spotlight NOUN
le <u>projecteur</u>
♦ **The universities have been in the spotlight recently.** Les universités ont été sous le feu des projecteurs ces derniers temps.

spotty ADJECTIVE
(*pimply*)
<u>boutonneux</u> MASC
<u>boutonneuse</u> FEM

spouse NOUN
l' <u>époux</u> MASC
l' <u>épouse</u> FEM

to **sprain** VERB
see also **sprain** NOUN
♦ **to sprain one's ankle** se faire une entorse à la cheville

sprain NOUN
see also **sprain** VERB
l' <u>entorse</u> FEM ◊ *It's just a sprain.* C'est juste une entorse.

spray NOUN
see also **spray** VERB
la <u>bombe</u> (*spray can*)

to **spray** VERB
see also **spray** NOUN
⓵ <u>vaporiser</u> ◊ *to spray perfume on one's hand* se vaporiser du parfum sur la main
⓶ <u>traiter</u> (*crops*)
⓷ <u>peindre avec une bombe</u> (*graffiti*) ◊ *Somebody had sprayed graffiti on the wall.* Quelqu'un avait peint des graffiti avec une bombe sur le mur.

spread NOUN
see also **spread** VERB
♦ **cheese spread** le fromage à tartiner
♦ **chocolate spread** le chocolat à tartiner

to **spread** VERB
see also **spread** NOUN
⓵ <u>étaler</u> ◊ *to spread butter on a slice of bread* étaler du beurre sur une tranche de pain
⓶ <u>se propager</u> (*disease, news*) ◊ *The news spread rapidly.* La nouvelle s'est propagée rapidement.
♦ **to spread out** (*people*) se disperser ◊ *The soldiers spread out across the field.* Les soldats se sont dispersés dans le champ.

spreadsheet NOUN
le <u>tableur</u> (*computer program*)

spring NOUN
⓵ le <u>printemps</u> (*season*)
♦ **in spring** au printemps
⓶ le <u>ressort</u> (*metal coil*)
⓷ la <u>source</u> (*water hole*)

spring-cleaning NOUN
le <u>grand nettoyage de printemps</u>

springtime NOUN
le <u>printemps</u>
♦ **in springtime** au printemps

sprinkler NOUN
l' <u>arroseur</u> MASC (*for lawn*)

sprint NOUN
see also **sprint** VERB
le <u>sprint</u>

to **sprint** VERB
see also **sprint** NOUN
<u>courir à toute vitesse</u> ◊ *She sprinted for the bus.* Elle a couru à toute vitesse pour attraper le bus.

sprinter NOUN
le <u>sprinteur</u>
la <u>sprinteuse</u>

sprouts PL NOUN
♦ **Brussels sprouts** les choux de Bruxelles MASC PL

spy NOUN
see also **spy** VERB

S

☞

l' espion MASC
l' espionne FEM

to spy VERB

> see also spy NOUN

♦to spy on somebody espionner quelqu'un

spying NOUN
l' espionnage MASC

to squabble VERB
se chamailler ◊ Stop squabbling! Arrêtez de vous chamailler!

square NOUN

> see also square ADJECTIVE

1 le carré ◊ a square and a triangle un carré et un triangle
2 la place ◊ the town square la place de l'hôtel de ville

square ADJECTIVE

> see also square NOUN

carré ◊ two square metres deux mètres carrés

♦It's 2 metres square. Ça fait deux mètres sur deux.

squash NOUN

> see also squash VERB

le squash (sport) ◊ I play squash. Je joue au squash.

♦a squash court un court de squash
♦a squash racket une raquette de squash
♦orange squash l' orangeade FEM
♦lemon squash la citronnade

to squash VERB

> see also squash NOUN

écraser ◊ You're squashing me. Tu m'écrases.

to squeak VERB
1 pousser un petit cri (mouse, child)
2 grincer (creak)

to squeeze VERB
1 presser (fruit, toothpaste)
2 serrer (hand, arm)

♦to squeeze into some tight jeans rentrer tout juste dans un jean serré

to squeeze in VERB
1 trouver une petite place ◊ It was a tiny car, but we managed to squeeze in. La voiture était toute petite, mais nous avons réussi à trouver une petite place.
2 caser (for appointment) ◊ I can squeeze you in tomorrow at two o'clock. Je peux vous caser demain à deux heures.

to squint VERB

> see also squint NOUN

loucher

squint NOUN

> see also squint VERB

♦He has a squint. Il louche.

squirrel NOUN
l' écureuil MASC

to stab VERB
poignarder

stable NOUN

> see also stable ADJECTIVE

l' écurie FEM

stable ADJECTIVE

> see also stable NOUN

stable ◊ a stable relationship une relation stable

stack NOUN
le pile ◊ a stack of books une pile de livres

stadium NOUN
le stade

staff NOUN
1 le personnel (in company)
2 les professeurs MASC PL (in school)

staffroom NOUN
la salle des professeurs

stage NOUN
1 la scène (in plays)
2 l' estrade FEM (for speeches, lectures)

♦at this stage (1) à ce stade ◊ at this stage in the negotiations à ce stade des négociations
♦at this stage (2) pour l'instant ◊ At this stage, it's too early to comment. Pour l'instant, il est trop tôt pour se prononcer.
♦to do something in stages faire quelque chose étape par étape

Be careful not to translate stage by the French word stage.

to stagger VERB
chanceler

stain NOUN

> see also stain VERB

la tache

to stain VERB

> see also stain NOUN

tacher

stainless steel NOUN
l' inox MASC

stain remover NOUN
le détachant

stair NOUN
la marche (step)

staircase NOUN
l' escalier MASC

stairs PL NOUN
l' escalier MASC SING

stale ADJECTIVE
rassis (bread)

stalemate NOUN
le pat (in chess)

stall NOUN
le <u>stand</u> MASC ◊ *He's got a market stall.* Il a un stand au marché.
♦**the stalls** (*in cinema, theatre*) l'orchestre MASC

stamina NOUN
l' <u>endurance</u> FEM

stammer NOUN
le <u>bégaiement</u>
♦**He's got a stammer.** Il bégaie.

to **stamp** VERB
see also **stamp** NOUN
<u>affranchir</u> (*letter*)
♦**to stamp one's foot** taper du pied

stamp NOUN
see also **stamp** VERB
[1] le <u>timbre</u> ◊ *My hobby is stamp collecting.* Je collectionne les timbres.
♦**a stamp album** un album de timbres
♦**a stamp collection** une collection de timbres
[2] le <u>tampon</u> (*rubber stamp*)

stamped ADJECTIVE
<u>affranchi</u> ◊ *The letter wasn't stamped.* La lettre n'était pas affranchie.
♦**Enclose a stamped addressed envelope.** Joindre une enveloppe affranchie à vos nom et adresse.

to **stand** VERB
[1] <u>être debout</u> (*be standing*) ◊ *He was standing by the door.* Il était debout à la porte.
[2] <u>se lever</u> (*stand up*)
[3] <u>supporter</u> (*tolerate, withstand*) ◊ *I can't stand all this noise.* Je ne supporte pas tout ce bruit.
♦**to stand for (1)** (*be short for*) être l'abréviation de ◊ *"BT" stands for "British Telecom".* "BT" est l'abréviation de "British Telecom".
♦**to stand for (2)** (*tolerate*) supporter ◊ *I won't stand for it!* Je ne supporterai pas ça!
♦**to stand in for somebody** remplacer quelqu'un
♦**to stand out** se distinguer ◊ *All the contestants were good, but none of them stood out.* Tous les concurrents étaient bons, mais aucun ne se distinguait.
♦**She really stands out in that orange coat.** Tout le monde la remarque avec ce manteau orange.
♦**to stand up** (*get up*) se lever
♦**to stand up for** défendre ◊ *Stand up for your rights!* Défendez vos droits!

standard ADJECTIVE
see also **standard** NOUN
[1] <u>courant</u> ◊ *standard French* le français courant
[2] <u>ordinaire</u> (*equipment*)
♦**the standard procedure** la procédure normale

standard NOUN
see also **standard** ADJECTIVE
le <u>niveau</u>
(les niveaux PL)
◊ *The standard is very high.* Le niveau est très haut.
♦**the standard of living** le niveau de vie
♦**She's got high standards.** Elle est très exigeante.

stand-by ticket NOUN
le <u>billet stand-by</u>

standpoint NOUN
le <u>point de vue</u>

stands PL NOUN
la <u>tribune</u> SING (*at sports ground*)

stank VERB see **stink**

staple NOUN
see also **staple** VERB
l' <u>agrafe</u> FEM

to **staple** VERB
see also **staple** NOUN
<u>agrafer</u>

stapler NOUN
l' <u>agrafeuse</u> FEM

star NOUN
see also **star** VERB
[1] l' <u>étoile</u> FEM (*in sky*)
[2] la <u>vedette</u> (*celebrity*) ◊ *He's a TV star.* C'est une vedette de la télé.
♦**the stars** (*horoscope*) l' horoscope MASC

to **star** VERB
see also **star** NOUN
<u>être la vedette</u> ◊ *to star in a film* être la vedette d'un film
♦**The film stars Glenda Jackson.** Le film a pour vedette Glenda Jackson.
♦**... starring Johnny Depp ...** avec Johnny Depp

to **stare** VERB
♦**to stare at something** fixer quelque chose

stark ADVERB
♦**stark naked** complètement nu

start NOUN
see also **start** VERB
[1] le <u>début</u> ◊ *It's not much, but it's a start.* Ce n'est pas grand chose, mais c'est un début.
♦**Shall we make a start on the washing-up?** On commence à faire la vaisselle?
[2] le <u>départ</u> (*of race*)

to **start** VERB
see also **start** NOUN

S

☞

1 commencer ◊ *What time does it start?* À quelle heure est-ce que ça commence?

♦ **to start doing something** commencer à faire quelque chose ◊ *I started learning French three years ago.* J'ai commencé à apprendre le français il y a trois ans.

2 créer (*organization*) ◊ *He wants to start his own business.* Il veut créer sa propre entreprise.

3 organiser (*campaign*) ◊ *She started a campaign against drugs.* Elle a organisé une campagne contre la drogue.

4 démarrer (*car*) ◊ *He couldn't start the car.* Il n'a pas réussi à démarrer la voiture. ◊ *The car wouldn't start.* La voiture ne voulait pas démarrer.

♦ **to start off** (*leave*) partir ◊ *We started off first thing in the morning.* Nous sommes partis en début de matinée.

starter NOUN
l' entrée FEM (*first course*)

to **starve** VERB
mourir de faim ◊ *People were literally starving.* Les gens mouraient littéralement de faim.

♦ **I'm starving!** Je meurs de faim!

state NOUN
see also **state** VERB
l' état MASC

♦ **he was in a real state** il était dans tous ses états

♦ **the state** (*government*) l'État

♦ **the States** (*USA*) les États-Unis MASC

to **state** VERB
see also **state** NOUN
1 déclarer (*say*) ◊ *He stated his intention to resign.* Il a déclaré son intention de démissionner.

2 donner (*give*) ◊ *Please state your name and address.* Veuillez donner vos nom et adresse.

stately home NOUN
le château
(les châteaux PL)

statement NOUN
la déclaration

station NOUN
la gare (*railway*)

♦ **the bus station** la gare routière

♦ **a police station** un poste de police

♦ **a radio station** une station de radio

stationer's NOUN
la papeterie

station wagon NOUN US
le break

statue NOUN
la statue

to **stay** VERB
see also **stay** NOUN
1 rester (*remain*) ◊ *Stay here!* Reste ici!

♦ **to stay in** (*not go out*) rester à la maison

♦ **to stay up** rester debout ◊ *We stayed up till midnight.* Nous sommes restés debout jusqu'à minuit.

2 loger (*spend the night*) ◊ *to stay with friends* loger chez des amis ◊ *Where are you staying?* Où est-ce que vous logez?

♦ **to stay the night** passer la nuit

♦ **We stayed in Belgium for a few days.** Nous avons passé quelques jours en Belgique.

stay NOUN
see also **stay** VERB
le séjour ◊ *my stay in France* mon séjour en France

steady ADJECTIVE
1 régulier MASC
régulière FEM
◊ *steady progress* des progrès réguliers

2 stable ◊ *a steady job* un emploi stable

3 (*voice, hand*)
ferme

4 (*person*)
calme

♦ **a steady boyfriend** un copain

♦ **a steady girlfriend** une copine

♦ **Steady on!** Doucement!

steak NOUN
le steak (*beef*) ◊ *steak and chips* un steak frites

to **steal** VERB
voler

steam NOUN
la vapeur ◊ *a steam engine* une locomotive à vapeur

steel NOUN
l' acier MASC ◊ *a steel door* une porte en acier

steep ADJECTIVE
raide (*slope*)

steeple NOUN
le clocher

steering wheel NOUN
le volant

step NOUN
see also **step** VERB
1 le pas (*pace*) ◊ *He took a step forward.* Il a fait un pas en avant.

2 la marche (*stair*) ◊ *She tripped over the step.* Elle a trébuché sur la marche.

to **step** VERB

see also **step** NOUN

♦**to step aside** faire un pas de côté

♦**to step back** faire un pas en arrière

stepbrother NOUN
le <u>demi-frère</u>

stepdaughter NOUN
la <u>belle-fille</u>
(les belles-filles PL)

stepfather NOUN
le <u>beau-père</u>
(les beaux-pères PL)

stepladder NOUN
l' <u>escabeau</u> MASC
(les escabeaux PL)

stepmother NOUN
la <u>belle-mère</u>
(les belles-mères PL)

stepsister NOUN
la <u>demi-sœur</u>

stepson NOUN
le <u>beau-fils</u>
(les beaux-fils PL)

stereo NOUN
la <u>chaîne stéréo</u>
(les chaînes stéréo PL)

sterling ADJECTIVE
♦**£5 sterling** cinq livres sterling

stew NOUN
le <u>ragoût</u>

steward NOUN
le <u>steward</u>

stewardess NOUN
l' <u>hôtesse de l'air</u> FEM

stick NOUN

see also **stick** VERB

1 le <u>bâton</u>
2 la <u>canne</u> (walking stick)

to **stick** VERB

see also **stick** NOUN

<u>coller</u> (with adhesive) ◊ Stick the stamps on the envelope. Collez les timbres sur l'enveloppe.

♦**I can't stick it any longer.** Je n'en peux plus.

to **stick out** VERB

<u>sortir</u> (project) ◊ A pen was sticking out of his pocket. Un stylo sortait de sa poche.

♦**Stick your tongue out and say "ah".** Tirez la langue et dites "ah".

sticker NOUN
l' <u>autocollant</u> MASC

sticky ADJECTIVE

1 <u>poisseux</u> MASC
<u>poisseuse</u> FEM
◊ to have sticky hands avoir les mains poisseuses

2 <u>adhésif</u> MASC

<u>adhésive</u> FEM
◊ a sticky label une étiquette adhésive

stiff ADJECTIVE, ADVERB
<u>rigide</u> (rigid)

♦**to have a stiff back** avoir mal au dos

♦**to feel stiff** avoir des courbatures

♦**to be bored stiff** s'ennuyer à mourir

♦**to be frozen stiff** être mort de froid

♦**to be scared stiff** être mort de peur

still ADVERB

see also **still** ADJECTIVE

1 <u>encore</u> ◊ I still haven't finished. Je n'ai pas encore fini. ◊ Are you still in bed? Tu es encore au lit?

♦**better still** encore mieux

2 <u>quand même</u> (even so) ◊ She knows I don't like it, but she still does it. Elle sait que je n'aime pas ça, mais elle le fait quand même.

3 <u>enfin</u> (after all) ◊ Still, it's the thought that counts. Enfin, c'est l'intention qui compte.

still ADJECTIVE

see also **still** ADVERB

♦**Keep still!** Ne bouge pas!

♦**Sit still!** Reste tranquille!

sting NOUN

see also **sting** VERB

la <u>piqûre</u> ◊ a bee sting une piqûre d'abeille

to **sting** VERB

see also **sting** NOUN

<u>piquer</u> ◊ I've been stung. J'ai été piqué.

stingy ADJECTIVE
<u>pingre</u>

to **stink** VERB

see also **stink** NOUN

<u>puer</u> ◊ It stinks! Ça pue!

stink NOUN

see also **stink** VERB

la <u>puanteur</u>

to **stir** VERB
<u>remuer</u>

to **stitch** VERB

see also **stitch** NOUN

<u>coudre</u> (cloth)

stitch NOUN

see also **stitch** VERB

1 le <u>point</u> (in sewing)
2 le <u>point de suture</u> (in wound) ◊ I had five stitches. J'ai eu cinq points de suture.

stock NOUN

see also **stock** VERB

1 la <u>réserve</u> (supply)
2 le <u>stock</u> (in shop) ◊ in stock en stock

♦**out of stock** épuisé

S

☞

3 le <u>bouillon</u> ◊ *chicken stock* du bouillon de volaille

to **stock** VERB

see also **stock** NOUN

<u>avoir</u> (*have in stock*) ◊ *Do you stock camping stoves?* Vous avez des camping-gaz?

♦**to stock up** s'approvisionner ◊ *to stock up with something* s'approvisionner en quelque chose

stock cube NOUN
le <u>cube de bouillon</u>

stocking NOUN
le <u>bas</u>

stole, stolen VERB *see* **steal**

stomach NOUN
l' <u>estomac</u> MASC

stomachache NOUN
♦**to have a stomachache** avoir mal au ventre

stone NOUN
1 (*rock*)
la <u>pierre</u> ◊ *a stone wall* un mur en pierre
2 (*in fruit*)
le <u>noyau</u>
(les noyaux PL)
◊ *a peach stone* un noyau de pêche

> *ⓘ In France, weight is expressed in kilos. A stone is about 6.3 kg.*

♦**I weigh eight stone.** Je pèse cinquante kilos.

stood VERB *see* **stand**

stool NOUN
le <u>tabouret</u>

to **stop** VERB

see also **stop** NOUN

1 <u>arrêter</u> ◊ *a campaign to stop whaling* une campagne pour arrêter la chasse à la baleine
2 <u>s'arrêter</u> ◊ *The bus doesn't stop there.* Le bus ne s'arrête pas là. ◊ *I think the rain's going to stop.* Je pense qu'il va s'arrêter de pleuvoir.

♦**to stop doing something** arrêter de faire quelque chose ◊ *to stop smoking* arrêter de fumer

♦**to stop somebody doing something** empêcher quelqu'un de faire quelque chose

♦**Stop!** Stop!

stop NOUN

see also **stop** VERB

l' <u>arrêt</u> MASC ◊ *a bus stop* un arrêt de bus

♦**This is my stop.** Je descends ici.

stopwatch NOUN

le <u>chronomètre</u>

store NOUN

see also **store** VERB

1 le <u>magasin</u> (*shop*) ◊ *a furniture store* un magasin de meubles
2 la <u>réserve</u> (*stock, storeroom*)

to **store** VERB

see also **store** NOUN

1 <u>garder</u> ◊ *They store potatoes in the cellar.* Ils gardent des pommes de terre dans la cave.
2 <u>enregistrer</u> (*information*)

storey NOUN
l' <u>étage</u> MASC ◊ *a three-storey building* un immeuble à trois étages

storm NOUN
1 la <u>tempête</u> (*gale*)
2 l' <u>orage</u> MASC (*thunderstorm*)

stormy ADJECTIVE
<u>orageux</u> MASC
<u>orageuse</u> FEM

story NOUN
l' <u>histoire</u> FEM

stove NOUN
1 la <u>cuisinière</u> (*in kitchen*)
2 le <u>réchaud</u> (*camping stove*)

straight ADJECTIVE
1 <u>droit</u> ◊ *a straight line* une ligne droite
2 <u>raide</u> ◊ *straight hair* les cheveux raides
3 <u>hétéro</u> (*heterosexual*)
♦**straight away** tout de suite
♦**straight on** tout droit

straightforward ADJECTIVE
<u>simple</u>

strain NOUN

see also **strain** VERB

le <u>stress</u>
♦**It was a strain.** C'était éprouvant.

to **strain** VERB

see also **strain** NOUN

<u>se faire mal à</u> ◊ *I strained my back.* Je me suis fait mal au dos.
♦**to strain a muscle** se froisser un muscle

strained ADJECTIVE
<u>froissé</u> (*muscle*)

stranded ADJECTIVE
♦**We were stranded.** Nous étions coincés.

strange ADJECTIVE
<u>bizarre</u> ◊ *That's strange!* C'est bizarre!

stranger NOUN
l' <u>inconnu</u> MASC
l' <u>inconnue</u> FEM

◊ *Don't talk to strangers.* Ne parle pas aux inconnus.

♦ **I'm a stranger here.** Je ne suis pas d'ici.

to **strangle** VERB
étrangler

strap NOUN
☐1 la courroie (*of bag, camera, suitcase*)
☐2 la bretelle (*of bra, dress*)
☐3 la lanière (*on shoe*)
☐4 le bracelet (*of watch*)

straw NOUN
la paille
♦ **That's the last straw!** Ça, c'est le comble!

strawberry NOUN
la fraise ◊ *strawberry jam* la confiture de fraises ◊ *a strawberry ice cream* une glace à la fraise

stray NOUN
♦ **a stray cat** un chat perdu

stream NOUN
le ruisseau
(les ruisseaux PL)

street NOUN
la rue ◊ *in the street* dans la rue

streetcar NOUN US
le tramway

streetlamp NOUN
le réverbère

street plan NOUN
le plan de la ville

streetwise ADJECTIVE
dégourdi

strength NOUN
la force

to **stress** VERB
see also **stress** NOUN
souligner ◊ *I would like to stress that ...* J'aimerais souligner que ...

stress NOUN
see also **stress** VERB
le stress

to **stretch** VERB
☐1 s'étirer (*person, animal*) ◊ *The dog woke up and stretched.* Le chien s'est réveillé et s'est étiré.
☐2 se détendre (*get bigger*) ◊ *My sweater stretched when I washed it.* Mon pull s'est détendu au lavage.
☐3 tendre (*stretch out*) ◊ *They stretched a rope between two trees.* Ils ont tendu une corde entre deux arbres.
♦ **to stretch out one's arms** tendre les bras

stretcher NOUN
le brancard

stretchy ADJECTIVE
élastique

strict ADJECTIVE
strict

strike NOUN
see also **strike** VERB
la grève
♦ **to be on strike** être en grève
♦ **to go on strike** faire grève

to **strike** VERB
see also **strike** NOUN
☐1 sonner (*clock*) ◊ *The clock struck three.* L'horloge a sonné trois heures.
☐2 faire grève (*go on strike*)
☐3 frapper (*hit*)
♦ **to strike a match** frotter une allumette

striker NOUN
☐1 le/la gréviste (*person on strike*)
☐2 le buteur (*footballer*)

striking ADJECTIVE
☐1 en grève (*on strike*) ◊ *striking miners* les mineurs en grève
☐2 frappant (*noticeable*) ◊ *a striking difference* une différence frappante

string NOUN
☐1 la ficelle ◊ *a piece of string* un bout de ficelle
☐2 la corde (*of violin, guitar*)

to **strip** VERB
see also **strip** NOUN
se déshabiller (*get undressed*)

strip NOUN
see also **strip** VERB
la bande
♦ **a strip cartoon** une bande dessinée

stripe NOUN
la rayure

striped ADJECTIVE
à rayures ◊ *a striped skirt* une jupe à rayures

stripper NOUN
le strip-teaseur
la strip-teaseuse

stripy ADJECTIVE
rayé ◊ *a stripy shirt* une chemise rayée

to **stroke** VERB
see also **stroke** NOUN
caresser

stroke NOUN
see also **stroke** VERB
l' attaque FEM ◊ *to have a stroke* avoir une attaque

stroll NOUN
♦ **to go for a stroll** aller faire une petite promenade

S

stroller NOUN [US]
la <u>poussette</u>

strong ADJECTIVE
1 <u>fort</u> ◊ *She's very strong.* Elle est très forte.
2 <u>résistant</u> (*material*)

strongly ADVERB
<u>fortement</u> ◊ *We recommend strongly that ...* Nous recommandons fortement que ...
♦ **He smelt strongly of tobacco.** Il sentait fort le tabac.
♦ **strongly built** solidement bâti
♦ **I don't feel strongly about it.** Ça m'est égal.

struck VERB *see* **strike**

to **struggle** VERB
| *see also* **struggle** NOUN |
<u>se débattre</u> (*physically*) ◊ *He struggled, but he couldn't escape.* Il s'est débattu, mais il n'a pas pu s'échapper.
♦ **to struggle to do something (1)** (*fight*) se battre pour faire quelque chose ◊ *He struggled to get custody of his daughter.* Il s'est battu pour obtenir la garde de sa fille.
♦ **to struggle to do something (2)** (*have difficulty*) avoir du mal à faire quelque chose

struggle NOUN
| *see also* **struggle** VERB |
la <u>lutte</u> (*for independence, equality*)
♦ **It was a struggle.** Ça a été laborieux.

stub NOUN
le <u>mégot</u> (*of cigarette*)

to **stub out** VERB
<u>écraser</u> (*cigarette*)

stubborn ADJECTIVE
<u>têtu</u>

stuck VERB *see* **stick**

stuck ADJECTIVE
<u>coincé</u> (*jammed*) ◊ *It's stuck.* C'est coincé.
♦ **to get stuck** rester coincé ◊ *We got stuck in a traffic jam.* Nous sommes restés coincés dans un embouteillage.

stuck-up ADJECTIVE
<u>coincé</u> (*informal*)

stud NOUN
1 la <u>boucle d'oreille</u> (*earring*)
2 le <u>clou</u> (*on football boots*)

student NOUN
l' <u>étudiant</u> MASC
l' <u>étudiante</u> FEM

studio NOUN
le <u>studio</u> ◊ *a TV studio* un studio de télévision
♦ **a studio flat** un studio

to **study** VERB
1 <u>faire des études</u> (*at university*) ◊ *I plan to study biology.* J'ai l'intention de faire des études de biologie.
2 <u>travailler</u> (*do homework*) ◊ *I've got to study tonight.* Je dois travailler ce soir.

stuff NOUN
1 le <u>truc</u> (*substance*) ◊ *I need some stuff for hay fever.* J'ai besoin d'un truc contre le rhume des foins.
2 les <u>trucs</u> MASC PL (*things*) ◊ *There's some stuff on the table for you.* Il y a des trucs sur la table pour toi.
3 les <u>affaires</u> FEM PL (*possessions*) ◊ *Have you got all your stuff?* Est-ce que tu as toutes tes affaires?

stuffy ADJECTIVE
<u>mal aéré</u> (*room*)
♦ **It's really stuffy in here.** On étouffe ici.

to **stumble** VERB
<u>trébucher</u>

stung VERB *see* **sting**

stunk VERB *see* **stink**

stunned ADJECTIVE
<u>sidéré</u> (*amazed*) ◊ *I was stunned.* J'étais sidéré.

stunning ADJECTIVE
<u>superbe</u>

stunt NOUN
la <u>cascade</u> (*in film*)

stuntman NOUN
le <u>cascadeur</u>

stupid ADJECTIVE
<u>stupide</u> ◊ *a stupid joke* une plaisanterie stupide
♦ **Me, go jogging? Don't be stupid!** Moi, faire du footing? Ne dis pas de bêtises!

to **stutter** VERB
| *see also* **stutter** NOUN |
<u>bégayer</u>

stutter NOUN
| *see also* **stutter** VERB |
♦ **He's got a stutter.** Il bégaie.

style NOUN
le <u>style</u> ◊ *That's not his style.* Ça n'est pas son style.

subject NOUN
1 le <u>sujet</u> ◊ *The subject of my project was the internet.* Le sujet de mon projet était l'Internet.
2 la <u>matière</u> (*at school*) ◊ *What's your favourite subject?* Quelle est ta matière préférée?

subjunctive NOUN

le subjonctif ◊ *in the subjunctive* au subjonctif

submarine NOUN
le sous-marin

subscription NOUN
l' abonnement MASC (*to paper, magazine*)
♦ **to take out a subscription to** s'abonner à

subsequently ADVERB
en conséquence

to **subsidize** VERB
subventionner

subsidy NOUN
la subvention

substance NOUN
la substance

substitute NOUN
see also **substitute** VERB
(*person*)
le remplaçant
la remplaçante

to **substitute** VERB
see also **substitute** NOUN
substituer ◊ *to substitute A for B* substituer A à B

subtitled ADJECTIVE
sous-titré

subtitles PL NOUN
les sous-titres MASC PL ◊ *a French film with English subtitles* un film français avec des sous-titres en anglais

subtle ADJECTIVE
subtil

to **subtract** VERB
retrancher ◊ *to subtract 3 from 5* retrancher trois de cinq

suburb NOUN
la banlieue ◊ *a suburb of Paris* une banlieue de Paris ◊ *They live in the suburbs.* Ils habitent en banlieue.

suburban ADJECTIVE
de banlieue ◊ *a suburban train* un train de banlieue

subway NOUN
le passage souterrain (*underpass*)

to **succeed** VERB
réussir ◊ *to succeed in doing something* réussir à faire quelque chose

success NOUN
le succès ◊ *The play was a great success.* La pièce a eu beaucoup de succès.

successful ADJECTIVE
réussi ◊ *a successful attempt* une tentative réussie

♦ **to be successful in doing something** réussir à faire quelque chose
♦ **He's a successful businessman.** Ses affaires marchent bien.

successfully ADVERB
avec succès

successive ADJECTIVE
♦ **on four successive occasions** quatre fois de suite

such ADJECTIVE, ADVERB
si ◊ *such nice people* des gens si gentils ◊ *such a long journey* un voyage si long
♦ **such a lot of** tellement de ◊ *such a lot of work* tellement de travail
♦ **such as** (*like*) comme ◊ *hot countries, such as India* les pays chauds, comme l'Inde
♦ **not as such** pas exactement ◊ *He's not an expert as such, but ...* Ce n'est pas exactement un expert, mais ...
♦ **There's no such thing.** Ça n'existe pas. ◊ *There's no such thing as the yeti.* Le yéti n'existe pas.

such-and-such ADJECTIVE
tel ou tel MASC
telle ou telle FEM
◊ *such-and-such a place* tel ou tel endroit

to **suck** VERB
sucer ◊ *to suck one's thumb* sucer son pouce

sudden ADJECTIVE
soudain ◊ *a sudden change* un changement soudain
♦ **all of a sudden** tout à coup

suddenly ADVERB
1 brusquement (*stop, leave, change*)
2 subitement (*die*)
3 soudain (*at beginning of sentence*)
◊ *Suddenly, the door opened.* Soudain, la porte s'est ouverte.

suede NOUN
le daim ◊ *a suede jacket* une veste en daim

to **suffer** VERB
souffrir ◊ *She was really suffering.* Elle souffrait beaucoup.
♦ **to suffer from a disease** avoir une maladie ◊ *I suffer from hay fever.* J'ai le rhume des foins.

to **suffocate** VERB
suffoquer

sugar NOUN
le sucre ◊ *Do you take sugar?* Est-ce que vous prenez du sucre?

to **suggest** VERB

S

☞

suggérer ◊ *I suggested they set off early.* Je leur ai suggéré de partir de bonne heure.

suggestion NOUN
la suggestion ◊ *to make a suggestion* faire une suggestion

suicide NOUN
le suicide
◆**to commit suicide** se suicider

suit NOUN
⎢see also **suit** VERB⎥
① le costume (*man's*)
② le tailleur (*woman's*)

to **suit** VERB
⎢see also **suit** NOUN⎥
① convenir à (*be convenient for*) ◊ *What time would suit you?* Quelle heure vous conviendrait?
◆ **That suits me fine.** Ça m'arrange.
◆ **Suit yourself!** Comme tu veux!
② aller bien à (*look good on*) ◊ *That dress really suits you.* Cette robe te va vraiment bien.

suitable ADJECTIVE
① convenable ◊ *a suitable time* une heure convenable
② approprié (*clothes*) ◊ *suitable clothing* des vêtements appropriés

suitcase NOUN
la valise

suite NOUN
la suite (*of rooms*)
◆ **a bedroom suite** une chambre à coucher

to **sulk** VERB
bouder

sulky ADJECTIVE
boudeur MASC
boudeuse FEM

sultana NOUN
le raisin sec
(les raisins secs PL)

sum NOUN
① le calcul (*calculation*) ◊ *She's good at sums.* Elle est bonne en calcul.
② la somme (*amount*) ◊ *a sum of money* une somme d'argent

to **sum up** VERB
résumer

to **summarize** VERB
résumer

summary NOUN
le résumé

summer NOUN
l' été MASC
◆**in summer** en été
◆**summer clothes** les vêtements d'été MASC

◆**the summer holidays** les vacances d'été FEM
◆**a summer camp** US une colonie de vacances US

summertime NOUN
l' été MASC
◆**in summertime** en été

summit NOUN
le sommet

sun NOUN
le soleil ◊ *in the sun* au soleil

to **sunbathe** VERB
se bronzer

sunblock NOUN
l' écran total MASC

sunburn NOUN
le coup de soleil

sunburnt ADJECTIVE
◆**I got sunburnt.** J'ai attrapé un coup de soleil.

Sunday NOUN
le dimanche ◊ *on Sunday* dimanche ◊ *on Sundays* le dimanche ◊ *every Sunday* tous les dimanches ◊ *last Sunday* dimanche dernier ◊ *next Sunday* dimanche prochain

Sunday school NOUN
le catéchisme

> **ⓘ** *le catéchisme*, the French equivalent of **Sunday school**, takes place during the week after school rather than on a Sunday.

◊ *to go to Sunday school* aller au catéchisme

sunflower NOUN
le tournesol

sung VERB *see* **sing**

sunglasses PL NOUN
les lunettes de soleil FEM PL

sunk VERB *see* **sink**

sunlight NOUN
le soleil

sunny ADJECTIVE
ensoleillé ◊ *a sunny morning* une matinée ensoleillée
◆**It's sunny.** Il fait du soleil.
◆**a sunny day** une belle journée

sunrise NOUN
le lever du soleil

sunroof NOUN
le toit ouvrant

sunscreen NOUN
la crème solaire

sunset NOUN
le coucher du soleil

sunshine NOUN

le soleil

sunstroke NOUN
l' insolation FEM ◊ *to get sunstroke*
attraper une insolation

suntan NOUN
le bronzage
♦ **suntan lotion** le lait solaire
♦ **suntan oil** l'huile solaire FEM

super ADJECTIVE
formidable

superb ADJECTIVE
superbe

supermarket NOUN
le supermarché

supernatural ADJECTIVE
surnaturel MASC
surnaturelle FEM

superstitious ADJECTIVE
superstitieux MASC
superstitieuse FEM

to **supervise** VERB
surveiller

supervisor NOUN
1 (*in factory*)
le surveillant
la surveillante
2 (*in department store*)
le chef de rayon

supper NOUN
le dîner

supplement NOUN
le supplément

supplies PL NOUN
les vivres MASC PL (*food*)

to **supply** VERB
see also **supply** NOUN
fournir (*provide*)
♦ **to supply somebody with something**
fournir quelque chose à quelqu'un
◊ *The centre supplied us with all the
equipment.* Le centre nous a fourni
tout l'équipement.

supply NOUN
see also **supply** VERB
la provision ◊ *a supply of paper* une
provision de papier
♦ **the water supply** (*to town*)
l'approvisionnement en eau MASC

supply teacher NOUN
le suppléant
la suppléante

to **support** VERB
see also **support** NOUN
1 soutenir ◊ *My mum has always
supported me.* Ma mère m'a toujours
soutenu.

2 être supporter de ◊ *What team
do you support?* Tu es supporter de
quelle équipe?
3 subvenir aux besoins de
(*financially*) ◊ *She had to support five
children on her own.* Elle a dû
subvenir toute seule aux besoins de
cinq enfants.

*Be careful not to translate **to support**
by **supporter**.*

support NOUN
see also **support** VERB
le soutien (*backing*)

supporter NOUN
1 le supporter ◊ *a Liverpool
supporter* un supporter de Liverpool
2 le sympathisant
la sympathisante
◊ *a supporter of the Labour Party* un
sympathisant du parti travailliste

to **suppose** VERB
imaginer ◊ *I suppose he's late.*
J'imagine qu'il est en retard.
◊ *Suppose you won the lottery.*
Imaginez que vous gagniez à la
loterie.
♦ **I suppose so.** J'imagine.
♦ **to be supposed to do something** être
censé faire quelque chose ◊ *You're
supposed to show your passport.* On
est censé montrer son passeport.

supposing CONJUNCTION
si ◊ *Supposing you won the lottery ...*
Si tu gagnais à la loterie ...

surcharge NOUN
la surcharge

sure ADJECTIVE
sûr ◊ *Are you sure?* Tu es sûr?
♦ **Sure!** Bien sûr!
♦ **to make sure that ...** vérifier que ...
◊ *I'm going to make sure the door's
locked.* Je vais vérifier que la porte
est fermée à clé.

surely ADVERB
♦ **Surely you've been to London?**
J'imagine que tu es allé à Londres,
non?
♦ **The shops are closed on Sundays,
surely?** J'imagine que les magasins
sont fermés le dimanche, non?

surf NOUN
see also **surf** VERB
le ressac

to **surf** VERB
see also **surf** NOUN
surfer
♦ **to go surfing** faire du surf
♦ **to surf the Net** surfer sur le Net

surface NOUN
la surface

S

surfboard NOUN
la planche de surf
(les planches de surf PL)

surfing NOUN
le surf ◊ *to go surfing* faire du surf

surgeon NOUN
le chirurgien ◊ *She's a surgeon.* Elle
est chirurgien.

surgery NOUN
le cabinet médical (*doctor's surgery*)
♦ **surgery hours** les heures de
consultation FEM

surname NOUN
le nom de famille
(les noms de famille PL)

surprise NOUN
la surprise

surprised ADJECTIVE
surpris ◊ *I was surprised to see him.*
J'ai été surpris de le voir.

surprising ADJECTIVE
surprenant

to **surrender** VERB
capituler

surrogate mother NOUN
la mère porteuse
(les mères porteuses PL)

to **surround** VERB
encercler ◊ *The police surrounded
the house.* La police a encerclé la
maison. ◊ *You're surrounded!* Vous
êtes encerclé!
♦ **surrounded by** entouré de ◊ *The
house is surrounded by trees.* La
maison est entourée d'arbres.

surroundings PL NOUN
le cadre SING ◊ *a hotel in beautiful
surroundings* un hôtel situé dans un
beau cadre

survey NOUN
l' enquête FEM (*research*)

surveyor NOUN
1 l' expert en bâtiment MASC (*of
buildings*)
2 le/la géomètre (*of land*)

to **survive** VERB
survivre

survivor NOUN
le survivant
la survivante
◊ *There were no survivors.* Il n'y a
pas eu de survivants.

to **suspect** VERB
see also **suspect** NOUN
soupçonner

suspect NOUN
see also **suspect** VERB
le suspect
la suspecte

to **suspend** VERB
1 exclure (*from school, team*) ◊ *He's
been suspended.* Il s'est fait exclure.
2 suspendre (*from job*)

suspenders PL NOUN US
les bretelles FEM PL (*braces*)

suspense NOUN
1 l' attente FEM (*waiting*) ◊ *The
suspense was terrible.* L'attente a été
terrible.
2 le suspense (*in story*) ◊ *a film with
lots of suspense* un film avec
beaucoup de suspense

suspension NOUN
1 l' exclusion FEM (*from school, team*)
2 la suspension (*from job*)

suspicious ADJECTIVE
1 méfiant ◊ *He was suspicious at
first.* Il était méfiant au début. ◊ *a
suspicious person* un individu louche

to **swallow** VERB
avaler

swam VERB *see* **swim**

swan NOUN
le cygne

to **swap** VERB
échanger ◊ *Do you want to swap?*
Tu veux échanger? ◊ *to swap A for B*
échanger A contre B

to **swat** VERB
écraser

to **sway** VERB
osciller

to **swear** VERB
jurer (*make an oath, curse*)

swearword NOUN
le gros mot

sweat NOUN
see also **sweat** VERB
la transpiration

to **sweat** VERB
see also **sweat** NOUN
transpirer

sweater NOUN
le pull

sweatshirt NOUN
le sweat

sweaty ADJECTIVE
1 en sueur (*person, face*) ◊ *I'm all
sweaty.* Je suis en sueur.
2 moite (*hands*)

Swede NOUN
(*person*)
le Suédois
la Suédoise

swede NOUN
le rutabaga (*vegetable*)

Sweden NOUN
la Suède
♦ **in Sweden** en Suède
♦ **to Sweden** en Suède

Swedish ADJECTIVE
see also **Swedish** NOUN
suédois ◊ She's Swedish. Elle est suédoise.

Swedish NOUN
see also **Swedish** ADJECTIVE
le suédois (language)

to **sweep** VERB
balayer
♦ **to sweep the floor** balayer

sweet NOUN
see also **sweet** ADJECTIVE
1 le bonbon (candy) ◊ a bag of sweets un paquet de bonbons
2 le dessert (pudding) ◊ What sweet did you have? Qu'est-ce que vous avez mangé comme dessert?

sweet ADJECTIVE
see also **sweet** NOUN
1 (not savoury)
sucré
2 (kind)
gentil MASC
gentille FEM
◊ That was really sweet of you. C'était vraiment gentil de ta part.
3 (cute)
mignon MASC
mignonne FEM
◊ Isn't she sweet? Comme elle est mignonne!
♦ **sweet and sour pork** le porc à la sauce aigre-douce

sweetcorn NOUN
le maïs doux

sweltering ADJECTIVE
♦ **It was sweltering.** Il faisait une chaleur étouffante.

swept VERB see **sweep**

to **swerve** VERB
faire une embardée ◊ He swerved to avoid the cyclist. Il a fait une embardée pour éviter le cycliste.

swim NOUN
see also **swim** VERB
♦ **to go for a swim** aller se baigner

to **swim** VERB
see also **swim** NOUN
nager ◊ Can you swim? Tu sais nager?
♦ **She swam across the river.** Elle a traversé la rivière à la nage.

swimmer NOUN
le nageur
la nageuse

◊ She's a good swimmer. C'est une bonne nageuse.

swimming NOUN
la natation ◊ Do you like swimming? Tu aimes la natation?
♦ **to go swimming** (in a pool) aller à la piscine
♦ **a swimming cap** un bonnet de bain
♦ **a swimming costume** un maillot de bain
♦ **a swimming pool** une piscine
♦ **swimming trunks** le maillot de bain

swimsuit NOUN
le maillot de bain

swing NOUN
see also **swing** VERB
la balançoire (in playground, garden)

to **swing** VERB
see also **swing** NOUN
1 se balancer ◊ A bunch of keys swung from his belt. Un trousseau de clés se balançait à sa ceinture.
♦ **Sam was swinging an umbrella as he walked.** Sam balançait son parapluie en marchant.
2 virer ◊ The canoe swung round sharply. Le canoë a viré brusquement.

Swiss ADJECTIVE
see also **Swiss** NOUN
suisse ◊ Sabine's Swiss. Sabine est suisse.

Swiss NOUN
see also **Swiss** ADJECTIVE
le/la Suisse (person)
♦ **the Swiss** les Suisses

switch NOUN
see also **switch** VERB
le bouton (for light, radio etc)

to **switch** VERB
see also **switch** NOUN
changer de ◊ We switched partners. Nous avons changé de partenaire.

to **switch off** VERB
1 éteindre (electrical appliance)
2 arrêter (engine, machine)

to **switch on** VERB
1 allumer (electrical appliance)
2 mettre en marche (engine, machine)

Switzerland NOUN
la Suisse
♦ **in Switzerland** en Suisse

swollen ADJECTIVE
enflé (arm, leg)

to **swop** VERB
échanger ◊ Do you want to swop? Tu veux échanger? ◊ to swop A for B échanger A contre B

S

sword NOUN
l' <u>épée</u> FEM

swore, sworn VERB *see* **swear**

swot NOUN
| *see also* **swot** VERB |
le <u>bûcheur</u>
la <u>bûcheuse</u>

to **swot** VERB
| *see also* **swot** NOUN |
<u>bosser dur</u> ◊ *I'll have to swot for my maths exam.* Je vais devoir bosser dur pour mon examen de maths.

swum VERB *see* **swim**

swung VERB *see* **swing**

syllabus NOUN
le <u>programme</u> ◊ *on the syllabus* au programme

symbol NOUN
le <u>symbole</u>

sympathetic ADJECTIVE
<u>compréhensif</u> MASC
<u>compréhensive</u> FEM
Be careful not to translate ***sympathetic** by* ***sympathique**.*

to **sympathize** VERB
♦**to sympathize with somebody**
comprendre quelqu'un

sympathy NOUN
la <u>compassion</u>

symptom NOUN
le <u>symptôme</u>

syringe NOUN
la <u>seringue</u>

system NOUN
le <u>système</u>

T

table NOUN
la <u>table</u> ◊ *to lay the table* mettre la table

tablecloth NOUN
la <u>nappe</u>

tablespoon NOUN
la <u>grande cuillère</u>
♦ **a tablespoonful of sugar** une cuillerée à soupe de sucre

tablet NOUN
le <u>comprimé</u>

table tennis NOUN
le <u>ping-pong</u> ◊ *to play table tennis* jouer au ping-pong

tabloid NOUN
le <u>quotidien populaire</u>

tackle NOUN
| see also **tackle** VERB |
1 le <u>tacle</u> (*in football*)
2 le <u>plaquage</u> (*in rugby*)
♦ **fishing tackle** le matériel de pêche

to **tackle** VERB
| see also **tackle** NOUN |
1 <u>tacler</u> (*in football*)
2 <u>plaquer</u> (*in rugby*)
♦ **to tackle a problem** s'attaquer à un problème

tact NOUN
le <u>tact</u>

tactful ADJECTIVE
<u>plein de tact</u>

tactics PL NOUN
la <u>tactique</u> SING

tactless ADJECTIVE
♦ **to be tactless** manquer de tact ◊ *a tactless remark* une remarque qui manque de tact

tadpole NOUN
le <u>têtard</u>

tag NOUN
l' <u>étiquette</u> FEM (*label*)

tail NOUN
la <u>queue</u>
♦ **Heads or tails?** Pile ou face?

tailor NOUN
le <u>tailleur</u>

to **take** VERB
1 <u>prendre</u> ◊ *Are you taking your new camera?* Tu prends ton nouvel appareil photo? ◊ *He took a plate from the cupboard.* Il a pris une assiette dans le placard. ◊ *It takes about an hour.* Ça prend environ une heure.

2 <u>emmener</u> (*person*) ◊ *He goes to London every week, but he never takes me.* Il va à Londres toutes les semaines, mais il ne m'emmène jamais.
♦ **to take something somewhere** emporter quelque chose quelque part ◊ *Do you take your exercise books home?* Vous emportez vos cahiers chez vous? ◊ *Don't take anything valuable with you.* N'emportez pas d'objets de valeur.
♦ **I'm going to take my coat to the cleaner's.** Je vais donner mon manteau à nettoyer.

3 <u>demander</u> (*effort, skill*) ◊ *that takes a lot of courage* cela demande beaucoup de courage
♦ **It takes a lot of money to do that.** Il faut beaucoup d'argent pour faire ça.

4 <u>supporter</u> (*tolerate*) ◊ *He can't take being criticized.* Il ne supporte pas d'être critiqué.

5 <u>passer</u> (*exam, test*) ◊ *Have you taken your driving test yet?* Est-ce que tu as déjà passé ton permis de conduire?

6 <u>faire</u> (*subject*) ◊ *I decided to take French instead of German.* J'ai décidé de faire du français au lieu de l'allemand.

to **take after** VERB
<u>ressembler à</u> ◊ *She takes after her mother.* Elle ressemble à sa mère.

to **take apart** VERB
♦ **to take something apart** démonter quelque chose

to **take away** VERB
1 <u>emporter</u> (*object*)
2 <u>emmener</u> (*person*)
♦ **to take something away** (*confiscate*) confisquer quelque chose
♦ **hot meals to take away** des plats chauds à emporter

to **take back** VERB
<u>rapporter</u> ◊ *I took it back to the shop.* Je l'ai rapporté au magasin.
♦ **I take it all back!** Je n'ai rien dit!

to **take down** VERB
1 <u>enlever</u> (*poster, sign*)
2 <u>décrocher</u> (*painting, curtains*)
3 <u>démonter</u> (*tent, scaffolding*)
4 <u>prendre en note</u> (*make a note of*) ◊ *He took down the details in his notebook.* Il a pris tous les détails en note dans son carnet.

to **take in** VERB
comprendre (*understand*) ◊ *I didn't really take it in.* Je n'ai pas bien compris.

to **take off** VERB
1 décoller (*plane*) ◊ *The plane took off twenty minutes late.* L'avion a décollé avec vingt minutes de retard.
2 enlever (*clothes*) ◊ *Take your coat off.* Enlevez votre manteau.

to **take out** VERB
sortir (*from container, pocket*)
♦ **He took her out to the theatre.** Il l'a emmenée au théâtre.

to **take over** VERB
prendre la relève ◊ *I'll take over now.* Je vais prendre la relève.
♦ **to take over from somebody** remplacer quelqu'un

takeaway NOUN
1 le plat à emporter (*meal*)
2 le restaurant qui vend des plats à emporter (*shop*) ◊ *a Chinese takeaway* un restaurant chinois qui vend des plats à emporter

taken VERB *see* **take**

takeoff NOUN
le décollage (*of plane*)

talcum powder NOUN
le talc

tale NOUN
le conte (*story*)

talent NOUN
le talent ◊ *She's got lots of talent.* Elle a beaucoup de talent.
♦ **to have a talent for something** être doué pour quelque chose ◊ *He's got a real talent for languages.* Il est vraiment doué pour les langues.

talented ADJECTIVE
♦ **She's a talented pianist.** C'est une pianiste de talent.

talk NOUN
see also **talk** VERB
1 l' exposé MASC (*speech*) ◊ *She gave a talk on rock climbing.* Elle a fait un exposé sur la varappe.
2 la conversation (*conversation*) ◊ *I had a talk with my Mum about it.* J'ai eu une petite conversation avec ma mère à ce sujet.
3 les racontars MASC PL (*gossip*) ◊ *It's just talk.* Ce sont des racontars.

to **talk** VERB
see also **talk** NOUN
parler ◊ *to talk about something* parler de quelque chose

♦ **to talk something over with somebody** discuter de quelque chose avec quelqu'un

talkative ADJECTIVE
bavard

tall ADJECTIVE
1 grand (*person, tree*)
♦ **to be 2 metres tall** mesurer deux mètres
2 haut (*building*)

tame ADJECTIVE
apprivoisé (*animal*) ◊ *They've got a tame hedgehog.* Ils ont un hérisson apprivoisé.

tampon NOUN
le tampon

tan NOUN
le bronzage ◊ *She's got an amazing tan.* Elle a un bronzage superbe.

tangerine NOUN
la mandarine

tangle NOUN
1 l' enchevêtrement MASC (*ropes, cables*)
2 le nœud (*hair*)
♦ **to be in a tangle (1)** être enchevêtré (*ropes, cables*)
♦ **to be in a tangle (2)** être emmêlé (*hair*)

tank NOUN
1 le réservoir (*for water, petrol*)
2 le char d'assaut (*military*)
♦ **a fish tank** un aquarium

tanker NOUN
1 le pétrolier (*ship*)
♦ **an oil tanker** un pétrolier
2 le camion-citerne (*truck*)
♦ **a petrol tanker** un camion-citerne

tap NOUN
1 le robinet (*water tap*)
2 la petite tape (*gentle blow*)

tap-dancing NOUN
les claquettes FEM PL ◊ *I do tap-dancing.* Je fais des claquettes.

to **tape** VERB
see also **tape** NOUN
enregistrer (*record*) ◊ *Did you tape that film last night?* As-tu enregistré le film hier soir?

tape NOUN
see also **tape** VERB
1 la cassette ◊ *a tape of Sinead O'Connor* une cassette de Sinead O'Connor
2 le scotch ® (*sticky tape*)

tape deck NOUN
le magnétophone

tape measure NOUN

le mètre à ruban

tape recorder NOUN
le magnétophone

target NOUN
la cible

tarmac NOUN
le macadam (on road)

tart NOUN
la tarte ◊ an apple tart une tarte aux
pommes

tartan ADJECTIVE
écossais ◊ a tartan scarf une écharpe
écossaise

task NOUN
la tâche

taste NOUN
| see also **taste** VERB |
le goût ◊ It's got a really strange
taste. Ça a un goût vraiment bizarre.
◊ a joke in bad taste une plaisanterie
de mauvais goût
♦**Would you like a taste?** Tu veux
goûter?

to **taste** VERB
| see also **taste** NOUN |
goûter ◊ Would you like to taste it?
Vous voulez y goûter?
♦**to taste of something** avoir un goût
de quelque chose ◊ It tastes of fish.
Ça a un goût de poisson.
♦**You can taste the garlic in it.** Ça a
bien le goût d'ail.

tasteful ADJECTIVE
de bon goût

tasteless ADJECTIVE
1 fade (food)
2 de mauvais goût (in bad taste) ◊ a
tasteless remark une remarque de
mauvais goût

tasty ADJECTIVE
savoureux MASC
savoureuse FEM

tattoo NOUN
le tatouage

taught VERB see **teach**

Taurus NOUN
le Taureau ◊ I'm Taurus. Je suis
Taureau.

tax NOUN
1 les impôts MASC PL (on income)
2 la taxe (on goods, alcohol)

taxi NOUN
le taxi
♦**a taxi driver** un chauffeur de taxi

taxi rank NOUN
la station de taxis

TB NOUN
la tuberculose

tea NOUN
1 le thé ◊ a cup of tea une tasse de
thé
♦**a tea bag** un sachet de thé
2 le dîner (evening meal)
♦**We were having tea.** Nous étions en
train de dîner.

to **teach** VERB
1 apprendre ◊ My sister taught me
to swim. Ma sœur m'a appris à
nager. ◊ That'll teach you! Ça
t'apprendra!
2 enseigner (in school) ◊ She teaches
physics. Elle enseigne la physique.

teacher NOUN
1 (in secondary school)
le professeur ◊ a maths teacher un
professeur de maths ◊ She's a
teacher. Elle est professeur.
2 (in primary school)
l' instituteur MASC
l' institutrice FEM
◊ He's a primary school teacher. Il est
instituteur.

teacher's pet NOUN
le chouchou
la chouchoute

tea cloth NOUN
le torchon

team NOUN
l' équipe FEM ◊ a football team une
équipe de football ◊ She was in my
team. Elle était dans mon équipe.

teapot NOUN
la théière

tear NOUN
| see also **tear** VERB |
la larme ◊ She was in tears. Elle
était en larmes.

to **tear** VERB
| see also **tear** NOUN |
1 déchirer ◊ Be careful or you'll tear
the page. Fais attention, tu vas
déchirer la page.
2 se déchirer ◊ It won't tear, it's
very strong. Ça ne se déchire pas,
c'est très solide.
♦**to tear up** déchirer ◊ He tore up the
letter. Il a déchiré la lettre.

tear gas NOUN
le gaz lacrymogène

to **tease** VERB
1 tourmenter (unkindly) ◊ Stop
teasing that poor animal! Arrête de
tourmenter cette pauvre bête!
2 taquiner (jokingly) ◊ He's teasing
you. Il te taquine.
♦**I was only teasing.** Je plaisantais.

teaspoon NOUN

T

☞

la petite cuillère
- **a teaspoonful of sugar** une cuillerée à café de sucre

teatime NOUN
l' heure du dîner FEM (*in evening*) ◊ *It was nearly teatime.* C'était presque l'heure du dîner.
- **Teatime!** À table!

tea towel NOUN
le torchon

technical ADJECTIVE
technique
- **a technical college** un lycée technique

technician NOUN
le technicien
la technicienne

technique NOUN
la technique

techno NOUN
la techno (*music*)

technological ADJECTIVE
technologique

technology NOUN
la technologie

teddy bear NOUN
le nounours

teenage ADJECTIVE
1 pour les jeunes ◊ *a teenage magazine* un magazine pour les jeunes
2 adolescent (*boys, girls*) ◊ *She has two teenage daughters.* Elle a deux filles adolescentes.

teenager NOUN
l' adolescent MASC
l' adolescente FEM

teens PL NOUN
- **She's in her teens.** C'est une adolescente.

tee-shirt NOUN
le tee-shirt

teeth PL NOUN
les dents MASC PL

to **teethe** VERB
faire ses dents

teetotal ADJECTIVE
- **I'm teetotal.** Je ne bois jamais d'alcool.

telecommunications PL NOUN
les télécommunications FEM PL

telephone NOUN
see also **phone** NOUN AND VERB
le téléphone ◊ *on the telephone* au téléphone
- **a telephone box** une cabine téléphonique
- **a telephone call** un coup de téléphone

- **the telephone directory** l'annuaire MASC
- **a telephone number** un numéro de téléphone

telesales PL NOUN
la vente par téléphone SING ◊ *She works in telesales.* Elle travaille dans la vente par téléphone.

telescope NOUN
le télescope

television NOUN
la télévision
- **on television** à la télévision
- **a television licence** une redevance de télévision
- **a television programme** une émission de télévision

to **tell** VERB
dire
- **to tell somebody something** dire quelque chose à quelqu'un ◊ *Did you tell your mother?* Tu l'as dit à ta mère? ◊ *I told him that I was going on holiday.* Je lui ai dit que je partais en vacances.
- **to tell somebody to do something** dire à quelqu'un de faire quelque chose ◊ *He told me to wait a moment.* Il m'a dit d'attendre un moment.
- **to tell lies** dire des mensonges
- **to tell a story** raconter une histoire
- **I can't tell the difference between them.** Je n'arrive pas à les distinguer.

to **tell off** VERB
gronder

telly NOUN
la télé ◊ *to watch telly* regarder la télé
- **on telly** à la télé

temper NOUN
le caractère ◊ *He's got a terrible temper.* Il a un sale caractère.
- **to be in a temper** être en colère
- **to lose one's temper** se mettre en colère ◊ *I lost my temper.* Je me suis mis en colère.

temperature NOUN
la température (*of oven, water, person*)
- **The temperature was 30 degrees.** Il faisait trente degrés.
- **to have a temperature** avoir de la fièvre

temple NOUN
le temple

temporary ADJECTIVE
temporaire

to **tempt** VERB
tenter ◊ *I'm very tempted!* Je suis très tenté!

- **to tempt somebody to do something**
persuader quelqu'un de faire quelque
chose

temptation NOUN
la tentation

tempting ADJECTIVE
tentant

ten NUMBER
dix ◊ *She's ten.* Elle a dix ans.

tenant NOUN
le locataire
la locataire

to **tend** VERB
- **to tend to do something** avoir
tendance à faire quelque chose ◊ *He
tends to arrive late.* Il a tendance à
arriver en retard.

tender ADJECTIVE
1 tendre (*food*)
2 sensible (*part of body*) ◊ *My feet
are really tender.* J'ai les pieds très
sensibles.

tennis NOUN
le tennis ◊ *Do you play tennis?* Vous
jouez au tennis?
- **a tennis ball** une balle de tennis
- **a tennis court** un court de tennis
- **a tennis racket** une raquette de tennis

tennis player NOUN
le joueur de tennis
la joueuse de tennis
◊ *He's a tennis player.* Il est joueur
de tennis.

tenor NOUN
le ténor

tenpin bowling NOUN
le bowling ◊ *to go tenpin bowling*
jouer au bowling

tense ADJECTIVE
see also **tense** NOUN
tendu

tense NOUN
see also **tense** ADJECTIVE
- **the present tense** le présent
- **the future tense** le futur

tension NOUN
la tension

tent NOUN
la tente
- **a tent peg** un piquet de tente
- **a tent pole** un montant de tente

tenth ADJECTIVE
dixième ◊ *the tenth floor* le dixième
étage
- **the tenth of August** le dix août

term NOUN
1 le trimestre (*at school*)

2 le terme ◊ *a short-term solution*
une solution à court terme
- **to come to terms with something**
accepter quelque chose

terminal ADJECTIVE
see also **terminal** NOUN
incurable (*illness, patient*)

terminal NOUN
see also **terminal** ADJECTIVE
le terminal (*of computer*)
- **an oil terminal** un terminal pétrolier
- **an air terminal** une aérogare

terminally ADVERB
- **to be terminally ill** être condamné

terrace NOUN
1 la terrasse (*patio*)
2 la rangée de maisons (*row of
houses*)
- **the terraces** (*at stadium*) les gradins
MASC

terraced ADJECTIVE
- **a terraced house** une maison
mitoyenne

terrible ADJECTIVE
épouvantable ◊ *My French is
terrible.* Mon français est
épouvantable.

terribly ADVERB
1 terriblement ◊ *He suffered terribly.*
Il a terriblement souffert.
2 vraiment ◊ *I'm terribly sorry.* Je
suis vraiment désolé.

terrier NOUN
le terrier

terrific ADJECTIVE
super (*wonderful*) ◊ *That's terrific!*
C'est super!
- **You look terrific!** Tu es superbe!

terrified ADJECTIVE
terrifié ◊ *I was terrified!* J'étais
terrifié!

terrorism NOUN
le terrorisme

terrorist NOUN
le/la terroriste
- **a terrorist attack** un attentat terroriste

test NOUN
see also **test** VERB
1 l' interrogation FEM (*at school*) ◊ *I've
got a test tomorrow.* J'ai une
interrogation demain.
2 l' essai MASC (*trial, check*) ◊ *nuclear
tests* les essais nucléaires
3 l' analyse FEM (*medical*) ◊ *a blood
test* une analyse de sang ◊ *They're
going to do some more tests.* Ils vont
faire d'autres analyses.
- **driving test** l'examen du permis de
conduire MASC ◊ *He's got his driving*

T

test tomorrow. Il passe son permis de conduire demain.

to **test** VERB

see also **test** NOUN

1 essayer ◊ *to test something out* essayer quelque chose

2 interroger (*class*) ◊ *He tested us on the new vocabulary.* Il nous a interrogés sur le nouveau vocabulaire.

♦**She was tested for drugs.** On lui a fait subir un contrôle antidopage.

test match NOUN

le match international

test tube NOUN

l' éprouvette FEM

tetanus NOUN

le tétanos ◊ *a tetanus injection* un vaccin contre le tétanos

textbook NOUN

le manuel ◊ *a French textbook* un manuel de français

textiles PL NOUN

les textiles MASC PL ◊ *a textiles factory* une usine textile

Thames NOUN

la Tamise

than CONJUNCTION

que ◊ *She's taller than me.* Elle est plus grande que moi. ◊ *I've got more books than him.* J'ai plus de livres que lui.

♦**more than ten years** plus de dix ans
♦**more than once** plus d'une fois

to **thank** VERB

remercier ◊ *Don't forget to write and thank them.* N'oublie pas de leur écrire pour les remercier.

♦**thank you** merci
♦**thank you very much** merci beaucoup

thanks EXCLAMATION

merci!

♦**thanks to** grâce à ◊ *Thanks to him, everything went OK.* Grâce à lui, tout s'est bien passé.

that ADJECTIVE, PRONOUN, CONJUNCTION

Use **ce** when **that** is followed by a masculine noun, and **cette** when **that** is followed by a feminine noun. **ce** changes to **cet** before a vowel and before most words beginning with "h".

1 ce ◊ *that book* ce livre
cet ◊ *that man* cet homme
cette ◊ *that woman* cette femme

♦**that road** cette route
♦**THAT road** cette route-là

♦**that one (1)** (*masculine*) celui-là ◊ *This man? – No, that one.* Cet homme-ci? – Non, celui-là.

♦**that one (2)** (*feminine*) celle-là ◊ *Do you like this photo? – No, I prefer that one.* Tu aimes cette photo? – Non, je préfère celle-là.

2 ça ◊ *You see that?* Tu vois ça?

♦**What's that?** Qu'est-ce que c'est?
♦**Who's that?** Qui est-ce?
♦**Is that you?** C'est toi?
♦**That's ...** C'est ... ◊ *That's my French teacher.* C'est mon prof de français. ◊ *That's what he said.* C'est ce qu'il a dit.

In relative phrases use **qui** when **that** refers to the subject of the sentence, and **que** when it refers to the object.

3 qui ◊ *the man that saw us* l'homme qui nous a vus ◊ *the man that spoke to us* l'homme qui nous a parlé ◊ *the dog that bit her* le chien qui l'a mordue

4 que ◊ *the man that we saw* l'homme que nous avons vu ◊ *the man that we spoke to* l'homme à qui nous avons parlé

que changes to **qu'** before a vowel and before most words beginning with "h".

◊ *the dog that she bought* le chien qu'elle a acheté ◊ *He thought that Henri was ill.* Il pensait qu'Henri était malade. ◊ *I know that she likes chocolate.* Je sais qu'elle aime le chocolat.

♦**It was that big.** Il était grand comme ça.
♦**It's about that high.** Il est à peu près haut comme ça.
♦**It's not that difficult.** Ça n'est pas si difficile que ça.

thatched ADJECTIVE

♦**a thatched cottage** une chaumière

the ARTICLE

Use **le** with a masculine noun, and **la** with a feminine noun. Use **l'** before a vowel and most words beginning with "h". For plural nouns always use **les**.

le ◊ *the boy* le garçon
l' ◊ *the man* l'homme MASC ◊ *the orange* l'orange FEM ◊ *the habit* l'habitude FEM
la ◊ *the girl* la fille
les ◊ *the children* les enfants

theatre NOUN (US **theater**)

le théâtre

theft NOUN

le vol

their ADJECTIVE
leur
(leurs PL)
◊ *their house* leur maison ◊ *their parents* leurs parents

theirs PRONOUN
le leur + MASC NOUN ◊ *It's not our garage, it's theirs.* Ce n'est pas notre garage, c'est le leur.
la leur + FEM NOUN ◊ *It's not our car, it's theirs.* Ce n'est pas notre voiture, c'est la leur.
les leurs + PL NOUN ◊ *They're not our ideas, they're theirs.* Ce ne sont pas nos idées, ce sont les leurs.
♦ **Is this theirs? (1)** (*masculine owners*) C'est à eux?
♦ **Is this theirs? (2)** (*feminine owners*) C'est à elles? ◊ *This car is theirs.* Cette voiture est à eux. ◊ *Whose is this? – It's theirs.* C'est à qui? – À eux.

them PRONOUN
1 les ◊ *I didn't see them.* Je ne les ai pas vus.
*Use **leur** when **them** means to them.*
2 leur ◊ *I gave them some brochures.* Je leur ai donné des brochures. ◊ *I told them the truth.* Je leur ai dit la vérité.
*Use **eux** or **elles** after a preposition.*
3 eux MASC ◊ *It's for them.* C'est pour eux.
elles FEM ◊ *Ann and Sophie came – Graham was with them.* Ann et Sophie sont venues – Graham était avec elles.

theme NOUN
le thème

theme park NOUN
le parc d'attractions

themselves PRONOUN
1 se ◊ *Did they hurt themselves?* Est-ce qu'ils se sont fait mal?
2 eux-mêmes MASC
elles-mêmes FEM
◊ *They did it themselves.* Ils l'ont fait eux-mêmes.

then ADVERB, CONJUNCTION
1 ensuite (*next*) ◊ *I get dressed. Then I have breakfast.* Je m'habille. Ensuite je prends mon petit déjeuner.
2 alors (*in that case*) ◊ *My pen's run out. – Use a pencil then!* Il n'y a plus d'encre dans mon stylo. – Alors utilise un crayon!
3 à l'époque (*at that time*) ◊ *There was no electricity then.* Il n'y avait pas l'électricité à l'époque.

♦ **now and then** de temps en temps ◊ *Do you play chess? – Now and then.* Vous jouez aux échecs? – De temps en temps.
♦ **By then it was too late.** Il était déjà trop tard.

therapy NOUN
la thérapie

there ADVERB
1 là ◊ *Put it there, on the table.* Mets-le là, sur la table.
♦ **over there** là-bas
♦ **in there** là
♦ **on there** là
♦ **up there** là-haut
♦ **down there** là-bas
♦ **There he is!** Le voilà!
2 y ◊ *He went there on Friday.* Il y est allé vendredi. ◊ *Paris? I've never been there.* Paris? Je n'y suis jamais allé.
♦ **There is ...** Il y a ... ◊ *There's a factory near my house.* Il y a une usine près de chez moi.
♦ **There are ...** Il y a ... ◊ *There are five people in my family.* Il y a cinq personnes dans ma famille.
♦ **There has been an accident.** Il y a eu un accident.

therefore ADVERB
donc

there's = there is, = there has

thermometer NOUN
le thermomètre

Thermos ® NOUN
le thermos ®

these ADJECTIVE, PRONOUN
1 ces ◊ *these shoes* ces chaussures
♦ **THESE shoes** ces chaussures-là
2 ceux-ci MASC ◊ *I want these!* Je veux ceux-ci!
celles-ci FEM ◊ *I'm looking for some sandals. Can I try these?* Je cherche des sandales. Je peux essayer celles-ci?

they PRONOUN
*Check if **they** stands for a masculine or feminine noun.*
ils ◊ *Are there any tickets left? – No, they're all sold.* Est-ce qu'il reste des billets? – Non, ils sont tous vendus.
elles ◊ *Do you like those shoes? – No, they're horrible.* Tu aimes ces chaussures? – Non, elles sont affreuses.
♦ **They say that ...** On dit que ...

they'd = they had, = they would
they'll = they will
they're = they are

T

they've = they have

thick ADJECTIVE
1 (*not thin*)
épais MASC
épaisse FEM
♦**The walls are one metre thick.** Les murs font un mètre d'épaisseur.
2 (*stupid*)
bête

thief NOUN
le voleur
la voleuse
♦**Stop thief!** Au voleur!

thigh NOUN
la cuisse

thin ADJECTIVE
1 mince (*person, slice*)
2 maigre (*skinny*)

thing NOUN
1 la chose ◊ *beautiful things* de belles choses
2 le truc (*thingy*) ◊ *What's that thing called?* Comment s'appelle ce truc?
♦**my things** (*belongings*) mes affaires FEM
♦**You poor thing!** Mon pauvre!

to **think** VERB
1 penser (*believe*) ◊ *I think you're wrong.* Je pense que vous avez tort. ◊ *What do you think about the death penalty?* Que pensez-vous de la peine de mort?
2 réfléchir (*spend time thinking*) ◊ *Think carefully before you reply.* Réfléchis bien avant de répondre. ◊ *What are you thinking about?* À quoi tu penses? ◊ *I'll think about it.* Je vais y réfléchir.
3 imaginer (*imagine*) ◊ *Think what life would be like without cars.* Imaginez la vie sans voitures.
♦**I think so.** Oui, je crois.
♦**I don't think so.** Je ne crois pas.
♦**I'll think it over.** Je vais y réfléchir.

third ADJECTIVE
see also **third** NOUN
troisième ◊ *the third day* le troisième jour ◊ *the third time* la troisième fois ◊ *I came third.* Je suis arrivé troisième.
♦**the third of March** le trois mars

third NOUN
see also **third** ADJECTIVE
le tiers ◊ *a third of the population* un tiers de la population

thirdly ADVERB
troisièmement

Third World NOUN
le tiers monde

thirst NOUN

la soif

thirsty ADJECTIVE
♦**to be thirsty** avoir soif

thirteen NUMBER
treize ◊ *I'm thirteen.* J'ai treize ans.

thirteenth ADJECTIVE
treizième ◊ *her thirteenth birthday* son treizième anniversaire ◊ *the thirteenth floor* le treizième étage
♦**the thirteenth of August** le treize août

thirty NUMBER
trente

this ADJECTIVE, PRONOUN
> Use **ce** when **this** is followed by a masculine noun, and **cette** when **this** is followed by a feminine noun. **ce** changes to **cet** before a vowel and before most words beginning with "h".

1 ce ◊ *this book* ce livre
cet ◊ *this man* cet homme
cette ◊ *this woman* cette femme
♦**this road** cette route
♦**THIS road** cette route-ci
♦**this one (1)** (*masculine*) celui-ci ◊ *Pass me that pen. – This one?* Passe-moi ce stylo. – Celui-ci?
♦**this one (2)** (*feminine*) celle-ci ◊ *Of the two photos, I prefer this one.* Des deux photos, c'est celle-ci que je préfère.
2 ça ◊ *You see this?* Tu vois ça?
♦**What's this?** Qu'est-ce que c'est?
♦**This is my mother.** (*introduction*) Je te présente ma mère.
♦**This is Gavin speaking.** (*on the phone*) C'est Gavin à l'appareil.

thistle NOUN
le chardon

thorough ADJECTIVE
minutieux MASC
minutieuse FEM
◊ *She's very thorough.* Elle est très minutieuse.

thoroughly ADVERB
à fond (*examine*)

those ADJECTIVE, PRONOUN
1 ces ◊ *those shoes* ces chaussures
♦**THOSE shoes** ces chaussures-là
2 ceux-là MASC ◊ *I want those!* Je veux ceux-là!
celles-là FEM ◊ *I'm looking for some sandals. Can I try those?* Je cherche des sandales. Je peux essayer celles-là?

though CONJUNCTION, ADVERB
bien que
> **bien que** has to be followed by a verb in the subjunctive.

◊ *Though it's raining ...* Bien qu'il pleuve ...
♦ **He's a nice person, though he's not very clever.** Il est sympa, mais pas très malin.

thought VERB *see* **think**

thought NOUN
l' **idée** FEM (*idea*) ◊ *I've just had a thought.* Je viens d'avoir une idée.
♦ **It was a nice thought, thank you.** C'est gentil de ta part, merci.

thoughtful ADJECTIVE
⬛1⬛ (*deep in thought*)
pensif MASC
pensive FEM
◊ *You look thoughtful.* Tu as l'air pensif.
⬛2⬛ (*considerate*)
prévenant ◊ *She's very thoughtful.* Elle est très prévenante.

thoughtless ADJECTIVE
♦ **He's completely thoughtless.** Il ne pense absolument pas aux autres.

thousand NUMBER
♦ **a thousand** mille ◊ *a thousand francs* mille francs
♦ **£2000** deux mille livres
♦ **thousands of people** des milliers de personnes

thousandth ADJECTIVE, NOUN
le millième

thread NOUN
le fil

threat NOUN
la menace

to **threaten** VERB
menacer ◊ *to threaten to do something* menacer de faire quelque chose

three NUMBER
trois ◊ *She's three.* Elle a trois ans.

three-dimensional ADJECTIVE
à trois dimensions

threw VERB *see* **throw**

thrifty ADJECTIVE
économe

thrill NOUN
l' **émotion** FEM (*excitement*)

thrilled ADJECTIVE
♦ **I was thrilled.** (*pleased*) J'étais absolument ravi.

thriller NOUN
le thriller

thrilling ADJECTIVE
palpitant

throat NOUN
la gorge ◊ *to have a sore throat* avoir mal à la gorge

to **throb** VERB
♦ **a throbbing pain** un élancement
♦ **My arm's throbbing.** J'ai des élancements dans le bras.

throne NOUN
le trône

through PREPOSITION, ADJECTIVE, ADVERB
⬛1⬛ par ◊ *through the window* par la fenêtre ◊ *I know her through my sister.* Je la connais par ma sœur.
◊ *to go through Birmingham* passer par Birmingham
♦ **to go through a tunnel** traverser un tunnel
⬛2⬛ à travers ◊ *through the mist* à travers la brume ◊ *through the crowd* à travers la foule ◊ *The window was dirty and I couldn't see through.* La fenêtre était sale et je n'arrivais pas à voir à travers.
♦ **a through train** un train direct
♦ **"no through road"** "impasse"

throughout PREPOSITION
♦ **throughout Britain** dans toute la Grande-Bretagne
♦ **throughout the year** pendant toute l'année

to **throw** VERB
lancer ◊ *He threw the ball to me.* Il m'a lancé le ballon.
♦ **to throw a party** organiser une soirée
♦ **That really threw him.** Ça l'a décontenancé.
♦ **to throw away (1)** (*rubbish*) jeter
♦ **to throw away (2)** (*chance*) perdre
♦ **to throw out (1)** (*throw away*) jeter
♦ **to throw out (2)** (*person*) mettre à la porte ◊ *I threw him out.* Je l'ai mis à la porte.
♦ **to throw up** vomir

thug NOUN
le voyou

thumb NOUN
le pouce

thumb tack NOUN ⬛US⬛
la punaise

to **thump** VERB
♦ **to thump somebody** donner un coup de poing à quelqu'un

thunder NOUN
le tonnerre

thunderstorm NOUN
l' **orage** MASC

thundery ADJECTIVE
orageux MASC
orageuse FEM

Thursday NOUN
le jeudi ◊ *on Thursday* jeudi ◊ *on Thursdays* le jeudi ◊ *every Thursday*

T

☞

tous les jeudis ◊ *last Thursday* jeudi dernier ◊ *next Thursday* jeudi prochain

thyme NOUN
le thym

tick NOUN
see also **tick** VERB
1 la coche (*mark*)
2 le tic-tac (*of clock*)
◆**I'll be back in a tick.** J'en ai pour une seconde.

to **tick** VERB
see also **tick** NOUN
1 cocher ◊ *Tick the appropriate box.* Cochez la case correspondante.
2 faire tic-tac (*clock*)

to **tick off** VERB
1 cocher (*check*) ◊ *He ticked off our names on the list.* Il a coché nos noms sur la liste.
2 passer un savon à (*tell off*) ◊ *She ticked me off for being late.* Elle m'a passé un savon à cause de mon retard.

ticket NOUN
Be careful to choose correctly between **le ticket** *and* **le billet**.
1 le ticket (*for bus, tube, cinema, museum*) ◊ *an underground ticket* un ticket de métro
2 le billet (*for plane, train, theatre, concert*)
◆**a parking ticket** un p.-v.

ticket inspector NOUN
le contrôleur
la contrôleuse

ticket office NOUN
le guichet

to **tickle** VERB
chatouiller

ticklish ADJECTIVE
chatouilleux MASC
chatouilleuse FEM
◊ *Are you ticklish?* Tu es chatouilleux?

tide NOUN
la marée
◆**high tide** la marée haute
◆**low tide** la marée basse

tidy ADJECTIVE
see also **tidy** VERB
1 bien rangé (*room*) ◊ *Your room's very tidy.* Ta chambre est bien rangée.
2 ordonné (*person*) ◊ *She's very tidy.* Elle est très ordonnée.

to **tidy** VERB
see also **tidy** ADJECTIVE
ranger ◊ *Go and tidy your room.* Va ranger ta chambre.

◆to **tidy up** ranger ◊ *Don't forget to tidy up afterwards.* N'oubliez pas de ranger après.

tie NOUN
see also **tie** VERB
la cravate (*necktie*)
◆**It was a tie.** (*in sport*) Ils ont fait match nul.

to **tie** VERB
see also **tie** NOUN
1 nouer (*ribbon, shoelaces*)
◆to **tie a knot in something** faire un nœud à quelque chose
2 faire match nul (*in sport*) ◊ *They tied three all.* Ils ont fait match nul, trois à trois.
◆to **tie up (1)** (*parcel*) ficeler
◆to **tie up (2)** (*dog, boat*) attacher
◆to **tie up (3)** (*prisoner*) ligoter

tiger NOUN
le tigre

tight ADJECTIVE
1 moulant (*tight-fitting*) ◊ *tight clothes* les vêtements moulants
2 juste (*too tight*) ◊ *This dress is a bit tight.* Cette robe est un peu juste.

to **tighten** VERB
1 tendre (*rope*)
2 resserrer (*screw*)

tightly ADVERB
fort (*hold*)

tights PL NOUN
le collant SING

tile NOUN
1 (*on roof*)
la tuile
2 (*on wall, floor*)
le carreau
(les carreaux PL)

tiled ADJECTIVE
1 en tuiles (*roof*)
2 carrelé (*wall, floor, room*)

till NOUN
see also **till** PREPOSITION
la caisse

till PREPOSITION, CONJUNCTION
see also **till** NOUN
1 jusqu'à ◊ *I waited till ten o'clock.* J'ai attendu jusqu'à dix heures.
◆**till now** jusqu'à présent
◆**till then** jusque-là

Use **avant** *if the sentence you want to translate contains a negative, such as "not" or "never".*

2 avant ◊ *It won't be ready till next week.* Ça ne sera pas prêt avant la semaine prochaine. ◊ *Till last year I'd*

never been to France. Avant l'année dernière, je n'étais jamais allé en France.

time NOUN

[1] l' heure FEM (*on clock*) ◇ *What time is it?* Quelle heure est-il? ◇ *What time do you get up?* À quelle heure tu te lèves? ◇ *It was two o'clock, French time.* Il était deux heures, heure française.

♦ **on time** à l'heure ◇ *He never arrives on time.* Il n'arrive jamais à l'heure.

[2] le temps (*amount of time*) ◇ *I'm sorry, I haven't got time.* Je suis désolé, je n'ai pas le temps.

♦ **from time to time** de temps en temps

♦ **in time** à temps ◇ *We arrived in time for lunch.* Nous sommes arrivés à temps pour le déjeuner.

♦ **just in time** juste à temps

♦ **in no time** en un rien de temps ◇ *It was ready in no time.* Ça a été prêt en un rien de temps.

♦ **It's time to go.** Il est temps de partir.

[3] le moment (*moment*) ◇ *This isn't a good time to ask him.* Ce n'est pas le bon moment pour lui demander.

♦ **for the time being** pour le moment

[4] la fois (*occasion*) ◇ *this time* cette fois-ci ◇ *next time* la prochaine fois ◇ *two at a time* deux à la fois

♦ **How many times?** Combien de fois?

♦ **at times** parfois

♦ **a long time** longtemps ◇ *Have you lived here for a long time?* Vous habitez ici depuis longtemps?

♦ **in a week's time** dans une semaine ◇ *I'll come back in a month's time.* Je reviendrai dans un mois.

♦ **Come and see us any time.** Venez nous voir quand vous voulez.

♦ **to have a good time** bien s'amuser ◇ *Did you have a good time?* Vous vous êtes bien amusés?

♦ **2 times 2 is 4** deux fois deux égalent quatre

time bomb NOUN
la bombe à retardement

time off NOUN
le temps libre

timer NOUN
le minuteur

time-share NOUN
l' appartement en multipropriété MASC

timetable NOUN
[1] l' horaire MASC (*for train, bus*)
[2] l' emploi du temps MASC (*at school*)

time zone NOUN
le fuseau horaire

tin NOUN
[1] la boîte ◇ *a tin of soup* une boîte de soupe ◇ *a biscuit tin* une boîte à biscuits
[2] la boîte de conserve ◇ *The bin was full of tins.* La poubelle était pleine de boîtes de conserve.
[3] l' étain MASC (*type of metal*)

tinned ADJECTIVE
en boîte (*food*) ◇ *tinned peaches* des pêches en boîte

tin opener NOUN
l' ouvre-boîte MASC

tinsel NOUN
les guirlandes de Noël FEM PL

tinted ADJECTIVE
teinté (*spectacles, glass*)

tiny ADJECTIVE
minuscule

tip NOUN

see also **tip** VERB

[1] (*money*)
le pourboire ◇ *Shall I give him a tip?* Je lui donne un pourboire?
[2] (*advice*)
le tuyau
(les tuyaux PL)
◇ *a useful tip* un bon tuyau (*informal*)
[3] (*end*)
le bout ◇ *It's on the tip of my tongue.* Je l'ai sur le bout de la langue.

♦ **a rubbish tip** une décharge

♦ **This place is a complete tip!** Quel fouillis!

to **tip** VERB

see also **tip** NOUN

donner un pourboire à ◇ *Don't forget to tip the taxi driver.* N'oubliez pas de donner un pourboire au chauffeur de taxi.

tipsy ADJECTIVE
pompette

tiptoe NOUN
♦ **on tiptoe** sur la pointe des pieds

tired ADJECTIVE
fatigué ◇ *I'm tired.* Je suis fatigué.

♦ **to be tired of something** en avoir assez de quelque chose

tiring ADJECTIVE
fatigant

tissue NOUN
le kleenex ® ◇ *Have you got a tissue?* Tu as un kleenex? ®

title NOUN
le titre

title role NOUN
le rôle principal

T

to PREPOSITION

> *à + le changes to* **au***. à + les changes to* **aux.**

[1] à ◊ *to go to Paris* aller à Paris ◊ *to go to school* aller à l'école ◊ *a letter to his mother* une lettre à sa mère ◊ *the answer to the question* la réponse à la question

au ◊ *to go to the theatre* aller au théâtre

aux ◊ *We said goodbye to the neighbours.* Nous avons dit au revoir aux voisins.

♦**ready to go** prêt à partir

♦**ready to eat** prêt à manger

♦**It's easy to do.** C'est facile à faire.

♦**something to drink** quelque chose à boire

♦**I've got things to do.** J'ai des choses à faire.

♦**from ... to ...** de ... à ... ◊ *from nine o'clock to half past three* de neuf heures à trois heures et demie

[2] de ◊ *the train to London* le train de Londres ◊ *the road to Edinburgh* la route d'Édimbourg ◊ *the key to the front door* la clé de la porte d'entrée

♦**It's difficult to say.** C'est difficile à dire.

♦**It's easy to criticize.** C'est facile de critiquer.

> *When referring to someone's house, shop or office, use* **chez.**

[3] chez ◊ *to go to the doctor's* aller chez le docteur ◊ *to go to the butcher's* aller chez le boucher ◊ *Let's go to Anne's house.* Si on allait chez Anne?

> *When* **to** *refers to a country which is feminine, use* **en***; when the country is masculine, use* **au.**

[4] en ◊ *to go to France* aller en France

au ◊ *to go to Portugal* aller au Portugal

[5] (*up to*)

jusqu'à ◊ *to count to ten* compter jusqu'à dix

[6] (*in order to*)

pour ◊ *I did it to help you.* Je l'ai fait pour vous aider. ◊ *She's too young to go to school.* Elle est trop jeune pour aller à l'école.

toad NOUN
le crapaud

toadstool NOUN
le champignon vénéneux

toast NOUN
[1] le pain grillé ◊ *a piece of toast* une tranche de pain grillé

[2] le toast (*speech*) ◊ *to drink a toast to somebody* porter un toast à quelqu'un

toaster NOUN
le grille-pain
(les grille-pain PL)

toastie NOUN
le sandwich chaud ◊ *a cheese and ham toastie* un croque-monsieur

tobacco NOUN
le tabac

tobacconist's NOUN
le bureau de tabac
(les bureaux de tabac PL)

toboggan NOUN
la luge

tobogganing NOUN
♦**to go tobogganing** faire de la luge

today ADVERB
aujourd'hui ◊ *What did you do today?* Qu'est-ce tu as fait aujourd'hui?

toddler NOUN
le bambin

toe NOUN
le doigt de pied

toffee NOUN
le caramel

together ADVERB
[1] ensemble ◊ *Are they still together?* Ils sont toujours ensemble?
[2] en même temps (*at the same time*) ◊ *Don't all speak together!* Ne parlez pas tous en même temps!

♦**together with** (*with person*) avec

toilet NOUN
les toilettes FEM PL

toilet paper NOUN
le papier hygiénique

toiletries PL NOUN
les articles de toilette MASC PL

toilet roll NOUN
le rouleau de papier hygiénique
(les rouleaux de papier hygiénique PL)

token NOUN
♦**a gift token** un bon-cadeau

told VERB *see* **tell**

tolerant ADJECTIVE
tolérant

toll NOUN
le péage (*on bridge, motorway*)

tomato NOUN
la tomate ◊ *tomato soup* la soupe à la tomate

tomboy NOUN
le garçon manqué ◊ *She's a real tomboy.* C'est un vrai garçon manqué.

tomorrow ADVERB
demain ◊ *tomorrow morning* demain matin ◊ *tomorrow night* demain soir
♦ **the day after tomorrow** après-demain

ton NOUN
la tonne ◊ *That old bike weighs a ton.* Ce vieux vélo pèse une tonne.

> ⓘ *In France measurements are in metric tonnes rather than tons. A ton is slightly more than a* **tonne**.

tongue NOUN
la langue
♦ **to say something tongue in cheek** dire quelque chose en plaisantant

tonic NOUN
le Schweppes ® (*tonic water*)
♦ **a gin and tonic** un gin tonic

tonight ADVERB
[1] ce soir (*this evening*) ◊ *Are you going out tonight?* Tu sors ce soir?
[2] cette nuit (*during the night*) ◊ *I'll sleep well tonight.* Je dormirai bien cette nuit.

tonsillitis NOUN
l' angine FEM

tonsils PL NOUN
les amygdales FEM PL

too ADVERB, ADJECTIVE
[1] aussi (*as well*) ◊ *My sister came too.* Ma sœur est venue aussi.
[2] trop (*excessively*) ◊ *The water's too hot.* L'eau est trop chaude. ◊ *We arrived too late.* Nous sommes arrivés trop tard.
♦ **too much (1)** (*with noun*) trop de ◊ *too much noise* trop de bruit
♦ **too much (2)** (*with verb*) trop ◊ *At Christmas we always eat too much.* À Noël nous mangeons toujours trop.
♦ **too much (3)** (*too expensive*) trop cher ◊ *Fifty francs? That's too much.* Cinquante francs? C'est trop cher.
♦ **too many** trop de ◊ *too many hamburgers* trop de hamburgers
♦ **too bad!** tant pis!

took VERB *see* **take**

tool NOUN
l' outil MASC
♦ **a tool box** une boîte à outils

tooth NOUN
la dent

toothache NOUN
le mal de dents ◊ *to have toothache* avoir mal aux dents

toothbrush NOUN
la brosse à dents

toothpaste NOUN
le dentifrice

top NOUN
see also **top** ADJECTIVE
[1] le haut (*of page, ladder, garment*) ◊ *at the top of the page* en haut de la page
♦ **a bikini top** un haut de bikini
[2] le sommet (*of mountain*)
[3] le dessus (*of table*)
♦ **on top of** (*on*) sur ◊ *on top of the fridge* sur le frigo
♦ **There's a surcharge on top of that.** Il a un supplément en plus.
♦ **from top to bottom** de fond en comble ◊ *I searched the house from top to bottom.* J'ai fouillé la maison de fond en comble.
[4] le couvercle (*of box, jar*)
[5] le bouchon (*of bottle*)

top ADJECTIVE
see also **top** NOUN
grand (*first-class*) ◊ *a top surgeon* un grand chirurgien
♦ **a top model** un top model
♦ **He always gets top marks in French.** Il a toujours d'excellentes notes en français.
♦ **the top floor** le dernier étage ◊ *on the top floor* au dernier étage

topic NOUN
le sujet ◊ *The essay can be on any topic.* Cette dissertation peut être sur n'importe quel sujet.

topical ADJECTIVE
d'actualité ◊ *a topical issue* un sujet d'actualité

topless ADJECTIVE
aux seins nus (*model*)
♦ **to go topless** enlever le haut

top-secret ADJECTIVE
top secret MASC
top secrète FEM
◊ *top-secret documents* des documents top secrets

torch NOUN
la lampe de poche

tore, torn VERB *see* **tear**

tortoise NOUN
la tortue

torture NOUN
see also **torture** VERB
la torture ◊ *It was pure torture.* C'était une vraie torture.

to **torture** VERB
see also **torture** NOUN
torturer ◊ *Stop torturing that poor animal!* Arrête de torturer cette pauvre bête!

Tory ADJECTIVE

T

☞

see also **Tory** NOUN
conservateur MASC
conservatrice FEM
◊ *the Tory government* le gouvernement conservateur

Tory NOUN
see also **Tory** ADJECTIVE
le conservateur
la conservatrice
♦ **the Tories** les conservateurs

to **toss** VERB
♦ **to toss pancakes** faire sauter les crêpes
♦ **Shall we toss for it?** On joue à pile ou face?

total ADJECTIVE
see also **total** NOUN
total
(totaux MASC PL)
♦ **the total amount** le total

total NOUN
see also **total** ADJECTIVE
le total
(les totaux PL)
♦ **the grand total** le total

totally ADVERB
complètement ◊ *He's totally useless.* Il est complètement nul.

touch NOUN
see also **touch** VERB
♦ **to get in touch with somebody** prendre contact avec quelqu'un
♦ **to keep in touch with somebody** ne pas perdre contact avec quelqu'un
♦ **Keep in touch!** Donne-moi de tes nouvelles!
♦ **to lose touch** se perdre de vue
♦ **to lose touch with somebody** perdre quelqu'un de vue

to **touch** VERB
see also **touch** NOUN
toucher
♦ **Don't touch that!** N'y touche pas!

touchdown NOUN
l' atterrissage MASC

touched ADJECTIVE
touché ◊ *I was really touched.* Ça m'a beaucoup touché.

touching ADJECTIVE
touchant

touchline NOUN
la ligne de touche

touchpad NOUN
le pavé tactile

touchy ADJECTIVE
susceptible ◊ *She's a bit touchy.* Elle est susceptible.

tough ADJECTIVE

[1] dur ◊ *It was tough, but I managed OK.* C'était dur, mais je m'en suis tiré. ◊ *It's a tough job.* C'est dur.
♦ **The meat's tough.** La viande est coriace.
[2] (*strong*)
solide ◊ *tough leather gloves* de solides gants en cuir ◊ *She's tough. She can take it.* Elle est solide. Elle tiendra le coup.
[3] (*rough, violent*)
dangereux MASC
dangereuse FEM
♦ **He thinks he's a tough guy.** Il se prend pour un gros dur.
♦ **Tough luck!** C'est comme ça!

toupee NOUN
le postiche

tour NOUN
see also **tour** VERB
[1] la visite (*of town, museum*) ◊ *We went on a tour of the city.* Nous avons visité la ville.
♦ **a package tour** un voyage organisé
[2] la tournée (*by singer, group*) ◊ *on tour* en tournée
♦ **to go on tour** faire une tournée

to **tour** VERB
see also **tour** NOUN
♦ **Paul Weller's touring Europe.** (*singer, artiste*) Paul Weller est en tournée en Europe.

tour guide NOUN
le/la guide

tourism NOUN
le tourisme

tourist NOUN
le/la touriste
♦ **tourist information office** l'office du tourisme MASC

tournament NOUN
le tournoi

tour operator NOUN
le tour-opérateur

towards PREPOSITION
[1] vers (*in the direction of*) ◊ *He came towards me.* Il est venu vers moi.
[2] envers (*of attitude*) ◊ *my feelings towards him* mes sentiments envers lui

towel NOUN
la serviette

tower NOUN
la tour
♦ **a tower block** une tour

town NOUN
la ville ◊ *a town plan* un plan de ville
♦ **the town centre** le centre-ville
♦ **the town hall** la mairie

tow truck NOUN US
 la dépanneuse

toy NOUN
 le jouet ◊ *a toy shop* un magasin de jouets
♦ **a toy car** une petite voiture

trace NOUN
 see also **trace** VERB
 la trace ◊ *There was no trace of the robbers.* Il n'y avait pas de trace des voleurs.

to **trace** VERB
 see also **trace** NOUN
 décalquer (*draw*)

tracing paper NOUN
 le papier calque

track NOUN
 [1] le chemin (*dirt road*)
 [2] la voie ferrée (*railway line*)
 [3] la piste (*in sport*) ◊ *two laps of the track* deux tours de piste
 [4] la chanson (*song*) ◊ *This is my favourite track.* C'est ma chanson préférée.
 [5] les traces FEM PL (*trail*) ◊ *They followed the tracks for miles.* Ils ont suivi les traces pendant des kilomètres.

to **track down** VERB
♦ **to track somebody down** retrouver quelqu'un ◊ *The police never tracked down the killer.* La police n'a jamais retrouvé l'assassin.

tracksuit NOUN
 le jogging

tractor NOUN
 le tracteur

trade NOUN
 le métier (*skill, job*) ◊ *to learn a trade* apprendre un métier

trade union NOUN
 le syndicat

trade unionist NOUN
 le/la syndicaliste

tradition NOUN
 la tradition

traditional ADJECTIVE
 traditionnel MASC
 traditionnelle FEM

traffic NOUN
 la circulation ◊ *The traffic was terrible.* Il y avait une circulation épouvantable.

traffic circle NOUN US
 le rond-point
 (les ronds-points PL)

traffic jam NOUN
 l' embouteillage MASC

traffic lights PL NOUN
 les feux MASC PL

traffic warden NOUN
 le contractuel
 la contractuelle

tragedy NOUN
 la tragédie

tragic ADJECTIVE
 tragique

trailer NOUN
 [1] la remorque (*vehicle*)
 [2] la bande-annonce (*film advert*)

train NOUN
 see also **train** VERB
 [1] le train
 [2] la rame (*on underground*)

to **train** VERB
 see also **train** NOUN
 s'entraîner (*sport*) ◊ *to train for a race* s'entraîner pour une course
♦ **to train as a teacher** suivre une formation d'enseignant
♦ **to train an animal to do something** dresser un animal à faire quelque chose

trained ADJECTIVE
♦ **She's a trained nurse.** Elle est infirmière diplômée.

trainee NOUN
 [1] (*in profession*)
 le/la stagiaire ◊ *She's a trainee.* Elle est stagiaire.
 [2] (*apprentice*)
 l' apprenti MASC
 l' apprentie FEM
 ◊ *a trainee plumber* un apprenti plombier

trainer NOUN
 [1] (*sports coach*)
 l' entraîneur MASC
 [2] (*of animals*)
 le dompteur
 la dompteuse

trainers PL NOUN
 les baskets FEM PL ◊ *a pair of trainers* une paire de baskets

training NOUN
 [1] la formation ◊ *a training course* un stage de formation
 [2] l' entraînement MASC (*sport*)

tram NOUN
 le tramway

tramp NOUN
 le clochard
 la clocharde

trampoline NOUN
 le trampoline

tranquillizer NOUN

T

☞

le tranquillisant ◊ *She's on
tranquillizers.* Elle prend des
tranquillisants.

transfer NOUN
la décalcomanie (*sticker*)

transfusion NOUN
la transfusion

transistor NOUN
le transistor

transit NOUN
le transit ◊ *in transit* en transit

transit lounge NOUN
la salle de transit

to **translate** VERB
traduire ◊ *to translate something into
English* traduire quelque chose en
anglais

translation NOUN
la traduction

translator NOUN
le traducteur
la traductrice
◊ *Anita's a translator.* Anita est
traductrice.

transparent ADJECTIVE
transparent

transplant NOUN
la greffe ◊ *a heart transplant* une
greffe du cardiaque

transport NOUN
  see also **transport** VERB
le transport ◊ *public transport* les
transports en commun

to **transport** VERB
  see also **transport** NOUN
transporter

trap NOUN
le piège

trash NOUN US
les ordures FEM PL
♦**the trash can** la poubelle

trashy ADJECTIVE
nul MASC
nulle FEM
◊ *a really trashy film* un film vraiment
nul

traumatic ADJECTIVE
traumatisant ◊ *It was a traumatic
experience.* Ça a été une expérience
traumatisante.

travel NOUN
  see also **travel** VERB
les voyages MASC PL

to **travel** VERB
  see also **travel** NOUN
voyager ◊ *I prefer to travel by train.*
Je préfère voyager en train.

♦**I'd like to travel round the world.**
J'aimerais faire le tour du monde.
♦**We travelled over 800 kilometres.**
Nous avons fait plus de huit cents
kilomètres.
♦**News travels fast!** Les nouvelles
circulent vite!

travel agency NOUN
l' agence de voyages FEM

travel agent NOUN
♦**She's a travel agent.** Elle travaille
dans une agence de voyages.

traveller NOUN (US **traveler**)
1 (*on bus, train, plane*)
le voyageur
la voyageuse
2 (*gypsy*)
le/la nomade

traveller's cheque NOUN (US **traveler's
check**)
le chèque de voyage

travelling NOUN (US **traveling**)
♦**I love travelling.** J'adore les voyages.

travel sickness NOUN
le mal des transports

tray NOUN
le plateau
(les plateaux PL)

to **tread** VERB
marcher ◊ *to tread on something*
marcher sur quelque chose

treasure NOUN
le trésor

treat NOUN
  see also **treat** VERB
1 le petit cadeau (*present*)
2 la gâterie (*food*)
♦**to give somebody a treat** faire plaisir
à quelqu'un

to **treat** VERB
  see also **treat** NOUN
traiter (*well, badly*)
♦**to treat somebody to something** offrir
quelque chose à quelqu'un ◊ *He
treated us to an ice cream.* Il nous a
offert une glace.

treatment NOUN
le traitement

to **treble** VERB
tripler ◊ *The cost of living there has
trebled.* Le coût de la vie y a triplé.

tree NOUN
l' arbre MASC

to **tremble** VERB
trembler

tremendous ADJECTIVE
énorme ◊ *a tremendous success* un
succès énorme

trend NOUN
la mode (fashion)

trendy ADJECTIVE
branché

trial NOUN
le procès (in court)

triangle NOUN
le triangle

tribe NOUN
la tribu

trick NOUN
see also **trick** VERB
[1] le tour ◊ to play a trick on
somebody jouer un tour à quelqu'un
[2] le truc FEM (knack) ◊ It's not easy:
there's a trick to it. Ce n'est pas
facile: il y a un truc.

to **trick** VERB
see also **trick** NOUN
♦to trick somebody rouler quelqu'un

tricky ADJECTIVE
délicat

tricycle NOUN
le tricycle

trifle NOUN
le diplomate (dessert)

to **trim** VERB
see also **trim** NOUN
[1] égaliser (hair)
[2] tondre (grass)

trim NOUN
see also **trim** VERB
la coupe d'entretien (haircut) ◊ to
have a trim se faire faire une coupe
d'entretien

trip NOUN
see also **trip** VERB
le voyage ◊ to go on a trip faire un
voyage ◊ Have a good trip! Bon
voyage!
♦a day trip une excursion d'une journée

to **trip** VERB
see also **trip** NOUN
trébucher (stumble)

triple ADJECTIVE
triple

triplets PL NOUN
les triplés MASC PL (boys)
les triplées FEM PL (girls)

trivial ADJECTIVE
insignifiant

trod, trodden VERB see **tread**

trolley NOUN
le chariot

trombone NOUN
le trombone ◊ I play the trombone.
Je joue du trombone.

troops PL NOUN
les troupes MASC PL ◊ British troops les
troupes britanniques

trophy NOUN
le trophée ◊ to win a trophy gagner
un trophée

tropical ADJECTIVE
tropical ◊ The weather was tropical.
Il faisait une chaleur tropicale.

to **trot** VERB
trotter

trouble NOUN
le problème ◊ The trouble is, it's too
expensive. Le problème, c'est que
c'est trop cher.
♦to be in trouble avoir des ennuis
♦What's the trouble? Qu'est-ce qui ne
va pas?
♦stomach trouble troubles gastriques
♦to take a lot of trouble over
something se donner beaucoup de
mal pour quelque chose
♦Don't worry, it's no trouble. Mais
non, ça ne me dérange pas du tout.

troublemaker NOUN
l' élément perturbateur MASC

trousers PL NOUN
le pantalon SING

trout NOUN
la truite

truant NOUN
♦to play truant faire l'école
buissonnière

truck NOUN
le camion
♦a truck driver un camionneur ◊ He's a
truck driver. Il est camionneur.

trucker NOUN US
le camionneur

true ADJECTIVE
vrai
♦That's true. C'est vrai.
♦to come true se réaliser ◊ I hope my
dream will come true. J'espère que
mon rêve se réalisera.
♦true love le grand amour

truly ADVERB
vraiment ◊ It was a truly remarkable
victory. C'était vraiment une victoire
remarquable.
♦Yours truly. Je vous prie d'agréer
mes salutations distinguées.

trumpet NOUN
la trompette ◊ She plays the
trumpet. Elle joue de la trompette.

trunk NOUN
[1] le tronc (of tree)
[2] la trompe (of elephant)
[3] la malle (luggage)

T

☞

4 le <u>coffre</u> (of car) US

trunks PL NOUN
♦**swimming trunks** le maillot de bain

trust NOUN
> see also **trust** VERB

la <u>confiance</u> ◊ to have trust in somebody avoir confiance en quelqu'un

to **trust** VERB
> see also **trust** NOUN

♦**to trust somebody** faire confiance à quelqu'un ◊ Don't you trust me? Tu ne me fais pas confiance? ◊ Trust me! Fais-moi confiance!

trusting ADJECTIVE
<u>confiant</u>

truth NOUN
la <u>vérité</u>

truthful ADJECTIVE
♦**She's a very truthful person.** Elle dit toujours la vérité.

try NOUN
> see also **try** VERB

l' <u>essai</u> MASC ◊ his third try son troisième essai
♦**to have a try** essayer
♦**It's worth a try.** Ça vaut la peine d'essayer.
♦**to give something a try** essayer quelque chose

to **try** VERB
> see also **try** NOUN

1 <u>essayer</u> (attempt) ◊ to try to do something essayer de faire quelque chose
♦**to try again** refaire un essai
2 <u>goûter</u> (taste) ◊ Would you like to try some? Voulez-vous goûter?
♦**to try on** essayer (clothes)
♦**to try something out** essayer quelque chose

T-shirt NOUN
le <u>tee-shirt</u>

tube NOUN
le <u>tube</u>
♦**the Tube** (underground) le métro

tuberculosis NOUN
la <u>tuberculose</u>

Tuesday NOUN
le <u>mardi</u> ◊ on Tuesday mardi ◊ on Tuesdays le mardi ◊ every Tuesday tous les mardis ◊ last Tuesday mardi dernier ◊ next Tuesday mardi prochain
♦**Shrove Tuesday, Pancake Tuesday** le mardi gras

tug-of-war NOUN
la <u>lutte à la corde</u>

tuition NOUN

les <u>cours</u> MASC PL
♦**private tuition** les cours particuliers

tulip NOUN
la <u>tulipe</u>

tumble dryer NOUN
le <u>sèche-linge</u>
(les sèche-linge PL)

tummy NOUN
le <u>ventre</u>

tuna NOUN
le <u>thon</u>

tune NOUN
l' <u>air</u> MASC (melody)
♦**to play in tune** jouer juste
♦**to sing out of tune** chanter faux

Tunisia NOUN
la <u>Tunisie</u>
♦**in Tunisia** en Tunisie

tunnel NOUN
le <u>tunnel</u>
♦**the Tunnel** (Chunnel) le tunnel sous la Manche

Turk NOUN
le <u>Turc</u>
la <u>Turque</u>

Turkey NOUN
la <u>Turquie</u>
♦**in Turkey** en Turquie
♦**to Turkey** en Turquie

turkey NOUN
1 la <u>dinde</u> (meat)
2 le <u>dindon</u> (live bird)

Turkish ADJECTIVE
> see also **Turkish** NOUN

<u>turc</u> MASC
<u>turque</u> FEM

Turkish NOUN
> see also **Turkish** ADJECTIVE

le <u>turc</u> (language)

turn NOUN
> see also **turn** VERB

1 le <u>tournant</u> (bend in road)
♦**"no left turn"** "défense de tourner à gauche"
2 le <u>tour</u> (go) ◊ It's my turn! C'est mon tour!

to **turn** VERB
> see also **turn** NOUN

1 <u>tourner</u> ◊ Turn right at the lights. Tournez à droite aux feux.
2 <u>devenir</u> (become) ◊ to turn red devenir rouge
♦**to turn into something** se transformer en quelque chose ◊ The frog turned into a prince. La grenouille s'est transformée en prince.

to **turn back** VERB
<u>faire demi-tour</u> ◊ We turned back. Nous avons fait demi-tour.

to **turn down** VERB
  1 refuser (offer)
  2 baisser (radio, TV, heating) ◊ *Shall I turn the heating down? Je baisse le chauffage?*

to **turn off** VERB
  1 éteindre (light, radio)
  2 fermer (tap)
  3 arrêter (engine)

to **turn on** VERB
  1 allumer (light, radio)
  2 ouvrir (tap)
  3 mettre en marche (engine)

to **turn out** VERB
  ♦ **It turned out to be a mistake.** Il s'est avéré que c'était une erreur.
  ♦ **It turned out that she was right.** Il s'est avéré qu'elle avait raison.

to **turn round** VERB
  1 faire demi-tour (car)
  2 se retourner (person)

to **turn up** VERB
  1 arriver (arrive)
  2 monter (heater)
  ♦ **Could you turn up the radio?** Tu peux monter le son de la radio?

turning NOUN
  ♦ **It's the third turning on the left.** C'est la troisième à gauche.
  ♦ **We took the wrong turning.** Nous n'avons pas tourné au bon endroit.

turnip NOUN
  le navet

turquoise ADJECTIVE
  turquoise MASC, FEM, PL (colour)

turtle NOUN
  la tortue

tutor NOUN
  le professeur particulier (private teacher)

tuxedo NOUN US
  le smoking

TV NOUN
  la télé

tweezers PL NOUN
  la pince à épiler SING

twelfth ADJECTIVE
  douzième ◊ *the twelfth floor* le douzième étage
  ♦ **the twelfth of August** le douze août

twelve NUMBER
  douze ◊ *She's twelve.* Elle a douze ans.
  ♦ **twelve o'clock (1)** (midday) midi
  ♦ **twelve o'clock (2)** (midnight) minuit

twentieth ADJECTIVE
  vingtième ◊ *the twentieth time* la vingtième fois
  ♦ **the twentieth of May** le vingt mai

twenty NUMBER
  vingt ◊ *He's twenty.* Il a vingt ans.

twice ADVERB
  deux fois
  ♦ **twice as much** deux fois plus ◊ *He gets twice as much pocket money as me.* Il a deux fois plus d'argent de poche que moi.

twin NOUN
  le jumeau (boy)
  la jumelle (girl)
  (les jumeaux PL)
  (les jumelles FEM PL)
  ♦ **my twin brother** mon frère jumeau
  ♦ **her twin sister** sa sœur jumelle
  ♦ **identical twins** les vrais jumeaux
  ♦ **a twin room** une chambre à deux lits

twinned ADJECTIVE
  jumelé ◊ *Stroud is twinned with Châteaubriant.* Stroud est jumelée avec Châteaubriant.

to **twist** VERB
  1 tordre (bend)
  2 déformer (distort) ◊ *You're twisting my words.* Tu déformes ce que j'ai dit.

twit NOUN
  le crétin
  la crétine

two NUMBER
  deux ◊ *She's two.* Elle a deux ans.

type NOUN
  see also **type** VERB
  le type ◊ *What type of camera have you got?* Quel type d'appareil photo as-tu?

to **type** VERB
  see also **type** NOUN
  taper à la machine ◊ *Can you type?* Tu sais taper à la machine?
  ♦ **to type a letter** taper une lettre

typewriter NOUN
  la machine à écrire

typical ADJECTIVE
  typique ◊ *That's just typical!* C'est typique!

tyre NOUN
  le pneu
  ♦ **the tyre pressure** la pression des pneus

T

U

UFO NOUN
l' <u>OVNI</u> MASC (= objet volant non identifié)

ugh EXCLAMATION
<u>pouah!</u>

ugly ADJECTIVE
<u>laid</u>

UK NOUN (= *United Kingdom*)
le <u>Royaume-Uni</u>
♦**from the UK** du Royaume-Uni
♦**in the UK** au Royaume-Uni
♦**to the UK** au Royaume-Uni

ulcer NOUN
l' <u>ulcère</u> MASC
♦**a mouth ulcer** un aphte

Ulster NOUN
l' <u>Irlande du Nord</u> FEM
♦**in Ulster** en Irlande du Nord

ultimate ADJECTIVE
<u>suprême</u> ◊ *the ultimate challenge* le défi suprême
♦**It was the ultimate adventure.** C'était la grande aventure.

ultimately ADVERB
<u>au bout du compte</u> ◊ *Ultimately, it's your decision.* Au bout du compte, c'est votre décision.

umbrella NOUN
1 le <u>parapluie</u>
2 le <u>parasol</u> (*for sun*)

umpire NOUN
1 l' <u>arbitre</u> MASC (*in cricket*)
2 le <u>juge de chaise</u> (*in tennis*)

UN NOUN
l' <u>ONU</u> FEM (= Organisation des Nations unies)

unable ADJECTIVE
♦**to be unable to do something** ne pas pouvoir faire quelque chose ◊ *I was unable to come.* Je n'ai pas pu venir.

unacceptable ADJECTIVE
<u>inacceptable</u>

unanimous ADJECTIVE
<u>unanime</u> ◊ *a unanimous decision* une décision unanime

unattended ADJECTIVE
♦**to leave something unattended** laisser quelque chose sans surveillance <u>laissé sans surveillance</u> ◊ *Never leave pets unattended in your car.* Ne laisser jamais d'animaux domestiques sans surveillance dans votre voiture.

unavoidable ADJECTIVE
<u>inévitable</u>

unaware ADJECTIVE
♦**to be unaware (1)** (*not know about*) ignorer ◊ *I was unaware of the regulations.* J'ignorais le règlement.
♦**to be unaware (2)** (*not notice*) ne pas se rendre compte ◊ *She was unaware that she was being filmed.* Elle ne s'était pas rendu compte qu'on la filmait.

unbearable ADJECTIVE
<u>insupportable</u>

unbeatable ADJECTIVE
<u>imbattable</u>

unbelievable ADJECTIVE
<u>incroyable</u>

unborn ADJECTIVE
♦**the unborn child** le fœtus

unbreakable ADJECTIVE
<u>incassable</u>

uncanny ADJECTIVE
<u>étrange</u> ◊ *That's uncanny!* C'est étrange!
♦**an uncanny resemblance** une ressemblance troublante

uncertain ADJECTIVE
<u>incertain</u> ◊ *The future is uncertain.* L'avenir est incertain.
♦**to be uncertain about something** ne pas être sûr de quelque chose

uncivilized ADJECTIVE
<u>barbare</u>

uncle NOUN
l' <u>oncle</u> MASC ◊ *my uncle* mon oncle

uncomfortable ADJECTIVE
<u>pas confortable</u> ◊ *The seats are rather uncomfortable.* Les sièges ne sont pas très confortables.

unconscious ADJECTIVE
<u>sans connaissance</u>

uncontrollable ADJECTIVE
<u>incontrôlable</u>

unconventional ADJECTIVE
<u>peu conventionnel</u> MASC
<u>peu conventionnelle</u> FEM

under PREPOSITION
1 <u>sous</u> ◊ *The cat's under the table.* Le chat est sous la table. ◊ *The tunnel goes under the Channel.* Le tunnel passe sous la Manche.
♦**under there** là-dessous ◊ *What's under there?* Qu'est-ce qu'il y a là-dessous?
2 <u>moins de</u> (*less than*) ◊ *under 20 people* moins de vingt personnes

◇ *children under 10* les enfants de moins de dix ans

underage ADJECTIVE
- ♦**He's underage.** Il n'a pas l'âge réglementaire.

undercover ADJECTIVE, ADVERB
secret MASC
secrète FEM
◇ *an undercover agent* un agent secret
- ♦**She was working undercover.** Elle travaillait sous une fausse identité.

to **underestimate** VERB
sous-estimer ◇ *I underestimated her.* Je l'ai sous-estimée.

to **undergo** VERB
subir (*operation, examination, change*)
- ♦**to be undergoing repairs** être en réparation

underground ADJECTIVE, ADVERB
see also **underground** NOUN
1 souterrain ◇ *an underground car park* un parking souterrain
2 sous terre ◇ *Moles live underground.* Les taupes vivent sous terre.

underground NOUN
see also **underground** ADJECTIVE
le métro ◇ *Is there an underground in Lille?* Est-ce qu'il y a un métro à Lille?

to **underline** VERB
souligner

underneath PREPOSITION, ADVERB
1 sous ◇ *underneath the carpet* sous la moquette
2 dessous ◇ *I got out of the car and looked underneath.* Je suis descendu de la voiture et j'ai regardé dessous.

underpaid ADJECTIVE
sous-payé ◇ *I'm underpaid.* Je suis sous-payé.

underpants PL NOUN
le slip SING

underpass NOUN
1 le passage souterrain (*for people*)
2 le passage inférieur (*for cars*)

undershirt NOUN US
le maillot de corps

underskirt NOUN
le jupon

to **understand** VERB
comprendre ◇ *Do you understand?* Vous comprenez? ◇ *I don't understand this word.* Je ne comprends pas ce mot. ◇ *Is that understood?* C'est compris?

understanding ADJECTIVE

compréhensif MASC
compréhensive FEM
◇ *She's very understanding.* Elle est très compréhensive.

understood VERB see **understand**

undertaker NOUN
l' entrepreneur des pompes funèbres MASC

underwater ADJECTIVE, ADVERB
sous l'eau ◇ *This sequence was filmed underwater.* Cette séquence a été filmée sous l'eau.
- ♦**an underwater camera** un appareil photographique de plongée
- ♦**underwater photography** la photographie subaquatique

underwear NOUN
les sous-vêtements MASC PL

underwent VERB see **undergo**

to **undo** VERB
1 défaire (*buttons, knot*)
2 déballer (*parcel*)

to **undress** VERB
se déshabiller (*get undressed*) ◇ *The doctor told me to undress.* Le médecin m'a dit de me déshabiller.

uneconomic ADJECTIVE
pas rentable

unemployed ADJECTIVE
au chômage ◇ *He's unemployed.* Il est au chômage. ◇ *He's been unemployed for a year.* Ça fait un an qu'il est au chômage.
- ♦**the unemployed** les chômeurs MASC

unemployment NOUN
le chômage

unexpected ADJECTIVE
inattendu ◇ *an unexpected visitor* un visiteur inattendu

unexpectedly ADVERB
à l'improviste ◇ *They arrived unexpectedly.* Ils sont arrivés à l'improviste.

unfair ADJECTIVE
injuste ◇ *It's unfair to girls.* C'est injuste pour les filles.

unfamiliar ADJECTIVE
- ♦**I heard an unfamiliar voice.** J'ai entendu une voix que je ne connaissais pas.

unfashionable ADJECTIVE
démodé

unfit ADJECTIVE
- ♦**I'm rather unfit at the moment.** Je ne suis pas en très bonne condition physique en ce moment.

to **unfold** VERB

U

déplier ◊ *She unfolded the map.* Elle a déplié la carte.

unforgettable ADJECTIVE
inoubliable

unfortunately ADVERB
malheureusement ◊ *Unfortunately, I arrived late.* Malheureusement, je suis arrivé en retard.

unfriendly ADJECTIVE
pas aimable ◊ *The waiters are a bit unfriendly.* Les serveurs ne sont pas très aimables.

ungrateful ADJECTIVE
ingrat

unhappy ADJECTIVE
malheureux MASC
malheureuse FEM
◊ *He was very unhappy as a child.* Il était très malheureux quand il était petit.
♦ **to look unhappy** avoir l'air triste

unhealthy ADJECTIVE
1 (*person*)
maladif MASC
maladive FEM
2 (*place, habit*)
malsain
3 (*food*)
pas sain

uni NOUN
la fac (*university*) ◊ *to go to uni* aller à la fac

uniform NOUN
l' uniforme MASC ◊ *the school uniform* l'uniforme scolaire

uninhabited ADJECTIVE
inhabité

union NOUN
le syndicat (*trade union*)

Union Jack NOUN
le drapeau du Royaume-Uni

unique ADJECTIVE
unique

unit NOUN
1 l' unité FEM ◊ *a unit of measurement* une unité de mesure
2 l' élément MASC (*piece of furniture*)
◊ *a kitchen unit* un élément de cuisine

United Kingdom NOUN
le Royaume-Uni

United Nations NOUN
l' O.N.U. FEM (= Organisation des Nations Unies)

United States PL NOUN
les États-Unis MASC PL
♦ **in the United States** aux États-Unis
♦ **to the United States** aux États-Unis

universe NOUN
l' univers MASC

university NOUN
l' université FEM ◊ *She's at university.* Elle va à l'université. ◊ *Do you want to go to university?* Tu veux aller à l'université? ◊ *Lancaster University* l'université de Lancaster

unleaded petrol NOUN
l' essence sans plomb FEM

unless CONJUNCTION
♦ **unless he leaves** à moins qu'il ne parte ◊ *I won't come unless you phone me.* Je ne viendrai pas à moins que tu ne me téléphones.

unlike PREPOSITION
contrairement à ◊ *Unlike him, I really enjoy flying.* Contrairement à lui, j'adore prendre l'avion.

unlikely ADJECTIVE
peu probable ◊ *It's possible, but unlikely.* C'est possible, mais peu probable.

unlisted ADJECTIVE US
♦ **an unlisted number** un numéro qui est sur la liste rouge

to **unload** VERB
décharger ◊ *We unloaded the car.* Nous avons déchargé la voiture.
◊ *The lorries go there to unload.* Les camions y vont pour être déchargés.

to **unlock** VERB
ouvrir ◊ *He unlocked the door of the car.* Il a ouvert la portière de la voiture.

unlucky ADJECTIVE
♦ **to be unlucky (1)** (*number, object*) porter malheur ◊ *They say thirteen is an unlucky number.* On dit que le nombre treize porte malheur.
♦ **to be unlucky (2)** (*person*) ne pas avoir de chance ◊ *Did you win? – No, I was unlucky.* Vous avez gagné? – Non, je n'ai pas eu de chance.

unmarried ADJECTIVE
célibataire (*person*) ◊ *an unmarried mother* une mère célibataire
♦ **an unmarried couple** un couple non marié

unnatural ADJECTIVE
pas naturel MASC
pas naturelle FEM

unnecessary ADJECTIVE
inutile

unofficial ADJECTIVE
1 (*meeting, leader*)
non officiel MASC
non officielle FEM
2 (*strike*)

sauvage

to **unpack** VERB

[1] défaire ◊ *I unpacked my suitcase.* J'ai défait ma valise.

[2] déballer ses affaires ◊ *I went to my room to unpack.* Je suis allé dans ma chambre pour déballer mes affaires. ◊ *I haven't unpacked my clothes yet.* Je n'ai pas encore déballé mes affaires.

unpleasant ADJECTIVE

désagréable

to **unplug** VERB

débrancher

unpopular ADJECTIVE

impopulaire

unpredictable ADJECTIVE

imprévisible

unreal ADJECTIVE

incroyable (*incredible*) ◊ *It was unreal!* C'était incroyable!

unrealistic ADJECTIVE

peu réaliste

unreasonable ADJECTIVE

pas raisonnable ◊ *Her attitude was completely unreasonable.* Son attitude n'était pas du tout raisonnable.

unreliable ADJECTIVE

pas fiable (*car, machine*) ◊ *It's a nice car, but a bit unreliable.* C'est une belle voiture, mais elle n'est pas très fiable.

♦ **He's completely unreliable.** On ne peut pas du tout compter sur lui.

to **unroll** VERB

dérouler

unsatisfactory ADJECTIVE

insatisfaisant

to **unscrew** VERB

dévisser ◊ *She unscrewed the top of the bottle.* Elle a dévissé le bouchon de la bouteille.

unshaven ADJECTIVE

mal rasé

unskilled worker ADJECTIVE

le manœuvre

unstable ADJECTIVE

instable

unsteady ADJECTIVE

mal assuré (*walk, voice*)

♦ **He was unsteady on his feet.** Il marchait d'un pas mal assuré.

unsuccessful ADJECTIVE

vain (*attempt*)

♦ **to be unsuccessful in doing something** ne pas réussir à faire

quelque chose ◊ *an unsuccessful artist* un artiste qui n'a pas réussi

unsuitable ADJECTIVE

inapproprié (*clothes, equipment*)

untidy ADJECTIVE

[1] en désordre ◊ *My bedroom's always untidy.* Ma chambre est toujours en désordre.

[2] débraillé (*appearance, person*) ◊ *He's always untidy.* Il est toujours débraillé.

[3] désordonné (*in character*) ◊ *He's a very untidy person.* Il est très désordonné.

to **untie** VERB

[1] défaire (*knot, parcel*)

[2] détacher (*animal*)

until PREPOSITION, CONJUNCTION

[1] jusqu'à ◊ *I waited until ten o'clock.* J'ai attendu jusqu'à dix heures.

♦ **until now** jusqu'à présent ◊ *It's never been a problem until now.* Ça n'a jamais été un problème jusqu'à présent.

♦ **until then** jusque-là ◊ *Until then I'd never been to France.* Jusque-là je n'étais jamais allé en France.

Use **avant** if the sentence you want to translate contains a negative, such as "not" or "never".

[2] avant ◊ *It won't be ready until next week.* Ça ne sera pas prêt avant la semaine prochaine. ◊ *Until last year I'd never been to France.* Avant l'année dernière, je n'étais jamais allé en France.

unusual ADJECTIVE

[1] insolite ◊ *an unusual shape* une forme insolite

[2] rare ◊ *It's unusual to get snow at this time of year.* Il est rare qu'il neige à cette époque de l'année.

unwilling ADJECTIVE

♦ **to be unwilling to do something** ne pas être disposé à faire quelque chose ◊ *He was unwilling to help me.* Il n'était pas disposé à m'aider.

to **unwind** VERB

se détendre (*relax*)

unwise ADJECTIVE

imprudent (*person*) ◊ *That was rather unwise of you.* C'était plutôt imprudent de votre part.

unwound VERB *see* **unwind**

to **unwrap** VERB

déballer ◊ *After the meal we unwrapped the presents.* Après le repas nous avons déballé les cadeaux.

up PREPOSITION, ADVERB

*For other expressions with **up**, see the verbs **go**, **come**, **put**, **turn** etc.*

en haut ◊ *up on the hill* en haut de la colline
- **up here** ici
- **up there** là-haut
- **up north** dans le nord
- **to be up** être levé (*out of bed*) ◊ *We were up at 6.* Nous étions levés à six heures. ◊ *He's not up yet.* Il n'est pas encore levé.
- **What's up?** Qu'est-ce qu'il y a? ◊ *What's up with her?* Qu'est-ce qu'elle a?
- **to get up** (*in the morning*) se lever ◊ *What time do you get up?* À quelle heure est-ce que tu te lèves?
- **to go up** monter ◊ *The bus went up the hill.* Le bus a monté la colline.
- **to go up to somebody** s'approcher de quelqu'un ◊ *She came up to me.* Elle s'est approchée de moi.
- **up to** (*as far as*) jusqu'à ◊ *to count up to fifty* compter jusqu'à cinquante ◊ *up to three hours* jusqu'à trois heures ◊ *up to now* jusqu'à présent
- **It's up to you.** C'est à vous de décider.

upbringing NOUN
l' éducation FEM

uphill ADVERB
- **to go uphill** monter

upper ADJECTIVE
supérieur ◊ *on the upper floor* à l'étage supérieur

upper sixth NOUN
- **the upper sixth** la terminale ◊ *She's in the upper sixth.* Elle est en terminale.

upright ADJECTIVE
- **to stand upright** se tenir droit

upset NOUN

see also **upset** ADJECTIVE, VERB

- **a stomach upset** une indigestion

upset ADJECTIVE

see also **upset** NOUN, VERB

contrarié ◊ *She's still a bit upset.* Elle est encore un peu contrariée.
- **I had an upset stomach.** J'avais l'estomac dérangé.

to **upset** VERB

see also **upset** NOUN, ADJECTIVE

- **to upset somebody** contrarier quelqu'un

upside down ADVERB
à l'envers ◊ *That painting is upside down.* Ce tableau est à l'envers.

upstairs ADVERB
en haut ◊ *Where's your coat? – It's upstairs.* Où est ton manteau? – Il est en haut.
- **to go upstairs** monter

uptight ADJECTIVE
tendu ◊ *She's really uptight.* Elle est très tendue.

up-to-date ADJECTIVE
1 moderne (*car, stereo*)
2 à jour (*information*) ◊ *an up-to-date timetable* un horaire à jour
- **to bring something up to date** moderniser quelque chose

upwards ADVERB
vers le haut ◊ *to look upwards* regarder vers le haut

urgent ADJECTIVE
urgent ◊ *Is it urgent?* C'est urgent?

urine NOUN
l' urine FEM

US NOUN
les USA MASC PL

us PRONOUN
nous ◊ *They helped us.* Ils nous ont aidés. ◊ *They gave us a map.* Ils nous ont donné une carte.

USA NOUN
les USA MASC PL

use NOUN

see also **use** VERB

- **It's no use.** Ça ne sert à rien. ◊ *It's no use shouting, she's deaf.* Ça ne sert à rien de crier, elle est sourde.
- **It's no use, I can't do it.** Il n'y a rien à faire, je n'y arrive pas.
- **to make use of something** utiliser quelque chose

to **use** VERB

see also **use** NOUN

utiliser ◊ *Can we use a dictionary in the exam?* Est-ce qu'on peut utiliser un dictionnaire à l'examen?
- **Can I use your phone?** Je peux téléphoner?
- **to use the toilet** aller aux W.C.
- **to use up** (1) finir ◊ *We've used up all the paint.* Nous avons fini la peinture.
- **to use up** (2) (*money*) dépenser
- **I used to live in London.** J'habitais à Londres autrefois.
- **I used not to like maths, but now ...** Avant, je n'aimais pas les maths, mais maintenant ...
- **to be used to something** avoir l'habitude de quelque chose ◊ *He wasn't used to driving on the right.* Il n'avait pas l'habitude de conduire à

droite. ◊ *Don't worry, I'm used to it.*
Ne t'inquiète pas, j'ai l'habitude.
♦ **a used car** une voiture d'occasion

useful ADJECTIVE
utile

useless ADJECTIVE
nul MASC
nulle FEM
◊ *This map is just useless.* Cette carte
est vraiment nulle. ◊ *You're useless!*
Tu es nul!
♦ **It's useless!** Ça ne sert à rien!

user NOUN
l' utilisateur MASC
l' utilisatrice FEM

user-friendly ADJECTIVE
facile à utiliser

usual ADJECTIVE
habituel MASC
habituelle FEM
♦ **as usual** comme d'habitude

usually ADVERB
[1] en général (*generally*) ◊ *I usually
get to school at about half past eight.*
En général, j'arrive à l'école vers huit
heures et demie.
[2] d'habitude (*when making a contrast*)
◊ *Usually I don't wear make-up, but
today is a special occasion.*
D'habitude je ne me maquille pas,
mais aujourd'hui c'est spécial.

utility room NOUN
la buanderie

U-turn NOUN
le demi-tour ◊ *to do a U-turn* faire
demi-tour

U

V

vacancy NOUN
1 le poste vacant (*job*)
2 la chambre disponible (*room in hotel*)
♦ **"no vacancies"** (*on sign*) "complet"

vacant ADJECTIVE
libre

vacation NOUN US
les vacances FEM PL ◇ *to be on vacation* être en vacances ◇ *to take a vacation* prendre des vacances

to **vaccinate** VERB
vacciner

to **vacuum** VERB
passer l'aspirateur ◇ *to vacuum the hall* passer l'aspirateur dans le couloir

vacuum cleaner NOUN
l' aspirateur MASC

vagina NOUN
le vagin

vague ADJECTIVE
vague

vain ADJECTIVE
vaniteux MASC
vaniteuse FEM
◇ *He's so vain!* Qu'est-ce qu'il est vaniteux!
♦ **in vain** en vain

Valentine card NOUN
la carte de la Saint-Valentin

Valentine's Day NOUN
la Saint-Valentin

valid ADJECTIVE
valable ◇ *This ticket is valid for three months.* Ce billet est valable trois mois.

valley NOUN
la vallée

valuable ADJECTIVE
1 de valeur ◇ *a valuable picture* un tableau de valeur
2 précieux MASC
précieuse FEM
◇ *valuable help* une aide précieuse

valuables PL NOUN
les objets de valeur MASC PL ◇ *Don't take any valuables with you.* N'emportez pas d'objets de valeur.

value NOUN
la valeur

van NOUN
la camionnette

vandal NOUN

le/la vandale

vandalism NOUN
le vandalisme

to **vandalize** VERB
saccager

vanilla NOUN
la vanille
♦ **vanilla ice cream** la glace à la vanille

to **vanish** VERB
disparaître

variable ADJECTIVE
variable

varied ADJECTIVE
varié

variety NOUN
la variété

various ADJECTIVE
plusieurs ◇ *We visited various villages in the area.* Nous avons visité plusieurs villages de la région.

to **vary** VERB
varier

vase NOUN
le vase

VAT NOUN (= *value added tax*)
la TVA (= taxe sur la valeur ajoutée)

VCR NOUN (= *video cassette recorder*)
le magnétoscope

VDU NOUN (= *visual display unit*)
la console

veal NOUN
le veau

vegan NOUN
le végétalien
la végétalienne
◇ *I'm a vegan.* Je suis végétalien.

vegetable NOUN
le légume ◇ *vegetable soup* la soupe aux légumes

vegetarian ADJECTIVE
see also **vegetarian** NOUN
végétarien MASC
végétarienne FEM
◇ *I'm vegetarian.* Je suis végétarien.
◇ *vegetarian lasagne* les lasagnes végétariennes

vegetarian NOUN
see also **vegetarian** ADJECTIVE
le végétarien
la végétarienne
◇ *I'm a vegetarian.* Je suis végétarien.

vehicle NOUN
le véhicule

vein NOUN
  la veine

velvet NOUN
  le velours

vending machine NOUN
  le distributeur automatique

Venetian blind NOUN
  le store vénitien

verb NOUN
  le verbe

verdict NOUN
  le verdict

vertical ADJECTIVE
  vertical
  (verticaux MASC PL)

vertigo NOUN
  le vertige ◊ *I get vertigo.* J'ai le vertige.

very ADVERB
  très ◊ *very tall* très grand ◊ *not very interesting* pas très intéressant
  ♦ **very much** beaucoup

vest NOUN
  1 le maillot de corps (*underclothing*)
  2 le gilet (*waistcoat*) US

vet NOUN
  le/la vétérinaire ◊ *She's a vet.* Elle est vétérinaire.

via PREPOSITION
  en passant par ◊ *We went to Paris via Boulogne.* Nous sommes allés à Paris en passant par Boulogne.

vicar NOUN
  le pasteur ◊ *He's a vicar.* Il est pasteur.

vice NOUN
  l' étau MASC (*for holding things*)

vice versa ADVERB
  vice versa

vicious ADJECTIVE
  1 brutal
  (brutaux MASC PL)
  ◊ *a vicious attack* une agression brutale
  2 (*dog, person*)
  méchant
  ♦ **a vicious circle** un cercle vicieux

victim NOUN
  la victime ◊ *He was the victim of a mugging.* Il a été victime d'une agression.

victory NOUN
  la victoire

to **video** VERB
  see also **video** NOUN
  1 enregistrer (*from TV*)
  2 filmer (*with video camera*)

video NOUN

see also **video** VERB
  1 la vidéo (*film*) ◊ *to watch a video* regarder une vidéo ◊ *a video of my family on holiday* une vidéo de ma famille en vacances ◊ *It's out on video.* C'est sorti en vidéo.
  2 la cassette vidéo (*video cassette*) ◊ *She lent me a video.* Elle m'a prêté une cassette vidéo.
  3 le magnétoscope (*video recorder*) ◊ *Have you got a video?* Tu as un magnétoscope?
  ♦ **a video camera** une caméra vidéo
  ♦ **a video cassette** une cassette vidéo
  ♦ **a video game** un jeu vidéo ◊ *He likes playing video games.* Il aime les jeux vidéo.
  ♦ **a video recorder** un magnétoscope
  ♦ **a video shop** un vidéoclub

Vietnam NOUN
  le Viêt-Nam
  ♦ **in Vietnam** au Viêt-Nam

Vietnamese ADJECTIVE
  vietnamien MASC
  vietnamienne FEM

view NOUN
  1 la vue ◊ *There's an amazing view.* Il y a une vue extraordinaire.
  2 l' avis MASC (*opinion*) ◊ *in my view* à mon avis

viewer NOUN
  le téléspectateur
  la téléspectatrice

viewpoint NOUN
  le point de vue

vile ADJECTIVE
  dégoûtant (*smell, food*)

villa NOUN
  la villa

village NOUN
  le village

villain NOUN
  1 le malfrat (*criminal*)
  2 le méchant (*in film*)

vine NOUN
  la vigne

vinegar NOUN
  le vinaigre

vineyard NOUN
  le vignoble

viola NOUN
  l' alto MASC ◊ *I play the viola.* Je joue de l'alto.

violence NOUN
  la violence

violent ADJECTIVE
  violent

violin NOUN

V

le violon ◊ *I play the violin.* Je joue du violon.

violinist NOUN
le/la violoniste

virgin NOUN
la vierge ◊ *to be a virgin* être vierge

Virgo NOUN
la Vierge ◊ *I'm Virgo.* Je suis Vierge.

virtual reality NOUN
la réalité virtuelle

virus NOUN
le virus (*also computing*)

visa NOUN
le visa

visible ADJECTIVE
visible

visit NOUN
see also **visit** VERB
1 la visite (*to museum*)
2 le séjour (*to country*) ◊ *Did you enjoy your visit to France?* Ton séjour en France s'est bien passé?
♦ **my last visit to my grandmother** la dernière fois que je suis allé voir ma grand-mère

to **visit** VERB
see also **visit** NOUN
1 rendre visite à (*person*) ◊ *to visit somebody* rendre visite à quelqu'un
2 visiter (*place*) ◊ *We'd like to visit the castle.* Nous voudrions visiter le château.

visitor NOUN
1 (*tourist*)
le visiteur
la visiteuse
2 (*guest*)
l' invité MASC
l' invitée FEM
♦ **to have a visitor** avoir de la visite

visual ADJECTIVE
visuel MASC
visuelle FEM

to **visualize** VERB
imaginer

vital ADJECTIVE
vital
(vitaux MASC PL)

vitamin NOUN
la vitamine

vivid ADJECTIVE
(*colour*)
vif MASC
vive FEM
♦ **to have a vivid imagination** avoir une imagination débordante

vocabulary NOUN
le vocabulaire

vocational ADJECTIVE
professionnel MASC
professionnelle FEM
♦ **a vocational course** un stage de formation professionnelle

vodka NOUN
la vodka

voice NOUN
la voix
(les voix PL)

voice mail NOUN
la messagerie vocale

volcano NOUN
le volcan

volleyball NOUN
le volley-ball ◊ *to play volleyball* jouer au volley-ball

volt NOUN
le volt

voltage NOUN
le voltage

voluntary ADJECTIVE
volontaire (*contribution, statement*)
♦ **to do voluntary work** travailler bénévolement

volunteer NOUN
see also **volunteer** VERB
le/la volontaire

to **volunteer** VERB
see also **volunteer** NOUN
♦ **to volunteer to do something** se proposer pour faire quelque chose

to **vomit** VERB
vomir

to **vote** VERB
voter

voucher NOUN
le bon ◊ *a gift voucher* un bon d'achat

vowel NOUN
la voyelle

vulgar ADJECTIVE
vulgaire

W

wafer NOUN
la gaufrette

wage NOUN
le salaire ◊ *He collected his wages.* Il a retiré son salaire.

waist NOUN
la taille

waistcoat NOUN
le gilet

to **wait** VERB
attendre
♦ **to wait for something** attendre quelque chose
♦ **to wait for somebody** attendre quelqu'un ◊ *I'll wait for you.* Je t'attendrai.
♦ **Wait for me!** Attends-moi!
♦ **Wait a minute!** Attends!
♦ **to keep somebody waiting** faire attendre quelqu'un ◊ *They kept us waiting for hours.* Ils nous ont fait attendre pendant des heures.
♦ **I can't wait for the holidays.** J'ai hâte d'être en vacances.
♦ **I can't wait to see him again.** J'ai hâte de le revoir.

to **wait up** VERB
attendre pour se coucher ◊ *My mum always waits up till I get in.* Ma mère attend toujours que je rentre pour se coucher.

waiter NOUN
le serveur
♦ **Waiter!** Garçon!

waiting list NOUN
la liste d'attente

waiting room NOUN
la salle d'attente

waitress NOUN
la serveuse

to **wake up** VERB
se réveiller ◊ *I woke up at six o'clock.* Je me suis réveillé à six heures.
♦ **to wake somebody up** réveiller quelqu'un ◊ *Please would you wake me up at seven o'clock?* Pourriez-vous me réveiller à sept heures?

Wales NOUN
le pays de Galles
♦ **in Wales** au pays de Galles
♦ **to Wales** au pays de Galles
♦ **I'm from Wales.** Je suis gallois.
♦ **the Prince of Wales** le prince de Galles

to **walk** VERB
see also **walk** NOUN
1 marcher ◊ *He walks fast.* Il marche vite.
2 aller à pied (go on foot) ◊ *Are you walking or going by bus?* Tu y vas à pied ou en bus? ◊ *We walked 10 kilometres.* Nous avons fait dix kilomètres à pied.
♦ **to walk the dog** promener le chien

walk NOUN
see also **walk** VERB
la promenade ◊ *to go for a walk* faire une promenade
♦ **It's 10 minutes' walk from here.** C'est à dix minutes d'ici à pied.

walkie-talkie NOUN
le talkie-walkie

walking NOUN
la randonnée ◊ *I did some walking in the Alps last summer.* J'ai fait de la randonnée dans les Alpes l'été dernier.

walking stick NOUN
la canne

Walkman ® NOUN
le baladeur

wall NOUN
le mur

wallet NOUN
le portefeuille

wallpaper NOUN
le papier peint

walnut NOUN
la noix
(les noix PL)

to **wander** VERB
♦ **to wander around** flâner ◊ *I just wandered around for a while.* J'ai flâné un peu.

to **want** VERB
vouloir ◊ *Do you want some cake?* Tu veux du gâteau?
♦ **to want to do something** vouloir faire quelque chose ◊ *I want to go to the cinema.* Je veux aller au cinéma. ◊ *What do you want to do tomorrow?* Qu'est-ce que tu veux faire demain?

war NOUN
la guerre

ward NOUN
la salle (*room in hospital*)

warden NOUN
(*of youth hostel*)

le directeur
la directrice

wardrobe NOUN
l' armoire FEM (*piece of furniture*)

warehouse NOUN
l' entrepôt MASC

warm ADJECTIVE
1 (*person*)
chaud ◊ *warm water* l'eau chaude
♦**It's warm in here.** Il fait chaud ici.
♦**to be warm** avoir chaud ◊ *I'm too warm.* J'ai trop chaud.
2 chaleureux MASC
chaleureuse FEM
◊ *a warm welcome* un accueil chaleureux
♦**to warm up (1)** (*for sport*) s'échauffer
♦**to warm up (2)** (*food*) réchauffer ◊ *I'll warm up some lasagne for you.* Je vais te réchauffer des lasagnes.

to **warn** VERB
prévenir ◊ *Well, I warned you!* Je t'avais prévenu!
♦**to warn somebody to do something** conseiller à quelqu'un de faire quelque chose

warning NOUN
l' avertissement MASC

Warsaw NOUN
Varsovie

wart NOUN
la verrue

was VERB *see* **be**

wash NOUN
see also **wash** VERB
♦**to have a wash** se laver ◊ *I had a wash.* Je me suis lavé.
♦**to give something a wash** laver quelque chose ◊ *He gave the car a wash.* Il a lavé la voiture.

to **wash** VERB
see also **wash** NOUN
1 laver ◊ *to wash something* laver quelque chose
2 se laver (*have a wash*) ◊ *Every morning I get up, wash and get dressed.* Tous les matins je me lève, je me lave et je m'habille.
♦**to wash one's hands** se laver les mains
♦**to wash one's hair** se laver les cheveux
♦**to wash up** faire la vaisselle

washbasin NOUN
le lavabo

washcloth NOUN US
le gant de toilette

washing NOUN
le linge ◊ *dirty washing* du linge sale

♦**Have you got any washing?** Tu as du linge à laver?
♦**to do the washing** faire la lessive

washing machine NOUN
la machine à laver

washing powder NOUN
la lessive

washing-up NOUN
♦**to do the washing-up** faire la vaisselle

washing-up liquid NOUN
le produit à vaisselle

wasn't = **was not**

wasp NOUN
la guêpe

waste NOUN
see also **waste** VERB
1 le gaspillage ◊ *It's such a waste!* C'est vraiment du gaspillage!
♦**It's a waste of time.** C'est une perte de temps.
2 les déchets MASC PL (*rubbish*)
◊ *nuclear waste* les déchets nucléaires

to **waste** VERB
see also **waste** NOUN
gaspiller ◊ *I don't like wasting money.* Je n'aime pas gaspiller de l'argent.
♦**to waste time** perdre du temps
◊ *There's no time to waste.* Il n'y a pas de temps à perdre.

wastepaper basket NOUN
la corbeille à papier

watch NOUN
see also **watch** VERB
la montre

to **watch** VERB
see also **watch** NOUN
1 regarder ◊ *to watch television* regarder la télévision ◊ *Watch me!* Regarde-moi!
2 surveiller (*keep a watch on*) ◊ *The police were watching the house.* La police surveillait la maison.
♦**to watch out** faire attention
♦**Watch out!** Attention!

water NOUN
see also **water** VERB
l' eau FEM

to **water** VERB
see also **water** NOUN
arroser ◊ *He was watering his tulips.* Il arrosait ses tulipes.

waterfall NOUN
la cascade

watering can NOUN
l' arrosoir MASC

watermelon NOUN
la pastèque

waterproof ADJECTIVE
imperméable ◊ *Is this jacket waterproof?* Ce blouson est-il imperméable?
♦ **a waterproof watch** une montre étanche

water-skiing NOUN
le ski nautique ◊ *to go water-skiing* faire du ski nautique

wave NOUN
see also **wave** VERB
⒈ la vague (*in water*)
⒉ le signe (*of hand*) ◊ *We gave him a wave.* Nous lui avons fait signe.

to **wave** VERB
see also **wave** NOUN
faire un signe de la main ◊ *to wave at somebody* faire un signe de la main à quelqu'un
♦ **to wave goodbye** faire au revoir de la main ◊ *I waved her goodbye.* Je lui ai fait au revoir de la main.

wavy ADJECTIVE
ondulé ◊ *wavy hair* les cheveux ondulés

wax NOUN
la cire

way NOUN
⒈ la façon (*manner*) ◊ *She looked at me in a strange way.* Elle m'a regardé d'une façon étrange.
♦ **This book tells you the right way to do it.** Ce livre explique comment il faut faire.
♦ **You're doing it the wrong way.** Ce n'est pas comme ça qu'il faut faire.
♦ **in a way** ... dans un sens ...
♦ **a way of life** un mode de vie
⒉ le chemin (*route*) ◊ *I don't know the way.* Je ne connais pas le chemin.
♦ **on the way** en chemin ◊ *We stopped for lunch on the way.* Nous nous sommes arrêtés pour déjeuner en chemin.
♦ **It's a long way.** C'est loin. ◊ *Paris is a long way from London.* Paris est loin de Londres.
♦ **Which way is it?** C'est par où?
♦ **The supermarket is this way.** Le supermarché est par ici.
♦ **Do you know the way to the station?** Est-ce que vous savez comment aller à la gare?
♦ **He's on his way.** Il arrive.
♦ **"way in"** "entrée"
♦ **"way out"** "sortie"
♦ **by the way** ... au fait ...

we PRONOUN
nous ◊ *We're staying here for a week.* Nous restons une semaine ici.

weak ADJECTIVE
faible

wealthy ADJECTIVE
riche

weapon NOUN
l' arme FEM

to **wear** VERB
porter (*clothes*) ◊ *She was wearing a hat.* Elle portait un chapeau.
♦ **She was wearing black.** Elle était en noir.

weather NOUN
le temps ◊ *What was the weather like?* Quel temps a-t-il fait? ◊ *The weather was lovely.* Il a fait un temps magnifique.

weather forecast NOUN
la météo

web browser NOUN
le navigateur

webmaster NOUN
le/la gestionnaire de site

website NOUN
le site web

webzine NOUN
le webzine

we'd = **we had**, = **we would**

wedding NOUN
le mariage
♦ **wedding anniversary** l'anniversaire de mariage MASC
♦ **wedding dress** la robe de mariée

Wednesday NOUN
le mercredi ◊ *on Wednesday* mercredi ◊ *on Wednesdays* le mercredi ◊ *every Wednesday* tous les mercredis ◊ *last Wednesday* mercredi dernier ◊ *next Wednesday* mercredi prochain

weed NOUN
la mauvaise herbe ◊ *The garden's full of weeds.* Le jardin est plein de mauvaises herbes.

week NOUN
la semaine ◊ *last week* la semaine dernière ◊ *every week* toutes les semaines ◊ *next week* la semaine prochaine ◊ *in a week's time* dans une semaine
♦ **a week on Friday** vendredi en huit

weekday NOUN
♦ **on weekdays** en semaine

weekend NOUN
le week-end ◊ *at weekends* le week-end ◊ *last weekend* le week-end

W

☞

dernier ◊ *next weekend* le week-end prochain

to **weep** VERB
pleurer

to **weigh** VERB
peser ◊ *How much do you weigh?* Combien est-ce que tu pèses? ◊ *First, weigh the flour.* Tout d'abord, pesez la farine.
♦ **to weigh oneself** se peser

weight NOUN
le poids
♦ **to lose weight** maigrir
♦ **to put on weight** grossir

weightlifter NOUN
l' haltérophile MASC

weightlifting NOUN
l' haltérophilie FEM

weird ADJECTIVE
bizarre

welcome NOUN
see also **welcome** VERB
l' accueil MASC ◊ *They gave her a warm welcome.* Ils lui ont fait un accueil chaleureux.
♦ **Welcome!** Bienvenue! ◊ *Welcome to France!* Bienvenue en France!

to **welcome** VERB
see also **welcome** NOUN
♦ **to welcome somebody** accueillir quelqu'un
♦ **Thank you! – You're welcome!** Merci! – De rien!

well ADJECTIVE, ADVERB
see also **well** NOUN
1 bien ◊ *You did that really well.* Tu as très bien fait ça.
♦ **to do well** réussir bien ◊ *She's doing really well at school.* Elle réussit vraiment bien à l'école.
♦ **to be well** (*in good health*) aller bien ◊ *I'm not very well at the moment.* Je ne vais pas très bien en ce moment.
♦ **get well soon!** remets-toi vite!
♦ **well done!** bravo!
2 enfin ◊ *It's enormous! Well, quite big anyway.* C'est énorme! Enfin, c'est assez grand.
♦ **as well** aussi ◊ *We worked hard, but we had some fun as well.* Nous avons travaillé dur, mais nous nous sommes bien amusés aussi. ◊ *We went to Chartres as well as Paris.* Nous sommes allés à Paris et à Chartres aussi.

well NOUN
see also **well** ADJECTIVE
le puits
(les puits PL)

we'll = **we will**

well-behaved ADJECTIVE
sage

well-dressed ADJECTIVE
bien habillé

wellingtons PL NOUN
les bottes en caoutchouc FEM PL

well-known ADJECTIVE
célèbre ◊ *a well-known film star* une vedette de cinéma célèbre

well-off ADJECTIVE
aisé

Welsh ADJECTIVE
see also **Welsh** NOUN
gallois ◊ *She's Welsh.* Elle est galloise.
♦ **Welsh people** les Gallois MASC

Welsh NOUN
see also **Welsh** ADJECTIVE
le gallois (*language*)

Welshman NOUN
le Gallois

Welshwoman NOUN
la Galloise

went VERB see **go**

wept VERB see **weep**

were VERB see **be**

we're = **we are**

weren't = **were not**

west NOUN
see also **west** ADJECTIVE
l' ouest MASC ◊ *in the west* dans l'ouest

west ADJECTIVE, ADVERB
see also **west** NOUN
1 ouest MASC, FEM, PL ◊ *the west coast* la côte ouest
♦ **west of** à l'ouest de ◊ *Stroud is west of Oxford.* Stroud est à l'ouest d'Oxford.
2 vers l'ouest ◊ *We were travelling west.* Nous allions vers l'ouest.
♦ **the West Country** le sud-ouest de l'Angleterre

westbound ADJECTIVE
♦ **The truck was westbound on the M5.** Le camion roulait sur la M5 en direction de l'ouest.
♦ **Westbound traffic is moving very slowly.** La circulation en direction de l'ouest est très ralentie.

western NOUN
see also **western** ADJECTIVE
le western (*film*)

western ADJECTIVE
see also **western** NOUN
♦ **the western part of the island** la partie ouest de l'île

♦ **Western Europe** l'Europe de l'Ouest

West Indian ADJECTIVE

see also **West Indian** NOUN

antillais ◊ *She's West Indian.* Elle est antillaise.

West Indian NOUN

see also **West Indian** ADJECTIVE

(*person*)
l' Antillais MASC
l' Antillaise FEM

West Indies PL NOUN
les Antilles FEM PL

♦ **in the West Indies** aux Antilles

wet ADJECTIVE
mouillé ◊ *wet clothes* les vêtements mouillés

♦ **to get wet** se faire mouiller

♦ **dripping wet** trempé

♦ **wet weather** le temps pluvieux

♦ **It was wet all week.** Il a plu toute la semaine.

wetsuit NOUN
la combinaison de plongée
(les combinaisons de plongée PL)

we've = **we have**

whale NOUN
la baleine

what ADJECTIVE, PRONOUN

[1] (*which*)
quel MASC
quelle FEM
◊ *What subjects are you studying?* Quelles matières est-ce que tu fais?
◊ *What colour is it?* C'est de quelle couleur? ◊ *What's the capital of Finland?* Quelle est la capitale de la Finlande? ◊ *What a mess!* Quel fouillis!

[2] qu'est-ce que ◊ *What are you doing?* Qu'est-ce que vous faites?
◊ *What did you say?* Qu'est-ce que vous avez dit? ◊ *What is it?* Qu'est-ce que c'est? ◊ *What's the matter?* Qu'est-ce qu'il y a?

[3] qu'est-ce qui ◊ *What happened?* Qu'est-ce qui s'est passé? ◊ *What's bothering you?* Qu'est-ce qui te préoccupe?

*In relative phrases use **ce qui** or **ce que** depending on whether **what** refers to the subject or the object of the sentence.*

[4] (*subject*)
ce qui ◊ *I saw what happened.* J'ai vu ce qui est arrivé. ◊ *I know what's bothering you.* Je sais ce qui te préoccupe.

[5] (*object*)
ce que ◊ *Tell me what you did.* Dites-moi ce que vous avez fait. ◊ *I*

heard what he said. J'ai entendu ce qu'il a dit.

♦ **What?** (*what did you say*) Comment?

♦ **What!** (*shocked*) Quoi!

wheat NOUN
le blé

wheel NOUN
la roue

♦ **the steering wheel** le volant

wheelchair NOUN
le fauteuil roulant

when ADVERB, CONJUNCTION
quand ◊ *When did he go?* Quand est-ce qu'il est parti? ◊ *She was reading when I came in.* Elle lisait quand je suis entré.

where ADVERB, CONJUNCTION
où ◊ *Where's Emma today?* Où est Emma aujourd'hui? ◊ *Where do you live?* Où habites-tu? ◊ *Where are you going?* Où vas-tu? ◊ *a shop where you can buy croissants* un magasin où l'on peut acheter des croissants

whether CONJUNCTION
si ◊ *I don't know whether to go or not.* Je ne sais pas si y aller ou non.

which ADJECTIVE, PRONOUN

[1] quel MASC
quelle FEM
◊ *Which flavour do you want?* Quel parfum est-ce que tu veux?

*When asking **which one** use **lequel** or **laquelle**, depending on whether the noun is masculine or feminine.*

♦ **I know his brother. – Which one?** Je connais son frère. – Lequel?

♦ **I know his sister. – Which one?** Je connais sa sœur. – Laquelle?

♦ **Which would you like?** Lequel est-ce que vous voulez?

♦ **Which of these are yours?** Lesquels sont à vous?

*In relative phrases use **qui** or **que** depending on whether **which** refers to the subject or the object of the sentence.*

[2] (*subject*)
qui ◊ *the CD which is playing now* le CD qui passe maintenant

[3] (*object*)
que ◊ *the CD which I bought today* le CD que j'ai acheté hier

while CONJUNCTION

see also **while** NOUN

[1] pendant que ◊ *You hold the torch while I look inside.* Tiens la lampe électrique pendant que je regarde à l'intérieur.

[2] alors que ◊ *Isobel is very dynamic, while Kay is more laid-back.*

W

Isobel est très dynamique, alors que Kay est plus relax.

while NOUN

> see also **while** CONJUNCTION

le moment ◊ *after a while* au bout d'un moment

♦ **a while ago** il y a un moment ◊ *He was here a while ago.* Il était là il y a un moment.

♦ **for a while** pendant quelque temps ◊ *I lived in London for a while.* J'ai vécu à Londres pendant quelque temps.

♦ **quite a while** longtemps ◊ *quite a while ago* il y a longtemps ◊ *I haven't seen him for quite a while.* Ça fait longtemps que je ne l'ai pas vu.

whip NOUN

> see also **whip** VERB

le fouet

to **whip** VERB

> see also **whip** NOUN

1 fouetter (*person, animal*)
2 battre (*eggs*)

whipped cream NOUN
la crème fouettée

whisk NOUN
le fouet

whiskers PL NOUN
les moustaches FEM PL

whisky NOUN
le whisky
(les whiskies PL)

to **whisper** VERB
chuchoter

whistle NOUN

> see also **whistle** VERB

le sifflet

♦ **The referee blew his whistle.** L'arbitre a sifflé.

to **whistle** VERB

> see also **whistle** NOUN

siffler

white ADJECTIVE
blanc MASC
blanche FEM
◊ *He's got white hair.* Il a les cheveux blancs.

♦ **white wine** le vin blanc
♦ **white bread** le pain blanc
♦ **white coffee** le café au lait
♦ **a white man** un Blanc
♦ **a white woman** une Blanche
♦ **white people** les Blancs

Whitsun NOUN
la Pentecôte

who PRONOUN
1 qui ◊ *Who said that?* Qui a dit ça?
◊ *Who is Jacques Chirac?* Qui est Jacques Chirac?

*In relative phrases use **qui** or **que** depending on whether **who** refers to the subject or the object of the verb.*

2 qui (*subject*) ◊ *the man who saw us* l'homme qui nous a vus ◊ *the man who spoke to us* l'homme qui nous a parlé

3 que (*object*) ◊ *the man who we saw* l'homme que nous avons vu ◊ *the man who she married* l'homme qu'elle a épousé

whole ADJECTIVE

> see also **whole** NOUN

tout ◊ *the whole class* toute la classe ◊ *the whole afternoon* tout l'après-midi

♦ **a whole box of chocolates** toute une boîte de chocolats
♦ **the whole world** le monde entier

whole NOUN

> see also **whole** ADJECTIVE

♦ **The whole of Wales was affected.** Le pays de Galles tout entier a été touché.
♦ **on the whole** dans l'ensemble

wholemeal ADJECTIVE
complet MASC
complète FEM

♦ **wholemeal bread** le pain complet

wholewheat ADJECTIVE US
complet MASC
complète FEM

whom PRONOUN
qui ◊ *Whom did you see?* Qui avez-vous vu? ◊ *the man to whom I spoke* l'homme à qui j'ai parlé

whose PRONOUN, ADJECTIVE
1 à qui ◊ *Whose is this?* À qui est-ce? ◊ *I know whose it is.* Je sais à qui c'est. ◊ *Whose book is this?* À qui est ce livre?

2 dont (*after noun*) ◊ *the girl whose picture was in the paper* la jeune fille dont la photo était dans le journal

why ADVERB
pourquoi ◊ *Why did you do that?* Pourquoi avez-vous fait ça? ◊ *That's why he did it.* Voilà pourquoi il a fait ça. ◊ *Tell me why.* Dis-moi pourquoi.

♦ **I've never been to France. – Why not?** Je ne suis jamais allé en France. – Pourquoi?
♦ **All right, why not?** D'accord, pourquoi pas?

wicked ADJECTIVE
1 (*evil*)
méchant
2 (*really great*)
génial
(géniaux MASC PL)

wicket NOUN
le guichet (*stumps*)

wide ADJECTIVE, ADVERB
large ◊ *a wide road* une route large
♦ **wide open** grand ouvert ◊ *The door was wide open.* La porte était grande ouverte. ◊ *The windows were wide open.* Les fenêtres étaient grandes ouvertes.
♦ **wide awake** complètement réveillé

widow NOUN
la veuve ◊ *She's a widow.* Elle est veuve.

widower NOUN
le veuf ◊ *He's a widower.* Il est veuf.

width NOUN
la largeur

wife NOUN
la femme ◊ *She's his wife.* C'est sa femme.

wig NOUN
la perruque

wild ADJECTIVE
1 (*not tame*)
sauvage ◊ *a wild animal* un animal sauvage
2 (*crazy*)
fou MASC
folle FEM
◊ *She's a bit wild.* Elle est un peu folle.

wildlife NOUN
la nature ◊ *I'm interested in wildlife.* Je m'intéresse à la nature.

will NOUN
see also **will** VERB
le testament ◊ *He left me some money in his will.* Il m'a laissé de l'argent dans son testament.

will VERB
see also **will** NOUN
♦ **I'll show you your room.** Je vais te montrer ta chambre.
♦ **I'll give you a hand.** Je vais t'aider.
Use the French future tense when referring to the more distant future.
♦ **I will finish it tomorrow.** Je le finirai demain.
♦ **It won't take long.** Ça ne prendra pas longtemps.
♦ **Will you wash up? – No, I won't.** Est-ce que tu peux faire la vaisselle? – Non.
♦ **Will you help me?** Est-ce que tu peux m'aider?
♦ **Will you be quiet!** Voulez-vous bien vous taire!
♦ **That will be the postman.** Ça doit être le facteur.

willing ADJECTIVE

♦ **to be willing to do something** être prêt à faire quelque chose

to **win** VERB
see also **win** NOUN
gagner ◊ *Did you win?* Est-ce que tu as gagné?
♦ **to win a prize** remporter un prix

win NOUN
see also **win** VERB
la victoire

to **wind** VERB
see also **wind** NOUN
1 enrouler (*rope, wool, wire*)
2 serpenter (*river, path*) ◊ *The road winds through the valley.* La route serpente à travers la vallée.

wind NOUN
see also **wind** VERB
le vent ◊ *There was a strong wind.* Il y avait beaucoup de vent.
♦ **a wind instrument** un instrument à vent
♦ **wind power** l'énergie éolienne FEM

windmill NOUN
le moulin à vent
(les moulins à vent PL)

window NOUN
1 (*of building*)
la fenêtre
2 (*in car, train*)
la vitre
♦ **a shop window** une vitrine
3 (*window pane*)
le carreau
(les carreaux PL)
◊ *to break a window* casser un carreau ◊ *a broken window* un carreau cassé

windscreen NOUN
le pare-brise
(les pare-brise PL)

windscreen wiper NOUN
l' essuie-glace MASC
(les essuie-glace PL)

windshield NOUN US
le pare-brise
(les pare-brise PL)

windshield wiper NOUN US
l' essuie-glace MASC
(les essuie-glace PL)

windy ADJECTIVE
(*place*)
venteux MASC
venteuse FEM
♦ **It's windy.** Il y a du vent.

wine NOUN
le vin ◊ *a bottle of wine* une bouteille de vin ◊ *a glass of wine* un verre de vin

W

♦ **white wine** le vin blanc
♦ **red wine** le vin rouge
♦ **a wine bar** un bar à vin
♦ **a wine glass** un verre à vin
♦ **the wine list** la carte des vins

wing NOUN
l' <u>aile</u> FEM

to **wink** VERB
♦ **to wink at somebody** faire un clin
d'œil à quelqu'un ◊ *He winked at me.*
Il m'a fait un clin d'œil.

winner NOUN
le <u>gagnant</u>
la <u>gagnante</u>

winning ADJECTIVE
♦ **the winning team** l'équipe gagnante
♦ **the winning goal** le but décisif

winter NOUN
l' <u>hiver</u> MASC
♦ **in winter** en hiver

winter sports PL NOUN
les <u>sports d'hiver</u> MASC PL

to **wipe** VERB
<u>essuyer</u>
♦ **to wipe one's feet** s'essuyer les pieds
◊ *Wipe your feet!* Essuie-toi les pieds!
♦ **to wipe up** essuyer

wire NOUN
le <u>fil de fer</u>

wisdom tooth NOUN
la <u>dent de sagesse</u>
(les dents de sagesse PL)

wise ADJECTIVE
<u>sage</u>

to **wish** VERB
see also **wish** NOUN
♦ **to wish for something** souhaiter
quelque chose ◊ *What more could
you wish for?* Que pourrais-tu
souhaiter de plus?
♦ **to wish to do something** désirer faire
quelque chose ◊ *I wish to make a
complaint.* Je désire porter plainte.
♦ **I wish you were here!** Si seulement
tu étais ici!
♦ **I wish you'd told me!** Si seulement tu
m'en avais parlé!

wish NOUN
see also **wish** VERB
le <u>vœu</u>
(les vœux PL)
◊ *to make a wish* faire un vœu
♦ **"best wishes"** (*on greetings card*)
"meilleurs vœux"
♦ **"with best wishes, Kathy"** "bien
amicalement, Kathy"

wit NOUN
l' <u>esprit</u> MASC (*humour*)

with PREPOSITION

1 <u>avec</u> ◊ *Come with me.* Venez avec
moi. ◊ *He walks with a stick.* Il
marche avec une canne.
♦ **a woman with blue eyes** une femme
aux yeux bleus
2 <u>chez</u> (*at the home of*) ◊ *We stayed
with friends.* Nous avons logé chez
des amis.
3 <u>de</u> ◊ *green with envy* vert de
jalousie ◊ *to shake with fear* trembler
de peur ◊ *Fill the jug with water.*
Remplis la carafe d'eau.

within PREPOSITION
♦ **The shops are within easy reach.** Les
magasins sont à proximité.
♦ **within the week** avant la fin de la
semaine

without PREPOSITION
<u>sans</u> ◊ *without a coat* sans manteau
◊ *without speaking* sans parler

witness NOUN
le <u>témoin</u> ◊ *There were no witnesses.*
Il n'a pas eu de témoins.

witty ADJECTIVE
<u>spirituel</u> MASC
<u>spirituelle</u> FEM

wives PL NOUN *see* **wife**

woke up, woken up VERB *see* **wake
up**

wolf NOUN
le <u>loup</u>

woman NOUN
la <u>femme</u> ◊ *a woman doctor* une
femme médecin

won VERB *see* **win**

to **wonder** VERB
<u>se demander</u> ◊ *I wonder why she
said that.* Je me demande pourquoi
elle a dit ça. ◊ *I wonder what that
means.* Je me demande ce que ça
veut dire. ◊ *I wonder where Caroline
is.* Je me demande où est Caroline.

wonderful ADJECTIVE
<u>formidable</u>

won't = will not

wood NOUN
le <u>bois</u> (*timber, forest*) ◊ *It's made of
wood.* C'est en bois. ◊ *We went for a
walk in the wood.* Nous sommes
allés nous promener dans le bois.

wooden ADJECTIVE
<u>en bois</u> ◊ *a wooden chair* une chaise
en bois

woodwork NOUN
la <u>menuiserie</u> ◊ *My hobby is
woodwork.* Je fais de la menuiserie.

wool NOUN

la <u>laine</u> ◊ *It's made of wool.* C'est en laine.

word NOUN
le <u>mot</u> ◊ *a difficult word* un mot difficile
♦ **What's the word for "shop" in German?** Comment dit-on "magasin" en allemand?
♦ **in other words** en d'autres termes
♦ **to have a word with somebody** parler avec quelqu'un
♦ **the words** (*lyrics*) les paroles FEM ◊ *I really like the words of this song.* J'adore les paroles de cette chanson.

word processing NOUN
le <u>traitement de texte</u>

word processor NOUN
la <u>machine de traitement de texte</u>

wore VERB *see* **wear**

work NOUN
| see also **work** VERB |
le <u>travail</u>
(les travaux PL)
◊ *She's looking for work.* Elle cherche du travail. ◊ *He's at work at the moment.* Il est au travail en ce moment.
♦ **It's hard work.** C'est dur.
♦ **to be off work** (*sick*) être malade ◊ *He's been off work for a week.* Il est malade depuis une semaine.
♦ **He's out of work.** Il est sans emploi.

to **work** VERB
| see also **work** NOUN |
[1] <u>travailler</u> (*person*) ◊ *She works in a shop.* Elle travaille dans un magasin. ◊ *to work hard* travailler dur
[2] <u>marcher</u> (*machine, plan*) ◊ *The heating isn't working.* Le chauffage ne marche pas. ◊ *My plan worked perfectly.* Mon plan a marché impeccablement.
♦ **to work out (1)** (*exercise*) faire de l'exercice ◊ *I work out twice a week.* Je fais de l'exercice deux fois par semaine.
♦ **to work out (2)** (*turn out*) marcher ◊ *In the end it worked out really well.* Au bout du compte, ça a très bien marché.
♦ **to work out (3)** (*figure out*) arriver à comprendre ◊ *I just couldn't work it out.* Je n'arrivais pas du tout à comprendre.
♦ **It works out at £10 each.** Ça fait dix livres chacun.

worker NOUN
(*in factory*)
l' <u>ouvrier</u> MASC

l' <u>ouvrière</u> FEM
♦ **He's a factory worker.** Il est ouvrier.
♦ **She's a good worker.** Elle travaille bien.

work experience NOUN
le <u>stage</u> ◊ *I'm going to do work experience in a factory.* Je vais faire un stage dans une usine.

working-class ADJECTIVE
<u>ouvrier</u> MASC
<u>ouvrière</u> FEM
◊ *a working-class family* une famille ouvrière

workman NOUN
l' <u>ouvrier</u> MASC

works NOUN
l' <u>usine</u> FEM (*factory*)

worksheet NOUN
la <u>feuille d'exercices</u>

workshop NOUN
l' <u>atelier</u> MASC ◊ *a drama workshop* un atelier de théâtre

workspace NOUN
l' <u>espace de travail</u> MASC (*computing*)

workstation NOUN
le <u>poste de travail</u>
(les postes de travail PL)

world NOUN
le <u>monde</u>
♦ **He's the world champion.** Il est champion du monde.

worm NOUN
le <u>ver</u>

worn VERB *see* **wear**

worn ADJECTIVE
<u>usé</u> ◊ *The carpet is a bit worn.* La moquette est un peu usée.
♦ **worn out** (*tired*) épuisé

worried ADJECTIVE
<u>inquiet</u> MASC
<u>inquiète</u> FEM
◊ *She's very worried.* Elle est très inquiète.
♦ **to be worried about something** s'inquiéter pour quelque chose ◊ *I'm worried about the exams.* Je m'inquiète pour les examens.
♦ **to look worried** avoir l'air inquiet ◊ *She looks a bit worried.* Elle a l'air un peu inquiète.

to **worry** VERB
s'<u>inquiéter</u>
♦ **Don't worry!** Ne t'inquiète pas!

worse ADJECTIVE, ADVERB
[1] <u>pire</u> ◊ *It was even worse than that.* C'était encore pire que ça. ◊ *My results were bad, but his were even worse.* Mes notes étaient mauvaises, mais les siennes étaient encore pires.

W

2 plus mal ◊ *I'm feeling worse.* Je me sens plus mal.

to **worship** VERB
vénérer (*God*)
♦He really worships her. Il est en adoration devant elle.

worst ADJECTIVE
see also **worst** NOUN
♦the worst le plus mauvais ◊ *the worst student in the class* le plus mauvais élève de la classe ◊ *He got the worst mark in the whole class.* Il a eu la plus mauvaise note de toute la classe.
♦my worst enemy mon pire ennemi
♦Maths is my worst subject. Je suis vraiment nul en maths.

worst NOUN
see also **worst** ADJECTIVE
le pire ◊ *The worst of it is that ...* Le pire c'est que ...
♦at worst au pire
♦if the worst comes to the worst au pire

worth ADJECTIVE
♦to be worth valoir ◊ *It's worth a lot of money.* Ça vaut très cher. ◊ *How much is it worth?* Ça vaut combien?
♦It's worth it. Ça vaut la peine. ◊ *Is it worth it?* Est-ce que ça vaut la peine? ◊ *It's not worth it.* Ça ne vaut pas la peine.

would VERB
♦Would you like a biscuit? Vous voulez un biscuit?
♦Would you like to go and see a film? Est-ce que tu veux aller voir un film?
♦Would you close the door please? Vous pouvez fermer la porte, s'il vous plaît?
♦I'd like ... J'aimerais ... ◊ *I'd like to go to America.* J'aimerais aller en Amérique. ◊ *Shall we go and see a film? – Yes, I'd like that.* Si on allait voir un film? – Oui, j'aimerais bien.
♦I said I would do it. J'ai dit que je le ferais.
♦If you asked him he'd do it. Si vous le lui demandiez, il le ferait.
♦If you had asked him he would have done it. Si vous le lui aviez demandé, il l'aurait fait.

wouldn't = would not

wound NOUN
see also **wound** VERB
la blessure

to **wound** VERB
see also **wound** NOUN
blesser ◊ *He was wounded in the leg.* Il a été blessé à la jambe.

to **wrap** VERB
emballer ◊ *She's wrapping her Christmas presents.* Elle est en train d'emballer ses cadeaux de Noël.
♦Can you wrap it for me please? (*in shop*) Vous pouvez me faire un papier cadeau, s'il vous plaît?
♦to wrap up emballer

wrapping paper NOUN
le papier cadeau

wreck NOUN
see also **wreck** VERB
1 le tas de ferraille (*vehicle, machine*) ◊ *That car is a wreck!* Cette voiture est un tas de ferraille!
2 la loque (*person*) ◊ *After the exams I was a complete wreck.* Après les examens j'étais une véritable loque.

to **wreck** VERB
see also **wreck** NOUN
1 démolir (*building, vehicle*) ◊ *The explosion wrecked the whole house.* L'explosion a démoli toute la maison.
2 ruiner (*plan, holiday*) ◊ *The trip was wrecked by bad weather.* Le voyage a été ruiné par le mauvais temps.

wreckage NOUN
1 les débris MASC PL (*of vehicle*)
2 les décombres MASC PL (*of building*)

wrestler NOUN
le lutteur
la lutteuse

wrestling NOUN
la lutte

wrinkled ADJECTIVE
ridé

wrist NOUN
le poignet

to **write** VERB
écrire ◊ *to write a letter* écrire une lettre
♦to write to somebody écrire à quelqu'un ◊ *I'm going to write to her in French.* Je vais lui écrire en français.
♦to write down noter ◊ *I wrote down the address.* J'ai noté l'adresse.
♦Can you write it down for me, please? Vous pouvez me l'écrire, s'il vous plaît?

writer NOUN
l' écrivain MASC ◊ *She's a writer.* Elle est écrivain.

writing NOUN
l' écriture FEM ◊ *I can't read your writing.* Je n'arrive pas à lire ton écriture.
♦in writing par écrit

written VERB *see* **write**

wrong ADJECTIVE, ADVERB

[1] (*incorrect*)

<u>faux</u> MASC

<u>fausse</u> FEM

◊ *The information they gave us was wrong.* Les renseignements qu'ils nous ont donnés étaient faux.

♦ **the wrong answer** la mauvaise réponse

♦ **You've got the wrong number.** Vous vous êtes trompé de numéro.

[2] (*morally bad*)

<u>mal</u> ◊ *I think hunting is wrong.* Je trouve que c'est mal de chasser.

♦ **to be wrong** (*mistaken*) se tromper

◊ *You're wrong about that.* Tu te trompes.

♦ **to do something wrong** se tromper

◊ *You've done it wrong.* Tu t'es trompé.

♦ **to go wrong** (*plan*) mal tourner ◊ *The robbery went wrong and they got caught.* Le cambriolage a mal tourné et ils ont été pris.

♦ **What's wrong?** Qu'est-ce qu'il y a?

♦ **What's wrong with her?** Qu'est-ce qu'elle a?

wrote VERB *see* **write**

WWW NOUN (= *World Wide Web*)

le <u>Web</u>

W

X

Xerox ® NOUN

see also **xerox** VERB

la <u>photocopie</u>

to **xerox** VERB

see also **Xerox** NOUN

<u>photocopier</u>

Xmas NOUN (= *Christmas*)

<u>Noël</u>

to **X-ray** VERB

see also **X-ray** NOUN

◆**to X-ray something** faire une radio de quelque chose ◊ *They X-rayed my arm.* Ils ont fait une radio de mon bras.

X-ray NOUN

see also **X-ray** VERB

la <u>radio</u> ◊ *to have an X-ray* passer une radio

Y

yacht NOUN

1 le <u>voilier</u> (*sailing boat*)
2 le <u>yacht</u> (*luxury motorboat*)

yard NOUN

1 la <u>cour</u> (*of building*) ◊ *in the yard* dans la cour
2 le <u>mètre</u>

> *i* *In France measurements are in metres rather than yards. A yard is slightly more than a metre.*

to **yawn** VERB

<u>bâiller</u>

year NOUN

l' <u>an</u> MASC ◊ *last year* l'an dernier ◊ *next year* l'an prochain
◆**to be 15 years old** avoir quinze ans
◆**an eight-year-old child** un enfant de huit ans

> *i* *In French secondary schools, years are counted from the **sixième** (youngest) to **première** and **terminale** (oldest).*

◊ *the first year* la sixième ◊ *the second year* la cinquième ◊ *the third year* la quatrième ◊ *the fourth year* la troisième ◊ *the fifth year* la seconde
◆**She's in the fifth year.** Elle est en seconde.
◆**He's a first-year.** Il est en sixième.

to **yell** VERB

<u>hurler</u>

yellow ADJECTIVE

<u>jaune</u>

yes ADVERB

1 <u>oui</u> ◊ *Do you like it? – Yes.* Tu aimes ça? – Oui.

◆**Would you like a cup of tea? – Yes please.** Voulez-vous une tasse de thé? – Je veux bien.

> *Use **si** when answering negative questions.*

2 <u>si</u> ◊ *Don't you like it? – Yes!* Tu n'aimes pas ça? – Si! ◊ *You're not Swiss, are you? – Yes I am!* Tu n'es pas suisse, si? – Si!

yesterday ADVERB

<u>hier</u> ◊ *yesterday morning* hier matin ◊ *yesterday afternoon* hier après-midi ◊ *yesterday evening* hier soir ◊ *all day yesterday* toute la journée d'hier

yet ADVERB

<u>encore</u>
◆**not yet** pas encore ◊ *It's not finished yet.* Ce n'est pas encore fini.
◆**not as yet** pas encore ◊ *There's no news as yet.* Nous n'avons pas encore de nouvelles.
◆**Have you finished yet?** Vous avez fini?

to **yield** VERB US

<u>céder le passage</u> (*on road sign*)

yob NOUN

le <u>loubard</u>

yoghurt NOUN

le <u>yaourt</u>

yolk NOUN

le <u>jaune d'œuf</u>
(les <u>jaunes d'œuf</u> PL)

you PRONOUN

> *Only use **tu** when speaking to one person of your own age or younger. If in doubt use **vous**.*

1 (*polite form or plural*)
<u>vous</u> ◊ *Do you like football?* Est-ce que vous aimez le football? ◊ *Can I*

help you? Est-ce que je peux vous aider? ◊ *It's for you.* C'est pour vous.
2 *(familiar singular)*
tu ◊ *Do you like football?* Tu aimes le football?

vous never changes, but tu has different forms. When you is the object of the sentence use te not tu. te becomes t' before a vowel sound.

3 te ◊ *I know you.* Je te connais. ◊ *I gave it you.* Je te l'ai donné.
t' ◊ *I saw you.* Je t'ai vu. ◊ *I'll help you.* Je vais t'aider.

toi is used instead of tu after a preposition and in comparisons.

4 toi ◊ *It's for you.* C'est pour toi. ◊ *I'll come with you.* Je viens avec toi. ◊ *She's younger than you.* Elle est plus jeune que toi.

young ADJECTIVE
jeune
♦ **young people** les jeunes

younger ADJECTIVE
plus jeune ◊ *He's younger than me.* Il est plus jeune que moi.
♦ **my younger brother** mon frère cadet
♦ **my younger sister** ma sœur cadette

youngest ADJECTIVE
le plus jeune
la plus jeune
◊ *my youngest brother* mon plus jeune frère ◊ *She's the youngest.* C'est la plus jeune.

your ADJECTIVE
Only use ton/ta/tes when speaking to one person of your own age or younger. If in doubt use votre/ vos.
1 *(polite form or plural)*
votre ◊ *your house* votre maison
vos PL ◊ *your seats* vos places
2 *(familiar singular)*
ton MASC ◊ *your brother* ton frère
ta FEM ◊ *your sister* ta sœur
tes PL ◊ *your parents* tes parents
ta becomes ton before a vowel sound
♦ **your friend (1)** *(male)* ton ami
♦ **your friend (2)** *(female)* ton amie
Do not use votre/vos or ton/ta/tes with parts of the body.
◊ *Would you like to wash your hands?* Est-ce que vous voulez vous laver les mains? ◊ *Do you want to wash your hair?* Tu veux te laver les cheveux?

yours PRONOUN
Only use le tien/la tienne/les tiens/ les tiennes when talking to one person of your own age or younger.

If in doubt use le vôtre/la vôtre/les vôtres. The same applies to à toi and à vous.
1 le vôtre + MASC NOUN ◊ *I've lost my pen. Can I use yours?* J'ai perdu mon stylo. Je peux utiliser le vôtre?
la vôtre + FEM NOUN ◊ *I like that car. Is it yours?* J'aime cette voiture-là. C'est la vôtre?
les vôtres + PL NOUN ◊ *my parents and yours* mes parents et les vôtres
♦ **Is this yours?** C'est à vous? ◊ *This book is yours.* Ce livre est à vous. ◊ *Whose is this? – It's yours.* C'est à qui? – À vous.
♦ **Yours sincerely ...** Veuillez agréer l'expression de mes sentiments les meilleurs ...
2 le tien + MASC NOUN ◊ *I've lost my pen. Can I use yours?* J'ai perdu mon stylo. Je peux utiliser le tien?
la tienne + FEM NOUN ◊ *I like that car. Is it yours?* J'aime cette voiture-là. C'est la tienne?
les tiens + MASC PL NOUN ◊ *my parents and yours* mes parents et les tiens
les tiennes + FEM PL NOUN ◊ *My hands are dirty, yours are clean.* Mes mains sont sales, les tiennes sont propres.
♦ **Is this yours?** C'est à toi? ◊ *This book is yours.* Ce livre est à toi. ◊ *Whose is this? – It's yours.* C'est à qui? – À toi.

yourself PRONOUN
Only use te when talking to one person of your own age or younger; use vous to everyone else. If in doubt use vous.
1 vous *(polite form)* ◊ *Have you hurt yourself?* Est-ce que vous vous êtes fait mal? ◊ *Tell me about yourself!* Parlez-moi de vous!
2 te *(familiar form)* ◊ *Have you hurt yourself?* Est-ce que tu t'es fait mal?
After a preposition, use toi instead of te.
3 toi *(familiar form)* ◊ *Tell me about yourself!* Parle-moi de toi!
4 toi-même ◊ *Do it yourself!* Fais-le toi-même!
5 vous-même ◊ *Do it yourself!* Faites-le vous-même!

yourselves PRONOUN
1 vous ◊ *Did you enjoy yourselves?* Vous vous êtes bien amusés?
2 vous-mêmes ◊ *Did you make it yourselves?* Vous l'avez fait vous-mêmes?

youth club NOUN
le centre de jeunes
youth hostel NOUN

Y

l' auberge de jeunesse FEM
(les auberges de jeunesse PL)
Yugoslavia NOUN
la Yougoslavie
♦ **in the former Yugoslavia** en ex-
Yougoslavie

Z

zany ADJECTIVE
loufoque
zebra NOUN
le zèbre
zebra crossing NOUN
le passage clouté
zero NOUN
le zéro
Zimbabwe NOUN
le Zimbabwe
♦ **in Zimbabwe** au Zimbabwe
Zimmer frame ® NOUN
le déambulateur
zip NOUN
la fermeture éclair ®
(les fermetures éclair PL)
zip code NOUN US

le code postal
zipper NOUN US
la fermeture éclair ®
(les fermetures éclair PL)
zit NOUN
le bouton
zodiac NOUN
le zodiaque ◊ *the signs of the zodiac*
les signes du zodiaque
zone NOUN
la zone
zoo NOUN
le zoo
zoom lens NOUN
le zoom
zucchini NOUN US
la courgette